KEY TO WORLD MAP PAGES

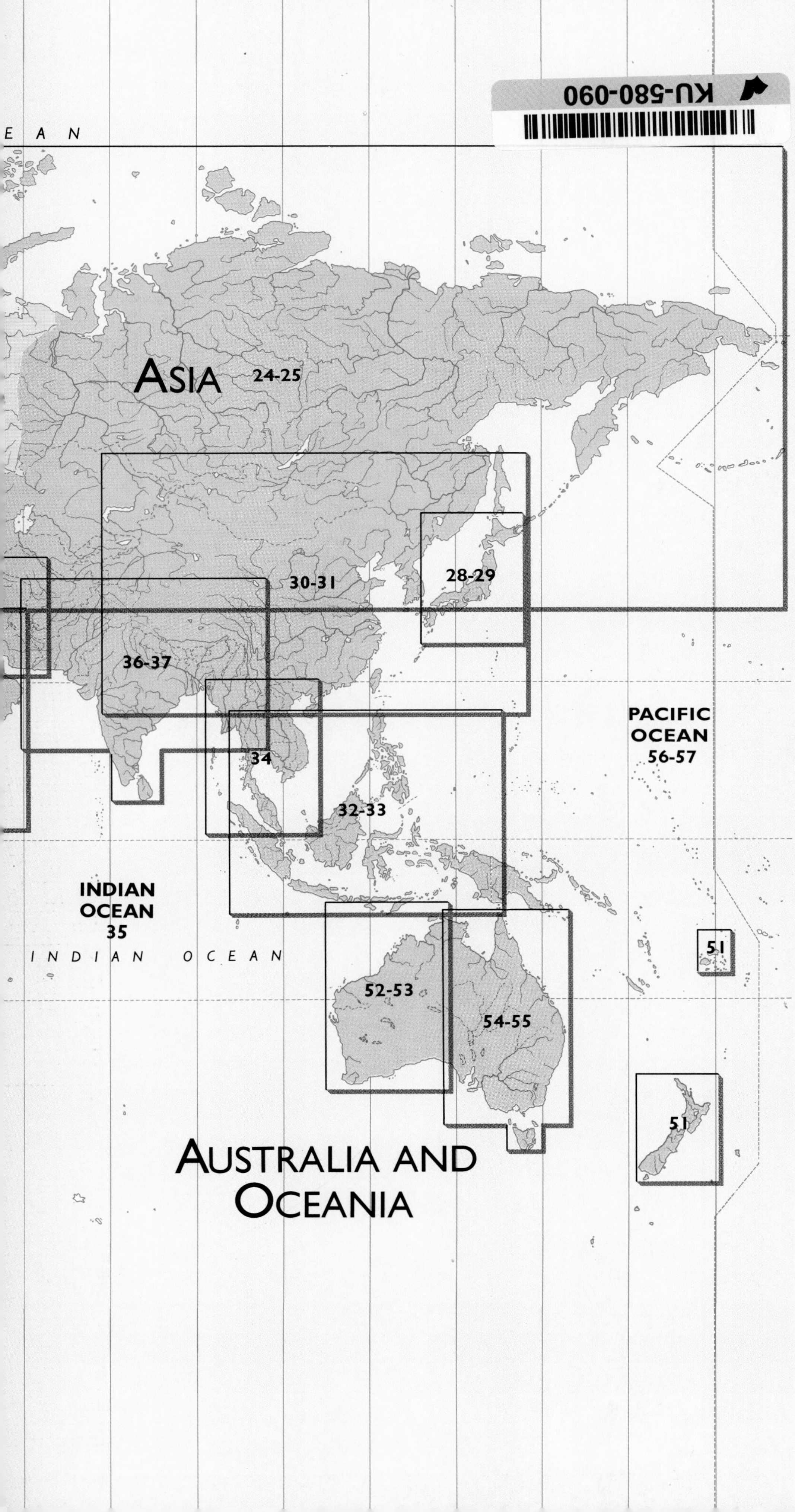

ASIA 24-25

PACIFIC
OCEAN
56-57

30-31

28-29

36-37

34

32-33

INDIAN
OCEAN
35

INDIAN OCEAN

51

52-53

54-55

51

AUSTRALIA AND
OCEANIA

COUNTRY INDEX

Country	Page	Country	Page
Afghanistan	36	Laos	34
Albania	21	Latvia	22
Algeria	44	Lebanon	41
Angola	46–47	Lesotho	47
Argentina	80	Liberia	44
Armenia	23	Libya	44–45
Australia	52–55	Lithuania	22
Austria	16	Luxembourg	15
Azerbaijan	23		
		Macedonia	21
Bahamas	75	Madagascar	47
Bahrain	39	Malawi	46–47
Bangladesh	37	Malaysia	32–34
Barbados	75	Mali	44
Belarus	22	Malta	20
Belgium	15	Mauritania	44
Belize	74	Mauritius	43
Benin	44	Mexico	74
Bhutan	37	Moldova	23
Bolivia	78	Mongolia	30–31
Bosnia-Herzegovina	20–21	Morocco	44
Botswana	47	Mozambique	46–47
Brazil	78–80		
Brunei	32	Namibia	47
Bulgaria	21	Nepal	37
Burkina Faso	44	Netherlands	15
Burma	37	New Zealand	51
Burundi	46	Nicaragua	74–75
		Niger	44–45
Cambodia	34	Nigeria	44–45
Cameroon	46	Northern Ireland	13
Canada	60–65	Norway	8–9
Central African			
Republic	46	Oman	40
Chad	45		
Chile	78, 80	Pakistan	36
China	30–31	Panama	75
Colombia	78	Papua New Guinea	50
Congo	46	Paraguay	78, 80
Costa Rica	74–75	Peru	78
Croatia	20–21	Philippines	33
Cuba	75	Poland	16–17
Cyprus	23	Portugal	19
Czech Republic	16–17	Puerto Rico	75
Denmark	9	Qatar	39
Djibouti	40		
Dominican Republic	75	Romania	17
		Russia	22–25
Ecuador	78	Rwanda	46
Egypt	45		
El Salvador	74	Saudi Arabia	40
England	10–11	Scotland	12
Equatorial Guinea	46	Senegal	44
Eritrea	40	Sierra Leone	44
Estonia	22	Singapore	34
Ethiopia	40	Slovak Republic	17
		Slovenia	20
Fiji	51	Somali Republic	40
Finland	8–9	South Africa	47
France	18	Spain	19
French Guiana	79	Sri Lanka	36
		Sudan	45
Gabon	46	Surinam	78–79
Gambia	44	Swaziland	47
Georgia	23	Sweden	8–9
Germany	16	Switzerland	16
Ghana	44	Syria	38, 41
Greece	21		
Greenland	4	Taiwan	31
Guatemala	74	Tajikistan	24
Guinea	44	Tanzania	46
Guinea-Bissau	44	Thailand	34
Guyana	78	Togo	44
		Trinidad and	
Haiti	75	Tobago	75
Honduras	74–75	Tunisia	44–45
Hong Kong	31	Turkey	23
Hungary	16–17	Turkmenistan	24
Iceland	8	Uganda	46
India	36–37	Ukraine	22–23
Indonesia	32–33	United Arab	
Iran	38–39	Emirates	39
Iraq	38–39	United Kingdom	10–14
Irish Republic	13	USA	66–73
Israel	41	Uruguay	80
Italy	20–21	Uzbekistan	24
Ivory Coast	44		
		Venezuela	78
Jamaica	75	Vietnam	34
Japan	28–29		
Jordan	41	Wales	10–11
Kazakhstan	24	Yemen	40
Kenya	46	Yugoslavia	21
Korea, North	31		
Korea, South	31	Zaïre	46–47
Kuwait	38–39	Zambia	46–47
Kyrgyzstan	24	Zimbabwe	47

PHILIP'S

NEW
WORLD
ATLAS

This 1995 edition published by Chancellor Press,
an imprint of Reed Books
Michelin House, 81 Fulham Road, London SW3 6RB,
and Auckland, Melbourne, Singapore and Toronto

Copyright © 1995 Reed International Books Limited

Cartography by Philip's

ISBN 1-85152-897-0

A CIP catalogue record for this book is available
from the British Library

Printed in Hong Kong

PHILIP'S

NEW WORLD ATLAS

CHANCELLOR
PRESS

CONTENTS

WORLD MAPS

Map Symbols
1:80 000 000
1

The World: Political
1:80 000 000
2–3

Arctic Ocean
1:35 000 000
4

Antarctica
1:35 000 000
5

EUROPE

Europe: Physical
1:20 000 000
6

Europe: Political
1:20 000 000
7

Scandinavia
1:5 000 000
8–9

England and Wales
1:2 000 000
10–11

Scotland
1:2 000 000
12

Ireland
1:2 000 000
13

British Isles
1:5 000 000
14

Netherlands, Belgium and Luxembourg
1:2 500 000
15

Middle Europe
1:5 000 000
16–17

France
1:5 000 000
18

Spain and Portugal
1:5 000 000
19

Italy and the Balkan States
1:5 000 000
20–21

Eastern Europe and Turkey
1:10 000 000
22–23

ASIA

Russia and Central Asia
1:20 000 000
24–25

Asia: Physical
1:50 000 000
26

Asia: Political
1:50 000 000
27

Japan
1:5 000 000
28–29

China and Korea
1:15 000 000
30–31

Indonesia and the Philippines
1:12 500 000
32–33

Mainland South-east Asia
1:10 000 000
34

Indian Ocean
1:50 000 000
35

South Asia
1:10 000 000
36–37

The Middle East
1:7 000 000
38–39

Arabia and the Horn of Africa
1:15 000 000
40

The Near East
1:2 500 000
41

AFRICA

Africa: Physical
1:42 000 000
42

Africa: Political
1:42 000 000
43

Northern Africa
1:15 000 000
44–45

Central and Southern Africa
1:15 000 000
46–47

Southern Africa
1:8 000 000
Madagascar 1:8 000 000
48–49

AUSTRALIA AND OCEANIA

Australia and Oceania: Physical and Political
1:50 000 000
50

New Zealand
1:6 000 000
51

Western Australia
1:8 000 000
52–53

Eastern Australia
1:8 000 000
54–55

Pacific Ocean
1:54 000 000
56–57

NORTH AMERICA

North America: Physical
1:35 000 000
58

North America: Political
1:35 000 000
59

Canada
1:15 000 000
Alaska 1:30 000 000
60–61

Eastern Canada
1:7 000 000
62–63

Western Canada
1:7 000 000
64–65

United States
1:12 000 000
Hawaii 1:10 000 000
66–67

Eastern United States
1:6 000 000
68–69

Middle United States
1:6 000 000
70–71

Western United States
1:6 000 000
72–73

Mexico, Central America and the West Indies
1:15 000 000
74–75

SOUTH AMERICA

South America: Physical
1:35 000 000
76

South America: Political
1:35 000 000
77

South America – North
1:16 000 000
78–79

South America – South
1:16 000 000
80

INDEX TO WORLD MAPS

81–128

World: Regions in the News 129

WORLD MAPS

SETTLEMENTS

⌂ **PARIS**   ■ **Berne**   ◉ **Livorno**   ◉ Brugge   ◉ *Algeciras*   ⊙ *Fréjus*   ○ *Oberammergau*   ○ *Thira*

Settlement symbols and type styles vary according to the scale of each map and indicate the importance
of towns on the map rather than specific population figures

∴ Ruins or Archæological Sites   ◡ Wells in Desert

ADMINISTRATION

———— International Boundaries

– – – International Boundaries
(Undefined or Disputed)

········· Internal Boundaries

National Parks

Country Names

NICARAGUA

Administrative
Area Names

KENT

CALABRIA

International boundaries show the *de facto* situation where there are rival claims to territory

COMMUNICATIONS

———— Principal Roads

⌒ Other Roads

⌒·⌒ Trails and Seasonal Roads

⌣ Passes

✧ Airfields

⌒ Principal Railways

–·–·– Railways
Under Construction

⌒ Other Railways

⌐---⌐ Railway Tunnels

············ Principal Canals

PHYSICAL FEATURES

⌒ Perennial Streams

······· Intermittent Streams

⬭ Perennial Lakes

⬭ Intermittent Lakes

Swamps and Marshes

Permanent Ice
and Glaciers

▲ 8848 Elevations in metres

▼ 8050 Sea Depths in metres

1134 Height of Lake Surface
Above Sea Level
in metres

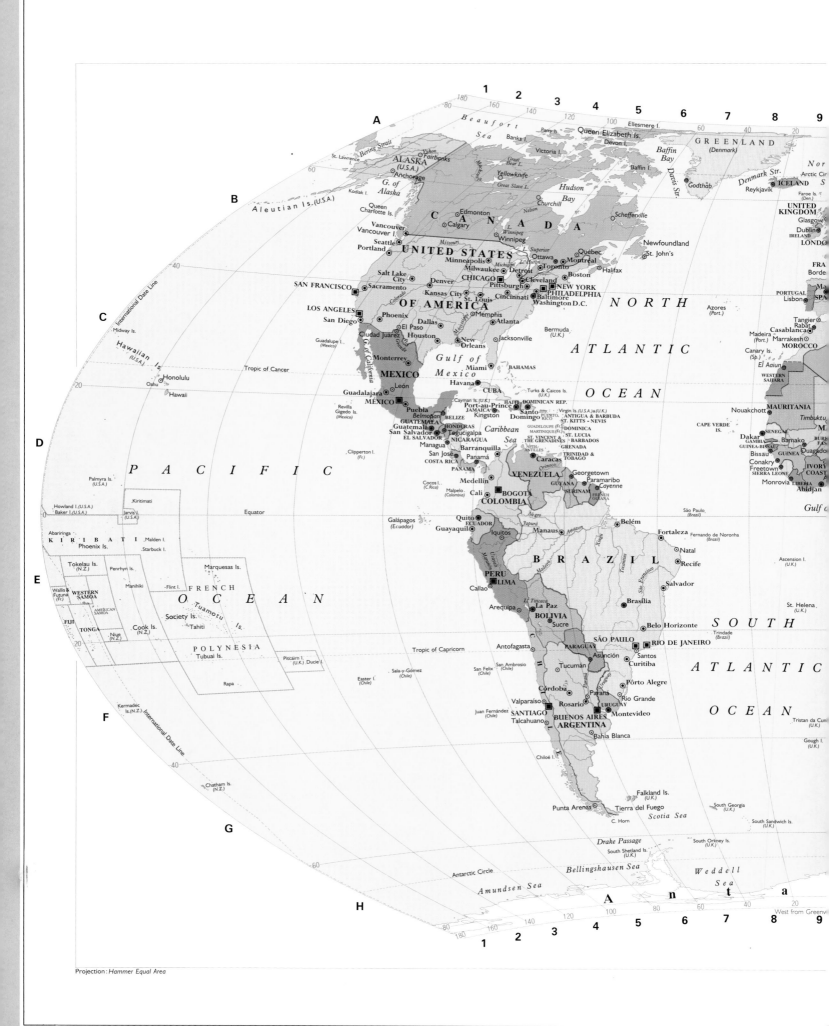

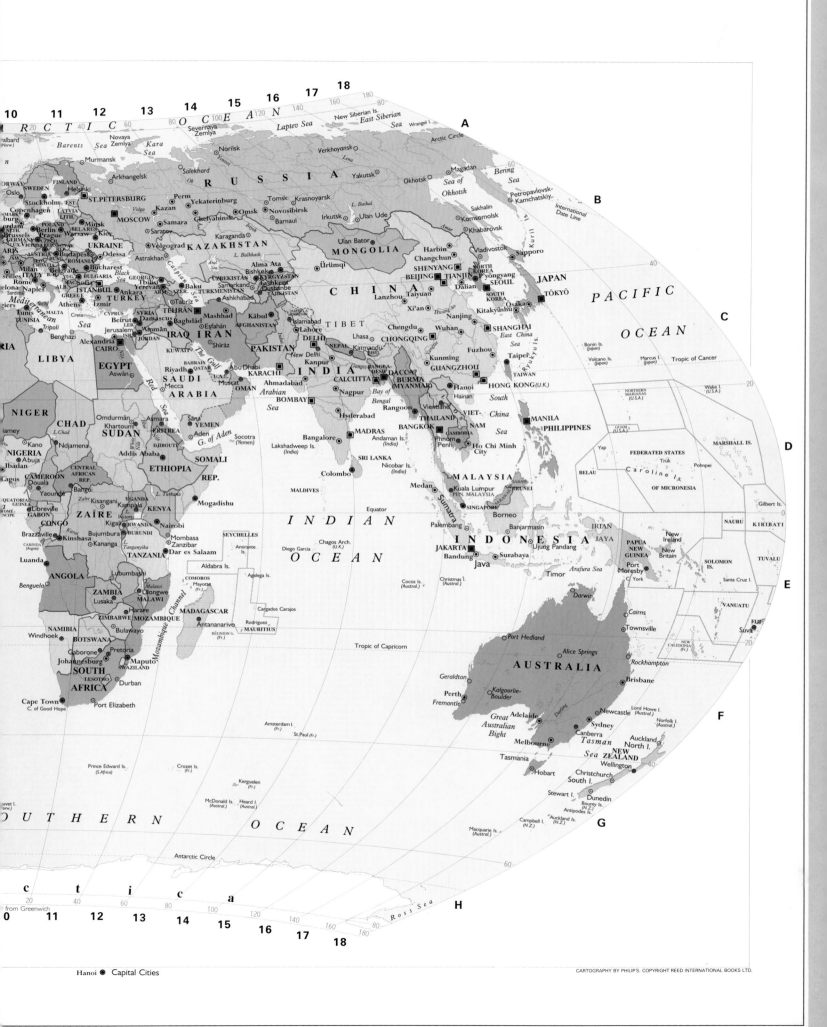

Hanoi ● Capital Cities

CARTOGRAPHY BY PHILIP'S. COPYRIGHT REED INTERNATIONAL BOOKS LTD.

1:80 000 000

3

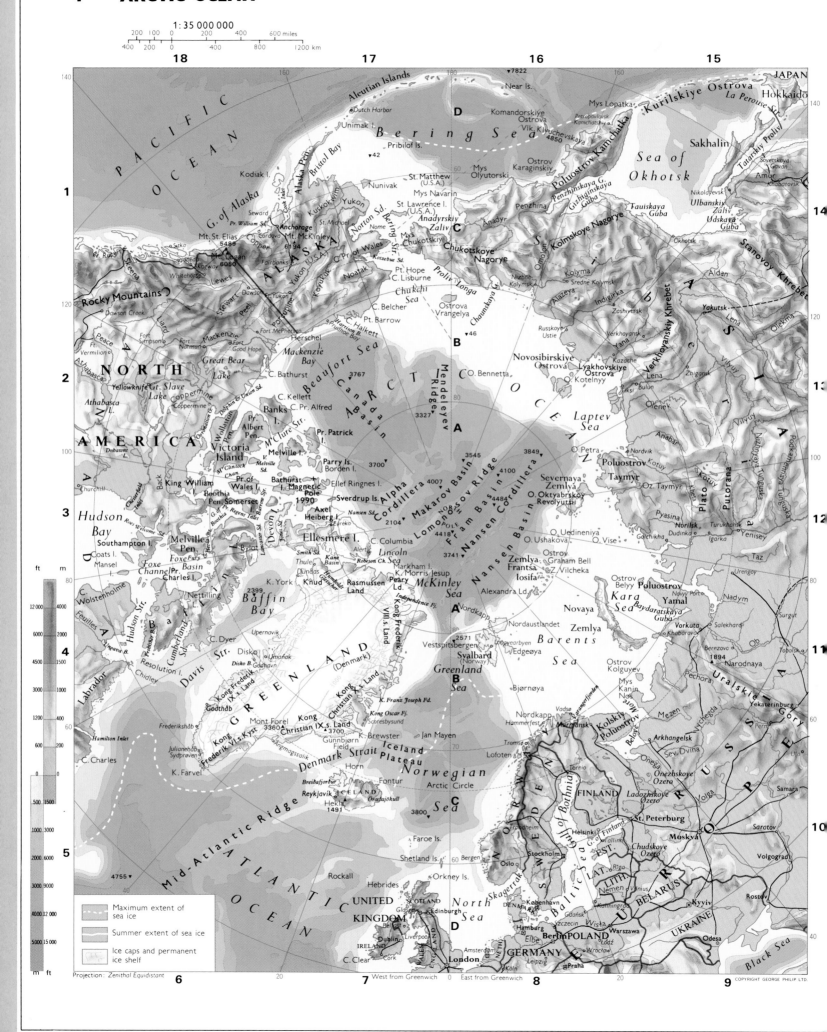

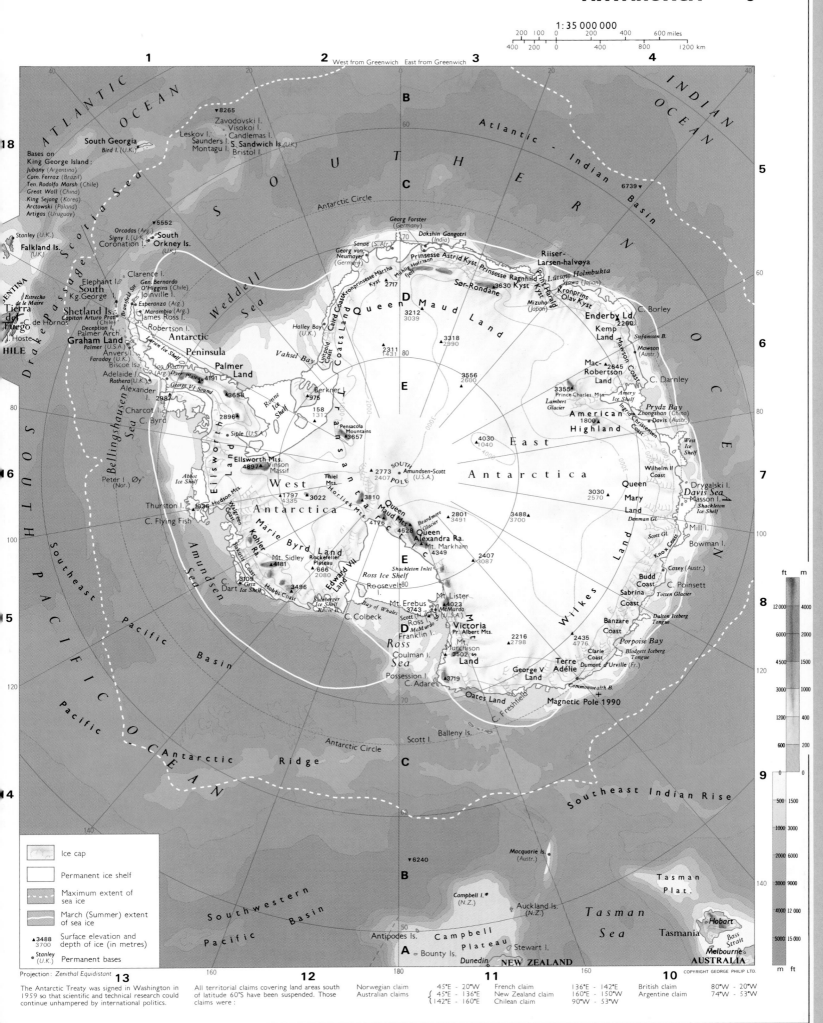

1:35 000 000

200 100 0 200 400 600 miles
400 200 0 400 800 1200 km

West from Greenwich | East from Greenwich

ATLANTIC OCEAN

INDIAN OCEAN

Atlantic - Indian Basin

▼8265

Zavodovski I.
Visokoi I.
Leskov I.
Candlemas I.
Saunders I.
S. Sandwich Is. (U.K.)
Montagu I.
Bristol I.

South Georgia
Bird I. (U.K.)

Bases on King George Island:
Jubany (Argentina)
Com. Ferraz (Brazil)
Ten. Rodolfo Marsh (Chile)
Great Wall (China)
King Sejong (Korea)
Arctowski (Poland)
Artigas (Uruguay)

SOUTHERN

Antarctic Circle

Georg Forster (Germany)
Dakshin Gangotri (India)
Sanae (S. Afr.)
Georg von Neumayer (Germany)

6739▼

Riiser-Larsen-halvøya

Prinsesse Astrid Kyst
Prinsesse Ragnhild Kyst
Prins Harald Kyst
Lützow Holmbukta
Syowa (Japan)
Kronprins Olav Kyst
Mizuho (Japan)

Stanley (U.K.)
Falkland Is. (U.K.)

▼5552
Orcadas (Arg.)
Signy I. (U.K.)
Coronation I.
South Orkney Is. (U.K.)

Möhling Hofmann
Jelbart
2717

Kronprinsesse Martha

Queen Maud Land

C. Borley

Enderby Ld.
2260

Kemp Land
Stefansson B.

Mawson (Austr.)

Mac-Robertson Land
2645

Prince Charles Mts.
3355▲
Amery Ice Shelf

Lambert Glacier

Prydz Bay
Zhongshan (China)
Davis (Austr.)

West Ice Shelf

Tierra del Fuego
C. de Hornos
I. Hoste
CHILE

ARGENTINA
Estrecho de le Maire
South Shetland Is.
Kg. George I.

Elephant I.
Gen. Bernardo O'Higgins (Chile)
Joinville I.
Esperanza (Arg.)
Clarence I.
Marambio (Arg.)
James Ross I.
Capitan Arturo Prat (Chile)
Deception I.
Robertson I.

Weddell Sea

Halley Bay (U.K.)

2311
1431

3318
2990

3556
2600

Graham Land
Palmer (U.S.A.)
Anvers I.
Faraday (U.K.)
Biscoe Is.
Adelaide I.
Rothera (U.K.)
Alexander I.

Antarctic Peninsula

Palmer Land

Larsen Ice Shelf
San Martin (Arg.)
Dyer Plateau
4191

Ronne Ice Shelf

Vahsel Bay

Berkner I.

Coats Land
Caird Coast
Luitpold Coast

975
158
1317

East Antarctica

3212
3039

3318
2990

4030
1040

3030
2570

3355
2600

Queen Mary Land

Wilhelm II Coast

Davis Sea
Drygalski I.
Masson I.
Shackleton Ice Shelf

2987▲

3658▲

Charcot I.
C. Byrd

2896▲

▲3657
Pensacola Mountains

Siple (U.S.A.)

Ellsworth Mts.
Vinson Massif 4897▲

SOUTH POLE
2773
2407

Amundsen-Scott (U.S.A.)

3488▲
3700

American Highland
1800
2600

Denman Gl.
Scott Gl.

Mill I.

Bowman I.

Peter I. Øy (Nor.)

Bellingshausen Sea

Thurston I.
1936 Hudson Mts.
C. Flying Fish

Abbot Ice Shelf

Thiel Mts.
3810

West Antarctica

1797
4335

3022

Horlick Mts.

3088

Queen Maud Mts.
4176
4528
Queen Alexandra Ra.
Mt. Markham
4349

2801
3491

2407
3087

Knox Coast

Casey (Austr.)
C. Poinsett

Budd Coast
Sabrina Coast
Totten Glacier

Dalton Iceberg Tongue

Amundsen Sea

Walgreen Coast

Marie Byrd Land

Kohler Ra.
Mt. Sidley
4181
3109
Getz
Dart Ice Shelf
Hobbs Coast
3496

Rockefeller Plateau
666
2080

Edward VII Land

Sulzberger Ice Shelf
Biscoe B.

Shackleton Inlet

Ross Ice Shelf

Roosevelt I.

Beardmore Glacier

Wilkes Land

3030
2570

Banzare Coast

Clarie Coast
Blodgett Iceberg Tongue

Porpoise Bay

C. Colbeck
Bay of Whales

Mt. Erebus
3743
McMurdo (U.S.A.)
Scott (N.Z.)
Ross I.
McMdo

Mt. Lister
4023

Victoria
Pr. Albert Mts.

Southeast Pacific Basin

Pacific Basin

Pacific Ocean

Antarctic Ridge

Coulman I.

Franklin I.

Mt. Murchison
3502

2216
2798

2435
4776

Budd Coast

Victoria Land

George V Land

Terre Adélie
Dumont d'Urville (Fr.)

Possession I.
C. Adare
3719

Ross Sea

Oates Land
C. Freshfield

Magnetic Pole 1990

Antarctic Circle

Scott I.

Balleny Is.

Southeast Indian Rise

▼6240

Macquarie Is. (Austr.)

Tasman Plat.

Southwestern Pacific Basin

Campbell I. (N.Z.)
Auckland Is. (N.Z.)

Tasman Sea

Antipodes Is.
Campbell Plateau

Bounty Is.

Stewart I.
Dunedin

Tasmania
Hobart
Bass Strait

Melbourne
AUSTRALIA

NEW ZEALAND

ft m
12 000 4000
6000 2000
4500 1500
3000 1000
1200 400
600 200
0 0
500 1500
1000 3000
2000 6000
3000 9000
4000 12 000
5000 15 000
m ft

Legend

- Ice cap
- Permanent ice shelf
- Maximum extent of sea ice
- March (Summer) extent of sea ice
- ▲3488 / 3700 Surface elevation and depth of ice (in metres)
- ● Stanley (U.K.) Permanent bases

Projection: *Zenithal Equidistant*

COPYRIGHT GEORGE PHILIP LTD.

The Antarctic Treaty was signed in Washington in 1959 so that scientific and technical research could continue unhampered by international politics.

All territorial claims covering land areas south of latitude 60°S have been suspended. Those claims were:

Norwegian claim	45°E – 20°W
Australian claims	45°E – 136°E
	142°E – 160°E
French claim	136°E – 142°E
New Zealand claim	160°E – 150°W
Chilean claim	90°W – 53°W
British claim	80°W – 20°W
Argentine claim	74°W – 53°W

1 : 20 000 000

100   0   100   200   300   400 miles
100   0   100   200   300   400   500   600 km

Map labels

Ob

Ural Mountains

Obschchi Syrt

Ural

Caspian Depression

Caspian Sea

U r a l

Pechora

Kama

Volga Hts.

Volga

Elbrus 5633

Caucasus

Terek

Kura

Kuban

Ararat 5165

Erops Dağ

Armenia

L. Van

Tigris

Kurdistan

Mesopotamia

Euphrates

Pontine Mts.

Black Sea

Anatolia (Asia Minor)

Taurus Mts.

Kizil Irmak

Sea of Marmara

Bosporus

Dardanelles

Str. of Ida

Nordkinn

Kanin Pen.

Mezen

N. Dvina

Pechora

White Sea

Kola Pen.

Onega

L. Onega

L. Ladoga

Neva

Finland

Rybinsk Res.

Don

Donets

Sea of Azov

Str. of Kerch

Crimea

Dnieper

Central Russian Uplands

Oka

W. Dvina

Dvina

Ukraine

Bug

Danube

Prut

Dniester

Pripet

Vistula

Carpathians

Wallachia

Transylvanian Alps

Balkans

Rhodope

Olympus 2917

Pindus

Aegean Sea

Morea

C. Matapan

Crete

Cyprus

Rhodes

North Cape

Lapland

Inari

Kebnekaise 2117

Torne

Vesterålen

Lofoten

Ume

Indals

Scandinavia

Norwegian Sea

Gulf of Bothnia

Finland Plain

G. of Finland

L. Chudskoye

Aland

Saaremaa

G. of Riga

Niemen

European Plain

North Sea

Baltic Sea

Gotland

Öland

Bornholm

Oder

Vistula

Tatra 2655

Plain of Hungary

Muresz

Tisza

Danube

Sava

Drava

Bavaria Forest

Danube

Sudeten

Moravia

Bohemian Forest

Erzgebirge

Inn

Dinaric Alps

Adriatic Sea

Gran Sasso d'Italia 2914

Apennines

Str. of Otranto

Ionian Is.

Ionian Sea

Nordkinn

Galdhøpiggen 2469

Kattegatt

Skagerrak

Jutland

Vänern

Mälaren

Helgoland

Elbe

Harz

Weser

Rhine

Westerwald

Taunus

Black Forest

Vosges

Jura

Alps

Mont Blanc 4807

Po

Vesuvius 1277

Tyrrhenian Sea

Corsica

Sardinia

Str. of Bonifacio

Str. of Messina

Sicily

Etna 3340

C. Bon

Pantelleria

Malta

Mediterranean Sea

Iceland

Hekla 1447

Öraefajökull 2119

Arctic Circle

Faroe Is.

Shetland Is.

Orkney Is.

Hebrides

British Isles

Ben Nevis 1347

Great Britain

Snowdon 1085

Ireland

Irish Sea

Thames

English Channel

Channel Is.

Brittany

Seine

Loire

Rockall

C. Clear

Celtic Sea

Land's End

Ushant

C. Finisterre

ATLANTIC OCEAN

Bay of Biscay

Gironde

Garonne

Massif Central

Puy de Dôme 1886

Cévennes

Rhône

G. of Lions

Ligurian Sea

Balearic Is.

Minorca

Majorca

Ibiza

Cantabrian Mts.

Pyrenees

Pico de Aneto 3404

Ebro

Iberian Peninsula

Old Castile

New Castile

Douro

Sierra de Estrela

Sierra Morena

Sierra Nevada 3478

Mulhacen 3478

Guadalquivir

Andalusia

Guadiana

Str. of Gibraltar

C. Trafalgar

C. de São Vicente

C. da Roca

Africa

Plateau of the Shotts

Projection: Bonne

West from Greenwich   0   East from Greenwich

CARTOGRAPHY BY PHILIP'S. COPYRIGHT REED INTERNATIONAL BOOKS LTD.

ft   m
15 000   5000
12 000   4000
6000   2000
3000   1000
600   200
0   0
200   600
3000   2000
6000   4000
12 000   m ft

1:20 000 000

100   0   100   200   300   400 miles
100   0   100   200   300   400   500   600 km

■ LONDON: Capital Cities 9

CARTOGRAPHY BY PHILIP'S. COPYRIGHT REED INTERNATIONAL BOOKS LTD.

Projection: Bonne   West from Greenwich   0   East from Greenwich

Seas and Oceans

ATLANTIC OCEAN
Norwegian Sea
North Sea
White Sea
Baltic Sea
G. of Bothnia
Mediterranean Sea
Black Sea
Caspian Sea
Adriatic Sea
Tyrrhenian Sea
Ionian Sea
Aegean Sea
Bay of Biscay
English Channel
Kattegatt
Skagerrak

Countries and Regions

ICELAND
UNITED KINGDOM
SCOTLAND
ENGLAND
WALES
IRELAND
NORWAY
SWEDEN
FINLAND
DENMARK
ESTONIA
LATVIA
LITHUANIA
RUSSIA
BELARUS
UKRAINE
MOLDOVA
POLAND
GERMANY
NETHERLANDS
BELGIUM
LUX.
FRANCE
SWITZERLAND
LIECH.
AUSTRIA
CZECH REP.
SLOVAK REP.
HUNGARY
SLOVENIA
CROATIA
BOSNIA-HERZ.
YUGOSLAVIA
SERBIA
MONTE-NEGRO
MACEDONIA
ALBANIA
ROMANIA
BULGARIA
GREECE
ITALY
SAN MARINO
MONACO
ANDORRA
SPAIN
PORTUGAL
GIBRALTAR (U.K.)
MALTA
TURKEY
CYPRUS
GEORGIA
ARMENIA
AZERBAIJAN
KAZAKHSTAN
SYRIA
IRAQ
IRAN
MOROCCO
ALGERIA
TUNISIA
Africa
Crete
Corsica
Sardinia
Sicily
Corfu
Crimea
Shetland Is.
Orkney Is.
Hebrides
Faroe Is. (Den.)
Channel Is.
Gotland
Öland
Balearic Is.
Minorca
Majorca
Ibiza
Rhodes
Pantelleria (Italy)

Cities and Towns

Reykjavík
Aberdeen
Dundee
Edinburgh
Glasgow
Newcastle-upon-Tyne
Leeds
Sheffield
Manchester
Liverpool
Birmingham
Bristol
Cardiff
Southampton
Plymouth
LONDON
Belfast
Dublin
Cork
Tromsø
Narvik
Bergen
Stavanger
Oslo
Trondheim
Göteborg
Stockholm
Uppsala
Örebro
Norrköping
Jönköping
Kiruna
Luleå
Umeå
Helsinki
Turku
Tampere
Vaasa
Murmansk
Arkhangelsk
St. Petersburg
MOSCOW
Vologda
Yaroslavl
Rybinsk Res.
Kostroma
Ivanovo
N. Novgorod
Kirov
Kotlas
Kazan
Simbirsk
Penza
Tambov
Voronezh
Tula
Orel
Kursk
Saratov
Volgograd
Astrakhan
Rostov
Krasnodar
Stavropol
Makhachkala
Baku
Tbilisi
Yerevan
Ufa
Magnitogorsk
Nizhniy Tagil
Chelyabinsk
Ob
Ishim
Uralsk
Kustanay
Atyrau
Copenhagen
Århus
Ålborg
Kiel
Hamburg
Bremen
Hanover
Berlin
Magdeburg
Leipzig
Halle
Dresden
Chemnitz
Cologne
Bonn
Essen
Dortmund
Frankfurt am Main
Nuremberg
Munich
Stuttgart
Wiesbaden
Mainz
Amsterdam
The Hague
Rotterdam
Antwerp
Brussels
Luxembourg
Strasbourg
Paris
Le Havre
Rouen
Lille
Brest
Nantes
Rennes
Tours
Dijon
Lyons
St-Étienne
Grenoble
Limoges
Bordeaux
Toulouse
Marseilles
Nice
Toulon
Geneva
Zürich
Bern
Basle
Innsbruck
Salzburg
Vienna
Linz
Graz
Prague
Plzeň
Brno
Ostrava
Bratislava
Budapest
Debrecen
Miskolc
Ljubljana
Zagreb
Trieste
Split
Sarajevo
Belgrade
Niš
Tirana
Skopje
Sofia
Plovdiv
Varna
Bucharest
Ploieşti
Galaţi
Braşov
Cluj-Napoca
Timişoara
Constanţa
Chişinău
Kishinev
Kiev
Lvov
Lublin
Warsaw
Łódź
Poznań
Wrocław
Katowice
Kraków
Gdańsk
Szczecin
Bydgoszcz
Białystok
Kaliningrad
Vilnius
Kaunas
Riga
Tallinn
Minsk
Vitebsk
Mogilev
Gomel
Chernigov
Zhitomir
Pripet
Brest
Smolensk
Dnepropetrovsk
Krivoy Rog
Zaporozhye
Donetsk
Taganrog
Kharkov
Nikolayev
Kherson
Odessa
Sevastopol
Istanbul
Bursa
Ankara
Izmir
Konya
Adana
Antalya
Kayseri
Samsun
Nicosia
Thessaloníki
Athens
Pátrai
Corfu
Madrid
Barcelona
Valencia
Alicante
Murcia
Granada
Málaga
Córdoba
Seville
Cádiz
Valladolid
Zaragoza
Bilbao
La Coruña
Vigo
Porto
Lisbon
Gibraltar
Ceuta (Sp.)
Melilla (Sp.)
Tangier
Tunis
Annaba
Constantine
Algiers
Oran
Rome
Naples
Turin
Milan
Genoa
Florence
Bologna
Venice
Bari
Taranto
Palermo
Messina
Catania
Cagliari
Sardinia
Ajaccio
Erzurum
Diyarbakir
Tabriz
Baghdad
Aleppo
Mosul
Tigris
Euphrates

Rivers

Volga
Don
Dnieper
Danube
Rhine
Rhône
Loire
Seine
Garonne
Ebro
Tagus
Guadiana
Guadalquivir
Douro
Elbe
Vistula
Oder
Tiber
Po
W. Dvina
N. Dvina
L. Onega
L. Ladoga
L. Chudskoye
Dniester
Bug
L. Peipus

Arctic Circle

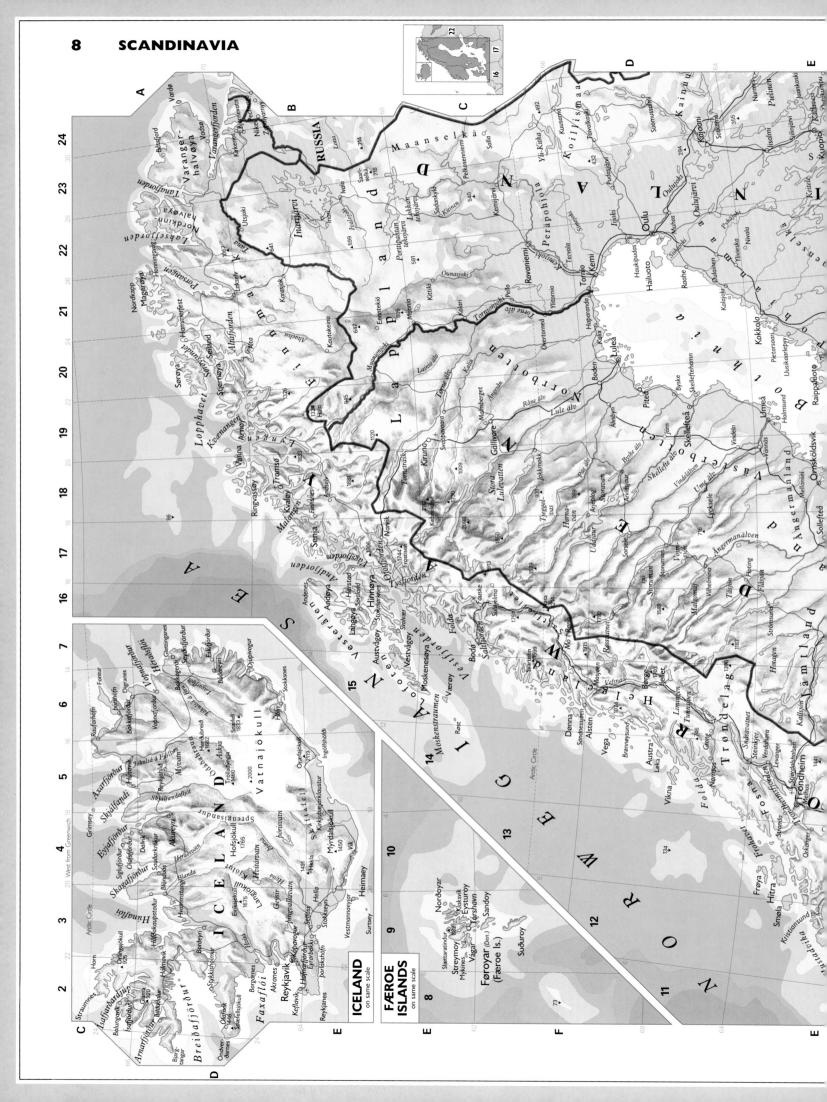

ICELAND
on same scale

FÆROE
ISLANDS
on same scale

Føroyar (Den.)
(Færoe Is.)

1 : 5 000 000

50   0   100 miles

50   0   50   100   150
km

East from Greenwich

Projection: Conical with two standard parallels

CARTOGRAPHY BY PHILIP'S. COPYRIGHT REED INTERNATIONAL BOOKS LTD

Finland area

Savonlinna
Jyväskylä
Tampere
Pori
Turku (Åbo)
Helsinki (Helsingfors)
Vantaa
Espoo

Gulf of Finland

Estonia

Tallinn
Tartu
Pärnu
Narva
Ozero Chudskoye

Latvia

Riga
Jūrmala
Daugava
Liepāja
Ventspils

Gulf of Riga
Hiiumaa (Dagö)
Saaremaa (Ösel)

Lithuania

Vilnius
Kaunas
Šiauliai
Panevėžys
Klaipėda
Kaliningrad (Russia)

BELARUS

Sweden

STOCKHOLM
Uppsala
Gävle
Sundsvall
Härnösand
Örebro
Norrköping
Linköping
Jönköping
Göteborg (Gothenburg)
Malmö
Karlskrona
Kalmar
Visby
Gotland
Öland
Falun
Mora
Östersund
Sveriges
Dalarna
Värmland
Bohuslän
Halland
Skåne
Blekinge
Småland
Gotaland
Vänern
Vättern
Svealand
Norrland
Uppland
Södermanland
Västmanland

Ålands hav
Åland (Ahvenanmaa)

BALTIC SEA

Bornholm
Rügen
Usedom

Norway

Oslo
Bergen
Stavanger
Kristiansand
Drammen
Hamar
Lillehammer
Hardangervidda
Telemark
Dovrefjell
Jotunheimen
Sognefjorden
Dalarna

Skagerrak
Oslofjorden

Denmark

KØBENHAVN (Copenhagen)
Århus
Ålborg
Odense
Esbjerg
Kolding
Roskilde
Helsingør
Sjælland
Fyn
Lolland
Falster
Bornholm

Kattegat
Store Bælt
Lille Bælt
Fehmarn Belt

Germany

Kiel
Lübeck
Rostock
Flensburg
Rendsburg
Schleswig
Holstein
Mecklenburger Bucht
Nordfriesische Inseln
Ostfriesische Inseln
Helgoland
Cuxhaven
Elbe

POLAND

Gdańsk
Gdynia
Słupsk
Koszalin
Kołobrzeg
Szczecin
Zatoka Gdańska
Malbork
Elbląg

m ft
6000 2000
3000 1000
1500 500
600 200
0
50-150
100-300
200-600
500-1500
1000-3000
2000-6000
m ft

NORTH SEA

IRISH SEA

North Channel

SCOTLAND

NORTHUMBERLAND

CUMBRIA

Cumbrian Mts.

DURHAM

TYNE & WEAR

CLEVELAND

NORTH YORKSHIRE

WEST YORKSHIRE

SOUTH YORKSHIRE

LANCASHIRE

MERSEYSIDE

GREATER MANCHESTER

CHESHIRE

DERBY

NOTTS.

LINCOLNSHIRE

HUMBERSIDE

CLWYD

GWYNEDD

STAFFORD

Pennines

Southern Uplands

Cheviot Hills

Galloway

ISLE OF MAN

Anglesey

Holy I.

Lincoln Wolds

Holderness

The Wash

Fife Ness
Anstruther
Kirkcaldy
Dunfermline
Firth of Forth
Edinburgh
Musselburgh
Haddington
Dunbar
North Berwick
Berwick
Bass Rock
St. Abb's Hd.
Eyemouth
Berwick-upon-Tweed
Holy I.
Farne Is.
Flodden
Coldstream
Kelso
Jedburgh
Hawick
Galashiels
Selkirk
Peebles
Moorfoot Hills
Lammermuir Hills
The Cheviot 816
Alnwick
Morpeth
Ashington
Blyth
Tynemouth
Newcastle
Gateshead
South Shields
Sunderland
Consett
Houghton-le-Spring
Hartlepool
Hexham
Durham
Bishop Auckland
Billingham
Stockton
Middlesbrough
Redcar
Darlington
Whitby
Scarborough
Filey
Flamborough Hd.
Bridlington
Hornsea
Withernsea
Spurn Hd.
Kingston upon Hull
Hull
Beverley
Cleethorpes
Grimsby
Mablethorpe
Alford
Louth
Skegness
Lincoln
Boston
Grantham
Newark
Retford
Gainsborough
Worksop
Mansfield
Sutton in Ashfield
Nottingham
Loughborough
Derby
Burton on Trent
Stoke on Trent
Newcastle-under-Lyme
Crewe
Chester
Wrexham
Chesterfield
Sheffield
Rotherham
Doncaster
Scunthorpe
Goole
Selby
York
Leeds
Bradford
Halifax
Huddersfield
Dewsbury
Wakefield
Barnsley
Harrogate
Knaresborough
Ripon
Thirsk
Northallerton
Richmond
Pickering
Malton
Driffield
Keighley
Nelson
Colne
Burnley
Skipton
Settle
Blackburn
Accrington
Preston
Chorley
Bolton
Bury
Rochdale
Oldham
Manchester
Salford
Stockport
Macclesfield
Wigan
St. Helens
Liverpool
Bootle
Wallasey
Birkenhead
Southport
Formby Pt.
Lytham St. Annes
Blackpool
Cleveleys
Fleetwood
Morecambe
Heysham
Lancaster
Kendal
Windermere
Ambleside
Penrith
Appleby
Brough
Keswick
Cockermouth
Workington
Maryport
Whitehaven
St. Bee's Hd.
Seascale
Millom
Barrow
Walney I.
Ulverston
Carlisle
Gretna Green
Annan
Dumfries
Dalbeattie
Castle Douglas
Kirkcudbright
Newton Stewart
Wigtown
Whithorn
Wigtown Bay
Luce Bay
Stranraer
Portpatrick
Mull of Galloway
Pt. of Ayre
Ramsey
Snaefell 620
Douglas
Castletown
Peel
Port Erin
Calf of Man
Glasgow
Paisley
Greenock
Port Glasgow
Dumbarton
Clydebank
Rutherglen
Hamilton
Motherwell
Wishaw
Airdrie
Coatbridge
Kilmarnock
Irvine
Saltcoats
Ayr
Girvan
Helensburgh
Stirling
Alloa
Falkirk
Inveraray
Campbeltown
Belfast
Belfast Lough
Bangor
Larne
Newtownards
Strangford L.
Downpatrick
Ardglass
Donaghadee
Newtownabbey
Arran
Goat Fell 874
Ailsa Craig
Holyhead
Amlwch
Beaumaris
Caernarfon
Bangor
Conwy
Colwyn Bay
Llandudno
Great Orme's Hd.
Rhyl
Prestatyn
Flint
Mold
Denbigh
Ruthin
Llangollen
Oswestry
Whitchurch
Nantwich
Northwich
Winsford
Leek
Buxton
Matlock
Belper
Heanor
Ilkeston
Shrewsbury
Snowdon 1085
Ffestiniog
Blaenau Ffestiniog
Harlech
Pwllheli
Nefyn

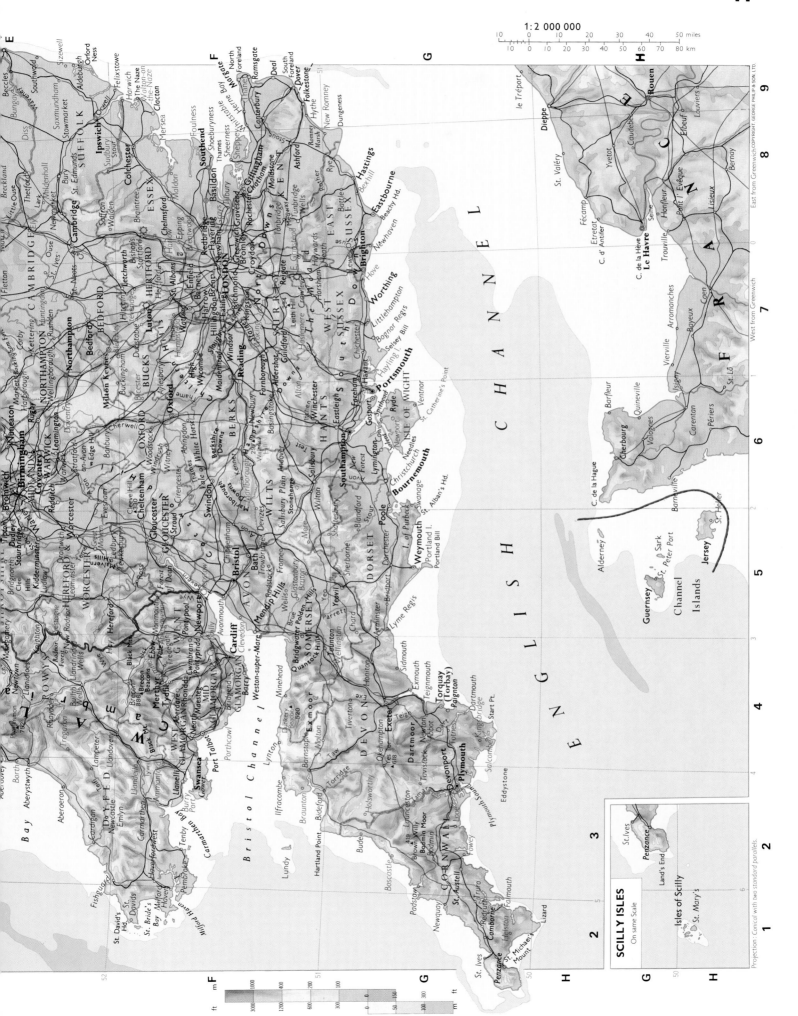

11

1 : 2 000 000

10 0 10 20 30 40 50 miles

10 5 0 10 20 30 40 50 60 70 80 km

SCILLY ISLES
On same Scale

Isles of Scilly
St. Mary's

Projection: Conical with two standard parallels.

East from Greenwich COPYRIGHT GEORGE PHILIP & SON LTD.

West from Greenwich

12 SCOTLAND

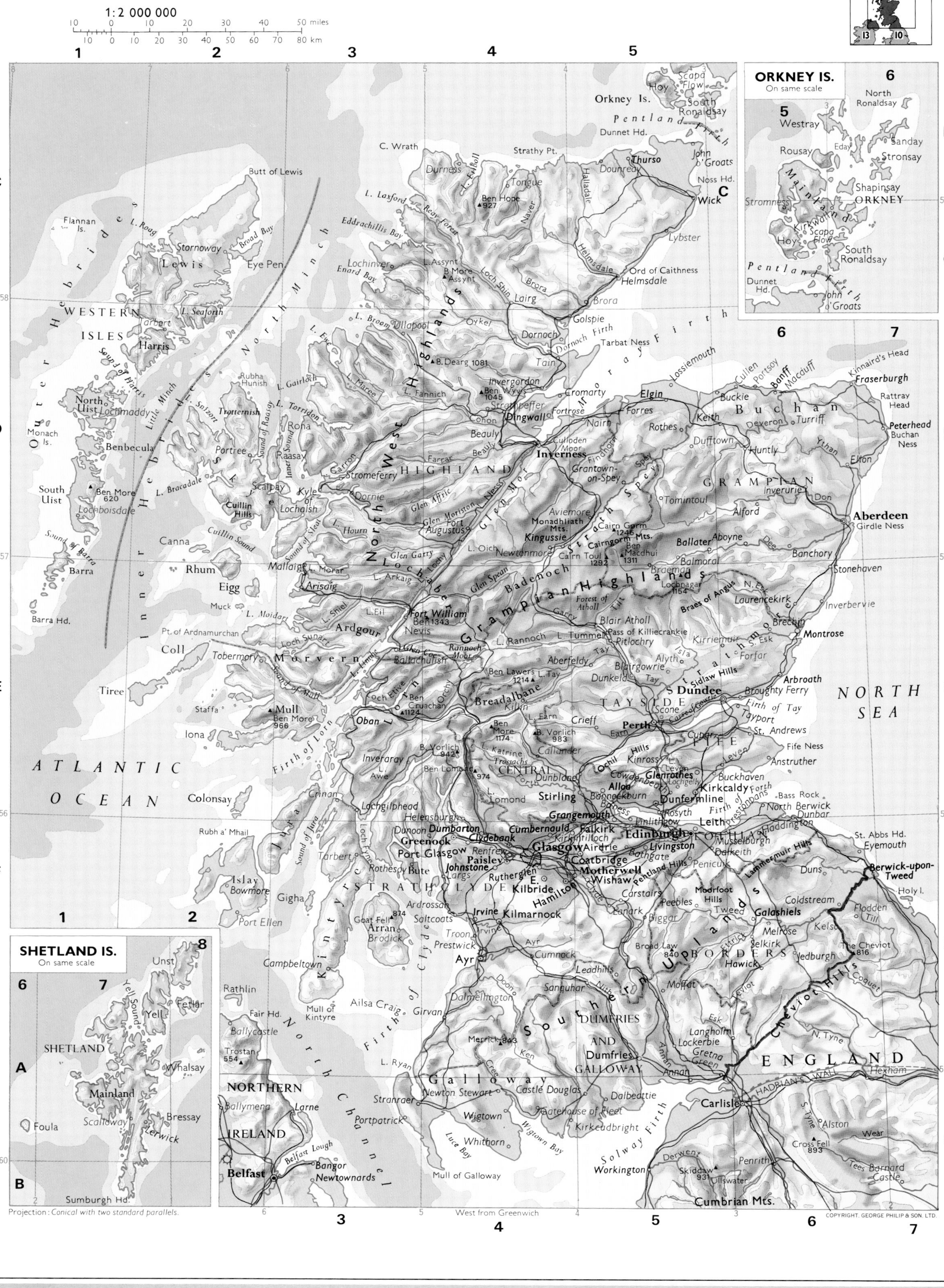

1 : 2 000 000

10   0   10   20   30   40   50 miles
10 0 10 20 30 40 50 60 70 80 km

1   2   3   4   5

ORKNEY IS.
On same scale

6

B

5

Westray
North Ronaldsay
Rousay   Eday   Sanday   Stronsay
Stromness   Mainland   Shapinsay   ORKNEY
Kirkwall   Scapa Flow
Hoy   Scapa Flow
South Ronaldsay
Pentland Firth
Dunnet Hd.   John o' Groats

C

59

6   7

SHETLAND IS.
On same scale

8

6   7

Unst
Fetlar
Yell   Yell Sound
Whalsay
A
SHETLAND
Mainland   Bressay
Foula   Scalloway   Lerwick
B
60
Sumburgh Hd.

ft   m
3000   1000
1200   400
600   200
300   100
0   0
50   150
100   300
m   ft

Projection: Conical with two standard parallels.

Main map labels

Orkney Is.   Hoy   Scapa Flow   South Ronaldsay   North Ronaldsay   Pentland Firth   Dunnet Hd.   John o' Groats   Noss Hd.   Duncansby   Thurso   Dounreay   Wick   Lybster

C. Wrath   Strathy Pt.   Halladale   Durness   L. Eriboll   Tongue   Naver   Rear Forest   Helmsdale   Ord of Caithness   Helmsdale   Brora   Brora   Golspie   Dornoch   Dornoch Firth   Tarbat Ness   Tain   Invergordon   Cromarty   Ben Hope 927   L. Laxford   Eddrachillis Bay   L. Assynt   B. More Assynt   Loch Shin   Lairg   Oykel   L. Broom   Ullapool   Dingwall   Strathpeffer   Fortrose   Ben Wyvis 1045   Beauly   Beauly   Nairn   Forres   Elgin   Lossiemouth   Buckie   Cullen   Portsoy   Banff   Macduff   Kinnaird's Head   Fraserburgh   Rattray Head   Peterhead   Buchan Ness

Butt of Lewis   Flannan Is.   L. Roag   Broad Bay   Stornoway   Eye Pen.   Lewis   Harris   Tarbert   L. Seaforth   North Uist   Lochmaddy   Benbecula   Monach Is.   South Uist   Ben More 620   Lochboisdale   Sound of Barra   Barra   Barra Hd.

WESTERN ISLES   Outer Hebrides   North Minch   Little Minch   Inner Sound   The Minch   Inner Hebrides

C. Wrath   Rubha Hunish   Trotternish   Rona   Raasay   Portree   Scalpay   Kyle of Lochalsh   Dornie   Stromeferry   Garron   L. Gairloch   L. Torridon   L. Maree   Loch Fannich   L. Ewe   Gairloch   Cuillin Hills   L. Bracadale   L. Dunvegan   Canna   Rhum   Eigg   Muck   Coll   Tiree   Staffa   Mull   Ben More 966   Iona   Tobermory   Ardnamurchan   Pt. of Ardnamurchan   L. Moidart   Arisaig   Morar   L. Shiel   L. Eil   Mallaig   Ardgour   Fort William   Ben Nevis 1343   L. Arkaig   Glen Spean

B. Dearg 1081   Strathspey   Invermoriston   Fort Augustus   Glen Moriston   Glen Affric   Glen Garry   Loch Ness   Inverness   Culloden Moor   Grantown-on-Spey   Aviemore   Monadhliath Mts.   Cairn Gorm 1246   Cairngorm Mts.   Ben Macdhui 1311   Cairn Toul 1292   Newtonmore   Kingussie   Badenoch   Glen Roy   Glen Spean   Spey   Tomintoul   Alford   Dufftown   Keith   Huntly   Rothes   Turriff   Deveron   Ythan   Ellon   BUCHAN   GRAMPIAN   Inverurie   Don   Aberdeen   Girdle Ness   Aboyne   Ballater   Balmoral   Braemar   Banchory   Stonehaven   Lochnagar 1154   Forest of Atholl   Braes of Angus   Laurencekirk   Inverbervie   Brechin   Montrose

NORTH WEST HIGHLANDS   Lochaber   Grampian Highlands   Glen Nevis   Rannoch Moor   Ballachulish   L. Rannoch   L. Tummel   Blair Atholl   Pass of Killiecrankie   Pitlochry   Aberfeldy   Ben Lawers 1214   L. Tay   Dunkeld   Blairgowrie   Alyth   Isla   Forfar   Kirriemuir   Ben More 1174   B. Vorlich 983   Crieff   Perth   Scone   Earn   Cupar   St. Andrews   Fife Ness   Anstruther   Tay   FIFE   TAYSIDE   Dundee   Broughty Ferry   Firth of Tay   Tayport   Arbroath

Morvern   Sound of Mull   Loch Linnhe   Ben Cruachan 1124   Oban   Loch Etive   Inveraray   L. Awe   B. Vorlich 943   L. Katrine   Trossachs   Ben Lomond 974   Callander   Dunblane   CENTRAL   L. Lomond   Stirling   Bannockburn   Alloa   Kinross   L. Leven   Glenrothes   Kirkcaldy   Buckhaven   Cowdenbeath   Dunfermline   Rosyth   Firth of Forth   Bass Rock   North Berwick   Dunbar   Preston pans   Leith   Edinburgh   Musselburgh   Dalkeith   Haddington   LOTHIAN   Pentland Hills   Penicuik

ATLANTIC OCEAN   Colonsay   Firth of Lorn   Crinan   Lochgilphead   Loch Fyne   Helensburgh   Dunoon   Dumbarton   Clydebank   Cumbernauld   Falkirk   Grangemouth   Linlithgow   Bathgate   Livingston   Renfrew   Greenock   Port Glasgow   Paisley   Glasgow   Airdrie   Coatbridge   Motherwell   Wishaw   Johnstone   Rutherglen   Kilbride   Hamilton   Carstairs   Carluke   Lanark   Biggar   Peebles   Moorfoot Hills   Lammermuir Hills   Duns   St. Abb's Hd.   Eyemouth   Berwick-upon-Tweed   Holy I.

Rubh' a' Mhail   Jura   Sound of Jura   Bute   Rothesay   Kintyre   STRATHCLYDE   Ardrossan   Saltcoats   Irvine   Kilmarnock   Troon   Prestwick   Ayr   Cumnock   Galashiels   Melrose   Selkirk   Tweed   BORDERS   SOUTHERN UPLANDS   Broad Law 840   Hawick   Jedburgh   The Cheviot 816   Coquet   Kelso   Coldstream   Flodden   Till   Cheviot Hills

Islay   Bowmore   Port Ellen   Gigha   Goat Fell 874   Arran   Brodick   Campbeltown   Mull of Kintyre   Rathlin   Fair Hd.   Ballycastle   Ailsa Craig   Trostan 554   Girvan   Dalmellington   Sanquhar   Leadhills   Moffat   Langholm   Lockerbie   Gretna Green   Esk   N. Tyne   Hexham   HADRIAN'S WALL   ENGLAND   Alston   Wear

NORTHERN IRELAND   Ballymena   Larne   Belfast   Belfast Lough   Bangor   Newtownards   North Channel   Stranraer   Portpatrick   Newton Stewart   Castle Douglas   Dalbeattie   Dumfries   DUMFRIES AND GALLOWAY   GALLOWAY   Merrick 843   Ken   Creetown   Gatehouse of Fleet   Kirkcudbright   Wigtown   Whithorn   Wigtown Bay   Luce Bay   L. Ryan   Mull of Galloway   Solway Firth   Annan   Carlisle   Workington   Skiddaw 931   Derwent   Penrith   Ullswater   Cross Fell 893   Tees   Barnard Castle   Cumbrian Mts.

NORTH SEA   ATLANTIC OCEAN   Firth of Clyde   North Channel

West from Greenwich

1 : 2 000 000

10 0 10 20 30 40 50 miles
10 0 10 20 30 40 50 60 70 80 km

Towns underlined in Northern Ireland give their
names to the Districts in which they stand
The remaining Districts are:—

1 Fermanagh	5 Castlereagh
2 Moyle	6 Ards
3 Newtownabbey	7 Down
4 North Down	8 Newry & Mourne

ATLANTIC OCEAN

NORTH Channel

IRISH SEA

St. George's Channel

Kintyre
Arran
Campbeltown
Mull of Kintyre
Ailsa Craig
Stranraer
Portpatrick

Malin Hd.
Tory I. Horn Hd.
Sheep Haven
Lough Swilly
Bloody Foreland
Gweedore
Carndonagh
Inishowen Pen.
Moville
Buncrana
Giant's Causeway
Rathlin I.
Portrush
Fair Hd.
Ballycastle
Ballymoney
Coleraine
Limavady
Londonderry
Ballymena
Larne
I. Magee
Trostan 554
Errigal 752
Derryveagh Mts.
Letterkenny
Strabane
Sperrin Mts.
Sawel 683
Magherafelt
Antrim
Carrickfergus
Belfast L.
Bangor
Donaghadee
Newtownards
Aran I.
DONEGAL
Gweebarra B.
Glenties
Bluestack 676
Finn
Lifford
Deie
Cookstown
Lough Neagh 16
Belfast
Lisburn
Ards Pen.
Rossan Pt.
Rathlin O Birne I.
Killybegs
Donegal
Ballyshannon
Omagh
ULSTER
NORTHERN IRELAND
Dungannon
Portadown
Lurgan (Craigavon)
Banbridge
Downpatrick
Strangford L.
Donegal Bay
Bundoran
Lower L. Erne
Irvinestown
Enniskillen
Upper L. Erne
Blackwater
Armagh
Dundrum
Newcastle
Slieve Donard 852
Mourne Mts.
Warrenpoint
Downpatrick Hd.
Killala B.
Sligo B.
Sligo
Collooney
L. Allen
Belturbet
Clones
Monaghan
Castleblayney
Newry
Sl. Gullion 577
Carlingford L.
Greenore
Broad Haven
Erris Hd.
Belmullet
Mullet Peninsula
Killala
Ballina
OX Mts.
Arrow
LEITRIM
Leitrim
Annalee
Cootehill
Carrickmacross
Louth
Dundalk
Blacksod Bay
Achill Hd.
Achill I.
Achill
L. Conn
Nephin 806
Moy
SLIGO
Boyle
Carrick-on-Shannon
CAVAN
Cavan
Kingscourt
Ardee
Dundalk Bay
Clare I.
Clew Bay
Croagh Patrick 765
Westport
Castlebar
MAYO
Claremorris
Castlerea
ROSCOMMON
Castlerea
L. Gowna
Granard
Oldcastle
L. Sheelin
Ceanannas Mor (Kells)
Blackwater
An Uaimh (Navan)
Drogheda
Balbriggan
Inishbofin
Clifden
Twelve Pins
CONNEMARA
Mweelrea 819
Killary Harbour
L. Mask
Ballinrobe
Robe
Roscommon
Suck
Longford
LONGFORD
L. Ree
Athboy
Trim
Boyne
MEATH
Swords
Lambay I.
Slyne Hd.
GALWAY
L. Corrib
Tuam
Athenry
Ballinasloe
IRELAND
Clara
Mullingar
WESTMEATH
Athlone
Maynooth
DUBLIN
Ireland's Eye
Howth Head
Galway
Clare
Loughrea
Inn
Edenderry
Celbridge
Dublin (Baile Atha Cliath)
Dublin Bay
Dun Laoghaire
Galway Bay
Inishmore
Aran Is.
Kilkieran B.
Slieve Aughty
Gort
Portumna
Brosna
Daingean
OFFALY
Tullamore
Birr
SL. BLOOM
Mountmellick
Portarlington
Nua
Naas
KILDARE
Kildare
Kippure 754
Poulaphouca Res.
Bray
Hags Hd.
Ennistymon
Liscannor Bay
L. Derg
Roscrea
Port Laoise
Athy
LEINSTER
WICKLOW
Lugnaquilla 923
Wicklow
Wicklow Hd.
Mal Bay
Miltown Malbay
Ennis
CLARE
Killaloe
Ballina
Nenagh
Templemore
LAOIS
Nore
Barrow
Carlow
CARLOW
Tullow
Shillelagh
Rathdrum
Mizen Hd.
Kilkee
Kilrush
Ardnacrusha
Keeper 694
Thurles
Callan
Gorey
Arklow
Avoca
Loop Hd.
Foynes
Rathkeale
Limerick
TIPPERARY Vale
Cashel
Kilkenny
KILKENNY
Muine Bheag
Mt. Leinster 796
Enniscorthy
Cahore Pt.
Listowel
Newcastle
LIMERICK
Golden Vale
Tipperary
Slievenamon 722
Carrick-on-Suir
New Ross
WEXFORD
Brandon Mt. 953
Tralee Bay
Fenit
Feale
Rath Luirc (Charleville)
Gallymore 920
Galty Mts.
Caher
Clonmel
Wexford
Wexford Harbour
Rosslare
Greenore Pt.
Tuscar Rock
Kerry Hd.
Brandon Hd.
Dingle
St. Mish
Maine
KERRY
Kanturk
Blackwater
Mallow
Newmarket
Mitchelstown
Knockmealdown Mts.
Comeragh Mts.
Dungarvan
Tramore
Carnsore Pt.
Gt. Blasket
Dunmore Hd.
Dingle Bay
Laune
Killarney
Boggeragh Mts.
Fermoy
Lismore
Dungarvan
WATERFORD
Waterford
Dungarvan Bay
Hook Hd.
Waterford Harbour
Saltee Is.
St. David's Hd.
Valencia Harbour
Valencia I.
Cahirciveen
Macgillycuddy's Reeks
Carrauntuohill 1040
Lakes of Killarney
Macroom
Lee
Blarney
Midleton
Youghal
Youghal Harbour
Skellig Rocks
Kenmare
Caha Mts.
Glengariff
CORK
Cork
Passage West
Cobh
Cork Harbour
Ballinskelligs B.
Kenmare River
Bantry
Clonakilty
Bandon
Crosshaven
Kinsale
Old Head of Kinsale
Castletown Bearhaven
Bear I.
Dunmanus Bay
Skull
Skibbereen
Clonakilty
Galley Hd.
Crow Hd.
Bantry Bay
Mizen Hd.
Baltimore
Clear I.
C. Clear
Fastnet Rock

ft   m
3000   1000
1200   400
600   200
300   100
0   0
100   300
200   600
m   ft

1 : 5 000 000

50 ... 50 ... 100 miles
50 ... 50 ... 100 ... 150 km

ATLANTIC OCEAN

Shetland Is.
Yell
Unst
Fetlar
Foula
Mainland
Lerwick

1224

316

Fair Isle

NORWAY
Askøy
Bergen
Osøyri
Stord
Bømlo
Haugesund
Kopervik
Åkrahamn
Bokno
Stavanger
Sandne
Bryne
Nærbø

Orkney Is.
Westray
Sanday
Stronsay
Mainland
Kirkwall
Hoy
South
Ronaldsay

Lewis
Stornoway
Outer Hebrides
Harris
St. Kilda
North Uist
Benbecula
South Uist
789
Portree
Skye
Barra
Rhum
Eigg
Coll
Tiree
Mull
Tobermory
Colonsay
Oban

C. Wrath
North West Highlands
North Minch
Ullapool
Thurso
Wick
Helmsdale
Laig
Golspie
Tain
Invergordon
Dingwall
L. Ness
1182
Inverness
Nairn
Aviemore
Ben Nevis
1342
Fort William

Pentland Firth

Moray Firth
Elgin
Buckie
Banff
Fraserburgh
Huntly
Peterhead
Inverurie

SCOTLAND
Grampian Mts.
1214
311
Dee
Aberdeen
Ballater
Stonehaven

Jura
Islay
973
Greenock
Glasgow
Edinburgh
Paisley
East Kilbride
Hamilton
Arran
Irvine
Kilmarnock
Campbeltown
Ayr

Mull
L. Lomond
Perth
St. Andrews
Stirling
Dunfermline
Kirkcaldy
Glenrothes
Clyde

Montrose
Forfar
Arbroath
Dundee

NORTH
SEA

238

Southern Uplands
Galashiels
Berwick-upon-Tweed
840
Jedburgh
Hawick
Cheviot Hills
816
Alnwick

Malin Hd.
Aran I.
Buncrana
Letterkenny
Coleraine
Ballymena
Larne
Lifford
Donegal
NORTHERN IRELAND
Omagh
Lough Neagh
Antrim
Bangor
Belfast
Lisburn
Lurgan
Lower L. Erne
Enniskillen
Portadown
Armagh
Clones
Newry
Bundoran
Sligo
Leitrim
Cavan
Castleblaney
Dundalk

North Channel
Firth of Clyde
Girvan
Stranraer
Kirkcudbright
Dumfries
Annan
Carlisle
Workington
Whitehaven

Dumfries
Hexham
893
Durham
Darlington
Cumbrian Mts.
978
Barrow-in-Furness

Newcastle-upon-Tyne
South Shields
Gateshead
Sunderland
Hartlepool
Redcar
Middlesbrough
Stockton-on-Tees
Scarborough

16

UNITED

KINGDOM

IRISH

Mull of Galloway
Douglas
I. of Man

Lancaster
Harrogate
York
Bridlington
Beverley
Kingston upon Hull

Achill I.
Ballina
L. Conn
Castlebar
Westport
Lough Mask
Connemara
Lough Corrib
Roscommon
Athlone
Lough Ree
Longford
Mullingar
Boyne
Ceanannus Mor
Drogheda

Dublin
Dun Laoghaire
Bray

Holyhead
Anglesey

Blackpool
Preston
Blackburn
Burnley
Keighley
Bradford
Leeds
Halifax
Huddersfield
Barnsley
Doncaster
Scunthorpe
Grimsby
Humber

SEA
Galway B.
Aran Is.
Galway
Ballinasloe
Birr
Tullamore
Port Laoise
Athy
Ennis
Lough Derg
Nenagh
Thurles
Carlow
Kilkenny
926
Arklow
Wicklow Mts.

IRELAND
Connacht
Limerick
Tipperary
Carrick-on-Suir
Clonmel
Wexford
Rosslare
Munster
Kilrush
Listowel
Tralee
Mallow
Blackwater
Youghal
Dungarvan
Waterford

953
1041
Dingle
Killarney
Carrauntoohill
Macgillycuddy's Reeks
Valencia I.
Bantry
Bandon
Kinsale
Cork
Cóbh

Anglesey
Bangor
Colwyn Bay
Chester
Crewe
1085
Snowdon
Wrexham
Pwllheli
Cambrian Mts.
Aberystwyth
Cardigan Bay

Liverpool
Warrington
Stockport
Manchester
Oldham
Chesterfield
636
Stoke on Trent
Stafford
Derby
Nottingham
Mansfield
Lincoln
Louth
Boston
Skegness
The Wash
Cromer

ENGLAND
Leicester
King's Lynn
Norwich
Great Yarmouth
Lowestoft
Shrewsbury
Telford
Nuneaton
Corby
Peterborough
Thetford
Welshpool
Wolverhampton
Coventry
Rugby
Northampton
Bury St. Edmunds
Ipswich
BIRMINGHAM
Redditch
Royal Leamington Spa
Bedford
Cambridge
Felixstowe
Worcester
Hereford
Milton Keynes
Stevenage
Harwich
Colchester

St. George's Channel
Fishguard
Haverfordwest
Milford Haven
Pembroke
Carmarthen
886
Brecon
Merthyr Tydfil
Neath
Llanelli
Swansea
Rhondda
Cwmbran
Newport
Port Talbot
Barry
Cardiff
Bristol

WALES
Cheltenham
Gloucester
Cotswold Hills
Oxford
High Wycombe
Slough
Watford
LONDON
Reading
Newbury
Basingstoke
Guildford
Reigate
Hemel Hempstead
Luton
Harlow
Chelmsford
Southend-on-Sea
Margate
Chatham
Maidstone
Canterbury
Dover

36

NETHERLAND
's-Gravenhage
(Den Haag)
ROTTERDAM
Dordrec
Hoek van Holland
Haarle
Den Held
Alkm
Te

Bristol Channel
Weston-super-Mare
Bath
Barnstaple
Exmoor
Taunton
Bude
618
Dartmoor
Exeter
Yeovil
Salisbury
Southampton
Winchester
Fareham
Bournemouth
Poole
Newport
Weymouth
Isle of Wight
Portsmouth
Worthing
Brighton
Eastbourne
Havant
Crawley
Hastings
Folkestone
Str. of Dover

CELTIC
SEA

Newquay
Truro
St. Austell
Plymouth
Falmouth
Land's End
Penzance
Isles of Scilly
Torbay
Exmouth

English Channel

C. de la Hague
Alderney
Pte. de Barfleur
Cotentin
Guernsey
St. Peter Port
Sark
Channel Is.
(U.K.)
St. Helier
Jersey
Cherbourg
Valognes
Bayeux
Caen

99

BELGIUM
BRUSSEL
(Bruxelles)
Antwerpe
Brugge
Gent
Oostende
Zeebrugge
Vlissingen
Meche
Tournai
Lille
Roubaix
Tourc
Dunkerque
Calais
C. Gris-Nez
St.-Omer
Boulogne-sur-Mer
Béthune
Lens
Bruay-en-Artois
Le Touquet-Paris-Plage
33
Abbeville
Le Tréport
Dieppe
Fécamp
Le Havre
Bolbec
Rouen
Seine
Elbeuf
Lisieux
Trouville-sur-Mer

FRANCE
Amiens
St. Quentin
Cambrai
Valenciennes
Picardie
Pays de Caux

East from Greenwich
West from Greenwich

Projection: Conical with two standard parallels

CARTOGRAPHY BY PHILIP'S.
COPYRIGHT REED INTERNATIONAL BOOKS LTD

Country and Region Labels

UNITED KINGDOM
NETHERLANDS
BELGIUM
LUXEMBOURG
FRANCE
GERMANY
DENMARK
SWITZERLAND
AUSTRIA
ITALY
SLOVENIA
CZECH
POLSKA

Seas and Water Bodies

NORTH SEA
BALTIC SEA
ADRIATIC SEA
Golfo di Génova
Golfo di Venézia

Major Cities and Places

Sylt, Abenrå, Svendborg, Næstved, Møn, Rügen, Sassnitz
Westerland, Föhr, Flensburg, Schleswig, Nakskov, Falster, Rødbyhavn, Gedser
Nordfriesische Inseln, Helgoland, Rendsburg, Kiel, Puttgarden, Fehmarn
Kieler Bucht, Fehmarn Bælt, Mecklenburger Bucht, Stralsund, Greifswald, Wolin, Świnoujście, Kołobrzeg, Kosz.
Ost-friesische Inseln, Norderney, Deutsche Bucht, Cuxhaven, Holstein, Neumünster, Travemünde, Rostock, Usedom, Białogard
Terschelling, Ameland, Schiermonnikoog, Borkum, Wilhelmshaven, Emden, Bremerhaven, Lübeck, Wismar, Schwerin, Güstrow, Neubrandenburg, Stettiner Haff, Police, Szczecin, Pojezier
Texel, Den Helder, Leeuwarden, Groningen, Assen, Oldenburg, Stade, Hamburg, Lüneburg, Müritzsee, Neustrelitz, Stargard Szczeciński, Wał.
Alkmaar, Hoorn, Sneek, Meppel, Emmen, Lingen, Delmenhorst, Bremen, Verden, Celle, Uelzen, Mecklenburg, Neuruppin, Oranienburg, Eberswalde-Finow, Gorzów Wielkopolski
Haarlem, AMSTERDAM, Zwolle, Almelo, Rheine, Osnabrück, Nienburg, Hannover, Wolfsburg, Stendal, Rathenow, Brandenburg, Potsdam, BERLIN, Fürstenwalde, Kostrzyn, Nowy Tomyśl
's-Gravenhage (Den Haag), Leiden, Gouda, Utrecht, Apeldoorn, Deventer, Enschede, Münster, Minden, Herford, Hildesheim, Braunschweig, Magdeburg, Frankfurt-Swiebodzin, Międzychód, Zielona Góra
Hoek van Holland, ROTTERDAM, Arnhem, Nijmegen, 's-Hertogenbosch, Bielefeld, Hamel, Salzgitter, Halberstadt, Bernburg, Dessau, Wittenberg, Luckenwalde, Cottbus, Nowa Sól
Dordrecht, Breda, Tilburg, Eindhoven, Duisburg, Krefeld, Dortmund, Paderborn, Göttingen, Nordhausen, Sangerhausen, Anhalt, Forst, Żagań, Głogów
Vlissingen, Antwerpen, Turnhout, Mönchengladbach, Essen, Bochum, Hagen, Kassel, Mühlhausen, Merseburg, Halle, Leipzig, Riesa, Hoyerswerda, Boleslawiec
Zeebrugge, Oostende, Brugge, Gent, Mechelen, Köln (Cologne), Solingen, Siegen, Marburg, Erfurt, Weimar, Zeitz, Gera, Meissen, Dresden, Görlitz, Zgorzelec, Legn.
Dover, Dunkerque, Calais, BRUSSEL (Bruxelles), Leuven, Liège, Bonn, Giessen, Fulda, Suhl, Gotha, Jena, Zwickau, Chemnitz, Liberec, Jelenia Góra
Boulogne-sur-Mer, Lille, Roubaix, Tournai, Namur, Verviers, Aachen, Düren, Koblenz, Wetzlar, Wasserkuppe, Plauen, Hof, Reichenbach, Greiz, Ústí nad Labem, Trutnov
Béthune, Lens, Valenciennes, Charleroi, Maubeuge, Dinant, Bastogne, Wiesbaden, Frankfurt, Hanau, Schweinfurt, Coburg, Bayreuth, Karlovy Vary, Teplice, Most, Litoměřice, Hradec Králové
Abbeville, Douai, Arras, Cambrai, Mons, Charleville-Mézières, Sedan, LUXEMBOURG, Trier, Mainz, Offenbach, Bamberg, Weiden, Cheb, Chomutov, Kladno, Mladá Boleslav, Pardub.
Amiens, St.-Quentin, Beauvais, Laon, Compiègne, Soissons, Thionville, Hagondange, Briey, Metz, Ludwigshafen, Darmstadt, Würzburg, Erlangen, Nürnberg, Amberg, PRAHA (Prague)
Beauvais, Noyon, Reims, Épernay, Verdun, Saarbrücken, Kaiserslautern, Speyer, Mannheim, Heidelberg, Ansbach, Fürth, Regensburg, Plzeň, Pribram, Kolín
île-de-France, Châlons-sur-Marne, Bar-le-Duc, Nancy, Haguenau, Karlsruhe, Pforzheim, Heilbronn, Crailsheim, Straubing, Deggendorf, Klatovy, Tábor, Jihlava
PARIS, Créteil, Evry, Melun, Provins, Troyes, Chaumont, Toul, Lunéville, Strasbourg, Baden-Baden, Stuttgart, Aalen, Ingolstadt, České Budějovice, Jindřichův Hradec
Sens, Fontainebleau, St.-Dizier, Épinal, Colmar, Offenburg, Tübingen, Göppingen, Donauwörth, Landshut, Passau, Gmünd, Znojmo
Auxerre, Langres, Vesoul, Belfort, Mulhouse, Freiburg, Villingen-Schwenningen, Biberach, Ulm, Augsburg, MÜNCHEN (Munich), Freising, Braunau, Linz, Krems
Avallon, Dijon, Montbéliard, Besançon, Basel, Winterthur, Sankt Gallen, Memmingen, Dachau, Rosenheim, Wels, Amstetten, Sankt Pölten
Nevers, Autun, Dole, Biel, Neuchâtel, Aarau, Zürich, Bregenz, Kempten, Garmisch-Partenkirchen, Chiemsee, Salzburg, Bad Ischl, Wiener Neustadt
Moulins, Beaune, Chalon-sur-Saône, Pontarlier, Solothurn, Luzern, Zug, Feldkirch, Dornbirn, Innsbruck, Kufstein, Gmunden, Eisenerz, Kapfenberg
Charolles, Lons-le-Saunier, Fribourg, BERN, Thun, Interlaken, Schwyz, Vaduz, LIECHTENSTEIN, Landeck, Bad Gastein, Leoben, Bruck an der Mur
Vichy, Mâcon, Bourg-en-Bresse, Lausanne, Montreux, Sion, SWITZERLAND, Chur, Davos, Merano, Bolzano, Lienz, Villach, Wolfsberg, Klagenfurt, Graz
Roanne, Thiers, Geneve, Martigny, Chamonix, Mont Blanc, Locarno, Bellinzona, Lugano, Como, Bressanone, Bruneck, Karnische Alpen, Kranj, Celje, Maribor
St.-Étienne, Annecy, Aosta, Domodossola, Verbania, Lugano, Varese, Bérgamo, Brescia, Trento, Rovereto, Belluno, Udine, Gorizia, Ljubljana, Novo Mesto
Lyon, Chambery, Albertville, Ivrea, Biella, Novara, Busto Arsizio, Monza, MILANO, Lodi, Verona, Vicenza, Padova, Treviso, Pordenone, Trieste, Koper, Rijeka, Karlovac
Grenoble, Voiron, Pinerolo, TORINO (Turin), Vercelli, Vigévano, Pavia, Cremona, Mántova, Lodi, Ferrara, Rovigo, Chióggia, Venézia (Venice), Rijeka, Krk
Valence, Romans-sur-Isère, Tournon, Briançon, Asti, Alessandria, Novi Ligure, Piacenza, Parma, Módena, Reno, Bologna, Ravenna, Senj, Gospić
Montélimar, Gap, Embrun, Cuneo, Savona, Fossano, Mondovi, Carpi, Reggio nell'Emilia, Imola, Faenza, Forlì, Cesena, Rímini, Pésaro, Pag
Montpellier, Nîmes, Avignon, Arles, Salon-de-Provence, Aix-en-Provence, Digne-les-Bains, San Remo, Impéria, Génova, La Spézia, Carrara, Massa, Lucca, Prato, Firenze (Florence), SAN MARINO, Fano
Aigues-Mortes, Istres, Martigues, Draguignan, Grasse, Cannes, Antibes, Nice, Monte-Carlo, MONACO, Menton, Riviera di Ponente, Viaréggio, Pisa, Scandicci, Marino
MARSEILLE, Aubagne, Fréjus, St.-Tropez, Toulon, La Seyne-sur-Mer, Hyères

Physiographic Labels

Niedersachsen, Nordrhein-Westfalen, Sauerland, Westerwald, Rheinland-Pfalz, Hunsrück, Taunus, Hessen, Vogelsberg, Rhön, Thüringer Wald, Fichtelgebirge, Erzgebirge, Böhmerwald
Franche-Comté, Bourgogne, Nivernais, Morvan, Jura, Alpes, Massif Central, Massif du Pelvoux, Provence, Piemonte, Lombárdia, Ligúria, Dolomiti, Karawanken
Bayern, Schwäbische Alb, Schwarzwald, Württemberg, Baden, Alsace, Lorraine, Ardenne
Brandenburg, Mecklenburg, Sachsen, Sachsen-Anhalt, Harz, Steiermark, Kärnten, Tirol
Lago di Garda, Lago di Como, Lago Maggiore, Lac Léman, Lago di Lugano

Map Margin Information

Projection: Conical with two standard parallels

Elevation Scale

ft / m
12000 / 4000
9000 / 3000
6000 / 2000
3000 / 1000
1500 / 500
600 / 200
150 / 50
0
150 / 50
300 / 100
1500 / 500
3000 / 1000
6000 / 2000
m ft

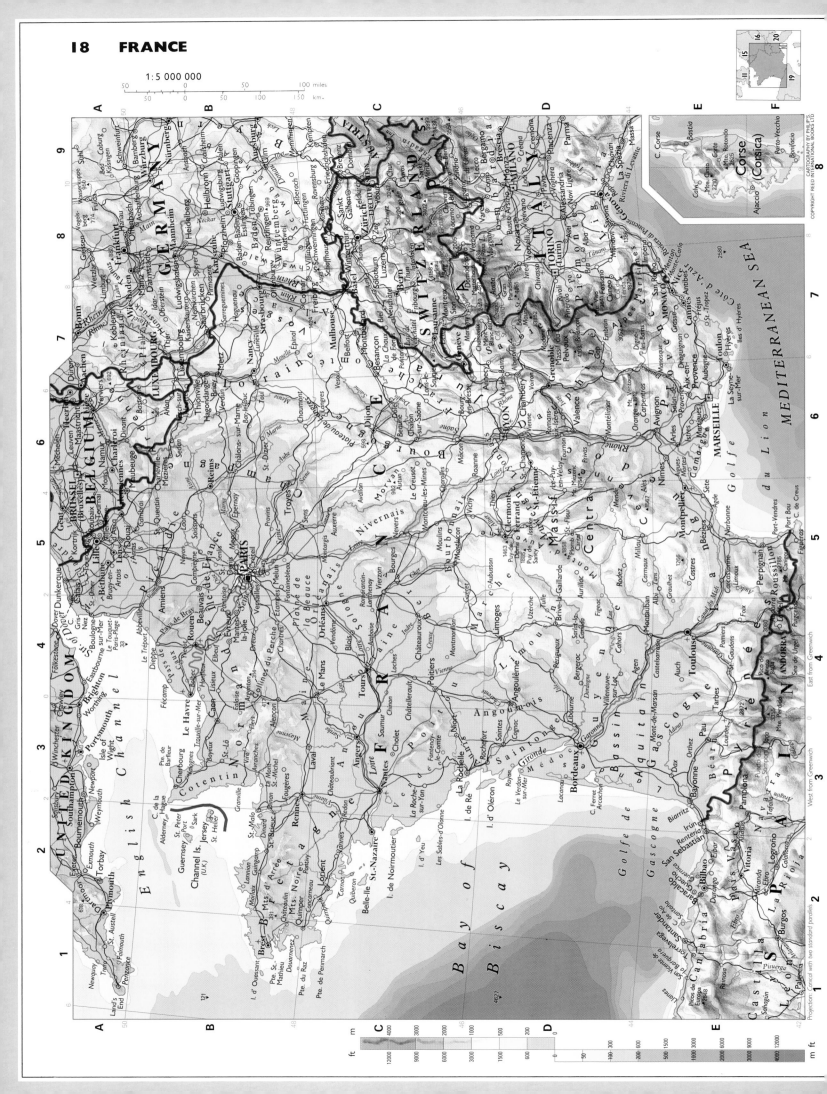

1:5 000 000

Corse (Corsica)

MEDITERRANEAN SEA

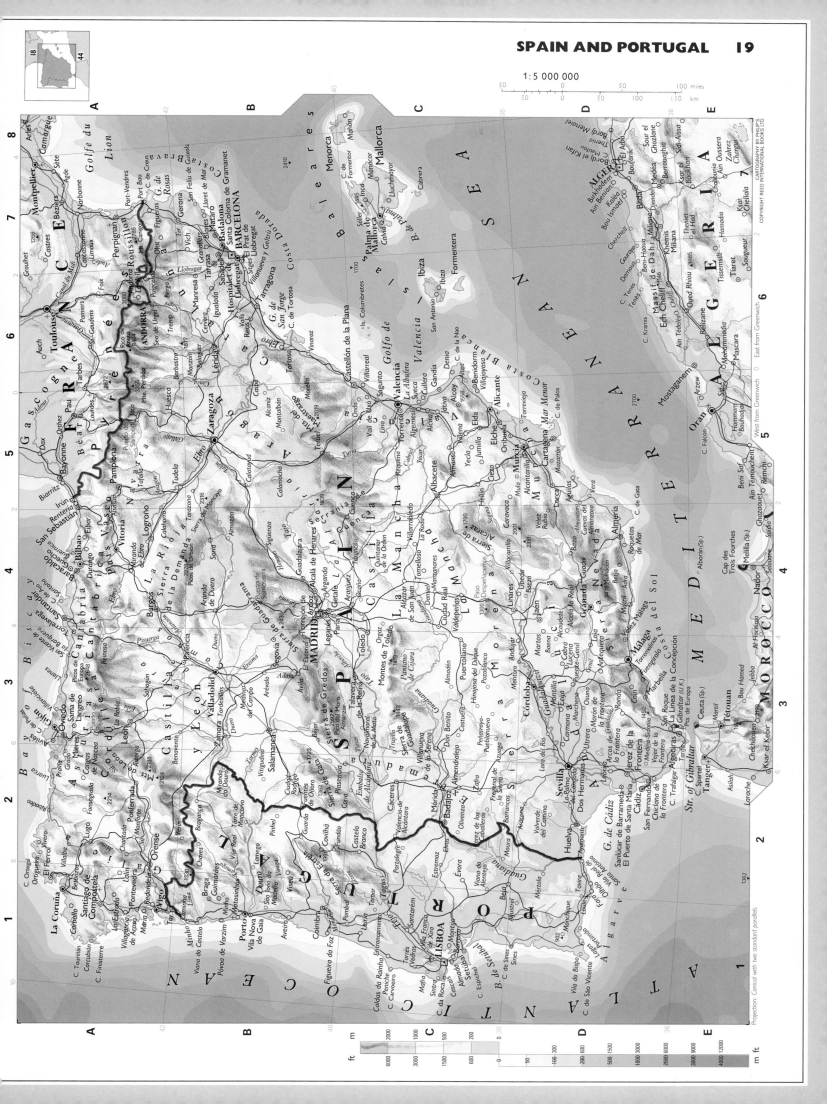

1:5 000 000

18 16 17
23
44 45

1:5 000 000

50　0　50　100 miles
50　0　50　100　150 km

8　9　22　10　24　11　26　12　28　13　30

East from Greenwich

HUNGARY

Szekszárd · Kalocsa · Kiskőrös · Kiskunhalas · Orosháza · Crișul Alb · Muntii Bihor 1848 · Arad · Odorheiu Secuiesc · Miercurea Ciuc · Onești · Bîrlad · Cedar-Lunga · Tatarbunary
Hódmezővásárhely · Makó · Arad · Brad · Alba-Iulia · Sighișoara · Sfîntu Gheorghe · Tecuci · Prut · Cahul · Kiliya · Ozero Sasyk
Szeged · Baja · Kikinda · Lugoj · Deva · Simeria · Sibiu · Mediaş · Tîrnăveni · Focșani · Galați · Reni · Izmayil · Volkove · **UKRAINE** · Bolhrad

Pécs · Mohács · Subotica · Senta · Sînnicolau Mare · Mureș · Timișoara · Caransebeș · Reșita · Hunedoara · Petroșani · Cîmpulung · Mt. Oituz 1783 · Rîmnicu Sărat · Galați · Brăila · Sulina

ROMANIA · Carpații Meridionali · Vf. Peleaga 2509 · Turnu Roșu · Mt. Oituz 2507 · Buzău · Dunărea (Danube) · Tulcea · Babadag

Osijek · Vojvodina · Zrenjanin · Bela Crkva · Porta Orientalis · Curtea de Argeș · Tîrgoviște · Cîmpina · Ploiești · Slobozia · Lacul Razelm

Slavonski Brod · Novi Sad · Pančevo · Orșova · Portile de Fier · Dobreta-Turnu-Severin · Drăgășani · Pitești · **BUCUREȘTI (Bucharest)** · Fetești · Năvodari

SNIA- · Vukovar · Sremska Mitrovica · Petrovaradin · Smederevo · Požarevac · Craiova · Slatina · Oltenița · Călărași · Medgidia · Constanța

Zenica · GOVINA · Bijeljina · Tuzla · Brčko · Šabac · **BEOGRAD (Belgrade)** · Dunav · Negotin · Bor · Băilești · Caracal · Rosiori-de-Vede · Vedea · Alexandria · Giurgiu · Silistra · Tutrakan · Mangalia

Sarajevo · Valjevo · Titovo Kragujevac · Svetozarevo · Vidin · Lom · Oryakhovo · Turnu Măgurele · Zimnicea · Ruse · Dobrich · Balchik

YUGOSLAVIA · Srebrnica · Han Pijesak · Užice · Čačak · Kruševac · Zaječar · Timok · Midžor 2168 · Mikhaylovgrad · Vratsa · Svishtov · Razgrad · Nos Kaliakra

Mostar · Durmitor 2522 · **SERBIA** · Kopaonik · Kraljevo · Niš · Pirot · Suva Planina · Pleven · Lovech · Gorna Oryakhovitsa · Veliko Tŭrnovo · Sumen · Varna

Konjic · Goražde · Novi Pazar · Leskovac · Prokuplje · Kopa 1409 · Stara Planina · Teteven · Sevlievo · Gabrovo · Tŭrgovishte · Kamchiya

Trebinje · Višegrad · Plevlja · Taru · **MONTENEGRO** · Titova Mitrovica · Uroševac · Vranje · Pernik · **SOFIYA** · Vezhen 2198 · Karlovo · Shipchenski P. 1636 · Sliven · Aytos · Burgas · **BLACK SEA**

Nikšić · Podgorica · Cetinje · **Kosovo** · Priština · Kyustendil · Stanke Dimitrov · Samokov · Pazardzhik · Kazanlŭk · Nova Zagora · Yambol · Nos Emine

Kotor · Bar · Skadarsko Jezero · Peć · Đakovica · Prizren · Kumanovo 2259 · Blagoevgrad · Musala 2925 · Plovdiv · Stara Zagora · Elkhovo · Michurin

Ulcinj · Shkodra · Kukës · Tetovo · **Skopje** · Kočani · Štip · Rhodopi Planina 2188 · Asenovgrad · Haskovo · Dimitrovgrad · Tundzha · **BULGARIA**

Lezha · **ALBANIA** · Debar · **MACEDONIA** · Titov Veles · Sandanski · Pirin Planina · Smolyan · Kŭrdzhali · Arda · Kŭrklareli · Edirne · Pınarhisar · Vize · Saray · İğneada Burnu 1018 · Istranca Dağları

Peshkopi · Solunska Glava 2540 · Prilep · Strumica · Petrich · Zlatograd · Momchilgrad · Orestiás · Bobaeski · Lüleburgaz · Çerkesköy · Çatalca · Karadeniz Boğazı (Bosporus)

Tirana · Jablanica 2242 · Ohrid · Bitola · Preshpansko Jezero · Valandovo · 2031 · Drama · Xánthi · Komotiní · Uzunköprü · Hayrabolu · Muratlı · Çorlu · Silivri · **İSTANBUL** · Kharta

Durrësi · Elbasani · Shkumbin · Ohridsko Jezero · Florína · Ptolemaís · Edhessa · Sérrai · Kaválla · Makedhonía · Enez · Keşan · Şarköy · Malkara · Tekirdağ · Büyükçekmece · Gebze 1220 · Darıca

Lushnja · Semani · Korça · Kastoria · Kozáni · Véroia · Yiannitsá · Kilkís · Strimón · Strimonikós Kólpos 1127 · Thásos · Alexandroúpolis · İpsala · Marmara · Marmara Denizi (Sea of Marmara) · Yalova · Orhangazi · İznik Gölü

Fieri · Berati 2480 · Tómoros · Smólikas 2637 · Thessaloniki · Polýiros · Singitikós Kólpos · Akra Pinnes · Samothráki 1600 · Gökçeada · Eceabat · Çanakkale Boğazı (Dardanelles) · Erdek · Bandırma · Mudanya · Gemlik · Bursa 2543

Vlóra · Gjirokastra 2495 · Píndos · Ossa 1978 · Thermaïkós Kólpos · Mt. Olympus 2917 · Toronaíos Kólpos · Athos 2033 · Móudhros · Boğaçada · Ezine · Bayramiç · Edremit · Balya · Uludağ · Dursunbey

Delvínë · Ioánnina 2469 · Tríkkala 2315 · Lárisa · Vólos · Pagastikós Kólpos · Akra Palioúrion · **Límnos** · Ayios Evstrátios · Baba Burnu · Ayvacık · Edremit Körfezi · Burhaniye · Bigadiç · Alaçam Dağları 2089 · Emet

IONIAN SEA · Kérkira (Corfu) · Igoumenitsa · Párga · Préveza · Árta · Tírnavot · Voríai Sporádhes 1280 · Ayvalık · Bergama · Soma · Demirci · Simav

Paxol · Kefallinía · Levkás · Agrínion 2510 · Óros Gióna 2510 · Skiathos · Skiatos · Skópelos · Istiaía · **AEGEAN SEA** · Lésvos · Mitilíni 968 · Kınık · **TURKEY** · Lydia

Itháki · Mesolóngion · Návpaktos · Parnassós 2457 · Dhírfis 1743 · Évvoia · Khalkís · Skíros · Psará · Foça · Karaburun · Manisa · Menemen · Turgutlu · Akhisar · SARDIS · Salihli · Alaşehir · Eşme · Uşak

Argostóllon · Erimanthos 2224 · Kýllini 2376 · Leivadhiá · Thívai · Akra Kafirévs 1398 · Khíos 1297 · Khíos · Çeşme · İZMİR (Smyrna) · Bayındır · Ödemiş · Boz Dağlar 2159 · Sarıgöl · Buldan

Zákinthos · Zákinthos 1628 · Pátrai · Aiyion · Korinthiakós Kólpos · Akharnaí · Mégara · **ATHÍNAI (Athens)** · Seferihisar · EPHESUS · Kuşadası · Aydın · Nazilli · Söke · Selçuk · İncirliova · Karacasu · Bozdoğan

Pyrgos · Olympia · Amaliás · Trípolis 1413 · Korinthos · Piraiévs · Salamis · Saronikós Kólpos · Lávrion · **Ándros** · Ándros · Tínos · Ikaría 1153 · Sámos · MILETUS · Milás · Muğla · Gö16eli Dağları

Pelopónnisos · Kiparissía · Kiparissiakós Kólpos 1421 · Árgos · MYCENE · Návplion · Ídhra · Kíthnos · Kéa · Tínos · Síros · Páros · Foúrnoi · Kálimnos · Bodrum · Örfez · Kerme Körfezi · Köyceğiz · Ortaca

Filiatrá · Messíni · Kalámai · Spárti · Taíyetos Óros 2407 · Argolikós Kólpos · Sérifos · Náxos · Náxos · Páros · Pátmos · Kos · Kárya · Datça · Marmaris · Bozburun

Pílos · Messiniakós Kólpos · Yíthion · Lakonikós Kólpos · Kíthira · Sífnos · Sikinos · Íos · Thíra · Amorgós · Astipálaia · Dhodhekánisos · Tílos · Sími · Ródhos

Akra Ákritas · Akra Maléa · Kíthira · Andikíthira 1480 · Mílos · **Ródhos (Rhodes)** 1215 · Líndhos

MEDITERRANEAN SEA 4070 · Akra Spátha · Kólpos Khanían · Kólpos Soudhás · **Kríti** · Iráklion · Kólpos Merabéllou · Akra Plaka · Kárpathos 1205 · Kásos

Khaniá · Réthimnon · KNOSSOS · Ídhi Óros 2453 · Dhíkti Óros 2148 · Sitía

Lévka Óri · Khóra Sfakíon · Lithinon · Ierápetra · Gávdhos

A B C D E F G
44 42 40 38 36

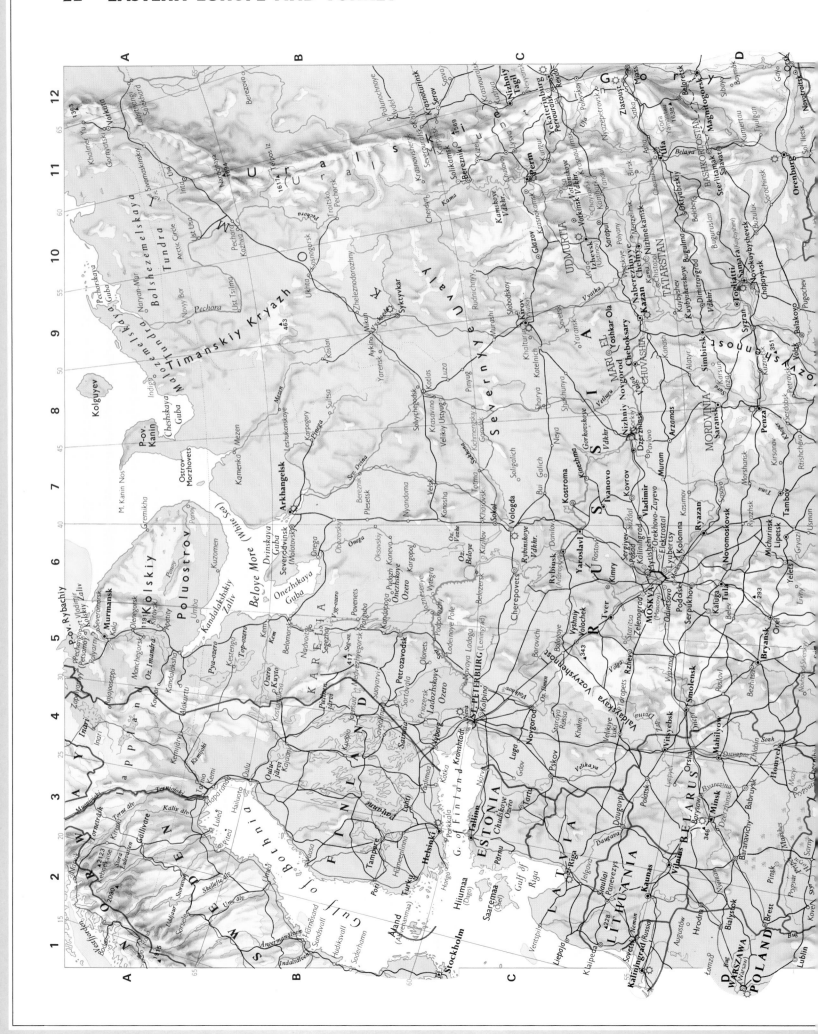

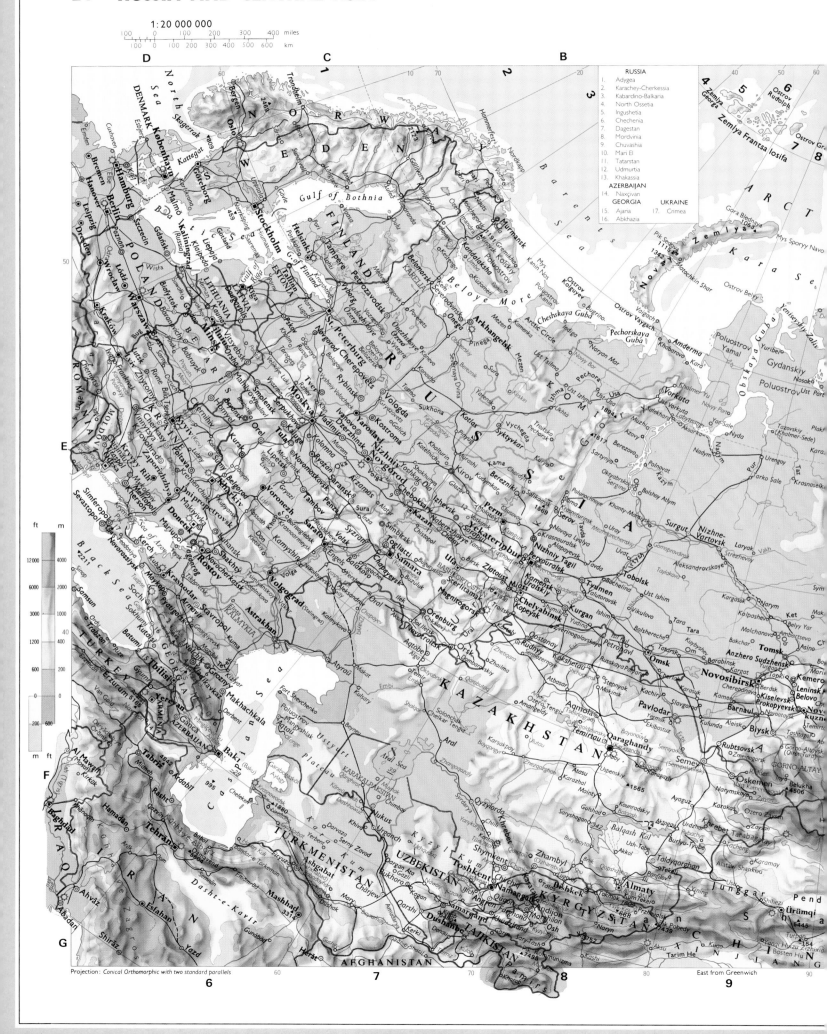

1 : 20 000 000

RUSSIA
1. Adygea
2. Karachey-Cherkessia
3. Kabardino-Balkaria
4. North Ossetia
5. Ingushetia
6. Chechenia
7. Dagestan
8. Mordvinia
9. Chuvashia
10. Mari El
11. Tatarstan
12. Udmurtia
13. Khakassia
AZERBAIJAN
14. Naxçivan
GEORGIA   UKRAINE
15. Ajana   17. Crimea
16. Abkhazia

Projection: Conical Orthomorphic with two standard parallels

East from Greenwich

Mys Dezhneva (East C.)

St. Lawrence I. (U.S.A.)

C

19

Chukchi Sea

Anadyrskiy Zaliv

B

A

D

E

F

17

18

16

15

14 3800

13

12

10 **11**
Mys Arkticheskiy

Ostrov Komsomolets

9 Ostrov
Pioner

Ostrov Oktyabrskoy
Revolyutsii
965

Ostrov Bolshevik

**Severnaya
Zemlya**

Proliv Vilkitskogo

OCEAN

Ostrov
Henrietta
Ostrova Delong
Ostrov
Jeanette

Ostrova
Ostrov Zhokhov

Novosibirskiye Ostrova

Ostrov Bennett

East Siberian Sea

Ostrov Vrangelya

Ostrova
Medvezhi

Bering
Sea

L a p t e v

Ostrov Belkovskiy

Ostrov Malyy
Lyakhovskiy
Ostrov Bolshoy
Lyakhovskiy

Ostrov Faddeyevskiy 374
Ostrov Kotelnyy

Ostrov Novaya Sibir

Lyakhovskiye Ostrova

Proliv Dmitriya Lapteva

Ostrov Ayon

Chukotskoye Nagorye

1843

1853

1562

S e a

Ostrov Stolbovoy

Kokuora

Nizhne Kolymsk

Pevek

Amguema

Uelen
Lavrentiya
Provideniya

Egvekinot

Anadyr

Markovo

Ust Olenek

Yuyung Kaya

Nordvik

**P o l u o s t r o v
T a y m y r**

Gory
Byranga
746

Ostrov Bolshoy
Begichev

Khatanga

Kazachye
Chokurdakh

Srednekolymsk

Kolyma

Nyzhne Kolymsk

Omolon

Omolon

Gizhiga

Penzhinskaya Guba

S r e d i n n y y

Kamandorskiye Ostrova

D

Nikolskoye Ust-Kamchatsk

Tiksi

Mys Buorkhaya

Kyusyur

Bulun

Zhilinda

Kheta

Volochanka

Pyasina

Novorybnoye

Popigay

Saskylakh

Anabar

Kel
(Bysyttakh)

Verkhoyansk
2389

Zashiversk

Ust Yansk

Ust Kuyga

Yana

Deputatskiy

Druzhina

Zyryanka

Srednekolymsk

Verkhnekolymsk

Seymchan

Balygychan

Taskan

Susuman

Ust-Omchug

Atka

Magadan

Ola

Gizhiginskaya
Guba

Tigil

Zaliv
Shelikhova

**P o l u o s t r o v
K a m c h a t k a**

**Petropavlovsk-
Kamchatskiy**

3621 4750

4688

2958

Norilsk
Gory
Putorana
1701

Yessey

Kotuy

Molyero

Zhiyansk

Olenek

Olenek

Lena

Zhigansk

Lepikha

Botamay

Kystatyam

Batagay

Gora Chen
2682

Pobeda
3147

Khongdo

Khandyga

Okhotskiy
Perevoz

Nelkan

Allakh Yun

Okhotsk

Ulya

S e a   o f
O k h o t s k

1780

Sakhalin

Zaliv

Ostrov
Paramushir

Nizhnyaya Tunguska

Tura

Vilyuy

Vilyuysk

Suntar

Nyurba
Verkhnevilyuysk

Sangar

Pokrovsk
Yelanskoye

Yakutsk

Mayya

Amga
Amga

Ust Maya

Maya

Nelkan

Ayon

Arctic Circle
962

Sholgontsy

Srednevilyuysk

Tuoy-Khaya

Chernyshevskiy

Mirnyy

Syul'dzhyukyor

Vanavara

Yukti

Simenga

Lensk
(Mukhtuya)

Olekminsk

Nokhtuysk

Khatyryk

Verkhnyaya Amga

Tommot

Aldan

Chagda

Uchur

Chasornaya
Uchurskaya

Ostrov Bolshoy
Shantar

R
Podkamennaya
Tunguska

Kuyumba

Baykit

Mutoray

Yerbogachen

Kurya

Roman

Vitim

Dikimdya

Aldan

Melyy Nimnyr
2246

Khatymal

Khulman

Nagornyy

Chumikan

Nemuy

Tugur

**Nikolayevsk-
na-Am.**

Okha

U

Severo-
Yeniseyskiy
1104

Artsevo

Ust-Ilimsk

Makarovo

Kezhma
Kata

Korshunovo

Mama

Kirensk

Bodaybo

Karalon
2999

Ust-Nyukzha

Tynda

Pavlovich

Skovorodino

Zeya

Selemdzha

Ekimchan imeni Polina
Osipenko

Amgun

Srednetambovskoye

Komsomolsk

2078

Khabarovsk

K

Yeniseysk
Angara

Strelka

Ust-Kut

Zheleznogorsk
Ilimskiy

Nizhneangarsk

Bagdarin

Vitim

Mogocha

Tupik

Dzhalinda

Yermakovo

Belogorsk

Svobodnyy
Zavitinsk
Obluchye

Birobidzhan

Srednetambovskoye

Kholmsk

Poronaysk

Yuzhno-Sakhalinsk

Ostrov Itunup

Ostrov
Simushir

Krasnoyarsk

Kansk

Kansk
Ilanskiy
Tayshet

Bratsk

Zayarsk

Magistralnyy

2840

Snovskaya

Ust-Ilga

Ust-Karenga

Aksenovo
Zilovskoye

A

Chernyshevsk

Nerchinsk

Shilka

Sretensk

Nerchinskiy
Zavod

Kocheya

Poyarkovo

Shimanovsk

Zavitinsk

Voznesenka

Nizhneudinsk

Tulun

Zima

Kardoy

Ust-Uda

Balagansk
Barguzin

Onguren

Cheremkhovo

Usolye Sibirskoye

Munku Sardyk
3491

Tulun

Zima

Irkutsk

Angarsk
1620

Ulan Ude

Petrovsk-
Zabaykalskiy

Khilok

Aginskoye

Olovyannaya

Borzya

Chita
Shilka
1054

Nerchinsk

Aleksandrovskiy
Zavod

Zabaykalsk

Hailar

Manzhouli

Olga

Plastun

Terney

Sovetskaya Gavan

Vanino

Hokkaidō

Sapporo

Hakodate

Vostochnyy
Sayan

Turan

Kyzyl
Toora-Khem

Hovsgol
Nuur

Hatgal

Slyudyanka

Krasnozersk

Zakamensk

Kyakhta

Kyusyur

Naushki
Khokhotolboy

Chingis
Khan

Nenjiang

Qiqihar

Anda

Harbin

Jiamusi

Mudanjiang

Muling

Daljnerechensk

Ussuriysk

Vladivostok
Nakhodka

Honshū

Niigata

JAPAN

Munku
Sardyk

Samagaltay

Ak-Dovurak

Ozero
Uvs Nuur

Hutag

Hentiyn
Nuruu

2800

Choybalsan

Tamsagbulag

Tao-an

Jilin

Unggi
Chongjin

Sea
of
Japan

Hangayn Nuruu

Uliastay
(Javhlant)

Hyargas Nuur

Har Nuur

Tsetserleg

Ulaanbaatar
(Ulan Bator)

Ondorhaan

Changchun
Siping

2274

Kilchu

MONGOLIA

Tsagaan Olom

Fushun
Anshan
Shenyang

Songhua
Yanji

Hunchun

Kanggye

Wŏnsan

Kansŏng

Kanazawa

To-yama

Akita

4266

Hami

Gaxun Nur

3957

Dalandzadgad

Saynshand

Linxi

Chifeng

Doulun

Chengde

Yingkou

Dandong

Anju

Pyongyang
Dalian

Namp'o

Sŏul
(Seoul)
Inch'ŏn

Wŏnsan

**NORTH
KOREA**

SOUTH KOREA
Taejon

Taegu

Pusan

Edrengiyn Nuruu

**S
E
R
E
P
U
B
L
I
C
GOBI**

Baotou

Hohhot
Zhangjiakou

Beijing

1949

Bengbu

Dongbei

Kurilskiye Ostrova

Ostrov
Kunashir

80 90 100 110 120 130 140 150 170 60

50

40

10 100 **11** 110 **12** 120 **13** 130 **14**

1 : 50 000 000

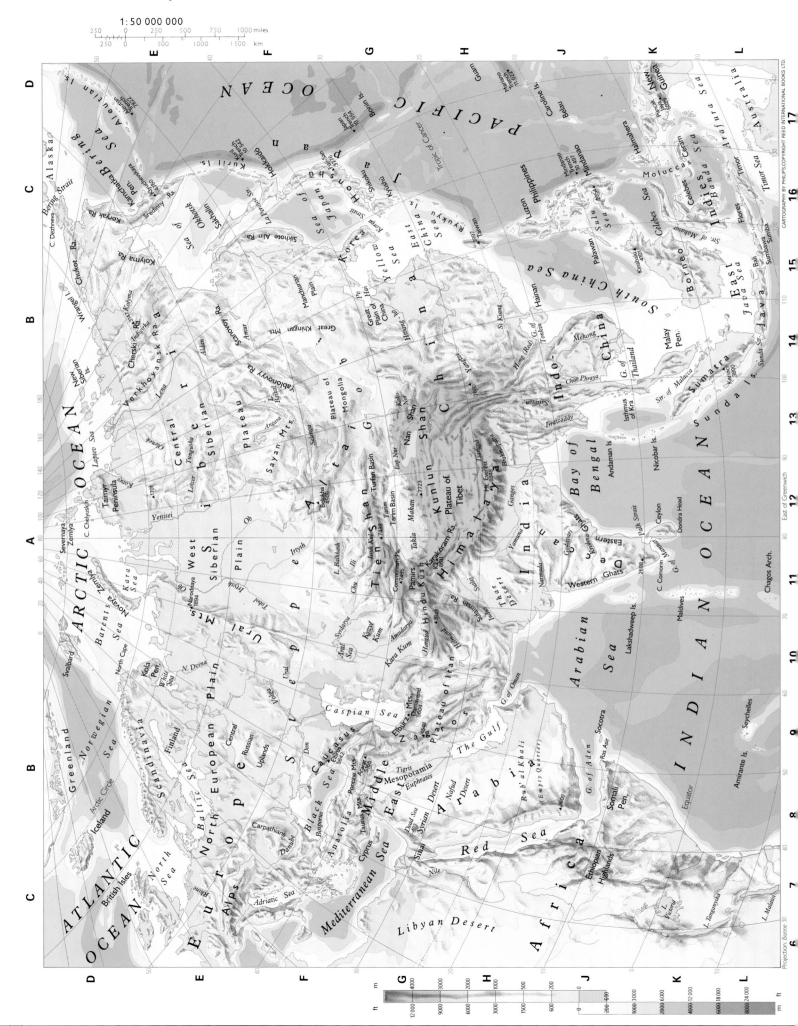

CARTOGRAPHY BY PHILIP'S. COPYRIGHT REED INTERNATIONAL BOOKS LTD.

Projection: Bonne 30

1:50 000 000

250 0 250 500 750 1000 miles
250 0 500 1000 1500 km

CARTOGRAPHY BY PHILIP'S. COPYRIGHT REED INTERNATIONAL BOOKS LTD.

PACIFIC OCEAN

ARCTIC OCEAN

ATLANTIC OCEAN

INDIAN OCEAN

R U S S I A

C H I N A

MONGOLIA

KAZAKHSTAN

INDIA

SAUDI ARABIA

IRAN

PAKISTAN

AFGHANISTAN

TURKEY

IRAQ

OMAN

YEMEN

JAPAN

SOUTH KOREA

NORTH KOREA

PHILIPPINES

TAIWAN

VIETNAM

THAILAND

LAOS

CAMBODIA

BURMA (MYANMAR)

MALAYSIA

SINGAPORE

INDONESIA

AUSTRALIA

BANGLADESH

NEPAL

BHUTAN

SRI LANKA

TIBET

SINKIANG

UIGHUR

JAMMU & KASHMIR

UZBEKISTAN

TURKMENISTAN

TAJIKISTAN

KYRGYZSTAN

AZERBAIJAN

GEORGIA

ARMENIA

SYRIA

LEBANON

ISRAEL

JORDAN

CYPRUS

KUWAIT

QATAR

BAHRAIN

UNITED ARAB EMIRATES

UKRAINE

EUROPE

GERMANY

FRANCE

ITALY

UNITED KINGDOM

ICELAND

NORWAY

SWEDEN

FINLAND

SUDAN

EGYPT

LIBYA

ETHIOPIA

ERITREA

DJIBOUTI

SOMALI REP.

KENYA

TANZANIA

UGANDA

ZAIRE

ZAMBIA

MALAWI

Bering Sea

Sea of Okhotsk

Sea of Japan

Yellow Sea

East China Sea

South China Sea

Philippine Sea

Java Sea

Banda Sea

Arafura Sea

Timor Sea

Celebes Sea

Sulu Sea

Bay of Bengal

Arabian Sea

Red Sea

Black Sea

Caspian Sea

Mediterranean Sea

North Sea

Aral Sea

Barents Sea

Kara Sea

Laptev Sea

The Gulf

G. of Oman

G. of Aden

G. of Thailand

Str. of Malacca

Arctic Circle

Tropic of Cancer

Equator

East from Greenwich

Cities: TOKYO, SEOUL, BEIJING, SHANGHAI, TIANJIN, SHENYANG, GUANGZHOU, HONG KONG (U.K.), CHONGQING, HANGZHOU, MANILA, BANGKOK, JAKARTA, KARACHI, BOMBAY, CALCUTTA, DACCA, MADRAS, New Delhi, TEHRAN, BAGHDAD, Riyadh, MOSCOW, ST. PETERSBURG, LONDON, PARIS, Berlin, Rome, CAIRO, Nairobi, Mogadishu

Hanoi ● Capital Cities

Projection: Bonne 30

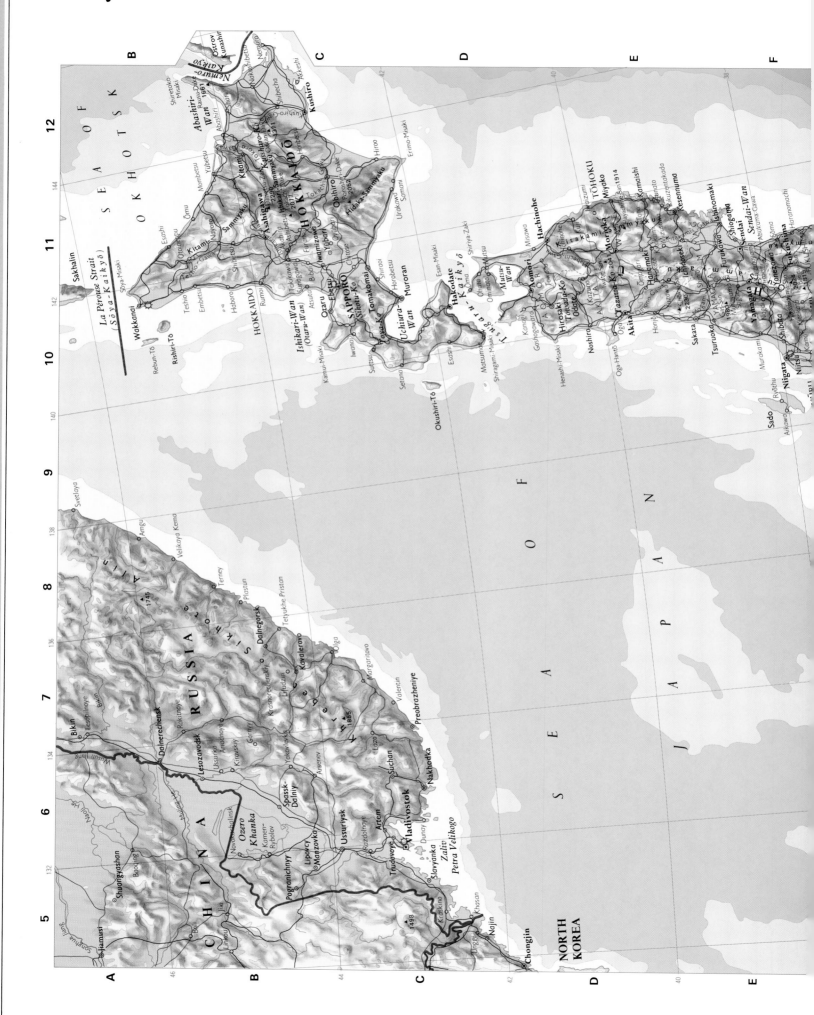

S E A   O F   O K H O T S K

Sakhalin

La Pérouse Strait
(Sōya-Kaikyō)

Ostrov
Kunashir

Nemuro-
Kaikyō

Shiretoko-
Misaki

Abashiri-
Wan

Rausu-Dake
1661

Nemuro

Akkeshi

Kushiro

Hiroo

Erimo-Misaki

HOKKAIDO

SAPPORO

Shikotsu-Ko

Tomakomai

Tōya-Ko

Uchiura-
Wan

Muroran

Esashi

Okushiri-Tō

Matsumae-Misaki

Shiragami-Misaki

Esan-Misaki

Hakodate

Tsugaru-Kaikyō

Oshima I.

Shiriya-Zaki

Mutsu-
Wan

Oma

Ominato

Misawa

Hachinohe

Aomori

Kuji

TŌHOKU

Miyako

Kamaishi

Kesennuma

Ishinomaki

Shiogama

Sendai-
Wan

Morioka

AKITA

Noshiro

Oga-Hantō

Akita

Honjo

Sakata

Tsuruoka

YAMAGATA

Shibata

Niigata

Sado

Ryōtsu

Wakkanai

Rebun-Tō

Rishiri-Tō

Teshio

Embetsu

Haboro

Rumoi

Otaru

Ishikari-Wan
(Otaru-Wan)

Iwanai

Suttsu

Setana

Kamui-Misaki

Asahigawa

Bibai

Furano

Iwamizawa

Obihiro

Tokachi

Kitami

Sammyaku

Hidaka-Sammyaku

Mombetsu

Yūbetsu

Nayoro

Esashi

Ōmu

Shibecha

Teshikaga

Kushiro

R U S S I A

C H I N A

NORTH
KOREA

S I K H O T E - A L I N

Svetlaya

Amgu

Velikaya Kema

Terney

Plastun

Tetyukhe Pristan

Olga

Margaritovo

Valentin

Preobrazheniye

Nakhodka

Vladivostok

Ussuriysk

Artem

Suchan

Kavalerovo

Dalnegorsk

Krasnorechenskiy

Lifudza

Luzo

Yakovlevka

Arsenev

Spassk-
Dalniy

Ozero
Khanka

Kamen-
Rybolov

Novocholinsk

Lipowcy

Matzovka

Pogranichnyy

Trudovoye

Slavyanka

Zaliv
Petra Velikogo

Dunay

Kraskino

Khasan

Unggi

Najin

Chongjin

Bikin

Lesozavodsk

Dalnerechensk

Rokitnoye

Gornyy

Kirovskiy

Ussuriysk

1745

1855

1498

S E A   O F   J A P A N

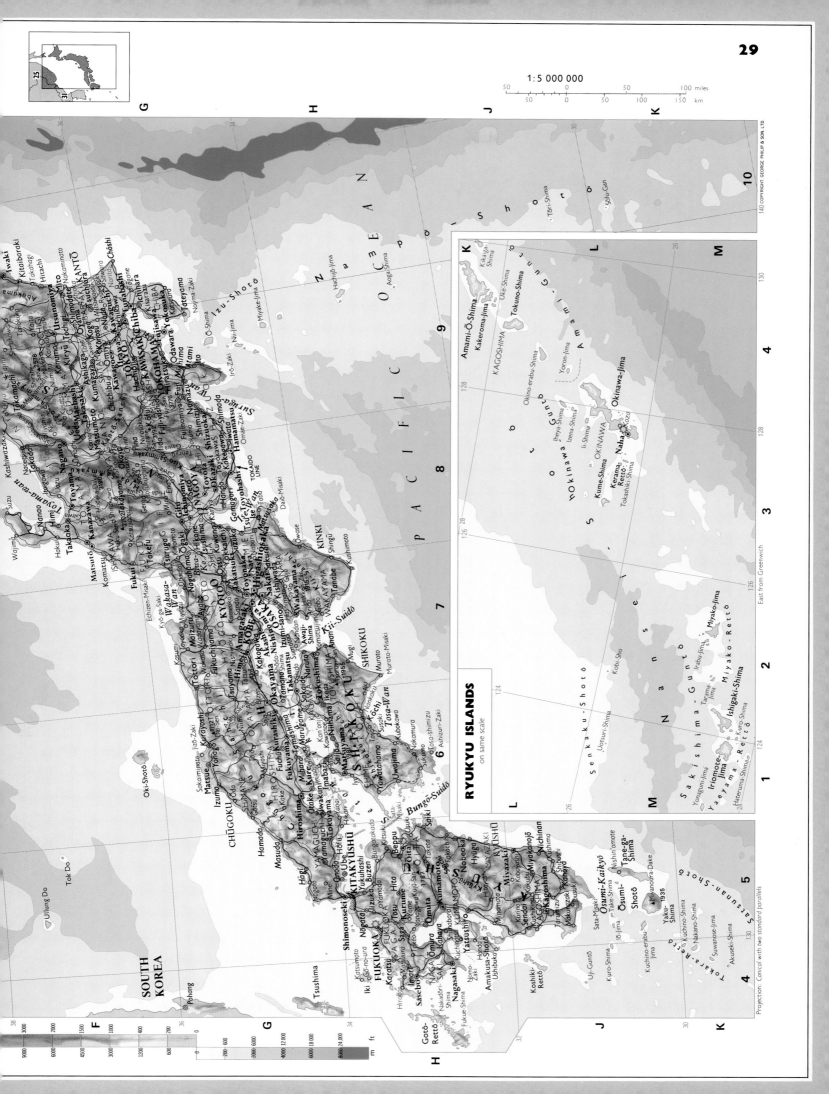

1:5 000 000

50   0   50   100 miles

50   0   50   100   150 km

RYUKYU ISLANDS

on same scale

Projection: Conical with two standard parallels

East from Greenwich

SOUTH
KOREA

PACIFIC OCEAN

KANTŌ

TOKYO
YOKOHAMA

NAGOYA

KYOTO
OSAKA
KOBE

SHIKOKU

KYŪSHŪ
KITAKYŪSHŪ
FUKUOKA
NAGASAKI

KAGOSHIMA

OKINAWA
Naha

Amami-Ō-Shima

Okinawa-Jima

Miyako-Rettō
Ishigaki-Shima

Sakishima-Guntō

Senkaku-Shotō

Nansei

Tokara-Rettō

Satsunan-Shotō

Ōsumi-Shotō

140 COPYRIGHT GEORGE PHILIP & SON, LTD.

Projection: Bonne

East from Greenwich

1:15 000 000

100   0   100   200   300   400 miles
100   0   100   200   300   400   500   600 km

25
36   34   33

B
C
D
E

Oz. Baykal
Ulan Ude
Chita
Sretensk
Nerchinsk
Oloyyannaya
Borzya
Manzhouli
Hailar
Hulun Nur
Buir Nur
Dutulun Shan
Dzamin Uud
Erenhot
Saynshand
Abagnar Qi
Duolun
Chaoyang
Chifeng
Hohhot
Jining
Zhangjiakou
Xuanhua
Datong
Yuanping
Baoding
BEIJING (Peking)
TIANJIN SHI
Tangshan
Qinhuangdao
Jinzhou
Yingkou
TIANJIN
Cangzhou
Shijiazhuang
Dezhou
TAIYUAN
Yangquan
Yuci
Fenyang
Linfen
Changzhi
Tongchuan
Sanmenxia
XI'AN
Luoyang
ZHENGZHOU
HENAN
Pingdingshan
Nanyang
Xiangfan
Zhumadian
Fuyang
Shangqiu
Xuzhou
Huaibei
Kaifeng
Shangshui
Bengbu
Hefei
NANJING
Ma'anshan
Wuhu
Tongling
Anqing
WUHAN
Huangshi
Shashi
Yichang
Changde
Yiyang
Nanchang
Changsha
Xiangtan
Pingxiang
Shaoyang
Hengyang
Guilin
Wuzhou
Shaoguan
Mei Xian
GUANGZHOU
Foshan
Macau (Port.)
HONG KONG (Br.)
Jiangmen
Maoming
Zhanjiang
Haikou
Hainan Dao
HAINAN
Yacheng

CHANGCHUN
HARBIN
Qiqihar
Jilin
Siping
Liaoyuan
Tongliao
Shuangliao
FUSHUN
SHENYANG
Liaoyang
Benxi
ANSHAN
Dandong
Mudanjiang
Vladivostok
Khabarovsk
Sakhalin
HOKKAIDO
SAPPORO
Hakodate
Aomori
Akita
Sendai
Niigata
TOKYO
YOKOHAMA
NAGOYA
KYOTO
KOBE
OSAKA
Hiroshima
KITAKYUSHU
FUKUOKA
Nagasaki
Kumamoto
Kagoshima
KYUSHU

P'YONGYANG
SOUL
SEOUL
Inch'on
NORTH
SOUTH
Taejon
TAEGU
PUSAN
Kwangju
Masan
Cheju Do

YELLOW SEA
QINGDAO
Jinan
Weifang
Yantai
Weihai
DALIAN
Bo Hai

EAST CHINA SEA
Shanghai
Hangzhou
Ningbo
Wenzhou
Fuzhou
Xiamen
TAIWAN
TAIBEI
Taizhong
Gaoxiong
Tainan

SEA OF JAPAN
PACIFIC OCEAN
Ryūkyū-rettō
Okinawa
Naha
Tropic of Cancer
SOUTH CHINA SEA

COPYRIGHT GEORGE PHILIP & SON LTD

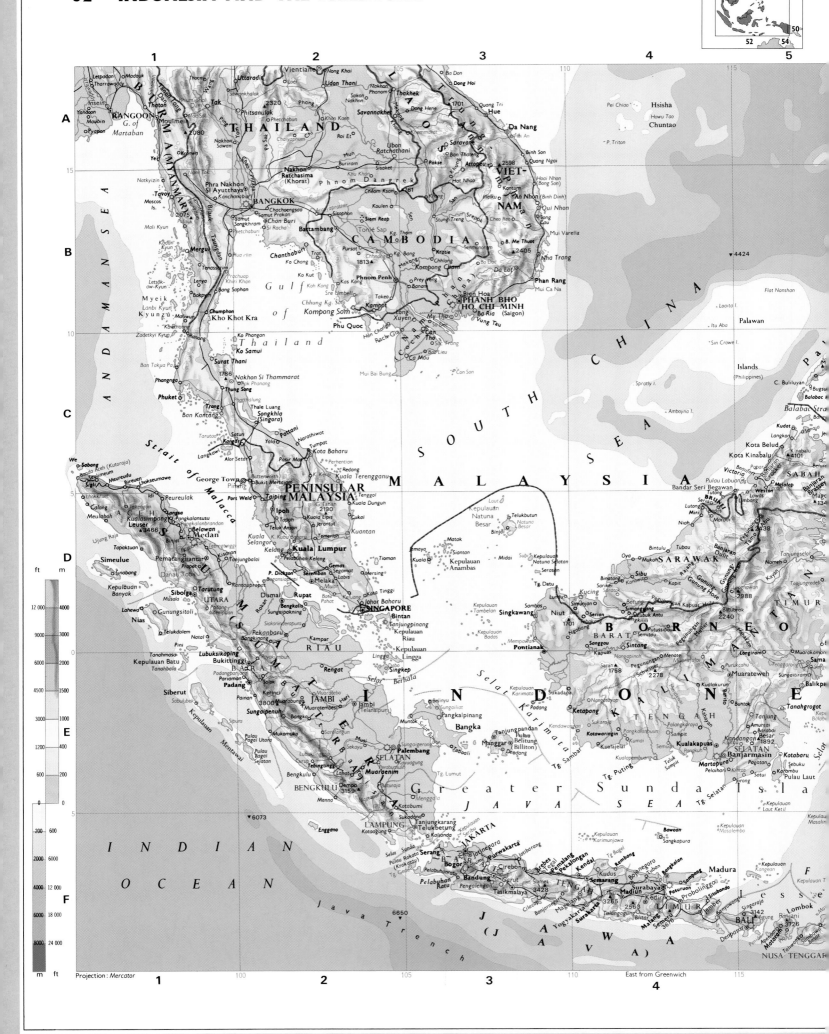

Projection: Mercator   East from Greenwich

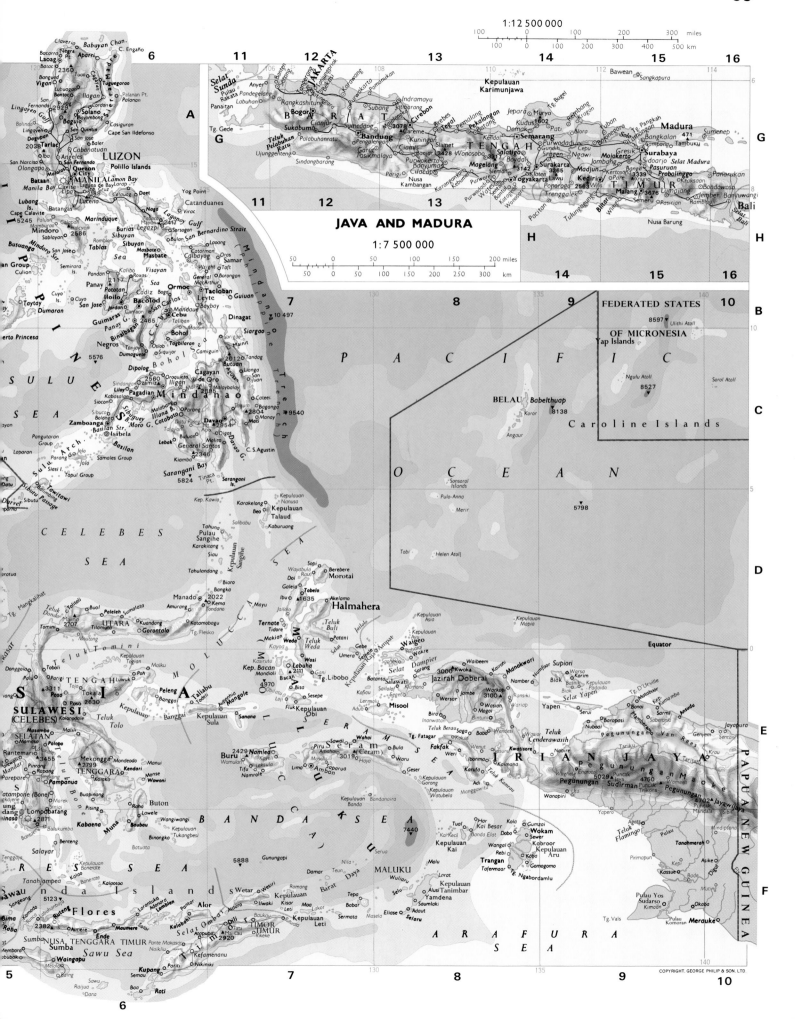

1:12 500 000

100   0   100   200   300 miles

100   0   100   200   300   400   500 km

JAVA AND MADURA

1:7 500 000

50   0   50   100   150   200 miles

50   0   50   100   150   200   250   300 km

PACIFIC

OCEAN

FEDERATED STATES

OF MICRONESIA

Yap Islands

Ulithi Atoll   8597

Ngulu Atoll

8527   Sorol Atoll

BELAU   Babelthuap

8138   Koror

Angaur

C a r o l i n e   I s l a n d s

Sonsorol Islands

Pulo-Anna

Merir   5798

Tobi   Helen Atoll

Equator

LUZON

MANILA

S U L U

S E A

C E L E B E S

S E A

M O L U C C A   S E A

Mindanao

S U L A W E S I
(CELEBES)

Halmahera

Kepulauan Talaud

B A N D A   S E A

Flores

TIMUR

NUSA TENGGARA TIMUR

MALUKU

A R A F U R A   S E A

IRIAN JAYA

P A P U A   N E W   G U I N E A

Jayapura

Merauke

COPYRIGHT. GEORGE PHILIP & SON. LTD.

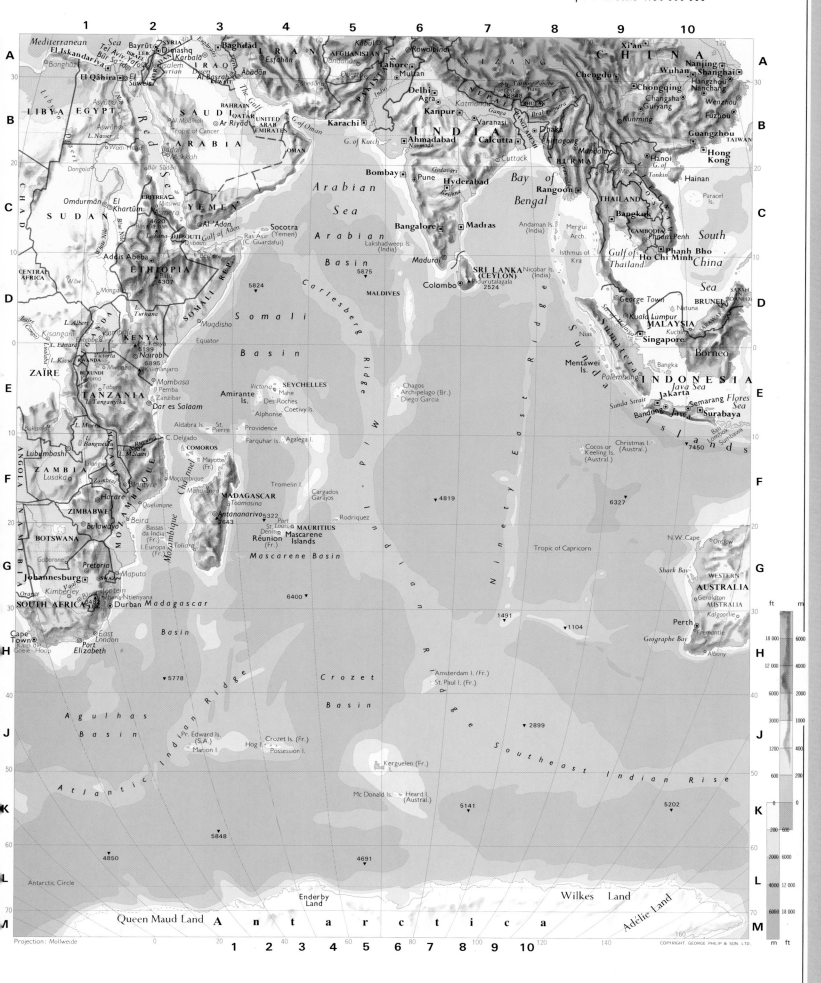

A B C D E F G H J K L M

1 2 3 4 5 6 7 8 9 10

Mediterranean Sea
El Iskandarîya
Banghāzî
Bayrūt
Tel Aviv-Yafo ISRAEL
Būr Sa'id
El Qâhira El Suweis
SYRIA
Dimashq
Karbalā
Baghdād
Al Basrah
Ābādān
IRAN
Kābul
AFGHANISTAN
Rawalpindi
Xi'an
CHINA
Chengdu
Wuhan Nanjing Shanghai
Chongqing Changsha Hangzhou Nanchang

LIBYA EGYPT
Asyūt
Aswān
L. Nasser
Wadi Halfa
SAUDI ARABIA
Al Madinah
BAHRAIN QATAR
Ar Riyad
UNITED ARAB EMIRATES
G. of Oman
Karachi
Delhi
Agra
Kanpur
INDIA
Varanasi
Kunming
Guiyang
Fuzhou
Guangzhou TAIWAN
Hong Kong

SUDAN
Omdurmân
El Khartûm
Dongola
Jiddah
Makkah
Būr Sūdan
OMAN
G. of Kutch
Ahmadabad
Narmada
Calcutta
Dhaka
Chittagong
BURMA
Mandalay
Hainan
Hanoi

CHAD
ERITREA
Mitsiwa
Asmera
4620
YEMEN
Al 'Adan
Gulf of Aden
Ras Asir
(C. Guardafui)
Socotra (Yemen)
Arabian Sea
Bombay
Pune
Hyderabad
Godavari
Krishna
Bay of Bengal
Rangoon
THAILAND
Bangkok
South China Sea
Paracel Is.

CENTRAL AFRICA
Wāw
Mongalla
Addis Abeba
ETHIOPIA
Raju 4307
DJIBOUTI
Djibouti
Berbera
Arabian Basin
Lakshadweep Is. (India)
5875
Bangalore
Madras
Andaman Is. (India)
Mergui Arch.
Isthmus of Kra
CAMBODIA
Phnom Penh
Gulf of Thailand
Phanh Bho
Ho Chi Minh

ZAIRE
Kisangani
L. Albert
Kampala
UGANDA
L. Edward
Mt. Kenya 5199
Nairobi
KENYA
5824
Somali Basin
Carlesberg Ridge
MALDIVES
Madurai
Colombo
SRI LANKA (CEYLON)
Pidurutalagala 2524
Nicobar Is. (India)
George Town
Kuala Lumpur
BRUNEI SABAH
Natuna
Nias
MALAYSIA
Kuching SARAWAK
Singapore
Borneo

Equator
L. Kivu RWANDA
BURUNDI
Kigoma
Mwanza
5895 Kilimanjaro
Mombasa
Pemba
Zanzibar
Victoria I.
SEYCHELLES
Mahe
Amirante Is.
Des Roches
Coetivy Is.
Chagos Archipelago (Br.)
Diego Garcia
Mentawei Is.
Palembang
Bangka
INDONESIA
Java Sea
Jakarta

Kisumu
TANZANIA
Tabora
Dar es Salaam
Aldabra Is.
St. Pierre
Providence
Alphonse
Sunda Strait
Bandung Semarang Flores Sea
Jawa Surabaya
Bali Lombok Sumbawa

Bukoba
L. Tanganyika
Farquhar Is. Agalega I.
Cocos or Keeling Is. (Austral.)
Christmas I. (Austral.)
7450

ANGOLA
Lubumbashi
ZAMBIA
Lusaka
L. Mweru
L. Bangweulu
L. Malawi
COMOROS
Mayotte (Fr.)
Moçambique
Tromelin I.
Cargados Garajos
4819
6327

Lilongwe
Blantyre
MOZAMBIQUE
Harare
ZIMBABWE
Bulawayo
Beira
Quelimane
MADAGASCAR
Toamasina
Antananarivo 2643
5322
Port
St. Louis
Denis
Réunion (Fr.)
MAURITIUS
Mascarene Islands
Rodriguez
Tropic of Capricorn
N.W. Cape
Onslow

BOTSWANA
Gaborone
Toliara
I. Europa (Fr.)
Bassas da India (Fr.)
Mascarene Basin
Shark Bay
WESTERN AUSTRALIA
AUSTRALIA
Geraldton

NAMIBIA
Pretoria
Johannesburg
Kimberley
Bloemfontein
SWAZ
Maputo
Madagascar Basin
6400
1491
1104
Perth
Geographe Bay
Fremantle
Kalgoorlie

SOUTH AFRICA
Cape Town
East London
Port Elizabeth
Durban
Kaap die Hoop
5778
Crozet Basin
Amsterdam I. (Fr.)
St. Paul I. (Fr.)
Albany

Agulhas Basin
Pr. Edward Is. (S.A.)
Marion I.
Crozet Is. (Fr.)
Hog I.
Possession I.
2899
Southeast Indian Rise

Atlantic Indian Ridge
Kerguelen (Fr.)
McDonald Is. Heard I. (Austral.)
5141
5202

5848
4691

Antarctic Circle
Enderby Land
Wilkes Land

Projection: Mollweide
Queen Maud Land A n t a r c t i c a Adélie Land

0 20 40 60 80 100 120 140 160

COPYRIGHT GEORGE PHILIP & SON LTD.

ft m
18 000 6000
12 000 4000
6000 2000
3000 1000
1200 400
600 200
0 0
200 600
2000 6000
4000 12 000
6000 18 000
m ft

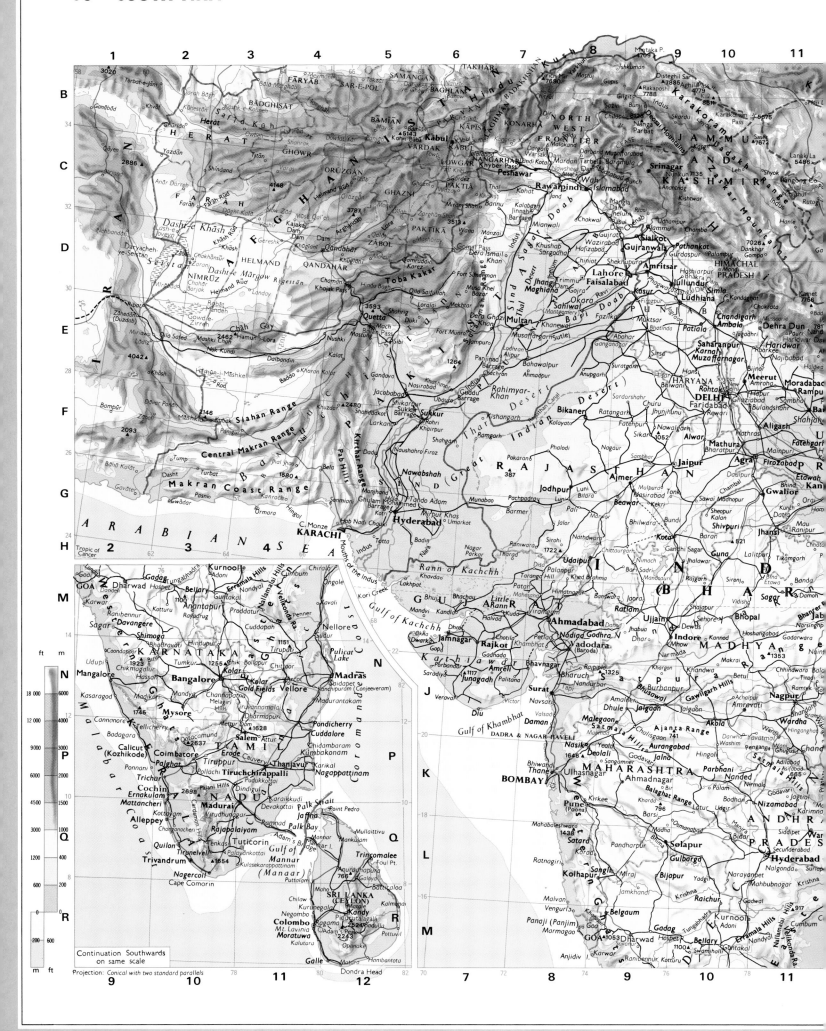

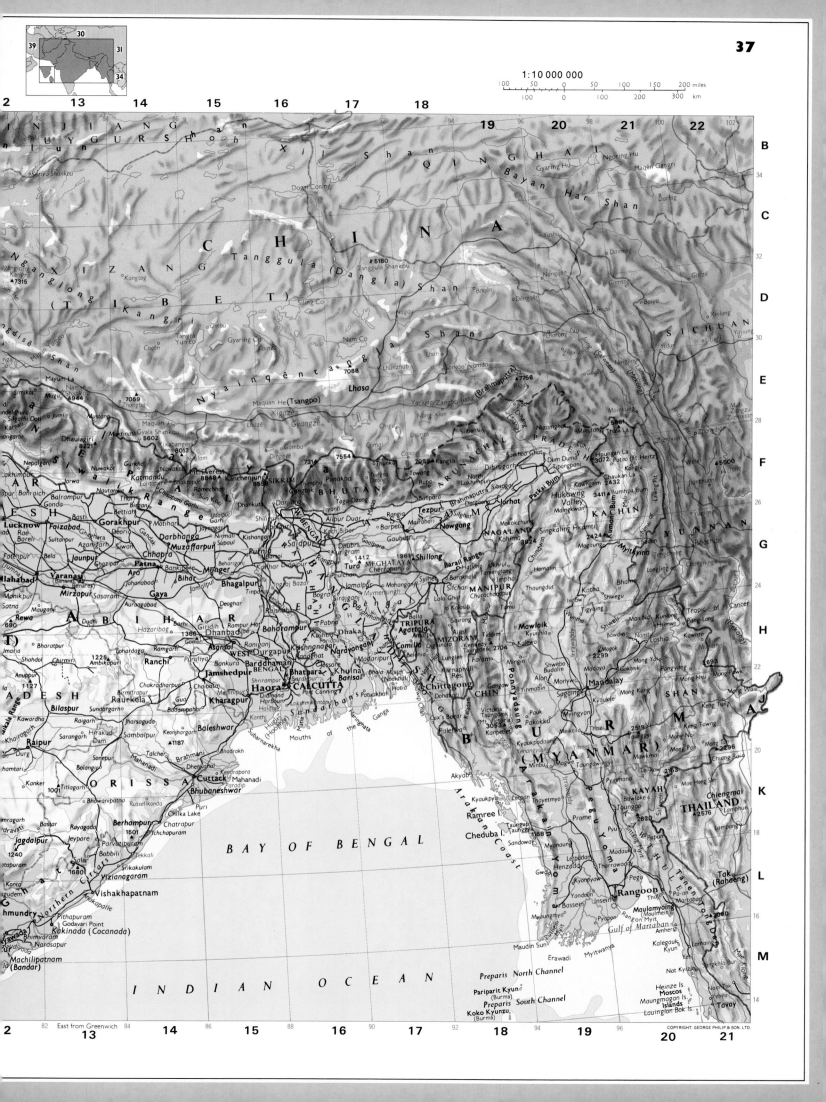

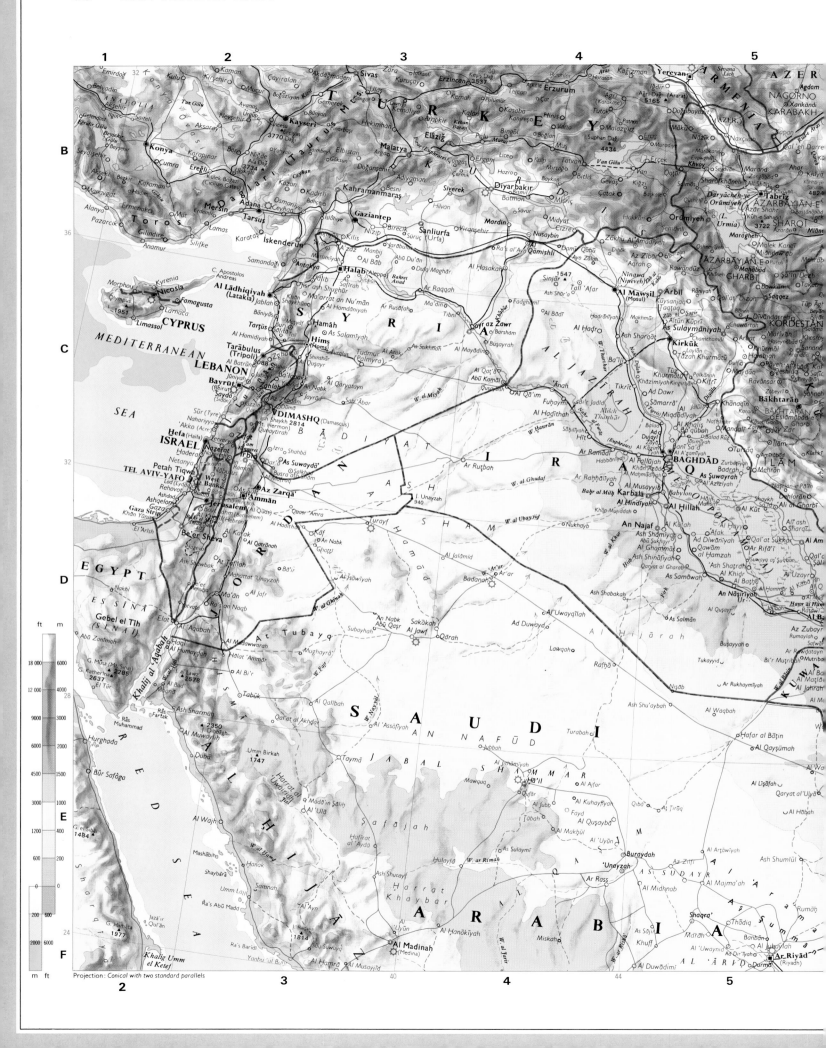

Projection: Conical with two standard parallels

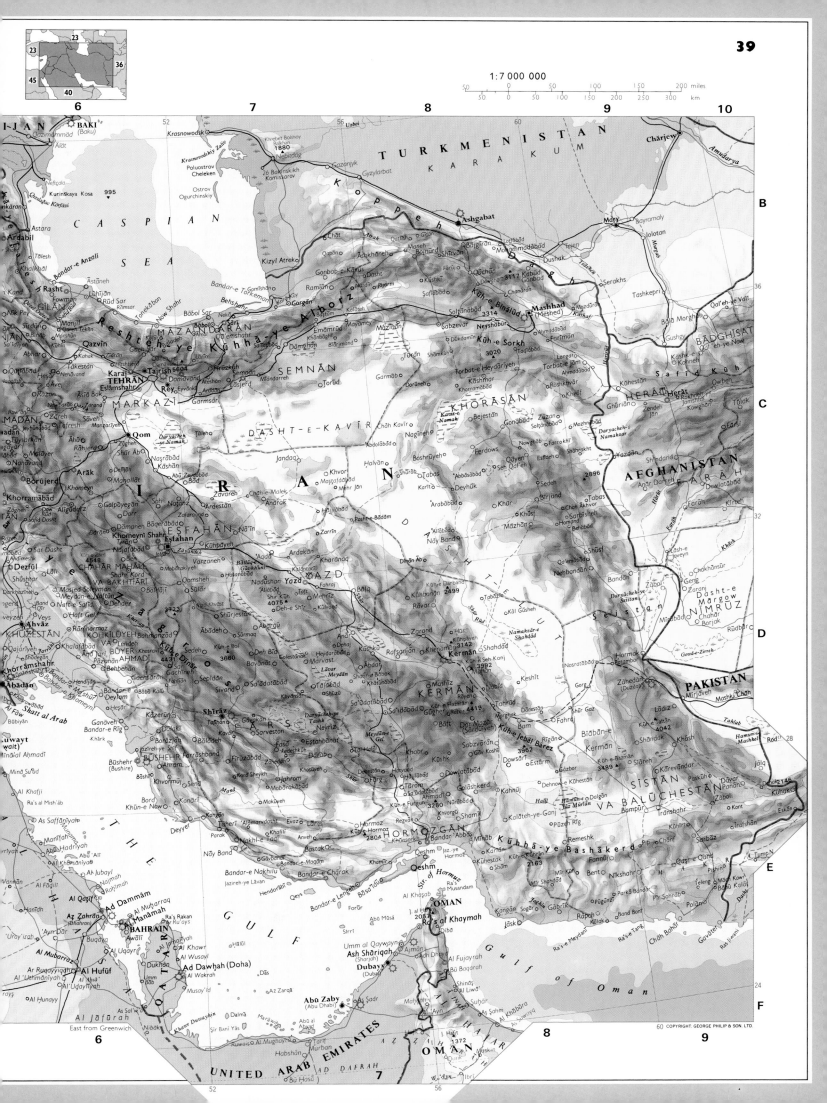

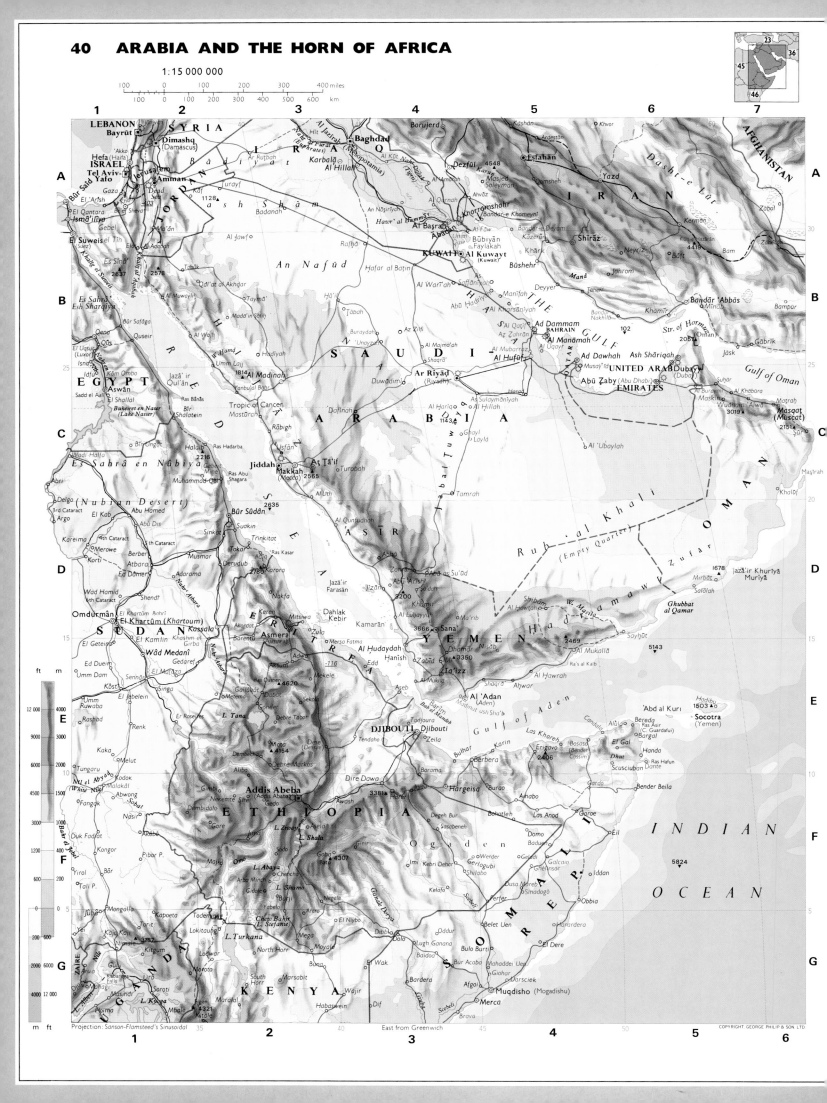

1:15 000 000

100   0   100   200   300   400 miles

100 0 100 200 300 400 500 600 km

1   2   3   4   5   6   7

LEBANON
Bayrūt
Hefa (Haifa)
ISRAEL
Tel Aviv-
Yafo
Jerusalem
Amman
Gaza
Būr Saïd
El 'Arîsh
Ismâ'ilîya
El Qantara
Gebel
El Suweis
(Suez)
El Tîh
Eilat
El 'Aqabah

SYRIA
Dimashq
(Damascus)
'Akko
Dead
Sea
JORDAN
Ma'ân
Bâdiyat
ash Shâm
Jurayf
Kaf
1128
403
2637
2578
Taḥūk

IRAQ
Al Jazirah
Hīt
Baghdad
Karbalā'
Al Hillah
Ar Ruţbah
Badanah
Nahr al Furāt
(Euphrates)
Mesopotamia)
Al Kūt
Naḥr Dijlah
(Tigris)
Al 'Amārah
An Nāşirīyah
Hawr al Hammar
At Başrah
Abadan
Khorramshahr

Borujerd
Kāshān
Ardestan
Khvor
Eşfahān
Dezfūl 4548
Yazd
Masjed
Soleymān
Aḥvāz
Būbiyān
Faylakah
Umm
Qaşr
Bandar-e Deylam
Bandar-e Khomeyni

AFGHANISTAN
IRAN
Dasht-e Lūt
Zābol
Kermān
4419
Kūh-e Hazārān
Bam
Zāhedān

An Nafūd
Ḥafar al Bāṭin
Al Warr'ah
Abū Ḥadrīyah
Manīfah
Al Khārsānīyah
S'Al Qaţīf
Az Zahrān
Ad Dammam
BAHRAIN
Al Manāmah
Al Mubarraz
Al 'Uqayr
Al Hufūf
Al 'Ubaylah

KUWAIT
Al Kuwayt
(Kuwait)
Būshehr
Deyyer
Tāheri
Khārk
Jahrom
Shīrāz
Neyrīz
Kāzerūn
Mand

THE GULF
QATAR
Ad Dawhah
Abū Ḥarīq
Musay'īd
UNITED ARAB
Abū Ẓaby (Abu Dhabi)
EMIRATES
Ash Shāriqah
Dubayy (Dubai)
Al Buraymi
Maskin
Wudham 3019
'Alwā

Bandar 'Abbās
Mīnāb
Khamīr
Bandar
Nakhīlū
Str. of Hormuz
(Oman)
205
Jask
Gābrik
Bampūr

102

Al Wajh
Al Muwaylih
Madā'in Şāliḥ
Taymā'
Ḥā'il
Ṭābah
Burayḍah
'Unayzah
Az Zilfī
Al Majma'ah
Shaqrā
As Sulaymānīyah
Al Ḥillah
1143

Būr Safāga
Es Sahrâ
Esh Sharqiya
Qena
Qūs
Būr Ungāt
Quseir

EGYPT
Aswân
El Uqsur
(Luxor)
Isna
Idfū
Kôm Ombo
Sadd el Aali
El Shallal
Buḥeiret en Naser
(Lake Nasser)

RED SEA
Jazâ'ir
Qul'ān
Al Madīnah 1814
Yanbu'al Baḥr
Ras Bānās
Bîr
Shalatein
Ras Hadarba
Halaib
2216
Mine
Ras Abu
Shagara
Muhammad Qol

SAUDI-
ARABIA
Ar Riyāḍ (Riyadh)
Duwādimi
'Dafīnah
Al Hārīq
As Sulaymānīyah
Al Ḥillah
Harad
Jabal Ṭuwayq
Ghayl
al Ḥillah
'Al 'Ubaylah

OMAN
Rub' al Khali
(Empty Quarter)
Zufār
W. Masīla
Shibām
Al Hawţah
Al Kharsānīyah
1678
Mirbaṭ
Salālah
Ghubbat
al Qamar
Khalūf
Maşīrah
Jazā'ir Khurīyā
Murīyā
2151
Şūr
Masqaṭ
(Muscat)
Al Khābūra
Maţraḥ
Maşkin
'Alwā
3019

Tropic of Cancer
Mastūrah
Rābigh
Usfān
Jiddah
Makkah (Mecca) 2565
Aţ Ṭā'if
Turabah
Al Līth
Al Qunfudhah
Abū 'Arīsh 3200
Jīzān
Ṣa'dah
Khamir 3666
Abā as Su'ūd
Zahrān
Al Lubayyih
Ma'rib
Nişāb 2469
Al Mukallā
5143

Bîr Ungāt
Wadi Halfa
Es Sahrâ en Nûbiya
(Nubian Desert)
Abri
Delgo
3rd Cataract
Argo
El Kab
Abu Hamed
Kareima
Merowe
4th Cataract
Korti
5th Cataract
Berber
Atbara
Ed Dâmer
Musmar
Derudub 2780
Adarama
Karora
Nahr 'Aṭbara
Shendî
6th Cataract
Wad Hamid

SUDAN
Omdurmân
El Khartûm Bnḥrî
El Khartûm (Khartoum)
Kassala
Khashm el Girba
El Kamlin
Wâd Medanî
El Geteina
El Matina
Gedaref
Sennâr
El Geteina
Singa
El Jebelein
Ed Dueim
Umm Dam
Kôstî
Er Roseires
Umm Ruwaba
Rashad
Kaka
Renk
Melut
Tungaru
Kodok
Malakâl
Abwong
Fangak
Nâsir
Sobat
Duk Fadiat
Bahr al Jebel
Kongor
Pibor P.
Bôr
Yirol
Tali P.
Jûba
Mongalla
Kapoeta
Torit
Yei
Kajo Kaji 3787
Kitgum
Gulu

ERITREA
Keren
Akordat
Barentū
Asmera (Asmara)
Mitsiwa
Dahlak
Kebir
Adwa -116
Aksum
Mekele
Zula
Mersa Fatma
Edd
Aseb

Suakin
Trinkitat
Tokar
Adîg
Ras Kasar
Jazâ'ir
Farasân
Kamarān
Ḥanīsh
Zabīd 3350
Ta'izz
Al Mukrā

YEMEN
Sana'
Dhamār 2469
Ḥaḍramawt
Saywūn
Ra's al Kalb
Al Ḥawrah
Ahwar
Shaqrā
Mīdnat ush Sha'b
Bāb el Mandeb
Al 'Adan (Aden)
Bārim
'Abd al Kuri
Hadibū 1503
Socotra
(Yemen)

Gallabat
Metema
Dabat
Dembecha
Sekota
Gonder
L. Tana
Debre Tabon
4620
Ras Dashan
Mota 4154
(Dessye)
Dese
Debre Markos
Alibo
Dembidolo
Gimbi
Nekemte
Sire
Gore
Jimma
Gobā 4307
Batu
L. Zïway
Asela
Ginir
L. Abaya
Chencha
Sodo
Arba Minch
L. Shamo
Gidole
Bùrji
Yabelo
Negele
Arero
Chew Bahir
L. Stefanie
Mega

ETHIOPIA
ADDIS ABEBA
(Addis Ababa)
Awash
Harer 3381
Dire Dawa
Degeh Bur
Sasaneneh
Imi
Kebri Dehar
Shilabo
Gode
Ginir
Kelafo
Ferfer
Dolo
Lugh Ganana
El Niybo
Moyale

DJIBOUTI
Djibouti
Tadjoura
Zeila
Tendaho
Dikhil
Borama
Hargeisa
Burao
Bulhar
Berbera
Karin
Las Khoreh
Erigavo
Bosaso (Bender Cassim)
Candala
Alūla
Bereda
Ras Asir
(C. Guardafui)
Bargal
El Gal
Dhut
Scusciuban
Dante
Handa
Ras Hafun

Gulf of Aden
INDIAN
OCEAN

SOMALI REP.
Ainabo
Las Anod
Gardo
Bohotleh
Domo
Baduen
Werder
Gerlogubi
Shilabo
Dusa Mareb
Sinadogò
Galcaio
Iddan
5824
Obbia
Garoe
Eil
Bender Beila

UGANDA
ZAIRE
Kaabong
Kitgum
Kasbagala
Falls
Moroto
Soroti
Mbale 4321
L. Kyoga
Gulu

KENYA
Lokitaung
L. Turkana
North Horr
Marsabit
Moyale
El Wak
Wajir
Habaswein
Dif
Marala l
Lodwar
Todenyang
South
Horr
Mega
El Niybo
Dibb
Dolo
Lugh Ganana
Bardera
Giohar
Varscick
Afgoi
Muqdisho (Mogadishu)
Merca
Brava
Belet Uen
Bur Acaba
Baidoa
Bulo Burti
Mahaddei Uen
Oddur
Hargeisa
El Dere
Bur Hakaba

Ogaden
Ghadir
Ginir
Scebeli
Bulhar

ft   m
12 000 4000
9000 3000
6000 2000
4500 1500
3000 1000
1200 400
600 200
0   0
200 600
2000 6000
4000 12 000
m   ft

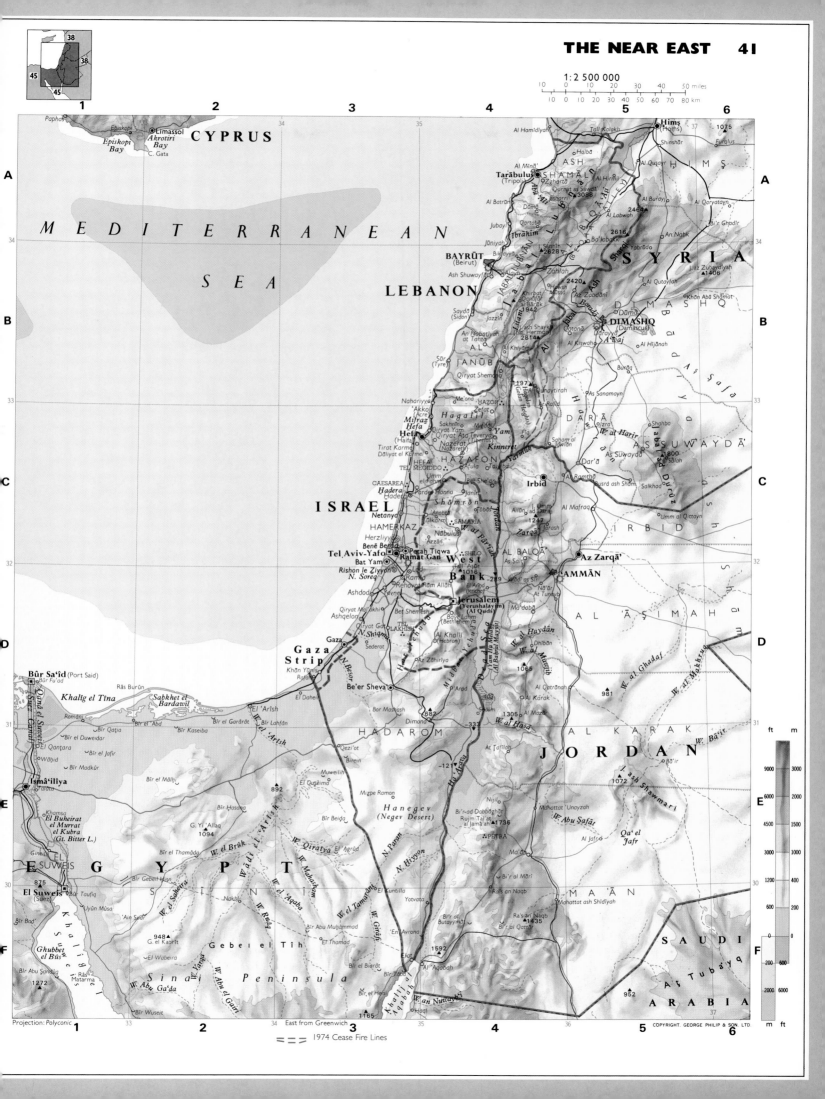

1:2 500 000

10 0 10 20 30 40 50 miles
10 0 10 20 30 40 50 60 70 80 km

CYPRUS

Paphos
Episkopi
Bay
Limassol
Akrotiri
Bay
C. Gata

M E D I T E R R A N E A N

S E A

Al Hamīdīyah Tall Kalakh Ḥimṣ (Homs)
Halbā Shinshār Furāilus
ASH Al Quṣayr
SHAMĀL HIMṢ
Al Mīnā' Al Ḥirmil Al Qaryatayn
Tarābulus Zgharta 3088 Al Buṛayj
(Tripoli) Bsharrī 2464 Bi'r Ghadīr
Al Batrūn 2616
Jubayl Dūmā An Nabk
Qarṭabā 2628 Ba'labakk
Ibrāhīm 2814 Yabrūd
Jūniyah J. az Zubaydīyah 1406
BAYRŪT Zaḥlah Al Quṭayfah
(Beirut) DIMASHQ
Ash Shuwayfāt 2420 Az Zabdānī DIMASHQ (Damascus)
Alayḥ Jdeideh Qaṭanā A'waj
LEBANON Khirbat Al Kiswah Al Ḥijānah
Ṣaydā Qanawāt el Barūk Būrāq
(Sidon) An Nabaṭīyah DAR'Ā Ṣafā
Jazzīn at Tahtā As Ṣanamayn
SYRIA
AL Sūr 1197 Qunayṭirah AS SUWAYDĀ'
JANŪB (Tyre) Ḥaghlan (Golan Heights) W. al Ḥarīr Shahbā
Qiryat Shemona Ḥūlah 1800
Nahariyya Me'ona Zefat Fiq Izra ṣalāh
Akko HAZOR Dar'ā
'Acre Ḥagalil Yam As Suwayda' JABAL AD DURŪZ
Miṭraz Sakhnīn Kinneret Saham el Jawlān Salkhad
Hefa Qiryat Yam Midday Busrā ash Sham
Hefa Qiryat Ata Teverya Irbid
(Haifa) Nazerat Afula Al Ramthā
Tirat Karmel (Nazareth) Umm al Qittayn
Dāliyat el Karmel HAZAFON Bet She'an IRBID
HEFA Allūn Al Mafraq
TEL MEGIDDO Umm Jarash
CAESAREA el Fahm 1247 Zarqā'
Hadera Janīn Ajlun ad Dārā
ISRAEL Shōmrōn Umm al Qittayn
Netanya SAMARIA Az Zarqā'
HAMERKAZ Anabta Nābulus AL BALQĀ'
Herzliyya Tūbās As Salt
Benē Beraq Azzūn W. al Fār'ah AMMĀN
Tel Aviv-Yafo Petah Tiqwa SHILO 289 Na'ūr
Ramat Gan W E S T Jordan Wādī as Sīr At Tunayb
Bat Yam 'Al Aṣūr Ma'daba
Rishon le Ziyyon B a n k 1016 ALʻĀṢIMAH
N. Soreq Rām Allāh 289
Rehovot (Jericho)
Ashdod Yavne Jerusalem
Qiryat Malʻakhi (Yerushalayim) Ma'daba
Rama (Al Quds)
Ashqelon Bet Shemesh Bayt Lahm (Bethlehem)
Qiryat Gat TEL Al Khalīl
Gaza N. Shiqma LAKHISH (Hebron)
Gaza Sederot Az Zāhirīya
Strip Khān Yūnis Bor Mashash AL KARAK
Rafah Arad W. al Haydān 981
El Dahel Be'er Sheva Dhibān
Būr Saʻīd (Port Said) 662 1065 W. Mawjib
Būr Fu'ād El 'Arīsh Dimona 1305 Al Mazār W. al Ghadaf
Rās Burūn Bir el 'Abd -333 W. al Ḥasā
Khalīg el Tīna Bīr el Garārāt HADAROM Al Qaṭrānah
Sabkhet el W. Lahfān JORDAN
Romāni Bardawil Qezi'ot At Tafīlah W. Bā'ir
Bīr Qaṭia Birein Ba'ir
Bīr el Duweidar Bīr Kaseiba -121 Al Karak
Bīr el Jafir W. al Arīsh Muweilih AL KARAK 1072 Mahattat ash Shawmari
Ismâ'îlîya Bīr Madkūr El Quseima Mizpe Ramon Al Jafr
Talata 892 Muzpe Ramon Bi'r Dabbāghāt Mahattat 'Unayzah
Khamsa Bīr Hasana Rujm Tal'at Qa' el
El Buheirat H a n e g e v al Jamā'ah 1736 W. Abu Şafā' Jafr
el Murrat G. Yi 'Allāq (Negev Desert) PETRA
el Kubra 1094 Bīr Beiḍa Ma'ān
(Gt. Bitter L.) N. Paran Bi'r al Mārī
Gineifa Bīr el Thamāda W. el Brūk W. Qirātya El Agrūd N. Ḥiyyon MA'ĀN Ra's an Naqb
EL SUWEIS Rafs an Naqb Mahaṭṭat ash Shidīyah
875 W. el Sheira El Kuntilla Bi'r al 1435
El Suweis Bīr Gebel Hasn Yotvata Butayyinat Bi'r al Qaṭṭār
(Suez) Bīr Taufîq 'Ain Sudr Nakhl 'En 'Avrona Ra's an Naqb
Bīr Bad 'Uyûn Mûsa W. el 'Aqaba 952 SAUDI
E G Y P T S I N A I W. el Tamārūd El Thamad 1592
Ghubbet 948 W. el Giraji El Qaṣrīn Al 'Aqabah
el Bûs G. el Kabrīt G e b e l e l T î h Elat Aṭ Ṭubāyq
Ras W. Abu Ga'da Bīr el Biarāt ARABIA
Matarma 1272 Bīr el Ḥenu Khalīg el 'Aqaba
Bīr Abu Şandîq W. Abu el Guarī 1165
Bīr Wuseit S i n a i P e n i n s u l a

Projection: Polyconic   East from Greenwich   COPYRIGHT. GEORGE PHILIP & SON. LTD.

= = = 1974 Cease Fire Lines

ft m
9000 3000
6000 2000
4500 1500
3000 1000
1200 400
600 200
0 0
200 600
2000 6000
m ft

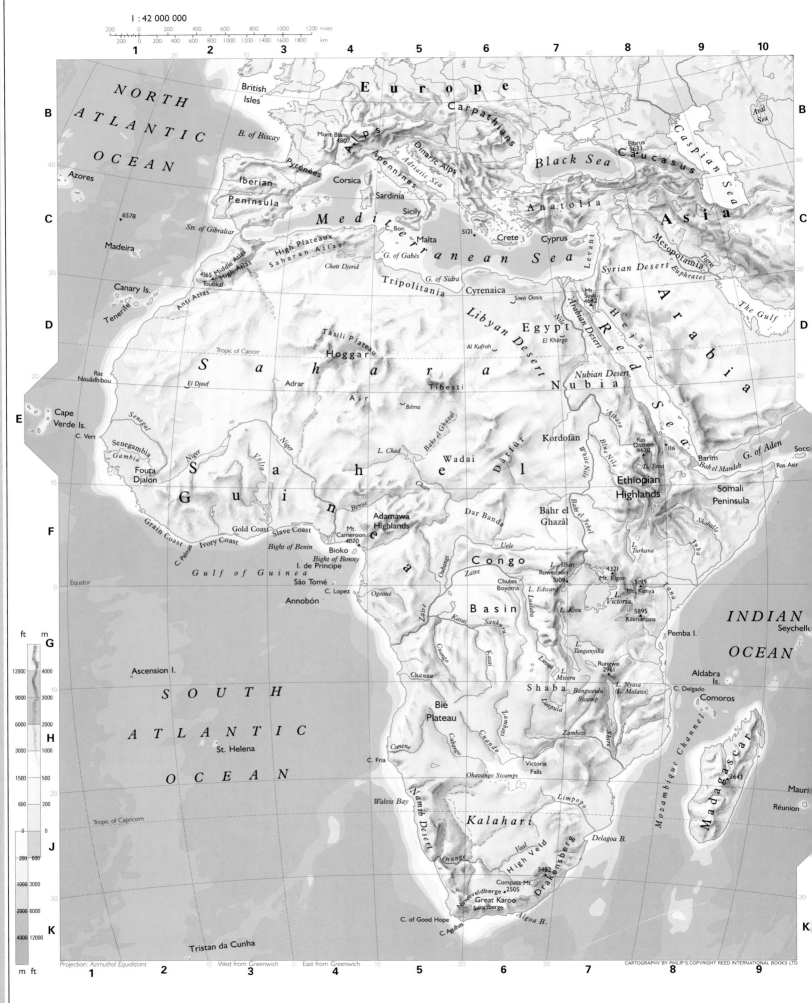

1 : 42 000 000

200   0   200   400   600   800   1000   1200 miles

200 0 200 400 600 800 1000 1200 1400 1600 1800
km

NORTH ATLANTIC OCEAN

SOUTH ATLANTIC OCEAN

British Isles

E u r o p e

Carpathians

Mont Blanc 4807

Alps

Dinaric Alps

Apennines

Adriatic Sea

Black Sea

Caucasus

Elbrus 5633

Caspian Sea

Aral Sea

B. of Biscay

Pyrénées

Corsica

Sardinia

Anatolia

Asia

Azores

Iberian Peninsula

Sicily

Crete

Cyprus

Levant

Mesopotamia

Tigris

Str. of Gibraltar

High Plateaux

Saharan Atlas

Malta

Bon

M e d i t e r r a n e a n   S e a

Syrian Desert

Euphrates

The Gulf

Madeira

6578

4165 Middle Atlas

High Atlas

Toubkal

Anti Atlas

Chott Djerid

G. of Gabès

G. of Sidra

Tripolitania

Cyrenaica

Siwa Oasis

Libyan Desert

Egypt

Nile

Arabian Desert

Mt. Sinai 4642

Red Sea

Hejaz

Arabia

Canary Is.

Tenerife

Tropic of Cancer

Tasili Plateau

Hoggar

Al Kufrah

El Khârga

Ras Nouâdhibou

El Djouf

Adrar

Air

Bilma

Tibesti

Bahr el Ghazal

Nubia

Nubian Desert

Atbara

Ras Dashen 4620

116

Cape Verde Is.

C. Vert

S a h a r a

Darfûr

Kordofân

Barim

Bab el Mandeb

Ras Asir

Soco

G. of Aden

Senegambia

Gambia

Senegal

Niger

Volta

Niger

L. Chad

Wadai

Chari

White Nile

Blue Nile

L. Tana

Ethiopian Highlands

Somali Peninsula

Fouta Djalon

S u d a n

G u i n e a

Benue

Adamawa Highlands

Dar Banda

Uele

Bahr el Ghazâl

Bahr el Jebel

Shaballe

Juba

Grain Coast

Gold Coast

Slave Coast

Ivory Coast

C. Palmas

Bight of Benin

Mt. Cameroon 4070

Bioko

Bight of Bonny

I. de Principe

São Tomé

C. Lopez

Annobón

Ogooué

Ubangi

Zaïre

Congo

Chutes Boyoma

L. Albert

Ruwenzori 5109

L. Edward

L. Kivu

4321

Mt. Elgon

L. Victoria

Mt. Kenya 5199

Tana

Equator

Gulf of Guinea

B a s i n

Kasai

Sankuru

Lualaba

L. Tanganyika

Kilimanjaro 5895

Pemba I.

INDIAN OCEAN

Seychelle

Ascension I.

SOUTH

Zaïre

Kasai

Cuango

Cuanza

L. Mweru

Lucua

Rungwe 2961

L. Nyasa (L. Malawi)

Aldabra Is.

C. Delgado

Comoros

ATLANTIC

St. Helena

Shaba

Bângweulu Swamp

Luapula

Zambezi

Shire

Mozambique Channel

Madagascar

2643

Mauri

Bié Plateau

Cunene

Cubango

Cuando

Zambezi

Victoria Falls

OCEAN

C. Fria

Okavango Swamps

Limpopo

Réunion

Walvis Bay

Namib Desert

Kalahari

Orange

Vaal

High Veld

Drakensberg

3482

Compass Mt. 2505

Nieuweldberge

Great Karoo

Swartberge

Delagoa B.

Tropic of Capricorn

C. of Good Hope

C. Agulhas

Algoa B.

Tristan da Cunha

ft	m
12000	4000
9000	3000
6000	2000
3000	1000
1500	500
600	200
0	0
200	600
1000	3000
2000	6000
4000	12000

m ft

West from Greenwich   East from Greenwich

Projection: Azimuthal Equidistant

CARTOGRAPHY BY PHILIP'S. COPYRIGHT REED INTERNATIONAL BOOKS LTD

1 : 42 000 000

200   0   200   400   600   800   1000   1200 miles
200   0   200   400   600   800   1000   1200 1400 1600 1800   km

NORTH ATLANTIC OCEAN

UNITED KINGDOM
LONDON
NETH.
BELG.
GERMANY
POLAND
Warsaw
RUSSIA
Kiev
UKRAINE
Volgograd
KAZAKHSTAN
Aral Sea
PARIS
FRANCE
SWITZ.
CZECH REP.
Prague
Vienna
SLOVAK REP.
AUSTRIA
HUNGARY
ROMANIA
Odessa
Black Sea
GEORGIA
ARM.
AZER.
Baku
Caspian Sea
TURKMEN.
B. of Biscay
CROATIA
BOS.-HERZ.
YUG.
ALB.
MAC.
BULGARIA
Ankara
TURKEY
Tehrān
Madrid
SPAIN
Lisbon
PORTUGAL
Corsica
Rome
ITALY
Sardinia
Adriatic Sea
GREECE
Athens
Crete
CYPRUS
Aleppo
SYRIA
Mosul
Tigris
Baghdad
Eşfahān
IRAN

Azores (Port.)

Mediterranean Sea
Algiers
Annaba
Constantine
Tunis
TUNISIA
MALTA
Sicily
Tel Aviv-Jaffa
Damascus
Jerusalem
ISRAEL
JORDAN
Euphrates
IRAQ
Basra
KUWAIT

Madeira (Port.)
Rabat
Tétouan
Casablanca
Fès
MOROCCO
Marrakesh
Tripoli
Misrātah
Benghazi
Alexandria
Port Said
Suez
CAIRO
El Faiyûm
Asyût
Nile
SAUDI
ARABIA
BAHRAIN
Riyadh
QATAR
The Gulf

Canary Is. (Sp.)
El Aaiún
WESTERN SAHARA
In Salah
ALGERIA
LIBYA
Marzūq
Al Jawf
EGYPT
Aswân
Medina
Mecca
Jedda

Dakhla
Sahara
Tropic of Cancer
Wadi Halfa
Port Sudan
Red Sea

Ras Nouâdhibou
Fdérik
MAURITANIA
Nouakchott
NIGER
Agadès
CHAD
Atbara
Omdurmân
Khartoum
ERITREA
Mesewa
Asmera
YEMEN
Socotra (Yemen)

VERDE IS.
Tombouctou
MALI
L. Chad
Abéché
El Fâsher
SUDAN
Wâd Medani
G. of Aden
Ras Asir

Praia
C. Vert
Dakar
SENEGAL
GAMBIA
Banjul
GUINEA-BISSAU
Bissau
St-Louis
Senegal
Bámako
Niamey
Kano
Maiduguri
Ndjamena
El Obeid
White Nile
Blue Nile
L. Tana
Addis Ababa
Harer
Berbera
DJIBOUTI
Djibouti

Conakry
Freetown
SIERRA LEONE
GUINEA
BURKINA FASO
Ouagadougou
Bobo-Dioulasso
BENIN
NIGERIA
Abuja
Chari
Benue
Wau
ETHIOPIA
Shabelle
SOMALI REP.

Monrovia
LIBERIA
IVORY COAST
GHANA
TOGO
Yamoussoukro
Bouaké
Kumasi
Lomé
Ibadan
Lagos
Enugu
CENTRAL AFRICAN REP.
Bangui
L. Turkana
Mogadishu

Abidjan
Sekondi-Takoradi
Accra
Porto Novo
Bight of Benin
Port Harcourt
CAMEROON
Douala
Yaoundé
Malabo
L. Albert
UGANDA
KENYA

Gulf of Guinea
EQUATORIAL GUINEA
SÃO TOMÉ & PRINCIPE
C. Lopez
GABON
Libreville
Mbandaka
Kisangani
L. Edward
RWANDA
Kigali
L. Kivu
Kampala
L. Victoria
Kisumu
Nairobi
Kismayu
INDIAN OCEAN

Equator
Annobón
CONGO
ZAÏRE
Zaïre
BURUNDI
Bujumbura
Mombasa
SEYCHELLES

Pointe Noire
Brazzaville
Kinshasa
Matadi
Kasai
Kananga
TANZANIA
Dodoma
Zanzibar
Dar es Salaam
L. Tanganyika

CABINDA (Angola)
Luanda
L. Mweru
Likasi
Lubumbashi
L. Malawi
C. Delgado
COMOROS
Antsiranana

SOUTH ATLANTIC OCEAN
Ascension I. (U.K.)
Lobito
Huambo
ANGOLA
Ndola
ZAMBIA
Lilongwe
MALAWI
Blantyre
Moçambique
Mayotte (Fr.)
Mahajanga

Namibe
Lusaka
MOZAMBIQUE
Zambezi
Mozambique Channel
Toamasina

St. Helena (U.K.)
Cunene
Cubango
ZIMBABWE
Livingstone
Harare
Beira
Antananarivo
MADAGASCAR
MAURITIUS

C. Fria
NAMIBIA
BOTSWANA
Bulawayo
Limpopo
Fianarantsoa
Réunion (Fr.)

Tropic of Capricorn
Windhoek
Gaborone
Pretoria
Maputo
Vaal
Johannesburg
Mbabane
SWAZ.

Orange
Kimberley
Maseru
LESOTHO
Durban

SOUTH AFRICA
Cape Town
C. of Good Hope
C. Agulhas
East London
Port Elizabeth

Tristan da Cunha (U.K.)

Projection: Azimuthal Equidistant

West from Greenwich   East from Greenwich

● Dakar Capital Cities

CARTOGRAPHY BY PHILIP'S. COPYRIGHT REED INTERNATIONAL BOOKS LTD

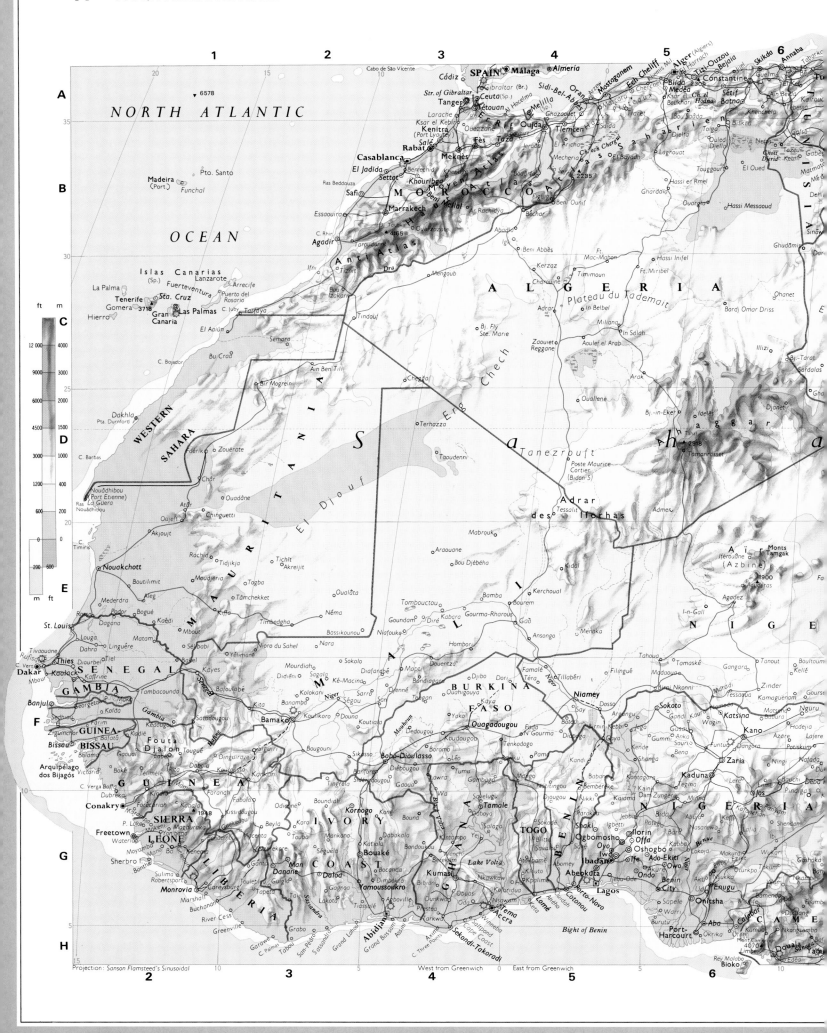

NORTH ATLANTIC

OCEAN

SPAIN ● Málaga ● Almería

Cabo de São Vicente
Cádiz
Str. of Gibraltar
Gibraltar (Br.)
Tanger
Ceuta (Sp.)
Tétouan
Al Hoceima
Melilla
Larache
Kenitra (Port Lyautey)
Salé
Rabat
Meknès
Fès
Taza
Casablanca
El Jadida
Berrechid
Settat
Khouribga
MOROCCO
Safi
Essaouira
Marrakech
Agadir
Taroudant
Anti Atlas
Ifni
Tiznit
Dra
Madeira (Port.)
Funchal
Pto. Santo
Ras Beddouza
C. Rhir

Oran
Mostaganem
Ech Cheliff
Arzew
Mascara
Sidi-Bel-Abbès
Tlemcen
Ghazaouet
Oujda
Saïda
El Aricha
Chott Chergui
Mecheria
El Bayadh
Bou Anane
Aïn Sefra
Béchar
Abadla
Igli
Beni Abbès
Mengoub

Alger (Algiers)
El Harrach
Tizi-Ouzou
Bejaia
Skikda
Annaba
Blida
Medéa
Ksar el Boukhari
Chlef
Hodna
Sétif
Batna
Constantine
Guelma
Aïn Beïda
Khenchela
Biskra
TUNISIA
Tozeur
Nefta
Chott Djerid
Kebili
Gabès
Matmata
Sfax
Sinaw

Laghouat
Djelfa
Touggourt
El Oued
Ghardaïa
Ouargla
Hassi er Rmel
Hassi Messaoud
Ghudāmis

ALGERIA

Plateau du Tademait
Charouine
Timimoun
Adrar
In Belbel
Miliana
In Salah
Zaouiet Reggane
Aoulef el Arab
Ohanet
Bordj Omar Driss
Illizi
Bj.-Tarat
Safdalas

Islas Canarias (Sp.)
Lanzarote
Fuerteventura
Arrecife
Puerto del Rosario
La Palma
Tenerife
Sta. Cruz
Gomera
Gran Canaria
Las Palmas
Hierro
El Aaiún
Tarfaya
C. Juby
Semara
Bu Craa
C. Bojador
Tindouf
Aïn Ben Tili
Chegga
Bir Mogrein

Chech
Erg
Tanezrouft
Bj. Fly Ste. Marie
Ouallene
Arak
Bj.-in-Eker
Idelas
Ahaggar
Tahat 2918
Tamanrasset
Djanet

WESTERN SAHARA

Dakhla
Pta. Durnford
C. Barbas
dérik
Zouérate
Chār
Ouadâne
C. Vert
Nouâdhibou (Port Étienne)
Ras Nouâdhibou
La Güera
Atâr
Chinguetti
Oujeft
Akjoujt

MAURITANIA
El Djouf
Terhazza
Taoudenni
Poste Maurice Cortier (Bidon 5)
Adrar des Iforhas
Tessalit
Admer

C. Timiris
Nouakchott
Boutilimit
Rachid
Tidjikja
Tichît
Akreijit
Boumdeid
Moudjéria
Tâmchekket
Kiffa
Mederdra
Aleg
Tagba
Oualâta

Araouane
Bou Djébéha
Mabrouk
Kidal
Aïr
Iférouane
Monts Tamgak (Azbine)
Iferouane
In-Gall
Agadez

St. Louis
Rosso
Podor
Bogué
Kaédi
M'bout
Néma
Bassikounou
Goundam
Diré
Kabara
Tombouctou
Bourem
Gourma-Rharous
Gao
I-n-Gall
NIGER

Louga
Dahra
Matam
Sélibabi
Yélimané
Nioro du Sahel
Nara
Niafouké
Timbedgha
Ansongo
Ménaka
Tahoua
Tamaské
Mdaoua
Gangara
Tanout

Tivaouane
Kaffrine
Linguère
Dagana
SENEGAL
Thies
Diourbel
Tiel
Matam
Homboti
Douentza
Famalé
Tillabéri
Filingué
Birni Nkonni
Maradi
Katsina
Zinder
Gourse

Dakar
Rufisque
Kaolack
Mbour
GAMBIA
Banjul
Georgetown
Kaffrine
Tambacounda
Kayes
Banamba
Kita
Koulikoro
Bamako
Ségou
San
Mopti
Bandiagara
Djibo
Dori
Téra
Say
Dosso
Argungu
Sokoto
Gandi
Kaura
Namoda
Gummi
Anka
Kamagueram
Nguru
Hadejia
Azare
Lafore
Potiskum

Bignona
Ziguinchor
GUINEA-BISSAU
Bissau
Bolama
Fouta Djalon
Labé
Tougué
Dinguiraye
Siguiri
Kankan
Bamako
Koutiala
Sikasso
Bobo-Dioulasso
BURKINA FASO
Ouahigouya
Kaya
Ouagadougou
Koudougou
Fada N'Gourma
Diapaga
Botou
Kande
Shonga
Zaria
Kaduna

Arquipélago dos Bijagós
C. Verga
Boffa
Boké
Télimélé
Pita
Mamou
Dabola
Faranah
Kouroussa
Kissidougou
Banfora
Sidéradougou
Gaoua
Diébougou
Lawra
Gambaga
Nalerigu
Diguou
Nikki
Kaiama
Dan Zungeru
Minna
Jos
GUINEA
Conakry
Dubréka
Kindia
Kabala
Beyla
Odienné
Kong
Bouna
Wa
Sokodé
Parakou
NIGERIA
Kontagora
Kaduna

SIERRA LEONE
Freetown
Waterloo
Makeni
Magburaka
Kambia
Port Loko
Bo
Kenema
Sefadu
IVORY COAST
Séguéla
Katiola
Bouaké
Bondoukou
Bole
GHANA
Tamale
Salaga
Yendi
TOGO
Blitta
BENIN
Shaki
Igbetti
Ilorin
Offa
Oshogbo
Ogbomosho
Iwo
Ibadan
Abeokuta
Lagos
Ife
Oyo
Ado-Ekiti
Owo
Akure
Ondo
Benin City
Sapele
Warri

LIBERIA
Monrovia
Marshall
Buchanan
River Cess
Greenville
Robertsport
Man
Danané
Guiglo
Duékoué
Yamoussoukro
Divo
Gagnoa
Lakota
Tiassalé
Abidjan
Grand Bassam
Assini
Aboisso
Kumasi
Obuasi
Dunkwa
Accra
Tema
Sekondi-Takoradi
Bight of Benin
Lomé
Cotonou
Porto-Novo
Aba
Onitsha
Enugu
Calabar
CAMEROON
Port-Harcourt
Okrika
Rey Malabo
Bioko
Douala
Limbe
Mont Cameroun 4070
Edéa

Sassandra
C. Palmas
Tabou
San Pédro
Grand Lahou

Projection: Sanson Flamsteed's Sinusoidal
West from Greenwich
East from Greenwich

40

46

7 8 9 10 11 12 13

1:15 000 000

100   0   100   200   300   400 miles
100   0   100   200   300   400   500   600 km

MEDITERRANEAN SEA

C. Bon
Pantelleria
Ragusa Sicily
C. Passero
MALTA
Lampedusa (It.)
Iles Kerkenna

Ròdhos
Karpathos
Iraklion
Kríti

Antalya
Antalya Körfezi
İskenderun Körfezi
İskenderun
TURKEY
CYPRUS
Nicosia
Limassol
Antakya
Al Ladhiqiya
Halab
Hamāh
Hims
Tarabulus
SYRIA
Al Mawsil (Mosul)
Nahr Dijla (Tigris)
Mesopotamia
Nahr al Furat

LEBANON
Bayrūt
Dimashq (Damascus)
'Akka
Haifa
Tel Aviv-Yafo
ISRAEL
Jerusalem (Al Quds)
Gaza
Amman
JORDAN
Ar Rutbah
IRAQ
Bādiyat ash Shām

Tarābulus (Tripoli)
Tājūrā
Al Khums
Zlitan
Misrātah
Al Qasabah
Gharyān
968
Bani Walid
Mizdah
Jādū
Zuwārah

Banghāzi (Benghazi)
Banīnah
878
Al Bayda
Darnah
Marsá Susah
Tūkrah
Al Marj
Tulmaythah
Khalīj Bunbah
Tubruq
Suluq
Az Zuwaytinah
Ajdābiyah
Marsa el Brega
Al 'Uqaylah
Ra's Al-Unuf
Khalīj Surt
Surt

LIBYA
Tripolitania
Cyrenaica
Sahrâ'
Hūn
Marādah
Awjilah
Zillah
1200
Sabhah
Fezzan
Tmassah
Marzūq
Tasāwah
Awbāri
Idehan
Marzûq
Waw al Kabir
Al Jaghbūb
Al Qatrūn
Rebiana
Al Jawf
Al Kufrah

Sha'b
Barqah
Bardīyah
Salūm
Sidi Barrâni
Ras al Milh
Marsá Matrûh
El 'Alamein
El Daba
Rashīd
Damanhūr
El Iskandarîya (Alexandria)
El Mahalla el Kubra
Dumyât
Mansûra
Būr Sa'id
El 'Arish
El Qantara
Ismâ'ilîya
Tanta
Zagazig
EL QÂHIRA (Cairo)
El Gîza
Helwân
El Suweis (Suez)
Gebel el Tih
Es Sînâ
Elat
Al 'Aqabah
Tabūk

Qâra
Munkhafed el Qattâra (Qattâra Depression)
Sîwa
El Faiyûm
Beni Suef
El Bowiti
Beni Mazâr
El Minya
Mallawi
Dairût
Asyût
Abu Tig
El Wâhât el-Dakhla
Mût
El Qasr
Bâris
El Wâhât el-Khârga
El Khârga
Qasr Farâfra
Sinnûris
Esh Sharqîya
Es Sahrâ
Akhmîm
Sohâg
Girga
Qena
Bûr Safâga
Quseir
El Uqsur (Luxor)
Isnâ
Qûs
Idfû
1st Cataract
Aswân (Aswân High Dam)
El Shallal
Ras Bânâs
Bîr Shalatein

SAUDI ARABIA
An Nafūd
Tayma'
Mada'in Salih
Al Wajh
Umm Lajj
Al Madinah
Yanbu'al Bahr
Rābigh Qasr
Jiddah
Makkah (Mecca)
At Tā'if
Al Lith

Buheiret en Naser (Lake Nasser)
Dunqul
Wadi Halfa
Es Sahrâ en Nûbiya
Bîr Ungat
Halaib
Ras Hadarba
RED SEA
Gebeit Mine
Bir Shalatein
Muhammad Qōl
Ras Abu Shagara
Bûr Sûdân (Port Sudan)
Suakin
Sawākin
Tokar
Trinkitat
'Aqiq
Ras Kasar

Toummo
Madama
Aozou
Wour
Bardaï
3150
Tarso Emissi
Zouar
TIBESTI
Emi Koussi 3415
Gouri
Anaye
Bilma
Ma'tan as Sarra
Uweinat 1893
Ayn al 'Uwaynat
El Wâhât el Selîma
Kosha
Abri
Nukheila
Laqiya Arba'in
Bir 'Atrun
(Nubian Desert)
Delgo
Abu Hamed
Derudub
Karora
ERITREA
Nakfa
Mitsiwa
Zula

Anaye
chirfa
Jado
Madama
BORKOU
Bahr el Ghazal (Soro)
Ounianga-Kébir
Ounianga Sérir
Dépression du Mourdi
Faya-Largeau
Fada
ENNEDI
Djourab
Oum Chalouba
3rd Cataract
Dongola
Argo
El Kab
Kareima
Merowe
Korti
Ed Debba
Dongola
El Khandaq
4th Cataract
5th Cataract
Berber
Atbara
Ed Dâmer
Adarama
Musmar
Haiya Junction
Sinkat
Asmera
Akordat
Keren
Barentu
Ras Dashen 4620
Metemu
Gonder
Debre Tabor
L. Tana
Lalibela
Mek'elē
Aksum
Mekele

CHAD
Zigey
Rig-Rig
Biltine
Arada
Tiné
Shigaita
Kutum
Malha
Hamrat esh Sheykh
Sodiri
Kagmar
El Geteina
Khashm el Girba
Gedaref
Gallâbat
Mao
L. Fitri
Ati
Moussoro
Massaguet
N'djamena
Massakory
Yao
Bokoro
Bitkine
Mongo
Abéché
Adré
Goz Beïda
Am Dam
Guéréda
El Junaynah
Kabkabiyah
El Fasher
Nyālā
Jebel Marrah 3088
Zalingei
Idd el Ghanam
Umm Keddada
Umm Bel
Wad Banda
En Nahud
Abū Zabad
Er Rahad
El Obeid
Kosti
Sennâr
Singa
Er Roseires
Kurmuk
Famaka
Dembecha
Debre Markos
Omdurmân
El Khartûm Bahri (Khartoum)
El Khartûm
El Kamlin
Wâd Medanî
El Managil
El Gezira
Rufa'a
Kassala
DARFUR
KORDOFAN
SUDAN
Lac Tchad
Bol
Kukawa
Marte
Dikwa
Makari
Kousséri
Maroua
Mora
Bama
Maïduguri
Dilling
Kadugli
Talodi
Kaka
Kodok
Malakâl
Abwong
Nasir
Gambela
Dembidolo
Nekemte
Gimbi
ETHIOPIA
Addis Abeba (Addis Ababa)
Addis Alem
Gore
Ghimbi
Jebelein
Renk
Melut
Tungaru
Heiban
Rashad
El Laqâwa
Muglad
Abu Matariq
Buram
Taweisha
El Odaiya
Dilling
Umm Ruwaba
Um Dam
Ed Dueim
Kaga Bandoro
Bangassou
Obo
CENTRAL AFRICAN REPUBLIC
Bangui
ZAÏRE
KENYA
L. Turkana
L. Stefanie (Chew Bahir)
Mega
Yabelo
L. Abaya 4200
L. Shala
L. Zway
Asela
Sodo
Gidole
Bunj
Bahr el Arab
Bahr el Ghazal
Wāw
Tonj
Rumbek
Bôr
Pibor P.
Juba
Yirol
Kapoeta
Torit
Lokichokio
Bahr el Jebel (White Nile)
El Abyad (White Nile)
Bahr el Azraq (Blue Nile)
Nahr 'Atbara
Jur
Bentiu
Fangak
Duk Fadiat
Kongor
Akōbo
Gambela
Sadd el Aali
Geili
6th Cataract
Shendi
Wad Hamid
El Wuz

Tropic of Cancer

COPYRIGHT GEORGE PHILIP & SON. LTD.

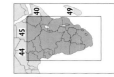

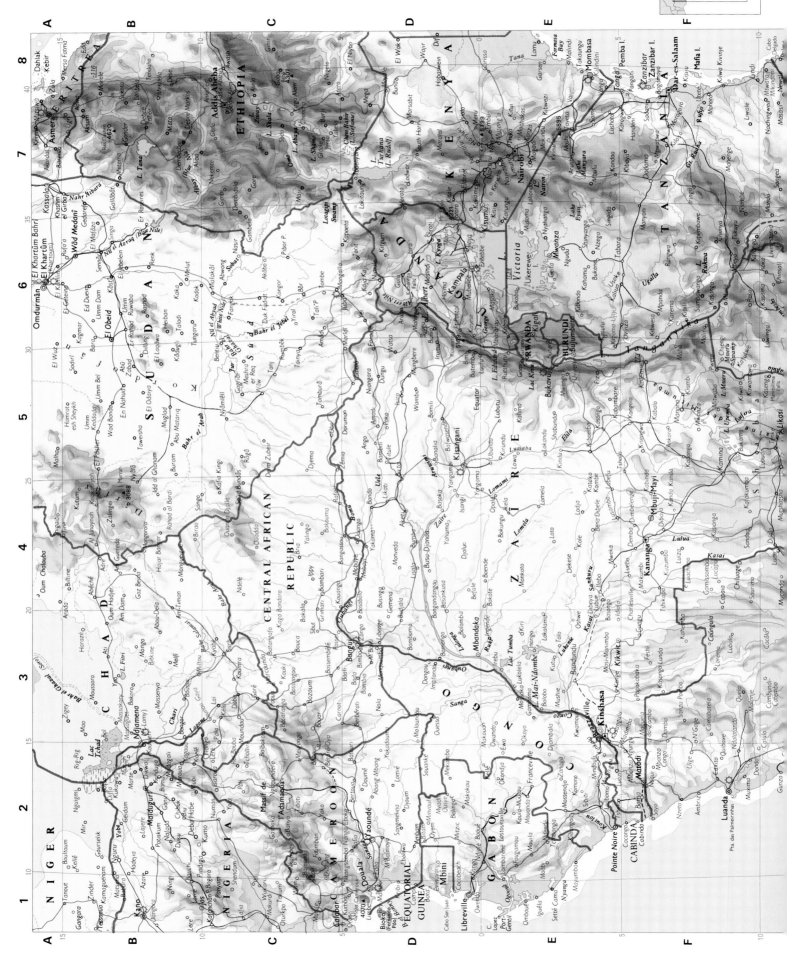

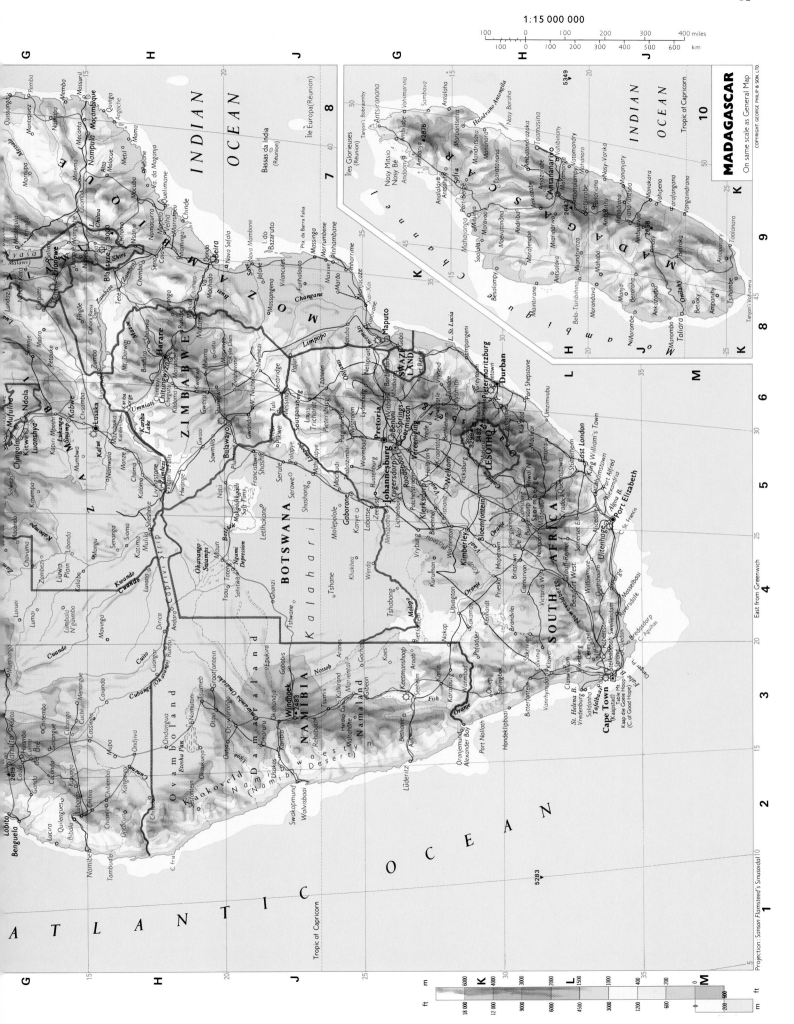

1:15 000 000

MADAGASCAR
On same scale as General Map

COPYRIGHT GEORGE PHILIP & SON LTD

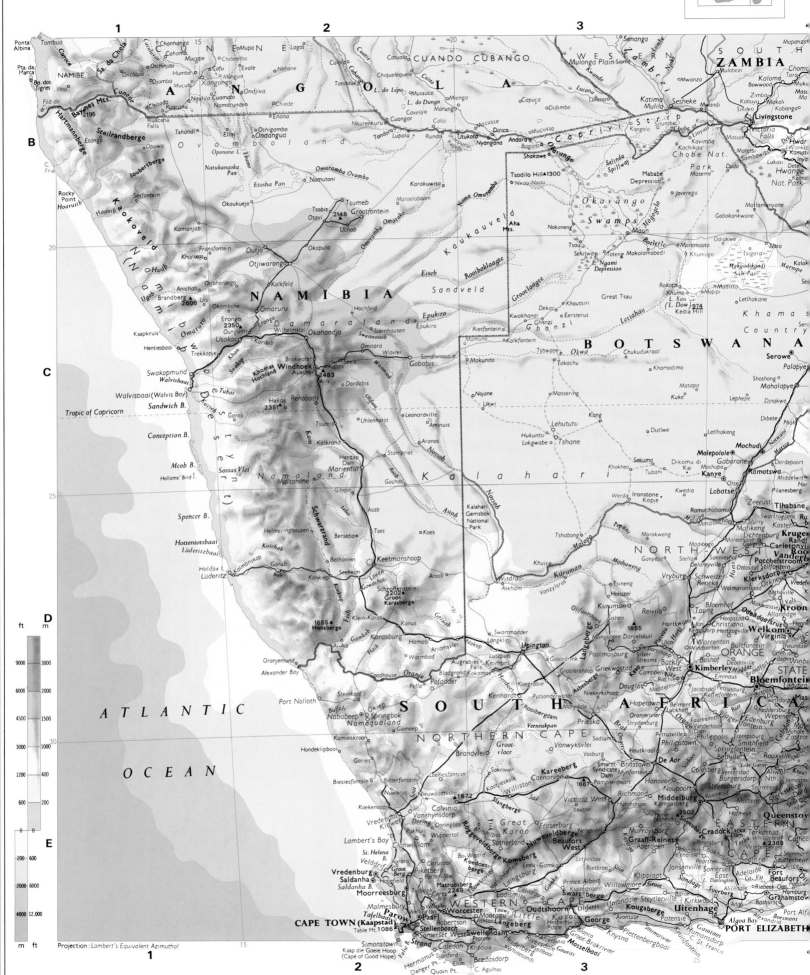

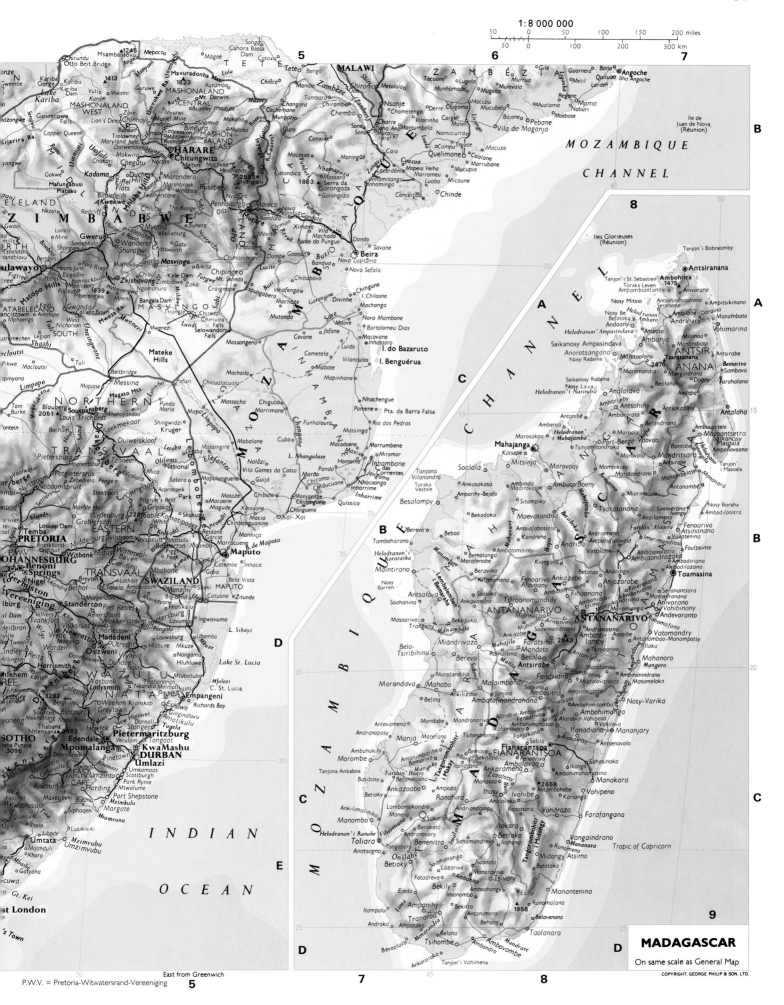

MADAGASCAR

On same scale as General Map

COPYRIGHT. GEORGE PHILIP & SON. LTD.

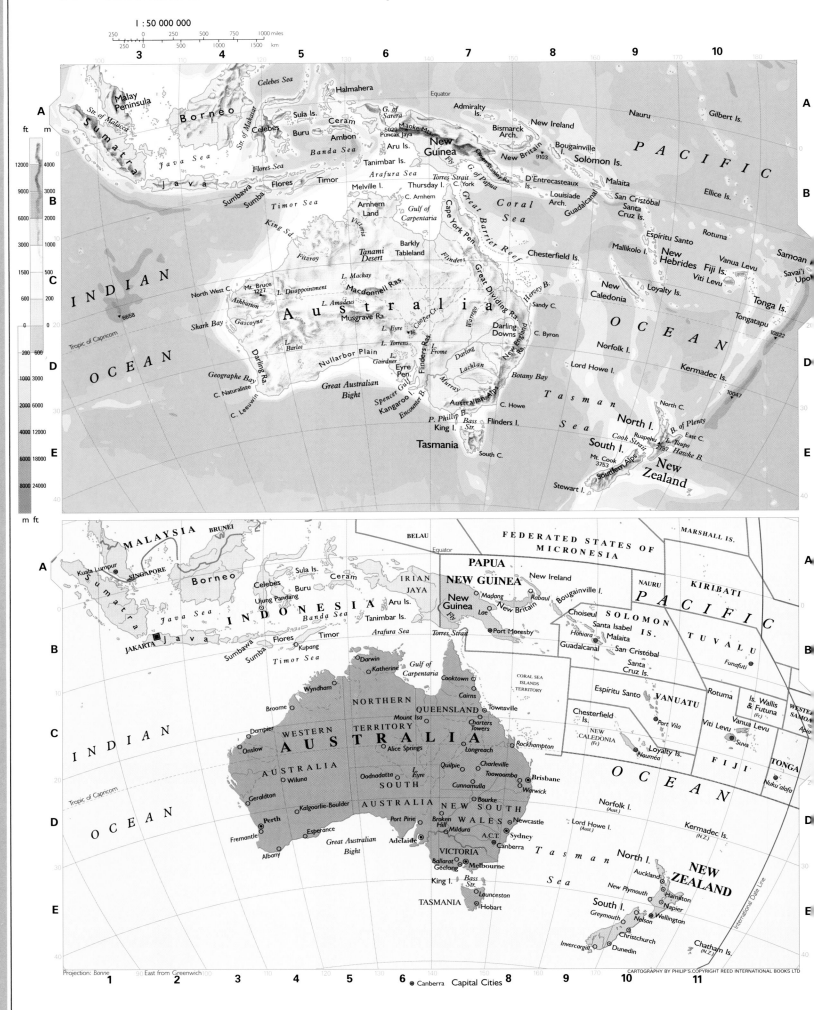

1:6 000 000
20 0 20 40 60 80 100 miles
20 0 40 80 120 160 km

56 56 56 56

NEW ZEALAND & S.W. PACIFIC
1:60 000 000
200 0 200 400 600 800 miles
200 0 400 800 1200 km

KIRIBATI

TUVALU (Ellice Is.)
Tokelau Is. (N.Z.)
Tongareva (Penrhyn) I.
Pukapuka
Rakahanga
Nassau
Manihiki
Suwarrow
Northern Group
WESTERN SAMOA
Savaii
Upolu
Tutuila
AMER. SAMOA (U.S.)
Cook Is. (N.Z.)
Îles de la Société
Wallis & Futuna (Fr.)
Rotuma
Vanua Levu
Lau or Eastern Group
Palmerston Atoll
Aitutaki
Mitiaro Mauke
FIJI
Viti Levu
TONGA (Friendly Is.)
Niue (N.Z.)
Lower Group
Atui
Rarotonga
Mangaia
FRENCH POLYNESIA
VAN-UATU

PACIFIC OCEAN

Tropic of Capricorn

Raoul (Sunday) I.
Macauley
Kermadec Is. (N.Z.)
Curtis
Three Kings Is.
Auckland
NORTH I.
Cook Strait
NEW ZEALAND
Wellington
SOUTH I.
Tasman Sea
Christchurch
Chatham I.
Chatham Is.
Pitt I.
Dunedin
Bounty Is.
Stewart I.
Antipodes Is.
Snares
Campbell I.
Auckland Is.
Macquarie I. (Austr.)
SOUTHERN OCEAN

SAMOA ISLANDS
1:12 000 000
WESTERN SAMOA
AMERICAN SAMOA
Savai'i
Apia
Upolu
Pago Pago
Manua Is.
Rose I.
Tutuila

Futuna
Wallis & Futuna (Fr.)
WESTERN SAMOA

ft m
12 000 4000
9000 3000
6000 2000
3000 1000
1200 400
600 200
0 0
200 600
m ft

NORTH ISLAND

Three Kings Is.
North C.
C. Reinga
C. Maria van Diemen
Houhora
Rangaunu Bay
Doubtless Bay
Mangonui
Whangaroa Bay
Ahipara B.
Kaitaia
Tauroa Pt.
B. of Islands
C. Brett
Rawene
Opua
Hokianga Harb.
Kaikohe
Hikurangi
Whangarei
Whangarei Harb.
Donnelly's Crossing
Bream Hd.
Bream Bay
Dargaville
Waipu
Lit. Barrier I.
Gt. Barrier I.
Kaipara Harb.
Waikworth
C. Rodney
Cuvier I.
Helensville
C. Colville
Coromandel
Hauraki Gulf
Whitianga
Takapuna
Devonport
Mayor I.
AUCKLAND
Onehunga
Manukau
Papakura
Thames
Tauranga Harb.
Waiuku
Pukekohe
Mercer
Paeroa
Waihi
Waikato
Huntly
Te Aroha
Bay of Plenty
Raglan
Morrinsville
Cambridge
Te Puke
Whakatane
Opotiki
White I.
C. Runaway
Hikurangi
Kawhia Harb.
Hamilton
Putaruru
Te Awamutu
Rotorua
Kawerau
Waipiro
Raukumara Ra.
Otorohanga
Kinleith
Kaingaroa Forest
Murupara
Matu
Tolaga Bay
Te Kuiti
Mokau
Makaki
L. Taupo
Tarawera
Ormond
North Taranaki Bight
New Plymouth
Ongarue
Taupo
Waikaremoana
Gisborne
Waitara
Whangamomona
Turangi
Kaimanawa Mts.
Poverty Bay
Inglewood
Mt. Egmont (Taranaki)
Stratford
Eltham
Ruapehu
Raetihi
Ohakune
Nuhaka
Wairoa
Mahia Peninsula
Opunake
Kaponga
Watotuu
Hawke Bay
Napier View
Hawera
Waverley
Taihape
Rangitikei
Ruahine
Napier
South Taranaki Bight
Patea
Mangaweka
Waipawa
Hastings
Wanganui
Marton Bulls
Halcombe
Hunterville
Waipukurau
Dannevirke
Palmerston N.
Feilding
Foxton
Woodville
Pahiatua
C. Turnagain
Shannon
Levin
Otaki
Eketahuna
Paraparaumu
Masterton
Kapiti I.
Featherston
Carterton
Greytown
Martinborough
Up. Hutt
Petone
Lr. Hutt
WELLINGTON
Eastbourne
Cook Strait

SOUTH ISLAND

C. Farewell
Golden Bay
D'Urville I.
Collingwood
Tasman Bay
Pelorus Sd.
Takaka
Tasman Mts.
Motueka
Picton
Nelson
Richmond
Wakefield
Havelock
Blenheim
Karamea Bight
Marlborough
Tadmor
Wairau
Seddon
Ward
Seddonville
Murchison
Granity
Matiri Ra.
Lyell
Tophouse
Westport
Inangahua Junction
Traversa 2038
2885 Tapuaenuku
Reefton
Spenser Mts.
Clarence
Blackball
Runanga
Hanmer
Kaikoura
Greymouth
Stillwater
L. Brunner
Amuri B.
Springs
Hokitika
Kumara
Jacksons
Arthur's P.
Waikari
Hurunui
Ross
Waiau
Culverden
Waiau
Waimakariri
Abut Hd.
Okarito
Amberley
Oxford
Waipara
Pegasus Bay
Kaiapoi
New Brighton
Christchurch
Springfield
Whitecliffs
Riccarton
Lincoln
Lyttelton
Mt. Cook 3753
Coleridge
Staveley
Little River
Akaroa
Banks Peninsula
Westland
Jackson B.
Rakaia
Southbridge
Ellesmere
Okuru
Haast
Rata
Ashburton
Canterbury Plains
Mt. Tasman
Fairlie
Ashburton Bight
Pukaki
Southern Alps
Ohau
Temuka
St. Andrews
Milford Sd.
Mt. Aspiring 2819
L. Hawea
L. Wanaka
Timaru
Bligh Sd.
George Sd.
Wanaka
Waimate
Secretary I.
Arrowtown
Cromwell
Maheno
Doubtful Sd.
Queenstown
Naseby
Tokarahi
Ngapara
Oamaru
Wakatipu
Clyde
Alexandra
Hampden
Breaksea Sd.
Kingston
Te Anau
Kakanui Mts.
Dunback
Palmerston
Resolution I.
Manapouri
Roxburgh
Otago Harbour
Waikouaiti
Mossburn
Lumsden
Dunedin
Port Chalmers
Dusky Sd.
Ohai
Edievale
Kelso
Lawrence
Mosgiel
C. Saunders
Chalky Inlet
Nightcaps
Tapanui
Waipori
St. Kilda
Preservation Inlet
Te Waewae B.
Riverton
Gore
Milton
Fairfield
Balclutha
Orepuki
Winton
Mataura
Kaitangata
Nugget Pt.
Tuatapere
Gorge Rd.
Edendale
Wyndham
Invercargill
Bluff
Oreti
Owaka
Tohakopa
Ruapuke I.
Halfmoon Bay
Foveaux Str.
Stewart I.
S.W. Cape
Port Pegasus

NORTH ISLAND

SOUTH ISLAND

TASMAN SEA

PACIFIC OCEAN

Cook Strait

FIJI AND TONGA ISLANDS
1:12 000 000
50 0 50 100 150 miles
50 0 50 100 150 200 250 km

Thikombia
Niuafo'ou (Tonga)
Yasawa Group
Lambasa
Vanua Levu
Taveuni
Koro
Vanua Balavu
FIJI
Lau or Eastern Group
Lautoka
Nandi
Levuka
Ovalau
Viti Levu
Suva
Ngau
Koro Sea
Lakemba
Moala
Kandavu
Vatoa
TONGA (Friendly Is.)
Vava'u
Tofua I.
Tongatapu
Nuku'alofa

NORTHERN TERRITORY

TIMOR SEA

INDONESIA

INDIAN OCEAN

Timor

Roti
Sawa
Semau
Danu
Raidjua
Sumba
Sumbawa
Lombok

Joseph Bonaparte Gulf
Cambridge Gulf
Dundas Str.
Van Diemen Gulf
Melville I.
Bathurst I.
Darwin
Port Darwin

C. Croker / McCluer I.
C. Don / Croker
Cobourg Pen.
P. Essington
Murgenella
Oenpelli
480
Jabiru
Field I.
Pt. Blaze
C. Gambier
Clarence Str.
C. Hotham
Peron Is.
Anson B.
C. Scott
Gordan B.
Pt. Fawcett
C. Van Diemen

Naongmuh
Batchelor
Rum Jungle
Adelaide River
Pine Creek
Daly
Katherine
Tindal
Willeroo
Birdum
Birdum Creek
Larrimah
Maranboy
Mataranka
Top Springs
Montejinnie

Koongra
Daly River
Dorisvale
Wingate Mts.
Fitzmaurice Ra.
Stokes Ra.
Coolibah
Victoria
Victoria River Downs
Humbert River
Wave Hill
Hooker Creek
Winnecke Cr.

Tanami Desert

Horden Hills
Tanami
Gordon Downs
Nicholson
Sturt Creek
Gregory Lake

Reynolds Ra.
Mt. Zeil 1510
Macdonell Ranges
Mt. Liebig 1524
Papunya
L. Macdonald
Mt. Leisler 901
Mt. Singleton 808
L. Bennett
Lake Mackay
Haasts Bluff
Hermannsburg
James Ranges
George Gill Ra.
Bonython Ra.
Angas Hills
L. Hopkins
L. Neale
L. Hazlett
L. White

Great Sandy Desert
Gibson Desert

Lake Disappointment
Percival Lakes
L. Auld
L. Dora
L. Blanche
L. George
L. Tobin
McKay Ra.
Broadhurst
Throssell
Poisonbush Ra.
Paterson Ra.
L. Waukarlycarly
L. Winifred
Robertson Ra.
Oldgatong

Cockburn
Carr Boyd Ra.
Ord
Turkey Creek
L. Argyle
Wyndham
Kununurra
Buckle Hd.
Dunstony Pt.

King Leopold Ranges
Durack
Gibb River
Mt. Hann 716
King Edward
Drysdale
Kalumburu
Prince Regent R.
Mt. Elizabeth
Hann
Mornington
Margaret Ct.
Mount Hart
Fitzroy
Christmas Creek
St. George Ra.
Mueller Ras.
Margaret
Mt. Ord 1007
Napier Downs
Kimberley Downs
Noonkanbah
Fitzroy Crossing
Halls Creek
Mabel Downs
Bohemia Downs
Billiluna
Carranya

McClintock Ra.
Albert Edward Ra.
Alice Downs
Springvale
Bedford Downs
Flora Valley

King Sound
Buccaneer Archipelago
Yampi Sd.
Collier B.
Pender B.
Beagle Bay
Lombadina
C. Leveque
King
Adele I.
Lacepede Is.
Carnot B.
C. Boileau
Roebuck Plains
Broome
Roebuck B.
Thangoo
Anna Plains
Frazer Downs
Wallal Downs
Ninety Mile Beach

Lagrange
Lagrange B.
C. Latouche Treville

De Grey
Shay Gap
Goldsworthy
Warrawagine
Nullagine
Marble Bar
Woodstock
Shaw
Hillside
Roy Hill
Marillana
Newman 1053
Ethel Creek
Ophthalmia
Hamersley Range
Wittenoom
Mt. Bruce 1235
Mt. Meharry 1251
Tom Price
Paraburdoo

Port Hedland
Poissonier Pt.
Pippingarra
C. Thouin
Depuch
Mallina
Yule
Yandeearra
Whim Creek
Roebourne
Dampier
Karratha
Cossack
C. Preston
C. Lambert
Enderby I.
Legendre I.
Delambre I.
Dampier Archipelago
Wickham
Pannawonica
Yarraloola
Mardie
Onslow
Ashburton
Barrow I.
Monte Bello Is.
North West C.
Exmouth
Learmonth
Exmouth Gulf
Pt. Cloates
Ningaloo

Rowley Shoals
Mermaid Reef
Imperieuse Reef
Clerke Reef
Scott Reef
Seringapatam Reef
Lynher Reef
Ashmore Reef
Hibernia Reef
Cartier I.
Browse I.
Adele I.

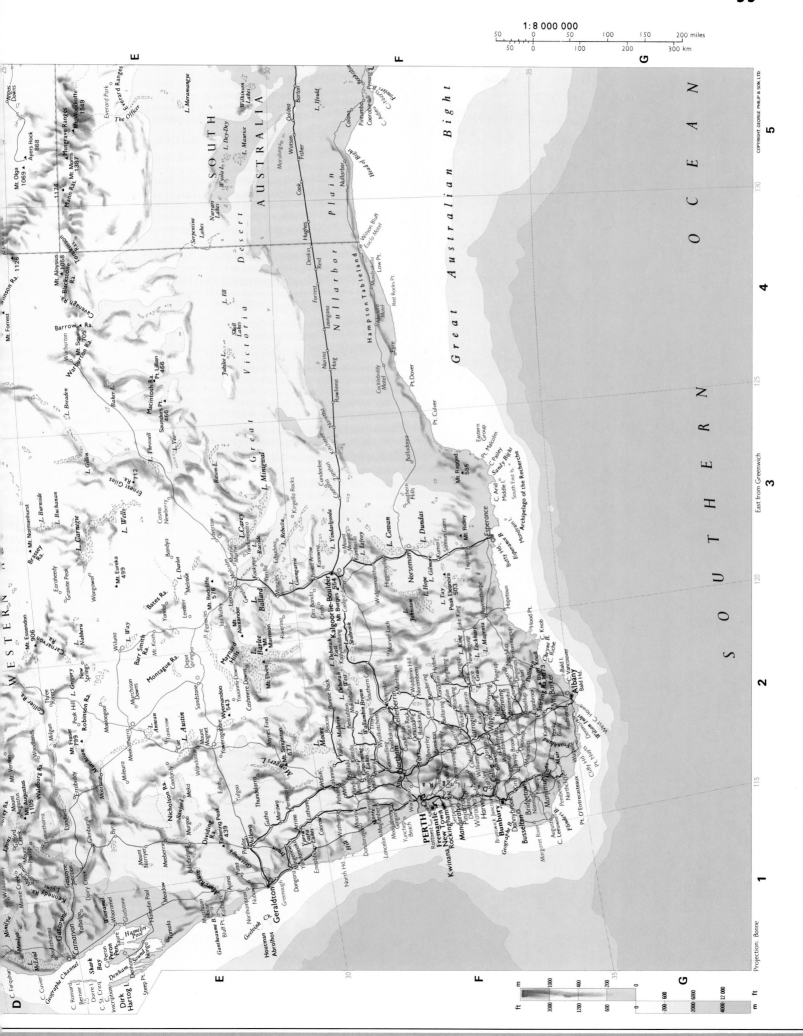

1 : 8 000 000

50   0   50   100   150   200 miles
50   0   100   200   300 km

D

E

F

G

WESTERN

SOUTH   AUSTRALIA

Great   Victoria   Desert

Nullarbor   Plain

Hampton Tableland

Great   Australian   Bight

S O U T H E R N   O C E A N

Musgrave Ranges
Mt.Woodroffe 1549
Mann Ra. Mt. Morris 1387
The Officer
Everard Park
Everard Ranges
Ayers Rock 868
Mt. Olga 1069

L. Meramangye
Wilkinson Lakes
L. Dey-Dey
L. Maurice
Serpentine Lakes
Nurrari Lakes
Wyola L.
L.Hyault
Ooldea
Barton
Cook
Maralinga
Watson
Fisher

Mt. Forrest
Winton Ra.
Mt. Aloysius 1058
Blackstone Ra.
Cavenagh Ra.
Tomkinson Ra. 1126

Barrow Ra.
Warburton Ra. 705
Warburton
Mt. Squires
L. Breaden
Baker L.
Macintosh Ra.
Pt. Lillian 466
Saunders Pt. 461

Shell Lakes
Jubilee L.
L. Ell

Deakin
Hughes
Forrest
Reid
Loongana
Cook
Coorabie
C. Adieu

L. Yeo
L. Throssell
Ernest Giles Ra. 712
L. Wells
L. Gillen

Mt. Normanhurst
Brassey Ra.
Eurobeedy
Mt. Eureka 499
Granite Peak
L. Carnegie
Wongowol
L. Darlot
Cosmo Newbery

L. Rebecca
L. Carey
Loverton
Yamarna
Edjudina
L. Minigwal
Raeside L.
Pinjin
Kirgella Rocks

Nurina
Haig
Rawlinna
Kitchener
Naretha
Zanthus
Cundeelee
Coonana

Wilson Bluff
Eucla Motel
Mundrabilla
Madura Motel
Cocklebiddy Motel
Low Pt.
Red Rocks Pt.
Eyre

Mt. Keith
Wiluna
Bates Ra.
Barr Smith Ra.
Mt. Essendon 906
Carnarvon Ra.
Nabberu
L. Way
Montague Ra.

Depot Springs
New Springs
L. Gregory
Murchison Downs
Cosmere Downs
Youanmi Downs Hills
Sandstone
Barlee Range
Maynard Hills
Mt. Elvire
Sir Samuel
Leonora
Mt. Alexander
Leinster
Mt. Clifford
Yundamindra

Mt. Redcliffe 576
L. Ballard
Menzies
Niagara
Kookynie
Goongarrie
Credo
Ora Banda
Broad Arrow
Kanowna

Mt. Margaret
Laverton
Mt. Morgans
Mt. Weld
Beria
Malcolm
Gwalia

Goongarrie
Kalgoorlie-Boulder 554
Kambalda
Mt. Burges
Coolgardie
Widgiemooltha
Kurnalpi
L. Lefroy
L. Cowan
L. Dundas
Solomon Gums
Mt. Ridley

Norseman
L. Hope
L. Johnston
Higginsville
L. Tay
Peak Eleanora 503

Mt. Ragged 585
Ballodonia
Pt. Culver
C. Arid
C. Pasley
Pt. Malcolm
Eastern Group
Sandy Bight
South East Is.
Middle I.
Archipelago of the Recherche
Esperance
Esperance B.
Butty Hd.
Mondrain I.

Southern Hills

Collier Ra.
Three Rivers
Peak Hill
Mt. Fraser 799
Robinson Ra.
Errabiddy
Mount Augustus 1105
Mt. Vernon
Waldburg Ra.
Mt. Gould
Woodlands
Nicholson Ra.
Sanford
Murgoo
Coodarby

L. Annean
Cue
Mt. Magnet
Mt. Singleton 677
Moore L.
Mongers L.
L. Austin
Mount
Sandstone
Yalgoo
Wyemandoo 543
Paynes Find
Beacon
Bonnie Rock
Mukinbudin

Meekatharra
Wandarrie
Meka
Field
Yowereerappe
Wondinong
Wiluna
Youanmi
Sandstone

Mileura
Austin Downs
Belele
Byro
Murchison
Beringarra
Twin Peaks
Murgoo
Pindar
Mullewa
Morawa

Geraldton
Northampton
Greenough
Dongara
Mingenew
Three Springs
Carnamah
Coorow
Moora
Watheroo
Dandaragan
Gingin

Houtman Abrolhos
North Hd.
Lancelin I.
Leeman

PERTH
Fremantle
Kwinana
Rockingham
Rottnest I.
Mandurah
Pinjarra
Harvey
Bunbury
Busselton
C. Naturaliste
C. Leeuwin
Margaret River
Pt. D'Entrecasteaux
Augusta
Nannup
Bridgetown
Manjimup
Pemberton
Northcliffe
Donnybrook
Collie
Boyup Brook
Kojonup

New Norcia
Toodyay
Northam
York
Beverley
Brookton
Pingelly
Narrogin
Wagin
Katanning
Broomehill
Kojonup
Cranbrook
Mt. Barker
Albany
King George Sd.
Bald I.
West C. Howe
Wilson Inlet
Denmark
Nornalup
Walpole

Southern Cross
Merredin
Kellerberrin
Quairading
Corrigin
Kondinin
Kulin
Lake Grace
Newdegate
Ravensthorpe
Hopetoun
Hood Pt.
Jerramungup
Gnowangerup
Ongerup
Borden
Needilup

Wodgina Hill
Mt. Holland
Hyden
Lake King
Newdegate
L. Magenta
Pallinup
Stirling Ra. 1073
Bluff Knoll
Chester Pass
Cheyne B.
C. Riche
C. Knob
C. Arid

Lake Brown
Trayning
Wyalkatchem
Dowerin
Goomalling
Cunderdin
Tammin
Kellerberrin
Bruce Rock
Narembeen
Bencubbin
Mukinbudin

Projection: Bonne

East from Greenwich

COPYRIGHT GEORGE PHILIP & SON LTD.

115   120   125   130

30   35

ft   m
3000   1000
1200   400
600   200
0   0
200   600
2000   6000
4000   12000
m   ft

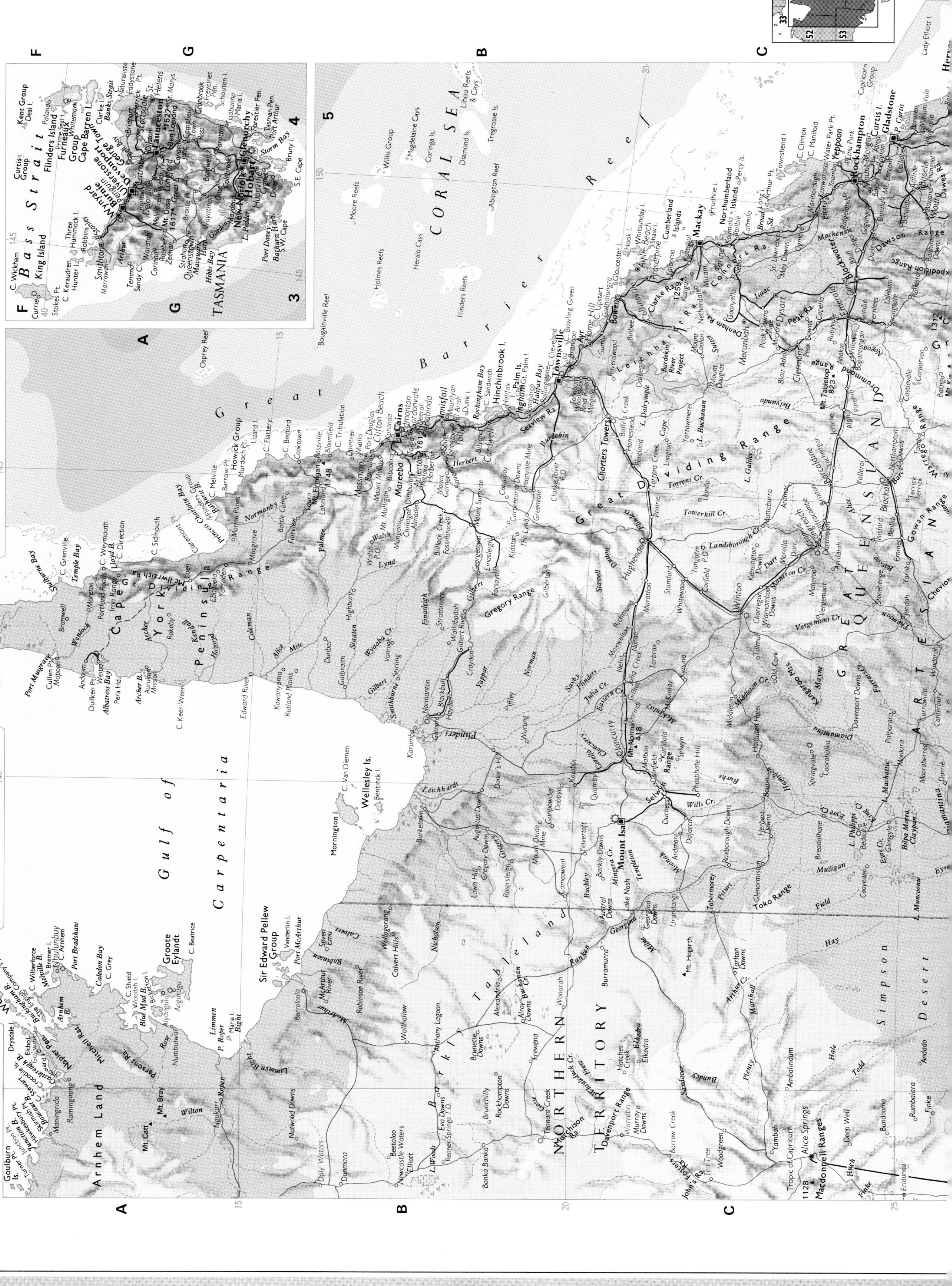

TASMANIA
Bass Strait
King Island
Flinders Island
Furneaux Group
Cape Barren I.
Launceston
Hobart
Devonport
Burnie
Storm Bay
Banks Strait
Kent Group
CORAL SEA
Great Barrier Reef
Gulf of Carpentaria
Cape York Peninsula
Great Dividing Range
QUEENSLAND
NORTHERN TERRITORY
GREAT ARTESIAN BASIN
Arnhem Land
Barkly Tableland
Simpson Desert
Groote Eylandt
Wellesley Is.
Mornington I.
Sir Edward Pellew Group
Wessel Is.
Cairns
Townsville
Mackay
Rockhampton
Gladstone
Mount Isa
Cloncurry
Charters Towers
Mareeba
Bowen
Hughenden
Winton
Longreach
Alice Springs
Macdonnell Ranges
Tennant Creek
Tropic of Capricorn
Thursday I.
Torres Strait
Cape York
Weipa
Cooktown
Normanton
Karumba
Burketown
Borroloola
Ngukurr
Emerald
Clermont
Yeppoon
Whitsunday I.
Hinchinbrook I.
Palm Is.
Ingham
Innisfail
Dawson Range
Gregory Range
Selwyn Range
Toko Range
Davenport Range
Mitchell
Gilbert
Flinders
Leichhardt
Burdekin
Diamantina
Georgina
Thomson
Barcoo
Roper
Willis Group
Magdelaine Cays
Coringa Is.
Lihou Reefs & Cays
Tregrosse Is.
Diamond Is.
Osprey Reef
Bougainville Reef
Flinders Reefs
Holmes Reefs
Moore Reefs
Herald Cays
Abington Reef
Howick Group
Lizard I.
C. Melville
C. Flattery
Princess Charlotte Bay
Temple Bay
Albatross Bay
Archer B.
Limmen Bight
Port McArthur
Caledon Bay
Blue Mud B.
Melville B.

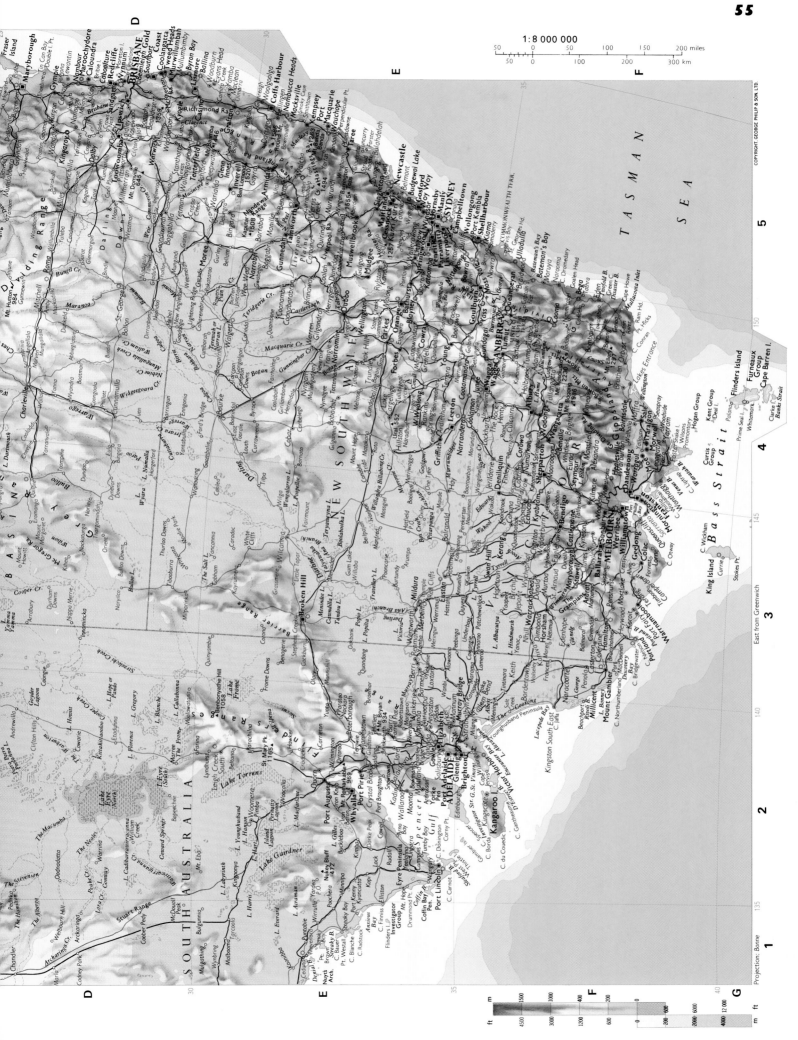

1:8 000 000

Projection: Bonne

East from Greenwich

TASMAN SEA

NEW SOUTH WALES

SOUTH AUSTRALIA

VICTORIA

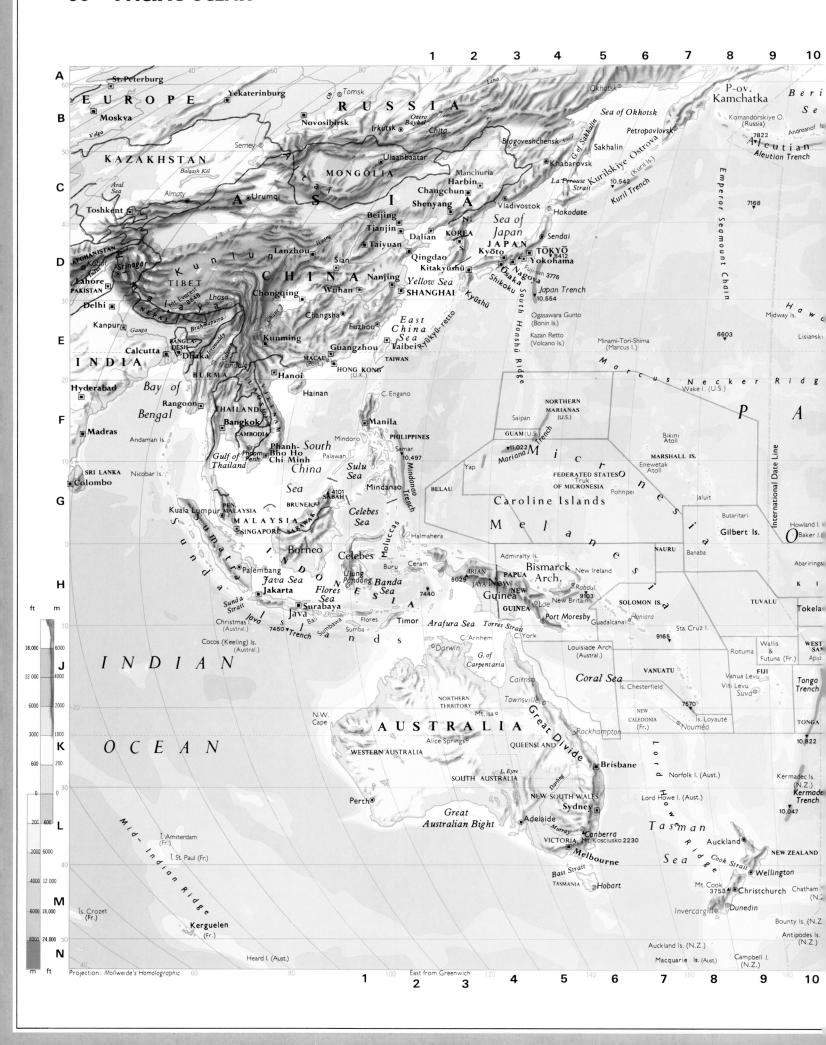

1 2 3 4 5 6 7 8 9 10

A

St.Peterburg
EUROPE   Yekaterinburg   RUSSIA   Okhotsk   P-ov.   Beri
B   Moskva   Tomsk   Kamchatka   Se
                    Novosibirsk   Ozero   Sea of Okhotsk
                              Irkutsk   Baykal   Chita   Komandorskiye O.
                    Semey   Blagoveshchensk   Petropavlovsk   (Russia)
KAZAKHSTAN   7822   Andreanof Is.
C   Balqash Köl   Ulaanbaatar   Manchuria   Sakhalin   A   Aleutian
     Aral   MONGOLIA   Harbin   La Perouse   Kurilskiye Ostrova   Aleutian Trench
     Sea   Almaty   Urumqi   A   S   Changchun   Strait   10,542   Kuril Trench
     Toshkent   I   A   Shenyang   Vladivostok   Hakodate   7168
D   Beijing   KOREA   Hakodate   Emperor Seamount Chain
AFGHANISTAN   Srinagar   Kunlun   Tianjin   Dalian   JAPAN   Sendai
     Kabul   Lanzhou   Taiyuan   Kyōto   TOKYO   8412
     Lahore   TIBET   Sian   Qingdao   Kitakyūshū   Nagoya   Yokohama   Japan Trench
PAKISTAN   Mt.Everest 8848   Lhasa   CHINA   Nanjing   Yellow Sea   Ōsaka   Fujisan 3776   10,554
     Delhi   NEPAL   Chongqing   Wuhan   SHANGHAI   Kyūshū   Shikoku   South   Ogasawara Gunto   Midway Is.   Hawa
E   Kanpur   Ganga   Brahmaputra   Changsha   East   Ryūkyū-retto   Honshū   (Bonin Is.)   6603   Lisianski
     Calcutta   BANGLA-   Mandalay   Kunming   Fuzhou   China   Taibei   Kazan Retto   Minami-Tori-Shima
     INDIA   DESH   Dhaka   Guangzhou   Sea   TAIWAN   (Volcano Is.)   (Marcus I.)
     Hyderabad   BURMA   Irrawaddy   MACAU   HONG KONG   Marcus   Necker   Ridge
                    Bay of   Hanoi   (Port.)   (U.K.)   Wake I. (U.S.)
F   Rangoon   THAILAND   Hainan   C. Engano   NORTHERN   P   A
     Madras   Bengal   Bangkok   MARIANAS
                    CAMBODIA   Manila   PHILIPPINES   Saipan   (U.S.)   Bikini
     Andaman Is.   Phanh-   South   Mindoro   Samar   GUAM (U.S.)   Atoll
                    Bho Ho   China   Palawan   10,497   11,022   MARSHALL IS.
     SRI LANKA   Phnom   Chi Minh   Sea   Mindanao   Yap   Mariana   Enewetak
     Colombo   Nicobar Is.   Penh   Gulf of   Sulu   Trench   Micro   Atoll
                    Thailand   Sea   FEDERATED STATES   Truk
G   4101   Mindanao Trench   BELAU   OF MICRONESIA   Pohnpei   Jaluit
     Kuala Lumpur   PEN.   SABAH   Celebes   Caroline Islands   n   Butaritari
     MALAYSIA   BRUNEI   Sea   Gilbert Is.
     SINGAPORE   SARAWAK   Moluccas   Halmahera   Mela   e   Howland I.
                    Borneo   Buru   Ceram   Baker I.
H   Palembang   I   Celebes   Admiralty Is.   Bismarck   New Ireland   NAURU   Abariring
     Sunda   Java Sea   Ujung   IRIAN   PAPUA   Arch.   Rabaul   Banaba   i
     Strait   Jakarta   N   Pandang   Banda   JAYA   New   NEW   New Britain   SOLOMON IS.   TUVALU   KI
                    D   Flores   Sea   5029   Guinea   GUINEA   9103   Lae   a
     Surabaya   O   Sea   7440   Port Moresby   Guadalcanal   Honiara
     Christmas I.   E   Java   Bali   Flores   Timor   Sta. Cruz I.   Tokelau
     (Austral.)   7450   Trench   Sumbawa   Sumba   Arafura Sea   Torres Strait   9165   Rotuma   Wallis   WEST
J   Cocos (Keeling) Is.   S   i   s   C. Arnhem   C. York   &   SAM
     (Austral.)   Darwin   G. of   Louisiade Arch.   VANUATU   Futuna (Fr.)   Apia
     INDIAN   Carpentaria   (Austral.)   Cairns   Coral Sea   Vanua Levu   FIJI   Tonga
                         NORTHERN   Is. Chesterfield   Viti Levu   Suva   Trench
K   OCEAN   N.W.   TERRITORY   Mt. Isa   Townsville   NEW   7670   TONGA   10,822
     Cape   AUSTRALIA   Great   CALEDONIA   Is. Loyauté
                    Alice Springs   QUEENSLAND   Divide   (Fr.)   Nouméa   Kermadec Is.
     WESTERN AUSTRALIA   Rockhampton   Norfolk I. (Aust.)   (N.Z.)
                              L. Eyre   SOUTH AUSTRALIA   Brisbane   L   Lord Howe I. (Aust.)   Kermadec
L   NEW SOUTH WALES   o   Tasman   Trench
     Perth   Great   Darling   Sydney   r   d   10,047
              Australian Bight   Adelaide   VICTORIA   Murray   Canberra   H   Auckland   Cook Strait   NEW ZEALAND
                         Mt. Kosciusko 2230   o   Ridge
M   Melbourne   w   Bass Strait   e   Mt. Cook   Wellington
                         TASMANIA   Hobart   Sea   3753   Christchurch   Chatham
                                                       Invercargill   Dunedin   (N.Z
                                             Bounty Is. (N.Z.
N   Auckland Is. (N.Z.)   Antipodes Is.
     Heard I. (Aust.)   East from Greenwich   Macquarie Is. (Aust.)   Campbell I.   (N.Z.)
Projection: Mollweide's Homolographic   60   1   100   2   3   (N.Z.)

ft   m
18,000   6000
12 000   4000
6000   2000
3000   1000
600   200
0   0
600   200
2000   600
6000   2000
12 000   4000
18,000   6000
24,000   8000
m   ft

Î. Amsterdam (Fr.)
Î. St. Paul (Fr.)
Mid-Indian Ridge
Îs. Crozet (Fr.)
Kerguelen (Fr.)

1   2   3   4   5   6   7   8   9   10

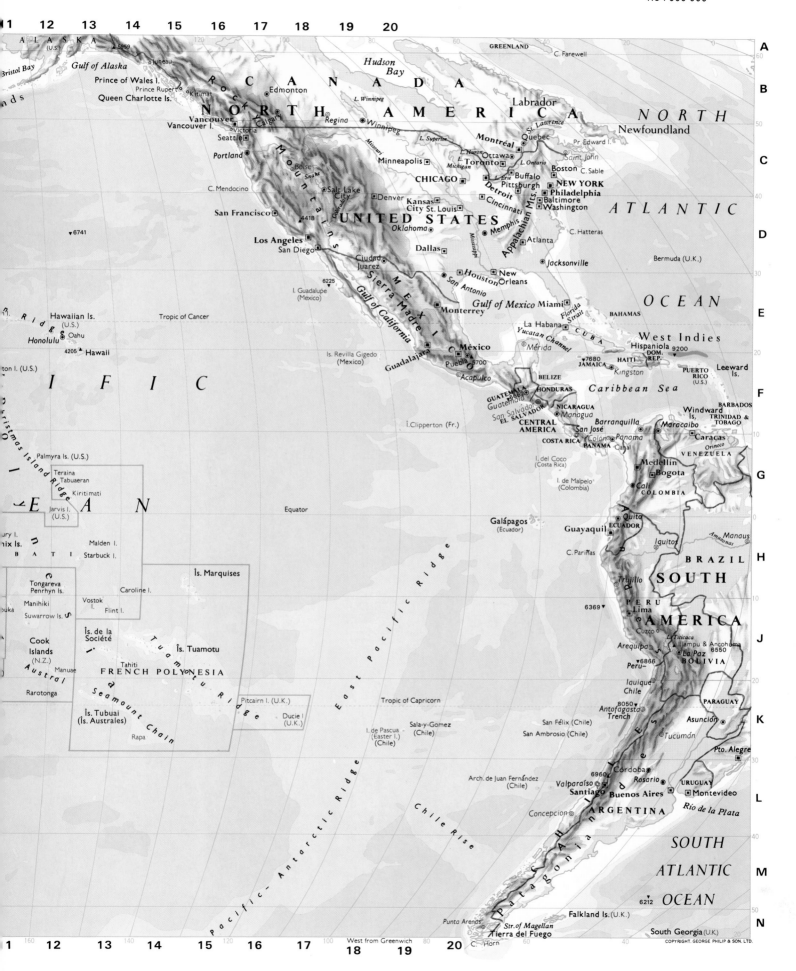

1:54 000 000

11 12 13 14 15 16 17 18 19 20

ALASKA
(U.S.)

Bristol Bay

Gulf of Alaska

Prince of Wales I.

Queen Charlotte Is.

°Juneau

5959

Prince Rupert° °Kitimat

Edmonton

C A N A D A

Hudson
Bay

GREENLAND
C. Farewell

NORTH

ROCKY

NORTH   AMERICA

Labrador

Newfoundland

Vancouver
Vancouver I.

°Victoria
Seattle°

Calgary

L. Winnipeg

Regina

Winnipeg

Montréal

Quebec

St. Lawrence

Pr. Edward I.

Saint John

Portland°

Boise°

Mountains

Minneapolis

L. Superior

L. Huron

L. Michigan

Ottawa°

Toronto°

L. Ontario

L. Erie

Buffalo°

Boston

C. Sable

A T L A N T I C

C. Mendocino

Snake

San Francisco°

Salt Lake
City°

4418

Denver°

CHICAGO

Kansas
City St. Louis°

Detroit°

Pittsburgh°

Cincinnati°

NEW YORK

Philadelphia

Baltimore°

Washington

6741

Los Angeles
San Diego°

U N I T E D   S T A T E S

Oklahoma°

Dallas°

Memphis°

Appalachian Mts.

Atlanta°

C. Hatteras

Jacksonville°

Bermuda (U.K.)

OCEAN

Ciudad
Juárez

SIERRA MADRE

M
E
X
I
C
O

8225

I. Guadalupe
(Mexico)

Gulf of California

San Antonio°

Houston°

New
Orleans°

Gulf of Mexico

Monterrey°

Miami°

BAHAMAS

Florida
Strait

Tropic of Cancer

Hawaiian Is.
(U.S.)

Honolulu° °Oahu

4205 °Hawaii

Ridge

I F I C

Is. Revilla Gigedo
(Mexico)

Guadalajara

México°

Puebla°

Acapulco°

5700

7680

La Habana°

Mérida°

Yucatan Channel

CUBA

Kingston°

HAITI

JAMAICA

Caribbean Sea

West Indies

Hispaniola 9200

DOM.
REP.

PUERTO
RICO
(U.S.)

Leeward
Is.

n I. (U.S.)

ton I. (U.S.)

Palmyra Is. (U.S.)

Teraina
Tabuaeran

Kiritimati

Î.Clipperton (Fr.)

GUATEMALA
Guatemala°

San Salvador°

EL SALVADOR

BELIZE

HONDURAS

NICARAGUA

°Managua

CENTRAL
AMERICA

San José°

COSTA RICA

Colón°

Panama°

PANAMA

Barranquilla°

Panama Canal

Maracaibo°

WINDWARD
Is.

TRINIDAD &
TOBAGO

BARBADOS

Caracas°

VENEZUELA

Orinoco

E   A   N

Jarvis I.
(U.S.)

Equator

B A T I

Malden I.

Starbuck I.

Galápagos
(Ecuador)

I. del Coco
(Costa Rica)

I. de Malpelo
(Colombia)

Medellín°

Cali°

Bogotá°

COLOMBIA

G

Quito°

ECUADOR

Guayaquil°

Manaus°

Iquitos°

Amazonas

BRAZIL

SOUTH

ix Is.

Manihiki

Suwarrow Is.

Tongareva
Penrhyn Is.

Vostok
I.

Caroline I.

Flint I.

Î. Marquises

C. Pariñas

6369

PERU

Lima°

Trujillo°

AMERICA

Cook
Islands
(N.Z.)

Manuae

Î. de la
Société

Tahiti

Î. Tuamotu

FRENCH POLYNESIA

Tuamotu Ridge

Cuzco°

Arequipa°

L. Titicaca

Illampu & Ancohoma
6550

La Paz°

BOLIVIA

6886

Peru

Rarotonga

Austral

Seamount Chain

Î. Tubuai
(Îs. Australes)

Rapa

Pitcairn I. (U.K.)

Ducie I.
(U.K.)

I. de Pascua
(Easter I.)
(Chile)

Iquique°

Chile

Antofagasta
Trench

8050

PARAGUAY

Tropic of Capricorn

Sala-y-Gomez
(Chile)

San Félix (Chile)

San Ambrosio (Chile)

Asunción°

Tucumán°

Pto. Alegre

East Pacific Ridge

Chile Rise

Arch. de Juan Fernández
(Chile)

Córdoba°

Rosario°

URUGUAY

6960

Valparaíso°

Santiago°

Buenos Aires°

Montevideo°

Concepción°

ARGENTINA

Río de la Plata

SOUTH

Pacific–Antarctic Ridge

Patagonia

ATLANTIC

6212

OCEAN

Punta Arenas°

Str. of Magellan

Tierra del Fuego

C. Horn

Falkland Is. (U.K.)

South Georgia (U.K.)

West from Greenwich

11 12 13 14 15 16 17 18 19 20

A B C D E F G H J K L M N

COPYRIGHT. GEORGE PHILIP & SON. LTD.

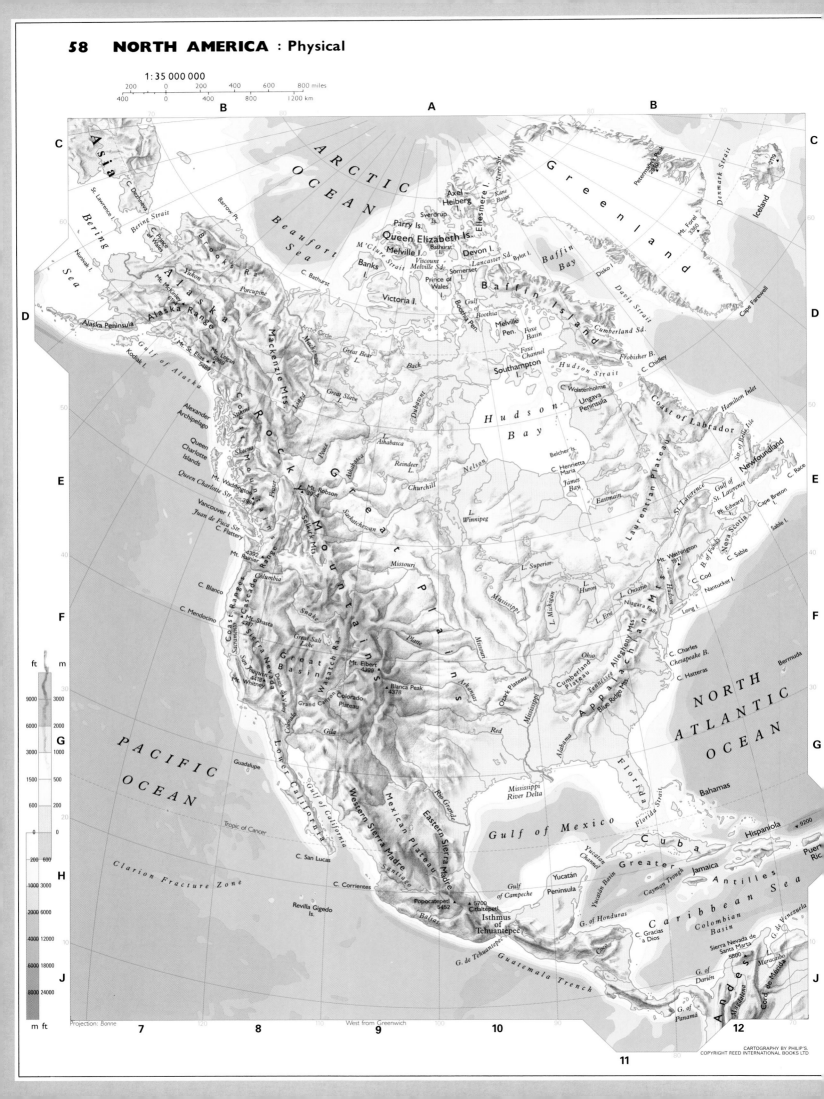

1 : 35 000 000

200   0   200   400   600   800 miles
400   0   400   800   1200 km

Projection: Bonne

West from Greenwich

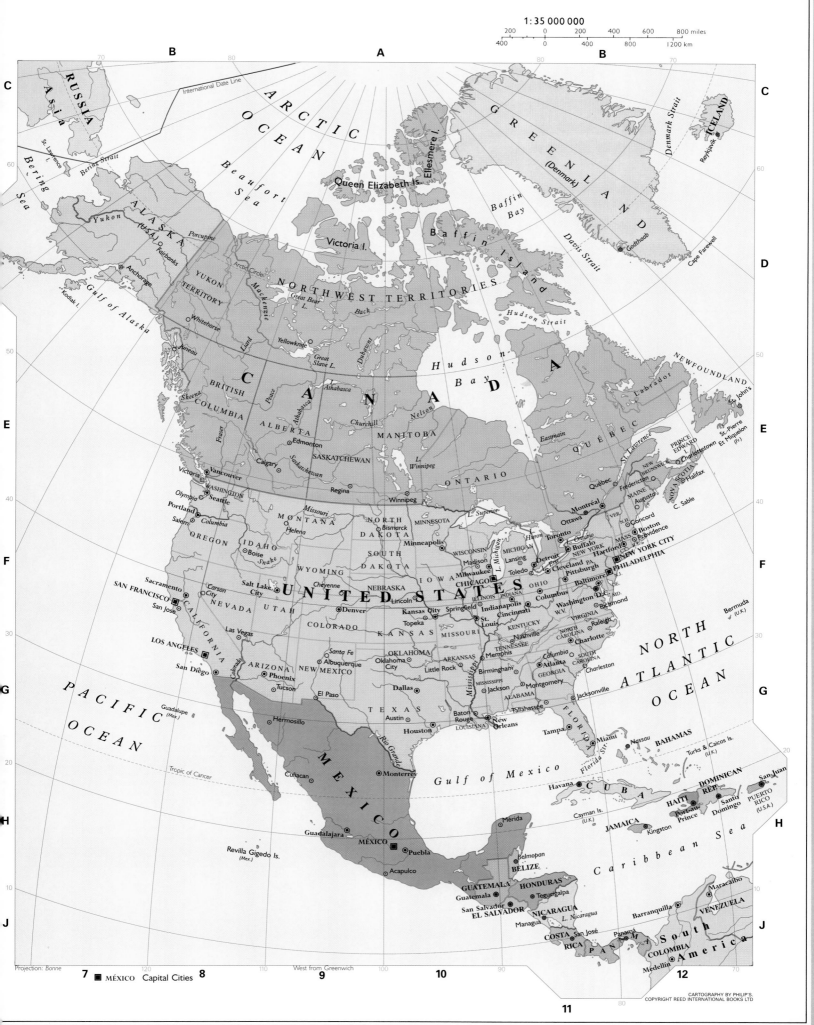

1 : 35 000 000

	200	0	200	400	600	800 miles
400		0	400	800		1200 km

B **A** **B**

C RUSSIA **C**
Asia
International Date Line

St. Lawrence
Bering Strait

ARCTIC OCEAN

GREENLAND
(Denmark)

Denmark Strait
ICELAND
Reykjavík

Bering Sea
Beaufort Sea
Queen Elizabeth Is.
Ellesmere I.

Baffin Bay
Davis Strait
Godthaab

ALASKA (USA)
Yukon
Porcupine
Victoria I.
Baffin Island
Cape Farewell

D Gulf of Alaska
Kodiak I.
Fairbanks
Anchorage
Arctic Circle
YUKON TERRITORY
Mackenzie
Great Bear L.
NORTHWEST TERRITORIES
Hudson Strait
Labrador
NEWFOUNDLAND **D**

Whitehorse
Juneau
Great Slave L.
Yellowknife
Liard
Dubawnt
Back

Hudson Bay

St. John's

E BRITISH COLUMBIA
Skeena
Athabasca
Peace
Churchill
Nelson
Eastmain
QUÉBEC
St. Lawrence
PRINCE EDWARD I.
St-Pierre Et. Miquelon (Fr.) **E**
CANADA
Fraser
ALBERTA
Athabasca
Edmonton
SASKATCHEWAN
MANITOBA
ONTARIO
NEW BRUNSWICK
Charlottetown
NOVA SCOTIA
Calgary
Victoria Vancouver
Saskatchewan
L. Winnipeg
Québec
Fredericton
Halifax
MAINE
C. Sable

Olympia
WASHINGTON
Seattle
Regina
Winnipeg
Montréal
Augusta

F Portland
Salem
Columbia
MONTANA
Missouri
NORTH DAKOTA
Bismarck
MINNESOTA
L. Superior
Ottawa
VER.
N.H.
Concord **F**
Helena
MICHIGAN
L. Huron
Toronto
L. Ontario
Buffalo
MASS. Boston
Providence
OREGON
IDAHO
Boise
Snake
WYOMING
SOUTH DAKOTA
WISCONSIN
Madison
Milwaukee
Lansing
Detroit
Cleveland
NEW YORK
Hartford
NEW YORK CITY
Sacramento
Carson City
Cheyenne
NEBRASKA
IOWA
L. Michigan
CHICAGO
Toledo
OHIO
PA
Pittsburgh
PHILADELPHIA
SAN FRANCISCO
San Jose
Salt Lake City
Lincoln
ILLINOIS
INDIANA
Columbus
Baltimore
DE.
Washington D.C.
MD.
UNITED STATES
Denver
Kansas City
Springfield
Indianapolis
Cincinnati
W.V.
Richmond
San Jose
NEVADA
UTAH
Topeka
St. Louis
KENTUCKY
VIRGINIA

G LOS ANGELES
CALIFORNIA
Las Vegas
COLORADO
KANSAS
MISSOURI
TENNESSEE
Nashville
NORTH CAROLINA
Raleigh
Charlotte
NORTH ATLANTIC OCEAN **G**
San Diego
Santa Fe
ARIZONA
NEW MEXICO
OKLAHOMA
Oklahoma City
ARKANSAS
Little Rock
Memphis
Birmingham
Mississippi
Columbia
SOUTH CAROLINA
Charleston
Bermuda (U.K.)
Colorado
Phoenix
Tucson
El Paso
Dallas
ATLANTA
GEORGIA
Jackson
Montgomery
ALABAMA
PACIFIC OCEAN
Guadalupe (Mex.)
Hermosillo
TEXAS
Austin
Baton Rouge
LOUISIANA
New Orleans
Tallahassee
Jacksonville

Rio Grande
Houston
Gulf of Mexico
FLORIDA
Tampa
Miami
Florida Str.
Nassau
BAHAMAS
Turks & Caicos Is. (U.K.)

Tropic of Cancer
Culiacan
MEXICO
Monterrey
Havana
CUBA
DOMINICAN REP.
San Juan
PUERTO RICO (U.S.A.)

H Revilla Gigedo Is. (Mex.)
Guadalajara
MÉXICO
Puebla
Mérida
Cayman Is. (U.K.)
HAITI
Port-au-Prince
Santo Domingo **H**
Acapulco
JAMAICA
Kingston
Caribbean Sea
Belmopan
BELIZE
Maracaibo

J GUATEMALA
Guatemala
HONDURAS
Tegucigalpa
VENEZUELA **J**
San Salvador
EL SALVADOR
NICARAGUA
Managua
L. Nicaragua
Barranquilla
COSTA RICA
San José
Panamá
PANAMA
South America
COLOMBIA
Medellín

Projection: Bonne

120
110
West from Greenwich
100
9 10

11

CARTOGRAPHY BY PHILIP'S.
COPYRIGHT REED INTERNATIONAL BOOKS LTD

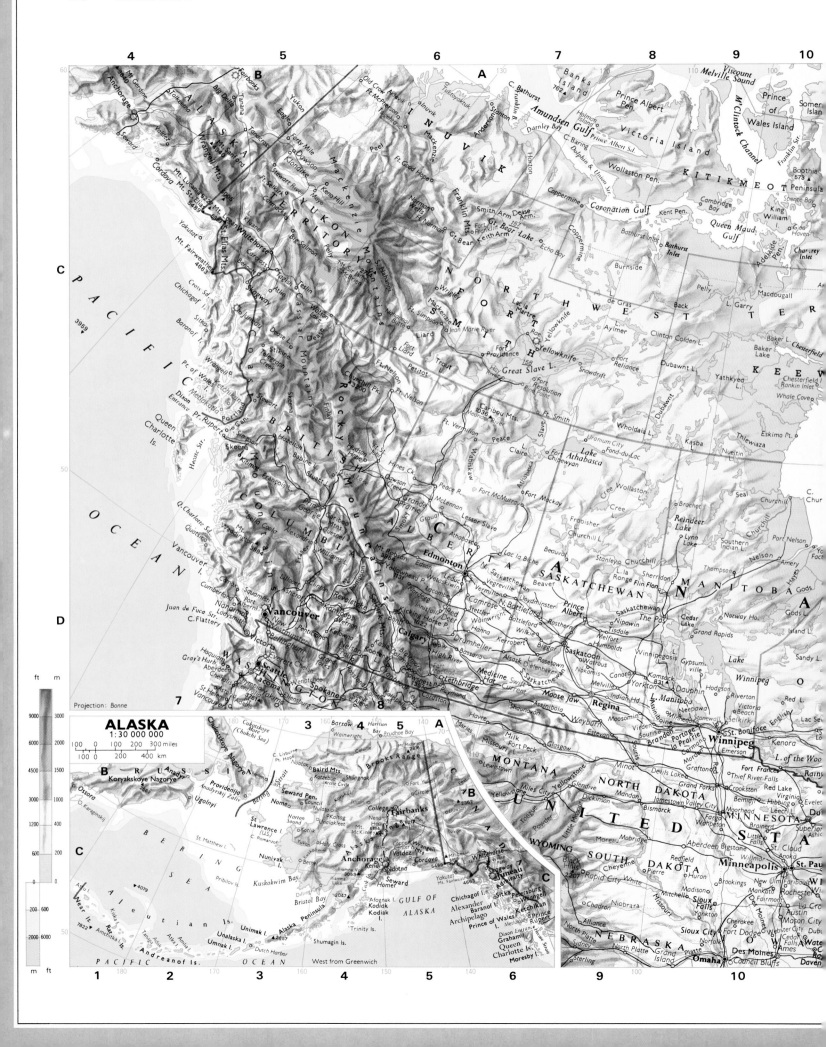

Projection: Bonne

ALASKA
1:30 000 000

| 100 | 0 | 100 | 200 | 300 miles |
| 100 | 0 | 200 | 400 km |

West from Greenwich

1:15 000 000

100 0 100 200 300 400 miles
100 0 100 200 300 400 500 600 km

B

Devon Island
Lancaster Sound

Baffin Bay

GREENLAND

• Angmagssalik

Arctic Bay   1890
Bylot I.

Pond Inlet
Brodeur   Milne   Scott I.
Peninsula   Inlet   Pond Inlet   Disko   2850

2136

Svartenhuk
Halvø

Christianshåb
Disko
B.

Clyde   Sandre Strømfjord

C. Hewett

Home B.   Holsteinsborg
Fury & Hecla Str.   • Sukkertoppen   Kong Frederik VI's Kyst

Igloolik   Hall
Island   Lake   2591   Godthåb
Melville   Cumberland   Broughton
Peninsula   Peninsula   Island   Fiskenæsset
Prince   Pangnirtung   Pagloping Island
Charles   C. Dyer   Frederikshåb
I.   Cape
Basin   Dyer   Ivigtut
Foxe   Hoare B.   Juliane håb   Sydbraven
Nettilling   C. Mercy
Rae Isthmus   Repulse   Nonortalik
Bay   Cumberland Sd.   Kap Farvel

Foxe   Amadjuak
Channel   L.   Igaluit
C. Dorchester   Amadjuak
Penin.   Lake
Coral Harbour   Harbour   3809
Southampton   Cape Dorset
I.   Frobisher Bay

Digges Is.   Resolution I.
Coats   Salluit
I.   Hudson   Strait
Mansel
I.   Ivujivik   Quaqtaq
(Notre Dame   C. Chidley
Hudson   de Koartac)   Akpatok
Kangiqsujuaq   I.

Bay   Arnaud
Ottawa   Kangirsuk   Kangiqsualujjuaq   1676
Isls.   Ungava Bay   Hebron
257   Ungava   Nutak

Sleeper Is.   Portland   Inukjuak   Feuilles   Nain
King   Promontory   Koksoak   George
George Is.   L. Minto   Kaniapiskau
King George Is.   Melezes   Whale   Hopedale
Baker's
Dozen   Is.   C. Harrison
Belcher   Indian Harbour
Is.   L. à l'Eau Claire   Lac Bienville   Bigolet

Big   C. Henrietta   Kuujjuarapik   Grand Baleine   COAST OF LABRADOR   Cartwright
Trout L.   Maria   Schefferville   North West   L. Melville
Ft. Severn   Pte.   A   Petitsikapau   River   Belle Isle
Louis-XIV   L.   Churchill   Goose
Falls   Bay   Str. of Belle Isle
Chisasibi   Kanaaupscow   Ashuanipi
Winisk   Kaniapiskau   L.   Natashquan   Notre Dame B.
James Bay   Chibougamau   St-Augustin-   Twillingate
Akimiski   Kuujjuarapik   Saguenay   Lewisporte
Attawapiskat   I.   Wemindji   Romaine   Bonavista
Eastmain   4128   Natashquan   Grand   Gander   Trinity B.
Eastmain   Gognon   Moisie   Corner   Falls   Carbonear
Ft. Albany   Charlton   QUEBEC   Mingan   Brook   St. John's
I.   Moisie   814   Buchans
Albany   Waskaganish   I. d'Anticosti   Harbour Grace   Placentia
Rupert   L.   NEWFOUNDLAND   B.
St. Joseph   L. Albanel   Sept Iles   Port-Cartier   Placentia   Trepassey
Moosonee   Mistassini   Port-Cartier   Pt. aux Basques   C. Race
Missinaibi   Manicouagan   Gulf of
Nakina   Matagami   Harricana   L.   Baie-Comeau   C. de Gaspé   St. Lawrence   Raye
Kenogami   Nottaway   Betsiamites   Is. de la Madeleine   Cabot Str.
Longlac   L. Abitibi   Rés. de Gouin   R. St. Lawrence   Matane   Pen. de Gaspé   Cabot
strong   Cochrane   Chibougamau   Dolbeau   St-Jean   Campbellton   Str.   C. North
L.   Timmins   Roberval   Rimouski   Cape Breton I.   Glace Bay
gon   Heron Bay   Norranda-   Senneterre   Saguenay   Bathurst   Chatham   ST-PIERRE
Nipigon   Oba   Rouyn   Chicoutimi   Rivière-   Newcastle   et MIQUELON   Sydney
Franz   Kirkland Lake   Val d'Or   1199   du-Loup   NEW   Northumberland   (Fr.)   Port Hawkesbury
Thunder Bay   La Tuque   Edmundston   BRUNSWICK   Str.   New Glasgow
Michipicoten   Haileybury   Shawinigan   St. Léonard   Moncton   Pictou   Mulgrave
Heron Bay   Cobalt   Trois-Rivières   Thetford Mines   Woodstock   Amherst   NOVA   Truro   Sable I.
Témiscamingue   Joliette   Québec   Springhill   Windsor   (Nova Scotia)
Copper Cliff   Rés. de   Lévis   Fredericton   Kentville   Dartmouth
Lake Superior   Cabonga   Sorel   Sherbrooke   Saint   SCOTIA   Halifax
Sault Ste. Marie   Sudbury   MONTRÉAL   St. Hyacinthe   John   Bridgewater
Calumet   North   Lachine   MAINE   B. of Fundy   Digby   Liverpool
Laurium   Bay   Granby   L. Champlain   Bangor   Yarmouth   Shelburne
Keweenaw   Sault Ste. Marie   Pembroke   1917   Augusta   C. Sable
Copper Cliff   North Chan.   Hull   Lewiston   6309
Port   Ottawa   Cornwall   Portland
Ironwood   Sound   Amprior   Belleville   Kingston   Burlington   Lewiston   PENNSYLVANIA
Cheboygan   Georgian   North   Watertown   Portland
elander   Manistique   Bay   Bay   Glens   Concord   Manchester
Menominee   Lake   Peterboro   VERMONT   Falls   NEW   Lowell
Iron Mt.   Huron   Orillia   Ontario   Utica   HAMPSHIRE   Manchester
Antigo   Traverse   Oshawa   Syracuse   C. Cod
WISCONSIN   City   Owen Sound   Rochester   Albany   Worcester   Boston
Wausau   Green   Cadillac   TORONTO   Springfield   MASS.   Providence
Appleton   Bay   Guelph   Niagara   NEW YORK   CONN.   New Haven
Sheboygan   Muskegon   Kitchener   Falls   Binghamton   Waterbury   R.I.
Milwaukee   Saginaw   Stratford   Buffalo   Elmira   Scranton   Bridgeport
Manitowoc   Lake Michigan   London   Brantford   Hamilton   Elmira   New Haven
Racine   Muskegon   Sarnia   St. Catharines   Lake Erie   PENNSYLVANIA   NEW YORK
Kenosha   Grand   Chatham   Jamestown   Williamsport   Allentown   NEW JERSEY
ford   Rapids   Windsor   Erie   Reading   Trenton
CHICAGO   Gary   Evanston   DETROIT   Cleveland   Youngstown   Jersey City
ILLINOIS   INDIANA   South Bend   Toledo   Akron   OHIO   Newark

ATLANTIC   OCEAN

West from Greenwich   COPYRIGHT. GEORGE PHILIP & SON. LTD.

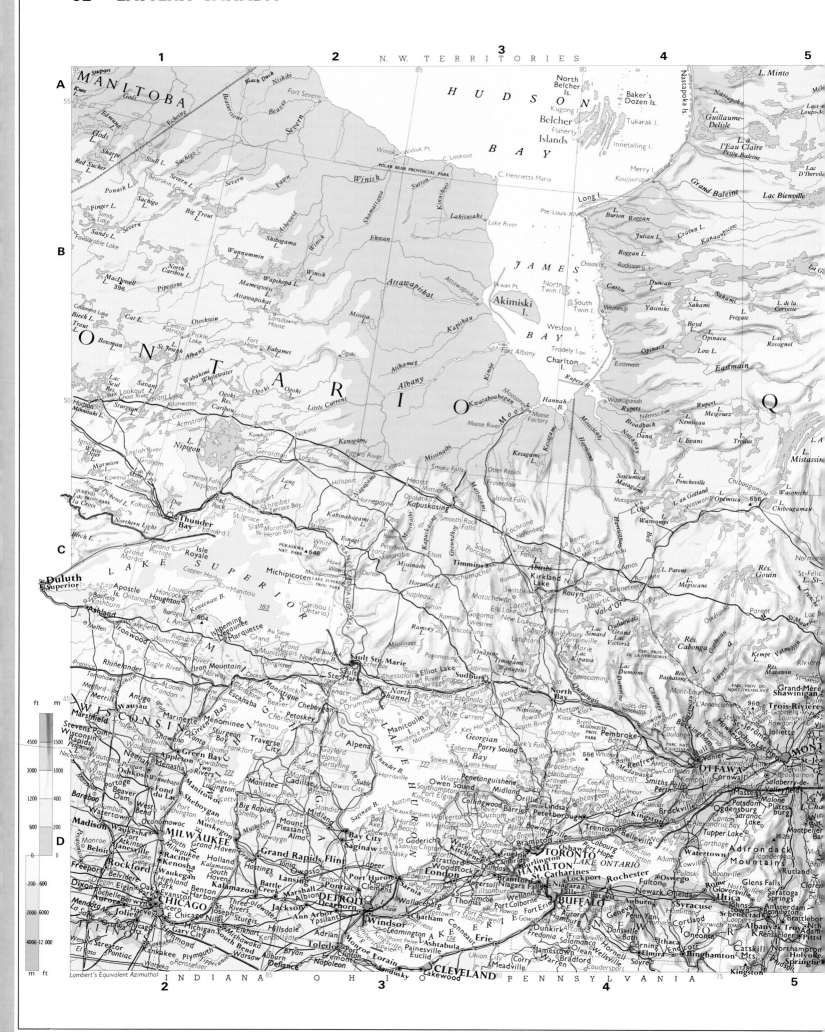

1:7 000 000

50 0 50 100 150 200 miles
50 0 50 100 150 200 250 300 km

6   7   8   9

A 55
B
C 50
D 45

NEWFOUNDLAND

COAST OF LABRADOR

QUEBEC

South Aulatsivik I.
Nain
High I.
Paul I.
Voisey's B.
Tunungayualok I.
Davis Inlet
Nunaksaluk I.
Hopedale
Kaipokok B.
Aillik
Mokkovik
Adlavik Is.
C. Harrison
Holton
Indian Harbour
Grosswater
Rigolet
Cartwright
Sandwich B.
Island of Ponds
Square Islands
Separation Point
Eagle
St. Lewis
Mary's Harbour
Battle Harbour
Red Bay
Belle I.
Str. of Belle Isle
St. Anthony
Flower's Cove
Hare B.
Groais I.
Conche
Englee
Bell I.
Horse Is.
C. St. John
White B.
Notre Dame B.
Fogo I.
Twillingate
Carmanville
C. Freels
Wesleyville
Bonavista
C. Bonavista
Catalina
Trinity
Bay de Verde
Conception B.
Carbonear
Harbour Grace
Trinity B.
St. John's
Avalon Peninsula
Ferryland
C. Race
C. Pine
St. Mary's B.
Placentia
St. Lawrence
Burin
Grand Bank
Fortune B.
Marystown
Harbour Breton
Burgeo
Ramea
Channel-Port aux Basques
C. Ray
St. Andrews B.
South Branch
St. David's
St. George's B.
Port au Port B.
Corner Brook
Bay of Islands
Trout River
GROS MORNE NAT. PARK
Deer Lake
Howley
Springdale
Baie Verte
Seal Cove
Gander
Grand Falls
Bishop's Falls
Botwood
Windsor
Badger
Buchans
Red Indian L.
Long Range Mts.
White Bear L.
Victoria Res.
Grey Res.
Meelpaeg L.
Gander L.
Glenwood
Glovertown
Dark Cove
Clarenville
Terrenceville
St. Alban's
Belleoram

LABRADOR

Smallwood Res.
Churchill Falls
North-West River
Goose
Happy Valley-Goose Bay
L. Melville
Mealy Mts.
Paradise
Alexis
Minipi
Little Mecatina
Burnt
St. Augustin
St. Paul
L. Anse-au-Loup
Forteau
Bradore Bay
Lourdes-de-Blanc-Sablon
St. Augustin-Saguenay
Harrington Harbour
I. du Petit-Mécatina
Daniel's Harbour
Port Saunders
Roddickton

Schefferville
Harp L.
Kogaluk
Big Bay
Attikamagen L.
Menihek Lakes
Woods L.
Whitegull L.
L. Tudor
Champdoré
610
Kanairiktok
Nackaupi
Seal L.
Nipishish
Grand L.
Ossokmanuan L.
Winokapau L.
Churchill

Erlandson
Whale
George
Fraser
L. de la Hutte Sauvage
Néret
Fort McKenzie
Kaniapiskau
Nachicapau
Chakonipau L.
Otelnuk L.
Wheeler
L. Bermen
Kaniapiskau Lake
Petitsikapau L.
Nitchequon
Naococane
Opiscoteo L.
Opiskotish L.
Shabogamo L.
Lac Joseph
Atikonak L.
Labrador City
Wabush
Ashuanipi L.
1128
Petit Lac Manicouagan
Monts
L. Plétipi
Péribonca
Manouane
Outardes
Betsiamites
Rés. Pipmuacan
Manicouagan
Gagnon
Rés. Manicouagan
1048
L. Manitou
Nipissis
Clarke City
Sept-Îles
Moisie
Port-Cartier
Rivière-Pentecôte
Walker
Godbout
Baie-Trinité
Forestville
Betsiamites
Baie-Comeau
Hauterive
Ste-Marguerite
St-Jean
Sheldrake
Mingan
Havre-St-Pierre
Magpie L.
Romaine
Aguanus
Natashquan
Nabisipi
Aguanish
Natashquan
Kegaska
Gethsémani
Etamamu
Musquaro
L. Musquaro
Nadispi
Olomane
Mecatina

Dét. de Jacques-Cartier
Î. d'Anticosti
Jupiter
Heath Pt.
Pte. Ouest
Port-Menier
Dét.
Cap-Chat
Ste-Anne-des-Monts
Mont-Louis
Grande-Vallée
Rivière-au-Renard
C. de Gaspé
Douglastown
Gaspé
Percé
Grande-Rivière
Chandler
Bonaventure
Paspébiac
Port-Cap
Petit-Cap
du Sud Ouest
Mont Jacques-Cartier
1268
PARC PROV. DE LA GASPÉSIE
Pén. de Gaspé
Mts. Chic-Chocs
Matane
Mont-Joli
Rimouski
Bic
Trois-Pistoles
Rivière-du-Loup
Cabano
St-Pascal
572

GULF OF ST. LAWRENCE

Î. Brion
Grande-Entrée
Îs. de la Madeleine (Quebec)
Cap-aux-Meules
Havre-Aubert
St. Paul
C. North
Cabot Strait

Miscou I.
Lamèque
Shippegan
Tracadie
Miramichi B.
North Pt.
Tignish
Alberton
Richibucto
Kouchibouguac
PRINCE EDWARD ISLAND
Summerside
Kensington
Charlottetown
Borden
Souris
East Pt.
Montague
Georgetown
Northumberland Str.
Cape Montague
Pictou
Pleasant Bay
CAPE BRETON NAT. PARK
Chéticamp
Ingonish
Inverness
Sydney Mines
New Waterford
N. Sydney
Sydney
Glace Bay
Louisbourg
Bras d'Or
Cape Breton Island
532
Port Hood
Mulgrave
Canso
Chedabucto B.
Guysborough
Sherbrooke

NEW BRUNSWICK
Campbellton
Dalhousie
Chaleur Bay
Bathurst
Redkwick
Atholville
St-Arthur
Heath Steele
Newcastle
Chatham
Neguac
Blackville
Plaster Rock
Grand Falls
St. Leonard
819
Edmundston
Van Buren
Caribou
Presque Isle
Houlton
Woodstock
Hartland
Stanley
Minto
Chipman
Grand L.
Fredericton
Oromocto
Gagetown
Sussex
Moncton
Shediac
Sackville
Amherst
Springhill
Parrsboro
Truro
Stellarton
New Glasgow
Antigonish
Havelock
Petitcodiac
Elgin
St. George
St. Martins
Saint John
Bay of Fundy
St. Stephen
Calais
Eastport
Grand Manan
St. Croix
St. Andrews

NOVA SCOTIA
Minas Basin
Windsor
Kentville
Middleton
Annapolis Royal
Digby
Bridgetown
Dartmouth
Halifax
Musquodoboit Hr.
Sheet Hr.
Upper Musquodoboit
Mahone Bay
Lunenburg
Bridgewater
Chester
Liverpool
Port Mouton
Rossignol Res.
Shelburne
Clark's Harbour
C. Sable
Yarmouth
Wedgeport
Weymouth
Freeport
St. Mary's B.
Lockeport

ATLANTIC OCEAN
Sable I. (Nova Scotia)

SAINT-PIERRE ET MIQUELON (Fr.)
Miquelon
Langlade
St. Pierre

MAINE
Mooselookmeguntic L.
Rangeley
Bingham
Skowhegan
Waterville
Augusta
Belfast
Camden
Rockland
Bar Harbor
Mt. Desert I.
Ellsworth
Bangor
Brewer
Old Town
Dover-Foxcroft
Millinocket
Mt. Katahdin
1606
Moosehead L.
Greenville
Jackman
Mattawamkeag
Lincoln
Guilford
Machias
Calais
Jonesport
Bath
Brunswick
Portland
Saco
Biddeford
Sanford
Dover
Portsmouth
Rochester
Concord
Manchester
Nashua
Haverhill
Lawrence
Lowell
Waltham
BOSTON
Brockton
Lynn
Gloucester
C. Ann

QUEBEC
Chicoutimi
Jonquière
Arvida
Alma
Saguenay
Bagotville
Port Alfred
La Malbaie
St-Siméon
Baie-St-Paul
PARC PROV. DES LAURENTIDES
Montmagny
Lévis
Lauzon
1190
St-Jean-Port-Joli
Rivière-du-Loup
Grandes-Bergeronnes
Tadoussac
Îs. d'Orléans
Beauceville
St-Georges
Thetford Mines
Plessisville
Asbestos
Sherbrooke
Coaticook
Lac-Mégantic
East Angus
Woburn
Lac-St-Jean
Péribonca

West from Greenwich

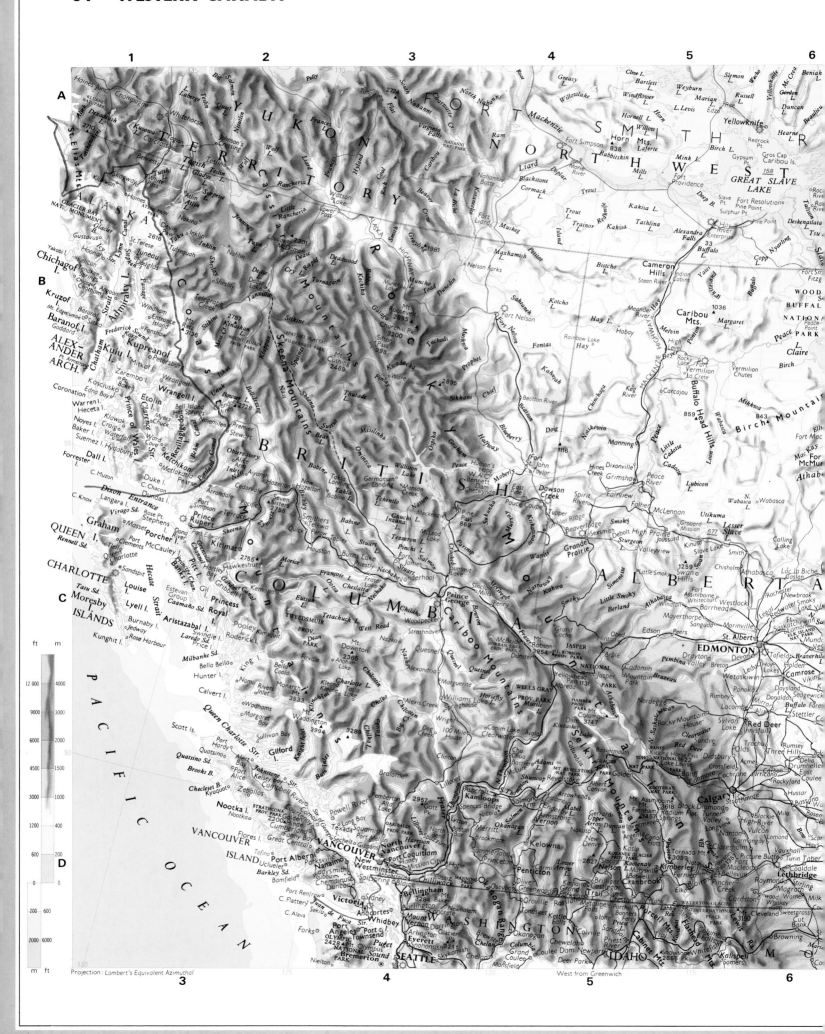

Projection: Lambert's Equivalent Azimuthal   West from Greenwich

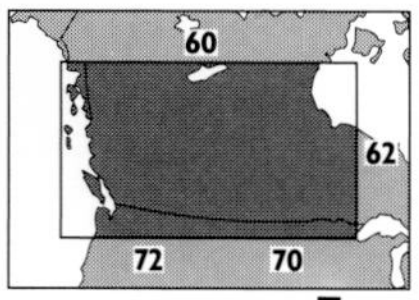

1:7 000 000

50   0   50   100   150   200 miles
50 0 50 100 150 200 250 300 km

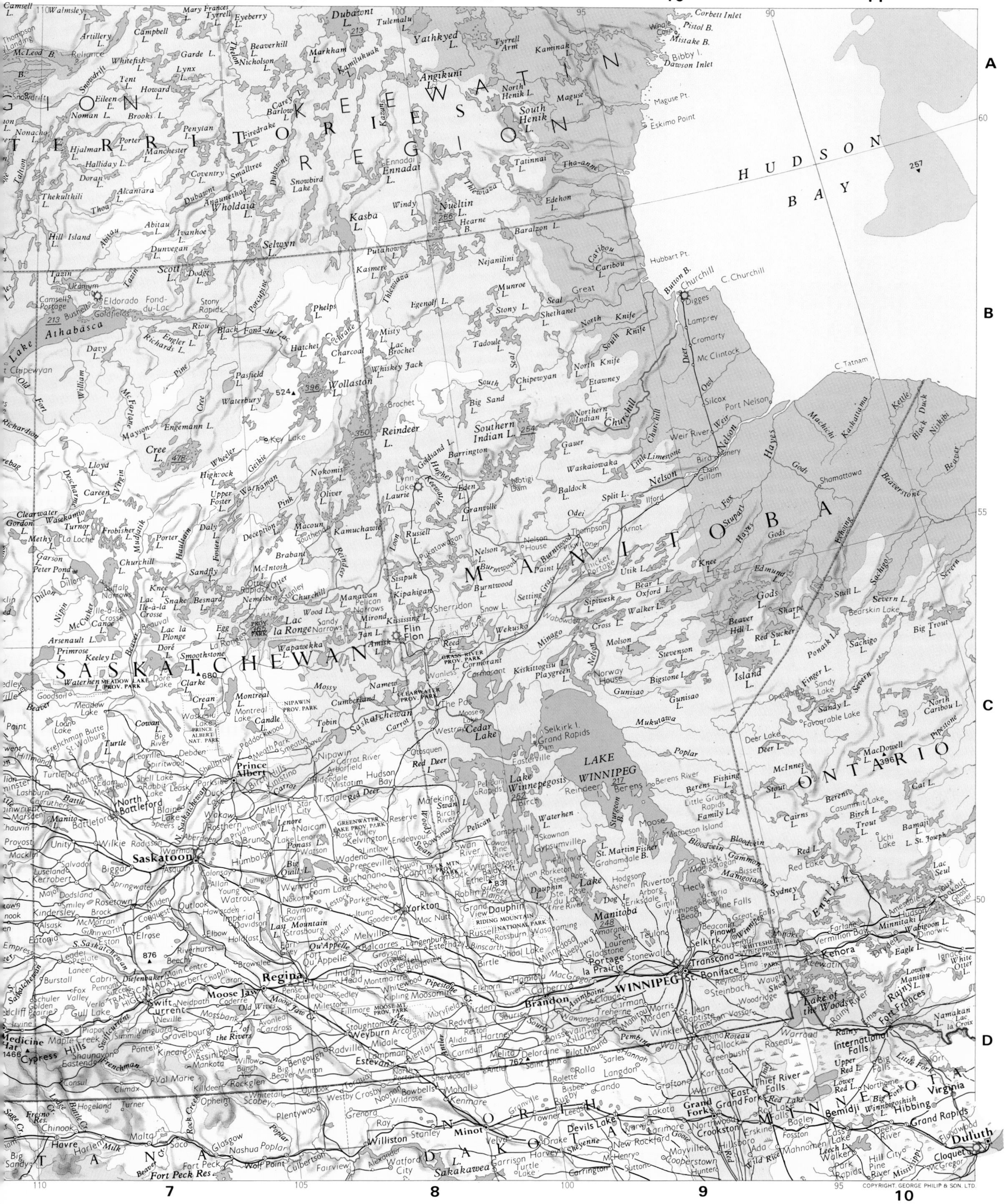

HUDSON BAY

KEEWATIN REGION

TERRITORIES

MANITOBA

SASKATCHEWAN

ONTARIO

NORTH DAKOTA

MINNESOTA

MONTANA

WINNIPEG

Regina

Saskatoon

Prince Albert

Brandon

Moose Jaw

Swift Current

Medicine Hat

Churchill

Duluth

Lake Athabasca

Reindeer L.

LAKE WINNIPEG

Lake Winnipegosis

Cedar Lake

Lac la Ronge

Flin Flon

The Pas

Grand Forks

Devils Lake

Williston

Minot

Bemidji

Hibbing

Grand Rapids

Fort Peck Res.

TRANS CANADA HIGHWAY

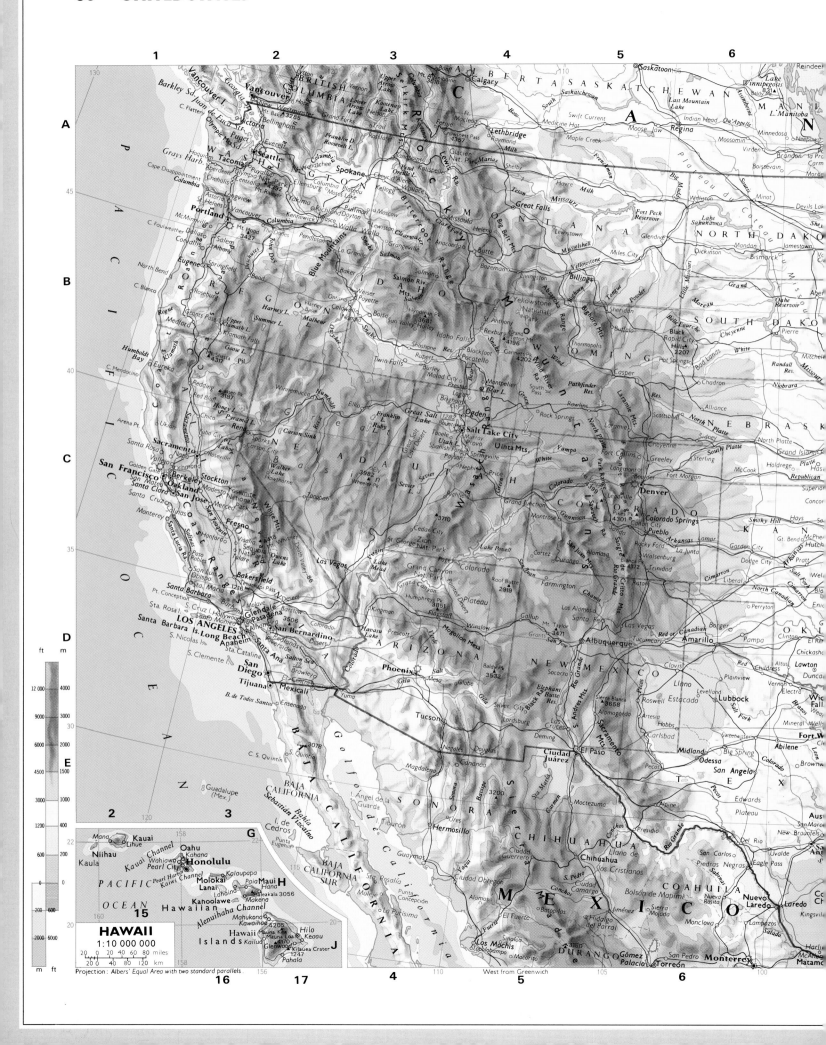

HAWAII
1:10 000 000
20 0 20 40 60 80 miles
20 0 40 80 120 km

Projection: Albers' Equal Area with two standard parallels

West from Greenwich

60 61
74 75

8 9 10 11 12 13

1:12 000 000

50 0 50 100 150 200 250 300 miles
50 0 50 100 150 200 250 300 350 400 450 km

A

B

C

D

E

F

8 9 10 11 12

CANADA

Lake Winnipeg
Trout Lake   L. St Joseph
English   L. Seul
Winnipeg   Kenora
Lake of the Woods   Rainy   Ignace   Seine
Fort Frances   Thief River Falls
Grand Forks   Red Lake   Bemidji   Hibbing   Virginia
Moorhead   Leech L.   Thunder Bay
Fergus Falls   Brainerd
Big Stone Lake   St Cloud   Anoka   Duluth   Superior   Ashland   Bessemer   Ironwood   Marquette
Willmar   Stillwater   MINNESOTA
Minneapolis   St Paul   Red Wing   Eau Claire   Green Bay   Appleton
Mankato   New Ulm   Faribault   Winona   La Crosse   WISCONSIN   Sheboygan
Fairmont   Albert Lea   Austin   Rochester   Madison   Milwaukee   Grand Rapids
Spencer   Mason City   Waterloo   Dubuque   Racine   Kenosha   Evanston
Fort Dodge   Cedar Rapids   Rockford   CHICAGO   Gary   Ft Wayne
Des Moines   Davenport   Rock Island   Aurora   Joliet   South Bend
Council Bluffs   Oskaloosa   Burlington   Peoria   Kankakee   Lima   Findlay
Omaha   Ottumwa   Galesburg   Bloomington   Champaign   Danville   Marion   Muncie   Anderson   Dayton   Columbus   Zanesville
Lincoln   Red Oak   Creston   Quincy   Springfield   Decatur   ILLINOIS   INDIANA   Indianapolis   Kettering   Chillicothe   OHIO
Beatrice   St Joseph   Hannibal   Jacksonville   Terre Haute   Cincinnati   Portsmouth
Atchison   Leavenworth   MISSOURI   St Louis   E St Louis   Vincennes   Louisville   Lexington   Huntington   Charleston
Topeka   Kansas City   Jefferson City   Evansville   KENTUCKY   Frankfort   WEST VIRGINIA
Lawrence   Ottawa   Sedalia   Columbia   St Louis   Owensboro   Bowling Green   Somerset
Emporia   El Dorado   Nevada   Rolla   Lebanon   Cape Girardeau   Paducah   Hopkinsville   Nashville   Knoxville
Wichita   Pittsburg   Springfield   Joplin   Carthage   Poplar Bluff   Mayfield   Clarksville   TENNESSEE   Chattanooga
Bartlesville   Carthage   Jonesboro   Dyersburg   Jackson   Columbia   Rome
Tulsa   Fayetteville   Boston Mts   Newport   Memphis   Florence   Huntsville   Decatur   Dalton   Gainesville
Cushing   Fort Smith   ARKANSAS   Russellville   Corinth   ALABAMA   GEORGIA
Oklahoma City   McAlester   Little Rock   Hot Springs   Tupelo   Birmingham   Atlanta   Athens   Augusta
Shawnee   Fort Smith   Pine Bluff   Greenwood   Columbus   Tuscaloosa   Macon   Milledgeville
Durant   Paris   Texarkana   El Dorado   Camden   MISSISSIPPI   Selma   Montgomery   Columbus   Savannah
Sherman   Greenville   Monroe   Jackson   Meridian   Phenix City   Dublin   Altamaha
Dallas   Tyler   Longview   Shreveport   Vicksburg   Brookhaven   Laurel   Troy   Albany   Fitzgerald   Brunswick
Waxahachie   Corsicana   Palestine   Nacogdoches   Alexandria   Natchez   LOUISIANA   Hattiesburg   Andalusia   Dothan   Thomasville   Valdosta   Jacksonville
Ennis   Lufkin   Baton Rouge   McComb   Mobile   Pensacola   Tallahassee   St Augustine
Houston   Beaumont   Lake Charles   Lafayette   New Orleans   Gulfport   FLORIDA   Daytona Beach
Pasadena   Port Arthur   Orange   Houma   Gainesville   Orlando
Galveston   Delta of the Mississippi   Tampa   Clearwater   Lakeland   Ft Pierce
Freeport   St Petersburg   Bradenton   West Palm Beach
Bay City   Sarasota   Arcadia   L. Okeechobee   Grand Bahama I.   Freeport
GULF OF MEXICO   Charlotte Harb.   Ft Myers   Fort Lauderdale   N.W. Providence Chan.   BAHAMAS
Matagorda I.   Miami   Coral Gables   Eleuthera I.
Key West   Florida Bay   Andros   New Providence   Exuma Sound   Cat I.   Long I.

Lake Superior
Lake Michigan
Lake Huron
Lake Erie
Lake Ontario

Sault Ste. Marie
Michipicoten
Wawa
Sudbury
North Bay
Sturgeon Falls
Parry Sound
Georgian Bay
Manitoulin
Owen Sound
Orangeville
Kitchener
London
TORONTO
Hamilton
Niagara Falls
Buffalo
Rochester
Syracuse
NEW YORK
Utica
Albany
Schenectady
Binghamton
Scranton
Wilkes Barre
PENNSYLVANIA
Allentown
Reading
PHILADELPHIA
Camden
Trenton
NEW JERSEY
Atlantic City
NEW YORK
Jersey City
Newark
Paterson
Bridgeport
New Haven
Hartford
Waterbury
Providence
Worcester
Springfield
Boston
MASS.
Brockton
Fall River
New Bedford
Martha's Vineyard
C. Cod

DETROIT
Windsor
Ann Arbor
Toledo
Lansing
Flint
Saginaw
Bay City
Pontiac
Cleveland
Akron
Youngstown
Canton
Pittsburgh
Wheeling
Columbus
PITTSBURGH
Altoona
Harrisburg
Johnstown
Cumberland
Washington
Baltimore
Wilmington
DELAWARE
Delaware Bay

Ottawa
Montréal
Québec
Sherbrooke
MAINE
Bangor
Bar Harbor
Penobscot Bay
Rockland
Portland
Biddeford
NEW HAMPSHIRE
Manchester
Concord
Nashua
Lowell
Lawrence
Lynn
VERMONT
Burlington
Rutland
Adirondack Mts
Watertown
Kingston
NEW BRUNSWICK

ATLANTIC OCEAN

Washington D.C.
VIRGINIA
Richmond
Lynchburg
Roanoke
Danville
Newport News
Norfolk
Portsmouth
NORTH CAROLINA
Greensboro
Winston Salem
Durham
Raleigh
Charlotte
Asheville
Greenville
Spartanburg
SOUTH CAROLINA
Columbia
Charleston
Charleston Harb.
Georgetown
Wilmington
C. Fear
C. Hatteras
Pamlico Sd.
Albemarle Sd.
Long Bay
Onslow Bay

COPYRIGHT. GEORGE PHILIP & SON, LTD

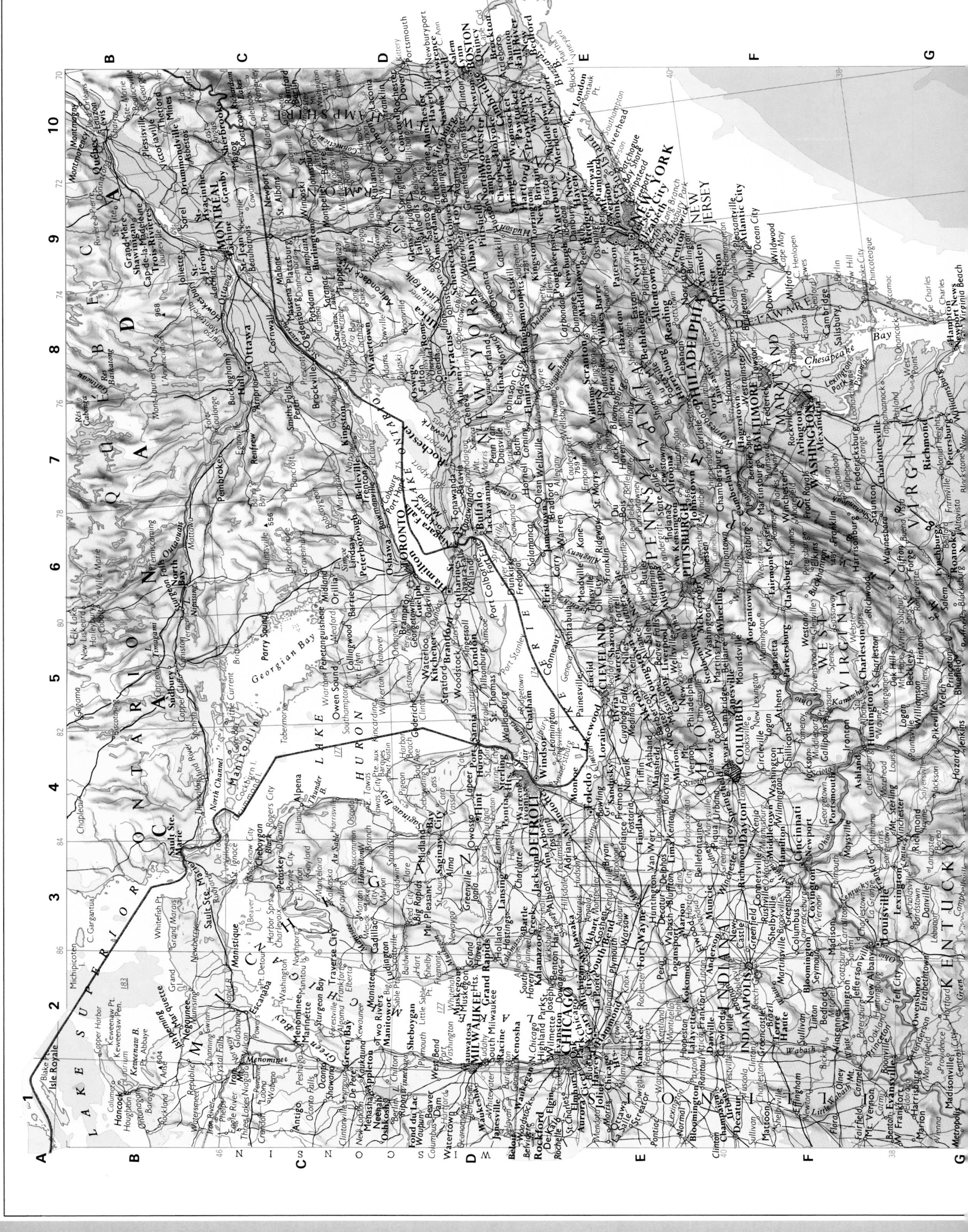
LAKE SUPERIOR
LAKE HURON
LAKE ONTARIO
LAKE ERIE
Georgian Bay
ONTARIO
QUEBEC
CHICAGO
DETROIT
TORONTO
MONTREAL
BOSTON
NEW YORK
PHILADELPHIA
PITTSBURGH
CLEVELAND
BALTIMORE
WASHINGTON D.C.
INDIANAPOLIS
COLUMBUS
MILWAUKEE
OTTAWA

1:6 000 000

50   0   50   100   150 miles
50   0   50   100   150   200 km

MAINE

NEW HAMPSHIRE

11 Continuation Eastwards On same scale.

12

TENNESSEE

NORTH CAROLINA

SOUTH CAROLINA

GEORGIA

ALABAMA

MISSISSIPPI

FLORIDA

GULF OF MEXICO

ATLANTIC OCEAN

BAHAMAS

Great Abaco I.

Grand Bahama I.

Freeport

Miami

Fort Lauderdale

Jacksonville

ATLANTA

Columbia

Charlotte

Raleigh

Wilmington

Charleston

Savannah

Tallahassee

Montgomery

Birmingham

Chattanooga

Knoxville

Nashville

Tampa

St. Petersburg

Orlando

Everglades

West from Greenwich

Projection: Alber's Equal Area with two standard parallels

COPYRIGHT. GEORGE PHILIP & SON LTD.

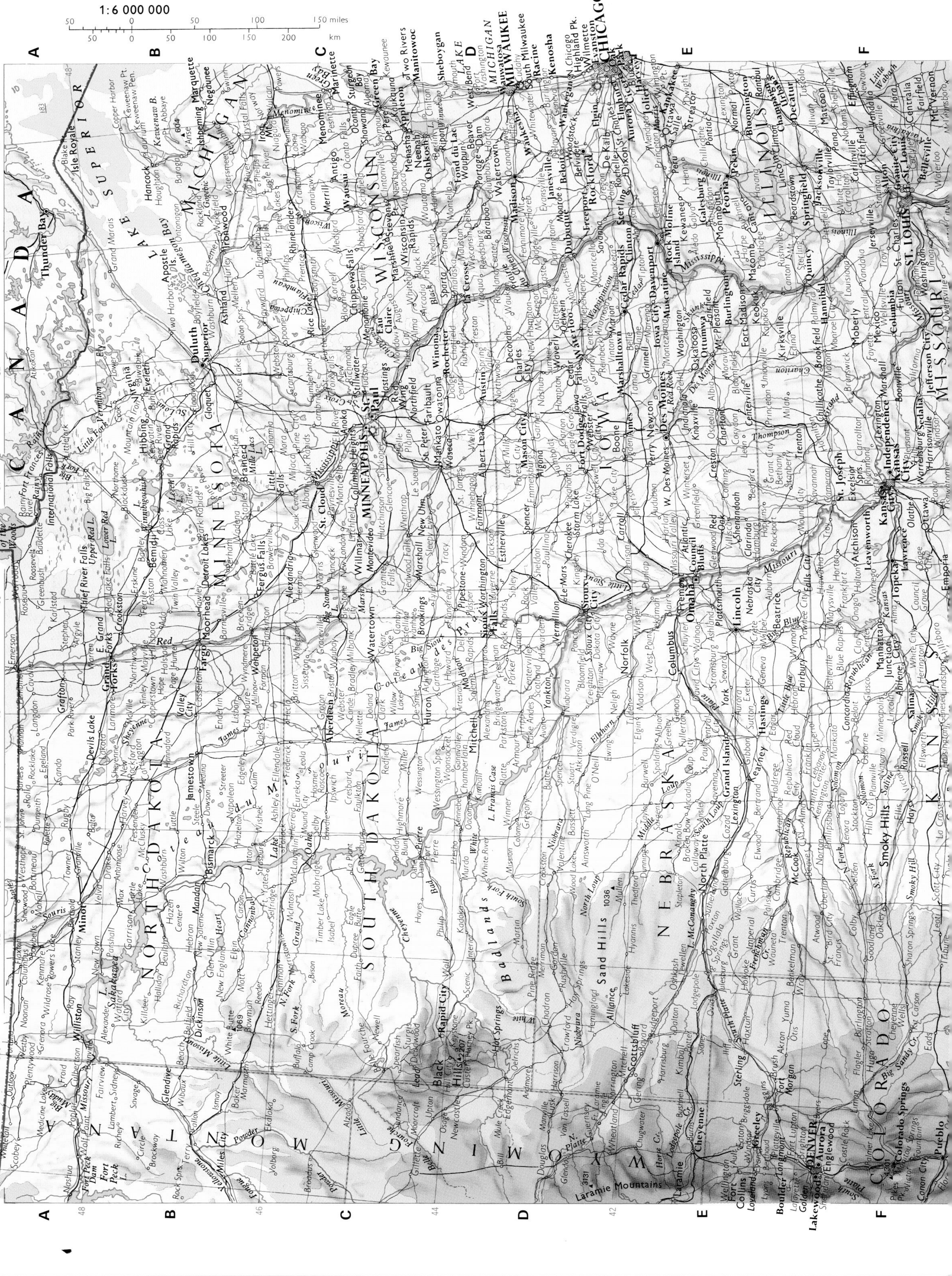

1:6 000 000
50 0 50 100 150 miles
50 0 50 100 150 200 km
CANADA
LAKE SUPERIOR
MINNESOTA
WISCONSIN
MICHIGAN
NORTH DAKOTA
SOUTH DAKOTA
IOWA
ILLINOIS
MISSOURI
NEBRASKA
KANSAS
COLORADO
WYOMING
MONTANA
CHICAGO
MILWAUKEE
MINNEAPOLIS
St. Paul
ST. LOUIS
Kansas City
Omaha
DENVER
Des Moines
Duluth
Lake of the Woods
Black Hills
Badlands
Sand Hills
Laramie Mountains

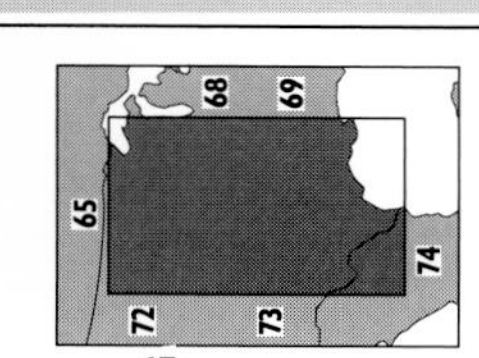

MEXICO

TENNESSEE

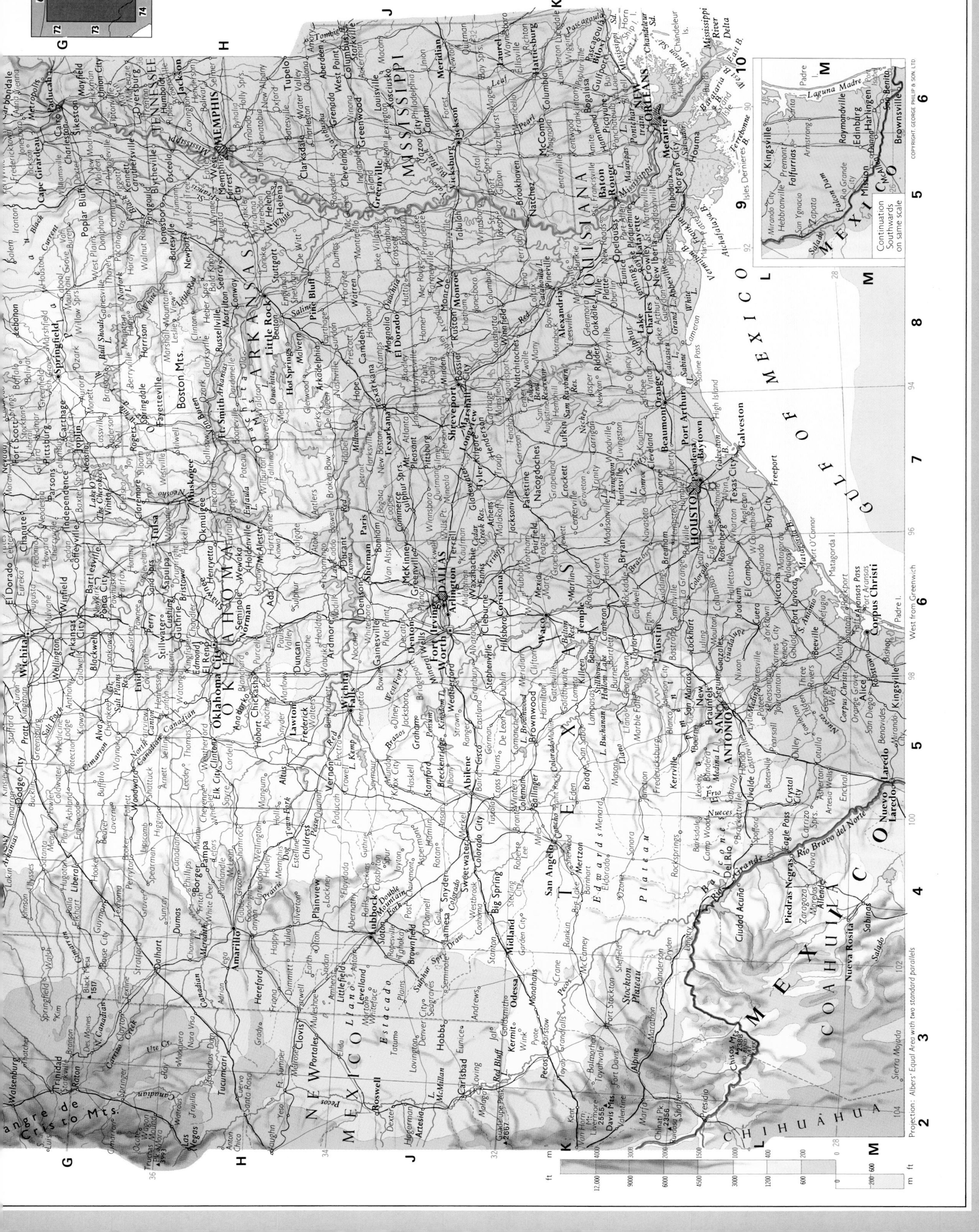

MISSISSIPPI

ARKANSAS

LOUISIANA

OKLAHOMA

TEXAS

NEW MEXICO

COAHUILA

CHIHUAHUA

GULF OF MEXICO

Laguna Madre

Projection: Albers' Equal Area with two standard parallels

West from Greenwich

Continuation Southwards on same scale

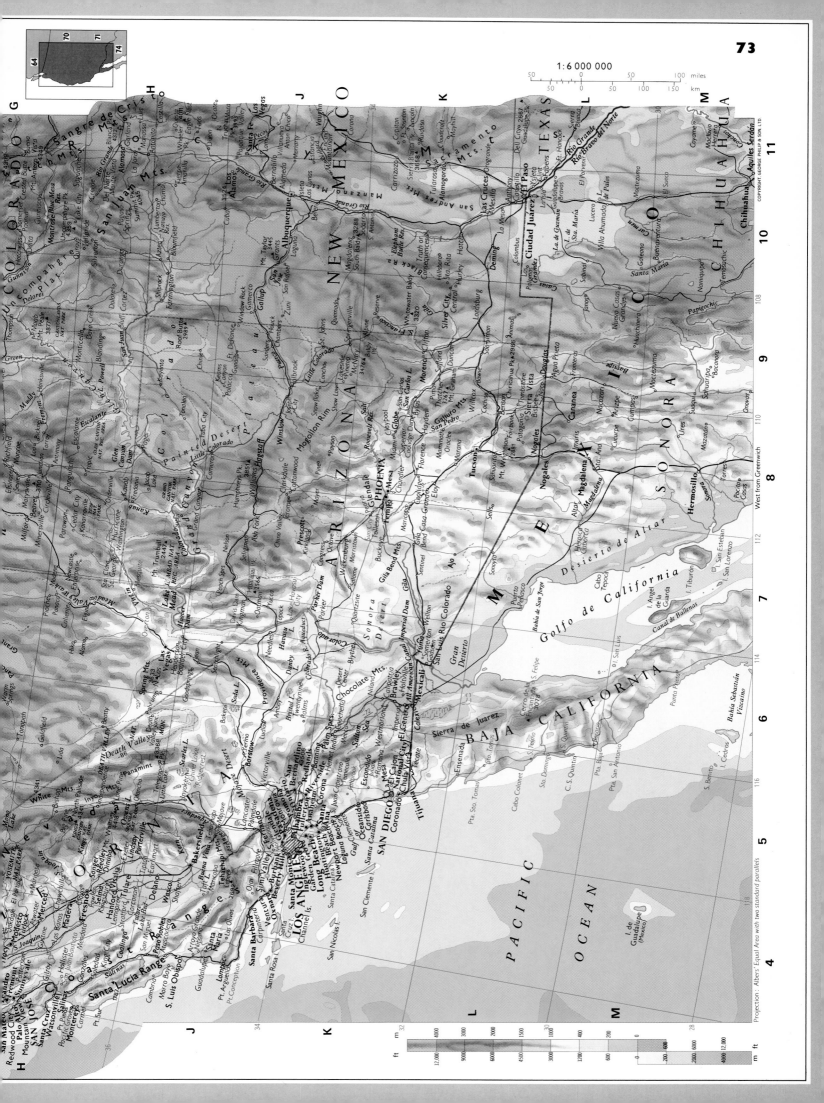

1:6 000 000

PANAMA CANAL
1 : 1 000 000

JAMAICA
1 : 5 000 000

TRINIDAD AND TOBAGO
1 : 5 000 000

LEEWARD ISLANDS
1 : 5 000 000

WINDWARD ISLANDS
1 : 5 000 000

66 67
78 79
8 9 10 11 12 13

1:15 000 000

100 0 100 200 300 400 miles
100 0 100 200 300 400 500 600 km

A

Columbia
Atlanta
Augusta
Macon
umbus
Savannah
C. Fear
Long Bay
C. Royal
Charleston

Bermuda
Hamilton

ahassee
Jacksonville

B

30

A T L A N T I C   O C E A N

Daytona Beach
Orlando
C. Canaveral
Tampa
sburg
Sarasota
Lakeland
L. Okeechobee
West Palm Beach
Grand Bahama I.
Freeport
Fort Lauderdale
Gt. Abaco I.

C

25

Miami
C. Sable
Key West
New Providence I.
Nassau
Eleuthera I.
Cat I.
S. Salvador or Watlings I.

BAHAMAS
Andros I.
Florida Str.

Tropic of Cancer

Habana (Havana)
rianao
Matanzas
Cárdenas
Colón
Sagua la Grande
Caibarién
Sta. Clara
Long I.
Acklins
Gt. Inagua
Mayaguana
Caicos I. (Br.)
Turks Is.(Br.)

20

G. de Batabanó
Cienfuegos
Trinidad
Sancti Spiritus
Ciego de Avila
Júcaro
Morón
Camagüey
Nuevitas
C U B A
Holguin
Antilla
Marti
Baracoa
Port de Paix
Cap Haitien
Monte Cristi
Valverde
Pto. Plata
S. Francisco de Macoris
Sanchez

PUERTO RICO (U.S.A.)
Aguadilla
Arecibo
San Juan

St. Thomas (U.S.A.)
Charlotte Amalie
Virgin Is. (Br.)
Sombrero (Br.)
Anguilla
St. Martin (Fr. & Neth.)

D

15

I. de Juventud
Manzanillo
Campechuela
Bayamo
Santiago de Cuba
Guantánamo
Paso de los Vientos
Gonaives
St. Marc
Jérémie
Leogane
La Vega
DOMINICAN REP.
La Romana
S. Pedro de Macoris
Santo Domingo
Canal de la Mona
Mayagüez
Ponce
Caguas
St. Croix (U.S.A.)
Christiansted
Basseterre
Charlestown
Nevis
St. John's
Plymouth
Montserrat
ST. CHRISTOPHER-NEVIS
ANTIGUA & BARBUDA
Guadeloupe (Fr.)
Pointe à Pitre
Marie Galante (Fr.)

Grand Cayman (Br.)
Montego Bay
St. Ann's Bay
P. Antonio
Savanna la Mar
Kingston
Spanish Town
JAMAICA
Les Cayes
Port au Prince
Jacmel
Barahona
Hispaniola
A N T I L L E S
Leeward Islands
DOMINICA
Roseau
LESSER

E

L. Caratasca
C. Gracias á Dios
Puerto Cabezas
Providencia (Col.)
San Andrés (Col.)
Bluefields

Pta. Gallinas
Pen. de la Guajira
Santa Marta
Gollo de Venezuela
Aruba (Neth.)
Curaçao (Neth.)
Willemstad
Bonaire (Neth.)
NETH. ANTILLES
Coro
Pto. Cabello
Maiquetia
La Tortuga (Ven.)
La Blanquilla (Ven.)
Margarita
La Asunción
Carúpano
Cumaná
G. de Paria
Port of Spain
San Fernando
TRINIDAD & TOBAGO
Tobago
ANTILLES Windward
ST. VINCENT
& Kingstown
THE GRENADINES Islands
The Grenadines
GRENADA
St. George's
Bridgetown
ST. LUCIA
BARBADOS
Fort de France
Castries
Martinique (Fr.)

C A R I B B E A N   S E A

10

Barranquilla
Soledad
Cartagena
Sierra Nevada de Santa Marta
Calamar
Riohacha
Dabajuro
Maracaibo
Cabimas
L. de Maracaibo
Trujillo
Maracay
San Felipe
Valencia
Caracas
Barcelona
Las Mercedes
El Tigre
Maturín
Tucupita
Ciudad Guayana
Ciudad Bolívar
Delta of the Orinoco
Georgetown

F

Limón
Colón
Vol. Chiriqui
Panama
La Palma
Arch. de las Perlas
Chitré
Pen. de Azuero
Coiba
G. del Darién
G. de Panama
G. de Cupica
Pta. Charambirá
Buenaventura
Turbo
El Real
Quibdó
Medellín
Barrancabermeja
El Banco
Corozal
Mompos
Plato
Sincelejo
Cauca
Ocaña
Cúcuta
Pamplona
Rubio
San Cristóbal
Bucaramanga
Cord. de Mérida
Portuguesa
Guanare
San Fernando de Apure
Apure
Arauca
Pto. Páez
Caicara
Pto. Carreño
Pto. Ayacucho
Orinoco
El Callao
Tumeremo
El Callao
Cuyuni
New Amsterdam
Wismare
SURINAM
GUYANA

Manizales
Pereira
Cartago
Armenia
Buga
Palmira
Cali
Neiva
Ibagué
Honda
Girardot
Tolima
Bogotá
Zipaquirá
Tunja
La Dorado
Berrio
Pto. Wilches
Arauca
Meta
VENEZUELA
Caura
Sierra Pacaraima
Roraima

G

Popayán
Guaviare
C O L O M B I A
Magdalena
Guaviare
Casiquiare
B R A Z I L

West from Greenwich
80 9 75 10 70 11 65 12

COPYRIGHT. GEORGE PHILIP & SON. LTD.

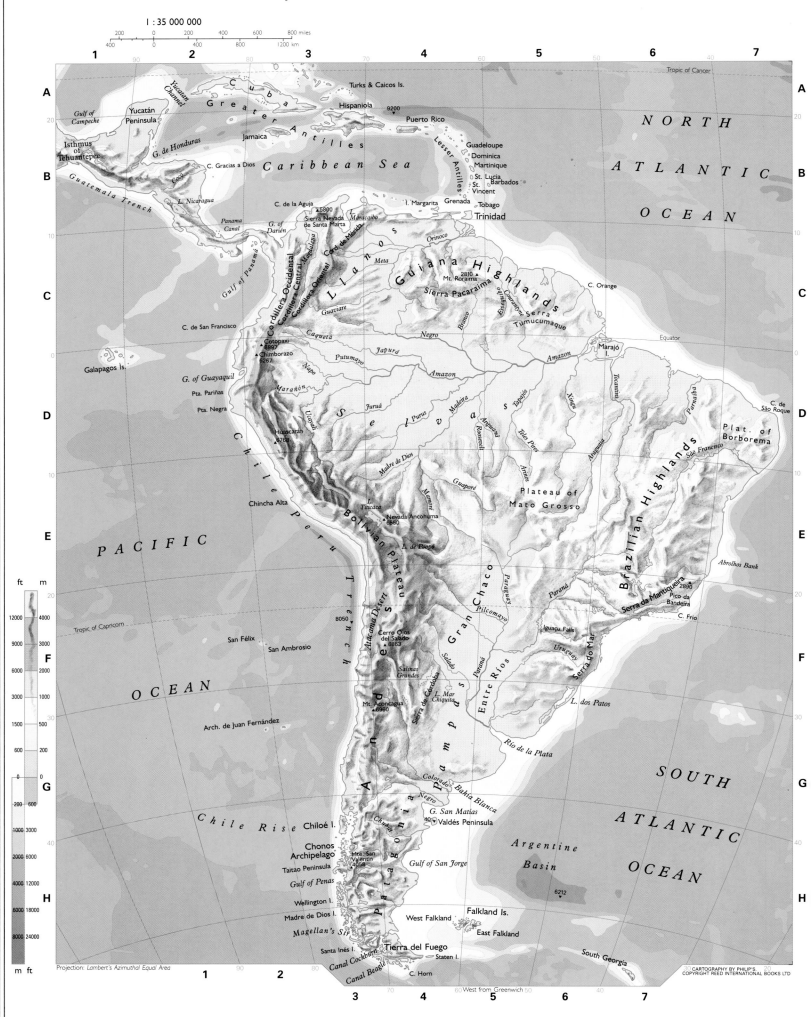

1 : 35 000 000

200   0   200   400   600   800 miles
400   0   400   800   1200 km

Tropic of Cancer

A

Gulf of Campeche
Yucatán Channel
Yucatán Peninsula
Cuba
Greater Antilles
Turks & Caicos Is.
Hispaniola
9200
Puerto Rico
Guadeloupe

20

Isthmus of Tehuantepec
G. de Honduras
Jamaica
Puerto Rico
Dominica
Martinique

NORTH
ATLANTIC
OCEAN

B

Guatemala Trench
Coco
C. Gracias a Dios
Caribbean Sea
St. Lucia
St. Vincent
Barbados
Grenada
Tobago

Panama Canal
L. Nicaragua
C. de la Aguja
5800
Sierra Nevada de Santa Marta
L. Maracaibo
I. Margarita
Trinidad

10

C

Gulf of Darién
G. of Panama
Cordillera Occidental
Cordillera Central
Cordillera Oriental
Cord de Merida
Orinoco
Meta
Llanos
Guiana Highlands
2810
Mt. Roraima
Sierra Pacaraima
Serra Tumucumaque
C. Orange

Guaviare
Essequibo
Caroní

D

C. de San Francisco
Caquetá
Napo
Putumayo
Japurá
Negro
Branco
Amazon
Equator
Marajó I.

Cotopaxi 5897
Chimborazo 6267
G. of Guayaquil
Marañón
Ucayali
Amazon
Juruá
Purus
Madeira
Tapajós
Araguaia
Roosevelt
Teles Pires
Tocantins
Xingú
Parnaíba
C. de São Roque

Pta. Pariñas
Pta. Negra
Selvas
Madre de Dios
Plat. of Borborema

10

E

Huascarán 6768
Chincha Alta
Titicaca
Nevada Ancohuma 6550
L. de Poopó
Guaporé
Mamoré
Pilcomayo
Plateau of Mato Grosso
Brazilian Highlands
São Francisco
Abrolhos Bank

PACIFIC

F

Tropic of Capricorn
San Félix
San Ambrosio
Atacama Desert
Cerro Ojos del Salado 6863
Salinas Grandes
Gran Chaco
Paraguay
Paraná
Uruguay
Serra da Mantiqueira 2890
Pico da Bandeira
C. Frio
Iguaçu Falls
Serra do Mar

8050
Bolivian Plateau
Andes
Chile Peru Trench

OCEAN

20

G

Arch. de Juan Fernández
Mt. Aconcagua 6960
Sierra de Córdoba
L. Mar Chiquita
Salado
Entre Ríos
Paraná
L. dos Patos
Río de la Plata

SOUTH
ATLANTIC
OCEAN

Pampas

Colorado
Negro
Bahía Blanca
G. San Matías
Valdés Peninsula
40

30

H

Chile Rise
Chiloé I.
Chonos Archipelago
Taitao Peninsula
Gulf of Penas
Wellington I.
Madre de Dios I.
Mte. San Valentín 4058
Chubut
Patagonia
Gulf of San Jorge
Argentine Basin
6212
Falkland Is.
West Falkland
East Falkland
South Georgia

40

Magellan's Str.
Santa Inés I.
Canal Cockburn
Canal Beagle
Tierra del Fuego
Staten I.
C. Horn
West from Greenwich

Projection: Lambert's Azimuthal Equal Area

30 CARTOGRAPHY BY PHILIP'S,
COPYRIGHT REED INTERNATIONAL BOOKS LTD

ft   m
12000 4000
9000   3000
6000   2000
3000   1000
1500   500
600   200
0   0
200   600
1000   3000
2000   6000
4000   12000
6000   18000
8000   24000
m   ft

1 : 35 000 000

200   0   200   400   600   800 miles
400   0   400   800   1200 km

Tropic of Cancer

Havana • CUBA
BAHAMAS
Turks & Caicos Is.
(U.K.)

NORTH

HAITI
DOMINICAN REP.
Port-au-Prince
San Juan
Virgin Is.
(U.K.)

ATLANTIC

JAMAICA   Kingston
PUERTO RICO
(U.S.A.)
ST. KITTS-NEVIS
ANTIGUA & BARBUDA
Basse-Terre GUADELOUPE (Fr.)

MEXICO
BELIZE
GUATEMALA
Caribbean Sea
DOMINICA
Fort-de-France MARTINIQUE (Fr.)
Castries ST. LUCIA
ST. VINCENT BARBADOS
Kingstown Bridgetown
GRENADA St. George's

OCEAN

Guatemala
HONDURAS
Tegucigalpa
San Salvador
EL SALVADOR
NICARAGUA
Managua
COSTA RICA San José
Panamá
PANAMA

Aruba
Curaçao
C. de la Aguja
Barranquilla
Cartagena
G. of Darién
Maracaibo
Caracas
Valencia
Port of Spain
TRINIDAD & TOBAGO

Cúcuta
San Cristóbal
Bárquisimeto
Orinoco
Ciudad Guayana
Georgetown
Paramaribo

Medellín
Bucaramanga
VENEZUELA
GUYANA
SURINAM
Cayenne
FRENCH GUIANA
C. Orange

Cali
Bógotá
COLOMBIA
RORAIMA
Branco
Essequibo

Galapagos Is.
(Ecuador)
Quito
ECUADOR
Japurá
AMAPÁ
Equator

Guayaquil
G. of Guayaquil
Napo
Putumayo
Amazon
Marajó I.
Belém

Iquitos
Marañón
Amazon
Manaus
Santarém
São Luís
Fortaleza

Chiclayo
Juruá
AMAZONAS
Madeira
Tapajós
PARÁ
MARANHÃO
Teresina
C. de São Roque
RIO G. DO NORTE
Natal

Trujillo
ACRE
Purus
Xingu
Tocantins
Parnaíba
PIAUÍ
CEARÁ
PARAÍBA
Campina Grande
Recife

Chimbote
PERU
Pôrto Velho
RONDÔNIA
BRAZIL
PERNAMBUCO
ALAGOAS
SERGIPE
Maceió

Callao LIMA
Madre de Dios
Cuzco
Mamoré
MATO GROSSO
TOCANTINS
BAHÍA
Aracaju
Salvador

L. Titicaca
BOLIVIA
Cuiabá
GOIÁS
São Francisco
Arequipa
La Paz
Cochabamba
Santa Cruz
DIS. FED. Brasília
Goiânia

Sucre
MINAS GERAIS
Iquique
MATO GROSSO DO SUL
Belo Horizonte
ESPÍRITO SANTO
Vitória

PACIFIC

Antofagasta
Salta
PARAGUAY
Pilcomayo
Asunción
Paraná
Ribeirão Prêto
SÃO PAULO
Juiz de Fora
Campos

San Félix (Chile)
San Ambrosio (Chile)
San Miguel de Tucumán
PARANÁ
SÃO PAULO
Campinas
RIO DE JANEIRO
Niterói

Resistencia
Corrientes
Uruguay
SANTA CATARINA

Tropic of Capricorn

OCEAN

Córdoba
Santa Fe
Paraná
RIO GRANDE DO SUL
Pôrto Alegre

Arch. de Juan Fernández
(Chile)
San Juan
Mendoza
Rosario
URUGUAY
Pelotas

Viña del Mar
Valparaíso
SANTIAGO
CHILE
BUENOS AIRES
Montevideo
La Plata
Río de la Plata

Talca
Concepción
ARGENTINA
Bahía Blanca
Colorado
Mar del Plata

SOUTH

Valdivia
Negro
Viedma

ATLANTIC

Puerto Montt
Chubut
Comodoro Rivadavia
Gulf of San Jorge

OCEAN

Gulf of Penas
Magellan's Str.
Punta Arenas
Tierra del Fuego
West Falkland
FALKLAND IS. (U.K.)
Stanley
East Falkland

C. Horn
South Georgia
(U.K.)

Projection: Lambert's Azimuthal Equal Area

■ LIMA Capital Cities

West from Greenwich

CARTOGRAPHY BY PHILIP'S.
COPYRIGHT REED INTERNATIONAL BOOKS LTD

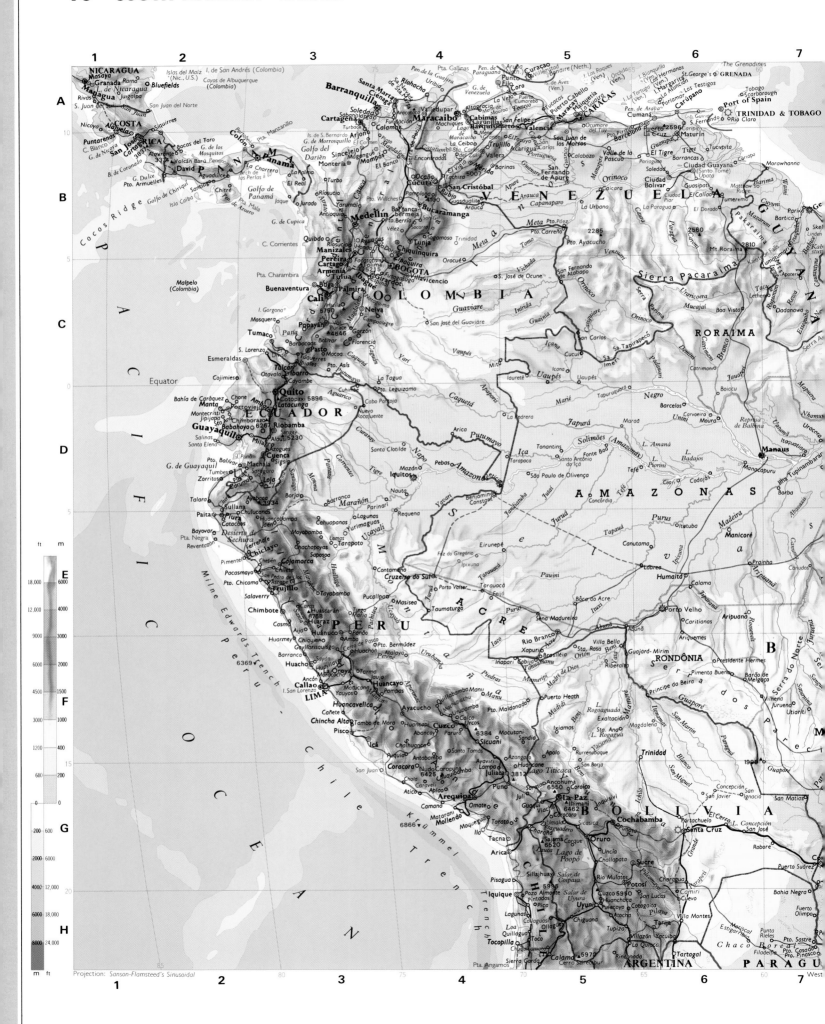

1:16 000 000

100 50 0 100 200 300 miles
100 0 100 200 300 400 km

A

B

C

D

E

F

G

H

A T L A N T I C   O C E A N

Equator

Suriname / Fr. Guiana area
Paramaribo · Nieuw Amsterdam · Albina · Mana · Iracoubo · Sinnamary · Kourou · Cayenne · Approuague · St. Laurent · Kaw · C. Orange · Oiapoque · Ouanary · St. Georges

FR. GUIANA · **SRINAM** (SURINAM) · Brokopondo · Tapanahoni · Litani · Tumucumaque · Serra Tumucumaque

AMAPÁ
Araguari · Serra do Navio · Rio Grande · Amapá · Ilha de Maracá · C. do Norte · Macapá · Mazagão · Afuá · Chaves · Souré · Salinópolis · Curuçá · Bragança · Vigia · Viseu · Ilha Caviana · Ilha Mexiana · Estuario do Rio Amazonas

PARÁ
Santarém · Belterra · Óbidos · Altamira · Itaituba · Brasília Legal · Pôrto de Móz · Gurupá · Breves · Ilha de Marajó · Anajás · Muaná · **Belém** · Abaetetuba · Cametá · Baião · Tucuruí · Represa de Tucuruí · Marabá · Imperatriz · Conceição do Araguaia · Araguacema · Serra dos Carajás · Xingu · Iriri · Tapajós · Amazonas

MARANHÃO
São Luís · Alcântara · Guimarães · B. de São Marcos · Turiaçu · Rosária · Bacabal · Coroatá · Codó · Caxias · Timon · Barra do Corda · Grajaú · Carolina · Riachão · Loreto · Balsas · Pôrto Franco · Tocantinópolis

PIAUÍ
Teresina · Parnaíba · Luís Correia · Piripiri · Campo Maior · União · Amarante · Floriano · Oeiras · Uruçuí · Picos · Nova Iorque · São João do Piauí · São Raimundo Nonato · Paulistana

CEARÁ
Fortaleza · Sobral · Camocim · Granja · Itapipoca · Cascavel · Aracati · Baturité · Quixadá · Maranguape · Crateús · Iguatu · Oros · Crato · Juazeiro do Norte · Russas · Mossoró · Areia Branca · Macau

RIO GRANDE DO NORTE
Natal · Nova Cruz · C. de São Roque · Ceará Mirim · Caicó

PARAÍBA
João Pessoa · Campina Grande · Cabedelo · Mamanguape · Conguaretama · Itabaiana

PERNAMBUCO
RECIFE · Olinda · Caruaru · Garanhuns · Palmares · Pesqueira · Arcoverde · Cabo de Santo Agostinho

ALAGOAS
Maceió · Arapiraca · Penedo · Palmeira dos Índios · Pal. dos Índios · Rio Largo

SERGIPE
Aracaju · Estância · São Cristóvão · Propriá · Capela

São Francisco · Juàzeiro · Petrolina · Paulo Afonso · Senhor do Bonfim

Fernando de Noronha (Braz.)
Rocas

TOCANTINS
Palmas · Pôrto Nacional · Natividade · Peixe · Paranã · Ilha do Bananal · Araguaia · Tocantins

BAHIA
Barreiras · Ibotirama · Xique-Xique · Jacobina · Barra · Irecê · Sta. Maria da Vitória · Bom Jesus da Lapa · Caetité · Brumado · Itaberaba · Feira de Santana · Santo Amaro · **Salvador** · Cachoeira · Alagoinhas · Nazaré · Valença · Jequié · Vitória da Conquista · Itabuna · Ilhéus · Canavieiras · Belmonte · Pôrto Seguro · Itacaré · Jequitinhonha · Januária · Represa de Sobradinho · Baía de Todos os Santos

1850

GOIÁS
Goiânia · Anápolis · Goiás · Catalão · Itumbiara · Rio Verde · Jataí · Luziânia

DIST. FED.
Brasília · Formosa · Paracatu

MINAS GERAIS
Belo Horizonte · Uberlândia · Uberaba · Araxá · Patos de Minas · Diamantina · Teófilo Otoni · Gov. Valadares · Ipatinga · Montes Claros · Janaúba · Salinas · Araçuaí · Pedra Azul · Nanuque · Conceição da Barra · Ouro Prêto · Divinópolis · São João del Rei · Barbacena · Juiz de Fora · Pirapora · Curvelo · Sete Lagoas · Caratinga · Aimorés · Lavras

ESPÍRITO SANTO
Vitória · Vila Velha · Cariacica · Linhares · São Mateus · Colatina · Cachoeiro de Itapemirim

Trindade (Braz.)

1340 · 1678 · 2890

RIO DE JANEIRO
Campos · Macaé · Cabo Frio · Niterói · Petrópolis · Nova Friburgo · Volta Redonda

SÃO PAULO
São Paulo · Campinas · Ribeirão Preto · Franca · Piracicaba · Bauru · Marília · Araçatuba · Pres. Prudente · São José do Rio Prêto · Araraquara · Botucatu · Assis

MATO GROSSO / MATO GROSSO DO SUL
Campo Grande · Três Lagoas · Dourados · Ponta Porã · Rondonópolis · Coxim · Aquidauana · Miranda

Planalto do Mato Grosso · Serra do Roncador · Serra do Espinhaço

B R A Z I L

6059

wich 55

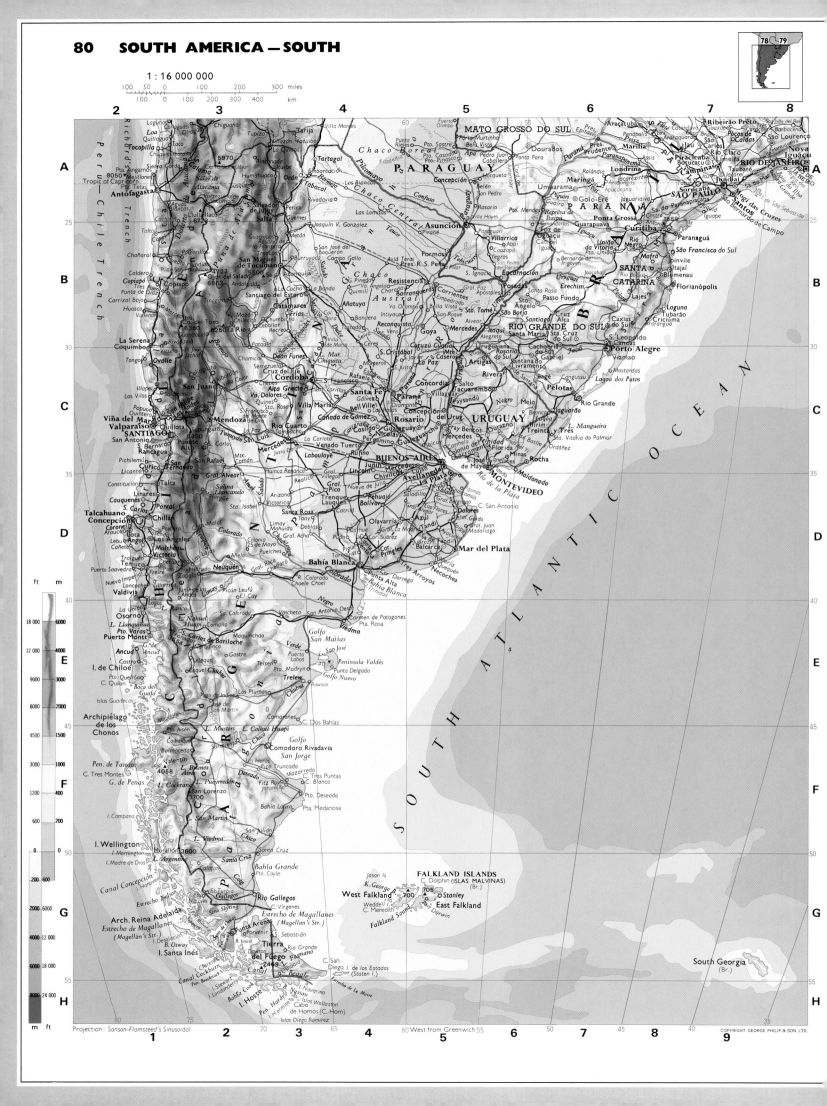

INDEX

The index contains the names of all the principal places and features shown on the World Maps. Each name is followed by an additional entry in italics giving the country or region within which it is located. The alphabetical order of names composed of two or more words is governed primarily by the first word and then by the second. This is an example of the rule:

Mīr Kūh, *Iran*	**39**	**E8**
Mīr Shahdād, *Iran*	**39**	**E8**
Miraj, *India*	**36**	**L9**
Miram Shah, *Pakistan*	**36**	**C7**
Miramar, *Mozam.*	**49**	**C6**

Physical features composed of a proper name (Erie) and a description (Lake) are positioned alphabetically by the proper name. The description is positioned after the proper name and is usually abbreviated:

Erie, L., *N. Amer.*	**68**	**D5**

Where a description forms part of a settlement or administrative name however, it is always written in full and put in its true alphabetic position:

Mount Morris, *U.S.A.*	**68**	**D7**

Names beginning with M' and Mc are indexed as if they were spelled Mac. Names beginning St. are alphabetised under Saint, but Sankt, Sint, Sant', Santa and San are all spelt in full and are alphabetised accordingly. If the same place name occurs two or more times in the index and all are in the same country, each is followed by the name of the administrative subdivision in which it is located. The names are placed in the alphabetical order of the subdivisions. For example:

Jackson, *Ky., U.S.A.*	**68**	**G4**
Jackson, *Mich., U.S.A.*	**68**	**D3**
Jackson, *Minn., U.S.A.*	**70**	**D7**

The number in bold type which follows each name in the index refers to the number of the map page where that feature or place will be found. This is usually the largest scale at which the place or feature appears. The letter and figure which are in bold type immediately after the page number give the grid square on the map page, within which the feature is situated. The letter represents the latitude and the figure the longitude.

In some cases the feature itself may fall within the specified square, while the name is outside. This is usually the case only with features which are larger than a grid square. Rivers are indexed to their mouths or confluences, and carry the symbol ➔ after their names. A solid square ■ follows the name of a country while, an open square □ refers to a first order administrative area.

Abbreviations used in the index

A.C.T. — Australian Capital Territory
Afghan. — Afghanistan
Ala. — Alabama
Alta. — Alberta
Amer. — America(n)
Arch. — Archipelago
Ariz. — Arizona
Ark. — Arkansas
Atl. Oc. — Atlantic Ocean
B. — Baie, Bahía, Bay, Bucht, Bugt
B.C. — British Columbia
Bangla. — Bangladesh
Barr. — Barrage
C. — Cabo, Cap, Cape, Coast
C.A.R. — Central African Republic
C. Prov. — Cape Province
Calif. — California
Cent. — Central
Chan. — Channel
Colo. — Colorado
Conn. — Connecticut
Cord. — Cordillera
Cr. — Creek
Czech. — Czech Republic
D.C. — District of Columbia
Del. — Delaware
Dep. — Dependency
Des. — Desert
Dist. — District
Dj. — Djebel
Domin. — Dominica
Dom. Rep. — Dominican Republic
E. — East
El Salv. — El Salvador

Eq. Guin. — Equatorial Guinea
Fla. — Florida
Falk. Is. — Falkland Is.
G. — Golfe, Golfo, Gulf, Guba, Gebel
Ga. — Georgia
Gt. — Great, Greater
Guinea-Biss. — Guinea-Bissau
H.K. — Hong Kong
H.P. — Himachal Pradesh
Hants. — Hampshire
Harb. — Harbor, Harbour
Hd. — Head
Hts. — Heights
I.(s). — Île, Ilha, Insel, Isla, Island, Isle
Ill. — Illinois
Ind. — Indiana
Ind. Oc. — Indian Ocean
Ivory C. — Ivory Coast
J. — Jabal, Jebel, Jazira
Junc. — Junction
K. — Kap, Kapp
Kans. — Kansas
Kep. — Kepulauan
Ky. — Kentucky
L. — Lac, Lacul, Lago, Lagoa, Lake, Limni, Loch, Lough
La. — Louisiana
Liech. — Liechtenstein
Lux. — Luxembourg
Mad. P. — Madhya Pradesh
Madag. — Madagascar
Man. — Manitoba
Mass. — Massachusetts

Md. — Maryland
Me. — Maine
Medit. S. — Mediterranean Sea
Mich. — Michigan
Minn. — Minnesota
Miss. — Mississippi
Mo. — Missouri
Mont. — Montana
Mozam. — Mozambique
Mt.(e). — Mont, Monte, Monti, Montaña, Mountain
N. — Nord, Norte, North, Northern, Nouveau
N.B. — New Brunswick
N.C. — North Carolina
N. Cal. — New Caledonia
N. Dak. — North Dakota
N.H. — New Hampshire
N.I. — North Island
N.J. — New Jersey
N. Mex. — New Mexico
N.S. — Nova Scotia
N.S.W. — New South Wales
N.W.T. — North West Territory
N.Y. — New York
N.Z. — New Zealand
Nebr. — Nebraska
Neths. — Netherlands
Nev. — Nevada
Nfld. — Newfoundland
Nic. — Nicaragua
O. — Oued, Ouadi
Occ. — Occidentale
O.F.S. — Orange Free State
Okla. — Oklahoma

Ont. — Ontario
Or. — Orientale
Oreg. — Oregon
Os. — Ostrov
Oz. — Ozero
P. — Pass, Passo, Pasul, Pulau
P.E.I. — Prince Edward Island
Pa. — Pennsylvania
Pac. Oc. — Pacific Ocean
Papua N.G. — Papua New Guinea
Pass. — Passage
Pen. — Peninsula, Péninsule
Phil. — Philippines
Pk. — Park, Peak
Plat. — Plateau
P-ov. — Poluostrov
Prov. — Province, Provincial
Pt. — Point
Pta. — Ponta, Punta
Pte. — Pointe
Qué. — Québec
Queens. — Queensland
R. — Rio, River
R.I. — Rhode Island
Ra.(s). — Range(s)
Raj. — Rajasthan
Reg. — Region
Rep. — Republic
Res. — Reserve, Reservoir
S. — San, South, Sea
Si. Arabia — Saudi Arabia
S.C. — South Carolina
S. Dak. — South Dakota
S.I. — South Island
S. Leone — Sierra Leone

Sa. — Serra, Sierra
Sask. — Saskatchewan
Scot. — Scotland
Sd. — Sound
Sev. — Severnaya
Sib. — Siberia
Sprs. — Springs
St. — Saint, Sankt, Sint
Sta. — Santa, Station
Ste. — Sainte
Sto. — Santo
Str. — Strait, Stretto
Switz. — Switzerland
Tas. — Tasmania
Tenn. — Tennessee
Tex. — Texas
Tg. — Tanjung
Trin. & Tob. — Trinidad & Tobago
U.A.E. — United Arab Emirates
U.K. — United Kingdom
U.S.A. — United States of America
Ut. P. — Uttar Pradesh
Va. — Virginia
Vdkhr. — Vodokhranilishche
Vf. — Vîrful
Vic. — Victoria
Vol. — Volcano
Vt. — Vermont
W. — Wadi, West
W. Va. — West Virginia
Wash. — Washington
Wis. — Wisconsin
Wlkp. — Wielkopolski
Wyo. — Wyoming
Yorks. — Yorkshire

A Coruña

A

A Coruña = La Coruña, Spain 19 A1
Aachen, Germany 16 C4
Aalborg = Ålborg, Denmark 9 H13
Aalen, Germany 16 D6
Aalsmeer, Neths. 15 B4
Aalst, Belgium 15 D4
Aalten, Neths. 15 C6
Äänekoski, Finland 9 E21
Aarau, Switz. 16 E5
Aare →, Switz. 16 E5
Aarhus = Århus, Denmark 9 H14
Aarschot, Belgium 15 D4
Aba, Nigeria 44 G6
Ābādān, Iran 39 D6
Ābādeh, Iran 39 D7
Abadla, Algeria 44 B4
Abaetetuba, Brazil 79 D9
Abakan, Russia 25 D10
Abancay, Peru 78 F4
Abariringa, Kiribati 56 H10
Abarqū, Iran 39 D7
Abashiri, Japan 28 B12
Abashiri-Wan, Japan 28 B12
Abay, Kazakhstan 24 E8
Abaya, L., Ethiopia 45 G12
Abaza, Russia 24 D10
'Abbāsābād, Iran 39 C8
Abbay = Nîl el Azraq →, Sudan 45 E11
Abbaye, Pt., U.S.A. 68 B1
Abbeville, France 18 A4
Abbeville, La., U.S.A. 71 K8
Abbeville, S.C., U.S.A. 69 H4
Abbieglassie, Australia 55 D4
Abbot Ice Shelf, Antarctica 5 D16
Abbotsford, Canada 64 D4
Abbotsford, U.S.A. 70 C9
Abbottabad, Pakistan 36 B8
Abd al Kūrī, Ind. Oc. 40 E5
Ābdar, Iran 39 D7
'Abdolābād, Iran 39 C8
Abéché, Chad 45 F9
Åbenrå, Denmark 9 J13
Abeokuta, Nigeria 44 G5
Aberaeron, U.K. 11 E3
Aberayron = Aberaeron, U.K. 11 E3
Abercorn = Mbala, Zambia 46 F6
Abercorn, Australia 55 D5
Aberdare, U.K. 11 F4
Aberdeen, Australia 55 E5
Aberdeen, Canada 65 C7
Aberdeen, S. Africa 48 E3
Aberdeen, U.K. 12 D6
Aberdeen, Ala., U.S.A. 69 J1
Aberdeen, Idaho, U.S.A. 72 E7
Aberdeen, S. Dak., U.S.A. 70 C5
Aberdeen, Wash., U.S.A. 72 C2
Aberdovey = Aberdyfi, U.K. 11 E3
Aberdyfi, U.K. 11 E3
Aberfeldy, U.K. 12 E5
Abergavenny, U.K. 11 F4
Abernathy, U.S.A. 71 J4
Abert, L., U.S.A. 72 E3
Aberystwyth, U.K. 11 E3
Abhar, Iran 39 B6
Abidjan, Ivory C. 44 G4
Abilene, Kans., U.S.A. 70 F6
Abilene, Tex., U.S.A. 71 J5
Abingdon, U.K. 11 F6
Abingdon, Ill., U.S.A. 70 E9
Abingdon, Va., U.S.A. 69 G5
Abington Reef, Australia 54 B4
Abitau →, Canada 65 B7
Abitau L., Canada 65 A7
Abitibi L., Canada 62 C4
Abkhaz Republic = Abkhazia □, Georgia 23 F7
Abkhazia □, Georgia 23 F7
Abkit, Russia 25 C16
Abminga, Australia 55 D1
Åbo = Turku, Finland 9 F20
Abohar, India 36 D9
Abomey, Benin 44 G5
Abong-Mbang, Cameroon 46 D2
Abou-Deïa, Chad 45 F8
Aboyne, U.K. 12 D6
Abri, Sudan 45 D11
Abrolhos, Banka, Brazil 79 G11
Abrud, Romania 17 E12
Absaroka Range, U.S.A. 72 D9
Abū al Khaṣīb, Iraq 39 D6
Abū 'Alī, Si. Arabia 39 E6
Abū 'Alī →, Lebanon 41 A4
Abu 'Arīsh, Si. Arabia 40 D3
Abu Dhabi = Abū Ẓāby, U.A.E. 39 E7
Abû Dis, Sudan 45 E11
Abū Du'ān, Syria 38 B3
Abu el Gairi, W. →, Egypt 41 F2
Abu Ga'da, W. →, Egypt 41 F1
Abū Ḥadrīyah, Si. Arabia 39 E6
Abu Hamed, Sudan 45 E11
Abū Kamāl, Syria 38 C4
Abū Madd, Ra's, Si. Arabia 38 E3
Abu Matariq, Sudan 45 F10
Abu Şafāt, W. →, Jordan 41 E5
Abū Şukhayr, Iraq 38 D5
Abu Tig, Egypt 45 C11
Abū Zabad, Sudan 45 F10
Abū Ẓāby, U.A.E. 39 E7
Abū Zeydābād, Iran 39 C6
Abuja, Nigeria 44 G6
Abukuma-Gawa →, Japan 28 E10
Abukuma-Sammyaku, Japan 28 F10
Abunã, Brazil 78 E5
Abunã →, Brazil 78 E5
Abut Hd., N.Z. 51 K3
Abwong, Sudan 45 G11
Acaponeta, Mexico 74 C3
Acapulco, Mexico 74 D5
Acarigua, Venezuela 78 B5
Accomac, U.S.A. 68 G8
Accra, Ghana 44 G4
Accrington, U.K. 10 D5
Aceh □, Indonesia 32 D1
Achalpur, India 36 J10
Achill, Ireland 13 C2
Achill Hd., Ireland 13 C1
Achill I., Ireland 13 C1
Achill Sd., Ireland 13 C2
Achinsk, Russia 25 D10
Acireale, Italy 20 F6
Ackerman, U.S.A. 71 J10
Acklins I., Bahamas 75 C10
Acme, Canada 64 C6
Aconcagua, Cerro, Argentina 80 C3
Aconquija, Mt., Argentina 80 B3
Açores, Is. dos = Azores, Atl. Oc. 2 C8
Acraman, L., Australia 55 E2
Acre = 'Akko, Israel 41 C4
Acre □, Brazil 78 E4
Acre →, Brazil 78 E5
Ad Dammām, Si. Arabia 39 E6
Ad Dawhah, Qatar 39 E6
Ad Dawr, Iraq 38 C4
Ad Dir'īyah, Si. Arabia 38 E5
Ad Dīwānīyah, Iraq 38 D5
Ad Dujayl, Iraq 38 C5
Ad Durūz, J., Jordan 41 C5
Ada, Minn., U.S.A. 70 B6
Ada, Okla., U.S.A. 71 H6
Adaja →, Spain 19 B3
Adamaoua, Massif de l', Cameroon 45 G7
Adamawa Highlands = Adamaoua, Massif de l', Cameroon 45 G7
Adamello, Mte., Italy 20 A4
Adaminaby, Australia 55 F4
Adams, N.Y., U.S.A. 68 D7
Adams, Wis., U.S.A. 70 D10
Adam's Bridge, Sri Lanka 36 Q11
Adams L., Canada 64 C5
Adams Mt., U.S.A. 72 C3
Adam's Peak, Sri Lanka 36 R12
Adana, Turkey 23 G6
Adapazarı, Turkey 23 F5
Adarama, Sudan 45 E11
Adare, C., Antarctica 5 D11
Adaut, Indonesia 33 F8
Adavale, Australia 55 D3
Adda →, Italy 20 B3
Addis Ababa = Addis Abeba, Ethiopia 45 G12
Addis Abeba, Ethiopia 45 G12
Addis Alem, Ethiopia 45 G12
Addo, S. Africa 48 E4
Ādeh, Iran 38 B5
Adel, U.S.A. 69 K4
Adelaide, Australia 55 E2
Adelaide, S. Africa 48 E4
Adelaide I., Antarctica 5 C17
Adelaide Pen., Canada 60 B10
Adelaide River, Australia 52 B5
Adele I., Australia 52 C3
Adélie, Terre, Antarctica 5 C10
Adélie Land = Adélie, Terre, Antarctica 5 C10
Aden = Al 'Adan, Yemen 40 E4
Aden, G. of, Asia 40 E4
Adendorp, S. Africa 48 E3
Adh Dhayd, U.A.E. 39 E7
Adi, Indonesia 33 E8
Adi Ugri, Eritrea 45 F12
Adieu, C., Australia 53 F5
Adieu Pt., Australia 52 C3
Adige →, Italy 20 B5
Adilabad, India 36 K11
Adin, U.S.A. 72 F3
Adin Khel, Afghan. 36 C6
Adirondack Mts., U.S.A. 68 D8
Adlavik Is., Canada 63 B8
Admer, Algeria 44 D6
Admiralty G., Australia 52 B4
Admiralty I., U.S.A. 60 C6
Admiralty Inlet, U.S.A. 72 C2
Admiralty Is., Papua N. G. 56 H6
Ado-Ekiti, Nigeria 44 G6
Adonara, Indonesia 33 F6
Adoni, India 36 M10
Adour →, France 18 E3
Adra, Spain 19 D4
Adrano, Italy 20 F6
Adrar, Algeria 44 C4
Adré, Chad 45 F9
Adrī, Libya 45 C7
Adrian, Mich., U.S.A. 68 E3
Adrian, Tex., U.S.A. 71 H3
Adriatic Sea, Medit. S. 20 C6
Adua, Indonesia 33 E7
Adwa, Ethiopia 45 F12
Adzhar Republic = Ajaria □, Georgia 23 F7
Ægean Sea, Medit. S. 21 E11
Æolian Is. = Eólie, Ís., Italy 20 E6
Aerhtai Shan, Mongolia 30 B4
'Afak, Iraq 38 C5
Afars & Issas, Terr. of = Djibouti ■, Africa 40 E3
Afghanistan ■, Asia 36 C4
Afgoi, Somali Rep. 40 G3
Afognak I., U.S.A. 60 C4
'Afrīn, Syria 38 B3
Afuá, Brazil 79 D8
Afula, Israel 41 C4
Afyonkarahisar, Turkey 23 G5
Agadès = Agadez, Niger 44 E6
Agadez, Niger 44 E6
Agadir, Morocco 44 B3
Agapa, Russia 25 B9
Agartala, India 37 H17
Agassiz, Canada 64 D4
Agats, Indonesia 33 F9
Agboville, Ivory C. 44 G4
Agde, France 18 E5
Agen, France 18 D4
Āgh Kand, Iran 39 B6
Aginskoye, Russia 25 D12
Agra, India 36 F10
Agri →, Italy 20 D7
Ağrı Dağı, Turkey 23 G7
Ağrı Karakose, Turkey 23 G7
Agrigento, Italy 20 F5
Agrinion, Greece 21 E9
Água Clara, Brazil 79 H8
Agua Prieta, Mexico 74 A3
Aguadas, Colombia 78 B3
Aguadilla, Puerto Rico 75 D11
Aguanish, Canada 63 B7
Aguanus →, Canada 63 B7
Aguarico →, Ecuador 78 D3
Aguas Blancas, Chile 80 A3
Aguascalientes, Mexico 74 C4
Aguilas, Spain 19 D5
Agulhas, C., S. Africa 48 E3
Agung, Indonesia 32 F5
Agusan →, Phil. 33 C7
Aha Mts., Botswana 48 B3
Ahaggar, Algeria 44 D6
Ahar, Iran 38 B5
Ahipara B., N.Z. 51 F4
Ahiri, India 36 K12
Ahmadabad, India 36 H8
Aḥmadābād, Khorāsān, Iran 39 C9
Aḥmadābād, Khorāsān, Iran 39 C8
Aḥmadī, Iran 39 E8
Ahmadnagar, India 36 K9
Ahmadpur, Pakistan 36 E7
Ahmedabad = Ahmadabad, India 36 H8
Ahmednagar = Ahmadnagar, India 36 K9
Ahram, Iran 39 D6
Āhū, Iran 39 C6
Ahvāz, Iran 39 D6
Ahvenanmaa = Åland, Finland 9 F19
Aḥwar, Yemen 40 E4
Aichi □, Japan 29 G8
Aigues-Mortes, France 18 E6
Aihui, China 31 A7
Aija, Peru 78 E3
Aikawa, Japan 28 E9
Aiken, U.S.A. 69 J5
Aillik, Canada 63 A8
Ailsa Craig, U.K. 12 F3
'Ailūn, Jordan 41 C4
Aim, Russia 25 D14
Aimere, Indonesia 33 F6
Aimorés, Brazil 79 G10
Aïn Beïda, Algeria 44 A6
Aïn Ben Tili, Mauritania 44 C3
Aïn-Sefra, Algeria 44 B4
'Ain Sudr, Egypt 41 F2
Ainabo, Somali Rep. 40 F4
Ainaži, Latvia 9 H21
Ainsworth, U.S.A. 70 D5
Aïr, Niger 44 E6
Airdrie, U.K. 12 F5
Aire →, U.K. 10 D7
Airlie Beach, Australia 54 C4
Aisne →, France 18 B5
Aitkin, U.S.A. 70 B8
Aiud, Romania 17 E12
Aix-en-Provence, France 18 E6
Aix-la-Chapelle = Aachen, Germany 16 C4
Aix-les-Bains, France 18 D6
Aiyansh, Canada 64 B3
Aiyion, Greece 21 E10
Aizawl, India 37 H18
Aizkraukle, Latvia 9 H21
Aizpute, Latvia 9 H19
Aizuwakamatsu, Japan 28 F9
Ajaccio, France 18 F8
Ajanta Ra., India 36 J9
Ajari Rep. = Ajaria □, Georgia 23 F7
Ajaria □, Georgia 23 F7
Ajdâbiyah, Libya 45 B9
Ajka, Hungary 17 E9
'Ajmān, U.A.E. 39 E7
Ajmer, India 36 F9
Ajo, U.S.A. 73 K7
Ajo, C. de, Spain 19 A4
Akabira, Japan 28 C11
Akaroa, N.Z. 51 K4
Akashi, Japan 29 G7
Akelamo, Indonesia 33 D7
Aketi, Zaïre 46 D4
Akharnaí, Greece 21 E10
Akhelóös →, Greece 21 E9
Akhisar, Turkey 21 E12
Akhmîm, Egypt 45 C11
Aki, Japan 29 H6
Akimiski I., Canada 62 B3
Akita, Japan 28 E10
Akita □, Japan 28 E10
Akjoujt, Mauritania 44 E2
Akkeshi, Japan 28 C12
'Akko, Israel 41 C4
Akkol, Kazakhstan 24 E8
Aklavik, Canada 60 B6
Akmolinsk = Aqmola, Kazakhstan 24 D8
Akō, Japan 29 G7
Akobo →, Ethiopia 45 G11
Akola, India 36 J10
Akordat, Eritrea 45 E12
Akpatok I., Canada 61 B13
Åkrahamn, Norway 9 G11
Akranes, Iceland 8 D2
Akreïjit, Mauritania 44 E3
Akron, Colo., U.S.A. 70 E3
Akron, Ohio, U.S.A. 68 E5
Aksai Chin, India 36 B11
Aksarka, Russia 24 C7
Aksay, Kazakhstan 22 D9
Aksenovo Zilovskoye, Russia 25 D12
Aksu, China 30 B3
Aksum, Ethiopia 45 F12
Aktogay, Kazakhstan 24 E8
Aktsyabrski, Belarus 17 B15
Aktyubinsk = Aqtöbe, Kazakhstan 23 D10
Aku, Nigeria 44 G6
Akure, Nigeria 44 G6
Akureyri, Iceland 8 D4
Akuseki-Shima, Japan 29 K4
Akyab = Sittwe, Burma 37 J18
Al 'Adan, Yemen 40 E4
Al Aḥsā, Si. Arabia 39 E6
Al Ajfar, Si. Arabia 38 E4
Al Amādīyah, Iraq 38 B4
Al Amārah, Iraq 38 D5
Al 'Aqabah, Jordan 41 F4
Al Arak, Syria 38 C3
Al 'Aramah, Si. Arabia 38 E5
Al Arṭāwīyah, Si. Arabia 38 E5
Al 'Āṣimah □, Jordan 41 D5
Al' Assāfīyah, Si. Arabia 38 D3
Al 'Ayn, Oman 39 E7
Al 'Ayn, Si. Arabia 38 E3
Al A'ẓamīyah, Iraq 38 C5
Al 'Azīzīyah, Iraq 38 C5
Al Bāb, Syria 38 B3
Al Bad', Si. Arabia 38 D2
Al Bādī, Iraq 38 C4
Al Baḥrah, Kuwait 38 D5
Al Balqā' □, Jordan 41 C4
Al Bārūk, J., Lebanon 41 B4
Al Başrah, Iraq 38 D5
Al Baṭḥā, Iraq 38 D5
Al Batrūn, Lebanon 41 A4
Al Bayḍā, Libya 45 B9
Al Biqā □, Lebanon 41 A5
Al Bi'r, Si. Arabia 38 D3
Al Bu'ayrāt al Ḥasūn, Libya 45 B8
Al Burayj, Syria 41 A5
Al Fallūjah, Iraq 38 C4
Al Fāw, Iraq 39 D6
Al Fujayrah, U.A.E. 39 E8
Al Ghadaf, W. →, Jordan 41 D5
Al Ghammās, Iraq 38 D5
Al Hābah, Si. Arabia 38 E5
Al Ḥadīthah, Iraq 38 C4
Al Ḥadīthah, Si. Arabia 38 D3
Al Ḥājānah, Syria 41 B5
Al Ḥāmad, Si. Arabia 38 D3
Al Hamdānīyah, Syria 38 C3
Al Ḥamīdīyah, Syria 41 A4
Al Ḥammār, Iraq 38 D5
Al Ḥamrā', Si. Arabia 38 E3
Al Ḥarīr, W. →, Syria 41 C4
Al Ḥasā, W. →, Jordan 41 D4
Al Ḥasakah, Syria 38 B4
Al Ḥawrah, Yemen 40 E4
Al Ḥaydān, W. →, Jordan 41 D4
Al Ḥayy, Iraq 38 C5
Al Ḥijāz, Si. Arabia 40 B2
Al Ḥillah, Iraq 38 C5
Al Ḥillah, Si. Arabia 40 C4
Al Hirmil, Lebanon 41 A5
Al Hoceïma, Morocco 44 A4
Al Ḥudaydah, Yemen 40 E3
Al Hufūf, Si. Arabia 39 E6
Al Ḥumayḍah, Si. Arabia 38 D2
Al Ḥunayy, Si. Arabia 39 E6
Al Īsāwīyah, Si. Arabia 38 D3
Al Ittihad = Madīnat ash Sha'b, Yemen 40 E3
Al Jafr, Jordan 41 E5
Al Jaghbūb, Libya 45 C9
Al Jahrah, Kuwait 38 D5
Al Jalāmīd, Si. Arabia 38 D3
Al Jamalīyah, Qatar 39 E6
Al Janūb □, Lebanon 41 B4
Al Jawf, Libya 45 D9
Al Jawf, Si. Arabia 38 D3
Al Jazirah, Iraq 38 C5
Al Jazirah, Libya 45 C9
Al Jithāmīyah, Si. Arabia 38 E4
Al Jubayl, Si. Arabia 39 E6
Al Jubaylah, Si. Arabia 38 E5
Al Jubb, Si. Arabia 38 E4
Al Junaynah, Sudan 45 F9
Al Kabā'ish, Iraq 38 D5
Al Karak, Jordan 41 D4
Al Karak □, Jordan 41 E5
Al Kāzim Tyah, Iraq 38 C5
Al Khalīl, West Bank 41 D4
Al Khawr, Qatar 39 E6
Al Khiḍr, Iraq 38 D5
Al Khiyām, Lebanon 41 B4
Al Kiswah, Syria 41 B5
Al Kufrah, Libya 45 D9
Al Kuhayfīyah, Si. Arabia 38 E4
Al Kūt, Iraq 38 C5
Al Kuwayt, Kuwait 38 D5
Al Labwah, Lebanon 41 A5
Al Lādhiqīyah, Syria 38 C2
Al Liwā', Oman 39 E8
Al Luḥayyah, Yemen 40 D3
Al Madīnah, Iraq 38 D5
Al Madīnah, Si. Arabia 40 C2
Al-Mafraq, Jordan 41 C5
Al Maḥmūdīyah, Iraq 38 C5
Al Majma'ah, Si. Arabia 38 E5
Al Makhruq, W. →, Jordan 41 D6
Al Makḥūl, Si. Arabia 38 E4
Al Manāmah, Bahrain 39 E6
Al Maqwa', Kuwait 38 D5
Al Marj, Libya 45 B9
Al Maṭlā, Kuwait 38 D5
Al Mawjib, W. →, Jordan 41 D4
Al Mawşil, Iraq 38 B4
Al Mayādin, Syria 38 C4
Al Mazār, Jordan 41 D4
Al Midhnab, Si. Arabia 38 E5
Al Minā', Lebanon 41 A4
Al Miqdādīyah, Iraq 38 C5
Al Mubarraz, Si. Arabia 39 E6
Al Mughayrā', U.A.E. 39 E7
Al Muḥarraq, Bahrain 39 E6
Al Mukallā, Yemen 40 E4
Al Mukhā, Yemen 40 E3
Al Musayjīd, Si. Arabia 38 E3
Al Musayyib, Iraq 38 C5
Al Muwayliḥ, Si. Arabia 38 E2
Al Qā'im, Iraq 38 C4
Al Qalībah, Si. Arabia 38 D3
Al Qaryatayn, Syria 41 A6
Al Qaşabát, Libya 45 B7
Al Qaṭ'ā, Syria 38 C4
Al Qaṭīf, Si. Arabia 39 E6
Al Qatrānah, Jordan 41 D5
Al Qaṭrūn, Libya 45 D8
Al Qayṣūmah, Si. Arabia 38 D5
Al Quds = Jerusalem, Israel 41 D4
Al Qunaytirah, Syria 41 C4
Al Qurnah, Iraq 38 D5
Al Quṣayr, Iraq 38 D5
Al Quṣayr, Syria 41 A5
Al Qutayfah, Syria 41 B5
Al' Uḍaylīyah, Si. Arabia 39 E6
Al 'Ulā, Si. Arabia 38 E3
Al Uqaylah ash Sharqīgah, Libya 45 B8
Al Uqayr, Si. Arabia 39 E6
Al 'Uwaynid, Si. Arabia 38 E5
Al 'Uwayqīlah, Si. Arabia 38 D4
Al 'Uyūn, Si. Arabia 38 E4
Al 'Uyūn, Si. Arabia 38 E3
Al Wajh, Si. Arabia 38 E3
Al Wakrah, Qatar 39 E6
Al Wannān, Si. Arabia 39 E6
Al Waqbah, Si. Arabia 38 D5
Al Wari'āh, Si. Arabia 38 E5
Al Wusayl, Qatar 39 E6
Ala Tau Shankou = Dzhungarskiye Vorota, Kazakhstan 30 B3
Alabama □, U.S.A. 69 J2
Alabama →, U.S.A. 69 K2
Alaçam Dağları, Turkey 21 E13
Alagoa Grande, Brazil 79 E11
Alagoas □, Brazil 79 E11
Alagoinhas, Brazil 79 F11
Alajuela, Costa Rica 75 E8
Alakamisy, Madag. 49 C8
Alakurtti, Russia 22 A5
Alameda, U.S.A. 73 J10
Alamo, U.S.A. 73 H6
Alamogordo, U.S.A. 73 K11
Alamosa, U.S.A. 73 H11
Åland, Finland 9 F19
Ålands hav, Sweden 9 F18
Alandur, India 36 N12
Alania = North Ossetia □, Russia 23 F7
Alanya, Turkey 23 G5
Alaotra, Farihin', Madag. 49 B8
Alapayevsk, Russia 24 D7
Alaşehir, Turkey 21 E13
Alaska □, U.S.A. 60 B5
Alaska, G. of, Pac. Oc. 60 C5
Alaska Highway, Canada 64 B3
Alaska Peninsula, U.S.A. 60 C4
Alaska Range, U.S.A. 60 B4
Älät, Azerbaijan 23 G8
Alatyr, Russia 22 D8
Alausi, Ecuador 78 D3
Alava, C., U.S.A. 72 B1
Alavus, Finland 9 E20
Alawoona, Australia 55 E3
'Alayh, Lebanon 41 B4
Alba, Italy 20 B3
Alba-Iulia, Romania 17 E12
Albacete, Spain 19 C5
Albacutya, L., Australia 55 F3
Albania ■, Europe 21 D9
Albany, Australia 53 G2
Albany, Ga., U.S.A. 69 K3
Albany, Minn., U.S.A. 70 C7
Albany, N.Y., U.S.A. 68 D9
Albany, Oreg., U.S.A. 72 D2
Albany, Tex., U.S.A. 71 J5
Albany →, Canada 62 B3
Albardón, Argentina 80 C3
Albatross B., Australia 54 A3
Albemarle, U.S.A. 69 H5
Albemarle Sd., U.S.A. 69 H7
Alberche →, Spain 19 C3
Albert, L., Australia 55 F2
Albert Canyon, Canada 64 C5
Albert Edward Ra., Australia 52 C4
Albert L., Africa 46 D6
Albert Lea, U.S.A. 70 D8
Albert Nile →, Uganda 46 D6
Alberta □, Canada 64 C6
Albertinia, S. Africa 48 E3
Alberton, Canada 63 C7
Albertville = Kalemie, Zaïre 46 F5
Albertville, France 18 D7
Albi, France 18 E5
Albia, U.S.A. 70 E8
Albina, Surinam 79 B8
Albina, Ponta, Angola 48 B1
Albion, Idaho, U.S.A. 72 E7
Albion, Mich., U.S.A. 68 D3
Albion, Nebr., U.S.A. 70 E5
Alborán, Medit. S. 19 E4
Ålborg, Denmark 9 H13
Alborz, Reshteh-ye Kūhhā-ye, Iran 39 C7
Albreda, Canada 64 C5
Albuquerque, U.S.A. 73 J10
Albury, Australia 55 F4
Alcalá de Henares, Spain 19 B4
Alcalá la Real, Spain 19 D4
Alcamo, Italy 20 F5
Alcañiz, Spain 19 B5
Alcântara, Brazil 79 D10
Alcántara, Embalse de, Spain 19 C2
Alcantara L., Canada 65 A7
Alcantarilla, Spain 19 D5
Alcaraz, Sierra de, Spain 19 C4
Alcaudete, Spain 19 D3
Alcázar de San Juan, Spain 19 C4
Alchevsk, Ukraine 23 E6
Alcira, Spain 19 C5
Alcoa, U.S.A. 69 H4
Alcova, U.S.A. 72 E10
Alcoy, Spain 19 C5
Aldabra Is., Seychelles 43 G8
Aldan, Russia 25 D13
Aldan →, Russia 25 C13
Aldeburgh, U.K. 11 E9
Alder, U.S.A. 72 D7
Alderney, U.K. 11 H5
Aldershot, U.K. 11 F7
Aledo, U.S.A. 70 E9
Aleg, Mauritania 44 E2
Alegrete, Brazil 80 B5
Aleisk, Russia 24 D9
Aleksandriya = Oleksandriya, Ukraine 17 C14
Aleksandrovsk-Sakhalinskiy, Russia 25 D15
Aleksandrovskiy Zavod, Russia 25 D12
Aleksandrovskoye, Russia 24 C8
Alemania, Argentina 80 B3
Alençon, France 18 B4
Alenuihaha Channel, U.S.A. 66 H17
Aleppo = Ḥalab, Syria 38 B3
Alert Bay, Canada 64 C3
Alès, France 18 D6
Alessándria, Italy 20 B3
Ålesund, Norway 9 E12
Aleutian Is., Pac. Oc. 60 C2
Aleutian Trench, Pac. Oc. 56 B10
Alexander, U.S.A. 70 B3
Alexander, Mt., Australia 53 E3
Alexander Arch., U.S.A. 64 B2
Alexander Bay, S. Africa 48 D2
Alexander City, U.S.A. 69 J3
Alexander I., Antarctica 5 C17
Alexandra, Australia 55 F4
Alexandra, N.Z. 51 L2
Alexandra Falls, Canada 64 A5
Alexandretta = İskenderun, Turkey 23 G6
Alexandria = El Iskandarîya, Egypt 45 B10
Alexandria, Australia 54 B2
Alexandria, B.C., Canada 64 C4
Alexandria, Ont., Canada 62 C5
Alexandria, Romania 17 G13
Alexandria, S. Africa 48 E4

Arapahoe

Alexandria, Ind., U.S.A. 68 E3
Alexandria, La., U.S.A. 71 K8
Alexandria, Minn., U.S.A. 70 C7
Alexandria, S. Dak., U.S.A. 70 D6
Alexandria, Va., U.S.A. 68 F7
Alexandria Bay, U.S.A. 68 C8
Alexandrina, L., Australia 55 F2
Alexandroúpolis, Greece 21 D11
Alexis →, Canada 63 B8
Alexis Creek, Canada 64 C4
Alford, U.K. 12 D6
Alfreton, U.K. 10 D6
Alga, Kazakhstan 23 E10
Algård, Norway 9 G11
Algarve, Portugal 19 D1
Algeciras, Spain 19 D3
Algemesí, Spain 19 C5
Alger, Algeria 44 A5
Algeria ■, Africa 44 C5
Alghero, Italy 20 D3
Algiers = Alger, Algeria 44 A5
Algoa B., S. Africa 48 E4
Algoma, U.S.A. 68 C2
Algona, U.S.A. 70 D7
Alhambra, U.S.A. 73 J4
Alhucemas = Al Hoceïma, Morocco 44 A4
'Alī al Gharbī, Iraq 38 C5
Alī ash Sharqī, Iraq 38 C5
'Alī Khēl, Afghan. 36 C6
Alī Shāh, Iran 38 B5
'Alīābād, Khorāsān, Iran 39 C8
'Alīābād, Kordestān, Iran 38 C5
'Alīābād, Yazd, Iran 39 D7
Aliağa, Turkey 21 E12
Aliákmon →, Greece 21 D10
Alibo, Ethiopia 45 G12
Alicante, Spain 19 C5
Alice, S. Africa 48 E4
Alice, U.S.A. 71 M5
Alice →, Queens., Australia 54 C3
Alice →, Queens., Australia 54 B3
Alice Arm, Canada 64 B3
Alice Downs, Australia 52 C4
Alice Springs, Australia 54 C1
Alicedale, S. Africa 48 E4
Aliceville, U.S.A. 69 J1
Alick Cr. →, Australia 54 C3
Alida, Canada 65 D8
Aligarh, India 36 F11
Alīgūdarz, Iran 39 C6
Alingsås, Sweden 9 H15
Alipur, Pakistan 36 E7
Alipur Duar, India 37 F16
Aliquippa, U.S.A. 68 E5
Alitus = Alytus, Lithuania 9 J21
Aliwal North, S. Africa 48 E4
Alix, Canada 64 C6
Aljustrel, Portugal 19 D1
Alkmaar, Neths. 15 B4
All American Canal, U.S.A. 73 K6
Allahabad, India 37 G12
Allakh-Yun, Russia 25 C14
Allan, Canada 65 C7
Allanmyo, Burma 37 K19
Allanridge, S. Africa 48 D4
Allanwater, Canada 62 B1
Allegan, U.S.A. 68 D3
Allegheny →, U.S.A. 68 E6
Allegheny Plateau, U.S.A. 68 G6
Allen, Bog of, Ireland 13 C4
Allen, L., Ireland 13 B3
Allentown, U.S.A. 68 E8
Alleppey, India 36 Q10
Aller →, Germany 16 B5
Alliance, Nebr., U.S.A. 70 D3
Alliance, Ohio, U.S.A. 68 E5
Allier →, France 18 C5
Alliston, Canada 62 D4
Alloa, U.K. 12 E5
Allora, Australia 55 D5
Alluitsup Paa = Sydprøven, Greenland 4 C5
Alma, Canada 63 C5
Alma, Ga., U.S.A. 69 K4
Alma, Kans., U.S.A. 70 F6
Alma, Mich., U.S.A. 68 D3
Alma, Nebr., U.S.A. 70 E5
Alma, Wis., U.S.A. 70 C9
Alma Ata = Almaty, Kazakhstan 24 E8
Almada, Portugal 19 C1
Almaden, Australia 54 B3
Almadén, Spain 19 C3
Almanor, L., U.S.A. 72 F3
Almansa, Spain 19 C5
Almanzor, Pico del Moro, Spain 19 B3
Almanzora →, Spain 19 D5
Almaty, Kazakhstan 24 E8
Almazán, Spain 19 B4
Almeirim, Brazil 79 D8
Almelo, Neths. 15 B6
Almendralejo, Spain 19 C2
Almería, Spain 19 D4
Almora, India 36 E11
Alnwick, U.K. 10 B6
Alon, Burma 37 H19
Alor, Indonesia 33 F6
Alor Setar, Malaysia 34 N13
Aloysius, Mt., Australia 53 E4
Alpena, U.S.A. 68 C4
Alpha, Australia 54 C4
Alphonse, Seychelles 35 E4
Alpine, Ariz., U.S.A. 73 K9
Alpine, Tex., U.S.A. 71 K3
Alps, Europe 16 E5
Alroy Downs, Australia 54 B2
Alsace, France 18 B7
Alsask, Canada 65 C7
Alsásua, Spain 19 A4
Alsten, Norway 8 D15
Alta, Norway 8 B20
Alta Gracia, Argentina 80 C4
Alta Lake, Canada 64 C4
Altaelva →, Norway 8 B20
Altafjorden, Norway 8 A20
Altagracia, Venezuela 78 A4
Altai = Aerhtai Shan, Mongolia 30 B4
Altamaha →, U.S.A. 69 K5
Altamira, Brazil 79 D8
Altamura, Italy 20 D7
Altanbulag, Mongolia 30 A5
Altavista, U.S.A. 68 G6
Altay, China 30 B3
Altea, Spain 19 C5
Alto Araguaia, Brazil 79 G8
Alto Molocue, Mozam. 47 H7
Alton, U.S.A. 70 F9
Alton Downs, Australia 55 D2
Altoona, U.S.A. 68 E6
Altūn Kūprī, Iraq 38 C5
Altun Shan, China 30 C3
Alturas, U.S.A. 72 F3
Altus, U.S.A. 71 H5
Alūksne, Latvia 9 H22
Alùla, Somali Rep. 40 E5
Alusi, Indonesia 33 F8
Al'Uzayr, Iraq 38 D5
Alva, U.S.A. 71 G5
Alvarado, Mexico 74 D5
Alvarado, U.S.A. 71 J6
Alvear, Argentina 80 B5
Alvesta, Sweden 9 H16
Alvie, Australia 55 F3
Alvin, U.S.A. 71 L7
Älvkarleby, Sweden 9 F17
Älvsbyn, Sweden 8 D19
Alwar, India 36 F10
Alxa Zuoqi, China 30 C5
Alyaskitovyy, Russia 25 C15
Alyata = Älät, Azerbaijan 23 G8
Alyth, U.K. 12 E5
Alytus, Lithuania 9 J21
Alzada, U.S.A. 70 C2
Am Dam, Chad 45 F9
Am-Timan, Chad 45 F9
Amadeus, L., Australia 53 D5
Amâdi, Sudan 45 G11
Amadi, Zaïre 46 D5
Amadjuak, Canada 61 B12
Amadjuak L., Canada 61 B12
Amagasaki, Japan 29 G7
Amakusa-Shotō, Japan 29 H5
Åmål, Sweden 9 G15
Amaliás, Greece 21 F9
Amalner, India 36 J9
Amambay, Cordillera de, S. Amer. 80 A5
Amami-Guntō, Japan 29 L4
Amami-Ō-Shima, Japan 29 L4
Amangeldy, Kazakhstan 24 D7
Amapá, Brazil 79 C8
Amapá □, Brazil 79 C8
Amarante, Brazil 79 E10
Amaranth, Canada 65 C9
Amargosa, Brazil 79 F11
Amarillo, U.S.A. 71 H4
Amaro, Mte., Italy 20 C6
Amatikulu, S. Africa 49 D5
Amazon = Amazonas →, S. Amer. 79 C9
Amazonas □, Brazil 78 E6
Amazonas →, S. Amer. 79 C9
Ambahakily, Madag. 49 C7
Ambala, India 36 D10
Ambalavao, Madag. 49 C8
Ambalindum, Australia 54 C2
Ambam, Cameroon 46 D2
Ambanja, Madag. 49 A8
Ambarchik, Russia 25 C17
Ambarijeby, Madag. 49 A8
Ambaro, Helodranon', Madag. 49 A8
Ambartsevo, Russia 24 D9
Ambato, Ecuador 78 D3
Ambato Boeny, Madag. 49 B8
Ambatofinandrahana, Madag. 49 C8
Ambatolampy, Madag. 49 B8
Ambatondrazaka, Madag. 49 B8
Ambatosoratra, Madag. 49 B8
Ambenja, Madag. 49 B8
Amberg, Germany 16 D6
Ambergris Cay, Belize 74 D7
Amberley, N.Z. 51 K4
Ambikapur, India 37 H13
Ambilobé, Madag. 49 A8
Ambinanindrano, Madag. 49 C8
Ambleside, U.K. 10 C5
Ambo, Peru 78 F3
Ambodifototra, Madag. 49 B8
Ambodilazana, Madag. 49 B8
Ambohimahasoa, Madag. 49 C8
Ambohimanga, Madag. 49 C8
Ambohitra, Madag. 49 A8
Amboise, France 18 C4
Ambon, Indonesia 33 E7
Ambositra, Madag. 49 C8
Ambovombé, Madag. 49 D8
Amboy, U.S.A. 73 J6
Amboyna I., S. China Sea 32 C4
Ambriz, Angola 46 F2
Amby, Australia 55 D4
Amchitka I., U.S.A. 60 C1
Amderma, Russia 24 C7
Ameca, Mexico 74 C4
Ameland, Neths. 15 A5
Amen, Russia 25 C18
American Falls, U.S.A. 72 E7
American Falls Reservoir, U.S.A. 72 E7
American Highland, Antarctica 5 D6
American Samoa ■, Pac. Oc. 51 B13
Americus, U.S.A. 69 J3
Amersfoort, Neths. 15 B5
Amersfoort, S. Africa 49 D4
Amery, Australia 53 F2
Amery, Canada 65 B10
Amery Ice Shelf, Antarctica 5 C6
Ames, U.S.A. 70 E8
Amga, Russia 25 C14
Amga →, Russia 25 C14
Amgu, Russia 25 E14
Amgun →, Russia 25 D14
Amherst, Burma 37 L20
Amherst, Canada 63 C7
Amherst, U.S.A. 71 H3
Amherstburg, Canada 62 D3
Amiata, Mte., Italy 20 C4
Amiens, France 18 B5
Amīrābād, Iran 38 C5
Amirante Is., Seychelles 35 E4
Amisk L., Canada 65 C8
Amite, U.S.A. 71 K9
Amlwch, U.K. 10 D3
'Ammān, Jordan 41 D4
Ammanford, U.K. 11 F3
Ammassalik = Angmagssalik, Greenland 4 C6
Āmol, Iran 39 B7
Amorgós, Greece 21 F11
Amory, U.S.A. 69 J1
Amos, Canada 62 C4
Åmot, Norway 9 G13
Amoy = Xiamen, China 31 D6
Ampanihy, Madag. 49 C7
Ampasindava, Helodranon', Madag. 49 A8
Ampasindava, Saikanosy, Madag. 49 A8
Ampenan, Indonesia 32 F5
Amper →, Germany 16 D6
Ampotaka, Madag. 49 D7
Ampoza, Madag. 49 C7
Amqui, Canada 63 C6
Amravati, India 36 J10
Amreli, India 36 J7
Amritsar, India 36 D9
Amroha, India 36 E11
Amsterdam, Neths. 15 B4
Amsterdam, U.S.A. 68 D8
Amsterdam, I., Ind. Oc. 35 H6
Amstetten, Austria 16 D8
Amudarya →, Uzbekistan 24 E6
Amundsen Gulf, Canada 60 A7
Amundsen Sea, Antarctica 5 D15
Amuntai, Indonesia 32 E5
Amur →, Russia 25 D15
Amurang, Indonesia 33 D6
Amuri Pass, N.Z. 51 K4
Amursk, Russia 25 D14
Amurzet, Russia 25 E14
Amyderya = Amudarya →, Uzbekistan 24 E6
An Nabatīyah at Tahta, Lebanon 41 B4
An Nabk, Si. Arabia 38 D3
An Nabk, Syria 41 A5
An Nabk Abū Qaşr, Si. Arabia 38 D3
An Nafūd, Si. Arabia 38 D4
An Najaf, Iraq 38 C5
An Nāşirīyah, Iraq 38 D5
An Nhon, Vietnam 34 F10
An Nu'ayrīyah, Si. Arabia 39 E6
An Nuwaybi', W. →, Si. Arabia 41 F3
An Uaimh, Ireland 13 C5
Anabar →, Russia 25 B12
'Anabtā, West Bank 41 C4
Anaconda, U.S.A. 72 C7
Anacortes, U.S.A. 72 B2
Anadarko, U.S.A. 71 H5
Anadolu, Turkey 23 G5
Anadyr, Russia 25 C18
Anadyr →, Russia 25 C18
Anadyrskiy Zaliv, Russia 25 C19
'Ānah, Iraq 38 C4
Anaheim, U.S.A. 73 K5
Anahim Lake, Canada 64 C3
Anakapalle, India 37 L13
Anakie, Australia 54 C4
Analalava, Madag. 49 A8
Anambas, Kepulauan, Indonesia 32 D3
Anambas Is. = Anambas, Kepulauan, Indonesia 32 D3
Anamoose, U.S.A. 70 B4
Anamosa, U.S.A. 70 D9
Anamur, Turkey 23 G5
Anan, Japan 29 H7
Anantnag, India 36 C9
Ananyiv, Ukraine 17 E15
Anápolis, Brazil 79 G9
Anār, Iran 39 D7
Anārak, Iran 39 C7
Anatolia = Anadolu, Turkey 23 G5
Anatone, U.S.A. 72 C5
Anatsogno, Madag. 49 C7
Añatuya, Argentina 80 B4
Anaunethad L., Canada 65 A8
Anaye, Niger 45 E7
Anchorage, U.S.A. 60 B5
Ancohuma, Nevada, Bolivia 78 G5
Ancón, Peru 78 F3
Ancona, Italy 20 C5
Ancud, Chile 80 E2
Ancud, G. de, Chile 80 E2
Anda, China 31 B7
Andado, Australia 54 D2
Andalgalá, Argentina 80 B3
Åndalsnes, Norway 9 E12
Andalucía □, Spain 19 D3
Andalusia, U.S.A. 69 K2
Andalusia = Andalucía □, Spain 19 D3
Andaman Is., Ind. Oc. 34 F2
Andaman Sea, Ind. Oc. 34 F3
Andaman Str., India 34 F2
Andara, Namibia 48 B3
Andenes, Norway 8 B17
Andenne, Belgium 15 D5
Anderson, Calif., U.S.A. 72 F2
Anderson, Ind., U.S.A. 68 E3
Anderson, Mo., U.S.A. 71 G7
Anderson, S.C., U.S.A. 69 H4
Anderson →, Canada 60 B7
Andes = Andes, Cord. de los, S. Amer. 78 F4
Andes, S. Amer. 78 F3
Andes, Cord. de los, S. Amer. 78 F4
Andfjorden, Norway 8 B17
Andhra Pradesh □, India 36 L11
Andijon, Uzbekistan 24 E8
Andikíthira, Greece 21 G10
Andīmeshk, Iran 39 C6
Andizhan = Andijon, Uzbekistan 24 E8
Andoany, Madag. 49 A8
Andorra ■, Europe 19 A6
Andorra La Vella, Andorra 19 A6
Andover, U.K. 11 F6
Andøya, Norway 8 B16
Andrahary, Mt., Madag. 49 A8
Andramasina, Madag. 49 B8
Andranopasy, Madag. 49 C7
Andreanof Is., U.S.A. 60 C2
Andrewilla, Australia 55 D2
Andrews, S.C., U.S.A. 69 J6
Andrews, Tex., U.S.A. 71 J3
Ándria, Italy 20 D7
Andriba, Madag. 49 B8
Androka, Madag. 49 C7
Andropov = Rybinsk, Russia 22 C6
Ándros, Greece 21 F11
Andros I., Bahamas 75 C9
Andselv, Norway 8 B18
Andújar, Spain 19 C3
Andulo, Angola 46 G3
Aného, Togo 44 G5
Aneto, Pico de, Spain 19 A6
Ang Thong, Thailand 34 E6
Angamos, Punta, Chile 80 A2
Angara →, Russia 25 D10
Angarsk, Russia 25 D11
Angas Downs, Australia 53 E5
Angas Hills, Australia 52 D4
Angaston, Australia 55 E2
Ånge, Sweden 9 E16
Angeles, Phil. 33 A6
Ängelholm, Sweden 9 H15
Angellala, Australia 55 D4
Angels Camp, U.S.A. 73 G3
Ångermanälven →, Sweden 8 E17
Ångermanland, Sweden 8 E18
Angers, France 18 C3
Ängesån →, Sweden 8 C20
Angikuni L., Canada 65 A9
Angkor, Cambodia 34 F7
Anglesey, U.K. 10 D3
Angleton, U.S.A. 71 L7
Angmagssalik, Greenland 4 C6
Ango, Zaïre 46 D5
Angola, U.S.A. 68 E3
Angola ■, Africa 47 G3
Angoon, U.S.A. 64 B2
Angoulême, France 18 D4
Angoumois, France 18 D3
Angra dos Reis, Brazil 80 A8
Angren, Uzbekistan 24 E8
Anguilla ■, W. Indies 74 J18
Angurugu, Australia 54 A2
Angus, Braes of, U.K. 12 E5
Anholt, Denmark 9 H14
Anhui □, China 31 C6
Anhwei = Anhui □, China 31 C6
Anichab, Namibia 48 C1
Animas, U.S.A. 73 L9
Anin, Burma 34 E4
Anivorano, Madag. 49 B8
Anjalankoski, Finland 9 F22
Anjidiv I., India 36 M9
Anjou, France 18 C3
Anjozorobe, Madag. 49 B8
Anka, Nigeria 44 F6
Ankaboa, Tanjona, Madag. 49 C7
Ankang, China 31 C5
Ankara, Turkey 23 G5
Ankaramena, Madag. 49 C8
Ankazoabo, Madag. 49 C7
Ankazobe, Madag. 49 B8
Ankisabe, Madag. 49 B8
Ankoro, Zaïre 46 F5
Ann, C., U.S.A. 68 D10
Ann Arbor, U.S.A. 68 D4
Anna, U.S.A. 71 G10
Anna Plains, Australia 52 C3
Annaba, Algeria 44 A6
Annalee →, Ireland 13 B4
Annam = Trung-Phan, Vietnam 34 D10
Annamitique, Chaîne, Asia 34 D9
Annan, U.K. 12 G5
Annan →, U.K. 12 G5
Annapolis, U.S.A. 68 F7
Annapolis Royal, Canada 63 D6
Annean, L., Australia 53 E2
Annecy, France 18 D7
Anning, China 30 D5
Anningie, Australia 52 D5
Anniston, U.S.A. 69 J3
Annobón, Atl. Oc. 43 G4
Annotto Bay, Jamaica 74 J17
Annuello, Australia 55 E3
Anoka, U.S.A. 70 C8
Anorotsangana, Madag. 49 A8
Anqing, China 31 C6
Ansbach, Germany 16 D6
Anshan, China 31 B7
Anshun, China 30 D5
Ansirabe, Madag. 49 B8
Ansley, U.S.A. 70 E5
Anson, U.S.A. 71 J5
Anson B., Australia 52 B5
Ansongo, Mali 44 E5
Anstruther, U.K. 12 E6
Ansudu, Indonesia 33 E9
Antabamba, Peru 78 F4
Antakya, Turkey 23 G6
Antalaha, Madag. 49 A9
Antalya, Turkey 23 G5
Antalya Körfezi, Turkey 23 G5
Antananarivo, Madag. 49 B8
Antananarivo □, Madag. 49 B8
Antanimbaribe, Madag. 49 C7
Antarctic Pen., Antarctica 5 C18
Antarctica 5 E3
Antequera, Spain 19 D3
Antero, Mt., U.S.A. 73 G10
Anthony, Kans., U.S.A. 71 G5
Anthony, N. Mex., U.S.A. 73 K10
Anthony Lagoon, Australia 54 B2
Anti Atlas, Morocco 44 C3
Anti-Lebanon = Ash Sharqi, Al Jabal, Lebanon 41 B5
Antibes, France 18 E7
Anticosti, I. d', Canada 63 C7
Antigo, U.S.A. 70 C10
Antigonish, Canada 63 C7
Antigua, W. Indies 74 L20
Antigua & Barbuda ■, W. Indies 74 K20
Antilla, Cuba 75 C9
Antimony, U.S.A. 73 G8
Antioch, U.S.A. 72 G3
Antioquia, Colombia 78 B3
Antipodes Is., Pac. Oc. 56 M9
Antler, U.S.A. 70 A4
Antler →, Canada 65 D8
Antlers, U.S.A. 71 H7
Antofagasta, Chile 80 A2
Antofagasta de la Sierra, Argentina 80 B3
Anton, U.S.A. 71 J3
Anton Chico, U.S.A. 73 J11
Antongila, Helodrano, Madag. 49 B8
Antonibé, Madag. 49 B8
Antonibé, Presqu'île d', Madag. 49 A8
Antonina, Brazil 80 B7
Antonito, U.S.A. 73 H10
Antrim, U.K. 13 B5
Antrim □, U.K. 13 B5
Antrim, Mts. of, U.K. 13 B5
Antrim Plateau, Australia 52 C4
Antsalova, Madag. 49 B7
Antsiranana, Madag. 49 A8
Antsohihy, Madag. 49 A8
Antsohimbondrona Seranana, Madag. 49 A8
Antwerp = Antwerpen, Belgium 15 C4
Antwerpen, Belgium 15 C4
Antwerpen □, Belgium 15 C4
Anupgarh, India 36 E8
Anuradhapura, Sri Lanka 36 Q12
Anveh, Iran 39 E7
Anvers = Antwerpen, Belgium 15 C4
Anvers I., Antarctica 5 C17
Anxi, China 30 B4
Anxious B., Australia 55 E1
Anyang, China 31 C6
Anzhero-Sudzhensk, Russia 24 D9
Ánzio, Italy 20 D5
Aoga-Shima, Japan 29 H9
Aomori, Japan 28 D10
Aomori □, Japan 28 D10
Aosta, Italy 20 B2
Aoudéras, Niger 44 E6
Aoulef el Arab, Algeria 44 C5
Apache, U.S.A. 71 H5
Apalachee B., U.S.A. 69 L3
Apalachicola, U.S.A. 69 L3
Apalachicola →, U.S.A. 69 L3
Apaporis →, Colombia 78 D5
Aparri, Phil. 33 A6
Apátity, Russia 22 A5
Apeldoorn, Neths. 15 B5
Apennines = Appennini, Italy 20 B4
Apia, W. Samoa 51 A13
Apiacás, Serra dos, Brazil 78 E7
Aplao, Peru 78 G4
Apo, Mt., Phil. 33 C7
Apollonia = Marsá Susah, Libya 45 B9
Apolo, Bolivia 78 F5
Apostle Is., U.S.A. 70 B9
Apostolos Andreas, C., Cyprus 38 C2
Apoteri, Guyana 78 C7
Appalachian Mts., U.S.A. 68 G6
Appennini, Italy 20 B4
Appleby-in-Westmorland, U.K. 10 C5
Appleton, U.S.A. 68 C1
Approuague, Fr. Guiana 79 C8
Aprília, Italy 20 D5
Apucarana, Brazil 80 A6
Apure →, Venezuela 78 B5
Apurimac →, Peru 78 F4
Aqabah = Al 'Aqabah, Jordan 41 F4
'Aqabah, Khalīj al, Red Sea 38 D2
'Aqdā, Iran 39 C7
Aqīq, Sudan 45 E12
Aqmola, Kazakhstan 24 D8
Aqrah, Iraq 38 B4
Aqtöbe, Kazakhstan 23 D10
Aquidauana, Brazil 79 H7
Aquitain, Bassin, France 18 D3
Ar Rachidiya, Morocco 44 B4
Ar Rafid, Syria 41 C4
Ar Raḩḩālīyah, Iraq 38 C4
Ar Ramādī, Iraq 38 C4
Ar Ramthā, Jordan 41 C5
Ar Raqqah, Syria 38 C3
Ar Rass, Si. Arabia 38 E4
Ar Rifā'ī, Iraq 38 D5
Ar Riyāḑ, Si. Arabia 40 C4
Ar Ru'ays, Qatar 39 E6
Ar Rukhaymīyah, Iraq 38 D5
Ar Ruqayyidah, Si. Arabia 39 E6
Ar Ruşāfah, Syria 38 C3
Ar Rutbah, Iraq 38 C4
Ara, India 37 G14
'Arab, Bahr el →, Sudan 45 G10
'Arabābād, Iran 39 C8
Arabia, Asia 40 C4
Arabian Desert = Es Sahrâ' Esh Sharqîya, Egypt 45 C11
Arabian Gulf = Gulf, The, Asia 39 E6
Arabian Sea, Ind. Oc. 27 H10
Aracaju, Brazil 79 F11
Aracataca, Colombia 78 A4
Aracati, Brazil 79 D11
Araçatuba, Brazil 79 H8
Aracena, Spain 19 D2
Araçuaí, Brazil 79 G10
'Arad, Israel 41 D4
Arad, Romania 17 E11
Arada, Chad 45 F9
Arafura Sea, E. Indies 33 F8
Aragón □, Spain 19 B5
Aragón →, Spain 19 A5
Araguacema, Brazil 79 E9
Araguaia →, Brazil 79 E9
Araguari, Brazil 79 G9
Araguari →, Brazil 79 C9
Arak, Algeria 44 C5
Arāk, Iran 39 C6
Arakan Coast, Burma 37 K19
Arakan Yoma, Burma 37 K19
Araks = Aras, Rūd-e →, Azerbaijan 38 B5
Aral, Kazakhstan 24 E7
Aral Sea, Asia 24 E7
Aral Tengizi = Aral Sea, Asia 24 E7
Aralsk = Aral, Kazakhstan 24 E7
Aralskoye More = Aral Sea, Asia 24 E7
Aramac, Australia 54 C4
Aran I., Ireland 13 B3
Aran Is., Ireland 13 C2
Aranda de Duero, Spain 19 B4
Arandān, Iran 38 C5
Aranjuez, Spain 19 B4
Aranos, Namibia 48 C2
Aransas Pass, U.S.A. 71 M6
Araouane, Mali 44 E4
Arapahoe, U.S.A. 70 E5

Arapiraca, *Brazil* 79 E11
Arapongas, *Brazil* 80 A6
Ar'ar, *Si. Arabia* 38 D4
Araranguá, *Brazil* 80 B7
Araraquara, *Brazil* ... 79 H9
Ararat, *Australia* 55 F3
Ararat, Mt. = Ağrı Dağı,
 Turkey 23 G7
Araripe, Chapada do,
 Brazil 79 E11
Aras, Rûd-e →,
 Azerbaijan 38 B5
Arauca, *Colombia* 78 B4
Arauca →, *Venezuela* . 78 B5
Arauco, *Chile* 80 D2
Araxá, *Brazil* 79 G9
Araya, Pen. de,
 Venezuela 78 A6
Arbat, *Iraq* 38 C5
Arbatax, *Italy* 20 E3
Arbīl, *Iraq* 38 B5
Arborfield, *Canada* ... 65 C8
Arborg, *Canada* 65 C9
Arbroath, *U.K.* 12 E6
Arbuckle, *U.S.A.* 72 G2
Arcachon, *France* 18 D3
Arcadia, *Fla., U.S.A.* .. 69 M5
Arcadia, *La., U.S.A.* .. 71 J8
Arcadia, *Nebr., U.S.A.* . 70 E5
Arcadia, *Wis., U.S.A.* . 70 C9
Arcata, *U.S.A.* 72 F1
Archangel =
 Arkhangelsk, *Russia* 22 B7
Archer →, *Australia* . 54 A3
Archer B., *Australia* . 54 A3
Arcila = Asilah,
 Morocco 44 A3
Arckaringa, *Australia* . 55 D1
Arckaringa Cr. →,
 Australia 55 D2
Arco, *U.S.A.* 72 E7
Arcola, *Canada* 65 D8
Arcos de la Frontera,
 Spain 19 D3
Arcot, *India* 36 N11
Arcoverde, *Brazil* 79 E11
Arctic Bay, *Canada* .. 61 A11
Arctic Ocean, *Arctic* . 4 B18
Arctic Red River,
 Canada 60 B6
Arda →, *Bulgaria* ... 21 D12
Ardabīl, *Iran* 39 B6
Ardakān = Sepīdān,
 Iran 39 D7
Ardee, *Ireland* 13 C5
Ardenne, *Belgium* ... 15 E5
Ardennes = Ardenne,
 Belgium 15 E5
Ardestān, *Iran* 39 C7
Ardgour, *U.K.* 12 E3
Ardlethan, *Australia* . 55 E4
Ardmore, *Australia* .. 54 C2
Ardmore, *Okla., U.S.A.* 71 H6
Ardmore, *S. Dak.,*
 U.S.A. 70 D3
Ardnacrusha, *Ireland* . 13 D3
Ardnamurchan, Pt. of,
 U.K. 12 E3
Ardrossan, *Australia* . 55 E2
Ardrossan, *U.K.* 12 F4
Ards □, *U.K.* 13 B6
Ards Pen., *U.K.* 13 B6
Arecibo, *Puerto Rico* . 75 D11
Areia Branca, *Brazil* .. 79 D11
Arendal, *Norway* 9 G13
Arequipa, *Peru* 78 G4
Arero, *Ethiopia* 45 H12
Arévalo, *Spain* 19 B3
Arezzo, *Italy* 20 C4
Argamakmur, *Indonesia* 32 E2
Arganda, *Spain* 19 B4
Argentan, *France* 18 B3
Argentário, Mte., *Italy* 20 C4
Argentia, *Canada* 63 C9
Argentina ■, *S. Amer.* 80 D3
Argentina Is., *Antarctica* 5 C17
Argentino, L., *Argentina* 80 G2
Argeş →, *Romania* .. 17 F14
Arghandab →,
 Afghan. 36 D4
Argo, *Sudan* 45 E11
Argolikós Kólpos,
 Greece 21 F10
Árgos, *Greece* 21 F10
Argostólion, *Greece* .. 21 E9
Arguello, Pt., *U.S.A.* . 73 J3
Argun →, *Russia* ... 25 D13
Argungu, *Nigeria* 44 F5
Argyle, *U.S.A.* 70 A6
Argyle, L., *Australia* . 52 C4
Århus, *Denmark* 9 H14
Ariadnoye, *Russia* ... 28 B7
Ariamsvlei, *Namibia* .. 48 D2
Arica, *Chile* 78 G4
Arica, *Colombia* 78 D4
Arid, C., *Australia* ... 53 F3
Arida, *Japan* 29 G7
Arīḥā, *Syria* 38 C3
Arima, *Trin. & Tob.* .. 74 S20
Arinos →, *Brazil* ... 78 F7
Aripuanã, *Brazil* 78 E6
Aripuanã →, *Brazil* . 78 E6
Ariquemes, *Brazil* ... 78 E6
Arisaig, *U.K.* 12 E3
Aristazabal I., *Canada* . 64 C3
Arivaca, *U.S.A.* 73 L8
Arivonimamo, *Madag.* 49 B8
Arizona, *Argentina* .. 80 D3
Arizona □, *U.S.A.* ... 73 J8
Arjeplog, *Sweden* ... 8 D18
Arjona, *Colombia* ... 78 A3
Arjuno, *Indonesia* ... 33 G15
Arka, *Russia* 25 C15

Arkadelphia, *U.S.A.* .. 71 H8
Arkaig, L., *U.K.* 12 E3
Arkalyk = Arqalyq,
 Kazakhstan 24 D7
Arkansas □, *U.S.A.* .. 71 H8
Arkansas →, *U.S.A.* . 71 J9
Arkansas City, *U.S.A.* 71 G6
Arkhangelsk, *Russia* . 22 B7
Arklow, *Ireland* 13 D5
Arktichoskiy, Mys,
 Russia 25 A10
Arlanzón →, *Spain* .. 19 A3
Arlberg P., *Austria* .. 16 E6
Arlee, *U.S.A.* 72 C6
Arles, *France* 18 E6
Arlington, *S. Africa* .. 49 D4
Arlington, *Oreg., U.S.A.* 72 D3
Arlington, *S. Dak.,*
 U.S.A. 70 C6
Arlington, *Va., U.S.A.* 68 F7
Arlington, *Wash.,*
 U.S.A. 72 B2
Arlon, *Belgium* 15 E5
Armagh, *U.K.* 13 B5
Armagh □, *U.K.* 13 B5
Armavir, *Russia* 23 E7
Armenia, *Colombia* .. 78 C3
Armenia ■, *Asia* ... 23 F7
Armidale, *Australia* .. 55 E5
Armour, *U.S.A.* 70 D5
Armstrong, *B.C.,*
 Canada 64 C5
Armstrong, *Ont.,*
 Canada 62 B2
Armstrong, *U.S.A.* .. 71 M6
Armstrong →,
 Australia 52 C5
Arnarfjörður, *Iceland* . 8 D2
Arnaud →, *Canada* .. 61 B12
Arnett, *U.S.A.* 71 G5
Arnhem, *Neths.* 15 C5
Arnhem, C., *Australia* 54 A2
Arnhem B., *Australia* 54 A2
Arnhem Land, *Australia* 54 A1
Arno →, *Italy* 20 C4
Arno Bay, *Australia* .. 55 E2
Arnold, *U.S.A.* 70 E4
Arnot, *Canada* 65 B9
Arnøy, *Norway* 8 A19
Arnprior, *Canada* ... 62 C4
Arnsberg, *Germany* .. 16 C5
Aroab, *Namibia* 48 D2
Arqalyq, *Kazakhstan* . 24 D7
Arrabury, *Australia* .. 55 D3
Arrah = Ara, *India* .. 37 G14
Arraiján, *Panama* ... 74 H14
Arran, *U.K.* 12 F3
Arrandale, *Canada* .. 64 C3
Arras, *France* 18 A5
Arrecife, *Canary Is.* . 44 C2
Arrée, Mts. d', *France* . 18 B2
Arrilalah P.O., *Australia* 54 C3
Arrino, *Australia* 53 E2
Arrow, L., *Ireland* ... 13 B3
Arrow Rock Res.,
 U.S.A. 72 E6
Arrowhead, *Canada* .. 64 C5
Arrowtown, *N.Z.* 51 L2
Arroyo Grande, *U.S.A.* 73 J3
Ars, *Iran* 38 B5
Arsenault L., *Canada* . 65 B7
Arsenev, *Russia* 28 B6
Árta, *Greece* 21 E9
Artem, *Russia* 28 C6
Artemovsk, *Russia* .. 25 D10
Artesia = Mosomane,
 Botswana 48 C4
Artesia, *U.S.A.* 71 J2
Artesia Wells, *U.S.A.* 71 L5
Artesian, *U.S.A.* 70 C6
Arthur →, *Australia* . 54 G3
Arthur Cr. →,
 Australia 54 C2
Arthur Pt., *Australia* . 54 C5
Arthur's Pass, *N.Z.* .. 51 K3
Arthur's Town, *Bahamas* 75 B4
Artigas, *Uruguay* ... 80 C4
Artillery L., *Canada* .. 65 A7
Artois, *France* 18 A5
Artsyz, *Ukraine* 17 E15
Artvin, *Turkey* 23 F7
Aru, Kepulauan,
 Indonesia 33 F8
Aru Is. = Aru,
 Kepulauan, *Indonesia* 33 F8
Arua, *Uganda* 46 D6
Aruanã, *Brazil* 79 F8
Aruba ■, *W. Indies* . 75 E11
Arumpo, *Australia* ... 55 E3
Arunachal Pradesh □,
 India 37 E19
Arusha, *Tanzania* ... 46 E7
Aruwimi →, *Zaïre* .. 46 D4
Arvada, *U.S.A.* 72 D10
Arvida, *Canada* 63 C5
Arvidsjaur, *Sweden* .. 8 D18
Arvika, *Sweden* 9 G15
Arxan, *China* 31 B6
Arys, *Kazakhstan* ... 24 E7
Arzamas, *Russia* 22 C7
Arzew, *Algeria* 44 A4
Aş Şadr, *U.A.E.* 39 E7
Aş Şafā, *Syria* 41 B6
'As Saffānīyah,
 Si. Arabia 39 D6
Aş Şafiīrah, *Syria* ... 38 B3
Aş Şahm, *Oman* 39 E8
As Salamīyah, *Syria* .. 38 C3
Aş Şalț, *Jordan* 41 C4
As Sal'w'a, *Qatar* ... 39 E6
As Samāwah, *Iraq* .. 38 D5
Aş Sanamayn, *Syria* . 41 B5

As Sukhnah, *Syria* ... 38 C3
As Sulaymānīyah, *Iraq* 38 C5
As Sulaymī, *Si. Arabia* 38 E4
As Summān, *Si. Arabia* 38 E5
As Suwaydā', *Syria* .. 41 C5
As Suwaydā □, *Syria* 41 C5
Aş Şuwayrah, *Iraq* .. 38 C5
Asab, *Namibia* 48 D2
Asahi-Gawa →, *Japan* 29 G6
Asahigawa, *Japan* ... 28 C11
Asansol, *India* 37 H15
Asbesberge, *S. Africa* 48 D3
Asbestos, *Canada* ... 63 C5
Asbury Park, *U.S.A.* . 68 E8
Ascension I., *Atl. Oc.* . 2 E9
Aschaffenburg,
 Germany 16 D5
Aschersleben, *Germany* 16 C6
Áscoli Piceno, *Italy* .. 20 C5
Ascope, *Peru* 78 E3
Aseb, *Eritrea* 40 E3
Asela, *Ethiopia* 45 G12
Asenovgrad, *Bulgaria* . 21 C11
Asfūn, *Egypt* 45 C11
Aţ Ţafilah, *Jordan* ... 41 E4
Aţ Ţa'if, *Si. Arabia* .. 40 C3
Aţ Ţirāq, *Si. Arabia* . 38 E5
Atacama, Desierto de,
 Chile 80 A3
Atacama, Salar de,
 Chile 80 A3
Atakpamé, *Togo* 44 G5
Atalaya, *Peru* 78 F4
Atami, *Japan* 29 G9
Atapupu, *Indonesia* .. 33 F6
Atâr, *Mauritania* 44 D2
Atascadero, *U.S.A.* .. 73 J3
Atasu, *Kazakhstan* .. 24 E8
Atauro, *Indonesia* ... 33 F7
Atbara, *Sudan* 45 E11
'Atbara →, *Sudan* .. 45 E11
Atbasar, *Kazakhstan* . 24 D7
Atchafalaya B., *U.S.A.* 71 L9
Atchison, *U.S.A.* 70 F7
Ath, *Belgium* 15 D3
Athabasca, *Canada* .. 64 C6
Athabasca →, *Canada* 65 B6
Athabasca, L., *Canada* 65 B7
Athboy, *Ireland* 13 C5
Athenry, *Ireland* 13 C3
Athens = Athínai,
 Greece 21 F10
Athens, *Ala., U.S.A.* . 69 H2
Athens, *Ga., U.S.A.* . 69 J4
Athens, *Ohio, U.S.A.* 68 F4
Athens, *Tenn., U.S.A.* 69 H3
Athens, *Tex., U.S.A.* 71 J7
Atherton, *Australia* .. 54 B4
Athínai, *Greece* 21 F10
Athlone, *Ireland* 13 C4
Atholl, Forest of, *U.K.* 12 E5
Atholville, *Canada* ... 63 C6
Áthos, *Greece* 21 D11
Athy, *Ireland* 13 D5
Ati, *Chad* 45 F8
Atico, *Peru* 78 G4
Atikokan, *Canada* ... 62 C1
Atikonak L., *Canada* . 63 B7
Atka, *Russia* 25 C16
Atkinson, *U.S.A.* 70 D5
Atlanta, *Ga., U.S.A.* . 69 J3
Atlanta, *Tex., U.S.A.* 71 J7
Atlantic, *U.S.A.* 70 E7
Atlantic City, *U.S.A.* . 68 F8
Atlantic Ocean, ... 2 E9
Atlas Mts. = Haut
 Atlas, *Morocco* 44 B3
Atlin, *Canada* 64 B2
Atlin, L., *Canada* ... 64 B2
Atmore, *U.S.A.* 69 K2
Atoka, *U.S.A.* 71 H6
Atrak = Atrek →,
 Turkmenistan 39 B8
Atrek →,
 Turkmenistan 39 B8
Atsuta, *Japan* 28 C10
Attalla, *U.S.A.* 69 H2
Attawapiskat, *Canada* 62 B3
Attawapiskat →,
 Canada 62 B3
Attawapiskat, L.,
 Canada 62 B2
Attica, *U.S.A.* 68 E5
Attikamagan L., *Canada* 63 A6
Attleboro, *U.S.A.* ... 68 E10
Attock, *Pakistan* 36 C8
Attopeu, *Laos* 34 E9
Attur, *India* 36 P11
Atuel →, *Argentina* . 80 D3
Atwater, *U.S.A.* 73 H3
Atwood, *U.S.A.* 70 F4
Atyraū, *Kazakhstan* . 23 E9
Au Sable →, *U.S.A.* . 68 C4
Aub, *Germany* 16 D6
Aubagne, *France* ... 18 E6
Aube →, *France* ... 18 B5
Aubenas, *France* ... 18 D6
Auburn, *Ala., U.S.A.* . 69 J3
Auburn, *Calif., U.S.A.* 72 G3
Auburn, *Ind., U.S.A.* 68 E3
Auburn, *N.Y., U.S.A.* 68 D7
Auburn, *Nebr., U.S.A.* 70 E7
Auburn Ra., *Australia* 55 D5
Auburndale, *U.S.A.* .. 69 L5
Aubusson, *France* ... 18 D5
Auch, *France* 18 E4
Auckland, *N.Z.* 51 G5
Auckland Is., *Pac. Oc.* 56 N8
Auden, *Canada* 62 B2
Audubon, *U.S.A.* ... 70 E7
Augathella, *Australia* . 55 D4
Augrabies Falls,
 S. Africa 48 D3

Augsburg, *Germany* .. 16 D6
Augusta, *Italy* 20 F6
Augusta, *Ark., U.S.A.* 71 H9
Augusta, *Ga., U.S.A.* 69 J5
Augusta, *Kans., U.S.A.* 71 G6
Augusta, *Maine, U.S.A.* 63 D6
Augusta, *Mont., U.S.A.* 72 C7
Augusta, *Wis., U.S.A.* 70 C9
Augustów, *Poland* ... 17 B12
Augustus, Mt.,
 Australia 52 D2
Augustus Downs,
 Australia 54 B2
Augustus I., *Australia* 52 C3
Auld, L., *Australia* ... 52 D3
Ault, *U.S.A.* 70 E2
Aunis, *France* 18 C3
Auponhia, *Indonesia* . 33 E7
Aurangabad, *Bihar,*
 India 37 G14
Aurangabad,
 Maharashtra, India . 36 K9
Aurich, *Germany* ... 16 B4
Aurillac, *France* 18 D5
Aurora, *S. Africa* ... 48 E2
Aurora, *Colo., U.S.A.* 70 F2
Aurora, *Ill., U.S.A.* .. 68 E1
Aurora, *Mo., U.S.A.* . 71 G8
Aurora, *Nebr., U.S.A.* 70 E6
Aurukun Mission,
 Australia 54 A3
Aus, *Namibia* 48 D2
Auschwitz = Oświęcim,
 Poland 17 C10
Austin, *Minn., U.S.A.* 70 D8
Austin, *Nev., U.S.A.* . 72 G5
Austin, *Tex., U.S.A.* . 71 K6
Austin, L., *Australia* . 53 E2
Austra, *Norway* 8 D14
Austral Downs,
 Australia 54 C2
Austral Is. = Tubuai Is.,
 Pac. Oc. 57 K12
Austral Seamount
 Chain, *Pac. Oc.* ... 57 K13
Australia ■, *Oceania* 56 K5
Australian Alps,
 Australia 55 F4
Australian Capital
 Territory □, *Australia* 55 F4
Austria ■, *Europe* .. 16 E8
Austvågøy, *Norway* . 8 B16
Autun, *France* 18 C6
Auvergne, *Australia* .. 52 C5
Auvergne, *France* ... 18 D5
Auvergne, Mts. d',
 France 18 D5
Auxerre, *France* 18 C5
Avallon, *France* 18 C5
Avalon Pen., *Canada* . 63 C9
Aveiro, *Brazil* 79 D7
Aveiro, *Portugal* 19 B1
Āvej, *Iran* 39 C6
Avellaneda, *Argentina* 80 C5
Avellino, *Italy* 20 D6
Aversa, *Italy* 20 D6
Avery, *U.S.A.* 72 C6
Avesta, *Sweden* 9 F17
Avezzano, *Italy* 20 C5
Aviá Terai, *Argentina* 80 B4
Avignon, *France* 18 E6
Ávila, *Spain* 19 B3
Avilés, *Spain* 19 A3
Avoca, *Ireland* 13 D5
Avoca →, *Australia* . 55 F3
Avola, *Canada* 64 C5
Avola, *Italy* 20 F6
Avon →, *U.S.A.* 70 D5
Avon □, *U.K.* 11 F5
Avon →, *Australia* . 53 F2
Avon →, *Avon, U.K.* 11 F5
Avon →, *Hants., U.K.* 11 G6
Avon →, *Warks., U.K.* 11 F5
Avonlea, *Canada* ... 65 D8
Avonmouth, *U.K.* ... 11 F5
Avranches, *France* .. 18 B3
A'waj →, *Syria* 41 B5
Awaji-Shima, *Japan* . 29 G7
'Awālī, *Bahrain* 39 E6
Awash, *Ethiopia* 40 F3
Awatere →, *N.Z.* ... 51 J5
Awbārī, *Libya* 45 C7
Awe, L., *U.K.* 12 E3
Awjilah, *Libya* 45 C9
Axarfjörður, *Iceland* . 8 C5
Axel Heiberg I., *Canada* 4 B3
Axim, *Ghana* 44 H4
Axiós →, *Greece* ... 21 D10
Axminster, *U.K.* 11 G4
Ayabaca, *Peru* 78 D3
Ayabe, *Japan* 29 G7
Ayacucho, *Argentina* 80 D5
Ayacucho, *Peru* 78 F4
Ayaguz, *Kazakhstan* . 24 E9
Ayamonte, *Spain* ... 19 D2
Ayan, *Russia* 25 D14
Ayaviri, *Peru* 78 F4
Aydın, *Turkey* 21 F12
Ayeritam, *Malaysia* .. 34 P13
Ayers Rock, *Australia* 53 E5
Áyios Evstrátios,
 Greece 21 E11
Aykino, *Russia* 22 B8
Aylesbury, *U.K.* 11 F7
Aylmer, L., *Canada* .. 60 B8
Ayon, Ostrov, *Russia* 25 C17
Ayr, *Australia* 54 B4
Ayr, *U.K.* 12 F4
Ayr →, *U.K.* 12 F4
Ayre, Pt. of, *U.K.* .. 10 C3
Aytos, *Bulgaria* 21 C12
Ayu, Kepulauan,
 Indonesia 33 D8

Ayutla, *Mexico* 74 D5
Ayvacık, *Turkey* 21 E12
Ayvalık, *Turkey* 21 E12
Az Zabdānī, *Syria* .. 41 B5
Az Ẓāhirīyah,
 West Bank 41 D3
Az Zahrān, *Si. Arabia* 39 E6
Az Zarqā, *Jordan* .. 41 B5
Az Zībār, *Iraq* 38 B5
Az-Zilfi, *Si. Arabia* .. 38 E5
Az Zubayr, *Iraq* 38 D5
Az Zuwaytīnah, *Libya* 45 B9
Azamgarh, *India* 37 F13
Āzār Shahr, *Iran* ... 38 B5
Āzarbāyjān =
 Azerbaijan ■, *Asia* 23 F8
Āzarbāyjān-e Gharbī □,
 Iran 38 B5
Āzarbāyjān-e Sharqī □,
 Iran 38 B5
Azare, *Nigeria* 44 F7
A'zāz, *Syria* 38 B3
Azbine = Aïr, *Niger* . 44 E6
Azerbaijan ■, *Asia* . 23 F8
Azerbaijchan =
 Azerbaijan ■, *Asia* 23 F8
Azogues, *Ecuador* ... 78 D3
Azores, *Atl. Oc.* 2 C8
Azov, *Russia* 23 E6
Azov, Sea of, *Europe* 23 E6
Azovskoye More =
 Azov, Sea of, *Europe* 23 E6
Azovy, *Russia* 24 C7
Aztec, *U.S.A.* 73 H10
Azúa, *Dom. Rep.* ... 75 D10
Azuaga, *Spain* 19 C3
Azuero, Pen. de,
 Panama 75 F8
Azul, *Argentina* 80 D5
'Azzūn, *West Bank* .. 41 C4

B

Ba Don, *Vietnam* 34 D9
Ba Ngoi = Cam Lam,
 Vietnam 34 G10
Ba Ria, *Vietnam* 34 G9
Baa, *Indonesia* 33 F6
Baarle Nassau, *Belgium* 15 C4
Baarn, *Neths.* 15 B5
Bab el Mandeb,
 Red Sea 40 E3
Baba Burnu, *Turkey* . 21 E12
Bābā Kalū, *Iran* 39 D6
Babadag, *Romania* .. 17 F15
Babadayhan,
 Turkmenistan 24 F7
Babaeski, *Turkey* ... 21 D12
Babahoyo, *Ecuador* . 78 D3
Babakin, *Australia* ... 53 F2
Babana, *Nigeria* 44 F5
Babar, *Indonesia* ... 33 F7
Babb, *U.S.A.* 72 B7
Babinda, *Australia* .. 54 B4
Babine, *Canada* 64 B3
Babine →, *Canada* . 64 B3
Babine L., *Canada* .. 64 C3
Babo, *Indonesia* 33 E8
Bābol, *Iran* 39 B7
Bābol Sar, *Iran* 39 B7
Baboua, *C.A.R.* 46 D2
Babruysk, *Belarus* .. 17 B15
Babuhri, *Nigeria* 44 F6
Babuyan Chan., *Phil.* 33 A6
Babylon, *Iraq* 38 C5
Bac Kan, *Vietnam* .. 34 A9
Bac Ninh, *Vietnam* .. 34 B9
Bac Phan, *Vietnam* . 34 A9
Bac Quang, *Vietnam* 34 A8
Bacabal, *Brazil* 79 D10
Bacan, Kepulauan,
 Indonesia 33 E7
Bacan, Pulau, *Indonesia* 33 E7
Bacarra, *Phil.* 33 A6
Bacău, *Romania* 17 E14
Bachelina, *Russia* ... 24 D7
Back →, *Canada* ... 60 B9
Backstairs Passage,
 Australia 55 F2
Bacolod, *Phil.* 33 B6
Bād, *Iran* 39 C7
Bad →, *U.S.A.* 70 C4
Bad Axe, *U.S.A.* ... 68 D4
Bad Ischl, *Austria* .. 16 E7
Bad Kissingen,
 Germany 16 C6
Bad Lands, *U.S.A.* .. 70 D3
Badagara, *India* 36 P9
Badajoz, *Spain* 19 C2
Badalona, *Spain* 19 B7
Badalzai, *Afghan.* ... 36 E1
Badampahar, *India* .. 37 H15
Badanah, *Si. Arabia* . 38 D4
Badarinath, *India* ... 36 D11
Badas, *Brunei* 32 D4
Badas, Kepulauan,
 Indonesia 32 D3
Baddo →, *Pakistan* . 36 F4
Bade, *Indonesia* 33 F9
Baden, *Austria* 16 D9
Baden-Baden, *Germany* 16 D5
Baden-Württemberg □,
 Germany 16 D5
Badenoch, *U.K.* 12 E4
Badgastein, *Austria* . 16 E7
Badger, *Canada* 63 C8
Bādghīsāt □, *Afghan.* 36 B3
Badin, *Pakistan* 36 G6
Baduen, *Somali Rep.* 40 F4
Badulla, *Sri Lanka* .. 36 R12

Baena, Spain 19 D3
Baeza, Spain 19 D4
Bafatá, Guinea-Biss. .. 44 F2
Baffin B., Canada 4 B4
Baffin I., Canada 61 B12
Bafia, Cameroon 44 H7
Bafing →, Mali 44 F2
Bafliyūn, Syria 38 B3
Bafoulabé, Mali 44 F2
Bāfq, Iran 39 D7
Bafwasende, Zaïre 46 D5
Bāft, Iran 39 D8
Baganga, Phil. 33 C7
Bagani, Namibia 48 B3
Bagansiapiapi,
  Indonesia 32 D2
Bagdarin, Russia 25 D12
Bagé, Brazil 80 C6
Bagenalstown = Muine
  Bheag, Ireland 13 D5
Baggs, U.S.A. 72 F10
Baghdād, Iraq 38 C5
Bagheria, Italy 20 E5
Baghlān, Afghan. 36 A6
Bagley, U.S.A. 70 B7
Bagotville, Canada ... 63 C5
Bagrationovsk, Russia . 9 J19
Baguio, Phil. 33 A6
Bahamas ■, N. Amer. . 75 C10
Baharampur, India ... 37 G16
Bahau, Malaysia 34 S15
Bahawalpur, Pakistan . 36 E7
Bahía = Salvador,
  Brazil 79 F11
Bahía □, Brazil 79 F10
Bahía Blanca, Argentina 80 D4
Bahía de Caráquez,
  Ecuador 78 D2
Bahía Laura, Argentina 80 F3
Bahía Negra, Paraguay 78 H7
Bahmanzād, Iran 39 D6
Bahr →, C.A.R. 46 C3
Bahr Salamat →,
  Chad 45 G8
Bahraich, India 37 F12
Bahrain ■, Asia 39 E6
Bāhū Kalāt, Iran 39 E9
Bai Bung, Mui, Vietnam 34 H8
Baia Mare, Romania .. 17 E12
Baïbokoum, Chad 45 G8
Baidoa, Somali Rep. .. 40 G3
Baie Comeau, Canada . 63 C6
Baie-St-Paul, Canada . 63 C5
Baie Trinité, Canada .. 63 C6
Baie Verte, Canada ... 63 C8
Ba'iji, Iraq 38 C4
Baikal, L. = Baykal, Oz.,
  Russia 25 D11
Baile Atha Cliath =
  Dublin, Ireland 13 C5
Băileşti, Romania 17 F12
Bailundo, Angola 47 G3
Bainbridge, U.S.A. ... 69 K3
Baing, Indonesia 33 F6
Bainville, U.S.A. 70 A2
Bā'ir, Jordan 41 E5
Baird, U.S.A. 71 J5
Baird Mts., U.S.A. ... 60 B3
Bairnsdale, Australia .. 55 F4
Baitadi, Nepal 37 E12
Baiyin, China 30 C5
Baja, Hungary 17 E10
Baja, Pta., Mexico ... 74 B1
Baja California, Mexico 74 B2
Bājgīrān, Iran 39 B8
Bajimba, Mt., Australia 55 D5
Bajool, Australia 54 C5
Bakala, C.A.R. 45 G9
Bakar, Russia 24 D9
Bakel, Senegal 44 F2
Baker, Calif., U.S.A. .. 73 J6
Baker, Mont., U.S.A. .. 70 B2
Baker, Oreg., U.S.A. .. 72 D5
Baker, L., Canada 60 B10
Baker I., Pac. Oc. 56 G10
Baker L., Australia ... 53 E4
Baker Lake, Canada .. 60 B10
Baker Mt., U.S.A. 72 B3
Bakers Creek, Australia 54 C4
Baker's Dozen Is.,
  Canada 62 A4
Bakersfield, U.S.A. ... 73 J4
Bākhtarān, Iran 38 C5
Bākhtarān □, Iran ... 38 C5
Bakı, Azerbaijan 23 F8
Bakkafjörður, Iceland . 8 C6
Bakkagerði, Iceland .. 8 D7
Bakony Forest =
  Bakony Hegyseg,
  Hungary 17 E9
Bakony Hegyseg,
  Hungary 17 E9
Bakouma, C.A.R. 45 G9
Baku = Bakı, Azerbaijan 23 F8
Bakutis Coast,
  Antarctica 5 D15
Baky = Bakı, Azerbaijan 23 F8
Bala, U.K. 10 E4
Balabac I., Phil. 32 C5
Balabac Str., E. Indies . 32 C5
Ba'labakk, Lebanon .. 41 A5
Balabalangan,
  Kepulauan, Indonesia 32 E5
Balad, Iraq 38 C5
Balad Rūz, Iraq 38 C5
Bālādeh, Fārs, Iran .. 39 D6
Bālādeh, Māzandarān,
  Iran 39 B6
Balaghat, India 36 J12
Balaghat Ra., India .. 36 K10
Balaguer, Spain 19 B6
Balaklava, Australia .. 55 E2

Balaklava, Ukraine ... 23 F5
Balakovo, Russia 22 D8
Balashov, Russia 22 D7
Balasore = Baleshwar,
  India 37 J15
Balaton, Hungary ... 17 E9
Balbina, Reprêsa de,
  Brazil 78 D7
Balboa, Panama 74 H14
Balboa Hill, Panama . 74 H14
Balbriggan, Ireland .. 13 C5
Balcarce, Argentina .. 80 D5
Balcarres, Canada ... 65 C8
Balchik, Bulgaria ... 21 C13
Balclutha, N.Z. 51 M2
Bald Hd., Australia .. 53 G2
Bald I., Australia 53 F2
Bald Knob, U.S.A. ... 71 H9
Baldock L., Canada .. 65 B9
Baldwin, Fla., U.S.A. . 69 K4
Baldwin, Mich., U.S.A. 68 D3
Baldwinsville, U.S.A. . 68 D7
Baldy Peak, U.S.A. .. 73 K9
Baleares, Is., Spain .. 19 C7
Balearic Is. = Baleares,
  Is., Spain 19 C7
Baler, Phil. 33 A6
Baleshwar, India ... 37 J15
Balfe's Creek, Australia 54 C4
Bali, Cameroon 44 G7
Bali, Indonesia 32 F5
Bali □, Indonesia ... 32 F5
Bali, Selat, Indonesia 33 H16
Balikeşir, Turkey ... 21 E12
Balikpapan, Indonesia 32 E5
Balimbing, Phil. 33 C5
Baling, Malaysia ... 34 P13
Balipara, India 37 F18
Baliza, Brazil 79 G8
Balkan Mts. = Stara
  Planina, Bulgaria .. 21 C10
Balkhash = Balqash,
  Kazakhstan 24 E8
Balkhash, Ozero =
  Balqash Köl,
  Kazakhstan 24 E8
Balla, Bangla. 37 G17
Ballachulish, U.K. ... 12 E3
Balladonia, Australia . 53 F3
Ballarat, Australia ... 55 F3
Ballard, L., Australia . 53 E3
Ballater, U.K. 12 D5
Balleny Is., Antarctica . 5 C11
Ballidu, Australia ... 53 F2
Ballina, Australia ... 55 D5
Ballina, Mayo, Ireland 13 B2
Ballina, Tipp., Ireland 13 D3
Ballinasloe, Ireland .. 13 C3
Ballinger, U.S.A. 71 K5
Ballinrobe, Ireland .. 13 C2
Ballinskelligs B., Ireland 13 E1
Ballycastle, U.K. 13 A5
Ballymena, U.K. 13 B5
Ballymena □, U.K. ... 13 B5
Ballymoney, U.K. ... 13 A5
Ballymoney □, U.K. .. 13 A5
Ballyshannon, Ireland 13 B3
Balmaceda, Chile ... 80 F2
Balmoral, Australia .. 55 F3
Balmoral, U.K. 12 D5
Balmorhea, U.S.A. .. 71 K3
Balonne →, Australia 55 D4
Balqash, Kazakhstan . 24 E8
Balqash Köl,
  Kazakhstan 24 E8
Balrampur, India ... 37 F13
Balranald, Australia . 55 E3
Balsas →, Mexico .. 74 D4
Balta, Ukraine 17 D15
Balta, U.S.A. 70 A4
Bălţi, Moldova 17 E14
Baltic Sea, Europe .. 9 H18
Baltimore, Ireland .. 13 E2
Baltimore, U.S.A. ... 68 F7
Baltiysk, Russia 9 J18
Baluchistan □, Pakistan 36 F4
Balvi, Latvia 9 H22
Balya, Turkey 21 E12
Balygychan, Russia .. 25 C16
Bam, Iran 39 D8
Bama, Nigeria 45 F7
Bamako, Mali 44 F3
Bamba, Mali 44 E4
Bambari, C.A.R. 45 G9
Bambaroo, Australia . 54 B4
Bamberg, Germany .. 16 D6
Bamberg, U.S.A. 69 J5
Bambili, Zaïre 46 D5
Bamenda, Cameroon . 44 G7
Bamfield, Canada ... 64 D3
Bāmīān □, Afghan. .. 36 B5
Bampūr, Iran 39 E9
Ban Aranyaprathet,
  Thailand 34 F7
Ban Ban, Laos 34 C7
Ban Bua Chum,
  Thailand 34 E6
Ban Don = Surat Thani,
  Thailand 34 H5
Ban Houei Sai, Laos . 34 B6
Ban Khe Bo, Vietnam . 34 C8
Ban Khun Yuam,
  Thailand 34 C4
Ban Mê Thuôt = Buon
  Me Thuot, Vietnam . 34 F10
Ban Phai, Thailand .. 34 D7
Ban Thateng, Laos .. 34 E9
Banalia, Zaïre 46 D5
Banam, Cambodia .. 34 G8
Banamba, Mali 44 F3
Banana, Australia ... 54 C5
Bananal, I. do, Brazil . 79 F8

Banaras = Varanasi,
  India 37 G13
Banbān, Si. Arabia .. 38 E5
Banbridge, U.K. 13 B5
Banbridge □, U.K. ... 13 B5
Banbury, U.K. 11 E6
Banchory, U.K. 12 D6
Bancroft, Canada ... 62 C4
Band Bonī, Iran 39 E8
Band Qīr, Iran 39 D6
Banda, India 36 G12
Banda, Kepulauan,
  Indonesia 33 E7
Banda Aceh, Indonesia 32 C1
Banda Banda, Mt.,
  Australia 55 E5
Banda Elat, Indonesia . 33 F8
Banda Is. = Banda,
  Kepulauan, Indonesia 33 E7
Banda Sea, Indonesia . 33 F7
Bandai-San, Japan .. 28 F10
Bandān, Iran 39 D9
Bandanaira, Indonesia 33 E7
Bandar =
  Machilipatnam, India 37 L12
Bandar 'Abbās, Iran . 39 E8
Bandar-e Anzalī, Iran . 39 B6
Bandar-e Bushehr =
  Büshehr, Iran 39 D6
Bandar-e Chārak, Iran . 39 E7
Bandar-e Deylam, Iran 39 D6
Bandar-e Khomeynī,
  Iran 39 D6
Bandar-e Lengeh, Iran 39 E7
Bandar-e Maqām, Iran 39 E7
Bandar-e Ma'shur, Iran 39 D6
Bandar-e Nakhīlū, Iran 39 E7
Bandar-e Rīg, Iran .. 39 D6
Bandar-e Torkeman,
  Iran 39 B7
Bandar Maharani =
  Muar, Malaysia ... 34 S15
Bandar Penggaram =
  Batu Pahat, Malaysia 34 T15
Bandar Seri Begawan,
  Brunei 32 C4
Bandawe, Malawi ... 47 G6
Bandeira, Pico da,
  Brazil 79 H10
Bandera, Argentina .. 80 B4
Bandera, U.S.A. 71 L5
Bandiagara, Mali ... 44 F4
Bandırma, Turkey ... 21 D13
Bandon, Ireland 13 E3
Bandon →, Ireland .. 13 E3
Bandundu, Zaïre 46 E3
Bandung, Indonesia . 33 G12
Bandya, Australia ... 53 E3
Bāneh, Iran 38 C5
Banff, Canada 64 C5
Banff, U.K. 12 D6
Banff Nat. Park, Canada 64 C5
Banfora, Burkina Faso 44 F4
Bang Hieng →, Laos . 34 D8
Bang Lamung, Thailand 34 F6
Bang Saphan, Thailand 34 G5
Bangalore, India ... 36 N10
Bangassou, C.A.R. .. 46 D4
Banggai, Kepulauan,
  Indonesia 33 E6
Banggi, P., Malaysia . 32 C5
Banghāzī, Libya 45 B9
Bangil, Indonesia ... 33 G15
Bangka, P., Sulawesi,
  Indonesia 33 D7
Bangka, P., Sumatera,
  Indonesia 32 E3
Bangka, Selat,
  Indonesia 32 E3
Bangkalan, Indonesia 33 G15
Bangkinang, Indonesia 32 D2
Bangko, Indonesia .. 32 E2
Bangkok, Thailand .. 34 F6
Bangladesh ■, Asia . 37 H17
Bangong Co, India .. 36 B11
Bangor, Down, U.K. . 13 B6
Bangor, Gwynedd, U.K. 10 D3
Bangor, U.S.A. 63 D6
Bangued, Phil. 33 A6
Bangui, C.A.R. 46 D3
Bangweulu, L., Zambia 46 G6
Bani, Dom. Rep. ... 75 D10
Banī Sa'd, Iraq 38 C5
Banī Walīd, Libya ... 45 B7
Banīnah, Libya 45 B9
Bāniyās, Syria 38 C3
Banja Luka, Bos.-H. . 20 B7
Banjar, Indonesia ... 33 G13
Banjarmasin, Indonesia 32 E4
Banjarnegara,
  Indonesia 33 G13
Banjul, Gambia 44 F1
Banka Banka, Australia 54 B1
Bankipore, India ... 37 G14
Banks I., B.C., Canada 64 C3
Banks I., N.W.T.,
  Canada 60 A7
Banks Pen., N.Z. ... 51 K4
Banks Str., Australia . 54 G4
Bankura, India 37 H15
Bann →, L'derry., U.K. 13 A5
Bann →, Tyrone, U.K. 13 B5
Banning, U.S.A. 73 K5
Banningville =
  Bandundu, Zaïre .. 46 E3
Bannockburn, U.K. .. 12 E5
Bannu, Pakistan 36 C7
Banská Bystrica,
  Slovak Rep. 17 D10
Banswara, India 36 H9
Banten, Indonesia .. 33 G12
Bantry, Ireland 13 E2
Bantry B., Ireland ... 13 E2

Bantul, Indonesia ... 33 G14
Banu, Afghan. 36 B6
Banyak, Kepulauan,
  Indonesia 32 D1
Banyo, Cameroon .. 44 G7
Banyumas, Indonesia 33 G13
Banyuwangi, Indonesia 33 H16
Banzare Coast,
  Antarctica 5 C9
Banzyville = Mobayi,
  Zaïre 46 D4
Baoding, China 31 C6
Baoji, China 30 C5
Baoshan, China 30 D4
Baotou, China 31 B6
Bapatla, India 37 M12
Bāqerābād, Iran 39 C6
Ba'qūbah, Iraq 38 C5
Bar, Montenegro, Yug. 21 C8
Bar, Ukraine 17 D14
Bar Harbor, U.S.A. .. 63 D6
Bar-le-Duc, France .. 18 B6
Barabai, Indonesia .. 32 E5
Barabinsk, Russia ... 24 D8
Baraboo, U.S.A. 70 D10
Baracaldo, Spain ... 19 A4
Baracoa, Cuba 75 C10
Barahona, Dom. Rep. 75 D10
Baraga, U.S.A. 70 B10
Barail Range, India .. 37 G18
Barakhola, India ... 37 G18
Barakpur, India 37 H16
Barakula, Australia .. 55 D5
Baralaba, Australia .. 54 C4
Baralzon L., Canada . 65 B9
Baramula, India 36 B9
Baran, India 36 G10
Baranavichy, Belarus 17 B14
Baranof I., U.S.A. ... 64 B1
Barão de Melgaço,
  Brazil 78 F6
Barapasi, Indonesia . 33 E9
Barat Daya, Kepulauan,
  Indonesia 33 F7
Barataria B., U.S.A. . 71 L10
Barbacena, Brazil ... 79 H10
Barbacoas, Colombia 78 C3
Barbados ■, W. Indies 74 P22
Barbastro, Spain ... 19 A6
Barberton, S. Africa . 49 D5
Barberton, U.S.A. ... 68 E5
Barbourville, U.S.A. . 69 G4
Barbuda, W. Indies .. 74 K20
Barcaldine, Australia . 54 C4
Barcellona Pozzo di
  Gotto, Italy 20 E6
Barcelona, Spain ... 19 B7
Barcelona, Venezuela 78 A6
Barcelos, Brazil 78 D6
Barcoo →, Australia . 54 D3
Bardai, Chad 45 D8
Barddhaman, India . 37 H15
Bardejov, Slovak Rep. 17 D11
Bardera, Somali Rep. 40 G3
Bardīyah, Libya 45 B9
Bardsey I., U.K. 10 E3
Bardstown, U.S.A. .. 68 G3
Bareilly, India 36 E11
Barents Sea, Arctic .. 4 B9
Barentu, Eritrea 45 E12
Barfleur, Pte. de, France 18 B3
Bargal, Somali Rep. . 40 E5
Bargara, Australia .. 54 C5
Barguzin, Russia ... 25 D11
Barhi, India 37 G14
Bari, Italy 20 D7
Bari Doab, Pakistan . 36 D8
Bariadi, Tanzania ...
Barīm, Yemen 40 E3
Barinas, Venezuela . 78 B4
Baring, C., Canada .. 60 B8
Baripada, India 37 J15
Bârîs, Egypt 45 D11
Barisal, Bangla. 37 H17
Barisan, Bukit,
  Indonesia 32 E2
Barito →, Indonesia . 32 E4
Barkley Sound, Canada 64 D3
Barkly Downs, Australia 54 C2
Barkly East, S. Africa . 48 E4
Barkly Tableland,
  Australia 54 B2
Barkly West, S. Africa . 48 D3
Barkol, China 30 B4
Barksdale, U.S.A. ... 71 L4
Barlee, L., Australia . 53 E2
Barlee, Mt., Australia 53 D4
Barletta, Italy 20 D7
Barlow L., Canada .. 65 A8
Barmedman, Australia 55 E4
Barmer, India 36 G7
Barmera, Australia .. 55 E3
Barmouth, U.K. 10 E3
Barnard Castle, U.K. . 10 C6
Barnato, Australia .. 55 E3
Barnaul, Russia 24 D9
Barnesville, U.S.A. .. 69 J3
Barnet, U.K. 11 F7
Barneveld, Neths. ... 15 B5
Barngo, Australia ... 54 D4
Barnhart, U.S.A. ... 71 K4
Barnsley, U.K. 10 D6
Barnstaple, U.K. ... 11 F3
Barnsville, U.S.A. ... 70 B6
Baro, Nigeria 44 G6
Baroda = Vadodara,
  India 36 H8
Baroe, S. Africa 48 E3
Baron Ra., Australia . 52 D4
Barpeta, India 37 F17
Barques, Pt. Aux,
  U.S.A. 68 C4
Barquísimeto,
  Venezuela 78 A5
Barra, Brazil 79 F10

Barra, U.K. 12 E1
Barra, Sd. of, U.K. ... 12 D1
Barra do Corda, Brazil 79 E9
Barra do Piraí, Brazil . 79 H10
Barra Falsa, Pta. da,
  Mozam. 49 C6
Barra Hd., U.K. 12 E1
Barraba, Australia ... 55 E5
Barrackpur = Barakpur,
  India 37 H16
Barranca, Lima, Peru . 78 F3
Barranca, Loreto, Peru 78 D3
Barrancabermeja,
  Colombia 78 B4
Barrancas, Venezuela 78 B6
Barrancos, Portugal . 19 C2
Barranqueras,
  Argentina 80 B5
Barranquilla, Colombia 78 A4
Barras, Brazil 79 D10
Barraute, Canada ... 62 C4
Barre, U.S.A. 68 C9
Barreiras, Brazil 79 F10
Barreiro, Portugal .. 19 C1
Barreiros, Brazil 79 E11
Barren, Nosy, Madag. 49 B7
Barretos, Brazil 79 H9
Barrhead, Canada .. 64 C6
Barrie, Canada 62 D4
Barrière, Canada ... 64 C4
Barrington L., Canada 65 B8
Barrington Tops,
  Australia 55 E5
Barringun, Australia . 55 D4
Barrow, U.S.A. 60 A4
Barrow →, Ireland .. 13 D4
Barrow Creek, Australia 54 C1
Barrow I., Australia . 52 D2
Barrow-in-Furness, U.K. 10 C4
Barrow Pt., Australia . 54 A3
Barrow Ra., Australia 53 E4
Barrow Str., Canada . 4 B3
Barry, U.K. 11 F4
Barry's Bay, Canada . 62 C4
Barsham, Syria 38 C4
Barsi, India 36 K9
Barsoi, India 37 G15
Barstow, Calif., U.S.A. 73 J5
Barstow, Tex., U.S.A. 71 K3
Bartica, Guyana 78 B7
Bartlesville, U.S.A. .. 71 G7
Bartlett, U.S.A. 71 K6
Bartlett, L., Canada . 64 A5
Barton, Australia ... 53 F5
Barton upon Humber,
  U.K. 10 D7
Bartow, U.S.A. 69 M5
Barysaw, Belarus ... 17 A15
Barzán, Iraq 38 B5
Bāsa'idū, Iran 39 E7
Basankusa, Zaïre ... 46 D3
Basarabeasca, Moldova 17 E15
Basel, Switz. 16 E4
Bāshī, Iran 39 D6
Bashkir Republic =
  Bashkortostan □,
  Russia 22 D10
Bashkortostan □,
  Russia 22 D10
Basilan, Phil. 33 C6
Basilan Str., Phil. ... 33 C6
Basildon, U.K. 11 F8
Basim = Washim, India 36 J10
Basin, U.S.A. 72 D9
Basingstoke, U.K. ... 11 F6
Baskatong, Rés.,
  Canada 62 C4
Basle = Basel, Switz. . 16 E4
Basoda, India 36 H10
Basoka, Zaïre 46 D4
Basongo, Zaïre 46 E4
Basque Provinces =
  País Vasco □, Spain 19 A4
Basra = Al Başrah, Iraq 38 D5
Bass Rock, U.K. 12 E6
Bass Str., Australia .. 54 F4
Bassano, Canada ... 64 C6
Bassano del Grappa,
  Italy 20 B4
Bassas da India,
  Ind. Oc. 47 J7
Basse-Terre,
  Guadeloupe 74 M20
Bassein, Burma 37 L19
Basseterre,
  St. Christopher-Nevis 74 K19
Bassett, Nebr., U.S.A. 70 D5
Bassett, Va., U.S.A. . 69 G6
Bassikounou,
  Mauritania 44 E3
Bastak, Iran 39 E7
Bastām, Iran 39 B7
Bastar, India 37 K12
Basti, India 37 F13
Bastia, France 18 E8
Bastogne, Belgium .. 15 D5
Bastrop, U.S.A. 71 K6
Bat Yam, Israel 41 C3
Bata, Eq. Guin. 46 D1
Bataan, Phil. 33 B6
Batabanó, Cuba 75 C8
Batabanó, G. de, Cuba 75 C8
Batac, Phil. 33 A6
Batagoy, Russia 25 C14
Batamay, Russia ... 25 C13
Batang, Indonesia .. 33 G13
Batangafo, C.A.R. .. 45 G8
Batangas, Phil. 33 B6
Batanta, Indonesia . 33 E8
Batavia, U.S.A. 68 D6

Batchelor, Australia .. 52 B5
Bateman's B., Australia 55 F5
Batemans Bay,
  Australia 55 F5
Bates Ra., Australia . 53 E3
Batesburg, U.S.A. ... 69 J5
Batesville, Ark., U.S.A. 71 H9
Batesville, Miss., U.S.A. 71 H10
Batesville, Tex., U.S.A. 71 L5
Bath, U.K. 11 F5
Bath, Maine, U.S.A. . 63 D6
Bath, N.Y., U.S.A. ... 68 D7
Bathgate, U.K. 12 F5
Bathurst = Banjul,
  Gambia 44 F1
Bathurst, Australia .. 55 E4
Bathurst, Canada ... 63 C6
Bathurst, S. Africa .. 48 E4
Bathurst, C., Canada 60 A7
Bathurst B., Australia 54 A3
Bathurst Harb.,
  Australia 54 G4
Bathurst I., Australia 52 B5
Bathurst I., Canada .. 4 B2
Bathurst Inlet, Canada 60 B9
Batlow, Australia ... 55 F4
Batman, Turkey 23 G7
Batna, Algeria 44 A6
Baton Rouge, U.S.A. . 71 K9
Batouri, Cameroon . 46 D2
Båtsfjord, Norway .. 8 A23
Battambang, Cambodia 34 F7
Batticaloa, Sri Lanka . 36 R12
Battipáglia, Italy ... 20 D6
Battle, U.K. 11 G8
Battle →, Canada .. 65 C7
Battle Camp, Australia 54 B3
Battle Creek, U.S.A. . 68 D3
Battle Harbour, Canada 63 B8
Battle Lake, U.S.A. .. 70 B7
Battle Mountain, U.S.A. 72 F5
Battleford, Canada .. 65 C7
Batu, Ethiopia 40 F2
Batu, Kepulauan,
  Indonesia 32 E1
Batu Gajah, Malaysia 34 Q14
Batu Is. = Batu,
  Kepulauan, Indonesia 32 E1
Batu Pahat, Malaysia 34 T15
Batuata, Indonesia .. 33 F6
Batumi, Georgia ... 23 F7
Baturaja, Indonesia . 32 E2
Baturité, Brazil 79 D11
Bau, Malaysia 32 D4
Baubau, Indonesia .. 33 F6
Bauchi, Nigeria 44 F6
Baudette, U.S.A. ... 70 A7
Bauer, C., Australia . 55 E1
Bauhinia Downs,
  Australia 54 C4
Baukau, Indonesia .. 33 F7
Bauru, Brazil 79 H9
Baús, Brazil 79 G8
Bauska, Latvia 9 H21
Bautzen, Germany .. 16 C8
Bavānāt, Iran 39 D7
Bavaria = Bayern □,
  Germany 16 D6
Bawdwin, Burma ... 37 H20
Bawean, Indonesia . 32 F4
Bawku, Ghana 44 F4
Bawlake, Burma ... 37 K20
Baxley, U.S.A. 69 K4
Baxter Springs, U.S.A. 71 G7
Bay, L. de, Phil. 33 B6
Bay Bulls, Canada .. 63 C9
Bay City, Mich., U.S.A. 68 D4
Bay City, Oreg., U.S.A. 72 D2
Bay City, Tex., U.S.A. 71 L7
Bay de Verde, Canada 63 C9
Bay Minette, U.S.A. . 69 K2
Bay St. Louis, U.S.A. 71 K10
Bay Springs, U.S.A. . 71 K10
Bay View, N.Z. 51 H6
Bayamo, Cuba 75 C9
Bayamón, Puerto Rico
Bayan Har Shan, China 30 C4
Bayan Hot = Alxa
  Zuoqi, China 30 C5
Bayanaūyl, Kazakhstan 24 D8
Bayanhongor,
  Mongolia 30 B5
Bayard, U.S.A. 70 E3
Baybay, Phil. 33 B6
Bayern □, Germany . 16 D6
Bayeux, France 18 B3
Bayfield, U.S.A. 70 B9
Bayındır, Turkey ... 21 E12
Baykal, Oz., Russia . 25 D11
Baykit, Russia 25 C10
Baykonur = Bayqongyr,
  Kazakhstan 24 E7
Baymak, Russia 22 D10
Baynes Mts., Namibia 48 B1
Bayombong, Phil. .. 33 A6
Bayonne, France ... 18 E3
Bayovar, Peru 78 E2
Bayqongyr, Kazakhstan 24 E7
Bayram-Ali =
  Bayramaly,
  Turkmenistan 24 F7
Bayramaly,
  Turkmenistan 24 F7
Bayramiç, Turkey ... 21 E12
Bayreuth, Germany . 16 D6
Bayrūt, Lebanon ... 41 B4
Bayt Lahm, West Bank 41 D4
Baytown, U.S.A. ... 71 L7
Baza, Spain 19 D4
Bazaruto, I. do, Mozam. 49 C6
Bazmān, Kūh-e, Iran . 39 D9
Beach, U.S.A. 70 B3
Beachport, Australia . 55 F2
Beachy Hd., U.K. ... 11 G8
Beacon, Australia ... 53 F2

Beacon, U.S.A.	68	E9
Beaconia, Canada	65	C9
Beagle, Canal, S. Amer.	80	G3
Beagle Bay, Australia	52	C3
Bealanana, Madag.	49	A8
Bear I., Ireland	13	E2
Bear L., B.C., Canada	64	B3
Bear L., Man., Canada	65	B9
Bear L., U.S.A.	72	E8
Bearcreek, U.S.A.	72	D9
Beardmore, Canada	62	C2
Beardmore Glacier, Antarctica	5	E11
Beardstown, U.S.A.	70	F9
Béarn, France	18	E3
Bearpaw Mts., U.S.A.	72	B9
Bearskin Lake, Canada	62	B1
Beatrice, U.S.A.	70	E6
Beatrice, C., Australia	54	A2
Beatton →, Canada	64	B4
Beatton River, Canada	64	B4
Beatty, U.S.A.	73	H5
Beauce, Plaine de la, France	18	B4
Beauceville, Canada	63	C5
Beaudesert, Australia	55	D5
Beaufort, Malaysia	32	C5
Beaufort, N.C., U.S.A.	69	H7
Beaufort, S.C., U.S.A.	69	J5
Beaufort Sea, Arctic	4	B1
Beaufort West, S. Africa	48	E3
Beauharnois, Canada	62	C5
Beaulieu →, Canada	64	A6
Beauly, U.K.	12	D4
Beauly →, U.K.	12	D4
Beaumaris, U.K.	10	D3
Beaumont, U.S.A.	71	K7
Beaune, France	18	C6
Beauséjour, Canada	65	C9
Beauvais, France	18	B5
Beauval, Canada	65	B7
Beaver, Alaska, U.S.A.	60	B5
Beaver, Okla., U.S.A.	71	G4
Beaver, Utah, U.S.A.	73	G7
Beaver →, B.C., Canada	64	B4
Beaver →, Ont., Canada	62	A2
Beaver →, Sask., Canada	65	B7
Beaver City, U.S.A.	70	E5
Beaver Dam, U.S.A.	70	D10
Beaver Falls, U.S.A.	68	E5
Beaver Hill L., Canada	65	C10
Beaver I., U.S.A.	68	C3
Beaverhill L., Alta., Canada	64	C6
Beaverhill L., N.W.T., Canada	65	A8
Beaverlodge, Canada	64	B5
Beavermouth, Canada	64	C5
Beaverstone →, Canada	62	B2
Beawar, India	36	F9
Beboa, Madag.	49	B7
Beccles, U.K.	11	E9
Bečej, Serbia, Yug.	21	B9
Béchar, Algeria	44	B4
Beckley, U.S.A.	68	G5
Bedford, Canada	62	C5
Bedford, S. Africa	48	E4
Bedford, U.K.	11	E7
Bedford, Ind., U.S.A.	68	F2
Bedford, Iowa, U.S.A.	70	E7
Bedford, Ohio, U.S.A.	68	E5
Bedford, Va., U.S.A.	68	G6
Bedford, C., Australia	54	B4
Bedford Downs, Australia	52	C4
Bedfordshire □, U.K.	11	E7
Bedourie, Australia	54	C2
Beech Grove, U.S.A.	68	F2
Beechy, Canada	65	C7
Beenleigh, Australia	55	D5
Be'er Menuha, Israel	38	D2
Be'er Sheva, Israel	41	D3
Beersheba = Be'er Sheva, Israel	41	D3
Beeston, U.K.	10	E6
Beetaloo, Australia	54	B1
Beeville, U.S.A.	71	L6
Befale, Zaïre	46	D4
Befandriana, Madag.	49	C8
Befotaka, Madag.	49	C8
Bega, Australia	55	F4
Behābād, Iran	39	C8
Behara, Madag.	49	C8
Behbehān, Iran	39	D6
Behshahr, Iran	39	B7
Bei Jiang →, China	31	D6
Bei'an, China	31	B7
Beihai, China	31	D5
Beijing, China	31	C6
Beilen, Neths.	15	B6
Beilpajah, Australia	55	E3
Beinn na Faoghla = Benbecula, U.K.	12	D1
Beira, Mozam.	47	H6
Beirut = Bayrūt, Lebanon	41	B4
Beitbridge, Zimbabwe	47	J6
Beja, Portugal	19	C2
Béja, Tunisia	44	A6
Bejaia, Algeria	44	A6
Béjar, Spain	19	B3
Bejestān, Iran	39	C8
Bekaa Valley = Al Biqā □, Lebanon	41	A5
Bekasi, Indonesia	33	G12
Békéscsaba, Hungary	17	E11
Bekily, Madag.	49	C8
Bekok, Malaysia	34	S16
Bela, India	37	G13

Bela, Pakistan	36	F5
Bela Crkva, Serbia, Yug.	21	B9
Bela Vista, Brazil	80	A5
Bela Vista, Mozam.	49	D5
Belarus ■, Europe	17	B14
Belau ■, Pac. Oc.	56	G5
Belavenona, Madag.	49	C8
Belawan, Indonesia	32	D1
Belaya →, Russia	22	C9
Belaya Tserkov = Bila Tserkva, Ukraine	17	D16
Belcher Is., Canada	61	C12
Belebey, Russia	22	D9
Belém, Brazil	79	D9
Belén, Paraguay	80	A5
Belen, U.S.A.	73	J10
Belet Uen, Somali Rep.	40	G4
Belev, Russia	22	D6
Belfast, S. Africa	49	D5
Belfast, U.K.	13	B6
Belfast, U.S.A.	63	D6
Belfast □, U.K.	13	B6
Belfast L., U.K.	13	B6
Belfield, U.S.A.	70	B3
Belfort, France	18	C7
Belfry, U.S.A.	72	D9
Belgaum, India	36	M9
Belgium ■, Europe	15	D5
Belgorod, Russia	23	D6
Belgorod-Dnestrovskiy = Bilhorod-Dnivstrovskyy, Ukraine	23	E5
Belgrade = Beograd, Serbia, Yug.	21	B9
Belgrade, U.S.A.	72	D8
Beli Drim →, Europe	21	C9
Belinga, Gabon	46	D2
Belinyu, Indonesia	32	E3
Beliton Is. = Belitung, Indonesia	32	E3
Belitung, Indonesia	32	E3
Belize ■, Cent. Amer.	74	D7
Belize City, Belize	74	D7
Belkovskiy, Ostrov, Russia	25	B14
Bell →, Canada	62	C4
Bell Bay, Australia	54	G4
Bell I., Canada	63	B8
Bell-Irving →, Canada	64	B3
Bell Peninsula, Canada	61	B11
Bell Ville, Argentina	80	C4
Bella Bella, Canada	64	C3
Bella Coola, Canada	64	C3
Bella Unión, Uruguay	80	C5
Bella Vista, Argentina	80	B5
Bellaire, U.S.A.	68	E5
Bellary, India	36	M10
Bellata, Australia	55	D4
Belle Fourche, U.S.A.	70	C3
Belle Fourche →, U.S.A.	70	C3
Belle Glade, U.S.A.	69	M5
Belle-Ile, France	18	C2
Belle Isle, Canada	63	B8
Belle Isle, Str. of, Canada	63	B8
Belle Plaine, Iowa, U.S.A.	70	E8
Belle Plaine, Minn., U.S.A.	70	C8
Belledune, Canada	63	C6
Bellefontaine, U.S.A.	68	E4
Bellefonte, U.S.A.	68	E7
Belleoram, Canada	63	C8
Belleville, Canada	62	D4
Belleville, Ill., U.S.A.	70	F10
Belleville, Kans., U.S.A.	70	F6
Bellevue, Canada	64	D6
Bellevue, U.S.A.	72	E6
Bellin = Kangirsuk, Canada	61	B13
Bellingen, Australia	55	E5
Bellingham, U.S.A.	72	B2
Bellingshausen Sea, Antarctica	5	C17
Bellinzona, Switz.	16	E5
Bellows Falls, U.S.A.	68	D9
Belluno, Italy	20	A5
Bellville, U.S.A.	71	L6
Belmont, Australia	55	E5
Belmont, S. Africa	48	D3
Belmonte, Brazil	79	G11
Belmopan, Belize	74	D7
Belmullet, Ireland	13	B2
Belo-sur-Mer, Madag.	49	C7
Belo-Tsiribihina, Madag.	49	B7
Belogorsk, Russia	25	D13
Beloha, Madag.	49	D8
Beloit, Kans., U.S.A.	70	F5
Beloit, Wis., U.S.A.	70	D10
Belokorovichi, Ukraine	17	C15
Belomorsk, Russia	22	B5
Belonia, India	37	H17
Beloretsk, Russia	22	D10
Belorussia = Belarus ■, Europe	17	B14
Belovo, Russia	24	D9
Beloye, Ozero, Russia	22	B6
Beloye More, Russia	22	A6
Belozersk, Russia	22	B6
Beltana, Australia	55	E2
Belterra, Brazil	79	D8
Belton, S.C., U.S.A.	69	H4
Belton, Tex., U.S.A.	71	K6
Belton Res., U.S.A.	71	K6
Beltsy = Bălți, Moldova	17	E14
Belturbet, Ireland	13	B4
Belukha, Russia	24	E9

Beluran, Malaysia	32	C5
Belvidere, U.S.A.	70	D10
Belyando →, Australia	54	C4
Belyy, Ostrov, Russia	24	B8
Belyy Yar, Russia	24	D9
Belzoni, U.S.A.	71	J9
Bemaraha, Lembalemban' i, Madag.	49	B7
Bemarivo, Madag.	49	C7
Bemarivo →, Madag.	49	B8
Bemavo, Madag.	49	C8
Bembéréke, Benin	44	F5
Bemidji, U.S.A.	70	B7
Ben, Iran	39	C6
Ben Cruachan, U.K.	12	E3
Ben Dearg, U.K.	12	D4
Ben Gardane, Tunisia	45	B7
Ben Hope, U.K.	12	C4
Ben Lawers, U.K.	12	E4
Ben Lomond, N.S.W., Australia	55	E5
Ben Lomond, Tas., Australia	54	G4
Ben Lomond, U.K.	12	E4
Ben Macdhui, U.K.	12	D5
Ben Mhor, U.K.	12	D1
Ben More, Central, U.K.	12	E4
Ben More, Strath., U.K.	12	E2
Ben More Assynt, U.K.	12	C4
Ben Nevis, U.K.	12	E4
Ben Vorlich, U.K.	12	E4
Ben Wyvis, U.K.	12	D4
Bena, Nigeria	44	F6
Bena Dibele, Zaïre	46	E4
Benagerie, Australia	55	E3
Benalla, Australia	55	F4
Benambra, Mt., Australia	55	F4
Benares = Varanasi, India	37	G13
Benavente, Spain	19	A3
Benavides, U.S.A.	71	M5
Benbecula, U.K.	12	D1
Benbonyathe, Australia	55	E2
Bencubbin, Australia	53	F2
Bend, U.S.A.	72	D3
Bender Beila, Somali Rep.	40	F5
Bendering, Australia	53	F2
Bendery = Tighina, Moldova	17	E15
Bendigo, Australia	55	F3
Benē Beraq, Israel	41	C3
Benenitra, Madag.	49	C8
Benevento, Italy	20	D6
Bengal, Bay of, Ind. Oc.	37	K16
Bengbu, China	31	C6
Benghazi = Banghāzī, Libya	45	B9
Bengkalis, Indonesia	32	D2
Bengkulu, Indonesia	32	E2
Bengkulu □, Indonesia	32	E2
Bengough, Canada	65	D7
Benguela, Angola	47	G2
Benguérua, I., Mozam.	49	C6
Beni, Zaïre	46	D5
Beni →, Bolivia	78	F5
Beni Abbès, Algeria	44	B4
Beni Mazâr, Egypt	45	C11
Beni Mellal, Morocco	44	B3
Beni Ounif, Algeria	44	B4
Beni Suef, Egypt	45	C11
Beniah L., Canada	64	A6
Benidorm, Spain	19	C5
Benin ■, Africa	44	G5
Benin, Bight of, W. Afr.	44	H5
Benin City, Nigeria	44	G6
Benjamin Constant, Brazil	78	D4
Benkelman, U.S.A.	70	E4
Benlidi, Australia	54	C3
Bennett, Canada	64	B2
Bennett, L., Australia	52	D5
Bennett, Ostrov, Russia	25	B15
Bennettsville, U.S.A.	69	H6
Bennington, U.S.A.	68	D9
Benoni, S. Africa	49	D4
Benson, U.S.A.	73	L8
Bent, Iran	39	E8
Benteng, Indonesia	33	F6
Bentinck I., Australia	54	B2
Benton, Ark., U.S.A.	71	H8
Benton, Ill., U.S.A.	70	F10
Benton Harbor, U.S.A.	68	D2
Bentung, Malaysia	34	R14
Benue →, Nigeria	44	G6
Benxi, China	31	B7
Beo, Indonesia	33	D7
Beograd, Serbia, Yug.	21	B9
Beowawe, U.S.A.	72	F5
Beppu, Japan	29	H5
Beqaa Valley = Al Biqā □, Lebanon	41	A5
Berati, Albania	21	D8
Berau, Teluk, Indonesia	33	E8
Berber, Sudan	45	E11
Berbera, Somali Rep.	40	E4
Berbérati, C.A.R.	46	D3
Berbice →, Guyana	78	B7
Berdichev = Berdychiv, Ukraine	17	D15
Berdsk, Russia	24	D9
Berdyansk, Ukraine	23	E6
Berdychiv, Ukraine	17	D15
Berea, U.S.A.	68	G3
Berebere, Indonesia	33	D7
Bereda, Somali Rep.	40	E5
Berekum, Ghana	44	G4
Berens →, Canada	65	C9
Berens I., Canada	65	C9
Berens River, Canada	65	C9

Berestechko, Ukraine	17	C13
Berevo, Mahajanga, Madag.	49	B7
Berevo, Toliara, Madag.	49	B7
Bereza, Belarus	17	B13
Berezhany, Ukraine	17	D13
Berezina = Byarezina →, Belarus	17	B16
Berezniki, Russia	24	D6
Berezovo, Russia	22	B11
Berga, Spain	19	A6
Bergama, Turkey	21	E12
Bérgamo, Italy	20	B3
Bergen, Neths.	15	B4
Bergen, Norway	9	F11
Bergen-op-Zoom, Neths.	15	C4
Bergerac, France	18	D4
Bergum, Neths.	15	A5
Bergville, S. Africa	49	D4
Berhala, Selat, Indonesia	32	E2
Berhampore = Baharampur, India	37	G16
Berhampur, India	37	K14
Bering Sea, Pac. Oc.	60	C1
Bering Strait, U.S.A.	60	B3
Beringen, Belgium	15	C5
Beringovskiy, Russia	25	C18
Berja, Spain	19	D4
Berkeley, U.K.	11	F5
Berkeley, U.S.A.	72	H2
Berkeley Springs, U.S.A.	68	F6
Berkner I., Antarctica	5	D18
Berkshire □, U.K.	11	F6
Berland →, Canada	64	C5
Berlin, Germany	16	B7
Berlin, Md., U.S.A.	68	F8
Berlin, N.H., U.S.A.	68	C10
Berlin, Wis., U.S.A.	68	D1
Bermejo →, Formosa, Argentina	80	B5
Bermejo →, San Juan, Argentina	80	C3
Bermuda ■, Atl. Oc.	75	A12
Bern, Switz.	16	E4
Bernado, U.S.A.	73	J10
Bernalillo, U.S.A.	73	J10
Bernam →, Malaysia	34	R14
Bernardo de Irigoyen, Argentina	80	B6
Bernburg, Germany	16	C6
Berne = Bern, Switz.	16	E4
Bernier I., Australia	53	D1
Bernina, Piz, Switz.	16	E5
Beroroha, Madag.	49	C8
Beroun, Czech.	16	D8
Berrechid, Morocco	44	B3
Berri, Australia	55	E3
Berry, Australia	55	E5
Berry, France	18	C5
Berryville, U.S.A.	71	G8
Bershad, Ukraine	17	D15
Berthold, U.S.A.	70	A4
Berthoud, U.S.A.	70	E2
Bertoua, Cameroon	46	D2
Bertrand, U.S.A.	70	E5
Berwick, U.S.A.	68	E7
Berwick-upon-Tweed, U.K.	10	B5
Berwyn Mts., U.K.	10	E4
Besalampy, Madag.	49	B7
Besançon, France	18	C7
Besar, Indonesia	32	E5
Beserah, Malaysia	34	R16
Besnard L., Canada	65	B7
Besor, N. →, Egypt	41	D3
Bessarabka = Basarabeasca, Moldova	17	E15
Bessemer, Ala., U.S.A.	69	J2
Bessemer, Mich., U.S.A.	70	B9
Bet She'an, Israel	41	C4
Bet Shemesh, Israel	41	D3
Betafo, Madag.	49	B8
Betancuria, Canary Is.		
Betanzos, Spain	19	A1
Bétaré Oya, Cameroon	46	C2
Bethal, S. Africa	49	D4
Bethanien, Namibia	48	D2
Bethany, U.S.A.	70	E7
Bethel, U.S.A.	60	B3
Bethlehem = Bayt Lahm, West Bank	41	D4
Bethlehem, S. Africa	49	D4
Bethlehem, U.S.A.	68	E8
Bethulie, S. Africa	48	E4
Béthune, France	18	A5
Bethungra, Australia	55	E4
Betioky, Madag.	49	C7
Betong, Thailand	34	P14
Betoota, Australia	54	D3
Betroka, Madag.	49	C8
Betsiamites, Canada	63	C6
Betsiamites →, Canada	63	C6
Betsiboka →, Madag.	49	B8
Bettiah, India	37	F14
Betul, India	36	J10
Betung, Malaysia	32	D4
Beulah, U.S.A.	70	B4
Beverley, Australia	53	F2
Beverley, U.K.	10	D7
Beverly, U.S.A.	72	C4
Beverly Hills, U.S.A.	73	J4
Beverwijk, Neths.	15	B4
Beyānlū, Iran	38	C5
Beyla, Guinea	44	G3
Beyneu, Kazakhstan	23	E10

Beypazan, Turkey	23	F5
Beyşehir Gölü, Turkey	23	G5
Bezhitsa, Russia	22	D5
Béziers, France	18	E5
Bezwada = Vijayawada, India	37	L12
Bhachau, India	36	H7
Bhadrakh, India	37	J15
Bhadravati, India	36	N9
Bhagalpur, India	37	G15
Bhakra Dam, India	36	D10
Bhamo, Burma	37	G20
Bhandara, India	36	J11
Bhanrer Ra., India	36	H11
Bharat = India ■, Asia	36	K11
Bharatpur, India	36	F10
Bhatpara, India	37	H16
Bhaunagar = Bhavnagar, India	36	J8
Bhavnagar, India	36	J8
Bhawanipatna, India	37	K12
Bhilsa = Vidisha, India	36	H10
Bhilwara, India	36	G9
Bhima →, India	36	L10
Bhimavaram, India	37	L12
Bhind, India	36	F11
Bhiwandi, India	36	K8
Bhiwani, India	36	E10
Bhola, Bangla.	37	H17
Bhopal, India	36	H10
Bhubaneshwar, India	37	J14
Bhuj, India	36	H6
Bhumiphol Dam = Phumiphon, Khuan, Thailand	32	A1
Bhusaval, India	36	J9
Bhutan ■, Asia	37	F17
Biafra, B. of = Bonny, Bight of, Africa	46	D1
Biak, Indonesia	33	E9
Biała Podlaska, Poland	17	B12
Białogard, Poland	16	A8
Białystok, Poland	17	B12
Biārjmand, Iran	39	B7
Biaro, Indonesia	33	D7
Biarritz, France	18	E3
Bibai, Japan	28	C10
Bibala, Angola	47	G2
Bibby I., Canada	65	A10
Biberach, Germany	16	D5
Bibiani, Ghana	44	G4
Biboohra, Australia	54	B4
Bic, Canada	63	C6
Bickerton I., Australia	54	A2
Bicknell, Ind., U.S.A.	68	F2
Bicknell, Utah, U.S.A.	73	G8
Bida, Nigeria	44	G6
Bidar, India	36	L10
Biddeford, U.S.A.	63	D5
Bideford, U.K.	11	F3
Bidon 5 = Poste Maurice Cortier, Algeria	44	D5
Bidor, Malaysia	34	Q14
Bié, Planalto de, Angola	47	G3
Bieber, U.S.A.	72	F3
Biel, Switz.	16	E4
Bielé Karpaty, Europe	17	D9
Bielefeld, Germany	16	B5
Biella, Italy	20	B3
Bielsk Podlaski, Poland	17	B12
Bielsko-Biała, Poland	17	D10
Bien Hoa, Vietnam	34	G9
Bienfait, Canada	65	D8
Bienne = Biel, Switz.	16	E4
Bienville, L., Canada	62	A5
Biesiesfontein, S. Africa	48	E2
Big B., Canada	63	A7
Big Beaver, Canada	65	D7
Big Belt Mts., U.S.A.	72	C8
Big Bend, Swaziland	49	D5
Big Bend National Park, U.S.A.	71	L3
Big Black →, U.S.A.	71	J9
Big Blue →, U.S.A.	70	F6
Big Cr. →, Canada	64	C4
Big Cypress Swamp, U.S.A.	69	M5
Big Falls, U.S.A.	70	A8
Big Fork →, U.S.A.	70	A8
Big Horn Mts. = Bighorn Mts., U.S.A.	72	D10
Big Lake, U.S.A.	71	K4
Big Muddy Cr. →, U.S.A.	70	A2
Big Pine, U.S.A.	73	H4
Big Piney, U.S.A.	72	E8
Big Quill L., Canada	65	C8
Big Rapids, U.S.A.	68	D3
Big River, Canada	65	C7
Big Sable Pt., U.S.A.	68	C2
Big Sand L., Canada	65	B9
Big Sandy, U.S.A.	72	B8
Big Sandy Cr. →, U.S.A.	70	F3
Big Sioux →, U.S.A.	70	D6
Big Spring, U.S.A.	71	J4
Big Springs, U.S.A.	70	E3
Big Stone City, U.S.A.	70	C6
Big Stone Gap, U.S.A.	69	G4
Big Stone L., U.S.A.	70	C6
Big Timber, U.S.A.	72	D9
Big Trout L., Canada	62	B1
Biga, Turkey	21	D12
Bigadiç, Turkey	21	E13
Bigfork, U.S.A.	72	B6
Biggar, Canada	65	C7
Biggar, U.K.	12	F5
Bigge I., Australia	52	B4
Biggenden, Australia	55	D5
Bighorn, U.S.A.	72	C10
Bighorn →, U.S.A.	72	C10

Bighorn Mts., U.S.A.	72	D10
Bigstone L., Canada	65	C9
Bihać, Bos.-H.	16	F8
Bihar, India	37	G14
Bihar □, India	37	G14
Bihor, Munţii, Romania	17	E12
Bijagós, Arquipélago dos, Guinea-Biss.	44	F1
Bijapur, Karnataka, India	36	L9
Bijapur, Mad. P., India	37	K12
Bījār, Iran	38	C5
Bijeljina, Bos.-H.	21	B8
Bijnor, India	36	E11
Bikaner, India	36	E8
Bikfayyā, Lebanon	41	B4
Bikin, Russia	25	E14
Bikin →, Russia	28	A7
Bikini Atoll, Pac. Oc.	56	F8
Bila Tserkva, Ukraine	17	D16
Bilara, India	36	F8
Bilaspur, India	37	H13
Bilauk Taungdan, Thailand	34	F5
Bilbao, Spain	19	A4
Bilbo = Bilbao, Spain	19	A4
Bíldudalur, Iceland	8	D2
Bilecik, Turkey	23	F5
Bilhorod-Dnivstrovskyy, Ukraine	23	E5
Bilibino, Russia	25	C17
Bilir, Russia	25	C14
Bill, U.S.A.	70	D2
Billabalong, Australia	53	E2
Billiluna, Australia	52	C4
Billingham, U.K.	10	C6
Billings, U.S.A.	72	D9
Billiton Is. = Belitung, Indonesia	32	E3
Bilma, Niger	45	E8
Biloela, Australia	54	C5
Biloxi, U.S.A.	71	K10
Bilpa Morea Claypan, Australia	54	D2
Biltine, Chad	45	F9
Bilyana, Australia	54	B4
Bima, Indonesia	33	F5
Bimbo, C.A.R.	46	D3
Bina-Etawah, India	36	G11
Bināb, Iran	39	B6
Binalbagan, Phil.	33	B6
Binalong, Australia	55	E4
Bīnālūd, Kūh-e, Iran	39	B8
Binatang, Malaysia	32	D4
Binbee, Australia	54	C4
Binche, Belgium	15	D4
Binda, Australia	55	D4
Bindle, Australia	55	D4
Bindura, Zimbabwe	47	H6
Bingara, N.S.W., Australia	55	D5
Bingara, Queens., Australia	55	D3
Bingham, U.S.A.	63	C6
Bingham Canyon, U.S.A.	72	F7
Binghamton, U.S.A.	68	D8
Binh Dinh = An Nhon, Vietnam	34	F10
Binh Son, Vietnam	34	E10
Binjai, Indonesia	32	D1
Binnaway, Australia	55	E4
Binongko, Indonesia	33	F6
Binscarth, Canada	65	C8
Bintan, Indonesia	32	D2
Bintulu, Malaysia	32	D4
Bintuni, Indonesia	33	E8
Binzert = Bizerte, Tunisia	44	A6
Bioko, Eq. Guin.	44	H6
Bir, India	36	K9
Bîr Abu Muḥammad, Egypt	41	F3
Bi'r ad Dabbāghāt, Jordan	41	E4
Bi'r al Butayyihāt, Jordan	41	F4
Bi'r al Mārī, Jordan	41	E4
Bi'r al Qaṭṭār, Jordan	41	F4
Bîr Autrun, Sudan	45	E10
Bîr Beida, Egypt	41	E3
Bîr el Biârât, Egypt	41	F3
Bîr el Duweidar, Egypt	41	E1
Bîr el Garârât, Egypt	41	D2
Bîr el Heisi, Egypt	41	F3
Bîr el Jafir, Egypt	41	E1
Bîr el Mâlḥi, Egypt	41	E2
Bîr el Thamâda, Egypt	41	E2
Bîr Gebeil Ḥiṣn, Egypt	41	E2
Bi'r Ghadir, Syria	41	A6
Bîr Ḥasana, Egypt	41	E2
Bi'r Jadîd, Iraq	38	C4
Bîr Kaseiba, Egypt	41	E2
Bîr Lahfân, Egypt	41	E2
Bîr Madkûr, Egypt	41	E1
Bîr Mogrein, Mauritania	44	C2
Bi'r Muṭribah, Kuwait	38	D5
Bîr Qaţia, Egypt	41	E1
Bîr Ungât, Egypt	45	D11
Bira, Indonesia	33	E8
Birao, C.A.R.	45	F9
Birch Hills, Canada	65	C7
Birch I., Canada	65	C9
Birch L., N.W.T., Canada	64	A5
Birch L., Ont., Canada	62	B1
Birch Mts., Canada	64	B6
Birch River, Canada	65	C8
Birchip, Australia	55	F3
Bird, Canada	65	B10
Bird City, U.S.A.	70	F4

Birdlip, U.K. 11 F5
Birdsville, Australia 54 D2
Birdum, Australia 52 C5
Birein, Israel 41 E3
Bireuen, Indonesia 32 C1
Birkenhead, U.K. 10 D4
Bîrlad, Romania 17 E14
Bîrlad →, Romania 17 F14
Birmingham, U.K. 11 E6
Birmingham, U.S.A. 69 J2
Birmitrapur, India 37 H14
Birni Nkonni, Niger 44 F6
Birnin Kebbi, Nigeria 44 F5
Birobidzhan, Russia 25 E14
Birr, Ireland 13 C4
Birrie →, Australia 55 D4
Birsk, Russia 22 C10
Birtle, Canada 65 C8
Birur, India 36 N9
Biržai, Lithuania 9 H21
Bisa, Indonesia 33 E7
Bisbee, U.S.A. 73 L9
Biscay, B. of, Atl. Oc. 18 D1
Biscayne B., U.S.A. 69 N5
Biscoe Bay, Antarctica 5 D13
Biscoe Is., Antarctica 5 C17
Biscostasing, Canada 62 C3
Bishkek, Kyrgyzstan 24 E8
Bisho, S. Africa 49 E4
Bishop, Calif., U.S.A. 73 H4
Bishop, Tex., U.S.A. 71 M6
Bishop Auckland, U.K. 10 C6
Bishop's Falls, Canada 63 C8
Bishop's Stortford, U.K. 11 F8
Biskra, Algeria 44 B6
Bislig, Phil. 33 C7
Bismarck, U.S.A. 70 B4
Bismarck Arch., Papua N. G. 56 H6
Bison, U.S.A. 70 C3
Bīsotūn, Iran 38 C5
Bissagos = Bijagós, Arquipélago dos, Guinea-Biss. 44 F1
Bissau, Guinea-Biss. 44 F1
Bissett, Canada 65 C9
Bistcho L., Canada 64 B5
Bistrița, Romania 17 E13
Bistrița →, Romania 17 E14
Bitam, Gabon 46 D2
Bitkine, Chad 45 F8
Bitlis, Turkey 23 G7
Bitola, Macedonia 21 D9
Bitolj = Bitola, Macedonia 21 D9
Bitter Creek, U.S.A. 72 F9
Bitter L. = Buheirat-Murrat-el-Kubra, Egypt 45 B11
Bitterfontein, S. Africa 48 E2
Bitterroot →, U.S.A. 72 C6
Bitterroot Range, U.S.A. 72 C6
Biu, Nigeria 45 F7
Biwa-Ko, Japan 29 G8
Biwabik, U.S.A. 70 B8
Biysk, Russia 24 D9
Bizana, S. Africa 49 E4
Bizen, Japan 29 G7
Bizerte, Tunisia 44 A6
Bjargtangar, Iceland 8 D1
Bjelovar, Croatia 20 B7
Bjørnevatn, Norway 8 B23
Bjørnøya, Arctic 4 B8
Black = Da →, Vietnam 34 B8
Black →, Ark., U.S.A. 71 H9
Black →, Wis., U.S.A. 70 D9
Black Diamond, Canada 64 C6
Black Forest = Schwarzwald, Germany 16 D5
Black Hills, U.S.A. 70 C3
Black I., Canada 65 C9
Black L., Canada 65 B7
Black L., U.S.A. 68 C3
Black Mesa, U.S.A. 71 G3
Black Mt. = Mynydd Du, U.K. 11 F4
Black Mts., U.K. 11 F4
Black Range, U.S.A. 73 K10
Black River, Jamaica 74 K16
Black River Falls, U.S.A. 70 C9
Black Sea, Eurasia 23 F6
Black Volta →, Africa 44 G4
Black Warrior →, U.S.A. 69 J2
Blackall, Australia 54 C4
Blackball, N.Z. 51 K3
Blackbull, Australia 54 B3
Blackburn, U.K. 10 D5
Blackduck, U.S.A. 70 B7
Blackfoot, U.S.A. 72 E7
Blackfoot →, U.S.A. 72 C7
Blackfoot River Reservoir, U.S.A. 72 E8
Blackie, Canada 64 C6
Blackpool, U.K. 10 D4
Blacks Harbour, Canada 63 C6
Blacksburg, U.S.A. 68 G5
Blacksod B., Ireland 13 B2
Blackstone, U.S.A. 68 G6
Blackstone →, Canada 64 A4
Blackstone Ra., Australia 53 E4
Blackville, Canada 63 C6
Blackwater, Australia 54 C4
Blackwater →, Ireland 13 D4
Blackwater →, U.K. 13 B5
Blackwater Cr. →, Australia 55 D3
Blackwell, U.S.A. 71 G6
Blaenau Ffestiniog, U.K. 10 E4

Blagodarnoye = Blagodarnyy, Russia 23 E7
Blagodarnyy, Russia 23 E7
Blagoevgrad, Bulgaria 21 C10
Blagoveshchensk, Russia 25 D13
Blaine, U.S.A. 72 B2
Blaine Lake, Canada 65 C7
Blair, U.S.A. 70 E6
Blair Athol, Australia 54 C4
Blair Atholl, U.K. 12 E5
Blairgowrie, U.K. 12 E5
Blairmore, Canada 64 D6
Blake Pt., U.S.A. 70 A10
Blakely, U.S.A. 69 K3
Blanc, Mont, Alps 18 D7
Blanca, B., Argentina 80 D4
Blanca Peak, U.S.A. 73 H11
Blanchard, U.S.A. 71 H6
Blanche, C., Australia 55 E1
Blanche, L., S. Austral., Australia 55 D2
Blanche, L., W. Austral., Australia 52 D3
Blanco, S. Africa 48 E3
Blanco, U.S.A. 71 K5
Blanco, C., U.S.A. 72 E1
Blanda →, Iceland 8 D3
Blandford Forum, U.K. 11 G5
Blanding, U.S.A. 73 H9
Blanes, Spain 19 B7
Blankenberge, Belgium 15 C3
Blantyre, Malawi 47 H6
Blarney, Ireland 13 E3
Blåvands Huk, Denmark 9 J13
Blaydon, U.K. 10 C6
Blayney, Australia 55 E4
Blaze, Pt., Australia 52 B5
Blednaya, Gora, Russia 24 B7
Blekinge, Sweden 9 H16
Blenheim, N.Z. 51 J4
Bletchley, U.K. 11 F7
Blida, Algeria 44 A5
Bligh Sound, N.Z. 51 L1
Blind River, Canada 62 C3
Blitar, Indonesia 33 H15
Blitta, Togo 44 G5
Block I., U.S.A. 68 E10
Blodgett Iceberg Tongue, Antarctica 5 C9
Bloemfontein, S. Africa 48 D4
Bloemhof, S. Africa 48 D4
Blois, France 18 C4
Blönduós, Iceland 8 D3
Bloodvein →, Canada 65 C9
Bloody Foreland, Ireland 13 A3
Bloomer, U.S.A. 70 C9
Bloomfield, Australia 54 B4
Bloomfield, Iowa, U.S.A. 70 E8
Bloomfield, N. Mex., U.S.A. 73 H10
Bloomfield, Nebr., U.S.A. 70 D6
Bloomington, Ill., U.S.A. 70 E10
Bloomington, Ind., U.S.A. 68 F2
Bloomsburg, U.S.A. 68 E7
Blora, Indonesia 33 G14
Blouberg, S. Africa 49 C4
Blountstown, U.S.A. 69 K3
Blue Island, U.S.A. 68 E2
Blue Lake, U.S.A. 72 F2
Blue Mesa Reservoir, U.S.A. 73 G10
Blue Mts., Oreg., U.S.A. 72 D4
Blue Mts., Pa., U.S.A. 68 E7
Blue Mud B., Australia 54 A2
Blue Nile = Nîl el Azraq →, Sudan 45 E11
Blue Rapids, U.S.A. 70 F6
Blue Ridge Mts., U.S.A. 69 G5
Blueberry →, Canada 64 B4
Bluefield, U.S.A. 68 G5
Bluefields, Nic. 75 E8
Bluff, Australia 54 C4
Bluff, N.Z. 51 M2
Bluff, U.S.A. 73 H9
Bluff Knoll, Australia 53 F2
Bluff Pt., Australia 53 E1
Bluffton, U.S.A. 68 E3
Blumenau, Brazil 80 B7
Blunt, U.S.A. 70 C4
Bly, U.S.A. 72 E3
Blyth, U.K. 10 B6
Blyth Bridge, U.K. 10 E5
Blythe, U.S.A. 73 K6
Bo, S. Leone 44 G2
Bo Duc, Vietnam 34 G9
Bo Hai, China 31 C6
Boa Vista, Brazil 78 C6
Boatman, Australia 55 D4
Bobadah, Australia 55 E4
Bobbili, India 37 K13
Bobcaygeon, Canada 62 D4
Bobo-Dioulasso, Burkina Faso 44 F4
Bóbr →, Poland 16 B8
Bobraomby, Tanjon' i, Madag. 49 A8
Bobruysk = Babruysk, Belarus 17 B15
Bôca do Acre, Brazil 78 E5
Boca Raton, U.S.A. 69 M5
Bocaiúva, Brazil 79 G10
Bocanda, Ivory C. 44 G4
Bocaranga, C.A.R. 45 G8
Bochnia, Poland 17 D11
Bochum, Germany 16 C4
Boda, C.A.R. 46 D3

Bodaybo, Russia 25 D12
Boddington, Australia 53 F2
Boden, Sweden 8 D19
Bodensee, Europe 16 E5
Bodhan, India 36 K10
Bodmin, U.K. 11 G3
Bodmin Moor, U.K. 11 G3
Bodø, Norway 8 C16
Bodrog →, Hungary 17 D11
Bodrum, Turkey 21 F12
Boende, Zaïre 46 E4
Boerne, U.S.A. 71 L5
Boffa, Guinea 44 F2
Bogalusa, U.S.A. 71 K10
Bogan Gate, Australia 55 E4
Bogantungan, Australia 54 C4
Bogata, U.S.A. 71 J7
Boggabilla, Australia 55 D5
Boggabri, Australia 55 E5
Boggeragh Mts., Ireland 13 D3
Bognor Regis, U.K. 11 G7
Bogo, Phil. 33 B6
Bogong, Mt., Australia 55 F4
Bogor, Indonesia 33 G12
Bogorodskoye, Russia 25 D15
Bogotá, Colombia 78 C4
Bogotol, Russia 24 D9
Bogra, Bangla. 37 G16
Boguchany, Russia 25 D10
Bogué, Mauritania 44 E2
Bohemia, Australia 52 C4
Bohemian Forest = Böhmerwald, Germany 16 D7
Bohena Cr. →, Australia 55 E4
Böhmerwald, Germany 16 D7
Bohol, Phil. 33 C6
Bohol Sea, Phil. 33 C6
Bohotleh, Somali Rep. 40 F4
Bohuslän, Sweden 9 G14
Boileau, C., Australia 52 C3
Boise, U.S.A. 72 E5
Boise City, U.S.A. 71 G3
Boissevain, Canada 65 D8
Bojador C., W. Sahara 44 C2
Bojana →, Albania 21 D8
Bojnürd, Iran 39 B8
Bojonegoro, Indonesia 33 G14
Boké, Guinea 44 F2
Bokhara →, Australia 55 D4
Boknafjorden, Norway 9 G11
Bokoro, Chad 45 F8
Bokote, Zaïre 46 E4
Bokpyin, Burma 34 G5
Bokungu, Zaïre 46 E4
Bol, Chad 45 F7
Bolama, Guinea-Biss. 44 F1
Bolan Pass, Pakistan 36 E5
Bolbec, France 18 B4
Boldājī, Iran 39 D6
Bole, China 30 B3
Bolekhiv, Ukraine 17 D12
Bolekhov = Bolekhiv, Ukraine 17 D12
Bolesławiec, Poland 16 C8
Bolgrad = Bolhrad, Ukraine 17 F15
Bolhrad, Ukraine 17 F15
Bolinao C., Phil. 33 A5
Bolívar, Argentina 80 D4
Bolívar, Colombia 78 C3
Bolivar, Mo., U.S.A. 71 G8
Bolivar, Tenn., U.S.A. 71 H10
Bolivia ■, S. Amer. 78 G6
Bolivian Plateau, S. Amer. 76 E4
Bollnäs, Sweden 9 F17
Bollon, Australia 55 D4
Bolmen, Sweden 9 H15
Bolobo, Zaïre 46 E3
Bologna, Italy 20 B4
Bologoye, Russia 22 C5
Bolomba, Zaïre 46 D3
Bolong, Phil. 33 C6
Boloven, Cao Nguyen, Laos 34 E9
Bolsena, L. di, Italy 20 C4
Bolshereche, Russia 24 D8
Bolshevik, Ostrov, Russia 25 B11
Bolshezemelskaya Tundra, Russia 22 A10
Bolshoi Kavkas = Caucasus Mountains, Eurasia 23 F7
Bolshoy Anyuy →, Russia 25 C17
Bolshoy Atlym, Russia 24 C7
Bolshoy Begichev, Ostrov, Russia 25 B12
Bolshoy Lyakhovskiy, Ostrov, Russia 25 B15
Bolshoy Tyuters, Ostrov, Russia 9 G22
Bolsward, Neths. 15 A5
Bolton, U.K. 10 D5
Bolu, Turkey 23 F5
Bolungavík, Iceland 8 C2
Bolvadin, Turkey 23 G5
Bolzano, Italy 20 A4
Bom Despacho, Brazil 79 G9
Bom Jesus da Lapa, Brazil 79 F10
Boma, Zaïre 46 F2
Bomaderry, Australia 55 E5
Bombala, Australia 55 F4
Bombay, India 36 K8
Bomboma, Zaïre 46 D3
Bomili, Zaïre 46 D5
Bømlo, Norway 9 G11

Bomongo, Zaïre 46 D3
Bomu →, C.A.R. 46 D4
Bon, C., Tunisia 45 A7
Bonang, Australia 55 F4
Bonaire, Neth. Ant. 75 E11
Bonaparte Arch., Australia 52 B3
Bonaventure, Canada 63 C6
Bonavista, Canada 63 C9
Bonavista, C., Canada 63 C9
Bondo, Zaïre 46 D4
Bondoukou, Ivory C. 44 G4
Bondowoso, Indonesia 33 G15
Bone, Teluk, Indonesia 33 E6
Bonerate, Indonesia 33 F6
Bonerate, Kepulauan, Indonesia 33 F6
Bo'ness, U.K. 12 E5
Bong Son = Hoai Nhon, Vietnam 34 E10
Bongandanga, Zaïre 46 D4
Bongor, Chad 45 F8
Bonham, U.S.A. 71 J6
Bonifacio, France 18 F8
Bonin Is. = Ogasawara Gunto, Pac. Oc. 56 E6
Bonn, Germany 16 C4
Bonne Terre, U.S.A. 71 G9
Bonners Ferry, U.S.A. 72 B5
Bonney, L., Australia 55 F3
Bonnie Downs, Australia 54 C3
Bonnie Rock, Australia 53 F2
Bonny, Bight of, Africa 46 D1
Bonnyville, Canada 65 C6
Bonoi, Indonesia 33 E9
Bontang, Indonesia 32 D5
Bonthain, Indonesia 33 F5
Bonthe, S. Leone 44 G2
Bontoc, Phil. 33 A6
Bookabie, Australia 53 F5
Booker, U.S.A. 71 G4
Boolaboolka L., Australia 55 E3
Booligal, Australia 55 E3
Boonah, Australia 55 D5
Boone, Iowa, U.S.A. 70 D8
Boone, N.C., U.S.A. 69 G5
Booneville, Ark., U.S.A. 71 H8
Booneville, Miss., U.S.A. 69 H1
Boonville, Ind., U.S.A. 68 F2
Boonville, Mo., U.S.A. 70 F8
Boonville, N.Y., U.S.A. 68 D8
Boorindal, Australia 55 E4
Boorowa, Australia 55 E4
Boothia, Gulf of, Canada 61 A11
Boothia Pen., Canada 60 A10
Bootle, U.K. 10 D4
Booué, Gabon 46 E2
Bor, Serbia, Yug. 21 B10
Bôr, Sudan 45 G11
Bor Mashash, Israel 41 D3
Borah Peak, U.S.A. 72 D7
Borama, Somali Rep. 40 F3
Borås, Sweden 9 H15
Borāzjān, Iran 39 D6
Borba, Brazil 78 D7
Bord Khūn-e Now, Iran 39 D6
Borda, C., Australia 55 F2
Bordeaux, France 18 D3
Borden, Australia 53 F2
Borden, Canada 63 C7
Borden I., Canada 4 B2
Borders □, U.K. 12 F6
Bordertown, Australia 55 F3
Borðeyri, Iceland 8 D3
Bordj Fly Ste. Marie, Algeria 44 C4
Bordj-in-Eker, Algeria 44 D6
Bordj Omar Driss, Algeria 44 C6
Bordj-Tarat, Algeria 44 C6
Borgå = Porvoo, Finland 9 F21
Borgarnes, Iceland 8 D3
Børgefjellet, Norway 8 D15
Borger, Neths. 15 B6
Borger, U.S.A. 71 H4
Borgholm, Sweden 9 H17
Borisoglebsk, Russia 23 D7
Borisov = Barysaw, Belarus 17 A15
Borja, Peru 78 D3
Borkou, Chad 45 E8
Borkum, Germany 16 B4
Borlänge, Sweden 9 F16
Borley, C., Antarctica 5 C5
Borneo, E. Indies 32 D5
Bornholm, Denmark 9 J16
Borobudur, Indonesia 33 G14
Borogontsy, Russia 25 C14
Boromo, Burkina Faso 44 F4
Borongan, Phil. 33 B7
Bororen, Australia 54 C5
Borovichi, Russia 22 C5
Borroloola, Australia 54 B2
Borșa, Romania 17 E13
Borth, U.K. 11 E3
Borūjerd, Iran 39 C6
Boryslav, Ukraine 17 D12
Borzya, Russia 25 D12
Bosa, Italy 20 D3
Bosanska Gradiška, Bos.-H. 20 B7
Bosaso, Somali Rep. 40 E4
Boscastle, U.K. 11 G3
Boshof, S. Africa 48 D4
Boshrūyeh, Iran 39 C8

Bosna →, Bos.-H. 21 B8
Bosna i Hercegovina = Bosnia-Herzegovina ■, Europe 20 B7
Bosnia-Herzegovina ■, Europe 20 B7
Bosnik, Indonesia 33 E9
Bosobolo, Zaïre 46 D3
Bosporus = Karadeniz Boğazı, Turkey 21 D13
Bossangoa, C.A.R. 45 G8
Bossembélé, C.A.R. 45 G8
Bossier City, U.S.A. 71 J8
Bosso, Niger 45 F7
Bostānābād, Iran 38 B5
Bosten Hu, China 30 B3
Boston, U.K. 10 E7
Boston, U.S.A. 68 D10
Boston Bar, Canada 64 D4
Boswell, Canada 64 D5
Boswell, U.S.A. 71 H7
Botany B., Australia 55 E5
Bothaville, S. Africa 48 D4
Bothnia, G. of, Europe 8 E19
Bothwell, Australia 54 G4
Botletle →, Botswana 48 C3
Botoşani, Romania 17 E14
Botswana ■, Africa 48 C3
Bottineau, U.S.A. 70 A4
Bottrop, Germany 15 C6
Botucatu, Brazil 80 A7
Botwood, Canada 63 C8
Bou Djébéha, Mali 44 E4
Bou Izakarn, Morocco 44 C3
Bouaké, Ivory C. 44 G3
Bouar, C.A.R. 46 C3
Bouârfa, Morocco 44 B4
Bouca, C.A.R. 45 G8
Boucaut B., Australia 54 A1
Bougainville, C., Australia 52 B4
Bougainville Reef, Australia 54 B4
Bougie = Bejaia, Algeria 44 A6
Bougouni, Mali 44 F3
Bouillon, Belgium 15 E5
Boulder, Colo., U.S.A. 70 E2
Boulder, Mont., U.S.A. 72 C7
Boulder City, U.S.A. 73 J6
Boulder Dam = Hoover Dam, U.S.A. 73 J6
Boulia, Australia 54 C2
Boulogne-sur-Mer, France 18 A4
Boultoum, Niger 44 F7
Bouna, Ivory C. 44 G4
Boundiali, Ivory C. 44 G3
Bountiful, U.S.A. 72 F8
Bounty Is., Pac. Oc. 56 M9
Bourbonnais, France 18 C5
Bourem, Mali 44 E4
Bourg-en-Bresse, France 18 C6
Bourg-St.-Maurice, France 18 D7
Bourges, France 18 C5
Bourgogne, France 18 C6
Bourke, Australia 55 E4
Bournemouth, U.K. 11 G6
Bousso, Chad 45 F8
Boutilimit, Mauritania 44 E2
Bouvet I. = Bouvetøya, Antarctica 3 G10
Bouvetøya, Antarctica 3 G10
Bovigny, Belgium 15 D5
Bovill, U.S.A. 72 C5
Bow Island, Canada 64 D6
Bowbells, U.S.A. 70 A3
Bowdle, U.S.A. 70 C5
Bowelling, Australia 53 F2
Bowen, Australia 54 C4
Bowen Mts., Australia 55 F4
Bowie, Ariz., U.S.A. 73 K9
Bowie, Tex., U.S.A. 71 J6
Bowkān, Iran 38 B5
Bowland, Forest of, U.K. 10 D5
Bowling Green, Ky., U.S.A. 68 G2
Bowling Green, Ohio, U.S.A. 68 E4
Bowling Green, C., Australia 54 B4
Bowman, U.S.A. 70 B3
Bowman I., Antarctica 5 C8
Bowmans, Australia 55 E2
Bowmanville, Canada 62 D4
Bowmore, U.K. 12 F2
Bowral, Australia 55 E5
Bowraville, Australia 55 E5
Bowron →, Canada 64 C4
Bowser L., Canada 64 B3
Bowsman, Canada 65 C8
Boxtel, Neths. 15 C5
Boyce, U.S.A. 71 K8
Boyer →, Canada 64 B5
Boyle, Ireland 13 C3
Boyne →, Ireland 13 C5
Boyne City, U.S.A. 68 C3
Boynton Beach, U.S.A. 69 M5
Boyup Brook, Australia 53 F2
Boz Dağları, Turkey 21 E13
Bozburun, Turkey 21 F13
Bozcaada, Turkey 21 E12
Bozdoğan, Turkey 21 F13
Bozeman, U.S.A. 72 D8
Bozen = Bolzano, Italy 20 A4
Bozoum, C.A.R. 45 G8
Bra, Italy 20 B2
Brabant □, Belgium 15 D4
Brabant L., Canada 65 B8

Brač, Croatia 20 C7
Bracadale, L., U.K. 12 D2
Bracciano, L. di, Italy 20 C5
Bracebridge, Canada 62 C4
Brach, Libya 45 C7
Bräcke, Sweden 9 E16
Brackettville, U.S.A. 71 L4
Brad, Romania 17 E12
Bradenton, U.S.A. 69 M4
Bradford, U.K. 10 D6
Bradford, U.S.A. 68 E6
Bradley, Ark., U.S.A. 71 J8
Bradley, S. Dak., U.S.A. 70 C6
Bradore Bay, Canada 63 B8
Bradshaw, Australia 52 C5
Brady, U.S.A. 71 K5
Braemar, Australia 55 E2
Braga, Portugal 19 B1
Bragança, Brazil 79 D9
Bragança, Portugal 19 B2
Brahmanbaria, Bangla. 37 H17
Brahmani →, India 37 J15
Brahmaputra →, India 37 H16
Braich-y-pwll, U.K. 10 E3
Braidwood, Australia 55 F4
Brăila, Romania 17 F14
Brainerd, U.S.A. 70 B7
Braintree, U.K. 11 F8
Brak →, S. Africa 48 D3
Brakwater, Namibia 48 C2
Bralorne, Canada 64 C4
Brampton, Canada 62 D4
Bramwell, Australia 54 A3
Branco →, Brazil 78 D6
Brandenburg = Neubrandenburg, Germany 16 B7
Brandenburg, Germany 16 B7
Brandenburg □, Germany 16 B6
Brandfort, S. Africa 48 D4
Brandon, Canada 65 D9
Brandon B., Ireland 13 D1
Brandon Mt., Ireland 13 D1
Brandvlei, S. Africa 48 E3
Braniewo, Poland 17 A10
Bransfield Str., Antarctica 5 C18
Branson, Colo., U.S.A. 71 G3
Branson, Mo., U.S.A. 71 G8
Brantford, Canada 62 D4
Branxholme, Australia 55 F3
Bras d'Or, L., Canada 63 C7
Brasiléia, Brazil 78 F5
Brasília, Brazil 79 G9
Braslaw, Belarus 9 J22
Brașov, Romania 17 F13
Brasschaat, Belgium 15 C4
Brassey, Banjaran, Malaysia 32 D5
Brassey Ra., Australia 53 E3
Brasstown Bald, U.S.A. 69 H4
Brastad, Sweden 9 G14
Bratislava, Slovak Rep. 17 D9
Bratsk, Russia 25 D11
Brattleboro, U.S.A. 68 D9
Braunau, Austria 16 D7
Braunschweig, Germany 16 B6
Braunton, U.K. 11 F3
Brava, Somali Rep. 40 G3
Bravo del Norte, R. = Grande, Rio →, U.S.A. 71 N6
Brawley, U.S.A. 73 K6
Bray, Ireland 13 C5
Bray, Mt., Australia 54 A1
Bray, Pays de, France 18 B4
Brazeau →, Canada 64 C5
Brazil, U.S.A. 68 F2
Brazil ■, S. Amer. 79 F9
Brazos →, U.S.A. 71 L7
Brazzaville, Congo 46 E3
Brčko, Bos.-H. 21 B8
Breadalbane, Australia 54 C2
Breadalbane, U.K. 12 E4
Breaden, L., Australia 53 E4
Breaksea Sd., N.Z. 51 L1
Bream B., N.Z. 51 F5
Bream Hd., N.Z. 51 F5
Brebes, Indonesia 33 G13
Brechin, U.K. 12 E6
Breckenridge, Colo., U.S.A. 72 G10
Breckenridge, Minn., U.S.A. 70 B6
Breckenridge, Tex., U.S.A. 71 J5
Breckland, U.K. 11 E8
Brecon, U.K. 11 F4
Brecon Beacons, U.K. 11 F4
Breda, Neths. 15 C4
Bredasdorp, S. Africa 48 E3
Bredbo, Australia 55 F4
Bregenz, Austria 16 E5
Breiðafjörður, Iceland 8 D2
Brejo, Brazil 79 D10
Bremen, Germany 16 B5
Bremer I., Australia 54 A2
Bremerhaven, Germany 16 B5
Bremerton, U.S.A. 72 C2
Brenham, U.S.A. 71 K6
Brenner P., Austria 16 E6
Brent, Canada 62 C4
Brent, U.K. 11 F7
Brentwood, U.K. 11 F8
Bréscia, Italy 20 B4
Breskens, Neths. 15 C3
Breslau = Wrocław, Poland 17 C9
Bressanone, Italy 20 A4
Bressay, U.K. 12 A7
Brest, Belarus 17 B12

Brest, France 18 B1
Brest-Litovsk = Brest, Belarus 17 B12
Bretagne, France 18 B2
Breton, Canada 64 C6
Breton Sd., U.S.A. .. 71 L10
Brett, C., N.Z. 51 F5
Brevard, U.S.A. 69 H4
Brewer, U.S.A. 63 D6
Brewarrina, Australia . 55 D4
Brewster, U.S.A. 72 B4
Brewster, Kap, Greenland 4 B6
Brewton, U.S.A. 69 K2
Breyten, S. Africa ... 49 D4
Brezhnev = Naberezhnyye Chelny, Russia 22 C9
Bria, C.A.R. 45 G9
Briançon, France 18 D7
Bribie I., Australia .. 55 D5
Bridgend, U.K. 11 F4
Bridgeport, Calif., U.S.A. 73 G4
Bridgeport, Conn., U.S.A. 68 E9
Bridgeport, Nebr., U.S.A. 70 E3
Bridgeport, Tex., U.S.A. 71 J6
Bridger, U.S.A. 72 D9
Bridgeton, U.S.A. ... 68 F8
Bridgetown, Australia . 53 F2
Bridgetown, Barbados 74 P22
Bridgetown, Canada .. 63 D6
Bridgewater, Canada . 63 D7
Bridgewater, U.S.A. . 70 D6
Bridgewater, C., Australia 55 F3
Bridgnorth, U.K. 11 E5
Bridgwater, U.K. 11 F4
Bridlington, U.K. 10 C7
Bridport, Australia .. 54 G4
Bridport, U.K. 11 G5
Brig, Switz. 16 E4
Brigg, U.K. 10 D7
Briggsdale, U.S.A. .. 70 E2
Brigham City, U.S.A. . 72 F7
Bright, Australia 55 F4
Brighton, Australia .. 55 F2
Brighton, Canada 62 D4
Brighton, U.K. 11 G7
Brighton, U.S.A. 70 F2
Brilliant, Canada 64 D5
Brindisi, Italy 21 D7
Brinkley, U.S.A. 71 H8
Brinkworth, Australia . 55 E2
Brion, I., Canada 63 C7
Brisbane, Australia .. 55 D5
Brisbane →, Australia 55 D5
Bristol, U.K. 11 F5
Bristol, Conn., U.S.A. . 68 E9
Bristol, S. Dak., U.S.A. 70 C5
Bristol, Tenn., U.S.A. . 69 G4
Bristol B., U.S.A. ... 60 C4
Bristol Channel, U.K. . 11 F3
Bristol I., Antarctica . 5 B1
Bristol L., U.S.A. ... 73 J5
Bristow, U.S.A. 71 H6
British Columbia □, Canada 64 C3
British Isles, Europe .. 6 D5
Brits, S. Africa 49 D4
Britstown, S. Africa .. 48 E3
Britt, Canada 62 C3
Brittany = Bretagne, France 18 B2
Britton, U.S.A. 70 C6
Brive-la-Gaillarde, France 18 D4
Brixen = Bressanone, Italy 20 A4
Brixton, Australia ... 54 C3
Brlik, Kazakhstan .. 24 E8
Brno, Czech. 17 D9
Broad →, U.S.A. ... 69 J5
Broad Arrow, Australia 53 F3
Broad B., U.K. 12 C2
Broad Haven, Ireland . 13 B2
Broad Law, U.K. 12 F5
Broad Sd., Australia . 54 C4
Broadhurst Ra., Australia 52 D3
Broads, The, U.K. ... 10 E9
Broadus, U.S.A. 70 C2
Broadview, Canada .. 65 C8
Brochet, Canada 65 B8
Brochet, L., Canada .. 65 B8
Brock, Canada 65 C7
Brocken, Germany .. 16 C6
Brockport, U.S.A. ... 68 D7
Brockville, Canada .. 62 D4
Brockway, U.S.A. ... 70 B2
Brodeur Pen., Canada 61 A11
Brodick, U.K. 12 F3
Brodnica, Poland ... 17 B10
Brody, Ukraine 17 C13
Brogan, U.S.A. 72 D5
Broken Bow, Nebr., U.S.A. 70 E5
Broken Bow, Okla., U.S.A. 71 H7
Broken Hill = Kabwe, Zambia 47 G5
Broken Hill, Australia . 55 E3
Bromfield, U.K. 11 E5
Bromley, U.K. 11 F8
Brønderslev, Denmark 9 H13
Bronkhorstspruit, S. Africa 49 D4
Brønnøysund, Norway 8 D15
Bronte, U.S.A. 71 K4
Bronte Park, Australia 54 G4
Brookfield, U.S.A. .. 70 F8

Brookhaven, U.S.A. .. 71 K9
Brookings, Oreg., U.S.A. 72 E1
Brookings, S. Dak., U.S.A. 70 C6
Brookmere, Canada .. 64 D4
Brooks, Canada 64 C6
Brooks B., Canada .. 64 C3
Brooks L., Canada .. 65 A7
Brooks Ra., U.S.A. .. 60 B5
Brooksville, U.S.A. .. 69 L4
Brookville, U.S.A. ... 68 F3
Brooloo, Australia ... 55 D5
Broom, L., U.K. 12 D3
Broome, Australia ... 52 C3
Broomehill, Australia . 53 F2
Brora, U.K. 12 C5
Brora →, U.K. 12 C5
Brosna →, Ireland .. 13 C4
Brothers, U.S.A. 72 E3
Brough, U.K. 10 C5
Broughton Island, Canada 61 B13
Broughty Ferry, U.K. . 12 E6
Brouwershaven, Neths. 15 C3
Browerville, U.S.A. .. 70 B7
Brown, Pt., Australia . 55 E1
Brown Willy, U.K. ... 11 G3
Brownfield, U.S.A. .. 71 J3
Browning, U.S.A. ... 72 B7
Brownlee, Canada ... 65 C7
Brownsville, Oreg., U.S.A. 72 D2
Brownsville, Tenn., U.S.A. 71 H10
Brownsville, Tex., U.S.A. 71 N6
Brownwood, U.S.A. .. 71 K5
Brownwood, L., U.S.A. 71 K5
Browse I., Australia .. 52 B3
Bruas, Malaysia ... 34 Q13
Bruay-en-Artois, France 18 A5
Bruce, Mt., Australia . 52 D2
Bruce Rock, Australia . 53 F2
Bruck an der Leitha, Austria 17 D9
Bruck an der Mur, Austria 16 E8
Brue →, U.K. 11 F5
Bruges = Brugge, Belgium 15 C3
Brugge, Belgium ... 15 C3
Brûlé, Canada 64 C5
Brumado, Brazil 79 F10
Brumunddal, Norway . 9 F14
Brunchilly, Australia . 54 B1
Brundidge, U.S.A. .. 69 K3
Bruneau, U.S.A. 72 E6
Bruneau →, U.S.A. . 72 E6
Brunei = Bandar Seri Begawan, Brunei . 32 C4
Brunei ■, Asia 32 D4
Brunette Downs, Australia 54 B2
Brunner, L., N.Z. ... 51 K3
Bruno, Canada 65 C7
Brunswick = Braunschweig, Germany 16 B6
Brunswick, Ga., U.S.A. 69 K5
Brunswick, Maine, U.S.A. 63 D6
Brunswick, Md., U.S.A. 68 F7
Brunswick, Mo., U.S.A. 70 F8
Brunswick, Pen. de, Chile 80 G2
Brunswick B., Australia 52 C3
Brunswick Junction, Australia 53 F2
Bruny I., Australia ... 54 G4
Brush, U.S.A. 70 E3
Brusque, Brazil 80 B7
Brussel, Belgium ... 15 D4
Brussels = Brussel, Belgium 15 D4
Bruthen, Australia .. 55 F4
Bruxelles = Brussel, Belgium 15 D4
Bryan, Ohio, U.S.A. . 68 E3
Bryan, Tex., U.S.A. . 71 K6
Bryan, Mt., Australia . 55 E2
Bryansk, Russia 22 D5
Bryant, U.S.A. 70 C6
Bryne, Norway 9 G11
Bryson City, U.S.A. . 69 H4
Bsharri, Lebanon ... 41 A5
Bū Baqarah, U.A.E. . 39 E8
Bu Craa, W. Sahara . 44 C2
Bū Ḥasā, U.A.E. ... 39 F7
Bua Yai, Thailand ... 34 E7
Buapinang, Indonesia 33 E6
Buayan, Phil. 33 C7
Būbiyān, Kuwait ... 39 D6
Bucaramanga, Colombia 78 B4
Buccaneer Arch., Australia 52 C3
Buchach, Ukraine .. 17 D13
Buchan, U.K. 12 D6
Buchan Ness, U.K. .. 12 D7
Buchanan, Canada .. 65 C8
Buchanan, Liberia .. 44 G2
Buchanan, L., Queens., Australia 54 C4
Buchanan, L., W. Austral., Australia 53 E3
Buchanan, L., U.S.A. 71 K5
Buchanan Cr. →, Australia 54 B2
Buchans, Canada ... 63 C8
Bucharest = București, Romania 17 F14
Buckeye, U.S.A. 73 K7

Buckhannon, U.S.A. .. 68 F5
Buckhaven, U.K. 12 E5
Buckie, U.K. 12 D6
Buckingham, Canada . 62 C4
Buckingham, U.K. ... 11 F7
Buckingham B., Australia 54 A2
Buckinghamshire □, U.K. 11 F7
Buckle Hd., Australia . 52 B4
Buckleboo, Australia . 55 E2
Buckley →, Australia 54 C2
Bucklin, U.S.A. 71 G5
Buctouche, Canada .. 63 C7
București, Romania . 17 F14
Bucyrus, U.S.A. 68 E4
Budalin, Burma 37 H19
Budapest, Hungary .. 17 E10
Budd Coast, Antarctica 5 C8
Bude, U.K. 11 G3
Budennovsk, Russia . 23 F7
Budgewoi, Australia . 55 E5
Búðareyri, Iceland .. 8 D6
Budjala, Zaïre 46 D3
Buena Vista, Colo., U.S.A. 73 G10
Buena Vista, Va., U.S.A. 68 G6
Buena Vista L., U.S.A. 73 J4
Buenaventura, Colombia 78 C3
Buenos Aires, Argentina 80 C5
Buenos Aires, L., Chile 80 F2
Buffalo, Mo., U.S.A. . 71 G8
Buffalo, N.Y., U.S.A. . 68 D6
Buffalo, Okla., U.S.A. . 71 G5
Buffalo, S. Dak., U.S.A. 70 C3
Buffalo, Wyo., U.S.A. . 72 D10
Buffalo →, Canada . 64 A5
Buffalo Head Hills, Canada 64 B5
Buffalo L., Canada .. 64 C6
Buffalo Narrows, Canada 65 B7
Buffels →, S. Africa . 48 D2
Buford, U.S.A. 69 H4
Bug →, Buh →, Ukraine 23 E5
Bug →, Poland ... 17 B11
Buga, Colombia 78 C3
Bugel, Tanjung, Indonesia 32 F4
Bugsuk, Phil. 32 C5
Bugulma, Russia ... 22 D9
Bugun Shara, Mongolia 30 B5
Buguruslan, Russia .. 22 D9
Buh →, Ukraine ... 23 E5
Buheirat-Murrat-el-Kubra, Egypt 45 B11
Buhl, Idaho, U.S.A. .. 72 E6
Buhl, Minn., U.S.A. . 70 B8
Buick, U.S.A. 71 G9
Builth Wells, U.K. ... 11 E4
Buir Nur, Mongolia .. 31 B6
Bujumbura, Burundi . 46 E5
Bukachacha, Russia . 25 D12
Bukama, Zaïre 46 F5
Bukavu, Zaïre 46 E5
Bukene, Tanzania ... 46 E6
Bukhara = Bukhoro, Uzbekistan 24 F7
Bukhoro, Uzbekistan . 24 F7
Bukittinggi, Indonesia 32 E2
Bukoba, Tanzania .. 46 E6
Bula, Indonesia 33 E8
Bulahdelah, Australia 55 E5
Bulan, Phil. 33 B6
Bulandshahr, India .. 36 E10
Bulawayo, Zimbabwe 47 J5
Buldan, Turkey 21 E13
Bulgaria ■, Europe . 21 C11
Bulgroo, Australia .. 55 D3
Bulgunnia, Australia . 55 E1
Bulhar, Somali Rep. . 40 E3
Buli, Teluk, Indonesia 33 D7
Buliluyan, C., Phil. .. 32 C5
Bulkley →, Canada . 64 B3
Bull Shoals L., U.S.A. 71 G8
Bullara, Australia ... 52 D1
Bullaring, Australia .. 53 F2
Bulli, Australia 55 E5
Bullock Creek, Australia 54 B3
Bulloo →, Australia 55 D3
Bulloo Downs, Queens., Australia 55 D3
Bulloo Downs, W. Austral., Australia 52 D2
Bulloo L., Australia . 55 D3
Bulls, N.Z. 51 J5
Bulo Burti, Somali Rep. 40 G4
Bulsar = Valsad, India 36 J8
Bultfontein, S. Africa . 48 D4
Bulu Karakelong, Indonesia 33 D7
Bulukumba, Indonesia 33 F6
Bulun, Russia 25 B13
Bulus, Russia 25 C13
Bumba, Zaïre 46 D4
Bumhpa Bum, Burma 37 F20
Buna, Kenya 46 D7
Bunbah, Khalīj, Libya 45 B9
Bunbury, Australia .. 53 F2
Buncrana, Ireland .. 13 A4
Bundaberg, Australia . 55 C5
Bundey →, Australia 54 C2
Bundi, India 36 G9
Bundooma, Australia 54 C1
Bundoran, Ireland .. 13 B3
Bungatakada, Japan . 29 H5
Bungil Cr. →, Australia 54 D4
Bungo-Suidō, Japan . 29 H6

Bunia, Zaïre 46 D6
Bunji, Pakistan 36 B9
Bunkie, U.S.A. 71 K8
Bunnell, U.S.A. 69 L5
Buntok, Indonesia .. 32 E4
Bunyu, Indonesia .. 32 D5
Buol, Indonesia 33 D6
Buon Me Thuot, Vietnam 34 F10
Buorkhaya, Mys, Russia 25 B14
Buqayq, Si. Arabia . 39 E6
Bur Acaba, Somali Rep. 40 G3
Bûr Safâga, Egypt .. 45 C11
Bûr Sa'îd, Egypt ... 45 B11
Bûr Sûdân, Sudan .. 45 E12
Burao, Somali Rep. .. 40 F4
Burāq, Syria 41 B5
Buras, U.S.A. 71 L10
Buraydah, Si. Arabia . 38 E5
Burbank, U.S.A. 73 J4
Burcher, Australia .. 55 E4
Burdekin →, Australia 54 B4
Burdett, Canada ... 64 D6
Burdur, Turkey 23 G5
Burdwan = Barddhaman, India 37 H15
Bure →, U.K. 10 E9
Bureya →, Russia . 25 E13
Burgas, Bulgaria ... 21 C12
Burgeo, Canada ... 63 C8
Burgersdorp, S. Africa 48 E4
Burges, Mt., Australia 53 F3
Burgos, Spain 19 A4
Burgsvik, Sweden .. 9 H18
Burgundy = Bourgogne, France 18 C6
Burhaniye, Turkey .. 21 E12
Burhanpur, India ... 36 J10
Burias, Phil. 33 B6
Burin, Canada 63 C8
Buriram, Thailand .. 34 E7
Burj Sāfītā, Syria .. 38 C3
Burji, Ethiopia 45 G12
Burkburnett, U.S.A. . 71 H5
Burke, U.S.A. 72 C6
Burke →, Australia . 54 C2
Burketown, Australia 54 B2
Burkina Faso ■, Africa 44 F4
Burk's Falls, Canada . 62 C4
Burley, U.S.A. 72 E7
Burlington, Colo., U.S.A. 70 F3
Burlington, Iowa, U.S.A. 70 E9
Burlington, Kans., U.S.A. 70 F7
Burlington, N.C., U.S.A. 69 G6
Burlington, N.J., U.S.A. 68 E8
Burlington, Vt., U.S.A. 68 C9
Burlington, Wash., U.S.A. 72 B2
Burlington, Wis., U.S.A. 68 D1
Burlyu-Tyube, Kazakhstan 24 E8
Burma ■, Asia 37 J20
Burnaby I., Canada . 64 C2
Burnet, U.S.A. 71 K5
Burney, U.S.A. 72 F3
Burngup, Australia .. 53 F2
Burnie, Australia ... 54 G4
Burnley, U.K. 10 D5
Burns, Oreg., U.S.A. . 72 E4
Burns, Wyo., U.S.A. . 70 E2
Burns Lake, Canada . 64 C3
Burnside →, Canada 60 B9
Burnside, L., Australia 53 E3
Burntwood →, Canada 65 B9
Burntwood L., Canada 65 B8
Burqān, Kuwait 38 D5
Burra, Australia 55 E2
Burramurra, Australia 54 C2
Burren Junction, Australia 55 E4
Burrendong Dam, Australia 55 E4
Burrinjuck Res., Australia 55 F4
Burruyacú, Argentina 80 B4
Burry Port, U.K. 11 F3
Bursa, Turkey 21 D13
Burstall, Canada ... 65 C7
Burton, Canada 62 D4
Burton upon Trent, U.K. 10 E6
Burtundy, Australia . 55 E3
Buru, Indonesia 33 E7
Burûn, Râs, Egypt .. 41 D2
Burundi ■, Africa .. 46 E5
Burutu, Nigeria 44 G6
Burwell, U.S.A. 70 E5
Burwick, U.K. 12 C5
Bury, U.K. 10 D5
Bury St. Edmunds, U.K. 11 E8
Buryatia □, Russia . 25 D11
Buşayrah, Syria 38 C4
Buşayyah, Iraq 38 D5
Büshehr, Iran 39 D6
Büshehr □, Iran ... 39 D6
Bushell, Canada ... 65 B7
Bushire = Büshehr, Iran 39 D6
Bushnell, Ill., U.S.A. . 70 E9
Bushnell, Nebr., U.S.A. 70 E3
Businga, Zaïre 46 D4
Busra ash Shām, Syria 41 C5
Busselton, Australia . 53 F2
Bussum, Neths. 15 B5
Busto Arsízio, Italy .. 20 B3
Busu-Djanoa, Zaïre . 46 D4
Busuanga, Phil. 33 B5
Buta, Zaïre 46 D4
Butare, Rwanda ... 46 E5
Butaritari, Kiribati .. 56 G9
Bute, U.K. 12 F3

Butembo, Zaïre 46 D5
Butha Qi, China 31 B7
Butler, Mo., U.S.A. . 70 F7
Butler, Pa., U.S.A. .. 68 E6
Butte, Mont., U.S.A. . 72 C7
Butte, Nebr., U.S.A. . 70 D5
Butterworth = Gcuwa, S. Africa 49 E4
Butterworth, Malaysia 34 P13
Buttfield, Mt., Australia 53 D4
Button B., Canada .. 65 B10
Butty Hd., Australia . 53 F3
Butuan, Phil. 33 C7
Butung = Buton, Indonesia 33 E6
Buturlinovka, Russia . 23 D7
Buxtehude, Germany . 16 B5
Buxton, U.K. 10 D6
Buy, Russia 22 C7
Büyük Menderes →, Turkey 21 F12
Büyükçekmece, Turkey 21 D13
Buzău, Romania ... 17 F14
Buzău →, Romania . 17 F14
Buzen, Japan 29 H5
Buzi →, Mozam. ... 47 H6
Buzuluk, Russia 22 D9
Buzzards Bay, U.S.A. 68 E10
Byarezina →, Belarus 17 B16
Bydgoszcz, Poland .. 17 B9
Byelarus = Belarus ■, Europe 17 B14
Byelorussia = Belarus ■, Europe . 17 B14
Byers, U.S.A. 70 F2
Byhalia, U.S.A. 71 H10
Bykhaw, Belarus ... 17 B16
Bykhov = Bykhaw, Belarus 17 B16
Bylas, U.S.A. 73 K8
Bylot I., Canada ... 61 A12
Byrd, C., Antarctica . 5 C17
Byro, Australia 53 E2
Byrock, Australia ... 55 E4
Byron Bay, Australia . 55 D5
Byrranga, Gory, Russia 25 B11
Byrranga Mts. = Byrranga, Gory, Russia 25 B11
Byske, Sweden 8 D19
Byske älv →, Sweden 8 D19
Bytom, Poland 17 C10
Bytów, Poland 17 A9

C

Ca Mau = Quan Long, Vietnam 34 H8
Ca Mau, Mui = Bai Bung, Mui, Vietnam 34 H8
Caála, Angola 47 G3
Caamano Sd., Canada 64 C3
Cabanatuan, Phil. .. 33 A6
Cabano, Canada ... 63 C6
Cabedelo, Brazil ... 79 E12
Cabimas, Venezuela . 78 A4
Cabinda, Angola ... 46 F2
Cabinda □, Angola . 46 F2
Cabinet Mts., U.S.A. 72 C6
Cabo Blanco, Argentina 80 F3
Cabo Frio, Brazil ... 79 H10
Cabo Pantoja, Peru . 78 D3
Cabonga, Réservoir, Canada 62 C4
Cabool, U.S.A. 71 G8
Caboolture, Australia 55 D5
Cabora Bassa Dam = Cahora Bassa Dam, Mozam. 47 H6
Cabot Str., Canada . 63 C8
Cabra, Spain 19 D3
Cabrera, Spain 19 C7
Cabri, Canada 65 C7
Cabriel →, Spain .. 19 C5
Čačak, Serbia, Yug. . 21 C9
Cáceres, Brazil 78 G7
Cáceres, Spain 19 C2
Cache Bay, Canada . 62 C4
Cachimbo, Serra do, Brazil 79 E7
Cachoeira, Brazil ... 79 F11
Cachoeira de Itapemirim, Brazil . 79 H10
Cachoeira do Sul, Brazil 80 C6
Cacólo, Angola 46 G3
Caconda, Angola ... 47 G3
Cacongo, Angola ... 46 F2
Caddo, U.S.A. 71 H6
Cadell Cr. →, Australia 54 C3
Cader Idris, U.K. ... 10 E4
Cadibarrawirracanna, L., Australia 55 D2
Cadillac, Canada ... 62 C4
Cadillac, U.S.A. 68 C3
Cadiz, Phil. 33 B6
Cádiz, Spain 19 D2
Cádiz, G. de, Spain . 19 D2
Cadney Park, Australia 55 D1
Cadomin, Canada .. 64 C5
Cadotte →, Canada 64 B5
Cadoux, Australia .. 53 F2
Caen, France 18 B3
Caernarfon, U.K. ... 10 D3
Caernarfon B., U.K. . 10 D3
Caernarvon = Caernarfon, U.K. .. 10 D3
Caerphilly, U.K. 11 F4

Caesarea, Israel 41 C3
Caeté, Brazil 79 G10
Caetité, Brazil 79 F10
Cafu, Angola 48 B2
Cagayan →, Phil. .. 33 A6
Cagayan de Oro, Phil. 33 C6
Cágliari, Italy 20 E3
Cágliari, G. di, Italy . 20 E3
Caguas, Puerto Rico . 75 D11
Caha Mts., Ireland .. 13 E2
Cahama, Angola ... 48 B1
Caher, Ireland 13 D4
Cahersiveen, Ireland . 13 E1
Cahora Bassa Dam, Mozam. 47 H6
Cahore Pt., Ireland .. 13 D5
Cahors, France 18 D4
Cahuapanas, Peru .. 78 E3
Cahul, Moldova 17 F15
Caia, Mozam. 47 H7
Caibarién, Cuba ... 75 C9
Caicara, Venezuela . 78 B5
Caicó, Brazil 79 E11
Caicos Is., W. Indies . 75 C10
Caird Coast, Antarctica 5 D1
Cairn Gorm, U.K. .. 12 D5
Cairn Toul, U.K. ... 12 D5
Cairngorm Mts., U.K. 12 D5
Cairns, Australia ... 54 B4
Cairo = El Qâhira, Egypt 45 B11
Cairo, Ga., U.S.A. .. 69 K3
Cairo, Ill., U.S.A. .. 71 G10
Caithness, Ord of, U.K. 12 C5
Caiundo, Angola ... 47 H3
Caiza, Bolivia 78 H5
Cajamarca, Peru ... 78 E3
Cajàzeiras, Brazil .. 79 E11
Calabar, Nigeria ... 44 H6
Calábria □, Italy ... 20 E7
Calafate, Argentina . 80 G2
Calahorra, Spain ... 19 A5
Calais, France 18 A4
Calais, U.S.A. 63 C6
Calama, Brazil 78 E6
Calama, Chile 80 A3
Calamar, Bolívar, Colombia 78 A4
Calamar, Vaupés, Colombia 78 C4
Calamian Group, Phil. 33 B5
Calamocha, Spain .. 19 B5
Calang, Indonesia .. 32 D1
Calapan, Phil. 33 B6
Călăraşi, Romania . 17 F14
Calauag, Phil. 33 B6
Calavite, C., Phil. .. 33 B6
Calbayog, Phil. 33 B6
Calca, Peru 78 F4
Calcasieu L., U.S.A. 71 L8
Calcutta, India 37 H16
Caldas da Rainha, Portugal 19 C1
Calder →, U.K. ... 10 D6
Caldera, Chile 80 B2
Caldwell, Idaho, U.S.A. 72 E5
Caldwell, Kans., U.S.A. 71 G6
Caldwell, Tex., U.S.A. 71 K6
Caledon, S. Africa .. 48 E2
Caledon →, S. Africa 48 E4
Caledon B., Australia 54 A2
Calemba, Angola ... 48 B2
Calexico, U.S.A. 73 K6
Calf of Man, U.K. .. 10 C3
Calgary, Canada ... 64 C6
Calhoun, U.S.A. ... 69 H3
Cali, Colombia 78 C3
Calicut, India 36 P9
Caliente, U.S.A. 73 H6
California, U.S.A. ... 70 F8
California □, U.S.A. . 73 H4
California, G. de, Mexico 74 B2
Calingasta, Argentina 80 C3
Calipatria, U.S.A. .. 73 K6
Calistoga, U.S.A. ... 72 G2
Calitzdorp, S. Africa . 48 E3
Callabonna, L., Australia 55 D3
Callan, Ireland 13 D4
Callander, U.K. 12 E4
Callao, Peru 78 F3
Callaway, U.S.A. ... 70 E5
Callide, Australia ... 54 C5
Calling Lake, Canada 64 B6
Calliope, Australia .. 54 C5
Calola, Angola 48 B2
Caloundra, Australia 55 D5
Calstock, Canada .. 62 C3
Caltagirone, Italy .. 20 F6
Caltanissetta, Italy .. 20 F6
Calulo, Angola 46 G2
Calumet, U.S.A. 68 B1
Calunda, Angola ... 47 G4
Calvert, U.S.A. 71 K6
Calvert →, Australia 54 B2
Calvert Hills, Australia 54 B2
Calvert I., Canada .. 64 C3
Calvert Ra., Australia 52 D3
Calvi, France 18 E8
Calvià, Spain 19 C7
Calvinia, S. Africa .. 48 E2
Cam →, U.K. 11 E8
Cam Lam, Vietnam . 34 G10
Cam Ranh, Vietnam . 34 G10
Camabatela, Angola 46 F3
Camacupa, Angola . 47 G3
Camagüey, Cuba ... 75 C9
Camaná, Peru 78 G4
Camargo, Bolivia ... 78 H5
Camargue, France .. 18 E6
Camarones, Argentina 80 E3

Camas, U.S.A. 72 D2
Camas Valley, U.S.A. . 72 E2
Cambay = Khambhat, India 36 H8
Cambay, G. of = Khambat, G. of, India 36 J8
Cambodia ■, Asia . . . 34 F8
Camborne, U.K. 11 G2
Cambrai, France 18 A5
Cambria, U.S.A. 73 J3
Cambrian Mts., U.K. . 11 E4
Cambridge, Canada . . 62 D3
Cambridge, N.Z. . . . 51 G5
Cambridge, U.K. . . . 11 E8
Cambridge, Idaho, U.S.A. 72 D5
Cambridge, Mass., U.S.A. 68 D10
Cambridge, Md., U.S.A. 68 F7
Cambridge, Minn., U.S.A. 70 C8
Cambridge, Nebr., U.S.A. 70 E4
Cambridge, Ohio, U.S.A. 68 E5
Cambridge Bay, Canada 60 B9
Cambridge G., Australia 52 B4
Cambridgeshire □, U.K. 11 E8
Cambundi-Catembo, Angola 46 G3
Camden, Ala., U.S.A. . 69 K2
Camden, Ark., U.S.A. . 71 J8
Camden, Maine, U.S.A. 63 D6
Camden, N.J., U.S.A. . 68 F8
Camden, S.C., U.S.A. . 69 H5
Camden Sd., Australia . 52 C3
Camdenton, U.S.A. . . 71 F8
Cameron, Ariz., U.S.A. 73 J8
Cameron, La., U.S.A. . 71 L8
Cameron, Mo., U.S.A. . 70 F7
Cameron, Tex., U.S.A. 71 K6
Cameron Falls, Canada 62 C2
Cameron Highlands, Malaysia 34 Q14
Cameron Hills, Canada 64 B6
Cameroon ■, Africa . . 45 G7
Cameroon, Mt., Cameroon 44 H6
Cametá, Brazil 79 D9
Caminha, Portugal . . 19 B1
Camino, U.S.A. 72 G3
Camira Creek, Australia 55 D5
Camissombo, Angola . 46 F4
Camocim, Brazil . . . 79 D10
Camooweal, Australia . 54 B2
Camopi, Fr. Guiana . . 79 C8
Camp Crook, U.S.A. . 70 C3
Camp Wood, U.S.A. . 71 L4
Campana, I., Chile . . 80 F1
Campánia □, Italy . . . 20 D6
Campbell, S. Africa . . 48 D3
Campbell I., Pac. Oc. . 56 N8
Campbell L., Canada . 65 A7
Campbell River, Canada 64 C3
Campbell Town, Australia 54 G4
Campbellsville, U.S.A. 68 G3
Campbellton, Canada . 63 C6
Campbelltown, Australia 55 E5
Campbeltown, U.K. . . 12 F3
Campeche, Mexico . . 74 D6
Campeche, B. de, Mexico 74 D6
Camperdown, Australia 55 F3
Camperville, Canada . 65 C8
Campina Grande, Brazil 79 E11
Campinas, Brazil . . . 80 A7
Campo, Cameroon . . 46 D1
Campo Belo, Brazil . . 79 H9
Campo Formoso, Brazil 79 F10
Campo Grande, Brazil . 79 H8
Campo Maíor, Brazil . 79 D10
Campo Mourão, Brazil 79 H8
Campoalegre, Colombia 78 C3
Campobasso, Italy . . 20 D6
Campos, Brazil 79 H10
Campos Belos, Brazil . 79 F9
Campuya, Peru 78 D4
Camrose, Canada . . . 64 C6
Camsell Portage, Canada 65 B7
Çan, Turkey 21 D12
Can Tho, Vietnam . . 34 G8
Canada ■, N. Amer. . 60 C10
Cañada de Gómez, Argentina 80 C4
Canadian, U.S.A. . . . 71 H4
Canadian →, U.S.A. . 71 H7
Canadian Shield, Canada 61 C10
Çanakkale, Turkey . . 21 D12
Çanakkale Boğazı, Turkey 21 D12
Canal Flats, Canada . . 64 C5
Canandaigua, U.S.A. . 68 D7
Cananea, Mexico . . . 74 A2
Canarias, Is., Atl. Oc. 44 C1
Canary Is. = Canarias, Is., Atl. Oc. 44 C1
Canaveral, C., U.S.A. . 69 L5
Canavieiras, Brazil . . 79 G11
Canbelego, Australia . 55 E4
Canberra, Australia . . 55 F4
Canby, Calif., U.S.A. . 72 F3
Canby, Minn., U.S.A. . 70 C6
Canby, Oreg., U.S.A. . 72 D2
Candala, Somali Rep. . 40 E4
Candelo, Australia . . 55 F4
Candia = Iráklion, Greece 21 G11

Candle L., Canada . . . 65 C7
Candlemas I., Antarctica 5 B1
Cando, U.S.A. 70 A5
Canea = Khaniá, Greece 21 G11
Canelones, Uruguay . . 80 C5
Cañete, Chile 80 D2
Cañete, Peru 78 F3
Cangas de Narcea, Spain 19 A2
Canguaretama, Brazil . 79 E11
Canguçu, Brazil 80 C6
Canicattì, Italy 20 F5
Canim Lake, Canada . 64 C4
Canipaan, Phil. 32 C5
Çankırı, Turkey 23 F5
Canmore, Canada . . . 64 C5
Cann River, Australia . 55 F4
Canna, U.K. 12 D2
Cannanore, India . . . 36 P9
Cannes, France 18 E7
Cannock, U.K. 10 E5
Cannon Ball →, U.S.A. 70 B4
Cannondale Mt., Australia 54 D4
Canoas, Brazil 80 B6
Canoe L., Canada . . . 65 B7
Canon City, U.S.A. . . 70 F2
Canora, Canada 65 C8
Canowindra, Australia 55 E4
Canso, Canada 63 C7
Cantabria □, Spain . . 19 A4
Cantabrian Mts. = Cantábrica, Cordillera, Spain 19 A3
Cantábrica, Cordillera, Spain 19 A3
Cantal, Plomb du, France 18 D5
Canterbury, Australia . 54 D3
Canterbury, U.K. . . . 11 F9
Canterbury □, N.Z. . . 51 K3
Canterbury Bight, N.Z. 51 L3
Canterbury Plains, N.Z. 51 K3
Canton = Guangzhou, China 31 D6
Canton, Ga., U.S.A. . . 69 H3
Canton, Ill., U.S.A. . . 70 E9
Canton, Miss., U.S.A. . 71 J9
Canton, Mo., U.S.A. . 70 E9
Canton, N.Y., U.S.A. . 68 C8
Canton, Ohio, U.S.A. . 68 E5
Canton, Okla., U.S.A. . 71 G5
Canton, S. Dak., U.S.A. 70 D6
Canton L., U.S.A. . . . 71 G5
Canudos, Brazil 78 E7
Canutama, Brazil . . . 78 E6
Canutillo, U.S.A. . . . 73 L10
Canyon, Tex., U.S.A. . 71 H4
Canyon, Wyo., U.S.A. 72 D8
Canyonlands National Park, U.S.A. 73 G9
Canyonville, U.S.A. . . 72 E2
Cap-aux-Meules, Canada 63 C7
Cap-Chat, Canada . . . 63 C6
Cap-de-la-Madeleine, Canada 63 C5
Cap-Haïtien, Haiti . . . 75 D10
Cap St.-Jacques = Vung Tau, Vietnam . 34 G9
Capaia, Angola 46 F4
Capanaparo →, Venezuela 78 B5
Cape →, Australia . . 54 C4
Cape Barren I., Australia 54 G4
Cape Breton Highlands Nat. Park, Canada . . 63 C7
Cape Breton I., Canada 63 C7
Cape Charles, U.S.A. . 68 G8
Cape Coast, Ghana . . 44 G4
Cape Dorset, Canada . 61 B12
Cape Dyer, Canada . . 61 B13
Cape Fear →, U.S.A. . 69 H6
Cape Girardeau, U.S.A. 71 G10
Cape Jervis, Australia . 55 F2
Cape May, U.S.A. . . . 68 F8
Cape May Point, U.S.A. 67 C12
Cape Tormentine, Canada 63 C7
Cape Town, S. Africa . 48 E2
Cape Verde Is. ■, Atl. Oc. 2 D8
Cape York Peninsula, Australia 54 A3
Capela, Brazil 79 F11
Capella, Australia . . . 54 C4
Capim →, Brazil . . . 79 D9
Capitan, U.S.A. 73 K11
Capraia, Italy 20 C3
Capreol, Canada . . . 62 C3
Caprera, Italy 20 D6
Capricorn Group, Australia 54 C5
Capricorn Ra., Australia 52 D2
Caprivi Strip, Namibia . 48 B3
Captain's Flat, Australia 55 F4
Caquetá →, Colombia 78 D5
Caracal, Romania . . . 17 F13
Caracas, Venezuela . . 78 A5
Caracol, Brazil 79 E10
Carajás, Serra dos, Brazil 79 E8
Carangola, Brazil . . . 79 H10
Carani, Australia . . . 53 F2
Caransebeş, Romania . 17 F12
Caratasca, L., Honduras 75 D8
Caratinga, Brazil . . . 79 G10
Caraúbas, Brazil . . . 79 E11

Caravaca, Spain 19 C5
Caravelas, Brazil . . . 79 G11
Caraveli, Peru 78 G4
Carballo, Spain 19 A1
Carberry, Canada . . . 65 D9
Carbon, Canada 64 C6
Carbonara, C., Italy . . 20 E3
Carbondale, Colo., U.S.A. 72 G10
Carbondale, Ill., U.S.A. 71 G10
Carbondale, Pa., U.S.A. 68 E8
Carbonear, Canada . . 63 C9
Carbonia, Italy 20 E3
Carcajou, Canada . . . 64 B5
Carcassonne, France . 18 E5
Carcross, Canada . . . 60 B6
Cardabia, Australia . . 52 D1
Cardamon Hills, India . 36 Q10
Cárdenas, Cuba 75 C8
Cardiff, U.K. 11 F4
Cardigan, U.K. 11 E3
Cardigan B., U.K. . . . 11 E3
Cardross, Canada . . . 65 D7
Cardston, Canada . . . 64 D6
Cardwell, Australia . . 54 B4
Careen L., Canada . . 65 B7
Carei, Romania 17 E12
Careme = Ceremai, Indonesia 33 G13
Carey, Idaho, U.S.A. . 72 E7
Carey, Ohio, U.S.A. . . 68 E4
Carey, L., Australia . . 53 E3
Carey L., Canada . . . 65 A8
Careysburg, Liberia . . 44 G2
Cargados Garajos, Ind. Oc. 35 F4
Carhué, Argentina . . . 80 D4
Caria, Turkey 21 F13
Cariacica, Brazil . . . 79 H10
Caribbean Sea, W. Indies 75 E10
Cariboo Mts., Canada . 64 C4
Caribou, U.S.A. 63 C6
Caribou →, Man., Canada 65 B10
Caribou →, N.W.T., Canada 64 A3
Caribou I., Canada . . 62 C2
Caribou Is., Canada . . 64 A6
Caribou L., Man., Canada 65 B9
Caribou L., Ont., Canada 62 B2
Caribou Mts., Canada . 64 B5
Carinda, Australia . . . 55 E4
Carinhanha, Brazil . . 79 F10
Carinthia = Kärnten □, Austria 16 E8
Caripito, Venezuela . . 78 A6
Caritianas, Brazil . . . 78 E6
Carleton Place, Canada 62 C4
Carletonville, S. Africa 48 D4
Carlin, U.S.A. 72 F5
Carlingford L., U.K. . . 13 B5
Carlinville, U.S.A. . . . 70 F10
Carlisle, U.K. 10 C5
Carlisle, U.S.A. 68 E7
Carlow, Ireland 13 D5
Carlow □, Ireland . . . 13 D5
Carlsbad, Calif., U.S.A. 73 K5
Carlsbad, N. Mex., U.S.A. 71 J2
Carlyle, Canada 65 D8
Carlyle, U.S.A. 70 F10
Carmacks, Canada . . 60 B6
Carman, Canada . . . 65 D9
Carmangay, Canada . . 64 C6
Carmanville, Canada . 63 C9
Carmarthen, U.K. . . . 11 F3
Carmarthen B., U.K. . 11 F3
Carmaux, France . . . 18 D5
Carmel-by-the-Sea, U.S.A. 73 H3
Carmel Coast, Canada 63 C7
Carmelo, Uruguay . . . 80 C5
Carmen, Colombia . . 78 B3
Carmen de Patagones, Argentina 80 E4
Carmi, U.S.A. 68 F1
Carmila, Australia . . . 54 C4
Carmona, Spain 19 D3
Carnac, France 18 C2
Carnarvon, Queens., Australia 54 C4
Carnarvon, W. Austral., Australia 53 D1
Carnarvon, S. Africa . 48 E3
Carnarvon Ra., Queens., Australia . . 54 D4
Carnarvon Ra., W. Austral., Australia 53 E3
Carndonagh, Ireland . 13 A4
Carnduff, Canada . . . 65 D8
Carnegie, U.S.A. . . . 68 F5
Carnegie, L., Australia 53 E3
Carnic Alps = Karnische Alpen, Europe 16 E7
Carniche Alpi = Karnische Alpen, Europe 16 E7
Carnot, C.A.R. 46 D3
Carnot, C., Australia . 55 E2
Carnot B., Australia . . 52 C3
Carnsore Pt., Ireland . 13 D5
Caro, U.S.A. 68 D4
Carol City, U.S.A. . . . 69 N5
Carolina, Brazil 79 E9
Carolina, S. Africa . . 49 D5
Caroline I., Kiribati . . 57 H12
Caroline Is., Pac. Oc. . 56 G6
Caron, Canada 65 C7
Caroni →, Venezuela . 78 B6
Caronie = Nébrodi, Monti, Italy 20 F6
Caroona, Australia . . 55 E5

Carpathians, Europe . 17 D11
Carpaţii Meridionali, Romania 17 F13
Carpentaria, G. of, Australia 54 A2
Carpentaria Downs, Australia 54 B3
Carpentras, France . . 18 D6
Carpi, Italy 20 B4
Carpinteria, U.S.A. . . 73 J4
Carpolac = Morea, Australia 55 F3
Carr Boyd Ra., Australia 52 C4
Carrabelle, U.S.A. . . . 69 L3
Carranya, Australia . . 52 C4
Carrara, Italy 20 B4
Carrauntoohill, Ireland 13 E2
Carrick-on-Shannon, Ireland 13 C3
Carrick-on-Suir, Ireland 13 D4
Carrickfergus, U.K. . . 13 B6
Carrickfergus □, U.K. . 13 B6
Carrickmacross, Ireland 13 C5
Carrieton, Australia . . 55 E2
Carrington, U.S.A. . . 70 B5
Carrizal Bajo, Chile . . 80 B2
Carrizo Cr. →, U.S.A. 71 G3
Carrizo Springs, U.S.A. 71 L5
Carrizozo, U.S.A. . . . 73 K11
Carroll, U.S.A. 70 D7
Carrollton, Ga., U.S.A. 69 J3
Carrollton, Ill., U.S.A. 70 F9
Carrollton, Ky., U.S.A. 68 F3
Carrollton, Mo., U.S.A. 70 F8
Carron →, U.K. . . . 12 D3
Carron, L., U.K. . . . 12 D3
Carrot →, Canada . . 65 C8
Carrot River, Canada . 65 C8
Carruthers, Canada . . 65 C7
Carse of Gowrie, U.K. 12 E5
Carson, U.S.A. 70 B4
Carson City, U.S.A. . . 72 G4
Carson Sink, U.S.A. . . 72 G4
Carstairs, U.K. 12 F5
Cartagena, Colombia . 78 A3
Cartagena, Spain . . . 19 D5
Cartago, Colombia . . 78 C3
Cartago, Costa Rica . . 75 F8
Cartersville, U.S.A. . . 69 H3
Carterton, N.Z. 51 J5
Carthage, Ark., U.S.A. 71 H8
Carthage, Ill., U.S.A. . 70 E9
Carthage, Mo., U.S.A. 71 G7
Carthage, S. Dak., U.S.A. 70 C6
Carthage, Tex., U.S.A. 71 J7
Cartier I., Australia . . 52 B3
Cartwright, Canada . . 63 B8
Caruaru, Brazil 79 E11
Carúpano, Venezuela . 78 A6
Caruthersville, U.S.A. . 71 G10
Carvoeiro, Brazil . . . 78 D6
Carvoeiro, C., Portugal 19 C1
Casa Grande, U.S.A. . 73 K8
Casablanca, Morocco . 44 B3
Cascade, Idaho, U.S.A. 72 D5
Cascade, Mont., U.S.A. 72 C8
Cascade Locks, U.S.A. 72 D3
Cascade Ra., U.S.A. . 72 C3
Cascais, Portugal . . . 19 C1
Cascavel, Brazil 80 A6
Cáscina, Italy 20 C4
Caserta, Italy 20 D6
Cashel, Ireland 13 D4
Cashmere, U.S.A. . . . 72 C3
Cashmere Downs, Australia 53 E2
Casiguran, Phil. 33 A6
Casilda, Argentina . . 80 C4
Casino, Australia . . . 55 D5
Casiquiare →, Venezuela 78 C5
Caslan, Canada 64 C6
Casma, Peru 78 E3
Caspe, Spain 19 B5
Casper, U.S.A. 72 E10
Caspian Depression, Eurasia 23 E8
Caspian Sea, Eurasia . 23 F9
Cass City, U.S.A. . . . 68 D4
Cass Lake, U.S.A. . . . 70 B7
Casselton, U.S.A. . . . 70 B6
Cassiar, Canada 64 B3
Cassiar Mts., Canada . 64 B2
Cassinga, Angola . . . 47 H3
Cassino, Italy 20 D5
Cassville, U.S.A. . . . 71 G8
Castellammare di Stábia, Italy 20 D6
Castellón de la Plana, Spain 19 C5
Castelo Branco, Portugal 19 C2
Castelsarrasin, France 18 E4
Castelvetrano, Italy . . 20 F5
Casterton, Australia . . 55 F3
Castilla La Mancha □, Spain 19 C4
Castilla y Leon □, Spain 19 B3
Castle Dale, U.S.A. . . 72 G8
Castle Douglas, U.K. . 12 G5
Castle Rock, Colo., U.S.A. 70 F2
Castle Rock, Wash., U.S.A. 72 C2
Castleblaney, Ireland . 13 B5
Castlegar, Canada . . 64 D5
Castlemaine, Australia 55 F3
Castlerea, Ireland . . . 13 C3
Castlereagh □, U.K. . . 13 B6

Castlereagh →, Australia 55 E4
Castlereagh B., Australia 54 A2
Castletown, U.K. . . . 10 C3
Castletown Bearhaven, Ireland 13 E2
Castlevale, Australia . . 54 C4
Castor, Canada 64 C6
Castres, France 18 E5
Castries, St. Lucia . . . 74 N21
Castro, Chile 80 E2
Castro Alves, Brazil . . 79 F11
Castroville, U.S.A. . . 71 L5
Castuera, Spain 19 C3
Casummit Lake, Canada 62 B1
Cat I., Bahamas 75 C9
Cat I., U.S.A. 71 K10
Cat L., Canada 62 B1
Catacáos, Peru 78 E2
Cataguases, Brazil . . 79 H10
Catalão, Brazil 79 G9
Çatalca, Turkey 21 D13
Catalina, Canada . . . 63 C9
Catalonia = Cataluña □, Spain 19 B6
Cataluña □, Spain . . . 19 B6
Catamarca, Argentina . 80 B3
Catanduanes, Phil. . . 33 B6
Catanduva, Brazil . . . 79 H9
Catánia, Italy 20 F6
Catanzaro, Italy 20 E7
Cataraman, Phil. . . . 33 B6
Cateel, Phil. 33 C7
Cathcart, S. Africa . . 48 E4
Cathlamet, U.S.A. . . . 72 C2
Cativa, Panama 74 H14
Catlettsburg, U.S.A. . 68 F4
Catoche, C., Mexico . 74 C7
Catrimani, Brazil . . . 78 C6
Catskill, U.S.A. 68 D9
Catskill Mts., U.S.A. . 68 D8
Catt, Mt., Australia . . 54 A1
Catuala, Angola 48 B2
Cauca →, Colombia . 78 B4
Caucaia, Brazil 79 D11
Caucasus Mountains, Eurasia 23 F7
Caúngula, Angola . . . 46 F3
Cauquenes, Chile . . . 80 D2
Caura →, Venezuela . 78 B6
Causapscal, Canada . . 63 C6
Caux, Pays de, France 18 B4
Cavalier, U.S.A. 70 A6
Cavan, Ireland 13 C4
Cavan □, Ireland . . . 13 C4
Cave City, U.S.A. . . . 68 G3
Cavenagh Ra., Australia 53 E4
Cavendish, Australia . 55 F3
Caviana, I., Brazil . . . 79 C8
Cavite, Phil. 33 B6
Cawndilla L., Australia 55 E3
Cawnpore = Kanpur, India 36 F12
Caxias, Brazil 79 D10
Caxias do Sul, Brazil . 80 B6
Caxito, Angola 46 F2
Cayambe, Ecuador . . 78 D3
Cayenne, Fr. Guiana . 79 B8
Cayuga L., U.S.A. . . . 68 D7
Cazombo, Angola . . . 47 G4
Ceanannus Mor, Ireland 13 C5
Ceará = Fortaleza, Brazil 79 D11
Ceará □, Brazil 79 E11
Ceará Mirim, Brazil . . 79 E11
Cebollar, Argentina . . 80 B3
Cebu, Phil. 33 B6
Cecil Plains, Australia . 55 D5
Cedar →, U.S.A. . . . 70 E9
Cedar City, U.S.A. . . 73 H7
Cedar Creek Reservoir, U.S.A. 71 J6
Cedar Falls, U.S.A. . . 70 D8
Cedar Key, U.S.A. . . . 69 L4
Cedar L., Canada . . . 65 C8
Cedar Rapids, U.S.A. . 70 E9
Cedartown, U.S.A. . . 69 H3
Cedarvale, Canada . . 64 B3
Cedarville, S. Africa . . 49 E4
Cedarville, U.S.A. . . . 72 F3
Cedro, Brazil 79 E11
Ceduna, Australia . . . 55 E1
Cefalù, Italy 20 E6
Cegléd, Hungary . . . 17 E10
Celaya, Mexico 74 C4
Celbridge, Ireland . . . 13 C5
Celebes = Sulawesi □, Indonesia 33 E6
Celebes Sea, Indonesia 33 D6
Celina, U.S.A. 68 E3
Celje, Slovenia 16 E8
Celle, Germany 16 B6
Cement, U.S.A. 71 H5
Center, N. Dak., U.S.A. 70 B4
Center, Tex., U.S.A. . 71 K7
Centerfield, U.S.A. . . 73 G8
Centerville, Iowa, U.S.A. 70 E8
Centerville, S. Dak., U.S.A. 70 D6
Centerville, Tenn., U.S.A. 69 H2
Centerville, Tex., U.S.A. 71 K7
Central □, U.K. 12 E4
Central, Cordillera, Colombia 78 C4
Central African Rep. ■, Africa 45 G9

Central City, Ky., U.S.A. 68 G2
Central City, Nebr., U.S.A. 70 E5
Central Makran Range, Pakistan 36 F4
Central Patricia, Canada 62 B1
Central Russian Uplands, Europe . . . 6 E13
Central Siberian Plateau, Russia . . . 26 C14
Centralia, Ill., U.S.A. . 70 F10
Centralia, Mo., U.S.A. 70 F8
Centralia, Wash., U.S.A. 72 C2
Centreville, Ala., U.S.A. 69 J2
Centreville, Miss., U.S.A. 71 K9
Cephalonia = Kefallinía, Greece . . 21 E9
Cepu, Indonesia 33 G14
Ceram = Seram, Indonesia 33 E7
Ceram Sea = Seram Sea, Indonesia . . . 33 E7
Ceres, Argentina . . . 80 B4
Ceres, S. Africa 48 E2
Cerignola, Italy 20 D6
Cerigo = Kithira, Greece 21 F10
Çerkeşköy, Turkey . . 21 D12
Cervera, Spain 19 B6
Cesena, Italy 20 B5
Cēsis, Latvia 9 H21
Česká Republika = Czech Rep. ■, Europe 16 D8
České Budějovice, Czech. 16 D8
Ceskomoravská Vrchovina, Czech. . . 16 D8
Çeşme, Turkey 21 E12
Cessnock, Australia . . 55 E5
Cetinje, Montenegro, Yug. . . . 21 C8
Cetraro, Italy 20 E6
Ceuta, N. Afr. 19 E3
Cévennes, France . . . 18 D5
Ceyhan, Turkey 23 G6
Ceylon = Sri Lanka ■, Asia 36 R12
Cha Pa, Vietnam . . . 34 A7
Chachapoyas, Peru . . 78 E3
Chachran, Pakistan . . 36 E7
Chad ■, Africa 45 E8
Chad, L. = Tchad, L., Chad 45 F7
Chadan, Russia 25 D10
Chadileuvú →, Argentina 80 D3
Chadron, U.S.A. . . . 70 D3
Chadyr-Lunga = Ceadâr-Lunga, Moldova 17 E15
Chagai Hills, Afghan. . 36 E3
Chagda, Russia 25 D14
Chagos Arch., Ind. Oc. 26 K11
Chágres →, Panama . 74 H14
Châh Ākhvor, Iran . . 39 C8
Châh Bahār, Iran . . . 39 E9
Châh-e-Malek, Iran . . 39 D8
Châh Kavīr, Iran . . . 39 D7
Chahar Burjak, Afghan. 36 D3
Chaibasa, India 37 H14
Chakhānsūr, Afghan. . 36 D3
Chakonipau, L., Canada 63 A6
Chakradharpur, India . 37 H14
Chakwal, Pakistan . . 36 C8
Chala, Peru 78 G4
Chalcis = Khalkís, Greece 21 E10
Chaleur B., Canada . . 63 C6
Chalhuanca, Peru . . . 78 F4
Chalisgaon, India . . . 36 J9
Chalky Inlet, N.Z. . . . 51 M1
Challapata, Bolivia . . 78 G5
Challis, U.S.A. 72 D6
Chalon-sur-Saône, France 18 C6
Châlons-sur-Marne, France 18 B6
Chama, U.S.A. 73 H10
Chaman, Pakistan . . 36 D5
Chamba, India 36 C10
Chamba, Tanzania . . 47 G7
Chambal →, India . . 36 F11
Chamberlain, U.S.A. . 70 D5
Chamberlain →, Australia 52 C4
Chambers, U.S.A. . . 73 J9
Chambersburg, U.S.A. 68 F7
Chambéry, France . . 18 D6
Chambord, Canada . . 63 C5
Chamchamal, Iraq . . 38 C5
Chamical, Argentina . 80 C3
Chamonix-Mont Blanc, France 18 D7
Champagne, Canada . 64 A1
Champagne, France . . 18 B6
Champaign, U.S.A. . . 68 E1
Champlain, Canada . . 68 B9
Champlain, U.S.A. . . 68 C9
Champlain, L., U.S.A. . 68 C9
Chañaral, Chile 80 B2
Chānārān, Iran 39 B8
Chandeleur Is., U.S.A. 71 L10
Chandeleur Sd., U.S.A. 71 L10
Chandigarh, India . . 36 D10
Chandler, Australia . . 55 D1
Chandler, Ariz., U.S.A. 73 K8
Chandler, Okla., U.S.A. 71 H6
Chandpur, Bangla. . . 37 H17
Chandrapur, India . . 36 K11
Chānf, Iran 39 E9

Ch'ang Chiang

Ch'ang Chiang = Chang Jiang →, China 31 C7
Chang Jiang →, China 31 C7
Changanacheri, India 36 Q10
Changane →, Mozam. 49 C5
Changchiak'ou = Zhangjiakou, China 31 B6
Ch'angchou = Changzhou, China 31 C6
Changchun, China 31 B7
Changde, China 31 D6
Changhai = Shanghai, China 31 C7
Changsha, China 31 D6
Changzhi, China 31 C6
Changzhou, China 31 C6
Chanhanga, Angola 48 B1
Channapatna, India 36 N10
Channel Is., U.K. 11 H5
Channel Is., U.S.A. 73 K4
Channel-Port aux Basques, Canada 63 C8
Channing, Mich., U.S.A. 68 B1
Channing, Tex., U.S.A. 71 H3
Chantada, Spain 19 A2
Chanthaburi, Thailand 34 F7
Chantrey Inlet, Canada 60 B10
Chanute, U.S.A. 71 G7
Chao Phraya →, Thailand 34 F6
Chao'an, China 31 D6
Chapala, L. de, Mexico 74 C4
Chapayev, Kazakhstan 23 D9
Chapayevsk, Russia 22 D8
Chapel Hill, U.S.A. 69 H6
Chapleau, Canada 62 C3
Chaplin, Canada 65 C7
Chapra = Chhapra, India 37 G14
Châr, Mauritania 44 D2
Chara, Russia 25 D12
Charadai, Argentina 80 B5
Charagua, Bolivia 78 G6
Charaña, Bolivia 78 G5
Charcoal L., Canada 65 B8
Chard, U.K. 11 G5
Chardara, Kazakhstan 24 E7
Chardzhou = Chärjew, Turkmenistan 24 F7
Charente →, France 18 D3
Chari →, Chad 45 F7
Chārīkār, Afghan. 36 B6
Chariton →, U.S.A. 70 F8
Chärjew, Turkmenistan 24 F7
Charleroi, Belgium 15 D4
Charles, C., U.S.A. 68 G8
Charles City, U.S.A. 70 D8
Charles L., Canada 65 B6
Charles Town, U.S.A. 68 F7
Charleston, Ill., U.S.A. 68 F1
Charleston, Miss., U.S.A. 71 H9
Charleston, Mo., U.S.A. 71 G10
Charleston, S.C., U.S.A. 69 J6
Charleston, W. Va., U.S.A. 68 F5
Charlestown, S. Africa 49 D4
Charlestown, U.S.A. 68 F3
Charlesville, Zaïre 46 F4
Charleville = Rath Luirc, Ireland 13 D3
Charleville, Australia 55 D4
Charleville-Mézières, France 18 B6
Charlevoix, U.S.A. 68 C3
Charlotte, Mich., U.S.A. 68 D3
Charlotte, N.C., U.S.A. 69 H5
Charlotte Amalie, Virgin Is. 75 D12
Charlotte Harbor, U.S.A. 69 M4
Charlottesville, U.S.A. 68 F6
Charlottetown, Canada 63 C7
Charlton, Australia 55 F3
Charlton, U.S.A. 70 E8
Charlton I., Canada 62 B4
Charny, Canada 63 C5
Charolles, France 18 C6
Charouine, Algeria 44 C4
Charters Towers, Australia 54 C4
Chartres, France 18 B4
Chascomús, Argentina 80 D5
Chasovnya-Uchurskaya, Russia 25 D14
Chāt, Iran 39 B7
Châteaubriant, France 18 C3
Châteaulin, France 18 B1
Châteauroux, France 18 C4
Châtellerault, France 18 C4
Chatfield, U.S.A. 70 D9
Chatham, N.B., Canada 63 C6
Chatham, Ont., Canada 62 D3
Chatham, U.K. 11 F8
Chatham, U.S.A. 71 J8
Chatham Is., Pac. Oc. 56 M10
Chatham Str., U.S.A. 64 B2
Chatrapur, India 37 K14
Chattahoochee →, U.S.A. 69 K3
Chattanooga, U.S.A. 69 H3
Chauk, Burma 37 J19
Chaukan La, Burma 37 F20
Chaumont, France 18 B6
Chauvin, Canada 65 C6
Chaves, Brazil 79 D9
Chaves, Portugal 19 B2
Chavuma, Zambia 47 G4
Chaykovskiy, Russia 22 C9
Cheb, Czech. 16 C7
Cheboksary, Russia 22 C8
Cheboygan, U.S.A. 68 C3
Chech, Erg, Africa 44 D4
Chechenia □, Russia 23 F8
Checheno-Ingush Republic = Chechenia □, Russia 23 F8
Chechnya = Chechenia □, Russia 23 F8
Checleset B., Canada 64 C3
Checotah, U.S.A. 71 H7
Chedabucto B., Canada 63 C7
Cheduba I., Burma 37 K18
Cheepie, Australia 55 D4
Chegdomyn, Russia 25 D14
Chegga, Mauritania 44 C3
Chegutu, Zimbabwe 47 H6
Chehalis, U.S.A. 72 C2
Cheju Do, S. Korea 31 C7
Chekiang = Zhejiang □, China 31 D7
Chela, Sa. da, Angola 48 B1
Chelan, U.S.A. 72 C4
Chelan, L., U.S.A. 72 C3
Cheleken, Turkmenistan 23 G9
Chelforó, Argentina 80 D3
Chelkar = Shalqar, Kazakhstan 24 E6
Chelkar Tengiz, Solonchak, Kazakhstan 24 E7
Chełm, Poland 17 C12
Chełmno, Poland 17 B10
Chelmsford, U.K. 11 F8
Chelsea, U.S.A. 71 G7
Cheltenham, U.K. 11 F5
Chelyabinsk, Russia 24 D7
Chelyuskin, C., Russia 26 B14
Chemainus, Canada 64 D4
Chemnitz, Germany 16 C7
Chemult, U.S.A. 72 E3
Chen, Gora, Russia 25 C15
Chenab →, Pakistan 36 D7
Chencha, Ethiopia 45 G12
Cheney, U.S.A. 72 C5
Chengchou = Zhengzhou, China 31 C6
Chengde, China 31 B6
Chengdu, China 30 C5
Chengjiang, China 30 D5
Ch'engtu = Chengdu, China 30 C5
Cheo Reo, Vietnam 34 F10
Cheom Ksan, Cambodia 34 E8
Chepén, Peru 78 E3
Chepes, Argentina 80 C3
Chequamegon B., U.S.A. 70 B9
Cher →, France 18 C4
Cheraw, U.S.A. 69 H6
Cherbourg, France 18 B3
Cherchell, Algeria 44 A5
Cherdyn, Russia 22 B10
Cheremkhovo, Russia 25 D11
Cherepanovo, Russia 24 D9
Cherepovets, Russia 22 C6
Chergui, Chott ech, Algeria 44 B5
Cherikov = Cherykaw, Belarus 17 B16
Cherkasy, Ukraine 23 E5
Cherlak, Russia 24 D8
Chernaya, Russia 25 B9
Chernigov = Chernihiv, Ukraine 22 D5
Chernihiv, Ukraine 22 D5
Chernikovsk, Russia 22 D10
Chernivtsi, Ukraine 17 D13
Chernobyl = Chornobyl, Ukraine 17 C16
Chernogorsk, Russia 25 D10
Chernovtsy = Chernivtsi, Ukraine 17 D13
Chernyakhovsk, Russia 9 J19
Chernyshovskiy, Russia 25 C12
Cherokee, Iowa, U.S.A. 70 D7
Cherokee, Okla., U.S.A. 71 G5
Cherokees, Lake O' The, U.S.A. 71 G7
Cherquenco, Chile 80 D2
Cherrapunji, India 37 G17
Cherry Creek, U.S.A. 72 G6
Cherryvale, U.S.A. 71 G7
Cherskiy, Russia 25 C17
Cherskogo Khrebet, Russia 25 C15
Cherven, Belarus 17 B15
Chervonohrad, Ukraine 17 C13
Cherwell →, U.K. 11 F6
Cherykaw, Belarus 17 B16
Chesapeake, U.S.A. 68 G7
Chesapeake B., U.S.A. 68 F7
Cheshire □, U.K. 10 D5
Cheshskaya Guba, Russia 22 A8
Cheslatta L., Canada 64 C3
Chester, U.K. 10 D5
Chester, Calif., U.S.A. 72 F3
Chester, Ill., U.S.A. 71 G10
Chester, Mont., U.S.A. 72 B8
Chester, Pa., U.S.A. 68 F8
Chester, S.C., U.S.A. 69 H5
Chesterfield, U.K. 10 D6
Chesterfield, Is., N. Cal. 56 J7
Chesterfield Inlet, Canada 60 B10
Chesterton Ra., Australia 55 D4
Chesuncook L., U.S.A. 63 C6
Chéticamp, Canada 63 C7
Chetwynd, Canada 64 B4
Cheviot, The, U.K. 10 B5
Cheviot Hills, U.K. 10 B5
Cheviot Ra., Australia 54 D3
Chew Bahir, Ethiopia 45 H12
Chewelah, U.S.A. 72 B5
Cheyenne, Okla., U.S.A. 71 H5
Cheyenne, Wyo., U.S.A. 70 E2
Cheyenne →, U.S.A. 70 C4
Cheyenne Wells, U.S.A. 70 F3
Cheyne B., Australia 53 F2
Chhapra, India 37 G14
Chhatarpur, India 36 G11
Chhindwara, India 36 H11
Chhlong, Cambodia 34 F8
Chi →, Thailand 34 E8
Chiai, Taiwan 31 D7
Chiamis, Indonesia 33 G13
Chiamussu = Jiamusi, China 31 B8
Chiang Mai, Thailand 34 C5
Chiange, Angola 47 H2
Chiapa →, Mexico 74 D6
Chiávari, Italy 20 B3
Chiavenna, Italy 20 A3
Chiba, Japan 29 G10
Chibabava, Mozam. 49 C5
Chibatu, Indonesia 33 G12
Chibemba, Cunene, Angola 47 H2
Chibemba, Huila, Angola 48 B2
Chibia, Angola 47 H2
Chibougamau, Canada 62 C5
Chibougamau L., Canada 62 C5
Chibuk, Nigeria 45 F7
Chic-Chocs, Mts., Canada 63 C6
Chicacole = Srikakulam, India 37 K13
Chicago, U.S.A. 68 E2
Chicago Heights, U.S.A. 68 E2
Chichagof I., U.S.A. 64 B1
Chichester, U.K. 11 G7
Chichibu, Japan 29 F9
Ch'ich'ihaerh = Qiqihar, China 25 E13
Chickasha, U.S.A. 71 H5
Chiclana de la Frontera, Spain 19 D2
Chiclayo, Peru 78 E3
Chico, U.S.A. 72 G3
Chico →, Chubut, Argentina 80 E3
Chico →, Santa Cruz, Argentina 80 G3
Chicomo, Mozam. 49 C5
Chicopee, U.S.A. 68 D9
Chicoutimi, Canada 63 C5
Chicualacuala, Mozam. 49 C5
Chidambaram, India 36 P11
Chidenguele, Mozam. 49 C5
Chidley, C., Canada 61 B13
Chiede, Angola 48 B2
Chiemsee, Germany 16 E7
Chiengi, Zambia 46 F5
Chiengmai = Chiang Mai, Thailand 34 C5
Chiese →, Italy 20 B4
Chieti, Italy 20 C6
Chignecto B., Canada 63 C7
Chiguana, Bolivia 78 H5
Chihli, G. of = Bo Hai, China 31 C6
Chihuahua, Mexico 74 B3
Chiili, Kazakhstan 24 E7
Chik Bollapur, India 36 N10
Chikmagalur, India 36 N9
Chilako →, Canada 64 C4
Chilapa, Mexico 74 D5
Chilas, Pakistan 36 B9
Chilaw, Sri Lanka 36 R11
Chilcotin →, Canada 64 C4
Childers, Australia 55 D5
Childress, U.S.A. 71 H4
Chile ■, S. Amer. 80 D2
Chile Rise, Pac. Oc. 57 L18
Chilete, Peru 78 E3
Chililabombwe, Zambia 47 G5
Chilin = Jilin, China 31 B7
Chilka L., India 37 K14
Chilko →, Canada 64 C4
Chilko, L., Canada 64 C4
Chillagoe, Australia 54 B3
Chillán, Chile 80 D2
Chillicothe, Ill., U.S.A. 70 E10
Chillicothe, Mo., U.S.A. 70 F8
Chillicothe, Ohio, U.S.A. 68 F4
Chilliwack, Canada 64 D4
Chiloane, I., Mozam. 49 C5
Chiloé, I. de, Chile 80 E2
Chilpancingo, Mexico 74 D5
Chiltern Hills, U.K. 11 F7
Chilton, U.S.A. 68 C1
Chiluage, Angola 46 F4
Chilung, Taiwan 31 D7
Chilwa, L., Malawi 47 H7
Chimay, Belgium 15 D4
Chimbay, Uzbekistan 24 E6
Chimborazo, Ecuador 78 D3
Chimbote, Peru 78 E3
Chimkent = Shymkent, Kazakhstan 24 E7
Chimoio, Mozam. 47 H6
Chin □, Burma 37 J18
China ■, Asia 31 C6
Chinan = Jinan, China 31 C6
Chinandega, Nic. 74 E7
Chinati Peak, U.S.A. 71 K2
Chincha Alta, Peru 78 F3
Chinchilla, Australia 55 D5
Chinchou = Jinzhou, China 31 B7
Chincoteague, U.S.A. 68 G8
Chinde, Mozam. 47 H7
Chindwin →, Burma 37 J19
Chingola, Zambia 47 G5
Ch'ingtao = Qingdao, China 31 C7
Chinguetti, Mauritania 44 D2
Chingune, Mozam. 49 C5
Chinhanguanine, Mozam. 49 D5
Chinhoyi, Zimbabwe 47 H6
Chiniot, Pakistan 36 D8
Chinle, U.S.A. 73 H9
Chino, Japan 29 G9
Chino Valley, U.S.A. 73 J7
Chinon, France 18 C4
Chinook, Canada 65 C6
Chinook, U.S.A. 72 B9
Chinsali, Zambia 46 G6
Chióggia, Italy 20 B5
Chíos = Khíos, Greece 21 E12
Chipata, Zambia 47 G6
Chipewyan L., Canada 65 B9
Chipley, U.S.A. 69 K3
Chipman, Canada 63 C6
Chippenham, U.K. 11 F5
Chippewa →, U.S.A. 70 C8
Chippewa Falls, U.S.A. 70 C9
Chiquián, Peru 78 F3
Chiquinquira, Colombia 78 B4
Chirala, India 36 M12
Chirchiq, Uzbekistan 24 E7
Chiricahua Peak, U.S.A. 73 L9
Chirmiri, India 37 H13
Chiromo, Malawi 47 H7
Chisamba, Zambia 47 G5
Chisapani Garhi, Nepal 37 F14
Chisasibi, Canada 62 B4
Chisholm, Canada 64 C6
Chişinău, Moldova 17 E15
Chisos Mts., U.S.A. 71 L3
Chistopol, Russia 22 C9
Chita, Russia 25 D12
Chitado, Angola 47 H2
Chitembo, Angola 47 G3
Chitose, Japan 28 C10
Chitral, Pakistan 36 B7
Chitré, Panama 75 F8
Chittagong, Bangla. 37 H17
Chittagong □, Bangla. 37 G17
Chittaurgarh, India 36 G9
Chittoor, India 36 N11
Chiusi, Italy 20 C4
Chivasso, Italy 20 B2
Chivilcoy, Argentina 80 D4
Chkalov = Orenburg, Russia 22 D10
Chobe National Park, Botswana 48 B3
Choctawhatchee B., U.S.A. 67 D9
Choele Choel, Argentina 80 D3
Chojnice, Poland 17 B9
Chōkai-San, Japan 28 E10
Chokurdakh, Russia 25 B15
Cholet, France 18 C3
Choluteca, Honduras 74 E7
Choma, Zambia 47 H5
Chomutov, Czech. 16 C7
Chon Buri, Thailand 34 F6
Chone, Ecuador 78 D2
Chŏngjin, N. Korea 31 B7
Chongqing, China 30 D5
Chonos, Arch. de los, Chile 80 F2
Chop, Ukraine 17 D12
Chorley, U.K. 10 D5
Chornobyl, Ukraine 17 C16
Chorregon, Australia 54 C3
Chortkiv, Ukraine 17 D13
Chorzów, Poland 17 C10
Chos-Malal, Argentina 80 D2
Choszczno, Poland 16 B8
Choteau, U.S.A. 72 C7
Chotila, India 36 H7
Chowchilla, U.S.A. 73 H3
Choybalsan, Mongolia 31 B6
Christchurch, N.Z. 51 K4
Christchurch, U.K. 11 G6
Christiana, S. Africa 48 D4
Christie B., Canada 65 A6
Christina →, Canada 65 B6
Christmas Cr. →, Australia 52 C4
Christmas Creek, Australia 52 C4
Christmas I. = Kiritimati, Kiribati 57 G12
Christmas I., Ind. Oc. 35 F9
Christopher L., Australia 53 D4
Chu = Shu, Kazakhstan 24 E8
Chu →, Vietnam 34 C8
Chu Chua, Canada 64 C4
Ch'uanchou = Quanzhou, China 31 D6
Chūbu □, Japan 29 F8
Chubut →, Argentina 80 E3
Chuchi L., Canada 64 B4
Chudskoye, Oz., Russia 9 G22
Chūgoku □, Japan 29 G6
Chūgoku-Sanchi, Japan 29 G6
Chugwater, U.S.A. 70 E2
Chukchi Sea, Russia 25 C19
Chukotskoye Nagorye, Russia 25 C18
Chula Vista, U.S.A. 73 K5
Chulman, Russia 25 D13
Chulucanas, Peru 78 E2
Chulym →, Russia 24 D9
Chumbicha, Argentina 80 B3
Chumikan, Russia 25 D14
Chumphon, Thailand 34 G5
Chuna →, Russia 25 D10
Chungking = Chongqing, China 30 D5
Chunya, Tanzania 46 F6
Chuquibamba, Peru 78 G4
Chuquicamata, Chile 80 A3
Chur, Switz. 16 E5
Churachandpur, India 37 G18
Churchill, Canada 65 B10
Churchill →, Man., Canada 65 B10
Churchill →, Nfld., Canada 63 B7
Churchill, C., Canada 65 B10
Churchill Falls, Canada 63 B7
Churchill L., Canada 65 B7
Churchill Pk., Canada 64 B3
Churu, India 36 E9
Chushal, India 36 C11
Chusovoy, Russia 22 C10
Chuvash Republic = Chuvashia □, Russia 22 C8
Chuvashia □, Russia 22 C8
Chuwārtah, Iraq 38 C5
Cianjur, Indonesia 33 G12
Cibadok, Indonesia 33 G12
Cibatu, Indonesia 33 G12
Cicero, U.S.A. 68 E2
Ciechanów, Poland 17 B11
Ciego de Avila, Cuba 75 C9
Ciénaga, Colombia 78 A4
Cienfuegos, Cuba 75 C8
Cieszyn, Poland 17 D10
Cieza, Spain 19 C5
Cijara, Pantano de, Spain 19 C3
Cijulang, Indonesia 33 G13
Cikajang, Indonesia 33 G12
Cikampek, Indonesia 33 G12
Cilacap, Indonesia 33 G13
Cill Chainnigh = Kilkenny, Ireland 13 D4
Cimahi, Indonesia 33 G12
Cimarron, Kans., U.S.A. 71 G4
Cimarron, N. Mex., U.S.A. 71 G2
Cimarron →, U.S.A. 71 G6
Cimişlia, Moldova 17 E15
Cimone, Mte., Italy 20 B4
Cîmpina, Romania 17 F13
Cîmpulung, Romania 17 F13
Cinca →, Spain 19 B6
Cincar, Bos.-H. 20 C7
Cincinnati, U.S.A. 68 F3
Çine, Turkey 21 F13
Ciney, Belgium 15 D5
Cinto, Mte., France 18 E8
Circle, Alaska, U.S.A. 60 B5
Circle, Mont., U.S.A. 70 B2
Circleville, Ohio, U.S.A. 68 F4
Circleville, Utah, U.S.A. 73 G7
Cirebon, Indonesia 33 G13
Cirencester, U.K. 11 F6
Cisco, U.S.A. 71 J5
Citlaltépetl, Mexico 74 D5
Citrusdal, S. Africa 48 E2
Città di Castello, Italy 20 C5
Ciudad Bolívar, Venezuela 78 B6
Ciudad Chetumal, Mexico 74 D7
Ciudad del Carmen, Mexico 74 D6
Ciudad Delicias = Delicias, Mexico 74 B3
Ciudad Guayana, Venezuela 78 B6
Ciudad Juárez, Mexico 74 A3
Ciudad Madero, Mexico 74 C5
Ciudad Mante, Mexico 74 C5
Ciudad Obregón, Mexico 74 B3
Ciudad Real, Spain 19 C4
Ciudad Rodrigo, Spain 19 B2
Ciudad Trujillo = Santo Domingo, Dom. Rep. 75 D11
Ciudad Victoria, Mexico 74 C5
Civitanova Marche, Italy 20 C5
Civitavécchia, Italy 20 C4
Cizre, Turkey 23 G7
Clacton-on-Sea, U.K. 11 F9
Claire, L., Canada 64 B6
Clairemont, U.S.A. 71 J4
Clanton, U.S.A. 69 J2
Clanwilliam, S. Africa 48 E2
Clara, Ireland 13 C4
Clara →, Australia 54 B3
Clare, Australia 55 E2
Clare, U.S.A. 68 D3
Clare □, Ireland 13 D3
Clare →, Ireland 13 C2
Clare I., Ireland 13 C2
Claremont, U.S.A. 68 D9
Claremont Pt., Australia 54 A3
Claremore, U.S.A. 71 G7
Claremorris, Ireland 13 C3
Clarence →, Australia 55 D5
Clarence →, N.Z. 51 K4
Clarence, I., Chile 80 G2
Clarence I., Antarctica 5 C18
Clarence Str., Australia 52 B5
Clarence Str., U.S.A. 64 B2
Clarendon, Ark., U.S.A. 71 H9
Clarendon, Tex., U.S.A. 71 H4
Clarenville, Canada 63 C9
Claresholm, Canada 64 C6
Clarie Coast, Antarctica 5 C9
Clarinda, U.S.A. 70 E7
Clarion, U.S.A. 70 D8
Clark, U.S.A. 70 C6
Clark Fork, U.S.A. 72 B5
Clark Fork →, U.S.A. 72 B5
Clark Hill Res., U.S.A. 69 J4
Clarkdale, U.S.A. 73 J7
Clarke City, Canada 63 B6
Clarke I., Australia 54 G4
Clarke L., Canada 65 C7
Clarke Ra., Australia 54 C4
Clark's Fork →, U.S.A. 72 D9
Clark's Harbour, Canada 63 D6
Clarksburg, U.S.A. 68 F5
Clarksdale, U.S.A. 71 H9
Clarkston, U.S.A. 72 C5
Clarksville, Ark., U.S.A. 71 H8
Clarksville, Tenn., U.S.A. 69 G2
Clarksville, Tex., U.S.A. 71 J7
Clatskanie, U.S.A. 72 C2
Claude, U.S.A. 71 H4
Claveria, Phil. 33 A6
Clay Center, U.S.A. 70 F6
Claypool, U.S.A. 73 K8
Clayton, Idaho, U.S.A. 72 D6
Clayton, N. Mex., U.S.A. 71 G3
Cle Elum, U.S.A. 72 C3
Clear, C., Ireland 13 E2
Clear I., Ireland 13 E2
Clear L., U.S.A. 72 G2
Clear Lake, S. Dak., U.S.A. 70 C6
Clear Lake, Wash., U.S.A. 72 B2
Clear Lake Reservoir, U.S.A. 72 F3
Clearfield, Pa., U.S.A. 68 E6
Clearfield, Utah, U.S.A. 72 F7
Clearmont, U.S.A. 72 D10
Clearwater, Canada 64 C4
Clearwater, U.S.A. 69 M4
Clearwater →, Alta., Canada 64 C6
Clearwater →, Alta., Canada 65 B6
Clearwater Cr. →, Canada 64 A3
Clearwater Mts., U.S.A. 72 C6
Clearwater Prov. Park, Canada 65 C8
Cleburne, U.S.A. 71 J6
Cleethorpes, U.K. 10 D7
Cleeve Hill, U.K. 11 F6
Clerke Reef, Australia 52 C2
Clermont, Australia 54 C4
Clermont-Ferrand, France 18 D5
Clervaux, Lux. 15 D6
Cleveland, Australia 55 D5
Cleveland, Miss., U.S.A. 71 J9
Cleveland, Ohio, U.S.A. 68 E5
Cleveland, Okla., U.S.A. 71 G6
Cleveland, Tenn., U.S.A. 69 H3
Cleveland, Tex., U.S.A. 71 K7
Cleveland □, U.K. 10 C9
Cleveland, C., Australia 54 B4
Clew B., Ireland 13 C2
Clewiston, U.S.A. 69 M5
Clifden, Ireland 13 C1
Clifden, N.Z. 51 M1
Clifton, Australia 55 D5
Clifton, Ariz., U.S.A. 73 K9
Clifton, Tex., U.S.A. 71 K6
Clifton Beach, Australia 54 B4
Clifton Forge, U.S.A. 68 G6
Clifton Hills, Australia 55 D2
Climax, Canada 65 D7
Clinch →, U.S.A. 69 H3
Clingmans Dome, U.S.A. 69 H4
Clint, U.S.A. 73 L10
Clinton, B.C., Canada 64 C4
Clinton, Ont., Canada 62 D3
Clinton, N.Z. 51 M2
Clinton, Ark., U.S.A. 71 H8
Clinton, Ill., U.S.A. 70 E10
Clinton, Ind., U.S.A. 68 F2
Clinton, Iowa, U.S.A. 70 E9
Clinton, Mass., U.S.A. 68 D10
Clinton, Mo., U.S.A. 70 F8
Clinton, N.C., U.S.A. 69 H6
Clinton, Okla., U.S.A. 71 H5
Clinton, S.C., U.S.A. 69 H5
Clinton, Tenn., U.S.A. 69 G3
Clinton C., Australia 54 C5
Clinton Colden L., Canada 60 B9
Clintonville, U.S.A. 70 C10
Clipperton, I., Pac. Oc. 57 F17
Clive L., Canada 64 A5
Cloates, Pt., Australia 52 D1
Clocolan, S. Africa 49 D4
Clonakilty, Ireland 13 E3
Clonakilty B., Ireland 13 E3
Cloncurry, Australia 54 C3
Cloncurry →, Australia 54 B3
Clones, Ireland 13 B4
Clonmel, Ireland 13 D4
Cloquet, U.S.A. 70 B8
Cloud Peak, U.S.A. 72 D10
Cloudcroft, U.S.A. 73 K11
Cloverdale, U.S.A. 72 G2
Clovis, Calif., U.S.A. 73 H4
Clovis, N. Mex., U.S.A. 71 H3
Cluj-Napoca, Romania 17 E12
Clunes, Australia 55 F3
Clutha →, N.Z. 51 M2
Clwyd □, U.K. 10 D4
Clwyd →, U.K. 10 D4
Clyde, N.Z. 51 L2
Clyde →, U.K. 12 F4
Clyde, Firth of, U.K. 12 F4
Clyde River, Canada 61 A13
Clydebank, U.K. 12 F4

Coachella, U.S.A. 73 K5
Coahoma, U.S.A. 71 J4
Coal →, Canada 64 B3
Coaldale, Canada 64 D6
Coalgate, U.S.A. 71 H6
Coalinga, U.S.A. 73 H3
Coalville, U.K. 10 E6
Coalville, U.S.A. 72 F8
Coari, Brazil 78 D6
Coast Mts., Canada ... 64 C3
Coast Ranges, U.S.A. . 72 F2
Coatbridge, U.K. 12 F4
Coatesville, U.S.A. ... 68 F8
Coaticook, Canada ... 63 C5
Coats I., Canada 61 B11
Coats Land, Antarctica . 5 D1
Coatzacoalcos, Mexico 74 D6
Cobalt, Canada 62 C4
Cobar, Australia 55 E4
Cóbh, Ireland 13 E3
Cobham, Australia ... 55 E3
Cobija, Bolivia 78 F5
Cobleskill, U.S.A. ... 68 D8
Cobourg, Canada 62 D4
Cobourg Pen., Australia 52 B5
Cobram, Australia ... 55 F4
Cobre, U.S.A. 72 F6
Cóbué, Mozam. 47 G6
Coburg, Germany 16 C6
Cocanada = Kakinada,
    India 37 L13
Cochabamba, Bolivia . 78 G5
Cochin, India 36 Q10
Cochin China = Nam-
    Phan, Vietnam 34 G9
Cochise, U.S.A. 73 K9
Cochran, U.S.A. 69 J4
Cochrane, Alta., Canada 64 C6
Cochrane, Ont., Canada 62 C3
Cochrane →, Canada . 65 B8
Cochrane, L., Chile .. 80 F2
Cockburn, Australia . 55 E3
Cockburn, Canal, Chile 80 G2
Cockburn, I., Canada . 62 C3
Cockburn Ra., Australia 52 C4
Cockbiddy Motel,
    Australia 53 F4
Coco →, Cent. Amer. . 75 E8
Coco Chan., India ... 34 F2
Coco Solo, Panama ... 74 H14
Cocoa, U.S.A. 69 L5
Cocobeach, Gabon ... 46 D1
Cocos, I. del, Pac. Oc. 57 G19
Cocos Is., Ind. Oc. ... 35 F8
Cod, C., U.S.A. 67 D13
Codajás, Brazil 78 D6
Coderre, Canada 65 C7
Codó, Brazil 79 D10
Cody, U.S.A. 72 D9
Coe Hill, Canada 62 D4
Coen, Australia 54 A3
Coetivy Is., Seychelles 35 E4
Cœur d'Alene, U.S.A. . 72 C5
Cœur d'Alene L., U.S.A. 72 C5
Coevorden, Neths. ... 15 B6
Coffeyville, U.S.A. ... 71 G7
Coffin B., Australia .. 55 E2
Coffin Bay Peninsula,
    Australia 55 E2
Coffs Harbour,
    Australia 55 E5
Cognac, France 18 D3
Cohagen, U.S.A. 72 C10
Cohoes, U.S.A. 68 D9
Cohuna, Australia ... 55 F4
Coiba, I., Panama ... 75 F8
Coig →, Argentina .. 80 G3
Coihaique, Chile 80 F2
Coimbatore, India ... 36 P10
Coimbra, Brazil 78 G7
Coimbra, Portugal ... 19 B1
Coin, Spain 19 D3
Cojimies, Ecuador ... 78 C2
Cokeville, U.S.A. 72 E8
Colac, Australia 55 F3
Colatina, Brazil 79 G10
Colbeck, C., Antarctica 5 D13
Colbinabbin, Australia 55 F4
Colby, U.S.A. 70 F4
Colchester, U.K. 11 F8
Coldstream, U.K. 12 F6
Coldwater, U.S.A. ... 71 G5
Colebrook, Australia . 54 G4
Colebrook, U.S.A. ... 68 C10
Coleman, Canada 64 D6
Coleman, U.S.A. 71 K5
Coleman →, Australia 54 B3
Colenso, S. Africa ... 49 D4
Coleraine, Australia . 55 F3
Coleraine, U.K. 13 A5
Coleraine □, U.K. 13 A5
Coleridge, L., N.Z. .. 51 K3
Colesberg, S. Africa .. 48 E4
Colfax, La., U.S.A. .. 71 K8
Colfax, Wash., U.S.A. 72 C5
Colhué Huapi, L.,
    Argentina 80 F3
Coligny, S. Africa ... 49 D4
Colima, Mexico 74 D4
Colinas, Brazil 79 E10
Coll, U.K. 12 E2
Collaguasi, Chile 78 H5
Collarenebri, Australia 55 D4
Collbran, U.S.A. 73 G10
College Park, U.S.A. . 69 J3
Collette, Canada 63 C6
Collie, Australia 53 F2
Collier B., Australia .. 52 C3
Collier Ra., Australia . 52 D2
Collingwood, Canada . 62 D3
Collingwood, N.Z. ... 51 J4
Collins, Canada 62 B2
Collinsville, Australia . 54 C4

Collooney, Ireland 13 B3
Colmar, France 18 B7
Colne, U.K. 10 D5
Colo →, Australia ... 55 E5
Cologne = Köln,
    Germany 16 C4
Colomb-Béchar =
    Béchar, Algeria ... 44 B4
Colômbia, Brazil 79 H9
Colombia ■, S. Amer. . 78 C4
Colombo, Sri Lanka .. 36 R11
Colome, U.S.A. 70 D5
Colón, Cuba 75 C8
Colón, Panama 74 H14
Colona, Australia ... 53 F5
Colonia, Uruguay ... 80 C5
Colonia Dora,
    Argentina 80 B4
Colonial Heights, U.S.A. 68 G7
Colonsay, Canada ... 65 C7
Colonsay, U.K. 12 E2
Colorado □, U.S.A. .. 73 G10
Colorado →,
    Argentina 80 D4
Colorado →, N. Amer. 73 L6
Colorado →, U.S.A. . 71 L7
Colorado, I., Panama . 74 H14
Colorado City, U.S.A. 71 J4
Colorado Desert, U.S.A. 66 D3
Colorado Plateau,
    U.S.A. 73 H8
Colorado River
    Aqueduct, U.S.A. . 73 J6
Colorado Springs,
    U.S.A. 70 F2
Colton, U.S.A. 72 C5
Columbia, La., U.S.A. . 71 J8
Columbia, Miss., U.S.A. 71 K10
Columbia, Mo., U.S.A. 70 F8
Columbia, Pa., U.S.A. 68 E7
Columbia, S.C., U.S.A. 69 H5
Columbia, Tenn., U.S.A. 69 H2
Columbia →, U.S.A. . 72 C1
Columbia, C., Canada . 4 A4
Columbia, District of □,
    U.S.A. 68 F7
Columbia, Mt., Canada 64 C5
Columbia Basin, U.S.A. 72 C4
Columbia Falls, U.S.A. 72 B6
Columbia Heights,
    U.S.A. 70 C8
Columbretes, Is., Spain 19 C6
Columbus, Ga., U.S.A. 69 J3
Columbus, Ind., U.S.A. 68 F3
Columbus, Kans.,
    U.S.A. 71 G7
Columbus, Miss.,
    U.S.A. 69 J1
Columbus, Mont.,
    U.S.A. 72 D9
Columbus, N. Dak.,
    U.S.A. 70 A3
Columbus, N. Mex.,
    U.S.A. 73 L10
Columbus, Nebr.,
    U.S.A. 70 E6
Columbus, Ohio, U.S.A. 68 F4
Columbus, Tex., U.S.A. 71 L6
Columbus, Wis., U.S.A. 70 D10
Colusa, U.S.A. 72 G2
Colville, U.S.A. 72 B5
Colville →, U.S.A. .. 60 A4
Colville, C., N.Z. 51 G5
Colwyn Bay, U.K. ... 10 D4
Comácchio, Italy 20 B5
Comallo, Argentina . 80 E2
Comanche, Okla.,
    U.S.A. 71 H6
Comanche, Tex., U.S.A. 71 K5
Combahee →, U.S.A. 69 J5
Comblain-au-Pont,
    Belgium 15 D5
Comeragh Mts., Ireland 13 D4
Comet, Australia 54 C4
Comilla, Bangla. 37 H17
Comino, C., Italy 20 D3
Commerce, Ga., U.S.A. 69 H4
Commerce, Tex., U.S.A. 71 J7
Committee B., Canada 61 B11
Commonwealth B.,
    Antarctica 5 C10
Commoron Cr. →,
    Australia 55 D5
Communism Pk. =
    Kommunizma, Pik,
    Tajikistan 24 F8
Como, Italy 20 B3
Como, L. di, Italy ... 20 B3
Comodoro Rivadavia,
    Argentina 80 F3
Comorin, C., India .. 36 Q10
Comoro Is. =
    Comoros ■, Ind. Oc. 43 H8
Comoros ■, Ind. Oc. . 43 H8
Comox, Canada 64 D4
Compiègne, France .. 18 B5
Compton Downs,
    Australia 55 E4
Comrat, Moldova ... 17 E15
Côn Dao, Vietnam ... 34 H9
Conakry, Guinea 44 G2
Conara Junction,
    Australia 54 G4
Concarneau, France . 18 C2
Conceição da Barra,
    Brazil 79 G11
Conceição do Araguaia,
    Brazil 79 E9
Concepción, Bolivia . 78 G6
Concepción, Chile ... 80 D2
Concepción, Paraguay 80 A5
Concepción, L., Bolivia 78 G6

Concepción del Oro,
    Mexico 74 C4
Concepción del
    Uruguay, Argentina 80 C5
Conception, Pt., U.S.A. 73 J3
Conception B., Namibia 48 C1
Conche, Canada 63 B8
Concho, U.S.A. 73 J9
Concho →, U.S.A. .. 71 K5
Conchos →, Mexico . 74 B3
Concord, Calif., U.S.A. 72 H2
Concord, N.C., U.S.A. 69 H5
Concord, N.H., U.S.A. 68 D10
Concordia, Argentina . 80 C5
Concórdia, Brazil ... 78 D5
Concordia, U.S.A. ... 70 F6
Concrete, U.S.A. 72 B3
Condamine, Australia 55 D5
Conde, U.S.A. 70 C5
Condeúba, Brazil ... 79 F10
Condobolin, Australia 55 E4
Condon, U.S.A. 72 D3
Conegliano, Italy ... 20 B5
Confuso →, Paraguay 80 B5
Congleton, U.K. 10 D5
Congo = Zaïre →,
    Africa 46 F2
Congo (Kinshasa) =
    Zaïre ■, Africa 46 E4
Congo ■, Africa 46 E3
Congo Basin, Africa . 42 G6
Congress, U.S.A. ... 73 J7
Coniston, Canada ... 62 C3
Conjeeveram =
    Kanchipuram, India 36 N11
Conjuboy, Australia . 54 B3
Conklin, Canada 65 B6
Conlea, Australia ... 55 E3
Conn, L., Ireland 13 B2
Connacht □, Ireland . 13 C3
Conneaut, U.S.A. ... 68 E5
Connecticut □, U.S.A. 68 E9
Connecticut →, U.S.A. 68 E9
Connell, U.S.A. 72 C4
Connellsville, U.S.A. . 68 E6
Connemara, Ireland . 13 C2
Connersville, U.S.A. . 68 F3
Connors Ra., Australia 54 C4
Conoble, Australia .. 55 E3
Cononaco →, Ecuador 78 D3
Cononbridge, U.K. .. 12 D4
Conquest, Canada ... 65 C7
Conrad, U.S.A. 72 B8
Conran, C., Australia 55 F4
Conroe, U.S.A. 71 K7
Conselheiro Lafaiete,
    Brazil 79 H10
Consort, Canada 65 C6
Constance = Konstanz,
    Germany 16 E5
Constance, L. =
    Bodensee, Europe . 16 E5
Constanţa, Romania . 17 F15
Constantine, Algeria . 44 A6
Constitución, Chile .. 80 D2
Consul, Canada 65 D7
Contact, U.S.A. 72 F6
Contai, India 37 J15
Contamana, Peru ... 78 E4
Contas →, Brazil ... 79 F11
Contra Costa, Mozam. 49 D5
Conway = Conwy, U.K. 10 D4
Conway →, U.K. 10 D4
Conway, Ark., U.S.A. 71 H8
Conway, N.H., U.S.A. 68 D10
Conway, S.C., U.S.A. 69 J6
Conway, L., Australia 55 D2
Conwy, U.K. 10 D4
Conwy →, U.K. 10 D4
Coober Pedy, Australia 55 D1
Cooch Behar = Koch
    Bihar, India 37 F16
Coodardy, Australia . 53 E2
Cook, Australia 53 F5
Cook, U.S.A. 70 B8
Cook, B., Chile 80 H3
Cook, Mt., N.Z. 51 K3
Cook Inlet, U.S.A. ... 60 C4
Cook Is., Pac. Oc. ... 57 J11
Cook Strait, N.Z. ... 51 J5
Cookeville, U.S.A. ... 69 G3
Cookhouse, S. Africa . 48 E4
Cookstown, U.K. 13 B5
Cookstown □, U.K. .. 13 B5
Cooktown, Australia . 54 B4
Coolabah, Australia . 55 E4
Cooladdi, Australia .. 55 D4
Coolah, Australia ... 55 E4
Coolamon, Australia . 55 E4
Coolangatta, Australia 55 D5
Coolgardie, Australia 53 F3
Coolibah, Australia .. 52 C5
Coolidge, U.S.A. 73 K8
Coolidge Dam, U.S.A. 73 K8
Cooma, Australia ... 55 F4
Coonabarabran,
    Australia 55 E4
Coonamble, Australia 55 E4
Coonana, Australia .. 53 F3
Coondapoor, India .. 36 N9
Coongie, Australia ... 55 D3
Coongoola, Australia 55 D4
Cooninie, L., Australia 55 D2
Cooper, U.S.A. 71 J7
Cooper →, U.S.A. .. 69 J6
Cooper Cr. →,
    Australia 55 D2
Cooperstown, N. Dak.,
    U.S.A. 70 B5
Cooperstown, N.Y.,
    U.S.A. 68 D8

Coorabie, Australia .. 53 F5
Coorabulka, Australia 54 C3
Coorow, Australia .. 53 E2
Cooroy, Australia ... 55 D5
Coos Bay, U.S.A. ... 72 E1
Cootamundra, Australia 55 E4
Cootehill, Ireland ... 13 B4
Cooyar, Australia ... 55 D5
Cope, U.S.A. 70 F3
Copenhagen =
    København, Denmark 9 J15
Copiapó, Chile 80 B2
Copiapó →, Chile ... 80 B2
Copley, Australia ... 55 E2
Copp L., Canada 64 A6
Copper Center, U.S.A. 60 B5
Copper Cliff, Canada . 62 C3
Copper Harbor, U.S.A. 68 B2
Coppermine, Canada . 60 B8
Coppermine →,
    Canada 60 B8
Coquet →, U.K. 10 B6
Coquilhatville =
    Mbandaka, Zaïre .. 46 D3
Coquille, U.S.A. 72 E1
Coquimbo, Chile 80 C2
Corabia, Romania ... 17 G13
Coracora, Peru 78 G4
Coral Gables, U.S.A. . 69 N5
Coral Harbour, Canada 61 B11
Coral Sea, Pac. Oc. . 56 J7
Corato, Italy 20 D7
Corbin, U.S.A. 68 G3
Corby, U.K. 11 E7
Corby Glen, U.K. 11 E7
Corcaigh = Cork,
    Ireland 13 E3
Corcoran, U.S.A. ... 73 H4
Corcubión, Spain ... 19 A1
Cordele, U.S.A. 69 K4
Cordell, U.S.A. 71 H5
Córdoba, Argentina . 80 C4
Córdoba, Spain 19 D3
Córdoba, Sierra de,
    Argentina 80 C4
Cordon, Phil. 33 A6
Cordova, Ala., U.S.A. 69 J2
Cordova, Alaska, U.S.A. 60 B5
Corella →, Australia 54 B3
Corfield, Australia .. 54 C3
Corfu = Kérkira, Greece 21 E8
Corigliano Cálabro,
    Italy 20 E7
Coringa Is., Australia 54 B4
Corinna, Australia .. 54 G4
Corinth = Kórinthos,
    Greece 21 F10
Corinth, U.S.A. 69 H1
Corinth, G. of =
    Korinthiakós Kólpos,
    Greece 21 E10
Corinto, Brazil 79 G10
Corinto, Nic. 75 E7
Cork, Ireland 13 E3
Cork □, Ireland 13 E3
Cork Harbour, Ireland 13 E3
Çorlu, Turkey 21 D12
Cormack L., Canada . 64 A4
Cormorant, Canada . 65 C8
Cormorant L., Canada 65 C8
Cornell, U.S.A. 70 C9
Corner Brook, Canada 63 C8
Corneşti, Moldova .. 17 E15
Corning, Ark., U.S.A. 71 G9
Corning, Calif., U.S.A. 72 G2
Corning, Iowa, U.S.A. 70 E7
Corning, N.Y., U.S.A. 68 D7
Cornwall, Canada ... 62 C5
Cornwall □, U.K. 11 G3
Corny Pt., Australia . 55 E2
Coro, Venezuela 78 A5
Coroatá, Brazil 79 D10
Corocoro, Bolivia ... 78 G5
Coroico, Bolivia 78 G5
Coromandel, N.Z. ... 51 G5
Coromandel Coast,
    India 36 N12
Corona, Australia ... 55 E3
Corona, Calif., U.S.A. 73 K5
Corona, N. Mex., U.S.A. 73 J11
Coronado, U.S.A. ... 73 K5
Coronado, B. de,
    Costa Rica 75 F8
Coronation, Canada . 64 C6
Coronation Gulf,
    Canada 60 B8
Coronation I.,
    Antarctica 5 C18
Coronation I., Canada 64 B2
Coronation Is.,
    Australia 52 B3
Coronel, Chile 80 D2
Coronel Dorrego,
    Argentina 80 D4
Coronel Pringles,
    Argentina 80 D4
Coronel Suárez,
    Argentina 80 D4
Corowa, Australia ... 55 F4
Corozal, Belize 74 H14
Corpus Christi, U.S.A. 71 M6
Corpus Christi, L.,
    U.S.A. 71 L6
Corque, Bolivia 78 G5
Corrèze →, France . 18 D4
Corrib, L., Ireland ... 13 C2
Corrientes, Argentina 80 B5
Corrientes →, Peru . 78 D4
Corrientes, C.,
    Colombia 78 B3
Corrientes, C., Mexico 74 C3
Corrigan, U.S.A. 71 K7
Corrigin, Australia .. 53 F2

Corry, U.S.A. 68 E6
Corse, France 18 F8
Corse, C., France ... 18 E8
Corsica = Corse,
    France 18 F8
Corsicana, U.S.A. ... 71 J6
Corte, France 18 E8
Cortez, U.S.A. 73 H9
Cortland, U.S.A. 68 D7
Çorum, Turkey 23 F5
Corumbá, Brazil 78 G7
Corumbá de Goiás,
    Brazil 79 G9
Corunna = La Coruña,
    Spain 19 A1
Corvallis, U.S.A. 72 D2
Corvette, L. de la,
    Canada 62 B5
Corydon, U.S.A. 70 E8
Cosenza, Italy 20 E7
Coshocton, U.S.A. .. 68 E5
Cosmo Newberry,
    Australia 53 E3
Costa Blanca, Spain . 19 C5
Costa Brava, Spain .. 19 B7
Costa del Sol, Spain . 19 D3
Costa Dorada, Spain . 19 B6
Costa Rica ■,
    Cent. Amer. 75 F8
Costilla, U.S.A. 73 H11
Cotabato, Phil. 33 C6
Cotagaita, Bolivia ... 78 H5
Côte d'Azur, France . 18 E7
Côte-d'Ivoire = Ivory
    Coast ■, Africa ... 44 G3
Coteau des Prairies,
    U.S.A. 70 C6
Coteau du Missouri,
    U.S.A. 70 B4
Cotentin, France 18 B3
Cotonou, Benin 44 G5
Cotopaxi, Ecuador .. 78 D3
Cotswold Hills, U.K. . 11 F5
Cottage Grove, U.S.A. 72 E2
Cottbus, Germany .. 16 C8
Cottingham, U.K. ... 10 D7
Cottonwood, U.S.A. . 73 J7
Cotulla, U.S.A. 71 L5
Coudersport, U.S.A. . 68 E6
Couedic, C. du,
    Australia 55 F2
Coulee City, U.S.A. . 72 C4
Coulman I., Antarctica 5 D11
Coulonge →, Canada 62 C4
Council, Alaska, U.S.A. 60 B3
Council, Idaho, U.S.A. 72 D5
Council Bluffs, U.S.A. 70 E7
Council Grove, U.S.A. 70 F6
Courantyne →,
    S. Amer. 78 B7
Courtenay, Canada .. 64 D3
Courtrai = Kortrijk,
    Belgium 15 D3
Coushatta, U.S.A. ... 71 J8
Coutts, Canada 64 D6
Coventry, U.K. 11 E6
Coventry L., Canada . 65 A7
Covilhã, Portugal ... 19 B2
Covington, Ga., U.S.A. 69 J4
Covington, Ky., U.S.A. 68 F3
Covington, Okla.,
    U.S.A. 71 G6
Covington, Tenn.,
    U.S.A. 71 H10
Cowal, L., Australia . 55 E4
Cowan, Canada 65 C8
Cowan, L., Australia . 53 F3
Cowan, L., Canada .. 65 C7
Cowangie, Australia . 55 F3
Cowarie, Australia .. 55 D2
Cowcowing Lakes,
    Australia 53 F2
Cowdenbeath, U.K. . 12 E5
Cowell, Australia ... 55 E2
Cowes, U.K. 11 G6
Cowra, Australia ... 55 E4
Coxim, Brazil 79 G8
Cox's Bazar, Bangla. 37 J17
Cox's Cove, Canada . 63 C8
Cozad, U.S.A. 70 E5
Cozumel, I. de, Mexico 74 C7
Craboon, Australia .. 55 E4
Cracow = Kraków,
    Poland 17 C10
Cracow, Australia ... 55 D5
Cradock, S. Africa .. 48 E4
Craig, Alaska, U.S.A. 64 B2
Craig, Colo., U.S.A. . 72 F10
Craigavon, U.K. 13 B5
Crailsheim, Germany 16 D6
Craiova, Romania ... 17 F12
Cramsie, Australia .. 54 C3
Cranberry Portage,
    Canada 65 C8
Cranbrook, Tas.,
    Australia 54 G4
Cranbrook, W. Austral.,
    Australia 53 F2
Cranbrook, Canada . 64 D5
Crandon, U.S.A. 70 C10
Crane, Oreg., U.S.A. 72 E4
Crane, Tex., U.S.A. . 71 K3
Crater L., U.S.A. 72 E2
Crateús, Brazil 79 E10
Crato, Brazil 79 E11
Crawford, U.S.A. ... 70 D3
Crawfordsville, U.S.A. 68 E2
Crawley, U.K. 11 F7
Crazy Mts., U.S.A. .. 72 C8
Crean L., Canada ... 65 C7
Credo, Australia 53 F3
Cree →, Canada ... 65 B7
Cree →, U.K. 12 G4

Cree L., Canada 65 B7
Creede, U.S.A. 73 H10
Creighton, U.S.A. ... 70 D6
Crema, Italy 20 B3
Cremona, Italy 20 B4
Cres, Croatia 16 F8
Cresbard, U.S.A. ... 70 C5
Crescent, Okla., U.S.A. 71 H6
Crescent, Oreg., U.S.A. 72 E3
Crescent City, U.S.A. 72 F1
Cressy, Australia ... 55 F3
Crested Butte, U.S.A. 73 G10
Creston, Canada 64 D5
Creston, Iowa, U.S.A. 70 E7
Creston, Wash., U.S.A. 72 C4
Crestview, U.S.A. ... 69 K2
Crete = Kríti, Greece 21 G11
Crete, U.S.A. 70 E6
Créteil, France 18 B5
Creus, C. de, Spain . 19 A7
Creuse →, France .. 18 C4
Crewe, U.K. 10 D5
Criciúma, Brazil 80 B7
Crieff, U.K. 12 E5
Crimean Pen. =
    Krymskyy Pivostriv,
    Ukraine 23 E5
Cristóbal, Panama .. 74 H14
Crişul Alb →,
    Romania 17 E11
Crişul Negru →,
    Romania 17 E11
Crna Gora =
    Montenegro □,
    Yugoslavia 21 C8
Crna Gora, Serbia, Yug. 21 C9
Crna Reka →,
    Macedonia 21 D9
Croagh Patrick, Ireland 13 C2
Croatia ■, Europe ... 16 F9
Crocker, Banjaran,
    Malaysia 32 C5
Crockett, U.S.A. 71 K7
Crocodile =
    Krokodil →, Mozam. 49 D5
Crocodile Is., Australia 54 A1
Croix, L. La, Canada . 62 C1
Croker, C., Australia . 52 B5
Croker I., Australia .. 52 B5
Cromarty, Canada ... 65 B10
Cromarty, U.K. 12 D4
Cromer, U.K. 10 E9
Cromwell, N.Z. 51 L2
Cronulla, Australia .. 55 E5
Crooked →, Canada . 64 C4
Crooked →, U.S.A. . 72 D3
Crookston, Minn.,
    U.S.A. 70 B6
Crookston, Nebr.,
    U.S.A. 70 D4
Crooksville, U.S.A. .. 68 F4
Crookwell, Australia . 55 E4
Crosby, Minn., U.S.A. 70 B8
Crosby, N. Dak., U.S.A. 65 D8
Crosbyton, U.S.A. ... 71 J4
Cross City, U.S.A. ... 69 L4
Cross Fell, U.K. 10 C5
Cross L., Canada 65 C9
Cross Plains, U.S.A. . 71 J5
Cross Sound, U.S.A. . 60 C6
Crossett, U.S.A. 71 J9
Crossfield, Canada .. 64 C6
Crosshaven, Ireland . 13 E3
Crotone, Italy 20 E7
Crow →, Canada ... 64 B4
Crow Agency, U.S.A. 72 D10
Crow Hd., Ireland ... 13 E1
Crowell, U.S.A. 71 J5
Crowley, U.S.A. 71 K8
Crown Point, U.S.A. . 68 E2
Crows Nest, Australia 55 D5
Crowsnest Pass,
    Canada 64 D6
Croydon, Australia . 54 B3
Croydon, U.K. 11 F7
Crozet Is., Ind. Oc. .. 35 J12
Cruz Alta, Brazil 80 B6
Cruz del Eje, Argentina 80 C4
Cruzeiro, Brazil 79 H10
Cruzeiro do Sul, Brazil 78 E4
Cry L., Canada 64 B3
Crystal Brook, Australia 55 E2
Crystal City, Mo.,
    U.S.A. 70 F9
Crystal City, Tex.,
    U.S.A. 71 L5
Crystal Falls, U.S.A. . 68 B1
Crystal River, U.S.A. 69 L4
Crystal Springs, U.S.A. 71 K9
Csongrád, Hungary . 17 E11
Cu Lao Hon, Vietnam 34 G10
Cuamato, Angola ... 48 B2
Cuamba, Mozam. ... 47 G7
Cuando →, Angola . 47 H4
Cuando Cubango □,
    Angola 48 B3
Cuangar, Angola ... 48 B2
Cuanza →, Angola . 42 G5
Cuarto →, Argentina 80 C4
Cuba, U.S.A. 73 J10
Cuba ■, W. Indies ... 75 C9
Cuballing, Australia . 53 F2
Cubango →, Africa . 48 B3
Cuchi, Angola 47 G3
Cúcuta, Colombia ... 78 B4
Cudahy, U.S.A. 68 D2
Cuddalore, India 36 P11
Cuddapah, India 36 M11
Cuddapan, L., Australia 54 D3
Cudgewa, Australia . 55 F4
Cue, Australia 53 E2
Cuenca, Ecuador ... 78 D3
Cuenca, Spain 19 B4

Cuenca, Serranía de,
  Spain 19 C5
Cuernavaca, Mexico . . 74 D5
Cuero, U.S.A. 71 L6
Cuervo, U.S.A. 71 H2
Cuevas del Almanzora,
  Spain 19 D5
Cuevo, Bolivia 78 H6
Cuiabá, Brazil 79 G7
Cuiabá →, Brazil 79 G7
Cuillin Hills, U.K. . . . 12 D2
Cuillin Sd., U.K. 12 D2
Cuima, Angola 47 G3
Cuito →, Angola 48 B3
Cukai, Malaysia 34 Q16
Culbertson, U.S.A. . . . 70 A2
Culcairn, Australia . . . 55 F4
Culgoa →, Australia . . 55 D4
Culiacán, Mexico 74 C3
Culion, Phil. 33 B6
Cullarin Ra., Australia . 55 E4
Cullen, U.K. 12 D6
Cullen Pt., Australia . . 54 A3
Cullera, Spain 19 C5
Cullman, U.S.A. 69 H2
Culloden, U.K. 12 D4
Culpeper, U.S.A. 68 F7
Culuene →, Brazil . . . 79 F8
Culver, Pt., Australia . . 53 F3
Culverden, N.Z. 51 K4
Cumaná, Venezuela . . 78 A6
Cumberland, Canada . . 64 D3
Cumberland, Md.,
  U.S.A. 68 F6
Cumberland, Wis.,
  U.S.A. 70 C8
Cumberland →,
  U.S.A. 69 G2
Cumberland I., U.S.A. . 69 K5
Cumberland Is.,
  Australia 54 C4
Cumberland L., Canada 65 C8
Cumberland Pen.,
  Canada 61 B13
Cumberland Plateau,
  U.S.A. 69 H3
Cumberland Sd.,
  Canada 61 B13
Cumborah, Australia . . 55 D4
Cumbria □, U.K. 10 C5
Cumbrian Mts., U.K. . . 10 C5
Cumbum, India 36 M11
Cummins, Australia . . 55 E2
Cumnock, Australia . . 55 E4
Cumnock, U.K. 12 F4
Cundeelee, Australia . . 53 F3
Cunderdin, Australia . . 53 F2
Cunene →, Angola . . . 48 B1
Cúneo, Italy 20 B2
Cunnamulla, Australia . 55 D4
Cupar, Canada 65 C8
Cupar, U.K. 12 E5
Cupica, G. de,
  Colombia 78 B3
Curaçao, Neth. Ant. . . 75 E11
Curaray →, Peru 78 D4
Curiapo, Venezuela . . 78 B6
Curicó, Chile 80 C2
Curitiba, Brazil 80 B7
Currabubula, Australia . 55 E5
Currais Novos, Brazil . 79 E11
Curralinho, Brazil . . . 79 D9
Currant, U.S.A. 72 G6
Curraweena, Australia . 55 E4
Currawilla, Australia . . 54 D3
Current →, U.S.A. . . . 71 G9
Currie, Australia 54 F3
Currie, U.S.A. 72 F6
Currituck Sd., U.S.A. . 69 G8
Curtea de Argeş,
  Romania 17 F13
Curtis, U.S.A. 70 E4
Curtis Group, Australia 54 F4
Curtis I., Australia . . . 54 C5
Curuápanema →,
  Brazil 79 D7
Curuçá, Brazil 79 D9
Çürüksu Çayi →,
  Turkey 23 G4
Curup, Indonesia 32 E2
Cururupu, Brazil 79 D10
Curuzú Cuatiá,
  Argentina 80 B5
Cushing, U.S.A. 71 H6
Cushing, Mt., Canada . 64 B3
Custer, U.S.A. 70 D3
Cut Bank, U.S.A. 72 B7
Cuthbert, U.S.A. 69 K3
Cuttaburra →,
  Australia 55 D3
Cuttack, India 37 J14
Cuvier, C., Australia . . 53 E1
Cuvier I., N.Z. 51 G5
Cuxhaven, Germany . . 16 B5
Cuyahoga Falls, U.S.A. 68 E5
Cuyo, Phil. 33 B6
Cuzco, Bolivia 78 H5
Cuzco, Peru 78 C4
Cwmbran, U.K. 11 F4
Cyclades = Kikládhes,
  Greece 21 F11
Cygnet, Australia 54 G4
Cynthiana, U.S.A. . . . 68 F3
Cypress Hills, Canada . 65 D7
Cyprus ■, Asia 38 C2
Cyrenaica, Libya 45 C9
Cyrene = Shaḥḥāt,
  Libya 45 B9
Czar, Canada 65 C6
Czech Rep. ■, Europe . 16 D8
Częstochowa, Poland . 17 C10

D

Da →, Vietnam 34 B8
Da Hinggan Ling, China 31 B7
Da Lat, Vietnam 34 G10
Da Nang, Vietnam . . . 34 D10
Da Qaidam, China . . . 30 C4
Daba Shan, China . . . 31 C5
Dabakala, Ivory C. . . . 44 G4
Dabo, Indonesia 32 E2
Dabola, Guinea 44 F2
Daboya, Ghana 44 G4
Dacca = Dhaka, Bangla. 37 H17
Dacca = Dhaka □,
  Bangla. 37 G17
Dachau, Germany . . . 16 D6
Dadanawa, Guyana . . 78 C7
Dade City, U.S.A. 69 L4
Dadra and Nagar
  Haveli □, India 36 J8
Dadu, Pakistan 36 F5
Daet, Phil. 33 B6
Dagana, Senegal 44 E1
Dagestan □, Russia . . 23 F8
Daghestan Republic =
  Dagestan □, Russia . 23 F8
Dagö = Hiiumaa,
  Estonia 9 G20
Dagupan, Phil. 33 A6
Dahlak Kebir, Eritrea . 40 D3
Dahlonega, U.S.A. . . . 69 H4
Dahod, India 36 H9
Dahomey = Benin ■,
  Africa 44 G5
Dahra, Senegal 44 E1
Dai-Sen, Japan 29 G6
Daingean, Ireland . . . 13 C4
Daintree, Australia . . . 54 B4
Daiō-Misaki, Japan . . 29 G8
Dairût, Egypt 45 C11
Daisetsu-Zan, Japan . 28 C11
Dajarra, Australia . . . 54 C2
Dakar, Senegal 44 F1
Dakhla, W. Sahara . . . 44 D1
Dakhla, El Wâhât el-,
  Egypt 45 C10
Dakhovskaya, Russia . 23 F7
Dakota City, U.S.A. . . 70 D6
Đakovica, Serbia, Yug. 21 C9
Đálaki, Iran 39 D6
Dalälven, Sweden . . . 9 F17
Dalaman →, Turkey . . 21 F13
Dalandzadgad,
  Mongolia 30 B5
Dalarna, Sweden 9 F16
Dālbandin, Pakistan . . 36 E4
Dalbeattie, U.K. 12 G5
Dalby, Australia 55 D5
Dalgán, Iran 39 E8
Dalhart, U.S.A. 71 G3
Dalhousie, Canada . . . 63 C6
Dali, China 30 D5
Dalian, China 31 C7
Daliang Shan, China . 30 D5
Daliyat el Karmel, Israel 41 C4
Dalkeith, U.K. 12 F5
Dall I., U.S.A. 64 C2
Dallarnil, Australia . . . 55 D5
Dallas, Oreg., U.S.A. . 72 D2
Dallas, Tex., U.S.A. . . 71 J6
Dalmacia = Dalmacija,
  Croatia 20 C7
Dalmatia = Dalmacija,
  Croatia 20 C7
Dalmellington, U.K. . . 12 F4
Dalnegorsk, Russia . . 25 E14
Dalnerechensk, Russia 25 E14
Daloa, Ivory C. 44 G3
Dalsland, Sweden . . . 9 G14
Dalton, Canada 62 C3
Dalton, Ga., U.S.A. . . 69 H3
Dalton, Nebr., U.S.A. . 70 E3
Dalton Iceberg Tongue,
  Antarctica 5 C9
Dalvík, Iceland 8 D4
Daly →, Australia 52 B5
Daly L., Canada 65 B7
Daly Waters, Australia 54 B1
Daman, India 36 J8
Dāmaneh, Iran 39 C6
Damanhûr, Egypt 45 B11
Damar, Indonesia . . . 33 F7
Damaraland, Namibia . 48 C2
Damascus = Dimashq,
  Syria 41 B5
Damāvand, Iran 39 C7
Damāvand, Qolleh-ye,
  Iran 39 C7
Damba, Angola 46 F3
Dāmghān, Iran 39 B7
Damiel, Spain 19 C4
Damietta = Dumyât,
  Egypt 45 B11
Damoh, India 36 H11
Dampier, Australia . . . 52 D2
Dampier, Selat,
  Indonesia 33 E8
Dampier Arch.,
  Australia 52 D2
Dana, Indonesia 33 F6
Dana, L., Canada 62 B4
Danbury, U.S.A. 68 E9
Danby L., U.S.A. 73 J6
Dandaragan, Australia 53 F2
Dandeldhura, Nepal . . 37 E12
Dandeli, India 36 M9
Dandenong, Australia . 55 F4
Dandong, China 31 B7
Danforth, U.S.A. 63 C6

Danger Is. = Pukapuka,
  Cook Is. 57 J11
Danger Pt., S. Africa . . 48 E2
Dangora, Nigeria 44 F6
Daniel, U.S.A. 72 E8
Daniel's Harbour,
  Canada 63 B8
Danielskuil, S. Africa . 48 D3
Danilov, Russia 22 C7
Dankhar Gompa, India 36 C11
Dannemora, U.S.A. . . 68 C9
Dannevirke, N.Z. 51 J6
Dannhauser, S. Africa . 49 D5
Dante, Somali Rep. . . 40 E5
Danube =
  Dunărea →, Europe . 17 F15
Danville, Ill., U.S.A. . . 68 E2
Danville, Ky., U.S.A. . 68 G3
Danville, Va., U.S.A. . 69 G6
Danzig = Gdańsk,
  Poland 17 A10
Dao, Phil. 33 B6
Daoud = Aïn Beïda,
  Algeria 44 A6
Dar el Beida =
  Casablanca, Morocco 44 B3
Dar es Salaam,
  Tanzania 46 F7
Dar Mazār, Iran 39 D8
Dar'ā, Syria 41 C5
Dar'ā □, Syria 41 C5
Dārāb, Iran 39 D7
Daraj, Libya 44 B7
Dārān, Iran 39 C6
Dārayyā, Syria 41 B5
Darband, Pakistan . . . 36 B8
Darband, Kūh-e, Iran . 39 D8
Darbhanga, India 37 F14
Darby, U.S.A. 72 C6
Dardanelle, U.S.A. . . . 71 H8
Dardanelles =
  Çanakkale Boğazı,
  Turkey 21 D12
Dārestān, Iran 39 D8
Dârfûr, Sudan 45 F9
Dargai, Pakistan 36 B7
Dargan Ata, Uzbekistan 24 E7
Dargaville, N.Z. 51 F4
Darica, Turkey 21 D13
Darien, Panama 74 H14
Darién, G. del,
  Colombia 78 B3
Darjeeling = Darjiling,
  India 37 F16
Darjiling, India 37 F16
Dark Cove, Canada . . 63 C9
Darkan, Australia 53 F2
Darkhazineh, Iran . . . 39 D6
Darling →, Australia . . 55 E3
Darling Downs,
  Australia 55 D5
Darling Ra., Australia . 53 F2
Darlington, U.K. 10 C6
Darlington, S.C., U.S.A. 69 H6
Darlington, Wis., U.S.A. 70 D9
Darlington, L., S. Africa 48 E4
Darlot, L., Australia . . 53 E3
Darłowo, Poland 16 A9
Darmstadt, Germany . 16 D5
Darnah, Libya 45 B9
Darnall, S. Africa 49 D5
Darnley, C., Antarctica 5 C6
Darnley B., Canada . . 60 B7
Darr, Australia 54 C3
Darr →, Australia 54 C3
Darrington, U.S.A. . . . 72 B3
Dart →, U.K. 11 G4
Dartmoor, U.K. 11 G4
Dartmouth, Australia . 54 C3
Dartmouth, Canada . . 63 D7
Dartmouth, U.K. 11 G4
Dartmouth, L., Australia 55 D4
Darvaza, Turkmenistan 24 E6
Darvel, Teluk, Malaysia 33 D5
Darwha, India 36 J10
Darwin, Australia 52 B5
Darwin River, Australia 52 B5
Daryoi Amu =
  Amudarya →,
  Uzbekistan 24 E6
Dās, U.A.E. 39 E7
Dashhowuz,
  Turkmenistan 24 E6
Dasht, Iran 39 B8
Dasht →, Pakistan . . . 36 G2
Dasht-e Mārgow,
  Afghan. 36 D3
Datça, Turkey 21 F12
Datia, India 36 G11
Datong, China 31 B6
Datu, Tanjung,
  Indonesia 32 D3
Datu Piang, Phil. 33 C6
Daugava →, Latvia . . . 9 H21
Daugavpils, Latvia . . . 9 J22
Daulpur, India 36 F10
Dauphin, Canada 65 C8
Dauphin I., U.S.A. . . . 69 K1
Dauphin L., Canada . . 65 C9
Dauphiné, France . . . 18 D6
Davangere, India 36 M9
Davao, Phil. 33 C7
Davao, G. of, Phil. . . . 33 C7
Davenport, Iowa, U.S.A. 70 E9
Davenport, Wash.,
  U.S.A. 72 C4
Davenport Downs,
  Australia 54 C3
Davenport Ra.,
  Australia 54 C1

David, Panama 75 F8
David City, U.S.A. . . . 70 E6
David Gorodok =
  Davyd Haradok,
  Belarus 17 B14
Davidson, Canada . . . 65 C7
Davis, U.S.A. 72 G3
Davis Dam, U.S.A. . . . 73 J6
Davis Inlet, Canada . . 63 A7
Davis Sea, Antarctica . 5 C7
Davis Str., N. Amer. . . 61 B14
Davos, Switz. 16 E5
Davy L., Canada 65 B7
Davyd Haradok, Belarus 17 B14
Dawes Ra., Australia . 54 C5
Dawson, Canada 60 B6
Dawson, Ga., U.S.A. . 69 K3
Dawson, N. Dak.,
  U.S.A. 70 B5
Dawson, I., Chile 80 G2
Dawson Creek, Canada 64 B4
Dawson Inlet, Canada . 65 A10
Dawson Ra., Australia . 54 C4
Dax, France 18 E3
Daxian, China 30 C5
Daxue Shan, China . . 30 C5
Dayr az Zawr, Syria . . 38 C4
Daysland, Canada . . . 64 C6
Dayton, Ohio, U.S.A. . 68 F3
Dayton, Tenn., U.S.A. . 69 H3
Dayton, Wash., U.S.A. 72 C4
Daytona Beach, U.S.A. 69 L5
Dayville, U.S.A. 72 D4
De Aar, S. Africa 48 E3
De Funiak Springs,
  U.S.A. 69 K2
De Grey, Australia . . . 52 D2
De Grey →, Australia . 52 D2
De Kalb, U.S.A. 70 E10
De Land, U.S.A. 69 L5
De Leon, U.S.A. 71 J5
De Pere, U.S.A. 68 C1
De Queen, U.S.A. . . . 71 H7
De Quincy, U.S.A. . . . 71 K8
De Ridder, U.S.A. . . . 71 K8
De Smet, U.S.A. 70 C6
De Soto, U.S.A. 70 F9
De Tour Village, U.S.A. 68 C4
De Witt, U.S.A. 71 H9
Dead Sea, Asia 41 D4
Deadwood, U.S.A. . . . 70 C3
Deadwood L., Canada . 64 B3
Deakin, Australia 53 F4
Deal, U.K. 11 F9
Deal I., Australia 54 F4
Dealesville, S. Africa . 48 D4
Dean, Forest of, U.K. . 11 F5
Deán Funes, Argentina 80 C4
Dearborn, U.S.A. 62 D3
Dease →, Canada . . . 64 B3
Dease L., Canada . . . 64 B2
Dease Lake, Canada . . 64 B2
Death Valley, U.S.A. . . 73 H5
Death Valley Junction,
  U.S.A. 73 H5
Death Valley National
  Monument, U.S.A. . . 73 H5
Deba Habe, Nigeria . . 44 F7
Debar, Macedonia . . . 21 D9
Debden, Canada 65 C7
Debica, Poland 17 C11
Debolt, Canada 64 B5
Deborah East, L.,
  Australia 53 F2
Deborah West, L.,
  Australia 53 F2
Debre Markos, Ethiopia 45 F12
Debre Tabor, Ethiopia . 45 F12
Debrecen, Hungary . . 17 E11
Decatur, Ala., U.S.A. . 69 H2
Decatur, Ga., U.S.A. . 69 J3
Decatur, Ill., U.S.A. . . 70 F10
Decatur, Ind., U.S.A. . 68 E3
Decatur, Tex., U.S.A. . 71 J6
Deccan, India 36 M10
Deception L., Canada . 65 B8
Děčín, Czech. 16 C8
Decorah, U.S.A. 70 D9
Dedéagach =
  Alexandroúpolis,
  Greece 21 D11
Dédougou,
  Burkina Faso 44 F4
Dee →, Clwyd, U.K. . . 10 D4
Dee →, Gramp., U.K. . 12 D6
Deep B., Canada 64 A5
Deep Well, Australia . 54 C1
Deepwater, Australia . 55 D5
Deer →, Canada 65 B10
Deer Lake, Nfld.,
  Canada 63 C8
Deer Lake, Ont.,
  Canada 65 C10
Deer Lodge, U.S.A. . . 72 C7
Deer Park, U.S.A. . . . 72 C5
Deer River, U.S.A. . . . 70 B8
Deeral, Australia 54 B4
Deerdepoort, S. Africa 48 C4
Defiance, U.S.A. 68 E3
Deggendorf, Germany . 16 D7
Deh Bīd, Iran 39 D7
Deh-e Shīr, Iran 39 D7
Dehaj, Iran 39 D7
Dehdez, Iran 39 D6
Dehestān, Iran 39 D7
Dehgolān, Iran 38 C5
Dehi Titan, Afghan. . . 36 C3
Dehibat, Tunisia 44 B7
Dehlorān, Iran 38 C5

Dehnow-e Kūhestān,
  Iran 39 E8
Dehra Dun, India 36 D11
Deinze, Belgium 15 D3
Dej, Romania 17 E12
Dekese, Zaïre 46 E4
Del Norte, U.S.A. 73 H10
Del Rio, U.S.A. 71 L4
Delano, U.S.A. 73 J4
Delareyville, S. Africa . 48 D4
Delavan, U.S.A. 70 D10
Delaware, U.S.A. 68 E4
Delaware □, U.S.A. . . 68 F8
Delaware →, U.S.A. . . 68 F8
Delaware B., U.S.A. . . 67 C12
Delegate, Australia . . 55 F4
Delft, Neths. 15 B4
Delfzijl, Neths. 15 A6
Delgado, C., Mozam. . 46 G8
Delgo, Sudan 45 D11
Delhi, India 36 E10
Delia, Canada 64 C6
Delice →, Turkey 23 G5
Delicias, Mexico 74 B3
Delījān, Iran 39 C6
Dell City, U.S.A. 73 L11
Dell Rapids, U.S.A. . . 70 D6
Delmenhorst, Germany 16 B5
Delmiro Gouveia, Brazil 79 E11
Delong, Ostrova, Russia 25 B15
Deloraine, Australia . . 54 G4
Deloraine, Canada . . . 65 D8
Delphi, U.S.A. 68 E2
Delphos, U.S.A. 68 E3
Delportshoop, S. Africa 48 D3
Delray Beach, U.S.A. . 69 M5
Delta, Colo., U.S.A. . . 73 G9
Delta, Utah, U.S.A. . . 72 G7
Delungra, Australia . . 55 D5
Delvinë, Albania 21 E9
Demanda, Sierra de la,
  Spain 19 A4
Demavand =
  Damāvand, Iran . . . 39 C7
Demba, Zaïre 46 F4
Dembecha, Ethiopia . . 45 F12
Dembidolo, Ethiopia . 45 G11
Demer →, Belgium . . . 15 D4
Demini →, Brazil 78 D6
Demirci, Turkey 21 E13
Demirköy, Turkey . . . 21 D12
Demopolis, U.S.A. . . . 69 J2
Dempo, Indonesia . . . 32 E2
Den Burg, Neths. 15 A4
Den Haag = 's-
  Gravenhage, Neths. 15 B4
Den Helder, Neths. . . 15 B4
Den Oever, Neths. . . . 15 B5
Denain, France 15 D3
Denau, Uzbekistan . . 24 F7
Denbigh, U.K. 10 D4
Dendang, Indonesia . . 32 E3
Dendermonde, Belgium 15 C4
Denham, Australia . . . 53 E1
Denham Ra., Australia 54 C4
Denham Sd., Australia 53 E1
Denia, Spain 19 C6
Denial B., Australia . . 55 E1
Deniliquin, Australia . . 55 F3
Denison, Iowa, U.S.A. 70 D7
Denison, Tex., U.S.A. . 71 J6
Denison Plains,
  Australia 52 C4
Denizli, Turkey 23 G4
Denman Glacier,
  Antarctica 5 C7
Denmark, Australia . . 53 F2
Denmark ■, Europe . . 9 J13
Denmark Str., Atl. Oc. 4 C6
Denpasar, Indonesia . 32 F5
Denton, Mont., U.S.A. 72 C9
Denton, Tex., U.S.A. . 71 J6
D'Entrecasteaux, Pt.,
  Australia 53 F2
Denver, U.S.A. 70 F2
Denver City, U.S.A. . . 71 J3
Deoghar, India 37 G15
Deolali, India 36 K8
Deoria, India 37 F13
Deosai Mts., Pakistan . 36 B9
Depot Springs,
  Australia 53 E3
Deputatskiy, Russia . . 25 C14
Dera Ghazi Khan,
  Pakistan 36 D7
Dera Ismail Khan,
  Pakistan 36 D7
Derbent, Russia 23 F8
Derby, Australia 52 C3
Derby, U.K. 10 E6
Derbyshire □, U.K. . . 10 E6
Derg →, Ireland 13 B4
Derg, L., Ireland 13 D3
Dergaon, India 37 F19
Dernieres, Isles, U.S.A. 71 L9
Derry = Londonderry,
  U.K. 13 B4
Derryveagh Mts.,
  Ireland 13 B3
Derudub, Sudan 45 E12
Derwent, Canada 64 C6
Derwent →, Derby,
  U.K. 10 E6
Derwent →, N. Yorks.,
  U.K. 10 D7
Derwent Water, U.K. . 10 C4

Desaguadero →,
  Bolivia 78 G5
Deschaillons, Canada . 63 C5
Descharme →,
  Canada 65 B7
Deschutes →, U.S.A. . 72 D3
Dese, Ethiopia 40 E2
Desert Center, U.S.A. . 73 K6
Deskenatlata L., Canada 64 A6
Desna →, Ukraine . . . 17 C16
Desolación, I., Chile . . 80 G2
Despeñaperros, Paso,
  Spain 19 C4
Dessau, Germany . . . 16 C7
Dessye = Dese,
  Ethiopia 40 E2
D'Estrees B., Australia 55 F2
Detmold, Germany . . . 16 C5
Detour, Pt., U.S.A. . . . 68 C2
Detroit, Mich., U.S.A. . 62 D3
Detroit, Tex., U.S.A. . 71 J7
Detroit Lakes, U.S.A. . 70 B7
Deurne, Belgium 15 C4
Deurne, Neths. 15 C5
Deutsche Bucht,
  Germany 16 A5
Deva, Romania 17 F12
Devakottai, India 36 Q11
Deventer, Neths. 15 B6
Deveron →, U.K. 12 D6
Devils Lake, U.S.A. . . 70 A5
Devils Paw, Canada . . 64 B2
Devizes, U.K. 11 F6
Devon, Canada 64 C6
Devon □, U.K. 11 G4
Devon I., Canada 4 B3
Devonport, Australia . 54 G4
Devonport, N.Z. 51 G5
Devonport, U.K. 11 G3
Dewas, India 36 H10
Dewetsdorp, S. Africa 48 D4
Dewsbury, U.K. 10 D6
Dexter, Mo., U.S.A. . . 71 G9
Dexter, N. Mex., U.S.A. 71 J2
Dey-Dey, L., Australia 53 E5
Deyhūk, Iran 39 C8
Deyyer, Iran 39 E6
Dezadeash L., Canada 64 A1
Dezfūl, Iran 39 C6
Dezhneva, Mys, Russia 25 C19
Dhahiriya = Aẕ
  Ẕāhirīyah, West Bank 41 D3
Dhahran = Aẕ Ẕahrān,
  Si. Arabia 39 E6
Dhaka, Bangla. 37 H17
Dhaka □, Bangla. . . . 37 G17
Dhamar, Yemen 40 E3
Dhamtari, India 37 J12
Dhanbad, India 37 H15
Dhangarhi, Nepal . . . 37 E12
Dhankuta, Nepal 37 F15
Dhar, India 36 H9
Dharmapuri, India . . . 36 N11
Dharwad, India 36 M9
Dhaulagiri, Nepal . . . 37 E13
Dhenkanal, India 37 J14
Dhībān, Jordan 41 D4
Dhíkti Óros, Greece . . 21 G11
Dhirfis, Greece 21 E10
Dhodhekánisos, Greece 21 F12
Dhrol, India 36 H7
Dhuburi, India 37 F16
Dhule, India 36 J9
Dhut →, Somali Rep. . 40 E5
Di Linh, Cao Nguyen,
  Vietnam 34 G10
Diablo Heights, Panama 74 H14
Diafarabé, Mali 44 F4
Diamantina, Brazil . . . 79 G10
Diamantina →,
  Australia 55 D2
Diamantino, Brazil . . . 79 F7
Diamond Harbour,
  India 37 H16
Diamond Is., Australia 54 B5
Diamond Mts., U.S.A. 72 G6
Diamondville, U.S.A. . 72 F8
Diapaga, Burkina Faso 44 F5
Dibā, Oman 39 E8
Dibaya, Zaïre 46 F4
Dibaya-Lubue, Zaïre . 46 E3
Dibbi, Ethiopia 40 G3
Dibete, Botswana . . . 48 C4
Dibrugarh, India 37 F19
Dickinson, U.S.A. . . . 70 B3
Dickson, Russia 24 B9
Dickson, U.S.A. 69 G2
Didiéni, Mali 44 F3
Didsbury, Canada . . . 64 C6
Diébougou,
  Burkina Faso 44 F4
Diefenbaker L., Canada 65 C7
Diego Garcia, Ind. Oc. 35 K11
Diekirch, Lux. 15 E6
Dien Bien, Vietnam . . 34 B7
Dieppe, France 18 B4
Dieren, Neths. 15 B6
Dierks, U.S.A. 71 H7
Diest, Belgium 15 D5
Differdange, Lux. 15 E5
Digby, Canada 63 D6
Digges, Canada 65 B10
Digges Is., Canada . . . 62 A4
Dighinala, Bangla. . . . 37 H18
Dighton, U.S.A. 70 F4
Digne-les-Bains, France 18 D7
Digos, Phil. 33 C7
Digranes, Iceland . . . 8 C6
Digul →, Indonesia . . 33 F9
Dihang →, India 37 F19
Dīhōk, Iraq 38 B4
Dijlah, Nahr →, Asia . 38 D5
Dijon, France 18 C6

Dikimdya, Russia . . . 25 D13
Dikomu di Kai, Botswana 48 C3
Diksmuide, Belgium . . 15 C2
Dikson = Dickson, Russia 24 B9
Dikwa, Nigeria 45 F7
Dili, Indonesia 33 F7
Dilley, U.S.A. 71 L5
Dilling, Sudan 45 F10
Dillingham, U.S.A. . . 60 C4
Dillon, Canada 65 B7
Dillon, Mont., U.S.A. . 72 D7
Dillon, S.C., U.S.A. . . 69 H6
Dillon →, Canada . . . 65 B7
Dilolo, Zaïre 46 G4
Dilston, Australia . . . 54 G4
Dimashq, Syria 41 B5
Dimashq □, Syria . . . 41 B5
Dimbaza, S. Africa . . . 49 E4
Dimbokro, Ivory C. . . . 44 G4
Dimboola, Australia . . 55 F3
Dîmbovița →, Romania 17 F14
Dimbulah, Australia . . 54 B4
Dimitrovgrad, Bulgaria 21 C11
Dimitrovgrad, Russia . 22 D8
Dimitrovo = Pernik, Bulgaria 21 C10
Dimmitt, U.S.A. 71 H3
Dimona, Israel 41 D4
Dinagat, Phil. 33 B7
Dinajpur, Bangla. . . . 37 G16
Dinan, France 18 B2
Dīnān Āb, Iran 39 C8
Dinant, Belgium 15 D4
Dīnār, Kūh-e, Iran . . . 39 D6
Dinara Planina, Croatia 20 C7
Dinard, France 18 B2
Dinaric Alps = Dinara Planina, Croatia . . 20 C7
Dindigul, India 36 P11
Dingle, Ireland 13 D1
Dingle B., Ireland . . . 13 D1
Dingo, Australia 54 C4
Dinguiraye, Guinea . . 44 F2
Dingwall, U.K. 12 D4
Dinokwe, Botswana . . 48 C4
Dinosaur National Monument, U.S.A. . 72 F9
Dinuba, U.S.A. 73 H4
Diourbel, Senegal . . . 44 F1
Dipolog, Phil. 33 C6
Dir, Pakistan 36 B7
Diré, Mali 44 E4
Dire Dawa, Ethiopia . . 40 F3
Dirico, Angola 47 H4
Dirk Hartog I., Australia 53 E1
Dirranbandi, Australia 55 D4
Disa, India 36 G8
Disappointment, C., U.S.A. 72 C1
Disappointment, L., Australia 52 D3
Disaster B., Australia . 55 F4
Discovery B., Australia 55 F3
Disko, Greenland 4 C5
Disko Bugt, Greenland 4 C5
Disteghil Sar, Pakistan 36 A9
Distrito Federal □, Brazil 79 G9
Diu, India 36 J7
Dīvāndarreh, Iran . . . 38 C5
Divide, U.S.A. 72 D7
Dividing Ra., Australia 53 E2
Divinópolis, Brazil . . . 79 H10
Divnoye, Russia 23 E7
Diwāl Kol, Afghan. . . . 36 B5
Dixon, Ill., U.S.A. . . . 70 E10
Dixon, Mont., U.S.A. . 72 C6
Dixon, N. Mex., U.S.A. 73 H11
Dixon Entrance, U.S.A. 64 C2
Dixonville, Canada . . 64 B5
Diyarbakır, Turkey . . . 23 G7
Djado, Niger 45 D7
Djakarta = Jakarta, Indonesia 33 G12
Djamba, Angola 47 B1
Djambala, Congo 46 E2
Djanet, Algeria 44 D6
Djawa = Jawa, Indonesia 33 G14
Djelfa, Algeria 44 B5
Djema, C.A.R. 46 C5
Djenné, Mali 44 F4
Djerba, I. de, Tunisia . 45 B7
Djerid, Chott, Tunisia . 44 B6
Djibo, Burkina Faso . . 44 F4
Djibouti, Djibouti 40 E3
Djibouti ■, Africa . . . 40 E3
Djolu, Zaïre 46 D4
Djougou, Benin 44 G5
Djoum, Cameroon . . . 46 D2
Djourab, Chad 45 E8
Djugu, Zaïre 46 D6
Djúpivogur, Iceland . . 8 D6
Dmitriya Lapteva, Proliv, Russia 25 B15
Dnepr = Dnipro →, Ukraine 23 E5
Dneprodzerzhinsk = Dniprodzerzhynsk, Ukraine 23 E5
Dnepropetrovsk = Dnipropetrovsk, Ukraine 23 E5
Dnestr = Dnister →, Europe 17 E16
Dnestrovski = Belgorod, Russia . . 23 D6
Dnieper = Dnipro →, Ukraine 23 E5

Dniester = Dnister →, Europe 17 E16
Dnipro →, Ukraine . . . 23 E5
Dniprodzerzhynsk, Ukraine 23 E5
Dnipropetrovsk, Ukraine 23 E5
Dnister →, Europe . . . 17 E16
Dnistrovskyy Lyman, Ukraine 17 E16
Dnyapro = Dnipro →, Ukraine 23 E5
Doba, Chad 45 G8
Dobbyn, Australia . . . 54 B3
Dobele, Latvia 9 H20
Doberai, Jazirah, Indonesia 33 E8
Doblas, Argentina . . . 80 D4
Dobo, Indonesia 33 F8
Doboj, Bos.-H. 21 B8
Dobreta-Turnu-Severin, Romania 17 F12
Dobrich, Bulgaria . . . 21 C12
Dobruja, Romania . . . 17 F15
Dobrush, Belarus 17 B16
Dodecanese = Dhodhekánisos, Greece 21 F12
Dodge Center, U.S.A. . 70 C8
Dodge City, U.S.A. . . . 71 G5
Dodge L., Canada . . . 65 B7
Dodgeville, U.S.A. . . . 70 D9
Dodoma, Tanzania . . . 46 F7
Dodsland, Canada . . . 65 C7
Dodson, U.S.A. 72 B9
Doetinchem, Neths. . . 15 C6
Dog Creek, Canada . . 64 C4
Dog L., Man., Canada . 65 C9
Dog L., Ont., Canada . 62 C2
Dogi, Afghan. 36 C3
Doha = Ad Dawhah, Qatar 39 E6
Dohazari, Bangla. . . . 37 H18
Doi, Indonesia 33 D7
Doi Luang, Thailand . . 34 C6
Doig →, Canada 64 B4
Dois Irmãos, Sa., Brazil 79 E10
Dokkum, Neths. 15 A5
Doland, U.S.A. 70 C5
Dolbeau, Canada . . . 63 C5
Dole, France 18 C6
Dolgellau, U.K. 10 E4
Dolgelley = Dolgellau, U.K. 10 E4
Dollart, Neths. 15 A7
Dolomites = Dolomiti, Italy 20 A4
Dolomiti, Italy 20 A4
Dolores, Argentina . . . 80 D5
Dolores, U.S.A. 73 H9
Dolores →, U.S.A. . . . 73 G9
Dolphin, C., Falk. Is. . 80 G5
Dolphin and Union Str., Canada 60 B8
Dombarovskiy, Russia 24 D6
Dombås, Norway 9 E13
Domburg, Neths. 15 C3
Domel I. = Letsôk-aw Kyun, Burma 34 G5
Dominica ■, W. Indies 74 M20
Dominican Rep. ■, W. Indies 75 D10
Domo, Ethiopia 40 F4
Domodóssola, Italy . . 20 A3
Domville, Mt., Australia 55 D5
Don →, Russia 23 E6
Don →, Gramp., U.K. . 12 D6
Don →, Humber., U.K. 10 D7
Don, C., Australia . . . 52 B5
Don Benito, Spain . . . 19 C3
Donaghadee, U.K. . . . 13 B6
Donald, Australia 55 F3
Donalda, Canada . . . 64 C6
Donaldsonville, U.S.A. 71 K9
Donalsonville, U.S.A. . 69 K3
Donau = Dunărea →, Europe 17 F15
Donauwörth, Germany 16 D6
Doncaster, U.K. 10 D6
Dondo, Angola 46 F2
Dondo, Mozam. 47 H6
Dondo, Teluk, Indonesia 33 D6
Dondra Head, Sri Lanka 36 S12
Donegal, Ireland 13 B3
Donegal □, Ireland . . . 13 B4
Donegal B., Ireland . . 13 B3
Donets →, Russia . . . 23 E7
Donetsk, Ukraine 23 E6
Dongara, Australia . . . 53 E1
Dongbei, China 31 B7
Dongchuan, China . . . 30 D5
Donggala, Indonesia . . 33 E5
Dongola, Sudan 45 E11
Dongou, Congo 46 D3
Dongting Hu, China . . 31 D6
Donington, C., Australia 55 E2
Doniphan, U.S.A. 71 G9
Donna, Norway 8 C15
Donna, U.S.A. 71 M5
Donnaconna, Canada . 63 C5
Donnelly's Crossing, N.Z. 51 F4
Donnybrook, Australia 53 F2
Donnybrook, S. Africa 49 D4
Donor's Hill, Australia . 54 B3
Donostia = San Sebastián, Spain . . . 19 A5
Doon →, U.K. 12 F4
Dora, L., Australia . . . 52 D3
Dora Báltea →, Italy . 20 B3
Doran L., Canada 65 A7
Dorchester, U.K. 11 G5

Dorchester, C., Canada 61 B12
Dordogne →, France . 18 D3
Dordrecht, Neths. . . . 15 C4
Dordrecht, S. Africa . . 48 E4
Doré Lake, Canada . . 65 C7
Dori, Burkina Faso . . . 44 F4
Doring →, S. Africa . . 48 E2
Doringbos, S. Africa . . 48 E2
Dorion, Canada 62 C5
Dornbirn, Austria 16 E5
Dornoch, U.K. 12 D4
Dornoch Firth, U.K. . . 12 D4
Dorohoi, Romania . . . 17 E14
Döröö Nuur, Mongolia 30 B4
Dorr, Iran 39 C6
Dorre I., Australia . . . 53 E1
Dorrigo, Australia . . . 55 E5
Dorris, U.S.A. 72 F3
Dorset □, U.K. 11 G5
Dortmund, Germany . . 16 C4
Doruma, Zaïre 46 D5
Dorūneh, Iran 39 C8
Dos Bahías, C., Argentina 80 E3
Dos Hermanas, Spain . 19 D3
Dosso, Niger 44 F5
Dothan, U.S.A. 69 K3
Douai, France 18 A5
Douala, Cameroon . . . 44 H6
Douarnenez, France . . 18 B1
Double Island Pt., Australia 55 D5
Doubs →, France 18 C6
Doubtful Sd., N.Z. . . . 51 L1
Doubtless B., N.Z. . . . 51 F4
Douentza, Mali 44 F4
Douglas, S. Africa . . . 48 D3
Douglas, U.K. 10 C3
Douglas, Alaska, U.S.A. 64 B2
Douglas, Ariz., U.S.A. . 73 L9
Douglas, Ga., U.S.A. . 69 K4
Douglas, Wyo., U.S.A. 70 D2
Douglastown, Canada . 63 C7
Douglasville, U.S.A. . . 69 J3
Doumé, Cameroon . . . 46 D2
Dounreay, U.K. 12 C5
Dourados, Brazil 80 A6
Douro →, Europe 19 B1
Dove →, U.K. 10 E6
Dove Creek, U.S.A. . . 73 H9
Dover, Australia 54 G4
Dover, U.K. 11 F9
Dover, Del., U.S.A. . . . 68 F8
Dover, N.H., U.S.A. . . 68 D10
Dover, Ohio, U.S.A. . . 68 E5
Dover, Pt., Australia . . 53 F4
Dover, Str. of, Europe . 18 A4
Dover-Foxcroft, U.S.A. 63 C11
Dovey = Dyfi →, U.K. 11 E4
Dovrefjell, Norway . . . 9 E13
Dow Rūd, Iran 39 C6
Dowagiac, U.S.A. 68 E2
Dowghā'i, Iran 39 B8
Dowlatābād, Iran 39 D8
Down □, U.K. 13 B6
Downey, U.S.A. 72 E7
Downham Market, U.K. 11 E8
Downieville, U.S.A. . . . 72 G3
Downpatrick, U.K. . . . 13 B6
Downpatrick Hd., Ireland 13 B2
Dowsāri, Iran 39 D8
Draa, Oued →, Morocco 44 C2
Drachten, Neths. 15 A6
Drăgăşani, Romania . . 17 F13
Dragichyn, Belarus . . . 17 B13
Dragoman, Prokhod, Bulgaria 21 C10
Draguignan, France . . 18 E7
Drain, U.S.A. 72 E2
Drake, Australia 55 D5
Drake, U.S.A. 70 B4
Drake Passage, S. Ocean 5 B17
Drakensberg, S. Africa 49 E4
Dráma, Greece 21 D11
Drammen, Norway . . . 9 G14
Drangajökull, Iceland . 8 C2
Drau = Drava →, Croatia 21 B8
Drava →, Croatia 21 B8
Drayton Valley, Canada 64 C6
Drenthe □, Neths. . . . 15 B6
Dresden, Germany . . . 16 C7
Dreux, France 18 B4
Driffield, U.K. 10 C7
Driggs, U.S.A. 72 E8
Drina →, Bos.-H. 21 B8
Drini →, Albania 21 C8
Drøbak, Norway 9 G14
Drochia, Moldova . . . 17 D14
Drogheda, Ireland . . . 13 C5
Drogichin = Dragichyn, Belarus 17 B13
Drogobych = Drohobych, Ukraine 17 D12
Drohobych, Ukraine . . 17 D12
Droichead Atha = Drogheda, Ireland . 13 C5
Droichead Nua, Ireland 13 C5
Droitwich, U.K. 11 E5
Dromedary, C., Australia 55 F5
Dronfield, Australia . . . 54 C3
Drumheller, Canada . . 64 C6
Drummond, U.S.A. . . . 72 C7
Drummond I., U.S.A. . 62 C3
Drummond Pt., Australia 55 E2
Drummond Ra., Australia 54 C4

Drummondville, Canada 62 C5
Drumright, U.S.A. 71 H6
Druskininkai, Lithuania 9 J20
Drut →, Belarus 17 B16
Druzhina, Russia 25 C15
Dryden, Canada 65 D10
Dryden, U.S.A. 71 K3
Drygalski I., Antarctica 5 C7
Drysdale →, Australia 52 B4
Drysdale I., Australia . 54 A2
Dschang, Cameroon . . 44 G7
Du Bois, U.S.A. 68 E6
Du Quoin, U.S.A. 70 G10
Duaringa, Australia . . 54 C4
Dubā, Si. Arabia 38 E2
Dubai = Dubayy, U.A.E. 39 E7
Dubāsari, Moldova . . . 17 E15
Dubăsari Vdkhr., Moldova 17 E15
Dubawnt →, Canada . 65 A8
Dubawnt, L., Canada . 65 A8
Dubayy, U.A.E. 39 E7
Dubbo, Australia 55 E4
Dublin, Ireland 13 C5
Dublin, Ga., U.S.A. . . 69 J4
Dublin, Tex., U.S.A. . . 71 J5
Dublin □, Ireland 13 C5
Dublin B., Ireland . . . 13 C5
Dubno, Ukraine 17 C13
Dubois, U.S.A. 72 D7
Dubossary = Dubăsari, Moldova 17 E15
Dubossary Vdkhr. = Dubăsari Vdkhr., Moldova 17 E15
Dubovka, Russia 23 E7
Dubréka, Guinea 44 G2
Dubrovitsa = Dubrovytsya, Ukraine 17 C14
Dubrovnik, Croatia . . . 21 C8
Dubrovskoye, Russia . 25 D12
Dubrovytsya, Ukraine . 17 C14
Dubuque, U.S.A. 70 D9
Duchesne, U.S.A. 72 F8
Duchess, Australia . . . 54 C2
Ducie I., Pac. Oc. . . . 57 K15
Duck Cr. →, Australia 52 D2
Duck Lake, Canada . . 65 C7
Duck Mountain Prov. Park, Canada 65 C8
Dudhi, India 37 G13
Dudinka, Russia 25 C9
Dudley, U.K. 11 E5
Duero = Douro →, Europe 19 B1
Dufftown, U.K. 12 D5
Dugi Otok, Croatia . . . 16 G8
Duifken Pt., Australia . 54 A3
Duisburg, Germany . . 16 C4
Duiwelskloof, S. Africa 49 C5
Dūkdamīn, Iran 39 C8
Duke I., U.S.A. 64 C2
Dukelský Průsmyk, Slovak Rep. 17 D11
Dukhān, Qatar 39 E6
Duki, Pakistan 36 D6
Duku, Nigeria 44 F7
Dulce →, Argentina . . 80 C4
Dulf, Iraq 38 C5
Dulit, Banjaran, Malaysia 32 D4
Dulq Maghār, Syria . . 38 B3
Dululu, Australia 54 C5
Duluth, U.S.A. 70 B8
Dum Duma, India . . . 37 F19
Dum Hadjer, Chad . . . 45 F8
Dūmā, Lebanon 41 A4
Dūmā, Syria 41 B5
Dumaguete, Phil. 33 C6
Dumai, Indonesia 32 D2
Dumaran, Phil. 33 B5
Dumas, Ark., U.S.A. . . 71 J9
Dumas, Tex., U.S.A. . . 71 H4
Dumbarton, U.K. 12 F4
Dumbleyung, Australia 53 F2
Dumfries, U.K. 12 F5
Dumfries & Galloway □, U.K. . . . 12 F5
Dumoine →, Canada . 62 C4
Dumoine L., Canada . 62 C4
Dumyât, Egypt 45 B11
Dún Dealgan = Dundalk, Ireland . . 13 B5
Dun Laoghaire, Ireland 13 C5
Duna = Dunărea →, Europe 17 F15
Dunaj = Dunărea →, Europe 17 F15
Dunakeszi, Hungary . . 17 E10
Dunărea →, Europe . . 17 F15
Dunaújváros, Hungary 17 E10
Dunav = Dunărea →, Europe 17 F15
Dunay, Russia 28 C6
Dunback, N.Z. 51 L3
Dunbar, Australia 54 B3
Dunbar, U.K. 12 E6
Dunblane, U.K. 12 E5
Duncan, Canada 64 D4
Duncan, Ariz., U.S.A. . 73 K9
Duncan, Okla., U.S.A. . 71 H6
Duncan L., Canada . . 64 A6
Duncan Passage, Ind. Oc. 34 G2
Dundalk, Ireland 13 B5
Dundalk Bay, Ireland . 13 C5
Dundas, Canada 62 D4
Dundas, L., Australia . 53 F3
Dundas I., Canada . . . 64 C2
Dundas Str., Australia . 52 B5
Dundee, S. Africa . . . 49 D5

Dundee, U.K. 12 E6
Dundoo, Australia . . . 55 D3
Dundrum, U.K. 13 B6
Dundrum B., U.K. . . . 13 B6
Dunedin, N.Z. 51 L3
Dunedin, U.S.A. 69 L4
Dunedin →, Canada . . 64 B4
Dunfermline, U.K. . . . 12 E5
Dungannon, U.K. 13 B5
Dungannon □, U.K. . . 13 B5
Dungarvan, Ireland . . 13 D4
Dungarvan Harbour, Ireland 13 D4
Dungeness, U.K. 11 G8
Dungo, L. do, Angola . 48 B2
Dungog, Australia . . . 55 E5
Dungu, Zaïre 46 D5
Dunhuang, China 30 B4
Dunk I., Australia 54 B4
Dunkeld, U.K. 12 E5
Dunkerque, France . . . 18 A5
Dunkery Beacon, U.K. 11 F4
Dunkirk = Dunkerque, France 18 A5
Dunkirk, U.S.A. 68 D6
Dunkwa, Ghana 44 G4
Dunlap, U.S.A. 70 E7
Dúnleary = Dun Laoghaire, Ireland . 13 C5
Dunmanus B., Ireland . 13 E2
Dunmara, Australia . . 54 B1
Dunmore, U.S.A. 68 E8
Dunmore Hd., Ireland . 13 D1
Dunn, U.S.A. 69 H6
Dunnellon, U.S.A. . . . 69 L4
Dunnet Hd., U.K. 12 C5
Dunning, U.S.A. 70 E4
Dunnville, Canada . . . 62 D4
Dunolly, Australia . . . 55 F3
Dunoon, U.K. 12 F4
Dunqul, Egypt 45 D11
Duns, U.K. 12 F6
Dunseith, U.S.A. 70 A4
Dunsmuir, U.S.A. 72 F2
Dunstable, U.K. 11 F7
Dunstan Mts., N.Z. . . 51 L2
Dunster, Canada 64 C5
Dunvegan L., Canada . 65 A7
Dupree, U.S.A. 70 C4
Dupuyer, U.S.A. 72 B7
Durack →, Australia . . 52 C4
Durack Ra., Australia . 52 C4
Durance →, France . . 18 E6
Durand, U.S.A. 68 D4
Durango = Victoria de Durango, Mexico . . 74 C4
Durango, Spain 19 A4
Durango, U.S.A. 73 H10
Duranillin, Australia . . 53 F2
Durant, U.S.A. 71 J6
Durazno, Uruguay . . . 80 C5
Durazzo = Durrësi, Albania 21 D8
Durban, S. Africa 49 D5
Düren, Germany 16 C4
Durg, India 37 J12
Durgapur, India 37 H15
Durham, Canada 62 D3
Durham, U.K. 10 C6
Durham, U.S.A. 69 G6
Durham □, U.K. 10 C6
Durham Downs, Australia 55 D4
Durmitor, Montenegro, Yug. 21 C8
Durness, U.K. 12 C4
Durrësi, Albania 21 D8
Durrie, Australia 54 D3
Dursunbey, Turkey . . . 21 E13
D'Urville, Tanjung, Indonesia 33 E9
D'Urville I., N.Z. 51 J4
Dusa Mareb, Somali Rep. 40 F4
Dushak, Turkmenistan 24 F7
Dushanbe, Tajikistan . 24 F7
Dusky Sd., N.Z. 51 L1
Dussejour, C., Australia 52 B4
Düsseldorf, Germany . 16 C4
Dutch Harbor, U.S.A. . 60 C3
Dutlwe, Botswana . . . 48 C3
Dutton →, Australia . . 54 C3
Duyun, China 30 D5
Duzdab = Zāhedān, Iran 39 D9
Dvina, Severnaya →, Russia 22 B7
Dvinsk = Daugavpils, Latvia 9 J22
Dvinskaya Guba, Russia 22 B6
Dwarka, India 36 H6
Dwellingup, Australia . 53 F2
Dwight, U.S.A. 68 E1
Dyatlovo = Dzyatlava, Belarus 17 B13
Dyer, C., Canada 61 B13
Dyer Plateau, Antarctica 5 D17
Dyersburg, U.S.A. . . . 71 G10
Dyfed □, U.K. 11 E3
Dyfi →, U.K. 11 E4
Dynevor Downs, Australia 55 D3
Dysart, Canada 65 C8
Dzamin Üüd, Mongolia 31 B6
Dzerzhinsk, Russia . . . 22 C7
Dzhalinda, Russia . . . 25 D13
Dzhambul = Zhambyl, Kazakhstan 24 E8
Dzhardzhan, Russia . . 25 C13
Dzhetygara = Zhetiqara, Kazakhstan 24 D7

Dzhezkazgan = Zhezqazghan, Kazakhstan 24 E8
Dzhizak = Jizzakh, Uzbekistan 24 E7
Dzhugdzur, Khrebet, Russia 25 D14
Dzhungarskiye Vorota, Kazakhstan 30 B3
Działdowa, Poland . . . 17 B11
Dzierzoniów, Poland . . 17 C9
Dzungaria = Junggar Pendi, China 30 B3
Dzungarian Gates = Dzhungarskiye Vorota, Kazakhstan . 30 B3
Dzuumod, Mongolia . . 30 B5
Dzyarzhynsk, Belarus . 17 B14
Dzyatlava, Belarus . . . 17 B13

E

Eabamet, L., Canada . . 62 B2
Eads, U.S.A. 70 F3
Eagle, U.S.A. 72 G10
Eagle →, Canada 63 B8
Eagle Butte, U.S.A. . . . 70 C4
Eagle Grove, U.S.A. . . 70 D8
Eagle L., Calif., U.S.A. . 72 F3
Eagle L., Maine, U.S.A. 63 B11
Eagle Lake, U.S.A. . . . 71 L6
Eagle Nest, U.S.A. . . . 73 H11
Eagle Pass, U.S.A. . . . 71 L4
Eagle Pt., Australia . . . 52 C3
Eagle River, U.S.A. . . . 70 C10
Ealing, U.K. 11 F7
Earaheedy, Australia . . 53 E3
Earl Grey, Canada . . . 65 C8
Earle, U.S.A. 71 H9
Earlimart, U.S.A. 73 J4
Earn →, U.K. 12 E5
Earn, L., U.K. 12 E4
Earnslaw, Mt., N.Z. . . 51 L2
Earth, U.S.A. 71 H3
Easley, U.S.A. 69 H4
East Angus, Canada . . 63 C5
East B., U.S.A. 71 L10
East Bengal, Bangla. . . 37 G17
East Beskids = Vychodné Beskydy, Europe 17 D11
East C., N.Z. 51 G7
East Chicago, U.S.A. . . 68 E2
East China Sea, Asia . . 31 C7
East Coulee, Canada . . 64 C6
East Falkland, Falk. Is. 80 G5
East Grand Forks, U.S.A. 70 B6
East Helena, U.S.A. . . . 72 C8
East Indies, Asia 33 E6
East Jordan, U.S.A. . . . 68 C3
East Lansing, U.S.A. . . 68 D3
East Liverpool, U.S.A. . 68 E5
East London, S. Africa . 49 E4
East Main = Eastmain, Canada 62 B4
East Orange, U.S.A. . . 68 E8
East Pacific Ridge, Pac. Oc. 57 J17
East Pakistan = Bangladesh ■, Asia 37 H17
East Pine, Canada . . . 64 B4
East Point, U.S.A. 69 J3
East Pt., Canada 63 C7
East Retford = Retford, U.K. 10 D7
East St. Louis, U.S.A. . 70 F9
East Schelde → = Oosterschelde, Neths. 15 C4
East Siberian Sea, Russia 25 B17
East Sussex □, U.K. . . 11 G8
East Tawas, U.S.A. . . . 68 C4
East Toorale, Australia 55 E4
Eastbourne, N.Z. 51 J5
Eastbourne, U.K. 11 G8
Eastend, Canada 65 D7
Easter Islands = Pascua, I. de, Pac. Oc. 57 K17
Eastern Cape □, S. Africa 48 E4
Eastern Cr. →, Australia 54 C3
Eastern Ghats, India . . 36 N11
Eastern Group = Lau Group, Fiji 51 C9
Eastern Group, Australia 53 F3
Eastern Transvaal □, S. Africa 49 D5
Easterville, Canada . . . 65 C9
Eastland, U.S.A. 71 J5
Eastleigh, U.K. 11 G6
Eastmain, Canada . . . 62 B4
Eastmain →, Canada . 62 B4
Eastman, U.S.A. 69 J4
Easton, Md., U.S.A. . . 68 F7
Easton, Pa., U.S.A. . . . 68 E8
Easton, Wash., U.S.A. . 72 C3
Eastport, U.S.A. 63 D6
Eaton, U.S.A. 70 E2
Eatonia, Canada 65 C7
Eatonton, U.S.A. 69 J4
Eau Claire, U.S.A. . . . 70 C9
Ebagoola, Australia . . 54 A3
Ebbw Vale, U.K. 11 F4
Ebeltoft, Denmark . . . 9 H14
Eberswalde-Finow, Germany 16 B7
Ebetsu, Japan 28 C10
Ebolowa, Cameroon . . 46 D2

Ebro →, *Spain* 19 B6
Eceabat, *Turkey* 21 D12
Ech Cheliff, *Algeria* 44 A5
Echigo-Sammyaku, *Japan* 29 F9
Echizen-Misaki, *Japan* 29 G7
Echo Bay, *N.W.T., Canada* 60 B8
Echo Bay, *Ont., Canada* 62 C3
Echoing →, *Canada* 65 B10
Echternach, *Lux.* 15 E6
Echuca, *Australia* 55 F3
Ecija, *Spain* 19 D3
Eclipse Is., *Australia* 52 B4
Ecuador ■, *S. Amer.* 78 D3
Ed Dâmer, *Sudan* 45 E11
Ed Debba, *Sudan* 45 E11
Ed Dueim, *Sudan* 45 F11
Edah, *Australia* 53 E2
Edam, *Canada* 65 C7
Edam, *Neths.* 15 B5
Eday, *U.K.* 12 B6
Edd, *Eritrea* 40 E3
Eddrachillis B., *U.K.* 12 C3
Eddystone, *U.K.* 11 G3
Eddystone Pt., *Australia* 54 G4
Ede, *Neths.* 15 B5
Édea, *Cameroon* 44 H7
Edehon L., *Canada* 65 A9
Eden, *Australia* 55 F4
Eden, *N.C., U.S.A.* 69 G6
Eden, *Tex., U.S.A.* 71 K5
Eden, *Wyo., U.S.A.* 72 E9
Eden →, *U.K.* 10 C4
Eden L., *Canada* 65 B8
Edenburg, *S. Africa* 48 D4
Edendale, *S. Africa* 49 D5
Edenderry, *Ireland* 13 C4
Edenton, *U.S.A.* 69 G7
Edenville, *S. Africa* 49 D4
Eder →, *Germany* 16 C5
Edgar, *U.S.A.* 70 E5
Edge Hill, *U.K.* 11 E6
Edgefield, *U.S.A.* 69 J5
Edgeley, *U.S.A.* 70 B5
Edgemont, *U.S.A.* 70 D3
Edgeøya, *Svalbard* 4 B9
Édhessa, *Greece* 21 D10
Edievale, *N.Z.* 51 L2
Edina, *U.S.A.* 70 E8
Edinburg, *U.S.A.* 71 M5
Edinburgh, *U.K.* 12 F5
Ediniţa, *Moldova* 17 D14
Edirne, *Turkey* 21 D12
Edithburgh, *Australia* 55 F2
Edjudina, *Australia* 53 E3
Edmond, *U.S.A.* 71 H6
Edmonds, *U.S.A.* 72 C2
Edmonton, *Australia* 54 B4
Edmonton, *Canada* 64 C6
Edmund L., *Canada* 65 C10
Edmundston, *Canada* 63 C6
Edna, *U.S.A.* 71 L6
Edna Bay, *U.S.A.* 64 B2
Edremit, *Turkey* 21 E12
Edremit Körfezi, *Turkey* 21 E12
Edson, *Canada* 64 C5
Edward →, *Australia* 55 F3
Edward, L., *Africa* 46 E5
Edward I., *Canada* 62 C2
Edward River, *Australia* 54 A3
Edward VII Land, *Antarctica* 5 E13
Edwards Plateau, *U.S.A.* 71 K4
Edzo, *Canada* 64 A5
Eekloo, *Belgium* 15 C3
Effingham, *U.S.A.* 68 F1
Égadi, Ísole, *Italy* 20 F5
Eganville, *Canada* 62 C4
Egeland, *U.S.A.* 70 A5
Egenolf L., *Canada* 65 B9
Eger = Cheb, *Czech.* 16 C7
Eger, *Hungary* 17 E11
Egersund, *Norway* 9 G12
Egg L., *Canada* 65 B7
Eginbah, *Australia* 52 D2
Egmont, C., *N.Z.* 51 H4
Egmont, Mt., *N.Z.* 51 H5
Eğridir, *Turkey* 23 G5
Eğridir Gölü, *Turkey* 23 G5
Egvekinot, *Russia* 25 C19
Egypt ■, *Africa* 45 C11
Ehime □, *Japan* 29 H6
Eibar, *Spain* 19 A4
Eidsvold, *Australia* 55 D5
Eidsvoll, *Norway* 9 F14
Eifel, *Germany* 16 C4
Eigg, *U.K.* 12 E2
Eighty Mile Beach, *Australia* 52 C3
Eil, *Somali Rep.* 40 F4
Eil, L., *U.K.* 12 E3
Eildon, L., *Australia* 55 F4
Eileen L., *Canada* 65 A7
Einasleigh, *Australia* 54 B3
Einasleigh →, *Australia* 54 B3
Eindhoven, *Neths.* 15 C5
Eire = Ireland ■, *Europe* 13 D4
Eiríksjökull, *Iceland* 8 D3
Eirunepé, *Brazil* 78 E5
Eisenach, *Germany* 16 C6
Eisenerz, *Austria* 16 E8
Eivissa = Ibiza, *Spain* 19 C6
Ekalaka, *U.S.A.* 70 C2
Eketahuna, *N.Z.* 51 J5
Ekibastuz, *Kazakhstan* 24 D8
Ekimchan, *Russia* 25 D14
Eksjö, *Sweden* 9 H16
Ekwan →, *Canada* 62 B3
Ekwan Pt., *Canada* 62 B3
El Aaiún, *W. Sahara* 44 C2
El 'Agrûd, *Egypt* 41 E3
El Alamein, *Egypt* 45 B10
El 'Aqaba, W. →, *Egypt* 41 E2
El Aricha, *Algeria* 44 B4
El Arīhā, *West Bank* 41 D4
El Arish, *Australia* 54 B4
El 'Arîsh, *Egypt* 41 D2
El 'Arîsh, W. →, *Egypt* 41 D2
El Asnam = Ech Cheliff, *Algeria* 44 A5
El Bawiti, *Egypt* 45 C10
El Bayadh, *Algeria* 44 B5
El Brûk, W. →, *Egypt* 41 E2
El Cajon, *U.S.A.* 73 K5
El Callao, *Venezuela* 78 B6
El Campo, *U.S.A.* 71 L6
El Centro, *U.S.A.* 73 K6
El Cerro, *Bolivia* 78 G6
El Cuy, *Argentina* 80 D3
El Cuyo, *Mexico* 74 C7
El Daheir, *Egypt* 41 D3
El Dere, *Somali Rep.* 40 G4
El Diviso, *Colombia* 78 C3
El Djouf, *Mauritania* 44 E3
El Dorado, *Ark., U.S.A.* 71 J8
El Dorado, *Kans., U.S.A.* 71 G6
El Dorado, *Venezuela* 78 B6
El Escorial, *Spain* 19 B3
El Faiyûm, *Egypt* 45 C11
El Fâsher, *Sudan* 45 F10
El Ferrol, *Spain* 19 A1
El Fuerte, *Mexico* 74 B3
El Gal, *Somali Rep.* 40 E5
El Geteina, *Sudan* 45 F11
El Gîza, *Egypt* 45 C11
El Iskandarîya, *Egypt* 45 B10
El Jadida, *Morocco* 44 B3
El Jebelein, *Sudan* 45 F11
El Kab, *Sudan* 45 E11
El Kabrît, G., *Egypt* 41 F2
El Kala, *Algeria* 44 A6
El Kamlin, *Sudan* 45 E11
El Kef, *Tunisia* 44 A6
El Khandaq, *Sudan* 45 E11
El Khârga, *Egypt* 45 C11
El Khartûm, *Sudan* 45 E11
El Khartûm Bahrî, *Sudan* 45 E11
El Kuntilla, *Egypt* 41 E3
El Laqâwa, *Sudan* 45 F10
El Mafâza, *Sudan* 45 F11
El Mahalla el Kubra, *Egypt* 45 B11
El Mansûra, *Egypt* 45 B11
El Minyâ, *Egypt* 45 C11
El Obeid, *Sudan* 45 F11
El Odaiya, *Sudan* 45 F10
El Oued, *Algeria* 44 B6
El Paso, *U.S.A.* 73 L10
El Portal, *U.S.A.* 73 H4
El Prat de Llobregat, *Spain* 19 B7
El Puerto de Santa María, *Spain* 19 D2
El Qâhira, *Egypt* 45 B11
El Qantara, *Egypt* 41 E1
El Qasr, *Egypt* 45 C10
El Quseima, *Egypt* 41 E3
El Reno, *U.S.A.* 71 H6
El Saheira, W. →, *Egypt* 41 E2
El Salvador ■, *Cent. Amer.* 74 E7
El Shallal, *Egypt* 45 D11
El Suweis, *Egypt* 45 C11
El Tamarâni, W. →, *Egypt* 41 E3
El Thamad, *Egypt* 41 F3
El Tigre, *Venezuela* 78 B6
El Tîh, G., *Egypt* 41 F2
El Tîna, Khalîg, *Egypt* 41 D1
El Tocuyo, *Venezuela* 78 B5
El Turbio, *Argentina* 80 G2
El Uqsur, *Egypt* 45 C11
El Vigía, *Venezuela* 78 B4
El Wabeira, *Egypt* 41 F2
El Wak, *Kenya* 46 D8
El Wuz, *Sudan* 45 E11
Elat, *Israel* 41 F3
Elâzığ, *Turkey* 23 G6
Elba, *Italy* 20 C4
Elba, *U.S.A.* 69 K2
Elbasani, *Albania* 21 D9
Elbe →, *Europe* 16 B5
Elbert, Mt., *U.S.A.* 73 G10
Elberta, *U.S.A.* 68 C2
Elberton, *U.S.A.* 69 H4
Elbeuf, *France* 18 B4
Elbing = Elbląg, *Poland* 17 A10
Elbląg, *Poland* 17 A10
Elbow, *Canada* 65 C7
Elbrus, *Asia* 23 F7
Elburg, *Neths.* 15 B5
Elburz Mts. = Alborz, Reshteh-ye Kūhhā-ye, *Iran* 39 C7
Elche, *Spain* 19 C5
Elcho I., *Australia* 54 A2
Elda, *Spain* 19 C5
Elde →, *Germany* 16 B6
Eldon, *U.S.A.* 70 F8
Eldora, *U.S.A.* 70 D8
Eldorado, *Canada* 65 B7
Eldorado, *Ill., U.S.A.* 68 G1
Eldorado, *Tex., U.S.A.* 71 K4
Eldorado Springs, *U.S.A.* 71 G8
Eldoret, *Kenya* 46 D7
Electra, *U.S.A.* 71 H5
Elefantes →, *Mozam.* 49 C5
Elektrostal, *Russia* 22 C6
Elephant Butte Reservoir, *U.S.A.* 73 K10
Elephant I., *Antarctica* 5 C18
Eleuthera, *Bahamas* 75 C9
Elgin, *Canada* 63 C6
Elgin, *U.K.* 12 D5
Elgin, *Ill., U.S.A.* 68 D1
Elgin, *N. Dak., U.S.A.* 70 B4
Elgin, *Nebr., U.S.A.* 70 E5
Elgin, *Nev., U.S.A.* 73 H6
Elgin, *Oreg., U.S.A.* 72 D5
Elgin, *Tex., U.S.A.* 71 K6
Elgon, Mt., *Africa* 46 D6
Eliase, *Indonesia* 33 F8
Elida, *U.S.A.* 71 J3
Elim, *S. Africa* 48 E2
Elisabethville = Lubumbashi, *Zaïre* 47 G5
Elista, *Russia* 23 E7
Elizabeth, *Australia* 55 E2
Elizabeth, *U.S.A.* 68 E8
Elizabeth City, *U.S.A.* 69 G7
Elizabethton, *U.S.A.* 69 G4
Elizabethtown, *U.S.A.* 68 G3
Ełk, *Poland* 17 B12
Elk City, *U.S.A.* 71 H5
Elk Island Nat. Park, *Canada* 64 C6
Elk Lake, *Canada* 62 C3
Elk Point, *Canada* 65 C6
Elk River, *Idaho, U.S.A.* 72 C5
Elk River, *Minn., U.S.A.* 70 C8
Elkedra, *Australia* 54 C2
Elkedra →, *Australia* 54 C2
Elkhart, *Ind., U.S.A.* 68 E3
Elkhart, *Kans., U.S.A.* 71 G4
Elkhorn, *Canada* 65 D8
Elkhorn →, *U.S.A.* 70 E6
Elkhovo, *Bulgaria* 21 C12
Elkin, *U.S.A.* 69 G5
Elkins, *U.S.A.* 68 F6
Elko, *Canada* 64 D5
Elko, *U.S.A.* 72 F6
Ell, L., *Australia* 53 E4
Ellef Ringnes I., *Canada* 4 B2
Ellendale, *Australia* 52 C3
Ellendale, *U.S.A.* 70 B5
Ellensburg, *U.S.A.* 72 C3
Ellenville, *U.S.A.* 68 E8
Ellery, Mt., *Australia* 55 F4
Ellesmere, L., *N.Z.* 51 M4
Ellesmere I., *Canada* 4 B4
Ellesmere Port, *U.K.* 10 D5
Ellice Is. = Tuvalu ■, *Pac. Oc.* 56 H9
Ellinwood, *U.S.A.* 70 F5
Elliot, *Australia* 54 B1
Elliot, *S. Africa* 49 E4
Elliot Lake, *Canada* 62 C3
Elliotdale = Xhora, *S. Africa* 49 E4
Ellis, *U.S.A.* 70 F5
Elliston, *Australia* 55 E1
Ellisville, *U.S.A.* 71 K10
Ellon, *U.K.* 12 D6
Ellore = Eluru, *India* 37 L12
Ells →, *Canada* 64 B6
Ellsworth, *U.S.A.* 70 F5
Ellsworth Land, *Antarctica* 5 D16
Ellsworth Mts., *Antarctica* 5 D16
Ellwood City, *U.S.A.* 68 E5
Elma, *Canada* 65 D9
Elma, *U.S.A.* 72 C2
Elmalı, *Turkey* 23 G4
Elmhurst, *U.S.A.* 68 E2
Elmira, *U.S.A.* 68 D7
Elmore, *Australia* 55 F3
Elmshorn, *Germany* 16 B5
Eloy, *U.S.A.* 73 K8
Elrose, *Canada* 65 C7
Elsas, *Canada* 62 C3
Elsinore = Helsingør, *Denmark* 9 H15
Elsinore, *U.S.A.* 73 G7
Eltham, *N.Z.* 51 H5
Eluru, *India* 37 L12
Elvas, *Portugal* 19 C2
Elverum, *Norway* 9 F14
Elvire →, *Australia* 52 C4
Elwood, *Ind., U.S.A.* 68 E3
Elwood, *Nebr., U.S.A.* 70 E5
Elx = Elche, *Spain* 19 C5
Ely, *U.K.* 11 E8
Ely, *Minn., U.S.A.* 70 B9
Ely, *Nev., U.S.A.* 72 G6
Elyria, *U.S.A.* 68 E4
Emāmrūd, *Iran* 39 B7
Emba = Embi, *Kazakhstan* 24 E6
Emba = Embi →, *Kazakhstan* 23 E9
Embarcación, *Argentina* 80 A4
Embarras Portage, *Canada* 65 B6
Embetsu, *Japan* 28 B10
Embi, *Kazakhstan* 24 E6
Embi →, *Kazakhstan* 23 E9
Embrun, *France* 18 D7
Embu, *Kenya* 46 E7
Emden, *Germany* 16 B4
Emerald, *Australia* 54 C4
Emerson, *Canada* 65 D9
Emery, *U.S.A.* 73 G8
Emet, *Turkey* 21 E13
Emi Koussi, *Chad* 45 E8
Emine, Nos, *Bulgaria* 21 C12
Emmeloord, *Neths.* 15 B5
Emmen, *Neths.* 15 B6
Emmet, *Australia* 54 C3
Emmetsburg, *U.S.A.* 70 D7
Emmett, *U.S.A.* 72 E5
Empalme, *Mexico* 74 B2
Empangeni, *S. Africa* 49 D5
Empedrado, *Argentina* 80 B5
Emperor Seamount Chain, *Pac. Oc.* 56 D9
Emporia, *Kans., U.S.A.* 70 F6
Emporia, *Va., U.S.A.* 69 G7
Emporium, *U.S.A.* 68 E6
Empress, *Canada* 65 C6
Empty Quarter = Rub' al Khali, *Si. Arabia* 40 D4
Ems →, *Germany* 16 B4
Emu Park, *Australia* 54 C5
'En 'Avrona, *Israel* 41 F3
En Nahud, *Sudan* 45 F10
Ena, *Japan* 29 G8
Enana, *Namibia* 48 B2
Enaratoli, *Indonesia* 33 E9
Enard B., *U.K.* 12 C3
Enare = Inarijärvi, *Finland* 8 B22
Encanto, C., *Phil.* 33 A6
Encarnación, *Paraguay* 80 B5
Encinal, *U.S.A.* 71 L5
Encino, *U.S.A.* 73 J11
Encounter B., *Australia* 55 F2
Endau →, *Malaysia* 34 S16
Ende, *Indonesia* 33 F6
Endeavour, *Canada* 65 C8
Endeavour Str., *Australia* 54 A3
Enderbury I., *Kiribati* 56 H10
Enderby, *Canada* 64 C5
Enderby I., *Australia* 52 D2
Enderby Land, *Antarctica* 5 C5
Enderlin, *U.S.A.* 70 B6
Endicott, *N.Y., U.S.A.* 68 D7
Endicott, *Wash., U.S.A.* 72 C5
Endyalgout I., *Australia* 52 B5
Enewetak Atoll, *Pac. Oc.* 56 F8
Enez, *Turkey* 21 D12
Enfield, *U.K.* 11 F7
Engadin, *Switz.* 16 E6
Engaño, C., *Phil.* 33 A6
Engcobo, *S. Africa* 49 E4
Engels, *Russia* 22 D8
Engemann L., *Canada* 65 B7
Enggano, *Indonesia* 32 F2
Enghien, *Belgium* 15 D4
Engkilili, *Malaysia* 32 D4
England, *U.S.A.* 71 H9
England □, *U.K.* 7 E5
Englee, *Canada* 63 B8
Englehart, *Canada* 62 C4
Engler L., *Canada* 65 B7
Englewood, *Colo., U.S.A.* 70 F2
Englewood, *Kans., U.S.A.* 71 G5
English →, *Canada* 65 C10
English Bazar = Ingraj Bazar, *India* 37 G16
English Channel, *Europe* 18 A3
English River, *Canada* 62 C1
Enid, *U.S.A.* 71 G6
Enkhuizen, *Neths.* 15 B5
Enna, *Italy* 20 F6
Ennadai, *Canada* 65 A8
Ennadai L., *Canada* 65 A8
Ennedi, *Chad* 45 E9
Enngonia, *Australia* 55 D4
Ennis, *Ireland* 13 D3
Ennis, *Mont., U.S.A.* 72 D8
Ennis, *Tex., U.S.A.* 71 J6
Enniscorthy, *Ireland* 13 D5
Enniskillen, *U.K.* 13 B4
Ennistimon, *Ireland* 13 D2
Enns →, *Austria* 16 D8
Enontekiö, *Finland* 8 B20
Enschede, *Neths.* 15 B6
Ensenada, *Mexico* 74 A1
Entebbe, *Uganda* 46 D6
Enterprise, *Canada* 64 A5
Enterprise, *Oreg., U.S.A.* 72 D5
Enterprise, *Utah, U.S.A.* 73 H7
Entroncamento, *Portugal* 19 C1
Enugu, *Nigeria* 44 G6
Enugu Ezike, *Nigeria* 44 G6
Enumclaw, *U.S.A.* 72 C3
Eólie, Ís., *Italy* 20 E6
Epe, *Neths.* 15 B5
Épernay, *France* 18 B5
Ephesus, *Turkey* 21 F12
Ephraim, *U.S.A.* 72 G8
Ephrata, *U.S.A.* 72 C4
Épinal, *France* 18 B7
Epping, *U.K.* 11 F8
Epukiro, *Namibia* 48 C2
Equatorial Guinea ■, *Africa* 46 D1
Er Rahad, *Sudan* 45 F11
Er Rif, *Morocco* 44 A4
Er Roseires, *Sudan* 45 F11
Erāwadī Myit = Irrawaddy →, *Burma* 37 M19
Erbil = Arbīl, *Iraq* 38 B5
Erciyaş Dağı, *Turkey* 23 G6
Érd, *Hungary* 17 E10
Erdek, *Turkey* 21 D12
Erebus, Mt., *Antarctica* 5 D11
Erechim, *Brazil* 80 B6
Ereğli, *Konya, Turkey* 23 G5
Ereğli, *Zonguldak, Turkey* 23 F5
Eresma →, *Spain* 19 B3
Erewadi Myitwanya, *Burma* 37 M19
Erfenisdam, *S. Africa* 48 D4
Erfurt, *Germany* 16 C6
Ergeni Vozvyshennost, *Russia* 23 E7
Ērgli, *Latvia* 9 H21
Eriboll, L., *U.K.* 12 C4
Érice, *Italy* 20 E5
Erie, *U.S.A.* 68 D5
Erie, L., *N. Amer.* 68 D5
Erigavo, *Somali Rep.* 40 E4
Eriksdale, *Canada* 65 C9
Erímanthos, *Greece* 21 F9
Erimo-misaki, *Japan* 28 D11
Eritrea ■, *Africa* 45 F12
Erlangen, *Germany* 16 D6
Erldunda, *Australia* 54 D1
Ermelo, *Neths.* 15 B5
Ermelo, *S. Africa* 49 D4
Ermoúpolis = Síros, *Greece* 21 F11
Ernakulam = Cochin, *India* 36 Q10
Erne →, *Ireland* 13 B3
Erne, Lower L., *U.K.* 13 B4
Erne, Upper L., *U.K.* 13 B4
Ernest Giles Ra., *Australia* 53 E3
Erode, *India* 36 P10
Eromanga, *Australia* 55 D3
Erongo, *Namibia* 48 C2
Errabiddy, *Australia* 53 E2
Erramala Hills, *India* 36 M11
Errigal, *Ireland* 13 A3
Erris Hd., *Ireland* 13 B1
Erskine, *U.S.A.* 70 B7
Ertis = Irtysh →, *Russia* 24 C7
Erwin, *U.S.A.* 69 G4
Erzgebirge, *Germany* 16 C7
Erzin, *Russia* 25 D10
Erzincan, *Turkey* 23 G6
Erzurum, *Turkey* 23 G7
Es Sahrâ' Esh Sharqîya, *Egypt* 45 C11
Es Sînâ', *Egypt* 45 C11
Esan-Misaki, *Japan* 28 D10
Esashi, *Hokkaidō, Japan* 28 B11
Esashi, *Hokkaidō, Japan* 28 D10
Esbjerg, *Denmark* 9 J13
Escalante, *U.S.A.* 73 H8
Escalante →, *U.S.A.* 73 H8
Escambia →, *U.S.A.* 69 K2
Escanaba, *U.S.A.* 68 C2
Esch-sur-Alzette, *Lux.* 18 B6
Escobal, *Panama* 74 H14
Escondido, *U.S.A.* 73 K5
Escuinapa, *Mexico* 74 C3
Eşfahān, *Iran* 39 C6
Esfideh, *Iran* 39 C8
Esh Sham = Dimashq, *Syria* 41 B5
Eshowe, *S. Africa* 49 D5
Esil = Ishim →, *Russia* 24 D8
Esk →, *Cumb., U.K.* 12 G5
Esk →, *N. Yorks., U.K.* 10 C7
Eskifjörður, *Iceland* 8 D7
Eskilstuna, *Sweden* 9 G17
Eskimo Pt., *Canada* 65 A10
Eskişehir, *Turkey* 23 G5
Esla →, *Spain* 19 B2
Eslāmābād-e Gharb, *Iran* 38 C5
Eşme, *Turkey* 21 E13
Esmeraldas, *Ecuador* 78 C3
Espanola, *Canada* 62 C3
Esperance, *Australia* 53 F3
Esperance B., *Australia* 53 F3
Esperanza, *Argentina* 80 C4
Espichel, C., *Portugal* 19 C1
Espinal, *Colombia* 78 C4
Espinazo, Sierra del = Espinhaço, Serra do, *Brazil* 79 G10
Espinhaço, Serra do, *Brazil* 79 G10
Espírito Santo □, *Brazil* 79 G10
Espoo, *Finland* 9 F21
Espungabera, *Mozam.* 49 C5
Esquel, *Argentina* 80 E2
Esquina, *Argentina* 80 C5
Essaouira, *Morocco* 44 B3
Essen, *Belgium* 15 C4
Essen, *Germany* 16 C4
Essendon, Mt., *Australia* 53 E3
Essequibo →, *Guyana* 78 B7
Essex □, *U.K.* 11 F8
Esslingen, *Germany* 16 D5
Estados, I. de Los, *Argentina* 80 G4
Eşţahbānāt, *Iran* 39 D7
Estância, *Brazil* 79 F11
Estancia, *U.S.A.* 73 J10
Estārm, *Iran* 39 D8
Estcourt, *S. Africa* 49 D4
Estelline, *S. Dak., U.S.A.* 70 C6
Estelline, *Tex., U.S.A.* 71 H4
Esterhazy, *Canada* 65 C8
Estevan, *Canada* 65 D8
Estevan Group, *Canada* 64 C3
Estherville, *U.S.A.* 70 D7
Eston, *Canada* 65 C7
Estonia ■, *Europe* 9 G21
Estrêla, Serra da, *Portugal* 19 B2
Estremoz, *Portugal* 19 C2
Estrondo, Serra do, *Brazil* 79 E9
Esztergom, *Hungary* 17 E10
Etadunna, *Australia* 55 D2
Etamamu, *Canada* 63 B8
Étampes, *France* 18 B5
Etanga, *Namibia* 48 B1
Etawah, *India* 36 F11
Etawah →, *U.S.A.* 69 H3
Etawney L., *Canada* 65 B9
Ethel Creek, *Australia* 52 D3
Ethelbert, *Canada* 65 C8
Ethiopia ■, *Africa* 40 F3
Ethiopian Highlands, *Ethiopia* 42 E7
Etive, L., *U.K.* 12 E3
Etna, *Italy* 20 F6
Etolin I., *U.S.A.* 64 B2
Etosha Pan, *Namibia* 48 B2
Etowah, *U.S.A.* 69 H3
Ettrick Water →, *U.K.* 12 F6
Euboea = Évvoia, *Greece* 21 E11
Eucla Motel, *Australia* 53 F4
Euclid, *U.S.A.* 68 E5
Eucumbene, L., *Australia* 55 F4
Eudora, *U.S.A.* 71 J9
Eufaula, *Ala., U.S.A.* 69 K3
Eufaula, *Okla., U.S.A.* 71 H7
Eufaula L., *U.S.A.* 71 H7
Eugene, *U.S.A.* 72 E2
Eugowra, *Australia* 55 E4
Eulo, *Australia* 55 D4
Eunice, *La., U.S.A.* 71 K8
Eunice, *N. Mex., U.S.A.* 71 J3
Eupen, *Belgium* 15 D6
Euphrates = Furāt, Nahr al →, *Asia* 38 D5
Eureka, *Canada* 4 B3
Eureka, *Calif., U.S.A.* 72 F1
Eureka, *Kans., U.S.A.* 71 G6
Eureka, *Mont., U.S.A.* 72 B6
Eureka, *Nev., U.S.A.* 72 G5
Eureka, *S. Dak., U.S.A.* 70 C5
Eureka, *Utah, U.S.A.* 72 G7
Eureka, Mt., *Australia* 53 E3
Euroa, *Australia* 55 F4
Europa, I., *Ind. Oc.* 47 J8
Europa, Picos de, *Spain* 19 A3
Europa, Pta. de, *Gib.* 19 D3
Europa Pt. = Europa, Pta. de, *Gib.* 19 D3
Europoort, *Neths.* 15 C4
Eustis, *U.S.A.* 69 L5
Eutsuk L., *Canada* 64 C3
Eva Downs, *Australia* 54 B1
Evale, *Angola* 48 B2
Evans, *U.S.A.* 70 E2
Evans Head, *Australia* 55 D5
Evans L., *Canada* 62 B4
Evanston, *Ill., U.S.A.* 68 D2
Evanston, *Wyo., U.S.A.* 72 F8
Evansville, *Ind., U.S.A.* 68 F2
Evansville, *Wis., U.S.A.* 70 D10
Evaz, *Iran* 39 E7
Eveleth, *U.S.A.* 70 B8
Evensk, *Russia* 25 C16
Everard, L., *Australia* 55 E1
Everard Park, *Australia* 53 E5
Everard Ras., *Australia* 53 E5
Everest, Mt., *Nepal* 37 E15
Everett, *U.S.A.* 72 C2
Everglades, The, *U.S.A.* 69 N5
Everglades City, *U.S.A.* 69 N5
Everglades National Park, *U.S.A.* 69 N5
Evergreen, *U.S.A.* 69 K2
Everson, *U.S.A.* 72 B2
Evesham, *U.K.* 11 E6
Evinayong, *Eq. Guin.* 46 D2
Evje, *Norway* 9 G12
Évora, *Portugal* 19 C2
Evowghlī, *Iran* 38 B5
Évreux, *France* 18 B4
Évros →, *Bulgaria* 21 D12
Evry, *France* 18 B5
Évvoia, *Greece* 21 E11
Ewe, L., *U.K.* 12 D3
Ewing, *U.S.A.* 70 D5
Ewo, *Congo* 46 E2
Exaltación, *Bolivia* 78 F5
Excelsior Springs, *U.S.A.* 70 F7
Exe →, *U.K.* 11 G4
Exeter, *U.K.* 11 G4
Exeter, *Calif., U.S.A.* 73 H4
Exeter, *Nebr., U.S.A.* 70 E6
Exmoor, *U.K.* 11 F4
Exmouth, *Australia* 52 D1
Exmouth, *U.K.* 11 G4
Exmouth G., *Australia* 52 D1
Expedition Ra., *Australia* 54 C4
Extremadura □, *Spain* 19 C2
Eyasi, L., *Tanzania* 46 E6
Eyeberry L., *Canada* 65 A8
Eyemouth, *U.K.* 12 F6
Eyjafjörður, *Iceland* 8 C4
Eyre, *Australia* 53 F4
Eyre (North), L., *Australia* 55 D2
Eyre (South), L., *Australia* 55 D2
Eyre Cr. →, *Australia* 55 D2
Eyre Mts., *N.Z.* 51 L2
Eyre Pen., *Australia* 55 E2
Eysturoy, *Færoe Is.* 8 E9
Eyvānkī, *Iran* 39 C6
Ezine, *Turkey* 21 E12

F

F.Y.R.O.M. =
Macedonia ■, *Europe* 21 D9
Fabens, *U.S.A.* 73 L10
Fabriano, *Italy* 20 C5
Facatativá, *Colombia* 78 C4
Fachi, *Niger* 44 E7
Fada, *Chad* 45 E9
Fada-n-Gourma,
Burkina Faso 44 F5
Faddeyevskiy, Ostrov,
Russia 25 B15
Fadghāmī, *Syria* 38 C4
Faenza, *Italy* 20 B4
Færoe Is. = Føroyar,
Atl. Oc. 8 F9
Făgăras, *Romania* 17 F13
Fagersta, *Sweden* 9 F16
Fagnano, L., *Argentina* 80 G3
Fahlīān, *Iran* 39 D6
Fahraj, *Kermān, Iran* 39 D8
Fahraj, *Yazd, Iran* 39 D7
Fair Hd., *U.K.* 13 A5
Fairbank, *U.S.A.* 73 L8
Fairbanks, *U.S.A.* 60 B5
Fairbury, *U.S.A.* 70 E6
Fairfax, *U.S.A.* 71 G6
Fairfield, *Ala., U.S.A.* 69 J2
Fairfield, *Calif., U.S.A.* 72 G2
Fairfield, *Idaho, U.S.A.* 72 E6
Fairfield, *Ill., U.S.A.* 68 F1
Fairfield, *Iowa, U.S.A.* 70 E9
Fairfield, *Mont., U.S.A.* 72 C8
Fairfield, *Tex., U.S.A.* 71 K7
Fairford, *Canada* 65 C9
Fairhope, *U.S.A.* 69 K2
Fairlie, *N.Z.* 51 L3
Fairmont, *Minn., U.S.A.* 70 D7
Fairmont, *W. Va.,*
U.S.A. 68 F5
Fairplay, *U.S.A.* 73 G11
Fairport, *U.S.A.* 68 D7
Fairview, *Australia* 54 B3
Fairview, *Canada* 64 B5
Fairview, *Mont., U.S.A.* 70 B2
Fairview, *Okla., U.S.A.* 71 G5
Fairview, *Utah, U.S.A.* 72 G8
Fairweather, Mt., *U.S.A.* 60 C6
Faisalabad, *Pakistan* 36 D8
Faith, *U.S.A.* 70 C3
Faizabad, *India* 37 F13
Fakfak, *Indonesia* 33 E8
Falaise, *France* 18 B3
Falam, *Burma* 37 H18
Falcon Dam, *U.S.A.* 71 M5
Falconara Maríttima,
Italy 20 C5
Falcone, C., *Italy* 20 D3
Faleshty = Fălești,
Moldova 17 E14
Fălești, *Moldova* 17 E14
Falfurrias, *U.S.A.* 71 M5
Falher, *Canada* 64 B5
Falkenberg, *Sweden* 9 H15
Falkirk, *U.K.* 12 F5
Falkland Is. ■, *Atl. Oc.* 80 G5
Falkland Sd., *Falk. Is.* 80 G5
Falköping, *Sweden* 9 G15
Fall River, *U.S.A.* 68 E10
Fall River Mills, *U.S.A.* 72 F3
Fallbrook, *U.S.A.* 73 K5
Fallon, *Mont., U.S.A.* 70 B2
Fallon, *Nev., U.S.A.* 72 G4
Falls City, *Nebr., U.S.A.* 70 E7
Falls City, *Oreg., U.S.A.* 72 D2
Falmouth, *Jamaica* 74 J16
Falmouth, *U.K.* 11 G2
Falmouth, *U.S.A.* 68 F3
False B., *S. Africa* 48 E2
Falster, *Denmark* 9 J14
Falsterbo, *Sweden* 9 J15
Fălticeni, *Romania* 17 E14
Falun, *Sweden* 9 F16
Famagusta, *Cyprus* 38 C2
Family L., *Canada* 65 C9
Fandriana, *Madag.* 49 C8
Fannich, L., *U.K.* 12 D4
Fannūj, *Iran* 39 E8
Fanny Bay, *Canada* 64 D4
Fanø, *Denmark* 9 J13
Fano, *Italy* 20 C5
Fanshaw, *U.S.A.* 64 B2
Fao = Al Fāw, *Iraq* 39 D6
Faradje, *Zaïre* 46 D5
Faradofay, *Madag.* 49 C8
Farāh, *Afghan.* 36 C3
Farāh □, *Afghan.* 36 C3
Farahalana, *Madag.* 49 A9
Faranah, *Guinea* 44 F2
Farasān, Jazā'ir,
Si. Arabia 40 D3
Farasan Is. = Farasān,
Jazā'ir, *Si. Arabia* 40 D3
Faratsiho, *Madag.* 49 B8
Fareham, *U.K.* 11 G6
Farewell, C., *N.Z.* 51 J4
Farewell C. = Farvel,
Kap, *Greenland* 4 D5
Farghona, *Uzbekistan* 24 E8
Fargo, *U.S.A.* 70 B6
Fār'iah, W. al →,
West Bank 41 C4
Faribault, *U.S.A.* 70 C8
Farim, *Guinea-Biss.* 44 F1
Farīmān, *Iran* 39 C8
Farina, *Australia* 55 E2
Farmerville, *U.S.A.* 71 J8
Farmington, *N. Mex.,*
U.S.A. 73 H9
Farmington, *Utah,*
U.S.A. 72 F8

Farmville, *U.S.A.* 68 G6
Farnborough, *U.K.* 11 F7
Farne Is., *U.K.* 10 B6
Faro, *Brazil* 79 D7
Faro, *Portugal* 19 D2
Fårö, *Sweden* 9 H18
Farquhar, C., *Australia* 53 D1
Farquhar Is., *Seychelles* 35 F4
Farrars Cr. →,
Australia 54 D3
Farrāshband, *Iran* 39 D7
Farrell, *U.S.A.* 68 E5
Farrell Flat, *Australia* 55 E2
Farrokhī, *Iran* 39 C8
Farrukhabad-cum-
Fatehgarh, *India* 36 F11
Fārs □, *Iran* 39 D7
Fársala, *Greece* 21 E10
Farsund, *Norway* 9 G12
Fartak, Rās, *Si. Arabia* 38 D2
Fārūj, *Iran* 39 B8
Farvel, Kap, *Greenland* 4 D5
Farwell, *U.S.A.* 71 H3
Fasā, *Iran* 39 D7
Fasano, *Italy* 20 D7
Fastiv, *Ukraine* 17 C15
Fastnet Rock, *Ireland* 13 E2
Fastov = Fastiv,
Ukraine 17 C15
Fatagar, Tanjung,
Indonesia 33 E8
Fatehgarh, *India* 36 F11
Fatehpur, *Raj., India* 36 F9
Fatehpur, *Ut. P., India* 37 G12
Fatima, *Canada* 63 C7
Faulkton, *U.S.A.* 70 C5
Faure I., *Australia* 53 E1
Fauresmith, *S. Africa* 48 D4
Fauske, *Norway* 8 C16
Favara, *Italy* 20 F5
Favignana, *Italy* 20 F5
Favourable Lake,
Canada 62 B1
Fawn →, *Canada* 62 A2
Faxaflói, *Iceland* 8 D2
Faya-Largeau, *Chad* 45 E8
Fayd, *Si. Arabia* 38 E4
Fayette, *Ala., U.S.A.* 69 J2
Fayette, *Mo., U.S.A.* 70 F8
Fayetteville, *Ark.,*
U.S.A. 71 G7
Fayetteville, *N.C.,*
U.S.A. 69 H6
Fayetteville, *Tenn.,*
U.S.A. 69 H2
Fazilka, *India* 36 D9
Fdérik, *Mauritania* 44 D2
Feale →, *Ireland* 13 D2
Fear, C., *U.S.A.* 69 J7
Feather →, *U.S.A.* 72 G3
Featherston, *N.Z.* 51 J5
Fécamp, *France* 18 B4
Fedeshküh, *Iran* 39 D7
Fehmarn, *Germany* 16 A6
Fehmarn Bælt,
Denmark 9 J14
Feilding, *N.Z.* 51 J5
Feira de Santana, *Brazil* 79 F11
Feldkirch, *Austria* 16 E5
Felipe Carrillo Puerto,
Mexico 74 D7
Felixstowe, *U.K.* 11 F9
Felton, *U.K.* 10 B6
Femunden, *Norway* 9 E14
Fengjie, *China* 31 C5
Fenit, *Ireland* 13 D2
Fennimore, *U.S.A.* 70 D9
Fenoarivo Afovoany,
Madag. 49 B8
Fenoarivo Atsinanana,
Madag. 49 B8
Fens, The, *U.K.* 10 E8
Fenton, *U.S.A.* 68 D4
Fenyang, *China* 31 C6
Feodosiya, *Ukraine* 23 E6
Ferdows, *Iran* 39 C8
Ferfer, *Somali Rep.* 40 F4
Fergana = Farghona,
Uzbekistan 24 E8
Fergus, *Canada* 62 D3
Fergus Falls, *U.S.A.* 70 B6
Ferland, *Canada* 62 B2
Fermanagh □, *U.K.* 13 B4
Fermo, *Italy* 20 C5
Fermoy, *Ireland* 13 D3
Fernandina Beach,
U.S.A. 69 K5
Fernando de Noronha,
Brazil 79 D12
Fernando Póo = Bioko,
Eq. Guin. 44 H6
Ferndale, *Calif., U.S.A.* 72 F1
Ferndale, *Wash., U.S.A.* 72 B2
Fernie, *Canada* 64 D5
Fernlees, *Australia* 54 C4
Fernley, *U.S.A.* 72 G4
Ferozepore = Firozpur,
India 36 D9
Ferrara, *Italy* 20 B4
Ferreñafe, *Peru* 78 E3
Ferret, C., *France* 18 D3
Ferriday, *U.S.A.* 71 K9
Ferrol = El Ferrol,
Spain 19 A1
Ferron, *U.S.A.* 73 G8
Ferryland, *Canada* 63 C9
Fertile, *U.S.A.* 70 B6
Fès, *Morocco* 44 B4
Feshi, *Zaïre* 46 F3
Fessenden, *U.S.A.* 70 B5
Fetești, *Romania* 17 F14
Fetlar, *U.K.* 12 A8
Feuilles →, *Canada* 61 C12

Fezzan, *Libya* 45 C8
Ffestiniog, *U.K.* 10 E4
Fianarantsoa, *Madag.* 49 C8
Fianarantsoa □, *Madag.* 49 B8
Fianga, *Cameroon* 45 G8
Ficksburg, *S. Africa* 49 D4
Field, *Canada* 62 C3
Field →, *Australia* 54 C2
Field I., *Australia* 52 B5
Fieri, *Albania* 21 D8
Fife □, *U.K.* 12 E5
Fife Ness, *U.K.* 12 E6
Figeac, *France* 18 D5
Figueira da Foz,
Portugal 19 B1
Figueras, *Spain* 19 A7
Figuig, *Morocco* 44 B4
Fihaonana, *Madag.* 49 B8
Fiherenana, *Madag.* 49 B8
Fiherenana →,
Madag. 49 C7
Fiji ■, *Pac. Oc.* 51 C8
Filer, *U.S.A.* 72 E6
Filey, *U.K.* 10 C7
Filiatrá, *Greece* 21 F9
Filipstad, *Sweden* 9 G16
Fillmore, *Canada* 65 D8
Fillmore, *Calif., U.S.A.* 73 J4
Fillmore, *Utah, U.S.A.* 73 G7
Findhorn →, *U.K.* 12 D5
Findlay, *U.S.A.* 68 E4
Finger L., *Canada* 65 C10
Fingōe, *Mozam.* 47 G6
Finisterre, C., *Spain* 19 A1
Finke, *Australia* 54 D1
Finke →, *Australia* 55 D2
Finland ■, *Europe* 8 E22
Finland, G. of, *Europe* 9 G21
Finlay →, *Canada* 64 B3
Finley, *Australia* 55 F4
Finley, *U.S.A.* 70 B6
Finn →, *Ireland* 13 B4
Finnigan, Mt., *Australia* 54 B4
Finniss, C., *Australia* 55 E1
Finnmark, *Norway* 8 B20
Finnsnes, *Norway* 8 B18
Finspång, *Sweden* 9 G16
Fiora →, *Italy* 20 C4
Fiq, *Syria* 41 C4
Firat = Furāt, Nahr
al →, *Asia* 38 D5
Fire River, *Canada* 62 C3
Firebag →, *Canada* 65 B6
Firedrake L., *Canada* 65 A8
Firenze, *Italy* 20 C4
Firk →, *Iraq* 38 D5
Firozabad, *India* 36 F11
Firozpur, *India* 36 D9
Fīrūzābād, *Iran* 39 D7
Fīrūzkūh, *Iran* 39 C7
Firvale, *Canada* 64 C3
Fish →, *Namibia* 48 D2
Fish →, *S. Africa* 48 E3
Fisher, *Australia* 53 F5
Fisher B., *Canada* 65 C9
Fishguard, *U.K.* 11 F3
Fishing L., *Canada* 65 C9
Fitchburg, *U.S.A.* 68 D10
Fitri, L., *Chad* 45 F8
Fitz Roy, *Argentina* 80 F3
Fitzgerald, *Canada* 64 B6
Fitzgerald, *U.S.A.* 69 K4
Fitzmaurice →,
Australia 52 B5
Fitzroy →, *Queens.,*
Australia 54 C5
Fitzroy →, *W. Austral.,*
Australia 52 C3
Fitzroy Crossing,
Australia 52 C4
Fiume = Rijeka, *Croatia* 16 F8
Fizi, *Zaïre* 46 E5
Flagler, *U.S.A.* 70 F3
Flagstaff, *U.S.A.* 73 J8
Flaherty I., *Canada* 62 A4
Flåm, *Norway* 9 F12
Flambeau →, *U.S.A.* 70 C9
Flamborough Hd., *U.K.* 10 C7
Flaming Gorge Dam,
U.S.A. 72 F9
Flaming Gorge
Reservoir, *U.S.A.* 72 F9
Flamingo, Teluk,
Indonesia 33 F9
Flanders = West-
Vlaanderen □,
Belgium 15 D3
Flandre, *Europe* 16 C2
Flandre Occidentale =
West-Vlaanderen □,
Belgium 15 D3
Flandre Orientale =
Oost-Vlaanderen □,
Belgium 15 C3
Flandreau, *U.S.A.* 70 C6
Flannan Is., *U.K.* 12 C1
Flåsjön, *Sweden* 8 D16
Flat →, *Canada* 64 A3
Flat River, *U.S.A.* 71 G9
Flathead L., *U.S.A.* 72 C6
Flattery, C., *Australia* 54 A4
Flattery, C., *U.S.A.* 72 B1
Flaxton, *U.S.A.* 70 A3
Fleetwood, *U.K.* 10 D4
Flekkefjord, *Norway* 9 G12
Flensburg, *Germany* 16 A5
Flers, *France* 18 B3
Flesko, Tanjung,
Indonesia 33 D6
Flevoland □, *Neths.* 15 B5
Flin Flon, *Canada* 65 C8
Flinders →, *Australia* 54 B3
Flinders B., *Australia* 53 F2
Flinders Group,
Australia 54 A3

Flinders I., *Australia* 54 F4
Flinders Ras., *Australia* 55 E2
Flinders Reefs,
Australia 54 B4
Flint, *U.K.* 10 D4
Flint, *U.S.A.* 68 D4
Flint →, *U.S.A.* 69 K3
Flint I., *Kiribati* 57 J12
Flinton, *Australia* 55 D4
Flodden, *U.K.* 10 B5
Floodwood, *U.S.A.* 70 B8
Flora, *U.S.A.* 68 F1
Florala, *U.S.A.* 69 K2
Florence = Firenze,
Italy 20 C4
Florence, *Ala., U.S.A.* 69 H2
Florence, *Ariz., U.S.A.* 73 K8
Florence, *Colo., U.S.A.* 70 F2
Florence, *Oreg., U.S.A.* 72 E1
Florence, *S.C., U.S.A.* 69 H6
Florence, L., *Australia* 55 D2
Florennes, *Belgium* 15 D4
Florenville, *Belgium* 15 E5
Flores, *Indonesia* 33 F6
Flores I., *Canada* 64 D3
Flores Sea, *Indonesia* 33 F6
Florești, *Moldova* 17 E15
Floriano, *Brazil* 79 E10
Florianópolis, *Brazil* 80 B7
Florida, *Uruguay* 80 C5
Florida □, *U.S.A.* 69 L5
Florida, Straits of,
U.S.A. 75 C9
Florida Keys, *U.S.A.* 67 F10
Flórina, *Greece* 21 D9
Florø, *Norway* 9 F11
Flower's Cove, *Canada* 63 B8
Floydada, *U.S.A.* 71 J4
Fluk, *Indonesia* 33 E7
Flushing = Vlissingen,
Neths. 15 C3
Flying Fish, C.,
Antarctica 5 D15
Foam Lake, *Canada* 65 C8
Foça, *Turkey* 21 E12
Focșani, *Romania* 17 F14
Fóggia, *Italy* 20 D6
Fogo, *Canada* 63 C9
Fogo I., *Canada* 63 C9
Föhr, *Germany* 16 A5
Foix, *France* 18 E4
Folda, *Nord-Trøndelag,*
Norway 8 D14
Folda, *Nordland,*
Norway 8 C16
Foleyet, *Canada* 62 C3
Folgefonni, *Norway* 9 F12
Foligno, *Italy* 20 C5
Folkestone, *U.K.* 11 F9
Folkston, *U.S.A.* 69 K5
Follett, *U.S.A.* 71 G4
Fond-du-Lac, *Canada* 65 B7
Fond du Lac, *U.S.A.* 70 D10
Fond-du-Lac →,
Canada 65 B7
Fondi, *Italy* 20 D5
Fonsagrada, *Spain* 19 A2
Fonseca, G. de,
Cent. Amer. 74 E7
Fontainebleau, *France* 18 B5
Fontas →, *Canada* 64 B4
Fonte Boa, *Brazil* 78 D5
Fontenay-le-Comte,
France 18 C3
Fontur, *Iceland* 8 C6
Foochow = Fuzhou,
China 31 D6
Forbes, *Australia* 55 E4
Forbes, Mt., *Canada* 64 C5
Førde, *Norway* 9 F11
Ford's Bridge, *Australia* 55 D4
Fordyce, *U.S.A.* 71 J8
Forécariah, *Guinea* 44 G2
Forel, Mt., *Greenland* 4 C6
Foremost, *Canada* 64 D6
Forest, *Canada* 62 D3
Forest City, *Iowa,*
U.S.A. 70 D8
Forest City, *N.C., U.S.A.* 69 H5
Forest Grove, *U.S.A.* 72 D2
Forestburg, *Canada* 64 C6
Forestier Pen., *Australia* 54 G4
Forestville, *Canada* 63 C6
Forestville, *U.S.A.* 68 C2
Forfar, *U.K.* 12 E6
Forks, *U.S.A.* 72 C1
Forlì, *Italy* 20 B5
Forman, *U.S.A.* 70 B6
Formby Pt., *U.K.* 10 D4
Formentera, *Spain* 19 C6
Formentor, C. de, *Spain* 19 C7
Former Yugoslav
Republic of
Macedonia =
Macedonia ■, *Europe* 21 D9
Fórmia, *Italy* 20 D5
Formosa = Taiwan ■,
Asia 31 D7
Formosa, *Argentina* 80 B5
Formosa, Serra, *Brazil* 79 F8
Formosa Bay, *Kenya* 46 E8
Føroyar, *Atl. Oc.* 8 F9
Forres, *U.K.* 12 D5
Forrest, *Vic., Australia* 55 F3
Forrest, *W. Austral.,*
Australia 53 F4
Forrest, Mt., *Australia* 53 D4
Forrest City, *U.S.A.* 71 H9
Forsayth, *Australia* 54 B3
Forssa, *Finland* 9 F20
Forst, *Germany* 16 C8

Forster, *Australia* 55 E5
Forsyth, *Ga., U.S.A.* 69 J4
Forsyth, *Mont., U.S.A.* 72 C10
Fort Albany, *Canada* 62 B3
Fort Apache, *U.S.A.* 73 K9
Fort Assiniboine,
Canada 64 C6
Fort Augustus, *U.K.* 12 D4
Fort Beaufort, *S. Africa* 48 E4
Fort Benton, *U.S.A.* 72 C8
Fort Bragg, *U.S.A.* 72 G2
Fort Bridger, *U.S.A.* 72 F8
Fort Chipewyan,
Canada 65 B6
Fort Clayton, *Panama* 74 H14
Fort Collins, *U.S.A.* 70 E2
Fort-Coulonge, *Canada* 62 C4
Fort Davis, *Panama* 74 H14
Fort Davis, *U.S.A.* 71 K3
Fort-de-France,
Martinique 74 N20
Fort de Possel =
Possel, *C.A.R.* 46 C3
Fort Defiance, *U.S.A.* 73 J9
Fort Dodge, *U.S.A.* 70 D7
Fort Frances, *Canada* 65 D10
Fort Franklin, *Canada* 60 B7
Fort Garland, *U.S.A.* 73 H11
Fort George =
Chisasibi, *Canada* 62 B4
Fort Good-Hope,
Canada 60 B7
Fort Hancock, *U.S.A.* 73 L11
Fort Hertz = Putao,
Burma 37 F20
Fort Hope, *Canada* 62 B2
Fort Jameson =
Chipata, *Zambia* 47 G6
Fort Kent, *U.S.A.* 63 C6
Fort Klamath, *U.S.A.* 72 E3
Fort-Lamy =
Ndjamena, *Chad* 45 F7
Fort Laramie, *U.S.A.* 70 D2
Fort Lauderdale, *U.S.A.* 69 M5
Fort Liard, *Canada* 64 A4
Fort Lupton, *U.S.A.* 70 E2
Fort Mackay, *Canada* 64 B6
Fort McKenzie, *Canada* 63 A6
Fort Macleod, *Canada* 64 D6
Fort MacMahon,
Algeria 44 C5
Fort McMurray, *Canada* 64 B6
Fort McPherson,
Canada 60 B6
Fort Madison, *U.S.A.* 70 E9
Fort Meade, *U.S.A.* 69 M5
Fort Miribel, *Algeria* 44 C5
Fort Morgan, *U.S.A.* 70 E3
Fort Myers, *U.S.A.* 69 M5
Fort Nelson, *Canada* 64 B4
Fort Nelson →,
Canada 64 B4
Fort Norman, *Canada* 60 B7
Fort Payne, *U.S.A.* 69 H3
Fort Peck, *U.S.A.* 72 B10
Fort Peck Dam, *U.S.A.* 72 C10
Fort Peck L., *U.S.A.* 72 C10
Fort Pierce, *U.S.A.* 69 M5
Fort Pierre, *U.S.A.* 70 C4
Fort Portal, *Uganda* 46 D6
Fort Providence,
Canada 64 A5
Fort Qu'Appelle,
Canada 65 C8
Fort Randolph, *Panama* 74 H14
Fort Resolution, *Canada* 64 A6
Fort Rosebery =
Mansa, *Zambia* 46 G5
Fort Rupert =
Waskaganish, *Canada* 62 B4
Fort St. James, *Canada* 64 C4
Fort St. John, *Canada* 64 B4
Fort Sandeman,
Pakistan 36 D6
Fort Saskatchewan,
Canada 64 C6
Fort Scott, *U.S.A.* 71 G7
Fort Severn, *Canada* 62 A2
Fort Sherman, *Panama* 74 H14
Fort Shevchenko,
Kazakhstan 23 F9
Fort Simpson, *Canada* 64 A4
Fort Smith, *Canada* 64 B6
Fort Smith, *U.S.A.* 71 H7
Fort Stanton, *U.S.A.* 73 K11
Fort Stockton, *U.S.A.* 71 K3
Fort Sumner, *U.S.A.* 71 H2
Fort Trinquet = Bir
Mogrein, *Mauritania* 44 C2
Fort Valley, *U.S.A.* 69 J4
Fort Vermilion, *Canada* 64 B5
Fort Walton Beach,
U.S.A. 69 K2
Fort Wayne, *U.S.A.* 68 E3
Fort William, *U.K.* 12 E3
Fort Worth, *U.S.A.* 71 J6
Fort Yates, *U.S.A.* 70 B4
Fort Yukon, *U.S.A.* 60 B5
Fortaleza, *Brazil* 79 D11
Forteau, *Canada* 63 B8
Forth →, *U.K.* 12 E5
Forth, Firth of, *U.K.* 12 E6
Fortrose, *U.K.* 12 D4
Fortuna, *Calif., U.S.A.* 72 F1
Fortuna, *N. Dak., U.S.A.* 70 A3
Fortune B., *Canada* 63 C8
Foshan, *China* 31 D6
Fossano, *Italy* 20 B2
Fossil, *U.S.A.* 72 D3
Fossilbrook, *Australia* 54 B3
Fosston, *U.S.A.* 70 B7

Foster →, *Canada* 65 B7
Fosters Ra., *Australia* 54 C1
Fostoria, *U.S.A.* 68 E4
Fougamou, *Gabon* 46 E2
Fougères, *France* 18 B3
Foul Pt., *Sri Lanka* 36 Q12
Foula, *U.K.* 12 A6
Foulness I., *U.K.* 11 F8
Foulpointe, *Madag.* 49 B8
Foumban, *Cameroon* 44 G7
Fountain, *Colo., U.S.A.* 70 F2
Fountain, *Utah, U.S.A.* 72 G8
Fourchu, *Canada* 63 C7
Fouriesburg, *S. Africa* 48 D4
Foúrnoi, *Greece* 21 F12
Fouta Djalon, *Guinea* 44 F2
Foveaux Str., *N.Z.* 51 M2
Fowey, *U.K.* 11 G3
Fowler, *Calif., U.S.A.* 73 H4
Fowler, *Colo., U.S.A.* 70 F2
Fowler, *Kans., U.S.A.* 71 G4
Fowlers B., *Australia* 53 F5
Fowlerton, *U.S.A.* 71 L5
Fox →, *Canada* 65 B10
Fox Valley, *Canada* 65 C7
Foxe Basin, *Canada* 61 B12
Foxe Chan., *Canada* 61 B11
Foxe Pen., *Canada* 61 B12
Foxpark, *U.S.A.* 72 F10
Foxton, *N.Z.* 51 J5
Foyle, Lough, *U.K.* 13 A4
Foynes, *Ireland* 13 D2
Fóz do Cunene, *Angola* 48 B1
Foz do Gregório, *Brazil* 78 E4
Foz do Iguaçu, *Brazil* 80 B6
Franca, *Brazil* 79 H9
Francavilla Fontana,
Italy 21 D7
France ■, *Europe* 18 C5
Frances, *Australia* 55 F3
Frances →, *Canada* 64 A3
Frances L., *Canada* 64 A3
Franceville, *Gabon* 46 E2
Franche-Comté, *France* 18 C6
Francistown, *Botswana* 49 C4
François, *Canada* 63 C8
François L., *Canada* 64 C3
Franeker, *Neths.* 15 A5
Frankfort, *S. Africa* 49 D4
Frankfort, *Ind., U.S.A.* 68 E2
Frankfort, *Kans., U.S.A.* 70 F6
Frankfort, *Ky., U.S.A.* 68 F3
Frankfort, *Mich., U.S.A.* 68 C2
Frankfurt, *Brandenburg,*
Germany 16 B8
Frankfurt, *Hessen,*
Germany 16 C5
Fränkische Alb,
Germany 16 D6
Frankland →,
Australia 53 G2
Franklin, *Ky., U.S.A.* 69 G2
Franklin, *La., U.S.A.* 71 L9
Franklin, *N.H., U.S.A.* 68 D10
Franklin, *Nebr., U.S.A.* 70 E5
Franklin, *Pa., U.S.A.* 68 E6
Franklin, *Tenn., U.S.A.* 69 H2
Franklin, *Va., U.S.A.* 68 G7
Franklin, *W. Va., U.S.A.* 68 F6
Franklin B., *Canada* 60 B7
Franklin D. Roosevelt
L., *U.S.A.* 72 B4
Franklin I., *Antarctica* 5 D11
Franklin L., *U.S.A.* 72 F6
Franklin Mts., *Canada* 60 B7
Franklin Str., *Canada* 60 A10
Franklinton, *U.S.A.* 71 K9
Franks Pk., *U.S.A.* 72 E9
Frankston, *Australia* 55 F4
Frantsa Iosifa, Zemlya,
Russia 24 A6
Franz, *Canada* 62 C3
Franz Josef Land =
Frantsa Iosifa,
Zemlya, *Russia* 24 A6
Fraser →, *B.C.,*
Canada 64 D4
Fraser →, *Nfld.,*
Canada 63 A7
Fraser, Mt., *Australia* 53 E2
Fraser I., *Australia* 55 D5
Fraser Lake, *Canada* 64 C4
Fraserburg, *S. Africa* 48 E3
Fraserburgh, *U.K.* 12 D6
Fraserdale, *Canada* 62 C3
Fray Bentos, *Uruguay* 80 C5
Frazier Downs,
Australia 52 C3
Fredericia, *Denmark* 9 J13
Frederick, *Md., U.S.A.* 68 F7
Frederick, *Okla., U.S.A.* 71 H5
Frederick, *S. Dak.,*
U.S.A. 70 C5
Frederick Sd., *U.S.A.* 64 B2
Fredericksburg, *Tex.,*
U.S.A. 71 K5
Fredericksburg, *Va.,*
U.S.A. 68 F7
Fredericktown, *U.S.A.* 71 G9
Fredericton, *Canada* 63 C6
Fredericton Junc.,
Canada 63 C6
Frederikshåb,
Greenland 4 C5
Frederikshavn,
Denmark 9 H14
Fredonia, *Ariz., U.S.A.* 73 H7
Fredonia, *Kans., U.S.A.* 71 G7
Fredonia, *N.Y., U.S.A.* 68 D6
Fredrikstad, *Norway* 9 G14
Freels, C., *Canada* 63 C9
Freeman, *U.S.A.* 70 D6
Freeport, *Bahamas* 75 B9

Freeport, *Canada* 63 D6
Freeport, *Ill., U.S.A.* . 70 D10
Freeport, *N.Y., U.S.A.* . 68 D9
Freeport, *Tex., U.S.A.* . 71 L7
Freetown, *S. Leone* ... 44 G2
Frégate, L., *Canada* ... 62 B5
Fregenal de la Sierra,
Spain 19 C2
Freibourg = Fribourg,
Switz. 16 E4
Freiburg, *Germany* 16 E4
Freire, *Chile* 80 D2
Freising, *Germany* 16 D6
Freistadt, *Austria* 16 D8
Fréjus, *France* 18 E7
Fremantle, *Australia* .. 53 F2
Fremont, *Calif., U.S.A.* . 73 H2
Fremont, *Mich., U.S.A.* . 68 D3
Fremont, *Nebr., U.S.A.* . 70 E6
Fremont, *Ohio, U.S.A.* . 68 E4
Fremont →, *U.S.A.* ... 73 G8
Fremont L., *U.S.A.* 72 E9
French Creek →,
U.S.A. 68 E6
French Guiana ■,
S. Amer. 79 C8
French Pass, *N.Z.* 51 J4
French Polynesia ■,
Pac. Oc. 57 J13
French Terr. of Afars &
Issas = Djibouti ■,
Africa 40 E3
Frenchglen, *U.S.A.* ... 72 E4
Frenchman Butte,
Canada 65 C7
Frenchman Cr. →,
Mont., U.S.A. 72 B10
Frenchman Cr. →,
Nebr., U.S.A. 70 E4
Fresco →, *Brazil* 79 E8
Freshfield, C.,
Antarctica 5 C10
Fresnillo, *Mexico* 74 C4
Fresno, *U.S.A.* 73 H4
Fresno Reservoir,
U.S.A. 72 B9
Frew →, *Australia* 54 C2
Frewena, *Australia* ... 54 B2
Freycinet Pen.,
Australia 54 G4
Fria, C., *Namibia* 48 B1
Frías, *Argentina* 80 B3
Fribourg, *Switz.* 16 E4
Friedrichshafen,
Germany 16 E5
Friendly Is. = Tonga ■,
Pac. Oc. 51 D11
Friesland □, *Neths.* ... 15 A5
Frijoles, *Panama* 74 H14
Frio →, *U.S.A.* 71 L5
Friona, *U.S.A.* 71 H3
Fritch, *U.S.A.* 71 H4
Frobisher B., *Canada* . 61 B13
Frobisher Bay = Iqaluit,
Canada 61 B13
Frobisher L., *Canada* . 65 B7
Frohavet, *Norway* 8 E13
Froid, *U.S.A.* 70 A2
Fromberg, *U.S.A.* 72 D9
Frome, *U.K.* 11 F5
Frome, L., *Australia* ... 55 E2
Frome Downs,
Australia 55 E2
Front Range, *U.S.A.* .. 72 G11
Front Royal, *U.S.A.* ... 68 F6
Frosinone, *Italy* 20 D5
Frostburg, *U.S.A.* 68 F6
Frostisen, *Norway* 8 B17
Frøya, *Norway* 8 E13
Frunze = Bishkek,
Kyrgyzstan 24 E8
Frutal, *Brazil* 79 G9
Frýdek-Místek, *Czech.* . 17 D10
Fuchou = Fuzhou,
China 31 D6
Fuchū, *Japan* 29 G6
Fuengirola, *Spain* 19 D3
Fuentes de Oñoro,
Spain 19 B2
Fuerte →, *Mexico* 74 B3
Fuerte Olimpo,
Paraguay 78 H7
Fuerteventura,
Canary Is. 44 C2
Fuhai, *China* 30 B3
Fuḥaymī, *Iraq* 38 C4
Fuji, *Japan* 29 G9
Fuji-San, *Japan* 29 G9
Fuji-yoshida, *Japan* ... 29 G9
Fujian □, *China* 31 D6
Fujinomiya, *Japan* 29 G9
Fujisawa, *Japan* 29 G9
Fukien = Fujian □,
China 31 D6
Fukuchiyama, *Japan* .. 29 G7
Fukue-Shima, *Japan* .. 29 H4
Fukui, *Japan* 29 F8
Fukui □, *Japan* 29 G8
Fukuoka, *Japan* 29 H5
Fukuoka □, *Japan* 29 H5
Fukushima, *Japan* 28 F10
Fukushima □, *Japan* .. 28 F10
Fukuyama, *Japan* 29 G6
Fulda, *Germany* 16 C5
Fulda →, *Germany* ... 16 C5
Fullerton, *Calif., U.S.A.* . 73 K5
Fullerton, *Nebr., U.S.A.* . 70 E5
Fulton, *Mo., U.S.A.* ... 70 F9
Fulton, *N.Y., U.S.A.* ... 68 D7
Fulton, *Tenn., U.S.A.* .. 69 G1
Funabashi, *Japan* 29 G10
Funchal, *Madeira* 44 B1
Fundación, *Colombia* . 78 A4

Fundão, *Portugal* 19 B2
Fundy, B. of, *Canada* . 63 D6
Funtua, *Nigeria* 44 F6
Furano, *Japan* 28 C11
Fürg, *Iran* 39 D7
Furneaux Group,
Australia 54 G4
Furness, *U.K.* 10 C4
Furqlus, *Syria* 41 A6
Furstenwalde, *Germany* 16 B8
Fürth, *Germany* 16 D6
Furukawa, *Japan* 28 E10
Fury and Hecla Str.,
Canada 61 B11
Fusagasuga, *Colombia* 78 C4
Fushun, *China* 31 B7
Futuna, *Wall. & F. Is.* . 51 B8
Fuxin, *China* 31 B7
Fuzhou, *China* 31 D6
Fylde, *U.K.* 10 D5
Fyn, *Denmark* 9 J14
Fyne, L., *U.K.* 12 F3

G

Gabela, *Angola* 46 G2
Gabès, *Tunisia* 44 B7
Gabès, G. de, *Tunisia* . 45 B7
Gabon ■, *Africa* 46 E2
Gaborone, *Botswana* . 48 C4
Gäbrīk, *Iran* 39 E8
Gabrovo, *Bulgaria* 21 C11
Gāch Sār, *Iran* 39 B6
Gachsārān, *Iran* 39 D6
Gadag, *India* 36 M9
Gadarwara, *India* 36 H11
Gadhada, *India* 36 J7
Gadsden, *Ala., U.S.A.* . 69 H2
Gadsden, *Ariz., U.S.A.* . 73 K6
Gadwal, *India* 36 L10
Gaffney, *U.S.A.* 69 H5
Gafsa, *Tunisia* 44 B6
Gagetown, *Canada* ... 63 C6
Gagnoa, *Ivory C.* 44 G3
Gagnon, *Canada* 63 B6
Gagnon, L., *Canada* .. 65 A6
Gail →, *U.S.A.* 71 J4
Gaillimh = Galway,
Ireland 13 C2
Gainesville, *Fla., U.S.A.* 69 L4
Gainesville, *Ga., U.S.A.* 69 H4
Gainesville, *Mo., U.S.A.* 71 G8
Gainesville, *Tex., U.S.A.* 71 J6
Gainsborough, *U.K.* .. 10 D7
Gairdner, L., *Australia* . 55 E2
Gairloch, L., *U.K.* 12 D3
Galangue, *Angola* 47 G3
Galápagos, *Pac. Oc.* . 57 H18
Galas →, *Malaysia* ... 34 Q14
Galashiels, *U.K.* 12 F6
Galați, *Romania* 17 F15
Galatina, *Italy* 21 D8
Galax, *U.S.A.* 69 G5
Galbraith, *Australia* .. 54 B3
Galcaio, *Somali Rep.* . 40 F4
Galdhøpiggen, *Norway* 9 F12
Galela, *Indonesia* 33 D7
Galesburg, *U.S.A.* 70 E9
Galich, *Russia* 22 C7
Galicia □, *Spain* 19 A2
Galilee = Hagalil, *Israel* 41 C4
Galilee, L., *Australia* .. 54 C4
Galilee, Sea of = Yam
Kinneret, *Israel* 41 C4
Galiuro Mts., *U.S.A.* .. 73 K8
Gallabat, *Sudan* 45 F12
Gallatin, *U.S.A.* 69 G2
Galle, *Sri Lanka* 36 R12
Gállego →, *Spain* 19 B5
Gallegos →,
Argentina 80 G3
Galley Hd., *Ireland* ... 13 E3
Gallinas, Pta., *Colombia* 78 A4
Gallipoli = Gelibolu,
Turkey 21 D12
Gallipoli, *Italy* 21 D8
Gallipolis, *U.S.A.* 68 F4
Gällivare, *Sweden* 8 C19
Galloway, *U.K.* 12 G4
Galloway, Mull of, *U.K.* 12 G4
Gallup, *U.S.A.* 73 J9
Galong, *Australia* 55 E4
Galoya, *Sri Lanka* 36 Q12
Galty Mts., *Ireland* ... 13 D3
Galtymore, *Ireland* ... 13 D3
Galva, *U.S.A.* 70 E9
Galveston, *U.S.A.* 71 L7
Galveston B., *U.S.A.* .. 71 L7
Gálvez, *Argentina* 80 C4
Galway, *Ireland* 13 C2
Galway □, *Ireland* 13 C2
Galway B., *Ireland* 13 C2
Gamagōri, *Japan* 29 G8
Gambaga, *Ghana* 44 F4
Gambela, *Ethiopia* 45 G11
Gambia ■, *W. Afr.* ... 44 F1
Gambia →, *W. Afr.* .. 44 F1
Gambier, C., *Australia* . 52 B5
Gambier Is., *Australia* . 55 F2
Gamboma, *Congo* 46 E3
Gamerco, *U.S.A.* 73 J9
Gamlakarleby =
Kokkola, *Finland* ... 8 E20
Gammon →, *Canada* . 65 C9
Gan Jiang →, *China* .. 31 D6
Ganado, *Ariz., U.S.A.* . 73 J9
Ganado, *Tex., U.S.A.* . 71 L6
Gananoque, *Canada* .. 62 D4
Ganāveh, *Iran* 39 D6

Gäncä, *Azerbaijan* 23 F8
Gand = Gent, *Belgium* 15 C3
Ganda, *Angola* 47 G2
Gandak →, *India* 37 G14
Gandava, *Pakistan* ... 36 E5
Gander, *Canada* 63 C9
Gander L., *Canada* ... 63 C9
Gandhi Sagar, *India* .. 36 G9
Gandi, *Nigeria* 44 F6
Gandía, *Spain* 19 C5
Ganedidalem = Gani,
Indonesia 33 E7
Ganga →, *India* 37 H17
Ganganagar, *India* ... 36 E8
Gangara, *Niger* 44 F6
Gangaw, *Burma* 37 H19
Gangdisê Shan, *China* 37 D12
Ganges = Ganga →,
India 37 H17
Gangtok, *India* 37 F16
Gani, *Indonesia* 33 E7
Gannett Peak, *U.S.A.* . 72 E9
Gannvalley, *U.S.A.* ... 70 C5
Gansu □, *China* 30 C5
Ganta, *Liberia* 44 G3
Gantheaume, C.,
Australia 55 F2
Gantheaume B.,
Australia 53 E1
Gantsevichy =
Hantsavichy, *Belarus* 17 B14
Ganyem, *Indonesia* ... 33 E10
Ganzhou, *China* 31 D6
Gao Bang, *Vietnam* .. 34 A9
Gaoua, *Burkina Faso* . 44 F4
Gaoual, *Guinea* 44 F2
Gaoxiong, *Taiwan* 31 D7
Gap, *France* 18 D7
Gar, *China* 30 C2
Garabogazköl Aylagy,
Turkmenistan 23 F9
Garanhuns, *Brazil* 79 E11
Garawe, *Liberia* 44 H3
Garber, *U.S.A.* 71 G6
Garberville, *U.S.A.* ... 72 F2
Gard, *Somali Rep.* ... 40 F4
Garda, L. di, *Italy* 20 B4
Garde L., *Canada* 65 A7
Garden City, *Kans.,
U.S.A.* 71 G4
Garden City, *Tex.,
U.S.A.* 71 K4
Garden Grove, *U.S.A.* . 73 K5
Gardez, *Afghan.* 36 C6
Gardiner, *U.S.A.* 72 D8
Gardner, *U.S.A.* 68 D10
Gardner Canal, *Canada* 64 C3
Gardnerville, *U.S.A.* .. 72 G4
Garfield, *U.S.A.* 72 C5
Gargano, Mte., *Italy* .. 20 D6
Garibaldi Prov. Park,
Canada 64 D4
Garies, *S. Africa* 48 E2
Garigliano →, *Italy* ... 20 D5
Garland, *U.S.A.* 72 F7
Garm, *Tajikistan* 24 F8
Garmāb, *Iran* 39 C8
Garmisch-
Partenkirchen,
Germany 16 E6
Garmsār, *Iran* 39 C7
Garner, *U.S.A.* 70 D8
Garnett, *U.S.A.* 70 F7
Garoe, *Somali Rep.* .. 40 F4
Garonne →, *France* .. 18 D3
Garoua, *Cameroon* ... 45 G7
Garrison, *Mont., U.S.A.* 72 C7
Garrison, *N. Dak.,
U.S.A.* 70 B4
Garrison, *Tex., U.S.A.* . 71 K7
Garrison Res. =
Sakakawea, L., *U.S.A.* 70 B3
Garry →, *U.K.* 12 E5
Garry, L., *Canada* 60 B9
Garsen, *Kenya* 46 E8
Garson L., *Canada* ... 65 B6
Garub, *Namibia* 48 D2
Garut, *Indonesia* 33 G12
Garwa = Garoua,
Cameroon 45 G7
Gary, *U.S.A.* 68 E2
Garzê, *China* 30 C5
Garzón, *Colombia* 78 C3
Gas-San, *Japan* 28 E10
Gasan Kuli = Hasan
Kuli, *Turkmenistan* . 24 F6
Gascogne, *France* ... 18 E4
Gascogne, G. de,
Europe 18 D2
Gascony = Gascogne,
France 18 E4
Gascoyne →,
Australia 53 D1
Gascoyne Junc. T.O.,
Australia 53 E2
Gashaka, *Nigeria* 44 G7
Gaspé, *Canada* 63 C7
Gaspé, C. de, *Canada* 63 C7
Gaspé, Pén. de, *Canada* 63 C6
Gaspésie, Parc Prov. de
la, *Canada* 63 C6
Gassaway, *U.S.A.* 68 F5
Gasteiz = Vitoria, *Spain* 19 A4
Gastonia, *U.S.A.* 69 H5
Gastre, *Argentina* 80 E3
Gata, C. de, *Spain* ... 19 D4
Gata, Sierra de, *Spain* 19 B2
Gataga →, *Canada* .. 64 B3
Gateshead, *U.K.* 10 C6
Gatesville, *U.S.A.* 71 K6
Gatineau →, *Canada* . 62 C4

Gatineau, Parc de la,
Canada 62 C4
Gatun, *Panama* 74 H14
Gatun, L., *Panama* ... 74 H14
Gatun Dam, *Panama* . 74 H14
Gatun Locks, *Panama* 74 H14
Gatyana, *S. Africa* 49 E4
Gau, *Fiji* 51 D8
Gauhati, *India* 37 F17
Gauja →, *Latvia* 9 H21
Gaula →, *Norway* 8 E14
Gausta, *Norway* 9 G13
Gauteng = P.W.V. □,
S. Africa 49 D4
Gāv Koshī, *Iran* 39 D8
Gāvakān, *Iran* 39 D7
Gävater, *Iran* 39 E9
Gāvbandī, *Iran* 39 E7
Gávdhos, *Greece* 21 G11
Gävle, *Sweden* 9 F17
Gawachab, *Namibia* .. 48 D2
Gawilgarh Hills, *India* . 36 J10
Gawler, *Australia* 55 E2
Gaxun Nur, *China* 30 B5
Gay, *Russia* 22 D10
Gaya, *India* 37 G14
Gaya, *Niger* 44 F5
Gaylord, *U.S.A.* 68 C3
Gayndah, *Australia* ... 55 D5
Gaysin = Haysyn,
Ukraine 17 D15
Gayvoron = Hayvoron,
Ukraine 17 D15
Gaza, *Gaza Strip* 41 D3
Gaza □, *Mozam.* 49 C5
Gaza Strip □, *Asia* ... 41 D3
Gāzbor, *Iran* 39 D8
Gaziantep, *Turkey* ... 23 G6
Gazli, *Uzbekistan* 24 E7
Gcuwa, *S. Africa* 49 E4
Gdańsk, *Poland* 17 A10
Gdańska, Zatoka,
Poland 17 A10
Gdov, *Russia* 9 G22
Gdynia, *Poland* 17 A10
Gebe, *Indonesia* 33 D7
Gebeit Mine, *Sudan* .. 45 D12
Gebze, *Turkey* 21 D13
Gede, Tanjung,
Indonesia 32 F3
Gediz →, *Turkey* 21 E12
Gedser, *Denmark* 9 J14
Geegully Cr. →,
Australia 52 C3
Geelong, *Australia* ... 55 F3
Geelvink Chan.,
Australia 53 E1
Geesthacht, *Germany* 16 B6
Geidam, *Nigeria* 45 F7
Geikie →, *Canada* ... 65 B8
Geili, *Sudan* 45 E11
Geita, *Tanzania* 46 E6
Gejiu, *China* 30 D5
Gela, *Italy* 20 F6
Geladi, *Ethiopia* 40 F4
Gelderland □, *Neths.* . 15 B6
Geldermalsen, *Neths.* . 15 C5
Geldrop, *Neths.* 15 C5
Geleen, *Neths.* 15 D5
Gelehun, *S. Leone* ... 44 G2
Gelibolu, *Turkey* 21 D12
Gelsenkirchen,
Germany 16 C4
Gemas, *Malaysia* 34 S15
Gembloux, *Belgium* .. 15 D4
Gemena, *Zaïre* 46 D3
Gemlik, *Turkey* 21 D13
Gendringen, *Neths.* .. 15 C6
General Acha,
Argentina 80 D4
General Alvear,
*Buenos Aires,
Argentina* 80 D5
General Alvear,
Mendoza, Argentina 80 D3
General Artigas,
Paraguay 80 B5
General Belgrano,
Argentina 80 D5
General Guido,
Argentina 80 D5
General Juan
Madariaga, *Argentina* 80 D5
General La Madrid,
Argentina 80 D4
General MacArthur,
Phil. 33 B7
General Martin Miguel
de Güemes,
Argentina 80 A4
General Paz, *Argentina* 80 B5
General Pico, *Argentina* 80 D4
General Pinedo,
Argentina 80 B4
General Santos, *Phil.* . 33 C7
General Villegas,
Argentina 80 D4
Genesee, *U.S.A.* 72 C5
Genesee →, *U.S.A.* .. 68 D7
Geneseo, *Ill., U.S.A.* .. 70 E9
Geneseo, *Kans., U.S.A.* 70 F5
Geneva = Genève,
Switz. 16 E4
Geneva, *Ala., U.S.A.* .. 69 K3
Geneva, *N.Y., U.S.A.* .. 68 D7
Geneva, *Nebr., U.S.A.* . 70 E6
Geneva, *Ohio, U.S.A.* . 68 E5
Geneva, L. = Léman,
L., *Europe* 16 E4
Genève, *Switz.* 16 E4

Genil →, *Spain* 19 D3
Genk, *Belgium* 15 D5
Gennargentu, Mti. del,
Italy 20 D3
Gennep, *Neths.* 15 C5
Genoa = Génova, *Italy* 20 B3
Genoa, *Australia* 55 F4
Genoa, *U.S.A.* 70 E6
Génova, *Italy* 20 B3
Génova, G. di, *Italy* .. 20 C3
Gent, *Belgium* 15 C3
Genteng, *Indonesia* .. 33 G13
Genyem, *Indonesia* .. 33 E10
Genzano di Lucania,
Italy 20 D7
Geographe B., *Australia* 53 F2
Geographe Chan.,
Australia 53 D1
George, *S. Africa* 48 E3
George →, *Canada* ... 63 A6
George, L., *N.S.W.,
Australia* 55 F4
George, L., *S. Austral.,
Australia* 55 F3
George, L., *W. Austral.,
Australia* 52 D3
George, L., *Uganda* .. 46 D6
George, L., *U.S.A.* 69 L5
George Gill Ra.,
Australia 52 D5
George River =
Kangiqsualujjuaq,
Canada 61 C13
George Sound, *N.Z.* .. 51 L1
George Town, *Malaysia* 34 P13
George V Land,
Antarctica 5 C10
George VI Sound,
Antarctica 5 D17
George West, *U.S.A.* .. 71 L5
Georgetown, *Australia* 54 B3
Georgetown, *Ont.,
Canada* 62 D4
Georgetown, *P.E.I.,
Canada* 63 C7
Georgetown, *Gambia* . 44 F2
Georgetown, *Guyana* . 78 B7
Georgetown, *Colo.,
U.S.A.* 72 G11
Georgetown, *Ky.,
U.S.A.* 68 F3
Georgetown, *S.C.,
U.S.A.* 69 J6
Georgetown, *Tex.,
U.S.A.* 71 K6
Georgia □, *U.S.A.* ... 69 J4
Georgia ■, *Asia* 23 F7
Georgia, Str. of,
Canada 64 D4
Georgian B., *Canada* . 62 C3
Georgina →, *Australia* 54 C2
Georgina Downs,
Australia 54 C2
Georgiu-Dezh = Liski,
Russia 23 D6
Georgiyevsk, *Russia* .. 23 F7
Gera, *Germany* 16 C7
Geraardsbergen,
Belgium 15 D3
Geral, Serra, *Brazil* ... 80 B7
Geral de Goiás, Serra,
Brazil 79 F9
Geraldine, *U.S.A.* 72 C8
Geraldton, *Australia* .. 53 E1
Geraldton, *Canada* ... 62 C2
Gereshk, *Afghan.* 36 D4
Gerik, *Malaysia* 34 P14
Gering, *U.S.A.* 70 E3
Gerlach, *U.S.A.* 72 F4
Gerlogubi, *Ethiopia* .. 40 F4
Germansen Landing,
Canada 64 B4
Germany ■, *Europe* .. 16 C6
Germiston, *S. Africa* .. 49 D4
Gero, *Japan* 29 G8
Gerona, *Spain* 19 B7
Gerrard, *Canada* 64 C5
Geser, *Indonesia* 33 E8
Getafe, *Spain* 19 B4
Gethsémani, *Canada* . 63 B7
Gettysburg, *Pa., U.S.A.* 68 F7
Gettysburg, *S. Dak.,
U.S.A.* 70 C5
Getz Ice Shelf,
Antarctica 5 D14
Geyser, *U.S.A.* 72 C8
Ghaghara →, *India* .. 37 G14
Ghana ■, *W. Afr.* 44 G4
Ghanzi, *Botswana* ... 48 C3
Ghanzi □, *Botswana* . 48 C3
Ghardaïa, *Algeria* 44 B5
Gharyān, *Libya* 45 B7
Ghat, *Libya* 44 D7
Ghatti, *Si. Arabia* 38 D3
Ghawdex = Gozo,
Malta 20 F6
Ghazal, Bahr el →,
Chad 45 F8
Ghazâl, Bahr el →,
Sudan 45 G11
Ghazaouet, *Algeria* ... 44 A4
Ghaziabad, *India* 36 E10
Ghazipur, *India* 37 G13
Ghaznī, *Afghan.* 36 C6
Ghaznī □, *Afghan.* ... 36 C6
Ghèlinsor, *Somali Rep.* 40 F4
Ghent = Gent, *Belgium* 15 C3
Ghizao, *Afghan.* 36 C4
Ghowr □, *Afghan.* ... 36 C4
Ghudaf, W. al →, *Iraq* 38 C4
Ghugus, *India* 36 K11
Ghūrīān, *Afghan.* 36 B2
Gia Lai = Pleiku,
Vietnam 34 F10
Gia Nghia, *Vietnam* .. 34 G9
Gian, *Phil.* 33 C7

Giants Causeway, *U.K.* 13 A5
Giarabub = Al
Jaghbūb, *Libya* 45 C10
Giarre, *Italy* 20 F6
Gibb River, *Australia* .. 52 C4
Gibbon, *U.S.A.* 70 E5
Gibraltar ■, *Europe* .. 19 D3
Gibraltar, Str. of,
Medit. S. 19 E3
Gibson Desert,
Australia 52 D4
Gibsons, *Canada* 64 D4
Giddings, *U.S.A.* 71 K6
Gidole, *Ethiopia* 45 G12
Giessen, *Germany* ... 16 C5
Gifan, *Iran* 39 B8
Gifford Creek, *Australia* 52 D2
Gifu, *Japan* 29 G8
Gifu □, *Japan* 29 G8
Gigha, *U.K.* 12 F3
Giglio, *Italy* 20 C4
Gijón, *Spain* 19 A3
Gil I., *Canada* 64 C3
Gila →, *U.S.A.* 73 K6
Gila Bend, *U.S.A.* 73 K7
Gila Bend Mts., *U.S.A.* 73 K7
Gīlān □, *Iran* 39 B6
Gilbert →, *Australia* .. 54 B3
Gilbert Is., *Kiribati* ... 56 G9
Gilbert Plains, *Canada* 65 C8
Gilbert River, *Australia* 54 B3
Gilberton, *Australia* ... 54 B3
Gilford I., *Canada* 64 C3
Gilgandra, *Australia* .. 55 E4
Gilgit, *India* 36 B9
Gillam, *Canada* 65 B10
Gillen, L., *Australia* ... 53 E3
Gilles, L., *Australia* ... 55 E2
Gillette, *U.S.A.* 70 C2
Gilliat, *Australia* 54 C3
Gillingham, *U.K.* 11 F8
Gilmer, *U.S.A.* 71 J7
Gilmore, *Australia* 55 F4
Gilmore, L., *Australia* . 53 F3
Gilmour, *Canada* 62 D4
Gilroy, *U.S.A.* 73 H3
Gimbi, *Ethiopia* 45 G12
Gimli, *Canada* 65 C9
Gin Gin, *Australia* 55 D5
Gindie, *Australia* 54 C4
Gingin, *Australia* 53 F2
Ginir, *Ethiopia* 40 F3
Giohar, *Somali Rep.* .. 40 G4
Gióna, Óros, *Greece* .. 21 E10
Girâfi, W. →, *Egypt* .. 41 F3
Girard, *U.S.A.* 71 G7
Girardot, *Colombia* ... 78 C4
Girdle Ness, *U.K.* 12 D6
Giresun, *Turkey* 23 F6
Girga, *Egypt* 45 C11
Giridih, *India* 37 G15
Girilambone, *Australia* 55 E4
Girne = Kyrenia,
Cyprus 38 C2
Girona = Gerona,
Spain 19 B7
Gironde →, *France* ... 18 D3
Giru, *Australia* 54 B4
Girvan, *U.K.* 12 F4
Gisborne, *N.Z.* 51 H7
Gisenyi, *Rwanda* 46 E5
Gislaved, *Sweden* 9 H15
Gitega, *Burundi* 46 E5
Giuba →, *Somali Rep.* 40 G3
Giurgiu, *Romania* 17 G13
Giza = El Gîza, *Egypt* . 45 C11
Gizhiga, *Russia* 25 C17
Gizhiginskaya Guba,
Russia 25 C16
Giżycko, *Poland* 17 A11
Gjirokastra, *Albania* .. 21 D9
Gjoa Haven, *Canada* . 60 B10
Gjøvik, *Norway* 9 F14
Glace Bay, *Canada* ... 63 C8
Glacier Bay, *U.S.A.* ... 64 C6
Glacier Nat. Park,
Canada 64 C5
Glacier Park, *U.S.A.* .. 72 B7
Glacier Peak, *U.S.A.* .. 72 B3
Gladewater, *U.S.A.* ... 71 J7
Gladstone, *Queens.,
Australia* 54 C5
Gladstone, *S. Austral.,
Australia* 55 E2
Gladstone, *W. Austral.,
Australia* 53 E1
Gladstone, *Canada* ... 65 C9
Gladstone, *U.S.A.* 68 C2
Gladwin, *U.S.A.* 68 D3
Gladys L., *Canada* ... 64 B2
Glâma = Glomma →,
Norway 9 G14
Gláma, *Iceland* 8 D2
Glasco, *U.S.A.* 70 F6
Glasgow, *U.K.* 12 F4
Glasgow, *Ky., U.S.A.* .. 68 G3
Glasgow, *Mont., U.S.A.* 72 B10
Glastonbury, *U.K.* 11 F5
Glazov, *Russia* 22 C9
Gleiwitz = Gliwice,
Poland 17 C10
Glen Affric, *U.K.* 12 D4
Glen Canyon Dam,
U.S.A. 73 H8
Glen Canyon National
Recreation Area,
U.S.A. 73 H8
Glen Coe, *U.K.* 12 E4
Glen Garry, *U.K.* 12 D3
Glen Innes, *Australia* . 55 D5
Glen Mor, *U.K.* 12 D4
Glen Moriston, *U.K.* .. 12 D4
Glen Orchy, *U.K.* 12 E4

Guasipati

Glen Spean, *U.K.* 12 E4
Glen Ullin, *U.S.A.* 70 B4
Glenburgh, *Australia* 53 E2
Glencoe, *S. Africa* 49 D5
Glencoe, *U.S.A.* 70 C7
Glendale, *Ariz., U.S.A.* 73 K7
Glendale, *Calif., U.S.A.* 73 J4
Glendale, *Oreg., U.S.A.* 72 E2
Glendive, *U.S.A.* 70 B2
Glendo, *U.S.A.* 70 D2
Glenelg, *Australia* 55 E2
Glenelg →, *Australia* 55 F3
Glenflorrie, *Australia* 52 D2
Glengarriff, *Ireland* 13 E2
Glengyle, *Australia* 54 C2
Glenmora, *U.S.A.* 71 K8
Glenmorgan, *Australia* 55 D4
Glenns Ferry, *U.S.A.* 72 E6
Glenorchy, *Australia* 54 G4
Glenore, *Australia* 54 B3
Glenormiston, *Australia* 54 C2
Glenreagh, *Australia* 55 E5
Glenrock, *U.S.A.* 72 E11
Glenrothes, *U.K.* 12 E5
Glens Falls, *U.S.A.* 68 D9
Glenties, *Ireland* 13 B3
Glenville, *U.S.A.* 68 F5
Glenwood, *Alta., Canada* 64 D6
Glenwood, *Nfld., Canada* 63 C9
Glenwood, *Ark., U.S.A.* 71 H8
Glenwood, *Hawaii, U.S.A.* 66 J17
Glenwood, *Iowa, U.S.A.* 70 E7
Glenwood, *Minn., U.S.A.* 70 C7
Glenwood Springs, *U.S.A.* 72 G10
Glettinganes, *Iceland* 8 D7
Gliwice, *Poland* 17 C10
Globe, *U.S.A.* 73 K8
Głogów, *Poland* 16 C9
Glomma →, *Norway* 9 G14
Glorieuses, Is., *Ind. Oc.* 49 A8
Glossop, *U.K.* 10 D6
Gloucester, *Australia* 55 E5
Gloucester, *U.K.* 11 F5
Gloucester I., *Australia* 54 C4
Gloucestershire □, *U.K.* 11 F5
Gloversville, *U.S.A.* 68 D8
Glovertown, *Canada* 63 C9
Glusk, *Belarus* 17 B15
Gmünd, *Austria* 16 D8
Gmunden, *Austria* 16 E7
Gniezno, *Poland* 17 B9
Gnowangerup, *Australia* 53 F2
Go Cong, *Vietnam* 34 G9
Gō-no-ura, *Japan* 29 H4
Goa, *India* 36 M8
Goa □, *India* 36 M8
Goalen Hd., *Australia* 55 F5
Goalpara, *India* 37 F17
Goat Fell, *U.K.* 12 F3
Goba, *Ethiopia* 40 F2
Goba, *Mozam.* 49 D5
Gobabis, *Namibia* 48 C2
Gobi, *Asia* 31 B6
Gobō, *Japan* 29 H7
Gochas, *Namibia* 48 C2
Godavari →, *India* 37 L13
Godavari Point, *India* 37 L13
Godbout, *Canada* 63 C6
Goderich, *Canada* 62 D3
Godhavn, *Greenland* 4 C5
Godhra, *India* 36 H8
Gods →, *Canada* 65 B10
Gods L., *Canada* 65 C10
Godthåb, *Greenland* 61 B14
Godwin Austen = K2, Mt., *Pakistan* 36 B10
Goeie Hoop, Kaap die = Good Hope, C. of, *S. Africa* 48 E2
Goéland, L. au, *Canada* 62 C4
Goeree, *Neths.* 15 C3
Goes, *Neths.* 15 C3
Gogama, *Canada* 62 C3
Gogango, *Australia* 54 C5
Gogebic, L., *U.S.A.* 70 B10
Gogland, Ostrov, *Russia* 9 F22
Gogra = Ghaghara →, *India* 37 G14
Goiânia, *Brazil* 79 G9
Goiás, *Brazil* 79 G8
Goiás □, *Brazil* 79 F9
Goio-Ere, *Brazil* 80 A6
Gojō, *Japan* 29 G7
Gojra, *Pakistan* 36 D8
Gökçeada, *Turkey* 21 D11
Gokteik, *Burma* 37 H20
Golan Heights = Hagolan, *Syria* 41 B4
Golāshkerd, *Iran* 39 E8
Golchikha, *Russia* 4 B12
Golconda, *U.S.A.* 72 F5
Gold Beach, *U.S.A.* 72 E1
Gold Coast, *Australia* 55 D5
Gold Coast, *W. Afr.* 42 F3
Gold Hill, *U.S.A.* 72 E2
Golden, *Canada* 64 C5
Golden, *U.S.A.* 70 F2
Golden B., *N.Z.* 51 J4
Golden Gate, *U.S.A.* 72 H2
Golden Hinde, *Canada* 64 D3
Golden Prairie, *Canada* 65 C7
Golden Vale, *Ireland* 13 D3
Goldendale, *U.S.A.* 72 D3
Goldfield, *U.S.A.* 73 H5
Goldfields, *Canada* 65 B7
Goldsand L., *Canada* 65 B8
Goldsboro, *U.S.A.* 69 H7
Goldsmith, *U.S.A.* 71 K3
Goldsworthy, *Australia* 52 D2
Goldthwaite, *U.S.A.* 71 K5
Golęniów, *Poland* 16 B8
Golestānak, *Iran* 39 D7
Golfo Aranci, *Italy* 20 D3
Goliad, *U.S.A.* 71 L6
Golpāyegān, *Iran* 39 C6
Golspie, *U.K.* 12 D5
Goma, *Rwanda* 46 E5
Gomel = Homyel, *Belarus* 17 B16
Gomera, *Canary Is.* 44 C1
Gómez Palacio, *Mexico* 74 B4
Gomīshān, *Iran* 39 B7
Gomogomo, *Indonesia* 33 F8
Gomoh, *India* 37 H15
Gompa = Ganta, *Liberia* 44 G3
Gonābād, *Iran* 39 C8
Gonaïves, *Haiti* 75 D10
Gonbab-e Kāvūs, *Iran* 39 B7
Gonda, *India* 37 F12
Gonder, *Ethiopia* 45 F12
Gondia, *India* 36 J12
Gönen, *Turkey* 21 D12
Gonghe, *China* 30 C5
Gongolgon, *Australia* 55 E4
Goniri, *Nigeria* 45 F7
Gonzales, *Calif., U.S.A.* 73 H3
Gonzales, *Tex., U.S.A.* 71 L6
Good Hope, C. of, *S. Africa* 48 E2
Gooderham, *Canada* 62 D4
Goodeve, *Canada* 65 C8
Gooding, *U.S.A.* 72 E6
Goodland, *U.S.A.* 70 F4
Goodnight, *U.S.A.* 71 H4
Goodooga, *Australia* 55 D4
Goodsoil, *Canada* 65 C7
Goodsprings, *U.S.A.* 73 J6
Goole, *U.K.* 10 D7
Goolgowi, *Australia* 55 E4
Goomalling, *Australia* 53 F2
Goombalie, *Australia* 55 D4
Goondiwindi, *Australia* 55 D5
Goongarrie, L., *Australia* 53 F3
Goonyella, *Australia* 54 C4
Goor, *Neths.* 15 B6
Gooray, *Australia* 55 D5
Goose →, *Canada* 63 B7
Goose L., *U.S.A.* 72 F3
Gop, *India* 36 H6
Göppingen, *Germany* 16 D5
Gorakhpur, *India* 37 F13
Goražde, *Bos.-H.* 21 C8
Gordan B., *Australia* 52 B5
Gordon, *U.S.A.* 70 D3
Gordon →, *Australia* 54 G4
Gordon Downs, *Australia* 52 C4
Gordon L., *Alta., Canada* 65 B6
Gordon L., *N.W.T., Canada* 64 A6
Gordonvale, *Australia* 54 B4
Gore, *Australia* 55 D5
Goré, *Chad* 45 G8
Gore, *Ethiopia* 45 G12
Gore, *N.Z.* 51 M2
Gore Bay, *Canada* 62 C3
Gorey, *Ireland* 13 D5
Gorg, *Iran* 39 D8
Gorgān, *Iran* 39 B7
Gorgona, I., *Colombia* 78 C3
Gorinchem, *Neths.* 15 C4
Gorízia, *Italy* 20 B5
Gorki = Nizhniy Novgorod, *Russia* 22 C7
Gorkiy = Nizhniy Novgorod, *Russia* 22 C7
Gorkovskoye Vdkhr., *Russia* 22 C7
Görlitz, *Germany* 16 C8
Gorlovka = Horlivka, *Ukraine* 23 E6
Gorman, *U.S.A.* 71 J5
Gorna Dzhumayo = Blagoevgrad, *Bulgaria* 21 C10
Gorna Oryakhovitsa, *Bulgaria* 21 C11
Gorno-Altay □, *Russia* 24 D9
Gorno-Altaysk, *Russia* 24 D9
Gorno Slinkino = Gornopravdinsk, *Russia* 24 C8
Gornopravdinsk, *Russia* 24 C8
Gornyatski, *Russia* 22 A11
Gornyi, *Russia* 28 B6
Gorodenka = Horodenka, *Ukraine* 17 D13
Gorodok = Horodok, *Ukraine* 17 D12
Gorokhov = Horokhiv, *Ukraine* 17 C13
Gorongose →, *Mozam.* 49 C5
Gorontalo, *Indonesia* 33 D6
Gort, *Ireland* 13 C3
Gorzów Wielkopolski, *Poland* 16 B8
Gosford, *Australia* 55 E5
Goshen, *U.S.A.* 68 E3
Goshogawara, *Japan* 28 D10
Goslar, *Germany* 16 C6
Gospič, *Croatia* 16 F8
Gosport, *U.K.* 11 G6
Gosse →, *Australia* 54 B1
Göta älv →, *Sweden* 9 H14
Göta kanal, *Sweden* 9 G16
Götaland, *Sweden* 9 G15
Göteborg, *Sweden* 9 H14
Gotha, *Germany* 16 C6
Gothenburg = Göteborg, *Sweden* 9 H14
Gothenburg, *U.S.A.* 70 E4
Gotland, *Sweden* 9 H18
Gotska Sandön, *Sweden* 9 G18
Gōtsu, *Japan* 29 G6
Göttingen, *Germany* 16 C5
Gottwaldov = Zlin, *Czech.* 17 D9
Gouda, *Neths.* 15 B4
Gough I., *Atl. Oc.* 2 G9
Gouin, Rés., *Canada* 62 C5
Goulburn, *Australia* 55 E4
Goulburn Is., *Australia* 54 A1
Gounou-Gaya, *Chad* 45 G8
Gouri, *Chad* 45 E8
Gourits →, *S. Africa* 48 E3
Gourma Rharous, *Mali* 44 E4
Gourock Ra., *Australia* 55 F4
Govan, *Canada* 65 C8
Governador Valadares, *Brazil* 79 G10
Gowan Ra., *Australia* 54 C4
Gowanda, *U.S.A.* 68 D6
Gowd-e Zirreh, *Afghan.* 36 E3
Gower, *U.K.* 11 F3
Gowna, L., *Ireland* 13 C4
Goya, *Argentina* 80 B5
Goyder Lagoon, *Australia* 55 D2
Goyllarisquisga, *Peru* 78 F3
Goz Beïda, *Chad* 45 F9
Gozo, *Malta* 20 F6
Graaff-Reinet, *S. Africa* 48 E3
Gračac, *Croatia* 16 F8
Grace, *U.S.A.* 72 E8
Graceville, *U.S.A.* 70 C6
Gracias a Dios, C., *Honduras* 75 E8
Grado, *Spain* 19 A2
Gradule, *Australia* 55 D4
Grady, *U.S.A.* 71 H3
Grafton, *Australia* 55 D5
Grafton, *U.S.A.* 70 A6
Graham, *Canada* 62 C1
Graham, *N.C., U.S.A.* 69 G6
Graham, *Tex., U.S.A.* 71 J5
Graham →, *Canada* 64 B4
Graham, Mt., *U.S.A.* 73 K9
Graham Bell, Os., *Russia* 24 A7
Graham I., *Canada* 64 C2
Graham Land, *Antarctica* 5 C17
Grahamdale, *Canada* 65 C9
Grahamstown, *S. Africa* 48 E4
Grain Coast, *W. Afr.* 42 F2
Grajaú, *Brazil* 79 E9
Grajaú →, *Brazil* 79 D10
Grampian □, *U.K.* 12 D6
Grampian Highlands = Grampian Mts., *U.K.* 12 E5
Grampian Mts., *U.K.* 12 E5
Gran Canaria, *Canary Is.* 44 C1
Gran Chaco, *S. Amer.* 80 B4
Gran Paradiso, *Italy* 20 B2
Gran Sasso d'Italia, *Italy* 20 C5
Granada, *Nic.* 74 E7
Granada, *Spain* 19 D4
Granada, *U.S.A.* 71 F3
Granard, *Ireland* 13 C4
Granbury, *U.S.A.* 71 J6
Granby, *Canada* 62 C5
Grand →, *Mo., U.S.A.* 70 F8
Grand →, *S. Dak., U.S.A.* 70 C4
Grand Bahama, *Bahamas* 75 B9
Grand Bank, *Canada* 63 C8
Grand Bassam, *Ivory C.* 44 G4
Grand-Bourg, *Guadeloupe* 74 M20
Grand Canyon, *U.S.A.* 73 H7
Grand Canyon National Park, *U.S.A.* 73 H7
Grand Cayman, *Cayman Is.* 75 D8
Grand Coulee, *U.S.A.* 72 C4
Grand Coulee Dam, *U.S.A.* 72 C4
Grand Falls, *Canada* 63 C8
Grand Forks, *Canada* 64 D5
Grand Forks, *U.S.A.* 70 B6
Grand Haven, *U.S.A.* 68 D2
Grand I., *U.S.A.* 68 B2
Grand Island, *U.S.A.* 70 E5
Grand Isle, *U.S.A.* 71 L10
Grand Junction, *U.S.A.* 73 G9
Grand L., *N.B., Canada* 63 C6
Grand L., *Nfld., Canada* 63 C8
Grand L., *Nfld., Canada* 63 B7
Grand L., *U.S.A.* 71 L8
Grand Lac Victoria, *Canada* 62 C4
Grand Lahou, *Ivory C.* 44 G3
Grand Lake, *U.S.A.* 72 F11
Grand Manan I., *Canada* 63 D6
Grand Marais, *Canada* 70 B9
Grand Marais, *U.S.A.* 68 B3
Grand-Mère, *Canada* 62 C5
Grand Portage, *U.S.A.* 62 C2
Grand Rapids, *Canada* 65 C9
Grand Rapids, *Mich., U.S.A.* 68 D2
Grand Rapids, *Minn., U.S.A.* 70 B8
Grand St.-Bernard, Col du, *Europe* 16 F4
Grand Teton, *U.S.A.* 72 E8
Grand Valley, *U.S.A.* 72 G9
Grand View, *Canada* 65 C8
Grande →, *Argentina* 80 A3
Grande →, *Bolivia* 78 G6
Grande →, *Bahia, Brazil* 79 F10
Grande →, *Minas Gerais, Brazil* 79 H8
Grande, B., *Argentina* 80 G3
Grande, Rio →, *U.S.A.* 71 N6
Grande Baie, *Canada* 63 C5
Grande Baleine, R. de la →, *Canada* 62 A4
Grande Cache, *Canada* 64 C5
Grande de Santiago →, *Mexico* 74 C3
Grande-Entrée, *Canada* 63 C7
Grande Prairie, *Canada* 64 B5
Grande-Rivière, *Canada* 63 C7
Grande-Vallée, *Canada* 63 C6
Grandes-Bergeronnes, *Canada* 63 C6
Grandfalls, *U.S.A.* 71 K3
Grandoe Mines, *Canada* 64 B3
Grandview, *U.S.A.* 72 C4
Grangemouth, *U.K.* 12 E5
Granger, *Wash., U.S.A.* 72 C3
Granger, *Wyo., U.S.A.* 72 F9
Grangeville, *U.S.A.* 72 D5
Granite City, *U.S.A.* 70 F9
Granite Falls, *U.S.A.* 70 C7
Granite Peak, *Australia* 53 E3
Granite Peak, *U.S.A.* 72 D9
Granity, *N.Z.* 51 J3
Granja, *Brazil* 79 D10
Granollers, *Spain* 19 B7
Grant, *U.S.A.* 70 E4
Grant, Mt., *U.S.A.* 72 G4
Grant City, *U.S.A.* 70 E7
Grant I., *Australia* 52 B5
Grant Range, *U.S.A.* 73 G6
Grantham, *U.K.* 10 E7
Grantown-on-Spey, *U.K.* 12 D5
Grants, *U.S.A.* 73 J10
Grants Pass, *U.S.A.* 72 E2
Grantsburg, *U.S.A.* 70 C8
Grantsville, *U.S.A.* 72 F7
Granville, *France* 18 B3
Granville, *N. Dak., U.S.A.* 70 A4
Granville, *N.Y., U.S.A.* 68 D9
Granville L., *Canada* 65 B8
Grapeland, *U.S.A.* 71 K7
Gras, L. de, *Canada* 60 B8
Graskop, *S. Africa* 49 C5
Grass →, *Canada* 65 B9
Grass Range, *U.S.A.* 72 C9
Grass River Prov. Park, *Canada* 65 C8
Grass Valley, *Calif., U.S.A.* 72 G3
Grass Valley, *Oreg., U.S.A.* 72 D3
Grasse, *France* 18 E7
Grassmere, *Australia* 55 E3
Graulhet, *France* 18 E4
Gravelbourg, *Canada* 65 D7
's-Gravenhage, *Neths.* 15 B4
Gravesend, *Australia* 55 D5
Gravesend, *U.K.* 11 F8
Grayling, *U.S.A.* 68 C3
Grayling →, *Canada* 64 B3
Grays Harbor, *U.S.A.* 72 C1
Grays L., *U.S.A.* 72 E8
Grayson, *Canada* 65 C8
Graz, *Austria* 16 E8
Greasy L., *Canada* 64 A4
Great Abaco I., *Bahamas* 75 B9
Great Artesian Basin, *Australia* 54 C3
Great Australian Bight, *Australia* 53 F5
Great Barrier I., *N.Z.* 51 G5
Great Barrier Reef, *Australia* 54 B4
Great Basin, *U.S.A.* 72 G5
Great Bear →, *Canada* 60 B7
Great Bear L., *Canada* 60 B7
Great Belt = Store Bælt, *Denmark* 9 J14
Great Bend, *U.S.A.* 70 F5
Great Blasket I., *Ireland* 13 D1
Great Britain, *Europe* 6 E5
Great Central, *Canada* 64 D3
Great Dividing Ra., *Australia* 54 C4
Great Driffield = Driffield, *U.K.* 10 C7
Great Falls, *Canada* 65 C9
Great Falls, *U.S.A.* 72 C8
Great Fish = Groot Vis →, *S. Africa* 48 E4
Great Harbour Deep, *Canada* 63 B8
Great I., *Canada* 65 B9
Great Inagua I., *Bahamas* 75 C10
Great Indian Desert = Thar Desert, *India* 36 F7
Great Karoo, *S. Africa* 48 E3
Great Lake, *Australia* 54 G4
Great Malvern, *U.K.* 11 E5
Great Ormes Head, *U.K.* 10 D4
Great Ouse →, *U.K.* 10 E8
Great Palm I., *Australia* 54 B4
Great Plains, *N. Amer.* 66 A6
Great Ruaha →, *Tanzania* 46 F7
Great Saint Bernard P. = Grand St.-Bernard, Col du, *Europe* 16 F4
Great Salt L., *U.S.A.* 72 F7
Great Salt Lake Desert, *U.S.A.* 72 F7
Great Salt Plains L., *U.S.A.* 71 G5
Great Sandy Desert, *Australia* 52 D3
Great Sangi = Sangihe, P., *Indonesia* 33 D7
Great Slave L., *Canada* 64 A5
Great Smoky Mts. Nat. Pk., *U.S.A.* 69 H4
Great Stour = Stour →, *U.K.* 11 F9
Great Victoria Desert, *Australia* 53 E4
Great Wall, *China* 31 C5
Great Whernside, *U.K.* 10 C6
Great Yarmouth, *U.K.* 10 E9
Greater Antilles, *W. Indies* 75 D10
Greater London □, *U.K.* 11 F7
Greater Manchester □, *U.K.* 10 D5
Greater Sunda Is., *Indonesia* 32 F4
Gredos, Sierra de, *Spain* 19 B3
Greece ■, *Europe* 21 E9
Greeley, *Colo., U.S.A.* 70 E2
Greeley, *Nebr., U.S.A.* 70 E5
Green →, *Ky., U.S.A.* 68 G2
Green →, *Utah, U.S.A.* 73 G9
Green B., *U.S.A.* 68 C2
Green Bay, *U.S.A.* 68 C2
Green C., *Australia* 55 F5
Green Cove Springs, *U.S.A.* 69 L5
Green River, *U.S.A.* 73 G8
Greenbush, *U.S.A.* 70 A6
Greencastle, *U.S.A.* 68 F2
Greenfield, *Ind., U.S.A.* 68 F3
Greenfield, *Iowa, U.S.A.* 70 E7
Greenfield, *Mass., U.S.A.* 68 D9
Greenfield, *Mo., U.S.A.* 71 G8
Greenland ■, *N. Amer.* 4 C5
Greenland Sea, *Arctic* 4 B7
Greenock, *U.K.* 12 F4
Greenore, *Ireland* 13 B5
Greenore Pt., *Ireland* 13 D5
Greenough →, *Australia* 53 E1
Greensboro, *Ga., U.S.A.* 69 J4
Greensboro, *N.C., U.S.A.* 69 G6
Greensburg, *Ind., U.S.A.* 68 F3
Greensburg, *Kans., U.S.A.* 71 G5
Greensburg, *Pa., U.S.A.* 68 E6
Greenville, *Liberia* 44 G3
Greenville, *Ala., U.S.A.* 69 K2
Greenville, *Calif., U.S.A.* 72 F3
Greenville, *Ill., U.S.A.* 70 F10
Greenville, *Maine, U.S.A.* 63 C6
Greenville, *Mich., U.S.A.* 68 D3
Greenville, *Miss., U.S.A.* 71 J9
Greenville, *N.C., U.S.A.* 69 H7
Greenville, *Ohio, U.S.A.* 68 E3
Greenville, *Pa., U.S.A.* 68 E5
Greenville, *S.C., U.S.A.* 69 H4
Greenville, *Tenn., U.S.A.* 69 G4
Greenville, *Tex., U.S.A.* 71 J6
Greenwater Lake Prov. Park, *Canada* 65 C8
Greenwich, *U.K.* 11 F8
Greenwood, *Canada* 64 D5
Greenwood, *Miss., U.S.A.* 71 J9
Greenwood, *S.C., U.S.A.* 69 H4
Greenwood, Mt., *Australia* 52 B5
Gregory, *U.S.A.* 70 D5
Gregory →, *Australia* 54 B2
Gregory, L., *S. Austral., Australia* 55 D2
Gregory, L., *W. Austral., Australia* 53 E2
Gregory Downs, *Australia* 54 B2
Gregory L., *Australia* 52 D4
Gregory Ra., *Queens., Australia* 54 B3
Gregory Ra., *W. Austral., Australia* 52 D3
Greifswald, *Germany* 16 A7
Greiz, *Germany* 16 C7
Gremikha, *Russia* 22 A6
Grenå, *Denmark* 9 H14
Grenada, *U.S.A.* 71 J10
Grenada ■, *W. Indies* 74 Q20
Grenadines, *W. Indies* 74 Q20
Grenen, *Denmark* 9 H14
Grenfell, *Australia* 55 E4
Grenfell, *Canada* 65 C8
Grenoble, *France* 18 D6
Grenora, *U.S.A.* 70 A3
Grenville, C., *Australia* 54 A3
Grenville Chan., *Canada* 64 C3
Gresham, *U.S.A.* 72 D2
Gresik, *Indonesia* 33 G15
Gretna Green, *U.K.* 12 F5
Grevenmacher, *Lux.* 15 E6
Grey →, *N.Z.* 51 K3
Grey, C., *Australia* 54 A2
Grey Ra., *Australia* 55 D3
Grey Res., *Canada* 63 C8
Greybull, *U.S.A.* 72 D9
Greymouth, *N.Z.* 51 K3
Greytown, *N.Z.* 51 J5
Greytown, *S. Africa* 49 D5
Gribbell I., *Canada* 64 C3
Gridley, *U.S.A.* 72 G3
Griekwastad, *S. Africa* 48 D3
Griffin, *U.S.A.* 69 J3
Griffith, *Australia* 55 E4
Grimari, *C.A.R.* 45 G9
Grimaylov = Hrymayliv, *Ukraine* 17 D14
Grimsby, *U.K.* 10 D7
Grímsey, *Iceland* 8 C5
Grimshaw, *Canada* 64 B5
Grimstad, *Norway* 9 G13
Grinnell, *U.S.A.* 70 E8
Gris-Nez, C., *France* 18 A4
Groais I., *Canada* 63 B8
Groblersdal, *S. Africa* 49 D4
Grodno = Hrodna, *Belarus* 17 B12
Grodzyanka = Hrodzyanka, *Belarus* 17 B15
Groesbeck, *U.S.A.* 71 K6
Grójec, *Poland* 17 C11
Grong, *Norway* 8 D15
Groningen, *Neths.* 15 A6
Groningen □, *Neths.* 15 A6
Groom, *U.S.A.* 71 H4
Groot →, *S. Africa* 48 E3
Groot Berg →, *S. Africa* 48 E2
Groot-Brakrivier, *S. Africa* 48 E3
Groot-Kei →, *S. Africa* 49 E4
Groot Vis →, *S. Africa* 48 E4
Groote Eylandt, *Australia* 54 A2
Grootfontein, *Namibia* 48 B2
Grootlaagte →, *Africa* 48 C3
Grootvloer, *S. Africa* 48 E3
Gros C., *Canada* 64 A6
Gross Glockner, *Austria* 16 E7
Grosser Arber, *Germany* 16 D7
Grosseto, *Italy* 20 C4
Groswater B., *Canada* 63 B8
Groton, *U.S.A.* 70 C5
Grouard Mission, *Canada* 64 B5
Groundhog →, *Canada* 62 C3
Grouse Creek, *U.S.A.* 72 F7
Groveton, *N.H., U.S.A.* 68 C10
Groveton, *Tex., U.S.A.* 71 K7
Groznyy, *Russia* 23 F8
Grudziądz, *Poland* 17 B10
Grundy Center, *U.S.A.* 70 D8
Gruver, *U.S.A.* 71 G4
Gryazi, *Russia* 22 D6
Gryazovets, *Russia* 24 D5
Gua, *India* 37 H14
Guadalajara, *Mexico* 74 C4
Guadalajara, *Spain* 19 B4
Guadalcanal, *Solomon Is.* 56 H8
Guadalete →, *Spain* 19 D2
Guadalquivir →, *Spain* 19 D2
Guadalupe = Guadeloupe ■, *W. Indies* 74 L20
Guadalupe, *U.S.A.* 73 J3
Guadalupe →, *U.S.A.* 71 L6
Guadalupe, Sierra de, *Spain* 19 C3
Guadalupe Peak, *U.S.A.* 73 L11
Guadarrama, Sierra de, *Spain* 19 B4
Guadeloupe ■, *W. Indies* 74 L20
Guadeloupe Passage, *W. Indies* 74 L19
Guadiana →, *Portugal* 19 D2
Guadix, *Spain* 19 D4
Guafo, Boca del, *Chile* 80 E2
Guaíra, *Brazil* 80 A6
Guaitecas, Is., *Chile* 80 E2
Guajará-Mirim, *Brazil* 78 F5
Guajira, Pen. de la, *Colombia* 78 A4
Gualeguay, *Argentina* 80 C5
Gualeguaychú, *Argentina* 80 C5
Guam ■, *Pac. Oc.* 56 F6
Guamúchil, *Mexico* 74 B3
Guanahani = San Salvador, *Bahamas* 75 C10
Guanajuato, *Mexico* 74 C4
Guandacol, *Argentina* 80 B3
Guane, *Cuba* 75 C8
Guangdong □, *China* 31 D6
Guangxi Zhuangzu Zizhiqu □, *China* 31 D5
Guangzhou, *China* 31 D6
Guanipa →, *Venezuela* 78 B6
Guantánamo, *Cuba* 75 C9
Guaporé →, *Brazil* 78 F5
Guaqui, *Bolivia* 78 G5
Guarapuava, *Brazil* 80 B6
Guarda, *Portugal* 19 B2
Guardafui, C. = Asir, Ras, *Somali Rep.* 40 E5
Guasdualito, *Venezuela* 78 B4
Guasipati, *Venezuela* 78 B6

Guatemala, *Guatemala* 74 E6
Guatemala ■,
  Cent. Amer. 74 D6
Guatire, *Venezuela* ... 78 A5
Guaviare □, *Colombia* 78 C4
Guaviare →,
  Colombia 78 C4
Guaxupé, *Brazil* 79 H9
Guayama, *Puerto Rico* 75 D11
Guayaquil, *Ecuador* .. 78 D3
Guayaquil, G. de,
  Ecuador 78 D2
Guaymas, *Mexico* 74 B2
Guchil, *Malaysia* 34 P15
Gudbrandsdalen,
  Norway 9 F14
Guddu Barrage,
  Pakistan 36 E6
Gudivada, *India* 37 L12
Gudur, *India* 36 M11
Guecho, *Spain* 19 A4
Guékédou, *Guinea* ... 44 G2
Guelma, *Algeria* 44 A6
Guelph, *Canada* 62 D3
Guéréda, *Chad* 45 F9
Guéret, *France* 18 C4
Guernica, *Spain* 19 A4
Guernsey, *U.K.* 11 H5
Guernsey, *U.S.A.* 70 D2
Gueydan, *U.S.A.* 71 K8
Gügher, *Iran* 39 D8
Guidónia-Montecélio,
  Italy 20 C5
Guiglo, *Ivory C.* 44 G3
Guijá, *Mozam.* 49 C5
Guildford, *U.K.* 11 F7
Guilford, *U.S.A.* 63 C6
Guilin, *China* 31 D6
Guimarães, *Brazil* ... 79 D10
Guimarães, *Portugal* . 19 B1
Guimaras, *Phil.* 33 B6
Guinea ■, *W. Afr.* .. 44 F2
Guinea, Gulf of, *Atl. Oc.* 42 F4
Guinea-Bissau ■, *Africa* 44 F2
Guingamp, *France* ... 18 B2
Güiria, *Venezuela* ... 78 A6
Guiuan, *Phil.* 33 B7
Guiyang, *China* 30 D5
Guizhou □, *China* ... 30 D5
Gujarat □, *India* 36 H7
Gujranwala, *Pakistan* . 36 C9
Gujrat, *Pakistan* 36 C9
Gulbarga, *India* 36 L10
Gulbene, *Latvia* 9 H22
Gulf, The, *Asia* 39 E6
Gulgong, *Australia* .. 55 E4
Gull Lake, *Canada* .. 65 C7
Güllük, *Turkey* 21 F12
Gulshad, *Kazakhstan* . 24 E8
Gulu, *Uganda* 46 D6
Gum Lake, *Australia* . 55 E3
Gumlu, *Australia* 54 B4
Gumma □, *Japan* ... 29 F9
Gummi, *Nigeria* 44 F6
Gumzai, *Indonesia* ... 33 F8
Guna, *India* 36 G10
Gundagai, *Australia* .. 55 F4
Gundih, *Indonesia* ... 33 G14
Gungu, *Zaïre* 46 F3
Gunisao →, *Canada* . 65 C9
Gunisao L., *Canada* . 65 C9
Gunnbjørn Fjeld,
  Greenland 4 C6
Gunnedah, *Australia* . 55 E5
Gunningbar Cr. →,
  Australia 55 E4
Gunnison, *Colo., U.S.A.* 73 G10
Gunnison, *Utah, U.S.A.* 72 G8
Gunnison →, *U.S.A.* . 73 G9
Gunpowder, *Australia* 54 B2
Guntakal, *India* 36 M10
Guntersville, *U.S.A.* .. 69 H2
Guntur, *India* 37 L12
Gunungapi, *Indonesia* 33 F7
Gunungsitoli, *Indonesia* 32 D1
Gunza, *Angola* 46 G2
Gupis, *Pakistan* 36 A8
Gurdaspur, *India* 36 C9
Gurdon, *U.S.A.* 71 J8
Gurgaon, *India* 36 E10
Gurkha, *Nepal* 37 E14
Gurley, *Australia* 55 D4
Gurun, *Malaysia* 34 P13
Gurupá, *Brazil* 79 D8
Gurupá, I. Grande de,
  Brazil 79 D8
Gurupi →, *Brazil* ... 79 D9
Guryev = Atyraū,
  Kazakhstan 23 E9
Gusau, *Nigeria* 44 F6
Gusev, *Russia* 9 J20
Gushgy, *Turkmenistan* 24 F7
Gusinoozersk, *Russia* . 25 D11
Gustine, *U.S.A.* 73 H3
Güstrow, *Germany* ... 16 B7
Gütersloh, *Germany* . 16 C5
Gutha, *Australia* 53 E2
Guthalongra, *Australia* 54 B4
Guthrie, *U.S.A.* 71 H6
Guttenberg, *U.S.A.* .. 70 D9
Guyana ■, *S. Amer.* . 78 C7
Guyane française =
  French Guiana ■,
  S. Amer. 79 C8
Guyenne, *France* 18 D4
Guymon, *U.S.A.* 71 G4
Guyra, *Australia* 55 E5
Gvardeysk, *Russia* ... 9 J19
Gwa, *Burma* 37 L19
Gwaai, *Zimbabwe* ... 47 H5
Gwabegar, *Australia* . 55 E4
Gwädar, *Pakistan* ... 36 G3

Gwalia, *Australia* 53 E3
Gwalior, *India* 36 F11
Gwanda, *Zimbabwe* . 47 J5
Gweebarra B., *Ireland* 13 B3
Gweedore, *Ireland* ... 13 A3
Gwent □, *U.K.* 11 F5
Gweru, *Zimbabwe* ... 47 H5
Gwinn, *U.S.A.* 68 B2
Gwydir →, *Australia* . 55 D4
Gwynedd □, *U.K.* .. 10 E4
Gyandzha = Gäncä,
  Azerbaijan 23 F8
Gyaring Hu, *China* .. 30 C4
Gydanskiy P-ov., *Russia* 24 C8
Gympie, *Australia* ... 55 D5
Gyöngyös, *Hungary* .. 17 E10
Györ, *Hungary* 17 E9
Gypsum Pt., *Canada* . 64 A6
Gypsumville, *Canada* 65 C9
Gyula, *Hungary* 17 E11
Gyumri, *Armenia* 23 F7
Gyzylarbat,
  Turkmenistan 24 F6

H

Ha 'Arava →, *Israel* . 41 E4
Haapsalu, *Estonia* ... 9 G20
Haarlem, *Neths.* 15 B4
Haast →, *N.Z.* 51 K2
Haast Bluff, *Australia* . 52 D5
Hab Nadi Chauki,
  Pakistan 36 G5
Habaswein, *Kenya* ... 46 D7
Habay, *Canada* 64 B5
Ḥabbānīyah, *Iraq* 38 C4
Haboro, *Japan* 28 B10
Hachijō-Jima, *Japan* . 29 H9
Hachinohe, *Japan* ... 28 D10
Hachiōji, *Japan* 29 G9
Hadarba, Ras, *Sudan* 45 D12
Hadarom □, *Israel* .. 41 E3
Haddington, *U.K.* ... 12 F6
Hadejia, *Nigeria* 44 F7
Haden, *Australia* 55 D5
Hadera, *Israel* 41 C3
Ḥadera, N. →, *Israel* . 41 C3
Haderslev, *Denmark* . 9 J13
Hadhramaut =
  Ḥaḍramawt, *Yemen* 40 D4
Ḥaḍramawt, *Yemen* . 40 D4
Ḥadīthah, *Iraq* 38 C4
Hadrian's Wall, *U.K.* . 10 C5
Haeju, *N. Korea* 31 C7
Haerhpin = Harbin,
  China 31 B7
Hafar al Bāṭin,
  Si. Arabia 38 D5
Ḥafirat al 'Aydā,
  Si. Arabia 38 E3
Hafizabad, *Pakistan* . 36 C8
Haflong, *India* 37 G18
Hafnarfjörður, *Iceland* 8 D3
Hafun, Ras,
  Somali Rep. 40 E5
Hagalil, *Israel* 41 C4
Hagen, *Germany* 16 C4
Hagerman, *U.S.A.* ... 71 J2
Hagerstown, *U.S.A.* . 68 F7
Hagfors, *Sweden* 9 F15
Hagi, *Japan* 29 G5
Hagolan, *Syria* 41 B4
Hagondange-Briey,
  France 18 B7
Hags Hd., *Ireland* ... 13 D2
Hague, C. de la, *France* 18 B3
Hague, The = 's-
  Gravenhage, *Neths.* 15 B4
Haguenau, *France* ... 18 B7
Haifa = Ḥefa, *Israel* . 41 C3
Haig, *Australia* 53 F4
Haikou, *China* 31 D6
Ḥā'il, *Si. Arabia* 38 E4
Hailar, *China* 31 B6
Hailey, *U.S.A.* 72 E6
Haileybury, *Canada* . 62 C4
Hailuoto, *Finland* 8 D21
Hainan □, *China* 31 E5
Hainaut □, *Belgium* . 15 D4
Haines, *U.S.A.* 72 D5
Haines City, *U.S.A.* .. 69 L5
Haines Junction,
  Canada 64 A1
Haiphong, *Vietnam* .. 30 D5
Haiti ■, *W. Indies* ... 75 D10
Haiya Junction, *Sudan* 45 E12
Hajar Bangar, *Sudan* . 45 F9
Hajdúböszörmény,
  Hungary 17 E11
Ḥājjī Muhsin, *Iraq* ... 38 C5
Ḥājjīābād, *Eṣfahan, Iran* 39 C7
Ḥājjīābād, *Hormozgān,
  Iran* 39 D7
Hajnówka, *Poland* ... 17 B12
Hakken-Zan, *Japan* .. 29 G7
Hakodate, *Japan* 28 D10
Haku-San, *Japan* 29 F8
Hakui, *Japan* 29 F8
Hala, *Pakistan* 36 G6
Ḥalab, *Syria* 38 B3
Ḥalabjah, *Iraq* 38 C5
Halaib, *Sudan* 45 D12
Ḥalāt 'Ammār,
  Si. Arabia 38 D3
Halba, *Lebanon* 41 A5
Halberstadt, *Germany* 16 C6
Halcombe, *N.Z.* 51 J5
Halcon, Mt., *Phil.* ... 33 B6
Halden, *Norway* 9 G14
Haldia, *India* 37 H16

Haldwani, *India* 36 E11
Hale →, *Australia* ... 54 C2
Haleakala Crater, *U.S.A.* 66 H16
Haleyville, *U.S.A.* ... 69 H2
Halfway →, *Canada* . 64 B4
Haliburton, *Canada* . 62 C4
Halifax, *Australia* 54 B4
Halifax, *Canada* 63 D7
Halifax, *U.K.* 10 D6
Halifax B., *Australia* . 54 B4
Halifax I., *Namibia* .. 48 D1
Halīl →, *Iran* 39 E8
Hall Beach, *Canada* . 61 B11
Hall Pt., *Australia* ... 52 C3
Halland, *Sweden* 9 H15
Halle, *Belgium* 15 D4
Halle, *Germany* 16 C6
Hällefors, *Sweden* ... 9 G16
Hallett, *Australia* 55 E2
Hallettsville, *U.S.A.* .. 71 L6
Halliday, *U.S.A.* 70 B3
Halliday L., *Canada* . 65 A7
Hallingdalselva →,
  Norway 9 F13
Hallock, *U.S.A.* 65 D9
Halls Creek, *Australia* 52 C4
Hallsberg, *Sweden* .. 9 G16
Halmahera, *Indonesia* 33 D7
Halmstad, *Sweden* .. 9 H15
Halq el Oued, *Tunisia* 45 A7
Hälsingborg =
  Helsingborg, *Sweden* 9 H15
Hälsingland, *Sweden* . 9 F16
Halstad, *U.S.A.* 70 B6
Halti, *Finland* 8 B19
Halul, *Qatar* 39 E7
Ḥalvān, *Iran* 39 C8
Ham Tan, *Vietnam* ... 34 G3
Hamab, *Namibia* 48 D2
Hamada, *Japan* 29 G6
Hamadān, *Iran* 39 C6
Hamadān □, *Iran* ... 39 C6
Hamāh, *Syria* 38 C3
Hamamatsu, *Japan* .. 29 G8
Hamar, *Norway* 9 F14
Hambantota, *Sri Lanka* 36 R12
Hamber Prov. Park,
  Canada 64 C5
Hamburg, *Germany* . 16 B5
Hamburg, *Ark., U.S.A.* 71 J9
Hamburg, *Iowa, U.S.A.* 70 E7
Ḥamḍ, W. al →,
  Si. Arabia 38 E3
Häme, *Finland* 9 F20
Hämeenlinna, *Finland* 9 F21
Hamelin Pool, *Australia* 53 E1
Hameln, *Germany* ... 16 B5
Hamerkaz □, *Israel* .. 41 C3
Hamersley Ra.,
  Australia 52 D2
Hami, *China* 30 B4
Hamilton, *Australia* .. 55 F3
Hamilton, *Bermuda* .. 75 A12
Hamilton, *Canada* ... 62 D4
Hamilton, *N.Z.* 51 G5
Hamilton, *U.K.* 12 F4
Hamilton, *Mo., U.S.A.* 70 F8
Hamilton, *Mont., U.S.A.* 72 C6
Hamilton, *N.Y., U.S.A.* 68 D8
Hamilton, *Ohio, U.S.A.* 68 F3
Hamilton, *Tex., U.S.A.* 71 K5
Hamilton →, *Australia* 54 C2
Hamilton Hotel,
  Australia 54 C3
Hamilton Inlet, *Canada* 63 B8
Hamiota, *Canada* ... 65 C8
Hamlet, *U.S.A.* 69 H6
Hamley Bridge,
  Australia 55 E2
Hamlin = Hameln,
  Germany 16 B5
Hamlin, *U.S.A.* 71 J4
Hamm, *Germany* 16 C4
Hammerfest, *Norway* . 8 A20
Hammond, *Ind., U.S.A.* 68 E2
Hammond, *La., U.S.A.* 71 K9
Hammonton, *U.S.A.* . 68 F8
Hampden, *N.Z.* 51 L3
Hampshire □, *U.K.* .. 11 F6
Hampshire Downs, *U.K.* 11 F6
Hampton, *Ark., U.S.A.* 71 J8
Hampton, *Iowa, U.S.A.* 70 D8
Hampton, *S.C., U.S.A.* 69 J5
Hampton, *Va., U.S.A.* 68 G7
Hampton Tableland,
  Australia 53 F4
Hamrat esh Sheykh,
  Sudan 45 F10
Han Pijesak, *Bos.-H.* .. 21 B8
Hana, *U.S.A.* 66 H17
Hanak, *Si. Arabia* ... 38 E3
Hanamaki, *Japan* 28 E10
Hanau, *Germany* 16 C5
Hancock, *Mich., U.S.A.* 70 B10
Hancock, *Minn., U.S.A.* 70 C7
Handa, *Japan* 29 G8
Handa, *Somali Rep.* . 40 E5
Handeni, *Tanzania* ... 46 F7
Handwara, *India* 36 B9
Hanegev, *Israel* 41 E4
Haney, *Canada* 64 D4
Hanford, *U.S.A.* 73 H4
Hangayn Nuruu,
  Mongolia 30 B4
Hangchou = Hangzhou,
  China 31 C7
Hangu, *China* 31 C6
Hangzhou, *China* 31 C7
Hangzhou Wan, *China* 31 C7
Ḥanīdh, *Si. Arabia* ... 39 E6
Ḥanīsh, *Yemen* 40 E3
Hankinson, *U.S.A.* ... 70 B6
Hanko, *Finland* 9 G20
Hanksville, *U.S.A.* ... 73 G8

Hanle, *India* 36 C11
Hanmer Springs, *N.Z.* 51 K4
Hann →, *Australia* .. 52 C4
Hann, Mt., *Australia* . 52 C4
Hanna, *Canada* 64 C6
Hannaford, *U.S.A.* ... 70 B5
Hannah, *U.S.A.* 70 A5
Hannah B., *Canada* . 62 B4
Hannibal, *U.S.A.* 70 F9
Hanoi, *Vietnam* 30 D5
Hanover = Hannover,
  Germany 16 B5
Hanover, *S. Africa* ... 48 E3
Hanover, *N.H., U.S.A.* 68 D9
Hanover, *Pa., U.S.A.* . 68 F7
Hanover, I., *Chile* ... 80 G2
Hansi, *India* 36 E9
Hanson, L., *Australia* . 55 E2
Hantsavichy, *Belarus* . 17 B14
Hanzhong, *China* 30 C5
Haora, *India* 37 H16
Haparanda, *Sweden* . 8 D21
Happy, *U.S.A.* 71 H4
Happy Camp, *U.S.A.* 72 F2
Happy Valley-Goose
  Bay, *Canada* 63 B7
Hapur, *India* 36 E10
Haql, *Si. Arabia* 41 F3
Har, *Indonesia* 33 F8
Har Hu, *China* 30 C4
Har Us Nuur, *Mongolia* 30 B4
Har Yehuda, *Israel* .. 41 D3
Ḥaraḍ, *Si. Arabia* ... 40 C4
Haranomachi, *Japan* . 28 F10
Harardera, *Somali Rep.* 40 G4
Harare, *Zimbabwe* ... 47 H6
Harazé, *Chad* 45 F8
Harbin, *China* 31 B7
Harbor Beach, *U.S.A.* 68 D4
Harbor Springs, *U.S.A.* 68 C3
Harbour Breton,
  Canada 63 C8
Harbour Grace, *Canada* 63 C9
Hardangerfjorden,
  Norway 9 F12
Hardangervidda,
  Norway 9 F12
Hardap Dam, *Namibia* 48 C2
Hardenberg, *Neths.* . 15 B6
Harderwijk, *Neths.* .. 15 B5
Hardey →, *Australia* . 52 D2
Hardin, *U.S.A.* 72 D10
Harding, *S. Africa* ... 49 E4
Harding Ra., *Australia* 52 C3
Hardisty, *Canada* 64 C6
Hardman, *U.S.A.* 72 D4
Hardoi, *India* 36 F12
Hardwar = Haridwar,
  India 36 E11
Hardy, *U.S.A.* 71 G9
Hardy, Pen., *Chile* ... 80 H3
Hare B., *Canada* 63 B8
Hareid, *Norway* 9 E12
Harer, *Ethiopia* 40 F3
Hargeisa, *Somali Rep.* 40 F3
Hari →, *Indonesia* ... 32 E2
Haridwar, *India* 36 E11
Haringhata →, *Bangla.* 37 J16
Ḥarīrūd →, *Asia* 36 A2
Härjedalen, *Sweden* . 9 E15
Harlan, *Iowa, U.S.A.* . 70 E7
Harlan, *Ky., U.S.A.* .. 69 G4
Harlech, *U.K.* 10 E3
Harlem, *U.S.A.* 72 B9
Harlingen, *Neths.* ... 15 A5
Harlingen, *U.S.A.* ... 71 M6
Harlowton, *U.S.A.* ... 72 C9
Harney Basin, *U.S.A.* 72 E4
Harney L., *U.S.A.* ... 72 E4
Harney Peak, *U.S.A.* . 70 D3
Härnösand, *Sweden* . 9 E17
Harp L., *Canada* 63 A7
Harrand, *U.S.A.* 69 H3
Harrington Harbour,
  Canada 63 B8
Harris, *U.K.* 12 D2
Harris L., *Australia* .. 55 E2
Harrisburg, *Ill., U.S.A.* 71 G10
Harrisburg, *Nebr.,
  U.S.A.* 70 E3
Harrisburg, *Oreg.,
  U.S.A.* 72 D2
Harrisburg, *Pa., U.S.A.* 68 E7
Harrismith, *S. Africa* . 49 D4
Harrison, *Ark., U.S.A.* 71 G8
Harrison, *Idaho, U.S.A.* 72 C5
Harrison, *Nebr., U.S.A.* 70 D3
Harrison, C., *Canada* . 63 B8
Harrison Bay, *U.S.A.* . 60 A4
Harrison L., *Canada* . 64 D4
Harrisonburg, *U.S.A.* 68 F6
Harrisonville, *U.S.A.* . 70 F7
Harriston, *Canada* ... 62 D3
Harrisville, *U.S.A.* ... 68 C4
Harrogate, *U.K.* 10 D6
Harrow, *U.K.* 11 F7
Harsin, *Iran* 38 C5
Harstad, *Norway* 8 B17
Hart, *U.S.A.* 68 D2
Hart, L., *Australia* ... 55 E2
Hartbees →, *S. Africa* 48 D3
Hartford, *Conn., U.S.A.* 68 E9
Hartford, *Ky., U.S.A.* . 68 G2
Hartford, *S. Dak.,
  U.S.A.* 70 D6
Hartford, *Wis., U.S.A.* 70 D10
Hartford City, *U.S.A.* . 68 E3
Hartland, *Canada* ... 63 C6
Hartland Pt., *U.K.* ... 11 F3
Hartlepool, *U.K.* 10 C6
Hartley Bay, *Canada* . 64 C3

Hartmannberge,
  Namibia 48 B1
Hartney, *Canada* 65 D8
Harts →, *S. Africa* .. 48 D3
Hartselle, *U.S.A.* 69 H2
Hartshorne, *U.S.A.* .. 71 H7
Hartsville, *U.S.A.* 69 H5
Hartwell, *U.S.A.* 69 H4
Harvand, *Iran* 39 D7
Harvey, *Australia* 53 F2
Harvey, *Ill., U.S.A.* .. 68 E2
Harvey, *N. Dak., U.S.A.* 70 B5
Harwich, *U.K.* 11 F9
Haryana □, *India* ... 36 E10
Haryn →, *Belarus* ... 17 B14
Harz, *Germany* 16 C6
Hasan Kiādeh, *Iran* .. 39 B6
Hasan Kuli,
  Turkmenistan 24 F6
Ḥasanābād, *Iran* 39 C7
Hashimoto, *Japan* ... 29 G7
Hashtjerd, *Iran* 39 C6
Hasian, *India* 36 E9
Haskell, *Okla., U.S.A.* 71 H7
Haskell, *Tex., U.S.A.* . 71 J5
Hasselt, *Belgium* 15 D5
Hassi Inifel, *Algeria* .. 44 C5
Hassi Messaoud,
  Algeria 44 B6
Hässleholm, *Sweden* . 9 H15
Hastings, *N.Z.* 51 H6
Hastings, *U.K.* 11 G8
Hastings, *Mich., U.S.A.* 68 D3
Hastings, *Minn., U.S.A.* 70 C8
Hastings, *Nebr., U.S.A.* 70 E5
Hastings Ra., *Australia* 55 E5
Hat Nhao, *Laos* 34 E9
Hatay = Antalya,
  Turkey 23 G5
Hatch, *U.S.A.* 73 K10
Hatches Creek,
  Australia 54 C2
Hatfield P.O., *Australia* 55 E3
Hatgal, *Mongolia* ... 30 A5
Hathras, *India* 36 F11
Hatia, *Bangla.* 37 H17
Hattah, *Australia* 55 E3
Hatteras, C., *U.S.A.* .. 69 H8
Hattiesburg, *U.S.A.* .. 71 K10
Hatvan, *Hungary* 17 E10
Hau Bon = Cheo Reo,
  Vietnam 34 F10
Haugesund, *Norway* . 9 G11
Haukipudas, *Finland* . 8 D21
Haultain →, *Canada* 65 B7
Hauraki G., *N.Z.* 51 G5
Haut Atlas, *Morocco* . 44 B3
Hauterive, *Canada* ... 63 C6
Hautes Fagnes = Hohe
  Venn, *Belgium* 15 D6
Hauts Plateaux, *Algeria* 44 A5
Havana = La Habana,
  Cuba 75 C8
Havana, *U.S.A.* 70 E9
Havant, *U.K.* 11 G7
Havasu, L., *U.S.A.* .. 73 J6
Havel →, *Germany* .. 16 B7
Havelange, *Belgium* . 15 D5
Havelock, *N.B., Canada* 63 C6
Havelock, *Ont., Canada* 62 D4
Havelock, *N.Z.* 51 J4
Havelock I., *India* 34 G2
Haverfordwest, *U.K.* . 11 F3
Haverhill, *U.S.A.* 68 D10
Havering, *U.K.* 11 F8
Havíŕov, *Czech Rep.* . 17 D10
Havlíčkův Brod, *Czech.* 16 D8
Havre, *U.S.A.* 72 B9
Havre-Aubert, *Canada* 63 C7
Havre-St.-Pierre,
  Canada 63 B7
Haw →, *U.S.A.* 69 H6
Hawaii □, *U.S.A.* ... 66 H16
Hawaii I., *Pac. Oc.* .. 66 J17
Hawaiian Is., *Pac. Oc.* 66 H17
Hawaiian Ridge,
  Pac. Oc. 57 E11
Hawarden, *Canada* .. 65 C7
Hawarden, *U.S.A.* ... 70 D6
Hawea, L., *N.Z.* 51 L2
Hawera, *N.Z.* 51 H5
Hawick, *U.K.* 12 F6
Hawk Junction, *Canada* 62 C3
Hawke, B., *N.Z.* 51 H6
Hawker, *Australia* ... 55 E2
Hawkesbury, *Canada* 62 C5
Hawkesbury I., *Canada* 64 C3
Hawkesbury Pt.,
  Australia 54 A1
Hawkinsville, *U.S.A.* . 69 J4
Hawkwood, *Australia* 55 D5
Hawley, *U.S.A.* 70 B6
Ḥawrān, *Syria* 41 C5
Ḥawsh Mūssá, *Lebanon* 41 B4
Hawthorne, *U.S.A.* .. 72 G4
Haxtun, *U.S.A.* 70 E3
Hay, *Australia* 55 E3
Hay →, *Australia* 54 C2
Hay, C., *Australia* ... 52 B4
Hay, L., *Canada* 64 B5
Hay Lakes, *Canada* .. 64 C6
Hay-on-Wye, *U.K.* ... 11 E4
Hay River, *Canada* .. 64 A5
Hay Springs, *U.S.A.* . 70 D3
Haya, *Indonesia* 33 E7
Hayachine-San, *Japan* 28 E10
Hayden, *Ariz., U.S.A.* 73 K8
Hayden, *Colo., U.S.A.* 72 F10
Haydon, *Australia* ... 54 B3
Hayes, *U.S.A.* 70 C4

Hayes →, *Canada* ... 65 B10
Haynesville, *U.S.A.* .. 71 J8
Hayrabolu, *Turkey* ... 21 D12
Hays, *Canada* 64 C6
Hays, *U.S.A.* 70 F5
Haysyn, *Ukraine* 17 D15
Hayvoron, *Ukraine* .. 17 D15
Hayward, *U.S.A.* 70 B9
Haywards Heath, *U.K.* 11 F7
Ḥazafon □, *Israel* ... 41 C4
Hazārām, Kūh-e, *Iran* 39 D8
Hazard, *U.S.A.* 68 G4
Hazaribag, *India* 37 H14
Hazelton, *Canada* ... 64 B3
Hazelton, *N. Dak., U.S.A.* 70 B4
Hazen, *N. Dak., U.S.A.* 70 B4
Hazen, *Nev., U.S.A.* . 72 G4
Hazlehurst, *Ga., U.S.A.* 69 K4
Hazlehurst, *Miss.,
  U.S.A.* 71 K9
Hazleton, *U.S.A.* 68 E8
Hazlett, L., *Australia* . 52 D4
Ḥazor, *Israel* 41 B4
Head of Bight, *Australia* 53 F5
Healdsburg, *U.S.A.* .. 72 G2
Healdton, *U.S.A.* 71 H6
Healesville, *Australia* . 55 F4
Heanor, *U.K.* 10 D6
Heard I., *Ind. Oc.* ... 35 K6
Hearne, *U.S.A.* 71 K6
Hearne B., *Canada* .. 65 A9
Hearne L., *Canada* .. 64 A6
Hearst, *Canada* 62 C3
Heart →, *U.S.A.* 70 B4
Heart's Content,
  Canada 63 C9
Heath Pt., *Canada* ... 63 C7
Heath Steele, *Canada* 63 C6
Heavener, *U.S.A.* 71 H7
Hebbronville, *U.S.A.* . 71 M5
Hebei □, *China* 31 C6
Hebel, *Australia* 55 D4
Heber, *U.S.A.* 73 K9
Heber Springs, *U.S.A.* 71 H9
Hebert, *Canada* 65 C7
Hebgen L., *U.S.A.* ... 72 D8
Hebrides, *U.K.* 12 D1
Hebron = Al Khalīl,
  West Bank 41 D4
Hebron, *Canada* 61 C13
Hebron, *N. Dak., U.S.A.* 70 B3
Hebron, *Nebr., U.S.A.* 70 E6
Hecate Str., *Canada* . 64 C2
Hechi, *China* 30 D5
Hechuan, *China* 30 C5
Hecla, *U.S.A.* 70 C5
Hecla I., *Canada* 65 C9
Hede, *Sweden* 9 E15
Hedemora, *Sweden* . 9 F16
Hedley, *U.S.A.* 71 H4
Heemstede, *Neths.* .. 15 B4
Heerde, *Neths.* 15 B6
Heerenveen, *Neths.* . 15 B5
Heerlen, *Neths.* 15 A6
Ḥefa, *Israel* 41 C3
Ḥefa □, *Israel* 41 C4
Hefei, *China* 31 C6
Hegang, *China* 31 B8
Heidelberg, *Germany* 16 D5
Heidelberg, *S. Africa* 48 E3
Heilbron, *S. Africa* ... 49 D4
Heilbronn, *Germany* . 16 D5
Heilongjiang □, *China* 31 B7
Heilunkiang =
  Heilongjiang □,
  China 31 B7
Heimaey, *Iceland* 8 E3
Heinola, *Finland* 9 F22
Heinze Is., *Burma* ... 34 E4
Hejaz = Al Ḥijāz,
  Si. Arabia 40 B2
Hekla, *Iceland* 8 E4
Hekou, *China* 30 D5
Helena, *Ark., U.S.A.* . 71 H9
Helena, *Mont., U.S.A.* 72 C7
Helensburgh, *U.K.* ... 12 E4
Helensville, *N.Z.* 51 G5
Helgeland, *Norway* .. 8 C15
Helgoland, *Germany* . 16 A4
Heligoland =
  Helgoland, *Germany* 16 A4
Heligoland B. =
  Deutsche Bucht,
  Germany 16 A5
Hella, *Iceland* 8 E3
Hellendoorn, *Neths.* . 15 B6
Hellevoetsluis, *Neths.* 15 C4
Hellín, *Spain* 19 C5
Helmand □, *Afghan.* . 36 D4
Helmand →, *Afghan.* 36 D2
Helmond, *Neths.* 15 C5
Helmsdale, *U.K.* 12 C5
Helper, *U.S.A.* 72 G8
Helsingborg, *Sweden* . 9 H15
Helsingfors = Helsinki,
  Finland 9 F21
Helsingør, *Denmark* . 9 H15
Helsinki, *Finland* 9 F21
Helston, *U.K.* 11 G2
Helvellyn, *U.K.* 10 C4
Helwân, *Egypt* 45 C11
Hemet, *U.S.A.* 73 K5
Hemingford, *U.S.A.* . 70 D3
Hemphill, *U.S.A.* 71 K8
Hempstead, *U.S.A.* .. 71 K6
Hemse, *Sweden* 9 H18
Henan □, *China* 31 C6
Henares →, *Spain* ... 19 B4
Henashi-Misaki, *Japan* 28 D9
Henderson, *Ky., U.S.A.* 68 G2
Henderson, *N.C., U.S.A.* 69 G6
Henderson, *Nev.,
  U.S.A.* 73 H6

Henderson, Tenn.,
U.S.A. 69 H1
Henderson, Tex., U.S.A. 71 J7
Hendersonville, U.S.A. 69 H4
Hendījān, Iran 39 D6
Hendon, Australia ... 55 D5
Hengelo, Neths. 15 B6
Hengyang, China 31 D6
Henlopen, C., U.S.A. .. 68 F8
Hennenman, S. Africa 48 D4
Hennessey, U.S.A. ... 71 G6
Henrietta, U.S.A. 71 J5
Henrietta, Ostrov,
Russia 25 B16
Henrietta Maria, C.,
Canada 62 A3
Henry, U.S.A. 70 E10
Henryetta, U.S.A. ... 71 H6
Hentiyn Nuruu,
Mongolia 31 B5
Henty, Australia 55 F4
Henzada, Burma 37 L19
Heppner, U.S.A. 72 D4
Héraðsflói, Iceland .. 8 D6
Héraðsvötn →,
Iceland 8 D4
Herald Cays, Australia 54 B4
Herāt, Afghan. 36 B3
Herāt □, Afghan. ... 36 B3
Herbert →, Australia 54 B4
Herbert Downs,
Australia 54 C2
Herberton, Australia 54 B4
Hercegnovi,
Montenegro, Yug. . 21 C8
Herðubreið, Iceland .. 8 D5
Hereford, U.K. 11 E5
Hereford, U.S.A. 71 H3
Hereford and
Worcester □, U.K. . 11 E5
Herentals, Belgium .. 15 C4
Herford, Germany ... 16 B5
Herington, U.S.A. ... 70 F6
Herkimer, U.S.A. ... 68 D8
Herman, U.S.A. 70 C6
Hermann, U.S.A. 70 F9
Hermannsburg Mission,
Australia 52 D5
Hermanus, S. Africa . 48 E2
Hermidale, Australia 55 E4
Hermiston, U.S.A. ... 72 D4
Hermitage, N.Z. 51 K3
Hermite, I., Chile ... 80 H3
Hermon, Mt. = Ash
Shaykh, J., Lebanon 41 B4
Hermosillo, Mexico ... 74 B2
Hernád →, Hungary . 17 D11
Hernandarias, Paraguay 80 B6
Hernando, U.S.A. ... 71 H10
Herne, Germany 15 C7
Herne Bay, U.K. 11 F9
Herning, Denmark ... 9 H13
Heroica Nogales =
Nogales, Mexico ... 74 A2
Heron Bay, Canada ... 62 C2
Herreid, U.S.A. 70 C4
Herrick, Australia ... 54 G4
Herrin, U.S.A. 71 G10
Herstal, Belgium ... 15 D5
Hertford, U.K. 11 F7
Hertfordshire □, U.K. . 11 F7
's-Hertogenbosch,
Neths. 15 C5
Hertzogville, S. Africa . 48 D4
Herzliyya, Israel 41 C3
Heşār, Fārs, Iran ... 39 D6
Heşār, Markazī, Iran . 39 C6
Hesse = Hessen □,
Germany 16 C5
Hessen □, Germany .. 16 C5
Hettinger, U.S.A. ... 70 C3
Hewett, C., Canada .. 61 A13
Hewitt, U.S.A. 70 C3
Hexham, U.K. 10 C5
Heydarābād, Iran ... 39 D7
Heyfield, Australia .. 55 F4
Heysham, U.K. 10 C5
Heywood, Australia .. 55 F3
Hialeah, U.S.A. 69 N5
Hiawatha, Kans., U.S.A. 70 F7
Hiawatha, Utah, U.S.A. 72 G8
Hibbing, U.S.A. 70 B8
Hibbs B., Australia .. 54 G4
Hibernia Reef, Australia 54 B3
Hickory, U.S.A. 69 H5
Hicks, Pt., Australia . 55 F4
Hida-Gawa →, Japan 29 G8
Hida-Sammyaku, Japan 29 F8
Hidaka-Sammyaku,
Japan 28 C11
Hidalgo del Parral,
Mexico 74 B3
Higashiōsaka, Japan . 29 G7
Higashiōsaka, Japan . 29 G7
Higgins, U.S.A. 71 G4
Higginsville, Australia 53 F3
High Atlas = Haut
Atlas, Morocco 44 B3
High I., Canada 63 A7
High Island, U.S.A. .. 71 L7
High Level, Canada .. 64 B5
High Point, U.S.A. ... 69 H6
High Prairie, Canada 64 B5
High River, Canada .. 64 C6
High Springs, U.S.A. . 69 L4
High Tatra = Tatry,
Slovak Rep. 17 D11
High Wycombe, U.K. . 11 F7
Highbury, Australia .. 54 B3
Highland □, U.K. ... 12 D4
Highland Park, U.S.A. 68 D2
Highmore, U.S.A. ... 70 C5
Highrock L., Canada 65 B7

Hiiumaa, Estonia 9 G20
Hijāz □, Si. Arabia ... 40 C2
Hijo = Tagum, Phil. . 33 C7
Hikari, Japan 29 H5
Hiko, U.S.A. 73 H6
Hikone, Japan 29 G8
Hikurangi, N.Z. 51 F5
Hikurangi, Mt., N.Z. 51 H6
Hildesheim, Germany . 16 B5
Hill →, Australia 53 F2
Hill City, Idaho, U.S.A. 72 E6
Hill City, Kans., U.S.A. 70 F5
Hill City, Minn., U.S.A. 70 B8
Hill City, S. Dak., U.S.A. 70 D3
Hill Island L., Canada 65 A7
Hillegom, Neths. ... 15 B4
Hillerød, Denmark ... 9 J15
Hillingdon, U.K. ... 11 F7
Hillman, U.S.A. 68 C4
Hillmond, Canada ... 65 C7
Hillsboro, Kans., U.S.A. 70 F6
Hillsboro, N. Dak.,
U.S.A. 70 B6
Hillsboro, N.H., U.S.A. 68 D10
Hillsboro, N. Mex.,
U.S.A. 73 K10
Hillsboro, Oreg., U.S.A. 72 D2
Hillsboro, Tex., U.S.A. 71 J6
Hillsdale, U.S.A. ... 68 E3
Hillside, Australia ... 52 D2
Hillsport, Canada ... 62 C2
Hillston, Australia .. 55 E4
Hilo, U.S.A. 66 J17
Hilversum, Neths. ... 15 B5
Himachal Pradesh □,
India 36 D10
Himalaya, Asia 37 E14
Himatnagar, India ... 36 H8
Himeji, Japan 29 G7
Himi, Japan 29 F8
Ḥimş, Syria 41 A5
Ḥimş □, Syria 41 A5
Hinchinbrook I.,
Australia 54 B4
Hinckley, U.K. 11 E6
Hinckley, U.S.A. 72 G7
Hindmarsh, L.,
Australia 55 F3
Hindu Kush, Asia ... 36 B7
Hindubagh, Pakistan . 36 D5
Hindupur, India 36 N10
Hines Creek, Canada 64 B5
Hinganghat, India ... 36 J11
Hingham, U.S.A. ... 72 B8
Hingoli, India 36 K10
Hinna = Imi, Ethiopia . 40 F3
Hinnøya, Norway ... 8 B16
Hinojosa del Duque,
Spain 19 C3
Hinsdale, U.S.A. ... 72 B10
Hinton, Canada 64 C5
Hinton, U.S.A. 68 G5
Hippolytushoef, Neths. 15 B4
Hirado, Japan 29 H4
Hirakud Dam, India . 37 J13
Hiratsuka, Japan ... 29 G9
Hiroo, Japan 28 C11
Hirosaki, Japan 28 D10
Hiroshima, Japan ... 29 G6
Hiroshima □, Japan . 29 G6
Hisar, India 36 E9
Hisb →, Iraq 38 D5
Ḥismá, Si. Arabia ... 38 D3
Hispaniola, W. Indies 75 D10
Hīt, Iraq 38 C4
Hita, Japan 29 H5
Hitachi, Japan 29 F10
Hitchin, U.K. 11 F7
Hitoyoshi, Japan ... 29 H5
Hitra, Norway 8 E13
Hiyyon, N. →, Israel . 41 E4
Hjalmar L., Canada .. 65 A7
Hjälmaren, Sweden .. 9 G16
Hjørring, Denmark .. 9 H13
Hluhluwe, S. Africa .. 49 D5
Hlyboka, Ukraine ... 17 D13
Ho, Ghana 44 G5
Ho Chi Minh City =
Phanh Bho Ho Chi
Minh, Vietnam 34 G9
Hoa Binh, Vietnam .. 34 B8
Hoai Nhon, Vietnam . 34 E10
Hoare B., Canada ... 61 B13
Hobart, Australia ... 54 G4
Hobart, U.S.A. 71 H5
Hobbs, U.S.A. 71 J3
Hobbs Coast, Antarctica 5 D14
Hoboken, Belgium ... 15 C4
Hobro, Denmark ... 9 H13
Hoburgen, Sweden .. 9 H18
Hodaka-Dake, Japan . 29 F8
Hodgson, Canada ... 65 C9
Hódmezővásárhely,
Hungary 17 E11
Hodna, Chott el, Algeria 44 A5
Hodonín, Czech. ... 17 D9
Hoek van Holland,
Neths. 15 C4
Hof, Germany 16 C6
Höfðakaupstaður,
Iceland 8 D3
Hofmeyr, S. Africa .. 48 E4
Höfn, Iceland 8 D6
Hofors, Sweden 9 F17
Hofsjökull, Iceland .. 8 D4
Höfu, Japan 29 G5
Hogan Group, Australia 54 F4
Hogansville, U.S.A. .. 69 J3
Hogeland, U.S.A. ... 72 B9
Hoggar = Ahaggar,
Algeria 44 D6

Hohenwald, U.S.A. .. 69 H2
Hohhot, China 31 B6
Hoi An, Vietnam ... 34 E10
Hoi Xuan, Vietnam .. 34 B8
Hoisington, U.S.A. .. 70 F5
Hōjō, Japan 29 H6
Hokianga Harbour, N.Z. 51 F4
Hokitika, N.Z. 51 K3
Hokkaidō □, Japan .. 28 C11
Holbrook, Australia .. 55 F4
Holbrook, U.S.A. ... 73 J8
Holden, Canada 64 C6
Holden, U.S.A. 72 G7
Holdenville, U.S.A. .. 71 H6
Holderness, U.K. ... 10 D7
Holdfast, Canada ... 65 C7
Holdrege, U.S.A. ... 70 E5
Holguín, Cuba 75 C9
Hollams Bird I.,
Namibia 48 C1
Holland, U.S.A. 68 D2
Hollandia = Jayapura,
Indonesia 33 E10
Hollidaysburg, U.S.A. 68 E6
Hollis, U.S.A. 71 H5
Hollister, Calif., U.S.A. 73 H3
Hollister, Idaho, U.S.A. 72 E6
Holly, U.S.A. 70 F3
Holly Hill, U.S.A. ... 69 L5
Holly Springs, U.S.A. 71 H10
Hollywood, Calif.,
U.S.A. 73 J4
Hollywood, Fla., U.S.A. 69 N5
Holman Island, Canada 60 A8
Hólmavík, Iceland ... 8 D3
Holmes Reefs, Australia 54 B4
Holmsund, Sweden .. 8 E19
Holroyd →, Australia 54 A3
Holstebro, Denmark . 9 H13
Holsworthy, U.K. ... 11 G3
Holton, Canada 63 B8
Holton, U.S.A. 70 F7
Holtville, U.S.A. ... 73 K6
Holwerd, Neths. ... 15 A5
Holy Cross, U.S.A. .. 60 B4
Holy I., Gwynedd, U.K. 10 D3
Holy I., Northumb., U.K. 10 B6
Holyhead, U.K. 10 D3
Holyoke, Colo., U.S.A. 70 E3
Holyoke, Mass., U.S.A. 68 D9
Holyrood, Canada .. 63 C9
Homalin, Burma 37 G19
Homand, Iran 39 C8
Hombori, Mali 44 E4
Home B., Canada ... 61 B13
Home Hill, Australia 54 B4
Homedale, U.S.A. ... 72 E5
Homer, Alaska, U.S.A. 60 C4
Homer, La., U.S.A. .. 71 J8
Homestead, Australia 54 C4
Homestead, Fla., U.S.A. 69 N5
Homestead, Oreg.,
U.S.A. 72 D5
Hominy, U.S.A. 71 G6
Homoine, Mozam. .. 49 C6
Homs = Ḥimş, Syria . 41 A5
Hon Chong, Vietnam . 34 G8
Honan = Henan □,
China 31 C6
Honbetsu, Japan ... 28 C11
Honda, Colombia ... 78 B4
Hondeklipbaai, S. Africa 48 E2
Hondo, Japan 29 H5
Hondo, U.S.A. 71 L5
Honduras ■,
Cent. Amer. 74 E7
Honduras, G. de,
Caribbean 74 D7
Hønefoss, Norway .. 9 F14
Honey L., U.S.A. ... 72 F3
Honfleur, France ... 18 B4
Hong Kong ■, Asia . 31 D6
Hongha →, Vietnam . 30 D5
Hongjiang, China ... 31 D5
Hongshui He →,
China 31 D5
Honguedo, Détroit d',
Canada 63 C7
Hongze Hu, China .. 31 C6
Honiara, Solomon Is. . 56 H7
Honiton, U.K. 11 G4
Honjō, Japan 28 E10
Honningsvåg, Norway . 8 A21
Honolulu, U.S.A. ... 66 H16
Honshū, Japan 29 G9
Hood, Mt., U.S.A. .. 72 D3
Hood, Pt., Australia . 53 F2
Hood River, U.S.A. .. 72 D3
Hoodsport, U.S.A. .. 72 C2
Hoogeveen, Neths. .. 15 B6
Hoogezand, Neths. .. 15 A6
Hooghly = Hughli →,
India 37 J16
Hook Hd., Ireland .. 13 D5
Hook I., Australia .. 54 C4
Hook of Holland =
Hoek van Holland,
Neths. 15 C4
Hooker, U.S.A. 71 G4
Hooker Creek, Australia 52 C5
Hoopeston, U.S.A. .. 68 E2
Hoopstad, S. Africa . 48 D4
Hoorn, Neths. 15 B5
Hoover Dam, U.S.A. 73 J6
Hope, Canada 64 D4
Hope, Ark., U.S.A. .. 71 J8
Hope, N. Dak., U.S.A. 70 B6
Hope, L., Australia .. 55 D2
Hope, Pt., U.S.A. ... 60 B3
Hopedale, Canada .. 63 A7
Hopefield, S. Africa . 48 E2

Hopei = Hebei □,
China 31 C6
Hopetoun, Vic.,
Australia 55 F3
Hopetoun, W. Austral.,
Australia 53 F3
Hopetown, S. Africa . 48 D3
Hopkins, U.S.A. 70 E7
Hopkins, L., Australia 52 D4
Hopkinsville, U.S.A. . 69 G2
Hopland, U.S.A. ... 72 G2
Hoquiam, U.S.A. ... 72 C2
Horden Hills, Australia 52 D5
Horlick Mts., Antarctica 5 E15
Horlivka, Ukraine ... 23 E6
Hormoz, Iran 39 E7
Hormoz, Jaz. ye, Iran . 39 E8
Hormuz, Str. of,
The Gulf 39 E8
Horn, Austria 16 D8
Horn, Iceland 8 C2
Horn →, Canada ... 64 A5
Horn, Cape = Hornos,
C. de, Chile 80 H3
Horn Head, Ireland .. 13 A3
Horn I., Australia ... 54 A3
Horn I., U.S.A. 69 K1
Horn Mts., Canada .. 64 A5
Hornavan, Sweden .. 8 C17
Hornbeck, U.S.A. ... 71 K8
Hornbrook, U.S.A. .. 72 F2
Horncastle, U.K. ... 10 D7
Hornell, U.S.A. 68 D7
Hornell L., Canada .. 64 A5
Hornepayne, Canada 62 C3
Hornos, C. de, Chile . 80 H3
Hornsby, Australia .. 55 E5
Hornsea, U.K. 10 D7
Horobetsu, Japan ... 28 C10
Horodenka, Ukraine . 17 D13
Horodok,
Khmelnytskyy,
Ukraine 17 D14
Horodok, Lviv, Ukraine 17 D12
Horokhiv, Ukraine 17 C13
Horqin Youyi Qianqi,
China 31 B7
Horqueta, Paraguay . 80 A5
Horse Creek, U.S.A. . 70 E3
Horse Is., Canada ... 63 B8
Horsefly L., Canada . 64 C4
Horsens, Denmark .. 9 J13
Horsham, Australia .. 55 F3
Horsham, U.K. 11 F7
Horten, Norway 9 G14
Horton, U.S.A. 70 F7
Horton →, Canada .. 60 B7
Horwood, L., Canada 62 C3
Hose, Gunung-Gunung,
Malaysia 32 D4
Ḥoseynābād,
Khuzestān, Iran ... 39 C6
Ḥoseynābād,
Kordestān, Iran ... 38 C5
Hoshangabad, India . 36 H10
Hoshiarpur, India ... 36 D9
Hosmer, U.S.A. 70 C5
Hospet, India 36 M10
Hospitalet de Llobregat,
Spain 19 B7
Hoste, I., Chile 80 H3
Hot, Thailand 34 C5
Hot Creek Range,
U.S.A. 72 G5
Hot Springs, Ark.,
U.S.A. 71 H8
Hot Springs, S. Dak.,
U.S.A. 70 D3
Hotagen, Sweden ... 8 E16
Hotan, China 30 C2
Hotazel, S. Africa ... 48 D3
Hotchkiss, U.S.A. .. 73 G10
Hotham, C., Australia 52 B5
Hoting, Sweden 8 D17
Hottentotsbaai,
Namibia 48 D1
Houck, U.S.A. 73 J9
Houffalize, Belgium . 15 D5
Houghton, U.S.A. .. 70 B10
Houghton L., U.S.A. 68 C3
Houghton-le-Spring,
U.K. 10 C6
Houhora Heads, N.Z. 51 F4
Houlton, U.S.A. ... 63 C6
Houma, U.S.A. 71 L9
Houston, Canada ... 64 C3
Houston, Mo., U.S.A. 71 G9
Houston, Tex., U.S.A. 71 L7
Houtman Abrolhos,
Australia 53 E1
Hov, Mongolia 30 B4
Hovd, Mongolia 30 B4
Hove, U.K. 11 G7
Hoveyzeh, Iran 39 D6
Hövsgöl Nuur,
Mongolia 30 A5
Howard, Australia .. 55 D5
Howard, Kans., U.S.A. 71 G6
Howard, S. Dak., U.S.A. 70 C6
Howard L., Canada .. 65 A7
Howe, U.S.A. 72 E7
Howe, C., Australia .. 55 F5
Howell, U.S.A. 68 D4
Howick, S. Africa ... 49 D5
Howick Group,
Australia 54 A4
Howitt, L., Australia 55 D2
Howland I., Pac. Oc. . 56 G10
Howrah = Haora, India 37 H16
Howth Hd., Ireland . 13 C5
Höxter, Germany ... 16 C5
Hoy, U.K. 12 C5

Høyanger, Norway .. 9 F12
Hoyerswerda, Germany 16 C8
Hpungan Pass, Burma 37 F20
Hradec Králové, Czech. 16 C8
Hrodna, Belarus 17 B12
Hrodzyanka, Belarus 17 B15
Hron →, Slovak Rep. 17 E10
Hrvatska = Croatia ■,
Europe 16 F9
Hrymayliv, Ukraine .. 17 D14
Hsenwi, Burma 37 H20
Hsiamen = Xiamen,
China 31 D6
Hsian = Xi'an, China . 31 C5
Hsinhailien =
Lianyungang, China 31 C6
Hsisha Chuntao,
Pac. Oc. 32 A4
Hsüchou = Xuzhou,
China 31 C6
Hua Hin, Thailand .. 34 F5
Huacho, Peru 78 F3
Huachón, Peru 78 F3
Huai He →, China .. 31 C6
Huainan, China 31 C6
Hualapai Peak, U.S.A. 73 J7
Huallaga →, Peru ... 78 E3
Huambo, Angola ... 47 G3
Huancabamba, Peru . 78 E3
Huancane, Peru 78 G5
Huancapi, Peru 78 F4
Huancavelica, Peru .. 78 F3
Huancayo, Peru 78 F3
Huang Hai = Yellow
Sea, China 31 C7
Huang He →, China . 31 C6
Huangshi, China ... 31 C6
Huánuco, Peru 78 E3
Huaraz, Peru 78 E3
Huarmey, Peru 78 F3
Huascarán, Peru ... 78 E3
Huasco, Chile 80 B2
Huatabampo, Mexico 74 B3
Huayllay, Peru 78 F3
Hubbard, U.S.A. ... 71 K6
Hubbart Pt., Canada . 65 B10
Hubei □, China 31 C6
Hubli-Dharwad =
Dharwad, India ... 36 M9
Huddersfield, U.K. .. 10 D6
Hudiksvall, Sweden . 9 F17
Hudson, Canada ... 65 C10
Hudson, Mich., U.S.A. 68 E3
Hudson, N.Y., U.S.A. 68 D9
Hudson, Wis., U.S.A. 70 C8
Hudson, Wyo., U.S.A. 72 E9
Hudson →, U.S.A. .. 68 E8
Hudson Bay, N.W.T.,
Canada 61 C11
Hudson Bay, Sask.,
Canada 65 C8
Hudson Falls, U.S.A. 68 D9
Hudson Mts., Antarctica 5 D16
Hudson Str., Canada . 61 B13
Hudson's Hope, Canada 64 B4
Hue, Vietnam 34 D9
Huelva, Spain 19 D2
Huesca, Spain 19 A5
Hugh →, Australia .. 54 D1
Hughenden, Australia 54 C3
Hughes, Australia .. 53 F4
Hughli →, India ... 37 J16
Hugo, U.S.A. 70 F3
Hugoton, U.S.A. ... 71 G4
Huila, Nevado del,
Colombia 78 C3
Huinca Renancó,
Argentina 80 C4
Huize, China 30 D5
Hukawng Valley, Burma 37 F20
Hukuntsi, Botswana . 48 C3
Ḥulayfā', Si. Arabia . 38 E4
Huld, Mongolia 30 B5
Hull = Kingston upon
Hull, U.K. 10 D7
Hull, Canada 62 C4
Hull →, U.K. 10 D7
Hulst, Neths. 15 C4
Hulun Nur, China .. 31 B6
Humahuaca, Argentina 80 A3
Humaitá, Brazil 78 E6
Humaitá, Paraguay .. 80 B5
Humansdorp, S. Africa 48 E3
Humbe, Angola 48 B1
Humber →, U.K. ... 10 D7
Humberside □, U.K. . 10 D7
Humble, U.S.A. 71 L8
Humboldt, Canada .. 65 C7
Humboldt, Iowa, U.S.A. 70 D7
Humboldt, Tenn.,
U.S.A. 71 H10
Humboldt →, U.S.A. 72 F4
Humboldt Gletscher,
Greenland 4 B4
Hume, L., Australia .. 55 F4
Humenné, Slovak Rep. 17 D11
Humphreys Peak,
U.S.A. 73 J8
Hūn, Libya 45 C8
Húnaflói, Iceland ... 8 D3
Hunan □, China 31 D6
Hundred Mile House,
Canada 64 C4
Hunedoara, Romania 17 F12
Hungary ■, Europe . 17 E10
Hungary, Plain of,
Europe 6 F9
Hungerford, Australia 55 D3
Hüngnam, N. Korea . 31 C14
Hunsberge, Namibia . 48 D2
Hunsrück, Germany . 16 D4

Hunstanton, U.K. ... 10 E8
Hunter, U.S.A. 70 B6
Hunter I., Australia .. 54 G3
Hunter I., Canada ... 64 C3
Hunter Ra., Australia 55 E5
Hunterville, N.Z. ... 51 H5
Huntingburg, U.S.A. 68 F2
Huntingdon, Canada 62 C5
Huntingdon, U.K. ... 11 E7
Huntingdon, U.S.A. . 68 E6
Huntington, Ind., U.S.A. 68 E3
Huntington, Oreg.,
U.S.A. 72 D5
Huntington, Utah,
U.S.A. 72 G8
Huntington, W. Va.,
U.S.A. 68 F4
Huntington Beach,
U.S.A. 73 K5
Huntington Park, U.S.A. 73 K4
Huntly, N.Z. 51 G5
Huntly, U.K. 12 D6
Huntsville, Canada .. 62 C4
Huntsville, Ala., U.S.A. 69 H2
Huntsville, Tex., U.S.A. 71 K7
Huonville, Australia . 54 G4
Hupeh = Hubei □,
China 31 C6
Hūr, Iran 39 D8
Hurley, N. Mex., U.S.A. 73 K9
Hurley, Wis., U.S.A. 70 B9
Huron, U.S.A. 70 C5
Huron, L., U.S.A. .. 68 C4
Hurricane, U.S.A. .. 73 H7
Hurunui →, N.Z. ... 51 K4
Húsavík, Iceland ... 8 C5
Huşi, Romania 17 E15
Huskvarna, Sweden . 9 H16
Hussar, Canada 64 C6
Hustadvika, Norway . 8 E12
Hutchinson, Kans.,
U.S.A. 71 F6
Hutchinson, Minn.,
U.S.A. 70 C7
Huttig, U.S.A. 71 J8
Hutton, Mt., Australia 55 D4
Huy, Belgium 15 D5
Hvammstangi, Iceland 8 D3
Hvar, Croatia 20 C7
Hvítá, Iceland 8 D3
Hvítá →, Iceland ... 8 D3
Hwang Ho = Huang
He →, China 31 C6
Hwange, Zimbabwe . 47 H5
Hwange Nat. Park,
Zimbabwe 48 B4
Hyannis, U.S.A. ... 70 E4
Hyargas Nuur,
Mongolia 30 B4
Hyden, Australia ... 53 F2
Hyderabad, India ... 36 L11
Hyderabad, Pakistan . 36 G6
Hyères, France 18 E7
Hyères, Is. d', France . 18 E7
Hyland →, Canada .. 64 B3
Hyōgo □, Japan ... 29 G7
Hyrum, U.S.A. 72 F8
Hysham, U.S.A. ... 72 C10
Hythe, U.K. 11 F9
Hyūga, Japan 29 H5
Hyvinge = Hyvinkää,
Finland 9 F21
Hyvinkää, Finland .. 9 F21

I-n-Gall, Niger 44 E6
Iaco →, Brazil 78 E5
Iakora, Madag. 49 C8
Ialomiţa →, Romania 17 F14
Iaşi, Romania 17 E14
Iba, Phil. 33 A6
Ibadan, Nigeria ... 44 G5
Ibagué, Colombia .. 78 C3
Ibar →, Serbia, Yug. 21 C9
Ibaraki □, Japan ... 29 F10
Ibarra, Ecuador 78 C3
Iberian Peninsula,
Europe 6 G5
Iberville, Canada ... 62 C5
Iberville, Lac d', Canada 62 A5
Ibi, Nigeria 44 G6
Ibiá, Brazil 79 G9
Ibicuy, Argentina .. 80 C5
Ibioapaba, Sa. da,
Brazil 79 D10
Ibiza, Spain 19 C6
Ibonma, Indonesia .. 33 E8
Ibotirama, Brazil ... 79 F10
Ibrāhīm →, Lebanon 41 A4
Ibu, Indonesia 33 D7
Ibusuki, Japan 29 J5
Içá →, Brazil 78 D5
Iça, Peru 78 F3
Içana, Brazil 78 C5
İçel = Mersin, Turkey 23 G5
Iceland ■, Europe .. 8 D4
Icha, Russia 25 D16
Ichchapuram, India . 37 K14
Ichihara, Japan 29 G10
Ichikawa, Japan ... 29 G9
Ichilo →, Bolivia ... 78 G6
Ichinohe, Japan 28 D10
Ichinomiya, Japan .. 29 G8
Ichinoseki, Japan .. 28 E10
Icy Str., U.S.A. 64 B1
Ida Grove, U.S.A. .. 70 D7
Ida Valley, Australia . 53 E3

Idabel, *U.S.A.* 71 J7
Idaho □, *U.S.A.* 72 D6
Idaho City, *U.S.A.* 72 E6
Idaho Falls, *U.S.A.* ... 72 E7
Idaho Springs, *U.S.A.* . 72 G11
Idar-Oberstein,
  Germany 16 D4
Idd el Ghanam, *Sudan* 45 F9
Iddan, *Somali Rep.* ... 40 F4
Idehan, *Libya* 45 D7
Idehan Marzûq, *Libya* 45 D7
Idelès, *Algeria* 44 D6
Idfû, *Egypt* 45 D11
Idhi Óros, *Greece* ... 21 G11
Idhra, *Greece* 21 F10
Idi, *Indonesia* 32 C1
Idiofa, *Zaïre* 46 E3
Idlib, *Syria* 38 C3
Idutywa, *S. Africa* ... 49 E4
Ieper, *Belgium* 15 D2
Ierápetra, *Greece* ... 21 G11
Ierissós, *Greece* 21 D11
Iesi, *Italy* 20 C5
'Ifál, W. al →,
  Si. Arabia 38 D2
Ifanadiana, *Madag.* .. 49 C8
Ife, *Nigeria* 44 G5
Iffley, *Australia* 54 B3
Ifni, *Morocco* 44 C2
Iforas, Adrar des, *Mali* 44 E5
Ifould, L., *Australia* .. 53 F5
Igarapava, *Brazil* 79 H9
Igarapé Açu, *Brazil* .. 79 D9
Igarka, *Russia* 24 C9
Igbetti, *Nigeria* 44 G5
Iggesund, *Sweden* ... 9 F17
Iglésias, *Italy* 20 E3
Igli, *Algeria* 44 B4
Igloolik, *Canada* 61 B11
Ignace, *Canada* 62 C1
İğneada Burnu, *Turkey* 21 D13
Igoumenítsa, *Greece* . 21 E9
Iguaçu →, *Brazil* 80 B6
Iguaçu, Cat. del, *Brazil* 80 B6
Iguaçu Falls = Iguaçu,
  Cat. del, *Brazil* ... 80 B6
Iguala, *Mexico* 74 D5
Igualada, *Spain* 19 B6
Iguassu = Iguaçu →,
  Brazil 80 B6
Iguatu, *Brazil* 79 E11
Iguéla, *Gabon* 46 E1
Iheya-Shima, *Japan* .. 29 L3
Ihosy, *Madag.* 49 C8
Ihotry, L., *Madag.* ... 49 C7
Ii, *Finland* 8 D21
Ii-Shima, *Japan* 29 L3
Iida, *Japan* 29 G8
Iijoki →, *Finland* 8 D21
Iisalmi, *Finland* 8 E22
Iiyama, *Japan* 29 F9
Iizuka, *Japan* 29 H5
Ijebu-Ode, *Nigeria* .. 44 G5
IJmuiden, *Neths.* 15 B4
IJssel →, *Neths.* 15 B5
IJsselmeer, *Neths.* ... 15 B5
Ikaría, *Greece* 21 F12
Ikeda, *Japan* 29 G6
Ikela, *Zaïre* 46 E4
Iki, *Japan* 29 H4
Ikopa →, *Madag.* ... 49 B8
Ilagan, *Phil.* 33 A6
Ilām, *Iran* 38 C5
Ilanskiy, *Russia* 25 D10
Iława, *Poland* 17 B10
Ilbilbie, *Australia* 54 C4
Ile-à-la-Crosse, *Canada* 65 B7
Ile-à-la-Crosse, Lac,
  Canada 65 B7
Île-de-France, *France* . 18 B5
Ilebo, *Zaïre* 46 E4
Ilek, *Russia* 24 D6
Ilek →, *Russia* 22 D9
Ilford, *Canada* 65 B9
Ilfracombe, *Australia* . 54 C3
Ilfracombe, *U.K.* 11 F3
Ilhéus, *Brazil* 79 F11
Ili →, *Kazakhstan* ... 24 E8
Ilich, *Kazakhstan* 24 E7
Iliff, *U.S.A.* 70 E3
Iligan, *Phil.* 33 C6
Ilion, *U.S.A.* 68 D8
Ilkeston, *U.K.* 10 E6
Illampu = Ancohuma,
  Nevada, *Bolivia* .. 78 G5
Illana B., *Phil.* 33 C6
Illapel, *Chile* 80 C2
Iller →, *Germany* 16 D6
Illimani, *Bolivia* 78 G5
Illinois □, *U.S.A.* 67 C9
Illinois →, *U.S.A.* ... 67 C8
Illium = Troy, *Turkey* 21 E12
Ilmajoki, *Finland* 9 E20
Ilmen, Ozero, *Russia* . 22 C5
Ilo, *Peru* 78 G4
Iloilo, *Phil.* 33 B6
Ilorin, *Nigeria* 44 G5
Ilwaki, *Indonesia* 33 F7
Imabari, *Japan* 29 G6
Imaloto →, *Madag.* .. 49 C8
Imandra, Ozero, *Russia* 22 A5
Imari, *Japan* 29 H4
Imbler, *U.S.A.* 72 D5
imeni 26 Bakinskikh
  Komissarov =
  Neftçala, *Azerbaijan* 23 G8
imeni 26 Bakinskikh
  Komissarov,
  Turkmenistan 23 G9
Imeni Poliny Osipenko,
  Russia 25 D14
Imeri, Serra, *Brazil* .. 78 C5
Imerimandroso, *Madag.* 49 B8
Imi, *Ethiopia* 40 F3

Imlay, *U.S.A.* 72 F4
Immingham, *U.K.* ... 10 D7
Immokalee, *U.S.A.* .. 69 M5
Imola, *Italy* 20 B4
Imperatriz, *Brazil* 79 E9
Impéria, *Italy* 20 C3
Imperial, *Canada* 65 C7
Imperial, *Calif., U.S.A.* 73 K6
Imperial, *Nebr., U.S.A.* 70 E4
Imperial Dam, *U.S.A.* 73 K6
Imperieuse Reef,
  Australia 52 C2
Impfondo, *Congo* 46 D3
Imphal, *India* 37 G18
Imroz = Gökçeada,
  Turkey 21 D11
Imuruan B., *Phil.* 33 B5
In Belbel, *Algeria* 44 C5
In Salah, *Algeria* 44 C5
Ina, *Japan* 29 G8
Inangahua Junction,
  N.Z. 51 J3
Inanwatan, *Indonesia* . 33 E8
Iñapari, *Peru* 78 F5
Inari, *Finland* 8 B22
Inarijärvi, *Finland* 8 B22
Inawashiro-Ko, *Japan* 28 F10
Inca, *Spain* 19 C7
Ince-Burnu, *Turkey* .. 23 F5
Inchon, *S. Korea* 31 C7
İncirliova, *Turkey* 21 F12
Incomáti →, *Mozam.* 49 D5
Indalsälven →,
  Sweden 9 E17
Indaw, *Burma* 37 G20
Independence, *Calif.,*
  U.S.A. 73 H4
Independence, *Iowa,*
  U.S.A. 70 D9
Independence, *Kans.,*
  U.S.A. 71 G7
Independence, *Mo.,*
  U.S.A. 70 F7
Independence, *Oreg.,*
  U.S.A. 72 D2
Independence Fjord,
  Greenland 4 A6
Independence Mts.,
  U.S.A. 72 F5
India ■, *Asia* 36 K11
Indian →, *U.S.A.* ... 69 M5
Indian Cabins, *Canada* 64 B5
Indian Harbour, *Canada* 63 B8
Indian Head, *Canada* . 65 C8
Indian Ocean 26 J10
Indiana, *U.S.A.* 68 E6
Indiana □, *U.S.A.* ... 68 E3
Indianapolis, *U.S.A.* .. 68 F2
Indianola, *Iowa, U.S.A.* 70 E8
Indianola, *Miss., U.S.A.* 71 J9
Indiga, *Russia* 22 A8
Indigirka →, *Russia* . 25 B15
Indio, *U.S.A.* 73 K5
Indonesia ■, *Asia* ... 32 F5
Indore, *India* 36 H9
Indramayu, *Indonesia* 33 G13
Indravati →, *India* ... 37 K12
Indre →, *France* 18 C4
Indus →, *Pakistan* .. 36 G5
İnebolu, *Turkey* 23 F5
Ingende, *Zaïre* 46 E3
Ingham, *Australia* 54 B4
Ingleborough, *U.K.* .. 10 C5
Inglewood, *Queens.,*
  Australia 55 D5
Inglewood, *Vic.,*
  Australia 55 F3
Inglewood, *N.Z.* 51 H5
Inglewood, *U.S.A.* ... 73 K4
Ingólfshöfði, *Iceland* . 8 E5
Ingolstadt, *Germany* . 16 D6
Ingomar, *U.S.A.* 72 C10
Ingonish, *Canada* 63 C7
Ingraj Bazar, *India* ... 37 G16
Ingrid Christensen
  Coast, *Antarctica* .. 5 C6
Ingulec = Inhulec,
  Ukraine 23 E5
Ingwavuma, *S. Africa* 49 D5
Inhaca, I., *Mozam.* ... 49 D5
Inhafenga, *Mozam.* .. 49 C5
Inhambane, *Mozam.* . 49 C6
Inhambane □, *Mozam.* 49 C5
Inhaminga, *Mozam.* .. 47 H7
Inharrime, *Mozam.* ... 49 C6
Inharrime →, *Mozam.* 49 C6
Inhulec, *Ukraine* 23 E5
Ining = Yining, *China* 24 E9
Inírida →, *Colombia* . 78 C5
Inishbofin, *Ireland* ... 13 C1
Inishmore, *Ireland* ... 13 C2
Inishowen Pen., *Ireland* 13 A4
Injune, *Australia* 55 D4
Inklin, *Canada* 64 B2
Inklin →, *Canada* 64 B2
Inkom, *U.S.A.* 72 E7
Inle L., *Burma* 37 J20
Inn →, *Austria* 16 D7
Innamincka, *Australia* 55 D3
Inner Hebrides, *U.K.* . 12 D2
Inner Mongolia = Nei
  Monggol Zizhiqu □,
  China 31 B6
Inner Sound, *U.K.* ... 12 D3
Innetalling I., *Canada* 62 A4
Innisfail, *Australia* 54 B4
Innisfail, *Canada* 64 C6
In'no-shima, *Japan* ... 29 G6
Innsbruck, *Austria* ... 16 E6
Inny →, *Ireland* 13 C4
Inongo, *Zaïre* 46 E3
Inoucdjouac =
  Inukjuak, *Canada* .. 61 C12
Inowrocław, *Poland* .. 17 B10

Inquisivi, *Bolivia* 78 G5
Inscription, C., *Australia* 53 E1
Insein, *Burma* 37 L20
Inta, *Russia* 22 A11
Interior, *U.S.A.* 70 D4
Interlaken, *Switz.* 16 E4
International Falls,
  U.S.A. 70 A8
Interview I., *India* 34 F2
Inthanon, Doi, *Thailand* 34 C5
Intiyaco, *Argentina* ... 80 B4
Inukjuak, *Canada* 61 C12
Inútil, B., *Chile* 80 G2
Inuvik, *Canada* 60 B6
Inveraray, *U.K.* 12 E3
Inverbervie, *U.K.* 12 E6
Invercargill, *N.Z.* 51 M2
Inverell, *Australia* 55 D5
Invergordon, *U.K.* ... 12 D4
Invermere, *Canada* ... 64 C5
Inverness, *Canada* ... 63 C7
Inverness, *U.K.* 12 D4
Inverness, *U.S.A.* 69 L4
Inverurie, *U.K.* 12 D6
Inverway, *Australia* ... 52 C4
Investigator Group,
  Australia 55 E1
Investigator Str.,
  Australia 55 F2
Inya, *Russia* 24 D9
Inyo Mts., *U.S.A.* 73 H5
Inyokern, *U.S.A.* 73 J5
Inza, *Russia* 22 D8
Iô-Jima, *Japan* 29 J5
Ioánnina, *Greece* 21 E9
Iola, *U.S.A.* 71 G7
Iona, *U.K.* 12 E2
Ione, *Calif., U.S.A.* ... 72 G3
Ione, *Wash., U.S.A.* .. 72 B5
Ionia, *U.S.A.* 68 D3
Ionian Is. = Iónioi
  Nísoi, *Greece* 21 E9
Ionian Sea, *Medit. S.* . 21 E7
Iónioi Nísoi, *Greece* .. 21 E9
Íos, *Greece* 21 F11
Iowa □, *U.S.A.* 70 D8
Iowa City, *U.S.A.* 70 D8
Iowa Falls, *U.S.A.* ... 70 D8
Ipameri, *Brazil* 79 G9
Ipatinga, *Brazil* 79 G10
Ipiales, *Colombia* 78 C3
Ipin = Yibin, *China* .. 30 D5
Ipixuna, *Brazil* 78 E4
Ipoh, *Malaysia* 34 Q14
Ippy, *C.A.R.* 45 G9
Ipsala, *Turkey* 21 D12
Ipswich, *Australia* ... 55 D5
Ipswich, *U.K.* 11 E9
Ipswich, *U.S.A.* 70 C5
Ipu, *Brazil* 79 D10
Iqaluit, *Canada* 61 B13
Iquique, *Chile* 78 H4
Iquitos, *Peru* 78 D4
Irabu-Jima, *Japan* 29 M2
Iracoubo, *Fr. Guiana* . 79 B8
Irafshān, *Iran* 39 E9
Iráklion, *Greece* 21 G11
Iran ■, *Asia* 39 C7
Iran, Gunung-Gunung,
  Malaysia 32 D4
Iran Ra. = Iran,
  Gunung-Gunung,
  Malaysia 32 D4
Īrānshahr, *Iran* 39 E9
Irapuato, *Mexico* 74 C4
Iraq ■, *Asia* 38 C5
Irbid, *Jordan* 41 C4
Irbid □, *Jordan* 41 C5
Irebu, *Zaïre* 46 E3
Ireland ■, *Europe* ... 13 D4
Ireland's Eye, *Ireland* . 13 C5
Iret, *Russia* 25 C16
Irian Jaya □, *Indonesia* 33 E9
Iringa, *Tanzania* 46 F7
Iriomote-Jima, *Japan* . 29 M1
Iriri →, *Brazil* 79 D8
Irish Republic ■,
  Europe 13 D4
Irish Sea, *U.K.* 10 D3
Irkineyeva, *Russia* ... 25 D10
Irkutsk, *Russia* 25 D11
Irma, *Canada* 65 C6
Irô-Zaki, *Japan* 29 G9
Iron Baron, *Australia* . 55 E2
Iron Gate = Portile de
  Fier, *Europe* 17 F12
Iron Knob, *Australia* . 55 E2
Iron Mountain, *U.S.A.* 68 C1
Iron Ra., *Australia* ... 54 A3
Iron River, *U.S.A.* ... 70 B10
Ironbridge, *U.K.* 11 E5
Ironstone Kopje,
  Botswana 48 D3
Ironton, *Mo., U.S.A.* . 71 G9
Ironton, *Ohio, U.S.A.* . 68 F4
Ironwood, *U.S.A.* 70 B9
Iroquois Falls, *Canada* 62 C3
Irpin, *Ukraine* 17 C16
Irrara Cr. →, *Australia* 55 D4
Irrawaddy □, *Burma* . 37 L19
Irrawaddy →, *Burma* 37 M19
Irtysh →, *Russia* 24 C7
Irumu, *Zaïre* 46 D5
Irún, *Spain* 19 A5
Irunea = Pamplona,
  Spain 19 A5
Irvine, *Canada* 65 D6
Irvine, *U.K.* 12 F4
Irvine, *U.S.A.* 68 G4
Irvinestown, *U.K.* 13 B4
Irving, *U.S.A.* 71 J6
Irwin →, *Australia* ... 53 E1
Irymple, *Australia* 55 E3

Isaac →, *Australia* ... 54 C4
Isabel, *U.S.A.* 70 C4
Isabella, *Phil.* 33 C6
Isabella Ra., *Australia* 52 D3
İsafjarðardjúp, *Iceland* 8 C2
İsafjörður, *Iceland* ... 8 C2
Isahaya, *Japan* 29 H5
Isangi, *Zaïre* 46 D4
Isar →, *Germany* 16 D7
Íschia, *Italy* 20 D5
Isdell →, *Australia* ... 52 C3
Ise, *Japan* 29 G8
Ise-Wan, *Japan* 29 G8
Isère □, *France* 18 D6
Isère →, *France* 18 D6
Isérnia, *Italy* 20 D6
Ishigaki-Shima, *Japan* 29 M2
Ishikari-Gawa →,
  Japan 28 C10
Ishikari-Sammyaku,
  Japan 28 C11
Ishikari-Wan, *Japan* .. 28 C10
Ishikawa □, *Japan* ... 29 F8
Ishim, *Russia* 24 D7
Ishim →, *Russia* 24 D8
Ishinomaki, *Japan* ... 28 E10
Ishioka, *Japan* 29 F10
Ishkuman, *Pakistan* .. 36 A8
Ishpeming, *U.S.A.* ... 68 B2
Isil Kul, *Russia* 24 D8
Isiolo, *Kenya* 46 D7
Isiro, *Zaïre* 46 D5
Isisford, *Australia* 54 C3
İskenderun, *Turkey* .. 23 G6
İskenderun Körfezi,
  Turkey 23 G6
Iskŭr →, *Bulgaria* ... 21 C11
Iskut →, *Canada* 64 B2
Isla →, *U.K.* 12 E5
Islamabad, *Pakistan* .. 36 C8
Island →, *Canada* ... 64 A4
Island Falls, *Canada* .. 62 C3
Island Falls, *U.S.A.* .. 63 C6
Island L., *Canada* 65 C10
Island Lagoon,
  Australia 55 E2
Island Pond, *U.S.A.* .. 68 C10
Islands, B. of, *Canada* 63 C8
Islay, *U.K.* 12 F2
Isle →, *France* 18 D3
Isle aux Morts, *Canada* 63 C8
Isle of Wight □, *U.K.* 11 G6
Isle Royale, *U.S.A.* ... 70 A10
Isleta, *U.S.A.* 73 J10
Ismail = Izmayil,
  Ukraine 17 F15
Ismâ'ilîya, *Egypt* 45 B11
Ismay, *U.S.A.* 70 B2
Isna, *Egypt* 45 C11
İsparta, *Turkey* 23 G5
İspica, *Italy* 20 F6
Israel ■, *Asia* 41 D3
Issoire, *France* 18 D5
Issyk-Kul, Ozero =
  Ysyk-Köl, Ozero,
  Kyrgyzstan 24 E8
Istaihah, *U.A.E.* 39 F7
İstanbul, *Turkey* 21 D13
Istiaía, *Greece* 21 E10
Istokpoga, L., *U.S.A.* . 69 M5
Istra, *Croatia* 16 F7
İstranca Dağları, *Turkey* 21 D12
Istres, *France* 18 E6
Istria = Istra, *Croatia* . 16 F7
Itabaiana, *Brazil* 79 E11
Itaberaba, *Brazil* 79 F10
Itabira, *Brazil* 79 G10
Itabuna, *Brazil* 79 F11
Itaipú, Reprêsa de,
  Brazil 80 B6
Itaituba, *Brazil* 79 D7
Itajaí, *Brazil* 80 B7
Italy ■, *Europe* 20 C5
Itampolo, *Madag.* 49 C7
Itapecuru-Mirim, *Brazil* 79 D10
Itaperuna, *Brazil* 79 H10
Itapicuru →, *Bahia,*
  Brazil 79 F11
Itapicuru →,
  Maranhão, Brazil .. 79 D10
Itapipoca, *Brazil* 79 D11
Itaquatiara, *Brazil* 78 D7
Itaquí, *Brazil* 80 B5
Itatuba, *Brazil* 78 E6
Itchen →, *U.K.* 11 G6
Ithaca = Itháki, *Greece* 21 E9
Ithaca, *U.S.A.* 68 D7
Itháki, *Greece* 21 E9
Ito, *Japan* 29 G9
Itoigawa, *Japan* 29 F8
Itonamas →, *Bolivia* . 78 F6
Ittoqqortoormiit =
  Scoresbysund,
  Greenland 4 B6
Ituaçu, *Brazil* 79 F10
Ituiutaba, *Brazil* 79 G9
Itumbiara, *Brazil* 79 G9
Ituna, *Canada* 65 C8
Iturbe, *Argentina* 80 A3
Iturup, Ostrov, *Russia* 25 E15
Itzehoe, *Germany* 16 B5
Ivaí →, *Brazil* 80 A6
Ivalo, *Finland* 8 B22
Ivalojoki →, *Finland* . 8 B22
Ivanava, *Belarus* 17 B13
Ivanhoe, *N.S.W.,*
  Australia 55 E3
Ivanhoe, *W. Austral.,*
  Australia 52 C4
Ivanhoe L., *Canada* .. 65 A7
Ivano-Frankivsk,
  Ukraine 17 D13
Ivano-Frankovsk =
  Ivano-Frankivsk,
  Ukraine 17 D13

Ivanovo = Ivanava,
  Belarus 17 B13
Ivanovo, *Russia* 22 C7
Ivato, *Madag.* 49 C8
Ivatsevichy, *Belarus* .. 17 B13
Ivdel, *Russia* 22 B11
Ivory Coast ■, *Africa* 44 G3
Ivrea, *Italy* 20 B2
Ivujivik, *Canada* 61 B12
Iwahig, *Phil.* 32 C5
Iwaizumi, *Japan* 28 E10
Iwaki, *Japan* 29 F10
Iwakuni, *Japan* 29 G6
Iwamizawa, *Japan* ... 28 C10
Iwanai, *Japan* 28 C10
Iwata, *Japan* 29 G8
Iwate □, *Japan* 28 E10
Iwate-San, *Japan* 28 E10
Iwo, *Nigeria* 44 G5
Ixiamas, *Bolivia* 78 F5
Ixopo, *S. Africa* 49 E5
Iyo, *Japan* 29 H6
Izegem, *Belgium* 15 D3
Izena-Shima, *Japan* .. 29 L3
Izhevsk, *Russia* 22 C9
Izmayil, *Ukraine* 17 F15
İzmir, *Turkey* 21 E12
İzmit, *Turkey* 23 F4
İznik Gölü, *Turkey* ... 21 D13
Izra, *Syria* 41 C5
Izu-Shotō, *Japan* 29 G10
Izumi-sano, *Japan* ... 29 G7
Izumo, *Japan* 29 G6
Izyaslav, *Ukraine* 17 C14

J

Jabal Lubnān, *Lebanon* 41 B4
Jabalpur, *India* 36 H11
Jabbūl, *Syria* 38 B3
Jablah, *Syria* 38 C3
Jablanica, *Macedonia* . 21 D9
Jablonec, *Czech.* 16 C8
Jaboatão, *Brazil* 79 E11
Jaburu, *Brazil* 78 E6
Jaca, *Spain* 19 A5
Jacareí, *Brazil* 80 A7
Jacarèzinho, *Brazil* ... 80 A7
Jackman, *U.S.A.* 63 C5
Jacksboro, *U.S.A.* 71 J5
Jackson, *Australia* ... 55 D4
Jackson, *Ala., U.S.A.* . 69 K2
Jackson, *Calif., U.S.A.* 72 G3
Jackson, *Ky., U.S.A.* .. 68 G4
Jackson, *Mich., U.S.A.* 68 D3
Jackson, *Minn., U.S.A.* 70 D7
Jackson, *Miss., U.S.A.* 71 J9
Jackson, *Mo., U.S.A.* . 71 G10
Jackson, *Ohio, U.S.A.* 68 F4
Jackson, *Tenn., U.S.A.* 69 H1
Jackson, *Wyo., U.S.A.* 72 E8
Jackson B., *N.Z.* 51 K2
Jackson L., *U.S.A.* 72 E8
Jacksons, *N.Z.* 51 K3
Jacksonville, *Ala.,*
  U.S.A. 69 J3
Jacksonville, *Fla.,*
  U.S.A. 69 K5
Jacksonville, *Ill., U.S.A.* 70 F9
Jacksonville, *N.C.,*
  U.S.A. 69 H7
Jacksonville, *Oreg.,*
  U.S.A. 72 E2
Jacksonville, *Tex.,*
  U.S.A. 71 K7
Jacksonville Beach,
  U.S.A. 69 K5
Jacmel, *Haiti* 75 D10
Jacob Lake, *U.S.A.* ... 73 H7
Jacobabad, *Pakistan* .. 36 E6
Jacobina, *Brazil* 79 F10
Jacques-Cartier, Mt.,
  Canada 63 C6
Jacundá →, *Brazil* ... 79 D8
Jadotville = Likasi,
  Zaïre 46 G5
Jādū, *Libya* 45 B7
Jaén, *Peru* 78 E3
Jaén, *Spain* 19 D4
Jaffa = Tel Aviv-Yafo,
  Israel 41 C3
Jaffa, C., *Australia* 55 F2
Jaffna, *Sri Lanka* 36 Q12
Jagadhri, *India* 36 D10
Jagdalpur, *India* 37 K12
Jagersfontein, *S. Africa* 48 D4
Jagraon, *India* 36 D9
Jagtial, *India* 36 K11
Jaguariaíva, *Brazil* 80 A7
Jaguaribe →, *Brazil* .. 79 D11
Jahrom, *Iran* 39 D7
Jailolo, *Indonesia* 33 D7
Jailolo, Selat, *Indonesia* 33 D7
Jaipur, *India* 36 F9
Jājarm, *Iran* 39 B8
Jakarta, *Indonesia* ... 33 G12
Jakobstad =
  Pietarsaari, *Finland* . 8 E20
Jal, *U.S.A.* 71 J3
Jalalabad, *Afghan.* ... 36 B7
Jalapa Enríquez,
  Mexico 74 D5
Jalasjärvi, *Finland* 9 E20
Jalgaon, *Maharashtra,*
  India 36 J10
Jalgaon, *Maharashtra,*
  India 36 J9
Jalíbah, *Iraq* 38 D5

Jalna, *India* 36 K9
Jalón →, *Spain* 19 B5
Jalpaiguri, *India* 37 F16
Jaluit I., *Pac. Oc.* 56 G8
Jalūlā, *Iraq* 38 C5
Jamaica ■, *W. Indies* . 74 J16
Jamalpur, *Bangla.* 37 G16
Jamalpur, *India* 37 G15
Jamanxim →, *Brazil* . 79 D7
Jambe, *Indonesia* 33 E8
Jambi, *Indonesia* 32 E2
Jambi □, *Indonesia* .. 32 E2
James →, *U.S.A.* 70 D6
James B., *Canada* 61 C11
James Ras., *Australia* . 52 D5
James Ross I.,
  Antarctica 5 C18
Jamestown, *Australia* . 55 E2
Jamestown, *S. Africa* . 48 E4
Jamestown, *Ky., U.S.A.* 68 G3
Jamestown, *N. Dak.,*
  U.S.A. 70 B5
Jamestown, *N.Y.,*
  U.S.A. 68 D6
Jamestown, *Tenn.,*
  U.S.A. 69 G3
Jamīlābād, *Iran* 39 C6
Jamkhandi, *India* 36 L9
Jammu, *India* 36 C9
Jammu & Kashmir □,
  India 36 B10
Jamnagar, *India* 36 H7
Jamrud, *Pakistan* 36 C7
Jämsä, *Finland* 9 F21
Jamshedpur, *India* ... 37 H15
Jämtland, *Sweden* 8 E15
Jan L., *Canada* 65 C8
Jan Mayen, *Arctic* ... 4 B7
Janakkala, *Finland* ... 9 F21
Jand, *Pakistan* 36 C8
Jandaq, *Iran* 39 C7
Jandowae, *Australia* .. 55 D5
Janesville, *U.S.A.* 70 D10
Janīn, *West Bank* 41 C4
Januária, *Brazil* 79 G10
Jaora, *India* 36 H9
Japan ■, *Asia* 29 G8
Japan, Sea of, *Asia* .. 28 E7
Japan Trench, *Pac. Oc.* 56 D6
Japen = Yapen,
  Indonesia 33 E9
Japurá →, *Brazil* 78 D5
Jaque, *Panama* 78 B3
Jarābulus, *Syria* 38 B3
Jarama →, *Spain* 19 B4
Jarash, *Jordan* 41 C4
Jargalant = Hovd,
  Mongolia 30 B4
Jarīr, W. al →,
  Si. Arabia 38 E4
Jarosław, *Poland* 17 C12
Jarrahdale, *Australia* . 53 F2
Jarso, *Ethiopia* 45 G12
Järvenpää, *Finland* ... 9 F21
Jarvis I., *Pac. Oc.* 57 H12
Jarwa, *India* 37 F13
Jāsimīyah, *Iraq* 38 C5
Jasin, *Malaysia* 34 S15
Jāsk, *Iran* 39 E8
Jasło, *Poland* 17 D11
Jasper, *Canada* 64 C5
Jasper, *Ala., U.S.A.* .. 69 J2
Jasper, *Fla., U.S.A.* ... 69 K4
Jasper, *Minn., U.S.A.* . 70 D6
Jasper, *Tex., U.S.A.* .. 71 K8
Jasper Nat. Park,
  Canada 64 C5
Jassy = Iaşi, *Romania* 17 E14
Jászberény, *Hungary* . 17 E10
Jataí, *Brazil* 79 G8
Jatibarang, *Indonesia* . 33 G13
Jatinegara, *Indonesia* . 33 G12
Játiva, *Spain* 19 C5
Jaú, *Brazil* 79 H9
Jauja, *Peru* 78 F3
Jaunpur, *India* 37 G13
Java = Jawa, *Indonesia* 33 G14
Java Sea, *Indonesia* .. 32 E3
Java Trench, *Ind. Oc.* . 56 H2
Javhlant = Ulyasutay,
  Mongolia 30 B4
Jawa, *Indonesia* 33 G14
Jay, *U.S.A.* 71 G7
Jaya, Puncak, *Indonesia* 33 E9
Jayanti, *India* 37 F16
Jayapura, *Indonesia* .. 33 E10
Jayawijaya,
  Pegunungan,
  Indonesia 33 E9
Jaynagar, *India* 37 F15
Jayrūd, *Syria* 38 C3
Jayton, *U.S.A.* 71 J4
Jazīreh-ye Shif, *Iran* . 39 D6
Jazzîn, *Lebanon* 41 B4
Jean, *U.S.A.* 73 J6
Jean Marie River,
  Canada 64 A4
Jeanerette, *U.S.A.* 71 L9
Jeannette, Ostrov,
  Russia 25 B16
Jebba, *Nigeria* 44 G5
Jebel, Bahr el →,
  Sudan 45 G11
Jedburgh, *U.K.* 12 F6
Jedda = Jiddah,
  Si. Arabia 40 C2
Jędrzejów, *Poland* ... 17 C11
Jedway, *Canada* 64 C2
Jefferson, *Iowa, U.S.A.* 70 D7
Jefferson, *Tex., U.S.A.* 71 J7
Jefferson, *Wis., U.S.A.* 70 D10
Jefferson, Mt., *Nev.,*
  U.S.A. 72 G5

Karatau

Jefferson, Mt., *Oreg., U.S.A.* 72 D3
Jefferson City, *Mo., U.S.A.* 70 F8
Jefferson City, *Tenn., U.S.A.* 69 G4
Jeffersonville, *U.S.A.* 68 F3
Jega, *Nigeria* 44 F5
Jēkabpils, *Latvia* 9 H21
Jelenia Góra, *Poland* 16 C8
Jelgava, *Latvia* 9 H20
Jellicoe, *Canada* 62 C2
Jemaja, *Indonesia* 32 D3
Jember, *Indonesia* 33 H15
Jembongan, *Malaysia* 32 C5
Jemeppe, *Belgium* 15 D5
Jena, *Germany* 16 C6
Jena, *U.S.A.* 71 K8
Jenkins, *U.S.A.* 68 G4
Jennings, *U.S.A.* 71 K8
Jennings →, *Canada* 64 B2
Jeparit, *Australia* 55 F3
Jequié, *Brazil* 79 F10
Jequitinhonha, *Brazil* 79 G10
Jequitinhonha →, *Brazil* 79 G11
Jerada, *Morocco* 44 B4
Jerantut, *Malaysia* 34 R15
Jérémie, *Haiti* 75 D10
Jerez de la Frontera, *Spain* 19 D2
Jerez de los Caballeros, *Spain* 19 C2
Jericho = Arīḩā, *Syria* 38 C3
Jericho = El Arīḩā, *West Bank* 41 D4
Jericho, *Australia* 54 C4
Jerilderie, *Australia* 55 F4
Jerome, *U.S.A.* 73 J8
Jersey, *U.K.* 11 H5
Jersey City, *U.S.A.* 68 E8
Jersey Shore, *U.S.A.* 68 E7
Jerseyville, *U.S.A.* 70 F9
Jerusalem, *Israel* 41 D4
Jervis B., *Australia* 55 F5
Jesselton = Kota Kinabalu, *Malaysia* 32 C5
Jessore, *Bangla.* 37 H16
Jesup, *U.S.A.* 69 K5
Jetmore, *U.S.A.* 71 F5
Jevnaker, *Norway* 9 F14
Jewett, *U.S.A.* 71 K6
Jeyḩūnābād, *Iran* 39 C6
Jeypore, *India* 37 K13
Jhal Jhao, *Pakistan* 36 F4
Jhalawar, *India* 36 G10
Jhang Maghiana, *Pakistan* 36 D8
Jhansi, *India* 36 G11
Jharsaguda, *India* 37 J14
Jhelum, *Pakistan* 36 C8
Jhelum →, *Pakistan* 36 D8
Jhunjhunu, *India* 36 E9
Jiamusi, *China* 31 B8
Ji'an, *China* 31 D6
Jiangcheng, *China* 30 D5
Jiangmen, *China* 31 D6
Jiangsu □, *China* 31 C7
Jiangxi □, *China* 31 D6
Jiaxing, *China* 31 C7
Jiayi, *Taiwan* 31 D7
Jibuti = Djibouti ■, *Africa* 40 E3
Jiddah, *Si. Arabia* 40 C2
Jido, *India* 37 E19
Jiggalong, *Australia* 52 D3
Jihlava, *Czech.* 16 D8
Jihlava →, *Czech.* 17 D9
Jijel, *Algeria* 44 A6
Jijiga, *Ethiopia* 40 F3
Jilin, *China* 31 B7
Jilin □, *China* 31 B7
Jilong, *Taiwan* 31 D7
Jima, *Ethiopia* 45 G12
Jiménez, *Mexico* 74 B4
Jinan, *China* 31 C6
Jindabyne, *Australia* 55 F4
Jindrichuv Hradeç, *Czech.* 16 D8
Jingdezhen, *China* 31 D6
Jinggu, *China* 30 D5
Jinhua, *China* 31 D6
Jining, *Nei Mongol Zizhiqu, China* 31 B6
Jining, *Shandong, China* 31 C6
Jinja, *Uganda* 46 D6
Jinnah Barrage, *Pakistan* 36 C7
Jinotega, *Nic.* 74 E7
Jinsha Jiang →, *China* 30 D5
Jinzhou, *China* 31 B7
Jiparaná →, *Brazil* 78 E6
Jipijapa, *Ecuador* 78 D2
Jisr ash Shughūr, *Syria* 38 C3
Jitarning, *Australia* 53 F2
Jitra, *Malaysia* 34 N13
Jiu →, *Romania* 17 F12
Jiujiang, *China* 31 D6
Jixi, *China* 31 B8
Jīzān, *Si. Arabia* 40 D3
Jizō-Zaki, *Japan* 29 G6
Jizzakh, *Uzbekistan* 24 E7
Joaçaba, *Brazil* 80 B6
João Pessoa, *Brazil* 79 E12
Joaquín V. González, *Argentina* 80 B4
Jodhpur, *India* 36 F8
Joensuu, *Finland* 22 B4
Jofane, *Mozam.* 49 C5
Jõgeva, *Estonia* 9 G22
Joggins, *Canada* 63 C7
Jogjakarta = Yogyakarta, *Indonesia* 33 G14
Johannesburg, *S. Africa* 49 D4
John Day, *U.S.A.* 72 D4
John Day →, *U.S.A.* 72 D3
John H. Kerr Reservoir, *U.S.A.* 69 G6
John o' Groats, *U.K.* 12 C5
John's Ra., *Australia* 54 C1
Johnson, *U.S.A.* 71 G4
Johnson City, *N.Y., U.S.A.* 68 D8
Johnson City, *Tenn., U.S.A.* 69 G4
Johnson City, *Tex., U.S.A.* 71 K5
Johnson's Crossing, *Canada* 64 A2
Johnston, L., *Australia* 53 F3
Johnston Falls = Mambilima Falls, *Zambia* 46 G5
Johnston I., *Pac. Oc.* 57 F11
Johnstone Str., *Canada* 64 C3
Johnstown, *N.Y., U.S.A.* 68 D8
Johnstown, *Pa., U.S.A.* 68 E6
Johor □, *Malaysia* 34 S16
Johor Baharu, *Malaysia* 34 T16
Jõhvi, *Estonia* 9 G22
Joinvile, *Brazil* 80 B7
Joinville I., *Antarctica* 5 C18
Jokkmokk, *Sweden* 8 C18
Jökulsá á Bru →, *Iceland* 8 D6
Jökulsá á Fjöllum →, *Iceland* 8 C5
Jolfā, *Āzarbājān-e Sharqī, Iran* 38 B5
Jolfā, *Eşfahan, Iran* 39 C6
Joliet, *U.S.A.* 68 E1
Joliette, *Canada* 62 C5
Jolo, *Phil.* 33 C6
Jombang, *Indonesia* 33 G15
Jome, *Indonesia* 33 E7
Jonava, *Lithuania* 9 J21
Jones Sound, *Canada* 4 B3
Jonesboro, *Ark., U.S.A.* 71 H9
Jonesboro, *Ill., U.S.A.* 71 G10
Jonesboro, *La., U.S.A.* 71 J8
Jonesport, *U.S.A.* 63 D6
Joniškis, *Lithuania* 9 H20
Jönköping, *Sweden* 9 H16
Jonquière, *Canada* 63 C5
Joplin, *U.S.A.* 71 G7
Jordan, *U.S.A.* 72 C10
Jordan ■, *Asia* 41 E5
Jordan →, *Asia* 41 D4
Jordan Valley, *U.S.A.* 72 E5
Jorhat, *India* 37 F19
Jörn, *Sweden* 8 D19
Jorong, *Indonesia* 32 E4
Jørpeland, *Norway* 9 G11
Jos, *Nigeria* 44 G6
Joseph, *U.S.A.* 72 D5
Joseph, L., *Canada* 63 B6
Joseph Bonaparte G., *Australia* 52 B4
Joseph City, *U.S.A.* 73 J8
Jostedalsbreen, *Norway* 9 F12
Jotunheimen, *Norway* 9 F13
Jourdanton, *U.S.A.* 71 L5
Joussard, *Canada* 64 B5
Juan de Fuca Str., *Canada* 72 B2
Juan de Nova, *Ind. Oc.* 49 B7
Juan Fernández, Arch. de, *Pac. Oc.* 57 L20
Juankoski, *Finland* 8 E23
Juárez, *Argentina* 80 D5
Juàzeiro, *Brazil* 79 E10
Juàzeiro do Norte, *Brazil* 79 E11
Jubayl, *Lebanon* 41 A4
Jubbah, *Si. Arabia* 38 D4
Jubbulpore = Jabalpur, *India* 36 H11
Jubilee L., *Australia* 53 E4
Juby, C., *Morocco* 44 C2
Júcar →, *Spain* 19 C5
Juchitán, *Mexico* 74 D5
Judaea = Har Yehuda, *Israel* 41 D3
Judith →, *U.S.A.* 72 C9
Judith Gap, *U.S.A.* 72 C9
Jugoslavia = Yugoslavia ■, *Europe* 21 B9
Juiz de Fora, *Brazil* 79 H10
Julesburg, *U.S.A.* 70 E3
Juli, *Peru* 78 G5
Julia Cr. →, *Australia* 54 C3
Julia Creek, *Australia* 54 C3
Juliaca, *Peru* 78 G4
Julian, *U.S.A.* 73 K5
Julianehåb, *Greenland* 4 C5
Jullundur, *India* 36 D9
Jumet, *Belgium* 15 D4
Jumilla, *Spain* 19 C5
Jumla, *Nepal* 37 E13
Jumna = Yamuna →, *India* 37 G12
Junagadh, *India* 36 J7
Junction, *Tex., U.S.A.* 71 K5
Junction, *Utah, U.S.A.* 73 G7
Junction B., *Australia* 54 A1
Junction City, *Kans., U.S.A.* 70 F6
Junction City, *Oreg., U.S.A.* 72 D2
Junction Pt., *Australia* 54 A1
Jundah, *Australia* 54 C3
Jundiaí, *Brazil* 80 A7
Juneau, *U.S.A.* 60 C6
Junee, *Australia* 55 E4
Jungfrau, *Switz.* 16 E4
Junggar Pendi, *China* 30 B3
Junín, *Argentina* 80 C4
Junín de los Andes, *Argentina* 80 D2
Jūniyah, *Lebanon* 41 B4
Juntura, *U.S.A.* 72 E4
Jupiter →, *Canada* 63 C7
Jur, Nahr el →, *Sudan* 45 G10
Jura = Schwäbische Alb, *Germany* 16 D5
Jura, *Europe* 16 E4
Jura, *U.K.* 12 F3
Jura, Sd. of, *U.K.* 12 F3
Jurado, *Colombia* 78 B3
Jurbarkas, *Lithuania* 9 J20
Jūrmala, *Latvia* 9 H20
Juruá →, *Brazil* 78 D5
Juruena →, *Brazil* 78 E7
Juruti, *Brazil* 79 D7
Justo Daract, *Argentina* 80 C3
Jutland = Jylland, *Denmark* 9 H13
Juventud, I. de la, *Cuba* 75 C8
Juwain, *Afghan.* 36 D2
Jūy Zar, *Iran* 38 C5
Jylland, *Denmark* 9 H13
Jyväskylä, *Finland* 9 E21

K

K2, Mt., *Pakistan* 36 B10
Kaap Plateau, *S. Africa* 48 D3
Kaapkruis, *Namibia* 48 C1
Kaapstad = Cape Town, *S. Africa* 48 E2
Kabaena, *Indonesia* 33 F6
Kabala, *S. Leone* 44 G2
Kabale, *Uganda* 46 E6
Kabalo, *Zaïre* 46 F5
Kabambare, *Zaïre* 46 E5
Kabanjahe, *Indonesia* 32 D1
Kabara, *Mali* 44 E4
Kabardino-Balkar Republic = Kabardino Balkaria □, *Russia* 23 F7
Kabardino Balkaria □, *Russia* 23 F7
Kabare, *Indonesia* 33 E8
Kabarega Falls, *Uganda* 46 D6
Kabasalan, *Phil.* 33 C6
Kabba, *Nigeria* 44 G6
Kabinakagami L., *Canada* 62 C3
Kabīr, Zab al →, *Iraq* 38 C4
Kabkabīyah, *Sudan* 45 F9
Kabompo →, *Zambia* 47 G4
Kabongo, *Zaïre* 46 F5
Kabra, *Australia* 54 C5
Kabūd Gonbad, *Iran* 39 B8
Kābul, *Afghan.* 36 B6
Kābul □, *Afghan.* 36 B6
Kabul →, *Pakistan* 36 C8
Kaburuang, *Indonesia* 33 D7
Kabwe, *Zambia* 47 G5
Kachchh, Gulf of, *India* 36 H6
Kachchh, Rann of, *India* 36 H7
Kachin □, *Burma* 37 F20
Kachiry, *Kazakhstan* 24 D8
Kaçkar, *Turkey* 23 F7
Kadan Kyun, *Burma* 34 F5
Kadina, *Australia* 55 E2
Kadiyevka = Stakhanov, *Ukraine* 23 E6
Kadoka, *U.S.A.* 70 D4
Kadoma, *Zimbabwe* 47 H5
Kâdugli, *Sudan* 45 F10
Kaduna, *Nigeria* 44 F6
Kaédi, *Mauritania* 44 E2
Kaelé, *Cameroon* 45 F7
Kaesŏng, *N. Korea* 31 C7
Kāf, *Si. Arabia* 38 D3
Kafakumba, *Zaïre* 46 F4
Kafan = Kapan, *Armenia* 23 G8
Kafanchan, *Nigeria* 44 G6
Kaffrine, *Senegal* 44 F1
Kafia Kingi, *Sudan* 45 G9
Kafirévs, Ákra, *Greece* 21 E11
Kafue →, *Zambia* 47 H5
Kafulwe, *Zambia* 46 F5
Kaga Bandoro, *C.A.R.* 45 G8
Kagan, *Uzbekistan* 24 F7
Kagawa □, *Japan* 29 G6
Kagoshima, *Japan* 29 J5
Kagoshima □, *Japan* 29 J5
Kagul = Cahul, *Moldova* 17 F15
Kahak, *Iran* 39 B6
Kahama, *Tanzania* 46 E6
Kahayan →, *Indonesia* 32 E4
Kahemba, *Zaïre* 46 F3
Kahniah →, *Canada* 64 B4
Kahnūj, *Iran* 39 E8
Kahoka, *U.S.A.* 70 E9
Kahoolawe, *U.S.A.* 66 H16
Kahramanmaraş, *Turkey* 23 G6
Kai, Kepulauan, *Indonesia* 33 F8
Kai Besar, *Indonesia* 33 F8
Kai Is. = Kai, Kepulauan, *Indonesia* 33 F8
Kai Kecil, *Indonesia* 33 F8
Kaiama, *Nigeria* 44 G5
Kaiapoi, *N.Z.* 51 K4
Kaieteur Falls, *Guyana* 78 B7
Kaifeng, *China* 31 C6
Kaikohe, *N.Z.* 51 F4
Kaikoura, *N.Z.* 51 K4
Kaikoura Ra., *N.Z.* 51 J4
Kailua Kona, *U.S.A.* 66 J17
Kaimana, *Indonesia* 33 E8
Kaimanawa Mts., *N.Z.* 51 H5
Kaingaroa Forest, *N.Z.* 51 H6
Kainji Res., *Nigeria* 44 F5
Kainuu, *Finland* 8 D23
Kaipara Harbour, *N.Z.* 51 G5
Kaipokok B., *Canada* 63 B8
Kaironi, *Indonesia* 33 E8
Kairouan, *Tunisia* 44 A7
Kaiserslautern, *Germany* 16 D4
Kaitaia, *N.Z.* 51 F4
Kaitangata, *N.Z.* 51 M2
Kaiwi Channel, *U.S.A.* 66 H16
Kajaani, *Finland* 8 D22
Kajabbi, *Australia* 54 B3
Kajana = Kajaani, *Finland* 8 D22
Kajang, *Malaysia* 34 S14
Kajo Kaji, *Sudan* 45 H11
Kaka, *Sudan* 45 F11
Kakabeka Falls, *Canada* 62 C2
Kakamas, *S. Africa* 48 D3
Kakamega, *Kenya* 46 D6
Kakanui Mts., *N.Z.* 51 L3
Kake, *Japan* 29 G6
Kakegawa, *Japan* 29 G9
Kakeroma-Jima, *Japan* 29 K4
Kakhovka, *Ukraine* 23 E5
Kakhovske Vdskh., *Ukraine* 23 E5
Kakinada, *India* 37 L13
Kakisa →, *Canada* 64 A5
Kakisa L., *Canada* 64 A5
Kakogawa, *Japan* 29 G7
Kakwa →, *Canada* 64 C5
Kāl Gūsheh, *Iran* 39 D8
Kal Safīd, *Iran* 38 C5
Kalabagh, *Pakistan* 36 C7
Kalabahi, *Indonesia* 33 F6
Kalabo, *Zambia* 47 G4
Kalach, *Russia* 23 D7
Kaladan →, *Burma* 37 J18
Kalahari, *Africa* 48 C3
Kalahari Gemsbok Nat. Park, *S. Africa* 48 D3
Kalajoki, *Finland* 8 D20
Kālak, *Iran* 39 E8
Kalakamati, *Botswana* 49 C4
Kalakan, *Russia* 25 D12
Kalakh, *Syria* 38 C3
Kalama, *U.S.A.* 72 D2
Kalámai, *Greece* 21 F10
Kalamata = Kalámai, *Greece* 21 F10
Kalamazoo, *U.S.A.* 68 D3
Kalamazoo →, *U.S.A.* 68 D2
Kalannie, *Australia* 53 F2
Kalāntarī, *Iran* 39 C7
Kalao, *Indonesia* 33 F6
Kalaotoa, *Indonesia* 33 F6
Kalasin, *Thailand* 34 D7
Kalat, *Pakistan* 36 E5
Kalāteh, *Iran* 39 B7
Kalāteh-ye-Ganj, *Iran* 39 E8
Kalbarri, *Australia* 53 E1
Kalce, *Slovenia* 16 F8
Kale, *Turkey* 21 F13
Kalegauk Kyun, *Burma* 37 M20
Kalemie, *Zaïre* 46 F5
Kalewa, *Burma* 37 H19
Kalgan = Zhangjiakou, *China* 31 B6
Kalgoorlie-Boulder, *Australia* 53 F3
Kaliakra, Nos, *Bulgaria* 21 C13
Kalianda, *Indonesia* 32 F3
Kalibo, *Phil.* 33 B6
Kalima, *Zaïre* 46 E5
Kalimantan, *Indonesia* 32 E4
Kalimantan Barat □, *Indonesia* 32 E4
Kalimantan Selatan □, *Indonesia* 32 E5
Kalimantan Tengah □, *Indonesia* 32 E4
Kalimantan Timur □, *Indonesia* 32 D5
Kálimnos, *Greece* 21 F12
Kalinin = Tver, *Russia* 22 C6
Kaliningrad, *Kaliningd., Russia* 9 J19
Kaliningrad, *Moskva, Russia* 22 C6
Kalinkavichy, *Belarus* 17 B15
Kalinkovichi = Kalinkavichy, *Belarus* 17 B15
Kalispell, *U.S.A.* 72 B6
Kalisz, *Poland* 17 C10
Kaliua, *Tanzania* 46 F6
Kalix, *Sweden* 8 D20
Kalix →, *Sweden* 8 D20
Kalkaska, *U.S.A.* 68 C3
Kalkfeld, *Namibia* 48 C2
Kalkfontein, *Botswana* 48 C3
Kalkrand, *Namibia* 48 C2
Kallavesi, *Finland* 8 E22
Kallsjön, *Sweden* 8 E15
Kalmar, *Sweden* 9 H17
Kalmyk Republic = Kalmykia □, *Russia* 23 E8
Kalmykia □, *Russia* 23 E8
Kalmykovo, *Kazakhstan* 23 E9
Kalocsa, *Hungary* 17 E10
Kalomo, *Zambia* 47 H5
Kaluga, *Russia* 22 D6
Kalundborg, *Denmark* 9 J14
Kalush, *Ukraine* 17 D13
Kalutara, *Sri Lanka* 36 R11
Kalya, *Russia* 22 B10
Kama →, *Russia* 22 C9
Kamaishi, *Japan* 28 E10
Kamaran, *Yemen* 40 D3
Kambalda, *Australia* 53 F3
Kambarka, *Russia* 22 C9
Kamchatka, P-ov., *Russia* 25 D16
Kamchatka Pen. = Kamchatka, P-ov., *Russia* 25 D16
Kamchiya →, *Bulgaria* 21 C12
Kamen, *Russia* 24 D9
Kamen-Rybolov, *Russia* 28 B6
Kamenjak, Rt., *Croatia* 16 F7
Kamenka, *Russia* 22 A7
Kamenka Bugskaya = Kamyanka-Buzka, *Ukraine* 17 C13
Kamensk Uralskiy, *Russia* 24 D7
Kamenskoye, *Russia* 25 C17
Kameoka, *Japan* 29 G7
Kamiah, *U.S.A.* 72 C5
Kamieskroon, *S. Africa* 48 E2
Kamilukuak, L., *Canada* 65 A8
Kamin-Kashyrskyy, *Ukraine* 17 C13
Kamina, *Zaïre* 46 F5
Kaminak L., *Canada* 65 A9
Kaminoyama, *Japan* 28 E10
Kamloops, *Canada* 64 C4
Kamo, *Japan* 28 F9
Kampala, *Uganda* 46 D6
Kampar, *Malaysia* 34 Q14
Kampar →, *Indonesia* 32 D2
Kampen, *Neths.* 15 B5
Kampot, *Cambodia* 34 G8
Kampuchea = Cambodia ■, *Asia* 34 F8
Kampung →, *Indonesia* 33 F9
Kampungbaru = Tolitoli, *Indonesia* 33 D6
Kamrau, Teluk, *Indonesia* 33 E8
Kamsack, *Canada* 65 C8
Kamskoye Vdkhr., *Russia* 22 C10
Kamuchawie L., *Canada* 65 B8
Kamui-Misaki, *Japan* 28 C10
Kamyanets-Podilskyy, *Ukraine* 17 D14
Kamyanka-Buzka, *Ukraine* 17 C13
Kāmyārān, *Iran* 38 C5
Kamyshin, *Russia* 23 D8
Kanaaupscow, *Canada* 62 B4
Kanab, *U.S.A.* 73 H7
Kanab →, *U.S.A.* 73 H7
Kanagi, *Japan* 28 D10
Kanairiktok →, *Canada* 63 A7
Kananga, *Zaïre* 46 F4
Kanarraville, *U.S.A.* 73 H7
Kanash, *Russia* 22 C8
Kanastraíon, Ákra = Palioúrion, Ákra, *Greece* 21 E10
Kanawha →, *U.S.A.* 68 F4
Kanazawa, *Japan* 29 F8
Kanchanaburi, *Thailand* 34 E5
Kanchenjunga, *Nepal* 37 F16
Kanchipuram, *India* 36 N11
Kanda Kanda, *Zaïre* 46 F4
Kandahar = Qandahār, *Afghan.* 36 D4
Kandalaksha, *Russia* 22 A5
Kandalakshkiy Zaliv, *Russia* 22 A5
Kandalu, *Afghan.* 36 E3
Kandangan, *Indonesia* 32 E5
Kandi, *Benin* 44 F5
Kandla, *India* 36 H7
Kandos, *Australia* 55 E4
Kandy, *Sri Lanka* 36 R12
Kane, *U.S.A.* 68 E6
Kane Basin, *Greenland* 4 B4
Kangān, *Fārs, Iran* 39 E7
Kangān, *Hormozgān, Iran* 39 E8
Kangar, *Malaysia* 34 N13
Kangaroo I., *Australia* 55 F2
Kangasala, *Finland* 9 F21
Kangāvar, *Iran* 39 C6
Kangean, Kepulauan, *Indonesia* 32 F5
Kangean Is. = Kangean, Kepulauan, *Indonesia* 32 F5
Kangiqsualujjuaq, *Canada* 61 C13
Kangiqsujuaq, *Canada* 61 B12
Kangirsuk, *Canada* 61 B13
Kango, *Gabon* 46 D2
Kangto, *India* 37 F18
Kaniapiskau →, *Canada* 63 A6
Kaniapiskau L., *Canada* 63 B6
Kanin, Poluostrov, *Russia* 22 A8
Kanin Nos, Mys, *Russia* 22 A7
Kanin Pen. = Kanin, Poluostrov, *Russia* 22 A8
Kaniva, *Australia* 55 F3
Kankaanpää, *Finland* 9 F20
Kankakee, *U.S.A.* 68 E2
Kankakee →, *U.S.A.* 68 E1
Kankan, *Guinea* 44 F3
Kankendy = Xankändi, *Azerbaijan* 23 G8
Kanker, *India* 37 J12
Kankunskiy, *Russia* 25 D13
Kannapolis, *U.S.A.* 69 H5
Kannauj, *India* 36 F11
Kannod, *India* 36 H10
Kano, *Nigeria* 44 F6
Kan'onji, *Japan* 29 G6
Kanowit, *Malaysia* 32 D4
Kanowna, *Australia* 53 F3
Kanoya, *Japan* 29 J5
Kanpetlet, *Burma* 37 J18
Kanpur, *India* 36 F12
Kansas □, *U.S.A.* 70 F6
Kansas →, *U.S.A.* 70 F7
Kansas City, *Kans., U.S.A.* 70 F7
Kansas City, *Mo., U.S.A.* 70 F7
Kansk, *Russia* 25 D10
Kansu = Gansu □, *China* 30 C5
Kantang, *Thailand* 34 J5
Kantō □, *Japan* 29 F9
Kantō-Sanchi, *Japan* 29 G9
Kanturk, *Ireland* 13 D3
Kanuma, *Japan* 29 F9
Kanus, *Namibia* 48 D2
Kanye, *Botswana* 48 C4
Kaohsiung = Gaoxiong, *Taiwan* 31 D7
Kaohsiung, *Taiwan* 31 D7
Kaokoveld, *Namibia* 48 B1
Kaolack, *Senegal* 44 F1
Kapan, *Armenia* 23 G8
Kapanga, *Zaïre* 46 F4
Kapchagai = Qapshaghay, *Kazakhstan* 24 E8
Kapfenberg, *Austria* 16 E8
Kapiri Mposhi, *Zambia* 47 G5
Kapiskau →, *Canada* 62 B3
Kapit, *Malaysia* 32 D4
Kapiti I., *N.Z.* 51 J5
Kapoeta, *Sudan* 45 H11
Kaposvár, *Hungary* 17 E9
Kapps, *Namibia* 48 C2
Kapsukas = Marijampolė, *Lithuania* 9 J20
Kapuas →, *Indonesia* 32 E3
Kapuas Hulu, Pegunungan, *Malaysia* 32 D4
Kapuas Hulu Ra. = Kapuas Hulu, Pegunungan, *Malaysia* 32 D4
Kapunda, *Australia* 55 E2
Kapuni, *N.Z.* 51 H5
Kapuskasing, *Canada* 62 C3
Kapuskasing →, *Canada* 62 C3
Kaputar, *Australia* 55 E5
Kara, *Russia* 24 C7
Kara Bogaz Gol, Zaliv = Garabogazköl Aylagy, *Turkmenistan* 23 F9
Kara Kalpak Republic = Karakalpakstan □, *Uzbekistan* 24 E6
Kara Kum, *Turkmenistan* 24 F6
Kara Sea, *Russia* 24 B7
Karabiğa, *Turkey* 21 D12
Karaburun, *Turkey* 21 E12
Karabutak = Qarabutaq, *Kazakhstan* 24 E7
Karacabey, *Turkey* 21 D13
Karacasu, *Turkey* 21 F13
Karachi, *Pakistan* 36 G5
Karad, *India* 36 L9
Karadeniz Boğazı, *Turkey* 21 D13
Karaganda = Qaraghandy, *Kazakhstan* 24 E8
Karagayly, *Kazakhstan* 24 E8
Karaginskiy, Ostrov, *Russia* 25 D17
Karagiye, Vpadina, *Kazakhstan* 23 F9
Karagiye Depression = Karagiye, Vpadina, *Kazakhstan* 23 F9
Karaikal, *India* 36 P11
Karaikkudi, *India* 36 P11
Karaj, *Iran* 39 C6
Karakalpakstan □, *Uzbekistan* 24 E6
Karakas, *Kazakhstan* 24 E9
Karakitang, *Indonesia* 33 D7
Karaklis = Vanadzor, *Armenia* 23 F7
Karakoram Pass, *Pakistan* 36 B10
Karakoram Ra., *Pakistan* 36 B10
Karalon, *Russia* 25 D12
Karaman, *Turkey* 23 G5
Karamay, *China* 30 B3
Karambu, *Indonesia* 32 E5
Karamea Bight, *N.Z.* 51 J3
Karand, *Iran* 38 C5
Karanganyar, *Indonesia* 33 G13
Karasburg, *Namibia* 48 D2
Karasino, *Russia* 24 C9
Karasjok, *Norway* 8 B21
Karasuk, *Russia* 24 D8
Karasuyama, *Japan* 29 F10
Karatau = Qarataū, *Kazakhstan* 24 E8

Karatau, Khrebet,
Kazakhstan 24 E7
Karawang, *Indonesia* . . 33 G12
Karawanken, *Europe* . . 16 E8
Karazhal, *Kazakhstan* . 24 E8
Karbalā, *Iraq* 38 C5
Karcag, *Hungary* 17 E11
Karda, *Russia* 25 D11
Kardhítsa, *Greece* . . . 21 E9
Kärdla, *Estonia* 9 G20
Kareeberge, *S. Africa* . 48 E3
Karelia □, *Russia* 22 A5
Karelian Republic =
Karelia □, *Russia* . . 22 A5
Karen, *India* 34 F2
Kārevāndar, *Iran* . . . 39 E9
Kargasok, *Russia* 24 D9
Kargat, *Russia* 24 D9
Kargil, *India* 36 B10
Kargopol, *Russia* 22 B6
Karī an, *Iran* 39 E8
Kariba, L., *Zimbabwe* 47 H5
Kariba Dam, *Zimbabwe* 47 H5
Kariba Gorge, *Zambia* 47 H5
Karibib, *Namibia* 48 C2
Karimata, Kepulauan,
Indonesia 32 E3
Karimata, Selat,
Indonesia 32 E3
Karimata Is. =
Karimata, Kepulauan,
Indonesia 32 E3
Karimnagar, *India* . . 36 K11
Karimunjawa,
Kepulauan, *Indonesia* 32 F3
Karin, *Somali Rep.* . . 40 E4
Karīt, *Iran* 39 C8
Kariya, *Japan* 29 G8
Karkaralinsk =
Qarqaraly,
Kazakhstan 24 E8
Karkinitska Zatoka,
Ukraine 23 E5
Karkinitskiy Zaliv =
Karkinitska Zatoka,
Ukraine 23 E5
Karl-Marx-Stadt =
Chemnitz, *Germany* 16 C7
Karlovac, *Croatia* . . . 16 F8
Karlovo, *Bulgaria* . . . 21 C11
Karlovy Vary, *Czech.* . 16 C7
Karlsbad = Karlovy
Vary, *Czech.* 16 C7
Karlsborg, *Sweden* . . . 9 G16
Karlshamn, *Sweden* . . 9 H16
Karlskoga, *Sweden* . . . 9 G16
Karlskrona, *Sweden* . . 9 H16
Karlsruhe, *Germany* . 16 D5
Karlstad, *Sweden* 9 G15
Karlstad, *U.S.A.* 70 A6
Karnal, *India* 36 E10
Karnali →, *Nepal* . 37 E12
Karnaphuli Res.,
Bangla. 37 H18
Karnataka □, *India* . 36 N10
Karnes City, *U.S.A.* . . 71 L6
Karnische Alpen,
Europe 16 E7
Kärnten □, *Austria* . 16 E8
Karonga, *Malawi* . . . 46 F6
Karoonda, *Australia* . . 55 F2
Karora, *Sudan* 45 E12
Kárpathos, *Greece* . . 21 G12
Karpinsk, *Russia* 22 C11
Karpogory, *Russia* . . . 22 B7
Karpuz Burnu =
Apostolos Andreas,
C., *Cyprus* 38 C2
Kars, *Turkey* 23 F7
Karsakpay, *Kazakhstan* 24 E7
Karshi = Qarshi,
Uzbekistan 24 F7
Karsun, *Russia* 22 D8
Kartaly, *Russia* 24 D7
Karufa, *Indonesia* . . . 33 E8
Karumba, *Australia* . . 54 B3
Karungu, *Kenya* 46 E6
Karviná, *Czech.* 17 D10
Karwar, *India* 36 M9
Kas Kong, *Cambodia* . 34 G7
Kasai →, *Zaïre* 46 E3
Kasama, *Zambia* 46 G6
Kasane, *Namibia* 48 B3
Kasanga, *Tanzania* . . 46 F6
Kasangulu, *Zaïre* . . . 46 E3
Kasaragod, *India* . . . 36 N9
Kasba L., *Canada* . . . 65 A8
Kāseh Garān, *Iran* . . 38 C5
Kasempa, *Zambia* . . . 47 G5
Kasenga, *Zaïre* 46 G5
Kashabowie, *Canada* . 62 C1
Kāshān, *Iran* 39 C6
Kashi, *China* 30 C2
Kashiwazaki, *Japan* . . 29 F9
Kashk-e Kohneh,
Afghan. 36 B3
Kāshmar, *Iran* 39 C8
Kashmir, *Asia* 36 B10
Kashun Noerh = Gaxun
Nur, *China* 30 B5
Kasimov, *Russia* 22 D7
Kasiruta, *Indonesia* . . 33 E7
Kaskaskia →, *U.S.A.* 70 G10
Kaskattama →,
Canada 65 B10
Kaskinen, *Finland* . . . 9 E19
Kaslo, *Canada* 64 D5
Kasmere L., *Canada* . . 65 B8
Kasongo, *Zaïre* 46 E5
Kasongo Lunda, *Zaïre* 46 F3
Kásos, *Greece* 21 G12
Kassalā, *Sudan* 45 E12
Kassel, *Germany* 16 C5

Kassue, *Indonesia* . . . 33 F9
Kastamonu, *Turkey* . . 23 F5
Kastoria, *Greece* 21 D9
Kasulu, *Tanzania* . . . 46 E6
Kasumi, *Japan* 29 G7
Kasur, *Pakistan* 36 D9
Kata, *Russia* 25 D11
Katako Kombe, *Zaïre* . 46 E4
Katamatite, *Australia* . 55 F4
Katanga = Shaba □,
Zaïre 46 F4
Katangi, *India* 36 J11
Katangli, *Russia* 25 D15
Kateríni, *Greece* 21 D10
Katha, *Burma* 37 G20
Katherine, *Australia* . . 52 B5
Kathiawar, *India* . . . 36 H7
Kathmandu, *Nepal* . . 37 F14
Katihar, *India* 37 G15
Katima Mulilo, *Zambia* 48 B3
Katingan =
Mendawai →,
Indonesia 32 E4
Katiola, *Ivory C.* . . . 44 G3
Katmandu, *Nepal* . . . 37 F14
Katoomba, *Australia* . . 55 E5
Katowice, *Poland* . . . 17 C10
Katrine, L., *U.K.* . . . 12 E4
Katrineholm, *Sweden* . 9 G17
Katsepe, *Madag.* 49 B8
Katsina, *Nigeria* 44 F6
Katsumoto, *Japan* . . . 29 H4
Katsuura, *Japan* 29 G10
Katsuyama, *Japan* . . . 29 F8
Kattegat, *Denmark* . . 9 H14
Katwijk-aan-Zee, *Neths.* 15 B4
Kauai, *U.S.A.* 66 H15
Kauai Channel, *U.S.A.* 66 H15
Kaufman, *U.S.A.* . . . 71 J6
Kauhajoki, *Finland* . . 9 E20
Kaukauna, *U.S.A.* . . . 68 C1
Kaukauveld, *Namibia* . 48 C3
Kaunas, *Lithuania* . . . 9 J20
Kaura Namoda, *Nigeria* 44 F6
Kautokeino, *Norway* . . 8 B20
Kavacha, *Russia* 25 C17
Kavalerovo, *Russia* . . 25 E14
Kavali, *India* 36 M12
Kaválla, *Greece* 21 D11
Kavār, *Iran* 39 D7
Kaw, *Fr. Guiana* 79 C8
Kawagoe, *Japan* 29 G9
Kawaguchi, *Japan* . . . 29 G9
Kawaihae, *U.S.A.* . . . 66 H17
Kawambwa, *Zambia* . . 46 F5
Kawanoe, *Japan* 29 G6
Kawardha, *India* 37 J12
Kawasaki, *Japan* 29 G9
Kawene, *Canada* 62 C1
Kawerau, *N.Z.* 51 H6
Kawhia Harbour, *N.Z.* 51 H5
Kawio, Kepulauan,
Indonesia 33 D7
Kawnro, *Burma* 37 H21
Kawthaung, *Burma* . . 34 G5
Kawthoolei =
Kawthule □, *Burma* 37 L20
Kawthule □, *Burma* . 37 L20
Kaya, *Burkina Faso* . . 44 F4
Kayah □, *Burma* . . . 37 K20
Kayan →, *Indonesia* . 32 D5
Kaycee, *U.S.A.* 72 E10
Kayeli, *Indonesia* . . . 33 E7
Kayenta, *U.S.A.* 73 H8
Kayes, *Mali* 44 F2
Kayoa, *Indonesia* . . . 33 D7
Kayrunnera, *Australia* . 55 E3
Kayseri, *Turkey* 23 G6
Kaysville, *U.S.A.* . . . 72 F8
Kayuagung, *Indonesia* 32 E2
Kazachye, *Russia* . . . 25 B14
Kazakhstan ■, *Asia* . . 24 E7
Kazan, *Russia* 22 C8
Kazan-Rettō, *Pac. Oc.* 56 E6
Kazanlŭk, *Bulgaria* . . 21 C11
Kazatin = Kozyatyn,
Ukraine 17 D15
Kazerūn, *Iran* 39 D6
Kazumba, *Zaïre* 46 F4
Kazuno, *Japan* 28 D10
Kazym →, *Russia* . . 24 C7
Ké-Macina, *Mali* . . . 44 F3
Kéa, *Greece* 21 F11
Keams Canyon, *U.S.A.* 73 J8
Kearney, *U.S.A.* 70 E5
Keban, *Turkey* 23 G6
Kebnekaise, *Sweden* . . 8 C18
Kebri Dehar, *Ethiopia* . 40 F3
Kebumen, *Indonesia* . 33 G13
Kecskemét, *Hungary* . 17 E10
Kedah □, *Malaysia* . . 34 P13
Kedgwick, *Canada* . . . 63 C6
Kedia Hill, *Botswana* . 48 C3
Kediniai, *Lithuania* . . 9 J21
Kediri, *Indonesia* . . . 33 G15
Kédougou, *Senegal* . . 44 F2
Keeley L., *Canada* . . . 65 C7
Keeling Is. = Cocos Is.,
Ind. Oc. 35 F8
Keelung = Chilung,
Taiwan 31 D7
Keene, *U.S.A.* 68 D9
Keeper Hill, *Ireland* . 13 D3
Keer-Weer, C., *Australia* 54 A3
Keetmanshoop,
Namibia 48 D2
Keewatin, *U.S.A.* . . . 70 B8
Keewatin □, *Canada* . 65 A9
Keewatin →, *Canada* 65 B8
Kefallinía, *Greece* . . . 21 E9
Kefamenanu, *Indonesia* 33 F6
Keffi, *Nigeria* 44 G6
Keflavík, *Iceland* . . . 8 D2

Keg River, *Canada* . . . 64 B5
Kegaska, *Canada* 63 B7
Keighley, *U.K.* 10 D6
Keila, *Estonia* 9 G21
Keimoes, *S. Africa* . . . 48 D3
Keitele, *Finland* 8 E22
Keith, *Australia* 55 F3
Keith, *U.K.* 12 D6
Keith Arm, *Canada* . . 60 B7
Kejser Franz Joseph
Fjord = Kong Franz
Joseph Fd.,
Greenland 4 B6
Kekri, *India* 36 G9
Kël, *Russia* 25 C13
Kelang, *Malaysia* . . . 34 R14
Kelantan □, *Malaysia* . 34 P15
Kelantan →, *Malaysia* 34 N15
Kelibia, *Tunisia* 45 A7
Kellé, *Congo* 46 E2
Keller, *U.S.A.* 72 B4
Kellerberrin, *Australia* 53 F2
Kellett, C., *Canada* . . 4 B1
Kellogg, *U.S.A.* 72 C5
Kells = Ceanannus
Mor, *Ireland* 13 C5
Kélo, *Chad* 45 G8
Kelowna, *Canada* . . . 64 D5
Kelsey Bay, *Canada* . . 64 C3
Kelso, *N.Z.* 51 L2
Kelso, *U.K.* 12 F6
Kelso, *U.S.A.* 72 C2
Keluang, *Malaysia* . . 34 S16
Kelvington, *Canada* . . 65 C8
Kelvin B., *U.S.A.* . . . 68 B1
Kem, *Russia* 22 B5
Kem →, *Russia* 22 B5
Kema, *Indonesia* 33 D7
Kemano, *Canada* 64 C3
Kemerovo, *Russia* . . . 24 D9
Kemi, *Finland* 8 D21
Kemi älv =
Kemijoki →, *Finland* 8 D21
Kemijärvi, *Finland* . . 8 C22
Kemijoki →, *Finland* . 8 D21
Kemmerer, *U.S.A.* . . . 72 F8
Kemp, L., *U.S.A.* . . . 71 J5
Kemp Land, *Antarctica* 5 C5
Kempsey, *Australia* . . 55 E5
Kempt, L., *Canada* . . 62 C5
Kempten, *Germany* . . 16 E6
Kemptville, *Canada* . . 62 C4
Kendal, *Indonesia* . . . 32 F4
Kendal, *U.K.* 10 C5
Kendall, *Australia* . . . 55 E5
Kendall →, *Australia* 54 A3
Kendallville, *U.S.A.* . . 68 E3
Kendari, *Indonesia* . . 33 E6
Kendawangan,
Indonesia 32 E4
Kende, *Nigeria* 44 F5
Kendenup, *Australia* . . 53 F2
Kendrapara, *India* . . 37 J15
Kendrew, *S. Africa* . . 48 E3
Kendrick, *U.S.A.* . . . 72 C5
Kenedy, *U.S.A.* 71 L6
Kenema, *S. Leone* . . . 44 G2
Keng Tawng, *Burma* . 37 J21
Keng Tung, *Burma* . . 37 J21
Kenge, *Zaïre* 46 E3
Kenhardt, *S. Africa* . . 48 D3
Kenitra, *Morocco* . . . 44 B3
Khān Ābū Shāmat,
Syria 41 B5
Kenmare, *Ireland* . . . 13 E2
Kenmare, *U.S.A.* . . . 70 A3
Kenmare →, *Ireland* . 13 E2
Kennebec, *U.S.A.* . . . 70 D5
Kennedy Ra., *Australia* 53 D2
Kennedy Taungdeik,
Burma 37 H18
Kennet →, *U.K.* . . . 11 F7
Kenneth Ra., *Australia* 52 D2
Kennett, *U.S.A.* 71 G9
Kennewick, *U.S.A.* . . 72 C4
Kénogami, *Canada* . . 63 C5
Kenogami →, *Canada* 62 B3
Kenora, *Canada* 65 D10
Kenosha, *U.S.A.* 68 D2
Kensington, *Canada* . . 63 C7
Kensington, *U.S.A.* . . 70 F5
Kensington Downs,
Australia 54 C3
Kent, *Ohio, U.S.A.* . . 68 E5
Kent, *Oreg., U.S.A.* . . 72 D3
Kent, *Tex., U.S.A.* . . . 71 K2
Kent □, *U.K.* 11 F8
Kent Group, *Australia* . 54 F4
Kent Pen., *Canada* . . 60 B9
Kentau, *Kazakhstan* . . 24 E7
Kentland, *U.S.A.* . . . 68 E2
Kenton, *U.S.A.* 68 E4
Kentucky □, *U.S.A.* . . 68 G3
Kentucky →, *U.S.A.* . 68 F3
Kentucky L., *U.S.A.* . . 69 G2
Kentville, *Canada* . . . 63 C7
Kentwood, *U.S.A.* . . . 71 K9
Kenya ■, *Africa* 46 D7
Kenya, Mt., *Kenya* . . 46 E7
Keokuk, *U.S.A.* 70 E9
Kepi, *Indonesia* 33 F9
Kerala □, *India* 36 P10
Kerama-Rettō, *Japan* . 29 L3
Kerang, *Australia* . . . 55 F3
Keraudren, C., *Australia* 52 C2
Kerava, *Finland* 9 F21
Kerch, *Ukraine* 23 E6
Kerchoual, *Mali* 44 E5
Kerguelen, *Ind. Oc.* . . 35 J5
Kericho, *Kenya* 46 E7
Kerinci, *Indonesia* . . . 32 E2
Kerki, *Turkmenistan* . 24 F7
Kérkira, *Greece* 21 E8
Kerkrade, *Neths.* . . . 15 D6
Kermadec Is., *Pac. Oc.* 56 K10

Kermadec Trench,
Pac. Oc. 56 L10
Kermān, *Iran* 39 D8
Kermān □, *Iran* 39 D8
Kermānshāh =
Bākhtarān, *Iran* . . 38 C5
Kerme Körfezi, *Turkey* 21 F12
Kermit, *U.S.A.* 71 K3
Kern →, *U.S.A.* 73 J4
Kerrobert, *Canada* . . . 65 C7
Kerrville, *U.S.A.* 71 K5
Kerry □, *Ireland* 13 D2
Kerry Hd., *Ireland* . . 13 D2
Kertosono, *Indonesia* . 33 G15
Kerulen →, *Asia* . . . 31 B6
Kerzaz, *Algeria* 44 C4
Kesagami →, *Canada* 62 B4
Kesagami L., *Canada* . 62 B3
Keşan, *Turkey* 21 D12
Kesennuma, *Japan* . . 28 E10
Keshit, *Iran* 39 D8
Kestell, *S. Africa* . . . 49 D4
Kestenga, *Russia* . . . 22 A5
Keswick, *U.K.* 10 C4
Ket →, *Russia* 24 D9
Keta, *Ghana* 44 G5
Ketapang, *Indonesia* . 32 E4
Ketchikan, *U.S.A.* . . . 60 C6
Ketchum, *U.S.A.* . . . 72 E6
Kętrzyn, *Poland* 17 A11
Kettering, *U.K.* 11 E7
Kettle →, *Canada* . . 65 B11
Kettle Falls, *U.S.A.* . . 72 B4
Keuruu, *Finland* 9 E21
Kevin, *U.S.A.* 72 B8
Kewanee, *U.S.A.* 70 E10
Kewaunee, *U.S.A.* . . . 68 C2
Keweenaw B., *U.S.A.* . 68 B1
Keweenaw Pen., *U.S.A.* 68 B2
Keweenaw Pt., *U.S.A.* 68 B2
Key Harbour, *Canada* . 62 C3
Key West, *U.S.A.* . . . 67 F10
Keyser, *U.S.A.* 68 F6
Keystone, *U.S.A.* . . . 70 D3
Kezhma, *Russia* 25 D11
Khabarovo, *Russia* . . 22 A12
Khabarovsk, *Russia* . . 25 E14
Khabr, *Iran* 39 D8
Khābūr →, *Syria* . . . 38 C4
Khairpur, *Pakistan* . . 36 F6
Khakassia □, *Russia* . 24 D9
Khakhea, *Botswana* . . 48 C3
Khalafābād, *Iran* . . . 39 D6
Khalīlī, *Iran* 39 E7
Khalkhāl, *Iran* 39 B6
Khalkís, *Greece* 21 E10
Khalmer-Sede =
Tazovskiy, *Russia* . . 24 C8
Khalmer Yu, *Russia* . 22 A12
Khalturin, *Russia* . . . 22 C8
Khalūf, *Oman* 40 C6
Kham Keut, *Laos* . . . 34 C8
Khamas Country,
Botswana 48 C4
Khambat, G. of, *India* 36 J8
Khambhat, *India* . . . 36 H8
Khamīr, *Iran* 39 E7
Khamir, *Yemen* 40 D3
Khamsa, *Egypt* 41 E1
Khān Azād, *Iraq* . . . 38 C5
Khān Mujiddah, *Iraq* 38 C4
Khān Shaykhūn, *Syria* 38 C3
Khān Yūnis, *Gaza Strip* 41 D3
Khānaqīn, *Iraq* 38 C5
Khānbāghī, *Iran* 39 B7
Khandwa, *India* 36 J10
Khandyga, *Russia* . . . 25 C14
Khāneh, *Iran* 38 B5
Khanewal, *Pakistan* . . 36 D7
Khaniá, *Greece* 21 G11
Khanión, Kólpos,
Greece 21 G10
Khanka, Ozero, *Asia* . 25 E14
Khankendy =
Xankändi, *Azerbaijan* 23 G8
Khanty-Mansiysk,
Russia 24 C7
Khapcheranga, *Russia* 25 E12
Kharagpur, *India* . . . 37 H15
Kharan Kalat, *Pakistan* 36 E4
Kharānaq, *Iran* 39 C7
Kharda, *India* 36 K9
Khārga, El Wâhât el,
Egypt 45 C11
Khargon, *India* 36 J9
Khārk, Jazireh, *Iran* . 39 D6
Kharkiv, *Ukraine* . . . 23 E6
Kharkov = Kharkiv,
Ukraine 23 E6
Kharovsk, *Russia* . . . 22 C7
Kharta, *Turkey* 21 D13
Khartoum = El
Khartûm, *Sudan* . . 45 E11
Khasan, *Russia* 28 C5
Khāsh, *Iran* 36 E2
Khashm el Girba,
Sudan 45 E12
Khaskovo, *Bulgaria* . . 21 D11
Khatanga, *Russia* . . . 25 B11
Khatanga →, *Russia* . 25 B11
Khātūnābād, *Iran* . . . 39 C6
Khatyrka, *Russia* . . . 25 C18
Khaybar, Harrat,
Si. Arabia 38 C4
Khāzimiyah, *Iraq* . . . 38 C4
Khed Brahma, *India* . 36 G8
Khemarak Phouminville
= Kampong Som,
Cambodia 34 G7
Khemelnik, *Ukraine* . 17 D14
Khemmarat, *Thailand* 34 D8
Khenāmān, *Iran* 39 D8
Khenchela, *Algeria* . . 44 A6
Khenifra, *Morocco* . . 44 B3

Kherson, *Ukraine* . . . 23 E5
Kheta →, *Russia* . . . 25 B11
Khilok, *Russia* 25 D12
Khíos, *Greece* 21 E12
Khirbat Qanāfār,
Lebanon 41 B4
Khiuma = Hiiumaa,
Estonia 9 G20
Khiva, *Uzbekistan* . . 24 E7
Khīyāv, *Iran* 38 B5
Khlong →, *Thailand* . 34 E5
Khmelnitskiy =
Khmelnytskyy,
Ukraine 17 D14
Khmelnytskyy, *Ukraine* 17 D14
Khmer Rep. =
Cambodia ■, *Asia* . 34 F8
Khodoriv, *Ukraine* . . 17 D13
Khodzent =
Khudzhand, *Tajikistan* 24 E7
Khojak P., *Afghan.* . . 36 D5
Kholm, *Russia* 22 C5
Kholmsk, *Russia* 25 E15
Khomas Hochland,
Namibia 48 C2
Khomeyn, *Iran* 39 C6
Khon Kaen, *Thailand* . 34 D7
Khong, *Cambodia* . . . 34 E8
Khong →, *Laos* 34 E9
Khonuu, *Russia* 25 C15
Khoper →, *Russia* . . 24 E5
Khóra Sfakíon, *Greece* 21 G11
Khorāsān □, *Iran* . . . 39 C8
Khorixas, *Namibia* . . 48 C1
Khorramābād,
Khorāsān, Iran . . . 39 C8
Khorramābād,
Lorestān, Iran . . . 39 C6
Khorramshahr, *Iran* . 39 D6
Khorugh, *Tajikistan* . . 24 F8
Khosravī, *Iran* 39 D6
Khosrowābād,
Khuzestān, Iran . . 39 D6
Khosrowābād,
Kordestān, Iran . . 38 C5
Khosūyeh, *Iran* 39 D7
Khotyn, *Ukraine* . . . 17 D14
Khouribga, *Morocco* . 44 B3
Khowai, *Bangla.* 37 G17
Khoyniki, *Belarus* . . . 17 C15
Khu Khan, *Thailand* . 34 E8
Khudzhand, *Tajikistan* 24 E7
Khuff, *Si. Arabia* . . . 38 E5
Khūgīānī, *Afghan.* . . 36 D4
Khulna, *Bangla.* 37 H16
Khulna □, *Bangla.* . . 37 H16
Khumago, *Botswana* . 48 C3
Khūnsorkh, *Iran* 39 E8
Khūr, *Iran* 39 C8
Khurayş, *Si. Arabia* . 39 E6
Khūrīyā Mūrīyā, Jazā
'ir, *Oman* 40 D6
Khūsf, *Iran* 39 C8
Khush, *Afghan.* 36 C3
Khushab, *Pakistan* . . 36 C8
Khust, *Ukraine* 17 D12
Khuzdar, *Pakistan* . . 36 F5
Khūzestān □, *Iran* . . 39 D6
Khvājeh, *Iran* 38 B5
Khvānsār, *Iran* 39 D7
Khvor, *Iran* 39 C7
Khvorgū, *Iran* 39 E8
Khvormūj, *Iran* 39 D6
Khvoy, *Iran* 38 B5
Khyber Pass, *Afghan.* 36 B7
Kiama, *Australia* 55 E5
Kiamba, *Phil.* 33 C6
Kiangsi = Jiangxi □,
China 31 D6
Kiangsu = Jiangsu □,
China 31 C7
Kibangou, *Congo* . . . 46 E2
Kibombo, *Zaïre* 46 E5
Kibondo, *Tanzania* . . 46 E6
Kibwesa, *Tanzania* . . 46 F5
Kibwezi, *Kenya* 46 E7
Kichiga, *Russia* 25 D17
Kicking Horse Pass,
Canada 64 C5
Kidal, *Mali* 44 E5
Kidderminster, *U.K.* . 11 E5
Kidnappers, C., *N.Z.* . 51 H6
Kidston, *Australia* . . . 54 B3
Kiel, *Germany* 16 A6
Kiel Kanal = Nord-
Ostsee-Kanal →,
Germany 16 A5
Kielce, *Poland* 17 C11
Kieler Bucht, *Germany* 16 A6
Kiev = Kyyiv, *Ukraine* 17 C16
Kiffa, *Mauritania* . . . 44 E2
Kifrī, *Iraq* 38 C5
Kigali, *Rwanda* 46 E6
Kigoma-Ujiji, *Tanzania* 46 E5
Kihee, *Australia* 55 D3
Kihnu, *Estonia* 9 G21
Kii-Sanchi, *Japan* . . . 29 G7
Kii-Suidō, *Japan* . . . 29 H7
Kiaga-Shima, *Japan* . 29 K4
Kikinda, *Serbia, Yug.* 21 F9
Kikládhes, *Greece* . . . 21 F11
Kikwit, *Zaïre* 46 E3
Kilauea Crater, *U.S.A.* 66 J17
Kilcoy, *Australia* 55 D5
Kildare, *Ireland* 13 C5
Kildare □, *Ireland* . . 13 C5
Kilgore, *U.S.A.* 71 J7
Kilimanjaro, *Tanzania* 46 E7
Kilindini, *Kenya* 46 E7

Kiliya, *Ukraine* 17 F15
Kilkee, *Ireland* 13 D2
Kilkenny, *Ireland* . . . 13 D4
Kilkenny □, *Ireland* . . 13 D4
Kilkieran B., *Ireland* . 13 C2
Kilkís, *Greece* 21 D10
Killala, *Ireland* 13 B2
Killala B., *Ireland* . . . 13 B2
Killaloe, *Ireland* 13 D3
Killam, *Canada* 64 C6
Killarney, *Australia* . . 55 D5
Killarney, *Canada* . . . 62 C3
Killarney, *Ireland* . . . 13 D2
Killarney, Lakes of,
Ireland 13 E2
Killary Harbour, *Ireland* 13 C2
Killdeer, *Canada* . . . 65 D7
Killdeer, *U.S.A.* 70 B3
Killeen, *U.S.A.* 71 K6
Killiecrankie, Pass of,
U.K. 12 E5
Killin, *U.K.* 12 E4
Killíni, *Greece* 21 F10
Killybegs, *Ireland* . . . 13 B3
Kilmarnock, *U.K.* . . . 12 F4
Kilmore, *Australia* . . . 55 F3
Kilosa, *Tanzania* 46 F7
Kilrush, *Ireland* 13 D2
Kilwa Kivinje, *Tanzania* 46 F7
Kim, *U.S.A.* 71 G3
Kimaam, *Indonesia* . . 33 F9
Kimba, *Australia* 55 E2
Kimball, *Nebr., U.S.A.* 70 E3
Kimball, *S. Dak., U.S.A.* 70 D5
Kimberley, *S. Africa* . 48 D3
Kimberley Downs,
Australia 52 C3
Kimberly, *U.S.A.* . . . 72 E6
Kimry, *Russia* 22 C6
Kimsquit, *Canada* . . . 64 C3
Kinabalu, Gunong,
Malaysia 32 C5
Kinaskan L., *Canada* . 64 B2
Kinbasket L., *Canada* . 64 C5
Kincaid, *Canada* 65 D7
Kincardine, *Canada* . . 62 D3
Kinder Scout, *U.K.* . . 10 D6
Kindersley, *Canada* . . 65 C7
Kindia, *Guinea* 44 G2
Kindu, *Zaïre* 46 E5
Kineshma, *Russia* . . . 22 C7
King, L., *Australia* . . . 53 F2
King, Mt., *Australia* . . 54 D4
King City, *U.S.A.* . . . 73 H3
King Cr. →, *Australia* 54 C2
King Edward →,
Australia 52 B4
King Frederick VI Land
= Kong Frederik VI.s
Kyst, *Greenland* . . . 4 C5
King George B., *Falk. Is.* 80 G4
King George I.,
Antarctica 5 C18
King George Is.,
Canada 61 C11
King I. = Kadan Kyun,
Burma 34 F5
King I., *Australia* . . . 54 F3
King I., *Canada* 64 C3
King Leopold Ras.,
Australia 52 C4
King Sd., *Australia* . . 52 C3
King William I., *Canada* 60 B10
King William's Town,
S. Africa 48 E4
Kingaroy, *Australia* . . 55 D5
Kingfisher, *U.S.A.* . . . 71 H6
Kingirbān, *Iraq* 38 C5
Kingisepp =
Kuressaare, *Estonia* 9 G20
Kingman, *Ariz., U.S.A.* 73 J6
Kingman, *Kans., U.S.A.* 71 G5
Kingoonya, *Australia* . 55 E2
Kings →, *U.S.A.* . . . 73 H4
Kings Canyon National
Park, *U.S.A.* 73 H4
King's Lynn, *U.K.* . . . 10 E8
Kings Mountain, *U.S.A.* 69 H5
King's Peak, *U.S.A.* . . 72 F8
Kingsbridge, *U.K.* . . . 11 G4
Kingsburg, *U.S.A.* . . . 73 H4
Kingscote, *Australia* . . 55 F2
Kingscourt, *Ireland* . . 13 C5
Kingsley, *U.S.A.* 70 D7
Kingsport, *U.S.A.* . . . 69 G4
Kingston, *Canada* . . . 62 D4
Kingston, *Jamaica* . . . 74 K17
Kingston, *N.Z.* 51 L2
Kingston, *N.Y., U.S.A.* 68 E8
Kingston, *Pa., U.S.A.* . 68 E8
Kingston South East,
Australia 55 F2
Kingston upon Hull,
U.K. 10 D7
Kingston-upon-Thames,
U.K. 11 F7
Kingstown, *St. Vincent* 74 P20
Kingstree, *U.S.A.* . . . 69 J6
Kingsville, *Canada* . . 62 D3
Kingsville, *U.S.A.* . . . 71 M6
Kingussie, *U.K.* 12 D4
Kınık, *Turkey* 21 E12
Kinistino, *Canada* . . . 65 C7
Kinkala, *Congo* 46 E2
Kinki □, *Japan* 29 H8
Kinleith, *N.Z.* 51 H5
Kinna, *Sweden* 9 H15
Kinnaird, *Canada* . . . 64 D5
Kinnairds Hd., *U.K.* . 12 D7
Kinnarodden, *Norway* 6 A11
Kinoje →, *Canada* . . 62 B3
Kinomoto, *Japan* . . . 29 G8

Kinross, U.K. 12 E5
Kinsale, Ireland 13 E3
Kinsale, Old Hd. of, Ireland 13 E3
Kinsha = Chang Jiang →, China 31 C7
Kinshasa, Zaïre 46 E3
Kinsley, U.S.A. 71 G5
Kinston, U.S.A. 69 H7
Kintampo, Ghana 44 G4
Kintap, Indonesia 32 E5
Kintore Ra., Australia 52 D4
Kintyre, U.K. 12 F3
Kintyre, Mull of, U.K. 12 F3
Kinushseo →, Canada 62 A3
Kinuso, Canada 64 B5
Kiosk, Canada 62 C4
Kiowa, Kans., U.S.A. 71 G5
Kiowa, Okla., U.S.A. 71 H7
Kipahigan L., Canada 65 B8
Kiparissía, Greece 21 F9
Kiparissiakós Kólpos, Greece 21 F9
Kipembawe, Tanzania 46 F6
Kipili, Tanzania 46 F6
Kipling, Canada 65 C8
Kippure, Ireland 13 C5
Kipushi, Zaïre 47 G5
Kirensk, Russia 25 D11
Kirgella Rocks, Australia 53 F3
Kirghizia = Kyrgyzstan ■, Asia 24 E8
Kirghizstan = Kyrgyzstan ■, Asia 24 E8
Kirgiziya Steppe, Eurasia 23 D10
Kiri, Zaïre 46 E3
Kiribati ■, Pac. Oc. 56 H10
Kırıkkale, Turkey 23 G5
Kirillov, Russia 22 C6
Kirin = Jilin, China 31 B7
Kirin = Jilin □, China 31 B7
Kiritimati, Kiribati 57 G12
Kirkcaldy, U.K. 12 E5
Kirkcudbright, U.K. 12 G4
Kirkee, India 36 K8
Kirkenes, Norway 8 B23
Kirkintilloch, U.K. 12 F4
Kirkjubæjarklaustur, Iceland 8 E4
Kirkkonummi, Finland 9 F21
Kirkland, U.S.A. 73 J7
Kirkland Lake, Canada 62 C3
Kırklareli, Turkey 21 D12
Kirksville, U.S.A. 70 E8
Kirkūk, Iraq 38 C5
Kirkwall, U.K. 12 C6
Kirkwood, S. Africa 48 E4
Kirov, Russia 24 D5
Kirovabad = Gäncä, Azerbaijan 23 F8
Kirovakan = Vanadzor, Armenia 23 F7
Kirovograd = Kirovohrad, Ukraine 23 E5
Kirovohrad, Ukraine 23 E5
Kirovsk = Babadayhan, Turkmenistan 24 F7
Kirovsk, Russia 22 A5
Kirovskiy, Kamchatka, Russia 25 D16
Kirovskiy, Sib., Russia 28 B6
Kirriemuir, U.K. 12 E6
Kirsanov, Russia 22 D7
Kırşehir, Turkey 23 G5
Kirthar Range, Pakistan 36 F5
Kiruna, Sweden 8 C19
Kirundu, Zaïre 46 E5
Kirup, Australia 53 F2
Kiryū, Japan 29 F9
Kisangani, Zaïre 46 D5
Kisar, Indonesia 33 F7
Kisaran, Indonesia 32 D1
Kisarazu, Japan 29 G9
Kiselevsk, Russia 24 D9
Kishanganj, India 37 F16
Kishangarh, India 36 F7
Kishinev = Chişinău, Moldova 17 E15
Kishiwada, Japan 29 G7
Kishtwar, India 36 C9
Kisii, Kenya 46 E6
Kisiju, Tanzania 46 F7
Kiska I., U.S.A. 60 C1
Kiskatinaw →, Canada 64 B4
Kiskittogisu L., Canada 65 C9
Kiskörös, Hungary 17 E10
Kiskunfélegyháza, Hungary 17 E10
Kiskunhalas, Hungary 17 E10
Kislovodsk, Russia 23 F7
Kiso-Gawa →, Japan 29 G8
Kiso-Sammyaku, Japan 29 G8
Kisofukushima, Japan 29 G8
Kissidougou, Guinea 44 G2
Kissimmee, U.S.A. 69 L5
Kissimmee →, U.S.A. 69 M5
Kississing L., Canada 65 B8
Kisumu, Kenya 46 E6
Kit Carson, U.S.A. 70 F3
Kita, Mali 44 F3
Kitab, Uzbekistan 24 F7
Kitaibaraki, Japan 29 F10
Kitakami, Japan 28 E10
Kitakami-Gawa →, Japan 28 E10
Kitakami-Sammyaku, Japan 28 E10
Kitakata, Japan 28 F9
Kitakyūshū, Japan 29 H5
Kitale, Kenya 46 D7
Kitami, Japan 28 C11
Kitami-Sammyaku, Japan 28 B11
Kitchener, Australia 53 F3
Kitchener, Canada 62 D3
Kitega = Gitega, Burundi 46 E5
Kitgum, Uganda 46 D6
Kíthira, Greece 21 F10
Kíthnos, Greece 21 F11
Kitikmeot □, Canada 60 A9
Kitimat, Canada 64 C3
Kitinen →, Finland 8 C22
Kitsuki, Japan 29 H5
Kittakittaooloo, L., Australia 55 D2
Kittanning, U.S.A. 68 E6
Kittery, U.S.A. 68 D10
Kittilä, Finland 8 C21
Kitui, Kenya 46 E7
Kitwe, Zambia 47 G5
Kivertsi, Ukraine 17 C13
Kivu, L., Zaïre 46 E5
Kiyev = Kyyiv, Ukraine 17 C16
Kiyevskoye Vdkhr. = Kyyivske Vdskh., Ukraine 17 C16
Kizel, Russia 22 C10
Kızıl Irmak →, Turkey 23 F6
Kizlyar, Russia 23 F8
Kizyl-Arvat = Gyzylarbat, Turkmenistan 24 F6
Kjölur, Iceland 8 D4
Kladno, Czech. 16 C8
Klagenfurt, Austria 16 E8
Klaipeda, Lithuania 9 J19
Klaksvík, Færoe Is. 8 E9
Klamath →, U.S.A. 72 F1
Klamath Falls, U.S.A. 72 E3
Klamath Mts., U.S.A. 72 F2
Klappan →, Canada 64 B3
Klarälven →, Sweden 9 G15
Klaten, Indonesia 33 G14
Klatovy, Czech. 16 D7
Klawer, S. Africa 48 E2
Klawock, U.S.A. 64 B2
Kleena Kleene, Canada 64 C4
Klein, U.S.A. 72 C9
Klein-Karas, Namibia 48 D2
Klerksdorp, S. Africa 48 D4
Kletsk = Klyetsk, Belarus 17 B14
Kletskiy, Russia 24 E5
Klickitat, U.S.A. 72 D3
Klin, Russia 24 D4
Klinaklini →, Canada 64 C3
Klipdale, S. Africa 48 E2
Klipplaat, S. Africa 48 E3
Kłodzko, Poland 17 C9
Klondike, Canada 60 B6
Klouto, Togo 44 G5
Kluane L., Canada 60 B6
Kluczbork, Poland 17 C10
Klyetsk, Belarus 17 B14
Klyuchevskaya, Gora, Russia 25 D17
Knaresborough, U.K. 10 C6
Knee L., Man., Canada 65 B10
Knee L., Sask., Canada 65 B7
Knight Inlet, Canada 64 C3
Knighton, U.K. 11 E4
Knights Landing, U.S.A. 72 G3
Knob, C., Australia 53 F2
Knockmealdown Mts., Ireland 13 D4
Knokke, Belgium 15 C3
Knossós, Greece 21 G11
Knox, U.S.A. 68 E2
Knox, C., Canada 64 C2
Knox City, U.S.A. 71 J5
Knox Coast, Antarctica 5 C8
Knoxville, Iowa, U.S.A. 70 E8
Knoxville, Tenn., U.S.A. 69 H4
Knysna, S. Africa 48 E3
Ko Chang, Thailand 34 F7
Ko Kut, Thailand 34 G7
Ko Phra Thong, Thailand 34 H5
Ko Tao, Thailand 34 G5
Koartac = Quaqtaq, Canada 61 B13
Koba, Aru, Indonesia 33 F8
Koba, Bangka, Indonesia 32 E3
Kobarid, Slovenia 16 E7
Kobayashi, Japan 29 J5
Kobdo = Hovd, Mongolia 30 B4
Kōbe, Japan 29 G7
København, Denmark 9 J15
Kōbi-Sho, Japan 29 M1
Koblenz, Germany 16 C4
Kobroor, Kepulauan, Indonesia 33 F8
Kobryn, Belarus 17 B13
Kocaeli = İzmit, Turkey 23 F4
Kočani, Macedonia 21 D10
Koch Bihar, India 37 F16
Kocheya, Russia 25 D13
Kōchi, Japan 29 H6
Kōchi □, Japan 29 H6
Kochiu = Gejiu, China 30 D5
Kodiak, U.S.A. 60 C4
Kodiak I., U.S.A. 60 C4
Kodiang, Malaysia 34 N13
Koes, Namibia 48 D2
Koffiefontein, S. Africa 48 D4
Kofiau, Indonesia 33 E7
Koforidua, Ghana 44 G4
Kōfu, Japan 29 G9
Koga, Japan 29 F9
Kogaluk →, Canada 63 A7
Kogan, Australia 55 D5
Køge, Denmark 9 J15
Koh-i-Bābā, Afghan. 36 B5
Kohat, Pakistan 36 C7
Kohima, India 37 G19
Kohkīlūyeh va Būyer Aḥmadi □, Iran 39 D6
Kohler Ra., Antarctica 5 D15
Kohtla-Järve, Estonia 9 G22
Koillismaa, Finland 8 D23
Kojonup, Australia 53 F2
Kojūr, Iran 39 B6
Kokand = Qŭqon, Uzbekistan 24 E8
Kokanee Glacier Prov. Park, Canada 64 D5
Kokas, Indonesia 33 E8
Kokchetav = Kökshetaū, Kazakhstan 24 D7
Kokemäenjoki →, Finland 9 F19
Kokkola, Finland 8 E20
Koko Kyunzu, Burma 34 E2
Kokomo, U.S.A. 68 E2
Kokonau, Indonesia 33 E9
Kökshetaū, Kazakhstan 24 D7
Koksoak →, Canada 61 C13
Kokstad, S. Africa 49 E4
Kokubu, Japan 29 J5
Kokuora, Russia 25 B15
Kola, Indonesia 33 F8
Kola, Russia 22 A5
Kola Pen. = Kolskiy Poluostrov, Russia 22 A6
Kolaka, Indonesia 33 E6
Kolar, India 36 N11
Kolar Gold Fields, India 36 N11
Kolari, Finland 8 C20
Kolayat, India 36 F8
Kolchugino = Leninsk-Kuznetskiy, Russia 24 D9
Kolda, Senegal 44 F2
Kolding, Denmark 9 J13
Kole, Zaïre 46 E4
Kolepom = Yos Sudarso, Pulau, Indonesia 33 F9
Kolguyev, Ostrov, Russia 22 A8
Kolhapur, India 36 L9
Kolín, Czech. 16 C8
Kolkas Rags, Latvia 9 H20
Kolmanskop, Namibia 48 D2
Köln, Germany 16 C4
Koło, Poland 17 B10
Kołobrzeg, Poland 16 A8
Kolokani, Mali 44 F3
Kolomna, Russia 22 C6
Kolomyya, Ukraine 17 D13
Kolonodale, Indonesia 33 E6
Kolosib, India 37 G18
Kolpashevo, Russia 24 D9
Kolpino, Russia 22 C5
Kolskiy Poluostrov, Russia 22 A6
Kolskiy Zaliv, Russia 22 A5
Kolwezi, Zaïre 46 G5
Kolyma →, Russia 25 C17
Kolymskoye, Okhotsko, Russia 25 C16
Kolymskoye Nagorye, Russia 25 C16
Komandorskiye Is. = Komandorskiye Ostrova, Russia 25 D17
Komandorskiye Ostrova, Russia 25 D17
Komárno, Slovak Rep. 17 E10
Komatipoort, S. Africa 49 D5
Komatsu, Japan 29 F8
Komatsujima, Japan 29 H7
Komi □, Russia 22 B10
Kommunarsk = Alchevsk, Ukraine 23 E6
Kommunizma, Pik, Tajikistan 24 F8
Komodo, Indonesia 33 F5
Komono, Congo 46 E2
Komoran, Pulau, Indonesia 33 F9
Komoro, Japan 29 F9
Komotini, Greece 21 D11
Kompasberg, S. Africa 48 E3
Kompong Cham, Cambodia 34 F8
Kompong Chhnang, Cambodia 34 F8
Kompong Som, Cambodia 34 G7
Kompong Speu, Cambodia 34 G8
Kompong Thom, Cambodia 34 F8
Komrat = Comrat, Moldova 17 E15
Komsberg, S. Africa 48 E3
Komsomolets, Ostrov, Russia 25 A10
Komsomolsk, Russia 25 D14
Konarhá □, Afghan. 36 B7
Konārī, Iran 39 D6
Konawa, U.S.A. 71 H6
Konch, India 36 G11
Kondakovo, Russia 25 C16
Kondinin, Australia 53 F2
Kondoa, Tanzania 46 E7
Kondopaga, Russia 22 B5
Kondratyevo, Russia 25 D10
Konduga, Nigeria 45 F7
Köneürgench, Turkmenistan 24 E6
Konevo, Russia 22 B6
Kong, Ivory C. 44 G4
Kong, Koh, Cambodia 34 G7
Kong Christian IX.s Land, Greenland 4 C6
Kong Christian X.s Land, Greenland 4 B6
Kong Franz Joseph Fd., Greenland 4 B6
Kong Frederik IX.s Land, Greenland 4 C5
Kong Frederik VI.s Kyst, Greenland 4 C5
Kong Frederik VIII.s Land, Greenland 4 B6
Kong Oscar Fjord, Greenland 4 B6
Konglu, Burma 37 F20
Kongolo, Zaïre 46 F5
Kongor, Sudan 45 G11
Kongsberg, Norway 9 G13
Kongsvinger, Norway 9 F15
Königsberg = Kaliningrad, Russia 9 J19
Konin, Poland 17 B10
Konjic, Bos.-H. 21 C7
Konkiep, Namibia 48 D2
Konosha, Russia 22 B7
Kōnosu, Japan 29 F9
Konotop, Ukraine 23 D5
Końskie, Poland 17 C11
Konstanz, Germany 16 E5
Kont, Iran 39 E9
Kontagora, Nigeria 44 F6
Kontum, Vietnam 34 E10
Konya, Turkey 23 G5
Konza, Kenya 46 E7
Kookynie, Australia 53 E3
Kooline, Australia 52 D2
Kooloonong, Australia 55 E3
Koolyanobbing, Australia 53 F2
Koondrook, Australia 55 F3
Koonibba, Australia 55 E1
Koorawatha, Australia 55 E4
Koorda, Australia 53 F2
Kooskia, U.S.A. 72 C6
Kootenai →, Canada 72 B5
Kootenay L., Canada 64 D5
Kootenay Nat. Park, Canada 64 C5
Kootjieskolk, S. Africa 48 E3
Kopaonik, Serbia, Yug. 21 C9
Kópavogur, Iceland 8 D3
Koper, Slovenia 16 F7
Kopervik, Norway 9 G11
Kopeysk, Russia 24 D7
Kopi, Australia 55 E2
Köping, Sweden 9 G17
Koppies, S. Africa 49 D4
Koprivnica, Croatia 20 A7
Kopychyntsi, Ukraine 17 D13
Korab, Macedonia 21 D9
Korça, Albania 21 D9
Korce = Korça, Albania 21 D9
Korčula, Croatia 20 C7
Kord Kūy, Iran 39 B7
Kord Sheykh, Iran 39 D7
Kordestān □, Iran 38 C5
Kordofân, Sudan 45 F10
Korea, North ■, Asia 31 C7
Korea, South ■, Asia 31 C7
Korea Bay, Korea 31 C7
Korea Strait, Asia 31 C7
Korets, Ukraine 17 C14
Korhogo, Ivory C. 44 G3
Korim, Indonesia 33 E9
Korinthiakós Kólpos, Greece 21 E10
Kórinthos, Greece 21 F10
Kōriyama, Japan 28 F10
Korla, China 30 B3
Korneshty = Corneşti, Moldova 17 E15
Koro, Fiji 51 C8
Koro, Ivory C. 44 G3
Koro, Mali 44 F4
Koro Sea, Fiji 51 C9
Korogwe, Tanzania 46 F7
Koroit, Australia 55 F3
Koror, Pac. Oc. 33 C8
Körös →, Hungary 17 E11
Korosten, Ukraine 17 C15
Korostyshev, Ukraine 17 C15
Korraraika, Helodranon' i, Madag. 49 B7
Korsakov, Russia 25 E15
Korshunovo, Russia 25 D12
Korsør, Denmark 9 J14
Korti, Sudan 45 E11
Kortrijk, Belgium 15 D3
Koryakskoye Nagorye, Russia 25 C18
Kos, Greece 21 F12
Koschagyl, Kazakhstan 23 E9
Kościan, Poland 17 B9
Kosciusko, U.S.A. 71 J10
Kosciusko, Mt., Australia 55 F4
Kosciusko I., U.S.A. 64 B2
Kosha, Sudan 45 D11
K'oshih = Kashi, China 30 C2
Koshiki-Rettō, Japan 29 J4
Košice, Slovak Rep. 17 D11
Koslan, Russia 22 B8
Kosovo □, Serbia, Yug. 21 C9
Kosovska-Mitrovica = Titova-Mitrovica, Serbia, Yug. 21 C9
Kostamuksa, Russia 22 B5
Koster, S. Africa 48 D4
Kôstî, Sudan 45 F11
Kostopil, Ukraine 17 C14
Kostroma, Russia 22 C7
Kostrzyn, Poland 16 B8
Koszalin, Poland 16 A9
Kota, India 36 G9
Kota Baharu, Malaysia 34 N15
Kota Belud, Malaysia 32 C5
Kota Kinabalu, Malaysia 32 C5
Kota Tinggi, Malaysia 34 T16
Kotaagung, Indonesia 32 F2
Kotabaru, Indonesia 32 E5
Kotabumi, Indonesia 32 E2
Kotagede, Indonesia 33 G14
Kotamobagu, Indonesia 33 D6
Kotaneelee →, Canada 64 A4
Kotawaringin, Indonesia 32 E4
Kotcho L., Canada 64 B4
Kotelnich, Russia 22 C8
Kotelnikovo, Russia 24 E5
Kotelnyy, Ostrov, Russia 25 B14
Kotka, Finland 9 F22
Kotlas, Russia 22 B8
Kotli, Pakistan 36 C8
Kotor, Montenegro, Yug. 21 C8
Kotovsk, Ukraine 17 E15
Kotri, Pakistan 36 G6
Kottayam, India 36 Q10
Kotturu, India 36 M10
Kotuy →, Russia 25 B11
Kotzebue, U.S.A. 60 B3
Kouango, C.A.R. 46 C4
Koudougou, Burkina Faso 44 F4
Kougaberge, S. Africa 48 E3
Kouilou →, Congo 46 E2
Kouki, C.A.R. 46 C3
Koula Moutou, Gabon 46 E2
Koulen, Cambodia 34 F8
Koulikoro, Mali 44 F3
Koumala, Australia 54 C4
Koumra, Chad 45 G8
Kounradskiy, Kazakhstan 24 E8
Kountze, U.S.A. 71 K7
Kouroussa, Guinea 44 F3
Kousseri, Cameroon 45 F7
Koutiala, Mali 44 F3
Kouvola, Finland 9 F22
Kovdor, Russia 22 A5
Kovel, Ukraine 17 C13
Kovrov, Russia 22 C7
Kowanyama, Australia 54 B3
Kowkash, Canada 62 B2
Köyceğiz, Turkey 21 F13
Koyuk, U.S.A. 60 B3
Koyukuk →, U.S.A. 60 B4
Koza, Japan 29 L3
Kozáni, Greece 21 D9
Kozhikode = Calicut, India 36 P9
Kozhva, Russia 22 A10
Kozyatyn, Ukraine 17 D15
Kpalimé, Togo 44 G5
Kra, Isthmus of = Kra, Kho Khot, Thailand 34 G5
Kra, Kho Khot, Thailand 34 G5
Kra Buri, Thailand 34 G5
Kragan, Indonesia 33 G14
Kragerø, Norway 9 G13
Kragujevac, Serbia, Yug. 21 B9
Krajina, Bos.-H. 20 B7
Krakatau = Rakata, Pulau, Indonesia 32 F3
Kraków, Poland 17 C10
Kraksaan, Indonesia 33 G15
Kraljevo, Serbia, Yug. 21 C9
Kramatorsk, Ukraine 23 E6
Kramfors, Sweden 9 E17
Kranj, Slovenia 16 E8
Krankskop, S. Africa 49 D5
Krasavino, Russia 22 B8
Kraskino, Russia 25 E14
Kraśnik, Poland 17 C12
Krasnoarmeysk, Russia 24 D5
Krasnodar, Russia 23 E6
Krasnokamsk, Russia 22 C10
Krasnoperekopsk, Ukraine 23 E5
Krasnorechenskiy, Russia 28 B7
Krasnoselkupsk, Russia 24 C9
Krasnoturinsk, Russia 22 C11
Krasnoufimsk, Russia 22 C10
Krasnouralsk, Russia 22 C11
Krasnovishersk, Russia 22 B10
Krasnovodsk = Krasnowodsk, Turkmenistan 23 F9
Krasnowodsk, Turkmenistan 23 F9
Krasnoyarsk, Russia 25 D10
Krasnyy Luch, Ukraine 23 E6
Krasnyy Yar, Russia 23 E8
Kratie, Cambodia 34 F9
Krau, Indonesia 33 E10
Kravanh, Chuor Phnum, Cambodia 34 G7
Krefeld, Germany 16 C4
Kremen, Croatia 16 F8
Kremenchug = Kremenchuk, Ukraine 23 E5
Kremenchuk, Ukraine 23 E5
Kremenchuksk Vdskh., Ukraine 23 E5
Kremenets, Ukraine 17 C13
Kremmling, U.S.A. 72 F10
Krems, Austria 16 D8
Kretinga, Lithuania 9 J19
Kribi, Cameroon 46 D1
Krichev = Krychaw, Belarus 17 B16
Krishna →, India 37 M12
Krishnanagar, India 37 H16
Kristiansand, Norway 9 G13
Kristianstad, Sweden 9 H16
Kristiansund, Norway 8 E12
Kristiinankaupunki, Finland 9 E19
Kristinehamn, Sweden 9 G16
Kristinestad = Kristiinankaupunki, Finland 9 E19
Kríti, Greece 21 G11
Krivoy Rog = Kryvyy Rih, Ukraine 23 E5
Krk, Croatia 16 F8
Krokodil →, Mozam. 49 D5
Kronprins Olav Kyst, Antarctica 5 C5
Kronshtadt, Russia 22 B4
Kroonstad, S. Africa 48 D4
Kropotkin, Irkutsk, Russia 25 D12
Kropotkin, Krasnodar, Russia 23 E7
Krosno, Poland 17 D11
Krotoszyn, Poland 17 C9
Kruger Nat. Park, S. Africa 49 C5
Krugersdorp, S. Africa 49 D4
Kruisfontein, S. Africa 48 E3
Krung Thep = Bangkok, Thailand 34 F6
Krupki, Belarus 17 A15
Kruševac, Serbia, Yug. 21 C9
Kruzof I., U.S.A. 64 B1
Krychaw, Belarus 17 B16
Krymskiy Poluostrov = Krymskyy Pivostriv, Ukraine 23 E5
Krymskyy Pivostriv, Ukraine 23 E5
Kryvyy Rih, Ukraine 23 E5
Ksar el Boukhari, Algeria 44 A5
Ksar el Kebir, Morocco 44 B3
Ksar es Souk = Ar Rachidiya, Morocco 44 B4
Kuala, Indonesia 32 D3
Kuala Kangsar, Malaysia 34 Q13
Kuala Kerai, Malaysia 34 P15
Kuala Kubu Baharu, Malaysia 34 R14
Kuala Lipis, Malaysia 34 Q15
Kuala Lumpur, Malaysia 34 R14
Kuala Sedili Besar, Malaysia 34 T17
Kuala Terengganu, Malaysia 32 C2
Kualajelai, Indonesia 32 E4
Kualakapuas, Indonesia 32 E4
Kualakurun, Indonesia 32 E4
Kualapembuang, Indonesia 32 E4
Kualasimpang, Indonesia 32 D1
Kuandang, Indonesia 33 D6
Kuangchou = Guangzhou, China 31 D6
Kuantan, Malaysia 34 R16
Kuba = Quba, Azerbaijan 23 F8
Kuban →, Russia 23 E6
Kubokawa, Japan 29 H6
Kuchino-eruba-Jima, Japan 29 J5
Kuchino-Shima, Japan 29 K4
Kuchinotsu, Japan 29 H5
Kucing, Malaysia 32 D4
Kuda, India 36 H7
Kudat, Malaysia 32 C5
Kudus, Indonesia 33 G14
Kudymkar, Russia 24 D6
Kueiyang = Guiyang, China 30 D5
Kufstein, Austria 16 E7
Kugong I., Canada 62 A4
Kūh-e-Hazārām, Iran 39 D8
Kūhak, Iran 36 F3
Kūhbonān, Iran 39 D8
Kūhestak, Iran 39 E8
Kūhīn, Iran 39 C6
Kūhīrī, Iran 39 E9
Kūhpāyeh, Eşfahan, Iran 39 C7
Kūhpāyeh, Kermān, Iran 39 D8
Kuito, Angola 47 G3
Kuji, Japan 28 D10
Kujū-San, Japan 29 H5
Kukawa, Nigeria 45 F7
Kukerin, Australia 53 F2
Kukësi, Albania 21 C9
Kula, Turkey 21 E13
Kulai, Malaysia 34 T16
Kulasekarappattinam, India 36 Q11
Kuldiga, Latvia 9 H19
Kuldja = Yining, China 24 E9
Kulin, Australia 53 F2
Kulja, Australia 53 F2
Kulm, U.S.A. 70 B5
Kŭlob, Tajikistan 24 F7
Kulsary, Kazakhstan 23 E9
Kulumbura, Australia 52 B4
Kulunda, Russia 24 D8
Kūlvand, Iran 39 D7
Kulwin, Australia 55 F3
Kulyab = Kŭlob, Tajikistan 24 F7
Kum Tekei, Kazakhstan 24 E8
Kuma →, Russia 23 F8

Kumagaya, Japan 29 F9
Kumai, Indonesia 32 E4
Kumamba, Kepulauan,
   Indonesia 33 E9
Kumamoto, Japan 29 H5
Kumamoto □, Japan . 29 H5
Kumanovo, Macedonia 21 C9
Kumara, N.Z. 51 K3
Kumarl, Australia ... 53 F3
Kumasi, Ghana 44 G4
Kumayri = Gyumri,
   Armenia 23 F7
Kumba, Cameroon .. 44 H6
Kumbakonam, India .. 36 P11
Kumbarilla, Australia . 55 D5
Kume-Shima, Japan . 29 L3
Kumertau, Russia 22 D10
Kumla, Sweden 9 G16
Kumo, Nigeria 44 F7
Kumon Bum, Burma .. 37 F20
Kunama, Australia ... 55 F4
Kunashir, Ostrov,
   Russia 25 E15
Kunda, Estonia 9 G22
Kungala, Australia ... 55 D5
Kunghit I., Canada .. 64 C2
Kungrad = Qŭnghirot,
   Uzbekistan 24 E6
Kungsbacka, Sweden . 9 H15
Kungur, Russia 22 C10
Kungurri, Australia .. 54 C4
Kuningan, Indonesia . 33 G13
Kunlong, Burma 37 H21
Kunlun Shan, Asia .. 30 C3
Kunming, China 30 D5
Kununurra, Australia . 52 C4
Kunwarara, Australia . 54 C5
Kunya-Urgench =
   Köneürgench,
   Turkmenistan 24 E6
Kuopio, Finland 8 E22
Kupa →, Croatia 16 F9
Kupang, Indonesia ... 33 F6
Kupyansk, Ukraine ... 24 E4
Kuqa, China 30 B3
Kür →, Azerbaijan .. 23 G8
Kura = Kür →,
   Azerbaijan 23 G8
Kuranda, Australia .. 54 B4
Kurashiki, Japan ... 29 G6
Kurayoshi, Japan ... 29 G6
Kürdzhali, Bulgaria .. 21 D11
Kure, Japan 29 G6
Kuressaare, Estonia . 9 G20
Kurgaldzhinskiy,
   Kazakhstan 24 D8
Kurgan, Russia 24 D7
Kuria Maria Is. =
   Khūriyā Mūriyā, Jazā
   'ir, Oman 40 D6
Kuridala, Australia .. 54 C3
Kurigram, Bangla. ... 37 G16
Kurikka, Finland 9 E20
Kuril Is. = Kurilskiye
   Ostrova, Russia .. 25 E15
Kuril Trench, Pac. Oc. 56 C7
Kurilsk, Russia 25 E15
Kurilskiye Ostrova,
   Russia 25 E15
Kurino, Japan 29 J5
Kurmuk, Sudan 45 F11
Kurnool, India 36 M10
Kuro-Shima,
   Kagoshima, Japan . 29 J4
Kuro-Shima, Okinawa,
   Japan 29 M2
Kurow, N.Z. 51 L3
Kurrajong, Australia . 55 E5
Kurri Kurri, Australia . 55 E5
Kurshskiy Zaliv, Russia 9 J19
Kursk, Russia 22 D6
Kuruktag, China 30 B3
Kuruman, S. Africa .. 48 D3
Kuruman →, S. Africa 48 D3
Kurume, Japan 29 H5
Kurunegala, Sri Lanka 36 R12
Kurya, Russia 25 C11
Kus Gölü, Turkey ... 21 D12
Kuşadası, Turkey ... 21 F12
Kusatsu, Japan 29 F9
Kusawa L., Canada .. 64 A1
Kushikino, Japan ... 29 J5
Kushima, Japan 29 J5
Kushimoto, Japan ... 29 H7
Kushiro, Japan 28 C12
Kushiro →, Japan .. 28 C12
Kūshk, Iran 39 D8
Kushka = Gushgy,
   Turkmenistan 24 F7
Kūshkī, Īlām, Iran .. 38 C5
Kūshkī, Khorāsān, Iran 39 B8
Kushkū, Iran 39 E7
Kushtia, Bangla. ... 37 H16
Kushva, Russia 22 C10
Kuskokwim →, U.S.A. 60 B3
Kuskokwim B., U.S.A. 60 C3
Kussharo-Ko, Japan . 28 C12
Kustanay = Qostanay,
   Kazakhstan 24 D7
Kütahya, Turkey ... 23 G5
Kutaisi, Georgia ... 23 F7
Kutaraja = Banda Aceh,
   Indonesia 32 C1
Kutch, Gulf of =
   Kachchh, Gulf of,
   India 36 H6
Kutch, Rann of =
   Kachchh, Rann of,
   India 36 H7
Kutno, Poland 17 B10
Kuttabul, Australia .. 54 C4
Kutu, Zaïre 46 E3
Kutum, Sudan 45 F9

Kuujjuaq, Canada ... 61 C13
Kuusamo, Finland ... 8 D23
Kuusankoski, Finland . 9 F22
Kuwait = Al Kuwayt,
   Kuwait 38 D5
Kuwait ■, Asia 38 D5
Kuwana, Japan 29 G8
Kuybyshev = Samara,
   Russia 22 D9
Kuybyshev, Russia .. 24 D8
Kuybyshevskoye
   Vdkhr., Russia ... 22 C8
Küyeh, Iran 38 B5
Küysanjaq, Iraq 38 B5
Kuyto, Ozero, Russia 22 B5
Kuyumba, Russia ... 25 C10
Kuzey Anadolu Dağları,
   Turkey 23 F6
Kuznetsk, Russia ... 22 D8
Kuzomen, Russia ... 22 A6
Kvænangen, Norway . 8 A19
Kvaløy, Norway 8 B18
Kvarner, Croatia ... 16 F8
Kvarnerič, Croatia .. 16 F8
Kwabhaca, S. Africa . 49 E4
Kwadacha →, Canada 64 B3
Kwakhanai, Botswana 48 C3
Kwakoegron, Surinam 79 B7
KwaMashu, S. Africa . 49 D5
Kwamouth, Zaïre ... 46 E3
Kwando →, Africa .. 48 B3
Kwangju, S. Korea .. 31 C7
Kwangsi-Chuang =
   Guangxi Zhuangzu
   Zizhiqu □, China . 31 D5
Kwangtung =
   Guangdong □, China 31 D6
Kwataboahegan →,
   Canada 62 B3
Kwatisore, Indonesia . 33 E8
KwaZulu Natal □,
   S. Africa 49 D5
Kweichow =
   Guizhou □, China . 30 D5
Kwekwe, Zimbabwe . 47 H5
Kwidzyn, Poland ... 17 B10
Kwinana New Town,
   Australia 53 F2
Kwoka, Indonesia ... 33 E8
Kyabé, Chad 45 G8
Kyabra Cr. →,
   Australia 55 D3
Kyabram, Australia .. 55 F4
Kyaikto, Burma 34 D4
Kyakhta, Russia 25 D11
Kyancutta, Australia . 55 E2
Kyangin, Burma 37 K19
Kyaukpadaung, Burma 37 J19
Kyaukpyu, Burma ... 37 K18
Kyaukse, Burma 37 J20
Kyle Dam, Zimbabwe 47 J6
Kyle of Lochalsh, U.K. 12 D3
Kymijoki →, Finland . 9 F22
Kyneton, Australia .. 55 F3
Kynuna, Australia ... 54 C3
Kyō-ga-Saki, Japan . 29 G7
Kyoga, L., Uganda .. 46 D6
Kyogle, Australia ... 55 D5
Kyongpyaw, Burma .. 37 L19
Kyōto, Japan 29 G7
Kyōto □, Japan 29 G7
Kyren, Russia 25 D11
Kyrenia, Cyprus ... 38 C2
Kyrgyzstan ■, Asia .. 24 E8
Kyrönjoki →, Finland 8 E19
Kystatyam, Russia ... 25 C13
Kytal Ktakh, Russia . 25 C13
Kyulyunken, Russia .. 25 C14
Kyunhla, Burma 37 H19
Kyuquot, Canada ... 64 C3
Kyūshū, Japan 29 H5
Kyūshū □, Japan ... 29 H5
Kyūshū-Sanchi, Japan 29 H5
Kyustendil, Bulgaria . 21 C10
Kyusyur, Russia 25 B13
Kywong, Australia .. 55 E4
Kyyiv, Ukraine 17 C16
Kyyivske Vdskh.,
   Ukraine 17 C16
Kyzyl, Russia 25 D10
Kyzyl Kum, Uzbekistan 24 E7
Kyzyl-Kyya, Kyrgyzstan 24 E8
Kzyl-Orda = Qyzylorda,
   Kazakhstan 24 E7

L

La Albufera, Spain ... 19 C5
La Alcarria, Spain ... 19 B4
La Asunción, Venezuela 78 A6
La Banda, Argentina . 80 B4
La Barge, U.S.A. 72 E8
La Belle, U.S.A. 69 M5
La Biche →, Canada 64 B4
La Boca, Panama ... 74 H14
La Calera, Chile 80 C2
La Carlota, Argentina 80 C4
La Ceiba, Honduras . 74 D7
La Chaux de Fonds,
   Switz. 16 E4
La Chorrera, Panama 74 H14
La Cocha, Argentina . 80 B3
La Conner, U.S.A. .. 72 B2
La Coruña, Spain ... 19 A1
La Crosse, Canada .. 64 B5
La Crosse, Kans.,
   U.S.A. 70 F5
La Crosse, Wis., U.S.A. 70 D9
La Dorada, Colombia 78 B4
La Estrada, Spain ... 19 A1

La Fayette, U.S.A. ... 69 H3
La Follette, U.S.A. .. 69 G3
La Grande, U.S.A. .. 72 D4
La Grange, Ga., U.S.A. 69 J3
La Grange, Ky., U.S.A. 68 F3
La Grange, Tex., U.S.A. 71 L6
La Guaira, Venezuela . 78 A5
La Güera, Mauritania . 44 D1
La Habana, Cuba ... 75 C8
La Harpe, U.S.A. ... 70 E9
La Jara, U.S.A. 73 H11
La Junta, U.S.A. ... 71 F3
La Línea de la
   Concepción, Spain . 19 D3
La Loche, Canada ... 65 B7
La Louvière, Belgium . 15 D4
La Malbaie, Canada . 63 C5
La Mancha, Spain ... 19 C4
La Mesa, Calif., U.S.A. 73 K5
La Mesa, N. Mex.,
   U.S.A. 73 K10
La Moure, U.S.A. ... 70 B5
La Palma, Canary Is. . 44 C1
La Palma, Panama .. 75 F9
La Palma del Condado,
   Spain 19 D2
La Paragua, Venezuela 78 B6
La Paz, Entre Ríos,
   Argentina 80 C5
La Paz, San Luis,
   Argentina 80 C3
La Paz, Bolivia 78 G5
La Paz, Mexico 74 C2
La Pedrera, Colombia . 78 D5
La Perouse Str., Asia . 28 B11
La Pine, U.S.A. 72 E3
La Plant, U.S.A. 70 C4
La Plata, Argentina .. 80 D5
La Porte, U.S.A. ... 68 E2
La Push, U.S.A. 72 C1
La Quiaca, Argentina . 80 A3
La Reine, Canada ... 62 C4
La Rioja, Argentina .. 80 B3
La Rioja □, Spain ... 19 A4
La Robla, Spain 19 A3
La Roche-sur-Yon,
   France 18 C3
La Rochelle, France .. 18 C3
La Roda, Spain 19 C4
La Romana, Dom. Rep. 75 D11
La Ronge, Canada .. 65 B7
La Salle, U.S.A. 70 E10
La Sarre, Canada ... 62 C4
La Scie, Canada 63 C8
La Serena, Chile 80 B2
La Seyne-sur-Mer,
   France 18 E6
La Spézia, Italy 20 B3
La Tortuga, Venezuela 75 E11
La Tuque, Canada ... 62 C5
La Unión, Chile 80 E2
La Urbana, Venezuela 78 B5
La Vega, Dom. Rep. . 75 D10
Labe = Elbe →,
   Europe 16 B5
Labé, Guinea 44 F2
Laberge, L., Canada . 64 A1
Labis, Malaysia 34 S16
Laboulaye, Argentina . 80 C4
Labrador, Coast of □,
   Canada 63 B7
Labrador City, Canada 63 B6
Lábrea, Brazil 78 E6
Labuan, Pulau,
   Malaysia 32 C5
Labuha, Indonesia ... 33 E7
Labuhan, Indonesia .. 33 G11
Labuhanbajo, Indonesia 33 F6
Labuk, Telok, Malaysia 32 C5
Labyrinth L., Australia 55 E2
Labytnangi, Russia .. 22 A12
Lac Allard, Canada .. 63 B7
Lac Bouchette, Canada 63 C5
Lac du Flambeau,
   U.S.A. 70 B10
Lac Édouard, Canada . 62 C5
Lac La Biche, Canada 64 C6
Lac la Martre, Canada 60 B8
Lac-Mégantic, Canada 63 C5
Lac Seul, Res., Canada 62 B1
Lacanau, France ... 18 D3
Laccadive Is. =
   Lakshadweep Is.,
   Ind. Oc. 26 H11
Lacepede B., Australia 55 F2
Lacepede Is., Australia 52 C3
Lachine, Canada ... 62 C5
Lachlan →, Australia 55 E3
Lachute, Canada ... 62 C5
Lackawanna, U.S.A. . 68 D6
Lacombe, Canada ... 64 C6
Laconia, U.S.A. 68 D10
Lacrosse, U.S.A. ... 72 C5
Ladakh Ra., India .. 36 C11
Ladismith, S. Africa . 48 E3
Lādīz, Iran 39 D9
Ladoga, L. =
   Ladozhskoye Ozero,
   Russia 22 B5
Ladozhskoye Ozero,
   Russia 22 B5
Lady Grey, S. Africa . 48 E4
Ladybrand, S. Africa . 48 D4
Ladysmith, Canada .. 64 D4
Ladysmith, S. Africa . 49 D4
Ladysmith, U.S.A. .. 70 C9
Lae, Papua N. G. ... 56 H6
Læsø, Denmark 9 H14
Lafayette, Colo., U.S.A. 70 F2
Lafayette, Ind., U.S.A. 68 E2
Lafayette, La., U.S.A. 71 K9
Lafayette, Tenn., U.S.A. 69 G3
Laferte →, Canada .. 64 A5

Lafia, Nigeria 44 G6
Lafleche, Canada ... 65 D7
Lagan →, U.K. 13 B6
Lagarfljót →, Iceland 8 D6
Lågen →, Oppland,
   Norway 9 F14
Lågen →, Vestfold,
   Norway 9 G14
Laghouat, Algeria ... 44 B5
Lagonoy Gulf, Phil. .. 33 B6
Lagos, Nigeria 44 G5
Lagos, Portugal ... 19 D1
Lagrange, Australia . 52 C3
Lagrange B., Australia 52 C3
Laguna, Brazil 80 B7
Laguna, U.S.A. 73 J10
Laguna Beach, U.S.A. 73 K5
Lagunas, Chile 78 H5
Lagunas, Peru 78 E3
Lahad Datu, Malaysia 33 C5
Lahat, Indonesia ... 32 E2
Lahewa, Indonesia .. 32 D1
Lāhījān, Iran 39 B6
Lahn →, Germany .. 16 C4
Laholm, Sweden ... 9 H15
Lahontan Reservoir,
   U.S.A. 72 G4
Lahore, Pakistan ... 36 D9
Lahti, Finland 9 F21
Lahtis = Lahti, Finland 9 F21
Laï, Chad 45 G8
Lai Chau, Vietnam .. 34 A7
Laidley, Australia ... 55 D5
Laingsburg, S. Africa . 48 E3
Lainio älv →, Sweden 8 C20
Lairg, U.K. 12 C4
Lajere, Nigeria 44 F7
Lajes, Brazil 80 B6
Lake Andes, U.S.A. . 70 D5
Lake Anse, U.S.A. .. 68 B1
Lake Arthur, U.S.A. . 71 K8
Lake Cargelligo,
   Australia 55 E4
Lake Charles, U.S.A. . 71 K8
Lake City, Colo., U.S.A. 73 G10
Lake City, Fla., U.S.A. 69 K4
Lake City, Iowa, U.S.A. 70 D7
Lake City, Mich., U.S.A. 68 C3
Lake City, Minn., U.S.A. 70 C8
Lake City, S.C., U.S.A. 69 J6
Lake Grace, Australia . 53 F2
Lake Harbour, Canada 61 B13
Lake Havasu City,
   U.S.A. 73 J6
Lake King, Australia . 53 F2
Lake Lenore, Canada . 65 C8
Lake Louise, Canada . 64 C5
Lake Mead National
   Recreation Area,
   U.S.A. 73 J6
Lake Mills, U.S.A. .. 70 D8
Lake Nash, Australia . 54 C2
Lake Providence, U.S.A. 71 J9
Lake River, Canada .. 62 B3
Lake Superior Prov.
   Park, Canada 62 C3
Lake Village, U.S.A. . 71 J9
Lake Wales, U.S.A. . 69 M5
Lake Worth, U.S.A. . 69 M5
Lakefield, Canada ... 62 D4
Lakeland, Australia .. 54 B3
Lakeland, U.S.A. ... 69 L5
Lakemba, Fiji 51 D9
Lakes Entrance,
   Australia 55 F4
Lakeside, Ariz., U.S.A. 73 J9
Lakeside, Nebr., U.S.A. 70 D3
Lakeview, U.S.A. ... 72 E3
Lakewood, Colo.,
   U.S.A. 70 F2
Lakewood, N.J., U.S.A. 68 E8
Lakewood, Ohio, U.S.A. 68 E5
Lakin, U.S.A. 71 G4
Lakitusaki →, Canada 62 B3
Lakonikós Kólpos,
   Greece 21 F10
Lakor, Indonesia ... 33 F7
Lakota, Ivory C. ... 44 G3
Lakota, U.S.A. 70 A5
Laksefjorden, Norway 8 A22
Lakselv, Norway ... 8 A21
Lakshadweep Is.,
   Ind. Oc. 26 H11
Lala Ghat, India ... 37 G18
Lalibela, Ethiopia .. 45 F12
Lalín, Spain 19 A1
Lalitapur = Patan,
   Nepal 37 F14
L'Aquila, Italy 20 C5
Lār, Āzarbājān-e Sharqī,
   Iran 38 B5
Lār, Fārs, Iran 39 E7
Larache, Morocco ... 44 A3
Laramie, U.S.A. 70 E2
Laramie Mts., U.S.A. . 70 E2
Larantuka, Indonesia . 33 F6
Larap, Phil. 33 B6
Larat, Indonesia ... 33 F8
Larder Lake, Canada . 62 C4
Laredo, U.S.A. 71 M5
Laredo Sd., Canada . 64 C3
Largs, U.K. 12 F4
Lariang, Indonesia .. 33 E5
Larimore, U.S.A. ... 70 B6
Larisa, Iran 39 C7
Lárisa, Greece 21 E10
Larnaca, Cyprus ... 38 C2
Larne, U.K. 13 B6
Larned, U.S.A. 70 F5
Larrimah, Australia .. 52 C5
Larsen Ice Shelf,
   Antarctica 5 C17
Larvik, Norway 9 G14
Laryak, Russia 24 C8

Las Animas, U.S.A. . 70 F3
Las Anod, Somali Rep. 40 F4
Las Cascadas, Panama 74 H14
Las Cruces, U.S.A. . 73 K10
Las Flores, Argentina . 80 D5
Las Khoreh,
   Somali Rep. 40 E4
Las Lajas, Argentina . 80 D2
Las Lomitas, Argentina 80 A4
Las Palmas, Canary Is. 44 C1
Las Pipinas, Argentina 80 D5
Las Plumas, Argentina 80 E3
Las Rosas, Argentina . 80 C4
Las Varillas, Argentina 80 C4
Las Vegas, N. Mex.,
   U.S.A. 73 J11
Las Vegas, Nev., U.S.A. 73 H6
Lashburn, Canada ... 65 C7
Lashio, Burma 37 H20
Lassen Pk., U.S.A. .. 72 F3
Last Mountain L.,
   Canada 65 C7
Lastoursville, Gabon . 46 E2
Lastovo, Croatia ... 20 C7
Latacunga, Ecuador . 78 D3
Latakia = Al
   Lādhiqiyah, Syria . 38 C2
Latchford, Canada .. 62 C4
Latham, Australia ... 53 E2
Latina, Italy 20 D5
Latium = Lazio □, Italy 20 C5
Latouche Treville, C.,
   Australia 52 C3
Latrobe, Australia .. 54 G4
Latvia ■, Europe ... 9 H20
Lau Group, Fiji 51 C9
Lauchhammer,
   Germany 16 C7
Laukaa, Finland ... 9 E21
Launceston, Australia 54 G4
Launceston, U.K. ... 11 G3
Laune →, Ireland .. 13 D2
Launglon Bok, Burma 34 F4
Laura, Australia ... 54 B3
Laurel, Miss., U.S.A. . 71 K10
Laurel, Mont., U.S.A. 72 D9
Laurencekirk, U.K. .. 12 E6
Laurens, U.S.A. ... 69 H4
Laurentian Plateau,
   Canada 63 B6
Laurentides, Parc Prov.
   des, Canada 63 C5
Lauria, Italy 20 E6
Laurie L., Canada .. 65 B8
Laurinburg, U.S.A. .. 69 H6
Laurium, U.S.A. ... 68 B1
Lausanne, Switz. ... 16 E4
Laut, Indonesia 32 D3
Laut Kecil, Kepulauan,
   Indonesia 32 E5
Lautoka, Fiji 51 C7
Lauzon, Canada ... 63 C5
Lava Hot Springs,
   U.S.A. 72 E7
Laval, France 18 B3
Laverne, U.S.A. ... 71 G5
Laverton, Australia .. 53 E3
Länkäran, Azerbaijan . 23 G8
Lávrion, Greece ... 21 F11
L'Annonciation, Canada 62 C5
Lansdowne, Australia . 55 E5
Lansdowne House,
   Canada 62 B2
L'Anse, U.S.A. 62 C2
L'Anse au Loup,
   Canada 63 B8
Lansing, U.S.A. 68 D3
Lanusei, Italy 20 E3
Lanzarote, Canary Is. 44 C2
Lanzhou, China 30 C5
Lao Cai, Vietnam ... 34 A7
Laoag, Phil. 33 A6
Laoang, Phil. 33 B7
Laois □, Ireland ... 13 D4
Laon, France 18 B5
Laona, U.S.A. 68 C1
Laos ■, Asia 34 D8
Lapa, Brazil 80 B7
Laparan, Phil. 33 C6
Lapeer, U.S.A. 68 D4
Lapland = Lappland,
   Europe 8 B21
Lappeenranta, Finland 9 F23
Lappland, Europe ... 8 B21
Laptev Sea, Russia .. 25 B13
Lapua, Finland 8 E20
Lār, Āzarbājān-e Sharqī,
   Iran 38 B5
Lär, Fārs, Iran 39 E7
Larache, Morocco ... 44 A3
Laramie, U.S.A. 70 E2
Laramie Mts., U.S.A. . 70 E2
Larantuka, Indonesia . 33 F6
Larap, Phil. 33 B6
Larat, Indonesia ... 33 F8
Larder Lake, Canada . 62 C4
Laredo, U.S.A. 71 M5
Laredo Sd., Canada . 64 C3
Largs, U.K. 12 F4
Lariang, Indonesia .. 33 E5
Larimore, U.S.A. ... 70 B6
Larisa, Iran 39 C7
Lárisa, Greece 21 E10
Larnaca, Cyprus ... 38 C2
Larne, U.K. 13 B6
Larned, U.S.A. 70 F5
Larrimah, Australia .. 52 C5
Larsen Ice Shelf,
   Antarctica 5 C17
Larvik, Norway 9 G14
Laryak, Russia 24 C8
Laaming, Burma 37 M20
Lamar, Colo., U.S.A. . 70 F3
Lamar, Mo., U.S.A. . 71 G7
Lamas, Peru 78 E3
Lambaréné, Gabon .. 46 E2
Lambay I., Ireland .. 13 C5
Lambert Glacier,
   Antarctica 5 D6
Lamberts Bay, S. Africa 48 E2
Lambi Kyun, Burma . 34 G5
Lame, Nigeria 44 F7
Lame Deer, U.S.A. .. 72 D10
Lamego, Portugal ... 19 B2
Lamèque, Canada ... 63 C7
Lameroo, Australia .. 55 F3
Lamia, Greece 21 E10
Lamon Bay, Phil. ... 33 B6
Lamont, Canada ... 64 C6
Lampa, Peru 78 G4
Lampang, Thailand .. 34 C5
Lampasas, U.S.A. .. 71 K5
Lampedusa, Medit. S. 20 G5
Lampeter, U.K. 11 E3
Lampione, Medit. S. .. 20 G5
Lampman, Canada .. 65 D8
Lamprey, Canada ... 65 B10
Lampung □, Indonesia 32 F2
Lamu, Kenya 46 E8
Lamy, U.S.A. 73 J11
Lanai I., U.S.A. 66 H16
Lanak La, India 36 B11
Lanak'o Shank'ou =
   Lanak La, India .. 36 B11
Lanao, L., Phil. 33 C6
Lanark, Canada ... 62 D4
Lanark, U.K. 12 F5
Lancang Jiang →,
   China 30 D5
Lancashire □, U.K. .. 10 D5
Lancaster, U.K. 10 C5
Lancaster, Calif., U.S.A. 73 J4
Lancaster, Ky., U.S.A. 68 G3
Lancaster, N.H., U.S.A. 68 C10
Lancaster, Pa., U.S.A. 68 E7
Lancaster, S.C., U.S.A. 69 H5
Lancaster, Wis., U.S.A. 70 D9
Lancaster Sd., Canada 61 A11
Lancer, Canada 65 C7
Lanchow = Lanzhou,
   China 30 C5
Lanciano, Italy 20 C6
Landeck, Austria ... 16 E6
Landen, Belgium ... 15 D5
Lander, U.S.A. 72 E9
Lander →, Australia 52 D5
Landes, France 18 D3
Landi Kotal, Pakistan . 36 B7
Landor, Australia ... 53 E2
Land's End, U.K. ... 11 G2
Landsborough Cr. →,
   Australia 54 C3
Landshut, Germany . 16 D7
Landskrona, Sweden . 9 J15
Lanett, U.S.A. 69 J3

104

Leask, Canada 65 C7
Leavenworth, Kans., U.S.A. 70 F7
Leavenworth, Wash., U.S.A. 72 C2
Lebak, Phil. 33 C6
Lebanon, Ind., U.S.A. 68 E2
Lebanon, Kans., U.S.A. 70 F5
Lebanon, Ky., U.S.A. 68 G3
Lebanon, Mo., U.S.A. 71 G8
Lebanon, Oreg., U.S.A. 72 D2
Lebanon, Pa., U.S.A. 68 E7
Lebanon, Tenn., U.S.A. 69 G2
Lebanon ■, Asia 41 B4
Lebec, U.S.A. 73 J4
Lebomboberge, S. Africa 49 C5
Lębork, Poland 17 A9
Lebrija, Spain 19 D2
Lebu, Chile 80 D2
Lecce, Italy 21 D8
Lecco, Italy 20 B3
Lech →, Germany 16 D6
Łęczyca, Poland 17 B10
Ledbury, U.K. 11 E5
Leduc, Canada 64 C6
Lee →, Ireland 13 E3
Leech →, U.S.A. 70 B7
Leedey, U.S.A. 71 H5
Leeds, U.K. 10 D6
Leeds, U.S.A. 69 J2
Leek, U.K. 10 D5
Leer, Germany 16 B4
Leesburg, U.S.A. 69 L5
Leesville, U.S.A. 71 K8
Leeton, Australia 55 E4
Leeu Gamka, S. Africa 48 E3
Leeuwarden, Neths. 15 A5
Leeuwin, C., Australia 53 F2
Leeward Is., Atl. Oc. 74 L18
Lefors, U.S.A. 71 H4
Lefroy, L., Australia 53 F3
Legal, Canada 64 C6
Leganés, Spain 19 B4
Legazpi, Phil. 33 B6
Legendre I., Australia 52 D2
Leghorn = Livorno, Italy 20 C4
Legionowo, Poland 17 B11
Legnago, Italy 20 B4
Legnica, Poland 16 C9
Legume, Australia 55 D5
Leh, India 36 B10
Lehi, U.S.A. 72 F8
Lehututu, Botswana 48 C3
Leicester, U.K. 11 E6
Leicestershire □, U.K. 11 E6
Leichhardt →, Australia 54 B2
Leichhardt Ra., Australia 54 C4
Leiden, Neths. 15 B4
Leie →, Belgium 15 C3
Leine →, Germany 16 B5
Leinster, Australia 53 E3
Leinster □, Ireland 13 C4
Leinster, Mt., Ireland 13 D5
Leipzig, Germany 16 C7
Leiria, Portugal 19 C1
Leirvik, Norway 9 G11
Leisler, Mt., Australia 52 D4
Leith, U.K. 12 F5
Leith Hill, U.K. 11 F7
Leitrim, Ireland 13 B3
Leitrim □, Ireland 13 B3
Leizhou Bandao, China 31 D6
Lek →, Neths. 15 C4
Leka, Norway 8 D14
Leksula, Indonesia 33 E7
Lékva Ori, Greece 21 G11
Leland, U.S.A. 71 J9
Leland Lakes, Canada 65 A6
Leleque, Argentina 80 E2
Lelystad, Neths. 15 B5
Léman, L., Europe 16 E4
Lemhi Ra., U.S.A. 72 D7
Lemmer, Neths. 15 B5
Lemmon, U.S.A. 70 C3
Lemoore, U.S.A. 73 H4
Lemvig, Denmark 9 H13
Lena →, Russia 25 B13
Lendeh, Iran 39 D6
Lenggong, Malaysia 34 P13
Leninabad = Khudzhand, Tajikistan 24 E7
Leninakan = Gyumri, Armenia 23 F7
Leningrad = Sankt-Peterburg, Russia 22 C5
Leninogorsk = Ridder, Kazakhstan 24 D9
Leninsk, Russia 23 E8
Leninsk-Kuznetskiy, Russia 24 D9
Leninskoye, Russia 25 E14
Lenkoran = Länkäran, Azerbaijan 23 G8
Lenmalu, Indonesia 33 E8
Lenoir, U.S.A. 69 H5
Lenoir City, U.S.A. 69 H3
Lenora, U.S.A. 70 F4
Lenore L., Canada 65 C8
Lens, France 18 A5
Lensk, Russia 25 C12
Lentini, Italy 20 F6
Leoben, Austria 16 E8
Leodhas = Lewis, U.K. 12 C2
Leola, U.S.A. 70 C5
Leominster, U.K. 11 E5
Leominster, U.S.A. 68 D10
León, Mexico 74 C4
León, Nic. 74 E7
León, Spain 19 A3

Leon, U.S.A. 70 E8
León, Montañas de, Spain 19 A2
Leonardtown, U.S.A. 68 F7
Leongatha, Australia 55 F4
Leonora, Australia 53 E3
Léopold II, Lac = Mai-Ndombe, L., Zaïre 46 E3
Leopoldsburg, Belgium 15 C5
Léopoldville = Kinshasa, Zaïre 46 E3
Leoti, U.S.A. 70 F4
Leova, Moldova 17 E15
Lepel = Lyepyel, Belarus 22 D4
Lepikha, Russia 25 C13
Leppävirta, Finland 9 E22
Léré, Chad 45 G7
Leribe, Lesotho 49 D4
Lérida, Spain 19 B6
Lerwick, U.K. 12 A7
Les Cayes, Haiti 75 D10
Les Étroits, Canada 63 C6
Les Sables-d'Olonne, France 18 C3
Lesbos = Lésvos, Greece 21 E12
Leshan, China 30 D5
Leshukonskoye, Russia 22 B8
Leskov I., Antarctica 5 B1
Leskovac, Serbia, Yug. 21 C9
Leslie, U.S.A. 71 H8
Lesopilnoye, Russia 28 A7
Lesotho ■, Africa 49 D4
Lesozavodsk, Russia 25 E14
Lesse →, Belgium 15 D4
Lesser Antilles, W. Indies 75 E12
Lesser Slave L., Canada 64 B5
Lesser Sunda Is., Indonesia 33 F6
Lessines, Belgium 15 D3
Lestock, Canada 65 C8
Lesuer I., Australia 52 B5
Lésvos, Greece 21 E12
Leszno, Poland 17 C9
Letchworth, U.K. 11 F7
Lethbridge, Canada 64 D6
Leti, Kepulauan, Indonesia 33 F7
Leti Is. = Leti, Kepulauan, Indonesia 33 F7
Letiahau →, Botswana 48 C3
Leticia, Colombia 78 D4
Letjiesbos, S. Africa 48 E3
Letlhakeng, Botswana 48 C3
Letpadan, Burma 37 L19
Letpan, Burma 37 K19
Letsôk-aw Kyun, Burma 34 G5
Letterkenny, Ireland 13 B4
Leuser, G., Indonesia 32 D1
Leuven, Belgium 15 D4
Leuze, Hainaut, Belgium 15 D3
Leuze, Namur, Belgium 15 D4
Levádhia, Greece 21 E10
Levan, U.S.A. 72 G8
Levanger, Norway 8 E14
Levelland, U.S.A. 71 J3
Leven, U.K. 12 E6
Leven, L., U.K. 12 E5
Leven, Toraka, Madag. 49 A8
Leveque C., Australia 52 C3
Levice, Slovak Rep. 17 D10
Levin, N.Z. 51 J5
Lévis, Canada 63 C5
Levis, L., Canada 64 A5
Levkás, Greece 21 E9
Levkôsia = Nicosia, Cyprus 38 C2
Levskigrad = Karlovo, Bulgaria 21 C11
Lewellen, U.S.A. 70 E3
Lewes, U.K. 11 G8
Lewes, U.S.A. 68 F8
Lewis, U.K. 12 C2
Lewis →, U.S.A. 72 C2
Lewis, Butt of, U.K. 12 C2
Lewis Ra., Australia 52 D4
Lewis Range, U.S.A. 72 B7
Lewisburg, U.S.A. 69 H2
Lewisporte, Canada 63 C8
Lewiston, Idaho, U.S.A. 72 C5
Lewiston, Maine, U.S.A. 69 C11
Lewistown, Mont., U.S.A. 72 C9
Lewistown, Pa., U.S.A. 68 E7
Lexington, Ill., U.S.A. 70 E10
Lexington, Ky., U.S.A. 68 F3
Lexington, Miss., U.S.A. 71 J9
Lexington, Mo., U.S.A. 70 F8
Lexington, N.C., U.S.A. 69 H5
Lexington, Nebr., U.S.A. 70 E5
Lexington, Oreg., U.S.A. 72 D4
Lexington, Tenn., U.S.A. 69 H1
Lexington Park, U.S.A. 68 F7
Leyte, Phil. 33 B6
Lezha, Albania 21 D8
Lhasa, China 30 D4
Lhazê, China 30 D3
Lhokkruet, Indonesia 32 D1
Lhokseumawe, Indonesia 32 C1
Lhuntsi Dzong, India 37 F17
Lianga, Phil. 33 C7
Lianyungang, China 31 C6
Liaoning □, China 31 B7
Liaoyang, China 31 B7
Liaoyuan, China 31 B7

Liard →, Canada 64 A4
Líbau = Liepāja, Latvia 9 H19
Libby, U.S.A. 72 B6
Libenge, Zaïre 46 D3
Liberal, Kans., U.S.A. 71 G4
Liberal, Mo., U.S.A. 71 G7
Liberec, Czech. 16 C8
Liberia ■, W. Afr. 44 G3
Liberty, Mo., U.S.A. 70 F7
Liberty, Tex., U.S.A. 71 K7
Libîya, Sahrâ', Africa 45 C9
Libobo, Tanjung, Indonesia 33 E7
Libode, S. Africa 49 E4
Libonda, Zambia 47 G4
Libourne, France 18 D3
Libramont, Belgium 15 E5
Libreville, Gabon 46 D1
Libya ■, N. Afr. 45 C8
Libyan Desert = Libîya, Sahrâ', Africa 45 C9
Licantén, Chile 80 D2
Licata, Italy 20 F5
Lichfield, U.K. 10 E6
Lichinga, Mozam. 47 G7
Lichtenburg, S. Africa 48 D4
Lida, Belarus 9 K21
Lida, U.S.A. 73 H5
Lidköping, Sweden 9 G15
Liebig, Mt., Australia 52 D5
Liechtenstein ■, Europe 16 E5
Liège, Belgium 15 D5
Liège □, Belgium 15 D5
Liegnitz = Legnica, Poland 16 C9
Lienyünchiangshih = Lianyungang, China 31 C6
Lienz, Austria 16 E7
Liepāja, Latvia 9 H19
Lier, Belgium 15 C4
Lièvre →, Canada 62 C4
Liffey →, Ireland 13 C5
Lifford, Ireland 13 B4
Lifudzin, Russia 28 B7
Lightning Ridge, Australia 55 D4
Liguria □, Italy 20 B3
Ligurian Sea, Medit. S. 20 C3
Lihou Reefs and Cays, Australia 54 B5
Lihue, U.S.A. 66 H15
Lijiang, China 30 D5
Likasi, Zaïre 46 G5
Likati, Zaïre 46 D4
Lille, France 18 A5
Lille Bælt, Denmark 9 J13
Lillehammer, Norway 9 F14
Lillesand, Norway 9 G13
Lilleshall, U.K. 11 E5
Lillian Point, Mt., Australia 53 E4
Lillooet →, Canada 64 C4
Lilongwe, Malawi 47 G6
Liloy, Phil. 33 C6
Lim →, Bos.-H. 21 C8
Lima, Indonesia 33 E7
Lima, Peru 78 F3
Lima, Mont., U.S.A. 72 D7
Lima, Ohio, U.S.A. 68 E3
Lima →, Portugal 19 B1
Limassol, Cyprus 38 C2
Limavady, U.K. 13 A5
Limavady □, U.K. 13 B5
Limay →, Argentina 80 D3
Limay Mahuida, Argentina 80 D3
Limbang, Brunei 32 D5
Limbaži, Latvia 9 H21
Limbe, Cameroon 44 H4
Limbri, Australia 55 E5
Limbunya, Australia 52 C4
Limburg, Germany 16 C5
Limburg □, Belgium 15 C5
Limburg □, Neths. 15 C5
Limeira, Brazil 80 A7
Limerick, Ireland 13 D3
Limerick □, Ireland 13 D3
Limestone →, Canada 65 B10
Limfjorden, Denmark 9 H13
Limia = Lima →, Portugal 19 B1
Limingen, Norway 8 D15
Limmen Bight, Australia 54 A2
Limmen Bight →, Australia 54 B2
Límnos, Greece 21 E11
Limoeiro do Norte, Brazil 79 E11
Limoges, France 18 D4
Limón, Costa Rica 75 F8
Limon, Panama 74 H14
Limón □, Panama 74 H14
Limousin, France 18 D4
Limoux, France 18 E5
Limpopo →, Africa 49 D5
Limuru, Kenya 46 E7
Linares, Chile 80 D2
Linares, Mexico 74 C5
Linares, Spain 19 C4
Lincoln, Argentina 80 C4
Lincoln, N.Z. 51 K4
Lincoln, U.K. 10 D7
Lincoln, Ill., U.S.A. 70 E10
Lincoln, Kans., U.S.A. 70 F5
Lincoln, Maine, U.S.A. 63 C6
Lincoln, N. Mex., U.S.A. 73 K11
Lincoln, Nebr., U.S.A. 70 E6
Lincoln Hav = Lincoln Sea, Arctic 4 A5
Lincoln Sea, Arctic 4 A5
Lincolnshire □, U.K. 10 D7

Lincolnshire Wolds, U.K. 10 D7
Lincolnton, U.S.A. 69 H5
Lind, U.S.A. 72 C4
Linden, Guyana 78 B7
Linden, U.S.A. 71 J7
Lindesnes, Norway 9 H12
Líndhos, Greece 21 F13
Lindi, Tanzania 46 F7
Lindsay, Canada 62 D4
Lindsay, Calif., U.S.A. 73 H4
Lindsay, Okla., U.S.A. 71 H6
Lindsborg, U.S.A. 70 F6
Lingayen, Phil. 33 A6
Lingayen G., Phil. 33 A6
Lingen, Germany 16 B4
Lingga, Indonesia 32 E2
Lingga, Kepulauan, Indonesia 32 E2
Lingga Arch. = Lingga, Kepulauan, Indonesia 32 E2
Lingle, U.S.A. 70 D2
Linguére, Senegal 44 E1
Linh Cam, Vietnam 34 C8
Linhai, China 31 D7
Linhares, Brazil 79 G10
Linköping, Sweden 9 G16
Linlithgow, U.K. 12 F5
Linnhe, L., U.K. 12 E3
Linosa, I., Medit. S. 20 G5
Lins, Brazil 80 A7
Linton, Canada 63 C5
Linton, Ind., U.S.A. 68 F2
Linton, N. Dak., U.S.A. 70 B4
Linville, Australia 55 D5
Linxia, China 30 C5
Linyanti →, Africa 48 B4
Linz, Austria 16 D8
Lion, G. du, France 18 E6
Lion's Head, Canada 62 D3
Lipa, Phil. 33 B6
Lípari, Italy 20 E6
Lipari, Is. = Eólie, Ís., Italy 20 E6
Lipcani, Moldova 17 D14
Lipetsk, Russia 22 D6
Lipkany = Lipcani, Moldova 17 D14
Lipovcy Manzovka, Russia 28 B6
Lipovets, Ukraine 17 D15
Lippe →, Germany 16 C4
Lipscomb, U.S.A. 71 G4
Liptrap, C., Australia 55 F4
Lira, Uganda 46 D6
Liria, Spain 19 C5
Lisala, Zaïre 46 D4
Lisboa, Portugal 19 C1
Lisbon = Lisboa, Portugal 19 C1
Lisbon, U.S.A. 70 B6
Lisburn, U.K. 13 B5
Lisburne, C., U.S.A. 60 B3
Liscannor, B., Ireland 13 D2
Lisianski I., Pac. Oc. 56 E10
Lisichansk = Lysychansk, Ukraine 23 E6
Lisieux, France 18 B4
Liski, Russia 23 D6
Lismore, Australia 55 D5
Lismore, Ireland 13 D4
Lisse, Neths. 15 B4
Lista, Norway 9 G12
Lister, Mt., Antarctica 5 D11
Liston, Australia 55 D5
Listowel, Canada 62 D3
Listowel, Ireland 13 D2
Litang, Malaysia 33 C5
Litani →, Lebanon 41 B4
Litchfield, Ill., U.S.A. 70 F10
Litchfield, Minn., U.S.A. 70 C7
Lithgow, Australia 55 E5
Líthinon, Ákra, Greece 21 G11
Lithuania ■, Europe 9 J20
Litoměřice, Czech. 16 C8
Little Andaman I., India 34 G2
Little Barrier I., N.Z. 51 G5
Little Belt Mts., U.S.A. 72 C8
Little Blue →, U.S.A. 70 F6
Little Cadotte →, Canada 64 B5
Little Churchill →, Canada 65 B9
Little Colorado →, U.S.A. 73 H8
Little Current, Canada 62 C3
Little Current →, Canada 62 B3
Little Falls, Minn., U.S.A. 70 C7
Little Falls, N.Y., U.S.A. 68 D8
Little Fork →, U.S.A. 70 A8
Little Grand Rapids, Canada 65 C9
Little Humboldt →, U.S.A. 72 F5
Little Karoo, S. Africa 48 E3
Little Lake, U.S.A. 73 J5
Little Laut Is. = Laut Kecil, Kepulauan, Indonesia 32 E5
Little Minch, U.K. 12 D2
Little Missouri →, U.S.A. 70 B3
Little Ouse →, U.K. 11 E8
Little Red →, U.S.A. 71 H9
Little River, N.Z. 51 K4
Little Rock, U.S.A. 71 H8
Little Sable Pt., U.S.A. 68 D2
Little Sioux →, U.S.A. 70 E6

Little Smoky →, Canada 64 C5
Little Snake →, U.S.A. 72 F9
Little Wabash →, U.S.A. 68 G1
Littlefield, U.S.A. 71 J3
Littlefork, U.S.A. 70 A8
Littlehampton, U.K. 11 G7
Littleton, U.S.A. 68 C10
Liukang Tenggaja, Indonesia 33 F5
Liuwa Plain, Zambia 47 G4
Liuzhou, China 31 D5
Live Oak, U.S.A. 69 K4
Liveringa, Australia 52 C3
Livermore, Mt., U.S.A. 71 K2
Liverpool, Australia 55 E5
Liverpool, Canada 63 D7
Liverpool, U.K. 10 D5
Liverpool Plains, Australia 55 E5
Liverpool Ra., Australia 55 E5
Livingston, Mont., U.S.A. 72 D8
Livingston, Tex., U.S.A. 71 K7
Livingstone, Zambia 47 H5
Livingstonia, Malawi 46 G6
Livny, Russia 22 D6
Livonia, U.S.A. 68 D4
Livorno, Italy 20 C4
Livramento, Brazil 80 C5
Liwale, Tanzania 46 F7
Lizard I., Australia 54 A4
Lizard Pt., U.K. 11 H2
Ljubljana, Slovenia 16 E8
Ljungan →, Sweden 9 E17
Ljungby, Sweden 9 H15
Ljusdal, Sweden 9 F17
Ljusnan →, Sweden 9 F17
Ljusne, Sweden 9 F17
Llancanelo, Salina, Argentina 80 D3
Llandeilo, U.K. 11 F3
Llandovery, U.K. 11 F4
Llandrindod Wells, U.K. 11 E4
Llandudno, U.K. 10 D4
Llanelli, U.K. 11 F3
Llanes, Spain 19 A3
Llangollen, U.K. 10 E4
Llanidloes, U.K. 11 E4
Llano, U.S.A. 71 K5
Llano →, U.S.A. 71 K5
Llano Estacado, U.S.A. 71 J3
Llanos, S. Amer. 78 C4
Lleida = Lérida, Spain 19 B6
Llobregat →, Spain 19 B7
Lloret de Mar, Spain 19 B7
Lloyd B., Australia 54 A3
Lloyd L., Canada 65 B7
Lloydminster, Canada 65 C6
Lluchmayor, Spain 19 C7
Llullaillaco, Volcán, S. Amer. 80 A3
Loa, U.S.A. 73 G8
Loa →, Chile 80 A2
Lobatse, Botswana 48 D4
Lobería, Argentina 80 D5
Lobito, Angola 47 G2
Loc Binh, Vietnam 34 B9
Loc Ninh, Vietnam 34 G9
Locarno, Switz. 16 E5
Loch Garman = Wexford, Ireland 13 D5
Lochaber, U.K. 12 E4
Locharron, U.K. 12 D3
Lochem, Neths. 15 B6
Loches, France 18 C4
Lochgelly, U.K. 12 E5
Lochgilphead, U.K. 12 E3
Lochinver, U.K. 12 C3
Lochnagar, Australia 54 C4
Lochnagar, U.K. 12 E5
Lochy →, U.K. 12 E3
Lock, Australia 55 E2
Lock Haven, U.S.A. 68 E7
Lockeford, U.S.A. 72 G5
Lockeport, Canada 63 D6
Lockerbie, U.K. 12 F5
Lockhart, U.S.A. 71 L6
Lockhart, L., Australia 53 F2
Lockney, U.S.A. 71 H4
Lockport, U.S.A. 68 D6
Lod, Israel 41 D3
Lodeinoye Pole, Russia 22 B5
Lodge Grass, U.S.A. 72 D10
Lodgepole, U.S.A. 70 E3
Lodgepole Cr. →, U.S.A. 70 E2
Lodhran, Pakistan 36 E7
Lodi, Italy 20 B3
Lodi, U.S.A. 72 G3
Lodja, Zaïre 46 E4
Lodwar, Kenya 46 D7
Łódź, Poland 17 C10
Loeriesfontein, S. Africa 48 E2
Lofoten, Norway 8 B15
Logan, Kans., U.S.A. 70 F5
Logan, Ohio, U.S.A. 68 F4
Logan, Utah, U.S.A. 72 F8
Logan, W. Va., U.S.A. 68 G5
Logan, Mt., Canada 60 B5
Logan Pass, U.S.A. 64 D6
Logansport, Ind., U.S.A. 68 E2
Logansport, La., U.S.A. 71 K8
Logone →, Chad 45 F8
Logroño, Spain 19 A4
Lohja, Finland 9 F21
Loi-kaw, Burma 37 K20
Loimaa, Finland 9 F20
Loir →, France 18 C3
Loire →, France 18 C2
Loja, Ecuador 78 D3
Loja, Spain 19 D3

Loji, Indonesia 33 E7
Lokandu, Zaïre 46 E5
Lokeren, Belgium 15 C3
Lokitaung, Kenya 46 D7
Lokkan tekojärvi, Finland 8 C22
Lokoja, Nigeria 44 G6
Lokolama, Zaïre 46 E3
Loliondo, Tanzania 46 E7
Lolland, Denmark 9 J14
Lolo, U.S.A. 72 C6
Lom, Bulgaria 21 C10
Lomami →, Zaïre 46 D4
Lombadina, Australia 52 C3
Lombárdia □, Italy 20 B3
Lombardy = Lombárdia □, Italy 20 B3
Lomblen, Indonesia 33 F6
Lombok, Indonesia 32 F5
Lomé, Togo 44 G5
Lomela, Zaïre 46 E4
Lomela →, Zaïre 46 E4
Lometa, U.S.A. 71 K5
Lomié, Cameroon 46 D2
Lomond, Canada 64 C6
Lomond, L., U.K. 12 E4
Lompobatang, Indonesia 33 F5
Lompoc, U.S.A. 73 J3
Łomza, Poland 17 B12
Loncoche, Chile 80 D2
Londa, India 36 M9
London, Canada 62 D3
London, U.K. 11 F7
London, Ky., U.S.A. 68 G3
London, Ohio, U.S.A. 68 F4
London, Greater □, U.K. 11 F7
Londonderry, U.K. 13 B4
Londonderry □, U.K. 13 B4
Londonderry, C., Australia 52 B4
Londonderry, I., Chile 80 H2
Londrina, Brazil 80 A6
Lone Pine, U.S.A. 73 H4
Long Beach, Calif., U.S.A. 73 K4
Long Beach, Wash., U.S.A. 72 C1
Long Branch, U.S.A. 68 E9
Long Creek, U.S.A. 72 D4
Long Eaton, U.K. 10 E6
Long I., Australia 54 C4
Long I., Bahamas 75 C9
Long I., U.S.A. 68 E9
Long L., Canada 62 C2
Long Pine, U.S.A. 70 D5
Long Pt., Canada 63 C8
Long Range Mts., Canada 63 C8
Long Reef, Australia 52 B4
Long Str. = Longa, Proliv, Russia 4 C16
Long Xuyen, Vietnam 34 G8
Longa, Proliv, Russia 4 C16
Longford, Australia 54 G4
Longford, Ireland 13 C4
Longford □, Ireland 13 C4
Longiram, Indonesia 32 E5
Longlac, Canada 62 C2
Longmont, U.S.A. 70 E2
Longnawan, Indonesia 32 D4
Longreach, Australia 54 C3
Longton, Australia 54 C4
Longtown, U.K. 11 F5
Longview, Canada 64 C6
Longview, Tex., U.S.A. 71 J7
Longview, Wash., U.S.A. 72 C2
Lonoke, U.S.A. 71 H9
Lons-le-Saunier, France 18 C6
Lookout, C., Canada 62 A3
Lookout, C., U.S.A. 69 H7
Loon →, Alta., Canada 64 B5
Loon →, Man., Canada 65 B8
Loon Lake, Canada 65 C7
Loongana, Australia 53 F4
Loop Hd., Ireland 13 D2
Lop Nor = Lop Nur, China 30 B4
Lop Nur, China 30 B4
Lopatina, G., Russia 25 D15
Lopez, C., Gabon 46 E1
Lopphavet, Norway 8 A19
Lora →, Afghan. 36 D4
Lora, Hamun-i-, Pakistan 36 E4
Lora →, Australia 55 D2
Lora del Río, Spain 19 D3
Lorain, U.S.A. 68 E4
Loralai, Pakistan 36 D3
Lorca, Spain 19 D5
Lord Howe I., Pac. Oc. 56 L7
Lord Howe Ridge, Pac. Oc. 56 L8
Lordsburg, U.S.A. 73 K9
Loreto, Brazil 79 E9
Lorient, France 18 C2
Lorn, U.K. 12 E3
Lorn, Firth of, U.K. 12 E3
Lorne, Australia 55 F3
Lorraine, France 18 B7
Lorrainville, Canada 62 C4
Los Alamos, U.S.A. 73 J10
Los Andes, Chile 80 C2
Los Angeles, Chile 80 D2
Los Angeles, U.S.A. 73 K4
Los Angeles Aqueduct, U.S.A. 73 J5
Los Banos, U.S.A. 73 H3
Los Blancos, Argentina 80 A4

Los Hermanos

Los Hermanos,
  Venezuela 78 A6
Los Lunas, *U.S.A.* 73 J10
Los Mochis, *Mexico* .. 74 B3
Los Olivos, *U.S.A.* ... 73 J3
Los Roques, *Venezuela* 78 A5
Los Testigos, *Venezuela* 78 A6
Los Vilos, *Chile* 80 C2
Loshkalakh, *Russia* .. 25 C15
Lošinj, *Croatia* 16 F8
Lossiemouth, *U.K.* ... 12 D5
Lot →, *France* 18 D4
Lotfābād, *Iran* 39 B8
Lothair, *S. Africa* ... 49 D5
Lothian □, *U.K.* 12 F5
Loubomo, *Congo* 46 E2
Loudon, *U.S.A.* 69 H3
Louga, *Senegal* 44 E1
Loughborough, *U.K.* .. 10 E6
Loughrea, *Ireland* ... 13 C3
Loughros More B.,
  Ireland 13 B3
Louis Trichardt,
  S. Africa 49 C4
Louis XIV, Pte., *Canada* 62 B4
Louisa, *U.S.A.* 68 F4
Louisbourg, *Canada* . 63 C8
Louise I., *Canada* 64 C2
Louiseville, *Canada* .. 62 C5
Louisiade Arch.,
  Papua N. G. 56 J7
Louisiana, *U.S.A.* ... 70 F9
Louisiana □, *U.S.A.* . 71 K9
Louisville, *Ky., U.S.A.* 68 F3
Louisville, *Miss., U.S.A.* 71 J10
Loulé, *Portugal* 19 D1
Loup City, *U.S.A.* ... 70 E5
Lourdes, *France* 18 E3
Lourdes-du-Blanc-
  Sablon, *Canada* ... 63 B8
Lourenço-Marques =
  Maputo, *Mozam.* .. 49 D5
Louth, *Australia* 55 E4
Louth, *Ireland* 13 C5
Louth, *U.K.* 10 D7
Louth □, *Ireland* 13 C5
Louvain = Leuven,
  Belgium 15 D4
Louwsburg, *S. Africa* . 49 D5
Love, *Canada* 65 C8
Lovech, *Bulgaria* ... 21 C11
Loveland, *U.S.A.* ... 70 E2
Lovell, *U.S.A.* 72 D9
Lovelock, *U.S.A.* ... 72 F4
Loviisa, *Finland* 9 F22
Loving, *U.S.A.* 71 J2
Lovington, *U.S.A.* .. 71 J3
Lovisa = Loviisa,
  Finland 9 F22
Low Pt., *Australia* .. 53 F4
Low Tatra = Nízké
  Tatry, *Slovak Rep.* . 17 D10
Lowell, *U.S.A.* 68 D10
Lower Arrow L.,
  Canada 64 D5
Lower California = Baja
  California, *Mexico* . 74 B2
Lower Hutt, *N.Z.* ... 51 J5
Lower L., *U.S.A.* 72 F3
Lower Lake, *U.S.A.* . 72 G2
Lower Post, *Canada* . 64 B3
Lower Red L., *U.S.A.* 70 B7
Lower Saxony =
  Niedersachsen □,
  Germany 16 B5
Lower Tunguska =
  Tunguska,
  Nizhnyaya →,
  Russia 25 C9
Lowestoft, *U.K.* 11 E9
Łowicz, *Poland* 17 B10
Lowville, *U.S.A.* 68 D8
Loxton, *Australia* ... 55 E3
Loxton, *S. Africa* ... 48 E3
Loyalty Is. = Loyauté,
  Is., *N. Cal.* 56 K8
Loyang = Luoyang,
  China 31 C6
Loyauté, Is., *N. Cal.* . 56 K8
Loyev = Loyew,
  Belarus 17 C16
Loyew, *Belarus* 17 C16
Luachimo, *Angola* .. 46 F4
Luacono, *Angola* ... 46 G4
Lualaba →, *Zaïre* ... 46 D5
Luan Chau, *Vietnam* . 34 B4
Luan He →, *China* .. 31 C6
Luanda, *Angola* 46 F2
Luang Prabang, *Laos* . 34 C7
Luangwa, *Zambia* .. 47 H6
Luangwa →, *Zambia* . 47 G6
Luanshya, *Zambia* .. 47 G5
Luapula →, *Africa* .. 46 F5
Luarca, *Spain* 19 A2
Luashi, *Zaïre* 46 G4
Luau, *Angola* 46 G4
Lubalo, *Angola* 46 F3
Lubana, Ozero =
  Lubānas Ezers, *Latvia* 9 H22
Lubānas Ezers, *Latvia* 9 H22
Lubang Is., *Phil.* 33 B6
Lubuk Antu, *Malaysia* . 32 D4
Lubbock, *U.S.A.* 71 J4
Lübeck, *Germany* ... 16 B6
Lubefu, *Zaïre* 46 E4
Lubero = Luofu, *Zaïre* 46 E5
Lubicon L., *Canada* . 64 B5
Lubin, *Poland* 16 C9
Lublin, *Poland* 17 C12
Lubnān, J., *Lebanon* . 41 B4
Lubny, *Ukraine* 24 D4
Lubuagan, *Phil.* 33 A6
Lubuk Antu, *Malaysia* 32 D4
Lubuklinggau,
  Indonesia 32 E2

Lubuksikaping,
  Indonesia 32 D2
Lubumbashi, *Zaïre* .. 47 G5
Lubutu, *Zaïre* 46 E5
Lucca, *Italy* 20 C4
Luce Bay, *U.K.* 12 G4
Lucea, *Jamaica* 74 J15
Lucedale, *U.S.A.* ... 69 K1
Lucena, *Phil.* 33 B6
Lucena, *Spain* 19 D3
Lučenec, *Slovak Rep.* . 17 D10
Lucerne = Luzern,
  Switz. 16 E5
Lucira, *Angola* 47 G2
Luckenwalde, *Germany* 16 B7
Lucknow, *India* 37 F12
Lüda = Dalian, *China* . 31 C7
Lüderitz, *Namibia* ... 48 D2
Ludhiana, *India* 36 D9
Ludington, *U.S.A.* .. 68 D2
Ludlow, *U.K.* 11 E5
Ludlow, *U.S.A.* 73 J5
Ludvika, *Sweden* ... 9 F16
Ludwigsburg, *Germany* 16 D5
Ludwigshafen,
  Germany 16 D5
Luebo, *Zaïre* 46 F4
Lufira →, *Zaïre* 46 F5
Lufkin, *U.S.A.* 71 K7
Luga, *Russia* 22 C4
Lugano, *Switz.* 16 E5
Lugansk = Luhansk,
  Ukraine 23 E6
Lugh Ganana =
  Lugh Ganana,
  Somali Rep. 40 G3
Lugnaquilla, *Ireland* . 13 D5
Lugo, *Italy* 20 B4
Lugo, *Spain* 19 A2
Lugoj, *Romania* 17 F11
Lugovoy, *Kazakhstan* . 24 E8
Luhansk, *Ukraine* ... 23 E6
Luiana, *Angola* 48 B3
Luimneach = Limerick,
  Ireland 13 D3
Luís Correia, *Brazil* .. 79 D10
Luitpold Coast,
  Antarctica 5 D1
Luiza, *Zaïre* 46 F4
Luján, *Argentina* 80 C5
Lukanga Swamp,
  Zambia 47 G5
Lukenie →, *Zaïre* ... 46 E3
Lukolela, *Zaïre* 46 E3
Łuków, *Poland* 17 C12
Lule älv →, *Sweden* . 8 D19
Luleå, *Sweden* 8 D20
Lüleburgaz, *Turkey* . 21 D12
Luling, *U.S.A.* 71 L6
Lulonga →, *Zaïre* ... 46 D3
Lulua →, *Zaïre* 46 E4
Luluabourg = Kananga,
  Zaïre 46 F4
Lumai, *Angola* 47 G4
Lumajang, *Indonesia* . 33 H15
Lumbala N'guimbo,
  Angola 47 G4
Lumberton, *Miss.,
  U.S.A.* 71 K10
Lumberton, *N.C., U.S.A.* 69 H6
Lumberton, *N. Mex.,
  U.S.A.* 73 H10
Lumsden, *N.Z.* 51 L2
Lumut, *Malaysia* ... 34 Q13
Lumut, Tg., *Indonesia* 32 E3
Lund, *Sweden* 9 J15
Lund, *U.S.A.* 72 G6
Lundazi, *Zambia* ... 47 G6
Lundu, *Malaysia* ... 32 D3
Lune →, *U.K.* 10 C5
Lüneburg, *Germany* . 16 B6
Lüneburg Heath =
  Lüneburger Heide,
  Germany 16 B6
Lüneburger Heide,
  Germany 16 B6
Lunenburg, *Canada* . 63 D7
Lunéville, *France* ... 18 B7
Lunglei, *India* 37 H18
Luni, *India* 36 G8
Luni →, *India* 36 G7
Luninets = Luninyets,
  Belarus 17 B14
Luning, *U.S.A.* 72 G4
Luninyets, *Belarus* .. 17 B14
Luofu, *Zaïre* 46 E5
Luoyang, *China* 31 C6
Luozi, *Zaïre* 46 E2
Lupanshui, *China* ... 30 D5
Luray, *U.S.A.* 68 F6
Luremo, *Angola* 46 F3
Lurgan, *U.K.* 13 B5
Lusaka, *Zambia* 47 H5
Lusambo, *Zaïre* 46 E4
Lusangaye, *Zaïre* ... 46 E5
Luseland, *Canada* .. 65 C7
Lushnja, *Albania* ... 21 D8
Lushoto, *Tanzania* .. 46 E7
Lusk, *U.S.A.* 70 D2
Luta = Dalian, *China* . 31 C7
Luton, *U.K.* 11 F7
Lutong, *Malaysia* ... 32 D4
Lutsk, *Ukraine* 17 C13
Lützow Holmbukta,
  Antarctica 5 C4
Lutzputs, *S. Africa* .. 48 D3
Luverne, *U.S.A.* 70 D6
Luwuk, *Indonesia* .. 33 E6
Luxembourg, *Lux.* .. 18 B7
Luxembourg □,
  Belgium 15 E5
Luxembourg ■, *Europe* 18 B7
Luxi, *China* 30 D4
Luxor = El Uqsur,
  Egypt 45 C11

Luza, *Russia* 22 B8
Luzern, *Switz.* 16 E5
Luzhou, *China* 30 D5
Luziânia, *Brazil* 79 G9
Luzon, *Phil.* 33 A6
Lviv, *Ukraine* 17 D13
Lvov = Lviv, *Ukraine* . 17 D13
Lyakhavichy, *Belarus* . 17 B14
Lyakhovskiye, Ostrova,
  Russia 25 B15
Lyallpur = Faisalabad,
  Pakistan 36 D8
Lycksele, *Sweden* ... 8 D18
Lydda = Lod, *Israel* . 41 D3
Lydenburg, *S. Africa* . 49 D5
Lydia, *Turkey* 21 E13
Lyell, *U.S.A.* 51 J4
Lyell I., *Canada* 64 C2
Lyepyel, *Belarus* 22 D4
Lyman, *U.S.A.* 72 F8
Lyme Regis, *U.K.* ... 11 G5
Lymington, *U.K.* 11 G6
Łyna →, *Poland* 9 J19
Lynchburg, *U.S.A.* .. 68 G6
Lynd →, *Australia* .. 54 B3
Lynd Ra., *Australia* .. 55 D4
Lynden, *U.S.A.* 72 B2
Lyndhurst, Queens.,
  Australia 54 B3
Lyndhurst, S. Austral.,
  Australia 55 E2
Lyndon →, *Australia* . 53 D1
Lyngen, *Norway* 8 B19
Lynher Reef, *Australia* 52 C3
Lynn, *U.S.A.* 68 D10
Lynn Canal, *U.S.A.* . 64 B1
Lynn Lake, *Canada* . 65 B8
Lynton, *U.K.* 11 F4
Lyntupy, *Belarus* 9 J22
Lynx L., *Canada* 65 A7
Lyon, *France* 18 D6
Lyonnais, *France* ... 18 D6
Lyons = Lyon, *France* 18 D6
Lyons, *Colo., U.S.A.* 70 E2
Lyons, *Ga., U.S.A.* .. 69 J4
Lyons, *Kans., U.S.A.* 70 F5
Lyons, *N.Y., U.S.A.* . 68 D7
Lys = Leie →,
  Belgium 15 C3
Lysva, *Russia* 22 C10
Lysychansk, *Ukraine* . 23 E6
Lytle, *U.S.A.* 71 L5
Lyttelton, *N.Z.* 51 K4
Lytton, *Canada* 64 C4
Lyubertsy, *Russia* .. 22 C6
Lyuboml, *Ukraine* .. 17 C13

M

Ma'adaba, *Jordan* ... 41 E4
Maamba, *Zambia* ... 48 B4
Ma'ān, *Jordan* 41 E4
Ma'ān □, *Jordan* ... 41 F5
Maanselkä, *Finland* . 8 C23
Ma'anshan, *China* .. 31 C6
Maarianhamina,
  Finland 9 F18
Ma'arrat an Nu'mān,
  Syria 38 C3
Maas →, *Neths.* ... 15 C4
Maaseik, *Belgium* ... 15 C5
Maassluis, *Neths.* ... 15 C4
Maastricht, *Neths.* .. 18 A6
Maave, *Mozam.* 49 C5
Mabel L., *Canada* ... 64 C5
Mablethorpe, *U.K.* .. 10 D8
Mabrouk, *Mali* 44 E4
Mabton, *U.S.A.* 72 C3
Macaé, *Brazil* 79 H10
McAlester, *U.S.A.* .. 71 H7
McAllen, *U.S.A.* 71 M5
Macamic, *Canada* .. 62 C4
Macao = Macau ■,
  China 31 D6
Macapá, *Brazil* 79 C8
McArthur →, *Australia* 54 B2
McArthur, Port,
  Australia 54 B2
McArthur River,
  Australia 54 B2
Macau, *Brazil* 79 E11
Macau ■, *China* 31 D6
McBride, *Canada* ... 64 C4
McCall, *U.S.A.* 72 D5
McCamey, *U.S.A.* .. 71 K3
McCammon, *U.S.A.* 72 E7
McCauley I., *Canada* . 64 C2
Macclesfield, *U.K.* .. 10 D5
McClintock, *Canada* . 65 B10
M'Clintock Chan.,
  Canada 60 A9
McClintock Ra.,
  Australia 52 C4
McCloud, *U.S.A.* ... 72 F2
McCluer I., *Australia* . 52 B5
M'Clure Str., *Canada* . 4 B2
McClusky, *U.S.A.* ... 70 B4
McComb, *U.S.A.* ... 71 K9
McConaughy, L., *U.S.A.* 70 E4
McCook, *U.S.A.* 70 E4
McCusker →, *Canada* 65 B7
McDame, *Canada* .. 64 B3
McDermitt, *U.S.A.* .. 72 F5
Macdonald, L.,
  Australia 52 D4
McDonald Is., *Ind. Oc.* 35 K6
Macdonnell Ras.,
  Australia 52 D5
McDouall Peak,
  Australia 55 D1

Macdougall L., *Canada* 60 B10
MacDowell L., *Canada* 62 B1
Macduff, *U.K.* 12 D6
Macedonia =
  Makedonía □,
  Greece 21 D10
Macedonia ■, *Europe* 21 D9
Maceió, *Brazil* 79 E11
Macenta, *Guinea* ... 44 G3
Macerata, *Italy* 20 C5
McFarlane →, *Canada* 65 B7
Macfarlane, L.,
  Australia 55 E2
McGehee, *U.S.A.* ... 71 J9
McGill, *U.S.A.* 72 G6
Macgillycuddy's Reeks,
  Ireland 13 D2
MacGregor, *Canada* . 65 D9
McGregor, *U.S.A.* .. 70 D9
McGregor →, *Canada* 64 B4
McGregor Ra., *Australia* 55 D3
Mach, *Pakistan* 36 E5
Māch Kowr, *Iran* ... 39 E9
Machado =
  Jiparaná →, *Brazil* 78 E6
Machakos, *Kenya* ... 46 E7
Machala, *Ecuador* .. 78 D3
Machanga, *Mozam.* . 49 C6
Machattie, L., *Australia* 54 C2
Machava, *Mozam.* .. 49 D5
Machevna, *Russia* .. 25 C18
Machichi →, *Canada* . 65 B10
Machilipatnam, *India* . 37 L12
Machiques, *Venezuela* 78 A4
Machupicchu, *Peru* . 78 F4
Machynlleth, *U.K.* .. 11 E4
McIlwraith Ra.,
  Australia 54 A3
McIntosh, *U.S.A.* ... 70 C4
McIntosh L., *Canada* . 65 B8
Macintosh Ra.,
  Australia 53 E4
Macintyre →,
  Australia 55 D5
Mackay, *Australia* .. 54 C4
Mackay, *U.S.A.* 72 E7
MacKay →, *Canada* . 64 B6
McKay Ra., *Australia* 52 D3
McKeesport, *U.S.A.* . 68 E6
Mackenzie, *Canada* . 64 B4
McKenzie, *U.S.A.* .. 69 G1
Mackenzie →,
  Australia 54 C4
Mackenzie →, *Canada* 60 B6
McKenzie →, *U.S.A.* 72 D2
Mackenzie Bay, *Canada* 4 B1
Mackenzie City =
  Linden, *Guyana* ... 78 B7
Mackenzie Highway,
  Canada 64 B5
Mackenzie Mts.,
  Canada 60 B6
Mackinaw City, *U.S.A.* 68 C3
McKinlay, *Australia* . 54 C3
McKinlay →, *Australia* 54 C3
McKinley, Mt., *U.S.A.* 60 B4
McKinley Sea, *Arctic* . 4 A7
McKinney, *U.S.A.* .. 71 J6
Macksville, *Australia* 55 E5
McLaughlin, *U.S.A.* . 70 C4
Maclean, *Australia* .. 55 D5
McLean, *U.S.A.* 71 H4
McLeansboro, *U.S.A.* 70 F10
Maclear, *S. Africa* ... 49 E4
Macleay →, *Australia* 55 E5
McLennan, *Canada* .. 64 B5
McLeod, B., *Canada* . 65 A7
McLeod, L., *Australia* 53 D1
MacLeod Lake, *Canada* 64 C4
McLoughlin, Mt., *U.S.A.* 72 E2
McLure, *Canada* 64 C4
McMillan, L., *U.S.A.* . 71 J2
McMinnville, *Oreg.,
  U.S.A.* 72 D2
McMinnville, *Tenn.,
  U.S.A.* 69 H3
McMorran, *Canada* . 65 C7
McMurdo Sd.,
  Antarctica 5 D11
McMurray = Fort
  McMurray, *Canada* 64 B6
McNary, *U.S.A.* 73 J9
MacNutt, *Canada* ... 65 C8
Macodoene, *Mozam.* 49 C6
Macomb, *U.S.A.* ... 70 E9
Mâcon, *France* 18 C6
Macon, *Ga., U.S.A.* . 69 J4
Macon, *Miss., U.S.A.* 69 J1
Macon, *Mo., U.S.A.* 70 F8
Macondo, *Angola* .. 47 G4
Macoun L., *Canada* . 65 B8
Macovane, *Mozam.* . 49 C6
McPherson, *U.S.A.* . 70 F6
McPherson Ra.,
  Australia 55 D5
Macquarie Harbour,
  Australia 54 G4
Macquarie Is., *Pac. Oc.* 56 N7
MacRobertson Land,
  Antarctica 5 D6
Macroom, *Ireland* .. 13 E3
Macroy, *Australia* ... 52 D2
Macusse, *Angola* ... 48 B3
McVille, *U.S.A.* 70 B5
Madadeni, *S. Africa* . 49 D5
Madagali, *Nigeria* ... 45 F7
Mada'in Sālih,
  Si. Arabia 38 E3
Madama, *Niger* 45 D7
Madame I., *Canada* . 63 C7

Madaoua, *Niger* 44 F6
Madaripur, *Bangla.* .. 37 H17
Madauk, *Burma* 37 L20
Madawaska →,
  Canada 62 C4
Madaya, *Burma* 37 H20
Madden Dam, *Panama* 74 H14
Madden L., *Panama* . 74 H14
Madeira, *Atl. Oc.* ... 44 B1
Madeira →, *Brazil* .. 78 D7
Madeleine, Is. de la,
  Canada 63 C7
Madera, *U.S.A.* 73 H3
Madha, *India* 36 L9
Madhya Pradesh □,
  India 36 H11
Madikeri, *India* 36 N9
Madill, *U.S.A.* 71 H6
Madimba, *Zaïre* 46 E3
Ma'din, *Syria* 38 C3
Madīnat ash Sha'b,
  Yemen 40 E3
Madingou, *Congo* .. 46 E2
Madirovalo, *Madag.* . 49 B8
Madison, *Fla., U.S.A.* 69 K4
Madison, *Ind., U.S.A.* 68 F3
Madison, *Nebr., U.S.A.* 70 E6
Madison, *S. Dak.,
  U.S.A.* 70 D6
Madison, *Wis., U.S.A.* 70 D10
Madison →, *U.S.A.* . 72 D8
Madisonville, *Ky.,
  U.S.A.* 68 G2
Madisonville, *Tex.,
  U.S.A.* 71 K7
Madista, *Botswana* . 48 C4
Madiun, *Indonesia* .. 33 G14
Madley, *U.K.* 11 E5
Madona, *Latvia* 9 H22
Madras = Tamil
  Nadu □, *India* 36 P10
Madras, *India* 36 N12
Madras, *U.S.A.* 72 D3
Madre, Laguna, *U.S.A.* 71 M6
Madre, Sierra, *Phil.* . 33 A6
Madre de Dios →,
  Bolivia 78 F5
Madre de Dios, I., *Chile* 80 G1
Madre Occidental,
  Sierra, *Mexico* 74 B3
Madre Oriental, Sierra,
  Mexico 74 C5
Madrid, *Spain* 19 B4
Madura, Selat,
  Indonesia 33 G15
Madura Motel,
  Australia 53 F4
Madurai, *India* 36 Q11
Madurantakam, *India* 36 N11
Mae Hong Son,
  Thailand 34 C5
Mae Sot, *Thailand* .. 34 D5
Maebashi, *Japan* ... 29 F9
Maestrazgo, Mts. del,
  Spain 19 B5
Maevatanana, *Madag.* 49 B8
Mafeking = Mafikeng,
  S. Africa 48 D4
Mafeking, *Canada* .. 65 C8
Mafeteng, *Lesotho* .. 48 D4
Maffra, *Australia* 55 F4
Mafia I., *Tanzania* ... 46 F7
Mafikeng, *S. Africa* . 48 D4
Mafra, *Brazil* 80 B7
Mafra, *Portugal* 19 C1
Magadan, *Russia* ... 25 D16
Magadi, *Kenya* 46 E7
Magaliesburg, *S. Africa* 49 D4
Magallanes, Estrecho
  de, *Chile* 80 G2
Magangué, *Colombia* 78 B4
Magburaka, *S. Leone* 44 G2
Magdalen Is. =
  Madeleine, Is. de la,
  Canada 63 C7
Magdalena, *Argentina* 80 D5
Magdalena, *Bolivia* . 78 F6
Magdalena, *Malaysia* 32 D5
Magdalena, *U.S.A.* . 73 J10
Magdalena →,
  Colombia 78 A4
Magdeburg, *Germany* 16 B6
Magdelaine Cays,
  Australia 54 B5
Magee, *U.S.A.* 71 K10
Magee, I., *U.K.* 13 B6
Magelang, *Indonesia* 33 G14
Magellan's Str. =
  Magallanes, Estrecho
  de, *Chile* 80 G2
Magenta, L., *Australia* 53 F2
Magerøya, *Norway* . 8 A21
Magherafelt, *U.K.* ... 13 B5
Magistralnyy, *Russia* 25 D11
Magnetic Pole (North)
  = North Magnetic
  Pole, *Canada* 4 B2
Magnetic Pole (South)
  = South Magnetic
  Pole, *Antarctica* .. 5 C9
Magnitogorsk, *Russia* 22 D10
Magnolia, *Ark., U.S.A.* 71 J8
Magnolia, *Miss., U.S.A.* 71 K9
Magog, *Canada* 63 C5
Magosa = Famagusta,
  Cyprus 38 C2
Magpie L., *Canada* . 63 B7
Magrath, *Canada* ... 64 D6
Maguarinho, C., *Brazil* 79 D9
Mağusa = Famagusta,
  Cyprus 38 C2

Maguse L., *Canada* . 65 A9
Maguse Pt., *Canada* . 65 A10
Magwe, *Burma* 37 J19
Mahābād, *Iran* 38 B5
Mahabo, *Madag.* ... 49 C7
Mahagi, *Zaïre* 46 D6
Mahajamba →,
  Madag. 49 B8
Mahajamba,
  Helodranon' i,
  Madag. 49 B8
Mahajanga, *Madag.* 49 B8
Mahajanga □, *Madag.* 49 B8
Mahajilo →, *Madag.* . 49 B8
Mahakam →,
  Indonesia 32 E5
Mahalapye, *Botswana* 48 C4
Mahallāt, *Iran* 39 C6
Māhān, *Iran* 39 D8
Mahanadi →, *India* . 37 J15
Mahanoro, *Madag.* . 49 B8
Maharashtra □, *India* 36 J9
Mahasham, W. →,
  Egypt 41 E3
Mahasolo, *Madag.* .. 49 B8
Mahattat ash Shīdīyah,
  Jordan 41 F4
Mahattat 'Unayzah,
  Jordan 41 E4
Mahbubnagar, *India* . 36 L10
Mahdah, *Oman* 39 E7
Mahdia, *Tunisia* 45 A7
Mahé, *Seychelles* ... 35 E4
Mahenge, *Tanzania* . 46 F7
Maheno, *N.Z.* 51 L3
Mahesana, *India* 36 H8
Mahia Pen., *N.Z.* ... 51 H6
Mahilyow, *Belarus* .. 17 B16
Mahnomen, *U.S.A.* . 70 B7
Mahón, *Spain* 19 C8
Mahone Bay, *Canada* 63 D7
Mai-Ndombe, L., *Zaïre* 46 E3
Maicurú →, *Brazil* .. 79 D8
Maidenhead, *U.K.* .. 11 F7
Maidstone, *Canada* . 65 C7
Maidstone, *U.K.* 11 F8
Maiduguri, *Nigeria* .. 45 F7
Maijdi, *Bangla.* 37 H17
Maikala Ra., *India* ... 37 J12
Main →, *Germany* .. 16 C5
Main →, *U.K.* 13 B5
Main Centre, *Canada* 65 C7
Maine, *France* 18 C3
Maine □, *U.S.A.* 63 C6
Maine →, *Ireland* ... 13 D2
Maingkwan, *Burma* . 37 F20
Mainit, L., *Phil.* 33 C7
Mainland, *Orkney, U.K.* 12 C5
Mainland, *Shet., U.K.* 12 A7
Maintirano, *Madag.* . 49 B7
Mainz, *Germany* 16 C5
Maipú, *Argentina* ... 80 D5
Maiquetía, *Venezuela* 78 A5
Mairabari, *India* 37 F18
Maitland, *N.S.W.,
  Australia* 55 E5
Maitland, *S. Austral.,
  Australia* 55 E2
Maizuru, *Japan* 29 G7
Majalengka, *Indonesia* 33 G13
Majene, *Indonesia* .. 33 E5
Maji, *Ethiopia* 45 G12
Major, *Canada* 65 C7
Majorca = Mallorca,
  Spain 19 C7
Maka, *Senegal* 44 F2
Makale, *Indonesia* .. 33 E5
Makari, *Cameroon* .. 46 B2
Makarikari =
  Makgadikgadi Salt
  Pans, *Botswana* ... 48 C4
Makarovo, *Russia* .. 25 D11
Makasar = Ujung
  Pandang, *Indonesia* 33 F5
Makasar, Selat,
  Indonesia 33 E5
Makasar, Str. of =
  Makasar, Selat,
  Indonesia 33 E5
Makat, *Kazakhstan* . 23 E9
Makedhonía □, *Greece* 21 D10
Makedonija =
  Macedonia ■, *Europe* 21 D9
Makena, *U.S.A.* 66 H16
Makeni, *S. Leone* ... 44 G2
Makeyevka =
  Makiyivka, *Ukraine* 23 E6
Makgadikgadi Salt
  Pans, *Botswana* ... 48 C4
Makhachkala, *Russia* 23 F8
Makhmūr, *Iraq* 38 C4
Makian, *Indonesia* .. 33 D7
Makindu, *Kenya* 46 E7
Makinsk, *Kazakhstan* 24 D8
Makiyivka, *Ukraine* . 23 E6
Makkah, *Si. Arabia* . 40 C2
Makkovik, *Canada* .. 63 B8
Makó, *Hungary* 17 E11
Makokou, *Gabon* ... 46 D2
Makoua, *Congo* 46 E3
Makrai, *India* 36 H10
Makran Coast Range,
  Pakistan 36 G4
Maksimkin Yar, *Russia* 24 D9
Mākū, *Iran* 38 B5
Makumbi, *Zaïre* 46 F4
Makunda, *Botswana* 48 C3
Makurazaki, *Japan* .. 29 J5
Makurdi, *Nigeria* ... 44 G6
Makūyeh, *Iran* 39 D7
Makwassie, *S. Africa* 48 D4
Mal B., *Ireland* 13 D2
Malabang, *Phil.* 33 C6

Mathura

Malabar Coast, India 36 P9
Malabo = Rey Malabo, Eq. Guin. 44 H6
Malacca, Str. of, Indonesia 34 S14
Malad City, U.S.A. 72 E7
Maladzyechna, Belarus 17 A14
Málaga, Spain 19 D3
Malaga, U.S.A. 71 J2
Malaimbandy, Madag. 49 C8
Malakâl, Sudan 45 G11
Malakand, Pakistan 36 B7
Malakoff, U.S.A. 71 J7
Malamyzh, Russia 25 E14
Malang, Indonesia 33 G15
Malangen, Norway 8 B18
Malanje, Angola 46 F3
Mälaren, Sweden 9 G17
Malargüe, Argentina 80 D3
Malartic, Canada 62 C4
Malaryta, Belarus 17 C13
Malatya, Turkey 23 G6
Malawi ■, Africa 47 G6
Malawi, L., Africa 47 G6
Malay Pen., Asia 34 J6
Malaybalay, Phil. 33 C7
Malāyer, Iran 39 C6
Malaysia ■, Asia 32 D4
Malazgirt, Turkey 23 G7
Malbon, Australia 54 C3
Malbooma, Australia 55 E1
Malbork, Poland 17 B10
Malcolm, Australia 53 E3
Malcolm, Pt., Australia 53 F3
Maldegem, Belgium 15 C3
Malden, U.S.A. 71 G10
Malden I., Kiribati 57 H12
Maldives ■, Ind. Oc. 27 J11
Maldonado, Uruguay 80 C6
Malé Karpaty, Slovak Rep. 17 D9
Maléa, Ákra, Greece 21 F10
Malegaon, India 36 J9
Malek Kandī, Iran 38 B5
Malema, Mozam. 47 G7
Malgomaj, Sweden 8 D17
Malha, Sudan 45 E10
Malheur →, U.S.A. 72 D5
Malheur L., U.S.A. 72 E4
Mali ■, Africa 44 E4
Mali →, Burma 37 G20
Mali Kyun, Burma 34 F5
Malik, Indonesia 33 E6
Malili, Indonesia 33 E6
Malin Hd., Ireland 13 A4
Malindi, Kenya 46 E8
Malines = Mechelen, Belgium 15 C4
Malino, Indonesia 33 D6
Malita, Phil. 33 C7
Malkara, Turkey 21 D12
Mallacoota, Australia 55 F4
Mallacoota Inlet, Australia 55 F4
Mallaig, U.K. 12 E3
Mallawi, Egypt 45 C11
Mallorca, Spain 19 C7
Mallow, Ireland 13 D3
Malmberget, Sweden 8 C19
Malmédy, Belgium 15 D6
Malmesbury, S. Africa 48 E2
Malmö, Sweden 9 J15
Malolos, Phil. 33 B6
Malone, U.S.A. 68 C8
Måløy, Norway 9 F11
Malozemelskaya Tundra, Russia 22 A9
Malpelo, Colombia 78 C2
Malta, Idaho, U.S.A. 72 E7
Malta, Mont., U.S.A. 72 B10
Malta ■, Europe 20 G6
Maltahöhe, Namibia 48 C2
Malton, U.K. 10 C7
Maluku, Indonesia 33 E7
Maluku □, Indonesia 33 E7
Maluku Sea = Molucca Sea, Indonesia 33 E6
Malvan, India 36 L8
Malvern, U.S.A. 71 H8
Malvern Hills, U.K. 11 E5
Malvinas, Is. = Falkland Is. □, Atl. Oc. 80 G5
Malyn, Ukraine 17 C15
Malyy Lyakhovskiy, Ostrov, Russia 25 B15
Malyy Nimnyr, Russia 25 D13
Mama, Russia 25 D12
Mamanguape, Brazil 79 E11
Mamasa, Indonesia 33 E5
Mamberamo →, Indonesia 33 E9
Mambilima Falls, Zambia 46 G5
Mamburao, Phil. 33 B6
Mameigwess L., Canada 62 B2
Mamfe, Cameroon 44 G6
Mammoth, U.S.A. 73 K8
Mamoré →, Bolivia 78 F5
Mamou, Guinea 44 F2
Mamuju, Indonesia 33 E5
Man, Ivory C. 44 G3
Man, I. of, U.K. 10 C3
Man Na, Burma 37 H20
Mana, Fr. Guiana 79 B8
Manaar, G. of = Mannar, G. of, Asia 36 Q11
Manacapuru, Brazil 78 D6
Manacor, Spain 19 C7
Manado, Indonesia 33 D6
Managua, Nic. 74 E7
Manakara, Madag. 49 C8
Manama = Al Manāmah, Bahrain 39 E6
Manambao →, Madag. 49 B7
Manambato, Madag. 49 A8
Manambolo →, Madag. 49 B7
Manambolosy, Madag. 49 B8
Mananara, Madag. 49 B8
Mananara →, Madag. 49 C8
Mananjary, Madag. 49 C8
Manantenina, Madag. 49 C8
Manaos = Manaus, Brazil 78 D7
Manapouri, N.Z. 51 L1
Manapouri, L., N.Z. 51 L1
Manas, China 30 B3
Manas →, India 37 F17
Manassa, U.S.A. 73 H11
Manaung, Burma 37 K18
Manaus, Brazil 78 D7
Manawan L., Canada 65 B8
Manay, Phil. 33 C7
Manbij, Syria 38 B3
Mancelona, U.S.A. 68 C3
Manchester, U.K. 10 D5
Manchester, Conn., U.S.A. 68 E9
Manchester, Ga., U.S.A. 69 J3
Manchester, Iowa, U.S.A. 70 D9
Manchester, Ky., U.S.A. 68 G4
Manchester, N.H., U.S.A. 68 D10
Manchester L., Canada 65 A7
Manchuria = Dongbei, China 31 B7
Mand →, Iran 39 D7
Manda, Tanzania 46 G6
Mandabé, Madag. 49 C7
Mandal, Norway 9 G12
Mandalay, Burma 37 J20
Mandale = Mandalay, Burma 37 J20
Mandalī, Iraq 38 C5
Mandan, U.S.A. 70 B4
Mandar, Teluk, Indonesia 33 E5
Mandasor = Mandsaur, India 36 G9
Mandaue, Phil. 33 B6
Mandi, India 36 D10
Mandimba, Mozam. 47 G7
Mandioli, Indonesia 33 E7
Mandla, India 37 H12
Mandoto, Madag. 49 B8
Mandrare →, Madag. 49 D8
Mandritsara, Madag. 49 B8
Mandsaur, India 36 G9
Mandurah, Australia 53 F2
Mandvi, India 36 H6
Mandya, India 36 N10
Maneh, Iran 39 B8
Maneroo, Australia 54 C3
Maneroo Cr. →, Australia 54 C3
Manfalût, Egypt 45 C11
Manfred, Australia 55 E3
Manfredónia, Italy 20 D6
Mangalia, Romania 17 G15
Mangalore, India 36 N9
Mangaweka, N.Z. 51 H5
Manggar, Indonesia 32 E3
Manggawitu, Indonesia 33 E8
Mangkalihat, Tanjung, Indonesia 33 D5
Mangla Dam, Pakistan 36 C8
Mangnai, China 30 C4
Mango, Togo 44 F5
Mangoche, Malawi 47 G7
Mangoky →, Madag. 49 C7
Mangole, Indonesia 33 E7
Mangonui, N.Z. 51 F4
Mangueigne, Chad 45 F9
Mangueira, L. da, Brazil 80 C6
Mangum, U.S.A. 71 H5
Mangyshlak Poluostrov, Kazakhstan 24 E6
Manhattan, U.S.A. 70 F6
Manhiça, Mozam. 49 D5
Manhuaçu, Brazil 79 H10
Mania →, Madag. 49 B8
Manica, Mozam. 49 B5
Manica e Sofala □, Mozam. 49 B5
Manicoré, Brazil 78 E6
Manicouagan →, Canada 63 C6
Manīfah, Si. Arabia 39 E6
Manifold, Australia 54 C5
Manifold, C., Australia 54 C5
Manigotagan, Canada 65 C9
Manihiki, Cook Is. 57 J11
Manila, Phil. 33 B6
Manila, U.S.A. 72 F9
Manila B., Phil. 33 B6
Manilla, Australia 55 E5
Maningrida, Australia 54 A1
Manipur □, India 37 G18
Manipur →, Burma 37 H19
Manisa, Turkey 21 E12
Manistee, U.S.A. 68 C2
Manistee →, U.S.A. 68 C2
Manistique, U.S.A. 68 C2
Manito L., Canada 65 C7
Manitoba □, Canada 65 B9
Manitoba, L., Canada 65 C9
Manitou, Canada 65 D9
Manitou I., U.S.A. 62 C2
Manitou Is., U.S.A. 68 C2
Manitou L., Canada 63 B6
Manitou Springs, U.S.A. 70 F2
Manitoulin I., Canada 62 C3
Manitowaning, Canada 62 C3
Manitowoc, U.S.A. 68 C2
Manizales, Colombia 78 B3
Manja, Madag. 49 C7
Manjacaze, Mozam. 49 C5
Manjakandriana, Madag. 49 B8
Manjhand, Pakistan 36 G6
Manjil, Iran 39 B6
Manjimup, Australia 53 F2
Manjra →, India 36 K10
Mankato, Kans., U.S.A. 70 F5
Mankato, Minn., U.S.A. 70 C8
Mankayane, Swaziland 49 D5
Mankono, Ivory C. 44 G3
Mankota, Canada 65 D7
Manly, Australia 55 E5
Manmad, India 36 J9
Mann Ras., Australia 53 E5
Manna, Indonesia 32 E2
Mannahill, Australia 55 E3
Mannar, Sri Lanka 36 Q11
Mannar, G. of, Asia 36 Q11
Mannar I., Sri Lanka 36 Q11
Mannheim, Germany 16 D5
Manning, Canada 64 B5
Manning, U.S.A. 69 J5
Manning Prov. Park, Canada 64 D4
Mannington, U.S.A. 68 F5
Mannum, Australia 55 E2
Mano, S. Leone 44 G2
Manokwari, Indonesia 33 E8
Manombo, Madag. 49 C7
Manono, Zaïre 46 F5
Manosque, France 18 E6
Manouane, L., Canada 63 B5
Manresa, Spain 19 B6
Mansa, Zambia 46 G5
Mansel I., Canada 61 B11
Mansfield, Australia 55 F4
Mansfield, U.K. 10 D6
Mansfield, La., U.S.A. 71 J8
Mansfield, Ohio, U.S.A. 68 E4
Mansfield, Wash., U.S.A. 72 C4
Manson Creek, Canada 64 B4
Manta, Ecuador 78 D2
Mantalingajan, Mt., Phil. 32 C5
Manteca, U.S.A. 73 H3
Manteo, U.S.A. 69 H8
Mantes-la-Jolie, France 18 B4
Manthani, India 36 K11
Manti, U.S.A. 72 G8
Mantiqueira, Serra da, Brazil 79 H10
Manton, U.S.A. 68 C3
Mántova, Italy 20 B4
Mänttä, Finland 9 E21
Mantua = Mántova, Italy 20 B4
Manu, Peru 78 F4
Manua Is., Amer. Samoa 51 B14
Manuae, Cook Is. 57 J12
Manuel Alves →, Brazil 79 F9
Manui, Indonesia 33 E6
Manville, U.S.A. 70 D2
Many, U.S.A. 71 K8
Manyara, L., Tanzania 46 E7
Manych-Gudilo, Ozero, Russia 23 E7
Manyoni, Tanzania 46 F6
Manzai, Pakistan 36 C7
Manzanares, Spain 19 C4
Manzanillo, Cuba 75 C9
Manzanillo, Mexico 74 D4
Manzano Mts., U.S.A. 73 J10
Manzarīyeh, Iran 39 C6
Manzhouli, China 31 B6
Manzini, Swaziland 49 D5
Mao, Chad 45 F8
Maoke, Pegunungan, Indonesia 33 E9
Maoming, China 31 D6
Mapam Yumco, China 30 C3
Mapia, Kepulauan, Indonesia 33 D8
Mapinhane, Mozam. 49 C6
Maple Creek, Canada 65 D7
Mapleton, U.S.A. 72 D2
Mapuera →, Brazil 78 D7
Maputo, Mozam. 49 D5
Maputo, B. de, Mozam. 49 D5
Maqnā, Si. Arabia 38 D2
Maquela do Zombo, Angola 46 F3
Maquinchao, Argentina 80 E3
Maquoketa, U.S.A. 70 D9
Mar, Serra do, Brazil 80 B7
Mar Chiquita, L., Argentina 80 C4
Mar del Plata, Argentina 80 D5
Mar Menor, Spain 19 D5
Maraã, Brazil 78 D5
Marabá, Brazil 79 E9
Maracá, I. de, Brazil 79 C8
Maracaibo, Venezuela 78 A4
Maracaibo, L. de, Venezuela 78 B4
Maracay, Venezuela 78 A5
Marādah, Libya 45 C8
Maradi, Niger 44 F6
Marāgheh, Iran 38 B5
Marāh, Si. Arabia 38 E5
Marajó, I. de, Brazil 79 D9
Marākand, Iran 38 B5
Maralal, Kenya 46 D7
Maralinga, Australia 53 F5
Marama, Australia 55 F3
Marampa, S. Leone 44 G2
Marana, U.S.A. 73 K8
Maranboy, Australia 52 B5
Marand, Iran 38 B5
Maranguape, Brazil 79 D11
Maranhão = São Luís, Brazil 79 D10
Maranhão □, Brazil 79 E9
Maranoa →, Australia 55 D4
Marañón →, Peru 78 D4
Marão, Mozam. 49 C5
Maraş = Kahramanmaraş, Turkey 23 G6
Marathon, Australia 54 C3
Marathon, Canada 62 C2
Marathon, U.S.A. 71 K3
Maratua, Indonesia 33 D5
Marāwih, U.A.E. 39 E7
Marbella, Spain 19 D3
Marble Bar, Australia 52 D2
Marble Falls, U.S.A. 71 K5
Marburg, Germany 16 C5
March, U.K. 11 E8
Marche, France 18 C4
Marche-en-Famenne, Belgium 15 D5
Marchena, Spain 19 D3
Marcus I. = Minami-Tori-Shima, Pac. Oc. 56 E7
Marcus Necker Ridge, Pac. Oc. 56 F9
Mardan, Pakistan 36 B8
Mardie, Australia 52 D2
Mardin, Turkey 23 G7
Maree, L., U.K. 12 D3
Mareeba, Australia 54 B4
Marek = Stanke Dimitrov, Bulgaria 21 C10
Marek, Indonesia 33 E6
Marengo, U.S.A. 70 E8
Marerano, Madag. 49 C7
Marfa, U.S.A. 71 K2
Margaret →, Australia 52 C4
Margaret Bay, Canada 64 C3
Margaret L., Canada 64 B5
Margaret River, Australia 52 C4
Margarita, Panama 74 H14
Margarita, I. de, Venezuela 78 A6
Margaritovo, Russia 28 C7
Margate, S. Africa 49 E5
Margate, U.K. 11 F9
Margelan = Marghilon, Uzbekistan 24 E8
Marghilon, Uzbekistan 24 E8
Marguerite, Canada 64 C4
Mari El □, Russia 22 C8
Mari Republic = Mari El □, Russia 22 C8
Maria I., N. Terr., Australia 54 A2
Maria I., Tas., Australia 54 G4
Maria van Diemen, C., N.Z. 51 F4
Marian L., Canada 64 A5
Mariana Trench, Pac. Oc. 56 F6
Marianao, Cuba 75 C8
Marianna, Ark., U.S.A. 71 H9
Marianna, Fla., U.S.A. 69 K3
Marias →, U.S.A. 72 C8
Ma'rib, Yemen 40 D4
Maribor, Slovenia 16 E8
Marico →, Africa 48 C4
Maricopa, Ariz., U.S.A. 73 K7
Maricopa, Calif., U.S.A. 73 J4
Maricourt, Canada 61 C12
Marîdî, Sudan 45 H10
Marie Byrd Land, Antarctica 5 D14
Marie-Galante, Guadeloupe 75 D12
Mariecourt = Kangiqsujuaq, Canada 61 B12
Marienberg, Neths. 15 B6
Marienbourg, Belgium 15 D4
Mariental, Namibia 48 C2
Mariestad, Sweden 9 G15
Marietta, Ga., U.S.A. 69 J3
Marietta, Ohio, U.S.A. 68 F5
Mariinsk, Russia 24 D9
Marijampolė, Lithuania 9 J20
Marília, Brazil 79 H8
Marillana, Australia 52 D2
Marín, Spain 19 A1
Marina Plains, Australia 54 A3
Marinduque, Phil. 33 B6
Marine City, U.S.A. 68 D4
Marinette, U.S.A. 68 C2
Maringá, Brazil 80 A6
Marion, Ala., U.S.A. 69 J2
Marion, Ill., U.S.A. 71 G10
Marion, Ind., U.S.A. 68 E3
Marion, Iowa, U.S.A. 70 D9
Marion, Kans., U.S.A. 70 F6
Marion, Mich., U.S.A. 68 C3
Marion, N.C., U.S.A. 69 H4
Marion, Ohio, U.S.A. 68 E4
Marion, S.C., U.S.A. 69 H6
Marion, Va., U.S.A. 69 G5
Marion, L., U.S.A. 69 J5
Marion I., Ind. Oc. 35 J2
Mariposa, U.S.A. 73 H4
Mariscal Estigarribia, Paraguay 78 H6
Maritime Alps = Maritimes, Alpes, Europe 16 F4
Maritimes, Alpes, Europe 16 F4
Maritsa = Évros →, Bulgaria 21 D12
Mariupol, Ukraine 23 E6
Marīvān, Iran 38 C5
Markazī □, Iran 39 C6
Marked Tree, U.S.A. 71 H9
Marken, Neths. 15 B5
Market Drayton, U.K. 10 E5
Market Harborough, U.K. 11 E7
Markham, Mt., Antarctica 5 E11
Markham L., Canada 65 A8
Markovo, Russia 25 C17
Marks, Russia 22 D8
Marksville, U.S.A. 71 K8
Marla, Australia 55 D1
Marlborough, Australia 54 C4
Marlborough Downs, U.K. 11 F6
Marlin, U.S.A. 71 K6
Marlow, U.S.A. 71 H6
Marmagao, India 36 M8
Marmara, Turkey 21 D12
Marmara, Sea of = Marmara Denizi, Turkey 21 D13
Marmara Denizi, Turkey 21 D13
Marmaris, Turkey 21 F13
Marmarth, U.S.A. 70 B3
Marmion, Mt., Australia 53 E2
Marmion L., Canada 62 C1
Marmolada, Mte., Italy 20 A4
Marmora, Canada 62 D4
Marne →, France 18 B5
Maroala, Madag. 49 B8
Maroantsetra, Madag. 49 B8
Maromandia, Madag. 49 A8
Marondera, Zimbabwe 47 H6
Maroni →, Fr. Guiana 79 B8
Maroochydore, Australia 55 D5
Maroona, Australia 55 F3
Marosakoa, Madag. 49 B8
Maroua, Cameroon 45 F7
Marovoay, Madag. 49 B8
Marquard, S. Africa 48 D4
Marquesas Is. = Marquises, Is., Pac. Oc. 57 H14
Marquette, U.S.A. 68 B2
Marquises, Is., Pac. Oc. 57 H14
Marracuene, Mozam. 49 D5
Marrakech, Morocco 44 B3
Marrawah, Australia 54 G3
Marree, Australia 55 D2
Marrilla, Australia 52 D1
Marrimane, Mozam. 49 C5
Marromeu, Mozam. 49 B6
Marrowie Cr. →, Australia 55 E4
Marrupa, Mozam. 47 G7
Marsá Matrûh, Egypt 45 B10
Marsá Susah, Libya 45 B9
Marsabit, Kenya 46 D7
Marsala, Italy 20 F5
Marsden, Australia 55 E4
Marseille, France 18 E6
Marseilles = Marseille, France 18 E6
Marsh I., U.S.A. 71 L9
Marsh L., U.S.A. 70 C6
Marshall, Liberia 44 G2
Marshall, Ark., U.S.A. 71 H8
Marshall, Mich., U.S.A. 68 D3
Marshall, Minn., U.S.A. 70 C7
Marshall, Mo., U.S.A. 70 F8
Marshall, Tex., U.S.A. 71 J7
Marshall →, Australia 54 C2
Marshall Is. ■, Pac. Oc. 56 G9
Marshalltown, U.S.A. 70 D8
Marshfield, Mo., U.S.A. 71 G8
Marshfield, Wis., U.S.A. 70 C9
Marshūn, Iran 39 B6
Märsta, Sweden 9 G17
Mart, U.S.A. 71 K6
Martaban, Burma 37 L20
Martaban, G. of, Burma 37 L20
Martapura, Kalimantan, Indonesia 32 E4
Martapura, Sumatera, Indonesia 32 E2
Marte, Nigeria 45 F7
Martelange, Belgium 15 E5
Martha's Vineyard, U.S.A. 68 E10
Martigny, Switz. 16 E4
Martigues, France 18 E6
Martin, Slovak Rep. 17 D10
Martin, S. Dak., U.S.A. 70 D4
Martin, Tenn., U.S.A. 71 G10
Martin L., U.S.A. 69 J3
Martina Franca, Italy 20 D7
Martinborough, N.Z. 51 J5
Martinique ■, W. Indies 75 E12
Martinique Passage, W. Indies 75 D12
Martinsburg, U.S.A. 68 F7
Martinsville, Ind., U.S.A. 68 F2
Martinsville, Va., U.S.A. 69 G6
Marton, N.Z. 51 J5
Martos, Spain 19 D4
Marudi, Malaysia 32 D4
Ma'ruf, Afghan. 36 D5
Marugame, Japan 29 G6
Marulan, Australia 55 E5
Marunga, Angola 48 B3
Marvast, Iran 39 D7
Marwar, India 36 G8
Mary, Turkmenistan 24 F7
Mary Frances L., Canada 65 A7
Mary Kathleen, Australia 54 C2
Maryborough = Port Laoise, Ireland 13 C4
Maryborough, Queens., Australia 55 D5
Maryborough, Vic., Australia 55 F3
Maryfield, Canada 65 D8
Maryland □, U.S.A. 68 F7
Maryport, U.K. 10 C4
Mary's Harbour, Canada 63 B8
Marystown, Canada 63 C8
Marysvale, U.S.A. 73 G7
Marysville, Canada 64 D5
Marysville, Calif., U.S.A. 72 G3
Marysville, Kans., U.S.A. 70 F6
Marysville, Ohio, U.S.A. 68 E4
Maryvale, Australia 55 D5
Maryville, U.S.A. 69 H4
Marzūq, Libya 45 C7
Masaka, Uganda 46 E6
Masalembo, Kepulauan, Indonesia 32 F4
Masalima, Kepulauan, Indonesia 32 F5
Masamba, Indonesia 33 E6
Masan, S. Korea 31 C7
Masasi, Tanzania 46 G7
Masaya, Nic. 74 E7
Masbate, Phil. 33 B6
Mascara, Algeria 44 A5
Mascarene Is., Ind. Oc. 35 G4
Masela, Indonesia 33 F7
Maseru, Lesotho 48 D4
Mashābih, Si. Arabia 38 E3
Mashhad, Iran 39 B8
Mashīz, Iran 39 D8
Mashkel, Hamun-i-, Pakistan 36 E3
Mashki Chāh, Pakistan 36 E3
Mashonaland Central □, Zimbabwe 49 B5
Mashonaland East □, Zimbabwe 49 B5
Mashonaland West □, Zimbabwe 49 B4
Masi Manimba, Zaïre 46 E3
Masindi, Uganda 46 D6
Masisea, Peru 78 E4
Masjed Soleyman, Iran 39 D6
Mask, L., Ireland 13 C2
Masoala, Tanjon' i, Madag. 49 B9
Masoarivo, Madag. 49 B7
Masohi, Indonesia 33 E7
Masomeloka, Madag. 49 C8
Mason, U.S.A. 71 K5
Mason City, U.S.A. 70 D8
Masqat, Oman 40 C6
Massa, Italy 20 B4
Massachusetts □, U.S.A. 68 D10
Massaguet, Chad 45 F8
Massakory, Chad 45 F8
Massangena, Mozam. 49 C5
Massawa = Mitsiwa, Eritrea 45 E12
Massena, U.S.A. 68 C8
Massénya, Chad 45 F8
Masset, Canada 64 C2
Massif Central, France 18 D5
Massillon, U.S.A. 68 E5
Massinga, Mozam. 49 C6
Masson I., Antarctica 5 C7
Mastanli = Momchilgrad, Bulgaria 21 D11
Masterton, N.Z. 51 J5
Mastuj, Pakistan 36 A8
Mastung, Pakistan 36 E5
Masty, Belarus 17 B13
Masuda, Japan 29 G5
Masvingo, Zimbabwe 47 J6
Maşyāf, Syria 38 C3
Mataboor, Indonesia 33 E9
Matachewan, Canada 62 C3
Matadi, Zaïre 46 F2
Matagalpa, Nic. 74 E7
Matagami, Canada 62 C4
Matagami, L., Canada 62 C4
Matagorda, U.S.A. 71 L7
Matagorda B., U.S.A. 71 L6
Matagorda I., U.S.A. 71 L6
Matak, P., Indonesia 32 D3
Matakana, Australia 55 E4
Matam, Senegal 44 E2
Matamoros, Coahuila, Mexico 74 B4
Matamoros, Tamaulipas, Mexico 74 B5
Ma'ţan as Sarra, Libya 45 D9
Matane, Canada 63 C6
Matanzas, Cuba 75 C8
Matapan, C. = Taínaron, Ákra, Greece 21 F10
Matapédia, Canada 63 C6
Matara, Sri Lanka 36 S12
Mataram, Indonesia 32 F5
Matarani, Peru 78 G4
Mataranka, Australia 52 B5
Matarma, Râs, Egypt 41 E1
Mataró, Spain 19 B7
Matatiele, S. Africa 49 E4
Mataura, N.Z. 51 M2
Matehuala, Mexico 74 C4
Matera, Italy 20 D7
Matheson Island, Canada 65 C9
Mathis, U.S.A. 71 L6
Mathura, India 36 F10

Mati, *Phil.* 33 C7
Matima, *Botswana* 48 C3
Matiri Ra., *N.Z.* 51 J4
Matlock, *U.K.* 10 D6
Matmata, *Tunisia* 44 B6
Mato Grosso □, *Brazil* 79 F8
Mato Grosso, Planalto do, *Brazil* 79 G8
Mato Grosso do Sul □, *Brazil* 79 G8
Matochkin Shar, *Russia* 24 B6
Matosinhos, *Portugal* 19 B1
Matsue, *Japan* 29 G6
Matsumae, *Japan* 28 D10
Matsumoto, *Japan* 29 F9
Matsusaka, *Japan* 29 G8
Matsuura, *Japan* 29 H4
Matsuyama, *Japan* 29 H6
Mattagami →, *Canada* 62 B3
Mattancheri, *India* 36 Q10
Mattawa, *Canada* 62 C4
Mattawamkeag, *U.S.A.* 63 C6
Matterhorn, *Switz.* 16 F4
Matthew's Ridge, *Guyana* 78 B6
Mattice, *Canada* 62 C3
Matuba, *Mozam.* 49 C5
Matucana, *Peru* 78 F3
Matun, *Afghan.* 36 C6
Maturín, *Venezuela* 78 B6
Mau Ranipur, *India* 36 G11
Maubeuge, *France* 18 A6
Maud, Pt., *Australia* 52 D1
Maude, *Australia* 55 E3
Maudin Sun, *Burma* 37 M19
Maués, *Brazil* 78 D7
Mauganj, *India* 37 G12
Maui, *U.S.A.* 66 H16
Maulamyaing = Moulmein, *Burma* 37 L20
Maumee, *U.S.A.* 68 E4
Maumee →, *U.S.A.* 68 E4
Maumere, *Indonesia* 33 F6
Maun, *Botswana* 48 B3
Mauna Kea, *U.S.A.* 66 J17
Mauna Loa, *U.S.A.* 66 J17
Maungmagan Kyunzu, *Burma* 34 E4
Maupin, *U.S.A.* 72 D3
Maurepas, L., *U.S.A.* 71 K9
Maurice, L., *Australia* 53 E5
Mauritania ■, *Africa* 44 D3
Mauritius ■, *Ind. Oc.* 43 J9
Mauston, *U.S.A.* 70 D9
Mavinga, *Angola* 47 H4
Mawk Mai, *Burma* 37 J20
Mawlaik, *Burma* 37 H19
Mawquq, *Si. Arabia* 38 E4
Mawson Coast, *Antarctica* 5 C6
Max, *U.S.A.* 70 B4
Maxesibeni, *S. Africa* 49 E4
Maxhamish L., *Canada* 64 B4
Maxixe, *Mozam.* 49 C6
Maxwelton, *Australia* 54 C3
May Downs, *Australia* 54 C4
May Pen, *Jamaica* 74 K16
Maya →, *Russia* 25 D14
Mayaguana, *Bahamas* 75 C10
Mayagüez, *Puerto Rico* 75 D11
Mayāmey, *Iran* 39 B7
Maybell, *U.S.A.* 72 F9
Maydān, *Iraq* 38 C5
Maydena, *Australia* 54 G4
Mayenne →, *France* 18 C3
Mayer, *U.S.A.* 73 J7
Mayerthorpe, *Canada* 64 C5
Mayfield, *U.S.A.* 69 G1
Mayhill, *U.S.A.* 73 K11
Maykop, *Russia* 23 F7
Maymyo, *Burma* 34 A4
Maynard Hills, *Australia* 53 E2
Mayne →, *Australia* 54 C3
Maynooth, *Ireland* 13 C5
Mayo, *Canada* 60 B6
Mayo □, *Ireland* 13 C2
Mayo L., *Canada* 60 B6
Mayon Volcano, *Phil.* 33 B6
Mayor I., *N.Z.* 51 G6
Mayotte, I., *Mayotte* 35 F3
Mayson L., *Canada* 65 B7
Maysville, *U.S.A.* 68 F4
Mayu, *Indonesia* 33 D7
Mayville, *U.S.A.* 70 B6
Mayya, *Russia* 25 C14
Mazabuka, *Zambia* 47 H5
Mazagán = El Jadida, *Morocco* 44 B3
Mazagão, *Brazil* 79 D8
Mazán, *Peru* 78 D4
Māzandarān □, *Iran* 39 B7
Mazara del Vallo, *Italy* 20 F5
Mazarredo, *Argentina* 80 F3
Mazarrón, *Spain* 19 D5
Mazaruni →, *Guyana* 78 B7
Mazatlán, *Mexico* 74 C3
Mažeikiai, *Lithuania* 9 H20
Māzhān, *Iran* 39 C8
Mazīnān, *Iran* 39 B8
Mazoe →, *Mozam.* 47 H6
Mazurian Lakes = Mazurski, Pojezierze, *Poland* 17 B11
Mazurski, Pojezierze, *Poland* 17 B11
Mazyr, *Belarus* 17 B15
Mbabane, *Swaziland* 49 D5
Mbaïki, *C.A.R.* 46 D3
Mbala, *Zambia* 46 F6
Mbale, *Uganda* 46 D6
Mbalmayo, *Cameroon* 46 D2
Mbamba Bay, *Tanzania* 46 G6
Mbandaka, *Zaïre* 46 D3
Mbanza Congo, *Angola* 46 F2
Mbanza Ngungu, *Zaïre* 46 F2
Mbarara, *Uganda* 46 E6
Mbashe →, *S. Africa* 49 E4
Mbeya, *Tanzania* 46 F6
Mbini □, *Eq. Guin.* 46 D2
Mbour, *Senegal* 44 F1
Mbout, *Mauritania* 44 E2
Mbuji-Mayi, *Zaïre* 46 F4
Mbulu, *Tanzania* 46 E7
Mchinji, *Malawi* 47 G6
Mead, L., *U.S.A.* 73 H6
Meade, *U.S.A.* 71 G4
Meadow, *Australia* 53 E1
Meadow Lake, *Canada* 65 C7
Meadow Lake Prov. Park, *Canada* 65 C7
Meadow Valley Wash →, *U.S.A.* 73 H6
Meadville, *U.S.A.* 68 E5
Meaford, *Canada* 62 D3
Mealy Mts., *Canada* 63 B8
Meander River, *Canada* 64 B5
Meares, C., *U.S.A.* 72 D2
Mearim →, *Brazil* 79 D10
Meath □, *Ireland* 13 C5
Meath Park, *Canada* 65 C7
Meaux, *France* 18 B5
Mebechi-Gawa →, *Japan* 28 D10
Mecca = Makkah, *Si. Arabia* 40 C2
Mecca, *U.S.A.* 73 K5
Mechelen, *Belgium* 15 C4
Mecheria, *Algeria* 44 B4
Mecklenburg, *Germany* 16 B6
Mecklenburger Bucht, *Germany* 16 A6
Meconta, *Mozam.* 47 G7
Meda, *Australia* 52 C3
Medan, *Indonesia* 32 D1
Medanosa, Pta., *Argentina* 80 F3
Medéa, *Algeria* 44 A5
Medellín, *Colombia* 78 B3
Medelpad, *Sweden* 9 E17
Medemblik, *Neths.* 15 B5
Mederdra, *Mauritania* 44 E1
Medford, *Oreg., U.S.A.* 72 E2
Medford, *Wis., U.S.A.* 70 C9
Medgidia, *Romania* 17 F15
Mediaş, *Romania* 17 E13
Medical Lake, *U.S.A.* 72 C5
Medicine Bow, *U.S.A.* 72 F10
Medicine Bow Pk., *U.S.A.* 72 F10
Medicine Bow Ra., *U.S.A.* 72 F10
Medicine Hat, *Canada* 65 D6
Medicine Lake, *U.S.A.* 70 A2
Medicine Lodge, *U.S.A.* 71 G5
Medina = Al Madīnah, *Si. Arabia* 40 C2
Medina, *N. Dak., U.S.A.* 70 B5
Medina, *N.Y., U.S.A.* 68 D6
Medina, *Ohio, U.S.A.* 68 E5
Medina →, *U.S.A.* 71 L5
Medina del Campo, *Spain* 19 B3
Medina L., *U.S.A.* 71 L5
Medina-Sidonia, *Spain* 19 D3
Medinipur, *India* 37 H15
Mediterranean Sea, *Europe* 42 C5
Medley, *Canada* 65 C6
Médoc, *France* 18 D3
Medstead, *Canada* 65 C7
Medveditsa →, *Russia* 23 E7
Medvezhi, Ostrava, *Russia* 25 B17
Medvezhyegorsk, *Russia* 22 B5
Medway →, *U.K.* 11 F8
Meeberrie, *Australia* 53 E2
Meekatharra, *Australia* 53 E2
Meeker, *U.S.A.* 72 F10
Meerut, *India* 36 E10
Meeteetse, *U.S.A.* 72 D9
Mega, *Ethiopia* 45 H12
Mégara, *Greece* 21 F10
Meghalaya □, *India* 37 G17
Mégiscane, L., *Canada* 62 C4
Mehr Jān, *Iran* 39 C7
Mehrābād, *Iran* 38 B5
Mehrān, *Iran* 38 C5
Mehrīz, *Iran* 39 D7
Mei Xian, *China* 31 D6
Meiganga, *Cameroon* 46 C2
Meiktila, *Burma* 37 J19
Meissen, *Germany* 16 C7
Mejillones, *Chile* 80 A2
Meka, *Australia* 53 E2
Mékambo, *Gabon* 46 D2
Mekdela, *Ethiopia* 45 F12
Mekhtar, *Pakistan* 36 D6
Meknès, *Morocco* 44 B3
Mekong →, *Asia* 34 H9
Mekongga, *Indonesia* 33 E6
Mekvari = Kür →, *Azerbaijan* 23 G8
Melagiri Hills, *India* 36 N10
Melaka, *Malaysia* 34 S15
Melaka □, *Malaysia* 34 S15
Melalap, *Malaysia* 32 C5
Melanesia, *Pac. Oc.* 56 H7
Melbourne, *Australia* 55 F3
Melbourne, *U.S.A.* 69 L5
Mélèzes →, *Canada* 61 C12
Melfi, *Chad* 45 F8
Melfort, *Canada* 65 C8
Melhus, *Norway* 8 E14
Melilla, *N. Afr.* 19 E4
Melita, *Canada* 65 D8
Melitopol, *Ukraine* 23 E6
Melk, *Austria* 16 D8
Mellansel, *Sweden* 8 E18
Mellen, *U.S.A.* 70 B9
Mellerud, *Sweden* 9 G15
Mellette, *U.S.A.* 70 C5
Melo, *Uruguay* 80 C6
Melolo, *Indonesia* 33 F6
Melrose, *N.S.W., Australia* 55 E4
Melrose, *W. Austral., Australia* 53 E3
Melrose, *U.K.* 12 F6
Melrose, *U.S.A.* 71 H3
Melstone, *U.S.A.* 72 C10
Melton Mowbray, *U.K.* 10 E7
Melun, *France* 18 B5
Melut, *Sudan* 45 F11
Melville, *Canada* 65 C8
Melville, C., *Australia* 54 A3
Melville, L., *Canada* 63 B8
Melville B., *Australia* 54 A2
Melville I., *Australia* 52 B5
Melville I., *Canada* 4 B2
Melville Pen., *Canada* 61 B11
Melvin →, *Canada* 64 B5
Memba, *Mozam.* 47 G8
Memboro, *Indonesia* 33 F5
Memel = Klaipėda, *Lithuania* 9 J19
Memel, *S. Africa* 49 D4
Memmingen, *Germany* 16 E6
Mempawah, *Indonesia* 32 D3
Memphis, *Tenn., U.S.A.* 71 H10
Memphis, *Tex., U.S.A.* 71 H4
Mena, *U.S.A.* 71 H7
Menai Strait, *U.K.* 10 D3
Ménaka, *Mali* 44 E5
Menan = Chao Phraya →, *Thailand* 34 F6
Menarandra →, *Madag.* 49 D7
Menard, *U.S.A.* 71 K5
Menasha, *U.S.A.* 68 C1
Menate, *Indonesia* 32 E4
Mendawai →, *Indonesia* 32 E4
Mende, *France* 18 D5
Mendip Hills, *U.K.* 11 F5
Mendocino, *U.S.A.* 72 G2
Mendocino, C., *U.S.A.* 72 F1
Mendota, *Calif., U.S.A.* 73 H3
Mendota, *Ill., U.S.A.* 70 E10
Mendoza, *Argentina* 80 C3
Mene Grande, *Venezuela* 78 B4
Menemen, *Turkey* 21 E12
Menen, *Belgium* 15 D3
Menggala, *Indonesia* 32 E3
Mengzi, *China* 30 D5
Menihek L., *Canada* 63 B6
Menin = Menen, *Belgium* 15 D3
Menindee, *Australia* 55 E3
Menindee L., *Australia* 55 E3
Meningie, *Australia* 55 F2
Menominee, *U.S.A.* 68 C2
Menominee →, *U.S.A.* 68 C2
Menomonie, *U.S.A.* 70 C9
Menongue, *Angola* 47 G3
Menorca, *Spain* 19 C8
Mentawai, Kepulauan, *Indonesia* 32 E1
Menton, *France* 18 E7
Menzelinsk, *Russia* 22 C9
Menzies, *Australia* 53 E3
Me'ona, *Israel* 41 B4
Meppel, *Neths.* 15 B6
Mer Rouge, *U.S.A.* 71 J9
Merabéllou, Kólpos, *Greece* 21 G11
Meramangye, L., *Australia* 53 E5
Meran = Merano, *Italy* 20 A4
Merano, *Italy* 20 A4
Merauke, *Indonesia* 33 F10
Merbabu, *Indonesia* 33 G14
Merbein, *Australia* 55 E3
Merca, *Somali Rep.* 40 G3
Merced, *U.S.A.* 73 H3
Mercedes, *Buenos Aires, Argentina* 80 C5
Mercedes, *Corrientes, Argentina* 80 B5
Mercedes, *San Luis, Argentina* 80 C3
Mercedes, *Uruguay* 80 C5
Merceditas, *Chile* 80 B2
Mercer, *N.Z.* 51 G5
Mercy C., *Canada* 61 B13
Meredith, C., *Falk. Is.* 80 G4
Meredith, L., *U.S.A.* 71 H4
Merga = Nukheila, *Sudan* 45 E10
Mergui Arch. = Myeik Kyunzu, *Burma* 34 G4
Mérida, *Mexico* 74 C7
Mérida, *Spain* 19 C2
Mérida, *Venezuela* 78 B4
Mérida, Cord. de, *Venezuela* 76 C3
Meriden, *U.S.A.* 68 E9
Meridian, *Idaho, U.S.A.* 72 E5
Meridian, *Miss., U.S.A.* 69 J1
Meridian, *Tex., U.S.A.* 71 K6
Meriruma, *Brazil* 79 C8
Merkel, *U.S.A.* 71 J4
Merksem, *Belgium* 15 C4
Mermaid Reef, *Australia* 52 C2
Merowe, *Sudan* 45 E11
Merredin, *Australia* 53 F2
Merrick, *U.K.* 12 F4
Merrill, *Oreg., U.S.A.* 72 E3
Merrill, *Wis., U.S.A.* 70 C10
Merriman, *U.S.A.* 70 D4
Merritt, *Canada* 64 C4
Merriwa, *Australia* 55 E5
Merriwagga, *Australia* 55 E4
Merry I., *Canada* 62 A4
Merrygoen, *Australia* 55 E4
Merryville, *U.S.A.* 71 K8
Mersa Fatma, *Eritrea* 40 E3
Mersch, *Lux.* 15 E6
Merseburg, *Germany* 16 C6
Mersey →, *U.K.* 10 D5
Merseyside □, *U.K.* 10 D5
Mersin, *Turkey* 23 G5
Mersing, *Malaysia* 34 S16
Merthyr Tydfil, *U.K.* 11 F4
Mértola, *Portugal* 19 D2
Mertzon, *U.S.A.* 71 K4
Meru, *Kenya* 46 D7
Mesa, *U.S.A.* 73 K8
Mesgouez, L., *Canada* 62 B4
Meshed = Mashhad, *Iran* 39 B8
Meshra er Req, *Sudan* 45 G10
Mesick, *U.S.A.* 68 C3
Mesilinka →, *Canada* 64 B4
Mesilla, *U.S.A.* 73 K10
Mesolóngion, *Greece* 21 E9
Mesopotamia = Al Jazirah, *Iraq* 38 C5
Mesquite, *U.S.A.* 73 H6
Mess Cr. →, *Canada* 64 B2
Messina, *Italy* 20 E6
Messina, *S. Africa* 49 C5
Messina, Str. di, *Italy* 20 F6
Messíni, *Greece* 21 F10
Messiniakós Kólpos, *Greece* 21 F10
Mesta →, *Bulgaria* 21 D11
Meta →, *S. Amer.* 78 B5
Metairie, *U.S.A.* 71 L9
Metaline Falls, *U.S.A.* 72 B5
Metán, *Argentina* 80 B4
Metangula, *Mozam.* 47 G6
Metema, *Ethiopia* 45 F12
Methven, *N.Z.* 51 K3
Methy L., *Canada* 65 B7
Metil, *Mozam.* 47 H7
Metlakatla, *U.S.A.* 64 B2
Metropolis, *U.S.A.* 71 G10
Mettur Dam, *India* 36 P10
Metz, *France* 18 B7
Meulaboh, *Indonesia* 32 D1
Meureudu, *Indonesia* 32 C1
Meuse →, *Europe* 18 A6
Mexborough, *U.K.* 10 D6
Mexia, *U.S.A.* 71 K6
Mexiana, I., *Brazil* 79 C9
Mexicali, *Mexico* 74 A1
México, *Mexico* 74 D5
Mexico, *U.S.A.* 70 F9
México □, *Mexico* 74 D5
Mexico ■, *Cent. Amer.* 74 C4
Mexico, G. of, *Cent. Amer.* 74 B7
Meymaneh, *Afghan.* 36 B4
Mezen, *Russia* 22 A7
Mezen →, *Russia* 22 A7
Mézene, *France* 18 D6
Mezőkövesd, *Hungary* 17 E11
Mezőtúr, *Hungary* 17 E11
Mhow, *India* 36 H9
Miallo, *Australia* 54 B4
Miami, *Ariz., U.S.A.* 73 K8
Miami, *Fla., U.S.A.* 69 N5
Miami, *Tex., U.S.A.* 71 H4
Miami →, *U.S.A.* 68 F3
Miami Beach, *U.S.A.* 69 N5
Miamisburg, *U.S.A.* 68 F3
Miāndowāb, *Iran* 38 B5
Miandrivazo, *Madag.* 49 B8
Miāneh, *Iran* 38 B5
Mianwali, *Pakistan* 36 C7
Miarinarivo, *Madag.* 49 B8
Miass, *Russia* 22 D11
Michalovce, *Slovak Rep.* 17 D11
Michigan □, *U.S.A.* 68 C3
Michigan, L., *U.S.A.* 68 C2
Michigan City, *U.S.A.* 68 E2
Michikamau L., *Canada* 63 B7
Michipicoten, *Canada* 62 C3
Michipicoten I., *Canada* 62 C2
Michurin, *Bulgaria* 21 C12
Michurinsk, *Russia* 22 D7
Miclere, *Australia* 54 C4
Micronesia, Federated States of ■, *Pac. Oc.* 56 G7
Mid Glamorgan □, *U.K.* 11 F4
Mid-Indian Ridge, *Ind. Oc.* 35 H6
Midai, P., *Indonesia* 32 D3
Midale, *Canada* 65 D8
Middelburg, *Neths.* 15 C3
Middelburg, *Eastern Cape, S. Africa* 48 E3
Middelburg, *Eastern Trans., S. Africa* 49 D4
Middelwit, *S. Africa* 48 C4
Middle Alkali L., *U.S.A.* 72 F3
Middle Andaman I., *India* 34 F2
Middle I., *Australia* 53 F3
Middle Loup →, *U.S.A.* 70 E5
Middleport, *U.S.A.* 68 F4
Middlesboro, *Ky., U.S.A.* 67 C10
Middlesboro, *Ky., U.S.A.* 69 G4
Middlesbrough, *U.K.* 10 C6
Middleton, *Australia* 54 C3
Middleton, *Canada* 63 D6
Middletown, *Conn., U.S.A.* 68 E9
Middletown, *N.Y., U.S.A.* 68 E8
Middletown, *Ohio, U.S.A.* 68 F3
Midi, Canal du →, *France* 18 E4
Midland, *Canada* 62 D4
Midland, *Mich., U.S.A.* 68 D3
Midland, *Tex., U.S.A.* 71 K3
Midleton, *Ireland* 13 E3
Midlothian, *U.S.A.* 71 J6
Midongy, Tangorombohitr' i, *Madag.* 49 C8
Midongy Atsimo, *Madag.* 49 C8
Midway Is., *Pac. Oc.* 56 E10
Midwest, *U.S.A.* 67 B9
Midwest, *Wyo., U.S.A.* 72 E10
Midzŏr, *Bulgaria* 21 C10
Mie □, *Japan* 29 G8
Międzychód, *Poland* 16 B8
Międzyrzec Podlaski, *Poland* 17 C12
Mielec, *Poland* 17 C11
Mienga, *Angola* 48 B2
Miercurea Ciuc, *Romania* 17 E13
Mieres, *Spain* 19 A3
Mifraz Ḥefa, *Israel* 41 C4
Migdāl, *Israel* 41 C4
Miguel Alves, *Brazil* 79 D10
Mihara, *Japan* 29 G6
Mikhaylovgrad, *Bulgaria* 21 C10
Mikkeli, *Finland* 9 F22
Mikkwa →, *Canada* 64 B6
Míkonos, *Greece* 21 F11
Mikun, *Russia* 22 B9
Milaca, *U.S.A.* 70 C8
Milagro, *Ecuador* 78 D3
Milan = Milano, *Italy* 20 B3
Milan, *Mo., U.S.A.* 70 E8
Milan, *Tenn., U.S.A.* 69 H1
Milang, *Australia* 55 E2
Milano, *Italy* 20 B3
Milâs, *Turkey* 21 F12
Milazzo, *Italy* 20 E6
Milbank, *U.S.A.* 70 C6
Milden, *Canada* 65 C7
Mildura, *Australia* 55 E3
Miles, *Australia* 55 D5
Miles, *U.S.A.* 71 K4
Miles City, *U.S.A.* 70 B2
Milestone, *Canada* 65 D8
Miletus, *Turkey* 21 F12
Mileura, *Australia* 53 E2
Milford, *Del., U.S.A.* 68 F8
Milford, *Utah, U.S.A.* 73 G7
Milford Haven, *U.K.* 11 F2
Milford Sd., *N.Z.* 51 L1
Milgun, *Australia* 53 D2
Milḩ, Baḩr al, *Iraq* 38 C4
Miliana, *Algeria* 44 C5
Miling, *Australia* 53 F2
Milk →, *U.S.A.* 72 B10
Milk River, *Canada* 64 D6
Mill City, *U.S.A.* 72 D2
Mill I., *Antarctica* 5 C8
Millau, *France* 18 D5
Mille Lacs, L. des, *Canada* 62 C1
Mille Lacs L., *U.S.A.* 70 B8
Milledgeville, *U.S.A.* 69 J4
Millen, *U.S.A.* 69 J5
Miller, *U.S.A.* 70 C5
Millicent, *Australia* 55 F3
Millinocket, *U.S.A.* 63 C6
Millmerran, *Australia* 55 D5
Mills L., *Canada* 64 A5
Milltown Malbay, *Ireland* 13 D2
Millville, *U.S.A.* 68 F8
Millwood L., *U.S.A.* 71 J8
Milne →, *Australia* 54 C2
Milne Inlet, *Canada* 61 A11
Milnor, *U.S.A.* 70 B6
Milo, *Canada* 64 C6
Mílos, *Greece* 21 F11
Milparinka P.O., *Australia* 55 D3
Milton, *N.Z.* 51 M2
Milton, *U.K.* 12 D4
Milton, *Fla., U.S.A.* 69 K2
Milton, *Pa., U.S.A.* 68 E7
Milton-Freewater, *U.S.A.* 72 D4
Milton Keynes, *U.K.* 11 E7
Miltou, *Chad* 45 F8
Milwaukee, *U.S.A.* 68 D2
Milwaukie, *U.S.A.* 72 D2
Min Chiang →, *China* 31 D6
Min Jiang →, *China* 30 D5
Mina, *U.S.A.* 73 G4
Mina Pirquitas, *Argentina* 80 A3
Mīnā Su'ud, *Si. Arabia* 39 D6
Mīnā'al Aḩmadī, *Kuwait* 39 D6
Mīnāb, *Iran* 39 E8
Minago →, *Canada* 65 C9
Minaki, *Canada* 65 D10
Minamata, *Japan* 29 H5
Minami-Tori-Shima, *Pac. Oc.* 56 E7
Minas, *Uruguay* 80 C5
Minas Basin, *Canada* 63 C7
Minas Gerais □, *Brazil* 79 G9
Minatitlán, *Mexico* 74 D6
Minbu, *Burma* 37 J19
Mindanao, *Phil.* 33 C6
Mindanao Sea = Bohol Sea, *Phil.* 33 C6
Mindanao Trench, *Pac. Oc.* 33 B7
Minden, *Germany* 16 B5
Minden, *U.S.A.* 71 J8
Mindiptana, *Indonesia* 33 F10
Mindoro, *Phil.* 33 B6
Mindoro Str., *Phil.* 33 B6
Mindouli, *Congo* 46 E2
Mine, *Japan* 29 G5
Minehead, *U.K.* 11 F4
Mineola, *U.S.A.* 71 J7
Mineral Wells, *U.S.A.* 71 J5
Minersville, *U.S.A.* 73 G7
Mingäçevir Su Anban, *Azerbaijan* 23 F8
Mingan, *Canada* 63 B7
Mingechaurskoye Vdkhr. = Mingäçevir Su Anban, *Azerbaijan* 23 F8
Mingela, *Australia* 54 B4
Mingenew, *Australia* 53 E2
Mingera Cr. →, *Australia* 54 C2
Mingin, *Burma* 37 H19
Mingt'iehkaitafan = Mintaka Pass, *Pakistan* 36 A9
Minho = Miño →, *Spain* 19 A2
Minho, *Portugal* 19 B1
Minidoka, *U.S.A.* 72 E7
Minigwal, L., *Australia* 53 E3
Minilya, *Australia* 53 D1
Minilya →, *Australia* 53 D1
Minipi, L., *Canada* 63 B7
Mink L., *Canada* 64 A5
Minna, *Nigeria* 44 G6
Minneapolis, *Kans., U.S.A.* 70 F6
Minneapolis, *Minn., U.S.A.* 70 C8
Minnedosa, *Canada* 65 C9
Minnesota □, *U.S.A.* 70 B7
Minnie Creek, *Australia* 53 D2
Minnipa, *Australia* 55 E2
Minnitaki L., *Canada* 62 C1
Mino, *Japan* 29 G8
Miño →, *Spain* 19 A2
Minorca = Menorca, *Spain* 19 C8
Minore, *Australia* 55 E4
Minot, *U.S.A.* 70 A4
Minsk, *Belarus* 17 B14
Mińsk Mazowiecki, *Poland* 17 B11
Mintaka Pass, *Pakistan* 36 A9
Minto, *U.S.A.* 60 B5
Minton, *Canada* 65 D8
Minturn, *U.S.A.* 72 G10
Minusinsk, *Russia* 25 D10
Minutang, *India* 37 E20
Minvoul, *Gabon* 46 D2
Mir, *Niger* 45 F7
Mīr Kūh, *Iran* 39 E8
Mīr Shahdād, *Iran* 39 E8
Mira, *Italy* 20 B5
Miraflores Locks, *Panama* 74 H14
Miraj, *India* 36 L9
Miram Shah, *Pakistan* 36 C7
Miramar, *Mozam.* 49 C6
Miramichi B., *Canada* 63 C7
Miranda, *Brazil* 79 H7
Miranda de Ebro, *Spain* 19 A4
Miranda do Douro, *Portugal* 19 B2
Mirando City, *U.S.A.* 71 M5
Mirani, *Australia* 54 C4
Mirbāţ, *Oman* 40 D5
Miri, *Malaysia* 32 D4
Miriam Vale, *Australia* 54 C5
Mirim, L., *S. Amer.* 80 C6
Mirnyy, *Russia* 25 C12
Mirond L., *Canada* 65 B8
Mirpur Khas, *Pakistan* 36 G6
Mirror, *Canada* 64 C6
Mirzapur, *India* 37 G13
Mirzapur-cum-Vindhyachal = Mirzapur, *India* 37 G13
Misawa, *Japan* 28 D10
Miscou I., *Canada* 63 C7
Mish'āb, Ra'as al, *Si. Arabia* 39 D6
Mishan, *China* 31 B8
Mishawaka, *U.S.A.* 68 E2
Mishima, *Japan* 29 G9
Miskah, *Si. Arabia* 38 E4
Miskolc, *Hungary* 17 D11
Misool, *Indonesia* 33 E8
Misrātah, *Libya* 45 B8
Missanabie, *Canada* 62 C3
Missinaibi →, *Canada* 62 B3
Missinaibi L., *Canada* 62 C3
Mission, *S. Dak., U.S.A.* 70 D4
Mission, *Tex., U.S.A.* 71 M5
Mission City, *Canada* 64 D4
Missisa L., *Canada* 62 B2
Missisagi →, *Canada* 62 C3
Mississippi □, *U.S.A.* 71 J10
Mississippi →, *U.S.A.* 71 L10
Mississippi River Delta, *U.S.A.* 71 L9
Mississippi Sd., *U.S.A.* 71 K10
Missoula, *U.S.A.* 72 C6
Missouri □, *U.S.A.* 70 F8
Missouri →, *U.S.A.* 70 F9
Missouri Valley, *U.S.A.* 70 E7
Mistake B., *Canada* 65 A10

Mozyr

Mistassini →, *Canada* 63 C5
Mistassini L., *Canada* . 62 B5
Mistastin L., *Canada* . . 63 A7
Mistatim, *Canada* 65 C8
Misty L., *Canada* 65 B8
Misurata = Misrātah, *Libya* 45 B8
Mitchell, *Australia* 55 D4
Mitchell, *Ind., U.S.A.* . . 68 F2
Mitchell, *Nebr., U.S.A.* 70 E3
Mitchell, *Oreg., U.S.A.* 72 D3
Mitchell, *S. Dak., U.S.A.* 70 D5
Mitchell →, *Australia* 54 B3
Mitchell, Mt., *U.S.A.* . . 69 H4
Mitchell Ras., *Australia* 54 A2
Mitchelstown, *Ireland* . 13 D3
Mitilíni, *Greece* 21 E12
Mito, *Japan* 29 F10
Mitrovica = Titova-Mitrovica, *Serbia, Yug.* 21 C9
Mitsinjo, *Madag.* 49 B8
Mitsiwa, *Eritrea* 45 E12
Mitsukaidō, *Japan* 29 F9
Mittagong, *Australia* . . 55 E5
Mitú, *Colombia* 78 C4
Mitumba, Chaîne des, *Zaïre* 46 F5
Mitumba Mts. = Mitumba, Chaîne des, *Zaïre* 46 F5
Mitwaba, *Zaïre* 46 F5
Mitzic, *Gabon* 46 D2
Miyagi □, *Japan* 28 E10
Miyah, W. el →, *Syria* 38 C3
Miyake-Jima, *Japan* . . 29 G9
Miyako, *Japan* 28 E10
Miyako-Jima, *Japan* . . 29 M2
Miyako-Rettō, *Japan* . . 29 M2
Miyakonojō, *Japan* . . . 29 J5
Miyanoura-Dake, *Japan* 29 J5
Miyazaki, *Japan* 29 J5
Miyazaki □, *Japan* . . . 29 H5
Miyazu, *Japan* 29 G7
Miyet, Bahr el = Dead Sea, *Asia* 41 D4
Miyoshi, *Japan* 29 G6
Mizamis = Ozamiz, *Phil.* 33 C6
Mizdah, *Libya* 45 B7
Mizen Hd., *Cork, Ireland* 13 E2
Mizen Hd., *Wick., Ireland* 13 D5
Mizoram □, *India* 37 H18
Mizpe Ramon, *Israel* . . 41 E3
Mizusawa, *Japan* 28 E10
Mjölby, *Sweden* 9 G16
Mjøsa, *Norway* 9 F14
Mkomazi →, *S. Africa* 49 E5
Mkuze, *S. Africa* 49 D5
Mladá Boleslav, *Czech.* 16 C8
Mława, *Poland* 17 B11
Mljet, *Croatia* 20 C7
Mmabatho, *S. Africa* . . 48 D4
Mo i Rana, *Norway* 8 C16
Moa, *Indonesia* 33 F7
Moab, *U.S.A.* 73 G9
Moabi, *Gabon* 46 E2
Moala, *Fiji* 51 D8
Moalie Park, *Australia* 55 D3
Moba, *Zaïre* 46 F5
Mobārakābād, *Iran* . . . 39 D7
Mobārakīyeh, *Iran* 39 C6
Mobaye, *C.A.R.* 46 D4
Mobayi, *Zaïre* 46 D4
Moberly, *U.S.A.* 70 F8
Moberly →, *Canada* . 64 B4
Mobile, *U.S.A.* 69 K1
Mobile B., *U.S.A.* 69 K2
Mobridge, *U.S.A.* 70 C4
Mobutu Sese Seko, L. = Albert L., *Africa* . . 46 D6
Moçambique, *Mozam.* 47 H8
Moçâmedes = Namibe, *Angola* 47 H2
Mochudi, *Botswana* . . 48 C4
Mocimboa da Praia, *Mozam.* 46 G8
Moclips, *U.S.A.* 72 C1
Mocoa, *Colombia* 78 C3
Mocuba, *Mozam.* 47 H7
Modane, *France* 18 D7
Modder →, *S. Africa* 48 D3
Modderrivier, *S. Africa* 48 D3
Módena, *Italy* 20 B4
Modena, *U.S.A.* 73 H7
Modesto, *U.S.A.* 73 H3
Módica, *Italy* 20 F6
Moe, *Australia* 55 F4
Moei →, *Thailand* . . . 34 D5
Moengo, *Surinam* 79 B8
Moffat, *U.K.* 12 F5
Mogadishu = Muqdisho, *Somali Rep.* 40 G4
Mogador = Essaouira, *Morocco* 44 B3
Mogalakwena →, *S. Africa* 49 C4
Mogami →, *Japan* . . 28 E10
Mogaung, *Burma* 37 G20
Mogi das Cruzes, *Brazil* 80 A7
Mogi-Mirim, *Brazil* . . . 80 A7
Mogilev = Mahilyow, *Belarus* 17 B16
Mogilev-Podolskiy = Mohyliv-Podilskyy, *Ukraine* 17 D14
Mogocha, *Russia* 25 D12
Mogoi, *Indonesia* 33 E8
Mogok, *Burma* 37 H20
Mogumber, *Australia* . 53 F2
Mohács, *Hungary* 17 F10
Mohales Hoek, *Lesotho* 48 E4
Mohall, *U.S.A.* 70 A4
Moḩammadābād, *Iran* 39 B8
Mohoro, *Tanzania* 46 F7
Mohyliv-Podilskyy, *Ukraine* 17 D14
Moidart, L., *U.K.* 12 E3
Mointy, *Kazakhstan* . . 24 E8
Moisaküla, *Estonia* . . . 9 G21
Moisie, *Canada* 63 B6
Moisie →, *Canada* . . 63 B6
Moïssala, *Chad* 45 G8
Mojave, *U.S.A.* 73 J4
Mojave Desert, *U.S.A.* 73 J5
Mojokerto, *Indonesia* . 33 G15
Mokai, *N.Z.* 51 H5
Mokhotlong, *Lesotho* . 49 D4
Mokokchung, *India* . . . 37 F19
Mokra Gora, *Serbia, Yug.* 21 C9
Mol, *Belgium* 15 C5
Molchanovo, *Russia* . . 24 D9
Mold, *U.K.* 10 D4
Moldavia = Moldova ■, *Europe* . 17 E15
Molde, *Norway* 8 E12
Moldova ■, *Europe* . . 17 E15
Moldoveana, *Romania* 17 F13
Molepolole, *Botswana* 48 C4
Molfetta, *Italy* 20 D7
Moline, *U.S.A.* 70 E9
Moliro, *Zaïre* 46 F6
Mollendo, *Peru* 78 G4
Mollerin, L., *Australia* . 53 F2
Mölndal, *Sweden* 9 H15
Molodechno = Maladzyechna, *Belarus* 17 A14
Molokai, *U.S.A.* 66 H16
Molong, *Australia* 55 E4
Molopo →, *Africa* . . . 48 D3
Molotov = Perm, *Russia* 22 C10
Moloundou, *Cameroon* 46 D3
Molson L., *Canada* . . . 65 C9
Molteno, *S. Africa* 48 E4
Molu, *Indonesia* 33 F8
Molucca Sea, *Indonesia* 33 E6
Moluccas = Maluku, *Indonesia* 33 E7
Moma, *Mozam.* 47 H7
Mombasa, *Kenya* 46 E7
Mombetsu, *Japan* 28 B11
Momchilgrad, *Bulgaria* 21 D11
Mompós, *Colombia* . . . 78 B4
Møn, *Denmark* 9 J15
Mon →, *Burma* 37 J19
Mona, Canal de la, *W. Indies* 75 D11
Monach Is., *U.K.* 12 D1
Monaco ■, *Europe* . . . 18 E7
Monadhliath Mts., *U.K.* 12 D4
Monaghan, *Ireland* . . . 13 B5
Monaghan □, *Ireland* . 13 B5
Monahans, *U.S.A.* 71 K3
Monarch Mt., *Canada* . 64 C3
Monastir = Bitola, *Macedonia* 21 D9
Monastir, *Tunisia* 45 A7
Moncayo, Sierra del, *Spain* 19 B5
Monchegorsk, *Russia* . 22 A5
Mönchengladbach, *Germany* 16 C4
Monchique, *Portugal* . . 19 D1
Monclova, *Mexico* 74 B4
Moncton, *Canada* 63 C7
Mondego →, *Portugal* 19 B1
Mondeodo, *Indonesia* 33 E6
Mondovì, *Italy* 20 B2
Mondovi, *U.S.A.* 70 C9
Mondrain I., *Australia* 53 F3
Monessen, *U.S.A.* 68 E6
Monett, *U.S.A.* 71 G8
Monforte de Lemos, *Spain* 19 A2
Mong Cai, *Vietnam* . . . 34 B9
Mong Hsu, *Burma* 37 J21
Mong Kung, *Burma* . . . 37 J20
Mong Lang, *Burma* . . . 34 B4
Mong Nai, *Burma* 37 J20
Mong Pawk, *Burma* . . 37 H21
Mong Ton, *Burma* 37 J21
Mong Wa, *Burma* 37 J22
Mong Yai, *Burma* 37 H21
Mongalla, *Sudan* 45 G11
Mongers, L., *Australia* 53 E2
Monghyr = Munger, *India* 37 G15
Mongibello = Etna, *Italy* 20 F6
Mongo, *Chad* 45 F8
Mongolia ■, *Asia* 25 E10
Mongororo, *Chad* 45 F9
Mongu, *Zambia* 47 H4
Môngua, *Angola* 48 B2
Monkira, *Australia* . . . 54 C3
Monkoto, *Zaïre* 46 E4
Monmouth, *U.K.* 11 F5
Monmouth, *U.S.A.* 70 E9
Mono L., *U.S.A.* 73 H4
Monópoli, *Italy* 20 D7
Monqoumba, *C.A.R.* . . 46 D3
Monroe, *Ga., U.S.A.* . . 69 J4
Monroe, *La., U.S.A.* . . 71 J8
Monroe, *Mich., U.S.A.* 68 E4
Monroe, *N.C., U.S.A.* . 69 H5
Monroe, *Utah, U.S.A.* . 73 G7
Monroe, *Wis., U.S.A.* . 70 D10
Monroe City, *U.S.A.* . . 70 F9
Monroeville, *U.S.A.* . . 69 K2
Monrovia, *Liberia* 44 G2
Monrovia, *U.S.A.* 73 J4
Mons, *Belgium* 15 D3
Monse, *Indonesia* 33 E6
Mont-de-Marsan, *France* 18 E3
Mont-Joli, *Canada* . . . 63 C6
Mont-Laurier, *Canada* . 62 C4
Mont-St.-Michel, Le = Le Mont-St.-Michel, *France* 18 B3
Mont Tremblant Prov. Park, *Canada* 62 C5
Montagu, *S. Africa* . . . 48 E3
Montagu I., *Antarctica* 5 B1
Montague, *Canada* . . . 63 C7
Montague, *U.S.A.* 72 F2
Montague Ra., *Australia* 53 E2
Montague Sd., *Australia* 52 B4
Montalbán, *Spain* 19 B5
Montaña, *Peru* 78 E4
Montana □, *U.S.A.* . . . 72 C9
Montargis, *France* 18 C5
Montauban, *France* . . . 18 D4
Montauk, *U.S.A.* 68 E10
Montbéliard, *France* . . 18 C7
Montceau-les-Mines, *France* 18 C6
Monte Alegre, *Brazil* . . 79 D8
Monte Azul, *Brazil* . . . 79 G10
Monte Bello Is., *Australia* 52 D2
Monte-Carlo, *Monaco* . 16 G4
Monte Caseros, *Argentina* 80 C5
Monte Comán, *Argentina* 80 C3
Monte Santu, C. di, *Italy* 20 D3
Monte Vista, *U.S.A.* . . 73 H10
Montebello, *Canada* . . 62 C5
Montecristi, *Ecuador* . . 78 D2
Montecristo, *Italy* 20 C4
Montego Bay, *Jamaica* 74 J16
Montejinnie, *Australia* 52 C5
Montélimar, *France* . . 18 D6
Montello, *U.S.A.* 70 D10
Montemorelos, *Mexico* 74 B5
Montenegro □, *Yugoslavia* 21 C8
Montepuez, *Mozam.* . . 47 G7
Monterey, *U.S.A.* 73 H3
Montería, *Colombia* . . 78 B3
Monterrey, *Mexico* . . . 74 B4
Montes Claros, *Brazil* . 79 G10
Montesano, *U.S.A.* . . . 72 C2
Montesilvano Marina, *Italy* 20 C6
Montevideo, *Uruguay* 80 C5
Montevideo, *U.S.A.* . . . 70 C7
Montezuma, *U.S.A.* . . . 70 E8
Montgomery = Sahiwal, *Pakistan* . . 36 D8
Montgomery, *U.K.* . . . 11 E4
Montgomery, *Ala., U.S.A.* 69 J2
Montgomery, *W. Va., U.S.A.* 68 F5
Monticello, *Ark., U.S.A.* 71 J9
Monticello, *Fla., U.S.A.* 69 K4
Monticello, *Ind., U.S.A.* 68 E2
Monticello, *Iowa, U.S.A.* 70 D9
Monticello, *Ky., U.S.A.* 69 G3
Monticello, *Minn., U.S.A.* 70 C8
Monticello, *Miss., U.S.A.* 71 K9
Monticello, *Utah, U.S.A.* 73 H9
Montijo, *Spain* 19 C1
Montilla, *Spain* 19 D3
Montluçon, *France* . . . 18 C5
Montmagny, *Canada* . . 63 C5
Montmartre, *Canada* . . 65 C8
Montmorency, *Canada* 63 C5
Montmorillon, *France* . 18 C4
Monto, *Australia* 54 C5
Montoro, *Spain* 19 C3
Montpelier, *Idaho, U.S.A.* 72 E8
Montpelier, *Ohio, U.S.A.* 68 E3
Montpelier, *Vt., U.S.A.* 68 C9
Montpellier, *France* . . . 18 E5
Montréal, *Canada* 62 C5
Montreal L., *Canada* . . 65 C7
Montreal Lake, *Canada* 65 C7
Montreux, *Switz.* 16 E4
Montrose, *U.K.* 12 E6
Montrose, *U.S.A.* 73 G10
Monts, Pte. des, *Canada* 63 C6
Montserrat ■, *W. Indies* 74 L19
Monveda, *Zaïre* 46 D4
Monywa, *Burma* 37 H19
Monza, *Italy* 20 B3
Monze, *Zambia* 47 H5
Monze, C., *Pakistan* . . 36 G5
Monzón, *Spain* 19 B6
Mooi River, *S. Africa* . 49 D4
Moolawatana, *Australia* 55 D2
Mooliabeenee, *Australia* 53 F2
Mooloogool, *Australia* 53 E2
Moomin Cr. →, *Australia* 55 D4
Moonah →, *Australia* 54 C2
Moonbeam, *Canada* . . 62 C3
Moonda, L., *Australia* . 54 D3
Moonie, *Australia* 55 D5
Moonie →, *Australia* 55 D4
Moonta, *Australia* 55 E2
Moora, *Australia* 53 F2
Mooraberree, *Australia* 54 D3
Moorarie, *Australia* . . . 53 E2
Moorcroft, *U.S.A.* 70 C2
Moore →, *Australia* . 53 F2
Moore, L., *Australia* . . 53 E2
Moore Reefs, *Australia* 54 B4
Moorefield, *U.S.A.* . . . 68 F6
Mooresville, *U.S.A.* . . . 69 H5
Moorfoot Hills, *U.K.* . . 12 F5
Moorhead, *U.S.A.* 70 B6
Mooroopna, *Australia* 55 F4
Moorreesburg, *S. Africa* 48 E2
Moose →, *Canada* . . 62 B3
Moose Factory, *Canada* 62 B3
Moose I., *Canada* 65 C9
Moose Jaw, *Canada* . . 65 C7
Moose Jaw →, *Canada* 65 C7
Moose Lake, *Canada* . 65 C8
Moose Lake, *U.S.A.* . . 70 B8
Moose Mountain Cr. →, *Canada* 65 D8
Moose Mountain Prov. Park, *Canada* 65 D8
Moose River, *Canada* . 62 B3
Moosehead L., *U.S.A.* . 63 C6
Moosomin, *Canada* . . 65 C8
Moosonee, *Canada* . . . 62 B3
Mopeia Velha, *Mozam.* 47 H7
Mopipi, *Botswana* 48 C3
Mopti, *Mali* 44 F4
Moquegua, *Peru* 78 G4
Mora, *Sweden* 9 F16
Mora, *Minn., U.S.A.* . . 70 C8
Mora, *N. Mex., U.S.A.* 73 J11
Moradabad, *India* 36 E11
Morafenobe, *Madag.* . 49 B7
Moramanga, *Madag.* . 49 B8
Moran, *Kans., U.S.A.* . 71 G7
Moran, *Wyo., U.S.A.* . 72 E8
Moranbah, *Australia* . . 54 C4
Morant Pt., *Jamaica* . . 74 K17
Morar, L., *U.K.* 12 E3
Moratuwa, *Sri Lanka* . 36 R11
Morava →, *Serbia, Yug.* 21 B9
Morava →, *Slovak Rep.* 17 D9
Moravia, *U.S.A.* 70 E8
Moravian Hts. = Ceskomoravská Vrchovina, *Czech.* . . 16 D8
Morawa, *Australia* . . . 53 E2
Morawhanna, *Guyana* 78 B7
Moray Firth, *U.K.* 12 D5
Morden, *Canada* 65 D9
Mordovian Republic = Mordvinia □, *Russia* 22 D7
Mordvinia □, *Russia* . . 22 D7
Morea, *Australia* 55 F3
Morea, *Greece* 6 H10
Moreau →, *U.S.A.* . . . 70 C4
Morecambe, *U.K.* 10 C5
Morecambe B., *U.K.* . . 10 C5
Moree, *Australia* 55 D4
Morehead, *U.S.A.* 68 F4
Morehead City, *U.S.A.* 69 H7
Morelia, *Mexico* 74 D4
Morella, *Australia* 54 C3
Morella, *Spain* 19 B5
Morena, Sierra, *Spain* 19 C3
Morenci, *U.S.A.* 73 K9
Moresby I., *Canada* . . . 64 C2
Moreton, *Australia* . . . 54 A3
Moreton I., *Australia* . 55 D5
Morgan, *Australia* 55 E2
Morgan, *U.S.A.* 72 F8
Morgan City, *U.S.A.* . . 71 L9
Morganfield, *U.S.A.* . . 68 G2
Morganton, *U.S.A.* . . . 69 H5
Morgantown, *U.S.A.* . . 68 F6
Morgenzon, *S. Africa* . 49 D4
Morghak, *Iran* 39 D8
Morice L., *Canada* . . . 64 C3
Morinville, *Canada* . . . 64 C6
Morioka, *Japan* 28 E10
Morlaix, *France* 18 B2
Mornington, *Vic., Australia* 55 F4
Mornington, *W. Austral., Australia* 52 C4
Mornington, I., *Chile* . . 80 F1
Mornington I., *Australia* 54 B2
Moro G., *Phil.* 33 C6
Morocco ■, *N. Afr.* . . . 44 B3
Morococha, *Peru* 78 F3
Morogoro, *Tanzania* . . 46 F7
Morombe, *Madag.* . . . 49 C7
Morón, *Cuba* 75 C9
Morón de la Frontera, *Spain* 19 D3
Morondava, *Madag.* . . 49 C7
Morotai, *Indonesia* . . . 33 D7
Moroto, *Uganda* 46 D6
Morpeth, *U.K.* 10 B6
Morphou, *Cyprus* 38 C2
Morrilton, *U.S.A.* 71 H8
Morrinhos, *Brazil* 79 G9
Morrinsville, *N.Z.* 51 G5
Morris, *Canada* 65 D9
Morris, *Ill., U.S.A.* . . . 68 E1
Morris, *Minn., U.S.A.* . 70 C7
Morris, Mt., *Australia* . 53 E5
Morrisburg, *Canada* . . 62 D4
Morrison, *U.S.A.* 70 E10
Morristown, *Ariz., U.S.A.* 73 K7
Morristown, *S. Dak., U.S.A.* 70 C4
Morristown, *Tenn., U.S.A.* 69 G4
Morro Bay, *U.S.A.* 73 J3
Morrumbene, *Mozam.* 49 C6
Mors Nykøbing, *Denmark* 9 H13
Morshansk, *Russia* . . . 22 D7
Morteros, *Argentina* . . 80 C4
Mortes, R. das →, *Brazil* 79 F8
Mortlake, *Australia* . . . 55 F3
Morton, *Tex., U.S.A.* . . 71 J3
Morton, *Wash., U.S.A.* 72 C2
Morundah, *Australia* . . 55 E4
Moruya, *Australia* 55 F5
Morvan, *France* 18 C6
Morven, *Australia* 55 D4
Morvern, *U.K.* 12 E3
Morwell, *Australia* 55 F4
Morzhovets, Ostrov, *Russia* 22 A7
Moscos Is., *Burma* . . . 34 F4
Moscow = Moskva, *Russia* 22 C6
Moscow, *U.S.A.* 72 C5
Mosel →, *Europe* . . . 18 A7
Moselle = Mosel →, *Europe* 18 A7
Moses Lake, *U.S.A.* . . 72 C4
Mosgiel, *N.Z.* 51 L3
Moshi, *Tanzania* 46 E7
Moshupa, *Botswana* . . 48 C4
Mosjøen, *Norway* 8 D15
Moskenesøya, *Norway* 8 C15
Moskenstraumen, *Norway* 8 C15
Moskva, *Russia* 22 C6
Moskva →, *Russia* . . 22 C6
Mosomane, *Botswana* 48 C4
Moson-magyaróvar, *Hungary* 17 E9
Mosquera, *Colombia* . 78 C3
Mosquero, *U.S.A.* 71 H3
Moss, *Norway* 9 G14
Moss Vale, *Australia* . . 55 E5
Mossaka, *Congo* 46 E3
Mossbank, *Canada* . . . 65 D7
Mossburn, *N.Z.* 51 L2
Mosselbaai, *S. Africa* . 48 E3
Mossendjo, *Congo* . . . 46 E2
Mossgiel, *Australia* . . . 55 E3
Mossman, *Australia* . . 54 B4
Mossoró, *Brazil* 79 E11
Mossuril, *Mozam.* 47 G8
Mossy →, *Canada* . . . 65 C8
Most, *Czech.* 16 C7
Moşţafáābād, *Iran* 39 C7
Mostaganem, *Algeria* . 44 A5
Mostar, *Bos.-H.* 21 C7
Mostardas, *Brazil* 80 C6
Mostiska = Mostyska, *Ukraine* 17 D12
Mosty = Masty, *Belarus* 17 B13
Mostyska, *Ukraine* . . . 17 D12
Mosul = Al Mawşil, *Iraq* 38 B4
Motala, *Sweden* 9 G16
Motherwell, *U.K.* 12 F5
Motihari, *India* 37 F14
Motril, *Spain* 19 D4
Mott, *U.S.A.* 70 B3
Motueka, *N.Z.* 51 J4
Motueka →, *N.Z.* 51 J4
Mouanda, *Gabon* 46 E2
Mouchalagane →, *Canada* 63 B6
Moúdhros, *Greece* . . . 21 E11
Moudjeria, *Mauritania* 44 E2
Mouila, *Gabon* 46 E2
Moulamein, *Australia* . 55 F3
Moulins, *France* 18 C5
Moulmein, *Burma* 37 L20
Moulton, *U.S.A.* 71 L6
Moultrie, *U.S.A.* 69 K4
Moultrie, L., *U.S.A.* . . . 69 J5
Mound City, *Mo., U.S.A.* 70 E7
Mound City, *S. Dak., U.S.A.* 70 C4
Moundou, *Chad* 45 G8
Moundsville, *U.S.A.* . . 68 F5
Mount Airy, *U.S.A.* . . . 69 G5
Mount Amherst, *Australia* 52 C4
Mount Angel, *U.S.A.* . 72 D2
Mount Augustus, *Australia* 52 D2
Mount Barker, *S. Austral., Australia* 55 F2
Mount Barker, *W. Austral., Australia* 53 F2
Mount Carmel, *U.S.A.* 68 F2
Mount Clemens, *U.S.A.* 62 D3
Mount Coolon, *Australia* 54 C4
Mount Darwin, *Zimbabwe* 47 H6
Mount Desert I., *U.S.A.* 63 D6
Mount Dora, *U.S.A.* . . 69 L5
Mount Douglas, *Australia* 54 C4
Mount Eba, *Australia* . 55 E2
Mount Edgecumbe, *U.S.A.* 64 B1
Mount Elizabeth, *Australia* 52 C4
Mount Fletcher, *S. Africa* 49 E4
Mount Forest, *Canada* 62 D3
Mount Gambier, *Australia* 55 F3
Mount Garnet, *Australia* 54 B4
Mount Hope, *N.S.W., Australia* 55 E4
Mount Hope, *S. Austral., Australia* 55 E2
Mount Hope, *U.S.A.* . . 68 G5
Mount Horeb, *U.S.A.* . 70 D10
Mount Howitt, *Australia* 55 D3
Mount Isa, *Australia* . . 54 C2
Mount Keith, *Australia* 53 E3
Mount Larcom, *Australia* 54 C5
Mount Lofty Ra., *Australia* 55 E2
Mount McKinley National Park, *U.S.A.* 60 B5
Mount Magnet, *Australia* 53 E2
Mount Margaret, *Australia* 55 D3
Mount Maunganui, *N.Z.* 51 G6
Mount Molloy, *Australia* 54 B4
Mount Monger, *Australia* 53 F3
Mount Morgan, *Australia* 54 C5
Mount Morris, *U.S.A.* . 68 D7
Mount Mulligan, *Australia* 54 B3
Mount Narryer, *Australia* 53 E2
Mount Olympus = Uludağ, *Turkey* 21 D13
Mount Oxide Mine, *Australia* 54 B2
Mount Pearl, *Canada* . 63 C9
Mount Perry, *Australia* 55 D5
Mount Phillips, *Australia* 52 D2
Mount Pleasant, *Iowa, U.S.A.* 70 E9
Mount Pleasant, *Mich., U.S.A.* 68 D3
Mount Pleasant, *S.C., U.S.A.* 69 J6
Mount Pleasant, *Tenn., U.S.A.* 69 H2
Mount Pleasant, *Tex., U.S.A.* 71 J7
Mount Pleasant, *Utah, U.S.A.* 72 G8
Mount Rainier National Park, *U.S.A.* 72 C3
Mount Revelstoke Nat. Park, *Canada* 64 C5
Mount Robson Prov. Park, *Canada* 64 C5
Mount Sandiman, *Australia* 53 D2
Mount Shasta, *U.S.A.* . 72 F2
Mount Sterling, *Ill., U.S.A.* 70 F9
Mount Sterling, *Ky., U.S.A.* 68 F4
Mount Surprise, *Australia* 54 B3
Mount Vernon, *Australia* 52 D2
Mount Vernon, *Ind., U.S.A.* 70 F10
Mount Vernon, *N.Y., U.S.A.* 68 E9
Mount Vernon, *Ohio, U.S.A.* 68 E4
Mount Vernon, *Wash., U.S.A.* 72 B2
Mountain City, *Nev., U.S.A.* 72 F6
Mountain City, *Tenn., U.S.A.* 69 G5
Mountain Grove, *U.S.A.* 71 G8
Mountain Home, *Ark., U.S.A.* 71 G8
Mountain Home, *Idaho, U.S.A.* 72 E6
Mountain Iron, *U.S.A.* 70 B8
Mountain Park, *Canada* 64 C5
Mountain View, *Ark., U.S.A.* 71 H8
Mountain View, *Calif., U.S.A.* 73 H2
Mountainair, *U.S.A.* . . 73 J10
Mountmellick, *Ireland* . 13 C4
Moura, *Australia* 54 C4
Moura, *Brazil* 78 D6
Moura, *Portugal* 19 C2
Mourdi, Dépression du, *Chad* 45 E9
Mourdiah, *Mali* 44 F3
Mourilyan, *Australia* . . 54 B4
Mourne →, *U.K.* 13 B4
Mourne Mts., *U.K.* . . . 13 B5
Mouscron, *Belgium* . . 15 D3
Moussoro, *Chad* 45 F8
Moutohara, *N.Z.* 51 H6
Moutong, *Indonesia* . . 33 D6
Moville, *Ireland* 13 A4
Moy →, *Ireland* 13 B3
Moyale, *Kenya* 40 G2
Moyamba, *S. Leone* . . 44 G2
Moyen Atlas, *Morocco* 44 B3
Moyle □, *U.K.* 13 A5
Moyo, *Indonesia* 32 F5
Moyobamba, *Peru* 78 E3
Moyyero →, *Russia* . 25 C11
Mozambique = Moçambique, *Mozam.* 47 H8
Mozambique ■, *Africa* 47 H7
Mozambique Chan., *Africa* 49 B7
Mozdok, *Russia* 23 F7
Mozdūrān, *Iran* 39 B9
Mozhnābād, *Iran* 39 C9
Mozyr = Mazyr, *Belarus* 17 B15

Mpanda, *Tanzania* . . . 46 F6
Mpika, *Zambia* 47 G6
Mpumalanga, *S. Africa* 49 D5
Mpwapwa, *Tanzania* . . 46 F7
Msaken, *Tunisia* 45 A7
Msoro, *Zambia* 47 G6
Mstislavl = Mstsislaw,
  Belarus 17 A16
Mstsislaw, *Belarus* . . . 17 A16
Mtubatuba, *S. Africa* . . 49 D5
Muaná, *Brazil* 79 D9
Muang Chiang Rai,
  Thailand 34 C5
Muang Lamphun,
  Thailand 34 C5
Muar, *Malaysia* 34 S15
Muar →, *Malaysia* . 34 S15
Muarabungo, *Indonesia* 32 E2
Muaraenim, *Indonesia* 32 E2
Muarajuloi, *Indonesia* . 32 E4
Muarakaman, *Indonesia* 32 E5
Muaratebo, *Indonesia* . 32 E2
Muaratembesi,
  Indonesia 32 E2
Muaratewe, *Indonesia* . 32 E4
Mubarraz = Al
  Mubarraz, *Si. Arabia* 39 E6
Mubende, *Uganda* . . . 46 D6
Mubi, *Nigeria* 45 F7
Muck, *U.K.* 12 E2
Muckadilla, *Australia* . 55 D4
Muconda, *Angola* 46 G4
Mucuri, *Brazil* 79 G11
Mucusso, *Angola* 48 B3
Mudanjiang, *China* . . . 31 B7
Mudanya, *Turkey* 21 D13
Muddy Cr. →, *U.S.A.* . 73 H8
Mudgee, *Australia* . . . 55 E4
Mudjatik →, *Canada* . 65 B7
Mueller Ra., *Australia* . 52 C4
Mufulira, *Zambia* 47 G5
Mughayrá', *Si. Arabia* 38 D3
Mugi, *Japan* 29 H7
Muğla, *Turkey* 21 F13
Mugu, *Nepal* 37 E13
Muhammad Qol, *Sudan* 45 D12
Mühlhausen, *Germany* 16 C6
Mühlig Hofmann fjella,
  Antarctica 5 D3
Muhos, *Finland* 8 D22
Muhu, *Estonia* 9 G20
Mui Bai Bung, *Vietnam* 34 H8
Mui Ron, *Vietnam* . . . 34 C9
Muikamachi, *Japan* . . 29 F9
Muine Bheag, *Ireland* . 13 D5
Muir, L., *Australia* . . . 53 F2
Mukacheve, *Ukraine* . . 17 D12
Mukachevo =
  Mukacheve, *Ukraine* 17 D12
Mukah, *Malaysia* 32 D4
Mukden = Shenyang,
  China 31 B7
Mukhtuya = Lensk,
  Russia 25 C12
Mukinbudin, *Australia* 53 F2
Mukomuko, *Indonesia* 32 E2
Muktsar, *India* 36 D9
Mukur, *Afghan.* 36 C6
Mukutawa →, *Canada* 65 C9
Mula, *Spain* 19 C5
Mulchén, *Chile* 80 D2
Mulde →, *Germany* . . 16 C7
Mule Creek, *U.S.A.* . . . 70 D2
Muleshoe, *U.S.A.* 71 H3
Mulgathing, *Australia* . 55 E1
Mulgrave, *Canada* . . . 63 C7
Mulhacén, *Spain* 19 D4
Mulhouse, *France* . . . 18 C7
Mull, *U.K.* 12 E3
Mullaittvu, *Sri Lanka* . 36 Q12
Mullen, *U.S.A.* 70 D4
Mullengudgery,
  Australia 55 E4
Mullens, *U.S.A.* 68 G5
Muller, Pegunungan,
  Indonesia 32 D4
Mullet Pen., *Ireland* . . 13 B1
Mullewa, *Australia* . . . 53 E2
Mulligan →, *Australia* 54 C2
Mullin, *U.S.A.* 71 K5
Mullingar, *Ireland* . . . 13 C4
Mullins, *U.S.A.* 69 H6
Mullumbimby,
  Australia 55 D5
Multan, *Pakistan* 36 D7
Mulvane, *U.S.A.* 71 G6
Mulwala, *Australia* . . . 55 F4
Mumbai = Bombay,
  India 36 K8
Mumbwa, *Zambia* 47 H5
Mun →, *Thailand* . . . 34 E7
Muna, *Indonesia* 33 F6
Munamagi, *Estonia* . . 9 H22
München, *Germany* . . 16 D6
Munchen-Gladbach =
  Mönchengladbach,
  Germany 16 C4
Muncho Lake, *Canada* 64 B3
Muncie, *U.S.A.* 68 E3
Muncoonie, L.,
  Australia 54 D2
Mundala, *Indonesia* . . 33 E10
Mundare, *Canada* . . . 64 C6
Munday, *U.S.A.* 71 J5
Münden, *Germany* . . . 16 C5
Mundiwindi, *Australia* 52 D3
Mundo Novo, *Brazil* . . 79 F10
Mundrabilla, *Australia* 53 F4
Mungallala, *Australia* . 55 D4
Mungallala Cr. →,
  Australia 55 D4
Mungana, *Australia* . . 54 B3

Mungbere, *Zaïre* 46 D5
Munger, *India* 37 G15
Mungindi, *Australia* . . 55 D4
Munhango, *Angola* . . . 47 G3
Munich = München,
  Germany 16 D6
Munising, *U.S.A.* 68 B2
Munku-Sardyk, *Russia* 25 D11
Muñoz Gamero, Pen.,
  Chile 80 G2
Munroe L., *Canada* . . . 65 B9
Münster, *Germany* . . . 16 C4
Munster □, *Ireland* . . 13 D3
Muntadgin, *Australia* . 53 F2
Muntok, *Indonesia* . . . 32 E3
Muon Pak Beng, *Laos* 34 C6
Muonio, *Finland* 8 C20
Muonionjoki →,
  Finland 8 C20
Mupa, *Angola* 47 H3
Muqdisho, *Somali Rep.* 40 G4
Mur →, *Austria* 17 E9
Murakami, *Japan* 28 E9
Murallón, Cuerro, *Chile* 80 F2
Murang'a, *Kenya* 46 E7
Murashi, *Russia* 22 C8
Muratlı, *Turkey* 21 D12
Murayama, *Japan* . . . 28 E10
Murban, *U.A.E.* 39 F7
Murchison →,
  Australia 53 E1
Murchison, Mt.,
  Antarctica 5 D11
Murchison Falls =
  Kabarega Falls,
  Uganda 46 D6
Murchison House,
  Australia 53 E1
Murchison Ra.,
  Australia 54 C1
Murcia, *Spain* 19 D5
Murcia □, *Spain* 19 D5
Murdo, *U.S.A.* 70 D4
Murdoch Pt., *Australia* 54 A3
Mureş →, *Romania* . . 17 E11
Mureşul = Mureş →,
  Romania 17 E11
Murfreesboro, *U.S.A.* . 69 H2
Murgab = Murghob,
  Tajikistan 24 F8
Murghob, *Tajikistan* . . 24 F8
Murgon, *Australia* . . . 55 D5
Murgoo, *Australia* . . . 53 E2
Muria, *Indonesia* 33 G14
Müritz-see, *Germany* . 16 B7
Murmansk, *Russia* . . . 22 A5
Murom, *Russia* 22 C7
Muroran, *Japan* 28 C10
Muroto, *Japan* 29 H7
Muroto-Misaki, *Japan* 29 H7
Murphy, *U.S.A.* 72 E5
Murphysboro, *U.S.A.* . 71 G10
Murray, Ky., *U.S.A.* . . . 69 G1
Murray, Utah, *U.S.A.* . 72 F8
Murray →, *Australia* . 55 F2
Murray →, *Canada* . . 64 B4
Murray, L., *U.S.A.* . . . 69 H5
Murray Bridge,
  Australia 55 F2
Murray Downs,
  Australia 54 C1
Murray Harbour,
  Canada 63 C7
Murraysburg, *S. Africa* 48 E3
Murree, *Pakistan* 36 C8
Murrin Murrin,
  Australia 53 E3
Murrumbidgee →,
  Australia 55 E3
Murrumburrah,
  Australia 55 E4
Murrurundi, *Australia* 55 E5
Murtazapur, *India* . . . 36 J10
Murtle L., *Canada* . . . 64 C5
Murtoa, *Australia* 55 F3
Murwara, *India* 37 H12
Murwillumbah,
  Australia 55 D5
Mürzzuschlag, *Austria* 16 E8
Muş, *Turkey* 23 G7
Mûsa, G., *Egypt* 45 C11
Musa Khel, *Pakistan* . 36 D6
Musá Qal'eh, *Afghan.* 36 C4
Musafargarh, *Pakistan* 36 D7
Musala, *Indonesia* . . . 32 D1
Musala, *Bulgaria* 21 C10
Musay'īd, *Qatar* 39 E6
Muscat = Masqat,
  Oman 40 C6
Muscat & Oman =
  Oman ■, *Asia* 40 C6
Muscatine, *U.S.A.* . . . 70 E9
Musgrave, *Australia* . . 54 A3
Musgrave Ras.,
  Australia 53 E5
Mushie, *Zaïre* 46 E3
Musi →, *Indonesia* . . 32 E2
Muskeg →, *Canada* . . 64 A4
Muskegon, *U.S.A.* . . . 68 D2
Muskegon →, *U.S.A.* . 68 D2
Muskegon Heights,
  U.S.A. 68 D2
Muskogee, *U.S.A.* . . . 71 H7
Muskwa →, *Canada* . 64 B4
Muslimiyah, *Syria* . . . 38 B3
Musmar, *Sudan* 45 E12
Musoma, *Tanzania* . . . 46 E6
Musquaro, L., *Canada* 63 B7
Musquodoboit Harbour,
  Canada 63 D7
Musselburgh, *U.K.* . . . 12 F5
Musselshell →, *U.S.A.* 72 C10
Mussoorie, *India* 36 D11
Mussuco, *Angola* 48 B2

Mustafakemalpaşa,
  Turkey 21 D13
Mustang, *Nepal* 37 E13
Musters, L., *Argentina* 80 F3
Muswellbrook,
  Australia 55 E5
Mût, *Egypt* 45 C10
Mutanda, *Mozam.* . . . 49 C5
Mutare, *Zimbabwe* . . . 47 H6
Muting, *Indonesia* . . . 33 F10
Mutoray, *Russia* 25 C11
Mutsu, *Japan* 28 D10
Mutsu-Wan, *Japan* . . . 28 D10
Muttaburra, *Australia* . 54 C3
Muweilih, *Egypt* 41 E3
Muxima, *Angola* 46 F2
Muynak, *Uzbekistan* . . 24 E6
Muzaffarabad, *Pakistan* 36 B8
Muzaffargarh, *Pakistan* 36 D7
Muzaffarnagar, *India* . 36 E10
Muzaffarpur, *India* . . . 37 F14
Muzhi, *Russia* 24 C7
Muzon, C., *U.S.A.* 64 C2
Mvuma, *Zimbabwe* . . . 47 H6
Mwanza, *Tanzania* . . . 46 E6
Mwanza, *Zaïre* 46 F5
Mweelrea, *Ireland* . . . 13 C2
Mweka, *Zaïre* 46 E4
Mwenezi, *Zimbabwe* . . 47 J6
Mwenga, *Zaïre* 46 E5
Mweru, L., *Zambia* . . . 46 F5
Mwinilunga, *Zambia* . . 47 G4
My Tho, *Vietnam* 34 G9
Myanaung, *Burma* . . . 37 K19
Myanmar = Burma ■,
  Asia 37 J20
Myaungmya, *Burma* . . 37 L19
Mycenæ, *Greece* 21 F10
Myeik Kyunzu, *Burma* 34 G4
Myingyan, *Burma* 37 J19
Myitkyina, *Burma* 37 G20
Mymensingh, *Bangla.* 37 G17
Mynydd Du, *U.K.* 11 F4
Mýrdalsjökull, *Iceland* 8 E4
Myroodah, *Australia* . . 52 C3
Myrtle Beach, *U.S.A.* . 69 J6
Myrtle Creek, *U.S.A.* . . 72 E2
Myrtle Point, *U.S.A.* . . 72 E1
Mysia, *Turkey* 21 E12
Mysore = Karnataka □,
  India 36 N10
Mysore, *India* 36 N10
Myszków, *Poland* 17 C10
Mytishchi, *Russia* . . . 22 C6
Myton, *U.S.A.* 72 F8
Mývatn, *Iceland* 8 D5
Mzimkulu →, *S. Africa* 49 E5
Mzimvubu →,
  S. Africa 49 E4

N

Na Hearadh = Harris,
  U.K. 12 D2
Naab →, *Germany* . . 16 D6
Naantali, *Finland* 9 F19
Naas, *Ireland* 13 C5
Nababiep, *S. Africa* . . . 48 D2
Nabari, *Japan* 29 G8
Nabawa, *Australia* . . . 53 E1
Nabberu, L., *Australia* . 53 E3
Naberezhnyye Chelny,
  Russia 22 C9
Nabeul, *Tunisia* 45 A7
Nabīd, *Iran* 39 D8
Nabire, *Indonesia* . . . 33 E9
Nabisipi →, *Canada* . 63 B7
Nablus = Nābulus,
  West Bank 41 C4
Naboomspruit,
  S. Africa 49 C4
Nābulus, *West Bank* . . 41 C4
Naches, *U.S.A.* 72 C3
Nachingwea, *Tanzania* 46 G7
Nackara, *Australia* . . . 55 E2
Naco, *U.S.A.* 73 L9
Nacogdoches, *U.S.A.* . 71 K7
Nacozari, *Mexico* 74 A3
Nadiad, *India* 36 H8
Nadüshan, *Iran* 39 C7
Nadvirna, *Ukraine* . . . 17 D13
Nadvoitsy, *Russia* . . . 22 B5
Nadvornaya =
  Nadvirna, *Ukraine* . 17 D13
Nadym, *Russia* 24 C8
Nadym →, *Russia* . . . 24 C8
Nærbø, *Norway* 9 G11
Næstved, *Denmark* . . . 9 J14
Nafada, *Nigeria* 44 F7
Naftshahr, *Iran* 38 C5
Nafud Desert = An
  Nafūd, *Si. Arabia* . . 38 D4
Naga, *Phil.* 33 B6
Nagagami →, *Canada* 62 C3
Nagahama, *Japan* . . . 29 G8
Nagai, *Japan* 28 E10
Nagaland □, *India* . . . 37 F19
Nagano, *Japan* 29 F9
Nagano □, *Japan* 29 F9
Nagaoka, *Japan* 29 F9
Nagappattinam, *India* . 36 P11
Nagar Parkar, *Pakistan* 36 G7
Nagasaki, *Japan* 29 H4
Nagasaki □, *Japan* . . . 29 H4
Nagato, *Japan* 29 G5
Nagaur, *India* 36 F8
Nagercoil, *India* 36 Q10
Nagīneh, *Iran* 39 C8
Nagoorin, *Australia* . . 54 C5

Nagornyy, *Russia* 25 D13
Nagoya, *Japan* 29 G8
Nagpur, *India* 36 J11
Nagykanizsa, *Hungary* 17 E9
Nagykőrös, *Hungary* . . 17 E10
Naha, *Japan* 29 L3
Nahanni Butte, *Canada* 64 A4
Nahanni Nat. Park,
  Canada 64 A3
Nahariyya, *Israel* 38 C2
Nahāvand, *Iran* 39 C6
Nahlin, *Canada* 64 B2
Naicam, *Canada* 65 C8
Na'īfah, *Si. Arabia* . . . 40 D5
Na'īn, *Iran* 39 C7
Nainpur, *India* 36 H12
Nairn, *U.K.* 12 D5
Nairobi, *Kenya* 46 E7
Naissaar, *Estonia* 9 G21
Naivasha, *Kenya* 46 E7
Najafābād, *Iran* 39 C6
Najibabad, *India* 36 E11
Najmah, *Si. Arabia* . . . 39 E6
Nakadōri-Shima, *Japan* 29 H4
Nakaminato, *Japan* . . 29 F10
Nakamura, *Japan* 29 H6
Nakano, *Japan* 29 F9
Nakano-Shima, *Japan* 29 K4
Nakashibetsu, *Japan* . 28 C12
Nakfa, *Eritrea* 45 E12
Nakhichevan =
  Naxçıvan, *Azerbaijan* 23 G8
Nakhichevan Republic
  = Naxçıvan □,
  Azerbaijan 23 G8
Nakhl, *Egypt* 41 F2
Nakhl-e Taqī, *Iran* . . . 39 E7
Nakhodka, *Russia* . . . 25 E14
Nakhon Phanom,
  Thailand 34 D8
Nakhon Ratchasima,
  Thailand 34 E7
Nakhon Sawan,
  Thailand 34 E6
Nakhon Si Thammarat,
  Thailand 34 H6
Nakina, B.C., *Canada* . 64 B2
Nakina, Ont., *Canada* . 62 B2
Nakskov, *Denmark* . . . 9 J14
Naku'u, *Kenya* 46 E7
Nakusp, *Canada* 64 C5
Nal →, *Pakistan* 36 G4
Nalchik, *Russia* 23 F7
Nalgonda, *India* 36 L11
Nallamalai Hills, *India* 36 M11
Nālūt, *Libya* 45 B7
Nam Co, *China* 30 C4
Nam Dinh, *Vietnam* . . 34 B9
Nam-Phan, *Vietnam* . . 34 G9
Nam Phong, *Thailand* 34 D7
Nam Tha, *Laos* 34 B6
Namacunde, *Angola* . . 48 B2
Namacurra, *Mozam.* . . 49 B6
Namak, Daryācheh-ye,
  Iran 39 C7
Namak, Kavir-e, *Iran* . . 39 C8
Namaland, *Namibia* . . 48 C2
Namangan, *Uzbekistan* 24 E8
Namapa, *Mozam.* 47 G7
Namaqualand, *S. Africa* 48 D2
Namber, *Indonesia* . . . 33 E8
Nambour, *Australia* . . 55 D5
Nambucca Heads,
  Australia 55 E5
Namcha Barwa, *China* 30 D4
Nameh, *Indonesia* . . . 32 D5
Namew L., *Canada* . . . 65 C8
Namib Desert =
  Namibwoestyn,
  Namibia 48 C2
Namibe, *Angola* 47 H2
Namibe □, *Angola* . . . 48 B1
Namibia ■, *Africa* . . . 48 C2
Namibwoestyn,
  Namibia 48 C2
Namlea, *Indonesia* . . . 33 E7
Namoi →, *Australia* . . 55 E4
Nampa, *U.S.A.* 72 E5
Nampō-Shotō, *Japan* . 29 J10
Nampula, *Mozam.* . . . 47 H7
Namrole, *Indonesia* . . 33 E7
Namse Shankou, *China* 37 E13
Namsen →, *Norway* . 8 D14
Namsos, *Norway* 8 D14
Namtsy, *Russia* 25 C13
Namtu, *Burma* 37 H20
Namu, *Canada* 64 C3
Namur, *Belgium* 15 D4
Namur □, *Belgium* . . . 15 D4
Namutoni, *Namibia* . . 48 B2
Namwala, *Zambia* . . . 47 H5
Nan, *Thailand* 34 C6
Nanaimo, *Canada* . . . 64 D4
Nanango, *Australia* . . 55 D5
Nanao, *Japan* 29 F8
Nanchang, *China* 31 D6
Nanching = Nanjing,
  China 31 C6
Nanchong, *China* 30 C5
Nancy, *France* 18 B7
Nanda Devi, *India* . . . 36 D11
Nandan, *Japan* 29 G7
Nanded, *India* 36 K10
Nandewar Ra.,
  Australia 55 E5
Nandi, *Fiji* 51 C7
Nandurbar, *India* 36 J9
Nandyal, *India* 36 M11
Nanga, *Australia* 53 E1
Nanga-Eboko,
  Cameroon 46 D2

Nanga Parbat, *Pakistan* 36 B9
Nangapinoh, *Indonesia* 32 E4
Nangarhár □, *Afghan.* 36 B7
Nangatayap, *Indonesia* 32 E4
Nanjing, *China* 31 C6
Nanking = Nanjing,
  China 31 C6
Nankoku, *Japan* 29 H6
Nanning, *China* 30 D5
Nannup, *Australia* . . . 53 F2
Nanping, *China* 31 D6
Nansei-Shotō =
  Ryūkyū-rettō, *Japan* 29 M2
Nansen Sd., *Canada* . . 4 A3
Nantes, *France* 18 C3
Nanticoke, *U.S.A.* 68 E7
Nanton, *Canada* 64 C6
Nantong, *China* 31 C7
Nantucket I., *U.S.A.* . . 58 E12
Nanuque, *Brazil* 79 G10
Nanutarra, *Australia* . . 52 D2
Nanyang, *China* 31 C6
Nanyuki, *Kenya* 46 D7
Nao, C. de la, *Spain* . . 19 C6
Naococane L., *Canada* 63 B5
Naoetsu, *Japan* 29 F9
Napa, *U.S.A.* 72 G2
Napanee, *Canada* . . . 62 D4
Napier, *N.Z.* 51 H6
Napier Broome B.,
  Australia 52 B4
Napier Downs,
  Australia 52 C3
Napier Pen., *Australia* 54 A2
Naples = Nápoli, *Italy* 20 D6
Naples, *U.S.A.* 69 M5
Napo →, *Peru* 78 D4
Napoleon, N. Dak.,
  U.S.A. 70 B5
Napoleon, Ohio, *U.S.A.* 68 E3
Nápoli, *Italy* 20 D6
Nappa Merrie, *Australia* 55 D3
Naqqāsh, *Iran* 39 C6
Nara, *Japan* 29 G7
Nara, *Mali* 44 E3
Nara □, *Japan* 29 G8
Nara Visa, *U.S.A.* 71 H3
Naracoorte, *Australia* . 55 F3
Naradhan, *Australia* . . 55 E4
Narasapur, *India* 37 L12
Narayanganj, *Bangla.* 37 H17
Narayanpet, *India* . . . 36 L10
Narbonne, *France* . . . 18 E5
Nardin, *Iran* 39 B7
Nardò, *Italy* 21 D8
Narembeen, *Australia* 53 F2
Nares Str., *Arctic* 58 B13
Naretha, *Australia* . . . 53 F3
Narew →, *Poland* . . . 17 B11
Narin, *Afghan.* 36 A6
Narindra, Helodranon'
  i, *Madag.* 49 A8
Narita, *Japan* 29 G10
Narmada →, *India* . . . 36 J8
Narmland, *Sweden* . . 9 F15
Narodnaya, *Russia* . . 22 A10
Narooma, *Australia* . . 55 F5
Narrabri, *Australia* . . . 55 E4
Narran →, *Australia* . 55 D4
Narrandera, *Australia* . 55 E4
Narraway →, *Canada* 64 B5
Narrogin, *Australia* . . . 53 F2
Narromine, *Australia* . 55 E4
Narsimhapur, *India* . . 36 H11
Naruto, *Japan* 29 G7
Narva, *Estonia* 22 C4
Narva →, *Russia* 9 G22
Narvik, *Norway* 8 B17
Naryan-Mar, *Russia* . . 22 A9
Naryilco, *Australia* . . . 55 D3
Narym, *Russia* 24 D9
Narymskoye,
  Kazakhstan 24 E9
Naryn, *Kyrgyzstan* . . . 24 E8
Nasa, *Norway* 8 C16
Nasarawa, *Nigeria* . . . 44 G6
Naseby, *N.Z.* 51 L3
Naser, Buheirat en,
  Egypt 45 D11
Nashua, Iowa, *U.S.A.* . 70 D8
Nashua, Mont., *U.S.A.* 72 B10
Nashua, N.H., *U.S.A.* . 68 D10
Nashville, Ark., *U.S.A.* 71 J8
Nashville, Ga., *U.S.A.* . 69 K4
Nashville, Tenn., *U.S.A.* 69 G2
Nasik, *India* 36 K8
Nasirabad, *India* 36 F9
Naskaupi →, *Canada* . 63 B7
Naşrīān-e Pā'īn, *Iran* . 38 C5
Nass →, *Canada* 64 B3
Nassau, *Bahamas* . . . 75 B4
Nassau, B., *Chile* 80 H3
Nasser, L. = Naser,
  Buheirat en, *Egypt* . 45 D11
Nässjö, *Sweden* 9 H16
Nat Kyizin, *Burma* . . . 34 E4
Natagaima, *Colombia* . 78 C3
Natal, *Brazil* 79 E11
Natal, *Canada* 64 D6
Natal, *Indonesia* 32 D1
Naţanz, *Iran* 39 C6
Natashquan, *Canada* . 63 B7
Natashquan →,
  Canada 63 B7
Natchez, *U.S.A.* 71 K9
Natchitoches, *U.S.A.* . 71 K8
Nathalia, *Australia* . . . 55 F4
Nathdwara, *India* 36 G8
Natimuk, *Australia* . . . 55 F3
Nation →, *Canada* . . 64 B4
National City, *U.S.A.* . . 73 K5

Natitingou, *Benin* 44 F5
Natoma, *U.S.A.* 70 F5
Natron, L., *Tanzania* . . 46 E7
Natuna Besar,
  Kepulauan, *Indonesia* 32 D3
Natuna Is. = Natuna
  Besar, Kepulauan,
  Indonesia 32 D3
Natuna Selatan,
  Kepulauan, *Indonesia* 32 D3
Naturaliste, C.,
  Australia 54 G4
Naubinway, *U.S.A.* . . . 62 C2
Naumburg, *Germany* . 16 C6
Nā'ūr at Tunayb,
  Jordan 41 D4
Nauru ■, *Pac. Oc.* . . . 56 H8
Naushahra =
  Nowshera, *Pakistan* 36 B8
Nauta, *Peru* 78 D4
Nautanwa, *India* 37 F13
Navahrudak, *Belarus* . 17 B13
Navajo Reservoir,
  U.S.A. 73 H10
Navalmoral de la Mata,
  Spain 19 C3
Navan = An Uaimh,
  Ireland 13 C5
Navarino, I., *Chile* . . . 80 H3
Navarra □, *Spain* . . . 19 A5
Navasota, *U.S.A.* 71 K6
Naver →, *U.K.* 12 C4
Năvodari, *Romania* . . 17 F15
Navoi = Nawoiy,
  Uzbekistan 24 E7
Navojoa, *Mexico* 74 B3
Návpaktos, *Greece* . . . 21 E9
Návplion, *Greece* 21 F10
Navsari, *India* 36 J8
Nawabshah, *Pakistan* 36 F6
Nawakot, *Nepal* 37 F14
Nawalgarh, *India* 36 F9
Nawoiy, *Uzbekistan* . . 24 E7
Naxçıvan, *Azerbaijan* . 23 G8
Naxçıvan □, *Azerbaijan* 23 G8
Náxos, *Greece* 21 F11
Nāy Band, *Iran* 39 E7
Nayakhan, *Russia* . . . 25 C16
Nayoro, *Japan* 28 B11
Nayyāl, W. →,
  Si. Arabia 38 D3
Nazareth = Nazerat,
  Israel 41 C4
Nazas, *Mexico* 74 B4
Nazas →, *Mexico* . . . 74 B4
Naze, The, *U.K.* 11 F9
Nazerat, *Israel* 41 C4
Nāzīk, *Iran* 38 B5
Nazilli, *Turkey* 21 F13
Nazir Hat, *Bangla.* . . . 37 H17
Nazko, *Canada* 64 C4
Nazko →, *Canada* . . . 64 C4
Ncheu, *Malawi* 47 G6
Ndalatando, *Angola* . . 46 F2
Ndélé, *C.A.R.* 45 G9
Ndendé, *Gabon* 46 E2
Ndjamena, *Chad* 45 F7
Ndjolé, *Gabon* 46 E2
Ndola, *Zambia* 47 G5
Neagh, Lough, *U.K.* . . 13 B5
Neah Bay, *U.S.A.* 72 B1
Neale, L., *Australia* . . . 52 D5
Near Is., *U.S.A.* 60 C1
Neath, *U.K.* 11 F4
Nebine Cr. →,
  Australia 55 D4
Nebitdag, *Turkmenistan* 23 G9
Nebraska □, *U.S.A.* . . 70 E5
Nebraska City, *U.S.A.* . 70 E7
Nébrodi, Monti, *Italy* . 20 F6
Necedah, *U.S.A.* 70 C9
Nechako →, *Canada* . 64 C4
Neches →, *U.S.A.* . . . 71 L8
Neckar →, *Germany* . 16 D5
Necochea, *Argentina* . 80 D4
Needles, *U.S.A.* 73 J6
Needles, The, *U.K.* . . . 11 G6
Neemuch = Nimach,
  India 36 G9
Neenah, *U.S.A.* 68 C1
Neepawa, *Canada* . . . 65 C9
Nefta, *Tunisia* 44 B6
Neftçala, *Azerbaijan* . . 23 G8
Neftyannyye Kamni,
  Azerbaijan 23 F9
Negapatam =
  Nagappattinam, *India* 36 P11
Negaunee, *U.S.A.* . . . 68 B2
Negele, *Ethiopia* 40 F2
Negeri Sembilan □,
  Malaysia 34 S15
Negev Desert =
  Hanegev, *Israel* . . . 41 E3
Negombo, *Sri Lanka* . 36 R11
Negotin, *Serbia, Yug.* 21 B10
Negra Pt., *Phil.* 33 A6
Negrais, C. = Maudin
  Sun, *Burma* 37 M19
Negro →, *Argentina* . 80 E4
Negro →, *Brazil* 78 D6
Negro →, *Uruguay* . . 80 C5
Negros, *Phil.* 33 C6
Nehāvand, *Iran* 39 C6
Nehbandān, *Iran* 39 D9
Nei Monggol Zizhiqu □,
  China 31 B6
Neidpath, *Canada* . . . 65 C7
Neihart, *U.S.A.* 72 C8
Neijiang, *China* 30 D5
Neilton, *U.S.A.* 72 C2
Neiva, *Colombia* 78 C3
Nejanilini L., *Canada* . 65 B9
Nekā, *Iran* 39 B7
Nekemte, *Ethiopia* . . . 45 G12

Neksø, Denmark 9 J16
Nelia, Australia 54 C3
Neligh, U.S.A. 70 D5
Nelkan, Russia 25 D14
Nellore, India 36 M11
Nelma, Russia 25 E14
Nelson, Canada 64 D5
Nelson, N.Z. 51 J4
Nelson, U.K. 10 D5
Nelson, U.S.A. 73 J7
Nelson →, Canada ... 65 C9
Nelson, C., Australia . 55 F3
Nelson, Estrecho, Chile 80 G2
Nelson Forks, Canada . 64 B4
Nelson House, Canada . 65 B9
Nelson L., Canada ... 65 B8
Nelspoort, S. Africa . 48 E3
Nelspruit, S. Africa . 49 D5
Néma, Mauritania ... 44 E3
Neman, Lithuania ... 9 J19
Nemeiben L., Canada . 65 B7
Nemunas =
  Neman →,
  Lithuania 9 J19
Nemuro, Japan 28 C12
Nemuro-Kaikyō, Japan 28 C12
Nemuy, Russia 25 D14
Nen Jiang →, China . 31 B7
Nenagh, Ireland ... 13 D3
Nenana, U.S.A. 60 B5
Nene →, U.K. 10 E8
Nenjiang, China ... 31 B7
Nenusa, Kepulauan,
  Indonesia 33 D7
Neodesha, U.S.A. ... 71 G7
Neosho, U.S.A. 71 G7
Neosho →, U.S.A. .. 71 H7
Nepal ■, Asia 37 F14
Nepalganj, Nepal ... 37 E12
Nephi, U.S.A. 72 G8
Nephin, Ireland ... 13 B2
Nerchinsk, Russia .. 25 D12
Nerchinskiy Zavod,
  Russia 25 D12
Néret L., Canada ... 63 B5
Neretva →, Croatia . 21 C7
Neringa, Lithuania . 9 J19
Ness, L., U.K. 12 D4
Nesterov, Ukraine .. 17 C12
Nesvizh = Nyasvizh,
  Belarus 17 B14
Netanya, Israel ... 41 C3
Nète →, Belgium ... 15 C4
Netherdale, Australia . 54 C4
Netherlands ■, Europe 15 C5
Netherlands Antilles ■,
  W. Indies 75 E11
Nettilling L., Canada . 61 B12
Neubrandenburg,
  Germany 16 B7
Neuchâtel, Switz. .. 16 E4
Neuchâtel, Lac de,
  Switz. 16 E4
Neufchâteau, Belgium . 15 E5
Neumünster, Germany 16 A5
Neunkirchen, Germany 16 D4
Neuquén, Argentina . 80 D3
Neuruppin, Germany . 16 B7
Neuse →, U.S.A. ... 69 H7
Neusiedler See, Austria 17 E9
Neuss, Germany 15 C6
Neustrelitz, Germany 16 B7
Neva →, Russia 22 C5
Nevada, U.S.A. 71 G7
Nevada □, U.S.A. ... 72 G5
Nevada, Sierra, Spain 19 D4
Nevada, Sierra, U.S.A. 72 G3
Nevada City, U.S.A. . 72 G3
Nevanka, Russia ... 25 D10
Nevers, France 18 C5
Nevertire, Australia . 55 E4
Neville, Canada ... 65 D7
Nevinnomyssk, Russia 23 F7
Nevis, W. Indies ... 75 D12
Nevyansk, Russia .. 22 C11
New Albany, Ind.,
  U.S.A. 68 F3
New Albany, Miss.,
  U.S.A. 71 H10
New Amsterdam,
  Guyana 78 B7
New Angledool,
  Australia 55 D4
New Bedford, U.S.A. . 68 E10
New Bern, U.S.A. ... 69 H7
New Boston, U.S.A. . 71 J7
New Braunfels, U.S.A. 71 L5
New Brighton, N.Z. . 51 K4
New Britain,
  Papua N. G. 56 H7
New Britain, U.S.A. . 68 E9
New Brunswick, U.S.A. 68 E8
New Brunswick □,
  Canada 63 C6
New Caledonia ■,
  Pac. Oc. 56 K8
New Castle, Ind., U.S.A. 68 F3
New Castle, Pa., U.S.A. 68 E5
New Castilla, Panama 74 H14
New Delhi, India ... 36 E10
New Denver, Canada . 64 D5
New England, U.S.A. . 70 B3
New England Ra.,
  Australia 55 E5
New Forest, U.K. ... 11 G6
New Glasgow, Canada 63 C7
New Guinea, Oceania 56 H5
New Hampshire □,
  U.S.A. 68 D10
New Hampton, U.S.A. 70 D8
New Hanover, S. Africa 49 D5
New Haven, U.S.A. . 68 E9
New Hazelton, Canada 64 B3

New Hebrides =
  Vanuatu ■, Pac. Oc. 56 J8
New Iberia, U.S.A. .. 71 K9
New Ireland,
  Papua N. G. 56 H7
New Jersey □, U.S.A. 68 E8
New Kensington,
  U.S.A. 68 E6
New Lexington, U.S.A. 68 F4
New Liskeard, Canada 62 C4
New London, Conn.,
  U.S.A. 68 E9
New London, Minn.,
  U.S.A. 70 C7
New London, Wis.,
  U.S.A. 70 C10
New Madrid, U.S.A. . 71 G10
New Meadows, U.S.A. 72 D5
New Mexico □, U.S.A. 73 J10
New Norcia, Australia 53 F2
New Norfolk, Australia 54 G4
New Orleans, U.S.A. 71 K9
New Philadelphia,
  U.S.A. 68 E5
New Plymouth, N.Z. . 51 H5
New Plymouth, U.S.A. 72 E5
New Providence,
  Bahamas 75 B9
New Radnor, U.K. .. 11 E4
New Richmond, U.S.A. 70 C8
New Roads, U.S.A. . 71 K9
New Rockford, U.S.A. 70 B5
New Ross, Ireland .. 13 D5
New Salem, U.S.A. . 70 B4
New Scone, U.K. ... 12 E5
New Siberian Is. =
  Novosibirskiye
  Ostrova, Russia ... 25 B15
New Smyrna Beach,
  U.S.A. 69 L5
New South Wales □,
  Australia 55 E4
New Springs, Australia 53 E3
New Town, U.S.A. .. 70 A3
New Ulm, U.S.A. ... 70 C7
New Waterford, Canada 63 C7
New Westminster,
  Canada 64 D4
New York □, U.S.A. . 68 D8
New York City, U.S.A. 68 E9
New Zealand ■,
  Oceania 51 J5
Newala, Tanzania .. 46 G7
Newark, Del., U.S.A. 68 F8
Newark, N.J., U.S.A. 68 E8
Newark, N.Y., U.S.A. 68 D7
Newark, Ohio, U.S.A. 68 E4
Newark-on-Trent, U.K. 10 D7
Newaygo, U.S.A. ... 68 D3
Newberg, U.S.A. ... 72 D2
Newberry, Mich.,
  U.S.A. 68 B3
Newberry, S.C., U.S.A. 69 H5
Newbridge =
  Droichead Nua,
  Ireland 13 C5
Newbrook, Canada .. 64 C6
Newburgh, U.S.A. .. 68 E8
Newbury, U.K. 11 F6
Newburyport, U.S.A. 68 D10
Newcastle, Australia 55 E5
Newcastle, Canada . 63 C6
Newcastle, S. Africa 49 D4
Newcastle, U.K. 13 B6
Newcastle, U.S.A. . 70 D2
Newcastle Emlyn, U.K. 11 E3
Newcastle Ra.,
  Australia 52 C5
Newcastle-under-Lyme,
  U.K. 10 D5
Newcastle-upon-Tyne,
  U.K. 10 C6
Newcastle Waters,
  Australia 54 B1
Newdegate, Australia 53 F2
Newell, U.S.A. 70 C3
Newfoundland □,
  Canada 63 B8
Newhalem, U.S.A. .. 64 D4
Newham, U.K. 11 F8
Newhaven, U.K. 11 G8
Newkirk, U.S.A. ... 71 G6
Newman, Australia . 52 D2
Newmarket, Ireland . 13 D3
Newmarket, U.K. ... 11 E8
Newnan, U.S.A. 69 J3
Newport, Gwent, U.K. 11 F5
Newport, I. of W., U.K. 11 G6
Newport, Ark., U.S.A. 71 H9
Newport, Ky., U.S.A. 68 F3
Newport, N.H., U.S.A. 68 D9
Newport, Oreg., U.S.A. 72 D1
Newport, R.I., U.S.A. 68 E10
Newport, Tenn., U.S.A. 69 H4
Newport, Vt., U.S.A. 68 C9
Newport, Wash., U.S.A. 72 B5
Newport Beach, U.S.A. 73 K5
Newport News, U.S.A. 68 G7
Newquay, U.K. 11 G2
Newry, U.K. 13 B5
Newry & Mourne □,
  U.K. 13 B5
Newton, U.S.A. 68 E5
Newton, Mass., U.S.A. 68 D10
Newton, Miss., U.S.A. 71 J10
Newton, N.C., U.S.A. 69 H5
Newton, N.J., U.S.A. 68 E8
Newton, Tex., U.S.A. 71 K8
Newton Abbot, U.K. . 11 G4
Newton Boyd, Australia 55 D5
Newton Stewart, U.K. 12 G4
Newtonmore, U.K. .. 12 D4
Newtown, U.K. 11 E4

Newtownabbey □, U.K. 13 B6
Newtownards, U.K. . 13 B6
Neya, Russia 22 C7
Neyrīz, Iran 39 D7
Neyshābūr, Iran ... 39 B8
Nezhin = Nizhyn,
  Ukraine 23 D5
Nezperce, U.S.A. .. 72 C5
Ngabang, Indonesia . 32 D3
Ngabordamlu, Tanjung,
  Indonesia 33 F8
Ngami Depression,
  Botswana 48 C3
Nganglong Kangri,
  China 37 C12
Nganjuk, Indonesia . 33 G14
Ngaoundéré, Cameroon 46 C2
Ngapara, N.Z. 51 L3
Ngawi, Indonesia .. 33 G14
Ngha Lo, Vietnam .. 34 B8
Ngoring Hu, China . 30 C4
Ngudu, Tanzania ... 46 E6
Nguigmi, Niger 45 F7
Ngukurr, Australia . 54 A1
Nguru, Nigeria 44 F7
Nha Trang, Vietnam . 34 F10
Nhacoongo, Mozam. . 49 C6
Nhangutazi, L., Mozam. 49 C5
Nhill, Australia 55 F3
Nhulunbuy, Australia 54 A2
Niafounké, Mali ... 44 E4
Niagara, U.S.A. ... 68 C1
Niagara Falls, Canada 62 D4
Niagara Falls, U.S.A. 68 D6
Niah, Malaysia 32 D4
Niamey, Niger 44 F5
Niangara, Zaïre 46 D5
Nias, Indonesia ... 32 D1
Nibong Tebal, Malaysia 34 P13
Nicaragua ■,
  Cent. Amer. 74 E7
Nicaragua, L. de, Nic. 74 E7
Nicastro, Italy 20 E7
Nice, France 18 E7
Niceville, U.S.A. ... 69 K2
Nichinan, Japan ... 29 J5
Nicholasville, U.S.A. 68 G3
Nicholson, Australia 52 C4
Nicholson →,
  Australia 54 B2
Nicholson Ra., Australia 53 E2
Nicobar Is., Ind. Oc. . 26 J13
Nicola, Canada 64 C4
Nicolet, Canada ... 62 C5
Nicosia, Cyprus ... 38 C2
Nicoya, Pen. de,
  Costa Rica 74 F7
Nidd →, U.K. 10 C6
Niedersachsen □,
  Germany 16 B5
Niekerkshoop, S. Africa 48 D3
Niemen = Neman →,
  Lithuania 9 J19
Nienburg, Germany . 16 B5
Nieu Bethesda,
  S. Africa 48 E3
Nieuw Amsterdam,
  Surinam 79 B7
Nieuw Nickerie,
  Surinam 79 B7
Nieuwoudtville,
  S. Africa 48 E2
Nieuwpoort, Belgium 15 C2
Niğde, Turkey 23 G5
Nigel, S. Africa 49 D4
Niger ■, W. Afr. ... 44 E6
Niger →, W. Afr. .. 44 G6
Nigeria ■, W. Afr. . 44 G6
Nightcaps, N.Z. 51 L2
Nii-Jima, Japan ... 29 G9
Niigata, Japan 28 F9
Niigata □, Japan ... 29 F9
Niihama, Japan 29 H6
Niihau, U.S.A. 66 H14
Niimi, Japan 29 G6
Niitsu, Japan 28 F9
Nijil, Jordan 41 E4
Nijkerk, Neths. 15 B5
Nijmegen, Neths. .. 15 C5
Nijverdal, Neths. .. 15 B6
Nik Pey, Iran 39 B6
Nikiniki, Indonesia . 33 F6
Nikki, Benin 44 G5
Nikkō, Japan 29 F9
Nikolayev = Mykolayiv,
  Ukraine 23 E5
Nikolayevsk, Russia 23 D8
Nikolayevsk-na-Amur,
  Russia 25 D15
Nikolskoye, Russia . 25 D17
Nikopol, Ukraine ... 23 E5
Nikshahr, Iran 39 E9
Nikšić,
  Montenegro, Yug. . 21 C8
Nîl, Nahr en →, Africa 45 B11
Nîl el Abyad →,
  Sudan 45 E11
Nîl el Azraq →, Sudan 45 E11
Niland, U.S.A. 73 K6
Nile = Nîl, Nahr
  en →, Africa 45 B11
Niles, U.S.A. 68 E5
Nimach, India 36 G9
Nîmes, France 18 E6
Nimfaíon, Ákra =
  Pinnes, Ákra, Greece 21 D11
Nimmitabel, Australia 55 F4
Nimule, Sudan 46 D6
Nīnawá, Iraq 38 B4
Nindigully, Australia 55 D4
Ninemile, U.S.A. ... 64 B2
Nineveh = Nīnawá,
  Iraq 38 B4

Ningaloo, Australia . 52 D1
Ningbo, China 31 D7
Ningjing Shan, China 30 C4
Ningpo = Ningbo,
  China 31 D7
Ningsia Hui A.R. =
  Ningxia Huizu
  Zizhiqu □, China . 30 C5
Ningxia Huizu
  Zizhiqu □, China . 30 C5
Ninh Binh, Vietnam . 34 B8
Ninove, Belgium ... 15 D4
Nioro du Sahel, Mali 44 E3
Niort, France 18 C3
Nipawin, Canada ... 65 C8
Nipawin Prov. Park,
  Canada 65 C8
Nipigon, Canada ... 62 C2
Nipigon, L., Canada . 62 C2
Nipin →, Canada .. 65 B7
Nipishish L., Canada . 63 B7
Nipissing L., Canada . 62 C4
Nipomo, U.S.A. 73 J3
Niquelândia, Brazil . 79 F9
Nir, Iran 38 B5
Nirasaki, Japan 29 G9
Nirmal, India 36 K11
Nirmali, India 37 F15
Niš, Serbia, Yug. .. 21 C9
Nişab, Si. Arabia .. 38 D5
Nişab, Yemen 40 E4
Nishinomiya, Japan . 29 G7
Nishin'omote, Japan 29 J5
Nishiwaki, Japan .. 29 G7
Niskibi →, Canada . 62 A2
Nissum Bredning,
  Denmark 9 H13
Nistru = Dnister →,
  Europe 17 E16
Nisutlin →, Canada . 64 A2
Nitchequon, Canada . 63 B5
Niterói, Brazil 79 H10
Nith →, U.K. 12 F5
Nitra, Slovak Rep. . 17 D10
Nitra →, Slovak Rep. 17 D10
Niuafo'ou, Tonga .. 51 B11
Niue, Cook Is. 57 J11
Niut, Indonesia 32 D4
Nivala, Finland 8 E21
Nivelles, Belgium .. 15 D4
Nivernais, France .. 18 C5
Nixon, U.S.A. 71 L6
Nizamabad, India .. 36 K11
Nizamghat, India .. 37 E19
Nizhne Kolymsk, Russia 25 C17
Nizhne-Vartovsk, Russia 24 C8
Nizhneangarsk, Russia 25 D11
Nizhnekamsk, Russia . 22 C9
Nizhneudinsk, Russia 25 D10
Nizhneyansk, Russia . 25 B14
Nizhniy Novgorod,
  Russia 22 C7
Nizhniy Tagil, Russia . 22 C10
Nizhyn, Ukraine ... 23 D5
Nízké Tatry,
  Slovak Rep. 17 D10
Njombe, Tanzania .. 46 F6
Nkambe, Cameroon 44 G7
Nkawkaw, Ghana .. 44 G4
Nkhata Bay, Malawi . 46 G6
Nkhota Kota, Malawi 47 G6
Nkongsamba,
  Cameroon 44 H6
Nkurenkuru, Namibia 48 B2
Nmai →, Burma ... 37 G20
Noakhali = Maijdi,
  Bangla. 37 H17
Noatak, U.S.A. 60 B3
Nobeoka, Japan 29 H5
Noblesville, U.S.A. . 68 E3
Nocera Inferiore, Italy 20 D6
Nockatunga, Australia 55 D3
Nocona, U.S.A. 71 J6
Noda, Japan 29 G7
Noel, U.S.A. 71 G7
Nogales, Mexico ... 74 A2
Nogales, U.S.A. 73 L8
Nōgata, Japan 29 H5
Noggerup, Australia 53 F2
Noginsk, Russia ... 25 C10
Nogoa →, Australia 54 C4
Noi →, Thailand ... 34 E6
Noire, Mts., France 18 B2
Noirmoutier, I. de,
  France 18 C2
Nojane, Botswana .. 48 C3
Nojima-Zaki, Japan 29 G9
Nok Kundi, Pakistan 36 E3
Nokaneng, Botswana 48 B3
Nokhtuysk, Russia . 25 C12
Nokia, Finland 9 F20
Nokomis, Canada .. 65 C8
Nokomis L., Canada 65 B8
Nola, C.A.R. 46 D3
Noma Omuramba →,
  Namibia 48 B3
Noman L., Canada . 65 A7
Nome, U.S.A. 60 B3
Nomo-Zaki, Japan . 29 H4
Nonacho L., Canada 65 A7
Nonda, Australia ... 54 C3
Nong Khae, Thailand 34 E6
Nong Khai, Thailand 34 D7
Nongoma, S. Africa 49 D5
Noonamah, Australia 52 B5
Noonan, U.S.A. 70 A3
Noondoo, Australia 55 D4
Noonkanbah, Australia 52 C3
Noord Brabant □,
  Neths. 15 C5
Noord Holland □,
  Neths. 15 B4

Noordbeveland, Neths. 15 C3
Noordoostpolder,
  Neths. 15 B5
Noordwijk aan Zee,
  Neths. 15 B4
Nootka, Canada 64 D3
Nootka I., Canada .. 64 D3
Nóqui, Angola 46 F2
Noranda, Canada .. 62 C4
Nord-Ostsee-Kanal →,
  Germany 16 A5
Nordaustlandet,
  Svalbard 4 B9
Nordegg, Canada .. 64 C5
Norderney, Germany 16 B4
Norderstedt, Germany 16 B5
Nordfjord, Norway . 9 F11
Nordfriesische Inseln,
  Germany 16 A5
Nordhausen, Germany 16 C6
Norðoyar, Færoe Is. . 8 E9
Nordkapp, Norway . 8 A21
Nordkapp, Svalbard . 4 A9
Nordkinn =
  Kinnarodden, Norway 6 A11
Nordkinn-halvøya,
  Norway 8 A22
Nordrhein-Westfalen □,
  Germany 16 C4
Nordvik, Russia ... 25 B12
Norembega, Canada 62 C3
Norfolk, Nebr., U.S.A. 70 D6
Norfolk, Va., U.S.A. 68 G7
Norfolk □, U.K. 10 E9
Norfolk Broads, U.K. 10 E9
Norfolk I., Pac. Oc. 56 K8
Norfork Res., U.S.A. 71 G8
Norilsk, Russia 25 C9
Norley, Australia ... 55 D3
Norma, Mt., Australia 54 C3
Normal, U.S.A. 70 E10
Norman, U.S.A. 71 H6
Norman →, Australia 54 B3
Norman Wells, Canada 60 B7
Normandie, France . 18 B4
Normandin, Canada 62 C5
Normandy =
  Normandie, France 18 B4
Normanhurst, Mt.,
  Australia 53 E3
Normanton, Australia 54 B3
Normanville, Australia 53 F2
Norquay, Canada .. 65 C8
Norquinco, Argentina 80 E2
Norrbotten □, Sweden 8 C19
Norris, U.S.A. 72 D8
Norristown, U.S.A. . 68 E8
Norrköping, Sweden 9 G17
Norrland, Sweden .. 9 E16
Norrtälje, Sweden .. 9 G18
Norseman, Australia 53 F3
Norsk, Russia 25 D14
North Adams, U.S.A. 68 D9
North Andaman I.,
  India 34 F2
North Battleford,
  Canada 65 C7
North Bay, Canada . 62 C4
North Belcher Is.,
  Canada 62 A4
North Bend, Canada 64 D4
North Bend, U.S.A. 72 E1
North Berwick, U.K. 12 E6
North C., Canada .. 63 C7
North C., N.Z. 51 F4
North Canadian →,
  U.S.A. 71 H7
North Cape =
  Nordkapp, Norway 8 A21
North Cape =
  Nordkapp, Svalbard 4 A9
North Caribou L.,
  Canada 62 B1
North Carolina □,
  U.S.A. 69 H5
North Channel, Canada 62 C3
North Channel, U.K. 12 G3
North Chicago, U.S.A. 68 D2
North Dakota □, U.S.A. 70 B5
North Dandalup,
  Australia 53 F2
North Down □, U.K. 13 B6
North Downs, U.K. . 11 F8
North East Frontier
  Agency = Arunachal
  Pradesh □, India . 37 E19
North Esk →, U.K. . 12 E6
North European Plain,
  Europe 6 D11
North Foreland, U.K. 11 F9
North Frisian Is. =
  Nordfriesische Inseln,
  Germany 16 A5
North Henik L., Canada 65 A9
North I., N.Z. 51 H5
North Knife →,
  Canada 65 B10
North Korea ■, Asia 31 C7
North Lakhimpur, India 37 F19
North Las Vegas,
  U.S.A. 73 H6
North Loup →, U.S.A. 70 E5
North Magnetic Pole,
  Canada 4 B2
North Minch, U.K. . 12 C3
North Nahanni →,
  Canada 64 A4
North Ossetia □, Russia 23 F7
North Palisade, U.S.A. 73 H4
North Platte, U.S.A. 70 E4

North Platte →, U.S.A. 70 E4
North Pole, Arctic .. 4 A
North Portal, Canada 65 D8
North Powder, U.S.A. 72 D5
North Pt., Canada .. 63 C7
North Rhine Westphalia
  = Nordrhein-
  Westfalen □,
  Germany 16 C4
North Ronaldsay, U.K. 12 B6
North
  Saskatchewan →,
  Canada 65 C7
North Sea, Europe . 6 D6
North Sentinel I., India 34 G2
North Sporades =
  Voriai Sporádhes,
  Greece 21 E10
North Sydney, Canada 63 C7
North Taranaki Bight,
  N.Z. 51 H5
North Thompson →,
  Canada 64 C4
North Tonawanda,
  U.S.A. 68 D6
North Truchas Pk.,
  U.S.A. 73 J11
North Twin I., Canada 62 B3
North Tyne →, U.K. 10 C5
North Uist, U.K. ... 12 D1
North Vancouver,
  Canada 64 D4
North Vernon, U.S.A. 68 F3
North Wabasca L.,
  Canada 64 B6
North Walsham, U.K. 10 E9
North-West □, S. Africa 48 D4
North West C.,
  Australia 52 D1
North West Christmas I.
  Ridge, Pac. Oc. .. 57 G11
North West Frontier □,
  Pakistan 36 B8
North West Highlands,
  U.K. 12 D3
North West River,
  Canada 63 B7
North West
  Territories □, Canada 60 B9
North York Moors, U.K. 10 C7
North Yorkshire □, U.K. 10 C6
Northallerton, U.K. . 10 C6
Northam, S. Africa . 48 C4
Northam, Australia . 53 E1
Northampton, Australia 53 E1
Northampton, U.K. . 11 E7
Northampton, U.S.A. 68 D9
Northampton Downs,
  Australia 54 C4
Northamptonshire □,
  U.K. 11 E7
Northcliffe, Australia 53 F2
Northern Cape □,
  S. Africa 48 D3
Northern Circars, India 37 L13
Northern Indian L.,
  Canada 65 B9
Northern Ireland □,
  U.K. 13 B5
Northern Light, L.,
  Canada 62 C1
Northern Marianas ■,
  Pac. Oc. 56 F6
Northern Territory □,
  Australia 52 D5
Northern Transvaal □,
  S. Africa 49 C4
Northfield, U.S.A. . 70 C8
Northland, N.Z. 51 F4
Northome, U.S.A. .. 70 B7
Northport, Ala., U.S.A. 69 J2
Northport, Mich.,
  U.S.A. 68 C3
Northport, Wash.,
  U.S.A. 72 B5
Northumberland □,
  U.K. 10 B5
Northumberland, C.,
  Australia 55 F3
Northumberland Is.,
  Australia 54 C4
Northumberland Str.,
  Canada 63 C7
Northwich, U.K. ... 10 D5
Northwood, Iowa,
  U.S.A. 70 D8
Northwood, N. Dak.,
  U.S.A. 70 B6
Norton, U.S.A. 70 F5
Norton Sd., U.S.A. . 60 B3
Norwalk, Conn., U.S.A. 68 E9
Norwalk, Ohio, U.S.A. 68 E4
Norway ■, Europe . 8 E14
Norway House, Canada 65 C9
Norwegian Sea, Atl. Oc. 4 C8
Norwich, U.K. 10 E9
Norwich, U.S.A. ... 68 D8
Noshiro, Japan 28 D10
Nosok, Russia 24 B9
Noss Hd., U.K. 12 C5
Nossob →, S. Africa 48 D3
Nosy Bé, Madag. .. 47 G9
Nosy Boraha, Madag. 49 B8
Nosy Mitsio, Madag. 47 G9
Nosy Varika, Madag. 49 C8
Noteć →, Poland .. 16 B8
Notigi Dam, Canada 65 B9
Notikewin →, Canada 64 B5
Notre-Dame, Canada 63 C7
Notre Dame B., Canada 63 C8
Notre Dame de Koartac
  = Quaqtaq, Canada 61 B13

111

Notre Dame d'Ivugivic
= Ivujivik, *Canada* . . 61 B12
Nottaway ➤, *Canada* 62 B4
Nottingham, *U.K.* 10 E6
Nottinghamshire □,
U.K. 10 D7
Nottoway ➤, *U.S.A.* 68 G7
Notwane ➤,
Botswana 48 C4
Nouâdhibou,
Mauritania 44 D1
Nouâdhibou, Ras,
Mauritania 44 D1
Nouakchott, *Mauritania* 44 E1
Nouméa, *N. Cal.* 56 K8
Noupoort, *S. Africa* . . 48 E3
Nouveau Comptoir =
Wemindji, *Canada* . . 62 B4
Nouvelle-Calédonie =
New Caledonia ■,
Pac. Oc. 56 K8
Nova Casa Nova, *Brazil* 79 E10
Nova Cruz, *Brazil* . 79 E11
Nova Friburgo, *Brazil* . 79 H10
Nova Gaia =
Cambundi-Catembo,
Angola 46 G3
Nova Iguaçu, *Brazil* . 79 H10
Nova Iorque, *Brazil* . 79 E10
Nova Lima, *Brazil* 79 G10
Nova Lisboa =
Huambo, *Angola* . . . 47 G3
Nova Mambone,
Mozam. 49 C6
Nova Scotia □, *Canada* 63 C7
Nova Sofala, *Mozam.* . 49 C5
Nova Venécia, *Brazil* . 79 G10
Nova Zagora, *Bulgaria* 21 C11
Novara, *Italy* 20 B3
Novaya Ladoga, *Russia* 22 B5
Novaya Lyalya, *Russia* 24 D7
Novaya Zemlya, *Russia* 24 B6
Nové Zámky,
Slovak Rep. 17 D10
Novgorod, *Russia* 22 C5
Novgorod-Severskiy =
Novhorod-Siverskyy,
Ukraine 22 D5
Novhorod-Siverskyy,
Ukraine 22 D5
Novi Lígure, *Italy* . . 20 B3
Novi Pazar,
Serbia, Yug. 21 C9
Novi Sad, *Serbia, Yug.* 21 B8
Novo Mesto, *Slovenia* 16 F8
Novo Remanso, *Brazil* 79 E10
Novoataysk, *Russia* . 24 D9
Novocherkassk, *Russia* 23 E7
Novogrudok =
Navahrudak, *Belarus* 17 B13
Novohrad-Volynskyy,
Ukraine 17 C14
Novokachalinsk, *Russia* 28 A6
Novokazalinsk =
Zhangaqazaly,
Kazakhstan 24 E7
Novokuybyshevsk,
Russia 22 D8
Novokuznetsk, *Russia* . 24 D9
Novomoskovsk, *Russia* 22 D6
Novorossiysk, *Russia* . 23 F6
Novorybnoye, *Russia* . 25 B11
Novoselytsya, *Ukraine* 17 D14
Novoshakhtinsk, *Russia* 23 E6
Novosibirsk, *Russia* . 24 D9
Novosibirskiye Ostrova,
Russia 25 B15
Novotroitsk, *Russia* . . 24 D6
Novouzensk, *Russia* . 23 D8
Novovolynsk, *Ukraine* 17 C13
Novska, *Croatia* 20 B7
Novyy Port, *Russia* . 24 C8
Now Shahr, *Iran* 39 B6
Nowa Sól, *Poland* 16 C8
Nowbarän, *Iran* 39 C6
Nowghâb, *Iran* 39 C8
Nowgong, *India* 37 F18
Nowra, *Australia* 55 E5
Nowshera, *Pakistan* . . 36 B8
Nowy Sącz, *Poland* . 17 D11
Nowy Targ, *Poland* . 17 D11
Nowy Tomyśl, *Poland* 16 B9
Noxon, *U.S.A.* 72 C6
Noyes I., *U.S.A.* 64 B2
Noyon, *France* 18 B5
Nsanje, *Malawi* 47 H7
Nsawam, *Ghana* 44 G4
Nsukka, *Nigeria* 44 G6
Nu Jiang ➤, *China* . . 30 D4
Nu Shan, *China* 30 D4
Nubian Desert =
Nûbîya, Es Sahrâ En,
Sudan 45 D11
Nûbîya, Es Sahrâ En,
Sudan 45 D11
Nuboai, *Indonesia* . . 33 E9
Nueces ➤, *U.S.A.* . . 71 M6
Nueltin L., *Canada* . . 65 A9
Nueva Imperial, *Chile* . 80 D2
Nueva Rosita, *Mexico* 74 B4
Nuéve de Julio,
Argentina 80 D4
Nuevitas, *Cuba* 75 C9
Nuevo, G., *Argentina* . 80 E4
Nuevo Laredo, *Mexico* 74 B5
Nugget Pt., *N.Z.* 51 M2
Nuhaka, *N.Z.* 51 H6
Nukey Bluff, *Australia* 55 E2
Nukheila, *Sudan* 45 E10
Nuku'alofa, *Tonga* . . 51 E11
Nukus, *Uzbekistan* . 24 E6
Nulato, *U.S.A.* 60 B4
Nullagine ➤, *Australia* 52 D3

Nullarbor, *Australia* . . 53 F5
Nullarbor Plain,
Australia 53 F4
Numalla, L., *Australia* 55 D3
Numan, *Nigeria* 45 G7
Numata, *Japan* 29 F9
Numazu, *Japan* 29 G9
Numbulwar, *Australia* 54 A2
Numfoor, *Indonesia* . 33 E8
Numurkah, *Australia* . 55 F4
Nunaksaluk I., *Canada* 63 A7
Nuneaton, *U.K.* 11 E6
Nunivak I., *U.S.A.* . . 60 B3
Nunkun, *India* 36 C10
Nunspeet, *Neths.* . . 15 B5
Núoro, *Italy* 20 D3
Nürâbâd, *Iran* 39 E8
Nuremburg =
Nürnberg, *Germany* 16 D6
Nurina, *Australia* . . 53 F4
Nuriootpa, *Australia* . 55 E2
Nurmes, *Finland* . . 8 E23
Nürnberg, *Germany* . 16 D6
Nurran, L. = Terewah,
L., *Australia* 55 D4
Nurrari Lakes, *Australia* 53 E5
Nusa Barung, *Indonesia* 33 H15
Nusa Kambangan,
Indonesia 33 G13
Nusa Tenggara
Barat □, *Indonesia* . 32 F5
Nusa Tenggara
Timur □, *Indonesia* . 33 F6
Nusaybin, *Turkey* . . 23 G7
Nushki, *Pakistan* . . 36 E5
Nutak, *Canada* 61 C13
Nutwood Downs,
Australia 54 B1
Nuuk = Godthåb,
Greenland 61 B14
Nuwakot, *Nepal* 37 E13
Nuweveldberge,
S. Africa 48 E3
Nuyts, C., *Australia* . 53 F5
Nuyts Arch., *Australia* 55 E1
Nxau-Nxau, *Botswana* 48 B3
Nyah West, *Australia* 55 F3
Nyahanga, *Tanzania* . 46 E6
Nyahururu, *Kenya* . . 46 D7
Nyainqentanglha Shan,
China 30 D3
Nyâlâ, *Sudan* 45 F9
Nyandoma, *Russia* . 22 B7
Nyangana, *Namibia* . 48 B3
Nyarling ➤, *Canada* . 64 A6
Nyasa, L. = Malawi, L.,
Africa 47 G6
Nyasvizh, *Belarus* . 17 B14
Nyazepetrovsk, *Russia* 22 C10
Nybro, *Sweden* 9 H16
Nyda, *Russia* 24 C8
Nyeri, *Kenya* 46 E7
Nyíregyháza, *Hungary* 17 E11
Nykøbing, Sjælland,
Denmark 9 J14
Nykøbing, Storstrøm,
Denmark 9 J14
Nyköping, *Sweden* . 9 G17
Nylstroom, *S. Africa* 49 C4
Nymagee, *Australia* . 55 E4
Nynäshamn, *Sweden* . 9 G17
Nyngan, *Australia* . . 55 E4
Nyoman = Neman ➤,
Lithuania 9 J19
Nysa, *Poland* 17 C9
Nysa ➤, *Europe* . . 16 B8
Nyssa, *U.S.A.* 72 E5
Nyurba, *Russia* 25 C12
Nzega, *Tanzania* . . 46 E6
N'Zérékoré, *Guinea* . 44 G3
Nzeto, *Angola* 46 F2

O

Ō-Shima, *Nagasaki,
Japan* 29 G4
Ō-Shima, *Shizuoka,
Japan* 29 G9
Oacoma, *U.S.A.* . . . 70 D5
Oahe, L., *U.S.A.* . . 70 C4
Oahe Dam, *U.S.A.* . . 70 C4
Oahu, *U.S.A.* 66 H16
Oak Creek, *U.S.A.* . 72 F10
Oak Harbor, *U.S.A.* . 72 B2
Oak Hill, *U.S.A.* . . 68 G5
Oak Park, *U.S.A.* . . 68 E2
Oak Ridge, *U.S.A.* . 69 G3
Oakan-Dake, *Japan* . 28 C12
Oakbank, *Australia* . 55 E3
Oakdale, Calif., *U.S.A.* 73 H3
Oakdale, La., *U.S.A.* . 71 K8
Oakengates, *U.K.* . . 10 E5
Oakes, *U.S.A.* 70 B5
Oakesdale, *U.S.A.* . . 72 C5
Oakey, *Australia* . . 55 D5
Oakham, *U.K.* 10 E7
Oakland, Calif., *U.S.A.* 73 H2
Oakland, Oreg., *U.S.A.* 72 E2
Oakland City, *U.S.A.* . 68 F2
Oakley, Idaho, *U.S.A.* 72 E7
Oakley, Kans., *U.S.A.* 70 F4
Oakover ➤, *Australia* 52 D3
Oakridge, *U.S.A.* . . 72 E2
Oamaru, *N.Z.* 51 L3
Oates Land, *Antarctica* 5 C11
Oatman, *U.S.A.* . . . 73 J6
Oaxaca, *Mexico* . . . 74 D5
Ob ➤, *Russia* 24 C7
Oba, *Canada* 62 C3
Obama, *Japan* 29 G7

Oban, *U.K.* 12 E3
Obbia, *Somali Rep.* . . 40 F4
Obed, *Canada* 64 C5
Oberhausen, *Germany* 16 C4
Oberlin, Kans., *U.S.A.* 70 F4
Oberlin, La., *U.S.A.* . 71 K8
Oberon, *Australia* . . 55 E4
Obi, Kepulauan,
Indonesia 33 E7
Obi Is. = Obi,
Kepulauan, *Indonesia* 33 E7
Óbidos, *Brazil* 79 D7
Obihiro, *Japan* 28 C11
Obilatu, *Indonesia* . . 33 E7
Obluchye, *Russia* . . 25 E14
Obo, *C.A.R.* 46 C5
Oboyan, *Russia* 24 D4
Obozerskaya =
Obozerskiy, *Russia* . 24 C5
Obozerskiy, *Russia* . 24 C5
Observatory Inlet,
Canada 64 B3
Obshchi Syrt, *Russia* . 6 D16
Obskaya Guba, *Russia* 24 C8
Obuasi, *Ghana* 44 G4
Ocala, *U.S.A.* 69 L4
Ocaña, *Spain* 19 C4
Ocanomowoc, *U.S.A.* . 70 D10
Ocate, *U.S.A.* 71 G2
Occidental, Cordillera,
Colombia 78 C3
Ocean City, *U.S.A.* . 68 F8
Ocean I. = Banaba,
Kiribati 56 H8
Ocean Park, *U.S.A.* . 72 C1
Oceanside, *U.S.A.* . 73 K5
Ochil Hills, *U.K.* . . 12 E5
Ochre River, *Canada* . 65 C9
Ocilla, *U.S.A.* 69 K4
Ocmulgee ➤, *U.S.A.* . 69 K4
Ocniţa, *Moldova* . . . 17 D14
Oconee ➤, *U.S.A.* . 69 K4
Oconto, *U.S.A.* . . . 68 C2
Oconto Falls, *U.S.A.* . 68 C1
Octave, *U.S.A.* . . . 73 J7
Ocumare del Tuy,
Venezuela 78 A5
Ōda, *Japan* 29 G6
Ódáðahraun, *Iceland* . 8 D5
Odate, *Japan* 28 D10
Odawara, *Japan* . . . 29 G9
Odda, *Norway* 9 F12
Oddur, *Somali Rep.* . 40 G3
Odei ➤, *Canada* . . . 65 B9
Ödemiş, *Turkey* . . . 21 E13
Odendaalsrus, *S. Africa* 48 D4
Odense, *Denmark* . . 9 J14
Oder ➤, *Germany* . 16 B8
Odesa, *Ukraine* . . . 23 E5
Odessa = Odesa,
Ukraine 23 E5
Odessa, Tex., *U.S.A.* . 71 K3
Odessa, Wash., *U.S.A.* 72 C4
Odiakwe, *Botswana* . 48 C4
Odienné, *Ivory C.* . . 44 G3
Odintsovo, *Russia* . 22 C6
O'Donnell, *U.S.A.* . . 71 J4
Odorheiu Secuiesc,
Romania 17 E13
Odra = Oder ➤,
Germany 16 B8
Odzi, *Zimbabwe* . . 49 B5
Oeiras, *Brazil* 79 E10
Oelrichs, *U.S.A.* . . 70 D3
Oelwein, *U.S.A.* . . 70 D9
Oenpelli, *Australia* . 52 B5
Ofanto ➤, *Italy* . . 20 D7
Offa, *Nigeria* 44 G5
Offaly □, *Ireland* . . 13 C4
Offenbach, *Germany* . 16 C5
Offenburg, *Germany* . 16 D4
Ofotfjorden, *Norway* . 8 B17
Ōfunato, *Japan* . . . 28 E10
Oga, *Japan* 28 E9
Oga-Hantō, *Japan* . . 28 E9
Ogahalla, *Canada* . . 62 B2
Ōgaki, *Japan* 29 G8
Ogallala, *U.S.A.* . . 70 E4
Ogasawara Gunto,
Pac. Oc. 56 E6
Ogbomosho, *Nigeria* . 44 G5
Ogden, Iowa, *U.S.A.* . 70 D7
Ogden, Utah, *U.S.A.* . 72 F7
Ogdensburg, *U.S.A.* . 68 C8
Ogeechee ➤, *U.S.A.* 69 K5
Oglio ➤, *Italy* . . . 20 B4
Ogmore, *Australia* . 54 C4
Ogoki ➤, *Canada* . 62 B2
Ogoki L., *Canada* . . 62 B2
Ogoki Res., *Canada* . 62 B2
Ogooué ➤, *Gabon* . 46 E1
Ogowe = Ogooué ➤,
Gabon 46 E1
Ogre, *Latvia* 9 H21
Ohai, *N.Z.* 51 L2
Ohakune, *N.Z.* . . . 51 H5
Ohanet, *Algeria* . . . 44 C6
Ohata, *Japan* 28 D10
Ohau, L., *N.Z.* . . . 51 L2
Ohey, *Belgium* . . . 15 D5
Ohio □, *U.S.A.* . . . 68 E3
Ohio ➤, *U.S.A.* . . 68 G1
Ohre ➤, *Czech.* . . 16 C8
Ohrid, *Macedonia* . 21 D9
Ohridsko Jezero,
Macedonia 21 D9
Ohrigstad, *S. Africa* . 49 C5
Oil City, *U.S.A.* . . . 68 E6
Oise ➤, *France* . . 18 B5
Ōita, *Japan* 29 H5
Ōita □, *Japan* 29 H5
Oiticica, *Brazil* . . . 79 E10
Ojai, *U.S.A.* 73 J4

Ojiya, *Japan* 29 F9
Ojos del Salado, Cerro,
Argentina 80 B3
Oka ➤, *Russia* . . . 24 D5
Okaba, *Indonesia* . . 33 F9
Okahandja, *Namibia* . 48 C2
Okahukura, *N.Z.* . . 51 H5
Okanagan L., *Canada* 64 C5
Okandja, *Gabon* . . 46 E2
Okanogan, *U.S.A.* . . 72 B4
Okanogan ➤, *U.S.A.* 72 B4
Okara, *Pakistan* . . . 36 D8
Okarito, *N.Z.* 51 K3
Okaukuejo, *Namibia* . 48 B2
Okavango Swamps,
Botswana 48 B3
Okaya, *Japan* 29 F9
Okayama, *Japan* . . 29 G6
Okayama □, *Japan* . 29 G6
Okazaki, *Japan* . . . 29 G8
Okeechobee, *U.S.A.* . 69 M5
Okeechobee, L., *U.S.A.* 69 M5
Okefenokee Swamp,
U.S.A. 69 K4
Okehampton, *U.K.* . 11 G3
Okha, *Russia* 25 D15
Okhotsk, *Russia* . . 25 D15
Okhotsk, Sea of, *Asia* 25 D15
Okhotskiy Perevoz,
Russia 25 C14
Okhotskiy Perevoz,
Japan 28 E10
Oki-Shotō, *Japan* . . 29 F6
Okiep, *S. Africa* . . 48 D2
Okinawa □, *Japan* . 29 L3
Okinawa-Guntō, *Japan* 29 L3
Okinawa-Jima, *Japan* 29 L4
Okino-erabu-Shima,
Japan 29 L4
Oklahoma □, *U.S.A.* . 71 H6
Oklahoma City, *U.S.A.* 71 H6
Okmulgee, *U.S.A.* . . 71 H7
Oknitsa = Ocniţa,
Moldova 17 D14
Okrika, *Nigeria* . . . 44 H6
Oksovskiy, *Russia* . 22 B6
Oktabrsk = Oktyabrsk,
Kazakhstan 23 E10
Oktyabrsk, Kazakhstan 23 E10
Oktyabrskiy =
Aktsyabrski, *Belarus* 17 B15
Oktyabrskiy, *Russia* . 22 D9
Oktyabrskoye
Revolyutsii, Os.,
Russia 25 B10
Oktyabrskoye, *Russia* . 24 C7
Oktyabrskōye, *Russia* 24 C7
Okuru, *N.Z.* 51 K2
Okushiri-Tō, *Japan* . 28 C9
Okwa ➤, *Botswana* . 48 C3
Ola, *U.S.A.* 71 H8
Ólafsfjörður, *Iceland* . 8 C4
Ólafsvík, *Iceland* . . 8 D2
Olancha, *U.S.A.* . . . 73 H4
Öland, *Sweden* . . . 9 H17
Olary, *Australia* . . . 55 E3
Olathe, *U.S.A.* . . . 70 F7
Olavarría, *Argentina* . 80 D4
Oława, *Poland* . . . 17 C9
Ólbia, *Italy* 20 D3
Old Cork, *Australia* . 54 C3
Old Crow, *Canada* . 60 B6
Old Fletton, *U.K.* . . 11 E7
Old Fort ➤, *Canada* 65 B6
Old Town, *U.S.A.* . . 63 D6
Old Wives L., *Canada* 65 C7
Oldbury, *U.K.* 11 F5
Oldcastle, *Ireland* . 13 C4
Oldenburg, *Germany* . 16 B5
Oldenzaal, *Neths.* . . 15 B6
Oldham, *U.K.* 10 D5
Oldman ➤, *Canada* . 64 D6
Olds, *Canada* 64 C6
Olean, *U.S.A.* 68 D6
Olekma ➤, *Russia* . 25 C13
Olekminsk, *Russia* . 25 C13
Oleksandriya, *Ukraine* 17 C14
Olenegorsk, *Russia* . 22 A5
Olenek, *Russia* . . . 25 C12
Olenek ➤, *Russia* . 25 B13
Oléron, I. d', *France* . 18 D3
Oleśnica, *Poland* . . 17 C9
Olevsk, *Ukraine* . . 17 C14
Olga, *Russia* 25 E14
Olga, L., *Canada* . . 62 C4
Olga, Mt., *Australia* . 53 E5
Olhão, *Portugal* . . . 19 D2
Olifants ➤, *Africa* . 49 C5
Olifantshoek, *S. Africa* 48 D3
Ólimbos, Óros, *Greece* 21 D10
Olinda, *Brazil* 79 E12
Oliveira, *Brazil* . . . 79 H10
Olivenza, *Spain* . . . 19 C2
Oliver, *Canada* . . . 64 D5
Oliver L., *Canada* . . 65 B8
Ollagüe, *Chile* . . . 78 H5
Olney, Ill., *U.S.A.* . . 68 F1
Olney, Tex., *U.S.A.* . 71 J5
Olomane ➤, *Canada* 63 B7
Olomouc, *Czech.* . . 17 D9
Olonets, *Russia* . . 22 B5
Olongapo, *Phil.* . . . 33 B6
Olot, *Spain* 19 A7
Olovyannaya, *Russia* . 25 D12
Oloy ➤, *Russia* . . 25 C16
Olsztyn, *Poland* . . 17 B11
Olt ➤, *Romania* . . 17 G13
Olteniţa, *Romania* . 17 F14
Olton, *U.S.A.* 71 H3
Olympia, *Greece* . . 21 F9
Olympia, *U.S.A.* . . 72 C2
Olympic Mts., *U.S.A.* 72 C2
Olympic Nat. Park,
U.S.A. 72 C2

Olympus, Mt. =
Ólimbos, Óros,
Greece 21 D10
Olympus, Mt., *U.S.A.* 72 C2
Om ➤, *Russia* 24 D8
Ōma, *Japan* 28 D10
Ōmachi, *Japan* 29 F8
Omae-Zaki, *Japan* . . 29 G9
Ōmagari, *Japan* . . . 28 E10
Omagh, *U.K.* 13 B4
Omagh □, *U.K.* . . . 13 B4
Omaha, *U.S.A.* . . . 70 E7
Omak, *U.S.A.* 72 B4
Oman ■, *Asia* 40 C6
Oman, G. of, *Asia* . . 39 E8
Omaruru, *Namibia* . 48 C2
Omaruru ➤, *Namibia* 48 C1
Omate, *Peru* 78 G4
Ombai, Selat, *Indonesia* 33 F6
Omboué, *Gabon* . . 46 E1
Ombrone ➤, *Italy* . 20 C4
Omdurmân, *Sudan* . 45 E11
Ometepec, *Mexico* . 74 D5
Omineca ➤, *Canada* 64 B4
Omitara, *Namibia* . . 48 C2
Ōmiya, *Japan* 29 G9
Ommen, *Neths.* . . . 15 B6
Omo ➤, *Ethiopia* . . 45 G12
Omolon ➤, *Russia* . 25 C16
Omono-Gawa ➤,
Japan 28 E10
Omsk, *Russia* 24 D8
Omsukchan, *Russia* . 25 C16
Ōmu, *Japan* 28 B11
Omul, Vf., *Romania* . 17 F13
Ōmura, *Japan* 29 H4
Omuramba
Omatako ➤,
Namibia 47 H4
Ōmuta, *Japan* 29 H5
Onaga, *U.S.A.* 70 F6
Onalaska, *U.S.A.* . . 70 D9
Onamia, *U.S.A.* . . . 70 B8
Onancock, *U.S.A.* . . 68 G8
Onang, *Indonesia* . . 33 E5
Onaping L., *Canada* . 62 C3
Onawa, *U.S.A.* . . . 70 D6
Onaway, *U.S.A.* . . . 68 C3
Oncócua, *Angola* . . 48 B1
Onda, *Spain* 19 C5
Ondangua, *Namibia* . 48 B2
Ondjiva, *Angola* . . 48 B2
Ondo, *Nigeria* 44 G5
Öndörhaan, *Mongolia* 31 B6
Öndverðarnes, *Iceland* 8 D1
Onega, *Russia* . . . 22 B6
Onega ➤, *Russia* . . 22 B6
Onega, G. of =
Onezhskaya Guba,
Russia 22 B6
Onega, L. =
Onezhskoye Ozero,
Russia 22 B6
Onehunga, *N.Z.* . . . 51 G5
Oneida, *U.S.A.* . . . 68 D8
Oneida L., *U.S.A.* . . 68 D8
O'Neill, *U.S.A.* . . . 70 D5
Onekotan, Ostrov,
Russia 25 E16
Oneonta, Ala., *U.S.A.* 69 J2
Oneonta, N.Y., *U.S.A.* 68 D8
Oneşti, *Romania* . . 17 E14
Onezhskaya Guba,
Russia 22 B6
Onezhskoye Ozero,
Russia 22 B6
Ongarue, *N.Z.* 51 H5
Ongerup, *Australia* . 53 F2
Ongole, *India* 36 M12
Onguren, *Russia* . . 25 D11
Onida, *U.S.A.* 70 C4
Onilahy ➤, *Madag.* . 49 C7
Onitsha, *Nigeria* . . 44 G6
Onoda, *Japan* 29 G5
Onslow, *Australia* . . 52 D2
Onslow B., *U.S.A.* . . 69 H7
Onstwedde, *Neths.* . 15 A7
Ontake-San, *Japan* . 29 G8
Ontario, Calif., *U.S.A.* 73 J5
Ontario, Oreg., *U.S.A.* 72 D5
Ontario □, *Canada* . 62 B2
Ontario, L., *U.S.A.* . 62 D4
Ontonagon, *U.S.A.* . 70 B10
Oodnadatta, *Australia* 55 D2
Ooldea, *Australia* . . 53 F5
Oombulgurri, *Australia* 52 C4
Oona River, *Canada* . 64 C2
Oorindi, *Australia* . . 54 C3
Oost-Vlaanderen □,
Belgium 15 C3
Oostende, *Belgium* . 15 C2
Oosterhout, *Neths.* . 15 C4
Oosterschelde, *Neths.* 15 C4
Ootacamund, *India* . 36 P10
Ootsa L., *Canada* . . 64 C3
Opala, *Russia* 25 D16
Opala, *Zaire* 46 E4
Opanake, *Sri Lanka* . 36 R12
Opasatika, *Canada* . 62 C3
Opasquia, *Canada* . 65 C10
Opava, *Czech.* . . . 17 D9
Opelousas, *U.S.A.* . 71 K8
Opémisca, L., *Canada* 62 C5
Opheim, *U.S.A.* . . . 72 B10
Ophthalmia Ra.,
Australia 52 D2
Opinaca ➤, *Canada* 62 B4
Opinaca, L., *Canada* . 62 B4
Opiskotish, L., *Canada* 63 B6
Opole, *Poland* 17 C9
Oporto = Porto,
Portugal 19 B1
Opotiki, *N.Z.* 51 H6

Opp, *U.S.A.* 69 K2
Oppdal, *Norway* . . 9 E13
Opua, *N.Z.* 51 F5
Opunake, *N.Z.* . . . 51 H4
Ora Banda, *Australia* . 53 F3
Oracle, *U.S.A.* . . . 73 K8
Oradea, *Romania* . . 17 E11
Öræfajökull, *Iceland* . 8 D5
Orai, *India* 36 G11
Oral = Zhayyq ➤,
Kazakhstan 23 E9
Oral, *Kazakhstan* . . 22 D9
Oran, *Algeria* 44 A4
Oran, *Argentina* . . 80 A4
Orange = Oranje ➤,
S. Africa 48 D2
Orange, *Australia* . . 55 E4
Orange, *France* . . . 18 D6
Orange, Tex., *U.S.A.* . 71 K8
Orange, Va., *U.S.A.* . 68 F6
Orange, C., *Brazil* . . 79 C8
Orange Free State □,
S. Africa 48 D4
Orange Grove, *U.S.A.* 71 M6
Orangeburg, *U.S.A.* . 69 J5
Orangeville, *Canada* . 62 D3
Oranienburg, *Germany* 16 B7
Oranje ➤, *S. Africa* . 48 D2
Oranje Vrystaat =
Orange Free State □,
S. Africa 48 D4
Oranjemund, *Namibia* 48 D2
Oranjerivier, *S. Africa* 48 D3
Oras, *Phil.* 33 B7
Oraşul Stalin = Braşov,
Romania 17 F13
Orbetello, *Italy* . . . 20 C4
Orbost, *Australia* . . 55 F4
Orchila, I., *Venezuela* 78 A5
Ord ➤, *Australia* . . 52 C4
Ord, Mt., *Australia* . 52 C4
Orderville, *U.S.A.* . 73 H7
Ordos = Mu Us
Shamo, *China* . . . 31 C5
Ordway, *U.S.A.* . . 70 F3
Ordzhonikidze =
Vladikavkaz, *Russia* 23 F7
Ore Mts. = Erzgebirge,
Germany 16 C7
Örebro, *Sweden* . . 9 G16
Oregon, *U.S.A.* . . . 70 D10
Oregon □, *U.S.A.* . 72 E3
Oregon City, *U.S.A.* . 72 D2
Orekhovo-Zuyevo,
Russia 22 C6
Orel, *Russia* 22 D6
Orem, *U.S.A.* 72 F8
Ören, *Turkey* 21 F12
Orenburg, *Russia* . . 22 D10
Orense, *Spain* 19 A2
Orepuki, *N.Z.* 51 M1
Orestiás, *Greece* . . 21 D12
Orford Ness, *U.K.* . 11 E9
Orgaz, *Spain* 19 C4
Orgeyev = Orhei,
Moldova 17 E15
Orhaneli, *Turkey* . . 21 E13
Orhangazi, *Turkey* . 21 D13
Orhei, *Moldova* . . . 17 E15
Orhon Gol ➤,
Mongolia 30 A5
Orient, *Australia* . . 55 D3
Oriental, Cordillera,
Colombia 78 B4
Orihuela, *Spain* . . . 19 C5
Orinoco ➤, *Venezuela* 78 B6
Orissa □, *India* . . . 37 K14
Orissaare, *Estonia* . 9 G20
Oristano, *Italy* . . . 20 E3
Oristano, G. di, *Italy* . 20 E3
Orizaba, *Mexico* . . 74 D5
Orkanger, *Norway* . 8 E13
Orkla ➤, *Norway* . 8 E13
Orkney, *S. Africa* . . 48 D4
Orkney □, *U.K.* . . . 12 C5
Orkney Is., *U.K.* . . 12 C6
Orland, *U.S.A.* . . . 72 G2
Orléanais, *France* . 18 C4
Orléans, *France* . . 18 C4
Orléans, I. d', *Canada* 63 C5
Ormara, *Pakistan* . . 36 G4
Ormoc, *Phil.* 33 B6
Ormond, *N.Z.* 51 H6
Ormond Beach, *U.S.A.* 69 L5
Örnsköldsvik, *Sweden* 8 E18
Orocué, *Colombia* . 78 C4
Orogrande, *U.S.A.* . 73 K10
Orol Dengizi = Aral Sea
, *Asia* 24 E7
Oromocto, *Canada* . 63 C6
Oroqen Zizhiqi, *China* 31 A7
Oroquieta, *Phil.* . . 33 C6
Orós, *Brazil* 79 E11
Orosháza, *Hungary* . 17 E11
Oroville, Calif., *U.S.A.* 72 G3
Oroville, Wash., *U.S.A.* 72 B4
Orroroo, *Australia* . 55 E2
Orsha, *Belarus* . . . 22 D5
Orsk, *Russia* 22 D10
Orşova, *Romania* . 17 F12
Ortaca, *Turkey* . . . 21 F13
Ortegal, C., *Spain* . 19 A2
Orthez, *France* . . . 18 E3
Ortigueira, *Spain* . . 19 A2
Ortles, *Italy* 20 A4
Ortón ➤, *Bolivia* . . 78 F5
Orümïyeh, *Iran* . . . 38 B5
Orümïyeh, Daryācheh-
ye, *Iran* 38 B5
Oruro, *Bolivia* . . . 78 G5
Orust, *Sweden* . . . 9 G14

Pauls Valley

Oruzgān □, Afghan. 36 C5
Orvieto, Italy 20 C5
Orwell —►, U.K. 11 E9
Oryakhovo, Bulgaria 21 C10
Osa, Russia 22 C10
Osage, Iowa, U.S.A. 70 D8
Osage, Wyo., U.S.A. 70 D2
Osage —►, U.S.A. 70 F9
Osage City, U.S.A. 70 F7
Ōsaka, Japan 29 G7
Osawatomie, U.S.A. 70 F7
Osborne, U.S.A. 70 F5
Osceola, Ark., U.S.A. 71 H10
Osceola, Iowa, U.S.A. 70 E8
Oscoda, U.S.A. 68 C4
Ösel = Saaremaa, Estonia 9 G20
Osh, Kyrgyzstan 24 E8
Oshawa, Canada 62 D4
Oshkosh, Nebr., U.S.A. 70 E3
Oshkosh, Wis., U.S.A. 70 C10
Oshmyany = Ashmyany, Belarus 9 J21
Oshnovīyeh, Iran 38 B5
Oshogbo, Nigeria 44 G5
Oshtorīnān, Iran 39 C6
Oshwe, Zaïre 46 E3
Osijek, Croatia 21 B8
Osipenko = Berdyansk, Ukraine 23 E6
Osipovichi = Asipovichy, Belarus 17 B15
Osizweni, S. Africa 49 D5
Oskaloosa, U.S.A. 70 E8
Oskarshamn, Sweden 9 H17
Oskélanéo, Canada 62 C4
Öskemen, Kazakhstan 24 E9
Oslo, Norway 9 G14
Oslob, Phil. 33 C6
Oslofjorden, Norway 9 G14
Osmanabad, India 36 K10
Osmaniye, Turkey 23 G6
Osnabrück, Germany 16 B5
Osorio, Brazil 80 B6
Osorno, Chile 80 E2
Osoyoos, Canada 64 D5
Osøyri, Norway 9 F11
Ospika —►, Canada 64 B4
Osprey Reef, Australia 54 A4
Oss, Neths. 15 C5
Ossa, Mt., Australia 54 G4
Óssa, Oros, Greece 21 E10
Ossabaw I., U.S.A. 69 K5
Ossining, U.S.A. 68 E9
Ossokmanuan L., Canada 63 B7
Ossora, Russia 25 D17
Ostend = Oostende, Belgium 15 C2
Oster, Ukraine 17 C16
Österdalälven, Sweden 9 F16
Østerdalen, Norway 9 F14
Östersund, Sweden 8 E16
Ostfriesische Inseln, Germany 16 B4
Ostrava, Czech. 17 D10
Ostróda, Poland 17 B10
Ostroh, Ukraine 17 C14
Ostrołęka, Poland 17 B11
Ostrów Mazowiecka, Poland 17 B11
Ostrów Wielkopolski, Poland 17 C9
Ostrowiec-Świętokrzyski, Poland 17 C11
Ostuni, Italy 21 D7
Ōsumi-Kaikyō, Japan 29 J5
Ōsumi-Shotō, Japan 29 J5
Osuna, Spain 19 D3
Oswego, U.S.A. 68 D7
Oswestry, U.K. 10 E4
Oświęcim, Poland 17 C10
Otago □, N.Z. 51 L2
Otago Harbour, N.Z. 51 L3
Ōtake, Japan 29 G6
Otaki, N.Z. 51 J5
Otaru, Japan 28 C10
Otaru-Wan = Ishikari-Wan, Japan 28 C10
Otavalo, Ecuador 78 C3
Otavi, Namibia 48 B2
Otchinjau, Angola 48 B1
Othello, U.S.A. 72 C4
Otira Gorge, N.Z. 51 K3
Otis, U.S.A. 70 E3
Otjiwarongo, Namibia 48 C2
Otoineppu, Japan 28 B11
Otorohanga, N.Z. 51 H5
Otoskwin —►, Canada 62 B2
Otosquen, Canada 65 C8
Otra —►, Norway 9 G13
Otranto, Italy 21 D8
Otranto, C. d', Italy 21 D8
Otranto, Str. of, Italy 21 D8
Otse, S. Africa 48 D4
Ōtsu, Japan 29 G7
Ōtsuki, Japan 29 G9
Ottawa = Outaouais —►, Canada 62 C5
Ottawa, Canada 62 C4
Ottawa, Ill., U.S.A. 70 E10
Ottawa, Kans., U.S.A. 70 F7
Ottawa Is., Canada 61 C11
Otter L., Canada 65 B8
Otter Rapids, Ont., Canada 62 B3
Otter Rapids, Sask., Canada 65 B8
Ottosdal, S. Africa 48 D4
Ottumwa, U.S.A. 70 E8
Oturkpo, Nigeria 44 G6
Otway, B., Chile 80 G2
Otway, C., Australia 55 F3
Otwock, Poland 17 B11
Ou —►, Laos 34 B7
Ou-Sammyaku, Japan 28 E10
Ouachita —►, U.S.A. 71 K9
Ouachita, L., U.S.A. 71 H8
Ouachita Mts., U.S.A. 71 H7
Ouadâne, Mauritania 44 D2
Ouadda, C.A.R. 45 G9
Ouagadougou, Burkina Faso 44 F4
Ouahran = Oran, Algeria 44 A4
Ouallene, Algeria 44 D5
Ouanda Djallé, C.A.R. 45 G9
Ouango, C.A.R. 46 D4
Ouargla, Algeria 44 B6
Ouarzazate, Morocco 44 B3
Oubangi —►, Zaïre 46 E3
Ouddorp, Neths. 15 C3
Oude Rijn —►, Neths. 15 B4
Oudenaarde, Belgium 15 D3
Oudtshoorn, S. Africa 48 E3
Ouessant, I. d', France 18 B1
Ouesso, Congo 46 D3
Ouest, Pte., Canada 63 C7
Ouezzane, Morocco 44 B3
Ouidah, Benin 44 G5
Oujda, Morocco 44 B4
Oujeft, Mauritania 44 D2
Oulainen, Finland 8 D21
Ouled Djellal, Algeria 44 B6
Oulu, Finland 8 D21
Oulujärvi, Finland 8 D22
Oulujoki —►, Finland 8 D21
Oum Chalouba, Chad 45 E9
Ounasjoki —►, Finland 8 C21
Ounguati, Namibia 48 C2
Ounianga-Kébir, Chad 45 E9
Ounianga Sérir, Chad 45 E9
Our —►, Lux. 15 E6
Ouray, U.S.A. 73 G10
Ourense = Orense, Spain 19 A2
Ouricuri, Brazil 79 E10
Ouro Prêto, Brazil 79 H10
Ourthe —►, Belgium 15 D5
Ouse, Australia 54 G4
Ouse —►, E. Susx., U.K. 11 G8
Ouse —►, N. Yorks., U.K. 10 C8
Outaouais —►, Canada 62 C5
Outardes —►, Canada 63 C6
Outer Hebrides, U.K. 12 D1
Outer I., Canada 63 B8
Outjo, Namibia 48 C2
Outlook, Canada 65 C7
Outlook, U.S.A. 70 A2
Outokumpu, Finland 8 E23
Ouyen, Australia 55 F3
Ovalau, Fiji 51 C8
Ovalle, Chile 80 C2
Ovamboland, Namibia 48 B2
Overflakkee, Neths. 15 C4
Overijssel □, Neths. 15 B6
Overpelt, Belgium 15 C5
Overton, U.S.A. 73 H6
Övertorneå, Sweden 8 C20
Ovid, U.S.A. 70 E3
Oviedo, Spain 19 A3
Oviši, Latvia 9 H19
Øvre Årdal, Norway 9 F12
Ovruch, Ukraine 17 C15
Owaka, N.Z. 51 M2
Owambo = Ovamboland, Namibia 48 B2
Owase, Japan 29 G8
Owatonna, U.S.A. 70 C8
Owbeh, Afghan. 36 B3
Owego, U.S.A. 68 D7
Owen Sound, Canada 62 D3
Owendo, Gabon 46 D1
Owens L., U.S.A. 73 H5
Owensboro, U.S.A. 68 G2
Owensville, U.S.A. 70 F9
Owl —►, Canada 65 B10
Owo, Nigeria 44 G6
Owosso, U.S.A. 68 D3
Owyhee, U.S.A. 72 F5
Owyhee —►, U.S.A. 72 E5
Owyhee, L., U.S.A. 72 E5
Oxelösund, Sweden 9 G17
Oxford, N.Z. 51 K4
Oxford, U.K. 11 F6
Oxford, Miss., U.S.A. 71 H10
Oxford, N.C., U.S.A. 69 G6
Oxford, Ohio, U.S.A. 68 F3
Oxford L., Canada 65 C9
Oxfordshire □, U.K. 11 F6
Oxley, Australia 55 E3
Oxnard, U.S.A. 73 J4
Oxus = Amudarya —►, Uzbekistan 24 E6
Oya, Malaysia 32 D4
Oyama, Japan 29 F9
Oyem, Gabon 46 D2
Oyen, Canada 65 C6
Oykel —►, U.K. 12 D4
Oymyakon, Russia 25 C15
Oyo, Nigeria 44 G5
Ōyūbari, Japan 28 C11
Ozamiz, Phil. 33 C6
Ozark, Ala., U.S.A. 69 K3
Ozark, Ark., U.S.A. 71 H8
Ozark, Mo., U.S.A. 71 G8
Ozark Plateau, U.S.A. 71 G9
Ozarks, L. of the, U.S.A. 70 F8
Ózd, Hungary 17 D11
Ozona, U.S.A. 71 K4

P

P.W.V. □, S. Africa 49 D4
Pa-an, Burma 37 L20
Pa Sak —►, Thailand 34 E6
Paamiut = Frederikshåb, Greenland 4 C5
Paarl, S. Africa 48 E2
Paauilo, U.S.A. 66 H17
Pab Hills, Pakistan 36 F5
Pabianice, Poland 17 C10
Pabna, Bangla. 37 G16
Pacaja —►, Brazil 79 D8
Pacaraima, Sierra, Venezuela 78 C6
Pacasmayo, Peru 78 E3
Pachpadra, India 36 G8
Pachuca, Mexico 74 C5
Pacific, Canada 64 C3
Pacific-Antarctic Ridge, Pac. Oc. 57 M16
Pacific Grove, U.S.A. 73 H3
Pacific Ocean, Pac. Oc. 57 G14
Pacitan, Indonesia 33 H14
Padaido, Kepulauan, Indonesia 33 E9
Padang, Indonesia 32 E2
Padang Endau, Malaysia 34 S16
Padangpanjang, Indonesia 32 E2
Padangsidempuan, Indonesia 32 D1
Paddockwood, Canada 65 C7
Paderborn, Germany 16 C5
Padloping Island, Canada 61 B13
Pádova, Italy 20 B4
Padre I., U.S.A. 71 M6
Padstow, U.K. 11 G3
Padua = Pádova, Italy 20 B4
Paducah, Ky., U.S.A. 68 G1
Paducah, Tex., U.S.A. 71 H4
Paeroa, N.Z. 51 G5
Pafúri, Mozam. 49 C5
Pag, Croatia 16 F8
Pagadian, Phil. 33 C6
Pagai Selatan, P., Indonesia 32 E2
Pagai Utara, Indonesia 32 E2
Pagalu = Annobón, Atl. Oc. 43 G4
Pagastikós Kólpos, Greece 21 E10
Pagatan, Indonesia 32 E5
Page, Ariz., U.S.A. 73 H8
Page, N. Dak., U.S.A. 70 B6
Pago Pago, Amer. Samoa 51 B13
Pagosa Springs, U.S.A. 73 H10
Pagwa River, Canada 62 B2
Pahala, U.S.A. 66 J17
Pahang □, Malaysia 34 R15
Pahang —►, Malaysia 34 R16
Pahiatua, N.Z. 51 J5
Pahokee, U.S.A. 69 M5
Pahrump, U.S.A. 73 H6
Paia, U.S.A. 66 H16
Paide, Estonia 9 G21
Paignton, U.K. 11 G4
Päijänne, Finland 9 F21
Pailin, Cambodia 34 F7
Painan, Indonesia 32 E2
Painesville, U.S.A. 68 E5
Paint Hills = Wemindji, Canada 62 B4
Paint L., Canada 65 B9
Paint Rock, U.S.A. 71 K5
Painted Desert, U.S.A. 73 J8
Paintsville, U.S.A. 68 G4
País Vasco □, Spain 19 A4
Paisley, U.K. 12 F4
Paisley, U.S.A. 72 E3
Paita, Peru 78 E2
Pajares, Puerto de, Spain 19 A3
Pak Lay, Laos 34 C6
Pakaraima Mts., Guyana 78 B6
Pakistan ■, Asia 36 E6
Pakistan, East = Bangladesh ■, Asia 37 H17
Pakokku, Burma 37 J19
Pakse, Laos 34 E8
Paktīā □, Afghan. 36 C6
Pala, Chad 45 G8
Palacios, U.S.A. 71 L6
Palagruža, Croatia 20 C7
Palam, India 36 K10
Palampur, India 36 C10
Palana, Australia 54 F4
Palana, Russia 25 D16
Palanan, Phil. 33 A6
Palanan Pt., Phil. 33 A6
Palanga, Lithuania 9 J19
Palangkaraya, Indonesia 32 E4
Palani Hills, India 36 P10
Palanpur, India 36 G8
Palanro, Indonesia 33 E5
Palapye, Botswana 48 C4
Palatka, Russia 25 C16
Palatka, U.S.A. 69 L5
Palau = Belau ■, Pac. Oc. 56 G5
Palauk, Burma 34 F5
Palawan, Phil. 32 C5
Palayankottai, India 36 Q10
Paldiski, Estonia 9 G21
Paleleh, Indonesia 33 D6
Palembang, Indonesia 32 E2
Palencia, Spain 19 A3
Palermo, Italy 20 E5
Palermo, U.S.A. 72 G3
Palestine, Asia 41 D4
Palestine, U.S.A. 71 K7
Paletwa, Burma 37 J18
Palghat, India 36 P10
Palgrave, Mt., Australia 52 D2
Pali, India 36 G8
Palioúrion, Ákra, Greece 21 E10
Palisade, U.S.A. 70 E4
Palitana, India 36 J7
Palk Bay, Asia 36 Q11
Palk Strait, Asia 36 Q11
Palkānah, Iraq 38 C5
Palla Road = Dinokwe, Botswana 48 C4
Pallanza = Verbánia, Italy 20 B3
Palm Beach, U.S.A. 69 M6
Palm Is., Australia 54 B4
Palm Springs, U.S.A. 73 K5
Palma, Mozam. 46 G8
Palma —►, Brazil 79 F9
Palma, B. de, Spain 19 C7
Palma de Mallorca, Spain 19 C7
Palmares, Brazil 79 E11
Palmas, C., Liberia 44 H3
Pálmas, G. di, Italy 20 E3
Palmdale, U.S.A. 73 J4
Palmeira dos Índios, Brazil 79 E11
Palmeirinhas, Pta. das, Angola 46 F2
Palmer, U.S.A. 60 B5
Palmer —►, Australia 54 B3
Palmer Arch., Antarctica 5 C17
Palmer Lake, U.S.A. 70 F2
Palmer Land, Antarctica 5 D18
Palmerston, N.Z. 51 L3
Palmerston North, N.Z. 51 J5
Palmetto, U.S.A. 69 M4
Palmi, Italy 20 E6
Palmira, Colombia 78 C3
Palmyra = Tudmur, Syria 38 C3
Palmyra, U.S.A. 70 F9
Palmyra Is., Pac. Oc. 57 G11
Palo Alto, U.S.A. 73 H2
Palopo, Indonesia 33 E6
Palos, C. de, Spain 19 D5
Palouse, U.S.A. 72 C5
Palparara, Australia 54 C3
Palu, Indonesia 33 E5
Palu, Turkey 23 G7
Paluan, Phil. 33 B6
Pama, Burkina Faso 44 F5
Pamanukan, Indonesia 33 G12
Pamekasan, Indonesia 33 G15
Pamiers, France 18 E4
Pamirs, Tajikistan 24 F8
Pamlico —►, U.S.A. 69 H7
Pamlico Sd., U.S.A. 69 H8
Pampa, U.S.A. 71 H4
Pampa de las Salinas, Argentina 80 C3
Pampanua, Indonesia 33 E6
Pampas, Argentina 80 D4
Pampas, Peru 78 F4
Pamplona, Colombia 78 B4
Pamplona, Spain 19 A5
Pampoenpoort, S. Africa 48 E3
Pana, U.S.A. 70 F10
Panaca, U.S.A. 73 H6
Panaitan, Indonesia 33 G11
Panaji, India 36 M8
Panamá, Panama 74 H14
Panama ■, Cent. Amer. 75 F9
Panamá, G. de, Panama 75 F9
Panama Canal, Panama 74 H14
Panama City, U.S.A. 69 K3
Panamint Range, U.S.A. 73 H5
Panão, Peru 78 E3
Panarukan, Indonesia 33 G15
Panay, Phil. 33 B6
Panay, G., Phil. 33 B6
Pancake Range, U.S.A. 73 G6
Pančevo, Serbia, Yug. 21 B9
Pandan, Phil. 33 B6
Pandegelang, Indonesia 33 G12
Pandharpur, India 36 L9
Pando, Uruguay 80 C5
Pando, L. = Hope, L., Australia 55 D2
Panevežys, Lithuania 9 J21
Panfilov, Kazakhstan 24 E8
Pang-Long, Burma 37 H21
Pang-Yang, Burma 37 H21
Pangalanes, Canal des, Madag. 49 C8
Pangani, Tanzania 46 F7
Pangfou = Bengbu, China 31 C6
Pangkah, Tanjung, Indonesia 33 G15
Pangkajene, Indonesia 33 E5
Pangkalanbrandan, Indonesia 32 D1
Pangkalanbuun, Indonesia 32 E4
Pangkalansusu, Indonesia 32 D1
Pangkalpinang, Indonesia 32 E3
Pangkoh, Indonesia 32 E4
Pangnirtung, Canada 61 B13
Pangrango, Indonesia 33 G12
Panguitch, U.S.A. 73 H7
Pangutaran Group, Phil. 33 C6
Panhandle, U.S.A. 71 H4
Panjgur, Pakistan 36 F4
Panjim = Panaji, India 36 M8
Panjinad Barrage, Pakistan 36 E7
Panna, India 36 G12
Panorama, Brazil 80 A6
Pantar, Indonesia 33 F6
Pante Macassar, Indonesia 33 F6
Pantelleria, Italy 20 F4
Pánuco, Mexico 74 C5
Panyam, Nigeria 44 G6
Paola, U.S.A. 70 F7
Paonia, U.S.A. 73 G10
Paoting = Baoding, China 31 C6
Paot'ou = Baotou, China 31 B6
Paoua, C.A.R. 45 G8
Pápa, Hungary 17 E9
Papakura, N.Z. 51 G5
Papantla, Mexico 74 C5
Papar, Malaysia 32 C5
Papien Chiang = Da —►, Vietnam 34 B8
Paposo, Chile 80 B2
Papua New Guinea ■, Oceania 56 H6
Papudo, Chile 80 C2
Papun, Burma 37 K20
Papunya, Australia 52 D5
Pará = Belém, Brazil 79 D9
Pará □, Brazil 79 D8
Paraburdoo, Australia 52 D2
Paracatu, Brazil 79 G9
Paracel Is. = Hsisha Chuntao, Pac. Oc. 32 A4
Parachilna, Australia 55 E2
Parachinar, Pakistan 36 C7
Paradip, India 37 J15
Paradise, U.S.A. 72 C6
Paradise —►, Canada 63 B8
Paradise Valley, U.S.A. 72 F5
Parado, Indonesia 33 F5
Paragould, U.S.A. 71 G9
Paragua —►, Venezuela 78 B6
Paraguaçu —►, Brazil 79 F11
Paraguaná, Pen. de, Venezuela 78 A4
Paraguarí, Paraguay 80 B5
Paraguay ■, S. Amer. 80 A5
Paraguay —►, Paraguay 80 B5
Paraíba = João Pessoa, Brazil 79 E12
Paraíba □, Brazil 79 E11
Paraíba do Sul —►, Brazil 79 H10
Parainen, Finland 9 F20
Parak, Iran 39 E7
Parakou, Benin 44 G5
Paramaribo, Surinam 79 B7
Paramushir, Ostrov, Russia 25 D16
Paran —►, Israel 41 E4
Paraná, Argentina 80 C4
Paranã, Brazil 79 F9
Paraná □, Brazil 80 A6
Paraná —►, Argentina 80 C5
Paranaguá, Brazil 80 B7
Paranaíba —►, Brazil 79 H8
Paranapanema —►, Brazil 80 A6
Paranapiacaba, Serra do, Brazil 80 A7
Parang, Jolo, Phil. 33 C6
Parang, Mindanao, Phil. 33 C6
Paratinga, Brazil 79 F10
Paratoo, Australia 55 E2
Parattah, Australia 54 G4
Parbhani, India 36 K10
Parchim, Germany 16 B6
Pardes Hanna, Israel 41 C3
Pardo —►, Bahia, Brazil 79 G11
Pardo —►, Mato Grosso, Brazil 79 H8
Pardo —►, São Paulo, Brazil 79 H9
Pardubice, Czech. 16 C8
Pare, Indonesia 33 G15
Parecis, Serra dos, Brazil 78 F7
Pareh, Iran 38 B5
Paren, Russia 25 C17
Parent, Canada 62 C5
Parent, L., Canada 62 C4
Parepare, Indonesia 33 E5
Párga, Greece 21 E9
Parguba, Russia 22 B5
Pariaguán, Venezuela 78 B6
Pariaman, Indonesia 32 E2
Parigi, Java, Indonesia 33 G13
Parigi, Sulawesi, Indonesia 33 E6
Parika, Guyana 78 B7
Parima, Serra, Brazil 78 C6
Parinari, Peru 78 D4
Parîngul Mare, Romania 17 F12
Parintins, Brazil 79 D7
Pariparit Kyun, Burma 37 M18
Paris, Canada 62 D3
Paris, France 18 B5
Paris, Idaho, U.S.A. 72 E8
Paris, Ky., U.S.A. 68 F3
Paris, Tenn., U.S.A. 69 G1
Paris, Tex., U.S.A. 71 J7
Pariti, Indonesia 33 F6
Park City, U.S.A. 72 F8
Park Falls, U.S.A. 70 C9
Park Range, U.S.A. 72 G10
Park Rapids, U.S.A. 70 B7
Park River, U.S.A. 70 A6
Park Rynie, S. Africa 49 E5
Parkā Bandar, Iran 39 E8
Parkano, Finland 9 E20
Parker, Ariz., U.S.A. 73 J6
Parker, S. Dak., U.S.A. 70 D6
Parker Dam, U.S.A. 73 J6
Parkersburg, U.S.A. 68 F5
Parkerview, Canada 65 C8
Parkes, Australia 55 E4
Parkside, Canada 65 C7
Parkston, U.S.A. 70 D5
Parksville, Canada 64 D4
Parla, Spain 19 B4
Parma, Italy 20 B4
Parma, U.S.A. 72 E5
Parnaguá, Brazil 79 F10
Parnaíba, Piauí, Brazil 79 D10
Parnaíba, São Paulo, Brazil 79 G8
Parnaíba —►, Brazil 79 D10
Parnassós, Greece 21 E10
Pärnu, Estonia 9 G21
Paroo —►, Australia 55 E3
Páros, Greece 21 F11
Parowan, U.S.A. 73 H7
Parral, Chile 80 D2
Parramatta, Australia 55 E5
Parrett —►, U.K. 11 F5
Parris I., U.S.A. 69 J5
Parrsboro, Canada 63 C7
Parry Is., Canada 4 B2
Parry Sound, Canada 62 C3
Parshall, U.S.A. 70 B3
Parsnip —►, Canada 64 B4
Parsons, U.S.A. 71 G7
Parsons Ra., Australia 54 A2
Partinico, Italy 20 E5
Paru —►, Brazil 79 D8
Paruro, Peru 78 F4
Parvān □, Afghan. 36 B6
Parvatipuram, India 37 K13
Parys, S. Africa 48 D4
Pasadena, Calif., U.S.A. 73 J4
Pasadena, Tex., U.S.A. 71 L7
Pasaje, Ecuador 78 D3
Pascagoula, U.S.A. 71 K10
Pascagoula —►, U.S.A. 71 K10
Paşcani, Romania 17 E14
Pasco, U.S.A. 72 C4
Pasco, Cerro de, Peru 78 F3
Pascua, I. de, Pac. Oc. 57 K17
Pasfield L., Canada 65 B7
Pashmakli = Smolyan, Bulgaria 21 D11
Pasir Mas, Malaysia 34 N15
Pasir Putih, Malaysia 34 P15
Pasirian, Indonesia 33 H15
Paskūh, Iran 39 E9
Pasley, C., Australia 53 F3
Pašman, Croatia 16 G8
Pasni, Pakistan 36 G3
Paso de Indios, Argentina 80 E3
Paso Robles, U.S.A. 73 J3
Paspébiac, Canada 63 C6
Passage West, Ireland 13 E3
Passau, Germany 16 D7
Passero, C., Italy 20 F6
Passo Fundo, Brazil 80 B6
Passos, Brazil 79 H9
Pastavy, Belarus 9 J22
Pastaza —►, Peru 78 D3
Pasto, Colombia 78 C3
Pasuruan, Indonesia 33 G15
Patagonia, Argentina 80 F3
Patagonia, U.S.A. 73 L8
Patambar, Iran 39 D9
Patan, India 36 H8
Patan, Nepal 37 F14
Patani, Indonesia 33 D7
Patchewollock, Australia 55 F3
Patchogue, U.S.A. 68 E9
Patea, N.Z. 51 H5
Pategi, Nigeria 44 G6
Patensie, S. Africa 48 E3
Paternò, Italy 20 F6
Pateros, U.S.A. 72 B4
Paterson, U.S.A. 68 E8
Paterson Ra., Australia 52 D3
Pathankot, India 36 C9
Pathfinder Reservoir, U.S.A. 72 E10
Pati, Indonesia 33 G14
Patiala, India 36 D10
Patkai Bum, India 37 F19
Pátmos, Greece 21 F12
Patna, India 37 G14
Patos, L. dos, Brazil 80 C6
Patos de Minas, Brazil 79 G9
Patquía, Argentina 80 C3
Pátrai, Greece 21 E9
Pátraikós Kólpos, Greece 21 E9
Patras = Pátrai, Greece 21 E9
Patrocínio, Brazil 79 G9
Pattani, Thailand 34 N14
Patten, U.S.A. 63 C6
Patterson, Calif., U.S.A. 73 H3
Patterson, La., U.S.A. 71 L9
Patuakhali, Bangla. 37 H17
Pau, France 18 E3
Pauini —►, Brazil 78 D6
Pauk, Burma 37 J19
Paul I., Canada 63 A7
Paulis = Isiro, Zaïre 46 D5
Paulistana, Brazil 79 E10
Paullina, U.S.A. 70 D7
Paulo Afonso, Brazil 79 E11
Paulpietersburg, S. Africa 49 D5
Pauls Valley, U.S.A. 71 H6

Pāveh

Pāveh, *Iran* 38 C5
Pavia, *Italy* 20 B3
Pāvilosta, *Latvia* 9 H19
Pavlodar, *Kazakhstan* . 24 D8
Pavlograd = Pavlohrad,
 Ukraine 23 E6
Pavlohrad, *Ukraine* ... 23 E6
Pavlovo, *Russia* 22 C7
Pavlovo, *Russia* 25 C12
Pavlovsk, *Russia* 23 D7
Pawhuska, *U.S.A.* 71 G6
Pawnee, *U.S.A.* 71 G6
Pawnee City, *U.S.A.* .. 70 E6
Pawtucket, *U.S.A.* ... 68 E10
Paxoí, *Greece* 21 E9
Paxton, *Ill., U.S.A.* .. 68 E1
Paxton, *Nebr., U.S.A.* . 70 E4
Paya Bakri, *Malaysia* . 34 S15
Payakumbuh, *Indonesia* 32 E2
Payette, *U.S.A.* 72 D5
Payne Bay =
 Kangirsuk, *Canada* . 61 B13
Paynes Find, *Australia* . 53 E2
Paynesville, *U.S.A.* ... 70 C7
Payson, *Ariz., U.S.A.* . 73 J8
Payson, *Utah, U.S.A.* . 72 F8
Paz, B. la, *Mexico* ... 74 C2
Pāzanān, *Iran* 39 D6
Pazardzhik, *Bulgaria* . 21 C11
Pe Ell, *U.S.A.* 72 C2
Pe →, *Canada* 64 B6
Peace Point, *Canada* .. 64 B6
Peace River, *Canada* .. 64 B5
Peach Springs, *U.S.A.* . 73 J7
Peak, The = Kinder
 Scout, *U.K.* 10 D6
Peak Downs, *Australia* . 54 C4
Peak Downs Mine,
 Australia 54 C4
Peak Hill, *N.S.W.,*
 Australia 55 E4
Peak Hill, *W. Austral.,*
 Australia 53 E2
Peak Ra., *Australia* ... 54 C4
Peake, *Australia* 55 F2
Peake Cr. →, *Australia* 55 D2
Peale, Mt., *U.S.A.* ... 73 G9
Pearl →, *U.S.A.* 71 K10
Pearl City, *U.S.A.* 66 H16
Pearsall, *U.S.A.* 71 L5
Pearse I., *Canada* 64 C2
Peary Land, *Greenland* . 4 A6
Pease →, *U.S.A.* 71 H5
Pebane, *Mozam.* 47 H7
Pebas, *Peru* 78 D4
Peć, *Serbia, Yug.* 21 C9
Pechenga, *Russia* 22 A5
Pechenizhyn, *Ukraine* . 17 D13
Pechora →, *Russia* .. 22 A9
Pechorskaya Guba,
 Russia 22 A9
Pečory, *Russia* 9 H22
Pecos, *U.S.A.* 71 K3
Pecos →, *U.S.A.* 71 L3
Pécs, *Hungary* 17 E10
Pedder, L., *Australia* .. 54 G4
Peddie, *S. Africa* 49 E4
Pedirka, *Australia* 55 D2
Pedra Azul, *Brazil* 79 G10
Pedreiras, *Brazil* 79 D10
Pedro Afonso, *Brazil* .. 79 E9
Pedro Juan Caballero,
 Paraguay 80 A5
Pedro Miguel Locks,
 Panama 74 H14
Peebinga, *Australia* ... 55 E3
Peebles, *U.K.* 12 F5
Peekskill, *U.S.A.* 68 E9
Peel, *U.K.* 10 C3
Peel →, *Australia* 55 E5
Peel →, *Canada* 60 B6
Peera Peera Poolanna
 L., *Australia* 55 D2
Peers, *Canada* 64 C5
Pegasus Bay, *N.Z.* ... 51 K4
Pegu, *Burma* 37 L20
Pegu Yoma, *Burma* ... 37 K19
Pehuajó, *Argentina* ... 80 D4
Peine, *Germany* 16 B6
Peip'ing = Beijing,
 China 31 C6
Peipus, L. =
 Chudskoye, Oz.,
 Russia 9 G22
Peixe, *Brazil* 79 F9
Pekalongan, *Indonesia* 33 G13
Pekan, *Malaysia* 34 R16
Pekanbaru, *Indonesia* . 32 D2
Pekin, *U.S.A.* 70 E10
Peking = Beijing, *China* 31 C6
Pelabuhan Kelang,
 Malaysia 34 S14
Pelabuhan Ratu, Teluk,
 Indonesia 33 G12
Pelabuhanratu,
 Indonesia 33 G12
Pelagie, Is., *Italy* 20 G5
Pelaihari, *Indonesia* .. 32 E4
Peleaga, Vf., *Romania* . 17 F12
Pelée, Mt., *Martinique* . 74 N20
Pelee, Pt., *Canada* ... 62 D3
Pelee I., *Canada* 62 D3
Peleng, *Indonesia* 33 E6
Pelham, *U.S.A.* 69 K3
Pelican L., *Canada* ... 65 C8
Pelican Narrows,
 Canada 65 B8
Pelican Rapids, *Canada* 65 C8
Pelješac, *Croatia* 20 C7
Pelkosenniemi, *Finland* 8 C22
Pella, *S. Africa* 48 D2
Pella, *U.S.A.* 70 E8

Pello, *Finland* 8 C21
Pelly →, *Canada* 60 B6
Pelly Bay, *Canada* ... 61 B11
Pelly L., *Canada* 60 B9
Peloponnese =
 Pelopónnisos □,
 Greece 21 F10
Pelopónnisos □,
 Greece 21 F10
Peloro, C., *Italy* 20 E6
Pelorus Sd., *N.Z.* 51 J4
Pelotas, *Brazil* 80 C6
Pelvoux, Massif du,
 France 18 D7
Pemalang, *Indonesia* . 33 G13
Pematangsiantar,
 Indonesia 32 D1
Pemba I., *Tanzania* ... 46 F7
Pemberton, *Australia* . 53 F2
Pemberton, *Canada* .. 64 C4
Pembina, *U.S.A.* 70 A6
Pembina →, *U.S.A.* . 65 D9
Pembine, *U.S.A.* 68 C2
Pembroke, *Canada* ... 62 C4
Pembroke, *U.K.* 11 F3
Pembroke, *U.S.A.* ... 69 J5
Pen-y-Ghent, *U.K.* ... 10 C5
Penang = Pinang,
 Malaysia 34 P13
Penápolis, *Brazil* 80 A6
Peñarroya-
 Pueblonuevo, *Spain* 19 C3
Peñas, C. de, *Spain* .. 19 A3
Penas, G. de, *Chile* ... 80 F2
Pench'i = Benxi, *China* 31 B7
Pend Oreille →,
 U.S.A. 72 B5
Pend Oreille L., *U.S.A.* 72 C5
Pendembu, *S. Leone* .. 44 G2
Pender B., *Australia* .. 52 C3
Pendleton, *U.S.A.* ... 72 D4
Penedo, *Brazil* 79 F11
Penetanguishene,
 Canada 62 D4
Pengalengan, *Indonesia* 33 G12
Penguin, *Australia* ... 54 G4
Peniche, *Portugal* 19 C1
Penicuik, *U.K.* 12 F5
Penida, *Indonesia* ... 32 F5
Peninsular Malaysia □,
 Malaysia 34 Q15
Penmarch, Pte. de,
 France 18 C1
Penn Yan, *U.S.A.* 68 D7
Pennant, *Canada* 65 C7
Penner →, *India* 36 M12
Pennines, *U.K.* 10 C5
Pennsylvania □, *U.S.A.* 68 E6
Penny, *Canada* 64 C4
Penola, *Australia* 55 F3
Penong, *Australia* 53 F5
Penrith, *Australia* 55 E5
Penrith, *U.K.* 10 C5
Pensacola, *U.S.A.* ... 69 K2
Pensacola Mts.,
 Antarctica 5 E1
Pense, *Canada* 65 C8
Penshurst, *Australia* .. 55 F3
Penticton, *Canada* ... 64 D5
Pentland, *Australia* ... 54 C4
Pentland Firth, *U.K.* .. 12 C5
Pentland Hills, *U.K.* .. 12 F5
Penylan L., *Canada* .. 65 A7
Penza, *Russia* 22 D8
Penzance, *U.K.* 11 G2
Penzhino, *Russia* 25 C17
Penzhinskaya Guba,
 Russia 25 C17
Peoria, *Ariz., U.S.A.* . 73 K7
Peoria, *Ill., U.S.A.* ... 70 E10
Pera Hd., *Australia* ... 54 A3
Perabumulih, *Indonesia* 32 E2
Perak →, *Malaysia* .. 34 P14
Peräpohjola, *Finland* . 8 C22
Percé, *Canada* 63 C7
Perche, Collines du,
 France 18 B4
Percival Lakes,
 Australia 52 D4
Percy Is., *Australia* ... 54 C5
Perdido, Mte., *Spain* . 19 A6
Perdu, Mt. = Perdido,
 Mte., *Spain* 19 A6
Pereira, *Colombia* 78 C3
Perekerten, *Australia* . 55 E3
Perenjori, *Australia* ... 53 E2
Pereyaslav-
 Khmelnytskyy,
 Ukraine 23 D5
Pergamino, *Argentina* 80 C4
Perham, *U.S.A.* 70 B7
Perhentian, Kepulauan,
 Malaysia 34 P15
Péribonca →, *Canada* 63 C5
Péribonca, L., *Canada* 63 B5
Perico, *Argentina* 80 A3
Périgueux, *France* ... 18 D4
Perijá, Sierra de,
 Colombia 78 B4
Perlas, Arch. de las,
 Panama 75 F9
Perlis □, *Malaysia* ... 34 N13
Perm, *Russia* 22 C10
Pernambuco = Recife,
 Brazil 79 E12
Pernambuco □, *Brazil* 79 E11
Pernatty Lagoon,
 Australia 55 E2
Pernik, *Bulgaria* 21 C10
Peron, C., *Australia* .. 53 E1
Peron Is., *Australia* ... 52 B5
Peron Pen., *Australia* . 53 E1
Perow, *Canada* 64 C3

Perpendicular Pt.,
 Australia 55 E5
Perpignan, *France* ... 18 E5
Perry, *Fla., U.S.A.* ... 69 K4
Perry, *Ga., U.S.A.* ... 69 J4
Perry, *Iowa, U.S.A.* .. 70 E7
Perry, *Maine, U.S.A.* . 69 C12
Perry, *Okla., U.S.A.* .. 71 G6
Perryton, *U.S.A.* 71 G4
Perryville, *U.S.A.* 71 G10
Pershotravensk,
 Ukraine 17 C14
Persia = Iran ■, *Asia* . 39 C7
Persian Gulf = Gulf,
 The, *Asia* 39 E6
Perth, *Australia* 53 F2
Perth, *Canada* 62 D4
Perth, *U.K.* 12 E5
Perth Amboy, *U.S.A.* . 68 E8
Peru, *Ill., U.S.A.* 70 E10
Peru, *Ind., U.S.A.* ... 68 E2
Peru ■, *S. Amer.* 78 E3
Peru-Chile Trench,
 Pac. Oc. 57 K20
Perúgia, *Italy* 20 C5
Pervomaysk, *Ukraine* . 23 E5
Pervouralsk, *Russia* .. 22 C10
Pésaro, *Italy* 20 C5
Pescara, *Italy* 20 C6
Peshawar, *Pakistan* .. 36 B7
Peshkopi, *Albania* ... 21 D9
Peshtigo, *U.S.A.* 68 C2
Pesqueira, *Brazil* 79 E11
Petah Tiqwa, *Israel* .. 41 C3
Petaling Jaya, *Malaysia* 34 R14
Petaluma, *U.S.A.* 72 G2
Petange, *Lux.* 15 E5
Petauke, *Zambia* 47 G6
Petawawa, *Canada* .. 62 C4
Peter I.s Øy, *Antarctica* 5 C16
Peter Pond L., *Canada* 65 B7
Peterbell, *Canada* ... 62 C3
Peterborough, *Australia* 55 E2
Peterborough, *Canada* 61 D12
Peterborough, *U.K.* .. 11 E7
Peterhead, *U.K.* 12 D7
Petermann Bjerg,
 Greenland 58 B17
Petersburg, *Alaska,*
 U.S.A. 64 B2
Petersburg, *Ind., U.S.A.* 68 F2
Petersburg, *Va., U.S.A.* 68 G7
Petersburg, *W. Va.,*
 U.S.A. 68 F6
Petford, *Australia* 54 B3
Petit Bois I., *U.S.A.* .. 69 K1
Petit-Cap, *Canada* ... 63 C7
Petit Lac Manicouagan,
 Canada 63 B6
Petitcodiac, *Canada* .. 63 C6
Petite Baleine →,
 Canada 62 A4
Petite Saguenay,
 Canada 63 C5
Petitsikapau, L., *Canada* 63 B6
Petlad, *India* 36 H8
Peto, *Mexico* 74 C7
Petone, *N.Z.* 51 J5
Petoskey, *U.S.A.* 68 C3
Petra, *Jordan* 41 E4
Petra, Ostrova, *Russia* 4 B13
Petra Velikogo, Zaliv,
 Russia 28 C5
Petrich, *Bulgaria* 21 D10
Petrikov = Pyetrikaw,
 Belarus 17 B15
Petrograd = Sankt-
 Peterburg, *Russia* .. 22 C5
Petrolândia, *Brazil* ... 79 E11
Petrolia, *Canada* 62 D3
Petrolina, *Brazil* 79 E10
Petropavl, *Kazakhstan* 24 D7
Petropavlovsk =
 Petropavl, *Kazakhstan* 24 D7
Petropavlovsk-
 Kamchatskiy, *Russia* 25 D16
Petrópolis, *Brazil* 79 H10
Petroşani, *Romania* .. 17 F12
Petrovaradin,
 Serbia, Yug. 21 B8
Petrovsk, *Russia* 22 D8
Petrovsk-Zabaykalskiy,
 Russia 25 D11
Petrozavodsk, *Russia* . 22 B5
Petrus Steyn, *S. Africa* 49 D4
Petrusburg, *S. Africa* . 48 D4
Peureulak, *Indonesia* . 32 D1
Pevek, *Russia* 25 C18
Pforzheim, *Germany* . 16 D5
Phagwara, *India* 36 D9
Phala, *Botswana* 48 C4
Phalodi, *India* 36 F8
Phan Rang, *Vietnam* . 34 G10
Phan Thiet, *Vietnam* . 34 G10
Phangan, Ko, *Thailand* 34 H6
Phangnga, *Thailand* .. 34 H5
Phanh Bho Ho Chi
 Minh, *Vietnam* 34 G9
Phatthalung, *Thailand* 34 J6
Phelps, *U.S.A.* 70 B10
Phelps L., *Canada* ... 65 B8
Phenix City, *U.S.A.* .. 69 J3
Phet Buri, *Thailand* .. 34 F5
Phetchabun, *Thailand* 34 D6
Phetchabun, Thiu Khao,
 Thailand 34 E6
Phetchaburi = Phet
 Buri, *Thailand* 34 F5
Phichai, *Thailand* ... 34 D6
Phichit, *Thailand* 34 D6
Philadelphia, *Miss.,*
 U.S.A. 71 J10
Philadelphia, *Pa.,*
 U.S.A. 68 E8

Philip, *U.S.A.* 70 C4
Philippeville, *Belgium* . 15 D4
Philippi L., *Australia* .. 54 C2
Philippines ■, *Asia* ... 33 B6
Philippolis, *S. Africa* .. 48 E4
Philippopolis = Plovdiv,
 Bulgaria 21 C11
Philipsburg, *U.S.A.* .. 72 C7
Philipstown =
 Daingean, *Ireland* . 13 C4
Philipstown, *S. Africa* . 48 E3
Phillip I., *Australia* ... 55 F4
Phillips, *Tex., U.S.A.* . 71 H4
Phillips, *Wis., U.S.A.* . 70 C9
Phillipsburg, *U.S.A.* .. 70 F5
Phillott, *Australia* 55 D4
Philomath, *U.S.A.* ... 72 D2
Phnom Dangrek,
 Thailand 34 E8
Phnom Penh,
 Cambodia 34 G8
Phnom Thbeng,
 Cambodia 34 F8
Phoenix, *U.S.A.* 73 K7
Phoenix Is., *Kiribati* .. 56 H10
Phong Saly, *Laos* 34 B7
Phosphate Hill,
 Australia 54 C2
Phra Chedi Sam Ong,
 Thailand 34 E5
Phra Nakhon Si
 Ayutthaya, *Thailand* 34 E6
Phrae, *Thailand* 34 C6
Phrao, *Thailand* 34 C5
Phuket, *Thailand* 34 J5
Phumiphon, Khuan,
 Thailand 32 A1
Piacenza, *Italy* 20 B3
Pialba, *Australia* 55 D5
Pian Cr. →, *Australia* 55 E4
Pianosa, *Italy* 20 C4
Piapot, *Canada* 65 D7
Piatra Neamţ, *Romania* 17 E14
Piauí □, *Brazil* 79 E10
Piave →, *Italy* 20 B5
Pibor Post, *Sudan* ... 45 G11
Pica, *Chile* 78 H5
Picardie □, *France* ... 18 B5
Picardy = Picardie,
 France 18 B5
Picayune, *U.S.A.* 71 K10
Pichilemu, *Chile* 80 C2
Pickerel L., *Canada* .. 62 C1
Pickle Lake, *Canada* . 62 B1
Pico Truncado,
 Argentina 80 F3
Picton, *Australia* 55 E5
Picton, *Canada* 62 D4
Picton, *N.Z.* 51 J5
Pictou, *Canada* 63 C7
Picture Butte, *Canada* 64 D6
Picún Leufú, *Argentina* 80 D3
Pidurutalagala,
 Sri Lanka 36 R12
Piedmont =
 Piemonte □, *Italy* .. 20 B2
Piedmont, *U.S.A.* ... 69 J3
Piedmont Plateau,
 U.S.A. 69 J5
Piedras, R. de las →,
 Peru 78 F5
Piedras Negras, *Mexico* 74 B4
Pieksämäki, *Finland* . 9 E22
Piemonte □, *Italy* ... 20 B2
Pierce, *U.S.A.* 72 C6
Pierre, *U.S.A.* 70 C4
Piet Retief, *S. Africa* . 49 D5
Pietarsaari, *Finland* .. 8 E20
Pietermaritzburg,
 S. Africa 49 D5
Pietersburg, *S. Africa* . 49 C4
Pietrosul, *Romania* .. 17 E13
Pietrosul, *Romania* .. 17 E13
Pigeon, *U.S.A.* 68 D4
Piggott, *U.S.A.* 71 G9
Pigüe, *Argentina* 80 D4
Pihlajavesi, *Finland* .. 9 F23
Pikes Peak, *U.S.A.* .. 70 F2
Piketberg, *S. Africa* .. 48 E2
Pikeville, *U.S.A.* 68 G4
Pikwitonei, *Canada* .. 65 B9
Piła, *Poland* 17 B9
Pilar, *Brazil* 79 E11
Pilar, *Paraguay* 80 B5
Pilas Group, *Phil.* ... 33 C6
Pilcomayo →,
 Paraguay 80 B5
Pilibhit, *India* 36 E11
Pilica →, *Poland* ... 17 C11
Pílos, *Greece* 21 F9
Pilot Mound, *Canada* 65 D9
Pilot Point, *U.S.A.* .. 71 J6
Pilot Rock, *U.S.A.* ... 72 D4
Pilsen = Plzeň, *Czech.* 16 D7
Pima, *U.S.A.* 73 K9
Pimba, *Australia* 55 E2
Pimenta Bueno, *Brazil* 78 F6
Pimentel, *Peru* 78 E3
Pinang, *Malaysia* 34 P13
Pinar del Río, *Cuba* .. 75 C8
Pınarhisar, *Turkey* ... 21 D12
Pincher Creek, *Canada* 64 D6
Pinchi L., *Canada* ... 64 C4
Pinckneyville, *U.S.A.* . 70 F10
Pińczów, *Poland* 17 C11
Pindar, *Australia* 53 E2
Pindiga, *Nigeria* 44 G7
Pindus Mts. = Píndos
 Óros, *Greece* 21 E9

Pine, *U.S.A.* 73 J8
Pine →, *Canada* 65 B7
Pine, C., *Canada* 63 C9
Pine Bluff, *U.S.A.* ... 71 H8
Pine City, *U.S.A.* 70 C8
Pine Falls, *Canada* ... 65 C9
Pine Pass, *Canada* ... 64 B4
Pine Point, *Canada* .. 64 A6
Pine Ridge, *U.S.A.* .. 70 D3
Pine River, *Canada* .. 65 C8
Pine River, *U.S.A.* ... 70 B7
Pinega →, *Russia* ... 22 B8
Pinehill, *Australia* ... 54 C4
Pinerolo, *Italy* 20 B2
Pinetop, *U.S.A.* 73 J9
Pinetown, *S. Africa* .. 49 D5
Pinetree, *U.S.A.* 72 E11
Pineville, *Ky., U.S.A.* . 69 G4
Pineville, *La., U.S.A.* . 71 K8
Ping →, *Thailand* ... 34 E6
Pingaring, *Australia* .. 53 F2
Pingdingshan, *China* . 31 C6
Pingdong, *Taiwan* ... 31 D7
Pingelly, *Australia* ... 53 F2
Pingliang, *China* 30 C5
Pingrup, *Australia* ... 53 F2
Pingxiang, *China* 30 D5
Pinhel, *Portugal* 19 B2
Pini, *Indonesia* 32 D1
Piniós →, *Greece* ... 21 E10
Pinjarra, *Australia* ... 53 F2
Pink →, *Canada* 65 B8
Pinnacles, *Australia* .. 53 E3
Pinnaroo, *Australia* .. 55 F3
Pínnes, Ákra, *Greece* 21 D11
Pinos Pt., *U.S.A.* 73 H3
Pinrang, *Indonesia* .. 33 E5
Pinsk, *Belarus* 17 B14
Pintados, *Chile* 78 H5
Pintumba, *Australia* .. 53 F5
Pinyug, *Russia* 22 B8
Pioche, *U.S.A.* 73 H6
Piombino, *Italy* 20 C4
Pioner, Os., *Russia* .. 25 B10
Piorini, L., *Brazil* 78 D6
Piotrków Trybunalski,
 Poland 17 C10
Pīp, *Iran* 39 E9
Pipestone, *U.S.A.* ... 70 D6
Pipestone →, *Canada* 62 B2
Pipestone Cr. →,
 Canada 65 D8
Pipmuacan, Rés.,
 Canada 63 C5
Pippingarra, *Australia* 52 D2
Piqua, *U.S.A.* 68 E3
Piquiri →, *Brazil* 80 A6
Piracicaba, *Brazil* 80 A7
Piracuruca, *Brazil* ... 79 D10
Piraeus = Piraiévs,
 Greece 21 F10
Piraiévs, *Greece* 21 F10
Pirané, *Argentina* ... 80 B5
Pirapora, *Brazil* 79 G10
Pírgos, *Greece* 21 F9
Pirin Planina, *Bulgaria* 21 D10
Piripiri, *Brazil* 79 D10
Pirmasens, *Germany* . 16 D4
Pirot, *Serbia, Yug.* ... 21 C10
Piru, *Indonesia* 33 E7
Pisa, *Italy* 20 C4
Pisagua, *Chile* 78 G4
Pisciotta, *Italy* 20 D6
Pisco, *Peru* 78 F3
Písek, *Czech.* 16 D7
Pishan, *China* 30 C2
Pising, *Indonesia* ... 33 F6
Pistóia, *Italy* 20 C4
Pistol B., *Canada* ... 65 A10
Pisuerga →, *Spain* .. 19 B3
Pitarpunga, L., *Australia* 55 E3
Pitcairn I., *Pac. Oc.* .. 57 K14
Pite älv →, *Sweden* . 8 D19
Piteå, *Sweden* 8 D19
Piteşti, *Romania* 17 F13
Pithapuram, *India* ... 37 L13
Pithara, *Australia* ... 53 F2
Pitlochry, *U.K.* 12 E5
Pitt I., *Canada* 64 C3
Pittsburg, *Kans., U.S.A.* 71 G7
Pittsburg, *Tex., U.S.A.* 71 J7
Pittsburgh, *U.S.A.* ... 68 E6
Pittsfield, *Ill., U.S.A.* . 70 F9
Pittsfield, *Mass., U.S.A.* 68 D9
Pittston, *U.S.A.* 68 E8
Pittsworth, *Australia* . 55 D5
Pituri →, *Australia* .. 54 C2
Piura, *Peru* 78 E2
Placentia, *Canada* ... 63 C9
Placentia B., *Canada* . 63 C9
Placerville, *U.S.A.* ... 72 G3
Plain Dealing, *U.S.A.* 71 J8
Plainfield, *U.S.A.* 68 E8
Plains, *Kans., U.S.A.* . 71 G4
Plains, *Mont., U.S.A.* . 72 C6
Plains, *Tex., U.S.A.* .. 71 J3
Plainview, *Nebr., U.S.A.* 70 D6
Plainview, *Tex., U.S.A.* 71 H4
Plainville, *U.S.A.* 70 F5
Plainwell, *U.S.A.* 68 D3
Pláka, Ákra, *Greece* . 21 G12
Plakhino, *Russia* 24 C9
Plankinton, *U.S.A.* .. 70 D5
Plano, *U.S.A.* 71 J6
Plant City, *U.S.A.* ... 69 L4
Plaquemine, *U.S.A.* . 71 K9
Plasencia, *Spain* 19 B2
Plaster Rock, *Canada* 63 C6
Plastun, *Russia* 28 B8
Plata, Río de la,
 S. Amer. 80 C5
Platani →, *Italy* 20 F5

Plateau du Coteau du
 Missouri, *U.S.A.* ... 70 B4
Plato, *Colombia* 78 B4
Platte, *U.S.A.* 70 D5
Platte →, *U.S.A.* ... 70 F7
Platteville, *U.S.A.* ... 70 D9
Plattsburg, *U.S.A.* ... 68 C9
Plattsmouth, *U.S.A.* . 70 E7
Plauen, *Germany* ... 16 C7
Plavinas, *Latvia* 9 H21
Playgreen L., *Canada* 65 C9
Pleasant Bay, *Canada* 63 C7
Pleasanton, *U.S.A.* .. 71 L5
Pleasantville, *U.S.A.* . 68 F8
Pleiku, *Vietnam* 34 F10
Plenty →, *Australia* . 54 C2
Plenty, B. of, *N.Z.* ... 51 G6
Plentywood, *U.S.A.* . 70 A2
Plesetsk, *Russia* 22 B7
Plessisville, *Canada* . 63 C5
Pletipi L., *Canada* ... 63 B5
Pleven, *Bulgaria* 21 C11
Plevlja,
 Montenegro, Yug. . 21 C8
Płock, *Poland* 17 B10
Plöckenstein, *Germany* 16 D7
Ploieşti, *Romania* ... 17 F14
Plonge, Lac la, *Canada* 65 B7
Plovdiv, *Bulgaria* 21 C11
Plummer, *U.S.A.* 72 C5
Plumtree, *Zimbabwe* . 47 J5
Plunge, *Lithuania* ... 9 J19
Plymouth, *U.K.* 11 G3
Plymouth, *Ind., U.S.A.* 68 E2
Plymouth, *N.C., U.S.A.* 69 H7
Plymouth, *Wis., U.S.A.* 68 D2
Plynlimon =
 Pumlumon Fawr,
 U.K. 11 E4
Plzeň, *Czech.* 16 D7
Po →, *Italy* 20 B5
Po Hai = Bo Hai, *China* 31 C6
Pobeda, *Russia* 25 C15
Pobedino, *Russia* ... 25 E15
Pobedy Pik, *Kyrgyzstan* 24 E8
Pocahontas, *Ark.,*
 U.S.A. 71 G9
Pocahontas, *Iowa,*
 U.S.A. 70 D7
Pocatello, *U.S.A.* ... 72 E7
Pocomoke City, *U.S.A.* 68 F8
Poços de Caldas, *Brazil* 79 H9
Podgorica,
 Montenegro, Yug. . 21 C8
Podilska Vysochyna,
 Ukraine 17 D14
Podkamennaya
 Tunguska →, *Russia* 25 C10
Podolsk, *Russia* 22 C6
Podor, *Senegal* 44 E1
Podporozhy, *Russia* . 22 B5
Pofadder, *S. Africa* .. 48 D2
Pogamasing, *Canada* 62 C3
Pogranitšnyi, *Russia* . 28 B5
Poh, *Indonesia* 33 E6
Pohjanmaa, *Finland* . 8 E20
Pohnpei, *Pac. Oc.* ... 56 G7
Poinsett, C., *Antarctica* 5 C8
Point Edward, *Canada* 62 D3
Point Pedro, *Sri Lanka* 36 Q12
Point Pleasant, *U.S.A.* 68 F4
Pointe-à-la-Hache,
 U.S.A. 71 L10
Pointe-à-Pitre,
 Guadeloupe 74 L20
Pointe Noire, *Congo* . 46 E2
Poisonbush Ra.,
 Australia 52 D3
Poitiers, *France* 18 C4
Poitou, *France* 18 C3
Pojoaque Valley, *U.S.A.* 73 J11
Pokaran, *India* 36 F7
Pokataroo, *Australia* . 55 D4
Pokrovsk = Engels,
 Russia 22 D8
Pokrovsk, *Russia* 25 C13
Pola = Pula, *Croatia* . 16 F7
Polacca, *U.S.A.* 73 J8
Polan, *Iran* 39 E9
Poland ■, *Europe* ... 17 C10
Polatsk, *Belarus* 22 C4
Polcura, *Chile* 80 D2
Polden Hills, *U.K.* ... 11 F5
Polessk, *Russia* 9 J19
Polesye = Pripet
 Marshes, *Europe* .. 17 B15
Polevskoy, *Russia* ... 22 C11
Poli, *Cameroon* 45 C2
Police, *Poland* 16 B8
Polillo Is., *Phil.* 33 B6
Políyiros, *Greece* ... 21 D10
Pollachi, *India* 36 P10
Pollock, *U.S.A.* 70 C4
Polnovat, *Russia* ... 24 C7
Polo, *U.S.A.* 70 E10
Polonne, *Ukraine* ... 17 C14
Polonnoye = Polonne,
 Ukraine 17 C14
Polson, *U.S.A.* 72 C6
Poltava, *Ukraine* 23 E5
Põltsamaa, *Estonia* . 9 G21
Polunochnoye, *Russia* 22 B11
Põlva, *Estonia* 9 G22
Polyarny, *Russia* 22 A5
Polynesia, *Pac. Oc.* . 57 H11
Polynésie française =
 French Polynesia ■,
 Pac. Oc. 57 J13
Pombal, *Brazil* 79 E11
Pombal, *Portugal* ... 19 C1
Pomeroy, *Ohio, U.S.A.* 68 F4
Pomeroy, *Wash., U.S.A.* 72 C5

Pomézia, Italy 20 D5
Pomona, U.S.A. 73 J5
Pomorski, Pojezierze, Poland 17 B9
Pompano Beach, U.S.A. 69 M5
Pompeys Pillar, U.S.A. 72 D10
Ponape = Pohnpei, Pac. Oc. 56 G7
Ponask, L., Canada .. 62 B1
Ponass L., Canada ... 65 C8
Ponca, U.S.A. 70 D6
Ponca City, U.S.A. ... 71 G6
Ponce, Puerto Rico ... 75 D11
Ponchatoula, U.S.A. .. 71 K9
Poncheville, L., Canada 62 B4
Pond Inlet, Canada ... 61 A12
Pondicherry, India ... 36 P11
Ponds, I. of, Canada .. 63 B8
Ponferrada, Spain ... 19 A2
Ponnani, India 36 P9
Ponnyadaung, Burma . 37 J19
Ponoka, Canada 64 C6
Ponorogo, Indonesia .. 33 G14
Ponoy, Russia 22 A7
Ponoy →, Russia 22 A7
Ponta Grossa, Brazil .. 80 B6
Ponta Pora, Brazil ... 80 A5
Pontarlier, France ... 18 C7
Ponte Nova, Brazil ... 79 H10
Pontefract, U.K. 10 D6
Ponteix, Canada 65 D7
Pontevedra, Spain ... 19 A1
Pontiac, Ill., U.S.A. .. 70 E10
Pontiac, Mich., U.S.A. 68 D4
Pontian Kecil, Malaysia 34 T16
Pontianak, Indonesia . 32 E3
Pontic Mts. = Kuzey Anadolu Dağları, Turkey 23 F6
Pontine Is. = Ponziane, Ísole, Italy 20 D5
Pontine Mts. = Kuzey Anadolu Dağları, Turkey 23 F6
Pontivy, France 18 B2
Pontoise, France 18 B5
Ponton →, Canada .. 64 B5
Pontypool, U.K. 11 F4
Pontypridd, U.K. 11 F4
Ponziane, Ísole, Italy . 20 D5
Poochera, Australia .. 55 E1
Poole, U.K. 11 G6
Pooley I., Canada 64 C3
Poona = Pune, India . 36 K8
Pooncarie, Australia .. 55 E3
Poopelloe L., Australia 55 E3
Poopó, L. de, Bolivia . 78 G5
Popanyinning, Australia 53 F2
Popayán, Colombia .. 78 C3
Poperinge, Belgium .. 15 D2
Popigay, Russia 25 B12
Popilta, L., Australia . 55 E3
Popio L., Australia ... 55 E3
Poplar, U.S.A. 70 A2
Poplar →, Man., Canada 65 C9
Poplar →, N.W.T., Canada 64 A4
Poplar Bluff, U.S.A. .. 71 G9
Poplarville, U.S.A. ... 71 K10
Popocatépetl, Volcán, Mexico 74 D5
Popokabaka, Zaïre ... 46 F3
Poprád, Slovak Rep. .. 17 D11
Porbandar, India 36 J6
Porcher I., Canada ... 64 C2
Porcupine →, Canada 65 B8
Porcupine →, U.S.A. 60 B5
Pordenone, Italy 20 B5
Pori, Finland 9 F19
Porlamar, Venezuela .. 78 A6
Poronaysk, Russia ... 25 E15
Poroshiri-Dake, Japan 28 C11
Porpoise B., Antarctica 5 C9
Porretta, Passo di, Italy 20 B4
Porsangen, Norway .. 8 A21
Porsgrunn, Norway .. 9 G13
Port Adelaide, Australia 55 E2
Port Alberni, Canada . 64 D4
Port Alfred, Canada .. 63 C5
Port Alfred, S. Africa . 48 E4
Port Alice, Canada ... 64 C3
Port Allegany, U.S.A. . 68 E6
Port Allen, U.S.A. ... 71 K9
Port Alma, Australia .. 54 C5
Port Angeles, U.S.A. . 72 B2
Port Antonio, Jamaica 74 J17
Port Aransas, U.S.A. . 71 M6
Port Arthur, Australia . 54 G4
Port Arthur, U.S.A. .. 71 L8
Port au Port B., Canada 63 C8
Port-au-Prince, Haiti . 75 D10
Port Augusta, Australia 55 E2
Port Augusta West, Australia 55 E2
Port Austin, U.S.A. .. 68 C4
Port Bergé Vaovao, Madag. 49 B8
Port Blair, India 34 G2
Port Blandford, Canada 63 C9
Port Bou, Spain 19 A7
Port Bradshaw, Australia 54 A2
Port Broughton, Australia 55 E2
Port Burwell, Canada . 62 D3
Port-Cartier, Canada . 63 B6
Port Chalmers, N.Z. .. 51 L3
Port Chester, U.S.A. . 68 E9
Port Clements, Canada 64 C2
Port Clinton, U.S.A. . 68 E4
Port Colborne, Canada 62 D4

Port Coquitlam, Canada 64 D4
Port Curtis, Australia . 54 C5
Port Darwin, Australia 52 B5
Port Darwin, Falk. Is. . 80 G5
Port Davey, Australia . 54 G4
Port Dickson, Malaysia 34 S14
Port Douglas, Australia 54 B4
Port Edward, Canada . 64 C2
Port Elgin, Canada ... 62 D3
Port Elizabeth, S. Africa 48 E4
Port Ellen, U.K. 12 F2
Port Erin, U.K. 10 C3
Port Essington, Australia 52 B5
Port Etienne = Nouâdhibou, Mauritania 44 D1
Port Fairy, Australia .. 55 F3
Port-Gentil, Gabon .. 46 E1
Port Gibson, U.S.A. .. 71 K9
Port Glasgow, U.K. .. 12 F4
Port Harcourt, Nigeria 44 H6
Port Hardy, Canada .. 64 C3
Port Harrison = Inukjuak, Canada ... 61 C12
Port Hawkesbury, Canada 63 C7
Port Hedland, Australia 52 D2
Port Henry, U.S.A. ... 68 C9
Port Hood, Canada .. 63 C7
Port Hope, Canada ... 62 D4
Port Huron, U.S.A. .. 68 D4
Port Isabel, U.S.A. ... 71 M6
Port Jefferson, U.S.A. 68 E9
Port Kelang = Pelabuhan Kelang, Malaysia 34 S14
Port Kembla, Australia 55 E5
Port Kenny, Australia . 55 E1
Port Laoise, Ireland .. 13 D4
Port Lavaca, U.S.A. .. 71 L6
Port Lincoln, Australia 55 E2
Port Loko, S. Leone .. 44 G2
Port Louis, Mauritius . 35 G4
Port Lyautey = Kenitra, Morocco 44 B3
Port MacDonnell, Australia 55 F3
Port Macquarie, Australia 55 E5
Port Maria, Jamaica .. 74 J17
Port Mellon, Canada . 64 D4
Port-Menier, Canada . 63 C7
Port Moresby, Papua N. G. 56 H6
Port Mouton, Canada 63 D7
Port Musgrave, Australia 54 A3
Port Nelson, Canada . 65 B10
Port Nolloth, S. Africa 48 D2
Port Nouveau-Québec = Kangiqsualujjuaq, Canada 61 C13
Port O'Connor, U.S.A. 71 L6
Port of Spain, Trin. & Tob. 74 S20
Port Orchard, U.S.A. . 72 C2
Port Orford, U.S.A. .. 72 E1
Port Pegasus, N.Z. ... 51 M1
Port Perry, Canada ... 62 D4
Port Phillip B., Australia 55 F3
Port Pirie, Australia .. 55 E2
Port Radium = Echo Bay, Canada 60 B8
Port Renfrew, Canada 64 D4
Port Roper, Australia . 54 A2
Port Rowan, Canada . 62 D3
Port Safaga = Bûr Safâga, Egypt 45 C11
Port Said = Bûr Sa'îd, Egypt 45 B11
Port St. Joe, U.S.A. .. 69 L3
Port St. Johns, S. Africa 49 E4
Port Sanilac, U.S.A. .. 62 D3
Port Saunders, Canada 63 B8
Port Shepstone, S. Africa 49 E5
Port Simpson, Canada 64 C2
Port Stanley = Stanley, Falk. Is. 80 G5
Port Stanley, Canada . 62 D3
Port Sudan = Bûr Sûdân, Sudan 45 E12
Port Talbot, U.K. 11 F4
Port Townsend, U.S.A. 72 B2
Port-Vendres, France . 18 E5
Port Vladimir, Russia . 22 A5
Port Wakefield, Australia 55 E2
Port Washington, U.S.A. 68 D2
Port Weld, Malaysia .. 34 Q13
Porta Orientalis, Romania 17 F12
Portachuelo, Bolivia .. 78 G6
Portadown, U.K. 13 B5
Portage, U.S.A. 70 D10
Portage La Prairie, Canada 65 D9
Portageville, U.S.A. .. 71 G10
Portalegre, Portugal . 19 C2
Portales, U.S.A. 71 H3
Portarlington, Ireland . 13 C4
Porter L., N.W.T., Canada 65 A7
Porter L., Sask., Canada 65 B7
Porterville, S. Africa .. 48 E2
Porterville, U.S.A. ... 73 H4
Porthcawl, U.K. 11 F4
Porthill, U.S.A. 72 B5
Portile de Fier, Europe 17 F12

Portimão, Portugal ... 19 D1
Portland, N.S.W., Australia 55 E4
Portland, Vic., Australia 55 F3
Portland, Maine, U.S.A. 63 D10
Portland, Mich., U.S.A. 68 D3
Portland, Oreg., U.S.A. 72 D2
Portland, I. of, U.K. .. 11 G5
Portland B., Australia . 55 F3
Portland Bill, U.K. ... 11 G5
Portland Prom., Canada 61 C12
Portlands Roads, Australia 54 A3
Portneuf, Canada ... 63 C5
Porto, Portugal 19 B1
Pôrto Alegre, Brazil .. 80 C6
Porto Amboim = Gunza, Angola 46 G2
Pôrto de Móz, Brazil . 79 D8
Porto Empédocle, Italy 20 F5
Porto Esperança, Brazil 78 G7
Pôrto Franco, Brazil . 79 E9
Pôrto Mendes, Brazil . 80 A6
Pôrto Murtinho, Brazil 78 H7
Pôrto Nacional, Brazil 79 F9
Porto Novo, Benin ... 44 G5
Porto Santo, Madeira . 44 B1
Pôrto Seguro, Brazil . 79 G11
Porto Tórres, Italy ... 20 D3
Pôrto União, Brazil .. 80 B6
Pôrto Válter, Brazil .. 78 E4
Pôrto-Vecchio, France 18 F8
Pôrto Velho, Brazil .. 78 E6
Portoferráio, Italy ... 20 C4
Portola, U.S.A. 72 G3
Portoscuso, Italy 20 E3
Portovíejo, Ecuador .. 78 D2
Portpatrick, U.K. 12 G3
Portree, U.K. 12 D2
Portrush, U.K. 13 A5
Portsmouth, Domin. . 74 M20
Portsmouth, U.K. 11 G6
Portsmouth, N.H., U.S.A. 68 D10
Portsmouth, Ohio, U.S.A. 68 F4
Portsmouth, Va., U.S.A. 68 G7
Portsoy, U.K. 12 D6
Porttipahtan tekojärvi, Finland 8 B22
Portugal ■, Europe .. 19 C1
Portumna, Ireland ... 13 C3
Porvenir, Chile 80 G2
Porvoo, Finland 9 F21
Posadas, Argentina .. 80 B5
Posht-e-Badam, Iran . 39 C7
Poso, Indonesia 33 E6
Posse, Brazil 79 F9
Possel, C.A.R. 46 C3
Possession I., Antarctica 5 D11
Post, U.S.A. 71 J4
Post Falls, U.S.A. 72 C5
Postavy = Pastavy, Belarus 9 J22
Poste Maurice Cortier, Algeria 44 D5
Postmasburg, S. Africa 48 D3
Postojna, Slovenia ... 16 F8
Potchefstroom, S. Africa 48 D4
Poteau, U.S.A. 71 H7
Poteet, U.S.A. 71 L5
Potenza, Italy 20 D6
Poteriteri, L., N.Z. ... 51 M1
Potgietersrus, S. Africa 49 C4
Poti, Georgia 23 F7
Potiskum, Nigeria ... 44 F7
Potomac →, U.S.A. . 68 F7
Potosí, Bolivia 78 G5
Potrerillos, Chile 80 B3
Potsdam, Germany .. 16 B7
Potsdam, U.S.A. 68 C8
Potter, U.S.A. 70 E3
Pottstown, U.S.A. ... 68 E8
Pottsville, U.S.A. 68 E7
Pottuvil, Sri Lanka ... 36 R12
Pouce Coupé, Canada 64 B4
Poughkeepsie, U.S.A. 68 E9
Poulaphouca Res., Ireland 13 C5
Poulsbo, U.S.A. 72 C2
Pouso Alegre, Brazil . 79 F7
Póvoa de Varzim, Portugal 19 B1
Powassan, Canada ... 62 C4
Powder →, U.S.A. .. 70 B2
Powder River, U.S.A. . 72 E10
Powell, U.S.A. 72 D9
Powell, L., U.S.A. 73 H8
Powell River, Canada 64 D4
Powers, Mich., U.S.A. 68 C2
Powers, Oreg., U.S.A. 72 E1
Powers Lake, U.S.A. . 70 A3
Powys □, U.K. 11 E4
Poyang Hu, China ... 31 D6
Poyarkovo, Russia ... 25 E13
Požarevac, Serbia, Yug. 21 B9
Poznań, Poland 17 B9
Pozo Almonte, Chile . 78 H5
Pozoblanco, Spain ... 19 C3
Pozzuoli, Italy 20 D6
Prachin Buri, Thailand 34 E6
Prachuap Khiri Khan, Thailand 34 G5
Prado, Brazil 79 G11
Prague = Praha, Czech. 16 C8
Praha, Czech. 16 C8

Prainha, Amazonas, Brazil 78 E6
Prainha, Pará, Brazil . 79 D8
Prairie, Australia 54 C3
Prairie →, U.S.A. ... 71 H5
Prairie City, U.S.A. .. 72 D4
Prairie du Chien, U.S.A. 70 D9
Prairies, Canada 60 C9
Prapat, Indonesia ... 32 D1
Prata, Brazil 79 G9
Prato, Italy 20 C4
Pratt, U.S.A. 71 G5
Prattville, U.S.A. 69 J2
Pravia, Spain 19 A2
Praya, Indonesia 32 F5
Preeceville, Canada .. 65 C8
Preili, Latvia 9 H22
Prelate, Canada 65 C7
Premier, Canada 64 B3
Premont, U.S.A. 71 M5
Prentice, U.S.A. 70 C9
Preobrazheniye, Russia 28 C6
Preparis North Channel, Ind. Oc. 34 E2
Preparis South Channel, Ind. Oc. ... 34 E2
Přerov, Czech. 17 D9
Prescott, Canada 62 D4
Prescott, Ariz., U.S.A. 73 J7
Prescott, Ark., U.S.A. 71 J8
Preservation Inlet, N.Z. 51 M1
Presho, U.S.A. 70 D4
Presidencia Roque Saenz Peña, Argentina 80 B4
Presidente Epitácio, Brazil 79 H8
Presidente Hermes, Brazil 78 F6
Presidente Prudente, Brazil 79 H8
Presidio, U.S.A. 71 L2
Prešov, Slovak Rep. .. 17 D11
Prespa, L. = Prespansko Jezero, Macedonia 21 D9
Prespansko Jezero, Macedonia 21 D9
Presque Isle, U.S.A. . 63 C6
Prestbury, U.K. 11 F5
Presteigne, U.K. 11 E5
Preston, U.K. 10 D5
Preston, Idaho, U.S.A. 72 E8
Preston, Minn., U.S.A. 70 D8
Preston, Nev., U.S.A. 72 G6
Preston, C., Australia . 52 D2
Prestonpans, U.K. ... 12 F6
Prestwick, U.K. 12 F4
Pretoria, S. Africa ... 49 D4
Préveza, Greece 21 E9
Prey-Veng, Cambodia 34 G8
Pribilof Is., Bering S. . 4 D17
Příbram, Czech. 16 D8
Price, U.S.A. 72 G8
Price I., Canada 64 C3
Prichard, U.S.A. 69 K1
Priekule, Latvia 9 H19
Prienai, Lithuania ... 9 J20
Prieska, S. Africa 48 D3
Priest →, U.S.A. 72 B5
Priest L., U.S.A. 72 B5
Priestly, Canada 64 C3
Prievidza, Slovak Rep. 17 D10
Prikaspiyskaya Nizmennost = Caspian Depression, Eurasia 23 E8
Prilep, Macedonia ... 21 D9
Priluki = Pryluky, Ukraine 23 D5
Prime Seal I., Australia 54 G4
Primrose L., Canada . 65 C7
Prince Albert, Canada 65 C7
Prince Albert, S. Africa 48 E3
Prince Albert Mts., Antarctica 5 D11
Prince Albert Nat. Park, Canada 65 C7
Prince Albert Pen., Canada 60 A8
Prince Albert Sd., Canada 60 A8
Prince Alfred, C., Canada 4 B1
Prince Charles I., Canada 61 B12
Prince Charles Mts., Antarctica 5 D6
Prince Edward I. □, Canada 63 C7
Prince Edward Is., Ind. Oc. 35 J2
Prince George, Canada 64 C4
Prince of Wales, C., U.S.A. 58 C3
Prince of Wales I., Australia 54 A3
Prince of Wales I., Canada 60 A10
Prince of Wales I., U.S.A. 64 B2
Prince Patrick I., Canada 4 B2
Prince Regent Inlet, Canada 4 B3
Prince Rupert, Canada 64 C2
Princess Charlotte B., Australia 54 A3
Princess May Ras., Australia 52 C4
Princess Royal I., Canada 64 C3
Princeton, Canada ... 64 D4

Princeton, Ill., U.S.A. . 70 E10
Princeton, Ind., U.S.A. 68 F2
Princeton, Ky., U.S.A. 68 G2
Princeton, Mo., U.S.A. 70 E8
Princeton, N.J., U.S.A. 68 E8
Princeton, W. Va., U.S.A. 68 G5
Principe, I. de, Atl. Oc. 42 F4
Principe Chan., Canada 64 C2
Principe da Beira, Brazil 78 F6
Prineville, U.S.A. 72 D3
Prins Harald Kyst, Antarctica 5 D4
Prinsesse Astrid Kyst, Antarctica 5 D3
Prinsesse Ragnhild Kyst, Antarctica .. 5 D4
Priozersk, Russia 22 B5
Pripet = Prypyat →, Europe 17 C16
Pripet Marshes, Europe 17 B15
Pripyat Marshes = Pripet Marshes, Europe 17 B15
Pripyats = Prypyat →, Europe 17 C16
Priština, Serbia, Yug. . 21 C9
Privas, France 18 D6
Privolzhskaya Vozvyshennost, Russia 23 D8
Prizren, Serbia, Yug. . 21 C9
Probolinggo, Indonesia 33 G15
Proddatur, India 36 M11
Progreso, Mexico ... 74 C7
Prokopyevsk, Russia . 24 D9
Prokuplje, Serbia, Yug. 21 C9
Prome = Pyè, Burma . 37 K19
Prophet →, Canada . 64 B4
Propriá, Brazil 79 F11
Proserpine, Australia . 54 C4
Prosser, U.S.A. 72 C4
Prostějov, Czech. 17 D9
Proston, Australia ... 55 D5
Protection, U.S.A. ... 71 G5
Provence, France 18 E6
Providence, Ky., U.S.A. 68 G2
Providence, R.I., U.S.A. 68 E10
Providence Bay, Canada 62 C3
Providence Mts., U.S.A. 73 J6
Providencia, I. de, Colombia 75 E8
Provideniya, Russia .. 25 C19
Provins, France 18 B5
Provo, U.S.A. 72 F8
Provost, Canada 65 C6
Prozna →, Poland ... 17 B9
Prud'homme, Canada 65 C7
Pruszków, Poland ... 17 B11
Prut →, Romania ... 17 F15
Pruzhany, Belarus ... 17 B13
Prydz B., Antarctica . 5 C6
Pryluky, Ukraine 23 D5
Pryor, U.S.A. 71 G7
Prypyat →, Europe .. 17 C16
Przemyśl, Poland 17 D12
Przhevalsk, Kyrgyzstan 24 E8
Psará, Greece 21 E11
Pskov, Russia 22 C4
Pskovskoye, Ozero, Russia 9 H22
Ptich = Ptsich →, Belarus 17 B15
Ptolemaís, Greece ... 21 D9
Ptsich →, Belarus ... 17 B15
Puán, Argentina 80 D4
Pucallpa, Peru 78 E4
Pudasjärvi, Finland .. 8 D22
Pudozh, Russia 22 B6
Pudukkottai, India ... 36 P11
Puebla, Mexico 74 D5
Pueblo, U.S.A. 70 F2
Pueblo Hundido, Chile 80 B2
Puelches, Argentina . 80 D3
Puente Alto, Chile ... 80 C2
Puente-Genil, Spain . 19 D3
Puerco →, U.S.A. .. 73 J10
Puerto Aisén, Chile .. 80 F2
Puerto Ayacucho, Venezuela 78 B5
Puerto Barrios, Guatemala 74 D7
Puerto Bermejo, Argentina 80 B5
Puerto Bermúdez, Peru 78 F4
Puerto Bolívar, Ecuador 78 D3
Puerto Cabello, Venezuela 78 A5
Puerto Cabezas, Nic. . 75 E8
Puerto Carreño, Colombia 78 B5
Puerto Chicama, Peru 78 E3
Puerto Coig, Argentina 80 G3
Puerto Cortés, Honduras 74 D7
Puerto Cumarebo, Venezuela 78 A5
Puerto del Rosario, Canary Is. 44 C2
Puerto Deseado, Argentina 80 F3
Puerto Heath, Bolivia 78 F5
Puerto La Cruz, Venezuela 78 A6
Puerto Leguízamo, Colombia 78 D4
Puerto Lobos, Argentina 80 E3
Puerto Maldonado, Peru 78 F5
Puerto Montt, Chile .. 80 E2

Puerto Morelos, Mexico 74 C7
Puerto Natales, Chile . 80 G2
Puerto Páez, Venezuela 78 B5
Puerto Pinasco, Paraguay 80 A5
Puerto Pirámides, Argentina 80 E4
Puerto Plata, Dom. Rep. 75 D10
Puerto Princesa, Phil. . 33 C5
Puerto Quellón, Chile . 80 E2
Puerto Rico ■, W. Indies 75 D11
Puerto Sastre, Paraguay 78 H7
Puerto Suárez, Bolivia 78 G7
Puerto Wilches, Colombia 78 B4
Puertollano, Spain ... 19 C3
Pueyrredón, L., Argentina 80 F2
Pugachev, Russia 22 D8
Puget Sound, U.S.A. . 72 C2
Pūgūnzī, Iran 39 E8
Puigcerdá, Spain 19 A6
Pukaki L., N.Z. 51 L3
Pukapuka, Cook Is. .. 57 J11
Pukatawagan, Canada 65 B8
Pukekohe, N.Z. 51 G5
Pula, Croatia 16 F7
Pulaski, N.Y., U.S.A. . 68 D7
Pulaski, Tenn., U.S.A. 69 H2
Pulaski, Va., U.S.A. .. 68 G5
Puławy, Poland 17 C11
Pulicat, L., India 36 N12
Pullman, U.S.A. 72 C5
Pulog, Phil. 33 A6
Pułtusk, Poland 17 B11
Pumlumon Fawr, U.K. 11 E4
Puna, Bolivia 78 G5
Puná, I., Ecuador 78 D2
Punakha, Bhutan 37 F16
Punata, Bolivia 78 G5
Punch, India 36 C9
Pune, India 36 K8
Punjab □, India 36 D9
Punjab □, Pakistan .. 36 D9
Puno, Peru 78 G4
Punta Alta, Argentina . 80 D4
Punta Arenas, Chile .. 80 G2
Punta de Díaz, Chile . 80 B2
Punta Gorda, U.S.A. . 69 M5
Puntabie, Australia .. 55 E1
Puntarenas, Costa Rica 75 F8
Punto Fijo, Venezuela 78 A4
Punxsatawney, U.S.A. 68 E6
Puquio, Peru 78 F4
Pur →, Russia 24 C8
Purace, Vol., Colombia 78 C3
Puralia = Puruliya, India 37 H15
Purbeck, Isle of, U.K. 11 G5
Purcell, U.S.A. 71 H6
Purcell Mts., Canada . 64 D5
Puri, India 37 K14
Purmerend, Neths. .. 15 B4
Purnia, India 37 G15
Pursat, Cambodia ... 34 F7
Purukcahu, Indonesia 32 E4
Puruliya, India 37 H15
Purus →, Brazil 78 D6
Purwakarta, Indonesia 33 G12
Purwodadi, Jawa, Indonesia 33 G14
Purwodadi, Jawa, Indonesia 33 G13
Purwokerto, Indonesia 33 G13
Purworejo, Indonesia 33 G14
Pusan, S. Korea 31 C7
Pushchino, Russia ... 25 D16
Pushkino, Russia 23 D8
Putao, Burma 37 F20
Putaruru, N.Z. 51 H5
Puthein Myit →, Burma 37 M19
Putignano, Italy 20 D7
Puting, Tanjung, Indonesia 32 E4
Putorana, Gory, Russia 25 C10
Puttalam, Sri Lanka .. 36 Q11
Putten, Neths. 15 B5
Puttgarden, Germany 16 A6
Putumayo →, S. Amer. 78 D5
Putussibau, Indonesia 32 D4
Puy-de-Dôme, France 18 D5
Puyallup, U.S.A. 72 C2
Pūzeh Rīg, Iran 39 E8
Pweto, Zaïre 46 F5
Pwllheli, U.K. 10 E3
Pya-ozero, Russia ... 22 A5
Pyapon, Burma 37 L19
Pyasina →, Russia .. 25 B9
Pyatigorsk, Russia ... 23 F7
Pyè, Burma 37 K19
Pyetrikaw, Belarus ... 17 B15
Pyhäjoki, Finland 8 D21
Pyinmana, Burma ... 37 K20
P'yŏngyang, N. Korea 31 C7
Pyote, U.S.A. 71 K3
Pyramid L., U.S.A. ... 72 G4
Pyrénées, Europe 19 A6
Pyu, Burma 37 K20

Q

Qaanaaq = Thule, Greenland 4 B4
Qachasnek, S. Africa . 49 E4
Qādib, Yemen 40 E5
Qa'el Jafr, Jordan ... 41 E5
Qa'emābād, Iran 39 D9

Qā'emshahr, *Iran* 39 B7
Qahremânshahr =
  Bâkhtarân, *Iran* 38 C5
Qaidam Pendi, *China* . . 30 C4
Qajarîyeh, *Iran* 39 D6
Qal'at al Akhḍar,
  Si. Arabia 38 E3
Qal'at Sukkar, *Iraq* . . . 38 D5
Qal'eh Darreh, *Iran* . . 38 B5
Qal'eh Shaharak,
  Afghan. 36 B4
Qamar, Ghubbat al,
  Yemen 40 D5
Qamdo, *China* 30 C4
Qamruddin Karez,
  Pakistan 36 D6
Qandahâr, *Afghan.* . . . 36 D4
Qandahâr □, *Afghan.* . 36 D4
Qapân, *Iran* 39 B7
Qapshaghay,
  Kazakhstan 24 E8
Qaqortoq =
  Julianehâb,
  Greenland 4 C5
Qâra, *Egypt* 45 C10
Qarabutaq, *Kazakhstan* 24 E7
Qaraghandy,
  Kazakhstan 24 E8
Qârah, *Si. Arabia* 38 D4
Qarataū, *Kazakhstan* . . 24 E8
Qareh →, *Iran* 38 B5
Qareh Tekân, *Iran* . . . 39 B6
Qarqan He →, *China* . . 30 C3
Qarqaraly, *Kazakhstan* 24 E8
Qarshi, *Uzbekistan* . . . 24 F7
Qartabâ, *Lebanon* 41 A4
Qaryat al Gharab, *Iraq* 38 D5
Qaryat al 'Ulyâ,
  Si. Arabia 38 E5
Qasr 'Amra, *Jordan* . . 38 D3
Qasr-e Qand, *Iran* . . . 39 E9
Qasr Farâfra, *Egypt* . . 45 C10
Qatanâ, *Syria* 41 B5
Qatar ■, *Asia* 39 E6
Qatlîsh, *Iran* 39 B8
Qattâra, Munkhafed el,
  Egypt 45 C10
Qattâra Depression =
  Qattâra, Munkhafed
  el, *Egypt* 45 C10
Qawâm al Ḥamzah, *Iraq* 38 D5
Qâyen, *Iran* 39 C8
Qazaqstan =
  Kazakhstan ■, *Asia* 24 E7
Qazvin, *Iran* 39 B6
Qena, *Egypt* 45 C11
Qeqertarsuaq = Disko,
  Greenland 4 C5
Qeqertarsuaq =
  Godhavn, *Greenland* . 4 C5
Qeshlâq, *Iran* 38 C5
Qeshm, *Iran* 39 E8
Qezi'ot, *Israel* 41 E3
Qibâ', *Si. Arabia* 38 E5
Qila Safed, *Pakistan* . . 36 E2
Qila Saifullâh, *Pakistan* 36 D6
Qilian Shan, *China* . . . 30 C4
Qingdao, *China* 31 C7
Qinghai □, *China* 30 C4
Qinghai Hu, *China* . . . 30 C5
Qingjiang, *China* 31 C6
Qinhuangdao, *China* . . 31 C6
Qinzhou, *China* 30 D5
Qiqihar, *China* 25 E13
Qiraîya, W. →, *Egypt* . 41 E3
Qiryat Ata, *Israel* 41 C4
Qiryat Gat, *Israel* 41 D3
Qiryat Mal'akhi, *Israel* 41 D3
Qiryat Shemona, *Israel* 41 B4
Qiryat Yam, *Israel* . . . 41 C4
Qitai, *China* 30 B3
Qojûr, *Iran* 38 B5
Qom, *Iran* 39 C6
Qomsheh, *Iran* 39 D6
Qostanay, *Kazakhstan* . 24 D7
Qu Xian, *China* 31 D6
Quairading, *Australia* . 53 F2
Qualeup, *Australia* . . . 53 F2
Quambatook, *Australia* 55 F3
Quambone, *Australia* . 55 E4
Quamby, *Australia* . . . 54 C3
Quan Long, *Vietnam* . 34 H8
Quanah, *U.S.A.* 71 H5
Quandialla, *Australia* . 55 E4
Quang Ngai, *Vietnam* . 34 E10
Quang Yen, *Vietnam* . 34 B9
Quantock Hills, *U.K.* . 11 F4
Quanzhou, *China* 31 D6
Quaqtaq, *Canada* 61 B13
Quarai, *Brazil* 80 C5
Quartu Sant'Elena, *Italy* 20 E3
Quartzsite, *U.S.A.* . . . 73 K6
Quatsino, *Canada* 64 C3
Quatsino Sd., *Canada* . 64 C3
Quba, *Azerbaijan* 23 F8
Qûchân, *Iran* 39 B8
Queanbeyan, *Australia* 55 F4
Québec, *Canada* 63 C5
Québec □, *Canada* . . . 63 B6
Queen Alexandra Ra.,
  Antarctica 5 E11
Queen Charlotte,
  Canada 64 C2
Queen Charlotte Is.,
  Canada 64 C2
Queen Charlotte Str.,
  Canada 64 C3
Queen Elizabeth Is.,
  Canada 58 B10
Queen Mary Land,
  Antarctica 5 D7
Queen Maud G.,
  Canada 60 B9

Queen Maud Land,
  Antarctica 5 D3
Queen Maud Mts.,
  Antarctica 5 E13
Queens Chan.,
  Australia 52 C4
Queenscliff, *Australia* . 55 F3
Queensland □,
  Australia 54 C3
Queenstown, *Australia* 54 G4
Queenstown, *N.Z.* . . . 51 L2
Queenstown, *S. Africa* 48 E4
Queimadas, *Brazil* . . . 79 F11
Quela, *Angola* 46 F3
Quelimane, *Mozam.* . . 47 H7
Quelpart = Cheju Do,
  S. Korea 31 C7
Quemado, N. Mex.,
  U.S.A. 73 J9
Quemado, Tex., *U.S.A.* 71 L4
Quequén, *Argentina* . . 80 D5
Querétaro, *Mexico* . . . 74 C4
Quesnel, *Canada* 64 C4
Quesnel →, *Canada* . . 64 C4
Quesnel L., *Canada* . . 64 C4
Questa, *U.S.A.* 73 H11
Quetico Prov. Park,
  Canada 62 C1
Quetta, *Pakistan* 36 D5
Quezon City, *Phil.* . . . 33 B6
Qufâr, *Si. Arabia* 38 E4
Qui Nhon, *Vietnam* . . 34 F10
Quibaxe, *Angola* 46 F2
Quibdo, *Colombia* . . . 78 B3
Quiberon, *France* 18 C2
Quick, *Canada* 64 C3
Quiet L., *Canada* 64 A2
Quilán, C., *Chile* 80 E2
Quilengues, *Angola* . . 47 G2
Quillabamba, *Peru* . . . 78 F4
Quillagua, *Chile* 78 H5
Quillota, *Chile* 80 C2
Quilon, *India* 36 Q10
Quilpie, *Australia* . . . 55 D3
Quimili, *Argentina* . . . 80 B4
Quimper, *France* 18 B1
Quimperlé, *France* . . . 18 C2
Quincy, Calif., *U.S.A.* . 72 G3
Quincy, Fla., *U.S.A.* . . 69 K3
Quincy, Ill., *U.S.A.* . . 70 F9
Quincy, Mass., *U.S.A.* 68 D10
Quincy, Wash., *U.S.A.* 72 C4
Quines, *Argentina* . . . 80 C3
Quinga, *Mozam.* 47 H8
Quintanar de la Orden,
  Spain 19 C4
Quintero, *Chile* 80 C2
Quinyambie, *Australia* 55 E3
Quirindi, *Australia* . . . 55 E5
Quissanga, *Mozam.* . . 47 G8
Quitilipi, *Argentina* . . 80 B4
Quitman, Ga., *U.S.A.* . 69 K4
Quitman, Miss., *U.S.A.* 69 J1
Quitman, Tex., *U.S.A.* 71 J7
Quito, *Ecuador* 78 D3
Quixadá, *Brazil* 79 D11
Qumbu, *S. Africa* 49 E4
Quneitra, *Syria* 41 B4
Qûnghirot, *Uzbekistan* 24 E6
Quoin I., *Australia* . . . 52 B4
Quoin Pt., *S. Africa* . . 48 E2
Quondong, *Australia* . 55 E3
Quorn, *Australia* 55 E2
Qûqon, *Uzbekistan* . . 24 E8
Qurnat as Sawdâ',
  Lebanon 41 A5
Qûs, *Egypt* 45 C11
Qusaybah, *Iraq* 38 C4
Quseir, *Egypt* 45 C11
Qûshchî, *Iran* 38 B5
Quthing, *Lesotho* 49 E4
Qûtîâbâd, *Iran* 39 C6
Qyzylorda, *Kazakhstan* 24 E7

R

Raahe, *Finland* 8 D21
Raasay, *U.K.* 12 D2
Raasay, Sd. of, *U.K.* . . 12 D2
Raba, *Indonesia* 33 F5
Rába →, *Hungary* 17 E9
Rabat, *Malta* 20 G6
Rabat, *Morocco* 44 B3
Rabaul, *Papua N. G.* . 56 H7
Rabbit →, *Canada* . . . 64 B3
Rabbit Lake, *Canada* . 65 C7
Rabbitskin →, *Canada* 64 A4
Râbor, *Iran* 39 D8
Race, C., *Canada* 63 C9
Rach Gia, *Vietnam* . . 34 G8
Racibórz, *Poland* 17 C10
Racine, *U.S.A.* 68 D2
Radama, Nosy, *Madag.* 49 A8
Radama, Saikanosy,
  Madag. 49 A8
Rădăuți, *Romania* . . . 17 E13
Radekhiv, *Ukraine* . . . 17 C13
Radekhov = Radekhiv,
  Ukraine 17 C13
Radford, *U.S.A.* 68 G5
Radisson, *Canada* . . . 65 C7
Radium Hot Springs,
  Canada 64 C5
Radnor Forest, *U.K.* . . 11 E4
Radom, *Poland* 17 C11
Radomsko, *Poland* . . . 17 C10
Radomyshl, *Ukraine* . 17 C15
Radstock, *U.K.* 11 F5
Radstock, C., *Australia* 55 E1

Radviliškis, *Lithuania* . 9 J20
Radville, *Canada* 65 D8
Rae, *Canada* 64 A5
Rae Bareli, *India* 37 F12
Rae Isthmus, *Canada* . 61 B11
Raeren, *Belgium* 15 D6
Raeside, L., *Australia* . 53 E3
Raetihi, *N.Z.* 51 H5
Rafaela, *Argentina* . . . 80 C4
Rafah, *Gaza Strip* . . . 41 D3
Rafai, *C.A.R.* 46 D4
Rafḥā, *Si. Arabia* 38 D4
Rafsanjân, *Iran* 39 D8
Raft Pt., *Australia* . . . 52 C3
Ragachow, *Belarus* . . 17 B16
Ragama, *Sri Lanka* . . . 36 R11
Ragged, Mt., *Australia* 53 F3
Raglan, *Australia* 54 C5
Raglan, *N.Z.* 51 G5
Ragusa, *Italy* 20 F6
Raha, *Indonesia* 33 E6
Rahad al Bardî, *Sudan* 45 F9
Rahaeng = Tak,
  Thailand 34 D5
Rahimyar Khan,
  Pakistan 36 E7
Râhjerd, *Iran* 39 C6
Raichur, *India* 36 L10
Raigarh, *India* 37 J13
Raijua, *Indonesia* 33 F6
Railton, *Australia* . . . 54 G4
Rainbow Lake, *Canada* 64 B5
Rainier, *U.S.A.* 72 D2
Rainier, Mt., *U.S.A.* . . 72 C3
Rainy L., *Canada* 65 D10
Rainy River, *Canada* . 65 D10
Raippaluoto, *Finland* . 8 E19
Raipur, *India* 37 J12
Raja, Ujung, *Indonesia* 32 D1
Raja Ampat,
  Kepulauan, *Indonesia* 33 E8
Rajahmundry, *India* . . 37 L12
Rajang →, *Malaysia* . . 32 D4
Rajapalaiyam, *India* . . 36 Q10
Rajasthan □, *India* . . . 36 F8
Rajasthan Canal, *India* 36 E8
Rajgarh, *India* 36 G10
Rajkot, *India* 36 H7
Rajpipla, *India* 36 J8
Rajshahi, *Bangla.* 37 G16
Rajshahi □, *Bangla.* . . 37 G16
Rakaia, *N.Z.* 51 K4
Rakaia →, *N.Z.* 51 K4
Rakan, Ra's, *Qatar* . . . 39 E6
Rakaposhi, *Pakistan* . . 36 A9
Rakata, Pulau,
  Indonesia 32 F3
Rakhiv, *Ukraine* 17 D13
Rakitnoye, *Russia* 28 B7
Rakops, *Botswana* . . . 48 C3
Rakvere, *Estonia* 9 G22
Raleigh, *U.S.A.* 69 H6
Raleigh B., *U.S.A.* . . . 69 H7
Ralls, *U.S.A.* 71 J4
Ram →, *Canada* 64 A4
Râm Allâh, *West Bank* 41 D4
Ram Hd., *Australia* . . 55 F4
Ramanathapuram, *India* 36 Q11
Ramanetaka, B. de,
  Madag. 49 A8
Ramat Gan, *Israel* . . . 41 C3
Ramatlhabama,
  S. Africa 48 D4
Rambipuji, *Indonesia* . 33 H15
Ramea, *Canada* 63 C8
Ramechhap, *Nepal* . . . 37 F15
Ramelau, *Indonesia* . . 33 F7
Ramgarh, Bihar, *India* 37 H14
Ramgarh, Raj., *India* . 36 F7
Râmhormoz, *Iran* . . . 39 D6
Râmiân, *Iran* 39 B7
Ramingining, *Australia* 54 A2
Ramla, *Israel* 41 D3
Ramnad =
  Ramanathapuram,
  India 36 Q11
Ramona, *U.S.A.* 73 K5
Ramore, *Canada* 62 C3
Ramotswa, *Botswana* . 48 C4
Rampur, *India* 36 E11
Rampur Hat, *India* . . . 37 G15
Ramree I. = Ramree
  Kyun, *Burma* 37 K18
Ramree Kyun, *Burma* . 37 K18
Râmsar, *Iran* 39 B6
Ramsey, *Canada* 62 C3
Ramsey, *U.K.* 10 C3
Ramsgate, *U.K.* 11 F9
Ramtek, *India* 36 J11
Ranaghat, *India* 37 H16
Ranau, *Malaysia* 32 C5
Rancagua, *Chile* 80 C2
Rancheria →, *Canada* . 64 A3
Ranchester, *U.S.A.* . . . 72 D10
Ranchi, *India* 37 H14
Randers, *Denmark* . . . 9 H14
Randfontein, *S. Africa* 49 D4
Randolph, *U.S.A.* 72 F8
Råne älv →, *Sweden* . 8 D20
Rangaunu B., *N.Z.* . . . 51 F4
Rangeley, *U.S.A.* 68 C10
Rangely, *U.S.A.* 72 F9
Rangia, *India* 37 F17
Rangiora, *N.Z.* 51 K4
Rangitaiki →, *N.Z.* . . . 51 G6
Rangitata →, *N.Z.* . . . 51 K3
Rangkasbitung,
  Indonesia 33 G12
Rangon →, *Burma* . . . 37 L20

Rangoon, *Burma* 37 L20
Rangpur, *Bangla.* 37 G16
Ranibennur, *India* . . . 36 M9
Raniganj, *India* 37 H15
Raniwara, *India* 36 G8
Râniyah, *Iraq* 38 B5
Ranken →, *Australia* . 54 C2
Rankin, *U.S.A.* 71 K4
Rankin Inlet, *Canada* . 60 B10
Rankins Springs,
  Australia 55 E4
Rannoch, L., *U.K.* . . . 12 E4
Rannoch Moor, *U.K.* . 12 E4
Ranobe, Helodranon' i,
  Madag. 49 C7
Ranohira, *Madag.* . . . 49 C8
Ranomafana,
  Toamasina, *Madag.* . 49 B8
Ranomafana, Toliara,
  Madag. 49 C8
Ranong, *Thailand* . . . 34 H5
Ransiki, *Indonesia* . . . 33 E8
Rantau, *Indonesia* . . . 32 E5
Rantauprapat,
  Indonesia 32 D1
Rantemario, *Indonesia* 33 E5
Rantoul, *U.S.A.* 68 E1
Rapa, *Pac. Oc.* 57 K13
Rapallo, *Italy* 20 B3
Râpch, *Iran* 39 E8
Rapid →, *Canada* 64 B3
Rapid City, *U.S.A.* . . . 70 D3
Rapid River, *U.S.A.* . . 68 C2
Rapides des Joachims,
  Canada 62 C4
Rapla, *Estonia* 9 G21
Rarotonga, *Cook Is.* . . 57 K12
Ra's al 'Ayn, *Syria* . . . 38 B4
Ra's al Khaymah,
  U.A.E. 39 E8
Ra's al-Unuf, *Libya* . . 45 B8
Ra's an Naqb, *Jordan* . 41 F4
Ras Bânâs, *Egypt* 45 D12
Ras Dashen, *Ethiopia* . 45 F12
Râs Timirist, *Mauritania* 44 E1
Rasa, Punta, *Argentina* 80 E4
Raseiniai, *Lithuania* . . 9 J20
Rashad, *Sudan* 45 F11
Rashîd, *Egypt* 45 B11
Rasht, *Iran* 39 B6
Rason L., *Australia* . . . 53 E3
Rat Buri, *Thailand* . . . 34 F5
Rat Islands, *U.S.A.* . . . 60 C1
Rat River, *Canada* . . . 64 A6
Ratangarh, *India* 36 E9
Raṭâwî, *Iraq* 38 D5
Rath Luirc, *Ireland* . . 13 D3
Rathdrum, *Ireland* . . . 13 D5
Rathenow, *Germany* . . 16 B7
Rathkeale, *Ireland* . . . 13 D3
Rathlin, *U.K.* 13 A5
Rathlin O'Birne I.,
  Ireland 13 B3
Ratibor = Racibórz,
  Poland 17 C10
Ratlam, *India* 36 H9
Ratnagiri, *India* 36 L8
Raton, *U.S.A.* 71 G2
Rattray Hd., *U.K.* 12 D7
Ratz, Mt., *Canada* . . . 64 B2
Raub, *Malaysia* 34 R14
Raufarhöfn, *Iceland* . . 8 C6
Raufoss, *Norway* 9 F14
Raukumara Ra., *N.Z.* . 51 H6
Rauma, *Finland* 9 F19
Raurkela, *India* 37 H14
Rausu-Dake, *Japan* . . 28 B12
Rava-Ruska, *Ukraine* . 17 C12
Rava Russkaya = Rava-
  Ruska, *Ukraine* 17 C12
Ravânsar, *Iran* 38 C5
Râvar, *Iran* 39 D8
Ravenna, *Italy* 20 B5
Ravenna, *U.S.A.* 70 E5
Ravensburg, *Germany* 16 E5
Ravenshoe, *Australia* . 54 B4
Ravensthorpe, *Australia* 53 F3
Ravenswood, *Australia* 54 C4
Ravenswood, *U.S.A.* . 68 F5
Ravi →, *Pakistan* 36 D7
Rawalpindi, *Pakistan* . 36 C8
Rawândûz, *Iraq* 38 B5
Rawang, *Malaysia* . . . 34 R14
Rawdon, *Canada* 62 C5
Rawene, *N.Z.* 51 F4
Rawlinna, *Australia* . . 53 F4
Rawlins, *U.S.A.* 72 F10
Rawlinson Ra.,
  Australia 53 D4
Rawson, *Argentina* . . 80 E3
Ray, *U.S.A.* 70 A3
Ray, C., *Canada* 63 C8
Rayadurg, *India* 36 M10
Rayagada, *India* 37 K13
Raychikhinsk, *Russia* . 25 E13
Râyen, *Iran* 39 D8
Raymond, *Canada* . . . 64 D6
Raymond, *U.S.A.* 72 C2
Raymondville, *U.S.A.* . 71 M6
Raymore, *Canada* . . . 65 C8
Rayne, *U.S.A.* 71 K8
Rayong, *Thailand* . . . 34 F6
Rayville, *U.S.A.* 71 J9
Raz, Pte. du, *France* . . 18 C1
Razan, *Iran* 39 C6
Razdel'naya =
  Rozdilna, *Ukraine* . . 17 E16
Razdolnoye, *Russia* . . 28 C5
Razeh, *Iran* 39 C6
Razelm, Lacul, *Romania* 17 F15
Razgrad, *Bulgaria* . . . 21 C12
Ré, I. de, *France* 18 C3

Reading, *U.K.* 11 F7
Reading, *U.S.A.* 68 E8
Realicó, *Argentina* . . . 80 D4
Ream, *Cambodia* 34 G7
Rebecca, L., *Australia* . 53 F3
Rebi, *Indonesia* 33 F8
Rebiana, *Libya* 45 D9
Rebun-Tô, *Japan* 28 B10
Recherche, Arch. of the,
  Australia 53 F3
Rechytsa, *Belarus* . . . 17 B16
Recife, *Brazil* 79 E12
Recklinghausen,
  Germany 15 C7
Reconquista, *Argentina* 80 B5
Recreo, *Argentina* . . . 80 B3
Red →, *La., U.S.A.* . . 71 K9
Red →, N. Dak.,
  U.S.A. 70 A6
Red Bay, *Canada* 63 B8
Red Bluff, *U.S.A.* 72 F2
Red Bluff L., *U.S.A.* . . 71 K3
Red Cliffs, *Australia* . 55 E3
Red Cloud, *U.S.A.* . . . 70 E5
Red Deer, *Canada* . . . 64 C6
Red Deer →, Alta.,
  Canada 65 C6
Red Deer →, Man.,
  Canada 65 C8
Red Deer L., *Canada* . 65 C8
Red Indian L., *Canada* 63 C8
Red Lake, *Canada* . . . 65 C10
Red Lake Falls, *U.S.A.* 70 B6
Red Lodge, *U.S.A.* . . . 72 D9
Red Oak, *U.S.A.* 70 E7
Red Rock, *Canada* . . . 62 C2
Red Rock, L., *U.S.A.* . 70 E8
Red Rocks Pt., *Australia* 53 F4
Red Sea, *Asia* 40 C2
Red Sucker L., *Canada* 65 C10
Red Tower Pass =
  Turnu Roşu, P.,
  Romania 17 F13
Red Wing, *U.S.A.* . . . 70 C8
Redbridge, *U.K.* 11 F8
Redcar, *U.K.* 10 C6
Redcliff, *Canada* 65 C6
Redcliffe, *Australia* . . 55 D5
Redcliffe, Mt., *Australia* 53 E3
Reddersburg, *S. Africa* 48 D4
Redding, *U.S.A.* 72 F2
Redditch, *U.K.* 11 E6
Redfield, *U.S.A.* 70 C5
Redknife →, *Canada* . 64 A5
Redlands, *U.S.A.* 73 K5
Redmond, *Australia* . . 53 F2
Redmond, *U.S.A.* 72 D3
Redon, *France* 18 C2
Redonda, *Antigua* . . . 74 L19
Redondela, *Spain* 19 A1
Redrock Pt., *Canada* . 64 A5
Redruth, *U.K.* 11 G2
Redvers, *Canada* 65 D8
Redwater, *Canada* . . . 64 C6
Redwood City, *U.S.A.* . 73 H2
Redwood Falls, *U.S.A.* 70 C7
Ree, L., *Ireland* 13 C4
Reed, L., *Canada* 65 C8
Reed City, *U.S.A.* 68 D3
Reeder, *U.S.A.* 70 B3
Reedley, *U.S.A.* 73 H4
Reedsburg, *U.S.A.* . . . 70 D9
Reedsport, *U.S.A.* . . . 72 E1
Reefton, *N.Z.* 51 K3
Refugio, *U.S.A.* 71 L6
Regensburg, *Germany* 16 D7
Réggio di Calábria, *Italy* 20 E6
Réggio nell'Emília, *Italy* 20 B4
Reghin, *Romania* 17 E13
Regina, *Canada* 65 C8
Rehoboth, *Namibia* . . 48 C2
Rehovot, *Israel* 41 D3
Rei-Bouba, *Cameroon* 45 G7
Reichenbach, *Germany* 16 C7
Reid, *Australia* 53 F4
Reid River, *Australia* . 54 B4
Reidsville, *U.S.A.* 69 G6
Reigate, *U.K.* 11 F7
Reims, *France* 18 B6
Reina Adelaida, Arch.,
  Chile 80 G2
Reinbeck, *U.S.A.* 70 D8
Reindeer →, *Canada* . 65 B8
Reindeer I., *Canada* . . 65 C9
Reindeer L., *Canada* . 65 B8
Reinga, C., *N.Z.* 51 F4
Reinosa, *Spain* 19 A3
Reitz, *S. Africa* 49 D4
Reivilo, *S. Africa* 48 D3
Rekinniki, *Russia* 25 C17
Reliance, *Canada* 65 A7
Remarkable, Mt.,
  Australia 55 E2
Rembang, *Indonesia* . 33 G14
Remeshk, *Iran* 39 E8
Remich, *Lux.* 15 E6
Rendsburg, *Germany* . 16 A5
Rene, *Russia* 25 C19
Renfrew, *Canada* 62 C4
Renfrew, *U.K.* 12 F4
Rengat, *Indonesia* . . . 32 E2
Reni, *Ukraine* 17 F15
Renk, *Sudan* 45 F11
Renkum, *Neths.* 15 C5
Renmark, *Australia* . . 55 E3
Rennell Sd., *Canada* . 64 C2
Renner Springs T.O.,
  Australia 54 B1
Rennes, *France* 18 B3
Reno, *U.S.A.* 72 G4
Reno →, *Italy* 20 B5
Renovo, *U.S.A.* 68 E7
Rensselaer, *U.S.A.* . . . 68 E2

Rentería, *Spain* 19 A5
Renton, *U.S.A.* 72 C2
Republic, Mich., *U.S.A.* 68 B2
Republic, Wash., *U.S.A.* 72 B4
Republican →, *U.S.A.* 70 F6
Republican City, *U.S.A.* 70 E5
Repulse Bay, *Canada* . 61 B11
Requena, *Peru* 78 E4
Requena, *Spain* 19 C5
Resadiye = Datça,
  Turkey 21 F12
Reserve, *Canada* 65 C8
Reserve, *U.S.A.* 73 K9
Resht = Rasht, *Iran* . . 39 B6
Resistencia, *Argentina* 80 B5
Reşiţa, *Romania* 17 F11
Resolution I., *Canada* . 61 B13
Resolution I., *N.Z.* . . . 51 L1
Ressano Garcia,
  Mozam. 49 D5
Reston, *Canada* 65 D8
Retford, *U.K.* 10 D7
Réthímnon, *Greece* . . 21 G11
Réunion ■, *Ind. Oc.* . 43 G21
Reus, *Spain* 19 B6
Reutlingen, *Germany* . 16 D5
Reval = Tallinn, *Estonia* 9 G21
Revda, *Russia* 22 C10
Revelstoke, *Canada* . . 64 C5
Revilla Gigedo, Is.,
  Pac. Oc. 57 F16
Revillagigedo I., *U.S.A.* 64 B2
Rewa, *India* 37 G12
Rewari, *India* 36 E10
Rexburg, *U.S.A.* 72 E8
Rey, *Iran* 39 C6
Rey Malabo, Eq. Guin. 44 H6
Reykjahlíð, *Iceland* . . 8 C5
Reykjanes, *Iceland* . . 8 E2
Reykjavík, *Iceland* . . . 8 D2
Reynolds, *Canada* . . . 65 D9
Reynolds Ra., *Australia* 52 C5
Reynosa, *Mexico* 74 B5
Rēzekne, *Latvia* 9 H22
Rezvân, *Iran* 39 E8
Rhayader, *U.K.* 11 E4
Rheden, *Neths.* 15 B6
Rhein, *Canada* 65 C8
Rhein →, *Europe* 15 C6
Rhein-Main-Donau-
  Kanal →, *Germany* . . 16 D6
Rheine, *Germany* 16 B4
Rheinland-Pfalz □,
  Germany 16 C4
Rhin = Rhein →,
  Europe 15 C6
Rhine = Rhein →,
  Europe 15 C6
Rhineland-Palatinate =
  Rheinland-Pfalz □,
  Germany 16 C4
Rhinelander, *U.S.A.* . . 70 C10
Rhode Island □, *U.S.A.* 68 E10
Rhodes = Ródhos,
  Greece 21 F13
Rhodesia =
  Zimbabwe ■, *Africa* 47 H5
Rhodope Mts. =
  Rhodopi Planina,
  Bulgaria 21 D11
Rhodopi Planina,
  Bulgaria 21 D11
Rhön = Hohe Rhön,
  Germany 16 C5
Rhondda, *U.K.* 11 F4
Rhône →, *France* 18 E6
Rhum, *U.K.* 12 E2
Rhyl, *U.K.* 10 D4
Rhymney, *U.K.* 11 F4
Riachão, *Brazil* 79 E9
Riasi, *India* 36 C9
Riau, *Indonesia* 32 D2
Riau, Kepulauan,
  Indonesia 32 D2
Riau Arch. = Riau,
  Kepulauan, *Indonesia* 32 D2
Ribadeo, *Spain* 19 A2
Ribble →, *U.K.* 10 C5
Ribe, *Denmark* 9 J13
Ribeirão Prêto, *Brazil* . 79 H9
Riberalta, *Bolivia* 78 F5
Ribniţa, *Moldova* 17 E15
Riccarton, *N.Z.* 51 K4
Rice Lake, *U.S.A.* 70 C9
Rich Hill, *U.S.A.* 71 F7
Richards Bay, *S. Africa* 49 D5
Richards L., *Canada* . 65 B7
Richardson →,
  Canada 65 B6
Richardton, *U.S.A.* . . . 70 B3
Riche, C., *Australia* . . 53 F2
Richey, *U.S.A.* 70 B2
Richfield, Idaho, *U.S.A.* 72 E6
Richfield, Utah, *U.S.A.* 73 G8
Richibucto, *Canada* . . 63 C7
Richland, Ga., *U.S.A.* . 69 J3
Richland, Oreg., *U.S.A.* 72 D5
Richland, Wash., *U.S.A.* 72 C4
Richland Center, *U.S.A.* 70 D9
Richlands, *U.S.A.* 68 G5
Richmond, N.S.W.,
  Australia 55 E5
Richmond, Queens.,
  Australia 54 C3
Richmond, *N.Z.* 51 J4
Richmond, *U.K.* 10 C6
Richmond, Calif., *U.S.A.* 72 H2
Richmond, Ind., *U.S.A.* 68 F3
Richmond, Ky., *U.S.A.* 68 G3
Richmond, Mo., *U.S.A.* 70 F8
Richmond, Tex., *U.S.A.* 71 L7
Richmond, Utah, *U.S.A.* 72 F8
Richmond, Va., *U.S.A.* 68 G7

St. Austell

Richmond Ra., Australia 55 D5
Richmond-upon-Thames, U.K. 11 F7
Richton, U.S.A. 69 K1
Richwood, U.S.A. 68 F5
Ridder, Kazakhstan 24 D9
Ridgedale, Canada 65 C8
Ridgeland, U.S.A. 69 J5
Ridgelands, Australia 54 C5
Ridgetown, Canada 62 D3
Ridgway, U.S.A. 68 E6
Riding Mountain Nat. Park, Canada 65 C8
Ridley, Mt., Australia 53 F3
Ried, Austria 16 D7
Riesa, Germany 16 C7
Riet →, S. Africa 48 D3
Rieti, Italy 20 C5
Rifle, U.S.A. 72 G10
Rig Rig, Chad 45 F7
Riga, Latvia 9 H21
Riga, G. of, Latvia 9 H20
Rīgān, Iran 39 D8
Rīgas Jūras Līcis = Riga, G. of, Latvia 9 H20
Rigby, U.S.A. 72 E8
Rīgestān □, Afghan. 36 D4
Riggins, U.S.A. 72 D5
Rigolet, Canada 63 B8
Riihimäki, Finland 9 F21
Riiser-Larsen-halvøya, Antarctica 5 C4
Rijeka, Croatia 16 F8
Rijn →, Neths. 15 B4
Rijssen, Neths. 15 B6
Rijswijk, Neths. 15 B4
Rikuzentakada, Japan 28 E10
Riley, U.S.A. 72 E4
Rimah, Wadi ar →, Si. Arabia 38 E4
Rimbey, Canada 64 C6
Rímini, Italy 20 B5
Rîmnicu Sărat, Romania 17 F14
Rîmnicu Vîlcea, Romania 17 F13
Rimouski, Canada 63 C6
Rinca, Indonesia 33 F5
Rinconada, Argentina 80 A3
Ringkøbing, Denmark 9 H13
Ringling, U.S.A. 72 C8
Ringvassøy, Norway 8 B18
Rinjani, Indonesia 32 F5
Rio Branco, Brazil 78 E5
Río Branco, Uruguay 80 C6
Rio Claro, Trin. & Tob. 74 S20
Río Colorado, Argentina 80 D4
Río Cuarto, Argentina 80 C4
Rio das Pedras, Mozam. 49 C6
Rio de Janeiro, Brazil 79 H10
Rio de Janeiro □, Brazil 79 H10
Rio do Sul, Brazil 80 B7
Río Gallegos, Argentina 80 G3
Río Grande, Argentina 80 G3
Rio Grande, Brazil 80 C6
Rio Grande →, U.S.A. 71 N6
Rio Grande City, U.S.A. 71 M5
Río Grande del Norte →, N. Amer. 67 E7
Rio Grande do Norte □, Brazil 79 E11
Rio Grande do Sul □, Brazil 80 B6
Rio Largo, Brazil 79 E11
Río Mulatos, Bolivia 78 G5
Río Muni = Mbini □, Eq. Guin. 46 D2
Rio Negro, Brazil 80 B7
Rio Verde, Brazil 79 G8
Rio Vista, U.S.A. 72 G3
Ríobamba, Ecuador 78 D3
Ríohacha, Colombia 78 A4
Ríosucio, Caldas, Colombia 78 B3
Ríosucio, Choco, Colombia 78 B3
Riou L., Canada 65 B7
Ripley, U.S.A. 71 H10
Ripon, U.K. 10 C6
Ripon, U.S.A. 68 D1
Rishā', W. ar →, Si. Arabia 38 E5
Rishiri-Tō, Japan 28 B10
Rishon le Ziyyon, Israel 41 D3
Rison, U.S.A. 71 J8
Risør, Norway 9 G13
Ritchies Archipelago, India 34 F2
Ritzville, U.S.A. 72 C4
Riva del Garda, Italy 20 B4
Rivadavia, Chile 80 B2
Rivera, Uruguay 80 C5
Riverhead, U.S.A. 68 E9
Riverhurst, Canada 65 C7
Riverina, Australia 53 E3
Rivers, Canada 65 C8
Rivers, L. of the, Canada 65 D7
Rivers Inlet, Canada 64 C3
Riversdale, S. Africa 48 E3
Riverside, Calif., U.S.A. 73 K5
Riverside, Wyo., U.S.A. 72 F10
Riversleigh, Australia 54 B2
Riverton, Australia 55 E2
Riverton, Canada 65 C9
Riverton, N.Z. 51 M1
Riverton, U.S.A. 72 E9
Riviera di Levante, Italy 20 B3
Riviera di Ponente, Italy 20 B3
Rivière-à-Pierre, Canada 63 C5
Rivière-au-Renard, Canada 63 C7
Rivière-du-Loup, Canada 63 C6
Rivière-Pentecôte, Canada 63 C6
Rivne, Ukraine 17 C14
Rívoli, Italy 20 B2
Rivoli B., Australia 55 F3
Riyadh = Ar Riyāḍ, Si. Arabia 40 C4
Rize, Turkey 23 F7
Rizzuto, C., Italy 20 E7
Rjukan, Norway 9 G13
Roag, L., U.K. 12 C2
Roanne, France 18 C6
Roanoke, Ala., U.S.A. 69 J3
Roanoke, Va., U.S.A. 68 G6
Roanoke →, U.S.A. 69 H7
Roanoke I., U.S.A. 69 H8
Roanoke Rapids, U.S.A. 69 G7
Robbins I., Australia 54 G4
Robe →, Australia 52 D2
Robe →, Ireland 13 C2
Robert Lee, U.S.A. 71 K4
Roberts, U.S.A. 72 E7
Robertson, S. Africa 48 E2
Robertson I., Antarctica 5 C18
Robertson Ra., Australia 52 D3
Robertsport, Liberia 44 G2
Robertstown, Australia 55 E2
Roberval, Canada 63 C5
Robeson Chan., Greenland 4 A4
Robinson →, Australia 54 B2
Robinson Ra., Australia 53 E2
Robinson River, Australia 54 B2
Robinvale, Australia 55 E3
Roblin, Canada 65 C8
Roboré, Bolivia 78 G7
Robson, Mt., Canada 64 C5
Robstown, U.S.A. 71 M6
Roca, C. da, Portugal 19 C1
Rocas, I., Brazil 79 D12
Rocha, Uruguay 80 C6
Rochdale, U.K. 10 D5
Rochefort, Belgium 15 D5
Rochefort, France 18 D3
Rochelle, U.S.A. 70 E10
Rocher River, Canada 64 A6
Rochester, Canada 64 C6
Rochester, U.K. 11 F8
Rochester, Ind., U.S.A. 68 E2
Rochester, Minn., U.S.A. 70 C8
Rochester, N.H., U.S.A. 68 D10
Rochester, N.Y., U.S.A. 68 D7
Rock →, Canada 64 A3
Rock Hill, U.S.A. 69 H5
Rock Island, U.S.A. 70 E9
Rock Rapids, U.S.A. 70 D6
Rock River, U.S.A. 72 F11
Rock Springs, Mont., U.S.A. 72 C10
Rock Springs, Wyo., U.S.A. 72 F9
Rock Valley, U.S.A. 70 D6
Rockall, Atl. Oc. 6 D3
Rockdale, U.S.A. 71 K6
Rockefeller Plateau, Antarctica 5 E14
Rockford, U.S.A. 70 D10
Rockglen, Canada 65 D7
Rockhampton, Australia 54 C5
Rockhampton Downs, Australia 54 B2
Rockingham, Australia 53 F2
Rockingham B., Australia 54 B4
Rockingham Forest, U.K. 11 E7
Rocklake, U.S.A. 70 A5
Rockland, Idaho, U.S.A. 72 E7
Rockland, Maine, U.S.A. 63 D6
Rockland, Mich., U.S.A. 70 B10
Rockmart, U.S.A. 69 H3
Rockport, Mo., U.S.A. 70 E7
Rockport, Tex., U.S.A. 71 L6
Rocksprings, U.S.A. 71 K4
Rockville, U.S.A. 68 F7
Rockwall, U.S.A. 71 J6
Rockwell City, U.S.A. 70 D7
Rockwood, U.S.A. 69 H3
Rocky Ford, U.S.A. 70 F3
Rocky Gully, Australia 53 F2
Rocky Lane, Canada 64 B5
Rocky Mount, U.S.A. 69 H7
Rocky Mountain House, Canada 64 C6
Rocky Mts., N. Amer. 64 C4
Rockyford, Canada 64 C6
Rod, Pakistan 36 E3
Rødbyhavn, Denmark 9 J14
Roddickton, Canada 63 B8
Roderick I., Canada 64 C3
Rodez, France 18 D5
Ródhos, Greece 21 F13
Rodney, C., N.Z. 51 G5
Rodriguez, Ind. Oc. 35 F5
Roe →, U.K. 13 A5
Roebourne, Australia 52 D2
Roebuck B., Australia 52 C3
Roebuck Plains, Australia 52 C3
Roermond, Neths. 15 C5
Roes Welcome Sd., Canada 61 B11
Roeselare, Belgium 15 D3
Rogachev = Ragachow, Belarus 17 B16
Rogagua, L., Bolivia 78 F5
Rogatyn, Ukraine 17 D13
Rogers, U.S.A. 71 G7
Rogers City, U.S.A. 68 C4
Rogerson, U.S.A. 72 E6
Rogersville, U.S.A. 69 G4
Roggan River, Canada 62 B4
Roggeveldberge, S. Africa 48 E3
Rogoaguado, L., Bolivia 78 F5
Rogue →, U.S.A. 72 E1
Rohri, Pakistan 36 F6
Rohtak, India 36 E10
Roi Et, Thailand 34 D7
Roja, Latvia 9 H20
Rojas, Argentina 80 C4
Rojo, C., Mexico 74 C5
Rokan →, Indonesia 32 D2
Rokeby, Australia 54 A3
Rokiškis, Lithuania 9 J21
Rolândia, Brazil 80 A6
Rolette, U.S.A. 70 A5
Rolla, Kans., U.S.A. 71 G4
Rolla, Mo., U.S.A. 71 G9
Rolla, N. Dak., U.S.A. 70 A5
Rolleston, Australia 54 C4
Rollingstone, Australia 54 B4
Roma, Australia 55 D4
Roma, Italy 20 D5
Roma, Sweden 9 H18
Roman, Romania 17 E14
Roman, Russia 25 C12
Romang, Indonesia 33 F7
Românî, Egypt 41 E1
Romania ■, Europe 17 F12
Romanovka = Basarabeasca, Moldova 17 E15
Romans-sur-Isère, France 18 D6
Romblon, Phil. 33 B6
Rome = Roma, Italy 20 D5
Rome, Ga., U.S.A. 69 H3
Rome, N.Y., U.S.A. 68 D8
Romney, U.S.A. 68 F6
Romney Marsh, U.K. 11 F8
Rømø, Denmark 9 J13
Romorantin-Lanthenay, France 18 C4
Romsdalen, Norway 9 E12
Rona, U.K. 12 D3
Ronan, U.S.A. 72 C6
Roncador, Serra do, Brazil 79 F8
Ronceverte, U.S.A. 68 G5
Ronda, Spain 19 D3
Rondane, Norway 9 F13
Rondônia □, Brazil 78 F6
Rondonópolis, Brazil 79 G8
Rong, Koh, Cambodia 34 G7
Ronge, L. la, Canada 65 B7
Rønne, Denmark 9 J16
Ronne Ice Shelf, Antarctica 5 D18
Ronsard, C., Australia 53 D1
Ronse, Belgium 15 D3
Roodepoort, S. Africa 49 D4
Roof Butte, U.S.A. 73 H9
Roorkee, India 36 E10
Roosendaal, Neths. 15 C4
Roosevelt, Minn., U.S.A. 70 A7
Roosevelt, Utah, U.S.A. 72 F8
Roosevelt →, Brazil 78 E6
Roosevelt, Mt., Canada 64 B3
Roosevelt I., Antarctica 5 D12
Roosevelt Res., U.S.A. 73 K8
Roper →, Australia 54 A2
Ropesville, U.S.A. 71 J3
Roquetas de Mar, Spain 19 D4
Roraima □, Brazil 78 C6
Roraima, Mt., Venezuela 78 B6
Rorketon, Canada 65 C9
Røros, Norway 9 E14
Rosa, Zambia 46 F6
Rosa, Monte, Europe 16 F4
Rosalia, U.S.A. 72 C5
Rosario, Argentina 80 C4
Rosário, Brazil 79 D10
Rosario, Mexico 74 C3
Rosario, Paraguay 80 A5
Rosario de la Frontera, Argentina 80 B4
Rosário do Sul, Brazil 80 C6
Rosas, G. de, Spain 19 A7
Roscoe, U.S.A. 70 C5
Roscommon, Ireland 13 C3
Roscommon, U.S.A. 68 C3
Roscommon □, Ireland 13 C3
Roscrea, Ireland 13 D4
Rose →, Australia 54 A2
Rose Blanche, Canada 63 C8
Rose Harbour, Canada 64 C2
Rose Pt., Canada 64 C2
Rose Valley, Canada 65 C8
Roseau, Domin. 74 M20
Roseau, U.S.A. 70 A7
Rosebery, Australia 54 G4
Rosebud, U.S.A. 71 K6
Roseburg, U.S.A. 72 E2
Rosedale, Australia 54 C5
Rosedale, U.S.A. 71 J9
Rosemary, Canada 64 C6
Rosenberg, U.S.A. 71 L7
Rosenheim, Germany 16 E7
Rosetown, Canada 65 C7
Rosetta = Rashîd, Egypt 45 B11
Roseville, U.S.A. 72 G3
Rosewood, N. Terr., Australia 52 C4
Rosewood, Queens., Australia 55 D5
Roshkhvār, Iran 39 C8
Rosignano Maríttimo, Italy 20 C4
Rosignol, Guyana 78 B7
Roşiori-de-Vede, Romania 17 F13
Roskilde, Denmark 9 J15
Roslavl, Russia 22 D5
Roslyn, Australia 55 E4
Rosmead, S. Africa 48 E4
Ross, Australia 54 G4
Ross, N.Z. 51 K3
Ross I., Antarctica 5 D11
Ross Ice Shelf, Antarctica 5 E12
Ross L., U.S.A. 72 B3
Ross-on-Wye, U.K. 11 F5
Ross Sea, Antarctica 5 D11
Rossan Pt., Ireland 13 B3
Rossano Cálabro, Italy 20 E7
Rossburn, Canada 65 C8
Rossignol, L., Canada 62 B5
Rossignol Res., Canada 63 D6
Rossland, Canada 64 D5
Rosslare, Ireland 13 D5
Rosso, Mauritania 44 E1
Rossosh, Russia 23 D6
Rossport, Canada 62 C2
Røssvatnet, Norway 8 D16
Rossville, Australia 54 B4
Røst, Norway 8 C15
Rosthern, Canada 65 C7
Rostock, Germany 16 A7
Rostov, Don, Russia 23 E6
Rostov, Yarosl, Russia 22 C6
Roswell, U.S.A. 71 J2
Rosyth, U.K. 12 E5
Rotan, U.S.A. 71 J4
Rother →, U.K. 11 G8
Rotherham, U.K. 10 D6
Rothes, U.K. 12 D5
Rothesay, Canada 63 C6
Rothesay, U.K. 12 F3
Roti, Indonesia 33 F6
Roto, Australia 55 E4
Rotondo Mte., France 18 E8
Rotoroa, L., N.Z. 51 J4
Rotorua, N.Z. 51 H6
Rotorua, L., N.Z. 51 H6
Rotterdam, Neths. 15 C4
Rottnest I., Australia 53 F2
Rottumeroog, Neths. 15 A6
Rottweil, Germany 16 D5
Rotuma, Fiji 56 J9
Roubaix, France 18 A5
Rouen, France 18 B4
Rouleau, Canada 65 C8
Round Mountain, U.S.A. 72 G5
Round Mt., Australia 55 E5
Roundup, U.S.A. 72 C9
Rousay, U.K. 12 B5
Roussillon, France 18 E5
Rouxville, S. Africa 48 E4
Rouyn, Canada 62 C4
Rovaniemi, Finland 8 C21
Rovereto, Italy 20 B4
Rovigo, Italy 20 B4
Rovinj, Croatia 16 F7
Rovno = Rivne, Ukraine 17 C14
Rovuma →, Tanzania 46 G8
Row'ān, Iran 39 C6
Rowena, Australia 55 D4
Rowley Shoals, Australia 52 C2
Roxas, Phil. 33 B6
Roxboro, U.S.A. 69 G6
Roxborough Downs, Australia 54 C2
Roxburgh, N.Z. 51 L2
Roy, Mont., U.S.A. 72 C9
Roy, N. Mex., U.S.A. 71 H2
Roy Hill, Australia 52 D2
Royal Leamington Spa, U.K. 11 E6
Royal Tunbridge Wells, U.K. 11 F8
Royan, France 18 D3
Rozdilna, Ukraine 17 E16
Rozhyshche, Ukraine 17 C13
Rtishchevo, Russia 22 C7
Ruacaná, Angola 48 B1
Ruahine Ra., N.Z. 51 H6
Ruapehu, N.Z. 51 H5
Ruapuke I., N.Z. 51 M2
Ruâq, W. →, Egypt 41 F2
Rub' al Khali, Si. Arabia 40 D4
Rubh a' Mhail, U.K. 12 F2
Rubha Hunish, U.K. 12 D2
Rubha Robhanais = Lewis, Butt of, U.K. 12 C2
Rubio, Venezuela 78 B4
Rubtsovsk, Russia 24 D9
Ruby L., U.S.A. 72 F6
Ruby Mts., U.S.A. 72 F6
Rūd Sar, Iran 39 B6
Rudall, Australia 55 E2
Rudall →, Australia 52 D3
Rudnichnyy, Russia 22 C9
Rudnogorsk, Russia 25 D11
Rudnyy, Kazakhstan 24 D7
Rudolf, Ostrov, Russia 24 A6
Rudyard, U.S.A. 68 B3
Rufa'a, Sudan 45 F11
Rufiji →, Tanzania 46 F7
Rufino, Argentina 80 C4
Rufisque, Senegal 44 F1
Rugby, U.K. 11 E6
Rugby, U.S.A. 70 A5
Rügen, Germany 16 A7
Ruhnu saar, Estonia 9 H20
Ruhr →, Germany 16 C4
Ruidosa, U.S.A. 71 L2
Ruidoso, U.S.A. 73 K11
Rujm Tal'at al Jamā'ah, Jordan 41 E4
Rukwa L., Tanzania 46 F6
Rulhieres, C., Australia 52 B4
Rum Jungle, Australia 52 B5
Rumāḥ, Si. Arabia 38 E5
Rumania = Romania ■, Europe 17 F12
Rumaylah, Iraq 38 D5
Rumbalara, Australia 54 D1
Rumbêk, Sudan 45 G10
Rumford, U.S.A. 68 C10
Rumia, Poland 17 A10
Rumoi, Japan 28 C10
Rumsey, Canada 64 C6
Rumula, Australia 54 B4
Runanga, N.Z. 51 K3
Runaway, C., N.Z. 51 G6
Runcorn, U.K. 10 D5
Rungwa, Tanzania 46 F6
Runton Ra., Australia 52 D3
Ruoqiang, China 30 C3
Rupa, India 37 F18
Rupat, Indonesia 32 D2
Rupert →, Canada 62 B4
Rupert House = Waskaganish, Canada 62 B4
Rurrenabaque, Bolivia 78 F5
Rusape, Zimbabwe 47 H6
Ruschuk = Ruse, Bulgaria 21 C12
Ruse, Bulgaria 21 C12
Rushden, U.K. 11 E7
Rushford, U.S.A. 70 D9
Rushville, Ill., U.S.A. 70 E9
Rushville, Ind., U.S.A. 68 F3
Rushville, Nebr., U.S.A. 70 D3
Rushworth, Australia 55 F4
Russas, Brazil 79 D11
Russell, Canada 65 C8
Russell, U.S.A. 70 F5
Russell L., Man., Canada 65 B8
Russell L., N.W.T., Canada 64 A5
Russellkonda, India 37 K14
Russellville, Ala., U.S.A. 69 H2
Russellville, Ark., U.S.A. 71 H8
Russellville, Ky., U.S.A. 69 G2
Russia ■, Eurasia 25 C11
Russkaya Polyana, Kazakhstan 24 D8
Russkoye Ustie, Russia 4 B15
Rustavi, Georgia 23 F8
Rustenburg, S. Africa 48 D4
Ruston, U.S.A. 71 J8
Ruteng, Indonesia 33 F6
Ruth, U.S.A. 72 G6
Rutherglen, U.K. 12 F4
Rutland I., India 34 G2
Rutland Plains, Australia 54 B3
Rutledge →, Canada 65 A6
Rutledge L., Canada 65 A6
Rutshuru, Zaïre 46 E5
Ruurlo, Neths. 15 B6
Ruwais, U.A.E. 39 E7
Ruwenzori, Africa 46 D5
Ružomberok, Slovak Rep. 17 D10
Rwanda ■, Africa 46 E5
Ryan, L., U.K. 12 G3
Ryazan, Russia 22 D6
Ryazhsk, Russia 22 D7
Rybache = Rybachye, Kazakhstan 24 E9
Rybachiy Poluostrov, Russia 22 A5
Rybachye, Kazakhstan 24 E9
Rybinsk, Russia 22 C6
Rybinskoye Vdkhr., Russia 22 C6
Rybnitsa = Rîbniţa, Moldova 17 E15
Ryde, U.K. 11 G6
Rye, U.K. 11 G8
Rye →, U.K. 10 C7
Rye Patch Reservoir, U.S.A. 72 F4
Ryegate, U.S.A. 72 C9
Rylstone, Australia 55 E4
Ryōthu, Japan 28 E9
Rypin, Poland 17 B10
Ryūgasaki, Japan 29 G10
Ryūkyū Is. = Ryūkyū-rettō, Japan 29 M2
Ryūkyū-rettō, Japan 29 M2
Rzeszów, Poland 17 C11
Rzhev, Russia 22 C5

S

Sa Dec, Vietnam 34 G8
Sa'ādatābād, Fārs, Iran 39 D7
Sa'ādatābād, Kermān, Iran 39 D7
Saale →, Germany 16 C6
Saalfeld, Germany 16 C6
Saar →, Europe 16 D4
Saarbrücken, Germany 16 D4
Saaremaa, Estonia 9 G20
Saarijärvi, Finland 9 E21
Saariselkä, Finland 8 B23
Saarland □, Germany 15 E7
Sab 'Ābar, Syria 38 C3
Saba, W. Indies 74 K18
Šabac, Serbia, Yug. 21 B8
Sabadell, Spain 19 B7
Sabah □, Malaysia 32 C5
Sábanalarga, Colombia 78 A4
Sabang, Indonesia 32 C1
Sabará, Brazil 79 G10
Saberania, Indonesia 33 E9
Sabhah, Libya 45 C7
Sabie, S. Africa 49 D5
Sabinal, U.S.A. 71 L5
Sabinas, Mexico 74 B4
Sabinas Hidalgo, Mexico 74 B4
Sabine →, U.S.A. 71 L8
Sabine L., U.S.A. 71 L8
Sabine Pass, U.S.A. 71 L8
Sabkhet el Bardawîl, Egypt 41 D2
Sablayan, Phil. 33 B6
Sable, C., Canada 63 D6
Sable, C., U.S.A. 67 E10
Sable I., Canada 63 D8
Sabrina Coast, Antarctica 5 C9
Sabulubek, Indonesia 32 E1
Sabzevār, Iran 39 B8
Sabzvārān, Iran 39 D8
Sac City, U.S.A. 70 D7
Săcele, Romania 17 F13
Sachigo →, Canada 62 A2
Sachigo, L., Canada 62 B1
Sachsen □, Germany 16 C7
Sachsen-Anhalt □, Germany 16 C7
Saco, Maine, U.S.A. 69 D10
Saco, Mont., U.S.A. 72 B10
Sacramento, U.S.A. 72 G3
Sacramento →, U.S.A. 72 G3
Sacramento Mts., U.S.A. 73 K11
Sadani, Tanzania 46 F7
Sadao, Thailand 34 N13
Sadd el Aali, Egypt 45 D11
Sado, Japan 28 E9
Sadon, Burma 37 G20
Sæby, Denmark 9 H14
Şafājah, Si. Arabia 38 E3
Säffle, Sweden 9 G15
Safford, U.S.A. 73 K9
Saffron Walden, U.K. 11 E8
Safi, Morocco 44 B3
Şafīābād, Iran 39 B8
Safīd Dasht, Iran 39 C6
Safīd Kūh, Afghan. 36 B3
Safwān, Iraq 38 D5
Saga, Indonesia 33 E8
Saga, Japan 29 H5
Saga □, Japan 29 H5
Sagae, Japan 28 E10
Sagala, Mali 44 F3
Sagar, India 36 M9
Saginaw, U.S.A. 68 D4
Saginaw B., U.S.A. 68 D4
Şagīr, Zāb aş →, Iraq 38 C4
Saglouc = Salluit, Canada 61 B12
Sagua la Grande, Cuba 75 C8
Saguache, U.S.A. 73 G10
Saguenay →, Canada 63 C5
Sagunto, Spain 19 C5
Sahagún, Spain 19 A3
Saḥam al Jawlān, Syria 41 C4
Sahand, Kūh-e, Iran 38 B5
Sahara, Africa 44 D5
Saharan Atlas = Saharien, Atlas, Algeria 44 B5
Saharanpur, India 36 E10
Saharien, Atlas, Algeria 44 B5
Sahasinaka, Madag. 49 C8
Şāḥilīyah, Iraq 38 C4
Sahiwal, Pakistan 36 D8
Şaḥneh, Iran 38 C5
Sahtaneh →, Canada 64 B4
Sahuarita, U.S.A. 73 L8
Sa'id Bundas, Sudan 45 G9
Saïda, Algeria 44 B5
Sa'īdābād, Kermān, Iran 39 D7
Sa'īdābād, Semnān, Iran 39 B7
Sa'īdīyeh, Iran 39 B6
Saidpur, Bangla. 37 G16
Saidu, Pakistan 36 B8
Saigon = Phanh Bho Ho Chi Minh, Vietnam 34 G9
Saijō, Japan 29 H6
Saikhoa Ghat, India 37 F19
Saiki, Japan 29 H5
Sailolof, Indonesia 33 E8
Saimaa, Finland 9 F23
Şa'in Dezh, Iran 38 B5
St. Abb's Head, U.K. 12 F6
St. Alban's, Canada 63 C8
St. Albans, U.K. 11 F7
St. Albans, Vt., U.S.A. 68 C9
St. Albans, W. Va., U.S.A. 68 F5
St. Alban's Head, U.K. 11 G5
St. Albert, Canada 64 C6
St. Andrew's, Canada 63 C8
St. Andrews, U.K. 12 E6
St. Ann B., Canada 63 C7
St. Anthony, Canada 63 B8
St. Anthony, U.S.A. 72 E8
St. Arnaud, Australia 55 F3
St. Arthur, Canada 63 C6
St. Asaph, U.K. 10 D4
St-Augustin-Saguenay, Canada 63 B8
St. Augustine, U.S.A. 69 L5
St. Austell, U.K. 11 G3

St.-Barthélemy, I.

St.-Barthélemy, I.,
  W. Indies 74 K19
St. Bee's Hd., *U.K.* . . . 10 C4
St. Boniface, *Canada* . . 65 D9
St. Bride's, *Canada* . . . 63 C9
St. Brides B., *U.K.* 11 F2
St.-Brieuc, *France* 18 B2
St. Catharines, *Canada* . 62 D4
St. Catherines I., *U.S.A.* 69 K5
St. Catherine's Pt., *U.K.* 11 G6
St.-Chamond, *France* . . 18 D6
St. Charles, *Ill., U.S.A.* . 68 E1
St. Charles, *Mo., U.S.A.* 70 F9
St. Christopher = St.
  Kitts, *W. Indies* 74 K19
St. Christopher-
  Nevis ■, *W. Indies* . . 74 K19
St. Clair, L., *Canada* . . 62 D3
St. Claude, *Canada* . . . 65 D9
St. Cloud, *Fla., U.S.A.* . 69 L5
St. Cloud, *Minn., U.S.A.* 70 C7
St-Coeur de Marie,
  Canada 63 C5
St. Cricq, C., *Australia* . 53 E1
St. Croix, *Virgin Is.* . . . 75 D12
St. Croix →, *U.S.A.* . . . 70 C8
St. Croix Falls, *U.S.A.* . 70 C8
St. David's, *Canada* . . . 63 C8
St. David's, *U.K.* 11 F2
St. David's Head, *U.K.* . 11 F2
St.-Denis, *France* 18 B5
St.-Denis, *Réunion* . . . 35 G4
St.-Dizier, *France* 18 B6
St. Elias, Mt., *U.S.A.* . . 60 B5
St. Elias Mts., *Canada* . 64 A1
St.-Étienne, *France* . . . 18 D6
St. Eustatius, *W. Indies* 74 K19
St-Félicien, *Canada* . . . 62 C5
St.-Flour, *France* 18 D5
St. Francis, *U.S.A.* 68 F2
St. Francis →, *U.S.A.* . . 71 H9
St. Francis, C., *S. Africa* 48 E3
St. Francisville, *U.S.A.* . 71 K9
St-Gabriel-de-Brandon,
  Canada 62 C5
St. Gallen = Sankt
  Gallen, *Switz.* 16 E5
St.-Gaudens, *France* . . 18 E4
St. George, *Australia* . . 55 D4
St. George, *Canada* . . . 63 C6
St. George, *S.C., U.S.A.* 69 J5
St. George, *Utah,*
  U.S.A. 73 H7
St. George, C., *Canada* . 63 C8
St. George, C., *U.S.A.* . 69 L3
St. George Ra.,
  Australia 52 C4
St-Georges, *Belgium* . . 15 D5
St.-Georges, *Canada* . . 63 C5
St-Georges, *Fr. Guiana* 79 C8
St. George's, *Grenada* . 74 Q20
St. George's B., *Canada* 63 C8
St. Georges Basin,
  Australia 52 C4
St. George's Channel,
  Europe 13 E6
St. Georges Hd.,
  Australia 55 F5
St. Gotthard P. = San
  Gottardo, P. del,
  Switz. 16 E5
St. Helena, *U.S.A.* 72 G2
St. Helena ■, *Atl. Oc.* . 2 E9
St. Helena B., *S. Africa* 48 E2
St. Helens, *Australia* . . 54 G4
St. Helens, *U.K.* 10 D5
St. Helens, *U.S.A.* 72 D2
St. Helier, *U.K.* 11 H5
St-Hubert, *Belgium* . . . 15 D5
St-Hyacinthe, *Canada* . 62 C5
St-Ignace, *U.S.A.* 68 C3
St. Ignace I., *Canada* . . 62 C2
St. Ignatius, *U.S.A.* . . . 72 C6
St. Ives, *Cambs., U.K.* . 11 E7
St. Ives, *Corn., U.K.* . . 11 G2
St. James, *U.S.A.* 70 D7
St-Jean, *Canada* 62 C5
St-Jean →, *Canada* . . . 63 B7
St-Jean, L., *Canada* . . . 63 C5
St. Jean Baptiste,
  Canada 65 D9
St-Jean-Port-Joli,
  Canada 63 C5
St-Jérôme, *Qué.,*
  Canada 62 C5
St-Jérôme, *Qué.,*
  Canada 63 C5
St. John, *Canada* 63 C6
St. John, *Kans., U.S.A.* . 71 G5
St. John, *N. Dak.,*
  U.S.A. 70 A5
St. John →, *U.S.A.* . . . 63 C6
St. John, C., *Canada* . . 63 B8
St. John's, *Antigua* . . . 74 K20
St. John's, *Canada* . . . 63 C9
St. Johns, *Ariz., U.S.A.* 73 J9
St. Johns, *Mich., U.S.A.* 68 D3
St. Johns →, *U.S.A.* . . 69 K5
St. Johnsbury, *U.S.A.* . 68 C9
St. Joseph, *La., U.S.A.* 71 K9
St. Joseph, *Mich.,*
  U.S.A. 68 D2
St. Joseph, *Mo., U.S.A.* 70 F7
St. Joseph →, *U.S.A.* . . 68 D2
St. Joseph, I., *Canada* . 62 C3
St. Joseph, L., *Canada* . 62 B1
St-Jovite, *Canada* 62 C5
St. Kilda, *U.K.* 8 C3
St. Kitts, *W. Indies* . . . 74 K19
St. Kitts-Nevis = St.
  Christopher-Nevis ■,
  W. Indies 74 K19

St. Laurent, *Canada* . . 65 C9
St. Laurent, *Fr. Guiana* 79 B8
St. Lawrence, *Australia* 54 C4
St. Lawrence, *Canada* . 63 C8
St. Lawrence →,
  Canada 63 C6
St. Lawrence, Gulf of,
  Canada 63 C7
St. Lawrence I., *U.S.A.* 60 B3
St. Leonard, *Canada* . . 63 C6
St. Lewis →, *Canada* . . 63 B8
St.-Lô, *France* 18 B3
St.-Louis, *Senegal* . . . 44 E1
St. Louis, *Mich., U.S.A.* 68 D3
St. Louis, *Mo., U.S.A.* . 70 F9
St. Louis →, *U.S.A.* . . . 70 B8
St. Lucia ■, *W. Indies* . 74 P21
St. Lucia, L., *S. Africa* . 49 D5
St. Lucia Channel,
  W. Indies 74 N21
St. Lunaire-Griquet,
  Canada 63 B8
St.-Malo, *France* 18 B2
St-Marc, *Haiti* 75 D10
St. Maries, *U.S.A.* 72 C5
St-Martin, *W. Indies* . . 74 J18
St. Martin, L., *Canada* . 65 C9
St. Martins, *Canada* . . 63 C6
St. Martinville, *U.S.A.* . 71 K9
St. Mary Pk., *Australia* 55 E2
St. Marys, *Australia* . . 54 G4
St. Marys, *U.K.* 11 H1
St. Marys, *U.S.A.* 68 E6
St. Mary's, C., *Canada* . 63 C9
St. Mary's B., *Canada* . 63 C9
St. Marys Bay, *Canada* 63 D6
St.-Mathieu, Pte.,
  France 18 B1
St. Matthews, I. =
  Zadetkyi Kyun,
  Burma 34 H5
St-Maurice →, *Canada* 62 C5
St. Michael's Mount,
  U.K. 11 G2
St.-Nazaire, *France* . . . 18 C2
St. Neots, *U.K.* 11 E7
St. Niklaas = Sint
  Niklaas, *Belgium* . . . 15 C4
St.-Omer, *France* 18 A5
St-Pacome, *Canada* . . . 63 C6
St-Pamphile, *Canada* . . 63 C6
St. Pascal, *Canada* . . . 63 C6
St. Paul, *Canada* 64 C6
St. Paul, *Minn., U.S.A.* . 70 C8
St. Paul, *Nebr., U.S.A.* . 70 E5
St. Paul, I., *Ind. Oc.* . . 35 H6
St. Paul I., *Canada* . . . 63 C7
St. Peter, *U.S.A.* 70 C8
St. Peter Port, *U.K.* . . . 11 H5
St. Peters, *N.S., Canada* 63 C7
St. Peters, *P.E.I.,*
  Canada 63 C7
St. Petersburg = Sankt-
  Peterburg, *Russia* . . 22 C5
St. Petersburg, *U.S.A.* . 69 M4
St.-Pierre, *St- P. & M.* . 63 C8
St. Pierre, *Seychelles* . 35 C5
St-Pierre, L., *Canada* . . 62 C5
St.-Pierre et
  Miquelon □,
  St- P. & M. 63 C8
St.-Quentin, *France* . . . 18 B5
St. Regis, *U.S.A.* 72 C6
St. Sebastien, Tanjon' i,
  Madag. 49 A8
St-Siméon, *Canada* . . . 63 C6
St. Stephen, *Canada* . . 63 C6
St. Thomas, *Canada* . . 62 D3
St. Thomas I., *Virgin Is.* 75 D12
St-Tite, *Canada* 62 C5
St.-Tropez, *France* 18 E7
St. Troud = Sint
  Truiden, *Belgium* . . . 15 D5
St. Vincent, G.,
  Australia 55 F2
St. Vincent & the
  Grenadines ■,
  W. Indies 74 Q20
St. Vincent Passage,
  W. Indies 74 P21
St-Vith, *Belgium* 15 D6
Ste-Agathe-des-Monts,
  Canada 62 C5
Ste-Anne de Beaupré,
  Canada 63 C5
Ste-Anne-des-Monts,
  Canada 63 C6
Ste. Genevieve, *U.S.A.* 70 G9
Ste-Marguerite →,
  Canada 63 B6
Ste.-Marie, *Martinique* 74 N20
Ste-Marie de la
  Madeleine, *Canada* . 63 C5
Ste.-Rose, *Guadeloupe* 74 L20
Ste. Rose du Lac,
  Canada 65 C9
Saintes, *France* 18 D3
Saintes, I. des,
  Guadeloupe 74 M20
Saintonge, *France* . . . 18 D3
Saipan, *Pac. Oc.* 56 F6
Sairang, *India* 37 H18
Sairecábur, Cerro,
  Bolivia 80 A3
Saitama □, *Japan* 29 F9
Sajama, *Bolivia* 78 G5
Sajó, *Hungary* 17 D11
Sak →, *S. Africa* 48 E3
Sakai, *Japan* 29 G7
Sakaide, *Japan* 29 G6
Sakaiminato, *Japan* . . 29 G6
Sakākah, *Si. Arabia* . . 38 D4

Sakami, L., *Canada* . . . 62 B4
Sakarya = Adapazan,
  Turkey 23 F5
Sakarya →, *Turkey* . . . 23 F5
Sakashima-Guntō,
  Japan 29 M2
Sakata, *Japan* 28 E9
Sakeny →, *Madag.* . . . 49 C8
Sakha □, *Russia* 25 C13
Sakhalin, *Russia* 25 D15
Sakhalinskiy Zaliv,
  Russia 25 D15
Šakiai, *Lithuania* 9 J20
Sakon Nakhon,
  Thailand 34 D8
Sakrivier, *S. Africa* . . . 48 E3
Sakuma, *Japan* 29 G8
Sakurai, *Japan* 29 G7
Sala, *Sweden* 9 G17
Sala Consilina, *Italy* . . 20 D6
Sala-y-Gómez, *Pac. Oc.* 57 K17
Salaberry-de-
  Valleyfield, *Canada* . 62 C5
Saladillo, *Argentina* . . 80 D5
Salado →,
  Buenos Aires,
  Argentina 80 D5
Salado →, *La Pampa,*
  Argentina 80 D3
Salado →, *Santa Fe,*
  Argentina 80 C4
Salaga, *Ghana* 44 G4
Sālah, *Syria* 41 C5
Salālah, *Oman* 40 D5
Salamanca, *Chile* 80 C2
Salamanca, *Spain* . . . 19 B3
Salamanca, *U.S.A.* . . . 68 D6
Salāmatābād, *Iran* . . . 38 C5
Salamís, *Greece* 21 F10
Salar de Atacama, *Chile* 80 A3
Salar de Uyuni, *Bolivia* 78 H5
Salatiga, *Indonesia* . . 33 G14
Salavat, *Russia* 22 D10
Salaverry, *Peru* 78 E3
Salawati, *Indonesia* . . 33 E8
Salayar, *Indonesia* . . . 33 F6
Salcombe, *U.K.* 11 G4
Saldanha, *S. Africa* . . . 48 E2
Saldanha B., *S. Africa* . 48 E2
Saldus, *Latvia* 9 H20
Sale, *Australia* 55 F4
Salé, *Morocco* 44 B3
Sale, *U.K.* 10 D5
Salekhard, *Russia* . . . 22 A12
Salem, *India* 36 P11
Salem, *Ind., U.S.A.* . . . 68 F2
Salem, *Mass., U.S.A.* . . 68 D10
Salem, *Mo., U.S.A.* . . . 71 G9
Salem, *N.J., U.S.A.* . . . 68 F8
Salem, *Ohio, U.S.A.* . . 68 E5
Salem, *Oreg., U.S.A.* . . 72 D2
Salem, *S. Dak., U.S.A.* . 70 D6
Salem, *Va., U.S.A.* . . . 68 G5
Salerno, *Italy* 20 D6
Salford, *U.K.* 10 D5
Salgótarján, *Hungary* . 17 D10
Salida, *U.S.A.* 66 C5
Salihli, *Turkey* 21 E13
Salihorsk, *Belarus* . . . 17 B14
Salima, *Malawi* 47 G6
Salina, *Italy* 20 E6
Salina, *U.S.A.* 70 F6
Salina Cruz, *Mexico* . . 74 D5
Salinas, *Brazil* 79 G10
Salinas, *Ecuador* 78 D2
Salinas, *U.S.A.* 73 H3
Salinas →, *U.S.A.* 73 H3
Salinas Ambargasta,
  Argentina 80 B4
Salinas Grandes,
  Argentina 80 B4
Saline →, *Ark., U.S.A.* . 71 J8
Saline →, *Kans.,*
  U.S.A. 70 F6
Salinópolis, *Brazil* . . . 79 D9
Salisbury = Harare,
  Zimbabwe 47 H6
Salisbury, *Australia* . . 55 E2
Salisbury, *U.K.* 11 F6
Salisbury, *Md., U.S.A.* . 68 F8
Salisbury, *N.C., U.S.A.* 69 H5
Salisbury Plain, *U.K.* . . 11 F6
Şalkhad, *Syria* 41 C5
Salla, *Finland* 8 C23
Sallisaw, *U.S.A.* 71 H7
Salluit, *Canada* 61 B12
Salmās, *Iran* 38 B5
Salmo, *Canada* 64 D5
Salmon, *U.S.A.* 72 D7
Salmon →, *Canada* . . . 64 C4
Salmon →, *U.S.A.* 72 D5
Salmon Arm, *Canada* . 64 C5
Salmon Falls, *U.S.A.* . . 72 E6
Salmon Gums,
  Australia 53 F3
Salmon Res., *Canada* . 63 C8
Salmon River Mts.,
  U.S.A. 72 D6
Salo, *Finland* 9 F20
Salome, *U.S.A.* 73 K7
Salon-de-Provence,
  France 18 E6
Salonica =
  Thessaloníki, *Greece* 21 D10
Salonta, *Romania* . . . 17 E11
Salpausselkä, *Finland* . 9 F22
Salsk, *Russia* 23 E7
Salso →, *Italy* 20 F5
Salt →, *Canada* 64 B6
Salt →, *U.S.A.* 73 K7
Salt Creek →, *U.S.A.* . . 70 F9
Salt Fork Arkansas →,
  U.S.A. 71 G6

Salt Lake City, *U.S.A.* . 72 F8
Salta, *Argentina* 80 A3
Saltcoats, *U.K.* 12 F4
Saltee Is., *Ireland* 13 D5
Saltfjellet, *Norway* . . . 8 C16
Saltfjorden, *Norway* . . 8 C16
Saltillo, *Mexico* 74 B4
Salto, *Uruguay* 80 C5
Salto →, *Italy* 20 C5
Salton Sea, *U.S.A.* . . . 73 K6
Saltpond, *Ghana* 44 G4
Saltville, *U.S.A.* 68 G5
Saluda →, *U.S.A.* 69 H5
Salûm, *Egypt* 45 B10
Salûm, Khâlig el, *Egypt* 45 B10
Salur, *India* 37 K13
Salvador, *Brazil* 79 F11
Salvador, *Canada* 65 C7
Salvador, L., *U.S.A.* . . . 71 L9
Salween →, *Burma* . . . 37 L20
Salyan, *Azerbaijan* . . . 23 G8
Salyersville, *U.S.A.* . . . 68 G4
Salzach →, *Austria* . . . 16 D7
Salzburg, *Austria* 16 E7
Salzgitter, *Germany* . . 16 B6
Salzwedel, *Germany* . . 16 B6
Sam Neua, *Laos* 34 B8
Sam Ngao, *Thailand* . . 34 D5
Sam Rayburn
  Reservoir, *U.S.A.* . . . 71 K7
Sama, *Russia* 24 C7
Sama de Langreo,
  Spain 19 A3
Samagaltay, *Russia* . . 25 D10
Samales Group, *Phil.* . 33 C6
Samani, *Japan* 28 C11
Samar, *Phil.* 33 B7
Samara, *Russia* 22 D9
Samaria = Shōmrōn,
  West Bank 41 C4
Samarinda, *Indonesia* . 32 E5
Samarkand =
  Samarqand,
  Uzbekistan 24 F7
Samarqand, *Uzbekistan* 24 F7
Sāmarrā, *Iraq* 38 C4
Sambalpur, *India* 37 J14
Sambar, Tanjung,
  Indonesia 32 E4
Sambas, *Indonesia* . . . 32 D3
Sambava, *Madag.* . . . 49 A9
Sambhal, *India* 36 E11
Sambhar, *India* 36 F9
Sambiase, *Italy* 20 E7
Sambir, *Ukraine* 17 D12
Sambor, *Cambodia* . . . 34 F9
Sambre →, *Europe* . . . 15 D4
Same, *Tanzania* 46 E7
Samnah, *Si. Arabia* . . 38 E3
Samokov, *Bulgaria* . . . 21 C10
Sámos, *Greece* 21 F12
Samothráki, *Évros,*
  Greece 21 D11
Samothráki, *Kérkira,*
  Greece 21 E8
Sampacho, *Argentina* . 80 C4
Sampang, *Indonesia* . . 33 G15
Sampit, *Indonesia* . . . 32 E4
Sampit, Teluk,
  Indonesia 32 E4
Samsø, *Denmark* 9 J14
Samsun, *Turkey* 23 F6
Samui, Ko, *Thailand* . . 34 H6
Samut Prakan, *Thailand* 34 F6
Samut Sakhon,
  Thailand 34 F6
Samut Songkhram →,
  Thailand 34 F6
San, *Mali* 44 F4
San →, *Poland* 17 C11
San Agustin, C., *Phil.* . 33 C7
San Ambrosio, *Pac. Oc.* 57 K20
San Andreas, *U.S.A.* . . 72 G3
San Andres, I. de,
  Caribbean 75 E8
San Andres Mts.,
  U.S.A. 73 K10
San Andrés Tuxtla,
  Mexico 74 D5
San Angelo, *U.S.A.* . . . 71 K4
San Antonio, *Chile* . . . 80 C2
San Antonio, *Spain* . . 19 C6
San Antonio, *N. Mex.,*
  U.S.A. 73 K10
San Antonio, *Tex.,*
  U.S.A. 71 L5
San Antonio →,
  U.S.A. 71 L6
San Antonio, C.,
  Argentina 80 D5
San Antonio, C., *Cuba* 74 C8
San Antonio Oeste,
  Argentina 80 E4
San Augustine, *U.S.A.* 71 K7
San Benedetto del
  Tronto, *Italy* 20 C5
San Benito, *U.S.A.* . . . 71 M6
San Bernardino, *U.S.A.* 73 J5
San Bernardino Str.,
  Phil. 33 B6
San Bernardo, *Chile* . . 80 C2
San Bernardo, I. de,
  Colombia 78 B3
San Blas, C., *U.S.A.* . . 69 L3
San Borja, *Bolivia* . . . 78 F5
San Carlos, *Argentina* . 80 C2
San Carlos, *Chile* 80 D2
San Carlos, *Phil.* 33 B6
San Carlos, *U.S.A.* . . . 73 K8
San Carlos, *Amazonas,*
  Venezuela 78 C5
San Carlos, *Cojedes,*
  Venezuela 78 B5

San Carlos de
  Bariloche, *Argentina* 80 E2
San Carlos del Zulia,
  Venezuela 78 B4
San Carlos L., *U.S.A.* . 73 K8
San Clemente, *U.S.A.* . 73 K5
San Clemente I., *U.S.A.* 73 K4
San Cristóbal,
  Argentina 80 C4
San Cristóbal, *Mexico* 74 D6
San Cristóbal,
  Venezuela 78 B4
San Diego, *Calif.,*
  U.S.A. 73 K5
San Diego, *Tex., U.S.A.* 71 M5
San Diego, C.,
  Argentina 80 G3
San Felipe, *Chile* 80 C2
San Felipe, *Venezuela* 78 A5
San Feliú de Guíxols,
  Spain 19 B7
San Félix, *Pac. Oc.* . . . 57 K20
San Fernando,
  La Union, Phil. 33 A6
San Fernando,
  Pampanga, Phil. . . . 33 A6
San Fernando, *Spain* . 19 D2
San Fernando,
  Trin. & Tob. 74 S20
San Fernando, *U.S.A.* . 73 J4
San Fernando de
  Apure, *Venezuela* . . 78 B5
San Fernando de
  Atabapo, *Venezuela* . 78 C5
San Francisco,
  Argentina 80 C4
San Francisco, *U.S.A.* . 73 H2
San Francisco →,
  U.S.A. 73 K9
San Francisco de
  Macorís, *Dom. Rep.* . 75 D10
San Francisco del
  Monte de Oro,
  Argentina 80 C3
San Gil, *Colombia* . . . 78 B4
San Gottardo, P. del,
  Switz. 16 E5
San Ignacio, *Bolivia* . . 78 G6
San Ignacio, *Paraguay* 80 B5
San Ildefonso, C., *Phil.* 33 A6
San Javier, *Argentina* . 80 C5
San Javier, *Bolivia* . . . 78 G6
San Joaquin →,
  U.S.A. 73 G3
San Jorge, B. de,
  Mexico 74 A2
San Jorge, G.,
  Argentina 80 F3
San Jorge, G. de, *Spain* 19 B6
San José, *Bolivia* 78 G6
San José, *Costa Rica* . 75 F8
San José, *Guatemala* . 74 E6
San José, *Phil.* 33 A6
San Jose, *U.S.A.* 73 H3
San Jose →, *U.S.A.* . . . 73 J10
San Jose de
  Buenovista, *Phil.* . . . 33 B6
San José de Jáchal,
  Argentina 80 C3
San José de Mayo,
  Uruguay 80 C5
San José de Ocune,
  Colombia 78 C4
San José del Guaviare,
  Colombia 78 C4
San Juan, *Argentina* . . 80 C3
San Juan, *Phil.* 33 C7
San Juan, *Puerto Rico* 75 D11
San Juan →, *Nic.* 75 E8
San Juan →, *U.S.A.* . . . 73 H8
San Juan, C., *Eq. Guin.* 46 D1
San Juan Bautista,
  U.S.A. 73 H3
San Juan Capistrano,
  U.S.A. 73 K5
San Juan de los
  Morros, *Venezuela* . 78 B5
San Juan Mts., *U.S.A.* . 73 H10
San Julián, *Argentina* . 80 F3
San Justo, *Argentina* . 80 C4
San Leandro, *U.S.A.* . . 73 H2
San Lorenzo, *Ecuador* 78 C3
San Lorenzo, I., *Peru* . 78 F3
San Lorenzo, Mt.,
  Argentina 80 F2
San Lucas, *Bolivia* . . . 78 H5
San Lucas, C., *Mexico* 74 C2
San Luis, *Argentina* . . 80 C3
San Luis, *U.S.A.* 73 H11
San Luis Obispo, *U.S.A.* 73 J3
San Luis Potosí, *Mexico* 74 C4
San Marcos, *U.S.A.* . . 71 L6
San Marino,
  San Marino 16 G7
San Marino ■, *Europe* 20 C5
San Martín, L.,
  Argentina 80 F2
San Mateo, *U.S.A.* . . . 73 H2
San Matías, *Bolivia* . . 78 G7
San Matías, G.,
  Argentina 80 E4
San Miguel, *El Salv.* . . 74 E7
San Miguel →, *Bolivia* 78 F6

San Pedro de las
  Colonias, *Mexico* . . . 74 B4
San Pedro de Lloc,
  Peru 78 E3
San Pedro de Macorís,
  Dom. Rep. 75 D11
San Pedro del Paraná,
  Paraguay 80 B5
San Pedro Sula,
  Honduras 74 D7
San Pieto, *Italy* 20 E3
San Rafael, *Argentina* 80 C3
San Rafael, *Calif.,*
  U.S.A. 72 H2
San Rafael, *N. Mex.,*
  U.S.A. 73 J10
San Ramón de la
  Nueva Orán,
  Argentina 80 A4
San Remo, *Italy* 20 C2
San Roque, *Argentina* 80 B5
San Roque, *Spain* . . . 19 D3
San Rosendo, *Chile* . . 80 D2
San Saba, *U.S.A.* 71 K5
San Salvador, *Bahamas* 75 C10
San Salvador, *El Salv.* 74 E7
San Salvador de Jujuy,
  Argentina 80 A4
San Sebastián,
  Argentina 80 G3
San Sebastián, *Spain* . 19 A5
San Severo, *Italy* 20 D6
San Simon, *U.S.A.* . . . 73 K9
San Valentin, Mte.,
  Chile 80 F2
San Vicente de la
  Barquera, *Spain* . . . 19 A3
San Ygnacio, *U.S.A.* . . 71 M5
Sana', *Yemen* 40 D3
Sana →, *Bos.-H.* 16 B7
Sanaga →, *Cameroon* 44 H6
Sanana, *Indonesia* . . . 33 E7
Sanandaj, *Iran* 38 C5
Sanco Pt., *Phil.* 33 C7
Sancti-Spíritus, *Cuba* . 75 C9
Sancy, Puy de, *France* 18 D5
Sand →, *S. Africa* 49 C5
Sand Springs, *U.S.A.* . 71 G6
Sanda, *Japan* 29 G7
Sandakan, *Malaysia* . . 32 C5
Sandan = Sambor,
  Cambodia 34 F9
Sandanski, *Bulgaria* . . 21 D10
Sanday, *U.K.* 12 G14
Sandefjord, *Norway* . . 9 G14
Sanders, *U.S.A.* 73 J9
Sanderson, *U.S.A.* . . . 71 K3
Sandfly L., *Canada* . . . 65 B7
Sandgate, *Australia* . . 55 D5
Sandía, *Peru* 78 F5
Sandnes, *Norway* 9 G11
Sandness, *U.K.* 12 A7
Sandnessjøen, *Norway* 8 C15
Sandoa, *Zaïre* 46 F4
Sandomierz, *Poland* . . 17 C11
Sandover →, *Australia* 54 C2
Sandoway, *Burma* . . . 37 K19
Sandoy, *Færoe Is.* . . . 8 F9
Sandpoint, *U.S.A.* . . . 72 B5
Sandringham, *U.K.* . . . 10 E8
Sandspit, *Canada* 64 C2
Sandstone, *Australia* . 53 E2
Sandusky, *Mich., U.S.A.* 62 D3
Sandusky, *Ohio, U.S.A.* 68 E4
Sandviken, *Sweden* . . 9 F17
Sandwich, C., *Australia* 54 B4
Sandwich B., *Canada* . 63 B8
Sandwich B., *Namibia* 48 C1
Sandwip Chan., *Bangla.* 37 H17
Sandy Bight, *Australia* 53 F3
Sandy C., *Queens.,*
  Australia 54 C5
Sandy C., *Tas.,*
  Australia 54 G3
Sandy Cr. →, *U.S.A.* . . 72 F9
Sandy L., *Canada* 62 B1
Sandy Lake, *Canada* . . 62 B1
Sandy Narrows,
  Canada 65 B8
Sanford, *Fla., U.S.A.* . . 69 L5
Sanford, *N.C., U.S.A.* . 69 H6
Sanford →, *Australia* . 53 E2
Sanford, Mt., *U.S.A.* . . 60 B5
Sanga →, *Congo* 46 E3
Sanga-Tolon, *Russia* . 25 C15
Sangamner, *India* . . . 36 K9
Sangar, *Russia* 25 C13
Sangasangadalam,
  Indonesia 32 E5
Sangeang, *Indonesia* . 33 F5
Sanger, *U.S.A.* 73 H4
Sangerhausen,
  Germany 16 C6
Sanggau, *Indonesia* . . 32 D4
Sanghe, Kepulauan,
  Indonesia 33 D7
Sanghe, P., *Indonesia* . 33 D7
Sangkapura, *Indonesia* 32 F4
Sangli, *India* 36 L9
Sangmélima, *Cameroon* 46 D2
Sangre de Cristo Mts.,
  U.S.A. 71 G2
Sangudo, *Canada* . . . 64 C6
Sanjo, *Japan* 28 F9
Sankt Gallen, *Switz.* . . 16 E5
Sankt Moritz, *Switz.* . . 16 E5
Sankt-Peterburg, *Russia* 22 C5
Sankt Pölten, *Austria* . 16 D8
Sankuru →, *Zaïre* 46 E4
Sanliurfa, *Turkey* 23 G6
Sanlúcar de
  Barrameda, *Spain* . . 19 D2
Sanmenxia, *China* . . . 31 C6

118

Sanming, China	31	D6
Sannaspos, S. Africa	48	D4
Sannicandro Gargánico, Italy	20	D6
Sannieshof, S. Africa	48	D4
Sannīn, J., Lebanon	41	B4
Sanok, Poland	17	D12
Sanquhar, U.K.	12	F5
Santa Ana, Bolivia	78	F5
Santa Ana, Ecuador	78	D2
Santa Ana, El Salv.	74	E7
Santa Ana, U.S.A.	73	K5
Santa Barbara, U.S.A.	73	J4
Santa Catalina, Gulf of, U.S.A.	73	K5
Santa Catalina I., U.S.A.	73	H3
Santa Clara, Cuba	75	C9
Santa Clara, Calif., U.S.A.	73	H3
Santa Clara, Utah, U.S.A.	73	H7
Santa Clotilde, Peru	78	D4
Santa Coloma de Gramanet, Spain	19	B7
Santa Cruz, Argentina	80	G3
Santa Cruz, Bolivia	78	G6
Santa Cruz, Phil.	33	B6
Santa Cruz, U.S.A.	73	H2
Santa Cruz →, Argentina	80	G3
Santa Cruz de Tenerife, Canary Is.	44	C1
Santa Cruz do Sul, Brazil	80	B6
Santa Cruz I., Solomon Is.	56	J8
Santa Cruz I., U.S.A.	73	K4
Santa Elena, Ecuador	78	D2
Santa Eugenia, Pta., Mexico	74	B1
Santa Fe, Argentina	80	C4
Santa Fe, U.S.A.	73	J11
Santa Filomena, Brazil	79	E9
Santa Inés, I., Chile	80	G2
Santa Isabel = Rey Malabo, Eq. Guin.	44	H6
Santa Isabel, Argentina	80	D3
Santa Isabel, Brazil	79	F8
Santa Lucia Range, U.S.A.	73	J3
Santa Maria, Brazil	80	B6
Santa Maria, U.S.A.	73	J3
Santa María →, Mexico	74	A3
Santa Maria da Vitória, Brazil	79	F10
Santa Maria di Leuca, C., Italy	21	E8
Santa Marta, Colombia	78	A4
Santa Marta, Sierra Nevada de, Colombia	78	A4
Santa Maura = Levkás, Greece	21	E9
Santa Monica, U.S.A.	73	K4
Santa Rita, La Pampa, Argentina	80	D4
Santa Rosa, San Luis, Argentina	80	C3
Santa Rosa, Bolivia	78	F5
Santa Rosa, Brazil	80	B6
Santa Rosa, Calif., U.S.A.	72	G2
Santa Rosa, N. Mex., U.S.A.	71	H2
Santa Rosa de Copán, Honduras	74	E7
Santa Rosa I., Calif., U.S.A.	73	K3
Santa Rosa I., Fla., U.S.A.	69	K2
Santa Rosa Range, U.S.A.	72	F5
Santa Vitória do Palmar, Brazil	80	C6
Santai, China	30	C5
Santana, Coxilha de, Brazil	80	C5
Santana do Livramento, Brazil	80	C5
Santander, Spain	19	A4
Sant'Antíoco, Italy	20	E3
Santaquin, U.S.A.	72	G8
Santarém, Brazil	79	D8
Santarém, Portugal	19	C1
Santiago, Brazil	80	B6
Santiago, Chile	80	C2
Santiago →, Peru	78	D3
Santiago de Compostela, Spain	19	A1
Santiago de Cuba, Cuba	75	D9
Santiago de los Cabelleros, Dom. Rep.	75	D10
Santiago del Estero, Argentina	80	B4
Santo Amaro, Brazil	79	F11
Santo Ângelo, Brazil	80	B6
Santo Antônio, Brazil	79	F11
Santo Corazón, Bolivia	78	G7
Santo Domingo, Dom. Rep.	75	D11
Santo Tomás, Peru	78	F4
Santo Tomé, Argentina	80	B5
Santo Tomé de Guayana = Ciudad Guayana, Venezuela	78	B6
Santoña, Spain	19	A4
Santorini = Thira, Greece	21	F11
Santos, Brazil	80	A7
Santos Dumont, Brazil	80	A8
Sanza Pombo, Angola	46	F3
São Anastácio, Brazil	80	A6
São Bernado de Campo, Brazil	79	H9
São Borja, Brazil	80	B5
São Carlos, Brazil	80	A7
São Cristóvão, Brazil	79	F11
São Domingos, Brazil	79	F9
São Francisco, Brazil	79	G10
São Francisco →, Brazil	79	F11
São Francisco do Sul, Brazil	80	B7
São Gabriel, Brazil	80	C6
São João da Madeira, Portugal	19	B1
São João del Rei, Brazil	79	H10
São João do Araguaia, Brazil	79	E9
São João do Piauí, Brazil	79	E10
São José do Rio Prêto, Brazil	80	A7
São Leopoldo, Brazil	80	B6
São Lourenço, Brazil	79	H9
São Lourenço →, Brazil	79	G7
São Luís, Brazil	79	D10
São Marcos →, Brazil	79	D10
São Marcos, B. de, Brazil	79	D10
São Mateus, Brazil	79	G11
São Paulo, Brazil	80	A7
São Paulo □, Brazil	80	A7
São Paulo, I., Atl. Oc.	2	D8
São Roque, C. de, Brazil	79	E11
São Sebastião, I. de, Brazil	80	A7
São Tomé, Atl. Oc.	42	F4
São Tomé & Principe ■, Africa	43	F4
São Vicente, C. de, Portugal	19	D1
Saône →, France	18	D6
Saonek, Indonesia	33	E8
Saparua, Indonesia	33	E7
Sapele, Nigeria	44	G6
Sapelo I., U.S.A.	69	K5
Saposoa, Peru	78	E3
Sapporo, Japan	28	C10
Sapudi, Indonesia	33	G16
Sapulpa, U.S.A.	71	G7
Saqqez, Iran	38	B5
Sar Dasht, Iran	39	C6
Sar Gachineh, Iran	39	D6
Sar Planina, Macedonia	21	C9
Sarāb, Iran	38	B5
Sarabadi, Iraq	38	C5
Sarada →, India	37	F12
Saragossa = Zaragoza, Spain	19	B5
Saraguro, Ecuador	78	D3
Sarajevo, Bos.-H.	21	C8
Saran, G., Indonesia	32	E4
Saranac Lake, U.S.A.	68	C8
Sarandí del Yi, Uruguay	80	C5
Sarangani B., Phil.	33	C7
Sarangani Is., Phil.	33	C7
Sarangarh, India	37	J13
Saransk, Russia	22	D8
Sarapul, Russia	22	C9
Sarasota, U.S.A.	69	M4
Saratoga, U.S.A.	72	F10
Saratoga Springs, U.S.A.	68	D9
Saratov, Russia	22	D8
Saravane, Laos	34	E9
Sarawak □, Malaysia	32	D4
Saray, Turkey	21	D12
Saraykóy, Turkey	21	F13
Sarbāz, Iran	39	E9
Sarbīsheh, Iran	39	C8
Sarda = Sarada →, India	37	F12
Sardalas, Libya	44	C7
Sardarshahr, India	36	E9
Sardegna □, Italy	20	D3
Sardinia = Sardegna □, Italy	20	D3
Sardis, Turkey	21	E12
Sārdūīyeh = Dar Mazār, Iran	39	D8
Sargent, U.S.A.	70	E5
Sargodha, Pakistan	36	C8
Sarh, Chad	45	G8
Sārī, Iran	39	B7
Sangöl, Turkey	21	E13
Sarikei, Malaysia	32	D4
Sarina, Australia	54	C4
Sarita, U.S.A.	71	M6
Sark, U.K.	11	H5
Şarköy, Turkey	21	D12
Sárlat-la-Canéda, France	18	D4
Sarles, U.S.A.	70	A5
Sarmi, Indonesia	33	E9
Sarmiento, Argentina	80	F3
Särna, Sweden	9	F15
Sarnia, Canada	62	D3
Sarny, Ukraine	17	C14
Sarolangun, Indonesia	32	E2
Saronikós Kólpos, Greece	21	F10
Saros Körfezi, Turkey	21	D12
Sarpsborg, Norway	9	G14
Sarre = Saar →, Europe	18	B7
Sarreguemines, France	18	B7
Sarro, Mali	44	F3
Sarthe →, France	18	C3
Sartynya, Russia	24	C7
Sarvestān, Iran	39	D7
Sary-Tash, Kyrgyzstan	24	F8
Saryshagan, Kazakhstan	24	E8
Sasabeneh, Ethiopia	40	F3
Sasaram, India	37	G14
Sasebo, Japan	29	H4
Saser, India	36	B10
Saskatchewan □, Canada	65	C7
Saskatchewan →, Canada	65	C8
Saskatoon, Canada	65	C7
Saskylakh, Russia	25	B12
Sasolburg, S. Africa	49	D4
Sasovo, Russia	22	D7
Sassandra, Ivory C.	44	H3
Sassandra →, Ivory C.	44	H3
Sássari, Italy	20	D3
Sassnitz, Germany	16	A7
Sassuolo, Italy	20	B4
Sasyk, Ozero, Ukraine	17	F15
Sata-Misaki, Japan	29	J5
Satadougou, Mali	44	F2
Satakunta, Finland	9	F20
Satanta, U.S.A.	71	G4
Satara, India	36	L8
Satilla →, U.S.A.	69	K5
Satka, Russia	22	C10
Satmala Hills, India	36	J9
Satna, India	37	G12
Sátoraljaújhely, Hungary	17	D11
Satpura Ra., India	36	J10
Satsuna-Shotō, Japan	29	K5
Satu Mare, Romania	17	E12
Satui, Indonesia	32	E5
Satun, Thailand	34	N13
Sauda, Norway	9	G12
Sauðarkrókur, Iceland	8	D4
Saudi Arabia ■, Asia	40	B3
Sauer →, Germany	15	E6
Sauerland, Germany	16	C4
Saugerties, U.S.A.	68	D9
Sauk Centre, U.S.A.	70	C7
Sauk Rapids, U.S.A.	70	C7
Sault Ste. Marie, Canada	62	C3
Sault Ste. Marie, U.S.A.	68	B3
Saumlaki, Indonesia	33	F8
Saumur, France	18	C3
Saunders, C., N.Z.	51	L3
Saunders I., Antarctica	5	B1
Saunders Point, Australia	53	E4
Sauri, Nigeria	44	F6
Saurimo, Angola	46	F4
Sava →, Serbia, Yug.	21	B9
Savage, U.S.A.	70	B2
Savage I. = Niue, Cook Is.	57	J11
Savai'i, W. Samoa	51	A12
Savalou, Benin	44	G5
Savanna, U.S.A.	70	D9
Savanna la Mar, Jamaica	74	J15
Savannah, Ga., U.S.A.	69	J5
Savannah, Mo., U.S.A.	70	F7
Savannah, Tenn., U.S.A.	69	H1
Savannah →, U.S.A.	69	J5
Savannakhet, Laos	34	D8
Savant L., Canada	62	B1
Savant Lake, Canada	62	B1
Savanur, India	36	M9
Savé, Benin	44	G5
Save →, Mozam.	49	C5
Sāveh, Iran	39	C6
Savelugu, Ghana	44	G4
Savo, Finland	8	E22
Savoie □, France	18	D7
Savona, Italy	20	B3
Savonlinna, Finland	22	B4
Sawahlunto, Indonesia	32	E2
Sawai, Indonesia	33	E7
Sawai Madhopur, India	36	F10
Sawara, Japan	29	G10
Sawatch Mts., U.S.A.	73	G10
Sawel Mt., U.K.	13	B4
Sawmills, Zimbabwe	47	H5
Sawu, Indonesia	33	F6
Sawu Sea, Indonesia	33	F6
Saxby →, Australia	54	B3
Saxony, Lower = Niedersachsen □, Germany	16	B5
Say, Niger	44	F5
Sayabec, Canada	63	C6
Sayán, Peru	78	F3
Sayan, Vostochnyy, Russia	25	D10
Sayan, Zapadnyy, Russia	25	D10
Saydā, Lebanon	41	B4
Sayḥut, Yemen	40	D5
Saynshand, Mongolia	31	B6
Sayre, Okla., U.S.A.	71	H5
Sayre, Pa., U.S.A.	68	E7
Sazanit, Albania	21	D8
Sázava →, Czech.	16	D8
Sazin, Pakistan	36	B8
Scafell Pike, U.K.	10	C4
Scalpay, U.K.	12	D2
Scandia, Canada	64	C6
Scandicci, Italy	20	C4
Scandinavia, Europe	6	C8
Scapa Flow, U.K.	12	C5
Scarborough, Trin. & Tob.	74	R21
Scarborough, U.K.	10	C7
Scebeli, Wabi →, Somali Rep.	40	G3
Scenic, U.S.A.	70	D3
Schaffhausen, Switz.	16	E5
Schagen, Neths.	15	B4
Schefferville, Canada	63	B6
Schelde →, Belgium	15	C4
Schell Creek Ra., U.S.A.	72	G6
Schenectady, U.S.A.	68	D9
Scheveningen, Neths.	15	B4
Schiedam, Neths.	15	C4
Schiermonnikoog, Neths.	15	A6
Schio, Italy	20	B4
Schleswig, Germany	16	A5
Schleswig-Holstein □, Germany	16	A5
Schofield, U.S.A.	70	C10
Schouten I., Australia	54	G4
Schouten Is. = Supiori, Indonesia	33	E9
Schouwen, Neths.	15	C3
Schreiber, Canada	62	C2
Schuler, Canada	65	C6
Schumacher, Canada	62	C3
Schurz, U.S.A.	72	G4
Schuyler, U.S.A.	70	E6
Schwäbische Alb, Germany	16	D5
Schwaner, Pegunungan, Indonesia	32	E4
Schwarzwald, Germany	16	D5
Schwedt, Germany	16	B8
Schweinfurt, Germany	16	C6
Schweizer-Reneke, S. Africa	48	D4
Schwenningen = Villingen-Schwenningen, Germany	16	D5
Schwerin, Germany	16	B6
Schwyz, Switz.	16	E5
Sciacca, Italy	20	F5
Scilla, Italy	20	E6
Scilly, Isles of, U.K.	11	H1
Scioto →, U.S.A.	68	F4
Scobey, U.S.A.	70	A2
Scone, Australia	55	E5
Scoresbysund = Greenland	4	B6
Scotia, U.S.A.	72	F1
Scotia Sea, Antarctica	5	B18
Scotland, U.S.A.	70	D6
Scotland □, U.K.	12	E5
Scotland Neck, U.S.A.	69	G7
Scott, C., Australia	52	B4
Scott City, U.S.A.	70	F4
Scott Glacier, Antarctica	5	C8
Scott I., Antarctica	5	C11
Scott Inlet, Canada	61	A12
Scott Is., Canada	64	C3
Scott L., Canada	65	B7
Scott Reef, Australia	52	B3
Scottburgh, S. Africa	49	E5
Scottsbluff, U.S.A.	70	E3
Scottsboro, U.S.A.	69	H2
Scottsburg, U.S.A.	68	F3
Scottsdale, Australia	54	G4
Scottsville, U.S.A.	69	G2
Scottville, U.S.A.	68	D2
Scranton, U.S.A.	68	E8
Scunthorpe, U.K.	10	D7
Scusciuban, Somali Rep.	40	E5
Scutari = Üsküdar, Turkey	23	F4
Seabrook, L., Australia	53	F2
Seaford, U.S.A.	68	F8
Seaforth, Canada	62	D3
Seagraves, U.S.A.	71	J3
Seal →, Canada	65	B10
Seal Cove, Canada	63	C8
Seal L., Canada	63	B7
Sealy, U.S.A.	71	L6
Searchlight, U.S.A.	73	J6
Searcy, U.S.A.	71	H9
Searles L., U.S.A.	73	J5
Seaside, U.S.A.	72	D2
Seaspray, Australia	55	F4
Seattle, U.S.A.	72	C2
Seaview Ra., Australia	54	B4
Sebastopol = Sevastopol, Ukraine	23	F5
Sebastopol, U.S.A.	72	G2
Sebewaing, U.S.A.	68	D4
Sebha = Sabhah, Libya	45	C7
Sebring, U.S.A.	69	M5
Sebta = Ceuta, N. Afr.	19	E3
Sebuku, Indonesia	32	E5
Sebuku, Teluk, Malaysia	32	D5
Sechelt, Canada	64	D4
Sechura, Desierto de, Peru	78	E2
Secretary I., N.Z.	51	L1
Secunderabad, India	36	L11
Sedalia, U.S.A.	70	F8
Sedan, Australia	55	E2
Sedan, France	18	B6
Sedan, U.S.A.	71	G6
Seddon, N.Z.	51	J5
Seddonville, N.Z.	51	J4
Sedeh, Fārs, Iran	39	D7
Sedeh, Khorāsān, Iran	39	C8
Sederot, Israel	41	D3
Sedgewick, Canada	64	C6
Sedhiou, Senegal	44	F1
Sedley, Canada	65	C8
Sedova, Pik, Russia	24	B7
Sedro-Woolley, U.S.A.	72	B2
Seeheim, Namibia	48	D2
Seekoei →, S. Africa	48	E4
Seferihisar, Turkey	21	E12
Seg-ozero, Russia	22	B5
Segamat, Malaysia	34	S15
Segesta, Italy	20	F5
Seget, Indonesia	33	E8
Segezha, Russia	22	B5
Ségou, Mali	44	F3
Segovia = Coco →, Cent. Amer.	75	E8
Segovia, Spain	19	B3
Segre →, Spain	19	B6
Séguéla, Ivory C.	44	G3
Seguin, U.S.A.	71	L6
Segura →, Spain	19	C5
Seh Qal'eh, Iran	39	C8
Sehitwa, Botswana	48	C3
Sehore, India	36	H10
Seiland, Norway	8	A20
Seiling, U.S.A.	71	G5
Seinäjoki, Finland	9	E20
Seine →, France	18	B4
Seistan, Iran	39	D9
Sekayu, Indonesia	32	E2
Sekondi-Takoradi, Ghana	44	H4
Sekuma, Botswana	48	C3
Selah, U.S.A.	72	C3
Selama, Malaysia	34	P13
Selangor □, Malaysia	34	R14
Selaru, Indonesia	33	F8
Selby, U.K.	10	D6
Selby, U.S.A.	70	C4
Selçuk, Turkey	21	F12
Selden, U.S.A.	70	F4
Sele →, Italy	20	D6
Selemdzha →, Russia	25	D13
Selenga = Selenge Mörön →, Asia	30	A5
Selenge Mörön →, Asia	30	A5
Seletan, Tg., Indonesia	32	E4
Selfridge, U.S.A.	70	B4
Sélibabi, Mauritania	44	E2
Seligman, U.S.A.	73	J7
Selîma, Ei Wâhât el, Sudan	45	D10
Selinda Spillway, Botswana	48	B3
Selkirk, Canada	65	C9
Selkirk, U.K.	12	F6
Selkirk I., Canada	65	C9
Selkirk Mts., Canada	64	C5
Sells, U.S.A.	73	L8
Selma, Ala., U.S.A.	69	J2
Selma, Calif., U.S.A.	73	H4
Selma, N.C., U.S.A.	69	H6
Selmer, U.S.A.	69	H1
Selpele, Indonesia	33	E8
Selsey Bill, U.K.	11	G7
Selu, Indonesia	33	F8
Selva, Argentina	80	B4
Selvas, Brazil	78	E5
Selwyn, Australia	54	C3
Selwyn L., Canada	65	A8
Selwyn Ra., Australia	54	C3
Semani →, Albania	21	D8
Semarang, Indonesia	33	G14
Semau, Indonesia	33	F6
Semeru, Indonesia	33	H15
Semey, Kazakhstan	24	D9
Seminoe Reservoir, U.S.A.	72	E10
Seminole, Okla., U.S.A.	71	H6
Seminole, Tex., U.S.A.	71	J3
Semiozernoye, Kazakhstan	24	D7
Semipalatinsk = Semey, Kazakhstan	24	D9
Semirara Is., Phil.	33	B6
Semisopochnoi I., U.S.A.	60	C2
Semitau, Indonesia	32	D4
Semiyarka, Kazakhstan	24	D8
Semiyarskoye = Semiyarka, Kazakhstan	24	D8
Semmering P., Austria	16	E8
Semnān, Iran	39	C7
Semnān □, Iran	39	C7
Semois →, Europe	15	E4
Semporna, Malaysia	33	D5
Semuda, Indonesia	32	E4
Sen →, Cambodia	34	F8
Senā, Iran	39	D6
Sena Madureira, Brazil	78	E5
Senador Pompeu, Brazil	79	E11
Senai, Malaysia	34	T16
Senaja, Malaysia	32	C5
Senanga, Zambia	48	B3
Senatobia, U.S.A.	71	H10
Sendai, Kagoshima, Japan	29	J5
Sendai, Miyagi, Japan	28	E10
Sendai-Wan, Japan	28	E10
Seneca, Oreg., U.S.A.	72	D4
Seneca, S.C., U.S.A.	69	H4
Seneca Falls, U.S.A.	68	D7
Seneca L., U.S.A.	68	D7
Senegal ■, W. Afr.	44	F2
Senegal →, W. Afr.	44	E1
Senegambia, Africa	42	E2
Senekal, S. Africa	49	D4
Senge Khambab = Indus →, Pakistan	36	G5
Sengkang, Indonesia	33	E6
Senhor-do-Bonfim, Brazil	79	F10
Senigállia, Italy	20	C5
Senj, Croatia	16	F8
Senja, Norway	8	B17
Senlis, France	18	B5
Senmonorom, Cambodia	34	F9
Sennâr, Sudan	45	F11
Senneterre, Canada	62	C4
Sens, France	18	B5
Senta, Serbia, Yug.	21	B9
Sentani, Indonesia	33	E10
Sentinel, U.S.A.	73	K7
Sentolo, Indonesia	33	G14
Seo de Urgel, Spain	19	A6
Seoul = Sŏul, S. Korea	31	C7
Separation Point, Canada	63	B8
Sepīdān, Iran	39	D7
Sepone, Laos	34	D9
Sept-Îles, Canada	63	B6
Sequim, U.S.A.	72	B2
Sequoia National Park, U.S.A.	73	H4
Seraing, Belgium	15	D5
Seram, Indonesia	33	E7
Seram Laut, Kepulauan, Indonesia	33	E8
Seram Sea, Indonesia	33	E7
Serang, Indonesia	33	G12
Serasan, Indonesia	32	D3
Serbia □, Yugoslavia	21	C9
Serdobsk, Russia	22	D7
Seremban, Malaysia	34	S14
Serenje, Zambia	47	G6
Sereth = Siret →, Romania	17	F14
Sergino, Russia	24	C7
Sergipe □, Brazil	79	F11
Sergiyev Posad, Russia	22	C6
Seria, Brunei	32	D4
Serian, Malaysia	32	D4
Seribu, Kepulauan, Indonesia	32	F3
Sérifos, Greece	21	F11
Seringapatam Reef, Australia	52	B3
Sermata, Indonesia	33	F7
Serny Zavod, Turkmenistan	24	F6
Serov, Russia	22	C11
Serowe, Botswana	48	C4
Serpentine, Australia	53	F2
Serpentine Lakes, Australia	53	E4
Serpukhov, Russia	22	D6
Sérrai, Greece	21	D10
Serrezuela, Argentina	80	C3
Serrinha, Brazil	79	F11
Sertânia, Brazil	79	E11
Serua, Indonesia	33	F8
Serui, Indonesia	33	E9
Serule, Botswana	48	C4
Sesepe, Indonesia	33	E7
Sesfontein, Namibia	48	B1
Sesheke, Zambia	48	B3
Setana, Japan	28	C9
Sète, France	18	E5
Sete Lagôas, Brazil	79	G10
Sétif, Algeria	44	A6
Seto, Japan	29	G8
Setonaikai, Japan	29	G6
Settat, Morocco	44	B3
Setté-Cama, Gabon	46	E1
Setting L., Canada	65	C9
Settle, U.K.	10	C5
Settlement Pt., Bahamas	69	M6
Setúbal, Portugal	19	C1
Setúbal, B. de, Portugal	19	C1
Seulimeum, Indonesia	32	C1
Sevan, Ozero = Sevana Lich, Armenia	23	F8
Sevana Lich, Armenia	23	F8
Sevastopol, Ukraine	23	F5
Seven Emu, Australia	54	B2
Seven Sisters, Canada	64	C3
Severn →, Canada	62	A2
Severn →, U.K.	11	F5
Severn L., Canada	62	B1
Severnaya Zemlya, Russia	25	B10
Severnyye Uvaly, Russia	22	C8
Severo-Kurilsk, Russia	25	D16
Severo-Yeniseyskiy, Russia	25	C10
Severodvinsk, Russia	22	B6
Severomorsk, Russia	22	A5
Severouralsk, Russia	22	B10
Sevier, U.S.A.	73	G7
Sevier →, U.S.A.	73	G7
Sevier L., U.S.A.	72	G7
Sevilla, Spain	19	D2
Seville = Sevilla, Spain	19	D2
Sevlievo, Bulgaria	21	C11
Seward, Alaska, U.S.A.	60	B5
Seward, Nebr., U.S.A.	70	E6
Seward Pen., U.S.A.	60	B3
Sewer, Indonesia	33	F8
Sexsmith, Canada	64	B5
Seychelles ■, Ind. Oc.	27	K9
Seyðisfjörður, Iceland	8	D6
Seydvān, Iran	38	B5
Seymchan, Russia	25	C16
Seymour, Australia	55	F4
Seymour, S. Africa	49	E4
Seymour, Ind., U.S.A.	68	F3
Seymour, Tex., U.S.A.	71	J5
Seymour, Wis., U.S.A.	68	C1
Sfax, Tunisia	45	B7
Sfîntu Gheorghe, Romania	17	F13
Shaanxi □, China	31	C5
Shaba □, Zaïre	46	F4
Shabunda, Zaïre	46	E5
Shache, China	30	C2
Shackleton Ice Shelf, Antarctica	5	C8
Shackleton Inlet, Antarctica	5	E11
Shādegān, Iran	39	D6
Shadrinsk, Russia	24	D7
Shafter, Calif., U.S.A.	73	J4
Shafter, Tex., U.S.A.	71	L2

Shaftesbury, *U.K.* 11 F5
Shahba, *Syria* 41 C5
Shahdād, *Iran* 39 D8
Shahdadkot, *Pakistan* . 36 F5
Shahgarh, *India* 36 F6
Shaḥḥāt, *Libya* 45 B9
Shahjahanpur, *India* . . 36 F11
Shahr Kord, *Iran* 39 C6
Shahr-e Bābak, *Iran* . . 36 D5
Shaikhabad, *Afghan.* . . 36 B6
Shajapur, *India* 36 H10
Shakawe, *Botswana* . . 48 B3
Shakhty, *Russia* 23 E7
Shakhunya, *Russia* . . . 22 C8
Shaki, *Nigeria* 44 G5
Shakopee, *U.S.A.* 70 C8
Shala, L., *Ethiopia* . . . 45 G12
Shalqar, *Kazakhstan* . . 24 E6
Shaluli Shan, *China* . . 30 C4
Shām, *Iran* 39 E8
Shamanovo, *Russia* . . 25 C15
Shamattawa, *Canada* . 65 B10
Shamattawa →,
  Canada 62 A2
Shamīl, *Iran* 39 E8
Shāmkūh, *Iran* 39 C8
Shamo = Gobi, *Asia* . . 31 B6
Shamo, L., *Ethiopia* . . 45 G12
Shamokin, *U.S.A.* 68 E7
Shamrock, *U.S.A.* 71 H4
Shamva, *Zimbabwe* . . 47 H6
Shan □, *Burma* 37 J21
Shandak, *Iran* 39 D9
Shandong □, *China* . . 31 C6
Shanghai, *China* 31 C7
Shangqiu, *China* 31 C6
Shangrao, *China* 31 D6
Shangshui, *China* 31 C6
Shaniko, *U.S.A.* 72 D3
Shannon, *N.Z.* 51 J5
Shannon →, *Ireland* . . 13 D2
Shansi = Shanxi □,
  China 31 C6
Shantar, Ostrov
  Bolshoy, *Russia* . . 25 D14
Shantou, *China* 31 D6
Shantung =
  Shandong □, *China* 31 C6
Shanxi □, *China* 31 C6
Shaoguan, *China* 31 D6
Shaoxing, *China* 31 C7
Shaoyang, *China* 31 D6
Shapinsay, *U.K.* 12 B6
Shaqra', *Si. Arabia* . . 38 E5
Shaqrā', *Yemen* 40 E4
Shari, *Japan* 28 C12
Sharjah = Ash
  Shāriqah, *U.A.E.* . . . 39 E7
Shark B., *Australia* . . . 53 E1
Sharon, *U.S.A.* 68 E5
Sharon Springs, *U.S.A.* 70 F4
Sharp Pt., *Australia* . . 54 A3
Sharpe, L., *Canada* . . 65 C10
Sharya, *Russia* 22 C8
Shashi, *Botswana* . . . 49 C4
Shashi, *China* 31 C6
Shasta, Mt., *U.S.A.* . . 72 F2
Shasta L., *U.S.A.* 72 F2
Shatt al'Arab →, *Iraq* 39 D6
Shattuck, *U.S.A.* 71 G5
Shaunavon, *Canada* . . 65 D7
Shaw →, *Australia* . . 52 D2
Shaw I., *Australia* . . . 54 C4
Shawano, *U.S.A.* 68 C1
Shawinigan, *Canada* . . 62 C5
Shawnee, *U.S.A.* 71 H6
Shaybārā, *Si. Arabia* . 38 E3
Shaykh Sa'īd, *Iraq* . . 38 C5
Shcherbakov =
  Rybinsk, *Russia* . . . 22 C6
Shchuchinsk,
  Kazakhstan 24 D8
Shebele = Scebeli,
  Wabi →,
  Somali Rep. 40 G3
Sheboygan, *U.S.A.* . . . 68 D2
Shediac, *Canada* 63 C7
Sheelin, L., *Ireland* . . 13 C4
Sheep Haven, *Ireland* 13 A4
Sheerness, *U.K.* 11 F8
Sheet Harbour, *Canada* 63 D7
Sheffield, *U.K.* 10 D6
Sheffield, Ala., *U.S.A.* 69 H2
Sheffield, Tex., *U.S.A.* 71 K4
Sheho, *Canada* 65 C8
Shekhupura, *Pakistan* 36 D8
Shelburne, N.S.,
  Canada 63 D6
Shelburne, Ont.,
  Canada 62 D3
Shelburne B., *Australia* 54 A3
Shelby, Mich., *U.S.A.* 68 D2
Shelby, Mont., *U.S.A.* 72 B8
Shelby, N.C., *U.S.A.* . 69 H5
Shelbyville, Ill., *U.S.A.* 70 F10
Shelbyville, Ind., *U.S.A.* 68 F3
Shelbyville, Tenn.,
  U.S.A. 69 H2
Sheldon, *U.S.A.* 70 D7
Sheldrake, *Canada* . . 63 B7
Shelikhova, Zaliv,
  Russia 25 D16
Shell Lake, *U.S.A.* . . . 70 C9
Shell Lakes, *Australia* 53 E4
Shellbrook, *Canada* . . 65 C7
Shellharbour, *Australia* 55 E5
Shelling Rocks, *Ireland* 13 E1
Shelton, *U.S.A.* 72 C2
Shenandoah, Iowa,
  U.S.A. 70 E7
Shenandoah, Pa.,
  U.S.A. 68 E7

Shenandoah, Va.,
  U.S.A. 68 F6
Shenandoah →,
  U.S.A. 68 F7
Shendam, *Nigeria* . . . 44 G6
Shendī, *Sudan* 45 E11
Shensi = Shaanxi □,
  China 31 C5
Shenyang, *China* 31 B7
Sheopur Kalan, *India* . 36 G10
Shepetivka, *Ukraine* . 17 C14
Shepetovka =
  Shepetivka, *Ukraine* 17 C14
Shepparton, *Australia* 55 F4
Sherborne, *U.K.* 11 G5
Sherbro I., *S. Leone* . . 44 G2
Sherbrooke, *Canada* . 63 C5
Sheridan, Ark., *U.S.A.* 71 H8
Sheridan, Wyo., *U.S.A.* 72 D10
Sherman, *U.S.A.* 71 J6
Sherridon, *Canada* . . . 65 B8
Sherwood, N. Dak.,
  U.S.A. 70 A4
Sherwood, Tex., *U.S.A.* 71 K4
Sherwood Forest, *U.K.* 10 D6
Sheslay, *Canada* 64 B2
Sheslay →, *Canada* . . 64 B2
Shethanei L., *Canada* . 65 B9
Shetland □, *U.K.* 12 A7
Shetland Is., *U.K.* . . . 12 A7
Sheyenne, *U.S.A.* . . . 70 B5
Sheyenne →, *U.S.A.* . 70 B6
Shibām, *Yemen* 40 D4
Shibata, *Japan* 28 F9
Shibecha, *Japan* 28 C12
Shibetsu, *Japan* 28 B11
Shibogama L., *Canada* 62 B2
Shibushi, *Japan* 29 J5
Shickshock Mts. =
  Chic-Chocs, Mts.,
  Canada 63 C6
Shido, *Japan* 29 G7
Shiel, L., *U.K.* 12 E3
Shield, C., *Australia* . 54 A2
Shiga □, *Japan* 29 G8
Shigaib, *Sudan* 45 E9
Shihchiachuangi =
  Shijiazhuang, *China* 31 C6
Shijiazhuang, *China* . . 31 C6
Shikarpur, *Pakistan* . . 36 F6
Shikoku □, *Japan* 29 H6
Shikoku-Sanchi, *Japan* 29 H6
Shilabo, *Ethiopia* . . . 40 F3
Shiliguri, *India* 37 F16
Shilka, *Russia* 25 D12
Shilka →, *Russia* 25 D13
Shillelagh, *Ireland* . . 13 D5
Shillong, *India* 37 G17
Shilo, *West Bank* 41 C4
Shimabara, *Japan* . . . 29 H5
Shimada, *Japan* 29 G9
Shimane □, *Japan* . . . 29 G6
Shimanovsk, *Russia* . . 25 D13
Shimizu, *Japan* 29 G9
Shimodate, *Japan* . . . 29 F9
Shimoga, *India* 36 N9
Shimonoseki, *Japan* . . 29 H5
Shimpuru Rapids,
  Angola 48 B2
Shin, L., *U.K.* 12 C4
Shin-Tone →, *Japan* . 29 G10
Shinano →, *Japan* . . 29 F9
Shindand, *Afghan.* . . 36 C3
Shingleton, *U.S.A.* . . . 62 C2
Shingū, *Japan* 29 H7
Shinjō, *Japan* 28 E10
Shinshār, *Syria* 41 A5
Shinyanga, *Tanzania* . 46 E6
Shiogama, *Japan* 28 E10
Shiojiri, *Japan* 29 F8
Ship I., *U.S.A.* 71 K10
Shipehenski Prohod,
  Bulgaria 21 C11
Shiping, *China* 30 D5
Shipki La, *India* 36 D11
Shippegan, *Canada* . . 63 C7
Shippensburg, *U.S.A.* 68 E7
Shiprock, *U.S.A.* 73 H9
Shiqma, N. →, *Israel* 41 D3
Shīr Kūh, *Iran* 39 D7
Shiragami-Misaki,
  Japan 28 D10
Shirakawa, Fukushima,
  Japan 29 F10
Shirakawa, Gifu, *Japan* 29 F8
Shirane-San, Gumma,
  Japan 29 F9
Shirane-San,
  Yamanashi, *Japan* . 29 G9
Shiraoi, *Japan* 28 C10
Shīrāz, *Iran* 39 D7
Shire →, *Africa* 47 H7
Shiretoko-Misaki, *Japan* 28 B12
Shiriya-Zaki, *Japan* . . 28 D10
Shiroishi, *Japan* 28 E10
Shīrvān, *Iran* 39 B8
Shirwa, L. = Chilwa, L.,
  Malawi 47 H7
Shivpuri, *India* 36 G10
Shizuoka, *Japan* 29 G9
Shizuoka □, *Japan* . . . 29 G9
Shklov = Shklow,
  Belarus 17 A16
Shklow, *Belarus* 17 A16
Shkoder = Shkodra,
  Albania 21 C8
Shkodra, *Albania* 21 C8
Shkumbini →, *Albania* 21 D8
Shmidta, O., *Russia* . . 25 A10
Shō-Gawa →, *Japan* . 29 F8
Shoal Lake, *Canada* . 65 C8
Shōdo-Shima, *Japan* . 29 G7
Shoeburyness, *U.K.* . . 11 F8

Sholapur = Solapur,
  India 36 L9
Shologontsy, *Russia* . 25 C12
Shōmrōn, *West Bank* . 41 C4
Shoshone, *U.S.A.* . . . 72 E6
Shoshone L., *U.S.A.* . 72 D8
Shoshone Mts., *U.S.A.* 72 G5
Shoshong, *Botswana* . 48 C4
Shoshoni, *U.S.A.* 72 E9
Show Low, *U.S.A.* . . . 73 J9
Shreveport, *U.S.A.* . . 71 J8
Shrewsbury, *U.K.* . . . 10 E5
Shrirampur, *India* . . . 37 H16
Shropshire □, *U.K.* . . 11 E5
Shu, *Kazakhstan* 24 E8
Shuangliao, *China* . . . 31 B7
Shuangyashan, *China* 31 B8
Shule, *China* 30 C2
Shumagin Is., *U.S.A.* . 60 C4
Shumikha, *Russia* . . . 24 D7
Shungnak, *U.S.A.* 60 B4
Shūr →, *Iran* 39 D7
Shūr Āb, *Iran* 39 C6
Shūr Gaz, *Iran* 39 D8
Shūrāb, *Iran* 39 C8
Shūrjestān, *Iran* 39 D7
Shurugwi, *Zimbabwe* . 47 H6
Shūsf, *Iran* 39 D9
Shūshtar, *Iran* 39 D6
Shuswap L., *Canada* . 64 C5
Shūzū, *Iran* 39 D7
Shwebo, *Burma* 37 H19
Shwegu, *Burma* 37 G20
Shweli →, *Burma* 37 H20
Shymkent, *Kazakhstan* 24 E7
Shyok, *India* 36 B11
Shyok →, *Pakistan* . . 36 B9
Si Kiang = Xi
  Jiang →, *China* . . . 31 D6
Si-ngan = Xi'an, *China* 31 C5
Si Racha, *Thailand* . . 34 F6
Siahan Range, *Pakistan* 36 F4
Siaksriindrapura,
  Indonesia 32 D2
Sialkot, *Pakistan* 36 C9
Siam = Thailand ■,
  Asia 34 D6
Siantan, P., *Indonesia* 32 D3
Siāreh, *Iran* 39 D9
Siargao, *Phil.* 33 C7
Siasi, *Phil.* 33 C6
Siau, *Indonesia* 33 D7
Šiauliai, *Lithuania* . . . 9 J20
Sibay, *Russia* 22 D10
Sibayi, L., *S. Africa* . . 49 D5
Šibenik, *Croatia* 20 C6
Siberia, *Russia* 4 D13
Siberut, *Indonesia* . . . 32 E1
Sibi, *Pakistan* 36 E5
Sibil, *Indonesia* 33 E10
Sibiti, *Congo* 46 E2
Sibiu, *Romania* 17 F13
Sibley, Iowa, *U.S.A.* . 70 D7
Sibley, La., *U.S.A.* . . . 71 J8
Sibolga, *Indonesia* . . . 32 D1
Sibsagar, *India* 37 F19
Sibu, *Malaysia* 32 D4
Sibuco, *Phil.* 33 C6
Sibuguey B., *Phil.* . . . 33 C6
Sibut, *C.A.R.* 45 G8
Sibutu, *Phil.* 33 D5
Sibutu Passage,
  E. Indies 33 D5
Sibuyan, *Phil.* 33 B6
Sibuyan Sea, *Phil.* . . . 33 B6
Sicamous, *Canada* . . 64 C5
Sichuan □, *China* . . . 30 C5
Sicilia, *Italy* 20 F6
Sicily = Sicilia, *Italy* . 20 F6
Sicuani, *Peru* 78 F4
Siddipet, *India* 36 K11
Sidéradougou,
  Burkina Faso 44 F4
Sîdi Barrâni, *Egypt* . . 45 B10
Sidi-bel-Abbès, *Algeria* 44 A5
Sidlaw Hills, *U.K.* . . . 12 E5
Sidley, Mt., *Antarctica* 5 D14
Sidmouth, *U.K.* 11 G4
Sidmouth, C., *Australia* 54 A3
Sidney, *Canada* 64 D4
Sidney, Mont., *U.S.A.* 70 B2
Sidney, N.Y., *U.S.A.* . 68 D8
Sidney, Nebr., *U.S.A.* 70 E3
Sidney, Ohio, *U.S.A.* . 68 E3
Sidoarjo, *Indonesia* . . 33 G15
Sidon = Saydā,
  Lebanon 41 B4
Sidra, G. of = Surt,
  Khalīj, *Libya* 45 B8
Siedlce, *Poland* 17 B12
Sieg →, *Germany* . . . 16 C4
Siegen, *Germany* . . . 16 C5
Siem Reap, *Cambodia* 34 F4
Siena, *Italy* 20 C4
Sieradz, *Poland* 17 C10
Sierra Blanca, *U.S.A.* 73 L11
Sierra Blanca Peak,
  U.S.A. 73 K11
Sierra City, *U.S.A.* . . 72 G3
Sierra Colorada,
  Argentina 80 E3
Sierra Gorda, *Chile* . . 80 A3
Sierra Leone ■, *W. Afr.* 44 G2
Sierra Madre,
  Mexico 74 D6

Siguiri, *Guinea* 44 F3
Sigulda, *Latvia* 9 H21
Sigurd, *U.S.A.* 73 G8
Sihanoukville =
  Kompong Som,
  Cambodia 34 G7
Siikajoki →, *Finland* . 8 D21
Siilinjärvi, *Finland* . . . 8 E22
Sikar, *India* 36 F9
Sikasso, *Mali* 44 F3
Sikeston, *U.S.A.* 71 G10
Sikhote Alin, Khrebet,
  Russia 25 E14
Sikhote Alin Ra. =
  Sikhote Alin, Khrebet,
  Russia 25 E14
Síkinos, *Greece* 21 F11
Sikkani Chief →,
  Canada 64 B4
Sikkim □, *India* 37 F16
Sikotu-Ko, *Japan* . . . 28 C10
Sil →, *Spain* 19 A2
Silchar, *India* 37 G18
Silcox, *Canada* 65 B10
Siler City, *U.S.A.* 69 H6
Silesia = Śląsk, *Poland* 16 C9
Silgarhi Doti, *Nepal* . 37 E12
Silghat, *India* 37 F18
Silifke, *Turkey* 23 G5
Siliguri = Shiliguri,
  India 37 F16
Siling Co, *China* 30 C3
Silistra, *Bulgaria* 21 B12
Silivri, *Turkey* 21 D13
Siljan, *Sweden* 9 F16
Silkeborg, *Denmark* . 9 H13
Sillajhuay, Cordillera,
  Chile 78 G5
Sillamäe, *Estonia* . . . 9 G22
Siloam Springs, *U.S.A.* 71 G7
Silsbee, *U.S.A.* 71 K7
Šilute, *Lithuania* 9 J19
Silva Porto = Kuito,
  Angola 47 G3
Silver City, *Panama* . . 74 H14
Silver City, N. Mex.,
  U.S.A. 73 K9
Silver City, Nev., *U.S.A.* 72 G4
Silver Cr. →, *U.S.A.* . 72 E4
Silver Creek, *U.S.A.* . 68 D6
Silver Lake, *U.S.A.* . . 72 E3
Silver Streams,
  S. Africa 48 D3
Silverton, Colo., *U.S.A.* 73 H10
Silverton, Tex., *U.S.A.* 71 H4
Silvies →, *U.S.A.* . . . 72 E4
Simanggang, *Malaysia* 32 D4
Simard, L., *Canada* . . 62 C4
Simav, *Turkey* 21 E13
Simbirsk, *Russia* 22 D8
Simcoe, *Canada* 62 D3
Simcoe, L., *Canada* . . 62 D4
Simenga, *Russia* 25 C11
Simeria, *Romania* . . . 17 F12
Simeulue, *Indonesia* . 32 D1
Simferopol, *Ukraine* . 23 F5
Simi, *Greece* 21 F12
Simikot, *Nepal* 37 E12
Simla, *India* 36 D10
Simmie, *Canada* 65 D7
Simojoki →, *Finland* . 8 D21
Simonette →, *Canada* 64 B5
Simonstown, *S. Africa* 48 E2
Simpang, *Malaysia* . . 34 Q13
Simplon P., *Switz.* . . . 16 E5
Simplon Pass =
  Simplon P., *Switz.* . 16 E5
Simpson Desert,
  Australia 54 D2
Simrishamn, *Sweden* . 9 J16
Simunjan, *Malaysia* . . 32 D4
Simushir, Ostrov,
  Russia 25 E16
Sinabang, *Indonesia* . 32 D1
Sinadogo, *Somali Rep.* 40 F4
Sinai = Es Sînâ', *Egypt* 45 C11
Sinai, Mt. = Mûsa, G.,
  Egypt 45 C11
Sinai Peninsula, *Egypt* 41 F2
Sinaloa de Levya,
  Mexico 74 B3
Sīnāwan, *Libya* 44 B7
Sincelejo, *Colombia* . 78 B3
Sinclair, *U.S.A.* 72 F10
Sinclair Mills, *Canada* 64 C4
Sincorá, Serra do,
  Brazil 79 F10
Sind □, *Pakistan* 36 F6
Sind Sagar Doab,
  Pakistan 36 D7
Sindangan, *Phil.* 33 C6
Sindangbarang,
  Indonesia 33 G12
Sines, *Portugal* 19 D1
Sines, C. de, *Portugal* 19 D1
Singa, *Sudan* 45 F11
Singapore ■, *Asia* . . . 34 T16
Singapore, Straits of,
  Asia 34 T17
Singaraja, *Indonesia* . 32 F5
Singida, *Tanzania* . . . 46 E6
Singitikós Kólpos,
  Greece 21 D11
Singkaling Hkamti,
  Burma 37 G19
Singkawang, *Indonesia* 32 D3
Singleton, *Australia* . 55 E5
Singleton, Mt., N. Terr.,
  Australia 52 D5
Singleton, Mt.,
  W. Austral., *Australia* 53 E2
Singora = Songkhla,
  Thailand 34 J6
Sînî □, *Egypt* 41 F2

Sinjai, *Indonesia* 33 F6
Sinjār, *Iraq* 38 B4
Sinkat, *Sudan* 45 E12
Sinkiang Uighur =
  Xinjiang Uygur
  Zizhiqu □, *China* . . 30 B3
Sinni →, *Italy* 20 D7
Sînnicolau Maré,
  Romania 17 E11
Sinnuris, *Egypt* 45 C11
Sinop, *Turkey* 23 F6
Sinsk, *Russia* 25 C13
Sint Niklaas, *Belgium* . 15 C4
Sint Truiden, *Belgium* 15 D5
Sintang, *Indonesia* . . 32 D4
Sinton, *U.S.A.* 71 L6
Sintra, *Portugal* 19 C1
Siocon, *Phil.* 33 C6
Siófok, *Hungary* 17 E10
Sioma, *Zambia* 48 B3
Sion, *Switz.* 16 E4
Sioux City, *U.S.A.* . . . 70 D6
Sioux Falls, *U.S.A.* . . 70 D6
Sioux Lookout, *Canada* 62 B1
Siping, *China* 31 B7
Sipiwesk L., *Canada* . 65 B9
Sipura, *Indonesia* . . . 32 E1
Siquijor, *Phil.* 33 C6
Sir Edward Pellew
  Group, *Australia* . . 54 B2
Sir Graham Moore Is.,
  Australia 52 B4
Sira →, *Norway* 9 G12
Siracusa, *Italy* 20 F6
Sirajganj, *Bangla.* . . . 37 G16
Sīrdān, *Iran* 39 B6
Sirdaryo =
  Syrdarya →,
  Kazakhstan 24 E7
Siret →, *Romania* . . . 17 F14
Sirohi, *India* 36 G8
Sironj, *India* 36 G10
Síros, *Greece* 21 F11
Sirsa, *India* 36 E9
Sisak, *Croatia* 16 F9
Sisaket, *Thailand* . . . 34 E8
Sishen, S. Africa 48 D3
Sisipuk L., *Canada* . . 65 B8
Sisophon, *Cambodia* . 34 F7
Sisseton, *U.S.A.* 70 C6
Sīstān va
  Balūchestān □, *Iran* 39 E9
Sisters, *U.S.A.* 72 D3
Sitapur, *India* 37 F12
Siteki, *Swaziland* . . . 49 D5
Sitges, *Spain* 19 B6
Sitía, *Greece* 21 G12
Sitka, *U.S.A.* 60 C6
Sitoti, *Botswana* 48 C3
Sittang Myit →,
  Burma 37 L20
Sittard, *Neths.* 15 C5
Sittwe, *Burma* 37 J18
Siuri, *India* 37 H15
Sīvand, *Iran* 39 D7
Sivas, *Turkey* 23 G6
Sivomaskinskiy, *Russia* 22 A11
Sivrihisar, *Turkey* . . . 23 G5
Sîwa, *Egypt* 45 C10
Siwalik Range, *Nepal* 37 F13
Siwan, *India* 37 F14
Sizewell, *U.K.* 11 E9
Sjælland, *Denmark* . . 9 J14
Sjumen = Šumen,
  Bulgaria 21 C12
Skadarsko Jezero,
  Montenegro, Yug. . 21 C8
Skaftafell, *Iceland* . . . 8 D5
Skagafjörður, *Iceland* . 8 D4
Skagastølstindane,
  Norway 9 F12
Skagen, *Denmark* . . . 9 H14
Skagerrak, *Denmark* . 9 H13
Skagway, *U.S.A.* 64 B1
Skala-Podilska, *Ukraine* 17 D14
Skala Podolskaya =
  Skala-Podilska,
  Ukraine 17 D14
Skalat, *Ukraine* 17 D13
Skåne, *Sweden* 9 J15
Skara, *Sweden* 9 G15
Skardu, *Pakistan* 36 B9
Skarzysko-Kamienna,
  Poland 17 C11
Skeena →, *Canada* . . 64 C2
Skeena Mts., *Canada* 64 B3
Skegness, *U.K.* 10 D8
Skeldon, *Guyana* . . . 78 B7
Skellefte älv →,
  Sweden 8 D19
Skellefteå, *Sweden* . . 8 D19
Skelleftehamn, *Sweden* 8 D19
Skerries, The, *U.K.* . . 10 D3
Ski, *Norway* 9 G14
Skiathos, *Greece* . . . 21 E10
Skibbereen, *Ireland* . 13 E2
Skiddaw, *U.K.* 10 C4
Skien, *Norway* 9 G13
Skierniewice, *Poland* . 17 C11
Skikda, *Algeria* 44 A6
Skipton, *Australia* . . . 55 F3
Skipton, *U.K.* 10 D5
Skirmish Pt., *Australia* 54 A1
Skíros, *Greece* 21 E11
Skjálfandafljót →,
  Iceland 8 D5
Skjálfandi, *Iceland* . . 8 C5
Skoghall, *Sweden* . . . 9 G15
Skole, *Ukraine* 17 D12
Skópelos, *Greece* . . . 21 E10
Skopje, *Macedonia* . . 21 C9
Skövde, *Sweden* 9 G15
Skovorodino, *Russia* . 25 D13

Skowhegan, *U.S.A.* . . 63 D6
Skownan, *Canada* . . . 65 C9
Skull, *Ireland* 13 E2
Skunk →, *U.S.A.* 70 E9
Skuodas, *Lithuania* . . 9 H19
Skvyra, *Ukraine* 17 D15
Skye, *U.K.* 12 D2
Skykomish, *U.S.A.* . . 72 C3
Skyros = Skíros,
  Greece 21 E11
Slættaratindur,
  Færoe Is. 8 E9
Slagelse, *Denmark* . . 9 J14
Slamet, *Indonesia* . . . 32 F3
Slaney →, *Ireland* . . . 13 D5
Śląsk, *Poland* 16 C9
Slate Is., *Canada* . . . 62 C2
Slatina, *Romania* . . . 17 F13
Slaton, *U.S.A.* 71 J4
Slave →, *Canada* . . . 64 A6
Slave Coast, W. Afr. . 42 F4
Slave Lake, *Canada* . 64 B6
Slave Pt., *Canada* . . . 64 A5
Slavgorod, *Russia* . . . 24 D8
Slavonski Brod, *Croatia* 21 B8
Slavuta, *Ukraine* 17 C14
Slavyanka, *Russia* . . . 28 C5
Slavyansk = Slovyansk,
  Ukraine 23 E6
Slawharad, *Belarus* . . 17 B16
Sleaford, *U.K.* 10 E7
Sleaford B., *Australia* 55 E2
Sleat, Sd. of, *U.K.* . . . 12 D3
Sleeper Is., *Canada* . 61 C11
Sleepy Eye, *U.S.A.* . . 70 C7
Sleman, *Indonesia* . . 33 G14
Slemon L., *Canada* . . 64 A5
Slidell, *U.S.A.* 71 K10
Sliedrecht, *Neths.* . . 15 C4
Slieve Aughty, *Ireland* 13 C3
Slieve Bloom, *Ireland* 13 C4
Slieve Donard, *U.K.* . 13 B6
Slieve Gullion, *U.K.* . 13 B5
Slieve Mish, *Ireland* . 13 D2
Slievenamon, *Ireland* 13 D4
Sligeach = Sligo,
  Ireland 13 B3
Sligo, *Ireland* 13 B3
Sligo □, *Ireland* 13 B3
Sligo B., *Ireland* 13 B3
Slite, *Sweden* 9 H18
Sliven, *Bulgaria* 21 C12
Slobodskoy, *Russia* . 22 C9
Slobozia, *Romania* . . 17 F14
Slocan, *Canada* 64 D5
Slochteren, *Neths.* . . 15 A6
Slonim, *Belarus* 17 B13
Slough, *U.K.* 11 F7
Slovak Rep. ■, *Europe* 17 D10
Slovakia = Slovak
  Rep. ■, *Europe* . . . 17 D10
Slovakian Ore Mts. =
  Slovenské Rudohorie,
  Slovak Rep. 17 D10
Slovenia ■, *Europe* . . 16 F8
Slovenija = Slovenia ■,
  Europe 16 F8
Slovenské Rudohorie,
  Slovak Rep. 17 D10
Slovenská Republika =
  Slovak Rep. ■,
  Europe 17 D10
Slovenské Rudohorie,
  Slovak Rep. 17 D10
Slovyansk, *Ukraine* . 23 E6
Sluch →, *Ukraine* . . . 17 C14
Sluis, *Neths.* 15 C3
Słupsk, *Poland* 17 A9
Slurry, S. Africa 48 D4
Slutsk, *Belarus* 17 B14
Slyne Hd., *Ireland* . . 13 C1
Slyudyanka, *Russia* . 25 D11
Småland, *Sweden* . . . 9 H16
Smalltree L., *Canada* . 65 A7
Smara, Morocco 44 C3
Smartt Syndicate Dam,
  S. Africa 48 E3
Smeaton, *Canada* . . . 65 C8
Smederevo,
  Serbia, Yug. 21 B9
Smidovich, *Russia* . . 25 E14
Smiley, *Canada* 65 C7
Smith, *Canada* 64 B6
Smith →, *Canada* . . . 64 B3
Smith Arm, *Canada* . 60 B7
Smith Center, *U.S.A.* 70 F5
Smith Sund, *Greenland* 4 B4
Smithburne →,
  Australia 54 B3
Smithers, *Canada* . . . 64 C3
Smithfield, S. Africa . 49 E4
Smithfield, N.C., *U.S.A.* 69 H6
Smithfield, Utah, *U.S.A.* 72 F8
Smiths Falls, *Canada* 62 D4
Smithton, *Australia* . 54 G4
Smithtown, *Australia* 55 E5
Smithville, *U.S.A.* . . . 71 K6
Smoky →, *Canada* . . 64 B5
Smoky Bay, *Australia* 55 E1
Smoky Falls, *Canada* 62 B3
Smoky Hill →, *U.S.A.* 70 F6
Smoky Lake, *Canada* 64 C6
Smøla, *Norway* 8 E13
Smolensk, *Russia* . . . 22 D4
Smolikas, Óros, *Greece* 21 D9
Smolyan, *Bulgaria* . . . 21 D11
Smooth Rock Falls,
  Canada 62 C3
Smoothstone L.,
  Canada 65 C7
Smorgon = Smarhon,
  Belarus 17 A14
Smyrna = İzmir, *Turkey* 21 E12
Snæfell, *Iceland* 8 D6
Snaefell, *U.K.* 10 C3

Strawberry Reservoir

Snæfellsjökull, *Iceland* 8 D2
Snake →, *U.S.A.* 72 C4
Snake I., *Australia* 55 F4
Snake L., *Canada* 65 B7
Snake Range, *U.S.A.* 72 G6
Snake River Plain, *U.S.A.* 72 E7
Snåsavatnet, *Norway* 8 D14
Sneek, *Neths.* 15 A5
Sneeuberge, *S. Africa* 48 E3
Sněžka, *Europe* 16 C8
Snizort, L., *U.K.* 12 D2
Snøhetta, *Norway* 9 E13
Snohomish, *U.S.A.* 72 C2
Snow Hill, *U.S.A.* 68 F8
Snow Lake, *Canada* 65 C8
Snowbird L., *Canada* 65 A8
Snowdon, *U.K.* 10 D3
Snowdrift, *Canada* 65 A6
Snowdrift →, *Canada* 65 A6
Snowflake, *U.S.A.* 73 J8
Snowshoe Pk., *U.S.A.* 72 B6
Snowtown, *Australia* 55 E2
Snowville, *U.S.A.* 72 F7
Snowy →, *Australia* 55 F4
Snowy Mts., *Australia* 55 F4
Snyatyn, *Ukraine* 17 D13
Snyder, *Okla., U.S.A.* 71 H5
Snyder, *Tex., U.S.A.* 71 J4
Soahanina, *Madag.* 49 B7
Soalala, *Madag.* 49 B8
Soanierana-Ivongo, *Madag.* 49 B8
Soap Lake, *U.S.A.* 72 C4
Sobat, Nahr →, *Sudan* 45 G11
Sobolevo, *Russia* 25 D16
Sobradinho, Reprêsa de, *Brazil* 79 E10
Sobral, *Brazil* 79 D10
Soc Trang, *Vietnam* 34 H8
Soch'e = Shache, *China* 30 C2
Sochi, *Russia* 23 F6
Société, Is. de la, *Pac. Oc.* 57 J12
Society Is. = Société, Is. de la, *Pac. Oc.* 57 J12
Socompa, Portezuelo de, *Chile* 80 A3
Socorro, *Colombia* 78 B4
Socorro, *U.S.A.* 73 J10
Socotra, *Ind. Oc.* 40 E5
Soda L., *U.S.A.* 73 J5
Soda Plains, *India* 36 B11
Soda Springs, *U.S.A.* 72 E8
Sodankylä, *Finland* 8 C22
Söderhamn, *Sweden* 9 F17
Söderköping, *Sweden* 9 G17
Södermanland, *Sweden* 9 G17
Södertälje, *Sweden* 9 G17
Sodiri, *Sudan* 45 F10
Sodo, *Ethiopia* 45 G12
Soekmekaar, *S. Africa* 49 C4
Soest, *Neths.* 15 B5
Sofia = Sofiya, *Bulgaria* 21 C10
Sofia →, *Madag.* 49 B8
Sofiya, *Bulgaria* 21 C10
Sofiysk, *Russia* 25 D14
Sōfu-Gan, *Japan* 29 K10
Sogamoso, *Colombia* 78 B4
Sogār, *Iran* 39 E8
Sogndalsfjøra, *Norway* 9 F12
Søgne, *Norway* 9 G12
Sognefjorden, *Norway* 9 F11
Soh, *Iran* 39 C6
Sohâg, *Egypt* 45 C11
Soignies, *Belgium* 15 D4
Soissons, *France* 18 B5
Sōja, *Japan* 29 G6
Sokal, *Ukraine* 17 C13
Söke, *Turkey* 21 F12
Sokhumi, *Georgia* 23 F7
Sokodé, *Togo* 44 G5
Sokol, *Russia* 22 C7
Sokółka, *Poland* 17 B12
Sokolo, *Mali* 44 F3
Sokołów Podlaski, *Poland* 17 B12
Sokoto, *Nigeria* 44 F6
Sol Iletsk, *Russia* 22 D10
Solano, *Phil.* 33 A6
Solapur, *India* 36 L9
Soledad, *U.S.A.* 73 H3
Soledad, *Venezuela* 78 B6
Solent, The, *U.K.* 11 G6
Solfonn, *Norway* 9 F12
Soligalich, *Russia* 22 C7
Soligorsk = Salihorsk, *Belarus* 17 B14
Solikamsk, *Russia* 22 C10
Solila, *Madag.* 49 C8
Solimões = Amazonas →, *S. Amer.* 79 C9
Solingen, *Germany* 15 C7
Sollefteå, *Sweden* 8 E17
Sóller, *Spain* 19 C7
Sologne, *France* 18 C4
Solok, *Indonesia* 32 E2
Solomon, N. Fork →, *U.S.A.* 70 F5
Solomon, S. Fork →, *U.S.A.* 70 F5
Solomon Is. ■, *Pac. Oc.* 56 H7
Solon, *China* 31 B7
Solon Springs, *U.S.A.* 70 B9
Solor, *Indonesia* 33 F6
Solothurn, *Switz.* 16 E4
Šolta, *Croatia* 20 C7
Soltānābād, *Khorāsān, Iran* 39 C8
Soltānābād, *Khorāsān, Iran* 39 B8
Soltānābād, *Markazī, Iran* 39 C6
Solunska Glava, *Macedonia* 21 D9
Solvay, *U.S.A.* 68 D7
Sölvesborg, *Sweden* 9 H16
Solvychegodsk, *Russia* 22 B8
Solway Firth, *U.K.* 10 C4
Solwezi, *Zambia* 47 G5
Sōma, *Japan* 28 F10
Soma, *Turkey* 21 E12
Somali Rep. ■, *Africa* 40 F4
Somalia = Somali Rep. ■, *Africa* 40 F4
Sombor, *Serbia, Yug.* 21 B8
Sombrerete, *Mexico* 74 C4
Sombrero, *Anguilla* 75 D12
Somers, *U.S.A.* 72 B6
Somerset, *Canada* 65 D9
Somerset, *Colo., U.S.A.* 73 G10
Somerset, *Ky., U.S.A.* 68 G3
Somerset □, *U.K.* 11 F5
Somerset East, *S. Africa* 48 E4
Somerset I., *Canada* 60 A10
Somerset West, *S. Africa* 48 E2
Somerton, *U.S.A.* 73 K6
Someş →, *Romania* 17 D12
Sommariva, *Australia* 55 D4
Somme →, *France* 18 A4
Somosierra, Puerto de, *Spain* 19 B4
Somport, Puerto de, *Spain* 18 E3
Son La, *Vietnam* 34 B7
Sondags →, *S. Africa* 48 E4
Sønderborg, *Denmark* 9 J13
Søndre Strømfjord, *Greenland* 61 B14
Sóndrio, *Italy* 20 A3
Sonepur, *India* 37 J13
Song Cau, *Vietnam* 34 F10
Songea, *Tanzania* 46 G7
Songhua Jiang →, *China* 31 B8
Songkhla, *Thailand* 34 J6
Songpan, *China* 30 C5
Sonipat, *India* 36 E10
Sonmiani, *Pakistan* 36 G5
Sono →, *Brazil* 79 E9
Sonora, *Calif., U.S.A.* 73 H3
Sonora, *Tex., U.S.A.* 71 K4
Sonora →, *Mexico* 74 B2
Sonsonate, *El Salv.* 74 E7
Soochow = Suzhou, *China* 31 C7
Sopi, *Indonesia* 33 D7
Sopot, *Poland* 17 A10
Sopron, *Hungary* 17 E9
Sop's Arm, *Canada* 63 C8
Sør-Rondane, *Antarctica* 5 D4
Sorata, *Bolivia* 78 G5
Sorel, *Canada* 62 C5
Soreq, N. →, *Israel* 41 D3
Sorgono, *Italy* 20 D3
Soria, *Spain* 19 B4
Sorkh, Kuh-e, *Iran* 39 C8
Soroca, *Moldova* 17 D15
Sorocaba, *Brazil* 80 A7
Sorochinsk, *Russia* 22 D9
Soroki = Soroca, *Moldova* 17 D15
Sorong, *Indonesia* 33 E8
Soroti, *Uganda* 46 D6
Sørøya, *Norway* 8 A20
Sørøysundet, *Norway* 8 A20
Sorrento, *Australia* 55 F3
Sorsele, *Sweden* 8 D17
Sorsogon, *Phil.* 33 B6
Sortavala, *Russia* 22 B5
Sortland, *Norway* 8 B16
Soscumica, L., *Canada* 62 B4
Sosnogorsk, *Russia* 22 B9
Sosnovka, *Russia* 25 D11
Sosnowiec, *Poland* 17 C10
Sosva, *Russia* 22 C11
Sotkamo, *Finland* 8 D23
Souanké, *Congo* 46 D2
Soúdhas, Kólpos, *Greece* 21 G11
Sŏul, *S. Korea* 31 C7
Sound, The, *U.K.* 11 G3
Sources, Mt. aux, *Lesotho* 49 D4
Soure, *Brazil* 79 D9
Souris, *Man., Canada* 65 D8
Souris, *P.E.I., Canada* 63 C7
Souris →, *Canada* 70 A5
Sousa, *Brazil* 79 E11
Sousel, *Brazil* 79 D8
Sousse, *Tunisia* 45 A7
South Africa ■, *Africa* 48 E3
South Aulatsivik I., *Canada* 63 A7
South Australia □, *Australia* 55 E2
South Baldy, *U.S.A.* 73 J10
South Bend, *Ind., U.S.A.* 68 E2
South Bend, *Wash., U.S.A.* 72 C2
South Boston, *U.S.A.* 69 G6
South Branch, *Canada* 63 C8
South Brook, *Canada* 63 C8
South Carolina □, *U.S.A.* 69 J5
South Charleston, *U.S.A.* 68 F5
South China Sea, *Asia* 32 C4
South Dakota □, *U.S.A.* 70 C5
South Downs, *U.K.* 11 G7
South East C., *Australia* 54 G4
South East Is., *Australia* 53 F3
South Esk →, *U.K.* 12 E5
South Foreland, *U.K.* 11 F9
South Fork →, *U.S.A.* 72 C7
South Gamboa, *Panama* 74 H14
South Georgia, *Antarctica* 5 B1
South Glamorgan □, *U.K.* 11 F4
South Haven, *U.S.A.* 68 D2
South Henik, L., *Canada* 65 A9
South Honshu Ridge, *Pac. Oc.* 56 E6
South Horr, *Kenya* 46 D7
South I., *N.Z.* 51 L3
South Invercargill, *N.Z.* 51 M2
South Knife →, *Canada* 65 B10
South Korea ■, *Asia* 31 C7
South Loup →, *U.S.A.* 70 E5
South Magnetic Pole, *Antarctica* 5 C9
South Milwaukee, *U.S.A.* 68 D2
South Molton, *U.K.* 11 F4
South Nahanni →, *Canada* 64 A4
South Natuna Is. = Natuna Selatan, Kepulauan, *Indonesia* 32 D3
South Orkney Is., *Antarctica* 5 C18
South Pagai, I. = Pagai Selatan, P., *Indonesia* 32 E2
South Pass, *U.S.A.* 72 E9
South Pittsburg, *U.S.A.* 69 H3
South Platte →, *U.S.A.* 70 E4
South Pole, *Antarctica* 5 E
South Porcupine, *Canada* 62 C3
South River, *Canada* 62 C4
South Ronaldsay, *U.K.* 12 C6
South Sandwich Is., *Antarctica* 5 B1
South Saskatchewan →, *Canada* 65 C7
South Seal →, *Canada* 65 B9
South Sentinel I., *India* 34 G2
South Shetland Is., *Antarctica* 5 C18
South Shields, *U.K.* 10 C6
South Sioux City, *U.S.A.* 70 D6
South Taranaki Bight, *N.Z.* 51 H5
South Thompson →, *Canada* 64 C4
South Twin I., *Canada* 62 B4
South Tyne →, *U.K.* 10 C5
South Uist, *U.K.* 12 D1
South West Africa = Namibia ■, *Africa* 48 C2
South West C., *Australia* 54 G4
South Yorkshire □, *U.K.* 10 D6
Southampton, *Canada* 62 D3
Southampton, *U.K.* 11 G6
Southampton, *U.S.A.* 68 E9
Southampton I., *Canada* 61 B11
Southbridge, *N.Z.* 51 K4
Southend, *Canada* 65 B8
Southend-on-Sea, *U.K.* 11 F8
Southern Alps, *N.Z.* 51 K3
Southern Cross, *Australia* 53 F2
Southern Hills, *Australia* 53 F3
Southern Indian L., *Canada* 65 B9
Southern Ocean, *Antarctica* 5 C6
Southern Pines, *U.S.A.* 69 H6
Southern Uplands, *U.K.* 12 F5
Southport, *Australia* 55 D5
Southport, *U.K.* 10 D4
Southport, *U.S.A.* 69 J6
Southwest C., *N.Z.* 51 M1
Southwold, *U.K.* 11 E9
Soutpansberg, *S. Africa* 49 C4
Sovetsk, *Kaliningd., Russia* 9 J19
Sovetsk, *Kirov, Russia* 22 C8
Sovetskaya Gavan, *Russia* 25 E15
Soweto, *S. Africa* 49 D4
Sōya-Kaikyō = La Perouse Str., *Asia* 28 B11
Sōya-Misaki, *Japan* 28 B10
Soyo, *Angola* 46 F2
Sozh →, *Belarus* 17 B16
Spa, *Belgium* 15 D5
Spain ■, *Europe* 19 B4
Spalding, *Australia* 55 E2
Spalding, *U.K.* 10 E7
Spalding, *U.S.A.* 70 E5
Spaniard's Bay, *Canada* 63 C9
Spanish, *Canada* 62 C3
Spanish Fork, *U.S.A.* 72 F8
Spanish Town, *Jamaica* 74 K17
Sparks, *U.S.A.* 72 G4
Sparta = Spárti, *Greece* 21 F10
Sparta, *Ga., U.S.A.* 69 J4
Sparta, *Wis., U.S.A.* 70 D9
Spartanburg, *U.S.A.* 69 H4
Spárti, *Greece* 21 F10
Spartivento, C., *Calabria, Italy* 20 F7
Spartivento, C., *Sard., Italy* 20 E3
Spassk Dalniy, *Russia* 25 E14
Spátha, Ákra, *Greece* 21 G10
Spatsizi →, *Canada* 64 B3
Spearfish, *U.S.A.* 70 C3
Spearman, *U.S.A.* 71 G4
Speers, *Canada* 65 C7
Speightstown, *Barbados* 74 P22
Spence Bay, *Canada* 60 B10
Spencer, *Idaho, U.S.A.* 72 D7
Spencer, *Iowa, U.S.A.* 70 D7
Spencer, *Nebr., U.S.A.* 70 D5
Spencer, *W. Va., U.S.A.* 68 F5
Spencer, C., *Australia* 55 F2
Spencer B., *Namibia* 48 D1
Spencer G., *Australia* 55 E2
Spences Bridge, *Canada* 64 C4
Spenser Mts., *N.Z.* 51 K4
Sperrin Mts., *U.K.* 13 B5
Spey →, *U.K.* 12 D5
Speyer, *Germany* 16 D5
Spirit Lake, *U.S.A.* 72 C5
Spirit River, *Canada* 64 B5
Spiritwood, *Canada* 65 C7
Spithead, *U.K.* 11 G6
Spitzbergen = Svalbard, *Arctic* 4 B8
Spjelkavik, *Norway* 9 E12
Split, *Croatia* 20 C7
Split L., *Canada* 65 B9
Spofford, *U.S.A.* 71 L4
Spokane, *U.S.A.* 72 C5
Spoleto, *Italy* 20 C5
Spooner, *U.S.A.* 70 C9
Sporyy Navolok, Mys, *Russia* 24 B7
Spragge, *Canada* 62 C3
Sprague, *U.S.A.* 72 C5
Sprague River, *U.S.A.* 72 E3
Spratly I., *S. China Sea* 32 C4
Spray, *U.S.A.* 72 D4
Spree →, *Germany* 16 B7
Sprengisandur, *Iceland* 8 D5
Spring City, *U.S.A.* 72 G8
Spring Mts., *U.S.A.* 73 H6
Spring Valley, *U.S.A.* 70 D8
Springbok, *S. Africa* 48 D2
Springdale, *Canada* 63 C8
Springdale, *Ark., U.S.A.* 71 G7
Springdale, *Wash., U.S.A.* 72 B5
Springer, *U.S.A.* 71 G2
Springerville, *U.S.A.* 73 J9
Springfield, *N.Z.* 51 K3
Springfield, *Colo., U.S.A.* 71 G3
Springfield, *Ill., U.S.A.* 70 F10
Springfield, *Mass., U.S.A.* 68 D9
Springfield, *Mo., U.S.A.* 71 G8
Springfield, *Ohio, U.S.A.* 68 F4
Springfield, *Oreg., U.S.A.* 72 D2
Springfield, *Tenn., U.S.A.* 69 G2
Springfontein, *S. Africa* 48 E4
Springhill, *Canada* 63 C7
Springhouse, *Canada* 64 C4
Springhurst, *Australia* 55 F4
Springs, *S. Africa* 49 D4
Springsure, *Australia* 54 C4
Springvale, *Queens., Australia* 54 C3
Springvale, *W. Austral., Australia* 52 C4
Springville, *N.Y., U.S.A.* 68 D6
Springville, *Utah, U.S.A.* 72 F8
Springwater, *Canada* 65 C7
Spur, *U.S.A.* 71 J4
Spurn Hd., *U.K.* 10 D8
Spuzzum, *Canada* 64 D4
Squamish, *Canada* 64 D4
Square Islands, *Canada* 63 B8
Squires, Mt., *Australia* 53 E4
Sragen, *Indonesia* 33 G14
Srbija = Serbia □, *Yugoslavia* 21 C9
Sre Umbell, *Cambodia* 34 G7
Srebrnica, *Bos.-H.* 21 B8
Sredinny Ra. = Sredinnyy Khrebet, *Russia* 25 D16
Sredinnyy Khrebet, *Russia* 25 D16
Sredne Tambovskoye, *Russia* 25 D14
Srednekolymsk, *Russia* 25 C16
Srednevilyuysk, *Russia* 25 C13
Śrem, *Poland* 17 B9
Sremska Mitrovica, *Serbia, Yug.* 21 B8
Sretensk, *Russia* 25 D12
Sri Lanka ■, *Asia* 36 R12
Srikakulam, *India* 37 K13
Srinagar, *India* 36 B9
Staaten →, *Australia* 54 B3
Stade, *Germany* 16 B5
Stadskanaal, *Neths.* 15 A6
Staffa, *U.K.* 12 E2
Stafford, *U.K.* 10 E5
Stafford, *U.S.A.* 71 G5
Staffordshire □, *U.K.* 10 E5
Staines, *U.K.* 11 F7
Stakhanov, *Ukraine* 23 E6
Stalingrad = Volgograd, *Russia* 23 E7
Staliniri = Tskhinvali, *Georgia* 23 F7
Stalino = Donetsk, *Ukraine* 23 E6
Stalinogorsk = Novomoskovsk, *Russia* 22 D6
Stalowa Wola, *Poland* 17 C12
Stalybridge, *U.K.* 10 D5
Stamford, *Australia* 54 C3
Stamford, *U.K.* 11 E7
Stamford, *Conn., U.S.A.* 68 E9
Stamford, *Tex., U.S.A.* 71 J5
Stamps, *U.S.A.* 71 J8
Stanberry, *U.S.A.* 70 E7
Standerton, *S. Africa* 49 D4
Standish, *U.S.A.* 68 D4
Stanford, *U.S.A.* 72 C8
Stanger, *S. Africa* 49 D5
Stanislav = Ivano-Frankivsk, *Ukraine* 17 D13
Stanke Dimitrov, *Bulgaria* 21 C10
Stanley, *Australia* 54 G4
Stanley, *N.B., Canada* 63 C6
Stanley, *Sask., Canada* 65 B8
Stanley, *Falk. Is.* 80 G5
Stanley, *Idaho, U.S.A.* 72 D6
Stanley, *N. Dak., U.S.A.* 70 A3
Stanley, *Wis., U.S.A.* 70 C9
Stanovoy Khrebet, *Russia* 25 D13
Stanovoy Ra. = Stanovoy Khrebet, *Russia* 25 D13
Stansmore Ra., *Australia* 52 D4
Stanthorpe, *Australia* 55 D5
Stanton, *U.S.A.* 71 J4
Staples, *U.S.A.* 70 B7
Stapleton, *U.S.A.* 70 E4
Star City, *Canada* 65 C8
Stara Planina, *Bulgaria* 21 C10
Stara Zagora, *Bulgaria* 21 C11
Starachowice, *Poland* 17 C11
Staraya Russa, *Russia* 22 C5
Starbuck I., *Kiribati* 57 H12
Stargard Szczeciński, *Poland* 16 B8
Staritsa, *Russia* 22 C5
Starke, *U.S.A.* 69 K4
Starkville, *Colo., U.S.A.* 71 G2
Starkville, *Miss., U.S.A.* 69 J1
Starogard Gdański, *Poland* 17 B10
Starokonstantinov = Starokonstyantyniv, *Ukraine* 17 D14
Starokonstyantyniv, *Ukraine* 17 D14
Start Pt., *U.K.* 11 G4
Staryy Chartoriysk, *Ukraine* 17 C13
Staryy Kheydzhan, *Russia* 25 C15
Staryy Oskol, *Russia* 22 D6
State College, *U.S.A.* 68 E7
Staten, I. = Estados, I. de Los, *Argentina* 80 G4
Statesboro, *U.S.A.* 69 J5
Statesville, *U.S.A.* 69 H5
Staunton, *Ill., U.S.A.* 70 F10
Staunton, *Va., U.S.A.* 68 F6
Stavanger, *Norway* 9 G11
Staveley, *N.Z.* 51 K3
Stavelot, *Belgium* 15 D5
Staveren, *Neths.* 15 B5
Stavern, *Norway* 9 G14
Stavropol, *Russia* 23 E7
Stawell, *Australia* 55 F3
Stawell →, *Australia* 54 C3
Steamboat Springs, *U.S.A.* 72 F10
Steele, *U.S.A.* 70 B5
Steelton, *U.S.A.* 68 E7
Steelville, *U.S.A.* 71 G9
Steen River, *Canada* 64 B5
Steenkool = Bintuni, *Indonesia* 33 E8
Steenwijk, *Neths.* 15 B6
Steep Pt., *Australia* 53 E1
Steep Rock, *Canada* 65 C9
Stefanie L. = Chew Bahir, *Ethiopia* 45 H12
Stefansson Bay, *Antarctica* 5 C5
Steiermark □, *Austria* 16 E8
Steinbach, *Canada* 65 D9
Steinfort, *Lux.* 15 E5
Steinkjer, *Norway* 8 D14
Steinkopf, *S. Africa* 48 D2
Stellarton, *Canada* 63 C7
Stellenbosch, *S. Africa* 48 E2
Stendal, *Germany* 16 B6
Steornabhaigh = Stornoway, *U.K.* 12 C2
Stepanakert = Xankändi, *Azerbaijan* 23 G8
Stephen, *U.S.A.* 70 A6
Stephens Creek, *Australia* 55 E3
Stephens I., *Canada* 64 C2
Stephenville, *Canada* 63 C8
Stephenville, *U.S.A.* 71 J5
Stepnoi = Elista, *Russia* 23 E7
Stepnyak, *Kazakhstan* 24 D8
Steppe, *Asia* 26 E7
Sterkstroom, *S. Africa* 48 E4
Sterling, *Colo., U.S.A.* 70 E3
Sterling, *Ill., U.S.A.* 70 E10
Sterling, *Kans., U.S.A.* 70 F5
Sterling City, *U.S.A.* 71 K4
Sterlitamak, *Russia* 22 D10
Stettin = Szczecin, *Poland* 16 B8
Stettiner Haff, *Germany* 16 B8
Stettler, *Canada* 64 C6
Steubenville, *U.S.A.* 68 E5
Stevens Point, *U.S.A.* 70 C10
Stevenson L., *Canada* 65 C9
Stewart, *B.C., Canada* 64 B3
Stewart, *N.W.T., Canada* 60 B6
Stewart, C., *Australia* 54 A1
Stewart, I., *Chile* 80 G2
Stewart I., *N.Z.* 51 M1
Stewiacke, *Canada* 63 C7
Steynsburg, *S. Africa* 48 E4
Steyr, *Austria* 16 D8
Steytlerville, *S. Africa* 48 E3
Stigler, *U.S.A.* 71 H7
Stikine →, *Canada* 64 B2
Stilfontein, *S. Africa* 48 D4
Stillwater, *N.Z.* 51 K3
Stillwater, *Minn., U.S.A.* 70 C8
Stillwater, *Okla., U.S.A.* 71 G6
Stillwater Range, *U.S.A.* 72 G4
Stilwell, *U.S.A.* 71 H7
Štip, *Macedonia* 21 D10
Stirling, *Australia* 54 B3
Stirling, *Canada* 64 D6
Stirling, *U.K.* 12 E5
Stirling Ra., *Australia* 53 F2
Stjernøya, *Norway* 8 A20
Stjørdalshalsen, *Norway* 8 E14
Stockerau, *Austria* 16 D9
Stockett, *U.S.A.* 72 C8
Stockholm, *Sweden* 9 G18
Stockport, *U.K.* 10 D5
Stockton, *Calif., U.S.A.* 73 H3
Stockton, *Kans., U.S.A.* 70 F5
Stockton, *Mo., U.S.A.* 71 G8
Stockton-on-Tees, *U.K.* 10 C6
Stoke on Trent, *U.K.* 10 D5
Stokes Bay, *Canada* 62 C3
Stokes Pt., *Australia* 54 G3
Stokes Ra., *Australia* 52 C5
Stokksnes, *Iceland* 8 D6
Stokmarknes, *Norway* 8 B16
Stolac, *Bos.-H.* 21 C7
Stolbovaya, *Russia* 25 C16
Stolbovoy, Ostrov, *Russia* 25 D17
Stolbtsy = Stowbtsy, *Belarus* 17 B14
Stolin, *Belarus* 17 C14
Stonehaven, *U.K.* 12 E6
Stonehenge, *Australia* 54 C3
Stonewall, *Canada* 65 C9
Stony L., *Canada* 65 B9
Stony Rapids, *Canada* 65 B7
Stony Tunguska = Podkamennaya Tunguska →, *Russia* 25 C10
Stora Lulevatten, *Sweden* 8 C18
Storavan, *Sweden* 8 D18
Stord, *Norway* 9 G11
Store Bælt, *Denmark* 9 J14
Store Creek, *Australia* 55 E4
Storm B., *Australia* 54 G4
Storm Lake, *U.S.A.* 70 D7
Stormberge, *S. Africa* 48 E4
Stormsrivier, *S. Africa* 48 E3
Stornoway, *U.K.* 12 C2
Storozhinets = Storozhynets, *Ukraine* 17 D13
Storozhynets, *Ukraine* 17 D13
Storsjön, *Sweden* 8 E16
Storuman, *Sweden* 8 D17
Storuman, sjö, *Sweden* 8 D17
Stoughton, *Canada* 65 D8
Stour →, *Dorset, U.K.* 11 G5
Stour →, *Here. & Worcs., U.K.* 11 E5
Stour →, *Kent, U.K.* 11 F9
Stour →, *Suffolk, U.K.* 11 F9
Stourbridge, *U.K.* 11 E5
Stout, L., *Canada* 65 C10
Stowbtsy, *Belarus* 17 B14
Stowmarket, *U.K.* 11 E9
Strabane, *U.K.* 13 B4
Strabane □, *U.K.* 13 B4
Strahan, *Australia* 54 G4
Stralsund, *Germany* 16 A7
Strand, *S. Africa* 48 E2
Stranda, *Møre og Romsdal, Norway* 9 E12
Stranda, *Nord-Trøndelag, Norway* 8 E14
Strangford L., *U.K.* 13 B6
Stranraer, *U.K.* 12 G3
Strasbourg, *Canada* 65 C8
Strasbourg, *France* 18 B7
Strasburg, *U.S.A.* 70 B4
Stratford, *Canada* 62 D3
Stratford, *N.Z.* 51 H5
Stratford, *Calif., U.S.A.* 73 H4
Stratford, *Tex., U.S.A.* 71 G3
Stratford-upon-Avon, *U.K.* 11 E6
Strath Spey, *U.K.* 12 D5
Strathalbyn, *Australia* 55 F2
Strathclyde □, *U.K.* 12 F4
Strathcona Prov. Park, *Canada* 64 D3
Strathmore, *Australia* 54 B3
Strathmore, *Canada* 64 C6
Strathmore, *U.K.* 12 E5
Strathnaver, *Canada* 64 C4
Strathpeffer, *U.K.* 12 D4
Strathroy, *Canada* 62 D3
Strathy Pt., *U.K.* 12 C4
Stratton, *U.S.A.* 70 F3
Straubing, *Germany* 16 D7
Straumnes, *Iceland* 8 C2
Strawberry Reservoir, *U.S.A.* 72 F8

Strawn, *U.S.A.* 71 J5
Streaky B., *Australia* . 55 E1
Streaky Bay, *Australia* . 55 E1
Streator, *U.S.A.* 70 E10
Streeter, *U.S.A.* 70 B5
Strelka, *Russia* 25 D10
Streymoy, *Færoe Is.* .. 8 E9
Strezhevoy, *Russia* ... 24 C8
Strimón →, *Greece* ... 21 D10
Strimonikós Kólpos,
   Greece 21 D11
Strómboli, *Italy* 20 E6
Stromeferry, *U.K.* 12 D3
Stromness, *U.K.* 12 C5
Stromsburg, *U.S.A.* .. 70 E6
Strömstad, *Sweden* .. 9 G14
Strömsund, *Sweden* .. 8 E16
Stronsay, *U.K.* 11 B6
Stroud, *U.K.* 11 F5
Stroud Road, *Australia* 55 E5
Struer, *Denmark* 9 H13
Strumica, *Macedonia* . 21 D10
Struthers, *Canada* 62 C2
Struthers, *U.S.A.* 68 E5
Stryker, *U.S.A.* 72 B6
Stryy, *Ukraine* 17 D12
Strzelecki Cr. →,
   Australia 55 D2
Stuart, *Fla., U.S.A.* .. 69 M5
Stuart, *Nebr., U.S.A.* . 70 D5
Stuart →, *Canada* ... 64 C4
Stuart Bluff Ra.,
   Australia 52 D5
Stuart L., *Canada* ... 64 C4
Stuart Ra., *Australia* . 55 D1
Stull, L., *Canada* 62 B1
Stung Treng, *Cambodia* 34 F8
Stupart →, *Canada* .. 65 B10
Sturgeon B., *Canada* . 65 C9
Sturgeon Bay, *U.S.A.* . 68 C2
Sturgeon Falls, *Canada* 62 C4
Sturgeon L., *Alta.,
   Canada* 64 B5
Sturgeon L., *Ont.,
   Canada* 62 B1
Sturgis, *Mich., U.S.A.* . 68 E3
Sturgis, *S. Dak., U.S.A.* 70 C3
Sturt Cr. →, *Australia* 52 C4
Sturt Creek, *Australia* . 52 C4
Stutterheim, *S. Africa* . 48 E4
Stuttgart, *Germany* .. 16 D5
Stuttgart, *U.S.A.* 71 H9
Stykkishólmur, *Iceland* 8 D2
Styria = Steiermark □,
   Austria 16 E8
Suakin, *Sudan* 45 E12
Subang, *Indonesia* .. 33 G12
Subansiri →, *India* .. 37 F18
Subayhah, *Si. Arabia* . 38 D3
Subi, *Indonesia* 32 D3
Subotica, *Serbia, Yug.* 21 A8
Success, *Canada* 65 C7
Suceava, *Romania* ... 17 E14
Suchan, *Russia* 28 C6
Suchou = Suzhou,
   China 31 C7
Süchow = Xuzhou,
   China 31 C6
Suck →, *Ireland* 13 C3
Sucre, *Bolivia* 78 G5
Sud, Pte., *Canada* ... 63 C7
Sud-Ouest, Pte. du,
   Canada 63 C7
Sudan, *U.S.A.* 71 H3
Sudan ■, *Africa* 45 E11
Sudbury, *Canada* 62 C3
Sudbury, *U.K.* 11 E8
Sûdd, *Sudan* 45 G11
Sudeten Mts. = Sudety,
   Europe 17 C9
Sudety, *Europe* 17 C9
Suðuroy, *Færoe Is.* ... 8 F9
Sudirman,
   Pegunungan,
   Indonesia 33 E9
Sueca, *Spain* 19 C5
Suez = El Suweis,
   Egypt 45 C11
Suez, G. of = Suweis,
   Khalîg el, *Egypt* . 45 C11
Suffield, *Canada* 65 C6
Suffolk, *U.S.A.* 68 G7
Suffolk □, *U.K.* 11 E9
Sugar City, *U.S.A.* ... 70 F3
Sugluk = Salluit,
   Canada 61 B12
Suhār, *Oman* 39 E8
Suhl, *Germany* 16 C6
Suihua, *China* 31 B7
Suir →, *Ireland* 13 D4
Sukabumi, *Indonesia* . 33 G12
Sukadana, *Kalimantan,
   Indonesia* 32 E3
Sukadana, *Sumatera,
   Indonesia* 32 F3
Sukagawa, *Japan* ... 29 F10
Sukaraja, *Indonesia* . 32 E4
Sukarnapura =
   Jayapura, *Indonesia* 33 E10
Sukhona →, *Russia* . 22 C6
Sukhumi = Sokhumi,
   Georgia 23 F7
Sukkur, *Pakistan* 36 F6
Sukkur Barrage,
   Pakistan 36 F6
Sukumo, *Japan* 29 H6
Sukunka →, *Canada* . 64 B4
Sula, Kepulauan,
   Indonesia 33 E7
Sulaiman Range,
   Pakistan 36 D6
Sülär, *Iran* 39 D6
Sulawesi □, *Indonesia* 33 E6

Sulawesi Sea =
   Celebes Sea,
   Indonesia 33 D6
Sulima, *S. Leone* 44 G2
Sulina, *Romania* 17 F15
Sulitjelma, *Norway* ... 8 C17
Sullana, *Peru* 78 D2
Sullivan, *Ill., U.S.A.* .. 70 F10
Sullivan, *Ind., U.S.A.* . 68 F2
Sullivan, *Mo., U.S.A.* . 70 F9
Sullivan Bay, *Canada* . 64 C3
Sullivan I. = Lambi
   Kyun, *Burma* 34 G5
Sulphur, *La., U.S.A.* .. 71 K8
Sulphur, *Okla., U.S.A.* 71 H6
Sulphur Pt., *Canada* . 64 A6
Sulphur Springs, *U.S.A.* 71 J7
Sulphur Springs
   Draw →, *U.S.A.* . 71 J4
Sultan, *Canada* 62 C3
Sultanpur, *India* 37 F13
Sultsa, *Russia* 22 B8
Sulu Arch. = *Phil.* ... 33 C6
Sulu Sea, *E. Indies* .. 33 C6
Suluq, *Libya* 45 B9
Sulzberger Ice Shelf,
   Antarctica 5 D10
Sumalata, *Indonesia* . 33 D6
Sumatera □, *Indonesia* 32 D2
Sumatra =
   Sumatera □,
   Indonesia 32 D2
Sumatra, *U.S.A.* 72 C10
Sumba, *Indonesia* ... 33 F5
Sumba, Selat,
   Indonesia 33 F5
Sumbawa, *Indonesia* . 32 F5
Sumbawa Besar,
   Indonesia 32 F5
Sumbe, *Angola* 46 G2
Sumburgh Hd., *U.K.* . 12 B7
Sumedang, *Indonesia* 33 G12
Šumen, *Bulgaria* 21 C12
Sumenep, *Indonesia* . 33 G15
Sumgait = Sumqayıt,
   Azerbaijan 23 F8
Summer L., *U.S.A.* ... 72 E3
Summerland, *Canada* . 64 D5
Summerside, *Canada* . 63 C7
Summerville, *Ga.,
   U.S.A.* 69 H3
Summerville, *S.C.,
   U.S.A.* 69 J5
Summit Lake, *Canada* 64 C4
Summit Peak, *U.S.A.* . 73 H10
Sumner, *U.S.A.* 70 D8
Sumoto, *Japan* 29 G7
Sumperk, *Czech.* 17 D9
Sumqayıt, *Azerbaijan* . 23 F8
Sumter, *U.S.A.* 69 J5
Sumy, *Ukraine* 23 D5
Sun City, *U.S.A.* 73 K7
Sunagawa, *Japan* ... 28 C10
Sunart, L., *U.K.* 12 E3
Sunburst, *U.S.A.* 72 B8
Sunbury, *Australia* ... 55 F3
Sunbury, *U.S.A.* 68 E7
Sunda, Selat, *Indonesia* 32 F3
Sunda Is., *Indonesia* . 26 K13
Sunda Str. = Sunda,
   Selat, *Indonesia* . 32 F3
Sundance, *U.S.A.* ... 70 C2
Sundarbans, The, *Asia* 37 J16
Sundargarh, *India* ... 37 H14
Sundays =
   Sondags →,
   S. Africa 48 E4
Sunderland, *U.K.* 10 C6
Sundre, *Canada* 64 C6
Sundridge, *Canada* .. 62 C4
Sundsvall, *Sweden* .. 9 E17
Sungai Patani, *Malaysia* 34 P13
Sungaigerong,
   Indonesia 32 E2
Sungailiat, *Indonesia* . 32 E3
Sungaipakning,
   Indonesia 32 D2
Sungaipenuh,
   Indonesia 32 E2
Sungaitiram, *Indonesia* 32 E5
Sungari = Songhua
   Jiang →, *China* .. 31 B8
Sungei Siput, *Malaysia* 34 Q14
Sungguminasa,
   Indonesia 33 F5
Sunghua Chiang =
   Songhua Jiang →,
   China 31 B8
Sunndalsøra, *Norway* . 9 E13
Sunnyside, *Utah,
   U.S.A.* 72 G8
Sunnyside, *Wash.,
   U.S.A.* 72 C4
Sunnyvale, *U.S.A.* ... 73 H2
Sunray, *U.S.A.* 71 G4
Suntar, *Russia* 25 C12
Suomenselkä, *Finland* 8 E21
Suomussalmi, *Finland* 8 D23
Suoyarvi, *Russia* 22 B5
Supai, *U.S.A.* 73 H7
Supaul, *India* 37 F15
Superior, *Ariz., U.S.A.* 73 K8
Superior, *Mont., U.S.A.* 72 C6
Superior, *Nebr., U.S.A.* 70 E5
Superior, *Wis., U.S.A.* 70 B8
Superior, L., *U.S.A.* .. 62 C2
Suphan Buri, *Thailand* 34 E6
Supiori, *Indonesia* ... 33 E9
Suq Suwayq, *Si. Arabia* 38 E3
Sûr, *Lebanon* 41 B4
Sur, Pt., *U.S.A.* 73 H3
Sura →, *Russia* 22 C8
Surabaja = Surabaya,
   Indonesia 33 G15

Surabaya, *Indonesia* .. 33 G15
Surakarta, *Indonesia* . 33 G14
Surat, *Australia* 55 D4
Surat, *India* 36 J8
Surat Thani, *Thailand* . 34 H5
Suratgarh, *India* 36 E9
Sûre = Sauer →,
   Germany 15 E6
Surgut, *Russia* 24 C8
Suriapet, *India* 36 L11
Surigao, *Phil.* 33 C7
Surin, *Thailand* 34 E7
Surinam ■,
   S. Amer. = Surinam 79 C7
Suriname = *Surinam* . 79 C7
Sûrmaq, *Iran* 39 D7
Surprise L., *Canada* . 64 B2
Surrey □, *U.K.* 11 F7
Surt, *Libya* 45 B8
Surt, Khalîj, *Libya* ... 45 B8
Surtsey, *Iceland* 8 E3
Suruga-Wan, *Japan* . 29 G9
Susaki, *Japan* 29 H6
Süsangerd, *Iran* 39 D6
Susanino, *Russia* ... 25 D15
Susanville, *U.S.A.* ... 72 F3
Susquehanna →,
   U.S.A. 68 F7
Susques, *Argentina* .. 80 A3
Sussex, *Canada* 63 C6
Sussex, E. □, *U.K.* .. 11 G8
Sussex, W. □, *U.K.* . 11 G7
Sustut →, *Canada* .. 64 B3
Susuman, *Russia* ... 25 C15
Susunu, *Indonesia* .. 33 E8
Susurluk, *Turkey* 21 E13
Sutherland, *S. Africa* . 48 E3
Sutherland, *U.S.A.* .. 70 E4
Sutherland Falls, *N.Z.* . 51 L1
Sutherlin, *U.S.A.* 72 E2
Sutlej →, *Pakistan* .. 36 E7
Sutton, *U.S.A.* 70 E6
Sutton →, *Canada* .. 62 A3
Sutton in Ashfield, *U.K.* 10 D6
Suttor →, *Australia* . 54 C4
Suttsu, *Japan* 28 C10
Suva, *Fiji* 51 D8
Suva Planina,
   Serbia, Yug. 21 C10
Suvorov Is. =
   Suwarrow Is.,
   Cook Is. 57 J11
Suwałki, *Poland* 17 A12
Suwannee →, *U.S.A.* 69 L4
Suwanose-Jima, *Japan* 29 K4
Suwarrow Is., *Cook Is.* 57 J11
Suwayq aş Şuqban,
   Iraq 38 D5
Suweis, Khalîg el,
   Egypt 45 C11
Suzdal, *Russia* 22 C7
Suzhou, *China* 31 C7
Suzu, *Japan* 29 F8
Suzu-Misaki, *Japan* .. 29 F8
Suzuka, *Japan* 29 G8
Svalbard, *Arctic* 4 B8
Svappavaara, *Sweden* 8 C19
Svartisen, *Norway* ... 8 C15
Svay Rieng, *Cambodia* 34 G8
Svealand □, *Sweden* . 9 G16
Sveg, *Sweden* 9 E16
Svendborg, *Denmark* . 9 J14
Sverdlovsk =
   Yekaterinburg, *Russia* 22 C11
Sverdrup Is., *Canada* . 4 B3
Svetlaya, *Russia* 28 A9
Svetlogorsk =
   Svyetlahorsk, *Belarus* 17 B15
Svetozarevo,
   Serbia, Yug. 21 C9
Svir →, *Russia* 22 B5
Svishtov, *Bulgaria* ... 21 C11
Svislach, *Belarus* ... 17 B13
Svobodnyy, *Russia* .. 25 D13
Svolvær, *Norway* 8 B16
Svyetlahorsk, *Belarus* 17 B15
Swabian Alps =
   Schwäbische Alb,
   Germany 16 D5
Swainsboro, *U.S.A.* .. 69 J4
Swakopmund, *Namibia* 48 C1
Swale →, *U.K.* 10 C6
Swan Hill, *Australia* .. 55 F3
Swan Hills, *Canada* .. 64 C5
Swan L., *Canada* 65 C8
Swan River, *Canada* . 65 C8
Swanage, *U.K.* 11 G6
Swansea, *Australia* .. 55 E5
Swansea, *U.K.* 11 F4
Swartberge, *S. Africa* . 48 E3
Swartmodder, *S. Africa* 48 D3
Swartruggens, *S. Africa* 48 D4
Swastika, *Canada* ... 62 C3
Swatow = Shantou,
   China 31 D6
Swaziland ■, *Africa* .. 49 D5
Sweden ■, *Europe* .. 9 G16
Sweet Home, *U.S.A.* . 72 D2
Sweetwater, *U.S.A.* .. 71 J4
Sweetwater →, *U.S.A.* 72 E10
Swellendam, *S. Africa* 48 E3
Świdnica, *Poland* ... 17 C9
Świdnik, *Poland* 17 C12
Świebodzin, *Poland* . 16 B8
Świecie, *Poland* 17 B10
Swift Current, *Canada* 65 C7
Swiftcurrent →,
   Canada 65 C7
Swilly, L., *Ireland* ... 13 A4
Swindle, I., *Canada* .. 64 C3
Swindon, *U.K.* 11 F6
Swinemünde =
   Świnoujście, *Poland* 16 B8

Świnoujście, *Poland* .. 16 B8
Switzerland ■, *Europe* 16 E5
Swords, *Ireland* 13 C5
Sydney, *Australia* ... 55 E5
Sydney, *Canada* 63 C7
Sydney Mines, *Canada* 63 C7
Sydprøven, *Greenland* 4 C5
Sydra, G. of = Surt,
   Khalîj, *Libya* 45 B8
Syktyvkar, *Russia* ... 22 B9
Sylacauga, *U.S.A.* ... 69 J2
Sylarna, *Sweden* 8 E15
Sylhet, *Bangla.* 37 G17
Sylt, *Germany* 16 A5
Sylvan Lake, *Canada* . 64 C6
Sylvania, *U.S.A.* 69 J5
Sylvester, *U.S.A.* 69 K4
Sym, *Russia* 24 C9
Synnott Ra., *Australia* 52 C4
Syracuse, *Kans., U.S.A.* 71 F4
Syracuse, *N.Y., U.S.A.* 68 D7
Syrdarya →,
   Kazakhstan 24 E7
Syria ■, *Asia* 38 C3
Syul'dzhyukyor, *Russia* 25 C12
Syzran, *Russia* 22 D8
Szczecin, *Poland* ... 16 B8
Szczecinek, *Poland* .. 17 B9
Szczytno, *Poland* ... 17 B11
Szechwan =
   Sichuan □, *China* . 30 C5
Szeged, *Hungary* 17 E11
Székesfehérvár,
   Hungary 17 E10
Szekszárd, *Hungary* . 17 E10
Szentes, *Hungary* ... 17 E11
Szolnok, *Hungary* ... 17 E11
Szombathely, *Hungary* 17 E9

T

Tabacal, *Argentina* ... 80 A4
Tabaco, *Phil.* 33 B6
Ţābah, *Si. Arabia* ... 38 E4
Tabarka, *Tunisia* 44 A6
Ţabas, *Khorāsān, Iran* 39 C9
Ţabas, *Khorāsān, Iran* 39 C8
Tabatinga, Serra da,
   Brazil 79 F10
Tabâzin, *Iran* 39 D8
Taber, *Canada* 64 D6
Tablas, *Phil.* 33 B6
Table B. = Tafelbaai,
   S. Africa 48 E2
Table B., *Canada* 63 B8
Table Mt., *S. Africa* .. 48 E2
Tableland, *Australia* .. 52 C4
Tabletop, Mt., *Australia* 54 C4
Tábor, *Czech.* 16 D8
Tabora, *Tanzania* 46 F6
Tabou, *Ivory C.* 44 H3
Tabrîz, *Iran* 38 B5
Tabuaeran, *Pac. Oc.* . 57 G12
Tabûk, *Si. Arabia* ... 38 D3
Tacheng, *China* 30 B3
Tacloban, *Phil.* 33 B6
Tacna, *Peru* 78 G4
Tacoma, *U.S.A.* 72 C2
Tacuarembó, *Uruguay* 80 C5
Tademaït, Plateau du,
   Algeria 44 C5
Tadjoura, *Djibouti* ... 40 E3
Tadmor, *N.Z.* 51 J4
Tadoule, L., *Canada* . 65 B9
Tadoussac, *Canada* . 63 C6
Tadzhikistan =
   Tajikistan ■, *Asia* . 24 F8
Taegu, *S. Korea* 31 C7
Taejŏn, *S. Korea* 31 C7
Tafalla, *Spain* 19 A5
Tafelbaai, *S. Africa* .. 48 E2
Tafermaar, *Indonesia* . 33 F8
Tafîhān, *Iran* 39 D7
Taft, *Iran* 39 D7
Taft, *Phil.* 33 B7
Taft, *Calif., U.S.A.* ... 73 J4
Taft, *Tex., U.S.A.* 71 M6
Taga Dzong, *Bhutan* . 37 F16
Taganrog, *Russia* ... 23 E6
Tagbilaran, *Phil.* 33 C6
Tagish, *Canada* 64 A2
Tagish L., *Canada* ... 64 A2
Tagliamento →, *Italy* 20 B5
Taguatinga, *Brazil* ... 79 F10
Tagum, *Phil.* 33 C7
Tagus = Tejo →,
   Europe 19 C1
Tahakopa, *N.Z.* 51 M2
Tahan, Gunong,
   Malaysia 34 Q15
Tahat, *Algeria* 44 D6
Tāheri, *Iran* 39 E7
Tahiti, *Pac. Oc.* 57 J13
Tahoe, L., *U.S.A.* 72 G3
Tahoe City, *U.S.A.* ... 72 G3
Tahoua, *Niger* 44 F6
Tahta, *Egypt* 45 C11
Tahulandang, *Indonesia* 33 D7
Tahuna, *Indonesia* .. 33 D7
Taï, *Ivory C.* 44 G3
Taï, *Taiwan* 31 D7
T'aichung = Taizhong,
   Taiwan 31 D7
Taieri →, *N.Z.* 51 M3
Taihape, *N.Z.* 51 H5
Tailem Bend, *Australia* 55 F2
Taimyr Peninsula =
   Taymyr, Poluostrov,
   Russia 25 B11
Tain, *U.K.* 12 D4
Tainan, *Taiwan* 31 D7

Taínaron, Ákra, *Greece* 21 F10
T'aipei = Taibei,
   Taiwan 31 D7
Taiping, *Malaysia* ... 34 Q13
Tairbeart = Tarbert,
   U.K. 12 D2
Taitao, Pen. de, *Chile* . 80 F2
Taivalkoski, *Finland* .. 8 D23
Taiwan ■, *Asia* 31 D7
Taïyetos Óros, *Greece* 21 F10
Taiyiba, *Israel* 41 C4
Taiyuan, *China* 31 C6
Taizhong, *Taiwan* ... 31 D7
Ta'izz, *Yemen* 40 E3
Tajikistan ■, *Asia* ... 24 F8
Tajima, *Japan* 29 F9
Tajo = Tejo →,
   Europe 19 C1
Tajrīsh, *Iran* 39 C6
Tājūrā, *Libya* 45 B7
Tak, *Thailand* 34 D5
Takāb, *Iran* 38 B5
Takachiho, *Japan* ... 29 H5
Takada, *Japan* 29 F9
Takahagi, *Japan* 29 F10
Takaka, *N.Z.* 51 J4
Takamatsu, *Japan* .. 29 G7
Takaoka, *Japan* 29 F8
Takapuna, *N.Z.* 51 G5
Takasaki, *Japan* 29 F9
Takatsuki, *Japan* 29 G7
Takaungu, *Kenya* ... 46 E7
Takayama, *Japan* ... 29 F8
Take-Shima, *Japan* .. 29 J5
Takefu, *Japan* 29 G8
Takengon, *Indonesia* . 32 D1
Takeo, *Cambodia* ... 34 G8
Takeo, *Japan* 29 H5
Takêstān, *Iran* 39 C6
Taketa, *Japan* 29 H5
Takikawa, *Japan* 28 C10
Takla →, *Canada* ... 64 B3
Takla Landing, *Canada* 64 B3
Takla Makan =
   Taklamakan Shamo,
   China 26 F12
Taklamakan Shamo,
   China 26 F12
Taku →, *Canada* ... 64 B2
Takum, *Nigeria* 44 G6
Tal Halâl, *Iran* 39 D7
Talara, *Peru* 78 D2
Talas, *Kyrgyzstan* ... 24 E8
Talâta, *Egypt* 41 E1
Talaud, Kepulauan,
   Indonesia 33 D7
Talaud Is. = Talaud,
   Kepulauan, *Indonesia* 33 D7
Talavera de la Reina,
   Spain 19 C3
Talawana, *Australia* .. 52 D3
Talayan, *Phil.* 33 C6
Talbot, C., *Australia* .. 52 B4
Talbragar →, *Australia* 55 E4
Talca, *Chile* 80 D2
Talcahuano, *Chile* ... 80 D2
Talcher, *India* 37 J14
Taldy Kurgan =
   Taldyqorghan,
   Kazakhstan 24 E8
Taldyqorghan,
   Kazakhstan 24 E8
Tålesh, *Iran* 39 B6
Tålesh, Kūhhā-ye, *Iran* 39 B6
Tali Post, *Sudan* 45 G11
Talibon, *Phil.* 33 B6
Talihina, *U.S.A.* 71 H7
Taling Sung, *Thailand* 34 E5
Taliwang, *Indonesia* . 32 F5
Tall 'Asūr, *West Bank* . 41 D4
Tall Kalakh, *Syria* ... 41 A5
Talladega, *U.S.A.* ... 69 J2
Tallahassee, *U.S.A.* .. 69 K3
Tallangatta, *Australia* . 55 F4
Tallarook, *Australia* .. 55 F4
Tallering Pk., *Australia* 53 E2
Tallinn, *Estonia* 9 G21
Tallulah, *U.S.A.* 71 J9
Talodi, *Sudan* 45 F11
Talsi, *Latvia* 9 H20
Taltal, *Chile* 80 B2
Taltson →, *Canada* . 64 A6
Talwood, *Australia* .. 55 D4
Talyawalka Cr. →,
   Australia 55 E3
Tama, *U.S.A.* 70 E8
Tamale, *Ghana* 44 G4
Tamano, *Japan* 29 G6
Tamanrasset, *Algeria* 44 D6
Tamar →, *U.K.* 11 G3
Tamarang, *Australia* . 55 E5
Tamashima, *Japan* .. 29 G6
Tamaské, *Niger* 44 F6
Tambacounda, *Senegal* 44 F2
Tambelan, Kepulauan,
   Indonesia 32 D3
Tambellup, *Australia* . 53 F2
Tambo, *Australia* 54 C4
Tambo de Mora, *Peru* 78 F3
Tambohorano, *Madag.* 49 B7
Tambora, *Indonesia* . 32 F5
Tambov, *Russia* 22 D7
Tambuku, *Indonesia* . 33 G15
Tamburâ, *Sudan* 45 G10
Tâmchekket, *Mauritania* 44 E2
Tamega →, *Portugal* 19 B1
Tamenglong, *India* .. 37 G18
Tamgak, Mts., *Niger* . 44 E6
Tamil Nadu □, *India* . 36 P10
Tammerfors =
   Tampere, *Finland* . 9 F20
Tammisaari, *Finland* . 9 F20

Tamo Abu,
   Pegunungan,
   Malaysia 32 D5
Tampa, *U.S.A.* 69 M4
Tampa B., *U.S.A.* 69 M4
Tampere, *Finland* ... 9 F20
Tampico, *Mexico* 74 C5
Tampin, *Malaysia* ... 34 S15
Tamrida = Qādib,
   Yemen 40 E5
Tamworth, *Australia* . 55 E5
Tamworth, *U.K.* 11 E6
Tana →, *Kenya* 46 E8
Tana →, *Norway* ... 8 A23
Tana, L., *Ethiopia* ... 45 F12
Tanabe, *Japan* 29 H7
Tanafjorden, *Norway* . 8 A23
Tanahbala, *Indonesia* . 32 E1
Tanahgrogot, *Indonesia* 32 E5
Tanahjampea,
   Indonesia 33 F6
Tanahmasa, *Indonesia* 32 E1
Tanahmerah, *Indonesia* 33 F10
Tanakura, *Japan* 29 F10
Tanami, *Australia* ... 52 C4
Tanami Desert,
   Australia 52 C5
Tanana, *U.S.A.* 60 B4
Tanana →, *U.S.A.* .. 60 B4
Tananarive =
   Antananarivo,
   Madag. 49 B8
Tánaro →, *Italy* 20 B3
Tanbar, *Australia* ... 54 D3
Tandag, *Phil.* 33 C7
Tandaué, *Angola* 48 B3
Tandil, *Argentina* 80 D5
Tandil, Sa. del,
   Argentina 80 D5
Tando Adam, *Pakistan* 36 G6
Tandou L., *Australia* . 55 E3
Tane-ga-Shima, *Japan* 29 J5
Taneatua, *N.Z.* 51 H6
Tanen Tong Dan,
   Burma 34 D5
Tanezrouft, *Algeria* .. 44 D5
Tanga, *Tanzania* 46 F7
Tanganyika, L., *Africa* 46 F6
Tanger, *Morocco* 44 A3
Tangerang, *Indonesia* 33 G12
Tanggula Shan, *China* 30 C4
Tangier = Tanger,
   Morocco 44 A3
Tangkak, *Malaysia* .. 34 S15
Tangorin P.O., *Australia* 54 C3
Tangshan, *China* 31 C6
Tanimbar, Kepulauan,
   Indonesia 33 F8
Tanimbar Is. =
   Tanimbar,
   Kepulauan, *Indonesia* 33 F8
Tanjay, *Phil.* 33 C6
Tanjore = Thanjavur,
   India 36 P11
Tanjung, *Indonesia* .. 32 E5
Tanjungbalai, *Indonesia* 32 D1
Tanjungbatu, *Indonesia* 32 D5
Tanjungkarang
   Telukbetung,
   Indonesia 32 F3
Tanjungpandan,
   Indonesia 32 E3
Tanjungpinang,
   Indonesia 32 D2
Tanjungpriok,
   Indonesia 33 G12
Tanjungredeb,
   Indonesia 32 D5
Tanjungselor, *Indonesia* 32 D5
Tannu-Ola, *Russia* .. 25 D10
Tanout, *Niger* 44 F6
Tanta, *Egypt* 45 B11
Tantung = Dandong,
   China 31 B7
Tanunda, *Australia* .. 55 E2
Tanzania ■, *Africa* .. 46 F6
Tanzilla →, *Canada* . 64 B2
Taolanaro, *Madag.* .. 49 D8
Taos, *U.S.A.* 73 H11
Taoudenni, *Mali* 44 D4
Taourirt, *Morocco* ... 44 B4
Tapa, *Estonia* 9 G21
Tapa Shan = Daba
   Shan, *China* 31 C5
Tapah, *Malaysia* 34 Q14
Tapajós →, *Brazil* .. 79 D8
Tapaktuan, *Indonesia* 32 D1
Tapanui, *N.Z.* 51 L2
Tapauá →, *Brazil* .. 78 E6
Tapeta, *Liberia* 44 G3
Tapi →, *India* 36 J8
Tapirapecó, Serra,
   Venezuela 78 C6
Tappahannock, *U.S.A.* 68 G7
Tapuaenuku, Mt., *N.Z.* 51 J4
Tapul Group, *Phil.* ... 33 C6
Taqīābād, *Iran* 39 C8
Taqtaq, *Iraq* 38 C5
Taquari →, *Brazil* ... 78 G7
Tara, *Australia* 55 D5
Tara, *Russia* 24 D8
Tara →,
   Montenegro, Yug. . 21 C8
Tara →, *Russia* 24 D8
Tarabagatay, Khrebet,
   Kazakhstan 24 E9
Tarābulus, *Lebanon* . 41 A4
Tarābulus, *Libya* 45 B7
Tarakan, *Indonesia* .. 32 D5
Taralga, *Australia* ... 55 E4
Tarama-Jima, *Japan* . 29 M2
Taran, Mys, *Russia* .. 9 J18
Taranaki □, *N.Z.* 51 H5

Tarancón, *Spain* 19 B4
Taranga Hill, *India* .. 36 H8
Táranto, *Italy* 20 D7
Táranto, G. di, *Italy* . 20 D7
Tarapacá, *Colombia* .. 78 D3
Tararua Ra., *N.Z.* 51 J5
Tarashcha, *Ukraine* .. 17 D16
Tarauacá, *Brazil* 78 E4
Tarauacá →, *Brazil* . 78 E5
Tarawera, *N.Z.* 51 H6
Tarawera L., *N.Z.* 51 H6
Tarazona, *Spain* 19 B5
Tarbat Ness, *U.K.* 12 D5
Tarbela Dam, *Pakistan* 36 B8
Tarbert, *Strath., U.K.* . 12 F3
Tarbert, *W. Isles, U.K.* 12 D2
Tarbes, *France* 18 E4
Tarboro, *U.S.A.* 69 H7
Tarbrax, *Australia* ... 54 C4
Tarcoon, *Australia* ... 55 E4
Taree, *Australia* 55 E5
Tarfaya, *Morocco* 44 C2
Tarifa, *Spain* 19 D3
Tarija, *Bolivia* 80 A4
Tariku →, *Indonesia* . 33 E9
Tarim Basin = Tarim
  Pendi, *China* 30 B3
Tarim He →, *China* .. 30 C3
Tarim Pendi, *China* .. 30 B3
Taritatu →, *Indonesia* 33 E9
Tarka →, *S. Africa* ... 48 E4
Tarkastad, *S. Africa* .. 48 E4
Tarkhankut, Mys,
  Ukraine 23 E5
Tarko Sale, *Russia* ... 24 C8
Tarkwa, *Ghana* 44 G4
Tarlac, *Phil.* 33 A6
Tarlton Downs,
  Australia 54 C2
Tarma, *Peru* 78 F3
Tarn →, *France* 18 E4
Tarnobrzeg, *Poland* .. 17 C11
Tarnów, *Poland* 17 C11
Tarnowskie Góry,
  Poland 17 C10
Taroom, *Australia* 55 D4
Taroudannt, *Morocco* . 44 B3
Tarpon Springs, *U.S.A.* 69 L4
Tarragona, *Spain* 19 B6
Tarrasa, *Spain* 19 B7
Tarshiha = Me'ona,
  Israel 41 B4
Tarso Emissi, *Chad* .. 45 D8
Tarsus, *Turkey* 23 G5
Tartagal, *Argentina* .. 80 A4
Tartu, *Estonia* 9 G22
Ţarţūs, *Syria* 38 C2
Tarumizu, *Japan* 29 J5
Tarutao, Ko, *Thailand* . 34 J5
Tarutung, *Indonesia* .. 32 D1
Tasāwah, *Libya* 45 C7
Taschereau, *Canada* .. 62 C4
Taseko →, *Canada* ... 64 C4
Tash-Kömür,
  Kyrgyzstan 24 E8
Tash-Kumyr = Tash-
  Kömür, *Kyrgyzstan* . 24 E8
Tashauz = Dashhowuz,
  Turkmenistan 24 E6
Tashi Chho Dzong =
  Thimphu, *Bhutan* . 37 F16
Tashkent = Toshkent,
  Uzbekistan 24 E7
Tashtagol, *Russia* 24 D9
Tasikmalaya, *Indonesia* 33 G13
Tåsjön, *Sweden* 8 D16
Taskan, *Russia* 25 C16
Tasman B., *N.Z.* 51 J4
Tasman Mts., *N.Z.* ... 51 J4
Tasman Pen., *Australia* 54 G4
Tasman Sea, *Pac. Oc.* 56 L8
Tasmania □, *Australia* 54 G4
Tasu Sd., *Canada* 64 C2
Tatabánya, *Hungary* .. 17 E10
Tatar Republic =
  Tatarstan □, *Russia* . 22 C9
Tatarbunary, *Ukraine* . 17 F15
Tatarsk, *Russia* 24 D8
Tatarstan □, *Russia* .. 22 C9
Tateyama, *Japan* 29 G9
Tathlina L., *Canada* .. 64 A5
Tathra, *Australia* 55 F4
Tatinnai L., *Canada* .. 65 A9
Tatnam, C., *Canada* .. 65 B10
Tatra = Tatry,
  Slovak Rep. 17 D11
Tatry, *Slovak Rep.* ... 17 D11
Tatsuno, *Japan* 29 G7
Tatta, *Pakistan* 36 G5
Tatuī, *Brazil* 80 A7
Tatum, *U.S.A.* 71 J3
Taʾung = Datong,
  China 31 B6
Tatvan, *Turkey* 23 G7
Taubaté, *Brazil* 80 A7
Tauern, *Austria* 16 E7
Taumarunui, *N.Z.* 51 H5
Taumaturgo, *Brazil* .. 78 E4
Taung, *S. Africa* 48 D3
Taungdwingyi, *Burma* . 37 J19
Taunggyi, *Burma* 37 J20
Taungup, *Burma* 37 K19
Taungup Pass, *Burma* 37 K19
Taungup Taunggya,
  Burma 37 K18
Taunton, *U.K.* 11 F4
Taunton, *U.S.A.* 68 E10
Taunus, *Germany* 16 C5
Taupo, *N.Z.* 51 H6
Taupo, L., *N.Z.* 51 H5
Tauranga, *N.Z.* 51 G6
Tauranga Harb., *N.Z.* . 51 G6

Taurianova, *Italy* 20 E7
Taurus Mts. = Toros
  Dağları, *Turkey* ... 23 G5
Tavda, *Russia* 24 D7
Tavda →, *Russia* 24 D7
Taveta, *Tanzania* 46 E7
Taveuni, *Fiji* 51 C9
Tavira, *Portugal* 19 D2
Tavistock, *U.K.* 11 G3
Tavoy, *Burma* 34 E5
Taw →, *U.K.* 11 F3
Tawas City, *U.S.A.* ... 68 C4
Tawau, *Malaysia* 32 D5
Tawitawi, *Phil.* 33 B6
Tay →, *U.K.* 12 E5
Tay, Firth of, *U.K.* ... 12 E5
Tay, L., *Australia* 53 F3
Tay, L., *U.K.* 12 E4
Tay Ninh, *Vietnam* ... 34 G9
Tayabamba, *Peru* 78 E3
Taylakova, *Russia* 24 D8
Taylakovy = Taylakova,
  Russia 24 D8
Taylor, *Canada* 64 B4
Taylor, *Nebr., U.S.A.* . 70 E5
Taylor, *Tex., U.S.A.* .. 71 K6
Taylor, Mt., *U.S.A.* ... 73 J10
Taylorville, *U.S.A.* ... 70 F10
Taymā, *Si. Arabia* ... 38 E3
Taymyr, Oz., *Russia* .. 25 B11
Taymyr, Poluostrov,
  Russia 25 B11
Tayport, *U.K.* 12 E6
Tayshet, *Russia* 25 D10
Tayside □, *U.K.* 12 E5
Taytay, *Phil.* 33 B5
Taz →, *Russia* 24 C8
Taza, *Morocco* 44 B4
Tāzah Khurmātū, *Iraq* 38 C5
Tazin L., *Canada* 65 B7
Tazovskiy, *Russia* 24 C8
Tbilisi, *Georgia* 23 F7
Tch'eng-tou =
  Chengdu, *China* ... 30 C5
Tchentlo L., *Canada* .. 64 B4
Tchibanga, *Gabon* ... 46 E2
Tch'ong-k'ing =
  Chongqing, *China* . 30 D5
Tczew, *Poland* 17 A10
Te Anau, L., *N.Z.* 51 L1
Te Aroha, *N.Z.* 51 G5
Te Awamutu, *N.Z.* ... 51 H5
Te Kuiti, *N.Z.* 51 H5
Te Puke, *N.Z.* 51 G6
Te Waewae B., *N.Z.* .. 51 M1
Tea Tree, *Australia* ... 54 C1
Teague, *U.S.A.* 71 K6
Tebakang, *Malaysia* .. 32 D4
Tébessa, *Algeria* 44 A6
Tebicuary →,
  Paraguay 80 B5
Tebingtinggi, *Indonesia* 32 D1
Tecuci, *Romania* 17 F14
Tecumseh, *U.S.A.* 68 D4
Tedzhen = Tejen,
  Turkmenistan 24 F7
Tees →, *U.K.* 10 C6
Teesside, *U.K.* 10 C6
Tefé, *Brazil* 78 D6
Tegal, *Indonesia* 33 G13
Tegelen, *Neths.* 15 C6
Tegid, L. = Bala, L.,
  U.K. 10 E4
Tegina, *Nigeria* 44 F6
Tegucigalpa, *Honduras* 74 E7
Tehachapi, *U.S.A.* 73 J4
Tehachapi Mts., *U.S.A.* 73 J4
Tehrān, *Iran* 39 C6
Tehuantepec, *Mexico* . 74 D5
Tehuantepec, G. de,
  Mexico 74 D5
Tehuantepec, Istmo de,
  Mexico 74 D6
Teifi →, *U.K.* 11 E3
Teign →, *U.K.* 11 G4
Teignmouth, *U.K.* 11 G4
Tejen, *Turkmenistan* .. 24 F7
Tejo →, *Europe* 19 C1
Tekamah, *U.S.A.* 70 E6
Tekapo, L., *N.Z.* 51 K3
Tekeli, *Kazakhstan* ... 24 E8
Tekirdağ, *Turkey* 21 D12
Tekkali, *India* 37 K14
Tekoa, *U.S.A.* 72 C5
Tel Aviv-Yafo, *Israel* . 41 C3
Tel Lakhish, *Israel* ... 41 D3
Tel Megiddo, *Israel* .. 41 C4
Tela, *Honduras* 74 D7
Telanaipura = Jambi,
  Indonesia 32 E2
Telavi, *Georgia* 23 F8
Telegraph Creek,
  Canada 64 B2
Telekhany =
  Tsyelyakhany,
  Belarus 17 B13
Telemark, *Norway* ... 9 G12
Teleng, *Iran* 39 E9
Teles Pires →, *Brazil* . 78 E7
Telescope Pk., *U.S.A.* . 73 H5
Telford, *U.K.* 10 E5
Télimélé, *Guinea* 44 F2
Telkwa, *Canada* 64 C3
Tell City, *U.S.A.* 68 G2
Tellicherry, *India* 36 P9
Telom →, *Malaysia* .. 34 Q14
Telpos Iz, *Russia* 22 B10
Telsen, *Argentina* 80 E3
Telšiai, *Lithuania* 9 H20
Teluk Anson, *Malaysia* 34 Q14

Teluk Betung =
  Tanjungkarang
  Telukbetung,
  Indonesia 32 F3
Teluk Intan = Teluk
  Anson, *Malaysia* .. 34 Q14
Telukbutun, *Indonesia* 32 D3
Telukdalem, *Indonesia* 32 D1
Tema, *Ghana* 44 G5
Temanggung,
  Indonesia 33 G14
Temax, *Mexico* 74 C7
Temba, *S. Africa* 49 D4
Tembeling →,
  Malaysia 34 Q15
Teme →, *U.K.* 11 E5
Temecula, *U.S.A.* 73 K5
Temerloh, *Malaysia* .. 34 R15
Temir, *Kazakhstan* ... 24 E6
Temirtau, *Kazakhstan* . 24 D8
Temirtau, *Russia* 24 D9
Témiscaming, *Canada* 62 C4
Temma, *Australia* 54 G3
Temora, *Australia* 55 E4
Tempe, *U.S.A.* 73 K8
Tempe Downs,
  Australia 52 D5
Temple, *U.S.A.* 71 K6
Temple B., *Australia* .. 54 A3
Templemore, *Ireland* . 13 D4
Templeton →,
  Australia 54 C2
Temuco, *Chile* 80 D2
Temuka, *N.Z.* 51 L3
Tenaha, *U.S.A.* 71 K7
Tenali, *India* 36 L12
Tenasserim, *Burma* .. 34 F5
Tenasserim □, *Burma* 34 F5
Tenby, *U.K.* 11 F3
Tenda, Col di, *France* . 20 D7
Tendaho, *Ethiopia* ... 40 E3
Tenerife, *Canary Is.* .. 44 C1
Teng →, *Burma* 34 B5
Tengah □, *Indonesia* . 33 E6
Tengah Kepulauan,
  Indonesia 32 F5
Tengchong, *China* 30 D4
Tenggara □, *Indonesia* 33 E6
Tenggarong, *Indonesia* 32 E5
Tengiz, Ozero =
  Chelkar Tengiz,
  Solonchak,
  Kazakhstan 24 E7
Tengiz, Ozero,
  Kazakhstan 24 D7
Tenkasi, *India* 36 Q10
Tenke, *Zaïre* 46 G5
Tenkodogo,
  Burkina Faso 44 F4
Tennant Creek,
  Australia 54 B1
Tennessee □, *U.S.A.* . 69 H2
Tennessee →, *U.S.A.* . 68 G1
Tennille, *U.S.A.* 69 J4
Tenom, *Malaysia* 32 C5
Tenryū-Gawa →,
  Japan 29 G8
Tent L., *Canada* 65 A7
Tenterfield, *Australia* . 55 D5
Teófilo Otoni, *Brazil* . 79 G10
Tepa, *Indonesia* 33 F7
Tepic, *Mexico* 74 C4
Teplice, *Czech.* 16 C7
Ter →, *Spain* 19 A7
Ter Apel, *Neths.* 15 B7
Téra, *Niger* 44 F5
Teraina, *Kiribati* 57 G11
Téramo, *Italy* 20 C5
Terang, *Australia* 55 F3
Terebovlya, *Ukraine* .. 17 D13
Terek →, *Russia* 23 F8
Terengganu □,
  Malaysia 34 Q16
Teresina, *Brazil* 79 E10
Terewah, L., *Australia* 55 D4
Terhazza, *Mali* 44 D3
Teridgerie Cr. →,
  Australia 55 E4
Termez = Termiz,
  Uzbekistan 24 F7
Términi Imerese, *Italy* 20 F5
Termiz, *Uzbekistan* .. 24 F7
Térmoli, *Italy* 20 C6
Ternate, *Indonesia* ... 33 D7
Terneuzen, *Neths.* ... 15 C3
Terney, *Russia* 25 E14
Terni, *Italy* 20 C5
Ternopil, *Ukraine* 17 D13
Ternopol = Ternopil,
  Ukraine 17 D13
Terowie, *N.S.W.,*
  Australia 55 E4
Terowie, *S. Austral.,*
  Australia 55 E2
Terrace, *Canada* 64 C3
Terrace Bay, *Canada* . 62 C2
Terracina, *Italy* 20 D5
Terralba, *Italy* 20 E3
Terranova = Ólbia, *Italy* 20 D3
Terrassa = Tarrasa,
  Spain 19 B7
Terre Haute, *U.S.A.* .. 68 F2
Terrebonne B., *U.S.A.* 71 L9
Terrell, *U.S.A.* 71 J6
Terrenceville, *Canada* 63 C9
Terrick Terrick,
  Australia 54 C4
Terry, *U.S.A.* 70 B2
Terschelling, *Neths.* .. 15 A5
Teruel, *Spain* 19 B5
Tervola, *Finland* 8 C21
Teryaweyna L.,
  Australia 55 E3
Teshio, *Japan* 28 B10

Teshio-Gawa →,
  Japan 28 B10
Tesiyn Gol →,
  Mongolia 30 A4
Teslin, *Canada* 64 A2
Teslin →, *Canada* ... 64 A2
Teslin L., *Canada* 64 A2
Tessalit, *Mali* 44 D5
Tessaoua, *Niger* 44 F6
Test →, *U.K.* 11 F6
Tetachuck L., *Canada* . 64 C3
Tetas, Pta., *Chile* 80 A2
Tete, *Mozam.* 47 H6
Teterev →, *Ukraine* .. 17 C16
Teteven, *Bulgaria* 21 C11
Tethul →, *Canada* ... 64 A6
Tetiyev, *Ukraine* 17 D15
Teton →, *U.S.A.* 72 C8
Tétouan, *Morocco* ... 44 A3
Tetovo, *Macedonia* ... 21 C9
Tetuán = Tétouan,
  Morocco 44 A3
Tetyukhe Pristan,
  Russia 28 B7
Teuco →, *Argentina* . 80 B4
Teulon, *Canada* 65 C9
Teun, *Indonesia* 33 F7
Teutoburger Wald,
  Germany 16 B5
Tévere →, *Italy* 20 D5
Teverya, *Israel* 41 C4
Teviot →, *U.K.* 12 F6
Tewantin, *Australia* .. 55 D5
Tewkesbury, *U.K.* 11 F5
Texada I., *Canada* ... 64 D4
Texarkana, *Ark., U.S.A.* 71 J8
Texarkana, *Tex., U.S.A.* 71 J7
Texas, *Australia* 55 D5
Texas □, *U.S.A.* 71 K5
Texas City, *U.S.A.* ... 71 L7
Texel, *Neths.* 15 A4
Texhoma, *U.S.A.* 71 G4
Texline, *U.S.A.* 71 G3
Texoma, L., *U.S.A.* ... 71 J6
Tezpur, *India* 37 F18
Tezzeron L., *Canada* . 64 C4
Tha-anne →, *Canada* 65 A10
Tha Nun, *Thailand* ... 34 H5
Thaba Putsoa, *Lesotho* 49 D4
Thabana Ntlenyana,
  Lesotho 49 D4
Thabazimbi, *S. Africa* . 49 C4
Thai Hoa, *Vietnam* .. 34 C8
Thai Nguyen, *Vietnam* 34 B8
Thailand ■, *Asia* 34 D6
Thailand, G. of, *Asia* . 34 G6
Thakhek, *Laos* 34 D8
Thal, *Pakistan* 36 C7
Thala La, *Burma* 37 E20
Thallon, *Australia* 55 D4
Thame →, *U.K.* 11 F6
Thames, *N.Z.* 51 G5
Thames →, *Canada* .. 62 D3
Thames →, *U.K.* 11 F8
Thane, *India* 36 K8
Thanet, I. of, *U.K.* ... 11 F9
Thang Binh, *Vietnam* . 34 E10
Thangoo, *Australia* ... 52 C3
Thangool, *Australia* .. 54 C5
Thanh Hoa, *Vietnam* . 34 C8
Thanh Pho Ho Chi
  Minh = Phanh Bho
  Ho Chi Minh,
  Vietnam 34 G9
Thanjavur, *India* 36 P11
Thar Desert, *India* ... 36 F7
Tharad, *India* 36 G7
Thargomindah,
  Australia 55 D3
Tharrawaddy, *Burma* . 37 L19
Tharthār, Mileh, *Iraq* . 38 C4
Tharthār, W. ath →,
  Iraq 38 C4
Thásos, *Greece* 21 D11
Thatcher, *Ariz., U.S.A.* 73 K9
Thatcher, *Colo., U.S.A.* 71 G2
Thaton, *Burma* 37 L20
Thaungdut, *Burma* ... 37 G19
Thayer, *U.S.A.* 71 G9
Thayetmyo, *Burma* .. 37 K19
Thazi, *Burma* 37 J20
The Alberga →,
  Australia 55 D2
The Coorong, *Australia* 55 F2
The Dalles, *U.S.A.* ... 72 D3
The English Company's
  Is., *Australia* 54 A2
The Frome →,
  Australia 55 D2
The Grampians,
  Australia 55 F3
The Great Divide =
  Great Dividing Ra.,
  Australia 54 C4
The Hague = 's-
  Gravenhage, *Neths.* 15 B4
The Hamilton →,
  Australia 55 D2
The Macumba →,
  Australia 55 D2
The Neales →,
  Australia 55 D2
The Officer →,
  Australia 53 E5
The Pas, *Canada* 65 C8
The Rock, *Australia* .. 55 F4
The Salt L., *Australia* . 55 E3
The Stevenson →,
  Australia 55 D2
The Warburton →,
  Australia 55 D2
Thebes = Thívai,
  Greece 21 E10
Thebes = Thívai,
  Greece 21 E10
Thedford, *U.S.A.* 70 E4

Theebine, *Australia* .. 55 D5
Thekulthili L., *Canada* . 65 A7
Thelon →, *Canada* .. 65 A8
Theodore, *Australia* .. 54 C5
Thermaïkós Kólpos,
  Greece 21 D10
Thermopolis, *U.S.A.* .. 72 E9
Thermopylae P., *Greece* 21 E10
Thessalon, *Canada* ... 62 C3
Thessaloníki, *Greece* . 21 D10
Thessaloníki, Gulf of =
  Thermaïkós Kólpos,
  Greece 21 D10
Thetford, *U.K.* 11 E8
Thetford Mines, *Canada* 63 C5
Theunissen, *S. Africa* . 48 D4
Thevenard, *Australia* . 55 E1
Thibodaux, *U.S.A.* ... 71 L9
Thicket Portage,
  Canada 65 B9
Thief River Falls, *U.S.A.* 70 A6
Thiel Mts., *Antarctica* 5 E16
Thiers, *France* 18 D5
Thies, *Senegal* 44 F1
Thika, *Kenya* 46 E7
Thikombia, *Fiji* 51 B9
Thimphu, *Bhutan* ... 37 F16
þingvallavatn, *Iceland* 8 D3
Thionville, *France* 18 B7
Thíra, *Greece* 21 F11
Thirsk, *U.K.* 10 C6
Thisted, *Denmark* 9 H13
Thistle I., *Australia* .. 55 F2
Thívai, *Greece* 21 E10
þjórsá →, *Iceland* ... 8 E3
Thlewiaza →, *Man.,*
  Canada 65 B8
Thlewiaza →, *N.W.T.,*
  Canada 65 A10
Thoa →, *Canada* 65 A7
Thomas, *Okla., U.S.A.* 71 H5
Thomas, *W. Va., U.S.A.* 68 F6
Thomas, L., *Australia* . 55 D2
Thomaston, *U.S.A.* ... 69 J3
Thomasville, *Ala.,*
  U.S.A. 69 K2
Thomasville, *Ga.,*
  U.S.A. 69 K3
Thomasville, *N.C.,*
  U.S.A. 69 H5
Thompson, *Canada* .. 65 B9
Thompson, *U.S.A.* ... 73 G9
Thompson →, *Canada* 64 C4
Thompson Falls, *U.S.A.* 72 C6
Thompson Landing,
  Canada 65 A6
Thompson Pk., *U.S.A.* 72 F2
Thomson's Falls =
  Nyahururu, *Kenya* . 46 D7
Thon Buri, *Thailand* .. 34 F6
þórisvatn, *Iceland* ... 8 D4
Thornaby on Tees, *U.K.* 10 C6
þórshöfn, *Iceland* 8 C6
Thouin, C., *Australia* . 52 D2
Thrace, *Turkey* 21 D12
Three Forks, *U.S.A.* .. 72 D8
Three Hills, *Canada* .. 64 C6
Three Hummock I.,
  Australia 54 G3
Three Lakes, *U.S.A.* .. 70 C10
Three Points, C., *Ghana* 44 H4
Three Rivers, *Australia* 53 E2
Three Rivers, *U.S.A.* .. 71 L5
Three Sisters, *U.S.A.* . 72 D3
Throssell, L., *Australia* 53 E3
Throssell Ra., *Australia* 52 D3
Thubun Lakes, *Canada* 65 A6
Thuin, *Belgium* 15 D4
Thule, *Greenland* 4 B4
Thun, *Switz.* 16 E4
Thunder B., *U.S.A.* ... 68 C4
Thunder Bay, *Canada* 62 C2
Thung Song, *Thailand* 34 H5
Thunkar, *Bhutan* 37 F17
Thüringer Wald,
  Germany 16 C6
Thurles, *Ireland* 13 D4
Thurloo Downs,
  Australia 55 D3
Thursday I., *Australia* 54 A3
Thurso, *Canada* 62 C4
Thurso, *U.K.* 12 C5
Thurston I., *Antarctica* 5 D16
Thutade L., *Canada* .. 64 B3
Thylungra, *Australia* .. 55 D3
Thysville = Mbanza
  Ngungu, *Zaïre* 46 F2
Ti-n-Barraï, *Algeria* .. —
Tia, *Australia* 55 E5
Tian Shan, *China* 30 B3
Tianjin, *China* 31 C6
Tianshui, *China* 30 C5
Tiaret, *Algeria* 44 A5
Tiassalé, *Ivory C.* 44 G4
Tibati, *Cameroon* 46 C2
Tiber = Tévere →,
  Italy 20 D5
Tiber Reservoir, *U.S.A.* 72 B8
Tiberias = Teverya,
  Israel 41 C4
Tiberias, L. = Yam
  Kinneret, *Israel* .. 41 C4
Tibesti, *Chad* 45 D8
Tibet = Xizang □,
  China 30 C3
Tibnī, *Syria* 38 C3
Tibooburra, *Australia* 55 D3
Tiburón, *Mexico* 74 B2
Tîchît, *Mauritania* ... 44 E3
Ticino →, *Italy* 20 B3
Ticonderoga, *U.S.A.* .. 68 D9
Tidaholm, *Sweden* ... 9 G15
Tiddim, *Burma* 37 H18

Tidjikja, *Mauritania* .. 44 E2
Tidore, *Indonesia* 33 D7
Tiel, *Neths.* 15 C5
Tiel, *Senegal* 44 F1
Tielt, *Belgium* 15 D3
Tien Shan, *Asia* 26 E11
Tien-tsin = Tianjin,
  China 31 C6
T'ienching = Tianjin,
  China 31 C6
Tienen, *Belgium* 15 D4
Tientsin = Tianjin,
  China 31 C6
Tierra Amarilla, *U.S.A.* 73 H10
Tierra de Campos,
  Spain 19 A3
Tierra del Fuego, I. Gr.
  de, *Argentina* 80 G3
Tiétar →, *Spain* 19 C3
Tieyon, *Australia* 55 D1
Tiffin, *U.S.A.* 68 E4
Tiflis = Tbilisi, *Georgia* 23 F7
Tifton, *U.S.A.* 69 K4
Tifu, *Indonesia* 33 E7
Tighina, *Moldova* 17 E15
Tigil, *Russia* 25 D16
Tignish, *Canada* 63 C7
Tigre →, *Peru* 78 D4
Tigris = Dijlah,
  Nahr →, *Asia* 38 D5
Tigyaing, *Burma* 37 H20
Tîh, Gebel el, *Egypt* .. 45 C11
Tijuana, *Mexico* 74 A1
Tikamgarh, *India* 36 G11
Tikhoretsk, *Russia* ... 23 E7
Tikrīt, *Iraq* 38 C4
Tiksi, *Russia* 25 B13
Tilamuta, *Indonesia* .. 33 D6
Tilburg, *Neths.* 15 C5
Tilbury, *Canada* 62 D3
Tilbury, *U.K.* 11 F8
Tilden, *Nebr., U.S.A.* . 70 D6
Tilden, *Tex., U.S.A.* .. 71 L5
Tilichiki, *Russia* 25 C17
Till →, *U.K.* 10 B5
Tillabéri, *Niger* 44 F5
Tillamook, *U.S.A.* ... 72 D2
Tillsonburg, *Canada* .. 62 D3
Tílos, *Greece* 21 F12
Tilpa, *Australia* 55 E3
Tilsit = Sovetsk, *Russia* 9 J19
Tilt →, *U.K.* 12 E5
Timagami L., *Canada* . 62 C3
Timanskiy Kryazh,
  Russia 22 A9
Timaru, *N.Z.* 51 L3
Timbedgha, *Mauritania* 44 E3
Timber Lake, *U.S.A.* .. 70 C4
Timboon, *Australia* ... 55 F3
Timbuktu =
  Tombouctou, *Mali* . 44 E4
Timimoun, *Algeria* ... 44 C5
Timişoara, *Romania* .. 17 F11
Timmins, *Canada* 62 C3
Timok →, *Serbia, Yug.* 21 B10
Timon, *Brazil* 79 E10
Timor, *Indonesia* 33 F7
Timor □, *Indonesia* .. 33 F7
Timor Sea, *Ind. Oc.* .. 52 B4
Tinaca Pt., *Phil.* 33 C7
Tindouf, *Algeria* 44 C3
Tingo Maria, *Peru* ... 78 E3
Tingrela, *Ivory C.* 44 F3
Tinjoub, *Algeria* 44 C3
Tinkurrin, *Australia* .. 53 F2
Tinnevelly =
  Tirunelveli, *India* .. 36 Q10
Tinogasta, *Argentina* . 80 B3
Tínos, *Greece* 21 F11
Tintinara, *Australia* .. 55 F3
Tioman, Pulau,
  Malaysia 34 S17
Tipongpani, *India* 37 F19
Tipperary, *Ireland* ... 13 D3
Tipperary □, *Ireland* . 13 D4
Tipton, *U.K.* 11 E5
Tipton, *Calif., U.S.A.* . 73 H4
Tipton, *Ind., U.S.A.* .. 68 E2
Tipton, *Iowa, U.S.A.* . 70 E9
Tiptonville, *U.S.A.* ... 71 G10
Tīrān, *Iran* 39 C6
Tirana, *Albania* 21 D8
Tiranë = Tirana,
  Albania 21 D8
Tiraspol, *Moldova* ... 17 E15
Tirat Karmel, *Israel* .. 41 C3
Tire, *Turkey* 21 E12
Tirebolu, *Turkey* 23 F6
Tiree, *U.K.* 12 E2
Tîrgoviște, *Romania* .. 17 F13
Tîrgu-Jiu, *Romania* ... 17 F12
Tîrgu Mureș, *Romania* 17 E13
Tirich Mir, *Pakistan* .. 36 A7
Tîrnăveni, *Romania* .. 17 E13
Tírnavos, *Greece* 21 E10
Tirodi, *India* 36 J11
Tirol □, *Austria* 16 E6
Tirso →, *Italy* 20 E3
Tiruchchirappalli, *India* 36 P11
Tirunelveli, *India* 36 Q10
Tirupati, *India* 36 N11
Tiruppur, *India* 36 P10
Tiruvannamalai, *India* 36 N11
Tisa →, *Serbia, Yug.* . 21 B9
Tisdale, *Canada* 65 C8
Tishomingo, *U.S.A.* .. 71 H6
Tisza = Tisa →,
  Serbia, Yug. 21 B9
Tit-Ary, *Russia* 25 B13
Titicaca, L., *S. Amer.* . 78 G5
Titograd = Podgorica,
  Montenegro, Yug. . 21 C8
Titov Veles, *Macedonia* 21 D9
Titova-Mitrovica,
  Serbia, Yug. 21 C9

Titovo Užice

Titovo Užice, *Serbia, Yug.* 21 C8
Titule, *Zaïre* 46 D5
Titusville, *Fla., U.S.A.* 69 L5
Titusville, *Pa., U.S.A.* 68 E6
Tivaouane, *Senegal* 44 F1
Tiverton, *U.K.* 11 G4
Tívoli, *Italy* 20 D5
Tizi-Ouzou, *Algeria* 44 A5
Tiznit, *Morocco* 44 C3
Tjeggelvas, *Sweden* 8 C17
Tjirebon = Cirebon, *Indonesia* 33 G13
Tjörn, *Sweden* 9 G14
Tlaxcala, *Mexico* 74 D5
Tlaxiaco, *Mexico* 74 D5
Tlell, *Canada* 64 C2
Tlemcen, *Algeria* 44 B4
Tmassah, *Libya* 45 C8
Toad →, *Canada* 64 B4
Toamasina, *Madag.* 49 B8
Toamasina □, *Madag.* 49 B8
Toay, *Argentina* 80 D4
Toba, *Japan* 29 G8
Toba Kakar, *Pakistan* 36 D6
Tobago, *W. Indies* 74 R21
Tobelo, *Indonesia* 33 D7
Tobermorey, *Australia* 54 C2
Tobermory, *Canada* 62 C3
Tobermory, *U.K.* 12 E2
Tobin, L., *Australia* 52 D4
Tobin L., *Canada* 65 C8
Toboali, *Indonesia* 32 E3
Tobol, *Kazakhstan* 24 D7
Tobol →, *Russia* 24 D7
Toboli, *Indonesia* 33 E6
Tobolsk, *Russia* 24 D7
Tobruk = Tubruq, *Libya* 45 B9
Tobyl = Tobol →, *Russia* 24 D7
Tocantinópolis, *Brazil* 79 E9
Tocantins □, *Brazil* 79 F9
Tocantins →, *Brazil* 79 D9
Toccoa, *U.S.A.* 69 H4
Tochigi, *Japan* 29 F9
Tochigi □, *Japan* 29 F9
Tocopilla, *Chile* 80 A2
Tocumwal, *Australia* 55 F4
Tocuyo →, *Venezuela* 78 A5
Todd →, *Australia* 54 C2
Todeli, *Indonesia* 33 E6
Todenyang, *Kenya* 46 D7
Todos os Santos, B. de, *Brazil* 79 F11
Tofield, *Canada* 64 C6
Tofino, *Canada* 64 D3
Tofua, *Tonga* 51 D11
Tōgane, *Japan* 29 G10
Togba, *Mauritania* 44 E2
Togian, Kepulauan, *Indonesia* 33 E6
Togliatti, *Russia* 22 D8
Togo ■, *W. Afr.* 44 G5
Tōhoku □, *Japan* 28 E10
Toinya, *Sudan* 45 G10
Tojikiston = Tajikistan ■, *Asia* 24 F8
Tojo, *Indonesia* 33 E6
Tōjō, *Japan* 29 G6
Tokachi-Dake, *Japan* 28 C11
Tokachi-Gawa →, *Japan* 28 C11
Tokala, *Indonesia* 33 E6
Tōkamachi, *Japan* 29 F9
Tokanui, *N.Z.* 51 M2
Tokar, *Sudan* 45 E12
Tokara-Rettō, *Japan* 29 K4
Tokarahi, *N.Z.* 51 L3
Tokashiki-Shima, *Japan* 29 L3
Tokelau Is., *Pac. Oc.* 56 H10
Tokmak, *Kyrgyzstan* 24 E8
Toko Ra., *Australia* 54 C2
Tokong, *Malaysia* 34 P13
Tokoro-Gawa →, *Japan* 28 B12
Tokuno-Shima, *Japan* 29 L4
Tokushima, *Japan* 29 G7
Tokushima □, *Japan* 29 H7
Tokuyama, *Japan* 29 G5
Tōkyō, *Japan* 29 G9
Tolaga Bay, *N.Z.* 51 H7
Tolbukhin = Dobrich, *Bulgaria* 21 C12
Toledo, *Spain* 19 C3
Toledo, *Ohio, U.S.A.* 68 E4
Toledo, *Oreg., U.S.A.* 72 D2
Toledo, *Wash., U.S.A.* 72 C2
Toledo, Montes de, *Spain* 19 C3
Tolga, *Algeria* 44 B6
Toliara, *Madag.* 49 C7
Toliara □, *Madag.* 49 C8
Tolima, *Colombia* 78 C3
Tolitoli, *Indonesia* 33 D6
Tolleson, *U.S.A.* 73 K7
Tolo, *Zaïre* 46 E3
Tolo, Teluk, *Indonesia* 33 E6
Toluca, *Mexico* 74 D5
Tom Burke, *S. Africa* 49 C4
Tom Price, *Australia* 52 D2
Tomah, *U.S.A.* 70 D9
Tomahawk, *U.S.A.* 70 C10
Tomakomai, *Japan* 28 C10
Tomar, *Portugal* 19 C1
Tomaszów Mazowiecki, *Poland* 17 C10
Tombé, *Sudan* 45 G11
Tombigbee →, *U.S.A.* 69 K2
Tombouctou, *Mali* 44 E4
Tombstone, *U.S.A.* 73 L8
Tombua, *Angola* 48 B1
Tomelloso, *Spain* 19 C4
Tomingley, *Australia* 55 E4
Tomini, *Indonesia* 33 D6
Tomini, Teluk, *Indonesia* 33 E6
Tomkinson Ras., *Australia* 53 E4
Tommot, *Russia* 25 D13
Tomnavoulin, *U.K.* 12 D5
Tomorit, *Albania* 21 D9
Tomsk, *Russia* 24 D9
Tonalea, *U.S.A.* 73 H8
Tonantins, *Brazil* 78 D5
Tonasket, *U.S.A.* 72 B4
Tonawanda, *U.S.A.* 68 D6
Tonbridge, *U.K.* 11 F8
Tondano, *Indonesia* 33 D6
Tonekābon, *Iran* 39 B6
Tonga ■, *Pac. Oc.* 51 D11
Tonga Trench, *Pac. Oc.* 56 J10
Tongaat, *S. Africa* 49 D5
Tongareva, *Cook Is.* 57 H12
Tongatapu, *Tonga* 51 E11
Tongchuan, *China* 31 C5
Tongeren, *Belgium* 15 D5
Tonghua, *China* 31 B7
Tongking, G. of = Tonkin, G. of, *Asia* 30 E5
Tongobory, *Madag.* 49 C7
Tongoy, *Chile* 80 C2
Tongres = Tongeren, *Belgium* 15 D5
Tongsa Dzong, *Bhutan* 37 F17
Tongue, *U.K.* 12 C4
Tongue →, *U.S.A.* 70 B2
Tonk, *India* 36 F9
Tonkawa, *U.S.A.* 71 G6
Tonkin = Bac Phan, *Vietnam* 34 A8
Tonkin, G. of, *Asia* 30 E5
Tonlé Sap, *Cambodia* 34 F8
Tono, *Japan* 28 E10
Tonopah, *U.S.A.* 73 G5
Tønsberg, *Norway* 9 G14
Tooele, *U.S.A.* 72 F7
Toompine, *Australia* 55 D3
Toonpan, *Australia* 54 B4
Toora, *Australia* 55 F4
Toora-Khem, *Russia* 25 D10
Toowoomba, *Australia* 55 D5
Top-ozero, *Russia* 22 A5
Topeka, *U.S.A.* 70 F7
Topki, *Russia* 24 D9
Topley, *Canada* 64 C3
Topock, *U.S.A.* 73 J6
Topol'čany, *Slovak Rep.* 17 D10
Topolobampo, *Mexico* 74 B3
Toppenish, *U.S.A.* 72 C3
Toraka Vestale, *Madag.* 49 B7
Torata, *Peru* 78 G4
Torbalı, *Turkey* 21 E12
Torbay, *Canada* 63 C9
Torbay, *U.K.* 11 G4
Tordesillas, *Spain* 19 B3
Torgau, *Germany* 16 C7
Torhout, *Belgium* 15 C3
Tori-Shima, *Japan* 29 J10
Torino, *Italy* 20 B2
Torit, *Sudan* 45 H11
Tormes →, *Spain* 19 B2
Tornado Mt., *Canada* 64 D6
Torne älv →, *Sweden* 8 D21
Torneå = Tornio, *Finland* 8 D21
Torneträsk, *Sweden* 8 B18
Tornio, *Finland* 8 D21
Tornionjoki →, *Finland* 8 D21
Tornquist, *Argentina* 80 D4
Toro, Cerro del, *Chile* 80 B3
Toro, Pta., *Panama* 74 H14
Toroníos Kólpos, *Greece* 21 D10
Toronto, *Australia* 55 E5
Toronto, *Canada* 62 D4
Toronto, *U.S.A.* 68 E5
Toropets, *Russia* 22 C5
Tororo, *Uganda* 46 D6
Toros Dağları, *Turkey* 23 G5
Torquay, *Canada* 65 D8
Torquay, *U.K.* 11 G4
Tôrre de Moncorvo, *Portugal* 19 B2
Torre del Greco, *Italy* 20 D6
Torrejón de Ardoz, *Spain* 19 B4
Torrelavega, *Spain* 19 A3
Torremolinos, *Spain* 19 D3
Torrens, L., *Australia* 55 E2
Torrens Cr. →, *Australia* 54 C4
Torrens Creek, *Australia* 54 C4
Torrente, *Spain* 19 C5
Torreón, *Mexico* 74 B4
Torres, *Mexico* 74 B2
Torres Strait, *Australia* 56 H6
Torres Vedras, *Portugal* 19 C1
Torrevieja, *Spain* 19 D5
Torrey, *U.S.A.* 73 G8
Torridge →, *U.K.* 11 G3
Torridon, L., *U.K.* 12 D3
Torrington, *Conn., U.S.A.* 68 E9
Torrington, *Wyo., U.S.A.* 70 D2
Tórshavn, *Færoe Is.* 8 E9
Tortosa, *Spain* 19 B6
Tortosa, C. de, *Spain* 19 B6
Torūd, *Iran* 39 C7
Toruń, *Poland* 17 B10
Tory I., *Ireland* 13 A3
Tosa, *Japan* 29 H6
Tosa-Shimizu, *Japan* 29 H6
Tosa-Wan, *Japan* 29 H6
Toscana □, *Italy* 20 C4
Toshkent, *Uzbekistan* 24 E7
Tostado, *Argentina* 80 B4
Tosu, *Japan* 29 H5
Toteng, *Botswana* 48 C3
Totma, *Russia* 22 C7
Totnes, *U.K.* 11 G4
Totten Glacier, *Antarctica* 5 C8
Tottenham, *Australia* 55 E4
Tottori, *Japan* 29 G7
Tottori □, *Japan* 29 G7
Touba, *Ivory C.* 44 G3
Toubkal, Djebel, *Morocco* 44 B3
Tougan, *Burkina Faso* 44 F4
Touggourt, *Algeria* 44 B6
Tougué, *Guinea* 44 F2
Toul, *France* 18 B6
Toulepleu, *Ivory C.* 44 G3
Toulon, *France* 18 E6
Toulouse, *France* 18 E4
Toummo, *Niger* 45 D7
Toungoo, *Burma* 37 K20
Touraine, *France* 18 C4
Tourane = Da Nang, *Vietnam* 34 D10
Tourcoing, *France* 18 A5
Touriñán, C., *Spain* 19 A1
Tournai, *Belgium* 15 D3
Tournon, *France* 18 D6
Tours, *France* 18 C4
Touwsrivier, *S. Africa* 48 E3
Towada, *Japan* 28 D10
Towada-Ko, *Japan* 28 D10
Towamba, *Australia* 55 F4
Towanda, *U.S.A.* 68 E7
Towang, *India* 37 F17
Tower, *U.S.A.* 70 B8
Towerhill Cr. →, *Australia* 54 C3
Towner, *U.S.A.* 70 A4
Townsend, *U.S.A.* 72 C8
Townshend I., *Australia* 54 C5
Townsville, *Australia* 54 B4
Towson, *U.S.A.* 68 F7
Toya-Ko, *Japan* 28 C10
Toyah, *U.S.A.* 71 K3
Toyahvale, *U.S.A.* 71 K3
Toyama, *Japan* 29 F8
Toyama □, *Japan* 29 F8
Toyama-Wan, *Japan* 29 F8
Toyohashi, *Japan* 29 G8
Toyokawa, *Japan* 29 G8
Toyonaka, *Japan* 29 G7
Toyooka, *Japan* 29 G7
Toyota, *Japan* 29 G8
Tozeur, *Tunisia* 44 B6
Trá Li = Tralee, *Ireland* 13 D2
Trabzon, *Turkey* 23 F6
Tracadie, *Canada* 63 C7
Tracy, *Calif., U.S.A.* 73 H3
Tracy, *Minn., U.S.A.* 70 C7
Trafalgar, C., *Spain* 19 D2
Trail, *Canada* 64 D5
Trainor L., *Canada* 64 A4
Tralee, *Ireland* 13 D2
Tralee B., *Ireland* 13 D2
Tramore, *Ireland* 13 D4
Tran Ninh, Cao Nguyen, *Laos* 34 C7
Tranås, *Sweden* 9 G16
Trancas, *Argentina* 80 B3
Trang, *Thailand* 34 J5
Trangahy, *Madag.* 49 B7
Trangan, *Indonesia* 33 F8
Trangie, *Australia* 55 E4
Trani, *Italy* 20 D7
Tranoroa, *Madag.* 49 C8
Transantarctic Mts., *Antarctica* 5 E12
Transcaucasia = Zakavkazye, *Asia* 23 F7
Transcona, *Canada* 65 D9
Transilvania, *Romania* 17 E12
Transilvanian Alps = Carpații Meridionali, *Romania* 17 F13
Transylvania = Transilvania, *Romania* 17 E12
Transylvanian Alps, *Romania* 6 F10
Trápani, *Italy* 20 E5
Trapper Pk., *U.S.A.* 72 D6
Traralgon, *Australia* 55 F4
Trasimeno, L., *Italy* 20 C5
Trat, *Thailand* 34 F7
Traun, *Austria* 16 D8
Traveller's L., *Australia* 55 E3
Travemünde, *Germany* 16 B6
Travers, Mt., *N.Z.* 51 K4
Traverse City, *U.S.A.* 68 C3
Travnik, *Bos.-H.* 21 B7
Trayning, *Australia* 53 F2
Trébbia →, *Italy* 20 B3
Třebíč, *Czech.* 16 D8
Trebinje, *Bos.-H.* 21 C8
Tredegar, *U.K.* 11 F4
Tregaron, *U.K.* 11 E4
Tregrosse Is., *Australia* 54 B5
Treherne, *Canada* 65 D9
Treinta y Tres, *Uruguay* 80 C6
Trelew, *Argentina* 80 E3
Trelleborg, *Sweden* 9 J15
Tremonton, *U.S.A.* 72 F7
Tremp, *Spain* 19 A6
Trenche →, *Canada* 62 C5
Trenčín, *Slovak Rep.* 17 D10
Trenggalek, *Indonesia* 33 H14
Trenque Lauquen, *Argentina* 80 D4
Trent →, *U.K.* 10 D7
Trento, *Italy* 20 A4
Trenton, *Canada* 62 D4
Trenton, *Mo., U.S.A.* 70 E8
Trenton, *N.J., U.S.A.* 68 E8
Trenton, *Nebr., U.S.A.* 70 E4
Trenton, *Tenn., U.S.A.* 71 H10
Trepassey, *Canada* 63 C9
Tres Arroyos, *Argentina* 80 D4
Três Corações, *Brazil* 79 H9
Três Lagoas, *Brazil* 79 H8
Tres Montes, C., *Chile* 80 F1
Tres Puentes, *Chile* 80 B2
Tres Puntas, C., *Argentina* 80 F3
Três Rios, *Brazil* 79 H10
Treviso, *Italy* 20 B5
Triabunna, *Australia* 54 G4
Tribulation, C., *Australia* 54 B4
Tribune, *U.S.A.* 70 F4
Trichinopoly = Tiruchchirappalli, *India* 36 P11
Trichur, *India* 36 P10
Trida, *Australia* 55 E4
Trier, *Germany* 16 D4
Trieste, *Italy* 20 B5
Triglav, *Slovenia* 16 E7
Tríkkala, *Greece* 21 E9
Trikora, Puncak, *Indonesia* 33 E9
Trim, *Ireland* 13 C5
Trincomalee, *Sri Lanka* 36 Q12
Trindade, I., *Atl. Oc.* 2 F8
Trinidad, *Bolivia* 78 F6
Trinidad, *Colombia* 78 B4
Trinidad, *Cuba* 75 C9
Trinidad, *Uruguay* 80 C5
Trinidad, *U.S.A.* 71 G2
Trinidad, I., *Argentina* 80 D4
Trinidad & Tobago ■, *W. Indies* 74 S20
Trinity, *Canada* 63 C9
Trinity, *U.S.A.* 71 K7
Trinity →, *Calif., U.S.A.* 72 F2
Trinity →, *Tex., U.S.A.* 71 L7
Trinity B., *Canada* 63 C9
Trinity Range, *U.S.A.* 72 F4
Trinkitat, *Sudan* 45 E12
Trion, *U.S.A.* 69 H3
Tripoli = Tarābulus, *Lebanon* 41 A4
Tripoli = Tarābulus, *Libya* 45 B7
Trípolis, *Greece* 21 F10
Tripp, *U.S.A.* 70 D6
Tripura □, *India* 37 H17
Tristan da Cunha, *Atl. Oc.* 2 F9
Trivandrum, *India* 36 Q10
Trnava, *Slovak Rep.* 17 D9
Trochu, *Canada* 64 C6
Trodely I., *Canada* 62 B4
Troglav, *Croatia* 20 C7
Troilus, L., *Canada* 62 B5
Trois-Pistoles, *Canada* 63 C6
Trois-Rivières, *Canada* 62 C5
Troitsk, *Russia* 24 D7
Troitsko Pechorsk, *Russia* 22 B10
Trölladyngja, *Iceland* 8 D5
Trollhättan, *Sweden* 9 G15
Trollheimen, *Norway* 8 E13
Tromelin I., *Ind. Oc.* 35 F4
Tromsø, *Norway* 8 B18
Tronador, *Argentina* 80 E2
Trøndelag, *Norway* 8 D14
Trondheim, *Norway* 8 E14
Trondheimsfjorden, *Norway* 8 E14
Troon, *U.K.* 12 F4
Tropic, *U.S.A.* 73 H7
Trossachs, The, *U.K.* 12 E4
Trostan, *U.K.* 13 A5
Trotternish, *U.K.* 12 D2
Troup, *U.S.A.* 71 J7
Trout →, *Canada* 64 A5
Trout L., *N.W.T., Canada* 64 A4
Trout L., *Ont., Canada* 65 C10
Trout Lake, *U.S.A.* 62 C2
Trout River, *Canada* 63 C8
Trouville-sur-Mer, *France* 18 B4
Trowbridge, *U.K.* 11 F5
Troy, *Turkey* 21 E12
Troy, *Ala., U.S.A.* 69 K3
Troy, *Idaho, U.S.A.* 72 C5
Troy, *Kans., U.S.A.* 70 F7
Troy, *Mo., U.S.A.* 70 F9
Troy, *Mont., U.S.A.* 72 B6
Troy, *N.Y., U.S.A.* 68 D9
Troy, *Ohio, U.S.A.* 68 E3
Troyes, *France* 18 B6
Trucial States = United Arab Emirates ■, *Asia* 39 F7
Truckee, *U.S.A.* 72 G3
Trudovoye, *Russia* 28 C6
Trujillo, *Honduras* 74 D7
Trujillo, *Peru* 78 E3
Trujillo, *Spain* 19 C3
Trujillo, *U.S.A.* 71 H2
Trujillo, *Venezuela* 78 B4
Truk, *Pac. Oc.* 56 G7
Trumann, *U.S.A.* 71 H9
Trumbull, Mt., *U.S.A.* 73 H7
Trundle, *Australia* 55 E4
Trung-Phan, *Vietnam* 34 D10
Truro, *Canada* 63 C7
Truro, *U.K.* 11 G2
Truskavets, *Ukraine* 17 D12
Truslove, *Australia* 53 F3
Truth or Consequences, *U.S.A.* 73 K10
Trutnov, *Czech.* 16 C8
Tryon, *U.S.A.* 69 H4
Tsaratanana, *Madag.* 49 B8
Tsaratanana, Mt. de, *Madag.* 49 A8
Tsarevo = Michurin, *Bulgaria* 21 C12
Tsau, *Botswana* 48 C3
Tselinograd = Aqmola, *Kazakhstan* 24 D8
Tsetserleg, *Mongolia* 30 B5
Tshabong, *Botswana* 48 D3
Tshane, *Botswana* 48 C3
Tshela, *Zaïre* 46 E2
Tshesebe, *Botswana* 49 C4
Tshikapa, *Zaïre* 46 F4
Tshofa, *Zaïre* 46 F5
Tshwane, *Botswana* 48 C3
Tsigara, *Botswana* 48 C4
Tsihombe, *Madag.* 49 D8
Tsimlyansk Res. = Tsimlyanskoye Vdkhr., *Russia* 23 E7
Tsimlyanskoye Vdkhr., *Russia* 23 E7
Tsinan = Jinan, *China* 31 C6
Tsineng, *S. Africa* 48 D3
Tsinghai = Qinghai □, *China* 30 C4
Tsingtao = Qingdao, *China* 31 C7
Tsinjomitondraka, *Madag.* 49 B8
Tsiroanomandidy, *Madag.* 49 B8
Tsivory, *Madag.* 49 C8
Tskhinvali, *Georgia* 23 F7
Tsna →, *Russia* 22 D7
Tsodilo Hill, *Botswana* 48 B3
Tsolo, *S. Africa* 49 E4
Tsomo, *S. Africa* 49 E4
Tsu, *Japan* 29 G8
Tsu L., *Canada* 64 A6
Tsuchiura, *Japan* 29 F10
Tsugaru-Kaikyō, *Japan* 28 D10
Tsumeb, *Namibia* 48 B2
Tsumis, *Namibia* 48 C2
Tsuruga, *Japan* 29 G8
Tsurugi-San, *Japan* 29 H7
Tsuruoka, *Japan* 28 E9
Tsushima, *Gifu, Japan* 29 G8
Tsushima, *Nagasaki, Japan* 29 G4
Tsyelyakhany, *Belarus* 17 B13
Tual, *Indonesia* 33 F8
Tuam, *Ireland* 13 C3
Tuamotu Arch. = Tuamotu Is., *Pac. Oc.* 57 J13
Tuamotu Is., *Pac. Oc.* 57 J13
Tuamotu Ridge, *Pac. Oc.* 57 K14
Tuao, *Phil.* 33 A6
Tuapse, *Russia* 23 F6
Tuatapere, *N.Z.* 51 M1
Tuba City, *U.S.A.* 73 H8
Tuban, *Indonesia* 33 G15
Tubarão, *Brazil* 80 B7
Tūbās, *West Bank* 41 C4
Tubau, *Malaysia* 32 D4
Tübingen, *Germany* 16 D5
Tubruq, *Libya* 45 B9
Tubuai Is., *Pac. Oc.* 57 K12
Tucacas, *Venezuela* 78 A5
Tuchodi →, *Canada* 64 B4
Tucson, *U.S.A.* 73 K8
Tucumcari, *U.S.A.* 71 H3
Tucupita, *Venezuela* 78 B6
Tucuruí, *Brazil* 79 D9
Tucuruí, Reprêsa de, *Brazil* 79 D9
Tudela, *Spain* 19 A5
Tudmur, *Syria* 38 C3
Tudor, L., *Canada* 63 A6
Tuen, *Australia* 55 D4
Tugela →, *S. Africa* 49 D5
Tuguegarao, *Phil.* 33 A6
Tugur, *Russia* 25 D14
Tukangbesi, Kepulauan, *Indonesia* 33 F6
Tukarak I., *Canada* 62 A4
Tukayyid, *Iraq* 38 D5
Tūkrah, *Libya* 45 B9
Tuktoyaktuk, *Canada* 60 B6
Tukums, *Latvia* 9 H20
Tukuyu, *Tanzania* 46 F6
Tula, *Mexico* 74 C5
Tula, *Russia* 22 D6
Tulancingo, *Mexico* 74 C5
Tulare, *U.S.A.* 73 H4
Tulare Lake Bed, *U.S.A.* 73 J4
Tularosa, *U.S.A.* 73 K10
Tulbagh, *S. Africa* 48 E2
Tulcán, *Ecuador* 78 C3
Tulcea, *Romania* 17 F15
Tulchyn, *Ukraine* 17 D15
Tūleh, *Iran* 39 C7
Tulemalu L., *Canada* 65 A9
Tuli, *Indonesia* 33 E6
Tuli, *Zimbabwe* 47 J5
Tulia, *U.S.A.* 71 H4
Ṭūlkarm, *West Bank* 41 C4
Tullahoma, *U.S.A.* 69 H2
Tullamore, *Australia* 55 E4
Tullamore, *Ireland* 13 C4
Tulle, *France* 18 D4
Tullibigeal, *Australia* 55 E4
Tullow, *Ireland* 13 D4
Tully, *Australia* 54 B4
Ṭulmaythah, *Libya* 45 B9
Tulmur, *Australia* 54 C3
Tulsa, *U.S.A.* 71 G7
Tulsequah, *Canada* 64 B2
Tulua, *Colombia* 78 C3
Tulun, *Russia* 25 D11
Tulungagung, *Indonesia* 32 F4
Tum, *Indonesia* 33 E8
Tumaco, *Colombia* 78 C3
Tumatumari, *Guyana* 78 B7
Tumba, *Sweden* 9 G17
Tumba, L., *Zaïre* 46 E3
Tumbarumba, *Australia* 55 F4
Túmbes, *Peru* 78 D2
Tumby Bay, *Australia* 55 E2
Tumeremo, *Venezuela* 78 B6
Tumkur, *India* 36 N10
Tummel, L., *U.K.* 12 E5
Tump, *Pakistan* 36 F3
Tumpat, *Malaysia* 34 N15
Tumu, *Ghana* 44 F4
Tumucumaque, Serra, *Brazil* 79 C8
Tumut, *Australia* 55 F4
Tumwater, *U.S.A.* 72 C2
Tunbridge Wells = Royal Tunbridge Wells, *U.K.* 11 F8
Tuncurry, *Australia* 55 E5
Tunduru, *Tanzania* 46 G7
Tundzha →, *Bulgaria* 21 C11
Tunga Pass, *India* 37 E19
Tungabhadra →, *India* 36 M11
Tungaru, *Sudan* 45 F11
Tungsten, *Canada* 64 A3
Tunguska, Nizhnyaya →, *Russia* 25 C9
Tunica, *U.S.A.* 71 H9
Tunis, *Tunisia* 44 A7
Tunisia ■, *Africa* 44 B6
Tunja, *Colombia* 78 B4
Tunnsjøen, *Norway* 8 D15
Tunungayualok I., *Canada* 63 A7
Tunuyán →, *Argentina* 80 C3
Tunxi, *China* 31 D6
Tuolumne, *U.S.A.* 73 H3
Tuoy-Khaya, *Russia* 25 C12
Tūp Āghāj, *Iran* 38 B5
Tupelo, *U.S.A.* 69 H1
Tupik, *Russia* 25 D12
Tupinambaranas, *Brazil* 78 D7
Tupiza, *Bolivia* 80 A3
Tupper, *Canada* 64 B4
Tupper Lake, *U.S.A.* 68 C8
Tupungato, Cerro, *S. Amer.* 80 C3
Túquerres, *Colombia* 78 C3
Tura, *Russia* 25 C11
Turabah, *Si. Arabia* 38 D4
Tūrān, *Iran* 39 C8
Turan, *Russia* 25 D10
Turayf, *Si. Arabia* 38 D3
Turda, *Romania* 17 E12
Turek, *Poland* 17 B10
Turfan = Turpan, *China* 30 B3
Tŭrgovishte, *Bulgaria* 21 C12
Turgutlu, *Turkey* 21 E12
Turia →, *Spain* 19 C5
Turiaçu, *Brazil* 79 D9
Turiaçu →, *Brazil* 79 D9
Turin = Torino, *Italy* 20 B2
Turin, *Canada* 64 D6
Turkana, L., *Africa* 46 D7
Turkestan = Türkistan, *Kazakhstan* 24 E7
Turkey ■, *Eurasia* 23 G6
Turkey Creek, *Australia* 52 C4
Türkistan, *Kazakhstan* 24 E7
Turkmenistan ■, *Asia* 24 F6
Turks & Caicos Is. ■, *W. Indies* 75 C10
Turku, *Finland* 9 F20
Turlock, *U.S.A.* 73 H3
Turnagain →, *Canada* 64 B3
Turnagain, C., *N.Z.* 51 J6
Turneffe Is., *Belize* 74 D7
Turner, *Australia* 52 C4
Turner, *U.S.A.* 72 B9
Turner Pt., *Australia* 54 A1
Turner Valley, *Canada* 64 C6
Turnhout, *Belgium* 15 C4
Turnor L., *Canada* 65 B7
Tŭrnovo = Veliko Tŭrnovo, *Bulgaria* 21 C11
Turnu Măgurele, *Romania* 17 G13
Turnu Roșu, P., *Romania* 17 F13
Turon, *U.S.A.* 71 G5
Turpan, *China* 30 B3
Turriff, *U.K.* 12 D6
Tursāq, *Iraq* 38 C5
Turtle Head I., *Australia* 54 A3
Turtle L., *Canada* 65 C7
Turtle Lake, *N. Dak., U.S.A.* 70 B4
Turtle Lake, *Wis., U.S.A.* 70 C8
Turtleford, *Canada* 65 C7
Turukhansk, *Russia* 25 C9
Tuscaloosa, *U.S.A.* 69 J2
Tuscany = Toscana □, *Italy* 20 C4
Tuscola, *Ill., U.S.A.* 68 F1
Tuscola, *Tex., U.S.A.* 71 J5
Tuscumbia, *U.S.A.* 69 H2
Tuskar Rock, *Ireland* 13 D5
Tuskegee, *U.S.A.* 69 J3
Tuticorin, *India* 36 Q11
Tutóia, *Brazil* 79 D10
Tutong, *Brunei* 32 D4
Tutrakan, *Bulgaria* 21 B12
Tutshi L., *Canada* 64 B2
Tuttle, *U.S.A.* 70 B5
Tuttlingen, *Germany* 16 E5
Tutuala, *Indonesia* 33 F7

Tutuila, *Amer. Samoa* 51 B13
Tuva □, *Russia* 25 D10
Tuvalu ■, *Pac. Oc.* .. 56 H9
Tuxpan, *Mexico* 74 C5
Tuxtla Gutiérrez,
 Mexico 74 D6
Tuy, *Spain* 19 A1
Tuy Hoa, *Vietnam* ... 34 F10
Tuya L., *Canada* 64 B2
Tuyen Hoa, *Vietnam* . 34 D9
Tūysarkān, *Iran* 39 C6
Tuz Gölü, *Turkey* ... 23 G5
Tūz Khurmātū, *Iraq* . 38 C5
Tuzla, *Bos.-H.* 21 B8
Tver, *Russia* 22 C6
Tweed ➜, *U.K.* 12 F7
Tweed Heads, *Australia* 55 D5
Tweedsmuir Prov. Park,
 Canada 64 C3
Twentynine Palms,
 U.S.A. 73 J5
Twillingate, *Canada* .. 63 C9
Twin Bridges, *U.S.A.* . 72 D7
Twin Falls, *U.S.A.* ... 72 E6
Twin Valley, *U.S.A.* .. 70 B6
Twisp, *U.S.A.* 72 B3
Two Harbors, *U.S.A.* . 70 B9
Two Hills, *Canada* ... 64 C6
Two Rivers, *U.S.A.* .. 68 C2
Twofold B., *Australia* . 55 F4
Tyachiv, *Ukraine* 17 D12
Tychy, *Poland* 17 C10
Tyler, *Minn., U.S.A.* . 70 C6
Tyler, *Tex., U.S.A.* .. 71 J7
Tynda, *Russia* 25 D13
Tyne ➜, *U.K.* 10 C6
Tyne & Wear □, *U.K.* . 10 C6
Tynemouth, *U.K.* 10 B6
Tyre = Sūr, *Lebanon* . 41 B4
Tyrifjorden, *Norway* .. 9 F14
Tyrol = Tirol □, *Austria* 16 E6
Tyrrell ➜, *Australia* . 55 F3
Tyrrell, L., *Australia* . 55 F3
Tyrrell Arm, *Canada* . 65 A9
Tyrrell L., *Canada* ... 65 A7
Tyrrhenian Sea,
 Medit. S. 20 E5
Tysfjorden, *Norway* .. 8 B17
Tyulgan, *Russia* 22 D10
Tyumen, *Russia* 24 D7
Tywi ➜, *U.K.* 11 F3
Tywyn, *U.K.* 11 E3
Tzaneen, *S. Africa* ... 49 C5
Tzukong = Zigong,
 China 30 D5

U

U.S.A. = United States
 of America ■,
 N. Amer. 66 C7
Uanda, *Australia* 54 C3
Uarsciek, *Somali Rep.* 40 G4
Uato-Udo, *Indonesia* . 33 F7
Uatumã ➜, *Brazil* ... 78 D7
Uaupés, *Brazil* 78 D5
Uaupés ➜, *Brazil* ... 78 C5
Ubá, *Brazil* 79 H10
Ubaitaba, *Brazil* 79 F11
Ubangi = Oubangi ➜,
 Zaïre 46 E3
Ubauro, *Pakistan* 36 E6
Ube, *Japan* 29 H5
Ubeda, *Spain* 19 C4
Uberaba, *Brazil* 79 G9
Uberlândia, *Brazil* ... 79 G9
Ubombo, *S. Africa* ... 49 D5
Ubon Ratchathani,
 Thailand 34 E8
Ubort ➜, *Belarus* ... 17 B15
Ubundu, *Zaïre* 46 E5
Ucayali ➜, *Peru* 78 D4
Uchi Lake, *Canada* .. 65 C10
Uchiura-Wan, *Japan* . 28 C10
Uchur ➜, *Russia* ... 25 D14
Ucluelet, *Canada* 64 D3
Uda ➜, *Russia* 25 D14
Udaipur, *India* 36 G8
Udaipur Garhi, *Nepal* . 37 F15
Uddevalla, *Sweden* .. 9 G14
Uddjaur, *Sweden* 8 D17
Udgir, *India* 36 K10
Udhampur, *India* 36 C9
Údine, *Italy* 20 A5
Udmurtia □, *Russia* .. 22 C9
Udon Thani, *Thailand* . 34 D7
Udupi, *India* 36 N9
Ueda, *Japan* 29 F9
Uedineniya, Os., *Russia* 4 B12
Uele ➜, *Zaïre* 46 D4
Uelen, *Russia* 25 C19
Uelzen, *Germany* 16 B6
Ufa, *Russia* 22 D10
Ufa ➜, *Russia* 22 D10
Ugab ➜, *Namibia* ... 48 C1
Ugalla ➜, *Tanzania* . 46 F6
Uganda ■, *Africa* ... 46 D6
Ugie, *S. Africa* 49 E4
Uglegorsk, *Russia* ... 25 E15
Uglich, *Russia* 22 C6
Ugolyak, *Russia* 25 C13
Uhrichsville, *U.S.A.* .. 68 E5
Uibhist a Deas = South
 Uist, *U.K.* 12 D1
Uibhist a Tuath =
 North Uist, *U.K.* .. 12 D1
Uíge, *Angola* 46 F2
Uinta Mts., *U.S.A.* ... 72 F8

Uitenhage, *S. Africa* . 48 E4
Uithuizen, *Neths.* 15 A6
Uji-guntō, *Japan* 29 J4
Ujjain, *India* 36 H9
Ujung Pandang,
 Indonesia 33 F5
Uka, *Russia* 25 D17
Uke-Shima, *Japan* ... 29 K4
Ukerewe I., *Tanzania* . 46 E6
Ukhrul, *India* 37 G19
Ukhta, *Russia* 22 B9
Ukiah, *U.S.A.* 72 G2
Ukmerge, *Lithuania* .. 9 J21
Ukraine ■, *Europe* .. 23 E5
Ukwi, *Botswana* 48 C3
Ulaanbaatar, *Mongolia* 25 E11
Ulaangom, *Mongolia* . 30 A4
Ulan Bator =
 Ulaanbaatar,
 Mongolia 25 E11
Ulan Ude, *Russia* 25 D11
Ulcinj,
 Montenegro, Yug. .. 21 D8
Ulco, *S. Africa* 48 D3
Ulefoss, *Norway* 9 G13
Ulhasnagar, *India* ... 36 K8
Uljadulla, *Australia* ... 55 F5
Ullapool, *U.K.* 12 D3
Ullswater, *U.K.* 10 C5
Ulm, *Germany* 16 D5
Ulmarra, *Australia* ... 55 E5
Ulongué, *Mozam.* 47 G6
Ulricehamn, *Sweden* . 9 H15
Ulster □, *U.K.* 13 B5
Ulubat Gölü, *Turkey* . 21 D13
Uludağ, *Turkey* 21 D13
Ulungur He ➜, *China* 30 B3
Uluru = Ayers Rock,
 Australia 53 E5
Ulutau, *Kazakhstan* .. 24 E7
Ulverston, *U.K.* 10 C4
Ulverstone, *Australia* . 54 G4
Ulya, *Russia* 25 D15
Ulyanovsk = Simbirsk,
 Russia 22 D8
Ulyasutay, *Mongolia* . 30 B4
Ulysses, *U.S.A.* 71 G4
Umala, *Bolivia* 78 G5
Uman, *Ukraine* 17 D16
Umaria, *India* 37 H12
Umarkot, *Pakistan* ... 36 G6
Umatilla, *U.S.A.* 72 D4
Umba, *Russia* 22 A5
Umbrella Mts., *N.Z.* .. 51 L2
Ume älv ➜, *Sweden* . 8 E19
Umeå, *Sweden* 8 E19
Umera, *Indonesia* 33 E7
Umkomaas, *S. Africa* . 49 E5
Umm ad Daraj, J.,
 Jordan 41 C4
Umm al Qaywayn,
 U.A.E. 39 E7
Umm al Qittayn,
 Jordan 41 C5
Umm Bāb, *Qatar* 39 E6
Umm Bel, *Sudan* 45 F10
Umm el Fahm, *Israel* . 41 C4
Umm Lajj, *Si. Arabia* . 38 E3
Umm Ruwaba, *Sudan* 45 F11
Umnak I., *U.S.A.* 60 C3
Umniati ➜, *Zimbabwe* 47 H5
Umpang, *Thailand* ... 34 D5
Umpqua ➜, *U.S.A.* .. 72 E1
Umtata, *S. Africa* 49 E4
Umuarama, *Brazil* ... 79 H8
Umzimvubu = Port St.
 Johns, *S. Africa* ... 49 E4
Umzinto, *S. Africa* ... 49 E5

Upper Arrow L.,
 Canada 64 C5
Upper Foster L.,
 Canada 65 B7
Upper Hutt, *N.Z.* 51 J5
Upper Klamath L.,
 U.S.A. 72 E3
Upper Lake, *U.S.A.* .. 72 G2
Upper Musquodoboit,
 Canada 63 C7
Upper Red L., *U.S.A.* . 70 A7
Upper Sandusky,
 U.S.A. 68 E4
Upper Volta = Burkina
 Faso ■, *Africa* 44 F4
Uppland, *Sweden* 9 F17
Uppsala, *Sweden* 9 G17
Upstart, C., *Australia* . 54 B4
Upton, *U.S.A.* 70 C2
Ur, *Iraq* 38 D5
Uracara, *Brazil* 78 D7
Urakawa, *Japan* 28 C11
Ural = Zhayyq ➜,
 Kazakhstan 23 E9
Ural, *Australia* 55 E4
Ural Mts. = Uralskie
 Gory, *Eurasia* 22 C10
Uralla, *Australia* 55 E5
Uralsk = Oral,
 Kazakhstan 22 D9
Uralskie Gory, *Eurasia* 22 C10
Urandangi, *Australia* . 54 C2
Uranium City, *Canada* 65 B7
Uranquinty, *Australia* . 55 F4
Urawa, *Japan* 29 G9
Uray, *Russia* 24 C7
'Uray'irah, *Si. Arabia* . 39 E6
Urbana, *Ill., U.S.A.* .. 68 E1
Urbana, *Ohio, U.S.A.* . 68 E4
Urbino, *Italy* 20 C5
Urbión, Picos de, *Spain* 19 A4
Urcos, *Peru* 78 F4
Urda, *Kazakhstan* 23 E8
Urdzhar, *Kazakhstan* . 24 E9
Ure ➜, *U.K.* 10 C6
Ures, *Mexico* 74 B2
Urfa = Sanliurfa,
 Turkey 23 G6
Urganch, *Uzbekistan* . 24 E7
Urgench = Urganch,
 Uzbekistan 24 E7
Uribia, *Colombia* 78 A4
Urk, *Neths.* 15 B5
Urla, *Turkey* 21 E12
Urmia = Orūmīyeh,
 Iran 38 B5
Urmia, L. = Orūmīyeh,
 Daryācheh-ye, *Iran* . 38 B5
Uroševac, *Serbia, Yug.* 21 C9
Uruana, *Brazil* 79 G9
Urubamba, *Peru* 78 F4
Urubamba ➜, *Peru* .. 78 F4
Uruçuí, *Brazil* 79 E10
Uruguai ➜, *Brazil* ... 80 B6
Uruguaiana, *Brazil* ... 80 B5
Uruguay ■, *S. Amer.* . 80 C5
Uruguay ➜, *S. Amer.* 80 C5
Urumchi = Ürümqi,
 China 24 E9
Ürümqi, *China* 24 E9
Urup, Os., *Russia* 25 E16
Usa ➜, *Russia* 22 A10
Uşak, *Turkey* 23 G4
Usakos, *Namibia* 48 C2
Usedom, *Germany* ... 16 B8
Ush-Tobe, *Kazakhstan* 24 E8
Ushakova, Os., *Russia* 4 A12
Ushant = Ouessant, I.
 d', *France* 18 B1
Ushibuka, *Japan* 29 H5
Ushuaia, *Argentina* .. 80 G3
Ushumun, *Russia* ... 25 D13
Usk ➜, *U.K.* 11 F5
Üsküdar, *Turkey* 23 F4
Usman, *Russia* 22 D6
Usoke, *Tanzania* 46 F6
Usolye Sibirskoye,
 Russia 25 D11
Uspallata, P. de,
 Argentina 80 C3
Uspenskiy, *Kazakhstan* 24 E8
Ussuri ➜, *Asia* 28 A7
Ussuriysk, *Russia* 25 E14
Ussurka, *Russia* 28 B6
Ust-Aldan = Batamay,
 Russia 25 C13
Ust Amginskoye =
 Khandyga, *Russia* .. 25 C14
Ust-Bolsheretsk, *Russia* 25 D16
Ust Chaun, *Russia* ... 25 C18
Ust'-Ilga, *Russia* 25 D11
Ust Ilimpeya = Yukti,
 Russia 25 C11
Ust-Ilimsk, *Russia* ... 25 D11
Ust Ishim, *Russia* 24 D8
Ust-Kamchatsk, *Russia* 25 D17
Ust-Kamenogorsk =
 Öskemen, *Kazakhstan* 24 E9
Ust-Karenga, *Russia* . 25 D12
Ust Khayryuzovo,
 Russia 25 D16
Ust-Kut, *Russia* 25 D11
Ust Kuyga, *Russia* ... 25 B14
Ust Maya, *Russia* 25 C14
Ust-Mil, *Russia* 25 D14
Ust Muya, *Russia* 25 D12
Ust-Nera, *Russia* 25 C15
Ust-Nyukzha, *Russia* . 25 D13
Ust Olenek, *Russia* .. 25 B12
Ust-Omchug, *Russia* . 25 C15
Ust Port, *Russia* 24 C9
Ust Tsilma, *Russia* ... 22 A9
Ust-Tungir, *Russia* ... 25 D13

Ust Urt = Ustyurt,
 Plateau, *Asia* 24 E6
Ust Usa, *Russia* 22 A10
Ust Vorkuta, *Russia* . 24 C7
Ústí nad Labem, *Czech.* 16 C8
Ustica, *Italy* 20 E5
Ustinov = Izhevsk,
 Russia 22 C9
Ustye, *Russia* 25 D10
Ustyurt, Plateau, *Asia* . 24 E6
Usu, *China* 30 B3
Usuki, *Japan* 29 H5
Usumacinta ➜,
 Mexico 74 D6
Usumbura =
 Bujumbura, *Burundi* 46 E5
Uta, *Indonesia* 33 E9
Utah □, *U.S.A.* 72 G8
Utah, L., *U.S.A.* 72 F8
Ute Creek ➜, *U.S.A.* . 71 H3
Utena, *Lithuania* 9 J21
Utete, *Tanzania* 46 F7
Uthai Thani, *Thailand* . 34 E6
Utiariti, *Brazil* 78 F7
Utica, *U.S.A.* 68 D8
Utik L., *Canada* 65 B9
Utikuma L., *Canada* .. 64 B5
Utrecht, *Neths.* 15 B5
Utrecht, *S. Africa* 49 D5
Utrecht □, *Neths.* ... 15 B5
Utrera, *Spain* 19 D3
Utsjoki, *Finland* 8 B22
Utsunomiya, *Japan* .. 29 F9
Uttar Pradesh □, *India* 36 F11
Uttaradit, *Thailand* ... 34 D6
Uttoxeter, *U.K.* 10 E6
Uummannarsuaq =
 Farvel, Kap,
 Greenland 4 D5
Uusikaarlepyy, *Finland* 8 E20
Uusikaupunki, *Finland* 9 F19
Uva, *Russia* 22 C9
Uvalde, *U.S.A.* 71 L5
Uvat, *Russia* 24 D7
Uvinza, *Tanzania* 46 F6
Uvira, *Zaïre* 46 E5
Uvs Nuur, *Mongolia* . 30 A4
Uwajima, *Japan* 29 H6
Uyandi, *Russia* 25 C15
Uyuni, *Bolivia* 78 H5
Uzbekistan ■, *Asia* .. 24 E7
Uzen, *Kazakhstan* ... 23 F9
Uzerche, *France* 18 D4
Uzh ➜, *Ukraine* 17 C16
Uzhgorod = Uzhhorod,
 Ukraine 17 D12
Uzhhorod, *Ukraine* .. 17 D12
Uzunköprü, *Turkey* .. 21 D12

V

Vaal ➜, *S. Africa* 48 D3
Vaal Dam, *S. Africa* .. 49 D4
Vaalwater, *S. Africa* .. 49 C4
Vaasa, *Finland* 8 E19
Vác, *Hungary* 17 E10
Vacaville, *U.S.A.* 72 G3
Vach = Vakh ➜,
 Russia 24 C8
Vadodara, *India* 36 H8
Vadsø, *Norway* 8 A23
Vaduz, *Liech.* 16 E5
Værøy, *Norway* 8 C15
Vágar, *Færoe Is.* 8 E9
Vågsfjorden, *Norway* . 8 B17
Váh ➜, *Slovak Rep.* . 17 D9
Vahsel B., *Antarctica* . 5 D1
Vaigach, *Russia* 24 B6
Vakh ➜, *Russia* 24 C8
Val d'Or, *Canada* 62 C4
Val Marie, *Canada* ... 65 D7
Valahia, *Romania* 17 F13
Valandovo, *Macedonia* 21 D10
Valcheta, *Argentina* .. 80 E3
Valdayskaya
 Vozvyshennost,
 Russia 22 C5
Valdepeñas, *Spain* ... 19 C4
Valdés, Pen., *Argentina* 80 E4
Valdez, *U.S.A.* 60 B5
Valdivia, *Chile* 80 D2
Valdosta, *U.S.A.* 69 K4
Valdres, *Norway* 9 F13
Vale, *U.S.A.* 72 E5
Valença, *Brazil* 79 F11
Valença do Piauí, *Brazil* 79 E10
Valence, *France* 18 D6
Valencia, *Spain* 19 C5
Valencia, *Venezuela* .. 78 A5
Valencia □, *Spain* ... 19 C5
Valencia de Alcántara,
 Spain 19 C2
Valencia Harbour,
 Ireland 13 E1
Valencia I., *Ireland* ... 13 E1
Valenciennes, *France* . 18 A5
Valentim, Sa. do, *Brazil* 79 E10
Valentin, *Russia* 28 C7
Valentine, *Tex., U.S.A.* 71 K2
Valera, *Venezuela* 78 B4
Valga, *Estonia* 9 H22
Valier, *U.S.A.* 72 B7
Valjevo, *Serbia, Yug.* . 21 B8
Valka, *Latvia* 9 H21
Valkeakoski, *Finland* . 9 F20
Valkenswaard, *Neths.* . 15 C5
Vall de Uxó, *Spain* ... 19 C5
Valladolid, *Mexico* ... 74 C7
Valladolid, *Spain* 19 B3

Valle de la Pascua,
 Venezuela 78 B5
Valledupar, *Colombia* . 78 A4
Vallejo, *U.S.A.* 72 G2
Vallenar, *Chile* 80 B2
Valletta, *Malta* 20 G6
Valley City, *U.S.A.* ... 70 B6
Valley Falls, *U.S.A.* .. 72 E3
Valleyview, *Canada* .. 64 B5
Valls, *Spain* 19 B6
Valmiera, *Latvia* 9 H21
Valognes, *France* 18 B3
Valona = Vlóra,
 Albania 21 D8
Valozhyn, *Belarus* ... 17 A14
Valparaíso, *Chile* 80 C2
Valparaiso, *U.S.A.* ... 68 E2
Vals ➜, *S. Africa* 48 D4
Vals, Tanjung,
 Indonesia 33 F9
Valsad, *India* 36 J8
Valverde del Camino,
 Spain 19 D2
Vammala, *Finland* ... 9 F20
Van, *Turkey* 23 G7
Van, L. = Van Gölü,
 Turkey 23 G7
Van Alstyne, *U.S.A.* .. 71 J6
Van Bruyssel, *Canada* 63 C5
Van Buren, *Canada* .. 63 C6
Van Buren, *Ark., U.S.A.* 71 H7
Van Buren, *Maine,
 U.S.A.* 69 B11
Van Buren, *Mo., U.S.A.* 71 G9
Van Diemen, C.,
 N. Terr., Australia .. 52 B5
Van Diemen, C.,
 Queens., Australia .. 54 B2
Van Diemen G.,
 Australia 52 B5
Van Gölü, *Turkey* 23 G7
Van Horn, *U.S.A.* ... 71 K2
Van Rees, Pegunungan,
 Indonesia 33 E9
Van Tassell, *U.S.A.* .. 70 D2
Van Wert, *U.S.A.* ... 68 E3
Vanadzor, *Armenia* .. 23 F7
Vanavara, *Russia* 25 C11
Vancouver, *Canada* .. 64 D4
Vancouver, *U.S.A.* ... 72 D2
Vancouver, C., *Australia* 53 G2
Vancouver I., *Canada* . 64 D3
Vandalia, *Ill., U.S.A.* . 70 F10
Vandalia, *Mo., U.S.A.* . 70 F9
Vanderbijlpark,
 S. Africa 49 D4
Vandergrift, *U.S.A.* ... 68 E6
Vanderhoof, *Canada* . 64 C4
Vanderkloof Dam,
 S. Africa 48 E3
Vanderlin I., *Australia* . 54 B2
Vandyke, *Australia* ... 54 C4
Vänern, *Sweden* 9 G15
Vänersborg, *Sweden* . 9 G15
Vang Vieng, *Laos* 34 C7
Vanga, *Kenya* 46 E7
Vangaindrano, *Madag.* 49 C8
Vanguard, *Canada* ... 65 D7
Vanier, *Canada* 62 C4
Vankleek Hill, *Canada* . 62 C5
Vanna, *Norway* 8 A18
Vännäs, *Sweden* 8 E18
Vannes, *France* 18 C2
Vanrhynsdorp, *S. Africa* 48 E2
Vanrook, *Australia* ... 54 B3
Vansbro, *Sweden* 9 F16
Vansittart B., *Australia* 52 B4
Vantaa, *Finland* 9 F21
Vanua Levu, *Fiji* 51 C8
Vanua Mbalavu, *Fiji* .. 51 C9
Vanuatu ■, *Pac. Oc.* . 56 J8
Vanwyksvlei, *S. Africa* 48 E3
Vanzylsrus, *S. Africa* . 48 D3
Vapnyarka, *Ukraine* .. 17 D15
Varanasi, *India* 37 G13
Varanger-halvøya,
 Norway 8 A23
Varangerfjorden,
 Norway 8 A23
Varaždin, *Croatia* 16 E9
Varberg, *Sweden* 9 H15
Vardar = Axiós ➜,
 Greece 21 D10
Varde, *Denmark* 9 J13
Vardø, *Norway* 8 A24
Varena, *Lithuania* 9 J21
Varese, *Italy* 20 B3
Variadero, *U.S.A.* 71 H2
Varkaus, *Finland* 9 E22
Varna, *Bulgaria* 21 C12
Värnamo, *Sweden* ... 9 H16
Vasa Barris ➜, *Brazil* 79 F11
Vascongadas = País
 Vasco □, *Spain* 19 A4
Vasht = Khāsh, *Iran* . 36 E2
Vasilevichi, *Belarus* .. 17 B15
Vasilkov = Vasylkiv,
 Ukraine 17 C16
Vaslui, *Romania* 17 E14
Vassar, *Canada* 65 D9
Vassar, *U.S.A.* 68 D4
Västeräs, *Sweden* ... 9 G17
Västerbotten, *Sweden* . 8 D18
Västerdalälven ➜,
 Sweden 9 F16
Västervik, *Sweden* ... 9 H17
Västmanland, *Sweden* 9 G16
Vasto, *Italy* 20 C6
Vasylkiv, *Ukraine* 17 C16
Vatican City ■, *Europe* 20 D5
Vatnajökull, *Iceland* .. 8 D5
Vatoa, *Fiji* 51 D9
Vatoloha, *Madag.* 49 B8

Vatomandry, *Madag.* . 49 B8
Vatra-Dornei, *Romania* 17 E13
Vättern, *Sweden* 9 G16
Vaughn, *Mont., U.S.A.* 72 C8
Vaughn, *N. Mex.,
 U.S.A.* 73 J11
Vaupés = Uaupés ➜,
 Brazil 78 C5
Vauxhall, *Canada* 64 C6
Vava'u, *Tonga* 51 D11
Vawkavysk, *Belarus* .. 17 B13
Växjö, *Sweden* 9 H16
Vaygach, Ostrov,
 Russia 24 C6
Vechte ➜, *Neths.* ... 15 B6
Vedea ➜, *Romania* .. 17 G13
Veendam, *Neths.* 15 A6
Veenendaal, *Neths.* .. 15 B5
Vefsna ➜, *Norway* .. 8 D15
Vega, *Norway* 8 D14
Vega, *U.S.A.* 71 H3
Veghel, *Neths.* 15 C5
Vegreville, *Canada* ... 64 C6
Vejer de la Frontera,
 Spain 19 D3
Vejle, *Denmark* 9 J13
Velddrif, *S. Africa* 48 E2
Velebit Planina, *Croatia* 16 F8
Vélez, *Colombia* 78 B4
Vélez Málaga, *Spain* .. 19 D3
Vélez Rubio, *Spain* ... 19 D4
Velhas ➜, *Brazil* 79 G10
Velika Kapela, *Croatia* . 16 F8
Velikaya ➜, *Russia* .. 22 C4
Velikaya Kema, *Russia* 28 B8
Veliki Ustyug, *Russia* . 22 B8
Velikiye Luki, *Russia* .. 22 C5
Veliko Tŭrnovo,
 Bulgaria 21 C11
Velikonda Range, *India* 36 M11
Velletri, *Italy* 20 D5
Vellore, *India* 36 N11
Velsen-Noord, *Neths.* . 15 B4
Velsk, *Russia* 22 B7
Velva, *U.S.A.* 70 A4
Venado Tuerto,
 Argentina 80 C4
Vendée □, *France* ... 18 C3
Vendôme, *France* 18 C4
Venézia, *Italy* 20 B5
Venézia, G. di, *Italy* .. 20 B5
Venezuela ■, *S. Amer.* 78 B5
Venezuela, G. de,
 Venezuela 78 A4
Vengurla, *India* 36 M8
Venice = Venézia, *Italy* 20 B5
Venkatapuram, *India* . 37 K12
Venlo, *Neths.* 15 C6
Vennesla, *Norway* ... 9 G12
Venraij, *Neths.* 15 C5
Ventana, Sa. de la,
 Argentina 80 D4
Ventersburg, *S. Africa* 48 D4
Venterstad, *S. Africa* . 48 E4
Ventnor, *U.K.* 11 G6
Ventotene, *Italy* 20 D5
Ventoux, Mt., *France* . 18 D6
Ventspils, *Latvia* 9 H19
Ventuarí ➜,
 Venezuela 78 C5
Ventura, *U.S.A.* 73 J4
Venus B., *Australia* ... 55 F4
Vera, *Argentina* 80 B4
Vera, *Spain* 19 D5
Veracruz, *Mexico* 74 D5
Veraval, *India* 36 J7
Verbánia, *Italy* 20 B3
Vercelli, *Italy* 20 B3
Verdalsøra, *Norway* .. 8 E14
Verde ➜, *Argentina* . 80 E3
Verden, *Germany* 16 B5
Verdigre, *U.S.A.* 70 D5
Verdun, *France* 18 B6
Vereeniging, *S. Africa* . 49 D4
Vérendrye, Parc Prov.
 de la, *Canada* 62 C4
Verga, C., *Guinea* 44 F2
Vergemont, *Australia* . 54 C3
Vergemont Cr. ➜,
 Australia 54 C3
Verín, *Spain* 19 B2
Verkhnevilyuysk, *Russia* 25 C13
Verkhneye Kalinino,
 Russia 25 D11
Verkhniy Baskunchak,
 Russia 23 E8
Verkhnyaya Amga,
 Russia 25 D13
Verkhoyansk, *Russia* . 25 C14
Verkhoyansk Ra. =
 Verkhoyanskiy
 Khrebet, *Russia* ... 25 C13
Verkhoyanskiy Khrebet,
 Russia 25 C13
Verlo, *Canada* 65 C7
Vermilion, *Canada* ... 65 C6
Vermilion ➜, *Alta.,
 Canada* 65 C6
Vermilion ➜, *Qué.,
 Canada* 62 C5
Vermilion, B., *U.S.A.* . 71 L9
Vermilion Bay, *Canada* 65 D10
Vermilion Chutes,
 Canada 64 B6
Vermilion L., *U.S.A.* .. 70 B8
Vermillion, *U.S.A.* ... 70 D6
Vermont □, *U.S.A.* .. 68 D9
Vernal, *U.S.A.* 72 F9
Verner, *Canada* 62 C3
Verneukpan, *S. Africa* 48 E3
Vernon, *Canada* 64 C5
Vernon, *U.S.A.* 71 H5
Vero Beach, *U.S.A.* .. 69 M5

Véroia, Greece 21 D10
Verona, Italy 20 B4
Versailles, France ... 18 B5
Vert, C., Senegal 44 F1
Verulam, S. Africa ... 49 D5
Verviers, Belgium ... 15 D5
Veselovskoye Vdkhr., Russia ... 23 E7
Vesoul, France 18 C7
Vesterålen, Norway .. 8 B16
Vestfjorden, Norway . 8 C15
Vestmannaeyjar, Iceland ... 8 E3
Vestspitsbergen, Svalbard ... 4 B8
Vestvågøy, Norway .. 8 B15
Vesuvio, Italy 20 D6
Vesuvius, Mte. = Vesuvio, Italy 20 D6
Veszprém, Hungary .. 17 E9
Vetlanda, Sweden ... 9 H16
Vetlugu →, Russia .. 24 D5
Vettore, Mte., Italy .. 20 C5
Veurne, Belgium 15 C2
Veys, Iran 39 D6
Vezhen, Bulgaria ... 21 C11
Viacha, Bolivia 78 G5
Viamão, Brazil 80 C6
Viana, Brazil 79 D10
Viana do Alentejo, Portugal ... 19 C2
Viana do Castelo, Portugal ... 19 B1
Vianópolis, Brazil ... 79 G9
Viaréggio, Italy 20 C4
Vibank, Canada 65 C8
Vibo Valéntia, Italy .. 20 E7
Viborg, Denmark ... 9 H13
Vicenza, Italy 20 B4
Vich, Spain 19 B7
Vichy, France 18 C5
Vicksburg, Mich., U.S.A. ... 68 D3
Vicksburg, Miss., U.S.A. 71 J9
Viçosa, Brazil 79 E11
Victor, India 36 J7
Victor, U.S.A. 70 F2
Victor Harbor, Australia 55 F2
Victoria, Canada 64 D4
Victoria, Chile 80 D2
Victoria, Guinea 44 F2
Victoria, Malaysia .. 32 C5
Victoria, Seychelles . 35 E4
Victoria, Kans., U.S.A. 70 F5
Victoria, Tex., U.S.A. 71 L6
Victoria □, Australia . 55 F3
Victoria →, Australia 52 C4
Victoria, Grand L., Canada ... 62 C4
Victoria, L., Africa .. 46 E6
Victoria, L., Australia 55 E3
Victoria Beach, Canada 65 C9
Victoria de Durango, Mexico ... 74 C4
Victoria Falls, Zimbabwe ... 47 H5
Victoria Harbour, Canada ... 62 D4
Victoria I., Canada .. 60 A8
Victoria Ld., Antarctica 5 D11
Victoria Res., Canada 63 C8
Victoria River Downs, Australia ... 52 C4
Victoria Taungdeik, Burma ... 37 J18
Victoria West, S. Africa 48 E3
Victorica, Argentina . 80 D3
Victoriaville, Canada . 63 C5
Victorville, U.S.A. ... 73 J5
Vicuña, Chile 80 C2
Vidalia, U.S.A. 69 J4
Vidin, Bulgaria 21 C10
Vidisha, India 36 H10
Vidzy, Belarus 9 J22
Viedma, Argentina .. 80 E4
Viedma, L., Argentina 80 F2
Vien Pou Kha, Laos . 34 B6
Vienna = Wien, Austria 16 D9
Vienna, U.S.A. 71 G10
Vienne, France 18 D6
Vienne →, France .. 18 C4
Vientiane, Laos 34 D8
Vierzon, France 18 C5
Vietnam ■, Asia 34 C9
Vigan, Phil. 33 A6
Vigévano, Italy 20 B3
Vigia, Brazil 79 D9
Vigo, Spain 19 A1
Vijayawada, India .. 37 L12
Vík, Iceland 8 E4
Vikeke, Indonesia .. 33 F7
Viking, Canada 64 C6
Vikna, Norway 8 D14
Vikulovo, Russia ... 24 D8
Vila da Maganja, Mozam. ... 47 H7
Vila de João Belo = Xai-Xai, Mozam. .. 49 D5
Vila do Bispo, Portugal 19 D1
Vila do Chibuto, Mozam. ... 49 C5
Vila Franca de Xira, Portugal ... 19 C1
Vila Gomes da Costa, Mozam. ... 49 C5
Vila Machado, Mozam. 47 H6
Vila Nova de Gaia, Portugal ... 19 B1
Vila Real, Portugal .. 19 B2
Vila Real de Santo António, Portugal . 19 D2
Vila Velha, Brazil ... 79 H10
Vilaine →, France ... 18 C2

Vilanandro, Tanjona, Madag. ... 49 B7
Vilanculos, Mozam. .. 49 C6
Vileyka, Belarus 17 A14
Vilhelmina, Sweden . 8 D17
Vilhena, Brazil 78 F6
Viliga, Russia 25 C16
Viliya →, Lithuania . 9 J21
Viljandi, Estonia ... 9 G21
Vilkitskogo, Proliv, Russia ... 25 B11
Vilkovo = Vylkove, Ukraine ... 17 F15
Villa Ahumada, Mexico 74 A3
Villa Ángela, Argentina 80 B4
Villa Bella, Bolivia ... 78 F5
Villa Bens = Tarfaya, Morocco ... 44 C2
Villa Cisneros = Dakhla, W. Sahara . 44 D1
Villa Colón, Argentina 80 C3
Villa de María, Argentina ... 80 B4
Villa Dolores, Argentina 80 C3
Villa Hayes, Paraguay 80 A5
Villa María, Argentina 80 C4
Villa Mazán, Argentina 80 B3
Villa Montes, Bolivia . 80 A4
Villa Ocampo, Argentina ... 80 B5
Villacarrillo, Spain ... 19 C4
Villach, Austria 16 E7
Villagarcía de Arosa, Spain ... 19 A1
Villaguay, Argentina . 80 C5
Villahermosa, Mexico 74 D6
Villajoyosa, Spain ... 19 C5
Villalba, Spain 19 A2
Villanueva, U.S.A. .. 73 J11
Villanueva de la Serena, Spain 19 C3
Villanueva y Geltrú, Spain ... 19 B6
Villarreal, Spain 19 C5
Villarrica, Chile 80 D2
Villarrica, Paraguay . 80 B5
Villarrobledo, Spain . 19 C4
Villavicencio, Colombia 78 C4
Villaviciosa, Spain .. 19 A3
Villazón, Bolivia 80 A3
Ville-Marie, Canada . 62 C4
Ville Platte, U.S.A. .. 71 K8
Villena, Spain 19 C5
Villeneuve-d'Ascq, France ... 18 A5
Villeneuve-sur-Lot, France ... 18 D4
Villiers, S. Africa ... 49 D4
Villingen-Schwenningen, Germany ... 16 D5
Villisca, U.S.A. 70 E7
Vilna, Canada 64 C6
Vilnius, Lithuania .. 9 J21
Vilvoorde, Belgium . 15 D4
Vilyuy →, Russia ... 25 C13
Vilyuysk, Russia ... 25 C13
Viña del Mar, Chile . 80 C2
Vinaroz, Spain 19 B6
Vincennes, U.S.A. .. 68 F2
Vindelälven →, Sweden ... 8 E18
Vindeln, Sweden ... 8 D18
Vindhya Ra., India . 36 H10
Vineland, U.S.A. ... 68 F8
Vinh, Vietnam 34 C8
Vinita, U.S.A. 71 G7
Vinkovci, Croatia ... 21 B8
Vinnitsa = Vinnytsya, Ukraine ... 17 D15
Vinnytsya, Ukraine . 17 D15
Vinton, Iowa, U.S.A. 70 D8
Vinton, La., U.S.A. . 71 K8
Virac, Phil. 33 B6
Virago Sd., Canada . 64 C2
Viramgam, India ... 36 H8
Virden, Canada 65 D8
Vire, France 18 B3
Vírgenes, C., Argentina 80 G3
Virgin →, Canada .. 65 B7
Virgin →, U.S.A. ... 73 H6
Virgin Is. (British) ■, W. Indies ... 75 D12
Virgin Is. (U.S.) ■, W. Indies ... 75 D12
Virginia, S. Africa .. 48 D4
Virginia, U.S.A. 70 B8
Virginia □, U.S.A. .. 68 G7
Virginia Beach, U.S.A. 68 G8
Virginia City, Mont., U.S.A. ... 72 D7
Virginia City, Nev., U.S.A. ... 72 G4
Virginia Falls, Canada 64 A3
Virginiatown, Canada 62 C4
Viroqua, U.S.A. 70 D9
Virovitica, Croatia .. 20 B7
Virton, Belgium 15 E5
Virudunagar, India . 36 Q10
Vis, Croatia 20 C7
Visalia, U.S.A. 73 H4
Visayan Sea, Phil. .. 33 B6
Visby, Sweden 9 H18
Viscount Melville Sd., Canada ... 4 B2
Visé, Belgium 15 D5
Višegrad, Bos.-H. .. 21 C8
Viseu, Brazil 79 D9
Viseu, Portugal 19 B2
Vishakhapatnam, India 37 L13
Viso, Mte., Italy 20 B2
Visokoi I., Antarctica 5 B1
Vistula = Wisła →, Poland ... 17 A10

Vitebsk = Vitsyebsk, Belarus ... 22 C5
Viterbo, Italy 20 C5
Viti Levu, Fiji 51 C7
Vitigudino, Spain .. 19 B2
Vitim, Russia 25 D12
Vitim →, Russia ... 25 D12
Vitória, Brazil 79 H10
Vitoria, Spain 19 A4
Vitória da Conquista, Brazil ... 79 F10
Vitsyebsk, Belarus . 22 C5
Vittória, Italy 20 F6
Vittório Véneto, Italy 20 B5
Vivero, Spain 19 A2
Vize, Turkey 21 D12
Vizianagaram, India 37 K13
Vjosa →, Albania .. 21 D8
Vlaardingen, Neths. 15 C4
Vladikavkaz, Russia 23 F7
Vladimir, Russia ... 22 C7
Vladimir Volynskiy = Volodymyr-Volynskyy, Ukraine ... 17 C13
Vladivostok, Russia 25 E14
Vlieland, Neths. ... 15 A4
Vlissingen, Neths. . 15 C3
Vlóra, Albania 21 D8
Vltava →, Czech. .. 16 D8
Vogelkop = Doberai, Jazirah, Indonesia 33 E8
Vogelsberg, Germany 16 C5
Voghera, Italy 20 B3
Vohibinany, Madag. 49 B8
Vohimarina, Madag. 49 A9
Vohimena, Tanjon' i, Madag. ... 49 D8
Vohipeno, Madag. . 49 C8
Voi, Kenya 46 E7
Voiron, France 18 D6
Voisey B., Canada . 63 A7
Vojmsjön, Sweden . 8 D17
Vojvodina □, Serbia, Yug. ... 21 B9
Volborg, U.S.A. 70 C2
Volcano Is. = Kazan-Rettō, Pac. Oc. .. 56 E6
Volchayevka, Russia 25 E14
Volda, Norway 9 E12
Volga →, Russia ... 23 E8
Volga Hts. = Privolzhskaya Vozvyshennost, Russia ... 23 D8
Volgodonsk, Russia 23 E7
Volgograd, Russia . 23 E7
Volgogradskoye Vdkhr., Russia ... 23 D8
Volkhov →, Russia . 22 B5
Volkovysk = Vawkavysk, Belarus 17 B13
Volksrust, S. Africa . 49 D4
Vollenhove, Neths. . 15 B5
Volochanka, Russia 25 B10
Volodymyr-Volynskyy, Ukraine ... 17 C13
Vologda, Russia ... 22 C6
Vólos, Greece 21 E10
Volovets, Ukraine .. 17 D12
Volozhin = Valozhyn, Belarus ... 17 A14
Volsk, Russia 22 D8
Volta →, Ghana ... 44 G5
Volta, L., Ghana ... 44 G5
Volta Redonda, Brazil 79 H10
Voltaire, C., Australia 52 B4
Volterra, Italy 20 C4
Volturno →, Italy .. 20 D6
Volvo, Australia ... 55 E3
Volzhskiy, Russia .. 23 E7
Vondrozo, Madag. . 49 C8
Voorburg, Neths. .. 15 B4
Vopnafjörður, Iceland 8 D6
Voríai Sporádhes, Greece ... 21 E10
Vorkuta, Russia ... 22 A11
Vormsi, Estonia ... 9 G20
Voronezh, Russia .. 22 D6
Voroshilovgrad = Luhansk, Ukraine . 23 E6
Voroshilovsk = Alchevsk, Ukraine . 23 E6
Vorovskoye, Russia 25 D16
Võrts Järv, Estonia . 9 G22
Võru, Estonia 9 H22
Vosges, France 18 B7
Voss, Norway 9 F12
Vostok I., Kiribati .. 57 J12
Votkinsk, Russia ... 22 C9
Votkinskoye Vdkhr., Russia ... 22 C10
Vouga →, Portugal 19 B1
Vozhe Ozero, Russia 22 B6
Voznesenka, Russia 25 D10
Voznesensk, Ukraine 23 E5
Voznesenye, Russia 22 B6
Vrangelya, Ostrov, Russia ... 25 B19
Vranje, Serbia, Yug. 21 C9
Vratsa, Bulgaria ... 21 C10
Vrbas →, Bos.-H. .. 20 B7
Vrede, S. Africa ... 49 D4
Vredefort, S. Africa . 48 D4
Vredenburg, S. Africa 48 E2
Vredendal, S. Africa 48 E2
Vršac, Serbia, Yug. . 21 B9
Vryburg, S. Africa .. 48 D3
Vryheid, S. Africa .. 49 D5
Vught, Neths. 15 C5
Vukovar, Croatia ... 21 B8
Vulcan, Canada 64 C6
Vulcan, Romania ... 17 F12
Vulcan, U.S.A. 68 C2

Vulcaneşti, Moldova . 17 F15
Vulcano, Italy 20 E6
Vulkaneshty = Vulcaneşti, Moldova 17 F15
Vung Tau, Vietnam .. 34 G9
Vyatka = Kirov, Russia 24 D5
Vyatka →, Russia .. 22 C9
Vyatskiye Polyany, Russia ... 22 C9
Vyazemskiy, Russia 25 E14
Vyazma, Russia ... 22 C5
Vyborg, Russia 22 B4
Vychegda →, Russia 22 B8
Vychodné Beskydy, Europe ... 17 D11
Vyg-ozero, Russia . 22 B5
Vylkove, Ukraine .. 17 F15
Vynohradiv, Ukraine 17 D12
Vyrnwy, L., U.K. ... 10 E4
Vyshniy Volochek, Russia ... 22 C5
Vyshzha = imeni 26 Bakinskikh Komissarov, Turkmenistan ... 23 G9
Vyškov, Czech. 17 D9
Vytegra, Russia 22 B6

W

W.A.C. Bennett Dam, Canada ... 64 B4
Wa, Ghana 44 F4
Waal →, Neths. 15 C5
Wabakimi L., Canada 62 B2
Wabana, Canada ... 63 C9
Wabasca, Canada .. 64 B6
Wabash, U.S.A. 68 E3
Wabash →, U.S.A. . 68 G1
Wabeno, U.S.A. 68 C1
Wabigoon L., Canada 65 D10
Wabowden, Canada 65 C9
Wabuk Pt., Canada . 62 A2
Wabush, Canada ... 63 B6
Wabuska, U.S.A. ... 72 G4
Waco, U.S.A. 71 K6
Waconichi, L., Canada 62 B5
Wad Banda, Sudan . 45 F10
Wad Hamid, Sudan . 45 E11
Wâd Medanî, Sudan 45 F11
Wadayama, Japan .. 29 G7
Waddeneilanden, Neths. ... 15 A5
Waddenzee, Neths. . 15 A5
Wadderin Hill, Australia 53 F2
Waddington, Mt., Canada ... 64 C3
Waddy Pt., Australia 55 C5
Wadena, Canada ... 65 C8
Wadena, U.S.A. 70 B7
Wadesboro, U.S.A. . 69 H5
Wadhams, Canada . 64 C3
Wādī as Sir, Jordan . 41 D4
Wadi Halfa, Sudan . 45 D11
Wadsworth, U.S.A. . 72 G4
Wafrah, Si. Arabia . 38 D5
Wageningen, Neths. 15 C5
Wager B., Canada .. 61 B11
Wager Bay, Canada 61 B10
Wagga Wagga, Australia ... 55 F4
Waghete, Indonesia 33 E9
Wagin, Australia ... 53 F2
Wagon Mound, U.S.A. 71 G2
Wagoner, U.S.A. ... 71 G7
Wah, Pakistan 36 C8
Wahai, Indonesia .. 33 E7
Wahiawa, U.S.A. ... 66 H15
Wahoo, U.S.A. 70 E6
Wahpeton, U.S.A. .. 70 B6
Waiau →, N.Z. 51 K4
Waibeem, Indonesia 33 E8
Waigeo, Indonesia . 33 E8
Waihi, N.Z. 51 G5
Waihou →, N.Z. ... 51 G5
Waikabubak, Indonesia 33 F5
Waikari, N.Z. 51 K4
Waikato →, N.Z. ... 51 G5
Waikerie, Australia . 55 E2
Waikokopu, N.Z. ... 51 H6
Waikouaiti, N.Z. ... 51 L3
Waimakariri →, N.Z. 51 K4
Waimate, N.Z. 51 L3
Waingapu, India ... 36 K11
Waingapu, Indonesia 33 F6
Wainwright, Canada 65 C6
Wainwright, U.S.A. . 60 A3
Waiouru, N.Z. 51 H5
Waipara, N.Z. 51 K4
Waipawa, N.Z. 51 H6
Waipiro, N.Z. 51 H7
Waipu, N.Z. 51 F5
Waipukurau, N.Z. .. 51 J6
Wairakei, N.Z. 51 H6
Wairarapa, L., N.Z. 51 J5
Wairoa, N.Z. 51 H6
Waitaki →, N.Z. ... 51 L3
Waitara, N.Z. 51 H5
Waitsburg, U.S.A. .. 72 C5
Waiuku, N.Z. 51 G5
Wajima, Japan 29 F8
Wajir, Kenya 46 D8
Wakasa, Japan 29 G7
Wakasa-Wan, Japan 29 G7
Wakatipu, L., N.Z. . 51 L2
Wakaw, Canada ... 65 C7
Wakayama, Japan .. 29 G7
Wakayama-ken □, Japan ... 29 H7

Wake Forest, U.S.A. . 69 H6
Wake I., Pac. Oc. ... 56 F8
Wakefield, N.Z. 51 J4
Wakefield, U.K. 10 D6
Wakefield, U.S.A. .. 70 B10
Wakeham Bay = Maricourt, Canada 61 C12
Wakema, Burma ... 37 L19
Wakkanai, Japan ... 28 B10
Wakkerstroom, S. Africa ... 49 D5
Wakool, Australia .. 55 F3
Wakool →, Australia 55 F3
Wakre, Indonesia .. 33 E8
Wakuach L., Canada 63 A6
Wałbrzych, Poland . 16 C9
Walbury Hill, U.K. .. 11 F6
Walcha, Australia .. 55 E5
Walcheren, Neths. . 15 C3
Walcott, U.S.A. 72 F10
Walden, U.S.A. 72 F10
Waldport, U.S.A. ... 72 D1
Waldron, U.S.A. 71 H7
Wales □, U.K. 11 E4
Walgett, Australia .. 55 E4
Walgreen Coast, Antarctica ... 5 D15
Walhalla, Australia . 55 F4
Walhalla, U.S.A. ... 65 D9
Walker, U.S.A. 70 B7
Walker L., Man., Canada ... 65 C9
Walker L., Qué., Canada 63 B6
Walker L., U.S.A. .. 72 G4
Walkerston, Australia 54 C4
Wall, U.S.A. 70 C3
Walla Walla, U.S.A. . 72 C4
Wallabadah, Australia 54 B3
Wallace, Idaho, U.S.A. 72 C6
Wallace, N.C., U.S.A. 69 H7
Wallace, Nebr., U.S.A. 70 E4
Wallaceburg, Canada 62 D3
Wallachia = Valahia, Romania ... 17 F13
Wallal, Australia ... 55 D4
Wallal Downs, Australia 52 C3
Wallambin, L., Australia 53 F2
Wallaroo, Australia . 55 E2
Wallasey, U.K. 10 D4
Wallerawang, Australia 55 E5
Wallhallow, Australia 54 B2
Wallis & Futuna, Is., Pac. Oc. ... 56 J10
Wallowa, U.S.A. ... 72 D5
Wallowa Mts., U.S.A. 72 D5
Wallsend, Australia . 55 E5
Wallsend, U.K. 10 C6
Wallula, U.S.A. 72 C4
Wallumbilla, Australia 55 D4
Walmsley, L., Canada 65 A7
Walney, I. of, U.K. .. 10 C4
Walnut Ridge, U.S.A. 71 G9
Walsall, U.K. 11 E6
Walsenburg, U.S.A. 71 G2
Walsh, U.S.A. 71 G3
Walsh →, Australia 54 B3
Walsh P.O., Australia 54 B3
Walterboro, U.S.A. . 69 J5
Walters, U.S.A. 71 H5
Waltham Station, Canada ... 62 C4
Waltman, U.S.A. ... 72 E10
Walvisbaai, Namibia 48 C1
Wamba, Zaïre 46 D5
Wamego, U.S.A. ... 70 F6
Wamena, Indonesia 33 E9
Wamulan, Indonesia 33 E7
Wana, Pakistan 36 C6
Wanaaring, Australia 55 D3
Wanaka, N.Z. 51 L2
Wanaka L., N.Z. ... 51 L2
Wanapiri, Indonesia 33 E9
Wanapitei L., Canada 62 C3
Wanbi, Australia ... 55 E3
Wandarrie, Australia 53 E2
Wandel Sea = McKinley Sea, Arctic 4 A7
Wandoan, Australia 55 D4
Wang Saphung, Thailand ... 34 D6
Wangal, Indonesia . 33 F8
Wanganella, Australia 55 F3
Wanganui, N.Z. 51 H5
Wangaratta, Australia 55 F4
Wangary, Australia . 55 E2
Wangerooge, Germany 16 B4
Wangiwangi, Indonesia 33 F6
Wanless, Canada .. 65 C8
Wanxian, China 31 C5
Wapakoneta, U.S.A. 68 E3
Wapato, U.S.A. 72 C3
Wapawekka L., Canada 65 C8
Wapikopa L., Canada 62 B2
Wapsipinicon →, U.S.A. ... 70 E9
Warangal, India 36 L11
Waratah, Australia . 54 G4
Waratah B., Australia 55 F4
Warburton, Vic., Australia ... 55 F4
Warburton, W. Austral., Australia ... 53 E4
Warburton Ra., Australia ... 53 E4
Ward, N.Z. 51 J5
Ward →, Australia . 55 D4
Ward Cove, U.S.A. . 64 B2
Warden, S. Africa .. 49 D4
Wardha, India 36 J11
Wardha →, India .. 36 K11
Wardlow, Canada .. 64 C6

Ware, Canada 64 B3
Warialda, Australia . 55 D5
Wariap, Indonesia . 33 E8
Warkopi, Indonesia 33 E8
Warley, U.K. 11 E6
Warm Springs, U.S.A. 73 G5
Warman, Canada ... 65 C7
Warmbad, Namibia . 48 D2
Warmbad, S. Africa 49 C4
Warnambool Downs, Australia ... 54 C3
Warner, Canada 64 D6
Warner Mts., U.S.A. 72 F3
Warner Robins, U.S.A. 69 J4
Waroona, Australia . 53 F2
Warracknabeal, Australia ... 55 F3
Warragul, Australia . 55 F4
Warrawagine, Australia 52 D3
Warrego →, Australia 55 E4
Warrego Ra., Australia 54 C4
Warren, Australia .. 55 E4
Warren, Ark., U.S.A. 71 J8
Warren, Mich., U.S.A. 68 D4
Warren, Minn., U.S.A. 70 A6
Warren, Ohio, U.S.A. 68 E5
Warren, Pa., U.S.A. 68 E6
Warrenpoint, U.K. .. 13 B5
Warrensburg, U.S.A. 70 F8
Warrenton, S. Africa 48 D3
Warrenton, U.S.A. . 72 C2
Warrenville, Australia 55 D4
Warri, Nigeria 44 G6
Warrina, Australia .. 55 D2
Warrington, U.K. ... 10 D5
Warrington, U.S.A. . 69 K2
Warrnambool, Australia 55 F3
Warroad, U.S.A. ... 70 A7
Warsa, Indonesia .. 33 E9
Warsaw = Warszawa, Poland ... 17 B11
Warsaw, U.S.A. 68 E3
Warszawa, Poland . 17 B11
Warta →, Poland .. 16 B8
Warthe = Warta →, Poland ... 16 B8
Waru, Indonesia ... 33 E8
Warwick, Australia . 55 D5
Warwick, U.K. 11 E6
Warwick, U.S.A. ... 68 E10
Warwickshire □, U.K. 11 E6
Wasatch Ra., U.S.A. 72 F8
Wasbank, S. Africa 49 D5
Wasco, Calif., U.S.A. 73 J4
Wasco, Oreg., U.S.A. 72 D3
Waseca, U.S.A. 70 C8
Wasekamio L., Canada 65 B7
Wash, The, U.K. ... 10 E8
Washburn, N. Dak., U.S.A. ... 70 B4
Washburn, Wis., U.S.A. 70 B9
Washim, India 36 J10
Washington, D.C., U.S.A. ... 68 F7
Washington, Ga., U.S.A. ... 69 J4
Washington, Ind., U.S.A. ... 68 F2
Washington, Iowa, U.S.A. ... 70 E9
Washington, Mo., U.S.A. ... 70 F9
Washington, N.C., U.S.A. ... 69 H7
Washington, Pa., U.S.A. 68 F5
Washington, Utah, U.S.A. ... 73 H7
Washington □, U.S.A. 72 C3
Washington, Mt., U.S.A. ... 68 C10
Washington I., U.S.A. 68 C2
Wasian, Indonesia . 33 E8
Wasior, Indonesia . 33 E8
Waskaganish, Canada 62 B4
Waskaiowaka, L., Canada ... 65 B9
Waskesiu Lake, Canada 65 C7
Wassenaar, Neths. . 15 B4
Wasserkuppe, Germany 16 C5
Waswanipi, Canada 62 C4
Waswanipi, L., Canada 62 C4
Watangpone, Indonesia 33 E6
Water Park Pt., Australia ... 54 C5
Water Valley, U.S.A. 71 H10
Waterberge, S. Africa 49 C4
Waterbury, U.S.A. . 68 E9
Waterbury L., Canada 65 B8
Waterford, Ireland . 13 D4
Waterford □, Ireland 13 D4
Waterford Harbour, Ireland ... 13 D5
Waterhen L., Man., Canada ... 65 C9
Waterhen L., Sask., Canada ... 65 C7
Waterloo, Belgium . 15 D4
Waterloo, Canada .. 62 D3
Waterloo, S. Leone 44 G2
Waterloo, Ill., U.S.A. 70 F9
Waterloo, Iowa, U.S.A. 70 D8
Watersmeet, U.S.A. 70 B10
Waterton-Glacier International Peace Park, U.S.A. ... 72 B7
Watertown, N.Y., U.S.A. 68 D8
Watertown, S. Dak., U.S.A. ... 70 C6
Watertown, Wis., U.S.A. ... 70 D10
Waterval-Boven, S. Africa ... 49 D5
Waterville, Maine, U.S.A. ... 63 D6

Waterville, Wash., U.S.A. 72 C3
Watervliet, U.S.A. 68 D9
Wates, Indonesia . . . 33 G14
Watford, U.K. 11 F7
Watford City, U.S.A. . 70 B3
Watheroo, Australia . . 53 F2
Watkins Glen, U.S.A. . 68 D7
Watling I. = San
 Salvador, Bahamas . 75 C10
Watonga, U.S.A. 71 H5
Watrous, Canada 65 C7
Watrous, U.S.A. 71 H2
Watsa, Zaïre 46 D5
Watseka, U.S.A. 68 E2
Watson, Australia . . . 53 F5
Watson, Canada 65 C8
Watson Lake, Canada . 64 A3
Watsonville, U.S.A. . . 73 H3
Wattiwarriganna
 Cr. →, Australia . . . 55 D2
Watuata = Batuata,
 Indonesia 33 F6
Watubela, Kepulauan,
 Indonesia 33 E8
Watubela Is. =
 Watubela, Kepulauan,
 Indonesia 33 E8
Waubay, U.S.A. 70 C6
Waubra, Australia . . . 55 F3
Wauchope, Australia . 55 E5
Wauchula, U.S.A. . . . 69 M5
Waugh, Canada 65 D9
Waukarlycarly, L.,
 Australia 52 D3
Waukegan, U.S.A. . . . 68 D2
Waukesha, U.S.A. . . . 68 D1
Waukon, U.S.A. 70 D9
Wauneta, U.S.A. 70 E4
Waupaca, U.S.A. 70 C10
Waupun, U.S.A. 70 D10
Waurika, U.S.A. 71 H6
Wausau, U.S.A. 70 C10
Wautoma, U.S.A. . . . 70 C10
Wauwatosa, U.S.A. . . 68 D2
Wave Hill, Australia . . 52 C5
Waveney →, U.K. . . . 11 E9
Waverley, N.Z. 51 H5
Waverly, Iowa, U.S.A. . 70 D8
Waverly, N.Y., U.S.A. . 68 D7
Wavre, Belgium 15 D4
Wâw, Sudan 45 G10
Wawa, Canada 62 C3
Wawanesa, Canada . . 65 D9
Waxahachie, U.S.A. . . 71 J6
Way, L., Australia . . . 53 E3
Wayabula Rau,
 Indonesia 33 D7
Wayatinah, Australia . 54 G4
Waycross, U.S.A. . . . 69 K4
Wayne, Nebr., U.S.A. . 70 D6
Wayne, W. Va., U.S.A. 68 F4
Waynesboro, Ga.,
 U.S.A. 69 J4
Waynesboro, Miss.,
 U.S.A. 69 K1
Waynesboro, Pa.,
 U.S.A. 68 F7
Waynesboro, Va.,
 U.S.A. 68 F6
Waynesburg, U.S.A. . . 68 F5
Waynesville, U.S.A. . . 69 H4
Waynoka, U.S.A. . . . 71 G5
Wazirabad, Pakistan . 36 C9
We, Indonesia 32 C1
Weald, The, U.K. . . . 11 F8
Wear →, U.K. 10 C6
Weatherford, Okla.,
 U.S.A. 71 H5
Weatherford, Tex.,
 U.S.A. 71 J6
Weaverville, U.S.A. . . 72 F2
Webb City, U.S.A. . . . 71 G7
Webster, S. Dak.,
 U.S.A. 70 C6
Webster, Wis., U.S.A. . 70 C8
Webster City, U.S.A. . 70 D8
Webster Green, U.S.A. 70 F9
Webster Springs,
 U.S.A. 68 F5
Weda, Indonesia 33 D7
Weda, Teluk, Indonesia 33 D7
Weddell I., Falk. Is. . . 80 G4
Weddell Sea, Antarctica 5 D1
Wedderburn, Australia 55 F3
Wedgeport, Canada . . 63 D6
Wee Waa, Australia . . 55 E4
Weed, U.S.A. 72 F2
Weemelah, Australia . 55 D4
Weenen, S. Africa . . . 49 D5
Weert, Neths. 15 C5
Weiden, Germany . . . 16 D7
Weifang, China 31 C6
Weimar, Germany . . . 16 C6
Weipa, Australia 54 A3
Weir →, Australia . . . 55 D4
Weir →, Canada 65 B10
Weir River, Canada . . 65 B10
Weiser, U.S.A. 72 D5
Wejherowo, Poland . . 17 A10
Wekusko L., Canada . 65 C9
Welbourn Hill, Australia 55 D1
Welch, U.S.A. 68 G5
Welkom, S. Africa . . . 48 D4
Welland, Canada . . . 62 D4
Welland →, U.K. 10 E7
Wellesley Is., Australia 54 B2
Wellin, Belgium 15 D5
Wellingborough, U.K. . 11 E7
Wellington, Australia . 55 E4
Wellington, Canada . . 62 D4

Wellington, N.Z. 51 J5
Wellington, S. Africa . 48 E2
Wellington, Shrops.,
 U.K. 10 E5
Wellington, Somst.,
 U.K. 11 G4
Wellington, Colo.,
 U.S.A. 70 E2
Wellington, Kans.,
 U.S.A. 71 G6
Wellington, Nev.,
 U.S.A. 72 G4
Wellington, Tex., U.S.A. 71 H4
Wellington, I., Chile . . 80 F1
Wellington, L., Australia 55 F4
Wells, U.K. 11 F5
Wells, Minn., U.S.A. . 70 D8
Wells, Nev., U.S.A. . . 72 F6
Wells, L., Australia . . 53 E3
Wells Gray Prov. Park,
 Canada 64 C4
Wells-next-the-Sea,
 U.K. 10 E8
Wellsboro, U.S.A. . . . 68 E7
Wellsville, Mo., U.S.A. 70 F9
Wellsville, N.Y., U.S.A. 68 D7
Wellsville, Ohio, U.S.A. 68 E5
Wellsville, Utah, U.S.A. 72 F8
Wellton, U.S.A. 73 K6
Wels, Austria 16 D8
Welshpool, U.K. 11 E4
Wem, U.K. 10 E5
Wemindji, Canada . . . 62 B4
Wenatchee, U.S.A. . . 72 C3
Wenchi, Ghana 44 G4
Wenchow = Wenzhou,
 China 31 D7
Wendell, U.S.A. 72 E6
Wendesi, Indonesia . . 33 E8
Wendover, U.S.A. . . . 72 F6
Wenlock →, Australia 54 A3
Wenshan, China 30 D5
Wensu, China 30 B3
Wentworth, Australia . 55 E3
Wenut, Indonesia . . . 33 E8
Wenzhou, China 31 D7
Weott, U.S.A. 72 F2
Wepener, S. Africa . . 48 D4
Werda, Botswana . . . 48 D3
Werder, Ethiopia . . . 40 F4
Weri, Indonesia 33 E8
Werra →, Germany . . 16 C5
Werribee, Australia . . 55 F3
Werrimull, Australia . . 55 E3
Werris Creek, Australia 55 E5
Wersar, Indonesia . . . 33 E8
Weser →, Germany . . 16 B5
Wesiri, Indonesia . . . 33 F7
Wesley Vale, U.S.A. . . 73 J10
Wesleyville, Canada . 63 C9
Wessel, C., Australia . 54 A2
Wessel Is., Australia . 54 A2
Wessington, U.S.A. . . 70 C5
Wessington Springs,
 U.S.A. 70 C5
West, U.S.A. 71 K6
West B., U.S.A. 71 L10
West Baines →,
 Australia 52 C4
West Bank □, Asia . . 41 C4
West Bend, U.S.A. . . 68 D1
West Bengal □, India . 37 H15
West Beskids =
 Západné Beskydy,
 Europe 17 D10
West Branch, U.S.A. . 68 C3
West Bromwich, U.K. . 11 E5
West Cape Howe,
 Australia 53 G2
West Chester, U.S.A. . 68 F8
West Columbia, U.S.A. 71 L7
West Des Moines,
 U.S.A. 70 E8
West Falkland, Falk. Is. 80 G4
West Fjord =
 Vestfjorden, Norway 8 C15
West Frankfort, U.S.A. 70 G10
West Glamorgan □,
 U.K. 11 F4
West Helena, U.S.A. . 71 H9
West Ice Shelf,
 Antarctica 5 C7
West Memphis, U.S.A. 71 H9
West Midlands □, U.K. 11 E6
West Monroe, U.S.A. . 71 J8
West Nicholson,
 Zimbabwe 47 J5
West Palm Beach,
 U.S.A. 69 M5
West Plains, U.S.A. . . 71 G9
West Point, Ga., U.S.A. 69 J3
West Point, Miss.,
 U.S.A. 69 J1
West Point, Nebr.,
 U.S.A. 70 E6
West Point, Va., U.S.A. 68 G7
West Pt. = Ouest, Pte.,
 Canada 63 C7
West Pt., Australia . . . 55 F2
West Road →, Canada 64 C4
West Rutland, U.S.A. . 68 D9
West Schelde =
 Westerschelde →,
 Neths. 15 C3
West Siberian Plain,
 Russia 26 C11
West Sussex □, U.K. . 11 G7
West-Terschelling,
 Neths. 15 A5
West Virginia □, U.S.A. 68 F5
West-Vlaanderen □,
 Belgium 15 D3
West Wyalong,
 Australia 55 E4

West Yellowstone,
 U.S.A. 72 D8
West Yorkshire □, U.K. 10 D6
Westall Pt., Australia . 55 E1
Westbrook, Maine,
 U.S.A. 69 D10
Westbrook, Tex., U.S.A. 71 J4
Westbury, Australia . . 54 G4
Westby, U.S.A. 70 A2
Westerland, Germany . 9 J13
Western Australia □,
 Australia 53 E2
Western Cape □,
 S. Africa 48 E3
Western Ghats, India . 36 N9
Western Isles □, U.K. . 12 D1
Western Sahara ■,
 Africa 44 D2
Western Samoa ■,
 Pac. Oc. 51 A13
Westernport, U.S.A. . . 68 F6
Westerschelde →,
 Neths. 15 C3
Westerwald, Germany . 16 C4
Westhope, U.S.A. . . . 70 A4
Westland Bight, N.Z. . 51 K3
Westlock, Canada . . . 64 C6
Westmeath □, Ireland 13 C4
Westminster, U.S.A. . 68 F7
Westmorland, U.S.A. . 73 K6
Weston, Malaysia . . . 32 C5
Weston, Oreg., U.S.A. 72 D4
Weston, W. Va., U.S.A. 68 F5
Weston I., Canada . . . 62 B4
Weston-super-Mare,
 U.K. 11 F5
Westport, Ireland . . . 13 C2
Westport, N.Z. 51 J3
Westport, U.S.A. 72 C1
Westray, Canada 65 C8
Westray, U.K. 12 B6
Westree, Canada 62 C3
Westville, Ill., U.S.A. . 68 E2
Westville, Okla., U.S.A. 71 G7
Westwood, U.S.A. . . . 72 F3
Wetar, Indonesia . . . 33 F7
Wetaskiwin, Canada . 64 C6
Wetteren, Belgium . . 15 D3
Wetzlar, Germany . . . 16 C5
Wewoka, U.S.A. 71 H6
Wexford, Ireland . . . 13 D5
Wexford □, Ireland . . 13 D5
Wexford Harbour,
 Ireland 13 D5
Weyburn, Canada . . . 65 D8
Weyburn L., Canada . 64 A5
Weymouth, Canada . . 63 D6
Weymouth, U.K. 11 G5
Weymouth, C.,
 Australia 54 A3
Whakatane, N.Z. 51 G6
Whale →, Canada . . . 63 A6
Whale Cove, Canada . 65 A10
Whales, B. of,
 Antarctica 5 D12
Whalsay, U.K. 12 A7
Whangamomona, N.Z. 51 H5
Whangarei, N.Z. 51 F5
Whangarei Harb., N.Z. 51 F5
Wharfe →, U.K. 10 D6
Wharfedale, U.K. . . . 10 C5
Wharton, U.S.A. 71 L6
Wheatland, U.S.A. . . 70 D2
Wheaton, U.S.A. . . . 70 C6
Wheeler, Oreg., U.S.A. 72 D2
Wheeler, Tex., U.S.A. 71 H4
Wheeler →, Canada . 65 B7
Wheeler Pk., N. Mex.,
 U.S.A. 73 H11
Wheeler Pk., Nev.,
 U.S.A. 73 G6
Wheeling, U.S.A. . . . 68 E5
Whernside, U.K. 10 C5
Whidbey I., U.S.A. . . 64 D4
Whiskey Gap, Canada 64 D6
Whiskey Jack L.,
 Canada 65 B8
Whistleduck Cr. →,
 Australia 54 C2
Whitby, U.K. 10 C7
White →, Ark., U.S.A. 71 J9
White →, Ind., U.S.A. 68 F2
White →, S. Dak.,
 U.S.A. 70 D5
White →, Utah, U.S.A. 72 F9
White, L., Australia . . 52 D4
White B., Canada . . . 63 B8
White Bear Res.,
 Canada 63 C8
White Bird, U.S.A. . . . 72 D5
White Butte, U.S.A. . . 70 B3
White City, U.S.A. . . . 70 F6
White Cliffs, Australia 55 E3
White Deer, U.S.A. . . 71 H4
White Hall, U.S.A. . . . 70 F9
White Horse, Vale of,
 U.K. 11 F6
White I., N.Z. 51 G6
White L., U.S.A. 71 L8
White Mts., Calif.,
 U.S.A. 73 H4
White Mts., N.H., U.S.A. 67 B12
White Nile = Nîl el
 Abyad →, Sudan . . 45 E11
White Otter L., Canada 62 C1
White Pass, Canada . 64 B1
White River, Canada . 62 C2
White River, S. Africa 49 D5
White River, U.S.A. . . 70 D4
White Russia =
 Belarus ■, Europe . 17 B14
White Sea = Beloye
 More, Russia 22 A6

White Sulphur Springs,
 Mont., U.S.A. 72 C8
White Sulphur Springs,
 W. Va., U.S.A. 68 G5
Whitecliffs, N.Z. 51 K3
Whitecourt, Canada . . 64 C5
Whiteface, U.S.A. . . . 71 J3
Whitefish, U.S.A. . . . 72 B6
Whitefish L., Canada . 65 A7
Whitefish Point, U.S.A. 68 B3
Whitegull, L., Canada . 63 A7
Whitehall, Mich., U.S.A. 68 D2
Whitehall, Mont.,
 U.S.A. 72 D7
Whitehall, N.Y., U.S.A. 68 D9
Whitehall, Wis., U.S.A. 70 C9
Whitehaven, U.K. . . . 10 C4
Whitehorse, Canada . 64 A1
Whitemark, Australia . 54 G4
Whitemouth, Canada . 65 D9
Whitesboro, U.S.A. . . 71 J6
Whiteshell Prov. Park,
 Canada 65 C9
Whitetail, U.S.A. 70 A2
Whiteville, U.S.A. . . . 69 H6
Whitewater, U.S.A. . . 68 D1
Whitewater Baldy,
 U.S.A. 73 K9
Whitewater L., Canada 62 B2
Whitewood, Australia . 54 C3
Whitewood, Canada . 65 C8
Whitfield, Australia . . 55 F4
Whithorn, U.K. 12 G4
Whitianga, N.Z. 51 G5
Whitmire, U.S.A. . . . 69 H5
Whitney, Canada . . . 62 C4
Whitney, Mt., U.S.A. . 73 H4
Whitstable, U.K. 11 F9
Whitsunday I., Australia 54 C4
Whittlesea, Australia . 55 F4
Whitwell, U.S.A. . . . 69 H3
Wholdaia L., Canada . 65 A8
Whyalla, Australia . . . 55 E2
Whyjonta, Australia . . 55 D3
Wiarton, Canada . . . 62 D3
Wiay, U.S.A. 70 B0
Wichita, U.S.A. 71 G6
Wichita Falls, U.S.A. . 71 J5
Wick, U.K. 12 C5
Wickenburg, U.S.A. . . 73 K7
Wickepin, Australia . . 53 F2
Wickham, C., Australia 54 F3
Wicklow, Ireland . . . 13 D5
Wicklow □, Ireland . . 13 D5
Wicklow Hd., Ireland . 13 D5
Widgiemooltha,
 Australia 53 F3
Widnes, U.K. 10 D5
Wieluń, Poland 17 C10
Wien, Austria 16 D9
Wiener Neustadt,
 Austria 16 E9
Wierden, Neths. 15 B6
Wiesbaden, Germany . 16 C5
Wigan, U.K. 10 D5
Wiggins, Colo., U.S.A. 70 E2
Wiggins, Miss., U.S.A. 71 K10
Wight, I. of □, U.K. . . 11 G6
Wigtown, U.K. 12 G4
Wigtown B., U.K. . . . 12 G4
Wilber, U.S.A. 70 E6
Wilberforce, C.,
 Australia 54 A2
Wilburton, U.S.A. . . . 71 H7
Wilcannia, Australia . 55 E3
Wildrose, U.S.A. . . . 70 A3
Wildspitze, Austria . . 16 E6
Wildwood, U.S.A. . . . 68 F8
Wilge →, S. Africa . . 49 D4
Wilhelm II Coast,
 Antarctica 5 C7
Wilhelmshaven,
 Germany 16 B5
Wilhelmstal, Namibia . 48 C2
Wilkes-Barre, U.S.A. . 68 E8
Wilkesboro, U.S.A. . . 69 G5
Wilkie, Canada 65 C7
Wilkinson Lakes,
 Australia 53 E5
Willamina, U.S.A. . . . 72 D2
Willandra Billabong
 Creek →, Australia . 55 E4
Willapa B., U.S.A. . . . 72 C2
Willard, N. Mex., U.S.A. 73 J10
Willard, Utah, U.S.A. . 72 F7
Willcox, U.S.A. 73 K9
Willemstad, Neth. Ant. 75 E11
Willeroo, Australia . . 52 C5
William →, Canada . . 65 B7
William Creek, Australia 55 D2
Williambury, Australia 53 D2
Williams, Australia . . 53 F2
Williams, U.S.A. 73 J7
Williams Lake, Canada 64 C4
Williamsburg, Ky.,
 U.S.A. 69 G3
Williamsburg, Va.,
 U.S.A. 68 G7
Williamson, U.S.A. . . 68 G4
Williamston, U.S.A. . . 69 H7
Williamstown, U.S.A. . 68 F3
Williamsville, U.S.A. . 71 G9
Willis Group, Australia 54 B5
Williston, S. Africa . . 48 E3
Williston, Fla., U.S.A. 69 L4
Williston, N. Dak.,
 U.S.A. 70 A3
Williston L., Canada . 64 B4
Willits, U.S.A. 72 G2
Willmar, U.S.A. 70 C7
Willow Bunch, Canada 65 D7
Willow L., Canada . . . 64 A5

Willow Lake, U.S.A. . . 70 C6
Willow Springs, U.S.A. 71 G8
Willowlake →, Canada 64 A4
Willowmore, S. Africa 48 E3
Willows, Australia . . . 54 C4
Willows, U.S.A. 72 G2
Willowvale = Gatyana,
 S. Africa 49 E4
Wills, L., Australia . . . 52 D4
Wills Cr. →, Australia 54 C3
Wills Point, U.S.A. . . 71 J7
Willunga, Australia . . 55 F2
Wilmette, U.S.A. . . . 68 D2
Wilmington, Australia 55 E2
Wilmington, Del.,
 U.S.A. 68 F8
Wilmington, Ill., U.S.A. 68 E1
Wilmington, N.C.,
 U.S.A. 69 H7
Wilmington, Ohio,
 U.S.A. 68 F4
Wilpena Cr. →,
 Australia 55 E2
Wilsall, U.S.A. 72 D8
Wilson, U.S.A. 69 H7
Wilson →, Queens.,
 Australia 55 D3
Wilson →,
 W. Austral., Australia 52 C4
Wilson Bluff, Australia 53 F4
Wilsons Promontory,
 Australia 55 F4
Wilton, U.K. 11 F6
Wilton, U.S.A. 70 B4
Wilton →, Australia . . 54 A1
Wiltshire □, U.K. . . . 11 F6
Wiltz, Lux. 15 E5
Wiluna, Australia . . . 53 E3
Wimmera →,
 Australia 55 F3
Winburg, S. Africa . . 48 D4
Winchester, U.K. . . . 11 F6
Winchester, Idaho,
 U.S.A. 72 C5
Winchester, Ind., U.S.A. 68 E3
Winchester, Ky., U.S.A. 68 G3
Winchester, Tenn.,
 U.S.A. 69 H2
Winchester, Va., U.S.A. 68 F6
Wind →, U.S.A. 72 E9
Wind River Range,
 U.S.A. 72 E9
Windau = Ventspils,
 Latvia 9 H19
Windber, U.S.A. 68 E6
Windermere, L., U.K. . 10 C5
Windfall, Canada . . . 64 C5
Windflower L., Canada 64 A5
Windhoek, Namibia . . 48 C2
Windom, U.S.A. 70 D7
Windorah, Australia . . 54 D3
Window Rock, U.S.A. . 73 J9
Windrush →, U.K. . . 11 F6
Windsor, Australia . . 55 E5
Windsor, N.S., Canada 63 D7
Windsor, Nfld., Canada 63 C8
Windsor, Ont., Canada 62 D3
Windsor, U.K. 11 F7
Windsor, Colo., U.S.A. 70 E2
Windsor, Mo., U.S.A. 70 F8
Windsor, Vt., U.S.A. . 68 D9
Windsorton, S. Africa 48 D3
Windward Is., W. Indies 74 P20
Windy L., Canada . . . 65 A8
Winefred L., Canada . 65 B6
Winfield, U.S.A. 71 G6
Wingate Mts., Australia 52 B5
Wingen, Australia . . . 55 E5
Wingham, Australia . . 55 E5
Wingham, Canada . . 62 D3
Winifred, U.S.A. 72 C9
Winisk, Canada 62 A2
Winisk →, Canada . . 62 A2
Winisk L., Canada . . . 62 B2
Wink, U.S.A. 71 K3
Winkler, Canada 65 D9
Winlock, U.S.A. 72 C2
Winnebago, U.S.A. . . 70 D7
Winnebago, L., U.S.A. 68 D1
Winnecke Cr. →,
 Australia 52 C5
Winnemucca, U.S.A. . 72 F5
Winnemucca L., U.S.A. 72 F4
Winner, U.S.A. 70 D5
Winnett, U.S.A. 72 C9
Winnfield, U.S.A. . . . 71 K8
Winnibigoshish, L.,
 U.S.A. 70 B7
Winning, Australia . . . 52 D1
Winnipeg, Canada . . 65 D9
Winnipeg →, Canada 65 C9
Winnipeg, L., Canada . 65 C9
Winnipeg Beach,
 Canada 65 C9
Winnipegosis, Canada 65 C9
Winnipegosis L.,
 Canada 65 C9
Winnsboro, La., U.S.A. 71 J9
Winnsboro, S.C., U.S.A. 69 H5
Winnsboro, Tex., U.S.A. 71 J7
Winokapau, L., Canada 63 B7
Winona, Minn., U.S.A. 70 C9
Winona, Miss., U.S.A. 71 J10
Winooski, U.S.A. . . . 68 C9
Winschoten, Neths. . . 15 A7
Winslow, U.S.A. 73 J8
Winston-Salem, U.S.A. 69 G5
Winter Garden, U.S.A. 69 L5
Winter Haven, U.S.A. 69 M5
Winter Park, U.S.A. . . 69 L5
Winters, U.S.A. 71 K5
Winterset, U.S.A. . . . 70 E7

Winterswijk, Neths. . . 15 C6
Winterthur, Switz. . . . 16 E5
Winthrop, Minn., U.S.A. 70 C7
Winthrop, Wash.,
 U.S.A. 72 B3
Winton, Australia . . . 54 C3
Winton, N.Z. 51 M2
Wirral, U.K. 10 D4
Wirrulla, Australia . . . 55 E1
Wisbech, U.K. 10 E8
Wisconsin □, U.S.A. . 70 C10
Wisconsin →, U.S.A. 70 D9
Wisconsin Dells, U.S.A. 70 D10
Wisconsin Rapids,
 U.S.A. 70 C10
Wisdom, U.S.A. 72 D7
Wishaw, U.K. 12 F5
Wishek, U.S.A. 70 B5
Wisła →, Poland . . . 17 A10
Wismar, Germany . . . 16 B6
Wisner, U.S.A. 70 E6
Witbank, S. Africa . . . 49 D4
Witdraai, S. Africa . . 48 D3
Witham →, U.K. 10 D7
Withernsea, U.K. . . . 10 D8
Witney, U.K. 11 F6
Witnossob →,
 Namibia 48 D3
Witten, Germany . . . 15 C7
Wittenberg, Germany . 16 C7
Wittenberge, Germany 16 B6
Wittenoom, Australia . 52 D2
Wkra →, Poland . . . 17 B11
Włocławek, Poland . . 17 B10
Włodawa, Poland . . . 17 C12
Wodonga, Australia . . 55 F4
Wokam, Indonesia . . 33 F8
Wolf →, Canada 64 A2
Wolf Creek, U.S.A. . . 72 C7
Wolf L., Canada 64 A2
Wolf Point, U.S.A. . . . 70 A2
Wolfe I., Canada 62 D4
Wolfsberg, Austria . . 16 E8
Wolfsburg, Germany . 16 B6
Wolin, Poland 16 B8
Wollaston, Is., Chile . 80 H3
Wollaston L., Canada . 65 B8
Wollaston Pen., Canada 60 B8
Wollogorang, Australia 54 B2
Wollongong, Australia 55 E5
Wolmaransstad,
 S. Africa 48 D4
Wolseley, Australia . . 55 F3
Wolseley, Canada . . . 65 C8
Wolseley, S. Africa . . 48 E2
Wolstenholme, C.,
 Canada 58 C12
Wolvega, Neths. 15 B6
Wolverhampton, U.K. . 11 E5
Wonarah, Australia . . 54 B2
Wondai, Australia . . . 55 D5
Wongalarroo L.,
 Australia 55 E3
Wongan Hills, Australia 53 F2
Wongawol, Australia . 53 E3
Wonosari, Indonesia . 33 G14
Wŏnsan, N. Korea . . 31 C7
Wonthaggi, Australia . 55 F4
Woocalla, Australia . . 55 E2
Wood Buffalo Nat.
 Park, Canada 64 B6
Wood Is., Australia . . 52 C3
Wood L., Canada . . . 65 B8
Wood Lake, U.S.A. . . 70 D4
Woodah I., Australia . 54 A2
Woodanilling, Australia 53 F2
Woodburn, Australia . 55 D5
Woodenbong, Australia 55 D5
Woodend, Australia . . 55 F3
Woodgreen, Australia 54 C1
Woodland, U.S.A. . . . 72 G3
Woodlands, Australia . 55 D4
Woodpecker, Canada . 64 C4
Woodridge, Canada . 65 D9
Woodroffe, Mt.,
 Australia 53 E5
Woodruff, Ariz., U.S.A. 73 J8
Woodruff, Utah, U.S.A. 72 F8
Woods, L., Australia . 54 B1
Woods, L., Canada . . 63 B6
Woods, L. of the,
 Canada 65 D10
Woodstock, Queens.,
 Australia 54 B4
Woodstock, W. Austral.,
 Australia 52 D2
Woodstock, N.B.,
 Canada 63 C6
Woodstock, Ont.,
 Canada 62 D3
Woodstock, U.K. . . . 11 F6
Woodstock, U.S.A. . . 70 D10
Woodsville, U.S.A. . . 68 C9
Woodville, N.Z. 51 J5
Woodville, U.S.A. . . . 71 K7
Woodward, U.S.A. . . 71 G5
Woolamai, C., Australia 55 F4
Woolgoolga, Australia 55 E5
Woombye, Australia . 55 D5
Woomera, Australia . . 55 E2
Woonsocket, R.I.,
 U.S.A. 68 E10
Woonsocket, S. Dak.,
 U.S.A. 70 C5
Wooramel, Australia . 53 E1
Wooramel →,
 Australia 53 E1
Wooroloo, Australia . 53 F2
Wooster, U.S.A. 68 E5
Worcester, S. Africa . 48 E2
Worcester, U.K. 11 E5

Worcester

Worcester, U.S.A. 68 D10
Workington, U.K. 10 C4
Worksop, U.K. 10 D6
Workum, Neths. 15 B5
Worland, U.S.A. 72 D10
Worms, Germany 16 D5
Worthing, U.K. 11 G7
Worthington, U.S.A. .. 70 D7
Wosi, Indonesia 33 E7
Wou-han = Wuhan,
  China 31 C6
Wour, Chad 45 D8
Wousi = Wuxi, China . 31 C7
Wowoni, Indonesia ... 33 E6
Woy Woy, Australia .. 55 E5
Wrangel I. = Vrangelya,
  Ostrov, Russia ... 25 B19
Wrangell, U.S.A. 60 C6
Wrangell I., U.S.A. .. 64 C6
Wrangell Mts., U.S.A. . 60 B5
Wrath, C., U.K. 12 C3
Wray, U.S.A. 70 E3
Wrekin, The, U.K. ... 10 E5
Wrens, U.S.A. 69 J4
Wrexham, U.K. 10 D4
Wright, Canada 64 C4
Wright, Phil. 33 B7
Wrightson Mt., U.S.A. . 73 L8
Wrigley, Canada 60 B7
Wrocław, Poland 17 C9
Września, Poland 17 B9
Wu Jiang →, China .. 30 D5
Wubin, Australia 53 F2
Wuhan, China 31 C6
Wuhsi = Wuxi, China . 31 C7
Wuhu, China 31 C6
Wukari, Nigeria 44 G6
Wuliaru, Indonesia ... 33 F8
Wuluk'omushih Ling,
  China 30 C3
Wulumuchi = Ürümqi,
  China 24 E9
Wum, Cameroon 44 G7
Wunnummin L.,
  Canada 62 B2
Wuntho, Burma 37 H19
Wuppertal, Germany . 16 C4
Wuppertal, S. Africa .. 48 E2
Wurung, Australia ... 54 B3
Würzburg, Germany . 16 D5
Wusuli Jiang =
  Ussuri →, Asia .. 28 A7
Wutongqiao, China .. 30 D5
Wuwei, China 30 C5
Wuxi, China 31 C7
Wuxing, China 31 C7
Wuyi Shan, China ... 31 D6
Wuzhong, China 30 C5
Wuzhou, China 31 D6
Wyaaba Cr. →,
  Australia 54 B3
Wyalkatchem, Australia 53 F2
Wyandotte, U.S.A. .. 68 D4
Wyandra, Australia .. 55 D4
Wyangala Res.,
  Australia 55 E4
Wyara, L., Australia .. 55 D3
Wycheproof, Australia 55 F3
Wye →, U.K. 11 F5
Wyemandoo, Australia 53 E2
Wymondham, U.K. .. 11 E7
Wymore, U.S.A. 70 E6
Wynbring, Australia .. 55 E1
Wyndham, Australia .. 52 C4
Wyndham, N.Z. 51 M2
Wyndmere, U.S.A. .. 70 B6
Wynne, U.S.A. 71 H9
Wynnum, Australia .. 55 D5
Wynyard, Australia .. 54 G4
Wynyard, Canada ... 65 C8
Wyola, L., Australia .. 53 E5
Wyoming □, U.S.A. .. 72 E10
Wyong, Australia ... 55 E5
Wytheville, U.S.A. .. 68 G5

X

Xai-Xai, Mozam. ... 49 D5
Xainza, China 30 C3
Xangongo, Angola ... 48 B2
Xankändi, Azerbaijan . 23 G8
Xánthi, Greece 21 D11
Xapuri, Brazil 78 F5
Xau, L., Botswana ... 48 C3
Xenia, U.S.A. 68 F4
Xhora, S. Africa 49 E4
Xhumo, Botswana ... 48 C3
Xi Jiang →, China .. 31 D6
Xiaguan, China 30 D5
Xiamen, China 31 D6
Xi'an, China 31 C5
Xiang Jiang →, China 31 D6
Xiangfan, China 31 C6
Xiangtan, China 31 D6
Xianyang, China 31 C5
Xiao Hinggan Ling,
  China 31 B7
Xichang, China 30 D5
Xieng Khouang, Laos . 34 C7
Xigazê, China 30 D3
Xinavane, Mozam. ... 49 D5
Xing'an, China 31 D6
Xingu →, Brazil ... 79 D8
Xining, China 30 C5
Xinjiang Uygur
  Zizhiqu □, China .. 30 C3
Xinxiang, China 31 C6
Xinyang, China 31 C6
Xique-Xique, Brazil .. 79 F10

Xisha Qundao = Hsisha
  Chuntao, Pac. Oc. .. 32 A4
Xixabangma Feng,
  China 37 E14
Xizang □, China ... 30 C3
Xuanhua, China 31 B6
Xuzhou, China 31 C6

Y

Yaamba, Australia ... 54 C5
Yaapeet, Australia ... 55 F3
Yabelo, Ethiopia ... 45 H12
Yablonovy Ra. =
  Yablonovyy Khrebet,
  Russia 25 D12
Yablonovyy Khrebet,
  Russia 25 D12
Yabrūd, Syria 41 B5
Yacheng, China 31 E5
Yacuiba, Bolivia 80 A4
Yadgir, India 36 L10
Yadkin →, U.S.A. .. 69 H5
Yagodnoye, Russia .. 25 C15
Yagoua, Cameroon .. 46 B3
Yahk, Canada 64 D5
Yahuma, Zaïre 46 D4
Yaita, Japan 29 F9
Yakima, U.S.A. 72 C3
Yakima →, U.S.A. .. 72 C3
Yakovlevka, Russia .. 28 B6
Yaku-Shima, Japan .. 29 J5
Yakutat, U.S.A. 60 C6
Yakutia = Sakha □,
  Russia 25 C13
Yakutsk, Russia 25 C13
Yala, Thailand 34 N14
Yalbalgo, Australia .. 53 E1
Yalboroo, Australia .. 54 C4
Yalgoo, Australia ... 53 E2
Yalinga, C.A.R. 45 G9
Yalleroi, Australia ... 54 C4
Yalobusha →, U.S.A. 71 J9
Yalong Jiang →,
  China 30 D5
Yalova, Turkey 21 D13
Yalta, Ukraine 23 F5
Yalutorovsk, Russia .. 24 D7
Yam Ha Melaḥ = Dead
  Sea, Asia 41 D4
Yam Kinneret, Israel . 41 C4
Yamada, Japan 29 H5
Yamagata, Japan ... 28 E10
Yamagata □, Japan . 28 E10
Yamaguchi, Japan ... 29 G5
Yamaguchi □, Japan . 29 G5
Yamal, Poluostrov,
  Russia 24 B8
Yamal Pen. = Yamal,
  Poluostrov, Russia . 24 B8
Yamanashi □, Japan . 29 G9
Yamantau, Gora,
  Russia 22 D10
Yamba, N.S.W.,
  Australia 55 D5
Yamba, S. Austral.,
  Australia 55 E3
Yambah, Australia .. 54 C1
Yambarran Ra.,
  Australia 52 C5
Yâmbiô, Sudan 45 H10
Yambol, Bulgaria ... 21 C12
Yamdena, Indonesia . 33 F8
Yame, Japan 29 H5
Yamethin, Burma ... 37 J20
Yamma-Yamma, L.,
  Australia 55 D3
Yamoussoukro, Ivory C. 44 G3
Yampa →, U.S.A. .. 72 F9
Yampi Sd., Australia . 52 C3
Yampil, Moldova 17 D15
Yampol = Yampil,
  Moldova 17 D15
Yamuna →, India .. 37 G12
Yamzho Yumco, China 30 D4
Yana →, Russia ... 25 B14
Yanac, Australia ... 55 F3
Yanagawa, Japan ... 29 H5
Yanai, Japan 29 H6
Yanaul, Russia 22 C10
Yanbu 'al Baḥr,
  Si. Arabia 38 F3
Yancannia, Australia . 55 E3
Yanco Cr. →,
  Australia 55 F4
Yandal, Australia ... 53 E3
Yandanooka, Australia 53 E2
Yandaran, Australia . 54 C5
Yandoon, Burma ... 37 L19
Yangambi, Zaïre ... 46 D4
Yangch'ü = Taiyuan,
  China 31 C6
Yangon = Rangoon,
  Burma 37 L20
Yangquan, China ... 31 C6
Yangtze Kiang = Chang
  Jiang →, China .. 31 C7
Yangzhou, China ... 31 C6
Yanhee Res., Thailand 34 D5
Yanji, China 31 B7
Yankton, U.S.A. 70 D6
Yanna, Australia ... 55 D4
Yanqi, China 30 B3
Yantabulla, Australia . 55 D4
Yantai, China 31 C7
Yanykurgan,
  Kazakhstan 24 E7
Yao, Chad 45 F8
Yaoundé, Cameroon . 44 H7
Yap I., Pac. Oc. 56 G5

Yapen, Indonesia 33 E9
Yapen, Selat, Indonesia 33 E9
Yappar →, Australia . 54 B3
Yaqui →, Mexico ... 74 B2
Yar-Sale, Russia 24 C8
Yaraka, Australia ... 54 C3
Yaransk, Russia 22 C8
Yardea P.O., Australia 55 E2
Yare →, U.K. 11 E9
Yaremcha, Ukraine .. 17 D13
Yarensk, Russia 22 B8
Yarí →, Colombia .. 78 D4
Yarkand = Shache,
  China 30 C2
Yarkhun →, Pakistan 36 A8
Yarmouth, Canada .. 63 D6
Yarmūk →, Syria .. 41 C4
Yaroslavl, Russia ... 22 C6
Yarqa, W. →, Egypt . 41 F2
Yarra Yarra Lakes,
  Australia 53 E2
Yarraden, Australia .. 54 A3
Yarraloola, Australia . 52 D2
Yarram, Australia ... 55 F4
Yarraman, Australia . 55 D5
Yarranvale, Australia . 55 D4
Yarras, Australia ... 55 E5
Yarrowmere, Australia 54 C4
Yartsevo, Russia 25 C10
Yasawa Group, Fiji .. 51 C7
Yaselda, Belarus ... 17 B14
Yasinski, L., Canada . 62 B4
Yasinya, Ukraine ... 17 D13
Yasothon, Thailand .. 34 E8
Yass, Australia 55 E4
Yatağan, Turkey ... 21 F13
Yates Center, U.S.A. . 71 G7
Yathkyed L., Canada . 65 A9
Yatsushiro, Japan ... 29 H5
Yauyos, Peru 78 F3
Yavari →, Peru ... 78 D4
Yavatmal, India 36 J11
Yavne, Israel 41 D3
Yavoriv, Ukraine ... 17 D12
Yavorov = Yavoriv,
  Ukraine 17 D12
Yawatahama, Japan . 29 H6
Yayama-Rettō, Japan . 29 M1
Yazd, Iran 39 D7
Yazd □, Iran 39 D7
Yazoo →, U.S.A. .. 71 J9
Yazoo City, U.S.A. .. 71 J9
Yding Skovhøj,
  Denmark 9 J13
Ye Xian, China 31 C6
Yealering, Australia . 53 F2
Yebyu, Burma 37 M21
Yecla, Spain 19 C5
Yedintsy = Edineţa,
  Moldova 17 D14
Yeeda, Australia ... 52 C3
Yeelanna, Australia . 55 E2
Yegros, Paraguay ... 80 B5
Yehuda, Midbar, Israel 41 D4
Yei, Sudan 45 H11
Yekaterinburg, Russia 22 C11
Yekaterinodar =
  Krasnodar, Russia .. 23 E6
Yelanskoye, Russia .. 25 C13
Yelarbon, Australia .. 55 D5
Yelets, Russia 22 D6
Yelizavetgrad =
  Kirovohrad, Ukraine 23 E5
Yell, U.K. 12 A7
Yell Sd., U.K. 12 A7
Yellow Sea, China .. 31 C7
Yellowhead Pass,
  Canada 64 C5
Yellowknife, Canada . 64 A6
Yellowknife →,
  Canada 64 A6
Yellowstone →,
  U.S.A. 70 B3
Yellowstone L., U.S.A. 72 D8
Yellowstone National
  Park, U.S.A. 72 D8
Yellowtail Res., U.S.A. 72 D9
Yelsk, Belarus 17 C15
Yelvertoft, Australia . 54 C2
Yemen ■, Asia 40 E3
Yenangyaung, Burma 37 J19
Yenbo = Yanbu 'al
  Baḥr, Si. Arabia .. 38 F3
Yenda, Australia ... 55 E4
Yenice, Turkey 21 E12
Yenisey →, Russia . 24 B9
Yeniseysk, Russia .. 25 D10
Yeniseyskiy Zaliv,
  Russia 24 B9
Yenyuka, Russia ... 25 D13
Yeo, L., Australia ... 53 E3
Yeola, India 36 J9
Yeovil, U.K. 11 G5
Yeppoon, Australia . 54 C5
Yerbent, Turkmenistan 24 F6
Yerbogachen, Russia 25 C11
Yerevan, Armenia .. 23 F7
Yerilla, Australia ... 53 E3
Yermak, Kazakhstan . 24 D8
Yermakovo, Russia .. 25 D13
Yermo, U.S.A. 73 J5
Yerofey Pavlovich,
  Russia 25 D13
Yeropol, Russia 25 C17
Yershov, Russia 23 D8
Yerushalayim =
  Jerusalem, Israel .. 41 D4
Yes Tor, U.K. 11 G4
Yeso, U.S.A. 71 H2
Yessey, Russia 25 C11
Yeu, Î. d', France ... 18 C2
Yevpatoriya, Ukraine 23 E5
Yeysk, Russia 23 E6

Yezd = Yazd, Iran .. 39 D7
Yi 'Allaq, G., Egypt .. 41 E2
Yiannitsa, Greece ... 21 D10
Yibin, China 30 D5
Yichang, China 31 C6
Yichun, China 31 B7
Yilehuli Shan, China . 31 A7
Yinchuan, China ... 30 C5
Yindarlgooda, L.,
  Australia 53 F3
Yingkou, China 31 B7
Yining, China 24 E9
Yinmabin, Burma ... 37 H19
Yinnietharra, Australia 52 D2
Yishan, China 30 D5
Yíthion, Greece ... 21 F10
Yiyang, China 31 D6
Ynykchanskiy, Russia 25 C14
Yoakum, U.S.A. 71 L6
Yog Pt., Phil. 33 B6
Yogyakarta, Indonesia 33 G14
Yoho Nat. Park, Canada 64 C5
Yokadouma, Cameroon 46 D2
Yokkaichi, Japan ... 29 G8
Yoko, Cameroon ... 45 G7
Yokohama, Japan ... 29 G9
Yokosuka, Japan ... 29 G9
Yokote, Japan 28 E10
Yola, Nigeria 45 G7
Yonago, Japan 29 G6
Yonaguni-Jima, Japan 29 M1
Yonezawa, Japan ... 28 F10
Yong Peng, Malaysia 34 T16
Yonibana, S. Leone . 44 G2
Yonkers, U.S.A. 68 E9
Yonne →, France .. 18 B5
York, Australia 53 F2
York, U.K. 10 D6
York, Ala., U.S.A. .. 69 J1
York, Nebr., U.S.A. . 70 E6
York, Pa., U.S.A. ... 68 F7
York, C., Australia .. 54 A3
York, Kap, Greenland . 4 B4
York Sd., Australia .. 52 C4
Yorke Pen., Australia . 55 E2
Yorkshire Wolds, U.K. 10 D7
Yorkton, Canada ... 65 C8
Yorktown, U.S.A. .. 71 L6
Yornup, Australia ... 53 F2
Yoron-Jima, Japan .. 29 L4
Yos Sudarso, Pulau,
  Indonesia 33 F9
Yosemite National Park,
  U.S.A. 73 H4
Yoshkar Ola, Russia . 22 C8
Yotvata, Israel 41 F4
Youbou, Canada ... 64 D4
Youghal, Ireland ... 13 E4
Youghal B., Ireland . 13 E4
Young, Australia ... 55 E4
Young, Canada 65 C7
Younghusband, L.,
  Australia 55 E2
Younghusband Pen.,
  Australia 55 F2
Youngstown, Canada 65 C6
Youngstown, U.S.A. . 68 E5
Yoweragabbie,
  Australia 53 E2
Yozgat, Turkey 23 G5
Ypres = Ieper, Belgium 15 D2
Ypsilanti, U.S.A. 68 D4
Yreka, U.S.A. 72 F2
Ysleta, U.S.A. 73 L10
Ysyk-Köl, Ozero,
  Kyrgyzstan 24 E8
Ythan →, U.K. 12 D7
Ytyk Kyuyel, Russia . 25 C14
Yu Jiang →, China . 31 D6
Yu Shan, Taiwan ... 31 D7
Yuan Jiang →, China 31 D6
Yuba City, U.S.A. .. 72 G3
Yūbari, Japan 28 C10
Yübetsu, Japan 28 B11
Yucatán □, Mexico . 74 C7
Yucatán, Canal de,
  Caribbean 74 C7
Yucatán, Península de,
  Mexico 74 D7
Yucatan Str. = Yucatán,
  Canal de, Caribbean 74 C7
Yucca, U.S.A. 73 J6
Yuci, China 31 C6
Yudino, Russia 24 D7
Yuendumu, Australia 52 D5
Yugoslavia ■, Europe 21 B9
Yukon →, U.S.A. .. 60 B3
Yukon Territory □,
  Canada 60 B6
Yukti, Russia 25 C11
Yukuhashi, Japan ... 29 H5
Yule →, Australia .. 52 D2
Yuma, Ariz., U.S.A. . 73 K6
Yuma, Colo., U.S.A. . 70 E3
Yumen, China 30 C4
Yundamindra, Australia 53 E3
Yunlin, Bolivia 78 G5
Yunnan □, China ... 30 D5
Yunta, Australia ... 55 E2
Yur, Russia 25 D14
Yurgao, Russia 24 D9
Yuribei, Russia 24 B8
Yurimaguas, Peru .. 78 E3
Yuryung Kaya, Russia 25 B12
Yushu, China 30 C4
Yuzawa, Japan 28 E10
Yuzhno-Sakhalinsk,
  Russia 25 E15
Yvetot, France 18 B4

Z

Zaandam, Neths. ... 15 B4
Zabaykalsk, Russia .. 25 E12
Zabid, Yemen 40 E3
Zābol, Iran 39 D9
Zābolī, Iran 39 E9
Zabrze, Poland 17 C10
Zacapa, Guatemala . 74 E7
Zacatecas, Mexico .. 74 C4
Zacoalco, Mexico ... 74 C4
Zadar, Croatia 16 F8
Zadetkyi Kyun, Burma 34 H5
Zafarqand, Iran 39 C7
Zafra, Spain 19 C2
Żagań, Poland 16 C8
Zagazig, Egypt 45 B11
Zāgheh, Iran 39 C6
Zagorsk = Sergiyev
  Posad, Russia 22 C6
Zagreb, Croatia 16 F9
Zãgros, Kühhã-ye, Iran 39 C6
Zagros Mts. = Zãgros,
  Kühhã-ye, Iran ... 39 C6
Zãhedãn, Fãrs, Iran . 39 D7
Zãhedãn,
  Sîstãn va Balüchestãn,
  Iran 39 D9
Zahlah, Lebanon ... 41 B4
Zaïre ■, Africa 46 E4
Zaïre →, Africa 46 F2
Zaječar, Serbia, Yug. . 21 C10
Zakamensk, Russia .. 25 D11
Zakavkazye, Asia ... 23 F7
Zakhodnaya Dzvina =
  Daugava →, Latvia 9 H21
Zãkhū, Iraq 38 B4
Zákinthos, Greece .. 21 F9
Zakopane, Poland ... 17 D10
Zalaegerszeg, Hungary 17 E9
Zalău, Romania 17 E12
Zaleshchiki =
  Zalishchyky, Ukraine 17 D13
Zalew Wiślany, Poland 17 A10
Zalingei, Sudan 45 F9
Zalishchyky, Ukraine . 17 D13
Zambeze →, Africa . 47 H7
Zambezi =
  Zambeze →, Africa 47 H7
Zambezi, Zambia ... 47 G4
Zambia ■, Africa ... 47 G5
Zamboanga, Phil. ... 33 C6
Zamora, Mexico 74 D4
Zamora, Spain 19 B3
Zamość, Poland 17 C12
Zanaga, Congo 46 E2
Zandvoort, Neths. .. 15 B4
Zanesville, U.S.A. .. 68 F4
Zangābād, Iran 38 B5
Zanjān, Iran 39 B6
Zanjān □, Iran 39 B6
Zante = Zákinthos,
  Greece 21 F9
Zanthus, Australia .. 53 F3
Zanzibar, Tanzania . 46 F7
Zaouiet El-Kala = Bordj
  Omar Driss, Algeria 44 C6
Zaouiet Reggane,
  Algeria 44 C5
Zap Suyu = Kabir, Zab
  al →, Iraq 38 C4
Zapadnaya Dvina,
  Russia 24 D4
Zapadnaya Dvina =
  Daugava →, Latvia 9 H21
Západné Beskydy,
  Europe 17 D10
Zapala, Argentina .. 80 D2
Zapata, U.S.A. 71 M5
Zapolyarnyy, Russia . 22 A5
Zaporizhzhya, Ukraine 23 E6
Zaporozhye =
  Zaporizhzhya,
  Ukraine 23 E6
Zaragoza, Spain ... 19 B5
Zarand, Kermān, Iran 39 C6
Zarand, Markazī, Iran 39 C6
Zaranj, Afghan. 36 D2
Zarasai, Lithuania .. 9 J22
Zárate, Argentina .. 80 C5
Zärd, Iran 39 D6
Zaria, Nigeria 44 F6
Zarneh, Iran 38 C5
Zarqā' →, Jordan .. 41 C4
Zarrin, Iran 39 C7
Zaruma, Ecuador ... 78 D3
Żary, Poland 16 C8
Zarzis, Tunisia 45 B7
Zashiversk, Russia .. 25 C15
Zaskar Mts., India .. 36 C10
Zastron, S. Africa .. 48 E4
Zãvareh, Iran 39 C7
Zavitinsk, Russia ... 25 D13
Zavodovski, I.,
  Antarctica 5 B1
Zawiercie, Poland .. 17 C10
Zãyã, Iraq 38 C5
Zaysan, Russia 25 D11
Zaysan, Kazakhstan . 24 E9
Zaysan, Oz., Kazakhstan 24 E9
Zayü, China 30 D4

Zeitz, Germany 16 C7
Zelenograd, Russia .. 22 C6
Zelenogradsk, Russia 9 J19
Zelzate, Belgium ... 15 C3
Zémio, C.A.R. 46 C5
Zemun, Serbia, Yug. . 21 B9
Zenica, Bos.-H. 21 B7
Żepče, Bos.-H. 21 B8
Zeya, Russia 25 D13
Zeya →, Russia ... 25 D13
Zêzere →, Portugal . 19 C1
Zghartâ, Lebanon .. 41 A4
Zgorzelec, Poland .. 16 C8
Zhabinka, Belarus .. 17 B13
Zhailma, Kazakhstan 24 D7
Zhambyl, Kazakhstan 24 E8
Zhangaqazaly,
  Kazakhstan 24 E7
Zhangjiakou, China . 31 B6
Zhangye, China 30 C5
Zhangzhou, China .. 31 D6
Zhanjiang, China ... 31 D6
Zhanyi, China 30 D5
Zhaotong, China ... 30 D5
Zhashkiv, Ukraine .. 17 D16
Zhayyq →,
  Kazakhstan 23 E9
Zhdanov = Mariupol,
  Ukraine 23 E6
Zhejiang □, China .. 31 D7
Zheleznodorozhny,
  Russia 22 B9
Zheleznogorsk-Ilimskiy,
  Russia 25 D11
Zhengzhou, China .. 31 C6
Zhetiqara, Kazakhstan 24 D7
Zhezqazghan,
  Kazakhstan 24 E7
Zhigansk, Russia ... 25 C13
Zhilinda, Russia ... 25 B12
Zhitomir = Zhytomyr,
  Ukraine 17 C15
Zhlobin, Belarus ... 17 B16
Zhmerinka =
  Zhmerynka, Ukraine 17 D15
Zhmerynka, Ukraine 17 D15
Zhodino = Zhodzina,
  Belarus 17 A15
Zhodzina, Belarus .. 17 A15
Zhokhova, Ostrov,
  Russia 25 B16
Zhongdian, China .. 30 D4
Zhumadian, China .. 31 C6
Zhupanovo, Russia . 25 D16
Zhytomyr, Ukraine .. 17 C15
Zîärän, Iran 39 B6
Zibo, China 31 C6
Zielona Góra, Poland 16 C8
Zierikzee, Neths. ... 15 C3
Zigey, Chad 45 F8
Zigong, China 30 D5
Ziguinchor, Senegal . 44 F1
Žilina, Slovak Rep. .. 17 D10
Zillah, Libya 45 C8
Zima, Russia 25 D11
Zimbabwe ■, Africa 47 H5
Zimnicea, Romania . 17 G13
Zinder, Niger 44 F6
Zion National Park,
  U.S.A. 73 H7
Zipaquirá, Colombia 78 C4
Zitundo, Mozam. ... 49 D5
Ziway, L., Ethiopia .. 45 G12
Zlatograd, Bulgaria . 21 D11
Zlatoust, Russia 22 C10
Zlín, Czech. 17 D9
Žlitan, Libya 45 B8
Zmeinogorsk,
  Kazakhstan 24 D9
Znojmo, Czech. 16 D9
Zobeyrī, Iran 38 C5
Zolochev = Zolochiv,
  Ukraine 17 D13
Zolochiv, Ukraine .. 17 D13
Zomba, Malawi 47 H7
Zongo, Zaïre 46 D3
Zonguldak, Turkey . 23 F5
Zorra I., Panama ... 74 H14
Zorritos, Peru 78 D2
Zouar, Chad 45 D8
Zouérate, Mauritania 44 D2
Zoutkamp, Neths. .. 15 A6
Zrenjanin, Serbia, Yug. 21 B9
Zuetina = Az
  Zuwaytinah, Libya . 45 B9
Zufar, Oman 40 D5
Zug, Switz. 16 E5
Zugspitze, Germany . 16 E6
Zuid-Holland □, Neths. 15 A5
Zuidhorn, Neths. ... 15 A6
Zula, Eritrea 40 D2
Zumbo, Mozam. ... 47 H6
Zungeru, Nigeria ... 44 G6
Zuni, U.S.A. 73 J9
Zunyi, China 30 D5
Zurbāṭīyah, Iraq ... 38 C5
Zürich, Switz. 16 E5
Zutphen, Neths. ... 15 B6
Zuwārah, Libya 45 B7
Zūzan, Iran 39 C8
Zvenigovsk,
  Russia 24 D7
Zverinogolovskoye,
  Russia 24 D7
Zvishavane, Zimbabwe 47 J6
Zvolen, Slovak Rep. . 17 D10
Zwettl, Austria 16 D8
Zwickau, Germany . 16 C7
Zwolle, Neths. 15 B6
Zwolle, U.S.A. 71 K8
Zymoetz →, Canada 64 C3
Żyrardów, Poland .. 17 B11
Zyryan, Kazakhstan . 24 E9
Zyryanka, Russia ... 25 C16
Zyryanovsk = Zyryan,
  Kazakhstan 24 E9
Żywiec, Poland 17 D10

WORLD : REGIONS IN THE NEWS

Maps show the situation in May 1995

THE BREAK UP OF YUGOSLAVIA
The former country of Yugoslavia comprised six republics. In 1991 Slovenia and Croatia declared independence. Bosnia-Herzegovina followed in 1992 and Macedonia in 1993. Yugoslavia now comprises the remaining two republics, Serbia and Montenegro.

YUGOSLAVIA
Population : 10,763,000 (Serb 62.6%, Albanian 16.5%, Montenegrin 5%, Hungarian 3.3%, Muslim 3.2%)

Serbia
Population : 5,824,211 (Serb 87.7%) excluding the former autonomous provinces of Kosovo and Vojvodina
  Kosovo
  Population : 1,956,196
  (Albanian 81.6%, Serb 9.9%)
  Vojvodina
  Population : 2,014,000
  (Serb 56.8%, Hungarian 16.9%)
Montenegro Population : 615,035 (Montenegrin 61.9%, Muslim 14.6%, Albanian 6.6%)

CROATIA
Population : 4,504,000 (Croat 78.1%, Serb 12.2%)

SLOVENIA
Population : 1,942,000 (Slovene 88%, Croat 3%, Serb 2%)

MACEDONIA (F.Y.R.O.M.)
Population : 2,142,000 (Macedonian 64%, Albanian 21.7%, Turkish 5%, Romanian 3%, Serb 2%)

BOSNIA - HERZEGOVINA
Population : 3,527,000 (Muslim 49%, Serb 31.2%, Croat 17.2%)

Civil war between Serbs and other ethnic groups continues in Bosnia-Herzegovina. The large scale map on the left shows the situation in early 1995.

FORMER YUGOSLAVIA
0   50   100   150   200 km

-·-·- International boundaries
-··-··- Republic boundaries
-·-·- Province boundaries
◎ Capital cities

BOSNIA-HERZEGOVINA
0   50   100 km

Under Croatian control
Under Serbian control
Under Muslim control

THE NEAR EAST
0   25   50km

ISRAEL Population : 5,458,000 (inc. East Jerusalem and Jewish settlers in the areas under Israeli administration. (Jewish 82%, Arab Muslim 13.8%, Arab Christian 2.5%, Druze 1.7%)

West Bank Population : 973,500 (Palestinian Arabs 97% [of whom Arab Muslim 85%, Jewish 7%, Christian 8%])

Gaza Strip Population : 658,200 (Arab Muslim 98%)

JORDAN Population : 5,198,000 (Arab 99% [of whom about 50% are Palestinian Arab])

-·-·- 1949 Armistice Line
- - - 1974 Cease-fire Lines

Efrata ● Main Jewish settlements in the West Bank and Gaza Strip

Halhul □ Main Palestinian Arab towns in the West Bank and Gaza Strip

THE CAUCASUS
0   100   200 km

-·-·- International boundaries
-··-··- Republic boundaries

Georgia, Armenia and Azerbaijan achieved independence in 1991. Abkhazia, Ajaria and South Ossetia seek independence from Georgia. Chechenia has been trying to break away from Russia since 1991, but Russia has resisted with military force. Hostility also continues between Armenia and Azerbaijan over the enclave of Nagorno-Karabakh.

RUSSIA
North Ossetia
Population : 695,000 (Ossetian 53%, Russian 29%, Chechen 5.2%, Ingush 5% [expelled in 1992])
Chechenia
Population : 1,308,000 (Chechen and Ingush 70.7%, Russian 23.1%)
Neighbouring **Ingushetia** (now split from Chechenia)
Population : 250,000 (mainly Ingush)
GEORGIA
Population : 5,450,000 (Georgian 70.1%, Armenian 8.1%, Russian 6.3%, Azerbaijani 5.7%, Ossetian 3%, Greek 2%, Abkhazian 2%)
Abkhazia
Population : 537,500 (Georgian 45.7%, Abkhazian 17.8%, Armenian 14.6%, Russian 14.3%)
Ajaria
Population : 382,000 (Georgian 82.8%, Russian 7.7%, Armenian 4%)
South Ossetia
Population : 99,800 (Ossetian 66.2%, Georgian 29%)
ARMENIA
Population : 3,548,000 (Armenian 93.3%, Azerbaijani 2.6%)
Nagorno-Karabakh
Population : 192,400 (Armenian 76.9%, Azerbaijani 21.5%)
AZERBAIJAN
Population : 7,472,000 (Azerbaijani 82.7%, Russian 5.6%, Armenian 5.6%, Lezgin 2.4%)
Naxçivan
Population : 300,400 (Azerbaijani 95.9%)

MOLDOVA
0   50   100   150 km

Separatist regions

Population : 4,420,000 (Moldovan 64.5%, Ukrainian 13.9%, Russian 14%, Gagauzi 3.5%, Jewish 2%, Bulgarian 2%)

ECUADOR AND PERU
0   100   200 km

▬▬▬ 1995 disputed border
Disputed territory allocated to Peru in 1942

CARTOGRAPHY BY PHILIP'S. COPYRIGHT REED INTERNATIONAL BOOKS LTD

KEY TO WORLD MAP PAGES

NORTH AMERICA

60-61

64-65

62-63

72-73 70-71 68-69

ATLANTIC

OCEAN

74-75

66

PACIFIC
OCEAN
56-57

SOUTH
AMERICA

78-79

80

PACIFIC   OCEAN

Arctic Circle

8

12

13 10-11

14

18

9

Tropic of Cancer

Equator

AFRIC

Tropic of Capricorn

4